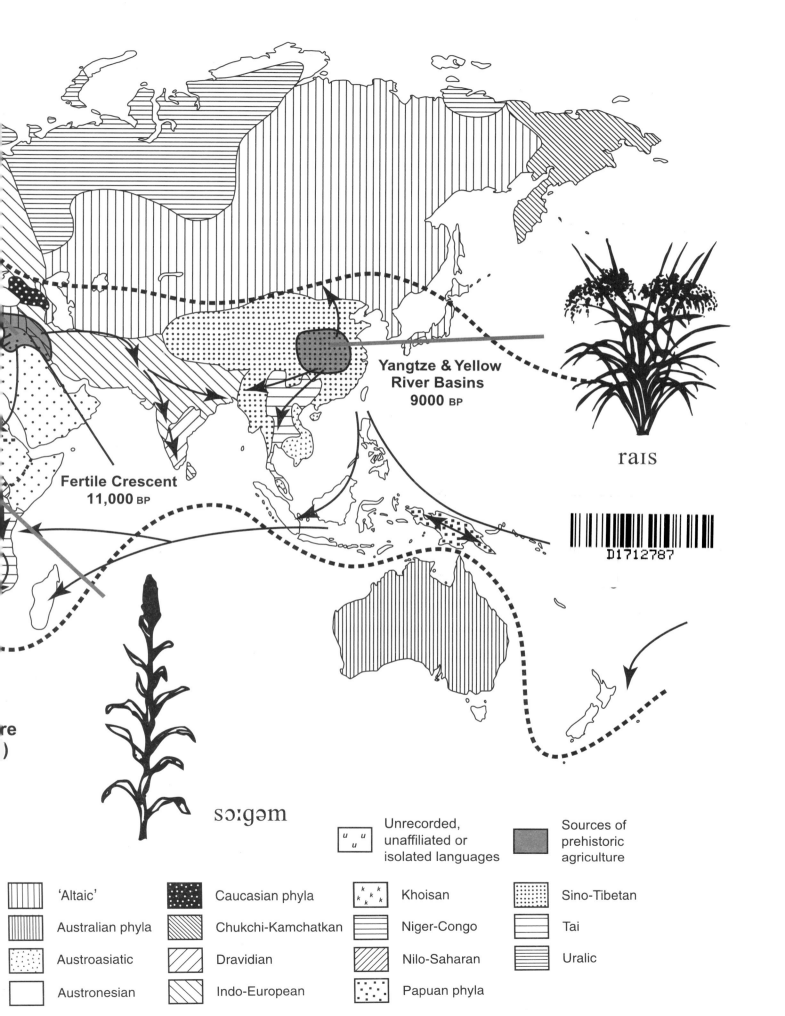

Yangtze & Yellow
River Basins
9000 BP

rais

D1712787

Fertile Crescent
11,000 BP

sɔːɡəm

ˈmeɪˌɡɪs

| | Unrecorded, unaffiliated or isolated languages | | Sources of prehistoric agriculture |

'Altaic'

Australian phyla

Austroasiatic

Austronesian

Caucasian phyla

Chukchi-Kamchatkan

Dravidian

Indo-European

Khoisan

Niger-Congo

Nilo-Saharan

Papuan phyla

Sino-Tibetan

Tai

Uralic

Delegates at the Farming/Language Dispersal Hypothesis symposium. From left to right: Back row - Ofer Bar-Yosef, Andrew Pawley, David Harris, Charles Higham, Christopher Ehret, David Phillipson, Martin Jones, Jane Renfrew, Colin Renfrew, Dorian Fuller, Fekri Hassan, Peter Bellwood, Alexander Militarev, Lounes Chikhi, Stephen LeBlanc, Marek Zvelebil, Søren Wichman, Richard Matson, Norman Hammond, Hans-Jürgen Bandelt, Richard Villems, Jane Hill, Toomas Kivisild, Chris Scarre, Mark Hudson; Middle row - Guido Barbujani, Franz Manni, Mark Cohen, Martin Richards, Stephen Oppenheimer, George Van Driem; Front row - Bernard Comrie, Lyle Campbell, Katie Boyle, Matthew Hurles, Graeme Barker, Victor Paz; Not in photograph - Roger Blench, Peter Forster, Erika Hagelberg, B.J. McDonald-Milne, Gregory Possehl and Peter Underhill.

MᴄDONALD INSTITUTE MONOGRAPHS

Examining the farming/ language dispersal hypothesis

Edited by Peter Bellwood & Colin Renfrew

Published by:

McDonald Institute for Archaeological Research
University of Cambridge
Downing Street
Cambridge, UK
CB2 3ER
(0)(1223) 339336

Distributed by Oxbow Books
 United Kingdom: Oxbow Books, Park End Place, Oxford, OX1 1HN, UK.
  Tel: (0)(1865) 241249; Fax: (0)(1865) 794449; http://www.oxbowbooks.com/
 USA: The David Brown Book Company, P.O. Box 511, Oakville, CT 06779, USA.
  Tel: 860-945-9329; FAX: 860-945-9468; http://www.oxbowbooks.com/

ISBN: 1-902937-20-1
ISSN: 1363-1349

Edited for the Institute by Chris Scarre (*Series Editor*) and Dora A. Kemp (*Production Editor*).

Film produced by Gary Reynolds Typesetting, 13 Sturton Street, Cambridge, CB1 2QG.
Printed and bound by Short Run Press, Bittern Rd, Sowton Industrial Estate, Exeter, EX2 7LW.

Contents

CONTRIBUTORS

HANS-JÜRGEN BANDELT
Fachbereich Mathematik, University of Hamburg, Bundesstr. 55, 20146 Hamburg, Germany.
Email: bandelt@math.uni-hamburg.de

OFER BAR-YOSEF
Peabody Museum, Harvard University, 11 Divinity Avenue, Cambridge, MA 02138, USA.
Email: obaryos@fas.harvard.edu

GUIDO BARBUJANI
Dipartimento di Biologia, Università di Ferrara, via L. Borsari, 46, I-44100 Ferrara, Italy.
Email: bjg@ifeuniv.unife.it

GRAEME BARKER
School of Archaeology and Ancient History, University of Leicester, Leicester, LE1 7RH, UK.
Email: gba@leicester.ac.uk

PETER BELLWOOD
School of Archaeology and Anthropology, Australian National University, Canberra ACT 0200, Australia.
Email: Peter.Bellwood@anu.edu.au

MARINA BERMISHEVA
Institute of Biochemistry and Genetics, Ufa Research Centre, 69 Oktyabrskaya Street, 450054 Ufa, Russia.
Email: marina_ber@omen.ru

LYLE CAMPBELL
Department of Linguistics, University of Canterbury, Private Bag 4800, Christchurch, New Zealand.
Email: l.campbell@ling.canterbury.ac.nz

LUCA CAVALLI-SFORZA
Department of Genetics, 300 Pasteur Drive, Stanford University, Stanford, CA 94305–5120, USA.
Email: cavalli@stanford.edu

LOUNÈS CHIKHI
UMR Evolution et Diversité Biologique, Equipe Structuration génétique des populations et évolution du génome, CESAC UMR C 5576 - Bat. IV R3, Université Paul Sabatier, 118 Route de Narbonne, 31062 - Toulouse cédex 4, France.

MARK NATHAN COHEN
Plattsburgh State University of New York, Anthropology Department, Redcay 103, Plattsburgh, NY 12901, USA.
Email: mark.cohen@plattsburgh.edu

BERNARD COMRIE
Max Planck Institute for Evolutionary Anthropology, Inselstrasse 22, D-04103 Leipzig, Germany.
Email: comrie@eva.mpg.de

LARISSA DAMBA
Institute of Genetics and Cytology, Siberian Branch of Russian Academy of Sciences, 10 Lavrentiev Avenue, 630090 Novosibirsk, Russia.
Email: damba@bionet.nsc.ru

ISABELLE DUPANLOUP
Dipartimento di Biologia, Universita' di Ferrara, via L. Borsari 46, I-44100 Ferrara, Italy.
Email: dpi@dns.unife.it

CHRISTOPHER EHRET
UCLA Department of History, 6265 Bunche Hall, Box 951473, Los Angeles, CA 90095-1473, USA.
Email: ehret@history.ucla.edu

PETER FORSTER
McDonald Institute for Archaeological Research, University of Cambridge, Downing Street, Cambridge, CB2 3ER, UK.
Email: pf223@cam.ac.uk

DORIAN FULLER
Institute of Archaeology, University College London, 31–34 Gordon Square, London, WC1H 0PY, UK.
Email: d.fuller@ucl.ac.uk

MARIA GOLUBENKO
Department of Experimental Cardiology, Max-Planck Institute for Physiological and Clinical Research, 2 Benekestrasse, D-61231 Bad Nauheim, Germany.
Email: m_goloubenko@yahoo.com

DAVID R. HARRIS
Professor Emeritus of Human Environment, Institute of Archaeology, University College London, 31–34 Gordon Square, London, WC1H 0PY, UK.
Email: david.harris@ucl.ac.uk

FEKRI A. HASSAN
Institute of Archaeology, University College London, 31–34 Gordon Square, London, WC1H 0PY, UK.
Email: f.hassan@ucl.ac.uk

CHARLES HIGHAM
Department of Anthropology, University of Otago, P.O. Box 56, Dunedin, New Zealand.
Email: charles.higham@stonebow.otago.ac.nz

JANE HILL
Department of Anthropology, University of Arizona, 1009 E South Campus Drive, Building #30A, Tucson, AZ 85721-0030, USA.
Email: jhill@u.arizona.edu

MARK HUDSON
Anthropology Program, College of Humanities, University of Tsukuba, Tsukuba Science City, Japan 305-8571.
Email: mhudson@first.tsukuba.ac.jp

MATTHEW HURLES
McDonald Institute for Archaeological Research, University of Cambridge, Downing Street, Cambridge, CB2 3ER, UK.
Email: meh32@cam.ac.uk

MARTIN JONES
Department of Archaeology, University of Cambridge, Downing Street, Cambridge, CB2 3DZ, UK.
Email: mkj12@hermes.cam.ac.uk

KATRIN KALDMA
Department of Evolutionary Biology, Tartu University and Estonian Biocentre, 23 Riia Street, 51010 Tartu, Estonia.
Email: kkaldma@ebc.ee

ELSA KHUSNUTDINOVA
Institute of Biochemistry and Genetics, Ufa Research Centre, 69 Oktyabrskaya Street, 450054 Ufa, Russia.
Email: ekkh@anrb.ru

TOOMAS KIVISILD
Estonian Biocentre and Department of Evolutionary Biology, Tartu University, 23 Riia Street, 51010 Tartu, Estonia.
Email: tkivisil@ebc.ee

STEVEN LEBLANC
Peabody Museum, Harvard University, 11 Divinity Avenue, Cambridge, MA 02138, USA.
Email: leblanc@fas.harvard.edu

VINCENT MACAULAY
Department of Statistics, 1 South Parks Road, Oxford, OX1 3TG, UK.
Email: macaulay@stats.ox.ac.uk

SARABJIT MASTANA
Human Genetics Laboratory, Department of Human Sciences, Loughborough University, Loughborough, LE11 3TU, UK.
Email: S.S.Mastana@lboro.ac.uk

R.G. MATSON
Anthropology and Sociology, University of British Columbia, 6303 N.W. Marine Drive, Vancouver, BC, V6T 1Z1, Canada.
Email: mesa@interchange.ubc.ca

ENE METSPALU
Estonia Biocentre and Department of Evolutionary Biology, Tartu University, 23 Riia Street, 51010 Tartu, Estonia.
Email: emetspal@ebc.ee

MAIT METSPALU
Department of Evolutionary Biology, Tartu University and Estonian Biocentre, 23 Riia Street, 51010 Tartu, Estonia.
Email: mait@ebc.ee

ALEXANDER MILITAREV
Oriental Institute, Russian State University for the Humanities, 6 Miusskaja pl., Moscow 125267, Russia.
Email: alex.mil@jum.ru

STEPHEN OPPENHEIMER
Green College, Woodstock Road, Oxford, OX2 6HG, UK.
Email: stephen.oppenheimer@ntlworld.com

SURINDER S. PAPIHA
Institute of Human Genetics, University of Newcastle upon Tyne, Central Parkway, Newcastle upon Tyne, NE1 3BZ, UK.
Email: S.S.Papiha@newcastle.ac.uk

JÜRI PARIK
Estonia Biocentre and Department of Evolutionary Biology, Tartu University, 23 Riia Street, 51010 Tartu, Estonia.
Email: jparik@ebc.ee

ANDREW PAWLEY
Research School of Pacific and Asian Studies, Department of Linguistics, Australian National University, Canberra, ACT, Australia 0200.
Email: apawley@coombs.anu.edu.au

VICTOR PAZ
Archaeological Studies Program, Palma Hall Basement, University of the Philippines, Diliman, Quezon City 1101, Philippines.
Email: victor.paz@up.edu.ph

DAVID W. PHILLIPSON
Museum of Archaeology & Anthropology, University of Cambridge, Downing Street, Cambridge, CB2 3DZ, UK.
Email: dwp1000@cus.cam.ac.uk

VALERY PUZYREV
Institute of Medical Genetics, Tomsk Research Centre, Siberian Branch of Russian Academy of Medical Sciences, 10 Nab. Ushayky, 634050 Tomsk, Russia.
Email: valery@img.tsu.ru

MAERE REIDLA
Estonia Biocentre and Department of Evolutionary Biology, Tartu University, 23 Riia Street, 51010 Tartu, Estonia.
Email: mreidla@ebc.ee

COLIN RENFREW
McDonald Institute for Archaeological Research, University of Cambridge, Downing Street, Cambridge, CB2 3ER, UK.
Email: acr10@cam.ac.uk

MARTIN RICHARDS
Department of Chemical and Biological Sciences, University of Huddersfield, Queensgate, Huddersfield, HD1 3DH, UK.
Email: m.b.richards@hud.ac.uk

SIIRI ROOTSI
Department of Evolutionary Biology, Tartu University and Estonian Biocentre, 23 Riia Street, 51010 Tartu, Estonia.
Email: sroots@ebc.ee

PAVAO RUDAN
Institute for Anthropological Research, 8 Amruceva Street, 10000 Zagreb, Croatia.
Email: pavao.rudan@inantro.hr

CHRIS SCARRE
McDonald Institute for Archaeological Research, University of Cambridge, Downing Street, Cambridge, CB2 3ER, UK.
Email: cjs16@cam.ac.uk

VADIM STEPANOV
Institute of Medical Genetics, Tomsk Research Centre, Siberian Branch of Russian Academy of Medical Sciences, 10 Nab. Ushayky, 634050 Tomsk, Russia.
Email: vadimst@img.tsu.ru

KRISTIINA TAMBETS
Department of Evolutionary Biology, Tartu University and Estonian Biocentre, 23 Riia Street, 51010 Tartu, Estonia.
Email: ktambets@ebc.ee

HELLE-VIIVI TOLK
Department of Evolutionary Biology, Tartu University and Estonian Biocentre, 23 Riia Street, 51010 Tartu, Estonia.
Email: htolk@ebc.ee

PETER A. UNDERHILL
Department of Genetics, 300 Pasteur Drive, Stanford University, Stanford, CA 94305 –5120, USA.
Email: under@stanford.edu

ESIEN USANGA
Department of Medical Laboratory Sciences, Faculty of Allied Health Sciences, Kuwait University, Shuwaikh Campus, Kuwait.
Email: usanga@hsc.kuniv.edu.kw

GEORGE VAN DRIEM
Himalayan Languages Project, Department of Comparative Linguistics, Leiden University, P.O. Box 9515, 2300 RA Leiden, The Netherlands.
Email: dzongkha@compuserve.com

RICHARD VILLEMS
Department of Evolutionary Biology, Tartu University and Estonian Biocentre, 23 Riia Street, 51010 Tartu, Estonia.
Email: rvillems@ebc.ee

MICHAEL VOEVODA
Institute of Genetics and Cytology, Siberian Branch of Russian Academy of Sciences, 10 Lavrentiev Avenue, 630090 Novosibirsk, Russia.
Email: voevoda@iim.nsu.ru

SØREN WICHMANN
Department of General and Applied Linguistics, University of Copenhagen, Njalsgade 80, DK-2300 Copenhagen S, Denmark.
Email: soerenw@hum.ku.dk

MAREK ZVELEBIL
Department of Prehistory and Archaeology, University of Sheffield, Sheffield, S10 2TN, UK.
Email: m.zvelebil@sheffield.ac.uk

Figures

Tables

Foreword

Peter Bellwood & Colin Renfrew

Suggestions that the spreads of early agricultural populations could have been responsible for the foundation spreads of language families have stimulated much debate in recent years. The two editors have both attempted to explain the early dispersals of the Austronesian and Indo-European languages in this way, and in the last few years have attempted to apply the hypothesis to agricultural populations and language families on a world-wide scale. These attempts reflect the apparent correlations between the homeland regions and dispersal histories of some of the major language families of agriculturalist latitudes, and the homeland regions and dispersals histories of early systems of food production.

We were certainly not the first to make such observations. For example, Robert Heine-Geldern almost 70 years ago placed the dispersals of the Austroasiatic and Austronesian language families firmly in the Southeast Asian Neolithic. Kimball Romney later suggested (1957) that the early Uto-Aztecan languages were spread northwards from Mesoamerica by early maize farmers (Heine-Geldern 1932; Romney 1957). But only in recent years has the farming/language dispersal hypothesis been examined cooperatively across the disciplines of archaeology, linguistics and genetics from a broad comparative perspective, rather than a perspective based upon a single region or language family. Perhaps surprisingly, Gordon Childe, despite his renowned intuition about the importance of the 'Neolithic Revolution', never suggested such a linkage for the Indo-European languages, preferring instead to locate their genesis in subsequent Bronze Age contexts.

Since the mid-1980s the farming/language dispersal hypothesis, which forms the core concept around which this book is structured, has become the focus of an ever-increasing intensity of debate. This debate has been fuelled in part by the reconstructions of the prehistories of major language families such as Indo-European, Austronesian and Bantu presented by both archaeologists and linguists, many

represented in the following chapters, and also by the concept of demic diffusion as developed within genetics by Luca Cavalli-Sforza and his colleagues (Cavalli-Sforza & Cavalli-Sforza 1995). Genetic research has since expanded to consider the non-recombining parts of the human genome (mitochondrial DNA and part of the Y chromosome), and it is these new frontiers that dominate the genetics papers published here. Linguists and archaeologists have likewise sharpened their research tools as language families have become better recorded, as methods of reconstructing genetic relationships in deep time have been refined, and as methods of archaeological data recovery, dating and environmental analysis have improved. AMS radiocarbon dating, for instance, has revolutionized understanding of the Neolithic in many parts of the world, as incidentally has the massive increase in construction-site rescue archaeology since the 1970s.

By 2000, the continuing intensity of debate circulating around the farming/language dispersal hypothesis indicated to the two editors the need for a focused meeting bringing together some of the leading scholars from the three major disciplines involved. The Wenner-Gren Foundation for Anthropological Research generously granted funding to both of us early in 2001, and the conference was held from 24–27 August 2001 in the McDonald Institute for Archaeological Research in Cambridge. A total of 43 delegates attended, several invited as discussants, and thirty-six pre-circulated papers tabled at the meeting have been revised and published here.

The bulk of the papers have been arranged into four major regional sections, namely Western Asia and North Africa, Asia and Oceania, Mesoamerica and the US Southwest, and Europe. These regional sections are located in Part III of the volume and are preceded by introductory papers by the two editors (Part I), and by four general papers on archaeological, linguistic and genetic issues (Part II).

It will be observed that some regions of early agriculture — especially the Eastern Woodlands of the USA and the Andean and Amazonian regions of South America — are missing from the contents list. In the final resort, it proved impossible to cover all regions, owing in part to reasons of space and funding, and in part to the difficulties of finding scholars both able to attend and in command of the necessary information. Nevertheless, we feel that those regions for which the hypothesis has been debated most fully in recent literature — Africa, Europe and Asia in particular — are very well covered. The Americas have been less involved in the debate than one might expect, particularly in view of the close relations between linguistics and anthropology in many North American universities, but the section on Meso-america and the Southwest in this volume helps to redress the situation.

It will also be observed that some of the authors in the volume express considerable disagreement with each other. This reflects the fact that the organizers deliberately invited not only those speakers known to agree with the farming/language dispersal hypothesis, but decided from the beginning to vary the field in terms of opinion. The hypothesis is not, and never will be, demonstrated to work to perfection for all times and places. Debate, some fairly acrimonious, is guaranteed to continue into the foreseeable future.

The editors hope, therefore, that this volume will stimulate further multidisciplinary debate on a series of developments which, while independent and of different date in different parts of the world, have in combination pushed humanity through one of the most significant transitions in its history, a transition in some ways almost as important as the achievement of modern humanness itself. The significance of this transition will ensure that it always attracts a kaleidoscope of interpretative opinion — one can regard it as the saviour or the bane of modern humanity, the source of wealth and comfort, or of disease and overpopulation. Like the debate about

the origins of modern humans, the fundamental questions which revolve around early farmers, their languages and their genes will exercise the minds of increasing numbers of scholars as the disciplines involved increase the accuracy and reliability of their research tools.

Last, but certainly not least, the organizers would like to thank the McDonald Institute for Archaeological Research for hosting and providing funding for the conference, the British Academy for awarding a British Conference Grant, the Wenner-Gren Foundation for Anthropological Research for generously granting us a conference award, the Publications Committee of the Australian National University for contributing towards the production costs of this volume, Selwyn College for accommodating the delegates, and Corpus Christi College for hosting the conference dinner. Katie Boyle provided invaluable assistance with organization both before and after the conference, inviting the delegates, organizing their accommodation, and contributing to the task of organizing and editing the papers for publication. Dora Kemp, the McDonald Institute's Production Editor, has played a major part in producing this volume of papers and the editors are duly grateful. The British Academy awarded Peter Bellwood a Visiting Professorship at the McDonald Institute from March to July 2001, while on leave from the Australian National University, enabling him to take part in the planning process.

References

Cavalli-Sforza, L.L. & F.C. Cavalli-Sforza, 1995. *The Great Human Diasporas*. Reading (MA): Addison-Wesley.

Heine-Geldern, R., 1932. Urheimat und früheste Wanderungen der Austronesier. *Anthropos* 27, 543–619.

Romney, A.K., 1957. The genetic model and Uto-Aztecan time perspective. *Davidson Journal of Anthropology* 3, 25–41.

Part I

Introduction

Chapter 1

'The Emerging Synthesis': the Archaeogenetics of Farming/Language Dispersals and other Spread Zones

Colin Renfrew

One of the enduring problems in anthropology, archaeology and historical linguistics is the origin of the world's major language families and of their distributions. It is a 'puzzle' which has proved problematic since the early recognition of language families, and which, over the years, has given rise to an extraordinary range of speculation. Some of that speculation, with its emphasis upon ethnicity and ethnic identity, has played its part in ethnic and national conflicts, and we should not forget that assertions about the past can be used in the present in a manipulative way, and form the basis for policies for which the present not the past should take responsibility.

The purpose of the symposium from which the present volume is derived was to examine the proposal, much discussed in recent years (Renfrew 1987; Bellwood 1989; 1991), which has been put forward to account for the present distribution of some of the world's largest language families: the 'farming/language dispersal hypothesis'. In short this proposes that some of these language families (such as the Niger-Kordofanian family (including Bantu), the Austronesian family, the Indo-European family, the Afroasiatic family, and several others) owe their current distributions, at least in part, to the demographic and cultural processes in different parts of the world which accompanied the dispersal in those areas of the practice of food production (and of the relevant domestic species) from the various key areas in which those plant and animal species were first domesticated. The approach has the undoubted merit, whatever the final outcome of the discussions and debates currently underway, of lifting the discussion out of and beyond the specifics of each individual case of a particular language family, and looking rather at the more general processes involved in the formation of language families, and at the correlates between the linguistic and the social or historical processes involved.

Such matters have been debated among archaeologists and historical linguists for some time. It is only over the past 20 years, however, that the findings of molecular genetics have been applied systematically to these questions, with the development of the new discipline of archaeogenetics, i.e. 'the study of the human past using the techniques of molecular genetics' (Renfrew & Boyle 2000, 3). Despite the evident problems involved in making the findings of one discipline cast light upon those of another, there are already indications that the approach will prove fruitful. Of course there is no suggestion that there is a direct relationship between specific genes or haplotypes and specific languages: languages are learnt, genes are inherited exclusively through the two parents. But already there are indications that in the field of population history, which is obviously of great relevance to historical linguistics as well as to prehistoric archaeology, the study of the molecular genetics of living populations as well as deceased ones, has a major role to play. Some years ago I spoke (Renfrew 1991, 20) of 'the emerging synthesis' between the three disciplines in question (historical linguistics, molecular genetics and archaeology). And although the 'emerging synthesis' has not yet fully taken shape, some of its outlines are perhaps becoming clear.

In what follows I should like first to review some of the underlying issues concerning the distribution of the world's language families, as they appear to an archaeologist, and then to address some of the emerging problems in the application of an archaeogenetic approach to these questions. First I should like to deal with aspects of spatial patterning,

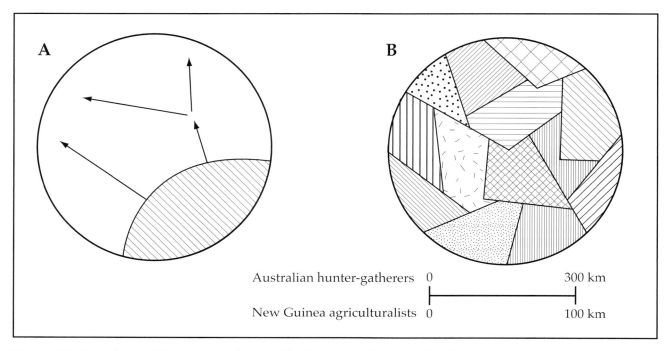

Figure 1.1. *Spread zone (A) versus mosaic zone (B). Contrasting language distribution patterns seen when there has been a language replacement following a rapid dispersal process or punctuation (case A), or when, after initial colonization, there has been a long period of uninterrupted local divergence (case B) resulting in a mosaic of small language units. In B one may compare the different scales for the language map for hunter-gatherers and for cases where the agricultural economy is indigenous, resulting in both cases in a mosaic of small language units. (The language units are for convenience separated by lines: this is not intended to suggest that they are discrete or bounded entities not to deny the existence of intermediate dialects.) (From Renfrew 1992, 59.)*

developing some points made in a recent paper (Renfrew 2000).

Spread zones and mosaic zones

Several linguists have remarked on the marked difference in the nature of the geographical distributions of language families, and Austerlitz (1980) has contrasted patterns of language-family density. In 1992 I suggested that there were contrasting geographical patterns (Renfrew 1992, 59) when a region had undergone language displacement as a result of some dispersal process (Fig. 1.1: case A), or when, after initial colonization, there was a long period of stability resulting in a mosaic of small language units (Fig. 1.1: case B).

This distinction is very similar to the one drawn by Nichols (1992) between what she terms linguistic 'spread zones' and 'residual zones', although the term 'mosaic zone' or 'retention zone' may be preferable to 'residual zone'. When a language family shows the 'spread-zone' pattern, it displays what one may term a low genetic density (i.e. only a limited number of linguistic units unrelated by descent from a common language ancestor) over a sizeable area, and with a relatively shallow time depth. The 'mosaic zone' (or residual zone') pattern shows more language families, greater linguistic diversity within the language family, and greater antiquity of the linguistic stocks there. The north Caucasus is a good example of a 'mosaic zone', and is sometimes regarded as a linguistic refugium, and north Australia offers a further example.

It should be noted that pattern B, the mosaic zone configuration, is seen both with hunter-gatherers and with agriculturalists in those cases where the agricultural economy does not seem to be the result of an agricultural dispersal but may be regarded as indigenous, as in the case of New Guinea with its very early horticulture and perhaps in regions of South America. But the interesting point is that the spatial scale of the language unit differs in the two cases, with a hunter-gatherer linguistic unit occupying a much larger area than an agricultural or horticultural one. This is no doubt related to the much greater population density in the agricultural case, so that the size of the speech community in the two cases may be more similar than the territorial extent. This is a point addressed much more fully by Nettle (1999).

> As I observed in 1992:

>> If we try to imagine a world whose language distribution was the product of initial colonization, followed by convergence and divergence effects, but without the effects of agricultural dispersal or élite dominance, might we perhaps imagine the linguistic configuration of Australia generalized for those areas with a hunter-gatherer economy, and that of New Guinea for those with an indigenous agricultural economy? (Renfrew 1992, 60).

In such a case as this the pattern does not in itself tell us whether the various languages involved are genetically related or not. For in the case of a mosaic zone, the time depth involved may be so great that through lapse of time most valid markers of relatedness, even if they existed initially, would have disappeared — we may be talking here of periods of stability enduring well over 10,000 years. And as Dixon (1997) has argued, the convergence effects operating over so long a period of time may produce a linguistic area or *Sprachbund* effect, with similarities developing between the languages which are not the product of genetic relatedness but simply of long-term interaction (on the model of Trubetzkoy 1939).

On the other hand, the configuration seen in pattern A suggests a relatively recent dispersal, in Dixon's recent terminology a punctuation. This may be due to a dispersal on the subsistence/demography model, or on the system collapse model (see Renfrew 1989). Or, as I have now come to realize, it may be the product of contact-induced language change (see below). In most cases, as Peter Bellwood has also suggested (Bellwood 1996; 1997; this volume), it is likely to be the product of farming dispersal. Other applications of the model have been suggested for the consequences of rice cultivation in southeast Asia (Glover & Higham 1996; Higham 1996; this volume), for the Afroasiatic languages (Diakonoff 1998; Militiarev this volume) and for some of the language families of Africa (Phillipson 1997; this volume; Ehret 1998).

The important implication of the evident distinction between 'spread zones' and 'mosaic zones' (or 'residual zones') is that they may in many cases be recognized by inspecting maps of language distributions, along with a basic classification of the languages in question into language families (or as isolates), following the work of linguists in the field.

It is possible in this way to suggest that in many cases the language distribution in a spread zone is likely to have been the result of a dispersal phenomenon, very possibly a farming dispersal, although that needs to be evaluated by closer examination including a consideration of the archaeological record. In cases where a mosaic zone is recognized, the pattern may well prove to be one of very early initial colonization, perhaps of the order of 15,000 years ago, followed by stability and local divergence. It is, of course, also possible that what may at first appear as a spread zone represents a point at the extreme right of Nettle's figure 3(b), where very long-term convergence processes have taken over in the manner proposed by Dixon, producing a language 'family' (but not in the genetic sense) through convergence. This, of course, is Dixon's proposal for the Pama-Nyungan language 'family' of Australia.

Although, as will be argued further below, farming/language dispersal is one of the appropriate explanations for the origin of a spread zone, other models are possible. In particular the distributions of the Altaic and Finno-Ugric language families — both giving every appearance of spread-zone characteristics — require other explanations (Janhunen 1996).

Models for language change and language replacement

It may be argued (Renfrew 1989, 110–12) that there are only four classes of model for spatio-linguistic change. Here one is considering the language or languages spoken over time within a well-defined geographical area. The treatment thus differs from many linguistic ones, where the focus of study is the language, which may have undergone spatial displacements. The models here are defined with respect to particular territories.

1. *Initial colonization.* Colonization models explain language distributions in terms of the colonization by human populations of previously uninhabited areas. They are particularly susceptible to archaeological investigation since the phenomenon of initial colonization usually offers abundant archaeological data with a secure chronology. The case of Polynesia has been extensively discussed (e.g. Terrell 1988).

2. *Linguistic replacement.* If a language within our given territory is replaced by another, different language, or by several, we may speak of linguistic replacement. A range of models may be formulated within this class. They are further

discussed below.

3. *Divergence models.* The phenomenon of linguistic divergence has been central to historical linguistics since its inception, just as genetic drift and the 'founder effect' are central concepts in biogeography. (Genetic drift may be a misleading analogy here precisely because mutations may well occur at a roughly constant rate.) More detailed aspects of specifically *spatial* variation through divergence seem not to have been intensively investigated, so far as long time periods are concerned. There have indeed been detailed studies over shorter time periods in dialectology (e.g. Labov 1965), but the broader problem of why Latin, for instance, should give rise to seven or eight rather than thirty daughter languages, and where their boundaries should lie has not been tackled in general, theoretical terms. Sociolinguistics has so far operated on the micro-scale, dealing in the main with single communities, or localized regions. Sociolinguistics on the macro-scale remains to be developed. It should be noted that all theories for the origin of the Indo-European language groups, except that of Trubetzkoy, have hitherto been largely dependent upon divergence models. Divergence models are generally expressed in family tree form.

4. *Convergence models.* The wave theory of Johannes Schmidt was the earliest and most widely discussed of these. The phenomenon of convergence is of course frequently considered (e.g. Hock 1986, ch. 16) and the notions of the koine, of the *Sprachbund* and of the creole have now a major role in linguistic theory, while many of the phenomena studies in the fields of dialectology and sociolinguistics fall within this class. That being so, as noted earlier, it is remarkable that convergence models have played so little part in analyses of language change viewed over the longer term. The highly original convergence theory of Trubetzkoy (1939; for the Indo-European languages) has been much criticized (see Dixon 1997).

It must be expected that convergence models will begin to play a larger role in the field of the historical linguistics of language formation than they have in the past (see Dixon 1997).

These four classes of model are not, of course, contradictory; initial colonization happens for every area just once (unless followed by biological extinction and consequent language death), and sets the scene for the processes of divergence and convergence that are always operating simultaneously in any area.

When we are contemplating a linguistic spread zone, except in the rare cases where this is the result of an episode of initial colonization, most linguists agree that the likely explanation is one of language replacement. There are very few cases of an extended spread zone where the most plausible explanation is one of initial colonization: Polynesia is about the only spread-zone case where the bearers of the languages in question had been unpopulated until the arrival of the first speakers of the ancestral language. As further discussed below, it is only in very northerly climes, where the retreat of the ice sheets in post-glacial times opened up vast tracts of land for occupation, where spread-zone phenomena are found which result from initial colonization. This may be true for the Eskimo-Aleut language family as also the Finno-Ugric (and perhaps also the Chukchi-Kamchatkan).

Models for language replacement

It is possible to suggest a number of distinct and coherent models within the language replacement category:

a. *Subsistence/demography model,* where large numbers of people speaking the new language move into the territory. They do not conquer by force of arms but are able to settle because they are possessed of a subsistence adaptation which either occupies a different ecological niche from that of the earlier population, or is significantly more effective and productive within the same niche through the possession of some technological advantage. The farming/language dispersal model is, at least in some respects, a model in this category.

b. *Élite dominance,* where an incoming minority élite is able, usually by military means, to seize control of the levers of power within the territory. This implies that the incoming group will have some centralized organization (that is, a stratified, or highly-ranked structure), and often that the group conquered will have some ranking also.

c. *System collapse,* where the collapse of a highly-centralized (state) society leads to instability on its perimeter and to significant local movements of people and of power. Such was the position in the late days of the Roman Empire and their aftermath, the so-called 'migration period'. Here again the pre-existence of a stratified or state society is a precondition.

d. *Lingua franca,* where a trading language (pidgin) develops within the territory as a result of intense trading or other activity by outsiders. The pidgin is usually a simplified version of the outsider language, and a creole may develop, spoken by many of the inhabitants as their natal tongue.

No doubt other such models can be devised, and these refined, but without an explicit theoretical basis of this kind, it is difficult to see how such phenomena can be coherently discussed.

Factors in world linguistic diversity

When the distribution of the world's language families is considered, it is in some cases possible to account for the spread-zone regions in terms of language replacement, or, in the extreme north of late initial colonization (or re-colonization). It would seem that the creation of an entire spread zone through élite dominance is rare: the most prominent case is that of the Altaic language family. But élite dominance has been significant at least in the case of some sub-families. For instance the distribution of the Romance languages is dependent upon the formation of the Roman Empire through processes of élite dominance. The same may be true for the Indo-Iranian sub-family of Indo-European, although the mechanisms by which Indo-European speech came to Iran and then the Indian sub-continent are not yet well understood.

In the case of the Americas, the picture is more complex. While some aspects of the distribution may go right back to the time of initial colonization there have been many subsequent processes at work, and it can be argued that there are indeed spread zones within the American continents. Golla (2000, 62) uses the term in a rather different way from that employed here, and it is clear that the theme of language replacement in the Americas is one which needs to be explored very much more carefully. If we express the reservation that the Americas need more complete treatment, the position may be summarized as follows:

'Mosaic zone' (Class A) and 'spread zone' (Class B) language families

The present distribution of each language area is accounted for by one of the following five processes:

CLASS A: MOSAIC ZONE (PLEISTOCENE)
I. *Initial colonization prior to 12,000 BP*:
'Khoisan', 'Nilo-Saharan' (plus later 'aquatic' expansion,) Northern Caucasian, South Caucasian, 'Indo-Pacific or Papuan' (plus later farming changes), North Australian, 'Amerind' (with subsequent spread-zone processes), Localized ancestral groups of II and III (below).

CLASS B: SPREAD ZONE (POST-PLEISTOCENE)
II. *Farming dispersal after 10,000 BP*:
Niger-Kordofanian (specifically the Bantu languages), Afroasiatic, Indo-European, Elamo-Dravidian, Early Altaic, Sino-Tibetan, Austronesian, Austroasiatic.

III. *Northern, climate-sensitive adjustments after 10,000 BP*:
Uralic-Yukaghir, Chukchi-Kamchatkan, Na-Dene, Eskimo-Aleut

IV. *Élite dominance*:
Indo-Iranian, Later Altaic, Southern Sino-Tibetan (Han).

V. *Long-distance maritime colonization since 1400 AD* (Élite dominance plus farming dispersal)
Mainly Indo-European (English, Spanish, Portuguese, French).

So brief a summary does no justice to any of the cases. The treatment offered by Janhunen (1996) for Manchuria and neighbouring areas, relevant for the Altaic and Finno-Ugrian languages as well as the Chukchi-Kamchatkan, is particularly illuminating.

It should be noted also that the maritime colonizations since 1400 AD also involve a number of special cases. For although at first sight the spread of the English language to North America and Australia, and of Spanish and Portuguese to Latin America seem examples of élite dominance, on closer examination it was the stability of the new, European farming regime (based on wheat and barley, and sheep and cattle) which ensured the survival of the colonists. This was what Nettle (1999) has aptly termed the 'after shock' of the farming revolution, begun some ten millennia earlier in the Near East, and then in Europe.

The farming/language dispersal model

Before considering the farming/language dispersal more carefully, along with its genetic implications, it is perhaps useful to summarize first the radical effects of the farming dispersal process. The following statement was conceived with western Asia and Europe in mind, and the 'hilly flanks of the Fertile Crescent' constitute one such nuclear area. The spatial effects have been neatly expressed in a diagram

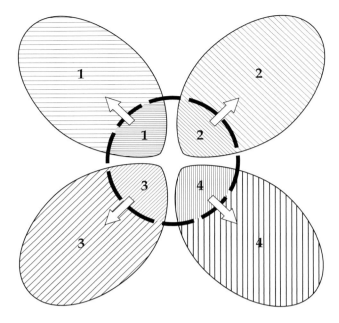

Figure 1.2. *Farming origins and language dispersal. When a transition to primary farming occurs within an area with some linguistic diversity (shown within the broken circle) the consequence of the ensuing agricultural dispersal is likely to be linguistic replacement in adjoining areas. The lobes represent the areas occupied by the subsequent language families derived from the corresponding proto-languages. Such processes may underlie the distribution of several of the world's linguistic macrofamilies. (After Sherratt & Sherratt 1988.)*

by Sherratt & Sherratt (1988) in which they show the initial process of spread-zone formation, which takes place adjacent to a 'nuclear area' of farming.

I have suggested that the distributions of the Indo-European, Afroasiatic and Elamo-Dravidian families seen today had their origins in this process, although the initial spread was in each case overlain by subsequent processes.

Farming dispersal
A nuclear area is defined supporting initially a specific range of wild plants (and sometimes animals) that later proved amenable to domestication. The farming 'package' of plants (and, where appropriate, animals), along with the appropriate exploitative techniques, becomes an expansive one dependent upon three factors:

1. *Suitability for* transplantation into new ecological niches of the plants (and animals), when sustained with the appropriate exploitative technol-

ogy by the accompanying human population, with propagation (i.e. seeding/planting or controlled breeding), protected growth (by weeding and manuring, or controlled feeding, e.g. by transhumance) and organized harvesting (or culling).

2. *Increased birth rate* and reduced rate of human infant mortality, and sometimes increased post-infantile life-expectancy, associated with aspects of the new subsistence regime. These accompany the sedentary life that farming facilitated.

3. *Greater intensity of production* as measured in terms of food (calories) per unit area, permitted by the new economy. Agricultural economies, even of a simple and non-intensive nature, are characteristically 50 times more productive in this sense than mobile hunter-gatherer economies, or have the capacity to be so.

In favourable cases the language or languages of the nuclear area are transmitted along with the plant and animal domesticates, either through demic diffusion of the farming population (the 'wave of advance model'), or through adoption by local hunter-gatherer groups of the new language along with the new agricultural economy (acculturation: the 'availability' model). The genetic effects of the two mechanisms are significantly different.

The statement above hints at the very large increase in population density which can result from the inception of farming in a given area. As implied above, the population density may increase by a factor of as much as 50 per cent, although this will not be the case for areas where special factors permitted a high population density in the hunter-gatherer economy, for instance when marine or riverine resources permitted high year-round productivity.

In some cases the incoming farmers may already outnumber the indigenous hunter-gatherer population, and in such cases there may be a fairly rapid language replacement. But in other cases the incoming farmers will be a minority. It is often assumed that they will initially undergo an exponential (and ultimately logistic) growth rate. But the point that has not yet been extensively discussed is that the local hunter-gatherer population may at the same time be taking up some of the new farming practices and itself undergoing population growth. But this means the languages of the indigenous population may continue to be spoken, and the language replacement process be of limited significance.

It is the case, however, that when farmers and hunter-gatherers occupy adjacent zones, and there is contact between them, the hunter-gatherers may in some cases come to speak the language of the incoming farmers (see Ehret 1988) by one of a number of possible processes of contact-induced language change (Zvelebil 1995; 1996; this volume). This situation is represented in Figure 1.3.

It should be recognized here that such a process is itself one of language replacement, although it is one which is not explicitly detailed in the discussion of élite dominance above, where it is subsumed (along with farming/language dispersal) under the subsistence/demography model. But the influence of the incoming language and its subsequent dominance is due less to demographic factors than to the social relations involved. This is not a matter of dominant war leaders or chiefs, for we are not necessarily speaking here of hierarchically ordered or stratified societies. The process can occur in the case of two neighbouring and essentially egalitarian societies, in cases where the farmer has greater success in winning a mate than does the hunter-gatherer.

What is needed here is a more careful sociolinguistic analysis, in which the differing roles of males and females are considered.

The archaeogenetics of farming dispersal

The first phase of research in the genetics of farming dispersal was dominated by the 'wave of advance' model of Ammerman & Cavalli-Sforza (1973) which, although very general in its formulation, has been applied primarily to Europe. The case of the possible spread of the Proto-Indo-European language, ancestral to the languages of the Indo-European language family, was put forward in a conference held in 1971 (Renfrew 1973), and developed subsequently (Renfrew 1987) laying emphasis upon the 'wave of advance' model. Its application to the whole of Europe was criticized on archaeological grounds by Zvelebil & Zvelebil (1988) and Whittle (1996). They suggested that the 'demic' diffusion' phase of the 'wave of advance' did not extend further than the Balkans and the Danubian Neolithic, and that to the north and west of that area contact-induced language change, with much less population movement, would be a more appropriate model.

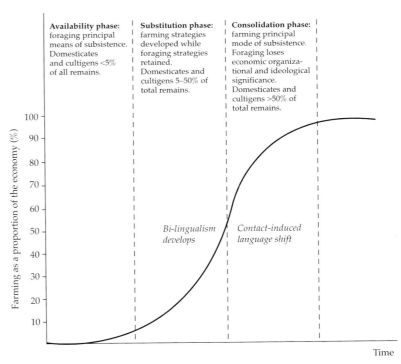

Figure 1.3. *Linguistic adjacency acceptance. The adoption by hunter-gatherers of the language of neighbouring cultivators through contact-induced language shift. (Based on Zvelebil 1996, 325, with additions.)*

Menozzi and colleagues (1978) first introduced genetic data into the discussion in their analysis of classical genetic markers for Europe (see also Cavalli-Sforza *et al.* 1994). The first principal component showed a marked cline from southeast to northwest which they explained as the product of the demic diffusion process associated with the farming 'wave of advance' from Anatolia to Europe. At first this seemed notable support from the view that Proto-Indo-European speech began in Anatolia, as originally argued in 1973 (Renfrew 1973; 2001).

The second phase of research (Richards *et al.* 1996), however, based upon the analysis of mitochondrial DNA, suggests that the greater part of the variability in mtDNA in Europe is to be dated back to the Late Upper Palaeolithic period (70 per cent), with a significant proportion to the Early Upper Palaeolithic (10 per cent) and only a limited proportion (20 per cent) to haplogroup J, associated by them with the arrival of farming at the beginning of the Neolithic period. This finding for mtDNA, which is passed down in the female line, has to a considerable extent been reinforced by recent work on Y-chromosome DNA, which is passed on down the male line (Underhill *et al.* 2000; Underhill this volume). At first sight, then, the findings of archaeogenetics do not support major gene flow at the onset of the Neolithic period in Europe. These results might at first be taken as calling into question the farming/language dispersal hypothesis in its application to Europe. Moreover a similar problem has arisen in the Pacific. What at first seemed a good correlation between the prehistoric archaeology and the historical linguistics for the Austronesian language family has recently been called into question (Oppenheimer & Richards 2001; Oppenheimer this volume) on the basis of the genetic data in an analogous way.

I will argue, however, that the wave of advance model has not been well understood by recent critics. Often the assumption is made that there is minimal or limited interaction (in terms of gene flow) between the incoming farmers and the indigenous hunter-gatherer population. In such a case a cline with an approximately linear decrease in gene frequency with distance from the area of farming origin would be expected — a pattern very much like that seen in the first Principal Component produced by Menozzi, Piazza and Cavalli-Sforza, in 1978 and in later work (Cavalli-Sforza *et al.* 1994).

The original wave of advance model, however (see Ammerman & Cavalli-Sforza 1984), did not make such an assumption, and allowed for significant gene flow between the incoming and pre-existing populations. Here this point is emphasized in what I have termed the Staged Population Interaction Wave of Advance (SPIWA). It produces a very different outcome, which is more in conformity with recent Y-chromosome studies (Semino *et al.* 2001).

Gene flow and farming dispersal: the Staged Population Interaction Wave of Advance model

It is arguable that progress in understanding the origins of the gene frequency distributions and the spatial distribution of DNA haplogroups has been facilitated in the case of Europe by the formulation of the explicit wave of advance model by Cavalli-Sforza and his colleagues. It will be recalled that the basis for the model is the postulated population growth accompanying the spread of farming, modelled as logistic in its growth pattern, with a population increase from hunter-gatherer to farming economy by a factor of as much as 100, although for modelling purposes a 50-fold increase (from 0.1 to 5 persons per sq.km) (Ammerman & Cavalli-Sforza 1973, 348; 1984, 63) was sometimes used.

In general the contrast was drawn between acculturation and demic diffusion:

Cultural diffusion would see the innovation of farm-

ing as being passed from one group to the next without subsequent movement of farming populations. According to the second explanation — demic diffusion — the spread of farming would derive from the local growth and expansion of Neolithic populations (Ammerman & Cavalli-Sforza 1984, 134).

In the initial formulation of the model the question of genetic interaction (i.e. interbreeding) between the incoming and the indigenous populations was not modelled. In subsequent modelling, acculturation (specifically taken as the transfer of hunter-gatherer individuals to the population of farmers) was considered, with values of B, the acculturation rate, from 0.001 to 0.0001 per generation. Simulation studies obtained were compared with the first six principal components resulting from an analysis of classical gene frequencies for Europe (Menozzi *et al.* 1978) and the resulting patterning was compared with that obtained from the 'wave of advance' simulation studies. The correspondence between the first principal component and the 'wave of advance' simulation found sufficiently good to support the hypothesis that the clinal patterning was largely the product of the Neolithic wave of advance.

Subsequent DNA studies have however suggested that the most frequent mtDNA (Richards *et al.* 1996) and Y-chromosome (Underhill *et al.* 2000) haplogroup frequencies were the result of demographic processes taking place in Upper Palaeolithic times. On the other hand, the mtDNA haplogroup J (Sykes 1999) and the Y-chromosome haplogroups 4, 9, 10 and 11 (Semino *et al.* 2001) are currently dated to the time when they could well be seen as the product of a Neolithic dispersal.

The SPIWA model
The purpose of this model is to show how the concept of a 'wave of advance' can give a valid insight into the way a relatively small-scale process of demic diffusion can have a massive linguistic effect — the effective replacement of the language of the indigenous hunter-gatherers by that of the incoming farmers — while at the same time showing the very limited (but discernible) impact upon the gene frequency, or haplotype frequency, distribution of haplotypes characteristic of the original incoming farmers which recent mtDNA and Y-chromosome researches have indicated in the case of Europe at the inception of the Neolithic. The model may usefully be compared with the simulation developed by Chikhi (this volume) with which it shares a number of assumptions.

The SPIWA model utilizes many of the insights

(and assumptions) of the original 'wave of advance' model for the spread of farming. In particular it assumes that the mean population density for hunter-gatherers in most territories will be exceeded by a large factor (of between 20 and 100) by that of a well-established farming economy on the same territories. At the same time it is recognized that some coastal, riverine or lacustrine locations will in favourable circumstances permit a much larger population density of fisher-hunter-gatherers than would otherwise be the case, and that such areas have to be treated with particular attention to this factor. It assumes also the random displacement behaviour assumed for all groups under the original model.

It differs, however, from the original model in assuming that gene flow will occur between the incomers and the local, indigenous population. Moreover it recognizes that there will be an asymmetry between male versus female and incomer versus indigene in the process. One may well imagine a situation where hunter-gatherer females would in some cases be assimilated to farming villages, but that the uptake of females of farming community origin by hunter-gatherer groups might be less. Again there might be arguments for suggesting that casual mating encounters between farming community males and hunter gatherer females might be more frequent than between hunter-gatherer males and farming community females.

Gene flow may come about in various ways, and is not well summarized by a single parameter. For instance a gene flow of 0 per cent between populations implies no mating between the incomer and the indigenous populations. The original 'wave of advance' model, where the incoming farmers steer clear of the local hunter-gatherers, would fulfill that. There the wave of advance accompanying the farming economy would take place without any hunter-gatherer participation. But a gene flow of 0 per cent may also be imagined for the sort of acculturation model where the indigenous population takes up the practices of farming from the incomers, along with the domesticates themselves, but without any intermarriage. There the hunter-gatherer population would experience the logistic growth inherent in the model, and the wave of advance would continue to be propagated. But the geographical distribution of gene frequency (in relative, percentile terms) might not change very much from the pattern of the original hunter-gatherers.

But in any case we shall wish to consider also those cases where the gene flow is not negligible. As we shall see, the resultant patternings may be very different.

It is often suggested that there were two principal routes for the dissemination of farming in Europe: up the Danube valley, and along the north coasts of the Mediterranean. For the purposes of argument we shall use the former in formulating the model, since maritime movements have a different logic to terrestrial ones.

With the model of van Andel & Runnels (1995) in mind, we shall imagine small groups of farming settlers arriving by sea from Anatolia on the eastern coasts of mainland Greece and soon settling in small enclaves in the plains of Macedonia, Thessaly and further south. Thessaly and Macedonia may be considered as one major region whose population becomes predominantly a farming one. The next stage envisaged is the transition to farming in southern Serbia. A further stage would be represented by the Great Hungarian Plain, and another by the loess lands of the Czech Republic, where the Danubian (Linearbandkeramik) culture became well-established. We shall consider the spread of this culture across Austria, Germany and the Low Countries to represent a further stage, and its dissemination to France and the Paris Basin the last of these.

In the first crude version of the model we postulate, then, a number of contiguous, cell-like territories. At this stage it is appropriate to imagine the farming population becoming established in one of these cells before pioneers move on to the next cell or region, having developed the further adaptive changes in farming techniques which that might entail. And since in the territories in question there is some evidence for early Neolithic farming villages, we shall speak in terms of villages. The pattern is then one of numerous, successive stages, in each of which the population grows to a certain level over a period of several generations before the next stage is colonized.

In the earliest version of the wave of advance model the local hunter-gatherer population was largely disregarded, and the population growth took place among the incoming farmers. Later an acculturation coefficient (Ammerman & Cavalli-Sforza 1984, 129) was added. But it may be helpful to think more carefully about the thinly scattered hunter-gatherer population. When the first farming groups enter this cell or region from its neighbour to the southeast there may initially be as few or fewer of the incoming farmers as there are hunter-gatherers. The farmers will begin with a few homesteads which gradually grow to villages perhaps with a population doubling approximately every five generations.

A hypothetical case

Take a linear series of adjacent territories, A to F etc., of equal size (say 2000 sq.km) each initially populated by indigenous hunter-gatherers of characteristically European (pre-farming) mtDNA and NRY haplogroups, with a population of 100 females and 100 males and hence an overall population density of 0.1 persons per sq.km. It is assumed that hunter-gatherer population growth is here zero or very small.

Allow groups of Neolithic farmers with characteristically 'Anatolian' mtDNA and NRY haplogroups to enter territory A in groups of 10, one group per 5-year interval, for 100 years: thus a total of 200 immigrants over the century.

Assuming a generation time of 25 years, allow one hunter-gatherer female or one hunter-gatherer male to join each farming group over 25 years, i.e. one per generation. (Strictly the figure should be 1.1 or 1.2 per generation. It is not particularly significant for this simple model whether 1 person per generation joins the hunter-gatherer population from the farming population, but we shall in the first instance assume that the exchanges are symmetrical.) And allow this to happen for two generations — i.e. twice.

Now assume that the farming population is undergoing rapid growth, with a doubling time of about 130 years (see Hassan 1981, 140), equivalent to a growth rate of roughly 0.5 per cent per annum (Ammerman & Cavalli-Sforza 1984, 71). After about 250 years the farming population will have increased fourfold to 800 persons, giving a farming population density of 0.4 persons per sq. km and a total population density (assuming roughly zero growth for the hunter-gatherers) of 0.5 persons per sq.km. After a further 250 years, if exponential growth continues, this would rise to 1.7 persons per sq.km.

Assume moreover that after 250 years there is some limited budding off of farmers who move from territory A to territory B: as before, in groups of 10, one group every five years for 100 years. There will be a population transfer of some 200 persons from area A to area B, so far populated only by hunter-gatherers at the same population density as was originally with the case with area A. The population density in A would be reduced thereby to 0.4 persons per sq.km, and after 500 years would have reached 1.3 persons per sq.km. Note that there is no suggestion here of high population densities approaching some notional carrying capacity: simply that after a few centuries' growth, some groups in each subsequent generation may find it more convenient to move a few tens of kilometres into virgin farming territory.

Now consider the genetic composition of the farming population which reaches B from A. For two generations in A each group of 10 farmers (slightly more after each generation) has had a young farmer (in genetic terms) replaced by a young hunter-gatherer, who is assumed to take up farming. Since initially the farmer and hunter-gatherer haplogroups were exclusive, there will now be a frequency of 80 per cent farming haplotypes and 20 per cent hunter-gatherer haplotypes in the population of farmers who transfer from A to B.

Now allow the entire process to be replicated (from B to C etc.). After a further 250 years, there will be a population transfer of 200 farmers from B to C. And crucially this will have 64 per cent (80 per cent of 80 per cent) 'farmer' genes and 36 per cent 'European' genes. By cell F, after 1250 years, there are only 33 per cent farming genes in the incoming 'farming' population and 67 per cent indigenous genes.

Of course such a model may be simulated with a variety of parameters. But I have chosen the figures so that after five episodes or stages the farming population contains only 33 per cent farming genes, and after 10 stages or 2500 years, in cell K it will contain only 10 per cent. (After 3750 years the farming population of cell P will contain only three per cent 'farming' genes.)

Now the point of this slightly laboured exercise is to illustrate the general case which a more sophisticated simulation will demonstrate: that a steady population growth can indeed sustain a 'wave of advance' (which nobody doubts) and to consider the genetic and linguistic implications. The incoming immigrant population of farmers is in this case modest: of the same order as the existing hunter-gatherer population. The simulation would work along similar lines if the incoming farmers were fewer in numbers than the hunter-gatherers, but the process would be slightly slower.

The outcome, however, is clear. In *linguistic* terms it seems evident that the farming population, assimilating only 10 per cent hunter-gatherers per generation for just a couple of generations, would continue to speak the parental language of the farmers, albeit with ongoing borrowings and modifications. We could expect this language to be propagated from cell A to cell B and so on. Even after many generations, in distant cells K or P, it will unequivocally be the daughter of the language spoken by the immigrant farmers in cell A. But look at the genetic picture. The 'wave of advance' has indeed propagated the incoming farming language, but the *genetic* signal is attenuated: after ten cell transfers down to just ten per cent of the incoming 'farming' haplotype frequencies, after fifteen stages to three per cent.

The consequences are evident. If we consider a series of successive stages, with significant population interaction (of the order of ten per cent per generation) — i.e. gene flow between hunter-gatherers and farmers — the signal of the original 'farming' genes becomes so attenuated after a few hundred kilometres and a millennium or two that it is scarcely to be distinguished from that of the hunter-gatherer background. Indeed the scale of decrement matches to a convenient extent the Y-chromosome haplotype frequencies reported by Semino *et al.* (2001) for the Anatolian 'farming' haplogroups which they identified (see Table 1.1).

The point of this argument is not to insist that the 'wave of advance' model is generally applicable. I agree with the comments of Zvelebil and others that it applies only in certain cases. But the point is that where it is applicable, we would not expect to see very high gene frequencies for the haplogroups identified as characteristic of an earlier stage of the process of the original immigrant farmers. We should predict, in the case of farming dispersal, that in some cases the incoming language will indeed be propagated over great areas while the incoming haplogroups rapidly fall with distance to very low frequencies.

Clearly in the model which I have adopted there are many parameters which may vary. In particular, if there is more admixture of female hunter-gatherer genes than male hunter-gatherer genes in successive populations of farmers — as many scholars have predicted — then we shall see more rapid attenuation with distance in mtDNA 'farming' haplogroup frequencies than in Y-chromosome haplogroup frequencies. This seems indeed to be the case with the data now available.

Implications
The point here is that the frequency of the incoming haplogroup is likely, on this model, to decline exponentially with distance, the decay curve being a decreasing step function which, with many steps, approximates to a declining exponential function. The variable here is of course the haplogroup frequency in percentage terms: absolute populations figures are not evaluated.

There is a parallel here with the monotonic decreasing decay curves for the quantities of a traded material, as distance from the source increases (Renfrew 1977, 78). If the attenuation is in two dimensions rather than linear as in the case described here, the fall-off is Gaussian rather than exponential (Renfrew 1977, 81).

Table 1.1. *The fall-off with increasing distance from Turkey of the 'Neolithic' Y-chromosome haplogroups. (After Semino et al. 2001.)*

Region	%Eu 4+9, 10, 11	Distance (miles) from Turkey (Konya)
Lebanese	74.1	400
Syrian	55.0	400
Turkish	63.2	0
Georgia	66.6	600
Greek	47.3	550
Albanian	51.1	750
Macedonia	35.0	600
Croatia	13.8	1050
Czech Republic	15.5	1200
Hungary	13.3	950
Ukraine*	14.0	1200
Germany	6.2	1350
Holland	3.7	1650
Poland	3.6	1200
Saami	0	2100
Calabria	53.9	900
Sardinia	35.0	1300
Central Italy	26.0	1200
France	26.0	1700
Andalusia	20.6	2200
Catalonia	16.7	1700
Spanish Basque	4.4	2200
French Basque	4.5	1800

* Ukraine 1200 miles by land (600 by sea)

Now of course it should be understood that this model allows one to discuss the haplogroup frequencies as they would have been immediately following the processes in question. As time passes subsequently, genetic drift may take place, but so will further admixture, so that there will be a tendency for frequency differences to diminish and for homogeneity to increase. The rate at which this occurs may vary as between male and female haplogroups depending on the differing behaviour patterns in relation to mating and translocating for males and females respectively.

It is notable that in their presentation of these data, Semino *et al.* (2001, fig. 2) find that a linear plot against distance is obtained when the ordinate is the logarithm of the gene frequency. This is the indicator of exponential fall-off and conforms in that respect with the model proposed here. The frequency data are given here in Table 1.1 along with the distance from Turkey (assumed to be the source both for the Mediterranean and Danubian farming dispersal routes). The Danubian distance is calculated following the path indicated by Renfrew (1987, 160), the maritime route assuming that Calabria is the first landfall after Greece. Chikhi (this volume) employs a comparable approach in discussing the same Y-chromosome data.

The essential point here is that a substantial wave of advance can indeed occur while leaving only quite limited genetic traces, although these are indeed there. When there are Palaeolithic demographic processes to take into account (i.e. unless the territories were uninhabited until post-Palaeolithic times) these will often be greater in magnitude than the later ones. This is a key point in seeking to reconcile genetic, archaeological and linguistic data. It may be particularly relevant for the western regions of Europe and for Austronesia.

What is needed, however, is an indicator of where a wave of advance peters out, and contact-induced language change and Neolithization through acculturation take over. The main point is that a substantial wave of advance makes only limited impact on haplogroup frequencies if there is population interaction during the process.

Cautionary observations

From these preliminary observations it would seem that there are arguments, certainly so far as the Y-chromosome data for Europe are concerned, for thinking that very strong demographic processes were involved in the spread of farming across Europe. This arose primarily from the circumstance that the spread of farming was a process accompanied by very pronounced population growth. There was, then, very marked gene flow from one area to the next. The crucial point, however, is that the growing population at the edge of the wave of advance had received only a limited percentage of genes, ultimately of Anatolian origin, representing different haplogroups from those previously present in Europe. This area soon changed in status from receptor to donor, as it passed on the techniques of farming and the plant and animal domesticates to the next area down the line.

By the time the 'wave of advance' reached northwest Europe, the proportion of ultimately Anatolian genes within it was very much attenuated. It is possible, for instance, to think of a situation where the population on the French side of the English Channel grew significantly in numbers first with the influx of farmers from eastern France and then with the demographic increase associated with the local adoption of farming. But the haplogroup frequencies of the population there were not much changed

in the process. If, at the outset, they did not differ significantly from those of the hunter-gatherer population of southern Britain, a significant influx of farmers from France, across the Channel, would not produce any significant change in gene frequencies. This point is well brought out in the paper by Chikhi (this volume), but he does not address himself to the concomittant phenomenon of the continuing transmission of the language of the early first farmers without radical attenuation (although word loss and lexical drift will have been a continuing part of the process).

Throughout this process, however, it is possible that in each local region along the line, the incoming population (now farmers) was actually greater in number than the local indigenous population in the region in question. In such circumstances it is perfectly possible that the language of the farmers, no doubt significantly modified in the transmission process, would be adopted also (even if not at once) by the numerically less significant hunter-gatherer population, some of whom will themselves have turned to farming.

The point of this rather long discussion is to emphasize that it is perfectly possible to envisage a 'wave of advance', with very local population displacements, in which the linguistic and genetic effects would be markedly different. We could certainly postulate a model where at least half of the population in any local area along the way would, at a crucial early stage, be composed of incoming farmers from the immediately previous area. The product of this 'down the line' phenomenon could be the transmission of the language of the incomers, and yet the significant attenuation of the signal carried on by their genes.

Ultimately the difference depends on the principle that a language does not get spoken by halves. It may be spoken or it may be dropped. But a language is a unity, and while there may be loan words and borrowings it cannot be treated in the same percentile terms as can gene frequencies.

References

Ammerman, A. & L.L Cavalli-Sforza, 1973. A population model for the diffusion of early farmers in Europe, in *The Explanation of Culture Change: Models in Prehistory*, ed. C. Renfrew. London: Duckworth, 343–58.

Ammerman, A. & L.L. Cavalli-Sforza, 1984. *The Neolithic Transition and the Genetics of Populations in Europe*. Princeton (NJ): Princeton University Press.

Austerlitz, R., 1980. Language family density in North

America and Eurasia. *Ural-Altäische Jahrbücher* 52, 1–10.

Bellwood, P., 1989. The colonization of the Pacific: some current hypotheses, in *The Colonization of the Pacific: a Genetic Trail*, eds. A.V.S. Hill & W. Serjeantson. Oxford: Oxford University Press, 1–59.

Bellwood, P., 1991. The Austronesian dispersal and the origin of languages. *Scientific American* 265(1), 88–93.

Bellwood, P., 1996. The origins and spread of agriculture in the Indo-Pacific region: gradualism and diffusion or revolution and colonization?, in Harris (ed.), 465–98.

Bellwood, P., 1997. Prehistoric cultural explanations for the existence of widespread language families, in *Archaeology and Linguistics: Aboriginal Australia in Global Perspective*, eds. P. McConvell & N. Evans. Melbourne: Oxford University Press, 123–34.

Cavalli-Sforza, L.L., P. Menozzi & A. Piazza, 1994. *The History and Geography of Human Genes*: Princeton (NJ): Princeton University Press.

Diakonoff, I., 1998, The earliest Semitic society. *Journal of Semitic Studies* 43, 209–17.

Dixon, R.M.W., 1997. *The Rise and Fall of Languages*. Cambridge: Cambridge University Press.

Ehret, C., 1988, Language change and the material correlates of languages and ethnic shift. *Antiquity* 62, 564–74.

Ehret, C., 1998. *An African Classical Age: Eastern and Southern Africa in World History, 1000 BC to AD 400*. Oxford: J. Currey.

Glover, I.C. & C.F.W. Higham, 1996. New evidence for early rice cultivation in South, Southeast and East Asia, in Harris (ed.), 413–42.

Golla, V., 2000. Language families of North America, in *America Past, America Present: Genes and Languages in the Americas and Beyond*, ed. C. Renfrew. (Papers in the Prehistory of Languages.) Cambridge: McDonald Institute for Archaeological Research, 59–76.

Harris, D.R. (ed.), 1996. *The Origins and Spread of Agriculture and Pastoralism in Eurasia*. London: UCL Press.

Hassan, F.A., 1981. *Demographic Archaeology*. London: Academic Press.

Higham, C.F.W., 1996. Archaeology and linguistics in Southeast Asia: implications of the Austric hypothesis. *Bulletin of the Indo-Pacific Prehistory Association* 14, 110–18.

Hock, H.H., 1986. *Principles of Historical Linguistics*. Berlin: Mouton de Gruyter.

Janhunen, J., 1996. *Manchuria: an Ethnic History*. Helsinki: The Finno-Ugrian Society.

Labov, W., 1965. On the mechanism of linguistic change, *Georgetown University Monographs on Language and Linguistics* 18, 91–114.

Menozzi, P., A. Piazza & L.L. Cavalli-Sforza, 1978. Synthetic map of human gene frequencies in Europe. *Science* 210, 786–92.

Nettle, D., 1999. *Linguistic Diversity*. Oxford: Oxford University Press.

Nichols, J., 1992. *Linguistic Diversity in Space and Time*.

Chicago (IL): University of Chicago Press.

Oppenheimer, S. & M. Richards, 2001. Slow boat to Melanesia? *Nature* 410, 166–7.

Phillipson, D.W., 1997. The spread of the Bantu languages. *Scientific American* 236(4), 106–14.

Renfrew, C., 1973. Problems in the general correlation of archaeological and linguistic strata in prehistoric Greece: the model of the autochthonous origin, in *Bronze Age Migrations in the Aegean*, eds. R.A. Crossland & A. Birchall. London: Duckworth, 263–76.

Renfrew, C., 1977. Alternative models for exchange and spatial distribution, in *Exchange Systems in Prehistory*, eds. T. Earle & J. Ericson. New York (NY): Academic Press, 71–90.

Renfrew, C., 1987. *Archaeology and Language: the Puzzle of Indo-European Origins*. London: Jonathan Cape.

Renfrew, C., 1989. Models of change in language and archaeology. *Transactions of the Philological Society*, 87(2), 103–55.

Renfrew, C., 1991. Before Babel, speculations on the origins of linguistic diversity. *Cambridge Archaeological Journal* 1(1), 3–23.

Renfrew, C., 1992. World languages and human dispersals, a minimalist view, in *Transition to Modernity*, eds. J.H. Hall & I.C. Jarvie. Cambridge: Cambridge University Press, 11–68.

Renfrew, C., 2000. At the edge of knowability: towards a prehistory of languages. *Cambridge Archaeological Journal* 10(1), 7–34.

Renfrew, C., 2001. The Anatolian origins of Proto-Indo-European and the autochthony of the Hittites, in *Greater Anatolia and the Indo-Hittite Language Family*, ed. R. Drews. (*Journal of Indo-European Studies* Monograph Series 38.) Washington (DC): Institute for the Study of Man, 36–63.

Renfrew, C. & K. Boyle (eds.), 2000. *Archaeogenetics: DNA and the Population Prehistory of Europe*. (McDonald Institute Monographs). Cambridge: McDonald Institute for Archaeological Research.

Richards, M.R., H. Corte-Real, P. Forster, V. Macaulay, H. Wilkinson-Herbots, A. Demaine, S. Papiha, R. Hedges, H.-J. Bandelt & B. Sykes, 1996. Paleolithic and Neolithic lineages in the European mitochondrial gene pool. *American Journal of Human Genetics* 59, 186–203.

Semino, O., G. Passarino, P.J. Oefner, A.A. Lin, S. Arbuzova, L.E. Beckman, G. De Benedictis, P. Francalacci, A. Kouvatsi, S. Limborska, M. Marcikiae, A. Mika, D. Primorac, A.S. Santachiara-Benerecetti, L.L. Cavalli-Sforza & P.A. Underhill, 2001. The genetic legacy of Palaeolithic *Homo sapiens sapiens* in extant Europeans: a Y-chromosome perspective. *Science* 290, 1155–9.

Sherratt A. & S. Sherratt, 1988. The archaeology of Indo-European, an alternative view. *Antiquity* 62, 584–94.

Sykes, B., 1999. The molecular genetics of European ancestry. *Philosophical Transactions of the Royal Society, Biological Sciences* 354, 131–40.

Terrell, J., 1988. *Prehistory in the Pacific Islands*. Cambridge:

Cambridge University Press.

Trubetzkoy, N.S., 1939. Gedanken über das Indogermanen problem. *Acta Linguistica 1*, 81–9. [Reprinted in Scherer, A. (ed.), 1968. *Die Urheimat der Indogermanen*. Darmstadt: Wissenschaftliche Buchgesellschaft, 214–23.]

Underhill, P.A., P. Shen, A.A. Lin, L. Jin, G. Passarino, W.H. Yang, E. Kauffman, B. Bonné-Tamir, J. Bertranpetit, P. Francalacci, M. Ibrahim, T. Jenkins, J.R. Kidd, S.Q. Mehdi, M.T. Seielstad, R.S. Wells, A. Piazza, R.W. Davis, M.W. Feldman, L.L. Cavalli-Sforza & P.J. Oefner, 2000. Y-chromosome sequence variation and the history of human populations. *Nature Genetics* 26, 358–61.

van Andel, T.H. & C.N. Runnels, 1995, The earliest farmers in Europe. *Antiquity* 69, 481–500.

Whittle, A., 1996. *Europe in the Neolithic: the Creation of New Worlds*. Cambridge: Cambridge University Press.

Zvelebil, M., 1995. Indo-European origins and the agricultural transition in Europe. *Journal of European Archaeology* 3(1), 33–70.

Zvelebil, M., 1996. The agricultural frontier and the transition to farming in the circum-Baltic region, in Harris (ed.), 323–45.

Zvelebil, M. & K.V. Zvelebil, 1988. Agricultural transition and Indo-European dispersals. *Antiquity* 62, 574–8.

Chapter 2

Farmers, Foragers, Languages, Genes:
the Genesis of Agricultural Societies

Peter Bellwood

The central hypothesis under discussion in this conference proposes that early farmers, by virtue of their healthy demographic and economic profiles, frequently colonized outwards from homeland regions, incorporating hunter-gatherer populations[1] and in the process spreading foundation trails of material culture, language and genetic distinctiveness.[2] An opposing hypothesis equates the spread of farming mainly with adoption by the descendants of *in situ* hunter-gatherers, without necessarily any spread of new languages or genes at all. The data that may be called upon to support or refute either of these hypotheses, or to promote a more comfortable middle way, relate to three major categories of dispersal phenomena:

a) the dispersal of Neolithic/Formative agricultural lifestyles and economies, as documented principally by the archaeological and natural science records (Fig. 2.1);

b) the dispersal of major agriculturalist language families (Figs. 2.2 & 2.3),[3] as documented mainly by the comparative study of existing languages (written documents in most parts of the world generally being too young to be of great assistance); and

c) the expansion of genetically distinctive human populations, or the dispersal by gene flow of certain genetic and phenotypic characteristics, as documented by population genetics and palaeo-anthropology.

Regardless of hypothesis or discipline, each of these three types of dispersal involves concepts of a homeland, followed by an expansion covering a specifiable geographical extent, often a very large one. Each dispersal progressed through time, sometimes measured in millennia, although some were clearly much faster than others and sometimes the rates of spread oscillated markedly. Each dispersal involved processes of phylogenetic differentiation, cross-cut by the results of reticulative interaction with contemporary external entities.[4] With the exception of previously uninhabited regions such as eastern Oceania, each dispersal progressed through pre-existing landscapes of archaeological, linguistic and genetic variation. Hence, we have a series of dynamic situations involving the dispersing entities themselves, with their internal driving forces, and the external social and natural environments to which they were obliged to adapt.

It is useful to think of these dispersal situations as finite processes of geographical spread with sloping trajectories through time. Our interest, for the purposes of this conference, is in the dispersals themselves, in their tempos, extents, densities of coverage and so forth, rather than in the myriad transformations that have muddled up, even buried traces of them in subsequent millennia. We must remember here that these dispersals occupied very small proportions of the total prehistoric chronology in any *specific* area, thus they have a certain ephemerality as events, combined with a far greater presence as contributors to subsequent cultural and biological patterning. As an example, it is the moving cusp of Austronesian language expansion from Taiwan and Island Southeast Asia into Oceania that is the topic of interest from the perspective of this conference, a cusp that evidently spread through many regions very rapidly (see Pawley, this volume). Events that occurred during the following millennia of phylogenetic differentiation and ethnogenetic interaction between Austronesian and other unrelated languages are of less interest for dispersal questions, although sometimes our understanding of any actual dispersal phenomenon will also require understanding of such subsequent transformations. This being the case, we must ask how the data corpus that survives for

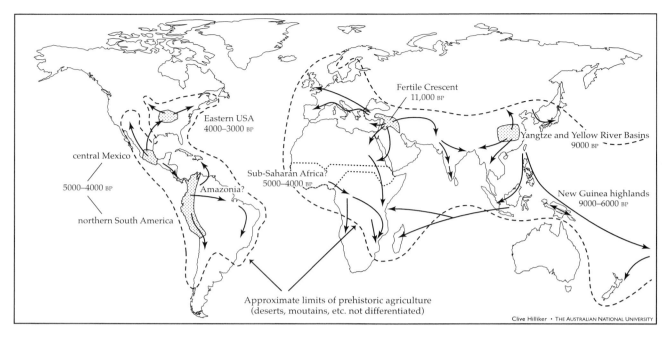

Figure 2.1. *Geographical trends in early agricultural dispersal out of regions of agricultural origin, according to the archaeological record.*

our perusal today — in the ground, in languages and in the bodies of the living — can reflect precisely on events, often very short-lived ones in terms of individual locations, that happened so many millennia ago.

How can we understand farming dispersals? Some considerations of language spread on a large scale

A number of observations about the large-scale spread of languages are of significance, and often overlooked by both archaeologists and linguists alike. From my own perspective, it is the linguistic evidence that gives the strongest support to the idea of agricultural dispersal as a population-based process involving farmer spread rather than hunter-gatherer adoption. This is because of the sheer weight of comparative evidence that suggests that long-distance agriculturalist proto-language spreads most probably occurred hand in hand with spreads of native speakers, rather than through language shift alone.

This comparative evidence is drawn from a historical perspective that suggests that conquest empires that did not invest in substantial programs of colonization never spread languages very far or very successfully, at least not on the long-term and whole-population level of the universal vernacular (short-lived trade or élite languages are of little interest in

this regard). One can quote many examples here — Latin beyond the inner provinces of the Roman Empire, Persian beyond the Achaemenid heartland, Greek beyond the Archaic and Hellenistic colonies (and even the latter were relatively ephemeral in a linguistic sense), Mongol beyond Mongolia, English and Dutch in the non-colonized (by Europeans) regions of Malaysia, India, Indonesia, and so forth. These examples suggest that successful language spread, over the long term, the long distance and at the level of the whole population, has always required a substantial spread of native speakers, as has the spread of English to Australasia and North America in the past two centuries.

Rather than examining at further length the historical documentation necessary to support these views, I will give one example — that of Arabic (Goldschmidt 1996; Levtzion 1979; Pentz 1992; Petry 1998). Contrary I think to some popular opinion, the Arabic language did not spread simply with Islam. In Jordan and Syria there were already widespread Arabic-speaking populations whose ancestors had migrated from Arabia long before the Arab conquest. In Iraq and Egypt, the Arabic language spread via garrison cities of settled Arab soldiers (about 40,000 in the case of Fustat near Cairo) and their families. The Arab conquests did not extend into South or Southeast Asia, thus the vast majority of Moslems in the world today, more in Indonesia than in any other

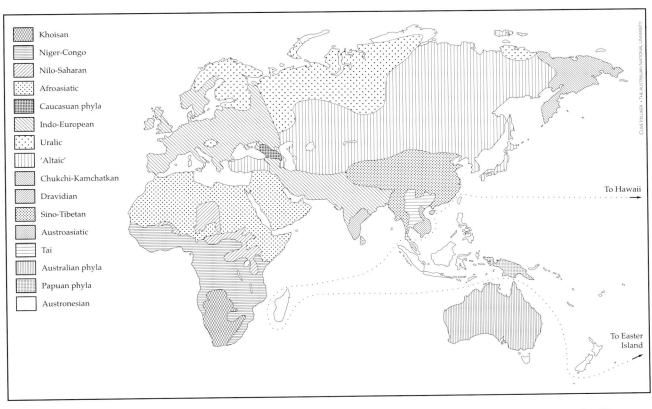

Figure 2.2. *The major language families of the Old World. After Ruhlen 1987. The major agriculturalist families as defined in this chapter are Indo-European, Afro-Asiatic (allowing for uncertainty in the agricultural status of Proto-Afro-Asiatic), Dravidian, Bantu (allowing for uncertainty in the agricultural status of pre-Bantu stages of Niger-Congo), Sino-Tibetan, Austroasiatic, Austronesian, Daic, and possibly Trans New Guinea (the most widespread Papuan family).*

country, speak not a word of Arabic (except in the form of lexical borrowings into other languages) unless they are reciting the Koran, in which case they use seventh-century rather than modern Arabic. This language thus spread essentially in the first place in the mouths of Arabic-speaking settlers, in the conquered areas of the Middle East and North Africa only, and in the early years it seems there was very little shift to the language on the part of other non-Arab populations. The whole process was no doubt assisted by the association of Arabic with the Koran, but even this was clearly not a driving factor behind *significant* language spread. In later centuries, of course, many Middle Eastern and North African populations not of Arab origin must have adopted the Arabic language, but this, from the viewpoint of this conference, is a little beside the point. Our interest here is in the original spread and its causation, and this was manifestly not a spread caused by language shift, but by native speaker movement.

If a cosmopolitan language such as Arabic (or Latin during the Roman Empire) had such difficulty in spreading into non-colonized regions, even aided by a document as linguistically-persuasive as the Koran, what hope can we have that Neolithic languages could have spread over the vast distances required to found language families by such means? It is worth noting also that Arabic has not spread through processes of language mixing; neither did any other language on a large geographical scale before the rise of forced translocation on the part of conquest powers (Bakker 2000).

The implication of all of this, in my opinion, is that the extents of the foundation geographical spreads required to explain the existences of the major language families (e.g. Madagascar to Easter Island for Austronesian, Ireland to Bangladesh for Indo-European, Cameroon to South Africa for Niger-Congo [mainly Bantu], and Central Mexico to Idaho for Uto-Aztecan), demand that native-speaker movement on a substantial scale, before literacy and before states, must come somehow into the equation.

Figure 2.3. *The major language families of the New World. The major agriculturalist families as defined in this chapter are Uto-Aztecan, Oto-Manguean, Mixe-Zoquean, Mayan, Chibchan, Tucanoan, Panoan, Quechumaran, Arawakan and Cariban. The language families of the eastern USA are less clearly agricultural in origin, although the eventual distributions of the latter (especially Iroquoian and Siouan) perhaps reflect the acquisition of maize agriculture within the past 2000 years.*

This is a very serious matter for archaeologists to consider. Languages cannot simply move by themselves (although Nichols 1997 appears to be suggesting that they can), and processes such as language shift, trade language formation and élite dominance, that seem to remove the need for native speaker penetration into a new region, are either far too restricted in geographical extent, or in their sociocultural and historical requirements, ever to have played more than minor roles. Somehow, in prehistory, both languages and their speakers moved, and some moved trans-generationally a very long way indeed.

The records of these movements must exist somewhere in the archaeological record, and for those language families that have convincing agricultural cognate sets in their foundation proto-languages it is not too difficult to suggest where in time many such movements might be located. The answer is along one of the major technological, economic and demographic unconformities in human history, that represented by the alteration of trajectory from Mesolithic/Archaic to Neolithic/Formative. I believe this set of linguistic observations to be of very high significance; indeed, they inform my perspective on farming dispersals perhaps more directly than the data from archaeology.

But, of course, native speakers over the whole extent of a language family need not be genetically or culturally identical. Indeed, any native speaker can always have one non-native parent. Yet one suspects that there are constraints to any *total* independence of biological trajectory from those of language and culture, especially in times of active population dispersal. It is possible that farming dispersals were relatively isomorphic in situations of resource competition, whether against hunter-gatherers or other farmers, and may have remained so for quite long periods until reticulation inexorably won the day. For instance, both Arabic (Levtzion 1979) and Proto-Oceanic (Blust 2000) are believed to have spread initially without interaction with the unrelated languages around them, only later coming into increasing contact as they became adopted by other groups as regional *lingua francas*.

There is one other very important observation I wish to make from a linguistic perspective. Some agriculturalist language families spread over vast areas leaving virtually no enclaves and very few indicators of the prior existence of other unrelated languages. Obvious examples here are Bantu (as by far the most extensive subgroup within the Niger-Congo family) and the Malayo-Polynesian (Austronesian) languages of most of Island Southeast Asia.

Both are agriculturalist language groupings and both represent fairly recent (post-3500 BP) spreads of language, evidently of farmers replacing or assimilating earlier hunter-gatherers. Despite obvious situations of biological admixture, in neither situation is there significant archaeological or linguistic evidence for any widespread survival of hunter-gatherer societies as separate cultural or linguistic entities over the long term. These spreads reflect farmer dispersal *par excellence*, through hunter-gatherer landscapes. Did Indo-European, Dravidian, Afroasiatic, Uto-Aztecan and Oto-Manguean (as examples drawn from many) also once have such early blanket-like distributions? For Indo-European, the answer for many fringe regions of western and northern Europe may be *no*, given the strong survival of non-Indo-European languages into historical times, but what of central and eastern Europe and much of northern India? These distributions do not offer much hope for a hypothesis of significant forager adoption of agriculture, a hypothesis that would require the survival of far more linguistic isolates than in fact exist in most regions, and some very substantial contact-induced change.

It may be protested that many agriculturalist language families do not reveal this kind of blanket spread, offering instead mosaic or intertwined distributions such as those we see in upland regions of mainland Southeast Asia or in Amazonia. But such mosaics in no way reflect hunter-gatherer survival. They simply reflect more complex histories of agriculturalist language spread, in which successive dispersals by farmers have occurred, none ever completely erasing the traces of its forebears. Even the much-vaunted spread of Thai through Thailand within the past millennium has not led to a linguistic blanketing on anything like the Austronesian scale in western and central Indonesia (see Smalley 1994 for the Thai/Lao, Austroasiatic and Hmong-Mien mosaic that makes up the real Thailand). Neither has the spread of Sinitic languages through China. Farmers simply do not normally replace other farmers on the Bantu or western Austronesian scale, but this does seem to be the scale on which they can replace or incorporate populations of foragers.

Some considerations of the archaeological record for early farming

Archaeological cultures *and* languages reflect processes both of phylogenetic descent and of borrowing from regions beyond their boundaries. But the items likely to survive in the archaeological record will generally be much fewer than those reconstructable in the vast majority of reconstructed proto-languages, with one important proviso. This is that proto-language vocabularies are rather more afflicted by the passage of deep time than are archaeological assemblages, which is why no coherent language families can be convincingly demonstrated to have existed for much more than 8000 to 10,000 years. But relatively young[5] language families can be classified phylogenetically more successfully than archaeological cultures, partly because of the larger number of reconstructable cognate forms.

All of this means that it is more difficult to organize archaeological cultures than languages into phylogenetic arrays, even though modern archaeology is starting to reveal a rather intense interest in the phylogeny of attributes and artefact classes (O'Brien & Lyman 2000; Shennan 2000; Collard & Shennan 2000). Since, for whole languages, phylogeny in the form of the family tree reflects dispersal history, the elusiveness of this interpretative aid in the archaeological record, at least at the whole-culture level, creates a problem. It means that archaeologists who wish to debate cultural phylogeny and origins with respect to something as complex as a continent-wide dispersal of agriculture are obliged to do so by means essentially of value judgements about whether or not there was some kind of regional continuity across the Mesolithic to Neolithic boundary. In theory, strong continuity will negate the importance of farmer spread, whereas lack of continuity will emphasize it. Admittedly, statistical techniques exist to aid such judgements, but their success is often in proportion to precision of chronology and the number of variables available for analysis. Hence, archaeology is subject to interminable arguments about whether farmers moved in, or hunters adopted agriculture and kept them out.

I do not have an immediate answer for this problem, but one way out may be to consider patterning rather than phylogeny. One can place archaeological cultures along a scale of coherence. Some are clearly defined and homogeneous over large regions. Others are not, indeed hardly qualifying as cultures at all, thus giving rise to the widespread negative view in modern archaeology that archaeological cultures in the Childean sense can *never* exist as anything identifiable or meaningful. To me this seems an extreme opinion since these patterns, and the range of intermediate stages between them, are significant. It is not a new observation that many early Neolithic/Formative cultures are rather more widespread and homogeneous than their successors,

or even their late hunter-gatherer forebears. If population expansion ever did occur in human prehistory, particularly of a population with a distinct ethnic identity, we can be sure that the resulting spread of material culture would have carried a high level of coherence and homogeneity. Interaction alone cannot lead to cultural homogeneity on the high levels of LBK or Lapita, *at least not in terms of the ethnographic record*. The coastal and island Melanesians formed some of the most interactive and exchange-conscious populations in the ethnographic corpus. But this situation did not lead to convergence of language and culture to a common form. Indeed, it appears to have encouraged the opposite situation, with conscious desires for cultural and linguistic identity promoting differentiation.

Indeed, if archaeological cultures in an early Neolithic/Formative context are seen to be unusually uniform and widespread, then our suspicions should be aroused. Hunter-gatherers generally lead mobile lives and practise group exogamy, hence people can sometimes move quite far during their lifetimes. Settled farmers with localized and unranked political structures, on the other hand, can often express much local variation in language and cultural style. This becomes apparent when one compares the small-scale patterns of cultural and linguistic variation in much of agriculturalist Melanesia with those in hunter-gatherer regions of mobility such as the Australian interior. As just noted for Melanesia, exchange by itself does not reduce this contrast. Independent local groups of subsistence farmers should be fairly parochial, not uniform, in their cultural expressions. When they are not, we need to ask pointed questions.

Having made these points, however, I wish to make it clear that a middle road, focusing on varying combinations of farmer expansion with hunter adoption of agriculture, is the best road for a great many prehistoric situations. In my view, it is just as unlikely that agriculture could have spread through a hunter-gatherer region without a presence of substantial numbers of already-committed farmers as it is to imagine, say, early Indo-European languages spreading only because 'native' Mesolithic or Neolithic speakers of non-Indo-European languages decided it was time for a change, time to switch language and join an attractive new club. Thus, elsewhere (Bellwood 2001a) I have outlined four environmental situations that offer a gradient of different opportunities to hunter-gatherers and farmers. These are defined as *homeland/starburst zones* of agricultural origin, *spread zones* of rapid and coherent farming dispersal, *friction zones* where human or

Table 2.1. *Simplified character states for the four conceptualized zones of agricultural origin and spread*

	Homeland/Starburst zones	Spread zones	Friction zones	Beyond (no agriculture)
Tempo of spread	Upwelling at varied rates	Fast	Slow	Variable
Extent of spread	Upwelling with radial spread	Great	Varies, generally limited	Variable
Suitability for agriculture	High	High	Low	Nil
Prior hunter-gatherer population densities	High (but hunters become farmers)	Low	Often high, especially along coastlines and rivers	Variable
Mesolithic–Neolithic continuity	Yes	Unlikely, except at entry point	Yes, to varying degrees	No

environmental factors restricted or induced strong interaction during farming dispersal, and the *beyond farming zones* where farmers continued into other, non-agricultural, adaptations. Their features are defined in Table 2.1.[6]

It is one of my major observations, as also for my co-editor (Renfrew 1991; 1992a,b; 1994; 1996; 2000), that *the homeland zones of agriculture and the homeland zones of the major agriculturalist language families are correlated geographically to a high degree*. In addition, the concept of the spread zone becomes more significant as the environment more closely resembles the homeland environment of the agricultural system concerned, as the intensity of agricultural dependence increases, as the demographic gradient between farmers and foragers becomes steeper, and as domesticated animals enter the equation. These variables perhaps inform us why spread zones should be *more* visible both in archaeology and in language in many parts of the Old World, where a large range of cereals and domestic animals was often available, than in the New, where production systems were in general not so powerful outside the immediate environs of the Mesoamerican and Andean civilizations.

I think it is also necessary for archaeologists to examine carefully the actual evidence, on a worldwide basis, for demonstrable and convincing *in situ* prehistoric transformations of hunters into farmers. One can hardly escape the conclusion that the only record with strong demonstration of such a continuous evolution is that from Natufian to Neolithic in the Levant (see Bar-Yosef in this volume). The Eastern Woodlands of the USA certainly come a very close second (Smith 1992). China, Mesoamerica, and the Andes are of course persuasive, and one presumes that, logically, there were independent transitions in these regions. Nevertheless, the actual 'concrete' evidence for transition, in the form of changes in settlement patterns, crop and animal morphologies and so forth, pales by comparison with

that from western Asia. This means that, in much of the world according to the archaeological record, Neolithic replacement can be as good a hypothesis, if not a better one, as Mesolithic to Neolithic internal evolution. If hunter adoption of agriculture was always, or even predominantly, the main means of agricultural spread, I would expect to find *substantially more* evidence for phylogenetic cultural continuity across the transition than in fact exists. We would have lots of sites where Archaic/Mesolithic hunters turn, *in situ*, into Formative/Neolithic farmers. Such sites are extremely rare, and I do not believe this merely reflects a hiatus in the archaeological record.

How do agricultural systems and languages spread? Issues of triangulation and isomorphism

Some interpretations of the past make more sense than others, particularly if they require a minimum of special pleading, and particularly if they receive independent (non-circular) support from the data of more than one discipline. Kirch & Green (2001) refer to this kind of multidisciplinary focusing down on particular human configurations in prehistory as 'triangulation', in their case using data mainly from archaeology and linguistics to reconstruct the nature of early Polynesian society. In my view, multidisciplinary thinking, the 'new synthesis' in Colin Renfrew's terms (Renfrew 1992b), is the crux of the matter. Reading a recent and excellent compilation of archaeological views on the Mesolithic to Neolithic transition/transformation in Europe (Price 2000), I was struck that, no matter how thoroughly each author discussed his/her chosen area, each one discussed the nature of the Mesolithic to Neolithic transition/shift *only* from the archaeological record. Yet this record alone can often be singularly unhelpful and frustratingly ambiguous on issues of real-world population spread.

For instance, some authors in Price 2000 favour the idea that agriculture spread through most of

Europe as a result of adoption by the existing Mesolithic populations. At face value, this proposition need cause little surprise. There is no infallible reason why hunters should not adopt farming, although it cannot be ignored that in the ethnographic record of agriculturally-feasible regions such as northern and eastern Australia, California and many other regions of the temperate USA, they never showed any interest in doing so. But could hunters really have adopted farming across a whole continent with absolutely no penetration by existing farmers with their 'foreign' genes and languages? I am very doubtful that this could ever have happened in a Mesolithic social context, but the archaeological record alone is unlikely to give a clear statement as to which perspective is correct.

The situation changes when we consider language history. Not only did agriculture spread across Europe, but so also did Indo-European languages. Without wishing to become embroiled in the many debates about the precise homeland of this family, it is still necessary to point out that its spread over the greater part of Europe, allowing for some survival of other languages around the peripheries (Sverdrup & Guardans 2000), and allowing that some subgroups (e.g. Romance, Slavic, Germanic) have expanded markedly in historical times, had still occurred to approximately its outer limits in Ireland and Scandinavia in full prehistory. Of course, if early Indo-European languages spread in the Bronze Age or even in the Palaeolithic, then we could legitimately decouple the Neolithic archaeology and the languages. But neither of these options provides a social mechanism for language spread. Renfrew (1987; 1991; 1994; 1996; 1999) has already asked how the enormous Indo-European spread could have occurred, and has argued strongly for the likelihood that it occupied the interface between the Mesolithic and the Neolithic as a result of the more rapid demographic-growth profiles of the farmers. This explanation removes the major problem facing any choice of a later (Bronze Age) spread, this being the problem of how a new language such as 'Proto-Indo-European'[7] or a group of its closely related daughters could spread so efficiently and so cleanly, without leaving messy enclaves, through such a vast area already occupied by complex agricultural societies with large populations. A Palaeolithic spread seems equally unconvincing, and would force us to assume that the PIE agro-pastoralist vocabulary was all borrowed from external sources.

We thus face the prospect that the most likely time for the spread of both agriculture and the foun-

dation Indo-European languages across Europe falls at the beginning of the Neolithic, in real time between about 7000 BC in Greece and 4000 BC in the British Isles. If we accept such a conjunction, then we must try to model the genetic situation. Did Mesolithic populations adopt both the farming and the Indo-European languages over huge areas without any significant genetic contact with 'native' Indo-European speakers? If they did, then of course all modern Europeans will essentially reveal a genetic ancestry based in the local Palaeolithic. But would it really be possible for hunter-gatherer groups in e.g. Britain to shift their economies and languages very rapidly into line with those of a population of Indo-European-speaking farmers far away on the continent of Europe? Even if they could do so, why on earth would they wish to?

It is true that there are groups of former hunters, such as some Agta (Negrito) groups in northwestern Luzon, who have clearly adopted agriculture and outsider languages (in this case Austronesian) in the past (Reid 1994), while maintaining some degree of biological separation from the surrounding dominant population. But such trajectories are rare. The main point about the agriculturalist Agta is that they occupy small territories marginal for lowland rice agriculture and are obviously an accretion around the edges of a much vaster dispersal of Austronesian peoples with their languages, cultures and Asian genotypes throughout the Philippines. The Agta situation does not explain the spread of farming or Austronesian languages into the Philippines at all. Had this process been purely a matter of hunter-gatherer adoption by Agta ancestors, then we would expect to find an Agta biological population far more prominent today. Equally, we would expect large numbers of non-Austronesian languages to survive today in Luzon, and there are none. We would also expect to find very clear traces of non-Austronesian substratum and contact-induced change, far stronger than we see in the encapsulated Agta world of reality. Indeed, Reid has suggested that original Agta-Austronesian creoles might have been 'Austronesianized' back into line by continuing contact with mainstream Austronesian languages, this process in itself indicating that the Austronesian dispersal cannot have occurred just through language shift.

The above argument suggests that if we allow for any combined spread of agriculture and language on any major scale, then we are pushed more and more into acceptance of farmer genetic dispersal, since as the combination increases in chronological and spatial extent so it renders hunter-gather adoption an increasingly unlikely prospect as the only mechanism of spread. Isomorphism on an increasing geographical scale between the archaeological and linguistic elements of a dispersal makes it very unlikely that genetic variation could be completely independent.

So what might 'Neolithicization' have required in varying prehistoric circumstances? I doubt that hunters anywhere in the world ever adopted agriculture by means of a chain-reactive process of emulation with absolutely no in-movement of farmers. But if we allow for farmer spread, we generate other questions — how many farmers moved, how many hunters were there before them, what role for the environmental mosaic, and so forth? In my view, the spread of farming, except in the most marginal situations, has always involved the spread of existing farmers. In some cases, farmers clearly assimilated previous hunters absolutely. In other cases, these prior occupants contributed far more to the resulting situation, as did Papuans in Austronesian Melanesia and perhaps Mesolithic populations in northern Europe. But Mesolithic adoption of agriculture across a continent, with no movement of existing farmers, is not a feasible scenario.

Some genetic observations, particularly concerning Polynesian ancestry

Genetic evidence is currently making the most exciting contributions to the early farmer debate. But it is also feeling its way to a consensus, and it is interesting to observe that many biological anthropologists are now asking how haplotype histories within the mtDNA and Y genomes, or multigene clines within the autosomal genome, actually relate to the histories of whole populations, of tens of thousands, even millions of people over several millennia. After all, if most of the major farming dispersals discussed in this conference took place between 9000 and even 1000 years ago (and all the significant Old World ones must have been underway by at least 3000 years ago, with the possible exception of the southern Bantu spread in Africa), then an awful lot of stirring of the pot has occurred since. Many countries suspected to be within or close to regions of agricultural origin now have quite different ethnolinguistic populations in residence, huge areas of the Near East (including Anatolia) and southern China, for instance. Civilizations have risen and fallen, millions have been translocated forcefully, diseases have taken massive tolls.

I am aware, of course, that many geneticists claim that haplotype histories in the non-recombining genomes should be relatively immune to all of this, and should reflect deep population histories anyway, regardless of what might have happened in later history. But my own research has placed me centrally in one debate, about Polynesian ancestry, which makes me wonder if all is so simple. Essentially, this debate brings us back to the issue of isomorphism between the movements through time and space of cultures, languages and human populations.

The growing mystery of Polynesian ancestry

The Polynesians are a very widely spread, but also very small population descended from a limited number of colonists who sailed into the central Pacific from the west about 3000 years ago (Bellwood 1987; Kirch 2000). According to Oppenheimer & Richards (2001; this volume), a specific and widespread mtDNA 'Polynesian motif' originated in eastern Indonesia between 5500 and 34,500 years ago, with the most likely age being 17,000 years. This motif, found today in a majority of the Polynesian population, is agreed by Oppenheimer & Richards to be of ultimate Asian ancestry. But their estimated date for its immediate mutation in eastern Indonesia makes it much older than the Austronesian linguistic and archaeological migration phase at about 4000–3000 years ago, by means of which many authors derive the Polynesian ancestors, at least in terms of archaeology and language, from an ultimate homeland in southern China and Taiwan (Bellwood 1991; 1997; Diamond 2001).

There are now Y-chromosome data which support the idea that Polynesians derived some of their genetic ancestry in eastern Indonesia or even coastal Melanesia (Su *et al.* 1999; Kayser *et al.* 2000; Gibbons 2001; Hurles *et al.* 2002; Hurles this volume), rather than directly from the Asian mainland, so there is no need to doubt Oppenheimer & Richards on the geographical region of origin of the Polynesian mtDNA motif. But the suggested age of the motif causes some interpretative problems. At 17,000 years ago, eastern Indonesia was inhabited by hunter-gatherers with cranial and facial characteristics very close to those of the modern inhabitants of Melanesia and New Guinea (see summary and references in Bellwood 1997). Admittedly, one could argue for Polynesian evolution out of such a population, an argument which would require a Polynesian evolution of 'Asian' phenotypic characters independently of the Southeast Asians themselves.

Even if one were to sustain such an argument there would still be major problems with the archaeology. Having worked extensively in eastern Indonesia in a range of sites covering the archaeology of the past 35,000 years, I can state unequivocally that archaeological assemblages related to those of the early Polynesians, necessarily including pottery related to the Lapita pottery of western Polynesia, polished stone adzes, shell ornaments, tattooing chisels and fishhooks, and bones of domesticated pigs, dogs and fowl, were all absent throughout eastern Indonesia until their fairly coherent introduction together, seemingly as a 'package', sometime in the second millennium BC. The archaeological record of Island Southeast Asia makes it fairly clear that artefact assemblages of this type spread southwards from Taiwan into the Philippines and Indonesia, a spread now established by hundreds of C14 dates and, in early sites in Taiwan, an unequivocal presence of agriculture by 3000 BC (see Paz this volume). This cultural assemblage did not evolve unaided in eastern Indonesia, even though a few items such as shell adzes and bone points might have been carried over into Neolithic cultures from local pre-Neolithic origins.

Linguistically, the suggestion of Dyen (1962) that the Austronesian languages could have evolved initially in Melanesia, a hypothesis based on lexicostatistical percentages, is no longer acceptable to Austronesian linguists. As Blust (2000) has shown, the high levels of lexical diversity in western Melanesia reflect accelerated contact-induced change rather than great time depth. Blust's (1995; 1999) innovation-based arguments for a Taiwan location for Proto-Austronesian, following older stages of linguistic evolution in southern China, seem to me to be very strong indeed. Admittedly, some linguists have challenged them (Dyen 1995; Wolff 1995), but neither Dyen nor Wolff locate specific homelands elsewhere, their arguments being essentially methodological.

Thus, neither the linguistic nor the archaeological evidence gives any hope to the idea that the Austronesian language family evolved in eastern Indonesia, or that Polynesian material culture was created here in isolation from regions such as China or Taiwan. Yet, in their 2001 publication, Oppenheimer & Richards suggest that the existence of the Polynesian mtDNA motif implies that the Austronesian population *as a whole* originated in Island Southeast Asia, not Taiwan or China. Today, the total Austronesian population consists of about 300 million people, of whom the Polynesians account for a small part of one per cent. This suggestion thus raises the question of how we derive the ancestry of 300 million Southeast Asian Austronesians with fairly transparent Asian phenotypes (except in eastern Indonesia and Melanesia) from a Pleistocene Australo-Melanesian population located in a region with no known indigenous development of agriculture, no internal transition from hunting to farming, and no presence until a relatively late date of the material culture known to characterize other Austronesian prehistories over a vast area.

At this point I should make it clear that my concern is more with the question of Austronesian origins in general, rather than with the origin of the Polynesian mtDNA motif in eastern Indonesia, which I have no reason to doubt. As far as the Polynesians are concerned, *if* the mutation of their mtDNA motif occurred 17,000 years ago (and I certainly do not believe that it did), then we must account for its presence in modern Polynesians by explanations involving factors such as language shift and in-marriage of females from native populations, combined with extreme founder effects, possibly natural selection, and also the very complex patterns of regional intermarriage during the 3000 years since initial Polynesian dispersal into Oceania occurred. All of this is no doubt possible. But is the date correct? Hagelberg (2001) casts doubt on it and notes that the precise nucleotide substitution that defines the Polynesian motif occurs on a background motif that manifestly *does* occur in China and Taiwan. Furthermore, while some Polynesian Y haplotypes perhaps originated in eastern Indonesia or Melanesia, the ones described as haplogroup M122 by Oppenheimer & Richards (2001) and as haplogroup L by Capelli *et al.* (2001) clearly dominate in Tonga, the Philippines, amongst the Amis of Taiwan and in southern China. To me, this implies a strong case for the Polynesians as being little different from other Austronesians, including Filipinos and some Formosans. The claim that Polynesians originated completely out of the Wallacean Palaeolithic is perhaps misplaced. A more balanced perspective on the whole issue is presented in this volume by Hurles.

In conclusion, I have written this paper around some background thoughts which are relevant for any consideration as to how the archaeological, linguistic and biological records might illuminate events of many millennia ago, and also of how those records are created and reconstructed out of the data that have survived to the present. Can we really expect, for instance, southern Chinese and Polynesians to reveal clear and unambiguous genetic relationships at the present day, perhaps 6000 years after archaeologists and linguists claim some degree of common origin, and after at least 3000 years of relentless sinicization and massive population movement in southern China (LaPolla 2001)? Likewise, should we really expect the genetic relationships between e.g.

modern Britons and modern Turks/Arabs to tell us much about Neolithic origins almost 9000 years ago? I hope the answer here is 'yes we can', but I suspect the historical and anthropological modelling needed to tease out the 'real' answers has yet to be applied. The chapters that follow (especially by Barbujani and Dupanloup, and by Chikhi) go a long way towards this goal.

Notes

1. No claim is being made that *only farmers* ever dispersed through already-inhabited areas in prehistoric times, or that *only farmers* ever spread large language families. Pama-Nyungan, Athabaskan, Eskimo-Aleut, Algonquian and Finno-Ugric all attest against the latter. In addition, no claim is being made that all early farmers were obliged to undergo expansion. Campbell's claim (this volume) that the existence of some 'stay-at-home' agriculturalist language families threatens the viability of the farming/language dispersal hypothesis is not significant in my view, since he overlooks the issue of historical contingency and opportunity. Like some ancient civilizations, some language families spread and some did not.

2. As favoured in a number of recent papers, e.g. Bellwood 1994; 1996a,b; 1997; 2000; 2001a,b,c; Renfrew 1991; 1992a,b; 1994; 1996; 2000.

3. For the purposes of this essay, agriculturalist language families have cognate agricultural vocabularies reconstructable as far back as their basal proto-languages. There are a remarkable number, some listed in Bellwood 1996a. Indeed, virtually all the major language families of agricultural latitudes, especially in the Old World, began their lives with partially agriculturalist as opposed to entirely hunter-gatherer proto-languages.

4. Except for the non-recombining genetic systems — mtDNA and the Y chromosome — that (presumably) only evolve phylogenetically.

5. By virtue of being recognizable as families at all, the majority of the world's language families are relatively young, as of course are the various spreads of agriculture. Most are solidly Holocene phenomena.

6. Although Campbell (this volume) criticizes the concept of the spread zone as defined by Johanna Nichols (1997), my own feeling is that this concept can work for ancient population spread in general, regardless of the specific linguistic uncertainties referred to by Campbell.

7. I have highlighted PIE deliberately here, since in reality no such 'language' ever spread far at all. The PIE concept reflects the earliest reconstructable layer of vocabulary and other linguistic features within the Indo-European family as a whole. It was probably quite restricted in geographical and chronological extent, and if we accept current phylogenies for Indo-European it relates to the time and place in which early Anatolian languages became linguistically separate from the rest of Indo-European. The first Indo-European settlers of e.g. the British Isles or Pakistan certainly did not speak Proto-Indo-European if it is defined precisely in this way.

Acknowledgements

I would like to thank the British Academy for awarding me a Visiting Professorship to the McDonald Institute from March to July 2001. Clive Hilliker of the Department of Geography at ANU prepared the maps.

References

Aikhenvald, A. & R. Dixon (eds.), 2001. *Areal Diffusion and Genetic Inheritance: Problems in Comparative Linguistics*. Oxford: Oxford University Press.

Bakker, P., 2000. Rapid language change: creolization, intertwining, convergence, in Renfrew *et al.* (eds.), vol. 2, 585–620.

Bellwood, P., 1987. *The Polynesians*. 2nd edition. London: Thames & Hudson.

Bellwood, P., 1991. The Austronesian dispersal and the origins of languages. *Scientific American* 265, 88–93.

Bellwood, P., 1994. An archaeologist's view of language macrofamily relationships. *Oceanic Linguistics* 33, 391–406.

Bellwood, P., 1996a. The origins and spread of agriculture in the Indo-Pacific region, in Harris (ed.), 465–98.

Bellwood, P., 1996b. Phylogeny and reticulation in prehistory. *Antiquity* 70, 881–90.

Bellwood, P., 1997. *Prehistory of the Indo-Malaysian Archipelago*. 2nd edition. Honolulu (HI): University of Hawaii Press.

Bellwood, P., 2000. The time depth of major language families: an archaeologist's perspective, in Renfrew *et al.* (eds.), vol. 1, 109–40.

Bellwood, P., 2001a. Early agricultural diasporas? Farming, languages, and genes. *Annual Review of Anthropology* 30, 181–207.

Bellwood, P., 2001b. Archaeology and the historical determinants of punctuation in language family origins, in Aikhenvald & Dixon (eds.), 27–43.

Bellwood, P., 2001c. Archaeology and the history of languages, in *International Encyclopaedia of the Social and Behavioral Sciences*, vol. 1, eds. N.J. Smelser & P.B. Baltes. Amsterdam: Pergamon, 617–22.

Blust, R., 1995. The position of the Formosan languages: method and theory in Austronesian comparative linguistics, in Li *et al.* (eds.), 585–650.

Blust, R., 1999. Subgrouping, circularity and extinction: some issues in Austronesian comparative linguistics, in *Selected Papers from the 8th International Conference on Austronesian Linguistics*, eds. E. Zeitoun & P.J. Li. Taipei: Symposium Series of the Institute of Linguistics, Academia Sinica, 31–94.

Blust, R., 2000. Why lexicostatistics doesn't work, in Renfrew *et al.* (eds.), vol. 2, 311–32.

Capelli, C., J.F. Wilsom, M. Richards, M.P.H. Stumpf, F. Gratrix, S. Oppenheimer, P. Underhill, V.L. Pascali, T.-M. Ko & D.B. Goldstein, 2001. A predominantly indigenous paternal heritage for the Austronesian-speaking peoples of Insular Southeast Asia and the pacific. *American Journal of Human Genetics* 68, 432–43.

Collard, M. & S. Shennan, 2000. Processes of culture change in prehistory, in *Archaeogenetics*, eds. C. Renfrew & K. Boyle. (McDonald Institute Monographs.) Cambridge: McDonald Institute for Archaeologial Research, 89–97.

Diamond, J., 2001. Response to Oppenheimer and Richards 2001. *Nature* 410, 167.

Dyen, I., 1962. Genetic classification of the Austronesian languages. *Language* 38, 38–46.

Dyen, I., 1995. Borrowing and inheritance in Austronesianistics, in Li *et al.* (eds.), 455–520.

Gibbons, A., 2001. The peopling of the Pacific. *Science* 291, 1735–8.

Goldschmidt, A., 1996. *A Concise History of the Middle East.* Boulder (CO): Westview.

Hagelberg, E., 2001. Genetic affinities of the principal human lineages in the Pacific, in *The Archaeology of Lapita Dispersal in Oceania,* eds G.R. Clark, A.J. Anderson & T. Vunidilo. (Terra Australis 17.) Canberra: Pandanus Books, 167–76.

Harris, D. (ed.), 1996. *The Origins and Spread of Agriculture and Pastoralism in Eurasia.* London: UCL Press.

Hurles, M.E., J. Nicholson, E. Bosch, C. Renfrew, B. Sykes & M. Jobling, 2002. Y-chromosomal evidence for the origins of Oceanic-speaking peoples. *Genetics* 160, 289–303.

Kayser, M., S. Brauer, G. Weiss, P. Underhill, L. Roewer, W. Schiefenhovel & M. Stoneking, 2000. Melanesian origin of Polynesian Y chromosomes. *Current Biology* 10, 1237–46.

Kirch, P., 2000. *On the Road of the Winds.* Berkeley (CA): University of California Press.

Kirch, P. & R. Green, 2001. *Hawaiki, Ancestral Polynesia.* Cambridge: Cambridge University Press.

LaPolla, R., 2001. The role of migration and language contact in the development of the Sino-Tibetan language family, in Aikhenvald & Dixon (eds.), 225–54.

Levtzion, N., 1979. Toward a comparative study of Islamization?, in *Conversion to Islam,* ed. N. Levtzion. New York (NY): Holmes and Meier, 1–23.

Li, P.J., C. Tsang, Y.-K. Huang, D. Ho & C. Tseng (eds.), 1995. *Austronesian Studies Relating to Taiwan.* Taipei: Institute of History and Philology, Academia Sinica.

Nichols, J., 1997. Modeling ancient population structures and movements in linguistics. *Annual Review of Anthropology* 26, 359–84.

O'Brien, M.J. & R.L. Lyman, 2000. *Applying Evolutionary Archaeology.* New York (NY): Kluwer.

Oppenheimer, S. & M. Richards, 2001. Slow boat to Melanesia? *Nature* 410, 166–7.

Pentz, P., 1992. *The Invisible Conquest.* Copenhagen: National Museum of Denmark.

Petry, C.F. (ed.), 1998. *The Cambridge History of Egypt.* Cambridge: Cambridge University Press.

Price, T.D. (ed.), 2000. *Europe's First Farmers.* Cambridge: Cambridge University Press.

Reid, L.R., 1994. Unravelling the linguistic histories of Philippine Negritos, in *Language Contact and Change in the Austronesian World,* eds. T. Dutton & D. Tryon. Berlin: Mouton de Gruyter, 443–76.

Renfrew, C., 1987. *Archaeology and Language.* London: Jonathan Cape.

Renfrew, C., 1991. Before Babel: speculations on the origins of linguistic diversity. *Cambridge Archaeological Journal* 1(1), 3–23.

Renfrew, C., 1992a. World languages and human dispersals: a minimalist view, in *Transition to Modernity,* eds J.A. Hall & I.C. Jarvie. Cambridge: Cambridge University Press, 11–68.

Renfrew, C., 1992b. Archaeology, genetics and linguistic diversity. *Man* 27, 445–78.

Renfrew, C., 1994. World linguistic diversity. *Scientific American* 270, 747–60.

Renfrew, C., 1996. Language families and the spread of farming, in Harris (ed.), 70–92.

Renfrew, C., 1999. Time depth, convergence theory, and innovation in Proto-Indo-European. *Journal of Indo-European Studies* 27, 257–93.

Renfrew, C., 2000. At the edge of knowability: towards a prehistory of languages. *Cambridge Archaeological Journal* 10(1), 7–34.

Renfrew, C., A. McMahon & L. Trask (eds.), 2000. *Time Depth in Historical Linguistics.* (Papers in the Prehistory of Languages.) Cambridge: McDonald Institute for Archaeological Research.

Ruhlen, M., 1987. *A Guide to the World's languages,* vol. 1. Stanford (CA): Stanford University Press.

Shennan, S., 2000. Population, culture history and the dynamics of culture change. *Current Anthropology* 41, 11–36.

Smalley, W.A., 1994. *Linguistic Diversity and National Unity.* Chicago (IL): University of Chicago Press.

Smith, B.D., 1992. *Rivers of Change.* Washington (DC): Smithsonian.

Su, B., L. Jin, P.A. Underhill, J. Martinson, N. Saha, S.T. McGarvey, M.D. Shriver, J. Chu, P. Oefner, R. Chakraborty & R. Deka, 1999. Polynesian origins: insights from the Y chromosome. *Proceedings of the National Academy of Sciences of the USA* 97, 8225–8.

Sverdrup, H. & R. Guardans, 1999. Compiling words from extinct non-Indo-European languages in Europe, in *Historical Linguistics and Lexicostatistics,* eds V. Shevoroshkin & P. Sidwell. (AHL Studies in the Science and History of Language 3.) Melbourne: AHL, 201–57.

Wolff, J., 1995. The position of the Austronesian languages of Taiwan within the Austronesian group, in Li *et al.* (eds.), 521–84.

Part II

Setting the Scene for the Farming/Language Dispersal Hypothesis

Chapter 3

The Expansion Capacity of Early Agricultural Systems: a Comparative Perspective on the Spread of Agriculture

David R. Harris

In AD 1500, on the eve of European expansion, most of the world's population depended for their food on the products of domesticated plants and animals, and agrarian societies occupied much of the cultivable land in all the habitable continents except Australia. Current archaeological evidence suggests that this extensive distribution of agriculture in Eurasia, Africa and the Americas was the result of expansion from a few core regions where primary transitions from hunting and gathering to agriculture took place.

In this paper my main aim is to show, by comparing their crops, livestock and nutritional status, that some early agricultural systems (EASs) were inherently more likely to expand spatially than others. I do not systematically address the question of to what extent languages may have spread with agriculture, although some correlations between agricultural and language expansions are suggested. By comparing the relative expansion capacity of different EASs I hope to provide linguists and geneticists, as well as archaeologists, with an analytical framework that will assist us in our joint endeavour to understand the distribution of the world's major agrarian societies and language families.

Introductory propositions

The following eight points underpin the argument developed in the paper.

1. There is a widespread tendency to refer to 'agriculture' as if it were an undifferentiated phenomenon, whereas EASs were diverse and varied greatly in their capacity to spread.
2. Although not all EASs spread extensively, they had a greater tendency to do so than hunter-gatherer (HG) subsistence systems[1] which depended on wild foods. In particular, dependence on wild plants in their natural habitats bound HGs to their territories and militated against large-scale dispersals.
3. The logistic and residential mobility practised by most HGs indirectly limited long-term population growth, as did the widespread practice of infanticide and other direct methods of population regulation (Kelly 1995, 232–59). Even among village-based sedentary HGs, some of whom engaged in 'proto-agriculture' (Keeley 1995), and/or systematically stored plant foods, continuing dependence on wild plants, fish and game animals inhibited territorial expansion.
4. Some extensive HG dispersals did, however, take place — not only the initial peopling of the continents by *Homo sapiens* but also later migrations associated with the exploitation of mobile game animals, such as antelopes and cattle in North Africa (Barker this volume) and caribou and marine mammals in arctic North America.
5. The nutritional potential and expansion capacity of EASs were strongly influenced by the presence or absence of domestic herd animals, cereals, pulses (herbaceous legumes), tree and root crops. Where herd animals were fully integrated into food production, as in western Southwest Asia (see below), they greatly enhanced both the nutritional status and the expansion capacity of the EAS. The co-cultivation of annual cereals and pulses as staple crops also conferred great nutritional benefits because they are suited to storage and provide abundant carbohydrate and protein, with the small amounts of some essential amino-acids, such as lysine, in the cereals being compensated by the larger amounts present in the pulses. Tree crops are nutritionally valuable, especially as a source of vegetable oils, but because they are long-lived perennials their cultivation has been inimical to agricultural expansion. So too has been

the cultivation of carbohydrate-yielding root crops, which is commonly complemented with protein obtained by fishing and hunting.

6. Agriculture expanded by the dispersal of individual crops, domestic animals, agricultural tools and techniques, and also by their spread as integrated assemblages or 'packages'. The creation of such packages is more likely to have led to the territorial expansion of agricultural populations and their languages than the dispersal of individual domesticates and techniques, which tends to occur through piecemeal adoption by HGs or by groups already practising some form of agriculture.

7. The routes and rates of spread of agricultural expansions were subject to physical, ecological and social barriers that impeded expansion by halting the spread of individual items or even causing packages to disaggregate.

8. The comparison of EASs provides some insights into the question (to which I return in the conclusion) of whether, in prehistoric times, agriculture was spread *mainly* by expanding populations of farmers or by HGs who adopted elements of the new way of life, but the question cannot be fully resolved without detailed regional case studies.

Identifying core regions of early agriculture

Before EASs can be compared, they must first be identified. This is difficult, but by synthesizing data from three main sources — ethnographic and historical accounts of 'traditional' (mainly pre-European) agriculture, biogeographical and genetic data on the areas of origin of plant and animal domesticates, and archaeological evidence — it is possible to identify several core regions where independent transitions to agriculture appear to have occurred.

The process of synthesis is impeded by regional disparities in the data available, in particular by inadequate knowledge of the antiquity of agricultural systems that pre-date AD 1500. Archaeological evidence capable of bridging the chronological gaps between ethnographic and historical data on agriculture, and much earlier time periods, is often inadequate or entirely absent. In three regions where early agriculture has been investigated quite intensively by archaeologists, western Southwest Asia, China and Mexico, we can trace with some confidence the origins and early development of their characteristic systems of food production, but in two other regions where biogeographical and ethnographic evidence suggests that EASs may have originated independently of external influence — the central Andes and the Sudanic zone of northern tropical Africa — the archaeological evidence is too meagre to allow more than speculative interpretations.

In what follows I briefly compare these five core regions in terms of their assemblages of domesticated plants and animals, their nutritional status, their expansion capacity, and what is known about the origins and prehistoric spread of their EASs. In all five, grain crops made a major contribution to the diet, with root crops also important in the Andes, less so in China, Mexico and northern Africa, and least in Southwest Asia. Other regions in which crop cultivation may have begun independently, but where large-scale transitions to grain-based agriculture did not occur, include eastern North America prior to the introduction of maize (Smith 1992), parts of South and Southeast Asia prior to the introduction of rice (Fuller *et al.* in press), the African forest-savanna zone along the northern fringe of the Congo basin, New Guinea and Amazonia. In the latter three regions there were no staple grain crops (prior to the introduction of maize in Amazonia) and instead root- and tree-crop cultivation was combined with hunting and fishing in horticultural/arboricultural/wild resource subsistence systems that, unlike the grain-crop systems of the five core regions, had no inherent tendency to expand into new environments. This contrast implies that language dispersals are much more likely to have been linked to expansion of the grain-based systems than to the root- and tree-crop systems (which, for lack of space, are not considered further in this paper).

Western Southwest Asia

The earliest known archaeological evidence, from anywhere in the world, for the cultivation of domesticated crops and the raising of domestic livestock comes from the so-called Fertile Crescent — the upland arc that extends around the Mesopotamian lowland from the southern Levant to the southern Zagros Mountains (Harris 1998a; Smith 1995, 48–89). Archaeobotanical evidence from the site of Abu Hureyra in Syria suggests that during the Late Palaeolithic, between 13,000 and 10,300 BP (uncalibrated radiocarbon years before present, equivalent to *c.* 15,400–11,800 cal BP), some Late Natufian sedentary HGs began to cultivate cereals and pulses, probably in response to the dry, cold conditions of the Younger Dryas climatic phase (*c.* 11,000–10,000 BP, *c.* 13,000–11,500 cal BP) which progressively reduced the availability of the wild-grass seeds that were an important source of food (Harris in press a; Hillman 1996, 193–5; Hillman *et al.* 2001; Moore & Hillman 1992).

During the succeeding Pre-Pottery Neolithic A (PPNA) period (*c.* 10,300–9500 BP, *c.* 11,800–10,500 cal BP) in the Levant, cereal and pulse cultivation expanded slowly, but there is no conclusive evidence of domestic animals other than the dog. It is only in the PPNB (*c.* 9500–7500 BP, *c.* 10,500–8200 cal BP) that we find evidence first of domestic goats and sheep and later of cattle and pigs, as well as of all the 'founder crops' (Zohary 1996): two-row and six-row barley, einkorn, emmer and free-threshing wheat, lentil, pea, chickpea, bitter vetch and flax. By the end of the PPNB agro-pastoralism had replaced hunting and gathering through much of the Fertile Crescent and had begun to spread west into Cyprus and across Anatolia towards Europe, southwest into Egypt, and east towards central and southern Asia (Bar-Yosef & Meadow 1995, 73–93; Harris 1998b; Meadow 1996; 1998; Peltenburg *et al.* 2000; Wetterstrom 1993, 199–202).

The emergence of agro-pastoralism ushered in a major change in human subsistence, and although the agro-pastoralists depended on a much narrower range of foods than their HG predecessors (Hillman *et al.* 1989, 258–61; Hillman 2000, 369–73), the crops and livestock that formed the foundation of the new economy (Bar-Yosef & Meadow 1995, 82–90; Garrard 1999) provided a sufficiently abundant and adequately balanced diet, without the need for continuing access to wild sources of protein and other nutrients, to sustain growing populations of farmers and herders. The cereals and pulses yielded staple supplies of carbohydrate and protein and some oil, while the domestic livestock provided large quantities of protein and fat, particularly after goats, sheep and cattle began to be routinely milked, probably during the later PPNB or perhaps the succeeding Pottery Neolithic period (*c.* 7500–6200 BP, *c.* 8200–7000 cal BP). Indeed, the introduction of livestock into the domestic economy, as draft animals and providers of milk as well as meat and many secondary products including dung (used for fuel and fertilizer), was crucial to the transformation of early agro-pastoralism into an integrated system of mixed grain-livestock farming (Harris in press b).

The combination of nutritious and readily-stored grain crops with mobile domestic livestock that could be managed in extensive pastoral systems, as well as being used as draft animals and fertilizing agents within the cultivated areas, made Southwest Asian agro-pastoralism more productive, nutritionally self-sufficient and ecologically adaptable than any other EAS. It had a unique capacity to

sustain human territorial expansion, and evidently did so both eastward and westward from the Fertile Crescent into central Asia and the northwest of the Indian subcontinent by 7000 BP (*c.* 7800 cal BP) (Harris 1998b; Meadow 1998, 12–13) and into central Europe by 6000 BP (*c.* 6800 cal BP) (Bogucki 2000). This massive latitudinal spread of 5000 km was, as Diamond (1997, 180–86) has pointed out, facilitated by the mainly east–west orientation of the major environmental zones of Eurasia, in particular the extensive warm-temperate zone of Mediterranean-type climate. Nevertheless, in marginal areas beyond that zone, the spread proceeded more hesitantly as elements of the Southwest Asian agro-pastoral package became selectively adapted to both cooler/wetter and hotter/drier conditions. At the northern and northwestern margins of Europe the spread continued slowly, as HGs adopted parts of the package (Zvelebil 1996), and by *c.* 4500 BP (*c.* 5100 cal BP) agro-pastoral economies were established in Scandinavia, Britain and Ireland (Price 1996; 2000; Woodman 2000). Whether this extraordinarily extensive agricultural expansion was the vehicle for the spread of Proto-Indo-European languages from Anatolia, as Renfrew (1987, 145–77; 1996, 76–84), Bellwood (1997) and others argue, continues to be debated, but it clearly was made possible by the integration in Neolithic Southwest Asia of a unique assemblage of nutritionally complementary and ecologically adaptable domestic plants and animals unmatched by any other of the world's EASs.

Central China

Although great advances have recently been made in the archaeological investigation of the beginnings of agriculture in China, we cannot yet trace the process there with as much confidence as in western Southwest Asia. It has long been inferred from ethnobiological data that central China (here defined as including the middle and lower reaches of both the Yangtze and Huanghe valleys) was an early centre of plant, and to a lesser extent animal, domestication (Crawford 1992; Li 1983), but until recently there was little bioarchaeological evidence available to confirm this view. Now, the investigation of plant and animal remains from Chinese Neolithic sites using modern methods of excavation, analysis and dating are making more comprehensive interpretations possible (Chen 1999; Cohen 1998; Crawford & Shen 1998). Grains of domestic rice from the site of Pengtoushan in the middle Yangtze valley have now been directly dated to *c.* 7000 BP (*c.* 7800 cal BP) and by 6000 BP (*c.* 6800 cal BP) there is abundant evidence of rice associated with the remains of pile dwellings, agricultural implements and pottery, together with bones of domesticated dog, pig, chicken and water buffalo (Glover & Higham 1996, 426–9; Underhill 1997, 141–4). In the middle Huanghe valley there is also evidence by 7000 BP (*c.* 7800 cal BP) for villages supported by a mixed economy of hunting, fishing, the cultivation of domesticated broomcorn and foxtail millet and the raising of domesticated dogs, pigs and probably chicken (Chang 1986, 87–95; Crawford 1992, 13–14; Lu 1999; Underhill 1997, 117–25).

As a whole, this evidence points to the emergence during the Chinese Early Neolithic of systems of mixed grain-livestock farming, with an emphasis in the northern cool-temperate Huanghe valley on millet cultivation and pig raising and in the southern warm-temperate Yangtze valley on rice cultivation, with water buffalo probably used as draft animals and pigs also raised. A variety of indigenous vegetables, fruits and one pulse (soybean) may well also have been cultivated, as they certainly were by early historical times, but this has not been confirmed from the bioarchaeological record. Nutritionally, Neolithic Chinese grain-livestock farming, like its Southwest Asian counterpart, had the capacity to provide an increasing human population with an abundant and adequately balanced food supply, with rice and the millets yielding staple supplies of carbohydrate and protein, and the pigs, chicken and water buffalo providing animal protein and fat. However, in the absence not only of goats and sheep but particularly of pulses, the founder crops and livestock of Chinese Neolithic agriculture did not constitute as diverse and nutritionally well-balanced a package as those of Southwest Asia — although if soybean was cultivated in the Neolithic it would have made an important additional contribution to the diet.

As in Southwest Asia, the development of mixed farming in China reduced the dependence of Neolithic populations on wild plant and animal foods and facilitated the spread of agriculture. But, in the absence of the mobile pastoral component which goats and sheep contributed in Southwest Asia, and because from central China agriculture spread mainly north and south across rather than along latitudinal climatic and vegetational zones, the process involved more complex ecological adaptations and was slower than in western Eurasia. This is borne out by, for example, the spread of rice north and south from the Yangtze valley, which depended on the selection of varieties adapted to different climatic and day-length regimes and was evidently a very slow process. The

earliest rice recovered archaeologically in Korea dates to *c.* 3200 BP (*c.* 3100 cal BP) (Choe 1982, 520) and it did not become a staple crop in Japan until the fourth century BC (Imamura 1996, 453–7). In mainland Southeast Asia its introduction, which may be associated with the expansion of early Austroasiatic languages (Higham 1998 and this volume), seems not to have occurred until after 5000 BP (*c.* 5700 cal BP), and its further spread in island Southeast Asia was eventually checked in the equatorial zone of eastern Indonesia (Glover & Higham 1996, 419–26). From there agriculture, with pigs and chickens and with root crops such as taro and yams as staples rather than rice, spread across the Pacific by a rapid process of maritime colonization that is thought to be represented archaeologically by the Lapita Culture and linguistically by Austronesian speakers (Bellwood 1991; Spriggs 1996; 1998).

Mexico

Mesoamerica, and in particular southern Mexico, is usually regarded as both the earliest and the most important region of agricultural origins in the Americas. The three main crops of indigenous Mesoamerican agriculture — maize, common bean and pepo squash — were domesticated in the region, as were some other important food plants such as avocado and chilli pepper. In pre-European times there were, however, no domesticated animals other than the dog, turkey and Muscovy duck, and none of these was a major food resource. The three principal crops were ecologically and nutritionally complementary. They were often planted together, the upright grass (maize) providing a robust support for the climber (bean), with the sprawling vine (squash) occupying spaces between the other two, thereby maximizing the use of light, moisture and soil nutrients above and below the ground surface. Nutritionally, both maize and common bean provide mainly carbohydrate and some protein, but more significantly the value of the maize protein is limited by the small amount of the essential amino acid lysine that it contains, which is compensated by the larger amount of lysine in common-bean protein. The co-cultivation of maize and beans thus yields high-quality protein as well as abundant carbohydrate, and the fleshy fruits, leaves and seeds of squash provide, respectively, carbohydrate, carotenes (a source of vitamin A), and protein and oil. Chilli peppers also provide carotenes, but their main nutritional value is as a source of ascorbic acid containing vitamin C, and the flesh of the avocado fruit is a major source of vegetable oil. These basic Mesoamerican crops, together with other carbohydrate- and vitamin-yielding tree fruits such as papaya and guava, have combined (in the absence of significant quantities of protein and fat from domesticated animals) to provide a well balanced vegetarian diet that was the mainstay of the inhabitants of Mesoamerica and parts of North America until Europeans introduced Eurasian crops and livestock after AD 1500.

Although there has been much less archaeological investigation of the beginnings of agriculture in Mesoamerica than in Southwest Asia — indeed most of what is known archaeologically about the early history of maize, beans and squash comes from only five dry caves in Mexico (Smith 2001, 1325–6) — a coherent if tentative interpretation of the domestication and spread of the three staple crops is now possible, largely as a result of the AMS-radiocarbon dating of a small number of well-preserved and identified specimens. What is most striking about these new results is that large time-gaps separate the earliest evidence for the three crops, with domesticated pepo squash attested at Guilá Naquitz cave in Oaxaca at *c.* 9000 BP (*c.* 10,000 cal BP) (Smith 1997), maize cobs also from Guilá Naquitz dated to *c.* 5500 BP (*c.* 6300 cal BP) (Piperno & Flannery 2001), and common beans, from Coxcatlán cave in the Tehuacán valley, no earlier than *c.* 2300 BP (*c.* 2300 cal BP) (Kaplan & Lynch 1999). While acknowledging that we lack archaeobotanical evidence of early crops over enormous areas of Mexico, these results do strongly suggest that several millennia (perhaps 6000 or even 7000 years) elapsed after the initial domestication of pepo squash before the three crops began to be cultivated together in the productive system familiar to us from historical and ethnographic accounts, and still widely practised today. In a recent overview of the new evidence Smith (2001) has charted and tabulated the present geographical ranges of the wild progenitor populations of the three crops and their radiocarbon-dated first appearances in the archaeological records of Oaxaca, Tehuacán, Tamaulipas and the American Southwest. This indicates that all three dispersed northwards from their south and west Mexican areas of origin, but that they did so at different periods and rates, with maize moving faster than squash and both reaching the Southwest about 3500 years ago, well before the common bean.

This pattern contrasts with the rapid latitudinal spread of the Southwest Asian agro-pastoral package and implies that in Mesoamerica dependence on agriculture developed even more gradually, from the earliest cultivation of a few useful plants such as squash and bottle gourd by HGs, to which maize and later common bean were added as agricultural economies slowly became established. Agriculture may initially have spread mainly through the piecemeal adoption of individual crops by HGs and only later by expanding populations of farmers more fully dependent on the Mesoamerican crop assemblage. Perhaps it was the latter who spread Proto-Uto-Aztecan from southern Mexico to the American Southwest (see Hill this volume).

The Andean highlands

The Andean highlands, especially in the central part of the cordillera, were the locale of a second biotically distinctive region of early agriculture in the Americas. Here an assemblage of indigenous plants and animals were domesticated that included grain crops (two species of *Chenopodium*: quinoa and cañihua; and two pulses: common and lima bean), tubers (the potato and other minor root crops), herd animals (two camelids: llama and alpaca) and one small mammal (guinea pig). Archaeological evidence of these domesticates is fragmentary, but it is possible to outline the sequence in which they appear in the record. Pre-agricultural subsistence in the region was largely based on the hunting of deer and wild camelids (guanaco and vicuña) and the gathering of wild plants. The earliest putative evidence of crop cultivation, for example potato at the cave site of Tres Ventanas (Ugent *et al.* 1982) and lima bean and chilli pepper at Guitarrero cave (Kaplan 1980; Kaplan & Lynch 1999; C.E. Smith 1980), comes from mid-altitude valleys and is indirectly dated to between 10,000 and 9500 BP (*c.* 11,500–10,500 cal BP). By *c.* 7800–6400 BP (*c.* 8500–7300 cal BP) there is evidence from these sites and from the Ayacucho valley for the cultivation of quinoa, squash, bottle gourd and some of the minor tubers, although the latter could be wild (Pearsall 1992).

The picture that emerges from this patchy archaeobotanical evidence is of crops domesticated at separate locations over the course of some 5000 years, and the sparse data on the camelids points to their having been domesticated in the high Andes at sites above 4000 m (Wing 1977), perhaps in association with cultivation of the chenopods and tubers (Pearsall 1989).

The fact that the early Andean agricultural assemblage included grains, tubers and herd animals (as well as the guinea pig) appears to imply that it had high nutritional potential for sustaining large and expanding human populations. However, closer examination shows that it did not develop into an integrated system of grain-livestock production on the Southwest Asian model. Although the camelids were an important source of meat for high-altitude populations they were valued as much or more as pack animals (llama) and wool producers (alpaca); they were managed in herds and neither milked nor used as draft animals in the cultivation of the grain and root crops (Gade 1969; Murra 1965). Furthermore, the emphasis on root crops, which are less easily stored for long periods than grain crops and the cultivation of which involved laborious hand tillage of heavy soils, would have militated against the territorial expansion of the food-producing system. Such evidence of expansion as there is relates to the movement of individual domesticates within and beyond the Andean highlands, especially to the desert zone along the Pacific coast, rather than to the system as a whole. Thus, despite the presence of a nutritionally comprehensive range of crops and livestock, an integrated agricultural package did not evolve in and spread outward from the Andean region.

Northern tropical Africa: the Sudanic (southern Sahara and Sahel) zone

The case for agriculture having developed independently in northern tropical Africa rather than as a result of diffusion from Southwest Asia via the Nile valley and the Sahara was first made on botanical and linguistic grounds (Baker 1962; Harlan et al. 1976; Harris 1998c; Portères 1950; Murdock 1959), when bioarchaeological evidence of early domesticates was — as it remains — very meagre.

The principal crops indigenous to the Sudanic zone comprise three cereals — sorghum, pearl and finger millet — and several pulses, of which cowpea is the most important (Harris 1976, 331). Finds of domesticated pearl millet at Tichitt in southern Mauritania dated to c. 3500 BP (c. 3800 cal BP) (Amblard 1996, 425; Holl 1985, 159), at Birini in northern Ghana dated to c. 3500–3000 BP (c. 3800–3200 cal BP) (D'Andrea et al. 2001) and at Ti-n-Akof in northern Burkina Faso and Kursakata in northeastern Nigeria dated to c. 3000–2500 BP (c. 3200–2600 cal BP) (Neumann 1999, 75–7; Neumann et al. 1996, 443) indicate that cereal, and probably also pulse, cultivation was underway by 4000 BP (c. 4500 BP).

There is uncertainty about when domesticated sheep and goats (from Southwest Asia) were introduced (Clutton-Brock 1993, 68–70), and when cattle were likewise, either from Southwest Asia or derived from wild cattle domesticated in the Sahara and/or the Nile valley (Barker this volume; Bradley et al. 1996; Clutton-Brock 1993, 66–7; A.B. Smith 1980; 1986). However, although domestic livestock have historically contributed protein and fat to the diets of local pastoralists and to a lesser extent grain farmers, they were never as closely integrated with cereal and pulse cultivation, as draft animals and providers of fertilizer, as they were in Southwest Asia. Nevertheless, the grain-crop agriculture of the Sudanic zone, supplemented by pastoralism, was capable of supporting large populations and of expanding into new areas, and it may have been the vehicle for the southerly expansion of language families of the Niger-Congo phylum including Bantu, and perhaps also of the Nilo-Saharan phylum (Blench 1993; Ehret 1993; this volume; Phillipson 1993, 198–205; this volume).

Conclusion

Among the regions of the world where independent transitions to agriculture may have taken place, it is only those which included grains among their staple crops, particularly cereals and pulses, and provided a sufficiently balanced diet to reduce substantially dependence on wild foods, that had an inherent capacity to expand territorially. Of the five such regions reviewed here, only the Andean highlands lacked a staple cereal (quinoa and cañihua, although seed crops, are not cereals), and even though the Andean system included domesticated camelids it did not expand on a large scale from its homeland. Conversely, although herd animals were lacking in both Mexico and northern tropical Africa (before the introduction of cattle, sheep and goats), the indigenous agricultural systems of both regions included staple cereals and pulses and both expanded over a large geographical area.

The central Chinese system represents another variant, in which the cultivation of staple cereals was combined with the raising of pigs and chickens (as household in contrast to herd animals) and possibly one pulse — soybean, although whether it was a Neolithic crop is uncertain. Despite the apparent lack of pulses to complement the millets and rice nutritionally, and the initial absence of a mobile pastoral component based on sheep and goat herding, indigenous Chinese agriculture spread extensively.

Comparison of the five regions highlights the distinctiveness of the Southwest Asian system of agro-pastoralism in its assemblage of domesticates and the nutritional self-sufficiency they provided. Given its unique productivity, and the opportunities for latitudinal expansion offered by the east–west orientation of Eurasia's main climatic, physiographic and vegetational zones, it is to be expected that it would spread farther, faster and as a more integrated package, introduced by farmers, than any of the world's other EASs. Whether any of the others were spread mainly as packages by expanding agricultural populations, or more through the small-scale, piecemeal dispersal of crops and domestic animals by cultivators and their adoption by HGs, is unclear. The limited bioarchaeological evidence for the spread of maize, beans and squash in the Americas, of rice, millets, pigs and water buffalo in eastern Asia, and of millets, pulses, cattle, sheep and goats in Africa, is open to either interpretation. However, the data available at present suggest (to me) that in most of tropical Africa agriculture was spread mainly by farmers and pastoralists and in eastern Asia also mainly by farmers, although in Southeast Asia the adoption of crops and domestic animals by HGs may have had a significant role in the process. In Mesoamerica, where the integration of maize, beans and squash cultivation appears to have taken place very slowly and there were no domestic herd animals, adoption of crops by HGs may have played a larger part in the spread of agriculture than it did elsewhere.

Few firm conclusions about whether language dispersals were linked to agricultural expansions can be drawn from this comparison of five EASs. The most convincing case for such a link is the expansion of Southwest Asian agro-pastoralism in Eurasia, which may well have fuelled the spread of Indo-European and possibly also Altaic and Elamo-Dravidian languages. In Africa the expansion of Niger-Congo and Nilo-Saharan languages was probably linked to the southerly spread of cultivation and pastoralism. In Southeast Asia the expansion of early Austroasiatic languages may have been driven by the spread of rice agriculture, as may also the expansion of Sino-Tibetan and Japanese in eastern Asia. In Mesoamerica, too, it is possible that the spread of Uto-Aztecan languages was associated with the northerly expansion of agriculture into the American Southwest.

Note

1. 'Hunter-gatherer' and 'early agricultural' subsistence systems are contrasted here for analytical purposes, but they are more realistically conceived as varying along a continuum from those wholly dependent on wild-food procurement to those almost entirely dependent on the products of domesticated crops and livestock (Harris 1996b, 444–56).

References

Amblard, S., 1996. Agricultural evidence and its interpretation on the Dhars Tichitt and Oualata, southeastern Mali, in Pwiti & Soper (eds.), 421–8.

Baker, H.G., 1962. Comments on the thesis that there was a major centre of plant domestication near the headwaters of the River Niger. *Journal of African History* 3, 229–33.

Bar-Yosef, O. & R.H. Meadow, 1995. The origins of agriculture in the Near East, in Price & Gebauer (eds.), 39–94.

Bellwood, P., 1991. The Austronesian dispersal and the origin of languages. *Scientific American* 265(1), 88–93.

Bellwood, P., 1997. Prehistoric cultural explanations for widespread language families, in *Archaeology and Linguistics*, eds. P. McConvell & N. Evans. Melbourne: Oxford University Press, 123–34.

Blench, R., 1993. Recent developments in African language classification and their implications for prehistory, in Shaw *et al.* (eds.), 126–38.

Blench, R. & M. Spriggs (eds.), 1998. *Archaeology and Language*, vol. II: *Correlating Archaeological and Linguistic Hypotheses*. London: Routledge.

Bogucki, P., 2000. How agriculture came to north-central Europe, in Price (ed.), 197–218.

Bradley, D.G., D.E. MacHugh, P. Cunningham & R.T. Loftus, 1996. Mitochondrial diversity and the origins of African and European cattle. *Proceedings of the National Academy of Sciences of the USA* 93, 5131–5.

Chang, K.C., 1986. *The Archaeology of Ancient China*. 4th edition. New Haven (CONN): Yale University Press.

Chen, X., 1999. On the earliest evidence for rice cultivation in China. *Bulletin of the Indo-Pacific Prehistory Association* 18, 81–93.

Choe, C.-P., 1982. The diffusion route and chronology of Korean plant domestication. *Journal of Asian Studies* 41, 19–29.

Clutton-Brock, J., 1993. The spread of domestic animals in Africa, in Shaw *et al.* (eds.), 61–70.

Cohen, D.J., 1998. The origins of domesticated cereals and the Pleistocene–Holocene transition in East Asia. *The Review of Archaeology* 19, 22–9.

Cowan, C.W. & P.J. Watson (eds.), 1992. *The Origins of Agriculture: an International Perspective*. Washington (DC): Smithsonian Institution Press.

Crawford, G.W., 1992. Prehistoric plant domestication in East Asia, in Cowan & Watson (eds.), 7–38.

Crawford, G.W. & C. Shen, 1998. The origins of rice agriculture: recent progress in East Asia. *Antiquity* 72, 858–66.

D'Andrea, A.C., M. Klee & J. Casey, 2001. Archaeobotanical evidence for pearl millet (*Pennisetum glaucum*) in sub-Saharan West Africa. *Antiquity* 75, 341–8.

Diamond, J., 1997. *Guns, Germs and Steel: the Fates of Human Societies*. London: Jonathan Cape.

Ehret, C., 1993. Nilo-Saharans and the Saharo-Sudanese

Neolithic, in Shaw *et al.* (eds.), 104–38.

Fuller, D.Q., R. Korisettar, P.C. Venkatasubbiah & M.K. Jones, in press. Early plant domestications in southern India: some preliminary archaeobotanical results. *Vegetation History and Archaeobotany.*

Gade, D.W., 1969. The llama, alpaca and vicuña: fact vs. fiction. *Journal of Geography* 68, 339–43.

Garrard, A., 1999. Charting the emergence of cereal and pulse domestication in South-west Asia. *Environmental Archaeology* 4, 67–86.

Glover, I.C. & C.F.W. Higham, 1996. New evidence for early rice cultivation in South, Southeast and East Asia, in Harris (ed.) 1996a, 413–41.

Harlan, J.R., J.M.J. de Wet & A.B.L. Stemler (eds.), 1976. *Origins of African Plant Domestication.* The Hague: Mouton.

Harris, D.R., 1976. Traditional systems of plant food production and the origins of agriculture in West Africa, in Harlan *et al.* (eds.), 311–56.

Harris, D.R. (ed.), 1996a. *The Origins and Spread of Agriculture and Pastoralism in Eurasia.* London: UCL Press & Washington (DC): Smithsonian Institution Press.

Harris, D.R., 1996b. Domesticatory relationships of people, plants and animals, in *Redefining Nature: Ecology, Culture and Domestication*, eds. R. Ellen & K. Fukui. Oxford: Berg, 437–63.

Harris, D.R., 1998a. The origins of agriculture in Southwest Asia. *The Review of Archaeology* 19, 5–11.

Harris, D.R., 1998b. The spread of Neolithic agriculture from the Levant to western Central Asia, in *The Origins of Agriculture and Crop Domestication: the Harlan Symposium*, eds. A.B. Damania, J. Valkoun, G. Willcox & C.O. Qualset. Aleppo, Syria: ICARDA, 65–82.

Harris, D.R., 1998c. Beginnings of agriculture in tropical Africa: retrospect and prospect, in *Africa: the Challenge of Archaeology*, eds. B.W. Andah, M.A. Sowunmi, A.I. Okpoko & C.A. Folorunso. Ibadan: Heinemann, 101–14.

Harris, D.R., in press a. Climatic change and the beginnings of agriculture: the case of the Younger Dryas, in *Evolution on Planet Earth: the Impact of the Physical Environment*, eds. A. Lister & L. Rothschild. New York (NY): Academic Press.

Harris, D.R., in press b. Development of the agro-pastoral economy in the Fertile Crescent during the Pre-Pottery Neolithic period, in *The Dawn of Farming in the Near East*, eds. R.J.T. Cappers & S. Bottema. Berlin: ex oriente.

Harris, D.R. & G.C. Hillman (eds.), 1989. *Foraging and Farming: the Evolution of Plant Exploitation.* London: Unwin Hyman.

Higham, C.F.W., 1998. Archaeology, linguistics and the expansion of the East and Southeast Asian Neolithic, in Blench & Spriggs (eds.), 103–14.

Hillman, G.C., 1996. Late Pleistocene changes in wild plantfoods available to hunter-gatherers of the northern Fertile Crescent: possible preludes to cereal cultivation, in Harris (ed.) 1996a, 159–203.

Hillman, G.C., 2000. The plant food economy of Abu Hureyra 1: the Epipalaeolithic, in Moore *et al.* (eds.), 327–99.

Hillman, G.C., S.M. Colledge & D.R. Harris, 1989. Plant-food economy during the Epipalaeolithic period at Tell Abu Hureyra, Syria: dietary diversity, seasonality, and modes of exploitation, in Harris & Hillman (eds.), 240–68.

Hillman, G.C., R. Hedges, A. Moore, S. Colledge & P. Pettitt, 2001. New evidence of Lateglacial cereal cultivation at Abu Hureyra on the Euphrates. *The Holocene* 11, 383–93.

Holl, A., 1985. Subsistence patterns of the Dhar Tichitt Neolithic, Mauritania. *African Archaeological Review* 3, 151–62.

Imamura, K., 1996. Jomon and Yayoi: the transition to agriculture in Japanese prehistory, in Harris (ed.) 1996a, 442–64.

Kaplan, L., 1980. Variation in the cultivated beans, in *Guitarrero Cave: Early Man in the Andes*, ed. T.F. Lynch. New York (NY): Academic Press, 145–8.

Kaplan, L. & T. Lynch, 1999. *Phaseolus* (Fabaceae) in archaeology: AMS radiocarbon dates and their significance for pre-Columbian agriculture. *Economic Botany* 53, 261–72.

Keeley, L.H., 1995. Protoagricultural practices among hunter-gatherers: a cross-cultural survey, in Price & Gebauer (eds.), 243–72.

Kelly, R.L., 1995. *The Foraging Spectrum: Diversity in Hunter-Gatherer Lifeways.* Washington (DC): Smithsonian Institution Press.

Li, H.-L., 1983. The domestication of plants in China: ecogeographical considerations, in *The Origins of Chinese Civilization*, ed. D.N. Keightley. Berkeley & Los Angeles (CA): University of California Press, 21–64.

Lu, T.L.-D., 1999. The transition from foraging to farming in China. *Bulletin of the Indo-Pacific Prehistory Association* 18, 77–80.

Meadow, R.H., 1996. The origins and spread of agriculture and pastoralism in northwestern South Asia, in Harris (ed.) 1996a, 390–412.

Meadow, R.H., 1998. Pre- and proto-historic agricultural and pastoral transformations in northwestern South Asia. *The Review of Archaeology* 19, 12–21.

Moore, A.M.T. & G.C. Hillman, 1992. The Pleistocene to Holocene transition and human economy in Southwest Asia: the impact of the Younger Dryas. *American Antiquity* 57, 482–94.

Moore, A.M.T., G.C. Hillman & A.J. Legge (eds.), 2000. *Village on the Euphrates: from Foraging to Farming at Abu Hureyra.* New York (NY): Oxford University Press.

Murdock, G.P., 1959. *Africa: its Peoples and their Culture History.* New York (NY): McGraw-Hill.

Murra, J.V., 1965. Herds and herders of the Inca state, in *Man, Culture and Animals*, eds. A. Leeds & A.P. Vayda. Washington (DC): American Association for the Advancement of Science, 185–215.

Neumann, K., 1999. Early plant food production in the

West African Sahel: new evidence, in *The Exploitation of Plant Resources in Ancient Africa*, ed. M. van der Veen. New York (NY): Kluwer Academic/Plenum Publishers, 73–80.

Neumann, K., A. Ballouche & M. Klee, 1996. The emergence of plant food production in the West African Sahel: new evidence from northeast Nigeria and northern Burkina Faso, in Pwiti & Soper (eds.), 441–8.

Pearsall, D.M., 1989. Adaptation of hunter-gatherers to the high Andes: the changing role of plant resources, in Harris & Hillman (eds.), 318–32.

Pearsall, D.M., 1992. The origins of plant cultivation in South America, in Cowan & Watson (eds.), 173–205.

Peltenburg, E., S. Colledge, P. Croft, A. Jackson, C. McCartney & M.A. Murray, 2000. Agro-pastoralist colonization of Cyprus in the 10th millennium BP: initial assessments. *Antiquity* 74, 844–53.

Phillipson, D.W., 1993. *African Archaeology*. 2nd edition. Cambridge: Cambridge University Press.

Piperno, D.R. & K.V. Flannery, 2001. The earliest archaeological maize (*Zea mays* L.) from highland Mexico: new accelerator mass spectrometry dates and their implications. *Proceedings of the National Academy of Sciences of the USA* 98, 2101–3.

Portères, R., 1950. Vieilles agricultures de l'Afrique intertropicale. *L'Agronomie Tropicale* 5, 489–507.

Price, T.D., 1996. The first farmers of southern Scandinavia, in Harris (ed.) 1996a, 346–62.

Price, T.D. (ed.), 2000. *Europe's First Farmers*. Cambridge: Cambridge University Press.

Price, T.D. & A.B. Gebauer (eds.), 1995. *Last Hunters–First Farmers: New Perspectives on the Prehistoric Transition to Agriculture*. Santa Fe (NM): School of American Research Press.

Pwiti, G. & R. Soper (eds.), 1996. *Aspects of African Archaeology*. Harare: University of Zimbabwe Publications.

Renfrew, C., 1987. *Archaeology and Language: the Puzzle of Indo-European Origins*. London: Cape.

Renfrew, C., 1996. Language families and the spread of farming, in Harris (ed.) 1996a, 70–92.

Shaw, T., P. Sinclair, B. Andah & A. Okpoko (eds.), 1993. *The Archaeology of Africa: Food, Metals and Towns*. London: Routledge.

Smith, A.B., 1980. Domesticated cattle in the Sahara and their introduction into West Africa, in *The Sahara and the Nile: Quaternary Environments and Prehistoric Occupation in Northern Africa*, eds. M.A.J. Williams & H. Faure. Rotterdam: Balkema, 489–503.

Smith, A.B., 1986. Review article: cattle domestication in North Africa. *African Archaeological Review* 4, 197–203.

Smith, B.D. (ed.), 1992. *Rivers of Change: Essays on Early Agriculture in Eastern North America*. Washington (DC): Smithsonian Institution Press.

Smith, B.D., 1995. *The Emergence of Agriculture*. New York (NY): Scientific American Library.

Smith, B.D., 1997. The initial domestication of Cucurbita pepo in the Americas 10,000 years ago. *Science* 276, 932–4.

Smith, B.D., 2001. Documenting plant domestication: the consilience of biological and archaeological approaches. *Proceedings of the National Academy of Sciences of the USA* 98, 1324–6.

Smith, C.E., Jr, 1980. Plant remains from Guitarrero Cave, in *Guitarrero Cave: Early Man in the Andes*, ed. T.F. Lynch. New York (NY): Academic Press, 87–119.

Spriggs, M., 1996. Early agriculture and what went before in Island Melanesia: continuity or intrusion?, in Harris (ed.) 1996a, 524–37.

Spriggs, M., 1998. From Taiwan to the Tuamotus: absolute dating of Austronesian language spread and major sub-groups, in Blench & Spriggs (eds.), 115–27.

Ugent, D., S. Pozorski & T. Pozorski, 1982. Archaeological potato tuber remains from the Casma Valley of Peru. *Economic Botany* 36, 417–32.

Underhill, A.P., 1997. Current issues in Chinese Neolithic archaeology. *Journal of World Prehistory* 11, 103–60.

Wetterstrom, W., 1993. Foraging and farming in Egypt: the transition from hunting and gathering to horticulture in the Nile valley, in Shaw *et al.* (eds.), 165–226.

Wing, E.S., 1977. Animal domestication in the Andes, in *Origins of Agriculture*, ed. C.A. Reed. The Hague: Mouton, 837–59.

Woodman, P., 2000. Getting back to basics: transitions to farming in Ireland and Britain, in Price (ed.), 219–59.

Zohary, D., 1996. The mode of domestication of the founder crops of Southwest Asian agriculture, in Harris (ed.) 1996a, 142–58.

Zvelebil, M., 1996. The agricultural frontier and the transition to farming in the circum-Baltic region, in Harris (ed.) 1996a, 323–45.

Chapter 4

The Economies of Late Pre-farming and Farming Communities and their Relation to the Problem of Dispersals

Mark Nathan Cohen

My contribution to this volume must be to provide an economic and ecological context in which to interpret patterns of population dispersal following the Neolithic revolution. Although I offer a few thoughts about dispersal *per se*, I largely leave it to other participants to interpret the relations of this information to the dispersal patterns observed.

In contrast to many other scholars who see strength in the detailed explication of individual data points, I believe that the most reliable data in archaeology are to be found in broad, large-scale parallels among data sets (i.e. multiple replications) and/or in conclusions that rest on the convergence of many samples. I also give extra weight to conclusions that result from the convergence of varied methods of analysis. If exceptions to the broad pattern become too numerous, of course, the generalization must be discarded. But as in the phrase, 'the exception *tests* (not 'proves') the rule', I consider individual exceptions not as disproof but as instances to be studied to explain why they diverge. If their exceptional nature can be explained, the generalization stands.

I would also argue that the explanation of a trend must match the size and breadth of the trend being explained, such that, for example, a broad trend cannot be explained by local or site-specific variables. If the adoption of agriculture is widespread in many regions, as it is, it cannot be explained by the detailed geographic features of the Fertile Crescent or by peculiarities of wheat. Conversely the domestication of wheat cannot be explained satisfactorily without reference to the broad patterns.

I have identified several general trends that are relevant to the discussions of this volume. The trends described, based on multiple replications and on the convergence of several types of analysis (theoretical considerations and widespread ethnographic and archaeological evidence), may be taken as trends roughly representative of the panhuman experience of broad-spectrum foraging and early farming. The data are hardly complete but the number of samples, their geographic distribution, the congruence of their results and the congruence of ethnographic, archaeological and theoretical considerations suggest that, despite occasional exceptions, these conclusions are now actually among the *best*-established major conclusions about prehistory.

My major points, as observed over a very large geographical scale, are as follows:
1. Farming, whether invented, dispersed, or diffused and adopted, is (almost?) universally preceded by what has come to be called the 'Broad-Spectrum Revolution' which is roughly synonymous with 'Mesolithic' economies in the Old World, and 'Archaic' in the New. Broad-spectrum foraging refers to increasingly intense utilization of the diverse resources of a small geographical area, including among other things an increased use of resources such as small game, riverine, coastal and lacustrine resources such as shellfish, and small seeded plants, often accompanied by increasing processing of foods (e.g. grindstones), storage, and (semi-) sedentary lifestyles. The 'invention' and/or adoption of farming builds on this basis in an incremental way, such that broad-spectrum foraging and farming are only two of a long sequence of economic changes and cannot be judged apart from this sequence.

I (Cohen 1977) have argued that changing balance between population and resources ('population pressure' or resource 'stress') must be at least one common ingredient in this sequence, because it is the only potential causative variable that is of sufficient geographical breadth to explain such a general phenomenon. This does not mean that population growth *per se* is always necessary or sufficient to induce population pressure, although the simultaneity of results over varied climate zones suggests that diffuse population growth along with effective population dispersal and pressure-balancing mechanisms ('flux') would have been a major factor in increasing the imbalance. Climate change may well have been involved at least in some zones, providing exceptions to general expectation; but climate change could only have been an agent in the specific way described below.

2. Farming was also preceded among Mesolithic or Archaic economies by widespread coalescing and fine definition of distinct local tool styles in archaeology, replacing the broad general horizons of tool styles in earlier prehistory. It has been suggested (Wobst 1974) that changes in tool-style distribution represented the shift from loose networks of population united by out-breeding (exogamy) to the development of tightly defined individual, independent, endogamous (in-breeding) groups. The change resulted from the fact that higher population densities made it possible for individual groups to find sufficient mates within a defined radius that they could afford to be selective. Endogamy would have increased the isolation of groups and helped halt the diffusion of styles beyond local groups. More importantly, it would have tended to isolate individual languages and individual gene pools. These narrowly defined style-groups suggest some points of relevance to this volume: late-pre agricultural groups, which provide the threshold of our discussions, must have been (among) the most narrowly-defined genetic and linguistic groups in human history.

3. The adoption of farming would have been at least loosely associated with an increase in sedentism, although not all farmers are sedentary and not all collectors of wild food are mobile.

4. The adoption of sedentary farming, and the broad-spectrum revolution which preceded it, clearly represent a *decline* in the efficiency of human labour (calories produced per hour of work), as measured in every region where 'broad-spectrum' efficiency studies have been undertaken.

5. The focus on seasonally-available crops would have necessitated storage and commitment to crops both before and after harvest. This in turn would have necessitated sedentism. But whether sedentism was necessitated or permitted by domestication, i.e. whether sedentism was a sought-after strategy or one to be avoided and adopted

only as necessary, remains unresolved. Its association with declining health and efficiency (see below) suggests the latter.

6. The adoption of sedentary farming clearly brought with it an overall decline in average nutrition and health and it probably resulted in a decline in life expectancy. These factors would have been disincentives to both sedentism and increased community size.

7. The adoption of farming probably brought with it an increase in human fertility.

8. The adoption of farming almost certainly brought with it an increase in *average* rates of population growth, but *on average,* the increase must have been trivial since the world-wide acceleration in growth must have been small. We cannot simply assume that a transition to farming resulted in a significant increase in population growth. It may well have done so in some regions, but we must then explain why such an increase occurred in a particular region and not in others (see Harris this volume).

9. The adoption of farming would have resulted in the increasingly efficient use of space (calories per acre) — probably its main economic advantage. In consequence:

10. The adoption of farming clearly resulted in an increase in general population density and increasing sizes of individual communities because larger groups of people could congregate without incurring excessive travel costs in the food quest.

11. The use of domesticated plants and animals probably *increased* the risk of 'crop failure', since domestication often resulted in the domesticates' loss of protections against natural enemies and crop dispersals often resulted in moving domesticates beyond their natural tolerance range. Moreover, the adoption of sedentary farming, preinvestment in food supplies, and storage would have made populations vulnerable to natural destruction of crops and foods from which they could not move, and/or human destruction and expropriation of food supplies. It would have increased both perceived and real insecurity about both personal safety and the security of food supplies. This vulnerability set the stage for class stratification and government by force ('civilization').

12. Increased community sizes would have been a major weapon of both attack and defense in a world in which military strength was largely synonymous with population size. This in turn may have been initially bound with both the need and ability of selective groups to disperse. But the

need for defense would have been a major disincentive toward dispersal.

Declining efficiency

In the last few decades, a great deal of attention has been focused on what are called 'optimal foraging' studies that have produced broad, generalized *expectations* of human perception, calculation and behaviour. Such studies observe and measure various food-getting and preparation strategies and rank them in terms of their efficiency, measured by caloric returns per individual hour of work, including not only the cost of killing or harvesting but of tool preparation and maintenance, travel time, food preparation, storage, storage losses and, although rarely considered, losses to human expropriation. One could also measure the efficiency with which other nutrients (e.g. protein, B-vitamins) are obtained, but the use of these would generally strengthen rather than weaken the conclusions drawn because farming seems to have focused on domesticates chosen for their ability to grow in high density, their affinity for human activity and their ability to be stored. Such resources typically are relatively low in their qualitative nutritive value.

Studies of comparative efficiency in various parts of the world repeatedly suggest that large game, once encountered, is by far the most efficient of resources to exploit (hence highly 'ranked'). Smaller game coastal resources, riverine and lacustrine resources and other 'gathered' animal and plant resources are of intermediate rank, and small seeded grains such as cereals typically rank very low on such lists. I report the relative rank order rather than specific numbers since the latter vary markedly from place to place and since it is the ranking that is most important. (Figures and original references are provided in Cohen 1989, 168–70. See also Simms 1987; Russell 1988.)

A significant distinction must be made between what is called 'search' time (pre-encounter time or the cost of locating a resource) and 'post-encounter' time (involving harvesting and conversion of a resource to food once it is located, storage and so forth.) Since the costs of post-encounter 'harvest' and processing of large animals are so small, and the overall value of large game is so high, the critical question is how many hours it takes to find an animal to kill, itself a reflection of the availability of large game. Figures from several studies suggest that big-game hunting is the most efficient strategy, even if it takes five to ten hours or even a few days to

find an animal. The implication is not that *Homo sapiens* populations would ever have been 'big-game hunters' in the old sense, but simply that when large game was more plentiful, more of it would have been included in the diet. (Most estimates suggest that animal foods would only rarely have exceeded 40 per cent of the diet.)

The same principle of availability does not apply to resources of lesser efficiency; but to make this point, the meaning of 'ranking' of resources must be explained. The point is that, when activities are ranked according to efficiency, *the availability of high-ranking resources dictates the use of those of lower rank.* If you can see a large animal, go for it. If you cannot see one it is still worth spending several hours in pursuit. But lower-ranking resources will not be exploited when higher-ranked resources are available, even if those of low rank are plentiful and visible. One eats grass seeds not because they are available, but only because higher-ranking resources have disappeared or become so scarce that search time is prohibitively high. *Grasses will enter the diet dependent only on the availability of better resources, not on their own availability.*

With specific reference to the productivity of early wheat farming in the Middle East, Russell (1988) estimates that neither foraging for, nor initial farming of, einkorn wheat would remotely have compared to the value of large-game hunting or even other 'Mesolithic' resources. As a low-ranking food choice, gathering and domestication of wild wheat, far from being 'discovered' or 'invented', would have entered the food quest and been deleted many times, depending on the availability of higher-ranking resources. As Bar Yosef pointed out to me (pers. comm. at the Cambridge conference), Russell's figures mispredict the sequence of animal domestication by suggesting that, on grounds of efficiency, cattle should have been domesticated before sheep and goats, which on present evidence is manifestly not the case. He implies that this error negates the general validity of Russell's results. But, since Russell's predictions are otherwise on target I suggest that we have to search for a reason for such deviance from the prediction rather than discarding the model. The relative safety of handling sheep and goats rather than cattle seems to me to be one fairly obvious reason for the discrepancy.

Declining health

Since parasites react strongly to changes in human activity, human health is very much a function of human behaviour — a function in turn of changing technology, changing social and political organization and/or a change in demographic parameters.

It is now clear also that growing population, higher density, sedentism, large concentrations of population, the loss of preferred resources and the intense use of low-ranking crops not only required more labour input but resulted in a declining quality of life through most of history. This general decline would have been exacerbated for most people by the emergence of class stratification and social control by force.

Work on prehistoric patterns of health demonstrates fairly clearly that the burden of infectious disease has increased throughout our history, as has the burden of malnutrition, beginning certainly as early as the adoption of farming and quite probably even in the stages of broad-spectrum foraging. One quick measure of the decline is that, beginning as early as the transition from Palaeolithic to Mesolithic economies, human stature, often considered the best and quickest shorthand measure of overall health, generally *declined* through most of the Old World.

Conclusions about broad similarities in health trends in different regions of the world are based on triangulation between three separate (but generally mutually reinforcing) sets of data. The three sets are:
1. the patterns of recorded diseases and appearance of new diseases in contemporary and historic societies of different scale (ethnography, ethnohistory, written history);
2. the appearance of disease and malnutrition in skeletons from prehistoric and historic sites (archaeology and palaeopathology); and
3. the known patterns of human, nutrient and pathogen biology that can be tentatively extrapolated to the past using uniformitarian principles.

Each source of knowledge has its own pitfalls; but together they often reinforce one another, offsetting the weaknesses of each alone, and leading to conclusions that, as suggested above, I consider to be among the strongest major conclusions we can draw about prehistory.

Perhaps the clearest example of such mutual reinforcement of the three legs of the tripod relates to the prehistoric and historic pattern of iron-deficiency anaemia. We know from ethnographic descriptions and actual iron measurements that the world's smallest and most mobile populations generally suffer less anaemia than more 'advanced' populations (Cohen 1989), in part because they take in a great deal of heme iron and protein from animal sources and in part because they are relatively infection free. Second, we know from uniformitarian rea-

soning that major sources of iron loss, including hookworm, should commonly be rare in small local bands, but increase both in prevalence and individual parasite load with population density. This is because people are infected by other peoples' stools, so parasite burden should increase with sedentism since the worms must develop in the soil and are left behind by mobile populations. We know also that infectious diseases such as TB have generally increased through history as the density of population has increased and as permanent living enclosures appear. We know that many of these infections force the body to sequester its own iron and induce anaemia as a defense against parasites that require iron for their own success. Third, we know that prehistoric skeletons of relatively small and mobile groups almost invariably show fewer skeletal signs of anaemia (porotic hyperostosis of the skull vault and cribra orbitalia of the eye sockets) than do later, larger, denser and more sedentary populations. The same skeletal populations show relatively low rates of other infections, particularly of tuberculosis.

Data from the three sources suggest that frequency of infection and of malnutrition generally increased through time. A comparison of 21 archaeological (palaeopathological) sequences summarized in Cohen & Armelagos (1984) (8 from North America, 4 from Latin America, 4 from Europe, 3 from the Middle East, one from India and one from North Africa, more recently supplemented by other studies cited in Cohen (1989) and Larsen (1995), provide strikingly parallel results involving the increase through time of anaemia (cribra orbitalia and porotic hyperostosis), infection (periostitis and osteomyelitis), specific infections such as yaws, syphilis, tuberculosis and leprosy, as well as an increase in general stress indicators such as enamel hypoplasia and enamel micro-defects of teeth (marking episodes of unspecified poor health), delayed juvenile growth, juvenile osteoporosis, and other measures. In short, they presented a striking and near universal pattern of declining health at the adoption of agriculture. Life expectancy probably also declined, but the justification for this statement must await further discussion (see below).

These conclusions concerning both comparative pathology rates and life expectancy have been questioned by a number of sources. In particular, Wood *et al.* (1992), describing what they call 'the osteological paradox', have argued that cemetery populations may not be fair representations of once-living groups because the proportion of the dead displaying a certain disease in a cemetery is not a reliable indicator of the prevalence of the disease in the once-living group. They suggest that, while the conclusions of Cohen & Armelagos (1984) and Cohen (1989) may be correct, many other interpretations might also be correct because deaths are not random but represent selective mortality. In fact, they argue that visible cemetery pathology might actually be *negatively* correlated with real health. The absence of pathology in the skeleton might be an indicator of death in the face of stress too rapid to be incorporated in bone. The presence of visible skeletal stress might be a sign of greater longevity, such that people lived long enough to record insults in their skeletons.

I believe that I have rebutted both arguments to the satisfaction of the critics involved (Cohen 1997). I have shown that, given the reinforcement of other lines of evidence (as in the case of anaemia and its skeletal manifestations discussed above), to apply any interpretation other than the direct one to changing rates of skeletal pathology involves a highly unlikely violation of Occam's Razor (principle of parsimony in scientific observations). I have shown that significant fallacies exist in their reference to 'selective mortality' and selective representation of individuals with pathology in cemeteries. However, the arguments of the osteological paradox also presume increases in both fertility and life expectancy, a premise that I can rebut for the origins of agriculture with reference to additional data presented below.

An increase in fertility

Several lines of evidence suggest that fertility is likely to have increased, on average very slightly as a function of sedentary farming. The arguments are partly theoretical. Biological arguments are based on the fact that two of nature's primary forms of natural birth control are breast-feeding (when done with a high frequency and on-demand schedule) and low body fat and high levels of exercise, particularly exercise related to carrying children. Hunter-gatherers are notoriously lean, based both on very low fat and caloric intake in an otherwise very well-balanced diet. Menstruation is commonly irregular and Ellison (1994) has pointed out that irregular menstruation is likely to be associated with far worse irregularity of ovulation. Hunter-gatherers often have prolonged breast-feeding related to the difficulty of finding other *qualitatively* satisfactory weaning food. Breast milk, bone marrow and pre-chewed meat are highly successful foods in qualitative terms, but are costly.

It has been suggested that sedentary farming, despite a probable decline in the quality of nutrients,

would have resulted in an increase in available calories and a decline in activity levels in child transport. Cereal gruel and other foods softened by boiling could have replaced breast-feeding, although providing a far poorer diet. The proximity of fields to homes might have made it easier for mothers to leave children behind in the care of other family members for parts of a day, reducing energy demands and cutting down on the frequency and regularity of nursing, thereby reducing its contraceptive effects. Others have argued that increased fertility might have resulted from relaxed birth control, resulting, for example, from changes in the availability of secondary caretakers and/or group vulnerability. (For general discussion of these issues see *Current Anthropology* 1973, 14.)

My observation is that hunter-gatherers generally have low rates of live-born children compared to third world populations (Cohen 1989), although Wood (1990) has argued that there is no difference in fertility cross-culturally between ethnographic hunter-gatherers and 'primitive' farmers. On the other hand, several hunter-gatherer groups have individually been shown to have enjoyed increased fertility when they became sedentary (Cohen 1989), with few or none showing the reverse trend.

Direct evidence from prehistoric cemeteries is ambiguous, but broad patterns of pathology in combination with known average rates of population growth before and after agriculture suggest an increase in fertility. Criticisms of the interpretations of palaeopathology, including those by Wood *et al.* (1992), are generally based on a presumption of increased fertility and increased life expectancy with the adoption of farming.

Accelerating population growth rates

The presumption of accelerating growth rates is based on the limits of possible growth from 100,000 or more BP until the adoption of agriculture (*c.* 10,000 BP), when world population has been variously estimated as 10–20 million people (see e.g. Hassan 1981). According to this model, generally espoused, the rate of compound 'interest' of population for the first 90,000 years, prior to the adoption of agriculture, had to be very near zero, perhaps only 0.003 per cent per annum, or it would have produced modern populations enormously in excess of those observed. Moreover, and for the same reasons, the rate of population growth sufficient to convert 20 million to the 500 million estimated for the time of Columbus is also extremely small (generally calculated as 0.1 per cent.) Again, a higher compounding rate would result in a historical population size immensely greater than it is.

It makes little difference if we take the inflection point associated with the adoption of farming as 5000 BP or even 3000 BP, or estimate Neolithic populations as 5, 10, 15, 20 or 30 million. That growth rate cannot have been significantly higher. It is for this reason that the osteological paradox can be rebutted. The increase in pathology is a very common world-wide trend requiring an explanation of equal magnitude. However, the osteological paradox requires a visible increase in both fertility and life expectancy after farming, which cannot possibly be accommodated by an increase in average growth rates to only 0.1 per cent. Individual populations of course could have grown faster, such that the low *average* rate is provided by the balance of successful and less successful populations. Yet all populations studied show the same increase in pathology.

Increased concentration of population and community size

There is little question that farming increases the number of calories produced per unit of space over the landscape. This, in turn, would allow higher population density and permit more people to live in any community within walking distance of their food sources.

However, sedentary farming may not only have permitted but also necessitated denser settlement, because sedentary farmers with planted and/or stored crops are vulnerable to conquest, expropriation and extermination to a far greater degree than mobile hunter-gatherers with little prior investment in resources and little need to store. Hunter-gatherers are hard to subdue and their resources are hard to expropriate, with the result that they can 'melt' into the surrounding landscape with the loss of no more than a few days food. As hunter-gatherers well know, moreover, disease is a disincentive for sedentism and aggregation, suggesting that the need for political strength must have been overpowering. This increase in community size, not health or efficiency or even population growth, I suspect, is by far the most important component of the subsequent political success and expansion of agriculturalist populations.

Some thoughts about the matter of dispersals

First, the success and dispersal of early farming communities was not based on increased health, effi-

ciency, longevity or quality of life. The reality and perception of the adoption of farming would not have been of great new success, but of declining productivity and declining health, suggesting that expansion would hardly have been exuberant and the force of territorial expansion may not have been as powerful as some of the dispersal models in this conference suggest. However, despite the importance of knowing when in a particular sequence declines in health would have occurred (for example, whether health declined immediately upon adoption of sedentism or only later as a result of the intensification of farming), such resolution is rarely available.

Agricultural cemetery samples, like all archaeological data, are only samples of prehistoric skeletons, mere snapshots of continuously changing behaviours. Rarely are there more than two to three snapshots spanning the transition from hunting and gathering to agriculture. To make matters worse, different sequences are sampled by different snapshots. As a result, existing data do not permit us to specify the precise chronology of the decline in any one location (whether, for example, it was an immediate consequence of sedentism and incipient cultivation or only of the increased intensity of farming.) The decline in health might have been evident to people adopting the new economy and should therefore have acted as a disincentive.

Second, the importance of climatic factors in the broad-spectrum revolution and the origins and spread of agriculture has probably been overstated. As a *zonal* variable, climate alone cannot explain a broad, multi-zonal pattern of intensification. More importantly, climate cannot have played a role simply by making certain resources such as cereals more available. The ranking of resources suggests that cereals would not have been utilized unless superior resources had been eliminated or their availability reduced. The significance of climate change, therefore, must have been the role it played in reducing the availability of higher-ranking resources, such as the disappearance of large game.

Third, many of the models presented at the Farming/Language Dispersals conference imply that the initial adoption of agriculture was a rare event, with most spreads of agriculture resulting from diffusion from a few centres. The arguments here strongly suggest that broad-spectrum foragers facing increased resource stress would have proceeded toward the intense use of small grains, whether or not crops or the farming concept diffused. The incentives would have been the same for all. It seems probable, therefore, that domestication would have occurred independently many times, and the distinction between domesticators and intense users of wild grains was probably a function of how human intervention did or did not change selective patterns and hence the spread of new mutations in the 'crop', regardless of any local inventiveness or the lack of it (Harris 1977). Mutations as convenient as the non-shattering rachis of some wheat plants may not have occurred among other wild foods.

Fourth, agriculture, if diffused, would not diffuse to collectors of wild foods simply because the principle was 'discovered', and it would not have diffused to those with superior wild crops. It would have been adopted independently with different local crops or diffused as the need arose. It would diffuse only because recipient cultures themselves were under stress and because the diffusing crops were superior (in terms of being better food sources, more tolerant of human presence and manipulation, more easily manipulated to suit human needs) to those local foods a group had been forced to gather intensively and/or domesticate and cultivate. As Harris (this volume) points out, diffusion of cultigens may also have occurred or failed based on the quality and balance of a particular *package* of resources.

Fifth, rather than being 'clean' events involving the spread of successful farming populations into a largely empty world populated by !Kung-like populations, the transformation must have been a complex blend of diffusion, displacement, population melding and so forth. The transition from selective hunting and gathering through broad-spectrum foraging to farming is in fact such a common and incremental trend that neighbouring populations would have been experiencing similar stresses related at least in part to population density. Farmers attempting to increase their territory would have been dispersing into a world of broad-spectrum economies with populations only slightly smaller/less dense and perhaps only slightly less sedentary than their own (e.g. Zvelebil this volume). This suggests that actual dispersal of a specific population may not have played as great a part in the spread of agriculture or of a language group as some papers presume.

Sixth, the success and dispersal of farming in any general way is unlikely to have resulted from population growth that, *on average*, must have been trivial in the short run and only very marginally greater than that of hunter-gatherers. The *average* rate of population growth by sedentary farming communities would have been far too low to confer either the reality or the perception of numerical superiority *per se*. Neither would it demand rapid disper-

sal. At the average 0.1 per cent compounding rate (0.001), a group of 500 would only grow to about 550 in a century and would need a thousand years to triple.

But that average rate of growth, of course, melds both populations of greater/lesser success and time periods of greater/lesser growth. Individual populations in specific time periods could have grown quite rapidly, at even 3 per cent per year. But if this was the case, of course, other populations/time periods must have been marked by failure to grow or even by abrupt decline. Success and dispersal were not automatic features of newly-invented farming economies. Dispersal must have been highly selective; the greater some successes the more marked had to be the failure of other populations. The problem then is to identify factors more local in time and space that permitted certain populations to succeed. Finally, physical dispersals, to the extent that they occurred, most probably would have been related to another ability of farmers — their ability to establish larger individual communities.

References

Cohen, M.N., 1977. *The Food Crisis in Prehistory*. New Haven (CT): Yale University Press.

Cohen, M.N., 1989. *Health and the Rise of Civilization*. New Haven (CT): Yale University Press.

Cohen, M.N., 1997. Does palaeopathology represent community health, in *Integrating Archaeological Demography*, ed. R. Payne. Carbondale (IL): Southern Illinois University Press, 242–62.

Cohen, M.N. & G. Armelagos (eds.), 1984. *Palaeopathology at the Origins of Agriculture*. New York (NY): Academic.

Ellison, P., 1994. Advances in human reproductive ecology. *Annual Review of Anthropology* 23, 255–75.

Harris, D., 1977. Alternative pathways to agriculture in *The Origins of Agriculture*, ed. C. Reed. Chicago (IL): Aldine, 179–243.

Hassan, F., 1981. *Demographic Archaeology*. New York (NY): Academic Press.

Larsen, C., 1995. Biological changes in human populations with agriculture. *Annual Review of Anthropology* 24, 185–214.

Russell, K., 1988. *After Eden*. (British Archaeological Reports International Series 391.) Oxford: BAR.

Simms, S., 1987. *Behavior Ecological Ecology and Hunter-gatherer Foraging*. (British Archaeological Reports International Series 381.) Oxford: BAR.

Wobst, M., 1974. Boundary conditions for Paleolithic social systems. *American Antiquity* 39, 1147–77.

Wood, J., 1990. Fertility in anthropological populations. *Annual Review of Anthropology* 19, 211–42.

Wood, J., G.R. Milner, H.C. Harpending & K.M. Weiss, 1992. The osteological paradox. *Current Anthropology* 33(4), 343–70.

Chapter 5

What Drives Linguistic Diversification and Language Spread?

Lyle Campbell

What is it that drives linguistic diversification? Why do languages split up into families of related languages? Why do languages spread? There have been numerous hypotheses about what causes languages to diversify, involving, among other things, migration, war, conquest, trade, technological advantage (from forms of food production, herding, navigation, metallurgy, military organization, etc.), and even divine retribution for the Tower of Babel. Communicative isolation is a commonly assumed cause, which has led to speculation about the cultural, geographical, demographic, ecological, economic, political, ideological and other factors that could bring communative isolation about. Earlier accounts of linguistic diversification typically lacked support, but do recent proposals fare better? My goal in this paper is to examine recent claims about why languages diversify and spread in hopes of clarifying the matter. I begin with claims about the role of agriculture.

1. The farming/language dispersal model

Renfrew and Bellwood (in various publications) emphasize agriculture — the farming/language dispersal model: 'farming dispersals, generally through the expansion of populations of farmers by a process of colonization or demic diffusion, are responsible for the distribution and areal extent of many of the world's language families' (Renfrew 1996, 70). Given its impact, it pays to scrutinize this model carefully.

Renfrew (1994; 1996) came to see language spreads as due to one of four processes:

1. *farming-language dispersals* through *demic diffusion* of the farming population, the 'wave of advance model' (Renfrew 2000, 26), that in the case of early farming expansion 'implies dispersals of real populations' (Bellwood 2001, 197);

2. *initial migrations* into previously unoccupied territory;

3. *climate-related colonizations* (late climate-related dispersals into zones not suitable for habitation until the ice receded); and

4. *élite dominance* (through adoption by local hunter-gatherer groups of the new language along with the new agricultural economy, i.e. *acculturation*: Renfrew 1992, 15–16; 1994, 120; 2000, 26; cf. 1988, 438–9).[1]

These 'processes' are discussed below.

1.1. Agriculture and population stability

Agriculture does not always motivate language expansions; rather, agriculture can allow a folk to stay put. Some examples of such stay-at-home agriculturalist language families are seen in Tables 5.1 and 5.2. Rather than expanding, some of these languages take a 'localist strategy', enforcing the linguistic boundaries that deny outsiders access to their resources (Golla 2000; Hill 2001a; cf. Ross 1996; 1997; Thurston 1987; 1989). Moreover, agriculture does not always lead to population pressure which exceeds of the carrying capacity of the land, forcing expansion.[2] Hill (2001a) asks, 'why did not Mixe-Zoqueans [bearers of Olmec civilization] expand at the expense of foraging neighbors, according to the models?' Her answer is,

> a very early adoption of agriculture with a consequent sense of entitlement would have permitted Mixe-Zoqueans to develop localist sociolinguistic strategies . . . As the new technologies of cultivation permitted a sense of trust in the reliability of local resources, new 'residual zones' could form, yielding the contemporary linguistic complexity of . . . Mesoamerica (Hill 2001a, 276).

Such non-expansionist agricultural languages (see Table 5.1) go against the farming/language dispersal model.

1.2. Distribution difficulties

To test the *farming/language dispersal* model, it is important to survey the language families of the world in order to see whether they have spread significantly and whether they have agriculture. A preliminary indication of language families both with and without agriculture is given in Table 5.1, distinguished according to significant spread or not. Language families listed as 'minus agriculture' are assumed not to have had agriculture at the time of their initial dispersal.

Table 5.1 contains a significant number of spread and non-spread languages both with and without agriculture. Simply stated, this means that the farming/language dispersal model alone is neither necessary nor sufficient to explain all these distributions — no one makes such a claim.[3] It is unnecessary since there are widespread non-agricultural language families, and it is not sufficient since there are non-spread agricultural languages. Therefore, other processes of spread must be invoked.

1.2.1. Exceptions and other 'processes'

We therefore need to ascertain whether the exceptions might be explained by Renfrew's (1997; 2000) other processes of spread: initial migrations, late climate-related dispersals and élite dominance. Since it is only spread languages which these processes address, the non-spread languages are less relevant (though an account is needed for why the non-spread agricultural languages did not spread). Among the widespread non-agricultural languages of Table 5.1, only Eskimo-Aleut, Athabaskan, Uralic (Samoyed) and Tungusic can be accounted for by one of these processes: late climate-related dispersals. The other exceptional languages are not explained by initial migrations, late climate-related dispersals, or élite dominance.

1.2.2. Linguistic diversity in agricultural zones

In zones of intensive agriculture, we often find great linguistic diversity. Agriculture in these zones has not necessarily led to language spreads, but has seemingly allowed the development and co-existence of numerous languages and language families. This calls for an explanation. Renfrew (1994, 122) relies on initial migration: 'such residual tongues, scattered in bits and pieces throughout the world map, must have arrived in their current ranges long ago, during the initial dispersal of modern humans'. He suggests (Renfrew 2000, 27) that 'many areas with mosaic-zone language distributions have not been subjected to a farming dispersal, but rather that the initial colonization took place during the Late Pleistocene period, and that there has been stability along with local divergence since that time' (cf. also Bellwood's 2001 'friction zones').

There are two difficulties with initial migration as an explanation. First, we do not know the real history of colonization and replacement in these 'mosaic areas'. In most areas of the world, humans arrived before 40,000 BP, and by at least 12,000 BP in the Americas. Given the very large time interval since initial colonization, numerous languages could have become extinct and been replaced. Thus, reference

Table 5.1. *Spread and non-spread language families with and without agriculture.*

	Plus agriculture	Minus agriculture (mostly)
Significantly spread families	Austronesian Bantu (Niger-Congo) Indo-European Semitic Dravidian Sino-Tibetan (Chinese) Tai Chibchan Cariban Tupian Otomanguean Arawakan Cushitic(?) (pastoralists)	Tungusic Uralic (Samoyed) Eskimo-Aleut Pama-Nyungan Salishan Uto-Aztecan Athabaskan Algonquian Siouan Yuman Chon (Tehuelche, Ona) Jê family
Relatively non-spread families	Some 25+ Papuan families Nakh-Dagastanian Kartvelian Munda Mixe-Zoquean Mayan Totonacan Xinkan Keresan Tanoan (Kiowa-Tanoan) Panoan Isolates: Zuni, Basque, Huave, Cuitlatec, Tarascan, Chitimacha, Tunica, Natchez, Burushaski Japanese, Korean, Sumerian, Etruscan	Some 25 N. Australian families Wakashan Tsimshian Chumashan Maiduan Pomoan Yukian Wintuan Khoi, San Chinookan Takelman Isolates: Kutenai, Haida, Alsea, Siuslaw, Washo, Yana, Esselen, Beothuk, etc.

to the time between original colonization and to-day's distribution of languages leaves far too much unknown and open to speculation. For example, Palaeoindians in the Great Lakes region are documented archaeologically from *c.* 11,000 BP, but the earliest language families of northeastern North America date glottochronologically to only about 4000 years ago: Algonquian *c.* 3000 BP, Iroquoian *c.* 4000 BP (Campbell 1997a, 104). Assuming initial immigration with Palaeoindians, we have 7000 years in which the linguistic landscape could have and probably did change in many ways.

Second, although the languages in 'mosaic zones' today may be agriculturalist, they had to have acquired agriculture sometime in their past. Reference to earliest colonization simply pushes the problem back in time: it is still necessary to explain why the first languages to acquire agriculture did not expand and swallow up others in the zone which did not yet have it, whenever the event took place. Whether agriculture is indigenous or not (Renfrew 2000, 24) seems to be a red herring — not all groups in these regions would have acquired agriculture simultaneously. For example, in Mesoamerica, agriculture is certainly indigenous, but it has also undeniably spread from one group to another so that all ethnic/linguistic groups now have it, though their language distribution seems to be mostly unaffected by this spread. To cite just one example, the linguistic evidence shows that formerly Xinkan speakers were not cultivators, but acquired agriculture from their Mayan neighbours. Virtually all Xinkan terms for cultivation and cultivated plants are borrowed from Mayan (Campbell 1972; 1997b). Thus, Xinkans maintained their distinct identity and language in face of the powerful Mayan agriculturalists, first as non-cultivators and later as cultivators, acquiring agriculture through acculturation, not as the model predicts. In short, there is also agricultural dispersal within mosaic zones, where languages are not displaced in the process.[4]

1.2.3. Small and big languages in the same territory

The agricultural dispersal model does not explain the co-existence of little languages (of few speakers or small geographical area) and large languages (widespread geographically, or of many speakers) within a region.

Bellwood (this volume, p. 21) has in mind 'agriculturalist language families [that] spread over vast areas leaving virtually no enclaves', with Bantu, Malayo-Polynesian [Austronesian] and Indo-Euro-pean as paradigm examples. The model predicts that the expanding larger agricultural languages should swallow up the small languages in the geographical domain of larger languages. The co-existence of such smaller languages with larger ones, thus, constitutes a difficulty for the model (see Table 5.2).

In short, widespread non-agricultural cases such as Pama-Nyungan and Uto-Aztecan and non-spread agricultural cases such as the 'Papuan' language families and Mixe-Zoquean which go against the predictions are serious problems for the farming/language dispersal model.[5]

1.3. Independent events?

Even in cases which might appear to fit the model there are problems of interpretation. For example, if

Table 5.2. *Larger and smaller agricultural languages in the same geographical area.*

Large	Small
Indo-European	Munda
Spanish, French	Basque
Italian	Friulian
German	Sorbian
Thai, Burmese	Mon
Japanese	Ainu
Chinese	Tujia (Tibeto-Burman), Ordos (Mongolian), Oroquen (Tungusic), etc.
Kmer	Cham (Chamic)
Bengali	Khasi (Mon-Khmer)
Hindi	Malto, Gondhi, Kurku (Dravidian), etc.
Oriya (Indo-Aryan)	Mundari (Munda)
Malayalam (Dravidian)	Tulu (Dravidian)
Arabic	various Berber languages
Amharic (Semitic)	Kemant (Cushitic)
Kwa (Niger-Congo)	Mpre (Mbre)
Adamawa (Niger-Congo)	Laal
Mande family (Niger-Congo)	Pre (Bere)
Cushitic (pastoralists)	Sandawe
Yoruba	(Benue-Congo) Chumbuli (Guang branch of Kwa)
Gonja (Kwa)	Safalaba (Gur)
Yucatec Maya	Mopan, Itzaj (Itzá), Lacandon
Zapotec	Huave, Tequistlatec, Pochutec, Papabuco
K'iche'	Uspanteko, Sipakapeño, Sakapulteko
K'iche'an	Xinkan
Nahuatl	Huastec
Muskogean	Natchez, Chitimacha
Quechua, Aymara	Jaqaru, Cauqui, Puquina
Tagalog	Sinauna
Far South (Dubea, Numèè)	Caac (in New Caladonia)
Magi ('Papuan')	Yoba (Austronesian, in Papua New Guinea)
Tetum/Timorese	Buruk ('Papuan')
Kakasi ('Papuan' of Timor)	Kairui-Midiki (Austronesian)

the Indo-Europeanization of Europe and northern India took several millennia, is it really appropriate to talk of it as a single expansion or dispersal, or a single cause? Most Indo-Europeanists insist on a number of independent movements scattered over centuries to account for the distribution of Indo-European languages. (See Vansina 1995, 191 for a similar view of Bantu 'expansion'.) This telescoping of events resulting in the distribution of the languages into a single spread with a single cause does disservice to the prehistory which we are attempting to understand.[6]

1.4. Is the New World different?

Both Bellwood (2000; 2001) and Renfrew (2000) see the New World, with many exceptions to the agricultural dispersal model, as different from the Old World. Following Crosby (1986) and Diamond (1997), they view differences as being due to the north–south axis, the absence of large domesticated animals and the lack of major cereals apart from maize, which may explain the exceptions. This overlooks, however, the fact that the geographical orientation of Mesoamerica is largely east–west and not north–south. Bellwood (2000, 28; this volume) says that New World production systems were not so powerful as those of the Old World. But Mesoamericans had maize, beans and squash (various species), chia (*Amaranthus salvia*), sweet manioc, sweet potatoes, tomatoes, peppers, cacao, guava, papaya, mamey (zapote), Mexican hawthorn, birdcherry, prickly pear, several kinds of *Chenopodium* (epazote, guazontle, verdolaga), turkeys, muscovy ducks and caged rabbits, supplemented with foraging, with extensive irrigation systems in various areas — capable of supporting cities of large population, states and empires.[7] The diet was not that powerless.[8]

These are insufficient grounds for setting the New World aside.

1.5. Application of the model: Uto-Aztecan

Stimulated by Bellwood (1997), Hill (2001b; this volume) re-interprets Uto-Aztecan (UA). She proposes a different Proto-Uto-Aztecan (PUA) homeland, in the south, postulating that PUAs were maize cultivators. This reinterpretation, however, fails to be convincing.

The hypothesis is plausible, but improbable. A southern PUA homeland, associated with Mesoamerica, would be consistent with Hill's claim of PUA maize agriculture. While reconstructed lexical evidence from PUA plant and animal terms is consistent with both the southern and the traditional

northern homeland hypotheses, the centre of gravity method (linguistic migration theory), based on minimum moves and maximum diversification, supports the traditional view, with the homeland in the southwestern US–northeastern Mexico area. Hill's southern homeland has difficulty explaining the distribution of the languages, with little diversification in the south and more in the north. Nahua (the only UA branch squarely in Mesoamerica) shows every sign of entering Mesoamerica later as a break away from its UA relatives. It underwent changes which make it like its Mesoamerican neighbours but set it off from other UA languages; it acquired several Mesoamerican structural traits (Campbell *et al.* 1986) missing from its sister languages, and it borrowed much vocabulary matching cultural traits diagnostic of the Mesoamerican culture area and its ecology, but not of the drier areas to the north (Campbell & Kaufman in prep.). These are not the earmarks of a language in its homeland whose sisters marched away to the north.

For Hill, most of the northern groups, except Hopi, lost agriculture, meaning that the argument for PUA agriculture rests heavily on Hopi evidence alone. Bellwood (1997; 2001) and Hill (2001b) assert that there are few known cases where foragers have adopted cultivation while maintaining their linguistic and ethnic integrity different from the donor community, as is assumed for the Southern UA (SUA) groups in the conventional view. But it is not true that hunter-gatherers do not adopt farming (as cases cited above show). For example, Xinkan and various smaller Mesoamerican groups took on cultivation while retaining their integrity. So did the maize-agricultural Zuni, Keresan, Tanoan, Chitimacha, Natchez and Iroquoian populations. Since these acquired agriculture by acculturation, why is Hopi not just one more in the list?[9]

Hill's principal evidence is nine presumed UA cognate sets as evidence of PUA maize cultivation, though the association which these words have with maize is limited primarily to Hopi and SUA languages. These are problematic: borrowing has been proposed as an explanation for some; for others, wide semantic difference among the languages casts doubt on the cognacy; most require the assumption of considerable semantic shift, though a shift from earlier non-agricultural meaning to later maize associations is more plausible. This evidence is too limited to support Hill's claim.

It is disturbing that so few proposed 'cognates' exist and that the argument depends so heavily on Hopi. I mention briefly some difficulties.

Set 1. SH '*Artemisia argentia*', Hopi 'sand grass' / some SUA languages 'corn, cornfield'. Hill indicates that this does not reconstruct to PUA with a sense of maize. Also, borrowing is not ruled out for the SUA forms.

Set 2. Hopi 'corn cob' / SUA forms 'corn leaf, cane, corn stubble, straw storage bin, granary (corn crib)'. Many of the SUA forms meaning 'storage (granary)' may be internally diffused; otherwise, 'stubble, leaf, cane, cob' have associations more with dry plant parts than agriculture.

Set 3. Hopi 'hominy' / 'seed, ear of corn', Guarijío 'seed but not of maize'. The PUA form is generally believed to have meant 'seed', not agricultural; Hill agrees that non-maize > maize is the most likely direction of semantic shift. The Hopi form *pa:cama* has some difficulties, a /c/ unexpected by regular sound correspondences and an unexplained /ma/.

Set 4. Tubatulabal 'to roast', other northern languages 'cook', 'to melt', 'to boil' / SUA forms 'to toast, parch', 'comal [griddle]', 'toasted corn', 'popcorn'. Probable direction: pre-agricultural 'toasting, roasting, parching' > SUA 'popcorn, parched corn'. (Some SUA forms are probably borrowed internally; compare also Zuni *saKo* 'corn meal', SUA *saki*, etc. 'parched corn, popcorn'.)

Set 5. Hopi 'corn gruel', Hopi 'be sifting (using wind), winnowing', Tumpisha Shoshone 'winnow', Cahuilla 'winnow, sift, blow something (like husks away from grain)' / SUA forms 'harvest, shell corn, shell, shelled, shelled corn kernels'. Probable direction: 'sift' (pre-agricultural) > 'shell'. Only the first syllable /wɨ/ is compared, leaving the rest unexplained, not valid etymological procedure. This syllable could be onomatopoeic, from 'blowing'. The semantic fit among these forms is poor, probably not true cognates; the medial consonant does not fit regular sound correspondences.

Set 6. Hopi 'dried ear of corn', Hopi 'butt end of corn cob', other northern languages 'hooked stick to pull down piñon cones', 'pine cone harvesting hook' / SUA forms 'corncob, corncob with kernels removed'. The semantic associations among the northern languages are strained; the more likely direction of semantic change would be 'pinecone harvesting hook' > 'pinecone' > 'cob'. The Hopi forms are problematic; an unattested /ö:/ 'cob' is extracted from /qaʔö/ 'dried ear of corn' and /o:vi(-ʔat)/ 'butt end of corn

cob', though the leftover parts are of doubtful status. It is too short to defy chance, and it lacks the *n : l* sound correspondence (cf. /l/ of Nahuatl /o:lo:-tl/ 'corn cob'), the basis for putting the other forms into this set.

Set 7. Hopi 'griddle', other northern languages 'to roast, bake, roast under ashes' / SUA forms 'tortilla, tamale'. Some of the SUA forms have been identified as loans. Probable direction: 'roast' > 'tortilla, tamale' (and 'roast' > 'griddle').

Set 8. Hopi 'oblong cake of baked sweet corn, flour' / SUA forms: 'flat and thin object, such as tortilla griddle, flat, a flat place, griddle'. Probable direction: 'flat' > 'griddle'. (Hopi may be 'flat' > 'oblong cake'.)

Set 9. Southern Paiute *qumia* 'corn (rare)', 'Zea mays' is compared to Hopi *kokoma* 'dark red, almost purple', *koko* '*Amaranthus cruentus* (for dye)', and SUA forms *ku:mi-*, *gumí*, etc. 'to eat, chew on something that comes in little pieces; corn cob; bite something hard and small like popcorn; eat small things, eat corn, ear of corn; chew; chew with small bites; mouse'. Since the glosses are so different, the phonetic similarity may be accidental. I believe the Southern Paiute form is a borrowing.

Set 10. 'digging stick'. Hill (2001b) sets this set aside, since foragers too use them.

Set 11. 'to plant' requires neither maize nor agriculture, as in the sense of 'to fix/hide/bury something in the ground'.

The wide semantic latitude in several of these forms calls them into question. All Hill's cases appear better interpreted as semantic shifts from foraging to cultivation and not vice versa.

In short, Hill's reinterpretation of UA is not convincing. The northern homeland and foraging culture of PUA have more support. The spread of non-agricultural UA remains a problem for the farming/language dispersal hypothesis.

1.6. Conclusions on agricultural dispersals

The farming/language dispersal model may work for parts of Austronesian, Bantu and perhaps similar cases, but these are insufficient for generalizing about language spread and diversification. Agriculture is, at best, only one factor driving linguistic diversification, in many cases not the most relevant one.

2. Dixon's approach

Dixon's (1997) characterizes his 'punctuated equilibrium' approach as:

> The hypothesis . . . is that there have been long periods of equilibrium during which a number of languages have coexisted — in a more or less harmonious way — within a given region without any major changes taking place. From time to time the state of equilibrium is punctuated by some cataclysmic event; this will engender sweeping changes in the linguistic situation and may trigger a multiple 'split and expansion' (which would be appropriately modelled by a family tree diagram) . . . After the events which caused the punctuation have run their course, a new state of equilibrium will come into being. (Dixon 1997, 67)

Dixon's book has become influential and therefore it is important to see whether it provides worthwhile insights. Where Dixon differs is in the degree of emphasis he places upon areal linguistics. He imagines that during a period of equilibrium,

> languages in contact will diffuse features between each other, becoming more and more similar. These similarities will gradually *converge*, towards a *common prototype*. We can thus say that language families are rapidly made during a period of punctuation . . . and slowly blurred during the long period of equilibrium . . . that follows (Dixon 1997, 70–71).

This makes classification in terms of language families difficult or impossible. There are problems with this conception.

2.1. Punctuated equilibrium in biology

Dixon's 'punctuated equilibrium' was inspired by Eldredge & Gould's (1972) popular notion which is, however, challenged in biology. As Dennett (1995) argues, there is nothing special about punctuated equilibrium; evolution continues even without punctuated events disrupting equilibrium. Language change and differentiation into language families also continue in periods of equilibrium (in the absence of disruptive events), as Dixon (1997, 9–70) acknowledges. The unrealistic assumptions about human society have been criticized (cf. Nettle 1999, 99).

2.2. Equilibrium without diffusion

Dixon (1997, 70–71) believes that in periods of equilibrium 'languages in contact will diffuse features between each other, becoming more and more similar. These similarities will gradually converge'. But linguistic diffusion does not always take place in situations of equilibrium. Languages in the same area over a long period of time may exhibit little evidence of contact-induced change. To cite just one of many examples, the Hano Tewa (Tanoan language) and Hopi (Uto-Aztecan) share the same very tiny mesa top harmoniously, yet extremely little borrowing or diffusion has taken place in either language (Kroskrity 1993). Diffusion is not a necessary outcome of equilibrium. This is a problem for the model's expectation that equilibrium gives diffusion.

2.3. Equilibrium with diversification

Contrary to expectations of the model, normal change leading to diversification into language families also takes place in equilibrium. There are many cases, with no evidence of punctuation, where the languages of a region continue to undergo normal change and to diversify into language families. Examples include: the Highland Mayan (K'ichean, Mamean subgroups), Zapotec (a complex of some 25 different languages recently diversified), Eskimoan, Nakh-Daghestanian, Lapp (Saami) languages (a subfamily of Finno-Ugric), various 'Papuan' families, etc. In short, a significant number of language families appear to have developed, in relative harmony, without punctuation, as Dixon (1997, 9–70) acknowledges.

2.4. Diffusion in punctuation

Linguistic diffusion can be caused by punctuation and does not take place just in equilibrium. Conquest and inequality are great promoters of structural diffusion among languages, and examples are common. For example, the history of English is mostly punctuated, with Scandinavian invasion and the Norman French conquest, but the outcome is that envisaged for equilibrium: English assimilated huge amounts of vocabulary, borrowed sounds and pronouns, and levelled morphosyntactic complexity. The impact of Spanish on the grammar of many indigenous languages of Latin America is a direct reflection of the inequality in the status of the languages involved and the punctuation that brought Spanish domination. Both forced-language contact (punctuation) and peaceful contact (equilibrium) can have similar outcomes.

Moreover, linguistic areas and areal phenomena shared across languages of a geographical region can arise as a response to punctuating factors (Hill 1978). Groups may join in areal associations in response to famine, resource failure, war and catastrophes of all sorts, structuring human organization at the areal level (see Hill 1978).

2.5. Caution about 'convergence'

Several scholars have interpreted Dixon's convergence with excessive enthusiasm. However, Dixon does not really see languages disappearing by convergence through long-term mutual influence in periods of equilibrium, just the opposite:

> It is instructive to enquire what the possibilities are for two languages in contact over a very long period of time. Could they conceivably merge? I believe that the answer to this question is 'no' . . . All our observation of normal linguistic development suggests that a language never has more than one parent (Dixon 1997, 71).

We know from the well-studied linguistic areas that:

1. typically few diffused structural features are actually found in established linguistic areas, usually less than a dozen main ones (cf. Campbell 1998, 300–306);
2. cases of profound language mixture are basically not found; clear cases of language mixture are truly rare, and these do not arise through normal mechanisms of borrowing in language contact; rather, invariably they are the results of extreme social circumstances, e.g. forced population removals, generally not found in pre-colonial settings (cf. Bakker 2000; Thomason & Kaufman 1988);
3. reference to the family membership of the languages involved is necessary in order to determine diffusion — you can't tell whether it's borrowed or inherited if you don't know where it came from.

It is of some concern that several scholars have understood Dixon to mean that so much convergence is possible that the comparative method is no longer valid and whole languages and families disappear through convergence with one another. What they fail to realize is that in documented linguistic areas wholesale convergence is not known. True, diffused traits across language boundaries can make the task of distinguishing inherited from diffused material very difficult in some cases, but the convergence of initially independent languages to the extent of obliteration of language family connections is not on offer.

It must be concluded, therefore, that the correlation envisaged, which equates equilibrium with convergence, and punctuation with divergence, is not supported — both kinds of change take place in both kinds of situations. The notion provides no real purchase on the questions of why and how languages diversify and spread. They diversify and spread in both punctuation and equilibrium.

3. Nichols' program

Nichols' (1990; 1992; 1993; 1995; 1997; Nichols & Peterson 1996; 1998) program is very complex; here I concentrate only on her treatment of language zones, the part of her work most closely connected with language spread (for a general evaluation, see Campbell & Poser in prep.). Nichols' intention is to use 'non-genetic structural comparison to show that structural affinities between large language areas can be mapped . . . to give us an unimpeded, if rather spare and abstract, view of language origins and ancient linguistic prehistory' (1996, 267). She bases her work on a sample of languages which contains one language representative for each of some 200 'lineages' (called 'stocks' in Nichols 1992) from the some 300 existing 'lineages'. Her method, largely statistical with a very large geographical component, is inspired by population studies in biology and genetics. She tries to find ties among language populations and to gauge the relative age of linguistic traits in large-scale geographical areas, attempting to infer what the source and direction of spread of these structural features is, and also how the languages involved came to have their geographical distributions.

Spread zones and *accretion zones* are an important part of Nichols' analysis' (Nichols 1992, 231; 1997, 369):

> An *accretion zone* (termed *residual zone* in previous works . . .) is an area where genetic and structural diversity of languages are high and increase over time through immigration. Examples are the Caucasus, the Himalayas, the Ethiopian highlands and the northern Rift Valley, California, the Pacific Northwest of North America, Amazonia, northern Australia, and of course New Guinea. Languages appear to move into these areas more often than they move out of them.

> A *spread zone* is an area of low density where a single language or family occupies a large range ('clean sweeps': Bellwood 2001, 195), and where diversity does not build up with immigration but is reduced by language shift and language spreading. A conspicuous spread zone is the grasslands of central Eurasia . . . Another spread zone is central and southern Australia, in which the Pama-Nyungan quasi-stock has undergone several spreads to cover most of the continent . . . Another is northern Africa. Another is the Great Basin of the western United States. (Nichols 1997, 369)

The notions of accretion zones and spread zones are quite relevant to the question of how languages and language families came to be distributed as they are. (The concepts figure in a number of papers in this volume.) There are, however, difficulties with these concepts.

3.1. Misassignment of 'zone' status

The accretion-spread zone distinction is central in Nichols' work, but it is misapplied in several instances. For example, she treats Mesoamerica as a 'spread zone', but by her criteria (Nichols 1992, 16–17) it is a residual (accretion) zone:

1. it has lots of linguistic diversity, not the low genetic diversity characteristic of spread zones;
2. it has lots of structural diversity, as opposed to the low structural diversity for spread zones;
3. the language families are not shallow, with Oto-Manguean calculated glottochronologically at 6400 BP, Uto-Aztecan at 5000 BP and Mayan at 4200 BP (see Kaufman 1974; 1976);
4. in opposition to rapid spread wiping out of existing families, Mesoamerican families stayed in place and rarely swallowed up other languages or took over anybody else's territory;
5. contrary to Nichols' criteria, there was no widespread *lingua franca* in Mesoamerica.

In short, Mesoamerica definitely conforms to Nichols' definition of an accretion/residual zone, not a spread zone. Mesoamerica is not the only 'zone' for which the label 'spread' or 'accretion (residual)' is questionable (see Campbell & Poser in prep.). This misassignment is serious. Nichols (1992) deals with only five spread zones (and five residual zones), so with even one of five misassigned (20 per cent), all the calculations involving these zones are seriously skewed, and all other calculations in which these zones play a role are distorted.

3.2. Problems of representatives

Some problems have to do with the geographic and linguistic composition of Nichols' (1992) zones. Of ten languages in the Mesoamerica zone, two (Chichimec, Miskito) fall outside Mesoamerica both geographically and linguistically. For example, both are SOV languages, while Mesoamerican languages typically lack SOV basic word order (Campbell *et al.* 1986). Chichimec is located beyond Mesoamerica to the north, Miskito outside to the south. Given that Nichols' Mesoamerica contains some non-Mesoamerican languages (20 per cent), all of her calculations concerning spread, stability, and the general character and distribution of linguistic traits in this area are skewed. Nichols' California area corresponds to the 'political boundaries' of the state. It includes

languages from the north (e.g. Yurok) to the south (e.g. Diegueño), but Yurok (Algic) and Diegueño (Yuman) share no significant features. Although there is a northern California linguistic area (with Yurok as a member) and a southern California–western Arizona linguistic area (where Diegueño is a member) (see Campbell 1997a, 335–8), these areas share no significant linguistic traits; there is no linguistic reason to place these languages together.

3.3. Spread zones and agriculture

There appears to be a tendency for scholars supporting the farming/language dispersal model to assume some association between agriculture and spread zones, since by the model, agriculture drives spreads. For example, Renfew (2000, 29) opines that 'it may be concluded that when a linguistic spread zone is observed, it will in many cases be the result of a farming dispersal process'. He acknowledges, however, that 'a linguistic spread zone can also be created by an episode of élite dominance . . . such is the explanation usually offered for the distribution of the Indo-Iranian languages of the Indo-European family, and for the distributions of the Turkic and Mongolian languages also' (Renfew 2000, 30). So, there is no necessary connection between a spread zone and agriculture.

Of the four spread zones originally identified in Nichols (1992), two involve no agriculture (interior North America, central and southern Australia), two do (Europe, Ancient Near East). Of those added later, the Great Basin lacks agriculture, and central Eurasia may have had it, but was focused on pastoralism and herding. central Eurasia is Nichols' best-defined spread zone, but she sees it as being produced not by farming dispersal, but by geographical determinism and political power (Nichols 1997; 1998). In short, a significant proportion of the few spread zones involves no agriculture; many agricultural dispersals are not found in spread zones, and even where there may be agriculture in a spread zone, the forces which shaped the zone in Nichols' view need have nothing to do with agricultural dispersal. So, caution about associating spread zones and agriculture is called for.

3.4. Do spread zones and accretion zones really exist?

Nichols (1992, 291) has four spread zones: ancient Near East, Europe, central Australia and interior North America (Mesoamerica, a residual zone, was eliminated from the list). These four are so different from one another that they raise doubts about the concept of the 'spread zone'. The ancient Near East is a recognized linguistic area (cf. Friedrich 1975;

Diakonoff 1990). It has considerable genetic diversity, with a number of unrelated language families and isolates. Central and southern Australia are entirely different in not being characterized by diffusion among genetically unrelated languages; rather, there is but a single widespread language family, Pama-Nyungan. As for Europe as a spread zone, it would appear that in her later work, Nichols (1997; 1998) considers it more the recipient of impact from the Eurasian zone than a proper zone of its own.

Interior North America appears to be arbitrary. It contains two members of the Northeast Linguistic Area (Seneca, Cree), four from the Plains Linguistic Area (Lakhota, Pawnee, Kiowa, Tonkawa), and one from the Plateau Linguistic Area (Kutenai) (cf. Campbell 1997a, 331–44). There is nothing in the linguistics, cultural anthropology or physical geography that would suggest that these languages ought to be grouped together. They have nothing in common (except the absence of coastline). Interior North America certainly does not match the spread zone definition of 'an area of low density where a single language or family occupies a large range, and where diversity does not to build up with immigration but is reduced by language shift and language spreading' (Nichols 1997, 369). Eight different 'lineages' are represented in interior North America, twice as many as for two of her five residual zones (Ethiopia-Kenya and Caucasus: Nichols 1992, 290–91). In several of her cases, including interior North America, the common assumption that spread zones reflect large migrations that reduce former diversity is not what we see.

Perhaps it is time to abandon the notion of 'spread zone' and simply take recourse in the non-controversial concept of linguistic area, for those that fit. For those instances of putative spread zones involving few but widely spread languages, it appears that there is no particular set of linguistic or other factors which unite them; rather, they appear to be arbitrary pieces of geography or mere artefacts of local political and social history, better understood on a case by case basis as products of contingent history involving language spread.

It is difficult to see that the notions of spread zone and accretion zone do anything more than restate the facts of language distribution while misleadingly suggesting that there is some underlying organizing principle or explanation that does not really exist. For residual (accretion) zones, there must always be linguistic diversity, by definition, otherwise they would be mistaken easily for spread zones or just not be identified at all. Many residual zones nevertheless have some language families which spread widely, behaving more like those thought to be confined to spread zones, while the other families in the zone do not. For example, in Mesoamerica (a residual zone by Nichols' criteria), Nahua (Uto-Aztecan) has spread far and wide, leaving Nahua-speaking communities from Nayarit to Panama. Similarly, Oto-Manguean stretches from above the Mesoamerican frontier to Nicaragua. However, the other language families of Mesoamerica mostly remain quite localized with very little outward spread. Similarly, while the Pueblo Linguistic Area fits Nichols' residual zone criteria, it also has incursions into it from the widespread Athabaskan family (Apachean: Navajo and Apache varieties: Bereznak 1995), and it could be argued that Hopi is intrusive, as well, while Kiowa (Kiowa-Tanoan) has moved out on to the Great Plains and spread out. While the Mayan languages seem to have stayed near to home, nevertheless Huastec is found separated by some 1000 kilometres to the north, though Huastec's closest sister, Chicomuceltec, is found among the other Mayan languages. Thus Huastec seems to suggest a spread while the bulk of Mayan languages fit residual zone traits.

At the same time, spread zones can have a number of residual pockets of surviving languages, giving a degree of linguistic diversity. If historical information were not available about movements and territorial take-overs, in some cases it would be difficult to determine whether a spread zone or residual zone were involved. In fact, given that the 'zones' Nichols (1992) works with are very large, covering continent-sized regions, it is not clear what independent criteria could be brought into the picture to show that the terrain involved is not included on a wholly arbitrary basis.

Nichols' residual zones are also not of a single consistent type. As Bellwood (2001, 195) points out, they can have 'two very distinct types of origin':

> They can be 'end-of-the-line' regions of inflow and substratum residue, as in the concept of the friction zone . . . On the other hand, many regions of great diversity at the level of whole language families — areas such as the Middle East, Mesoamerica, East Asia in general and central Africa — cannot really be considered residual zones, but rather 'upwelling' or 'starburst' zones of net population increase and outflow. These regions are all agricultural homelands and all have linguistic profiles which reflect language family genesis and outflow rather than residual accretion.

Bellwood proposes 'three concepts: (1) the homeland starburst zone of language outflow and non-replacement; (2) the spread zone of rapid language flow and widespread replacement; and (3) the friction zone of reticulation'. This responds to a problem in Nichols' definition, but requires clarification. Most of the problems with Nichols' spread zones remain for Bellwood's spread zones. The other two categories face the problem of how to distinguish them. Is the crucial difference really that 'starburst zones' are all 'agricultural homelands' and 'friction zones' are 'where hunter-gatherers lived in high densities'? If so, extremely few pristine friction zones will exist. If the crucial distinction is 'outflow and non-replacement' (starburst zones) and 'linguistic diversity without languages being lost in spreads' (friction zones), then, since both are characterized by linguistic diversity, how can one be distinguished from the other by purely linguistic means? Why would a starburst outflow and non-replacement of language not produce a friction zone's linguistic diversity without languages being lost in spreads? What would the linguistic difference be?

The terminological terrain dealing with the geographical distribution of linguistic diversity is becoming very complex. Renfrew's (2000) 'mosaic zone' appears to overlap Bellwood's 'starburst zone'; Bellwood's 'starburst zones' no doubt overlap Hill's (2001a) languages with 'localist stance' and Golla's (2000) 'compact language families' (below), though agriculture is not crucial to these other dichotomies. In the end, it is the questions of have linguistic traits diffused and have languages spread or not which matter. These are individual historical events which do not consult these various proposed kinds of zones to see whether or not they should proceed. The types of zone proposed by Bellwood and Renfrew seem to be more imposed on language diversity after the fact to try to save the farming/language dispersal model from cases that do not fit it rather than to explain the distribution of the languages.

In sum, Nichol's accretion–spread zone distinction is at best a misleading idealization. Moreover, Nichols' calculations concerning spread, stability, and the general character and distribution of linguistic traits for the zones with which she deals are called into question by the problems mentioned here. Her conclusions are not supported. In particular, the notion of spread zones and accretion/residual zones should be abandoned, and definitely should not be used in studies aimed at the questions addressed here.

4. Social factors

The farming/language dispersal model and Nichols' program both leave social factors mostly out of the picture, while they are treated unrealistically in Dixon's approach. Nevertheless, many social factors are highly relevant to questions of language spread and diversification (see Hassan this volume).

4.1. Language shift and maintenance

The abundant literature on language shift ('replacement') and maintenance and on language endangerment shows that no approach to linguistic diversification and language spread which emphasizes only geography and economy will be adequate by itself. In general, language shift or maintenance boils down to people's social behaviour, speakers making choices, sometimes under duress and perhaps channelled by economic and other considerations, but also mediated by ideology and social factors. In the interest of space, suffice it here merely to list some of the factors contributing to language shift: discrimination and repression, exogamous marriage patterns, acculturation, military service, cultural disintegration, war and slavery, famine and epidemics, religious proselytizing, lack of social cohesion, lack of physical proximity among speakers, symbolism of the dominant language (e.g. political symbol of nation, cultural symbol of civilization), stigmatization and low prestige, absence of institutions that establish norms (political hierarchy, schools, academies, texts), rapid population collapse, communication with outside regions, resettlement and migration, literacy, compulsory education and official language policies. In addition there are economic factors such as resource depletion and forced changes in subsistence patterns, lack of economic opportunities, rapid economic transformations, shifting subsistence patterns, migrant labour, etc.

Social stratification, class and prestige must not be ignored. To mention just one example, Latin was not imposed in Gaul, but rather came to have a prestige role in various aspects of social life, in the military, administration, commerce and education, which led the local population to replace Gaulish over a period of several centuries (Bauer 1995) — no wave of advance brought Latin, rather the choice to acculturate did.

4.2. 'Esoterogeny', distributed vs localists stances and spread vs compact languages

Recent work by Thurston (1987; 1989), Ross (1996; 1997), Hill (2001a) and Golla (2000) appears to converge as they address different kinds of language distributions, incorporating social and cultural factors and speakers' choices, which mediate them, investigating what this means for theories of language diversification and language spread.

Thurston (1987; 1989) and Ross (1996; 1997) speak of 'esoterogeny' in New Guinea: 'a sociolinguistic development in which speakers of a language add linguistic innovations that increase the complexity of their language in order to highlight their distinctiveness from neighboring groups' (Foley 2000, 359); 'esoterogeny arises through a group's desire for exclusiveness' (Ross 1996, 184). In this way, the community language, which Ross (1996) calls the 'emblematic' language, emblematic of ethnic identity in a multilingual situation, becomes the 'in-group' code which serves to exclude outsiders (cf. Thurston 1989, 556–7; Ross 1997, 232). As Foley (2000, 359) observes, 'such a process would add significantly to linguistic diversity'.

In the case of Thurston's and Ross' 'esoteric' languages, it is attractive to imagine that these languages have undergone the various changes which differentiate them in order for their speakers to distinguish themselves from and exclude outsiders. It is not clear, however, how this hypothesized cultural motive for these changes could be tested or how the investigator might distinguish changes motivated for this purpose from changes which take place without such motives. That such cultural factors were necessarily involved would be difficult to prove since it is possible to cite many situations where other languages have undergone rather extensive changes, leaving them looking 'esoteric', but where no such motive seems to be behind the changes. Languages can undergo changes which consequently but not on purpose keep outsiders from understanding them without necessarily having the cultural teleology of intention to exclude outsiders.

Nevertheless, in spite of the questions I raise about the testability of the claim about cultural motives, recent work by Hill (2001b) and Golla (2000) goes in a direction similar to the Thurston–Ross line of thought, bringing in factors which potentially could make the thesis testable, or at least more tangible.

Golla addresses different kinds of language distributions, incorporating social and cultural factors. For Golla (2000, 60), *spread languages* are:

> language communities all or most of whose constituent dialect communities are sufficiently distant from one another geographically and socially to make social contact sporadic and relatively unstructured. Such language communities are usually the result of the dispersal of speakers of related dialect communities across a wide territory, often by migration.

Examples include Inuit, Dene (northern Athabaskan Slavey, Mountain, Bearlake, Dogrib, Hare), Sahaptin, Ojibway, etc. Spread languages often constitute chains of intelligibility.

Compact languages are:

> language communities whose constituent dialect communities are closely adjacent and share a common interaction sphere (connected by trade, intermarriage, ritual and intergroup alliances and hostilities. (Golla 2000, 60)

Compact language communities were common along the West Coast, from Alaska to California, in the Pueblo southwest and along the Gulf Coast from Texas to Florida (Golla 2000, 60–61).

Examples include the nine divisions of Achomawi in northern California and the dialects of the Keresan pueblos of New Mexico. Golla cites Hill's (2001a) 'localist' strategy of closed groups whose 'insider/outsider' boundaries are marked by correspondingly abrupt linguistic discontinuity. Characteristic of compact language communities are phonological and grammatical differences among dialects that focus on a salient and easily dichotomized feature (Golla 2000, 60).

In similar fashion, Golla distinguishes two kinds of language families. *Spread families* are:

> those that have largely developed in the geographical and social contexts that are conducive to the development of spread languages. Dialect communities develop into language communities with mutually unintelligible linguistic patterns owing to lack of contact and the independent 'drift' of their linguistic systems. Boundaries among these groups remain informal, and where contact exists multilingualism is common, even encouraged, and innovations are rapidly transmitted. This frequently results in the language-level equivalent of dialect chains, where adjacent languages share more features than more distant languages, although the time depth of their split may be the same. Such language chains are typical of Northern Athabaskan languages . . . and Sahaptain languages. (Golla 2000, 62)

Examples of spread families in North America include Eskimo-Aleut, Algic, Na-Dene (Tlingit-Eyak-Athabaskan), Salishan, Cochimi-Yuman, Uto-Aztecan, Siouan, Caddoan, Muskogean and Iroquoian.

Compact families are:

> those that have largely developed in the geographical and social contexts that are conducive to the development of compact languages. Dialect communities develop into language communities in areas where the social boundaries are rigid and stable and where close contact with neighboring groups is the norm . . . patterns of interaction be-

tween adjacent dialect communities appear to have remained stable over many generations, with steadily increasing differentiation of linguistic systems. An important factor in this process is the social advantage of maintaining distinct adaptive systems focused on the exploitation of a relatively circumscribed territory. The continuance of such small-scale social units would appear to be dependent on encouraging monolingualism. (Golla 2000, 63)

Most examples of compact language families in North America are found along the Pacific Coast: Wakashan, Chimakuan, Tsimshianic, Chinookan, Coosan, Takelma-Kalapuyan, Wintuan, Maiduan, Miwok-Costanoan, Yokutsan, Shastan, Achumawi-Atsugewi, Pomoan, Salinan and Yukian (cf. Nettle 1999, 59).

The localist-distributed strategies and the spread-versus-compact languages and language families are not primarily about economics. Rather, they are about people's choices and how they restrict group membership and rights to participate in the cultural life of the group, about who gets to marry whom and where they will live — about the whole fabric of social life. These choices affect the diversification and spread of languages.

5. Conclusions

Agricultural dispersal is only one factor in the bigger picture of what drives language diversification and spread. There are many cases where the distribution of languages does not fit the farming / language dispersal model's predictions — there are many unexplained language spreads without agriculture and cases of linguistic diversity in spite of agricultural spread. The dichotomy between punctuation and equilibrium appears not to be relevant and, in any case, since both diffusion and diversification take place in both situations, in both states of equilibrium and of punctuation, it has no revealing role to play in addressing questions of language diversification and spread. The spread zone–accretion zone distinction is also neither useful nor reliable. The spread zones are so different from each another that nothing unites them and the concept should be abandoned.

On the other hand, the social behaviour of speakers is highly significant, as seen in factors contributing to language shift and maintenance, distributed versus localist strategies and spread versus compact languages and language families. These influence markedly the diversification and spread of languages and language families, and must be given a strong role in explaining these distributions.

Linguistic diversification and language spread appear to be the results of linguistic change mediated by social factors (speakers' choices) and contingent historical events (migration, conquest, climate change, choice to shift languages, etc.). Agriculture, geography, ecology and economics, to the extent that they play a role, are also mediated by social behaviour and particular historical events. It is doubtful that the non-linguistic, non-social generalizations discussed in this paper take us more than a short distance towards answering the questions raised here.

Notes

1. The diversification into families of related languages and the spread of language across territory are typically not distinguished in the works surveyed in this paper, though clearly they are not the same thing. They may be related, but they are not causally connected and can be independent of one another. In this paper, when the scholars discussed do not make this distinction, then neither do I, although clearly sometimes diversification is more at stake, other times it is spread.

   Also, in work surveyed here, the distinction between a language and its speakers is often not made, so, for example, we see 'agricultural languages'. I assume the distinction, but find it convenient to continue to speak of languages having agriculture as shorthand for speakers of a particular language having agriculture.

2. For example, Bellwood (2001) asserts that 'whether the agriculture was being spread by converting hunter-gatherers or range-expanding farmers — both groups would have become subject to population increase in good environments'; LeBlanc (this volume) has it that 'all societies, except for a few in terrible environments, quickly approach the carrying capacity' (cf. Renfrew this volume). Contrary to such claims, however, a difference in population pressures is not visible in all instances, given numerous agricultural language communities which did not expand (see Hill 2001a). Zvelebil (this volume) argues persuasively against the assumption of rapid population growth in farming populations, pointing out that this 'would remove the central assumption underpinning the spread of farming into Europe by demic diffusion' (Zvelebil & Zvelebil 1988, 579).

3. Supporters of the farming / language dispersal hypothesis do not insist it must work in all cases to be accepted. As Peter Bellwood points out (pers. comm.), lots of farmers stayed at home, such as the Egyptians, and some hunters have adopted agriculture, such as the Agta, so, 'the hypothesis is meant to explain some deep-lying patterns, not all aspects of farmer distribution'. Nevertheless, so many exceptions on both sides of the equation do make it difficult to test the hypothesis.

4. Peter Bellwood (pers. comm.) appears to accept this

as a counter-example to the general trend of the farming/language dispersal hypothesis, but does not think Xinkans adopting agriculture is especially relevant for the whole hypothesis, which does not require that all farmers spread instantly and absorb everyone else. Thus the question becomes, how many examples of this sort which go against the predictions of the assumed general tendency expressed in the farming/language dispersal hypothesis would be necessary for doubts about the overall hypothesis to be raised? Since all the Mesoamerican groups, on the whole, fits the Xinkan pattern of agriculture by acculturation rather than by language spread, it would seem that these, together with other known cases, as seen in the charts in this paper, are sufficient to raise doubts.

5. For the majority of historical linguists, the assumption of disputed macrofamilies in works by Bellwood and Renfrew casts doubt on the farming/language model. How one views language diversity and spread around the world differs markedly if one counts only some 20 or less super-families (cf. Renfrew 1992) instead of the 300 or so independent language families that most recognize. If the disputed Amerind, Austric, Altaic, Indo-Pacific, Nostratic and the like have failed to convince linguists, then notions of agricultural dispersals built on such entities obviously will not be found very attractive. Since the model does not depend on these doubtful linguistic entities, they should be dropped.

6. Thanks to Linda Manzanilla (pers. comm.) for discussing cultivation at Teotihuacan with me.

7. For another difference, Bellwood (2000, 129–30) believes that American families have shorter time-depths than major Old World language families. With (glottochronological) dates from 5000 to 6000 BP, however, several of these are as old as established language families anywhere. After Afroasiatic (not entirely uncontroversial) no demonstrated Old World family is relatively older than the New World families Bellwood lists.

8. Renfrew and Bellwood do not say that hunter-gatherers never adopt farming, but do assert that it is extremely rare. The question is, again, as in note 4, how many counter-examples would be considered sufficient to constitute a serious problem for the hypothesis? I believe that the cases cited in this paper are abundant enough to call the hypothesis into question, though Peter Bellwood (pers. comm.) does not.

9. Also, 'spread zones are to be expected at high latitudes and in dry and/or seasonal continental interiors, conditions under which population density has generally been low' (Nichols 1998, 229), but Mesoamerica is not at a high latitude, not dry nor in a seasonal continental interior, and not low in populations density.

References

Bakker, P., 2000. Rapid language change: creolization, intertwining, convergence, in Renfrew *et al.* (eds.), 585–620.

Bauer, B.L.M., 1995. Language Loss in Gaul: a Case Study of Language Conflict. Unpublished paper presented at the Symposium on Language Loss and Public Policy, University of New Mexico Linguistics Institute, Albuquerque, NM, July 1995.

Bellwood, P., 1989. The colonisation of the Pacific: some current hypotheses, in Hill & Serjeantson (eds.), 1–59.

Bellwood, P., 1991. The Austronesian dispersal and the origin of languages. *Scientific American* 265(1), 88–93.

Bellwood, P., 1994. An archeologist's view of language macrofamily relationships. *Oceanic Linguistics* 33, 391–406.

Bellwood, P., 1995. Language families and human dispersal. *Cambridge Archaeological Journal* 5(2), 271–4.

Bellwood, P., 1996. The origins and spread of agriculture in the Indo-Pacific region: gradualism and diffusion or revolution and colonization?, in Harris (ed.), 465–98.

Bellwood, P., 1997. The prehistoric cultural explanations for the existence of widespread language families, in McConvell & Evans (ed.), 23–34.

Bellwood, P., 2000. The time depth of major language families: an archaeologist's perspective, in Renfrew *et al.* (eds.), 109–40.

Bellwood, P., 2001. Early agriculturalist population diasporas? Farming, languages and genes. *Annual Review of Anthropology* 30, 181–207.

Bereznak, C., 1995. The Pueblo Region as a Linguistic Area. Unpublished PhD dissertation, Louisiana State University, Baton Rouge, LA.

Blench, R. & M. Spriggs (eds.), 1997. *Archaeology and Language*, vol. I: *Theoretical and Methodological Orientations*. London: Routledge.

Blench, R. & M. Spriggs (eds.), 1998. *Archaeology and Language*, vol. II: *Archaeological Data and Linguistic Hypotheses*. London: Routledge.

Campbell, L., 1972. Mayan loan words in Xinca. *International Journal of American Linguistics* 38, 187–90.

Campbell, L., 1997a. *American Indian Languages: the Historical Linguistics of Native America*. Oxford: Oxford University Press.

Campbell, L., 1997b. The Linguistic prehistory of Guatemala, in Hill *et al.* (eds.), 183–92.

Campbell, L., 1998. *Historical Linguistics: an Introduction*. Edinburgh: Edinburgh University Press. [American rights edition 1999, Cambridge, MA: MIT Press.]

Campbell, L. & T. Kaufman, in prep. *Linguistic Diffusion in Mesoamerica*.

Campbell, L. & W. Poser, in prep. *How to Show that Languages are Related*.

Campbell, L., T. Kaufman, & T. Smith-Stark, 1986. Mesoamerica as a linguistic area. *Language* 62, 530–70.

Crosby, A.W., 1986. *Ecological Imperialism*. Cambridge: Cambridge University Press.

Crossland, R.A. & A. Birchall (eds.), 1973. *Bronze Age Migrations and Prehistoric Europe*. London: Duckworth.

Dennett, D.C., 1995. *Darwin's Dangerous Idea: Evolution*

and the Meanings of Life. London: Penguin Books.

Diakonoff, I.M., 1990. Language contacts in the Caucasus and the Near East, in Markey & Greppin (eds.), 53–65.

Diamond, J., 1997. *Guns, Germs and Steel*. London: Jonathan Cape

Dixon, R.M.W., 1997. *The Rise and Fall of Languages*. Cambridge: Cambridge University Press.

Durie, M. & M. Ross (eds.), 1996. *The Comparative Method Reviewed: Regularity and Irregularity in Language Change*. Oxford: Oxford University Press.

Eldredge, N. & S.J. Gould, 1972. Punctuated equilibria: an alternative to phyletic gradualism, in Schopf (ed.), 82–115.

Foley, W.A., 2000. The languages of New Guinea. *Annual Review of Anthropology* 29, 357–404.

Friedrich, P., 1975. *Proto-Indo-European syntax: the Order of Meaningful Elements*. (*Journal of Indo-European Studies*, Memoir 1.) Butte (MT): College of Mineral Science.

Golla, V., 2000. Language families of North America, in Renfrew (ed.), 59–73.

Hall, J.A. & I.C. Jarvie (eds.), 1992. *Transition to Modernity*. Cambridge: Cambridge University Press.

Harlow, R. & R. Hooper, 1989. *VICAL 1: Oceanic Languages: Papers of the 5th International Conference of Austronesian Linguistics*. Auckland: Linguistic Society of New Zealand.

Harris, D.R. (ed.), 1996. *The Origins and Spread of Agriculture and Pastoralism in Eurasia*. London: University College London Press.

Hill, A.V.S. & W. Serjeantson (eds.), 1989. *The Colonisation of the Pacific: a Genetic Trail*. Oxford: Oxford University Press.

Hill, J., 1978. Language contact systems and human adaptations. *Journal of Anthropological Research* 34, 1–26.

Hill, J., 2001a. Language on the land: towards an anthropological dialectology, in Terrell (ed.), 257–82.

Hill, J., 2001b. Proto-Uto-Aztecan: a community of cultivators in central Mexico? *American Anthropologist* 103, 913–14.

Hill, J., P.J. Mistry, & L. Campbell (eds.), 1997. *Papers in Honor of William Bright*. Berlin: Mouton de Gruyter.

Kaufman, T., 1974. Middle American languages. 15th edition. *Encyclopaedia Britannica* 11, 959–63.

Kaufman, T., 1976. Archaeological and linguistic correlations in Mayaland and associated areas of Meso-America. *World Archaeology* 8, 101–18.

Kroskrity, P.V., 1993. *Language, History, and Identity: Ethnolinguistic Studies of the Arizona Tewa*. Tucson (AZ): University of Arizona Press.

McConvell, P & N. Evans (ed.), 1997. *Archaeology and Linguistics: Aboriginal Australia in Global Perspective*. Melbourne: Oxford University Press.

Markey, T. & J. Greppin (eds.), 1990. *When Worlds Collide*. Ann Arbor (MI): Karoma.

Nettle, D., 1999. *Linguistic Diversity*. Oxford: Oxford University Press.

Nichols, J., 1990. Linguistic diversity and the first settlement of the New World. *Language* 66, 475–521.

Nichols, J., 1992. *Linguistic Diversity in Time and Space*. Chicago (IL): University of Chicago Press.

Nichols, J., 1993. Ergativity and linguistic geography. *Australian Journal of Linguistics* 13, 39–89.

Nichols, J., 1995. Diachronically stable structural features, in *Historical Linguistics 1993: Selected Papers from the 11th International Conference on Historical Linguistics*, ed. H. Andersen. Amsterdam: John Benjamins, 337–56.

Nichols, J., 1996. The geography of language origins. *Berkeley Linguistics Society* 22, 267–78.

Nichols, J., 1997. Modeling ancient population structures and movement in linguistics. *Annual Review of Anthropology* 26, 359–84.

Nichols, J., 1998. The Eurasian spread zone and the Indo-European dispersal, in Blench & Spriggs (eds.), 220–66.

Nichols, J. & D.A. Peterson, 1996. The Amerind personal pronouns. *Language* 72, 336–71.

Nichols, J. & D.A. Peterson, 1998. Amerind personal pronouns: a reply to Campbell. *Language* 74, 605–14.

Renfrew, C. (ed.), 1973a. *The Explanation of Cultural Change: Models in Prehistory*. London: Duckworth.

Renfrew, C., 1973b. Problems in the general correlations of archaeological and linguistic strata in prehistoric Greece: the model of autochthonous origin, in Crossland & Birchall (eds.), 263–76.

Renfrew, C., 1987. *Archaeology and Language: the Puzzle of Indo-European Origins*. London: Jonathan Cape.

Renfrew, C., 1988. Author's précis. *Current Anthropology* 29, 437–41.

Renfrew, C., 1989. Models of change in language and archaeology. *Transactions of the Philological Society* 87, 103–55.

Renfrew, C., 1991. Before Babel: speculations on the origins of linguistic diversity. *Cambridge Archaeological Journal* 1(1), 3–23.

Renfrew, C., 1992. World languages and human dispersals: a minimalist view, in Hall & Jarvie (eds.), 11–68.

Renfrew, C., 1994. World linguistic diversity. *Scientific American* 270, 116–23.

Renfrew, C., 1996. Language families and the spread of farming, in Harris (ed.), 70–92.

Renfrew, C., 1997. World linguistic diversity and farming dispersals, in Blench & Spriggs (eds.), 82–90.

Renfrew, C., 2000. At the edge of knowability: towards a prehistory of languages. *Cambridge Archaeological Journal* 10(1), 7–34.

Renfrew, C. (ed.), 2000. *America Past, America Present: Genes and Languages in the Americas and Beyond*. (Papers in the Prehistory of Languages.) Cambridge: The McDonald Institute for Archaeological Research.

Renfrew, C., A. McMahon & L. Trask (eds.), 2000. *Time Depth in Historical Linguistics*. Cambridge: McDonald Institute for Archaeological Research.

Ross, M., 1996. Contact-induced change and the comparative method: cases from Papua New Guinea, in

Durie & Ross (eds.), 180–217.

Ross, M., 1997. Social networks and kinds of speech community events, in Blench & Spriggs (eds.), 209–61.

Schopf, T.J.M. (ed.), 1972. *Methods in Paleobiology*. San Francisco (CA): Freeman, Cooper.

Terrell, J.E. (ed.), 2001. *Archaeology, Language, and History: Essays on Culture and Ethnicity*. Westport (CT): Bergin & Garvey.

Thomason S.G. & T. Kaufman, 1988. *Language Contact, Creolization, and Genetic Linguistics*. Berkeley & Los Angeles (CA): University of California Press.

Thurston, W., 1987. Processes of change in the languages of northwestern New Britain. *Pacific Linguistics* B99, 1–163.

Thurston, W.R., 1989. How exoteric languages build a lexicon, in Harlow & Hooper (eds.), 555–80.

Vansina, J., 1995. New linguistic evidence and 'the Bantu expansion'. *Journal of African History* 36, 173–95.

Zvelebil, M. & K.V. Zvelebil, 1988. Agricultural transition and Indo-European dispersals. *Antiquity* 62, 574–83.

Chapter 6

Inference of Neolithic Population Histories using Y-chromosome Haplotypes

Peter A. Underhill

The impact of the development of plant and animal domesticates and domestication economies during the Neolithic/Formative period has been highly influential, both culturally and demographically. Agriculture has no simple single origin. It arose independently in multiple places, although at different times, during the improving climatic regime of the Holocene (Cavalli-Sforza *et al.* 1994; Bar-Yosef this volume). There were at least two significant factors which initially catalyzed these geographically diverse and independent localized transitions from food-collection to food-production. First was an increase in population density to levels that began to approach the carrying capacity of the environment for foragers. Second was the chance availability of exploitable native species amenable to domestication in the geographically diverse origination zones of the incipient agricultural communities. The mechanism(s) of the spread of agriculture and the development of resultant social complexity, settlement and civilization underlies the central theme of this volume and the conference on which it is based.

The contemporary genetic landscape is the manifestation of the differential survival of populations which have participated in multiple evolutionary and demographic processes (Underhill *et al.* 2001a). These include successful migration and settlement episodes, fluctuations in population sizes and succeeding demographic and range expansions, all overlain upon previous population ranges (except in cases of settling new landscapes). The aim here is to summarize salient geographic patterns of extant Y-chromosome binary DNA haplotype variation in an attempt to evaluate two diametrical concepts concerning the spread of agriculture. One proposition states that agriculturist mediated gene flow, driven by an expanding population size (i.e. by demic diffusion) was the major factor propelling the

dispersal of agriculture and language. The rival model claims that the transmission and adaptation of innovations associated with the agricultural revolution to indigenous people (i.e. by cultural diffusion) was the major forcing factor. Recent progress in Y-chromosome molecular genetic studies of contemporary human populations provides new clues to the relative effects of both processes.

The global Y phylogeny indicates a non-random clustering of haplotypes with geography (Underhill *et al.* 2001a). The pattern of Y-chromosome DNA sequence variation differentiation varies greatly with geographic distance, both between and within a continental framework (Fig. 6.1). The ability of the non-recombining portion of the Y chromosome to maintain evolutionarily stable binary marker-defined haplotype signatures, coupled with more rapidly mutating microsatellite loci, provides a powerful system for understanding diversity across both meso- and micro-time scales (de Knijff 2000). Thus, the transparent and irregular patterns of Y-chromosome haplotype geography, affinity and diversification provide an exciting additional metric to this chapter of human evolution.

This new knowledge of the Y-chromosome genealogy permits the inference of candidate haplotypes pertinent to the Neolithic period. The correspondence between Y-chromosome lineages and the geographically asymmetric radiation pattern of demographic phenomena inferred from archaeological, linguistic and other genetic evidence is suggestive of a mixture of reciprocal influences; a continuum that accommodates both models, i.e. demic and cultural diffusion. While the clinal patterns of haplotypes mark trajectories of the movement of genes and by inference, populations other factors can create genetic clines (Barbujani & Dupanloup this volume).

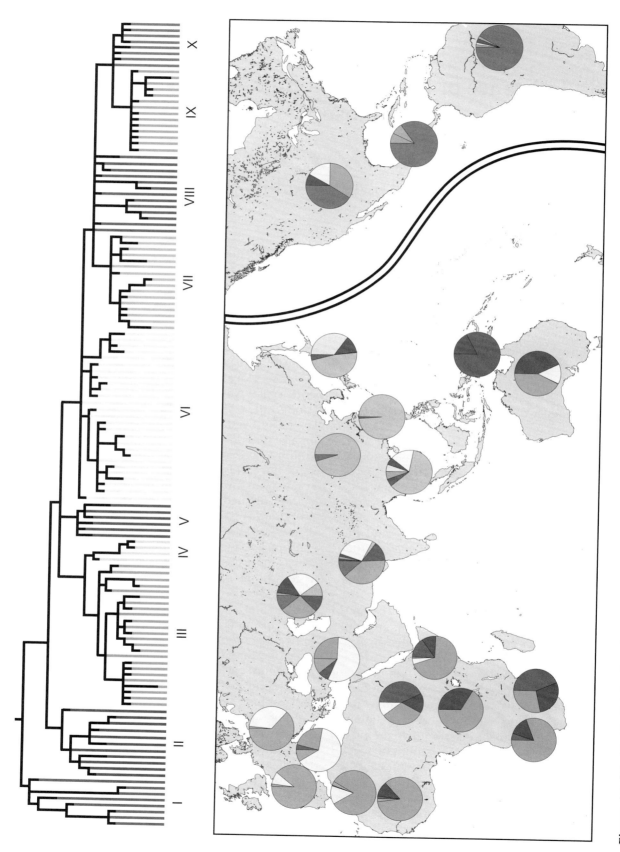

Figure 6.1. *Worldwide distribution of 10 clusters of Y-chromosome haplotypes in 22 regions. (From Underhill et al. 2001a, 47, fig. 2.)*

Molecular genetics and history: some considerations and caveats

Progress in understanding the spectrum of human DNA sequence variation and its causes, especially when integrated with other knowledge from historians, archaeologists, anthropologists and linguists can help illuminate human population histories (Owens & King 1999). The dynamics of evolution involve both extinction and diversification of survivors, both of entire organisms and individual genes. Thus, any inferences deduced from the history of a single gene must be viewed cautiously. Human evolution has been shaped by a constellation of evolutionary processes. Both natural selection and/or drift (random chance) can shape patterns of genetic variation. The sex-specific inherited non-recombining haploid mtDNA and the Y-chromosome loci, with their smaller effective population sizes relative to the autosomes, are particularly sensitive to the influences of drift, especially founder effect. Consequently, these loci are valuable for inferring migration patterns and provide context for hypothesis testing from a number of different disciplines. Although analysis of ancient DNA holds exciting promise (Krings *et al.* 1997; Ovchinnikov *et al.* 2000), most molecular work still involves contemporary populations, and potential sampling bias.

Thus, the picture that emerges, no matter how detailed, is representative of only those molecular genetic variants found that have survived to the present. Like the palaeoanthropological record, the molecular fossil record is also incomplete. An additional complication involves the likelihood that males and females may have different population histories modulated by differential reproductive success related to non-random mating phenomena. It is unlikely that panmixia is a valid assumption, especially regarding sex-specific loci (Hammer *et al.* 2001). Since both genes and humans experienced bottlenecks, followed by rapid population growth during the Neolithic, calculated molecular dates reflect only the origin of the clades based upon the common ancestor. Thus, actually one estimates the molecular age of a demographic event (or coalescence age), e.g. exponential population growth following a bottleneck (de Knijff 2000), not the age of the true divergence which may have occurred considerably earlier. Thus one can have lineages with considerably deep phylogenetic heritage which participated in a recent demographic event involving a founder event followed by an expansion (Tambets *et al.* this volume).

Recent comparative sequencing results indicate that NRY sequences show reduced variability compared to other genetic loci (Shen *et al.* 2000). Whether this is due to localized natural selection, differential gender-related survivorship and/or migration factors, rather than localized natural selection, remains uncertain. Whatever the cause of this discrepancy, it is useful since it accounts for the characteristic high stratification of NRY diversity with geography relative to other genes. Any evolutionary forces which reduce the effective male population size relative to females, such as polygamy (Torroni *et al.* 1990), coupled with gender-specific migration patterns that suggest women move more than men (Seielstad *et al.* 1998), will influence genetic clines observed on the geographic landscape.

The Neolithic period represents just a small portion of the overall history of anatomically modern humans. The question remains; just how much informative genetic variation accumulated within this window of time that can provide resolution of associated demographic events? While the Y chromosome is finite in physical size, the majority of its landscape has not yet been surveyed for polymorphisms. There must be tens of thousands of binary markers and a considerable number of potential polymorphic microsatellite loci to be revealed as a result of the completion of the human genome sequencing project. Thus, there is reason to believe that more Y-chromosome distinctive variation, with geographic specificity, can eventually be retrieved from the genealogical interval spanning the Neolithic to the present. The following summaries are predicated on the underlying assumption that there is a correspondence between the overall distribution of haplotypes and past human movements. The Y-chromosome data are consistent with this assumption and often find support from climatic, palaeoanthropological, linguistic and other genetic knowledge.

The Near East

The geographic arc encompassing the Fertile Crescent is considered the cradle of agricultural innovation that spread to other regions of the Near East. A variety of plant and animal species were domesticated at different times and places during the Neolithic in an unfolding mosaic of agriculture and pastoral lifestyles (Bar-Yosef 1998; and this volume). For example, genetic fingerprinting of plant varieties indicates that the domestication of wild einkorn wheat began near the Karacadag mountains in southeast Turkey (Heun *et al.* 1997).

Extant Y-chromosome haplotype diversity provides fascinating clues to these complex historical events. The non-random distribution of haplotypes observed in Europe has been proposed to be mainly a function of re-colonization episodes by descendents of earlier Palaeolithic foragers from various refugia following the Last Glacial Maximum (Semino *et al.* 2000). However, a different subset of lineages, that likely trace their heritage to Anatolia and the Near East, suggest the possible genetic contribution of patrilineages associated with demographic events during the transition to agriculture. Perhaps the most predominant Y haplotypes associated with the Neolithic in the Fertile Crescent and adjacent regions involves one of the first RFLP-based polymorphisms ever described. Casanova *et al.* (1985) reported that clone p12f detected a Taq I polymorphism in the genomic region assigned as locus DYS11 (Mitchell 1996). Southern blot data indicated high frequencies in populations associated with the Mediterranean basin (Santachiara-Bererecetti *et al.* 1993). Subsequently, Semino *et al.* (1996) proposed that the distribution of the p12f 8 kb allele coincided with the demic expansion of agriculturists from the Fertile Crescent. This contrasted in distribution to another RFLP haplotype, 49a,f ht 15, which is generally European-specific and was suggested as a possible signature of pre-Neolithic heritage. Additional support for this rendition has been reported recently (Hill *et al.* 2000; Wilson *et al.* 2001).

The recent conversion of the p12f locus to a PCR compatible assay (Sun *et al.* 2000; Rosser *et al.* 2000) has yielded considerable additional population frequency data (Hammer *et al.* 2000; Rosser *et al.* 2000; Quintana-Murci *et al.* 2001). This haplotype has often being called by the moniker 'Med' (Hammer *et al.* 2000), and has been attributed to the expansion of agriculture from the Fertile Crescent into Northeast Africa, southern Europe, coastal regions adjoining the Mediterranean basin, and Central and Western Asia. It has been associated with the 'Cohen modal' haplotype (Thomas *et al.* 1998), which has a distinctive pattern of large size alleles at the trinucleotide microsatellite locus DYS388. The large DYS388 alleles are associated with the 12f2 8 kb allele (Nebel *et al.* 2001a). One can cautiously interpret DYS388 large allele size data from the Near East (Thomas *et al.* 2000; Nebel *et al.* 2000) as a proxy for 12f2 8kb.

Semino *et al.* 2000 identified a collection of both putative Palaeolithic and other lineages that they attributed to demographic events. The proposed trajectories of these lineages are summarized in Figure 6.2. The lineages suggested to be associated with the Neolithic agricultural event in the Fertile Crescent

and peripheral regions include the haplotypes defined by M89, M89/M201, M89/M172 and YAP/M35. These authors also noted that M89/M172 lineages composed a major subset of 12f2 8 kb allele haplotypes. The genealogical relationship of all these haplotypes to one another has been recently shown (Underhill *et al.* 2001a). Considerable numbers of Middle Eastern chromosomes are either 12f2 8 kb or its major M172 sublineage, defined by M172, that appear to have a source in the southern and northern regions of the Fertile Crescent respectively (Nebel *et al.* 2001b). Figure 6.3 shows the global Y-chromosome binary polymorphism phylogeny previously reported (Underhill *et al.* 2001a). Key haplotypes inferred as participatory in Neolithic (e.g. Holocene) global demographically driven events are indicated and discussed further below.

The M172 mutation defines a diverse subset of 12f2 8 kb haplotypes which provide potential future opportunities for further resolution of the complex Neolithic events in the Mediterranean region, Africa and Asia. Using the data from Semino *et al.* (2000), a correlation between certain types of material culture and some Y-chromosome lineages was observed, suggesting a shared history of dispersal and cultural ideas (King & Underhill 2002). Specifically M172 related lineages successfully predicted the distribution of both Neolithic figurines (88 per cent accuracy) and painted pottery (80 per cent accuracy). The recent availability of a PCR assay for the 12f2 polymorphism has allowed us to demonstrate that the majority of the lineages previously defined as just having the M89 mutation are positive for the 12f2 mutation. It was pointed out that a direct relationship most likely exists between the M201 haplotype and the 12f2 8 kb allele sub-clade, indicating apparent shared common ancestry manifested by RFLP 49a,f ht 8 (Semino *et al.* 2000). A very small percentage of lineages, however, remain uncharacterized beyond M89 and these may represent the earliest spread of the M89 lineage. It is worth noting that the common M170 lineage diversified from an M89 lineage, *in situ* in Europe. The M170 lineage has been proposed as being associated with the Palaeolithic gene pool (Semino *et al.* 2000) and appears uncommon in populations from the Fertile Crescent region. It may be reflective of at least some of the Mesolithic foragers.

Another group of haplotypes, although phylogenetically distinct from the subset of M89-related putative Neolithic lineages, also appear to be associated with a demic expansion from the general area of the Middle East. Their geographic distribution in the Mid-East and Europe provides an additional sig-

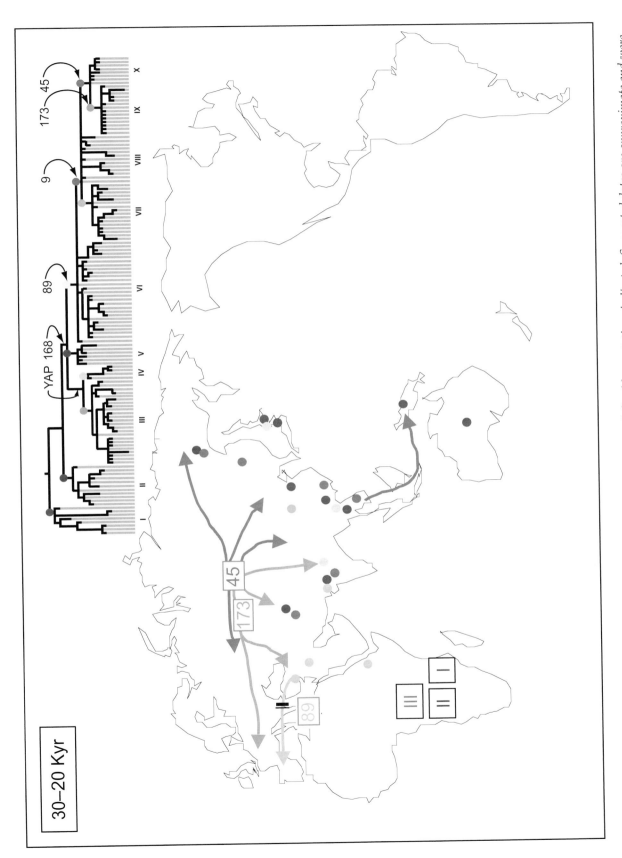

Figure 6.2. *Hypothesized trajectories of Y-chromosome haplotypes in Europe defined by mutations indicated. Suggested dates are approximate and were deduced mainly from non-genetic knowledge.*

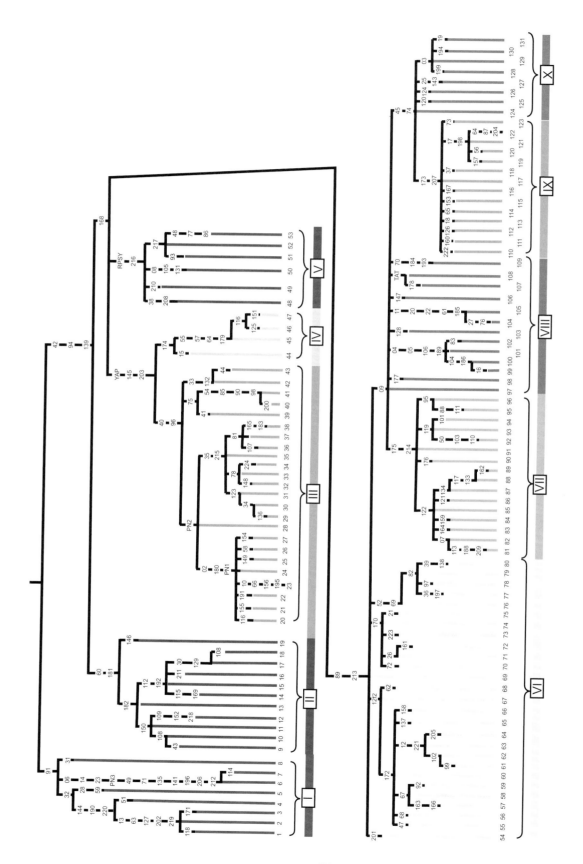

Figure 6.3. *Maximum parsimony phylogeny of 218 Y-chromosome binary polymorphisms. Tree is rooted with respect to great ape sequences. (From Underhill et al. 2001a, 45, fig. 1.)*

nal of a range expansion. These were defined as YAP/M35-related lineages (Semino *et al.* 2000). It should be recognized that M35 most likely comprises the majority of YAP+ chromosomes previously designated as ht 4 in a previous study of the global distribution of YAP (Hammer *et al.* 1997), and as hg21 in a study of Europe (Rosser *et al.* 2000). Following the Last Glacial Maximum (LGM), people moved into previously uninhabited areas. Some may have come from the Nile Valley (Henry 1989). The high frequency of hg21 observed in Northwest Africa in Rosser *et al.* (2000) has been further resolved using two M35-related binary mutations, M78 and M81 (Bosch *et al.* 2001). Considerable binary haplotype substructure exists within the M35 sub-clade with distinctive lineages in North Africa, the Mediterranean Basin and Western Asia. These provide additional reagents with which to infer specific episodes of population histories associated with the Neolithic agricultural expansion.

A significant correlation was observed when the entire collection of Neolithic lineages was compared to the first principal component (PC) analysis of 95 classical polymorphisms from Europe which has been previously interpreted as evidence of a demic expansion catalyzed by the spread of agriculture (Semino *et al.* 2000). The first PC of the 95 genes accounts for 28 per cent of the overall genetic variation. While there is a pronounced southeast to northwest clinal distribution of Y-chromosome lineages proposed as representative of Neolithic history, they occur at 22 per cent overall in Europe. This observation supports the concept that Y-chromosome lineages alone can be representative of the movement of multiple genes (i.e. populations) and reinforces the assignment of known or surmised population movements to Y-chromosome haplotype gradients. The interpretation of second PC in Europe was vague (Cavalli-Sforza *et al.* 1994). Y-chromosome haplotypes indicated, however, that one pole was the result of M173-defined haplotypes emerging from the Iberian Peninsula following the LGM and outlier Uralic Y-chromosome lineages in northern Europe at the opposite pole (Semino *et al.* 2000). The third PC in Europe significantly correlated with M17 lineages (Semino *et al.* 2000), which have been interpreted as the dispersal of nomadic people from the steppe territory around present-day Ukraine (Cavalli-Sforza *et al.* 1994; Quintana-Murci *et al.* 2001). Additional verification that the cataloging of major Y-chromosome binary haplotypes is correct comes from mtDNA data which contend that approximately 20 per cent of mtDNA lineages with internally consistent geographic proximity have Neolithic ancestry (Richards

et al. 2000; this volume). A recent re-analysis of the Semino *et al.* (2000) Y-chromosome data suggested that there was a greater genetic contribution by Neolithic farmers (Chikhi *et al.* 2002). I would caution against accepting the higher levels proposed too quickly. The computer simulation model employed has non-trivial inadequacies. For example, it ignores the significance of high-frequency autochthonous lineages like those defined by the M170 mutation. This creates a bias towards over-estimating admixture from the Middle East. Nonetheless, whatever the actual percentage of the agriculturalist influence, the genetic data support the concept of the demic diffusion model. The congruence of Y-chromosome haplotypes, mtDNA haplogroups and the first three PCs of classical genetic markers underscore the utility of using the contemporary gene pool to recover aspects of human history. The greater resolution of the Y-binary haplotypes with geography reinforces the likelihood that the Y provides the most detailed roadmap of human affinity, diversification and migration yet from a genetic perspective. Integrating microsatellite data to construct compound Y-chromosome haplotypes will provide additional temporal and spatial resolution.

Africa

The deepest roots of the Y-chromosome phylogeny are found in African populations, consistent with an 'Out of Africa' scenario. The collection of haplotypes comprising Groups I and II in Figures 6.1 and 6.3 are restricted to Africa and are distinguished from other African and non-African populations by the M168 transition mutation (Underhill *et al.* 2000; 2001a). The Group I and II lineages are dispersed across Africa, usually at low frequencies. These lineages represent survivorship of chromosomes with a deeper genealogical heritage than all the other haplotypes. It is interesting to note that Group I and II representatives include some Khosian and Bantu speakers from South Africa as well as some men from Sudan and Ethiopia. While numerous markers within Groups I and II show geographic specificity, some markers like M32 and M182 indicate preservation of a heritage from a more distant past, when the initial African population occupied a wider range (Cavalli-Sforza *et al.* 1994). Although there is genetic evidence of Palaeolithic expansions within Africa (Reisch & Goldstein 1998), the influence of demographic processes related to the recent spreads of agriculture, and later iron technology and the Bantu languages, left a major imprint on the continent (Cavalli-Sforza *et al.* 1994).

Demic expansions from the Middle East spread genes, agricultural innovations and languages into Northeast Africa (Passarino *et al.* 1998). Early agriculture first appeared in the Nile Valley by 6000 BC, although established farming communities probably did not exist until 5000 BC. It is unclear which lineages participated in this event. However, the high prevalence of YAP+ chromosomes in Egypt (Salem *et al.* 1996; Hammer *et al.* 1997), likely of M35 ancestry, as well as Ethiopian Y chromosomes with the 12f2 mutation, provide important clues (Semino *et al.* 1996). On the basis of data from the fourth PC in Africa, which accounts for 7 per cent of the total variation, Cavalli-Sforza *et al.* (1994) has postulated that the development of agriculture also occurred in Mali, Niger and Burkina Faso, beginning 4000–5000 years ago. This should be viewed cautiously because archeological data remain scarce. Although the distribution of Y-haplotype diversity in Africa is considerable, some lineages associated with Group III, defined by YAP/M40 (= SRY4064) mutations, participated greatly in this recent demographic expansion. Several studies have shown that the M2 mutation (Seielstad *et al.* 1994) and its molecular mimic, PN1, characterize many sub-Saharan populations (Hammer *et al.* 1997; Scozzari *et al.* 1999; Thomas *et al.* 2000). These appear to have participated in the last and best-known African agricultural expansion involving migration flows of Bantu speakers who originated near present-day Cameroon.

While M2 lineages are the major component of the Bantu expansion (Passarino *et al.* 1998; Thomas *et al.* 2000), another major derivative of M2 (M191) has recently been identified (Underhill *et al.* 2001a), which underscores the sensitivity of Y variants in delimiting bottleneck events. Additional non-M2 lineages related to Group III haplotypes also probably co-participated in the Bantu expansion event. Comparing published haplotype designations (Hammer *et al.* 1998; Scozzari *et al.* 1999), it is now possible to deduce likely additional resolution. The designated haplotype 3A lineages likely correspond to M33 and M75 associated lineages. Some YAP– haplotypes (IB) correlate with Underhill's Group II. The PN2 lineages without PN1 or M2 correspond to M35 associated lineages.

The widespread Bantu expansion is a recent event from a discreet homeland. We now have the capability to define high-resolution Y-chromosome binary and microsatellite defined haplotypes, in both putative regions of origin and destination. Thus, it appears promising that it will be possible to eventually provide additional resolution to any earlier de-

mographic events, as well as the more recent Bantu east and west migration streams.

East Asia

The earliest evidence of the formative, independent development of agriculture in East Asia traces to about 8000 years ago in the middle Yangtze River region of China (Cavalli-Sforza *et al.* 1994). Before considering the Neolithic period, however, a summation of the entire extant Y-chromosome gene pool provides a useful contextual framework.

Representative lineages associated with all three major non-African sub-clusters of M168 (i.e. YAP/M145/M203, RPS4Y/M216 and M89/M213) are found in East Asian populations (Underhill *et al.* 2001a). Using these markers, it was shown in a study of over 12,000 Y chromosomes that there is no evidence of any hybridization of archaic and modern humans in Asia (Ke *et al.* 2001). This tripartite pattern of paternal heritage represents different population compositions and histories. It has been recently noted that all East Asian YAP/M145/M203 haplotypes share the M174 mutation and these lineages are confined to peripheral or isolated geographical regions, consistent with a relic distribution (Underhill *et al.* 2001a). While East Asian-associated RPS4Y/M216 lineages are more frequent and widespread (Karafet *et al.* 1999; Underhill *et al.* 2000; Ke *et al.* 2001), these also are considered to reflect descendents of the early pioneers into the region (Underhill *et al.* 2001a). RPS4Y/M216 lineages also occur in insular Southeast Asia, Melanesia, New Guinea, Australia and Polynesia (Kayser *et al.* 2000; Capelli *et al.* 2001), but without the common M217 transversion (Underhill *et al.* 2001b).

The M217 sub-clade of RPS4Y/M216 occurs in West, Central, East Asians and North Americans with its highest frequency in northern Asia (Underhill *et al.* 2001a; Karafet *et al.* 2001; Lell *et al.* 2002). The gene geography suggests that its representatives participated to a greater extent in East Asian range and population size expansion than the Asian-specific M174 marked YAP/M145/M203 group. It is worth noting that the null haplotype (H1) of (Su *et al.* 1999; 2000a,b) actually represents RPS4Y/M216/M217 lineages that occur at considerably higher frequencies in northern than southern populations. The most prevalent assemblage of East Asian lineages, however, is those defined by M175/M214 that diversified in East Asia from an earlier M89/M213 ancestor, that also accumulated M9 elsewhere. Several haplotypes have diversified from a common M175/M214 ancestor that has a centre of gravity clearly placed in East Asia. Many of these associated haplotypes are widely distributed throughout the region at high frequency (Su *et al.* 1999; 2000 a,b), especially in southern populations. The M175 cluster of haplotypes defines a major subset of lineages whose distribution and frequency is consistent with the spread of rice and millet agriculture and possibly the Sino-Tibetan (or Tibeto-Burman, see van Driem this volume) languages (Su *et al.* 2000b).

Using dental characteristics, Turner (1989) observed a higher distribution of sinodonts in northern Mongoloids, versus southern Mongoloids who are more likely to display sundadont features. Although completely unlinked from a molecular perspective, and nothing is known about the role of natural selection in dentition, it is tempting to consider whether or not a similar dichotomy can be observed in the Y-chromosome record. Using predominantly M175 associated Y-chromosome data, a reduced Y-chromosome haplotype diversity was observed in the north, and every northern haplotype also occurred in the south. Based upon this evidence, it has been proposed that there was a Palaeolithic northerly migration into East Asia from the south (Su *et al.* 1999), although others have suggested that the data rather reflect isolation by distance (Ding *et al.* 2000).

Whatever the migration directionality, the data strongly imply an East Asian *in situ* origin of the M175/M214 clade. The presence of numerous M175/M214 differentiated lineages suggests that a very large population size participated in the population expansion which resulted from agricultural development. The presence of undifferentiated RPS4Y/M216 lineages in insular Southeast Asia (Underhill *et al.* 2001b), and associated lineages elsewhere, suggest a Palaeolithic bottleneck event represented by M217 which radiated towards North, Central and South Asia as well eventually to North America. Lastly, some 12f2-related lineages appear to have penetrated from the West via the Silk Road (see ht 4 in Su *et al.* 1999 and 2000b for candidate populations), best explained as a trace of Neolithic genes arriving from the Near East. A recent Eurasian study of Y-chromosome lineages supports the hypothesis that 12f2-related lineages arrived in East Asia from the Middle East via Central Asia (Wells *et al.* 2001)

Australasia and Oceania

Generally, this region (along with aboriginal Taiwan) is dominated by a single language family, Austronesian (Bellwood 1989; Gray & Jordan 2000), whose distribution is thought to be associated with the spread of agriculture. There is no evidence of an early agricultural economy in Australia, but it appears to have developed rather early in New Guinea (Cavalli-Sforza *et al.* 1994). Mitochondrial DNA evidence has provided an independent assessment that is consistent with a Southeast Asian Austronesian influence (Hertzberg *et al.* 1989; Murray-McIntosh *et al.* 1998). A 9 bp deletion motif (haplogroup B) and its derivatives almost singularly dominate the mtDNA landscape.

The mtDNA data have been used to support either a rapid expansion of Polynesians from Southeast Asia (Sykes *et al.* 1995; Melton *et al.* 1995), or Australo-Melanesian ancestry (Richards *et al.* 1998). Recent progress relating to Y-chromosome variation has revealed a more diverse genetic heritage (Kayser *et al.* 2000; 2001; Capelli *et al.* 2001; Underhill *et al.* 2001b), with the major representatives being RPS4Y/M216 lineages, M9 lineages and M175 lineages. It has been proposed that RPS4Y/M216 and M9 lineages reflect contributions initially arriving during the Pleistocene, with M175 lineages arriving later, possibly as one component of the recent Polynesian expansion (Underhill *et al.* 2001a,b). It should be emphasized that these diverse groups of Y-binary lineages all participated in the Neolithic expansions, including the colonization of Polynesia.

In contrast to some interpretations of mtDNA data and linguistic data, the Y data suggest a deep genetic contribution to the Polynesian gene pool by Australo-Melanesians. Some important markers include the RPS4Y/M216 derived M38 mutation which occurs in Indonesia, New Guinea and New Zealand. The M9 associated derivative, M4, has been observed in New Guinea (Underhill *et al.* 1997; 2000) and other Melanesian populations (Kayser *et al.* 2001), but not in Polynesians (Su *et al.* 2000a; Kayser *et al.* 2001). Lineages associated with M175 have been observed in Oceania. Interestingly, M119, which has a high frequency in Taiwan, is also observed in East and Southeast Asian populations but not in Polynesia (Su *et al.* 2000a) or Australia (Kayser *et al.* 2001). Another M175 derivative, M122, widely distributed in Asia (Su *et al.* 1999; 2000b; Underhill *et al.* 2000), has been observed in Polynesia and may have been brought to the region by the recent Austronesian expansion (Kayser *et al.* 2000).

The Americas

Although the date of entry into the Americas via the Beringian land bridge remains uncertain, it was the last continental landmass to be colonized (Cavalli-Sforza *et al.* 1994). Two distinctive genetic signatures have been observed in the Americas. One is associated with the M45 lineage, proposed to have originated in Central Asia (Underhill *et al.* 2001a). An important derivative of M45, called M3 (Underhill *et al.* 1996), occurs at high frequencies in both North and South America but is virtually absent elsewhere (Karafet *et al.* 1997; Lell *et al.* 1997). The M3 lineage probably originated *in situ* and dispersed through the Americas, possibly with Amerind population expansions catalyzed by the development of maize, bean and squash agriculture. M3 is found today through North and South American populations ranging from 25 per cent to 100 per cent. The first appearance of permanent settlements was about 4000 years ago, but the beginnings of agriculture predate this by a millennium or so.

The origins of pre-Columbian agriculture trace to different regions within Mexico and the Andes (Smith 2001). A haplotype proposed to be the precursor genetic background upon which M3 originated has been observed in the Lake Baikal region of Siberia (Santos *et al.* 1999). Other M45 lineages observed in the Americas, but without M3, are probably related to this putative Siberian paternal ancestor (Lell *et al.* 2002). North American groups also show small frequencies of RPS4Y lineages (Bergen *et al.* 1999; Karafet *et al.* 1999), associated with the NaDene-speaking populations (Ruhlen 1998), which arrived by a migration subsequent to those that developed into Amerind populations.

The transition to an agricultural economy was not rapid in the Americas, where a nomadic, forager way of life persisted in many regions until recently. Perhaps language was a partial impediment. While much remains to be understood, the continued development of Y markers provides one avenue of exploration. For example, the continued identification of binary mutations associated with M3, like M194 which appears confined to Mayan populations from Central America, and M19 which occurs in South American populations from Colombia, provide another level of resolution amenable to investigating localized Neolithic events.

Conclusion

While variation in any single gene can only reflect a small portion of human diversity, the unique nature of NRY chromosome haplotypic variation provides an elegant narrative of human population histories by genealogical inference. By merging other genetic and non-genetic knowledge it should be possible to improve our understanding of population histories, including the revolutionary impact of agricultural innovation during the Neolithic. Although much of the 'low hanging fruit' regarding Y-chromosome markers and human history is being rapidly harvested, more specific stories can be addressed. Some examples include the following:

1. a correlation between the TAT Y-chromosome polymorphism and the recent arrival of Uralic speakers in northern Europe (Zerjal *et al.* 1997);
2. a European gypsy (Roma) founder lineage with a linguistic association to the Indian subcontinent, marked by M52 and more rapidly mutating repetitive length polymorphisms (Kalaydjieva *et al.* 2001);
3. using Y markers to clarify the population genetic structure of Sardinians (Passarino *et al.* 2001), a population generally considered a genetic outlier (Cavalli-Sforza *et al.* 1994).

In conclusion, the association of geography and Y-chromosome haplotypes provides a transparent view of the dispersal of agriculturists via both demic expansion and cultural transmission mechanisms.

Acknowledgements

I thank L. Luca Cavalli-Sforza and Giuseppe Passarino for helpful discussions.

References

Bar-Yosef, O., 1998. On the nature of transitions: the middle to upper Paleolithic and the Neolithic revolution. *Cambridge Archaeological Journal* 8(2), 141–63.

Bellwood, P., 1989. The colonization of the Pacific: some current hypotheses, in *The Colonization of the Pacific: a Genetic Trail*, eds. A.V.S. Hill & S.W. Serjeantson. Oxford: Oxford University Press, 1–59.

Bergen, A.W., C.-Y. Wang, J. Tsai, K. Jefferson, C. Dey, K.D. Smith, S.-C. Park, S.-J. Tsai & D. Goldman, 1999. An Asian–native American paternal lineage identified by RPS4Y resequencing and by microsatellite haplotyping. *Annal of Human Genetics* 63, 63–80.

Bosch, E., F. Calafell, D. Comas, P.J. Oefner, P.A. Underhill & J. Bertranpetit, 2001. High resolution analysis of human Y-chromosome variation shows a sharp discontinuity and limited gene flow between northwestern Africa and the Iberian Peninsula. *American Journal of Human Genetics* 68, 1019–29.

Capelli, C., J.F. Wilson, M. Richards, M.P.H. Stumpf, F. Gratrix, S. Oppenheimer, P.A. Underhill, V.L. Pascali, T.-M. Ko & D.B. Goldstein, 2001. A predominantly indigenous paternal heritage for the Austronesian speaking peoples of insular South East Asia and

Oceania. *American Journal of Human Genetics* 68, 432–43.

Casanova, M., P. Leroy, C. Boucekine, J. Weissenbach, C. Bishop, M. Purello, G. Firoi & M. Siniscalco, 1985. A human Y-linked DNA polymorphism and its potential for estimating genetic and evolutionary distance. *Science* 230, 1402–6.

Cavalli-Sforza, L.L., P. Menozzi & A. Piazza, 1994. *The History and Geography of Human Genes*. Princeton (NJ): Princeton University Press.

Chikhi, L., R.A. Nichols, G. Barbujani & M.A. Beaumont, 2002. Y genetic data support the Neolithic demic diffusion model. *Proceedings of the National Academy of Sciences of the USA* 99, 11,008–13.

de Knijff, P., 2000. Messages through bottlenecks: on the combined use of slow and fast evolving polymorphic markers on the human Y chromosome. *American Journal of Human Genetics* 67, 1055–61.

Ding, Y.-C., S. Wooding, H.C. Harpending, H.-C. Chi, H.-P. Li, Y.-X. Fu, J.-F. Pang, Y.-G. Yao, J.-G.X. Yu, R. Moyzis & Y. Zhang, 2000. Population structure and history in East Asia. *Proceedings of the National Academy of Sciences of the USA* 97, 14,003–6.

Gray, R.D. & F.M. Jordan, 2000. Language trees support the express-train sequence of Austronesian expansion. *Nature* 405, 1052–5.

Hammer, M.F., A.B. Spurdle, T. Karafet, M.R. Bonner, E.T. Wood, A. Novelletto, P. Malaspina, R.J. Mitchel, S. Horai, T. Jenkins & S.L. Zegura, 1997. The geographic distribution of human Y chromosomes. *Genetics* 145, 787–805.

Hammer, M.F., T. Karafet, A. Rasanayagam, E.T. Wood, T.K. Altheide, T. Jenkins, R.C. Griffiths, A.R. Templeton & S.L. Zegura, 1998. Out of Africa and back again: nested cladistic analysis of human Y chromosome variation. *Molecular Biology and Evolution* 15, 427–41.

Hammer, M.F., A.J. Redd, E.T. Wood, M.R. Bonner, H. Jarjanazi, T. Karafet, S. Santachiara-Benerecetti, A. Oppenhiem, M.A. Jobling, T. Jenkins, H. Ostrer & B. Bonné-Tamir, 2000. Jewish and middle eastern non-Jewish populations share a common pool of Y-chromosome biallelic haplotypes. *Proceedings of the National Academy of Sciences of the USA* 97, 6769–74.

Hammer, M.F., T. Karafet, A.J. Redd, H. Jarjanazi, S. Santachiara-Benerecetti, M. Soodyall & S.L. Zegura, 2001. Hierarchical patterns of global human Y-chromosome diversity. *Molecular Biology and Evolution* 18, 1189–203.

Henry, D.O., 1989. *From Foraging to Agriculture: the Levant at the End of the Ice Age*. Philadelphia (PA): University of Pennsylvania Press.

Hertzberg, M., K.N.P. Mickleson, S.W. Serjeantson, J.F. Prior & R.J. Trent, 1989. An Asian-specific 9-bp deletion of mitochondrial DNA is frequently found in Polynesians. *American Journal of Human Genetics* 44, 504–10.

Heun, M., R. Schäfer-Pregl, D. Klawan, R. Castagna, M. Accerbi, B. Borghi & F. Salamini, 1997. Site of einkorn wheat domestication identified by DNA fingerprinting. *Science* 278, 1312–14.

Hill, E.W., M.A. Jobling & D.G. Bradley, 2000. Y-chromosome variation and Irish origins. *Nature* 404, 351–2.

Kalaydjieva, L., F. Calafell, M.A. Jobling, D. Angelicheva, P. de Knijff, Z.H. Rosser, M.E. Hurles, P. Underhill, I. Tournev, E. Marushiakova & V. Popov, 2001. Patterns of inter- and intra-group genetic diversity in the Vlax Roma as revealed by Y chromosome and mitochondrial DNA lineages. *European Journal of Human Genetics* 9, 97–104.

Karafet, T.M., S.L. Zegura, J. Vuturo-Brady, O. Posukh, L. Osipova, V. Weibe, F. Romero, J.C. Long, S. Harihara, F. Jin, B. Dashnyam, T. Gerelsaikhan, K. Omoto & M.F. Hammer, 1997. Y-chromosome markers and trans-Bering Strait dispersals. *American Journal of Physical Anthropology* 102, 301–14.

Karafet, T.M., S.L. Zegura, O. Posukh, L. Osipova, A. Bergen, J. Long, D. Goldman, W. Klitz, S. Harihara, P. de Knijff, V. Wiebe, R.C. Griffiths, A.R. Templeton, & M.F. Hammer, 1999. Ancestral Asians source(s) of new world Y-chromosome founder haplotypes. *American Journal of Human Genetics* 64, 817–31.

Karafet, T., L. Xu, R. Du, W. Wang, S. Feng, R.S. Wells, A.J. Redd, S.L. Zegura & M.F. Hammer, 2001. Paternal population history of East Asia: sources, patterns, and microevolutionary processes. *American Journal of Human Genetics* 69, 615–28.

Kayser, M., S. Brauer, G. Weiss, P.A. Underhill, L. Roewer, W. Schiefenhovel & M. Stoneking, 2000. Melanesian origin of Polynesian Y chromosomes. *Current Biology* 10, 1237–46.

Kayser, M., S. Brauer, G. Weiss, W. Schiefenhövel, P.A. Underhill & M. Stoneking, 2001. Independent histories of human Y chromosomes from Melanesia and Australia. *American Journal of Human Genetics* 68, 173–90.

Ke, Y., B. Su, X. Song, D. Lu, L. Chen, H. Li, C. Qi, S. Marzuki, R. Deka, P.A. Underhill, P.J. Oefner, C. Xiao, M. Shriver, J. Lell, D. Wallace, R.S. Wells, M. Seielstad, D. Zhu, J. Jin, W. Huang, R. Chakraborty, Z. Zhu Chen & L. Jin, 2001. African origin of modern humans in East Asia: a tale of 12,000 Y chromosomes. *Science* 292, 1151–3.

King, R. & P.A. Underhill, 2002. Congruent distribution of Neolithic painted pottery and ceramic figurines with Y-chromosome lineages. *Antiquity* 76, 707–14.

Krings, M., A. Stone, R.W. Schmitz, H. Krainitzki, M. Stoneking & S. Pääbo, 1997. Neanderthal mtDNA sequences and the origin of modern humans. *Cell* 90, 19–30.

Lell, J.T., M.D. Brown, T.G. Schurr, R.I. Sukernik, Y.B. Starikovskaya, A. Torroni, L.G. Moore, G.M. Troup & D.C. Wallace, 1997. Y chromosome polymorphisms in native American and Siberian populations: identification of native American Y haplotypes. *Human Genetics* 100, 536–43.

Lell, J.T., R.I. Sukernik, Y.B. Starikovskaya, B. Su, L. Jin, T.G. Schurr, P.A. Underhill & D.C. Wallace, 2002.

The duel origin and Siberian affinities of Native American Y chromosomes. *American Journal of Human Genetics* 70, 192–206.

Melton, T., S. Clifford, J. Martinson, J. Batzer & M. Stoneking, 1995. Polynesian genetic affinities with Southeast asian populations identified by mtDNA analysis. *American Journal of Human Genetics* 57, 403–14.

Mitchell, R.J., 1996. Y-chromosome-specific restriction fragment length polymorphisms (RFLPs): relevance to human evolution and human variation. *American Journal of Human Biology* 8, 573–86.

Murray-McIntosh, R.P., B.J. Scrimshaw, P.J. Hatfield & D. Penny, 1998. Testing migration patterns and estimating founding population size in Polynesia by using human mtDNA sequences. *Proceedings of the National Academy of Sciences of the USA* 95, 9047–52.

Nebel, A., D. Filon, D.A. Weiss, M. Weale, M. Faerman, A. Oppenheim & M.G. Thomas, 2000. High-resolution Y-chromosome haplotypes of Israeli and Palestinian Arabs reveal geographic substructure and substantial overlap with haplotypes of Jews. *Human Genetics* 107, 630–41.

Nebel, A., D. Filon, C. Hohoff, M. Faerman, B. Brinkmann, & A. Oppenheim, 2001a. Haplogroup-specfic deviation from the stepwisw mutation model at the microsatellite loci DYS388 and DYS392. *European Journal of Human Genetics* 9, 22–6.

Nebel, A., D. Filon, B. Brinkman, P. Majumder, M. Faerman & A. Oppenheim, 2001b. The Y-chromosome pool of Jews as part of the genetic landscape of the Middle East. *American Journal of Human Genetics* 69, 1095–112.

Ovchinnikov, I.V., A. Götherström, G.P. Romanova, V.M. Kharitonov, K. Lidén & W. Goodwin, 2000. Molecular analysis of Neanderthal DNA from the northern Caucasus. *Nature* 404, 490–93.

Owens, K. & M.-C. King, 1999. Genomic views of human history. *Science* 286, 451–6.

Passarino, G., O. Semino, L. Quintana-Murci, L. Excoffier, M. Hammer & A.S. Santachiara-Benerecetti, 1998. Different genetic components in the Ethiopian population, identified by mtDNA and Y-chromosome polymorphisms. *American Journal of Human Genetics* 62, 420–34

Passarino, G., P.A. Underhill, L.L. Cavalli-Sforza, O. Semino, G. Pes, C. Carru, L. Ferrucci, C. Franceschi, L. Deiana, G. Baggio & G. De Benedictis, 2001. Use of Y-chromosome binary markers to study the high prevalence of males in Sardinian Centenarians and the genetic structure of the Sardinian population. *Human Heredity* 52, 136–9.

Quintana-Murci, L., C. Krausz, T. Zerjal, S.H. Sayar, M.F. Hammer, S.Q. Mehdi, Q. Ayub, R. Oamar, A. Mohyuddin, U. Radhakrishna, M.A. Jobling, C. Tyler-Smith & K. McElreavey, 2001. Y-chromosome lineages trace diffusion of people and languages in southwestern Asia. *American Journal of Human Genetics* 68, 537–42.

Reisch, D.E. & D.B. Goldstein, 1998. Genetic evidence for a Paleolithic human population expansion in Africa. *Proceedings of the National Academy of Sciences of the USA* 95, 8119–23.

Richards, M., S. Oppenheimer & B. Sykes, 1998. MtDNA suggests Polynesian origins in Eastern Pacific. *American Journal of Human Genetics* 63, 1234–6.

Richards, M., V. Macaulay, E. Hickey, E. Vega, B. Sykes, V. Guida, C. Rengo, D. Sellitto, F. Cruciani, T. Kivisild, R. Villems, M. Thomas, S. Rychkov, O. Rychkov, Y. Rychkov, M. Golge, D. Dimitrov, E. Hill, D. Bradley, V. Romano, F. Cali, G. Vona, A. Demaine, S. Papiha, C. Triantaphyllidis, G. Stefanescu, J. Hatina, M. Belledi, A. Di Rienzo, A. Oppenheim, S. Norby, N. Al-Zaheri, S. Santachiara-Benerecetti, R. Scozzari, A. Torroni, H.-J. Bandelt, 2000. Tracing European founder lineages in the Near Eastern mtDNA Pool. *American Journal of Human Genetics* 67, 1251–76.

Rosser, Z.H., T. Zerjal, M.E. Hurles, M. Adojaan, D. Alavantic, A. Amorim, W. Amos, M. Armenteros, E. Arroyo, G. Barbujani, G. Beckman, L. Beckman, J. Bertranpetit, E. Bosch, D.G. Bradley, G. Brede, G. Cooper, H.B.S.M. Côrte-Real, P. de Knijff, R. Decorte, Y.E. Dubrova, O. Evgrafov, A. Gilissen, S. Glisic, M. Gölge, E.M. Hill, A. Jeziorowska, L. Kalaydjieva, M. Kayser, T. Kivisild, S.A. Kravchenko, A. Krumina, V. Kuinskas, J. Lavinha, L.A. Livshits, P. Malaspina, M. Syrrou, K. McElreavey, T.A. Meitinger, A.-V. Mikelsaar, R.J. Mitchell, K. Nafa, J. Nicholson, S. Nørby, A. Pandya, J. Parik, P.C. Patsalis, L. Pereira, B. Peterlin, G. Pielberg, M.J. Prata, C. Previderé, L. Roewer, S. Rootsi, D.C. Rubinsztein, J. Saillard, F.R. Santos, G. Stefanescu, B.C. Sykes, A. Tolun, R. Villems, C. Tyler-Smith & M.A. Jobling, 2000. Y-chromosomal diversity in Europe is clinal and influenced primarily by geography, rather than by language. *American Journal of Human Genetics* 67, 1526–34.

Ruhlen, M., 1998. The origin of the Na-Dene. *Proceedings of the National Academy of Sciences of the USA* 95, 13,994–6.

Salem, A.H., F.M. Bard, M.F. Gaballah & S. Pääbo, 1996. The genetics of traditional living: Y-chromosomal and mitochondrial lineages in the Sinai Peninsula *American Journal of Human Genetics* 59, 741–3.

Santachiara-Benerecetti, A.S., O. Semino, G. Passarino, A. Torroni, R. Brdicka, M. Fellous & G. Modiano, 1993. The common near-eastern origin of Ashkenazi and Sephardi Jews supported by Y-chromosome similarity. *Annal of Human Genetics* 57, 55–64.

Santos, F.R., A. Pandya, C. Tyler-Smith, S.D. Pena, M. Schanfield, W.R. Leonard, L. Osipova, M.H. Crawford & R.J. Mitchell, 1999. The central Siberian origin for native American Y chromosomes. *American Journal of Human Genetics* 64, 619–28.

Scozzari, R., F. Cruciani, P. Santolamazza, P. Malaspina, A. Torroni, D. Sellitto, B. Arredi, G. Destro-Bisol, G. De Stefano, O. Rickards, C. Martinez-Labarga, D.

Modiano, G. Biondi, P. Moral, A. Olckers, D.C. Wallace & A. Novelletto, 1999. Combined use of biallelic and microsatellite Y-chromosome polymorphisms to infer affinities among African populations. *American Journal of Human Genetics* 65, 829–46.

Seielstad, M.T., J.M. Hebert, A.A. Lin, P.A. Underhill, M.D. Ibrahim, D. Vollrath & L.L. Cavalli-Sforza, 1994. Construction of human Y-chromosomal haplotypes using a new polymorphic A to G transition. *Human Molecular Genetics* 3, 2159–61.

Seielstad, M.T., E. Minch & L.L. Cavalli-Sforza, 1998. Genetic evidence for a higher female migration rate in humans. *Nature Genetics* 20, 278–80.

Semino, O., G. Passarino, A. Brega, M. Fellous & A.S. Santachiara-Benerecetti, 1996. A view of the Neolithic demic-diffusion in Europe through two Y-chromosome-specific markers. *American Journal of Human Genetics* 59, 964–8.

Semino, O., G. Passarino, P. Oefner, A.A. Lin, S. Arbuzova, L.E. Beckman, G. De Benedictis, P. Francalacci, A. Kouvatsi, S. Limborska, M. Marcikiæ, A. Mika, B. Mika, D. Primorac, A.S. Santachiara-Benerecetti, L.L. Cavalli-Sforza & P.A. Underhill, 2000. The genetic legacy of Palaeolithic *Homo sapiens sapiens* in extant Europeans: a Y-chromosome perspective. *Science* 290, 1155–9.

Shen, P., F. Wang, P.A. Underhill, C. Franco, W.-H. Yang, A. Roxas, R. Sun, A.A. Lin, R.W. Hyman, D. Vollrath, R.W. Davis, L.L. Cavalli-Sforza & P.J. Oefner, 2000. Population genetic implications from sequence variation in four Y-chromosome genes. *Proceedings of the National Academy of Sciences of the USA* 97, 7354–9.

Smith, B.D., 2001. Documenting plant domestication: the consilience of biological and archaeological approaches. *Proceedings of the National Academy of Sciences of the USA* 98, 1324–6.

Su, B., J. Xiao, P. Underhill, R. Deka, W. Zhang, J. Akey, W. Huang, D. Shen, D. Lu, J. Luo, J. Chu, J. Tan, P. Shen, R. Davis, L. Cavalli-Sforza, R. Chakraborty, M. Xiong, R. Du, P. Oefner, Z. Chen & L. Jin, 1999. Y-chromosome evidence for a northward migration of modern humans into eastern Asia during the last ice age. *American Journal of Human Genetics* 65, 1718–24.

Su, B., L. Jin, P.A. Underhill, J. Martinson, N. Saha, S.T. McGarvey, M.D. Shriver, J. Chu, P. Oefner, R. Chakraborty & R. Deka, 2000a. Polynesian origins: insights from the Y chromosome. *Proceedings of the National Academy of Sciences of the USA* 97, 8225–8.

Su, B., C. Xiao, R. Deka, M.T. Seielstad, D. Kangwanpong, J. Xiao, D. Lu, P. Underhill, L. Cavalli-Sforza, R. Chakraborty & L. Jin, 2000b. Y-chromosome haplotypes reveal prehistorical migrations to the Himalayas. *Human Genetics* 107, 582–90.

Sun, C., H. Skaletsky, S. Rozen, J. Gromoll, E. Nieschlag, R. Oates & D.C. Page, 2000. Deletion of azoospermia factor a (AZFa) region of human Y chromosome caused by recombination between HERV15 proviruses. *Human Molecular Genetics* 9, 2291–6.

Sykes, B., A. Leiboff, J. Low-Beer, S. Tetzner & M. Richards, 1995. The origins of the Polynesians: an interpretation from mitochondrial lineage analysis. *American Journal of Human Genetics* 57, 1463–75.

Thomas, M.G., K. Skorecki, H. Ben-Ami, T. Parfitt, N. Bradman & D.B. Goldstein, 1998. Origins of Old Testament priests. *Nature* 394, 138–40.

Thomas, M.G., T. Parfitt, D.A. Weiss, K. Skorecki, J.F. Wilson, M. le Roux, N. Bradman & D.B. Goldstein, 2000. Y chromosomes traveling south: the Cohen model haplotype and the origins of the Lemba — the 'Black Jews of southern Africa'. *American Journal of Human Genetics* 66, 674–86.

Torroni, A., O. Semino, R. Scozzari, G. Sirugo, G. Spedini, N. Abbas, M. Fellous & A.S. Santachiara Benerecetti, 1990. Y-chromosome DNA polymorphisms in human populations: differences between Caucasoids and Africans detected by 49a and 49f probes. *Annals of Human Genetics* 54, 287–96.

Turner, C.G., 1989. Teeth and prehistory in Asia. *Scientific American* 260, 88–96.

Underhill, P.A., L. Jin, R. Zemans, P.J. Oefner & L.L. Cavalli-Sforza, 1996. A pre-Columbian human Y-chromosome-specific C to T transition and its implications for human evolution. *Proceedings of the National Academy of Sciences of the USA* 93, 196–200.

Underhill, P.A., L. Jin, A.A. Lin, S.Q. Mehdi, T. Jenkins, D. Vollrath, R.W. Davis, L.L. Cavalli-Sforza & P.J. Oefner, 1997. Detection of numerous Y-chromosome biallelic polymorphisms by denaturing high performance liquid chromatography (DHPLC). *Genome Research* 7, 996–1005.

Underhill, P.A., P. Shen, A.A. Lin, L. Jin, G. Passarino, W.H. Yang, E. Kauffman, B. Bonné-Tamir, J. Bertranpetit, P. Francalacci, M. Ibrahim, T. Jenkins, J.R. Kidd, S.Q. Mehdi, M.T. Seielstad, R.S. Wells, A. Piazza, R.W. Davis, M.W. Feldman, L.L. Cavalli-Sforza & P.J. Oefner, 2000. Y chromosome sequence variation and the history of human populations. *Nature Genetics* 26, 358–61.

Underhill, P.A., G.P. Passarino, A.A. Lin, P. Shen, M. Mirazon-Lahr, R.A. Foley, P.J. Oefner & L.L. Cavalli-Sforza, 2001a. The phylogeography of Y-chromosome binary haplotypes and the origins of modern human populations. *Annals of Human Genetics* 65, 43–62.

Underhill, P.A., G. Passarino, A.A. Lin, S. Marzuki, L.L. Cavalli-Sforza & G. Chambers, 2001b. Maori origins, Y-chromosome haplotypes and implications for human history in the Pacific. *Human Mutation* 17, 271–80.

Wells, R.S., N. Yuldasheva, R. Ruslan Ruzibakiev, P.A. Underhill, I. Evseeva, J. Blue-Smith, L. Jin, B. Su, R. Pitchappan, S. Shanmugalakshmi, K. Balakrishnan, M. Read, N. Pearson, T. Zerjal, M. Webster, I. Zholoshvili, E. Jamarashvili, S. Gambarov, B. Nikbin, A. Dostiev, O. Ogonazar Akhnazarov, P. Zalloua, I. Tsoy, M. Kitaev & W.F. Bodmer, 2001. The Eurasian Heartland: a continental perspective on Y-chromosome diversity. *Proceedings of the National Academy of Sciences of the USA* 98, 10,244–9.

Wilson, J.F., D.A. Weiss, M. Richards, M.G. Thomas, N. Bradman & D.B. Goldstein, 2001. Genetic evidence for different male and female roles during cultural transitions in the British Isles. *Proceedings of the Na-*

tional Academy of Sciences of the USA 98, 5078–83.

Zerjal, T., B. Dashnyam, A. Pandya, M. Kayser, L. Rower & F.R. Santos, 1997. Genetic relationships of Asians and Northern Europeans revealed by Y-chromosomal DNA analysis. *American Journal of Human Genetics* 60, 1174–83.

Chapter 7

Demic Diffusion as the Basic Process of Human Expansions

Luca Cavalli-Sforza

Renfrew (1987) is responsible for stressing the tie between the demic expansion of farmers and language families, especially for the spread of Middle Eastern farming and Indo-European languages. Bellwood (1991) has emphasized another remarkable example involving the radiation of the Austronesian-speaking peoples. I remember discussing with Albert Ammerman, at the time we started working on the demic diffusion hypothesis, the similarity between the geographic map of Indo-European and the archaeological maps of the spread of farming from the Middle East. Ammerman replied that, unfortunately, archaeologists are helpless about languages spoken by people living before the introduction of writing. This difficulty was remembered repeatedly at the Cambridge meeting, and its truth is supported by the heat of the published discussion that followed Renfrew's original proposal. In spite of this, I believe the bold 1987 attempt by Renfrew was very useful, and the confrontations to which it gave rise will in the long run prove constructive.

The real trouble with any historical problem is that history cannot be repeated, and, *pace* Giovan Battista Vico, even if repetitions are available of some processes in different times and places, they are usually imperfect. This takes much strength out of that technique that Aristotle recommended as useful in science, namely analogy. I am very aware of the weaknesses of comparisons of independent repetitions of history, and of their usefulness as evidence, but it was difficult for me to not be influenced by the close look I had at another joint demographic and linguistic expansion — that of the Bantu languages.

The Bantu expansion is much closer in time than that of the European Neolithic and the transition to agriculture of foragers in Africa is not yet complete. There still live hunter-gatherers at the fringes of the expansion of farmers. Perhaps for this reason, very few Anglo-American archaeologists have taken the same indigenist attitude towards it

that dominated the discussion of the expansion of agriculture to Europe. The transition to Sub-Saharan agriculture must have begun before the Bantu expansion, in West Africa, where archaeological information is still scanty. It is therefore easy to overlook demic diffusion in West Africa and take a sceptical attitude about it (MacEachern 2000). The Bantu expansion started later, and is postulated, on the basis of linguistic evidence by Greenberg, to have originated along the border between Nigeria and Cameroon. This is reasonably close to the implications of the archaeological evidence. The Bantu expansion then moved from the area of origin towards East and South Africa. Although it began somewhat before the use of iron, most of the movement occurred after iron appeared and was certainly helped by its presence.

My work on the genetics and anthropology of African Pygmies (Cavalli-Sforza 1986) brought me into direct contact with the continuing Central African transition from hunting-gathering to agriculture, in the vast forest tracts not yet fully penetrated by farmers. I found the living evidence of Bantu expansion into the forests of Central Africa extremely instructive. Archaeologists interested in the problem of transition should use the vantage point offered by studying the few Pygmies or Bushmen or other foragers still living in areas which are almost totally Bantu. Of course, the few remaining foragers live today under conditions somewhat changed by prolonged contact. But long-lasting, residual ecological diversity helped to keep some degree of separation between these peoples and the invading farmers for three thousand years. Now, local foragers are forced by the almost total disappearance of their resources to shift to agriculture, so that the time left for study is rather short. It is interesting that, at the time Renfrew wrote his seminal 1987 book, he had little respect or interest for biology, an attitude he has certainly changed. From conversations with him I gather he perhaps equated biology at that time mainly with physical anthropological (skeletal) data, and I would concur with his scepticism. His persuasion that demic diffusion had an important role in the transition to agriculture was based, he stated, on what he called anthropological process.

In more recent years Renfrew has somewhat receded from his enthusiasm for demic diffusion, yielding to arguments from Zvelebil. Actually, Zvelebil seems to accept that demic diffusion was of some importance in the south and east of Europe (how could one ignore the evidence from Linear Pottery!), but maintains a strict indigenist position for the north of Europe, and it is more difficult to argue with him on this point. It is inevitable that demic diffusion is least at the extreme of the range. Evidence for genetic admixture must be at its lowest in that region, and time has advanced by 3000 years compared with the beginning of the process, so that everything has changed. But I believe, as I will also discuss at the end of this paper, that as is frequently the case in anthropology, Zvelebil does not pay sufficient attention to demographic process. Doubts were expressed by some participants at the Cambridge meeting about the validity or usefulness of the concept of demic diffusion. Some of these are based on misunderstandings and misstatements of the concept, and therefore it is necessary to consider it in some detail in what follows.

Some considerations on demic diffusion

The process of demic diffusion seems to me a major mechanism for the spread of successful species. It probably lies behind any evolutionary radiation, and behind any major stars in trees (as exemplified by the Y-chromosome tree of modern humans: Underhill *et al.* 2000). The process is therefore not limited to the spread of agriculture. Similar processes most probably are to be found in all the critical phases of the last two million years of human evolution. We know very little about the first Out-of-Africa spread, and only little more about the much more dramatic, global and rapid Out of Africa 2 (Stringer 2000), but I see no reason to exclude them *a priori*. Demic diffusion is a specific process of geographic expansion of a group from a place of origin, unleashed by major innovation/s, that permit or even stimulate population growth and expansion to new areas. The innovations may be biological, and then the process may be rarer because major biological novelties are rare. In the case of the human species they were mostly technological. They probably do not have to be, bio-

logically or culturally, an effective response to a serious need or limitation, but they always are highly acceptable demographically or culturally. The development of agriculture, or more generally of the agro-pastoral economy, is a perfect and major example, but is far from being the only one in human history. It has been debated if this development was a response to considerable, maybe even excessive, population growth, or if it was a cause of it (e.g. Cohen this volume), but it most probably was both. Innovations causing expansion usually permit greater availability of food, but may include or even depend entirely on improved means of transportation, communication, social organization or warfare. In human society, the increase of communication made possible by language made the contribution of technological innovation take the lead. One observes demic diffusion instead of cultural diffusion especially if the innovations require the learning of multiple new techniques that are not easily acquired, and if they require important changes of customs and way of life. This is true of agriculture. When the innovations are easier to learn, one may have more simply cultural diffusion, which usually is much more rapid than demic diffusion. Nobody among the sceptics of demic diffusion of agriculture seems, however, to have tried to explain why it took four thousand years for agriculture to spread from the West Asian centre of origin to the north of Europe. But if it was also demic then we can easily explain its slow pace, and in fact our first contribution with Ammerman was to show that it was compatible with the slow mechanism and rates of population increase dictated for demic diffusion by demographic realities (Ammerman & Cavalli-Sforza 1971; 1973; 1984). By contrast, the diffusion of pottery in the earliest stages of the European Neolithic is an excellent example of cultural diffusion. It is well known that the first period of Middle Eastern agriculture was aceramic, but when pottery started in the Middle East more than one thousand years after the beginning of the agro-pastoral economy, ceramics spread very rapidly to Anatolian and Greek farmers. Another, earlier example of probable cultural diffusion might be that of the bow and arrow. By contrast, the transition from foraging to farming demands much learning and a radical change of customs, including the likelihood of an increase in the birth rate. But even in these cases, it is likely that demic diffusion will always be accompanied by some degree of cultural diffusion. Moreover, in order to observe the genetic gradients which we detected in Europe (Menozzi *et al.* 1978), it seemed necessary that there was either some cultural diffusion, i.e. learning of agro-pastoral techniques and customs by neighbouring Mesolithic people, or genetic admixture between Neolithic and Mesolithic groups and acceptance of spouses of Mesolithic origin into the Neolithic culture. Ammerman and I insisted on this point in our 1984 book (see also Rendine *et al.* 1986). Genetic gradients alone, however, do not necessarily guarantee that demic diffusion was responsible for the genetic gradients, because they may have been generated by other causes, related to selection due to environmental variation (Fisher 1950; Haldane 1948).

Population growth, permitted or stimulated by some technological innovation, will start in regions where there are conditions favourable for it. Arctic regions in Asia and America permitted only minor expansions compared with the more temperate zones, where major agricultural expansions started. Growth may involve decreased mortality and/or increased fertility, and can continue until the population reaches local saturation in the new environmental conditions created by the innovation. At that point, excess growth will almost automatically feed emigration of individuals, families or small groups. Migrants may often be represented heavily by the new generations, and they will usually move to the nearest places where one can export the new mode of life. The association between population growth and migration is not just an accident: population growth that comes near to, or overshoots the carrying capacity of the land has the natural consequence of emigration, if this is at all possible and easy. It also stimulates more innovation and technological development, as growth will hardly stop suddenly and spontaneously as soon as a minor degree of overcrowding develops. But resettlement elsewhere is an easier response than new technological developments, or decrease of birth rates. It is possible within the individual's lifetime, and may have other advantages. In a new environment growth can continue, sometimes even faster than in the original location.

Demic diffusion thus involves the joint participation of the two major demographic ingredients: population growth and migration. Migration is not there by coincidence, but as a consequence of population growth. Although colonization is a form of demic diffusion, Ammerman and I avoided the term because there are standard historical paradigms that go under this name, like the Greek and Phoenician colonizations of the Mediterranean in the first millennium BC. They presuppose the existence of city states or equivalent social entities, and the organized movement of relatively large groups well pre-

pared to fight local opposition in the areas newly settled, if necessary. Most probably, the Neolithic did not follow that paradigm, or at least there is no evidence of such complex social organization in Neolithic villages and early dispersal contexts. Much, perhaps all of it, may have been a slow infiltration of individuals or small groups. One still sees this kind of creation of small, new, individual plantations which I witnessed inside the forest by Bantus living on the fringe of the tropical forest in Central Africa. Similarly, in the extension of Linear Pottery in Central Europe towards the north, forest had to be cleared for making new settlements, but no big villages were usually formed and there is no clear evidence of organized resistance, although there may well have been episodes of local conflict. There was perhaps more often cooperation and exchange with local foragers, made easier by the tendency of foragers and farmers to prefer geologically different types of terrain (as exemplified by Scarre in this volume), as there still is between Pygmies and Bantu farmers. This would certainly limit opportunities of conflict between Mesolithic and Neolithic groups, and favour genetic exchange between them. It would also favour cultural exchange, although in the case of African Pygmies they often prefer to continue their traditional life, whenever possible.

I agree entirely with Bar-Yosef (this volume) when he distinguishes between the essential 'wave of advance' model, that draws the large picture and the average rate of movement, and the 'saltatory jumps' (leapfrogging) model of detailed on-the-ground reality proposed by van Andel & Runnels (1995), but concludes 'that they are essentially the same'. The wave of advance is a macro-model, leapfrogging is a micro-model. Is the wave of advance really 'a thing of the past', as suggested by Richards *et al.* (this volume)? Are macro-models really useless? Is it not useful to evaluate average rates of advance of settlers, whether the individual behaviour escapes us or not? Should we look only at the tree, never at the forest?

It seems strange that the importance of the process was not immediately perceived. Perhaps one might try the following cure for the total sceptic. Consider two recent, historical, undeniable examples: the spreads of European settlers in French Canada and in South Africa. Both were started around 1650 by a few thousand original colonists. Both extended to a substantial area and involved a multiplication of the population by a factor of almost one thousand in *c.* 300 years. Until the nineteenth century, South African whites were almost entirely the descendants of the original Dutch farmers. Both groups seem to have reached local saturation today, for a variety of different reasons. It is interesting that the multiplication factor is about the same as for the European Neolithic farmers: approximately a 1000-times increase, but in 300 rather than in 10,000 years. The differences in the rates of growth and geographic expansion (the geographic expansion rate is perhaps ten to twenty times greater for French Canadians and Afrikaners compared to the European Neolithic) is clearly due to improvement of food quality, means of transportation and weaponry, and perhaps also the decreased mortality and somewhat higher growth rates in the modern examples. The great progress of medicine has taken place only in the last 100 years and cannot have contributed to the expansion of French Canadians or South African Whites. But life in a dry climate, at very low population density and with an excellent diet, must have been favourable enough to keep mortality low. Hygienic conditions may have been especially good in the growing fringe of farmers' settlements located in virgin territory. Perhaps this was true, though to a lesser extent, also of primitive farmers.

Because of the basic importance of population growth in the demic diffusion process, it is erroneous to call it a 'migrationist' or 'immigrationist' model. Migration alone is not necessarily a sufficient explanation for what is discussed here, whether we discuss farming or linguistics. A migration is often the movement of a whole population that may leave very few or no people behind. It does not need to involve population growth, but simply a desire to move to new territory which offers some advantages. It is likely that the migrations of Visigoths from the Baltic region to southeast Europe, Italy and finally to Aquitania and Spain were mostly of this type, and can properly be called migrations. Other examples are perhaps the numerous resettlements planned by Chinese emperors.

Another misunderstanding of demic diffusion is that it is meant to be a total substitute for cultural diffusion and/or admixture. On the contrary, Ammerman and I tried to make it clear from the beginning that demic diffusion cannot be detected by geographical gene gradients, as revealed by principal components, unless there has also been cultural diffusion and/or admixture with local foragers. The most complete statement is in our 1984 book. At least one of these two processes is necessary in order to generate a genetic gradient, and it is likely that both normally contribute. The slope of a demic cline will depend on the rates of population growth and

environmental carrying capacity, the rates of local migration of both farmers and foragers, local genetic admixture between foragers and farmers, and cultural diffusion. The differences in carrying capacity supported by the two major economies, the rates of admixture of farmers with local foragers, and rates of cultural diffusion are the most important quantities determining genetic gradients. A gradient can be observed only if the rates of admixture plus cultural diffusion have been intermediate between extreme values. In our simulations we used a single parameter that included both the process of genetic admixture (followed by absorption into the agricultural economy) and that of true cultural diffusion, because they have the same effect on the genetic landscape (Sgaramella-Zonta & Cavalli-Sforza 1973; Rendine et al. 1986). The simulations show a gradient, measured by the proportion of the original genetic types as a function of the distance from the nuclear area, that decreases exponentially and flattens out at the extreme periphery. Thus, with a demic diffusion model with an intermediate degree of genetic admixture and/or partial cultural diffusion one would observe that at the western and northern edges of Europe the indigenous types may remain more or less unmixed. This is exactly what is observed in Europe, a circumstance that should reassure the extreme indigenists. Had there been demic diffusion with very little or no survival of the former foragers no genetic gradient would be found in the area of farmers' expansion. This is the situation observed in the USA or Canada, where the average gene frequencies of North American Whites are those of the European settlers, with very little residue of the original Amerindian genes. With the opposite hypothesis, of cultural diffusion alone, the gene frequencies will remain those of the previous settlers, the foragers, with no contribution of the farmers. Thus, gene frequency and principal component gradients will form only when demic and cultural diffusion have both occurred and the slope of the gradient will depend on the ratio of the two. This has been elaborated by Rendine et al. (1986) to study the time behaviour of the gradient, another important aspect of the process.

In this volume, Marek Zvelebil accepts that most of Central and southern Europe was populated by Neolithic farmers by a process of demic diffusion, but some of his conclusions concerning the Mesolithic, at least in his original paper, seem unacceptable from the demographic point of view. For instance, his suggestion that palynological work shows that the impact of agriculture is not evident until 6000 BP is used to deny the possible importance of a 'demographic explosion' in Europe. It is an explosion that caused a 1000-times increase in population size in 10,000 years, and it is an explosion compared with the slow increase of the genus *Homo* in 2.5 million years. But the 'explosion' of agriculture took many thousands of years, and until 6000 BP agriculture was a newcomer in most of Europe. Demographic explosions can be ecologically evident only in their later stages. Forests decreased very substantially in England only in the last thousand years.

In addition, population densities can reach enormous peaks in very small areas, but what matters are average population densities over sufficiently vast areas. Zvelebil quotes Hassan (1985) on hunter-gatherer population densities ranging from 0.01 to 34 per square kilometre, although the maximum is limited to the mouths of rivers where salmon can be taken by hand in certain seasons and smoked — such areas are very limited in extent. There seem to be two confusions here: one between anthropological, recent estimates and true archaeological population estimates, and a more serious one between point densities and the densities that count for demographic growth evaluations, which must be estimated over adequately wide areas. Zvelebil also refers to recent genetic studies in Africa that are purported to show the lack of any great differences in population dynamics between hunter-gatherers and subsistence farmers. But these studies rely on methods that are profoundly indirect (DNA mismatch distributions: Bandelt & Forster 1997), and are useful at best only for dating very approximately the beginning of major expansions. I may add that unpublished results with this method show late Palaeolithic/Neolithic population growths in Europe.

But the pearl of misquotations regarding the role of demic diffusion belongs to Brian Sykes. In his recent book *The Seven Daughters of Eve* (Sykes 2001) he describes in his flamboyant style how he nailed down Walter Bodmer in a recent meeting in Barcelona. Sykes had declared, on the basis of his recent mtDNA data, that there was little or no contribution of demic diffusion to the spread of farming. This derived from a statement first made in a paper by Richards *et al.* (1996); the statement was later withdrawn, after a criticism of the statistical significance of the Richards *et al.* (1996) data by Cavalli-Sforza *et al.* (1997) and after new data were presented (Richards *et al.* 1997) which indicated a contribution of 20 per cent. On page 151 of his book Sykes claims that Bodmer & Cavalli-Sforza (1976) stated that there was only demic diffusion and Europeans are in essence

all descendants of Middle Eastern farmers, using the following quotation:

> [Bodmer] insisted that they (he and Luca) had never said that the farmers had overwhelmed Europe and replaced the hunter-gatherers. I had brought along a copy of their jointly written textbook *Genetics Evolution and Man* . . . and read out: 'If the population of Europe is largely composed of farmers who gradually immigrated from the Near East, the genes of the original Near Easterners were diluted out progressively with local genes as the farmers advanced westward. However, the density of hunters-gatherers was probably small and the dilution [of Near Eastern genes, that is] would thus be relatively modest.' There it was in black and white, in their own words. This was massive replacement in all but name.

Careful readers will perhaps suspect that some of the context was omitted. Note that the cited sentence (Bodmer & Cavalli-Sforza 1976, 548) starts with an 'If'. Two lines before, we stated: 'Probably, both phenomena [demic and cultural diffusion] have occurred, but their relative importance remains a problem.' And, three lines below the piece Sykes cited, we wrote: 'The problem of the relative importance of demic and cultural diffusion of agriculture, however, is not yet settled and requires further investigation.'

Sykes also omits to note that the book was printed in 1976 and was written in 1974. The first paper with Ammerman on demic diffusion, based entirely on radiocarbon dates for the arrival of wheat in Europe, was published in 1971. In 1976 there had been no real analysis of the genetic data, but two genetic systems gave a qualitative impression in favour of demic diffusion: the west to east gradient of RH negative genes, and evidence from a number of HLA genes. In the first principal component analysis, published in 1978, the HLA evidence in favour of demic diffusion was stronger than that from other autosomal genes. Later, new evidence that had accumulated for several autosomal genes, other than HLA or RH, was shown to be equally strong by Sokal *et al.* (1991), even though each gene was taken in isolation. I was present at Barcelona, but I have no recollection of the reading of our text referred to by Sykes.

Palaeolithic vs Neolithic contributions to Europe

The question of estimating the proportion of Palaeolithic vs Neolithic contributions to the peopling of Europe is of some interest, but is not as easy to resolve as some have thought. For one thing, Palaeolithic preglacial contributions came from various origins. It is often assumed that most came through the Middle East (Richards *et al.* 1996; 1997; 2000), but Y-chromosome evidence (Underhill *et al.* 2001), which is ordinarily sharper than that coming from mitochondrial DNA, indicates that a greater fraction came from Central Asia above the Black Sea. Estimating the fraction of the truly Middle Eastern contribution at different times is not easy. There were also direct contributions from Africa across the Mediterranean, and some of these may have been non-trivial. There has been a relatively recent contribution from Northwest Asia, clearly shown by the Y-chromosome haplotypes marked by TAT (corresponding to Eu 13 and Eu 14 by Semino *et al.* 2000) and by linguistic coevolution (the Finno-Ugric branch of the Uralic family). This is probably post-Paleolithic, dated genetically at about 4000 years ago, but whether it should be considered Neolithic may involve an archaeological classification problem. In any case, it is most probably unrelated to the Middle Eastern Neolithic.

For Europe especially, there are disagreements between the mtDNA and Y-chromosome data relating to relatively recent language replacements. The dating of Y-chromosome contributions depends mostly on microsatellites and is not always as sharp as one would like. Dating of mtDNA seems even more subject to doubt.

The variance of the first principal component estimate of the Neolithic contribution to Europe is 26–28 per cent of the total variance of autosomal markers. I have been trying to think of the actual meaning of this estimate. It seems a reasonable intuition that the variance of a principal component is largely determined, in this case, by the slope of the first principal component gradient. In the long run, the slope will decrease and, with it, also the estimate of the contribution to the variance. But the rate of decrease is slow (Rendine *et al.* 1986). The next highest principal component, the second, explains about 20 per cent of the total variance. This was originally interpreted by us as possibly including genetic variation correlated with climate. This may still be true, at least in part, though difficult to prove. On the basis of mtDNA data, Torroni *et al.* (1998) put forward the hypothesis that the second principal component expressed the postglacial Mesolithic expansion from the glacial refugium in southwestern France. This seems very reasonable, and the later published evidence on the Y-chromosome haplotype Eu 18 (Semino *et al.* 2000) has corroborated it. The second principal component, however, probably does not distinguish between this Mesolithic expansion and

the Uralic one from the northeast of Europe, which does not appear in isolation in independent principal components but is clearly expressed by haplotypes Eu 13 and Eu 14 of the Y chromosome. The two unrelated expansions took place at different times and were in opposite directions, but the available autosomal markers seem unable to distinguish them and therefore the second principal component has one pole in the Basque region (like the mtDNA evidence cited by Torroni) while the opposite pole is clearly visible in northern Scandinavia and corresponds to Y chromosomes marked by TAT.

Other more recent estimates of the Middle Eastern Neolithic contribution to Europe include those from mtDNA, stated to be 20 per cent (Sykes 1999), and those from the Y chromosome that give a similar estimate (20 per cent: Semino *et al.* 2000). They are only slightly lower than that obtained from the first principal component. It seems cautious to think that the data available are still too few and not sufficiently representative. That demic diffusion of farmers did occur in Europe has been qualitatively acknowledged even by many of its strongest opponents, including Zvelebil (see Ammerman & Biagi in press). Genetics gives a chance to make quantitative estimates, but the low numbers tested, the poor representativeness of the samples, the uncertainties of the methods available and the rush to publish make the majority of current statements rather unsatisfactory. Some more years, perhaps even a decade, will be necessary before the dust can settle. The temperature of the discussions measures, among other things, the uncertainty of the conclusions, and also the difficulty in relinquishing one's beloved persuasions, like the early statement by Richards *et al.* (1996) that demic diffusion did not take place in Neolithic Europe at all. My view is that we do not yet have really good estimates of the Palaeolithic and Neolithic contributions to Europe, but we should carefully distinguish different Palaeolithic, as well as post-Palaeolithic contributions (e.g. that of the Uralic language speakers). In the first version of this manuscript, I wrote:

> I would not be surprised if the contribution of the demic diffusion tied with agriculture should turn out to be greater than 20%. But at the moment it would seem that numbers and attitudes are influenced more by sentiments than by facts. It is well known that the heart has reasons that reason itself cannot comprehend.

It happens that, with the help of a new method, more advanced than earlier ones, Chikhi *et al.* (2002) have just reached the conclusion that the contribution of mideastern farmers to Europe is not far from

50 per cent, and is definitely higher in south Europe, while it is lower, but not zero, in north Europe.

There are many potential sources of error in the analysis of this problem. We will need better data than those currently available, which can hardly be considered truly representative of the present European population. A more thorough study of methods will be necessary before one can reach final conclusions. At this point, it seems that the validity of the hypothesis of demic diffusion is beyond doubt, at least in the spread of the European Neolithic, and that its contribution to the extant European genome is not at all trivial. Other factors not considered so far include the poor accuracy of mutation dating. Mutation dates are seriously affected by the low accuracy of mutation rate estimates, as well as by the assumption usually made, and usually erroneous, that all rates are the same. They ignore the fact that expansion dates are likely to be definitely younger than those of mutations used to date them (Rosenberg & Feldman in prep.). Genetic dating of past events needs further efforts to increase its accuracy and reliability.

Some recent progress on the wave of advance theory and its application

There has been some progress recently in estimating the rate of advance of Neolithic expansion in Europe. Fisher's original formula (Fisher 1937) predicts it to be proportional to the geometric mean of the rates of population growth (a) and migration (m), that is, the square root of the product of a and m. One thing to keep in mind is that the population growth rate a is the *initial* rate in a 'logistic' growth curve, the usual curve observed in the growth of a population, which has an s-shape. This is the highest rate throughout the whole process, and is difficult to estimate, especially from archaeological data. Fort & Mendez (1999) have developed a correction of this formula that incorporates the effect of a cause of delay not previously considered: generation time. It decreases the expected rate given by the original Fisher formula. Earlier analysis by Ammerman & Cavalli-Sforza (1984) showed that the rate of advance of farming, calculated on the basis of archaeological dates of first arrival of agriculture in over 100 archaeological sites, was compatible with a fairly wide range of ethnological observations of growth and migration rates. Repeating calculations on the radiocarbon dates for the European Neolithic, with the inclusion of some more recent archaeological observations, Fort & Mendez obtained an observed

rate of 1.1 km/year, very similar to the earliest estimates. But taking into account generation time by their formula, they showed that a migration rate m equal to that of observations on recent shifting agriculturalists in Ethiopia (the Majangir, an example used in our earlier analysis in 1984), and the population growth rate a published by Birdsell for various historical populations generated a narrow range for the expected value of the rate of advance, which did include the observed rate. It is reassuring that Birdsell's a values are very similar to those of South Africa and French Canada mentioned above.

The archaeology of the Bantu expansion does not yet supply enough data for a similar analysis. But if one considers that expansion rates have so far been based on distances calculated as the crow flies, a first rough estimate of the distance covered can be derived from that between the starting point, which we will take to be in south Cameroon, and the location of the most southern Bantu tribe, the !Xhosa, about 500 km northeast of Capetown at the time of arrival of the Dutch settlers. This distance was covered in about 2700 years. These very approximate values suggest a 1.5 km/yr rate of advance, roughly 50 per cent faster than the European Neolithic. Most probably for at least two-thirds of the time involved, the advance into the forest enjoyed the use of iron instead of stone tools. Moreover, the southern part of the settled area was not, or not entirely, forested.

A further analysis of archaeological information on the speed of expansions was dedicated to the Austronesian one. The data used were limited to the later part of the expansion in Melanesia and Polynesia, starting with the earliest example of Lapita pottery (c. 3300 BP). Assuming that the expansion was uninterrupted, its rate was calculated to be about 3.3–6.3 km/year (95 per cent fiducial interval, personal communication by Fort). Such a rate is 4–5 times higher than that of the Neolithic European expansion. Bellwood, to whom this result was communicated, noted, however, that it does not take account of a period of standstill of about 1000–1500 years in western Polynesia. So this was really a 2-stage expansion, and this estimate is therefore too low and must be revised.

The Austronesian expansion took place almost entirely by boat. In the European agricultural expansion, the genetic component of diffusion was 3 times more efficient in the Mediterranean part than in the expansion to Central Europe (Semino *et al.* 2000). It is known that here boats were also widely used, as exemplified for instance by the diffusion of obsidian available only in some Mediterranean islands, and the archaeological recovery of Neolithic boats in Italy and France. But in the Pacific Ocean, especially in the later part of the expansion, jumps from island to island and especially from archipelago to archipelago were much longer. They demanded greater nautical wisdom and means, but may have involved also more trials and failures.

Radiocarbon dates for the postglacial expansion from the southwestern European refuge were published by Housley *et al.* (1997), who calculated various speeds of advance. A preliminary reanalysis of these data, using the new formula by Fort and Mendez (Fort *et al.* in prep.), gave an estimate of 0.4–1.1 km/year (95 per cent fiducial interval). This was in good agreement with a prediction of 0.7 km/yr, based on ethnographic estimates of population growth and migration, which is also similar to one of the rates calculated by Housley and colleagues. The interest of this estimate is that a very rough evaluation for the earlier Palaeolithic expansions across Eurasia around 50,000 years ago suggests only slightly lower values.

Demic and linguistic diffusion

The major stimulus to this meeting came from the need to understand the correlations between genes and languages, and especially the usefulness of Renfrew's hypothesis (1987) that anthropological processes like demic diffusion or the extension of political power to a specific area (the élite dominance process) may have expanded languages or groups of them. If demic diffusions never occurred, as some of the members of this meeting choose to suggest, then this is a non-problem. But this leaves the need to understand why the distribution of languages is so highly clustered geographically, and the original suggestion by Renfrew that demic diffusions are the origin of major linguistic clusters (families, superfamilies or subfamilies) seems the natural explanation.

In the last 20 years, the historical and evolutionary analysis of modern humans has made substantial progress, mostly thanks to the analysis of uniparentally transmitted genetic systems like mitochondrial DNA and the Y chromosome, free from the embarrassment of recombination. Such systems, and in particular the male-transmitted Non Recombinant portion of the Y chromosome (NRY), have provided us with genealogies of individuals that give precise information about their evolutionary origin. These results correlate well with archaeological information, some of which seems to support the approximate dates obtained by indirect genetic methods. They are also in excellent agreement with 80 years of genetic analysis on the rest of the genome, beginning in 1919. This earlier research was inevitably less precise, being affected by the complexity of biparental transmission and the need to analyze the protein products of genes. It was only after 1980 that it became possible to analyze the genes themselves. The study of single nucleotide polymorphisms of the NRY, in particular, begun in 1994 has supplied a very detailed and most probably error-free genealogy that generated what we believe gives the most satisfactory picture of human evolution, summarized below.

Modern humans are descendants of a small population from eastern Africa that started expanding in Africa around 100,000 years ago. From approximately the same area, 40–60,000 years later, a small subset entered Asia and started a second, faster expansion, probably in two major directions. One direction was along the southern coast of Asia, from where it reached Southeast Asia, western Oceania, and continued along the coast of East Asia. This was probably the earlier expansion. The second direction was towards the centre of Asia, from where the expansion radiated westwards to Europe, eastwards to East Asia, and northwards to Siberia, eventually mixing with the southern stream in East Asia and reaching also America. A major factor in this expansion was communication, made possible by what was probably the latest major step in the genesis of human language. It is reasonable to assume, on diverse but increasing linguistic evidence, that there was a single origin of language. The linguistic evidence is supported by genetics, since the fact that only a small population, probably of the size of a small tribe, seems to have been involved in the expansion makes it likely that modern extant languages have a single origin. A tribe typically speaks a single language, almost by definition. Further factors that contributed to make this sequence of expansions possible were the development of better tools (the Aurignacian) and of nautical means enabling the crossing of sea tracts, e.g. through eastern Indonesia to New Guinea and Australia.

My own fascination with the correlation of genes and languages began serendipitously when we decided, with Paolo Menozzi and Alberto Piazza, to extend to the rest of the world our analysis of European gene frequencies for the study of demic diffusion in the Neolithic. At the beginning we were interested in using languages in order to have a list of human populations organized in a hierarchy, simply as a help to establish a data base of human gene frequencies. Languages provide still today the only complete classification of human populations. We used the linguistic classification provided by Merritt Ruhlen (1991), based largely on Greenberg's taxonomic work, and I would like to acknowledge much generous help from Ruhlen, who made available to us his unpublished material. It included at the time 17 major families, some of which had been already grouped into two controversial superfamilies (Nostratic/Eurasiatic, two different linguistic families that largely overlap, and Austric). The genetic tree we built was based on 42 populations and showed three main branches, corresponding to the three main expansions just mentioned — an early one within Africa, and later ones to southern and northern Asia, visible also in the NRY genealogy (Underhill *et al.* 2000). It was quite a surprise to find such a good correlation with the linguistic families. We published these correlations between genes and language families in a short paper (Cavalli-Sforza *et al.* 1988), which preceded the publication of a much more detailed presentation (Cavalli-Sforza *et al.* 1994). There clearly were exceptions to a parallel expansion of genes and languages, which were listed with their likely historical explanations. They were mainly examples of 'élite dominance', the mechanism suggested by Renfrew for the relatively sudden replacement of a language by another.

Why should there be a correlation between the linguistic and genetic classifications? Any traits transmitted vertically (from parent to child, or more generally in the family), whether biological or cultural, are bound to show a strong correlation with each other. But horizontal transmission (between unrelated people: Cavalli-Sforza & Feldman 1981) will generate exceptions. Élite dominance is a major mechanism of such horizontal cultural transmission and produces the major exceptions that erode the correlation. Anyhow, the correlation of the genetic and linguistic trees is clearly significantly different from zero — as was tested only later because of the original lack of reliable methods (Cavalli-Sforza *et al.* 1992). An independent method for testing significance of the correlation between two trees, developed by Penny *et al.* (1993), gave the same result.

Today, a few linguists interested in the evolution of language are laboriously generating more superfamilies and a complete linguistic tree is developing. It is too early to make strong statements, but it would seem that the correlation between genetic and linguistic evolution is invigorated by these results. It should be acknowledged that Darwin had

already predicted this. A full citation of the relevant passage in *The Origin of Species*, second edition, can be found in my book *Genes, Peoples and Language* (2001, 167). Darwin's statement may seem exceedingly optimistic, but may turn out to be more prophetic than more people would like to concede today. Another conclusion that seems inescapable is that the Out-of-Africa 2 expansion was determined, especially in the last 50,000 years, by a substantial population growth rate, presumably because of a change in reproductive customs. By contrast, the older fraction of the African populations that are today still largely foraging (Y-chromosome haplogroups I and II) is now almost stationary, as might be expected given that they are restricted to a shrinking territory. Inevitably, socioeconomic and ecological conditions strongly determine reproductive behaviour. Thus, our knowledge of modern humans evolution is developing, largely thanks to genetic analysis, and shows good promise of integration with information from other related disciplines.

References

Ammerman, A. & P. Biagi (eds.), in press. *The Widening Harvest*. Boston (MA): Archaeological Institute of America.

Ammerman, A. & L.L. Cavalli-Sforza, 1971. Measuring the rate of spread of early farming in Europe. *Man* 6, 674–88.

Ammerman, A. & L.L. Cavalli-Sforza, 1973. A population model for the diffusion of early farming in Europe, in *The Explanation of Cultural Change*, ed. C. Renfrew. London: Duckworth, 343–57.

Ammerman, A. & L.L. Cavalli-Sforza, 1984. *The Neolithic Transition and the Population Genetics of Europe*. Princeton (NJ): Princeton University Press.

Bandelt, H.-J. & P. Forster, 1997. The myth of hunter-gatherer mismatch distributions. *American Journal of Human Genetics* 61, 980–83.

Bellwood, P., 1991. The Austronesian dispersal and the origins of languages. *Scientific American* 265, 88–93.

Bodmer, W. & L.L. Cavalli-Sforza, 1976. *Genetics, Evolution and Man*. San Francisco (CA): Freeman.

Cavalli-Sforza, L.L. (ed.), 1986. *African Pygmies*. Orlando (FL): Academic.

Cavalli-Sforza, L.L., 2001. *Genes, Peoples and Languages*. New York (NY): Farrar, Straus and Giroux.

Cavalli-Sforza, L.L. & M.W.F. Feldman, 1981. *Cultural Transmission and Evolution: a Quantitative Approach*. Princeton (NJ): Princeton University Press.

Cavalli-Sforza, L.L. & E. Minch, 1997. Paleolithic and Neolithic lineages in the European mitochondrial gene pool. *American Journal of Human Genetics* 61, 247–51.

Cavalli-Sforza, L.L., A. Piazza, P. Menozzi & J.L. Mountain, 1988. Reconstruction of human evolution: bringing together genetic, archeological and linguistic data. *Proceedings of the National Academy of Sciences of the USA* 85, 6002–6.

Cavalli-Sforza L.L., E. Minch & J. Mountain, 1992. Co-evolution of genes and languages revisited. *Proceedings of the National Academy of Sciences of the USA* 89, 5620–24.

Cavalli-Sforza, L.L., P. Menozzi & A. Piazza, 1994. *History and Geography of Human Genes*. Princeton (NJ): Princeton University Press.

Chikhi, L., R.A. Nichols, G. Barbujani & M.A. Beaumont, 2002. Y genetic data support the Neolithic demic diffusion model. *Proceedings of the National Academy of Sciences of the USA* 99, 11,008–103.

Fisher, R.A., 1937. The wave of advance of advantageous genes. *Annals of Eugenics* 7, 355–69.

Fisher, R.A., 1950. Gene frequencies in a cline determined by selection and diffusion. *Biometrics* 6, 356–61.

Fort, J. & L.L. Cavalli-Sforza, submitted. Wave of advance model for the Austronesian population expansion. *Antiquity*.

Fort, J. & V. Mendez, 1999. Time delayed theory of the Neolithic transition in Europe. *Physical Review Letters* 82, 867–71.

Fort, J., T. Pujol & L.L. Cavalli-Sforza, in prep. Paleolithic population waves of advance.

Haldane, J.B.S., 1948. The theory of a cline. *Journal of Genetics* 48, 277–84.

Hassan, F.A., 1985. *Demographic Archeology*. New York (NY): Academic.

Housley, R.A., C.S. Gamble, M. Street & P. Pettitt, 1997. Radiocarbon evidence for the late glacial human recolonization of northern Europe. *Proceedings of the Prehistoric Society* 63, 25–54.

MacEachern, S., 2000. Genes, tribes and African history. *Current Anthropology* 41, 357–84.

Menozzi, P.A., A. Piazza & L. Cavalli-Sforza, 1978. Synthetic maps of human gene frequencies in Europe. *Science* 201, 786–92.

Penny, D., E.E. Watson & M.A. Steel, 1993. Trees from genes and languages are very similar. *Systematic Biology* 42, 382–4.

Rendine, S., A. Piazza & L.L. Cavalli-Sforza, 1986. Simulation and separation by principal components of multiple demic expansions in Europe. *American Naturalist* 128, 681–706.

Renfrew, C., 1987. *Archaeology and Language*. Cambridge: Cambridge University Press.

Richards, M., H. Côrte-Real, P. Forster, V. Macaulay, H. Wilkinson-Herbots, A. Demaine, S. Papiha, R. Hedges, H.-J. Bandelt & B.C. Sykes, 1996. Palaeolithic and Neolithic lineages in the European mitochondrial gene pool. *American Journal of Human Genetics* 59, 185–203.

Richards, M., V. Macaulay, B. Sykes, P. Pettitt, R. Hedges, P. Forster & H.-J. Bandelt, 1997. Letter: reply to Cavalli-Sforza and Minch. *American Journal of Human Genetics* 61, 251–4.

Richards, M., V. Macaulay, E. Hickey, E. Vega, B. Sykes, V. Guida, C. Rengo, D. Sellitto, F. Cruciani, T. Kivisild, R. Villems, M. Thomas, S. Rychkov, O. Rychkov, Y. Rychkov, M. Golge, D. Dimitrov, E. Hill, D. Bradley, V. Romano, F. Calí, G. Vona, A. Demaine, S. Papiha, C. Triantaphyllidis, G. Stefanescu, J. Hatina, M. Belledi, A. di Rienzo, A. Novelletto, A. Oppenheim, S. Norby, N. Al-Zaheri, S. Santachiara-Benerecetti, R. Scozzari, A. Torroni & H.-J. Bandelt, 2000. Tracing European founder lineages in the near eastern mtDNA pool. *American Journal of Human Genetics* 67, 1251–76.

Rosenberg, N.A. & M.W. Feldman, in prep. Chapter in *Modern Developments in Theoretical Population Genetics*, eds. M. Slatkin & M. Veuille.

Ruhlen, M., 1991. *A Guide to the World's Languages*. Stanford (CA): Stanford University Press.

Semino, O., G. Passarino, P.J. Oefner, A.A. Lin, S. Arbuzova L.E. Beckman, G. de Benedictis, P. Francalacci, A. Kouvatsi, S. Limborska, M. Marcikiae, A. Mika, B. Mika, D. Primorac, A.S. Santachiara-Benerecetti, L.L. Cavalli-Sforza & P.A. Underhill, 2000 The genetic legacy of paleolithic *Homo sapiens sapiens* in extant Europeans: a Y-chromosome perspective. *Science* 290, 1155–9.

Sgaramella-Zonta, L.A. & L.L. Cavalli-Sforza, 1973. A method for the detection of a demic cline, in *Genetic Structure of Populations*, ed. N.E. Morton. (Population Genetics Monographs 3.) Honolulu (HI): University of Hawaii Press, 128–35.

Sokal, R.R., N.L. Oden & C. Wilson, 1991. Genetic evidence for the spread of agriculture in Europe by demic diffusion. *Nature* 351, 143–5.

Stringer, C., 2000. Coasting out of Africa. *Nature* 405, 24–7.

Sykes, B., 1999. The molecular genetics of European ancestry. *Philosophical Transactions of the Royal Society of London* 354, 131–9.

Sykes, B., 2001. *The Seven Daughters of Eve*. London: Bantam.

Torroni, A., H.-J. Bandelt, L. d'Urbano, P. Lahermo, P. Moral, D. Sellitto, C. Rengo, P. Forster, M.-L. Savontaus, B. Bonné-Tamir & R. Scozzari, 1998. MtDNA analysis reveals a major late Palaeolithic population expansion from southwestern to northeastern Europe. *American Journal of Human Genetics* 62, 1137–52.

Underhill, P.A., P.D. Shen, A.A. Lin, L. Jin, G. Passarino, W.H. Yang, E. Kauffman, B. Bonné-Tamir, J. Bertranpetit, P. Francalacci, M. Ibrahim, T. Jenkins, J.R. Kidd, S.Q. Mehdi, M.T. Seielstad, R.S. Wells, A. Piazza, R.W. Davis, M.W. Feldman, L.L. Cavalli-Sforza & P.J. Oefner, 2000. Y-chromosome sequence variation and the history of human populations. *Nature Genetics* 26, 358–61.

van Andel, T.H. & C. Runnels, 1995. The earliest farmers in Europe. *Antiquity* 69, 481–500.

Chapter 8

The DNA Chronology of Prehistoric Human Dispersals

Peter Forster & Colin Renfrew

Agriculture developed in the remarkably stable climate of the Holocene lasting from 11,400 calendar years ago until today (Dansgaard *et al.* 1993; Björck *et al.* 1996), and is thus a very recent phenomenon within the prehistory of anatomically modern humans. It is therefore worthwhile to assess the genetic record of mankind in its full time depth before focusing on potential connections between agriculture on the one hand, and genes, languages and climate on the other. It has now become evident that the genetic record, as documented in modern humans, owes many of its features to events and processes taking place long before the Holocene. In order therefore to seek to find traces in that genetic record of aspects of demographic history assignable to the Holocene period, it is desirable first to establish a clear picture of the earlier history of the human spe-

cies, including the patterning of early dispersals and expansions, so that the understanding of those earlier processes offers a backdrop against which more recent dispersals can effectively be studied. Such is the purpose of the present paper where aspects of that earlier history are delineated, and the impact of earlier and more severe climatic episodes (notably the glacial maximum of *c.* 20,000 years ago) are assessed.

Maternally inherited mitochondrial DNA (mtDNA) can be analyzed in living humans to yield a chronology of ancient genetic prehistory (Wilson *et al.* 1985). This approach has confirmed a recent African origin for the human species (Vigilant *et al.* 1991) previously suggested by 130,000-year-old African fossils transitional to anatomically modern humans (Day & Stringer 1982; Bräuer 1989). Soon after, an early expansion across Africa left its footsteps in the mitochondria particularly of the Bushmen and the West Pygmies (Watson *et al.* 1997) and possibly in the remains of Skhul/Qafzeh. Subsequently an east African reexpansion 60–80,000 years ago repopulated Africa, and ultimately led to a migration out of Africa of possibly only one (Watson *et al.* 1997) major mtDNA type, indicating a small number of emigrant women. Their descendants appear to have replaced all preexisting Eurasian *Homo erectus* or *Homo neanderthalensis* mtDNA types, given that no divergent mtDNA type has been found in any survey of modern humans (e.g. Torroni *et al.* 1994b; Richards *et al.* 1996). According to the mtDNA sequences recovered from Neanderthal bones (Krings *et al.* 1997; Ovchinnikov *et al.* 2000), Neanderthal mtDNA diverged from the modern human mtDNA lineage about 500,000 years ago.

While this overall picture of mitochondrial prehistory came into focus, Harpending *et al.* (1993) shifted their attention to the question of whether modern European, Asian, Papuan, and Australian mtDNA types derive from an uninterrupted demographic expansion of the Out-of-Africa founders

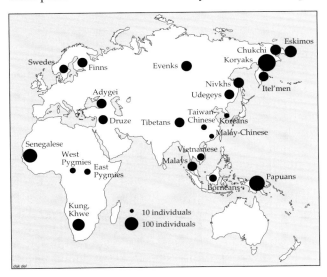

Figure 8.1. *MtDNA samples typed by 14-enzyme RFLP analysis as of August 2000. The 1221 samples shown on the map, as well as 381 native Americans, were typed and published by the research groups of Douglas Wallace, Antonio Torroni and Allan Wilson.*

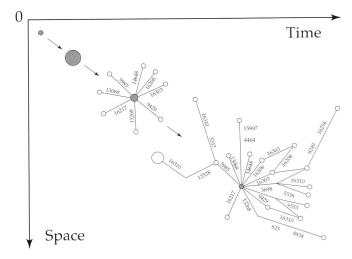

Figure 8.2. *Starlike cluster of mtDNA types resulting from a successful prehistoric maternal lineage. The cluster at the bottom right is one of the major Papuan clusters P/p94 today. The original phase of breeding success (top left) occurred roughly 30,000 years ago, probably after the arrival in Papua New Guinea. Numbers refer to positions (1–16,569) on the DNA at which mutations have occurred.*

(strong Garden of Eden model), or whether an initial expansion was followed by the formation of regional gene pools, which, after a period of isolation and drift, expanded demographically and geographically to form the present mtDNA variation in different continents and regions (weak Garden of Eden model). Worldwide studies on mtDNA (Fig. 8.1) confirmed the weak Garden of Eden model by finding distinct and phylogenetically deep mtDNA branches in each continent or region.

To visualize the genetic link between prehistoric events and current DNA variation, the reader may consider a woman living, say, 30,000 years ago. This woman, located in space and time, would have had a particular mtDNA type, which we indicate by a small circle in Figure 8.2. Imagine further that this woman enjoyed greater breeding success than most of her contemporaries anywhere in the world. Whatever the cause for this success (favourable climatic conditions, penetration of new and unexploited territory, discovery of food production, high social status, an advantageous mutation etc.), if the favourable conditions persisted over several generations, then her mtDNA, passed on to her daughters and granddaughters, would increase in frequency (indicated by the enlarged circle in Fig. 8.2). After thousands of years, some descendants carrying this successful

DNA would inevitably acquire a mutation (indicated by the starlike branches in the figure), and the original type would become less and less common. At this stage it is no longer the original type, but the entire starlike cluster which testifies to the favourable conditions thousands of years earlier. Hence we quantify the success of a type by today's frequency of such a cluster. Technical difficulties set in after tens of thousands of years of mutation: the original type can become extinct, or at least so infrequent that it is not likely to be sampled (see the fourth phase in Fig. 8.2). Furthermore, mutations may hit the same DNA position in different individuals, making it difficult to decide from which particular ancestral type a descendant type is derived. If unresolvable, these ambiguities need to be identified and displayed as reticulations (Fig. 8.2). Moreover, a descendant type might become exposed to favourable breeding conditions and become a successful type in its own right (cf. the large peripheral circle in phase 4) without any causal connection to the original expansion success of the cluster. To address these three problems, we have previously published phylogenetic network and star contraction algorithms (Forster *et al.* 2001), and we here summarize the application of these tools in producing a chronology for the Out-of-Africa migration and the onset of demographic expansions in the rest of the world.

Subjects and methods

MtDNA data
Extensive mtDNA analyses and scenarios for Africa, America, and Europe already exist, so in the following we focus on recent advances in the understanding of Asian and Papuan DNA evolution, based on mtDNA RFLP data (Forster *et al.* 2001). The RFLP method of typing DNA is to expose it to enzymes which recognize mutations at certain DNA positions, at which the enzymes then cut to yield fragments of distinctive lengths. The mutated positions can thus be indirectly pinpointed on the DNA. MtDNA RFLP data was taken from the literature, after extensive proofreading and correcting (Forster *et al.* 2001). The samples analyzed here comprised 119 Papuans and 707 central and east Asians, detailed in Figure 8.1. A file (asiapng.tor) of the revised Asian data is available free within the Network package at http://www.fluxus-engineering.com.

Star contraction algorithm
The aim of the star contraction algorithm (Forster *et al.* 2001) is to identify starlike clusters of sequences

in a given sequence set, and contract any such clusters to a single ancestral sequence. The resulting contracted sequence set can be entered into a phylogenetic algorithm to generate a tree or network. There are two potential applications for this method. First, large population data sets (several hundred to over a thousand) are rapidly becoming the norm in population genetic studies, and it is becoming increasingly difficult to display the corresponding phylogeny as a figure in a publication or even to visually analyze it on a computer screen. The star contraction algorithm in conjunction with a phylogenetic analysis can display the much smaller 'skeleton' of the tree, with the clusters indicated as single nodes. The second application of the star contraction method is rigorously to define dense starlike clusters which are potentially diagnostic for demographic expansions. The age of such phylogenetic clusters can then be dated via the molecular clock, and compared to historic or prehistoric records of other disciplines.

RFLP mutation rate and genetic dating

The mutation rate of the 14-enzyme RFLP typing system for the whole mtDNA molecule has been estimated as 1 RFLP mutation every 21,800 years (Forster *et al.* 2001) in good agreement with the calibration of Horai *et al.* (1995) using primate mtDNA. As a time measure for dating nodes in the phylogeny we use the demographically unbiased parameter ρ, which is the average mutational distance to the node of interest. For estimating the standard error σ of ρ we employ the method of Saillard *et al.* (2000). The values for ρ and σ are converted into years by multiplication with the mutation rate. The standard error σ does not include uncertainty in the mutation rate. However, any future improved calibration for the mutation rate can directly be multiplied with the ρ and σ values presented throughout this paper to obtain improved absolute time estimates. Thus for example, if the Out-of-Africa migration date were doubled from 55,000 years to 110,000 years (e.g. to accommodate the Skhul/Qafzeh remains as our ancestors), then the mtDNA date for the migration into the Americas would correspondingly increase from 25,000 to 50,000 years.

Results

Three rounds of star contraction applied to the 826 east Asian and Papuan RFLP sequences (encompassing 245 types) contracted the number of types to 83 ancestral types. The algorithm searched at a radius

Figure 8.3. *Star-contracted phylogenetic network of Asian and Papuan mtDNA. The larger circles indicate contracted clusters, comprising >1 per cent of the total sample. The smaller circles represent single, multiple, or star-contracted mtDNA types comprising <1 per cent of the sample. Some types are named according to standard mtDNA clade nomenclature A, B, C etc. (Forster et al. 2001; Kivisild et al. 2002). Note that any type derived from e.g. a C type is itself within clade C. The asterisk denotes the empty African root.*

of 5 mutations to avoid overlooking relevant outlying lineages. The contracted data set is displayed as a phylogenetic network in Figure 8.3. The root node was determined by comparison with African mtDNA and is marked with an asterisk.

Next, we defined those nodes in the Asian–Papuan phylogeny (Fig. 8.3) which contained more than 1 per cent of the sample as demographic expansion clusters. In other words, for the detection of smaller demographic expansions, much larger sample sizes would be necessary. The expansion nodes are listed in Table 8.1, along with their age estimates. The estimates are based on detailed networks (not shown) which together display all 826 individuals and resolve some ambiguities and inaccuracies, concerning for example the M7 branch. The current

Table 8.1. *Time estimates for mtDNA expansion clusters.*

cluster*	distribution	n	ρ	σ	age (years)	error (years)
P	PNG	13	3.0000	1.0686	65,400	23,300
M	S&C Asia	59	1.5932	0.2570	34,700	5600
F/v51	S&C Asia	16	1.5625	0.4881	34,100	10,600
P/p94	PNG	19	1.5263	0.3722	33,300	8100
N	Asia	33	1.3636	0.4525	29,700	9900
B/asia	S&C Asia	18	1.3333	0.3239	29,100	7100
A1	S&C Asia	12	1.2500	0.3891	27,300	8500
D	N&C Asia	26	0.7692	0.5189	16,800	11,300
Q	PNG	37	0.7027	0.1622	15,300	3500
D/chu49	N Asia	19	0.6842	0.6338	14,900	13,800
B/png	coastal PNG	21	0.5714	0.3927	12,500	8600
E/s106	SE Asia	9	0.5556	0.3685	12,100	8000
A2	N Asia	117	0.5128	0.2961	11,200	6500
C	N&C Asia	110	0.4955	0.2303	10,800	5000
F/ma33	SE Asia	12	0.4167	0.2205	9100	4800
Z	N Asia	9	0.2222	0.1571	4800	3400
Y	N Asia	59	0.2203	0.1137	4800	2500
G/ky37	N Asia	102	0.2157	0.1009	4700	2200
M7	N Asia	9	0.1250	0.1111	2700	2400
C/e30	N Asia	16	0	0	0	0

*Defined in Fig. 8.3, not to be confused with entire clades of the same name.

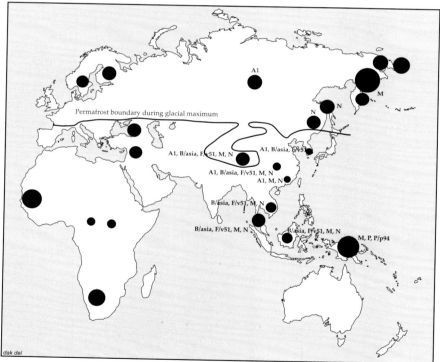

Figure 8.4. *Current distribution of Asian mtDNA expansion clusters older than 20,000 years. The permafrost boundary at the glacial maximum about 20,000 years ago is drawn according to Frenzel et al. (1992). Cluster labels refer to the local presence or absence of clusters without specifying local frequency. A single coastal Papuan has a F/v51 type which is omitted here as it presumably represents recent Austronesian contribution.*

geographic distributions of the expansion clusters are shown in Figures 8.4 and 8.5.

Discussion

All 826 Asian and Papuan sequences (as in fact most non-African sequences) belong to the African subcluster L3 (Watson *et al.* 1997), and the African root of the Asian–Papuan network is indicated by an asterisk between M and N in Figure 8.3. The diversity ρ for M and N, and thus the minimum age for the Out-of-Africa migration, amounts to 2.4861±0.5232 mutations (corresponding to 54,200±11,400 years) for mtDNA clade M and 2.4512±0.5364 mutations (corresponding to 53,400±11,700 years) for mtDNA clade N. These values are in excellent agreement with the dentochronological date of 60,000±6100 years (Turner 1986) for the Out-of-Africa migration, and with the age of the L3 expansion within Africa, dated at 60–80,000 years (Watson *et al.* 1997), which is necessarily expected to predate the Out-of-Africa migration. Note that the founding ages of 54,000 years for M and N precedes their expansion during the Neanderthals' demise 30,000 years ago which we discuss below. As nearly all non-African mtDNA types are descended from those two sequences it is possible that only a small number of women carrying closely related mtDNA types migrated out of Africa according to the following considerations. The estimated founder ages of M and N are very similar (54,000±11,500 years), raising the possibility that these two mtDNA types are derived from a single African migration. Furthermore, the fact that the M and N founder types differ by only two mutations from each other, while the average difference in the ancestral African L1 group is about 10 mutations (Chen *et al.* 1995), indicates that they may have belonged to a genetically closely-knit group.

The oldest expansion in Eurasia occurred 65,000±23,000 years ago (Table 8.1) and is witnessed by mitochondrial descendants preserved in Papua New Guinea; the age estimate can be narrowed somewhat by considering that the Papuan node is derived from a Eurasian founder, so it should not be older than 54,000±12,000 years. This is still about 20,000 years older than any mainland Asian cluster, although both the Papuans and the Asians are derived from the same two Eurasian founders. On the basis of this time difference, we tentatively propose the following scenario to account for the obvious phenotypic differences between Papuans and Eurasians despite sharing a common mitochondrial ancestry. The M and N founders derive from a single African migration, but split at an early stage (possibly before reaching Europe, which lacks M) into Proto-Papuan and Proto-Eurasian. The Proto-Papuan M and N immediately expanded demographically and geographically along a southern route until reaching Papua New Guinea, thus allowing Papuans to retain their overall genetic similarity to Africans (Stoneking et al. 1997). Meanwhile, small Proto-Eurasian founder groups spent 20 or more millennia genetically drifting to their present distinct European, Indian and east Asian M and N types as well as phenotypes long before expanding. The Papuan network of Figure 8.3 shows that it may still be possible to trace the proposed southern route taken by Proto-Papuan mtDNA. As had already been noted by Ballinger et al. (1992), one Malay Malaysian (MM90) has two diagnostic mutations, 15606a and 207o, in common with the Papuan P/p94 clade. If Malaysian MM90 turns out to be representative for southeast Asian P-types, then 12528k (Fig. 8.3) would have mutated in or near Papua New Guinea, yielding a minimum age of about 33,000 years (Table 8.1) for the settlement of Papua New Guinea, and a maximum age of 51,000± 17,000 years (i.e. the age of the P-node ancestral to MM90). Another interesting point to resolve

would be the genetic relationship of Australians to Papuans and Eurasians. Unfortunately, published Australian RFLP data had to be discarded for this study (Forster et al. 2001), but other studies on mtDNA control region sequences (Redd & Stoneking 1999) and Y STRs (Forster et al. 1998) have shown that Papuans and Australians are not closely related as far as these loci are concerned. The oldest Australian human remains are found at Lake Mungo and dated to 62,000±6000 years (Thorne et al. 1999). Ancient DNA extracted from these remains (Adcock et al. 2001) may be genuine (although experimental reproduction and details are lacking) as it appears to be related to an ancient mtDNA type found to be inserted in nuclear DNA of modern humans (Zischler et al. 1995). The absence of this mtDNA lineage in any mitochondria in over 17,000 published modern human mtDNA sequences (Röhl et al. 2001), including aboriginal Australians, would mean that the Lake Mungo mtDNA lineage was replaced by modern mtDNA (Adcock et al. 2001) at some time in the past 60,000 years.

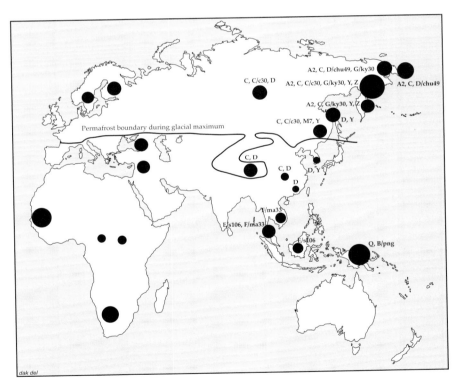

Figure 8.5. *Current distribution of Asian mtDNA expansion clusters younger than 20,000 years. The permafrost boundary at the glacial maximum about 20,000 years ago is drawn according to Frenzel et al. (1992). Cluster labels refer to the local presence or absence of clusters without specifying local frequency. Within Papua New Guinea the B/png cluster is found only in Austronesian-speaking coastal areas.*

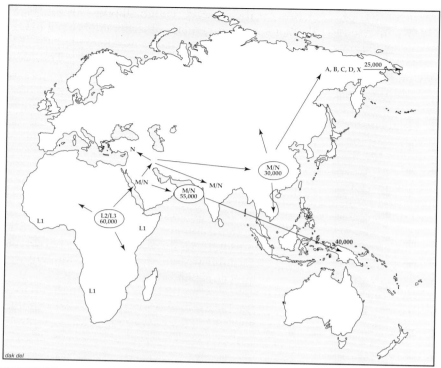

Figure 8.6a. *Out-of-Africa migration and establishment of regional founding mtDNA pools (Weak Garden of Eden scenario) 60,000 to 20,000 years ago. The labels A, B, C etc. denote mtDNA clades, and are not listed exhaustively for each area. Dates within ellipses refer to demographic expansions, other dates to migration events; the dates may vary by more than 10,000 years within and between studies.*

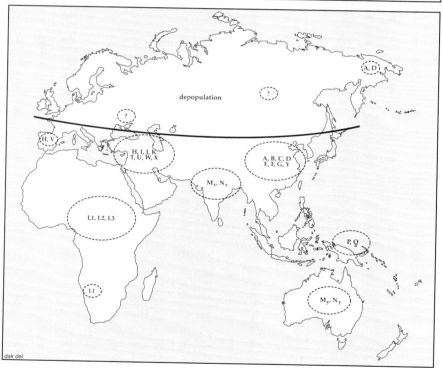

Figure 8.6b. *Glacial refugia about 20,000 years ago as detected by mtDNA analysis. Question marks indicate lack of mitochondrial data for some representative areas. The postglacial reexpansion from the Iberian refugium was postulated by Torroni et al. (1998), and mtDNA analyses on the Polynesian expansion of clade B are reviewed by Richards et al. (1998). The presence of further Near Eastern mtDNA clades in Europe is postulated by Richards et al. (2000). The ancient presence of N in India is testified by its Indian subclade of U (Kivisild et al. 1999).*

At the next time level in Table 8.1, six expansion nodes date to 27–35,000 years, coinciding with the disappearance of Neanderthals in Europe. If we take the mean value of 31,000 years as a lower limit for the arrival in east Asia of the African founders (a distance of about 8000 km) and 54,000 years as the starting date, then the minimal eastward migration speed would have amounted to about 300 metres per year. This rate appears plausible as it is the same order of magnitude as the minimal southward migration speed of Amerinds from Beringia to Chile of about 1 km per year, assuming an Alaskan entry date of 25,000 years and an arrival in Monte Verde by at least 14,000 calendar years ago (Forster *et al.* 1996). Similarly, the arrival of the east African L2/L3 expansion (60,000 years old) in west Africa by 30,000 years ago (Watson *et al.* 1997) implies a westward migration speed of at least 200 metres per year.

Inspection of the geographic distributions of the six oldest east Asian expansion clusters reveals that they are mainly located south of the permafrost boundary of the Last Glacial Maximum 20,000 years ago (Fig. 8.4). A link with the Ice Age is strengthened by the gap in Table 8.1 of 10,000 years during the Last Glacial Maximum before the next demographic expansion clusters occurred, all younger than 17,000 years and thus post-glacial maximum. Most of these post-glacial clusters are found today in northern Asia (Fig. 8.5), excepting a few southeast Asian expansion clusters, notably the Polynesian mtDNA clade B expansion to coastal Papua New Guinea (Stoneking *et al.* 1990). Taken together, this evidence strongly suggests that northern Asia was depopulated during the last glacial maximum (Fig. 8.6). The early expansions starting about 30,000 years ago in Asia did however reach America before they were swept back again, as is seen in the widespread presence of mtDNA clade B in America and central Asia, but not in northern Asia (Shields *et al.* 1993; Torroni *et al.* 1993a,b). According to the time estimates in Table 8.1 and the geographic distributions in Figures 8.4 and 8.5, northern Asia was resettled partly from central Asia (from approximately the latitude of Korea according to Fig. 8.4) and partly from the Beringian glacial refuge whence the Na Dene and Eskimo derive their mtDNA clade A2 types (Forster *et al.* 1996). The reexpansions from these two refugia may have contributed to the geographic patterns of the second principal component of autosomal variation in Asia (fig. 4.17.2. in Cavalli-Sforza *et al.* 1994). Any attempt to search for the Amerind ancestors in modern Mongolians (Neel *et al.* 1994) or elsewhere is thus going to overlook the actual ancestral Amerind population which crossed the Bering land bridge more than 20,000 years ago, presumably from northeast Asia, and then had most of its genetic traces in Asia obliterated by the ensuing glacial conditions. The depopulation of northern latitudes during the last glacial maximum has also left striking genetic signatures in America and Europe. Among the north American Na Dene and Eskimo-Aleut speakers, four of the five major American founding mtDNA types are extinct, and the surviving A-type is only half as

diverse as its parent A type in all other Amerindians further south. Here again, the diversity of the northern A-type corresponds to the onset of climatic stabilization after the Ice Age, which may also have facilitated the establishment of the Clovis, Monte Verde and Monte Alegre cultures to the south. Europe seems to have been depopulated to roughly the same latitude as Asia, with genetic evidence for a major glacial refugium in Iberia (Fig. 8.6). From this, much of western and northern Europe was repopulated, spreading, amongst others, H and V mtDNA types, which alone account for about 50 per cent of western European types today (Torroni *et al.* 1998). It is thought that Neolithic immigration brought few female newcomers to Europe (Richards *et al.* 1996) on the assumption that today's Basques, who share mostly the same mtDNA lineages with all other Europeans, represent pre-Neolithic mtDNA arrivals to Europe.

Both archaeologists and linguists take an interest in the possible connection between agriculture, language and genes. The earliest evidence of agriculture in east Asia appears to be rice cultivation in the middle Yangtze River Valley dated to 11,500 years ago (Normile 1997), well within the area of our 30,000-year-old demographic expansion clusters. Younger dates up to 8000 years old, but also in central China, are reviewed by Bellwood (1997, 205), see also Higham (this volume). As outlined above, the same pattern holds true for the other continents in that the inception of agriculture is younger than the Ice Age genetic signatures of colonization and growth. Does this mean that the effect of agriculture on prehistoric colonization within continents has been comparatively minor, and that regional genetic continuity from the Palaeolithic until today has been the rule? This is plausible in a scenario where continuing gene flow between an indigenous hunter-gatherer population caused an exponential fall-off with distance of the allele frequencies of the alleles characteristic of the earliest farmers (Renfrew this volume). However, it could reasonably be argued that a significant demographic growth and spread of farmers from a nuclear area, harbouring the mtDNA signatures of Palaeolithic events, would be invisible if the farmers had quantitatively eliminated hunter-gatherer populations. This is not impossible, but would contrast for example with the European conquest of America, where the victors considerably reduced the proportion of native Y chromosomes but less so that of native mtDNA (e.g. Torroni *et al.* 1994a). Another claim might be that input of incoming farmers' genes could have been considerable, but would be invisible if the recipient population had had a similar gene pool. This may well have been the case on a regional scale, but the current existence of the latitudinal discontinuity between northern and southern mtDNA types in east Asia suggests that migrations of farmers were not extensive enough to affect this demarcation. Higher-resolution mtDNA data are being compiled in order to analyze regional, possibly Neolithic, migration and demographic growth and to explore alternative connections between climate, language, genes, and archaeology during and since the Ice Age.

References

Adcock, G.J., E.S. Dennis, S. Easteal, G.A. Huttley, L.S. Jermiin, W.J. Peacock & A. Thorne. 2001. Mitochondrial DNA sequences in ancient Australians: implications for modern human origins. *Proceedings of the National Academy of Sciences of the USA* 98, 537–42.

Ballinger, S.W, T.G. Schurr, A. Torroni, Y.Y. Gan, J.A. Hodge, K. Hassan, K.-H. Chen & D.C. Wallace, 1992. Southeast Asian mitochondrial DNA analysis reveals genetic continuity of ancient Mongoloid migrations. *Genetics* 130, 139–52.

Bellwood, P., 1997. *Prehistory of the Indo-Malaysian Archipelago*. Honolulu (HI): University of Hawaii Press.

Björck, S., B. Kromer, S. Johnsen, O. Bennike, D. Hammarlund, G. Lemdahl, G. Possnert, T. Lander Rasmussen, B. Wohlfahrt, C.U. Hammer & M. Spurk, 1996. Synchronised terrestrial-atmospheric deglacial records around the north Atlantic. *Science* 274, 1155–60.

Bräuer, G., 1989. The evolution of modern humans: a comparison of the African and non-African evidence, in *The Human Revolution: Behavioural and Biological Perspectives in the Origins of Modern Humans*, eds. P. Mellars & C. Stringer. Edinburgh: Edinburgh University Press, 123–54.

Cavalli-Sforza, L.L., P. Menozzi & A. Piazza, 1994. *The History and Geography of Human Genes*. Princeton (NJ): Princeton University Press.

Chen, Y.-S., A. Torroni, L. Excoffier, A.S. Santachiara-Benerecetti & D.C. Wallace, 1995. Analysis of mtDNA variation in African populations reveals the most ancient of all human continent-specific haplogroups. *American Journal of Human Genetics* 57, 133–49.

Dansgaard, W., S.J. Johnsen, H.B. Clausen, D. Dahl-Jensen, N.S. Gundestrup, C.U. Hammer, C.S. Hvidberg, J.P. Steffensen, A.E. Sveinbjörnsdottir, J. Jouzel & G. Bond, 1993. Evidence for general instability of past climate from a 250-kyr ice-core record. *Nature* 364, 218–20.

Day, M.H. & C.B. Stringer, 1982. A reconsideration of the Omo Kibish remains and the erectus-sapiens transition, in *L'Homo erectus et la place de l'homme de Tautavel parmi les hominidés fossiles*, ed. H. De Lumley.

Nice: Centre National de la Recherche Scientifique/ Louis-Jean Scientific and Literary, 814–46.

Forster, P., R. Harding, A. Torroni & H.-J. Bandelt, 1996. Origin and evolution of native American mtDNA variation: a reappraisal. *American Journal of Human Genetics* 59, 935–45.

Forster, P., M. Kayser, E. Meyer, L. Roewer, H. Pfeiffer, H. Benkmann & B. Brinkmann, 1998. Phylogenetic resolution of complex mutational features at Y-STR DYS390 in aboriginal Australians and Papuans. *Molecular Biology and Evolution* 15, 1108–14.

Forster, P., A. Torroni, C. Renfrew & A. Röhl, 2001. Phylogenetic star contraction applied to Asian and Papuan mtDNA evolution. *Molecular Biology and Evolution* 18, 1864–81.

Frenzel, B., M. Pécsi & A. Velichko, 1992. *Atlas of Paleoclimates and Paleoenvironments of the Northern Hemisphere: Late Pleistocene–Holocene*. Budapest/ Stuttgart: Hungarian Academy of Sciences, Gustav-Fischer-Verlag.

Harpending, H.C., S.T. Sherry, A.R. Rogers & M. Stoneking, 1993. The genetic structure of ancient human populations. *Current Anthropology* 34, 483–96.

Horai, S., K. Hayasaka, R. Kondo, K. Tsugane & N. Takahata, 1995. Recent African origin of modern humans revealed by complete sequences of hominoid mitochondrial DNAs. *Proceedings of the National Academy of Sciences of the USA* 92, 532–6.

Kivisild, T., M.J. Bamshad, K. Kaldma, M. Metspalu, E. Metspalu, M. Reidla, S. Laos, J. Parik, W.S. Watkins, M.E. Dixon, S.S. Papiha, S.S. Mastana, M.R. Mir, V. Ferak & R. Villems. 1999. Deep common ancestry of Indian and western-Eurasian mitochondrial DNA lineages. *Current Biology* 9, 1331–4.

Kivisild, T., H.-V. Tolk, J. Parik, Y. Wang, S.S. Papiha, H.-J. Bandelt & R. Villems, 2002. The emerging limbs and twigs of the East Asian mtDNA tree. *Molecular Biology and Evolution* 19, 1737–51.

Krings, M., A. Stone, R.W. Schmitz, H. Krainitzki, M. Stoneking & S. Pääbo, 1997. Neandertal DNA sequences and the origin of modern humans. *Cell* 90, 19–30.

Neel, J.V., R.J. Biggar & R.I. Sukernik. 1994. Virologic and genetic studies relate Amerind origins to the indigenous people of the Mongolia/Manchuria/southeastern Siberia region. *Proceedings of the National Academy of Sciences of the USA* 91, 10,737–41.

Normile, D., 1997. Yangtze seen as earliest rice site. *Science* 275, 309.

Ovchinnikov, I.V., A. Götherström, G.P. Romanova, V.M. Kharitonov, K. Lidén & W Goodwin, 2000. Molecular analysis of Neanderthal DNA from the northern Caucasus. *Nature* 404, 490–93.

Redd, A.J. & M. Stoneking, 1999. Peopling of Sahul: mtDNA variation in aboriginal Australian and Papua New Guinean populations. *American Journal of Human Genetics* 65, 808–28.

Richards, M.B., H. Côrte-Real, P. Forster, V. Macaulay, H. Wilkinson-Herbots, A. Demaine, S. Papiha, R.

Hedges, H.-J. Bandelt & B.C. Sykes. 1996. Palaeolithic and Neolithic lineages in the European mitochondrial gene pool. *American Journal of Human Genetics* 59, 185–203.

Richards, M., S. Oppenheimer & B. Sykes, 1998. MtDNA suggests Polynesian origins in eastern Indonesia. *American Journal of Human Genetics* 63, 1234–6.

Richards, M., V. Macaulay, E. Hickey, E. Vega, B. Sykes, V. Guida, C. Rengo, D. Sellitto, F. Cruciani, T. Kivisild, R. Villems, M. Thomas, S. Rychkov, O. Rychkov, Y. Rychkov, M. Golge, D. Dimitrov, E. Hill, D. Bradley, V. Romano, F. Calí, G. Vona, A. Demaine, S. Papiha, C. Triantaphyllidis, G. Stefanescu, J. Hatina, M. Belledi, A. di Rienzo, A. Novelletto, A. Oppenheim, S. Norby, N. Al-Zaheri, S. Santachiara-Benerecetti, R. Scozzari, A. Torroni & H.-J. Bandelt, 2000. Tracing European founder lineages in the Near Eastern mtDNA gene pool. *American Journal of Human Genetics* 67, 1251–76.

Röhl, A., B. Brinkmann, L. Forster & P. Forster, 2001. An annotated mtDNA database. *International Journal of Legal Medicine* 115, 29–39.

Saillard, J., P. Forster, N. Lynnerup, H.-J. Bandelt & S. Nørby, 2000. mtDNA variation among Greenland Eskimos: the edge of the Beringian expansion. *American Journal of Human Genetics* 67, 718–26.

Shields, G.F., A.M. Schmiechen, B.L. Frazier, A. Redd, M. I. Voevoda, J.K. Reed & R.H. Ward, 1993. MtDNA sequences suggest a recent evolutionary divergence for Beringian and northern North American populations. *American Journal of Human Genetics* 53, 549–62.

Stoneking, M., L.B. Jorde, K. Bhatia & A.C. Wilson, 1990. Geographic variation in human mitochondrial DNA from Papua New Guinea. *Genetics* 124, 717–33.

Stoneking, M., J.J. Fontius, S.L. Clifford, H. Soodyall, S.S. Arcot, N. Saha, T. Jenkins, M.A. Tahir, P.L. Deininger & M.A. Batzer, 1997. *Alu* insertion polymorphisms and human evolution: evidence for a larger population size in Africa. *Genome Research* 7, 1061–71.

Thorne, A., R. Grün, G. Mortimer, N.A. Spooner, J.J. Simpson, M. McCulloch, L. Taylor & D. Curnoe, 1999. Australia's oldest human remains: age of the Lake Mungo 3 skeleton. *Journal of Human Evolution* 36, 591–612.

Torroni, A., T.G. Schurr, M.F. Cabell, M.D. Brown, J.V. Neel, M. Larsen, D.G. Smith, C.M. Vullo & D.C. Wallace, 1993a. Asian affinities and continental radiation of the four founding native American mtDNAs. *American Journal of Human Genetics* 53, 563–90.

Torroni, A., R.I. Sukernik, T.G. Schurr, Y.B. Starikovskaya, M.F. Cabell, M.H. Crawford, A.S.G. Comuzzie & D.C. Wallace, 1993b. MtDNA variation of aboriginal Siberians reveals distinct genetic affinities with Native Americans. *American Journal of Human Genetics* 53, 591–608.

Torroni, A., Y.-S. Chen, O. Semino, A.S. Santachiara-Benerecetti, C.R. Scott, M.T. Lott, M. Winter & D.C. Wallace, 1994a. MtDNA and Y-chromosome polymorphisms in four native American populations from southern Mexico. *American Journal of Human Genetics* 54, 303–48.

Torroni, A., M.T. Lott, M.F. Cabell, Y.-S. Chen, L. Lavergne & D.C. Wallace, 1994b. MtDNA and the origin of Caucasians: identification of ancient Caucasian-specific haplogroups, one of which is prone to a recurrent somatic duplication in the D-loop region. *American Journal of Human Genetics* 55, 760–76.

Torroni, A., H.-J. Bandelt, L. d'Urbano, P. Lahermo, P. Moral, D. Sellitto, C. Rengo, P. Forster, M.-L. Savontaus, B. Bonné-Tamir & R. Scozzari, 1998. MtDNA analysis reveals a major late Palaeolithic population expansion from southwestern to northeastern Europe. *American Journal of Human Genetics* 62, 1137–52.

Turner, C.G., 1986. Dentochronological separation estimates for Pacific rim populations. *Science* 232, 1140–42.

Vigilant, L., M. Stoneking, H. Harpending, K. Hawkes & A.C. Wilson, 1991. African populations and the evolution of human mitochondrial DNA. *Science* 253, 1503–7.

Watson, E., P. Forster, M. Richards & H.-J. Bandelt, 1997. Mitochondrial footprints of human expansions in Africa. *American Journal of Human Genetics* 61, 691–704.

Wilson, A.C., R.L. Cann, S.M. Carr, M. George, U.B. Gyllensten, K.M. Helm-Bychowski, R.G. Higuchi, S.R. Palumbi, E.M. Prager, R.D. Sage & M. Stoneking. 1985. Mitochondrial DNA and two perspectives on evolutionary genetics. *Biological Journal of the Linnean Society* 26, 375–400.

Zischler, H., H. Geisert, A. von Haeseler & S. Pääbo, 1995. A nuclear 'fossil' of the mitochondrial D-loop and the origin of modern humans. *Nature* 378, 489–92.

Chapter 9

What Molecules Can't Tell Us about the Spread of Languages and the Neolithic

Hans-Jürgen Bandelt, Vincent Macaulay & Martin Richards

A wealth of molecular sequence data seems to have revolutionized our knowledge about the distant past, so what can molecular geneticists tell us about the spread of languages and the Neolithic? How does inference proceed — from data to tales? Is the genetic approach the key to a new synthesis? We will retell some stories of past and recent publications, briefly comment on them and discuss the potential of the future and the limits of the genetic programme.

The 'archaeogenetic' enterprise

Following Amorim (1999), and echoing the 'genetical archaeology' of von Haeseler *et al.* (1996), Renfrew (2000) coined the term 'archaeogenetics' for 'the newly-emerged discipline which applies molecular genetics to the study of the human past'. His earlier suggestion of 'historical genetics' (Renfrew 1992) never really gained currency amongst geneticists, despite the elegant evocation of historical linguistics. To be awkward, we will adopt the latter expression, which we have only just discovered; this can serve to remind us of the delay in communications that often hinders relations between archaeologists and geneticists.

It was in the late eighties that molecules such as mtDNA began to tell stories, with the 'Out-of-Africa' narrative (Cann *et al.* 1987). This wave of advance soon reached Europe: Richards *et al.* (1996), putting molecules rather than populations into an archaeological context, saw the Neolithic arriving with members of one major mitochondrial haplogroup (J). The context of discovery for most geneticists at the time was, of course, the demic-diffusion model of Cavalli-Sforza and his colleagues (Menozzi *et al.* 1978). This had gradually been interpreted as a tidal wave of farmers swelling into Europe from the Near East, engulfing small bands of

hapless hunter-gatherers as it flooded in. Curiously though, for us (being familiar with our Dennell, Barker and Whittle), the initial interest lay in the discovery that there were some Neolithic immigrants after all. It even seemed that an estimate of ~20 per cent Near Eastern Neolithic ancestry in Europe might actually be taken as rather strongly confirming (at least one interpretation of) the Cavalli-Sforza *et al.* picture, *viz.* the colonization model of farming origins.

It soon became clear, though, that there might be more mileage in taking on the demic-diffusionists rather than the indigenists, especially as it seemed that a certain dogmatism had set in amongst the former camp. But it was not clear that such a low Neolithic input was incompatible with demic diffusion, or even a 'wave of advance'. So it was not simply 'new data' that moved this debate forward, but a consideration of those data in the context of, for example, arguments such as those of Zvelebil (1986) concerning the archaeological context, and a consideration of how seriously the more rigid interpretations of the classical marker gradients needed to be taken. Indeed, in 1996 the evidence for which mtDNAs arrived when was rather weak, because of the paucity of Near Eastern data. A minor subhaplogroup (T1) was subsequently shunted into the Neolithic component (Richards *et al.* 1998), and the distinction between 'Palaeolithic' and 'Neolithic' lineages eventually became somewhat fuzzier, as more Near Eastern data were considered (Richards *et al.* 2000), moving us away from a rather simplistic 'one haplogroup–one migration' model.

In any case, more than three quarters of the mtDNA remain firmly rooted in the European Palaeolithic. But there is clearly some flexibility in the way in which stories about such data can be told. Can we be sure that the ancestors of the 'Neolithic' mtDNAs were carried into Europe along with the very first cereals and goats? Hardly, although exactly this inference was the fallback position at the time, when the predominant view among geneticists was that of Neolithic replacement or waves of advance, so that any molecules which could be tied to the spread of the Neolithic were greeted with enthusiasm. A molecule entering in the Early Neolithic could well have had a Mesolithic carrier — it depends on the archaeological reconstruction whether Neolithic or Mesolithic affiliation is more likely. Once the Neolithic became established, exchange networks broadened, allowing for introgression of molecules during subsequent stages. Perhaps a number of mitochondria rolled along with the secondary-products revolution (Sherratt 1981)?

Molecular genetics, however, is conventionally seen to fuel a 'new synthesis' centred on 'population history' (Renfrew 1999b). A prime example of a (far from grand) synthesis attempted by human geneticists in this spirit is laid out next.

The Finnish Adam and Eve story

Why are Finns so alike physically? A commentary in th journal 'Science' (Holden 1996) revealed the exciting reasons uncovered by molecular geneticists: the Finns descended from a small band of people who settled in what is now Finland some 4000 years ago (Sajantila et al. 1996). Their language was originally Indo-European but later these people switched to Finnish, which they learnt from their Saami neighbours (Sajantila & Pääbo 1995). The Saami, on the other hand, appear to have been separated from the other European populations for tens of thousands of years (Sajantila et al. 1995). The data on which these sweeping claims were based were a meagre handful of Y-chromosome microsatellites and the mitochondrial hypervariable segment I (HVS-I).

None of those assertions has had a long half-life as more data from Finland accumulated; cf. Kittles et al. (1999), Peltonen et al. (2000, Box 2), and Finnilä et al. (2001). As to the question of potential language replacement in Scandinavia, most scholars prefer to believe that Proto-Finnic, ancestral to the present-day languages Saami, Finnish, Estonian etc., spread into the eastern Baltic area during the Eastern Bronze Age, thus eventually leading to a complete replacement of the languages spoken earlier in the area of Finland. In particular, Kallio (2000) suggests (in modifying Posti's theory) that the Proto-Baltic and Proto-Germanic speakers in the area became Finnic speakers (Finnic notabene, not Finnish).

Since the methodology of this classic series of papers on Saami/Finnish mtDNA still lives on, one needs to take a closer look at how data were turned into tales in this case. The HVS-I data were processed by Sajantila et al. (1996) in a quite peculiar way, discarding most of the polymorphic sites as recently mutated. The 'rationale' for this was an erroneously-presumed statistical sorting, in that slow sites preferably changed in the distant past while fast sites did so relatively recently. For the distinction of slow vs fast, they appealed to Hasegawa et al. (1993), who reconstructed multiple hits at the HVS-I sites for the worldwide mtDNA data set available at the time. Sajantila et al. (1996) regarded those sites listed with exactly one hit as the potentially most conservative sites — thus ignoring the most conservative candidates, viz. the sites unvaried (i.e. zero hits) in the test data of Hasegawa et al. (1993). Heterozygosity values calculated with respect to those 'one-hit' sites then were apparently much smaller for the Finnish sample compared to the samples from most other European sources. This effect, however, completely disappears when the zero-hit sites are also taken into consideration.

Now comes the dating of the perceived mitochondrial bottleneck that should account for the low-seeming diversity of the Finnish mtDNA pool. The average nucleotide difference in the 360-bp segment of HVS-I was calculated as 3.9 substitutions (all sites having been put back for this exercise). One unit of pairwise difference scaled with the divergence rate of Ward et al. (1991) would then correspond to 8,300 years, but Sajantila et al. (1995, 1996) enigmatically cited this as 13,000 years. On top of this, they confounded divergence rate (the rate at which two lineages diverge from a common ancestor) with substitution rate (the rate at which a lineage diverges from an ancestor), so that they effectively turned the false 13,000 years into 6500 years (a lab-specific blunder; see Bandelt & Forster 1997). Even then the perceived bottleneck came out too old for the story to be told. So, a substitution rate faster by more than an order of magnitude was invoked (gleaned from maternal pedigree studies; cf. Pääbo 1996): this gave an age reported as 3900 years, which again has to be halved (now, however, turning out to be too young) because of the substitution/divergence confusion.

The slightly earlier published story about the Saami (Sajantila et al. 1995) uses the conventional mutation rate and genetic distances in the form of net nucleotide differences, which are the averaged nucleotide differences between two populations minus the average of the averaged nucleotide differences within the respective two populations. Although no attempt was made to scale these genetic distances to absolute time (using the assumed mutation rate), Sajantila *et al.* (1995) tacitly assumed that the ages of typical population splits in Europe were of the order of a few thousand years, so that the genetic distances of the Saami to the other European populations would correspond to tens of thousands of years. Note that the authors regard the Saami as a constant-size population whereas all other European populations are seen as having expanded in size. This, however, clashes with the theory behind the distance measure employed (see below).

The contrast between the mtDNA pools of Saami and Finns was interpreted by von Haeseler *et al.* (1996) in the same way (under the roof of coalescent theory) as the typical genetic contrast between hunter-gatherers and agriculturalists. What was evidently overlooked is that both mtDNA samples share some basal branches of the Eurasian mtDNA phylogeny and coalesce on the same Eurasian founder haplotype. This ancestral type cannot at the same time be tens of thousands of years old and four (or two) thousand years old. The message for archaeologists and linguists interested in what geneticists have to say about Finno-Ugric prehistory must be: don't believe everything you read in the papers.

Split the difference

Genetic distances (*viz.* net nucleotide differences) between several European populations, Turkey, and the Near East based on mitochondrial HVS-I sequences were listed in table 2 of Richards *et al.* (1996) for the sake of demonstrating their futility. The distances between the Near East and the other populations would be scaled to times within the range of 1000–4000 years, whereas all other distances fall into the range of 0–1000 years. Curiously, the former values have been taken seriously as evidence for 'Neolithic' population splits by Barbujani *et al.* (1998). But what about the latter values? For instance, the split between Bavaria and Turkey receives an entertaining age of under 100 years. It seems wise at this point to consult the theoretical basis of the distance measure employed.

The net nucleotide difference distance (Nei & Li 1979), when scaled by twice the mutation rate, is an unbiased estimator of the time of a clean population split - but only under very limiting circumstances. In particular, the (constant) population sizes of both the ancestral and each of the two daughter populations are required to be equal. While this is theoretically convenient (it means that each gene copy throughout the history of the sample is a part of a population of the same size), it could not be said to be useful. Even under (marginally) more realistic scenarios of different population sizes in the three populations, linearity in the time of the split is lost, unless the daughter populations have been going their separate ways for a very long time. For real data, which typically show imprints of founder/expansion events, this distance measure is therefore rather meaningless. As an illustration, consider the Basque sample (of size 156; Richards *et al.* 2000) and the Korean sample (of size 124; Horai *et al.* 1996; Pfeiffer *et al.* 1998): then the net nucleotide difference (when scoring only transitions in 16090 to 16365, without reconstruction of recurrent events) equals $5.094 - (2.769 + 5.670)/2 = 0.874$, which corresponds to a time of 8800 years (Forster *et al.* 1996). This may seduce the working historical geneticist to conclude that Koreans and Basques originally spoke a Proto-Basque–Korean language and arrived with the Neolithic from the Fertile Crescent.

In order to address phenomena of historical or recent prehistorical times, one may study the number of matching haplotypes across regional or ethnic groups. For reflecting ancient events dating to the Palaeolithic, however, matching coefficients would be so small that subsequent fluctuations in population sizes and gene flow would likely destroy any potentially meaningful relationship to real time. This did not hinder Barbujani & Bertorelle (2001) from taking matching coefficients as time estimators for putative population splits back to 40,000 years. When comparing European and Near Eastern populations, they observed two major modes (at coefficient values of 3 per cent and 0.6 per cent, respectively) in the pairwise population comparisons, which they interpreted as pointing to splits at 4000 years ago (referred to as 'Neolithic divergence', although this date sits rather in the Bronze Age) and at 40,000 years ago (equated with 'Palaeolithic divergence', although the Palaeolithic ended only about 12,000 years ago).

Before jumping on any desired interpretation, one should first consider the numerical cause for having greatly differing matching coefficients. In the European mtDNA pool, one HVS-I haplotype is absolutely predominant, *viz.* the Cambridge reference sequence (CRS), which accounts for 20 per cent and more of the regional mtDNA pools in western Europe. The matching between such pools is thus overwhelmed by shared CRS haplotypes, which essentially determine the matching coefficient. The pattern of CRS sharing runs counter to any 'Neolithic' interpretation as the CRS frequency cline runs opposite to a putative Neolithic cline from the Near East, from ~20 per cent in the west to ~12–16 per cent in central and eastern Europe, through ~10 per cent in the southeast and ~6 per cent in the Near East (Richards *et al.* 2000). Relatively low CRS frequency, though, is not always a 'Neolithic marker', but may be due to founder events in historical time (Saami, Icelanders) or simply due to poor sequencing (Ladins) that carried phantom mutations into innocent CRS (and other) sequences (see Bandelt *et al.* 2001; 2002).

Note that the European story told by Barbujani & Bertorelle (2001) requires the assumption of exponential growth after population splitting in order to make the dates fit. In contrast, the above stories told by Barbujani *et al.* (1998) from net nucleotide differences require constant sizes throughout. One cannot have both demographic scenarios at the same time, unless one adheres to research programmes such as those described in the next two sections.

Populations as æther

The desire to date population splits closely follows the paradigm set forth by the mentor of human population geneticists, Cavalli-Sforza (1998), who emphasized that 'it is the date of population splits, not the birth of individuals carrying the first mutation, that is of interest for comparison with archaeological dates, which usually refer to the early settlement of new areas'. The relationship of dating with population models has become so intimate that there is a widespread belief that any rate of accumulation of genetic changes is based on the assumption of demographically stable populations, so that 'the dating of genetic changes have very broad confidence limits and may be in error altogether' (Zvelebil 2000). Although age estimation for a mutational event does rely on a molecular clock, it does not have to be channelled through doubtful *a priori* assumptions of demographic scenarios.

The concept of the population, even at the synchronic level, is absolutely vague, although it appears that most geneticists think they have an intuitive (nationally inspired?) feeling of what a population really is. The list of European populations in the compendium of Cavalli-Sforza *et al.* (1994) apparently equates populations with nation states except for a few 'tribes' that are delineated as different, such as the Basques, Saami, and Sardinians. The history of the thus (un)defined populations then becomes the centre of interest to the population geneticist (Barbujani & Bertorelle 2001). There seems to be

no limit to the diachronic perspective, as long as the genetic polymorphisms under study have existed for long enough. In the case of a uniparental marker such as mtDNA the limit is the coalescence time of the sample. Coalescent theory allows exercises such as the ones enjoyed by Weiss & von Haeseler (1998), who discovered that 'the population of the Basques has expanded, whereas that of the Biaka pygmies is most likely decreasing. The Nuu-Chah-Nulth data are consistent with a model of constant population'. In these cases, the populations are considered as viable isolated genetic units, well-delineated from the rest of the world since between 50,000 and 150,000 years ago. This clearly does not sit easily with the results of modern ethnographic research (e.g. Hodder 1982).

Cutting down the information contained in mtDNA, the Y chromosome, or autosomal genes to the population level did not prove conclusive even in the (outdated) debate of multiregionalism versus Out-of-Africa. It is instructive and discouraging to see that even with the wealth of new data hardly any progress could be achieved in discriminating clearly between the two alternative models when the population remains the target of investigation; see Harpending & Rogers (2000) and Relethford (2001).

Concepts that were introduced in the early development of a discipline where they actually may have played a useful role may cease to be useful, just as did the concept of the æther in physics. Even the constant elaboration of models of the æther could not reconcile the observations with the theory (Einstein 1905); so too with the theoretical unit at the heart of classical population genetics, the population. To dismiss the concept of a population does not, of course, mean that one should, for example, turn mtDNA molecules into fictive Ur-mothers, complete with names and absurd birthplaces in space and time, not to mention a mystical bond with their descendants (Sykes 2001).

Alchemy

In a way similar to the tale about Finnish and Saami origins, contrasting so-called hunter-gatherers to agriculturalists, mtDNA data have been (ab)used to adduce the demographic impact of food-production in Africa (Watson *et al.* 1996). Bandelt & Forster (1997) have rejected 'the superficial assertion that the adoption of agriculture is the key to mismatch distributions, without reference to a particular cultural/ethnic population with an identifiable mixture of genotypes with a defined statistical shape and the archaeological/ethnographic data that addresses when that particular population may be inferred to have settled in a region and farmed in a way distinctive enough (specific stylized tool kit) to be associated with that particular group. In effect, Watson *et al.* (1996) provided no internal calibration to their system. This lack of calibration leads to a confusion between population and lineage identity. Many African populations actually coalesce at the deepest nodes of the global human tree, if one is paying attention to tribal/linguistic affiliations. Languages change, food preferences change, but genotypes persist, sometimes, under different population structures. How long they persist is a matter of drift and effective population size. The persistence of the same mtDNA allelic lineages in hunter-gatherer populations and farming populations implies that mismatch distributions are insensitive to very recent demographic expansion, as argued by Rogers (1995). How then can the effects of agriculture, as opposed to infectious disease, be seen with any accuracy? It seems like alchemy' (edited from an anonymous referee report, January 1997).

The analogy to alchemy suggests yet another feature in common: you make grand claims to the funding body — then, it was king; now, the national science foundation. One of the main problems using genetics to answer prehistoric questions is that the geneticist is expected to get a grant to do something stupendous, and then quickly solve it and move on to do something else. Thus, there has been an overemphasis on superficial population-genetics formalizations and insufficient attention to the resources of other disciplines.

The tale goes on

Coalescence times are still being calculated using the (theoretically convenient) model of random-mating populations of constant sizes. For instance, Su *et al.* (1999) used this model for estimating coalescence times of Y-chromosome haplogroups in eastern Asia. They explicitly claim that the estimation is robust even under a 'strong bottleneck event followed by a rapid population expansion'. This issue, however, is not really relevant here since the major departure from the model is the presence of geographic substructure — random mating was never possible in an area as huge as China — and several phases of considerable expansion, leading to potentially dramatic miscalculations of coalescence times. Bounds on the effective population size — a spurious lower limit that is clearly not robust to departures from the

simplistic model and an upper limit distilled from a hand-waving contrast with Africa — were effectively plucked from the air. This sort of *post hoc* accommodation is set up just in order to make the ages of founder haplogroups match the archaeological dates.

Data are often regarded as 'storytellers' (Bertranpetit 2000). 'This reflects the culture history view that new data, rather than new frameworks, are the most important aspect in the development of historical genetics. The framework allows the data to 'speak for themselves' and what they tell the 'listening' geneticist is when change took place and from what direction it came. Very often any further interpretation is regarded as speculation and if it occurs it will only be found hidden away in the closing remarks rather than the body of the report' (cited from Gamble 2001 by substituting 'archaeology' and 'archaeologist' by the genetic counterparts). This, nonetheless, does not exclude a situation where it may be fairly pedestrian, with appropriate genetic data in hand, to reject simple tales (such as the speedboat-to-Polynesia story of Diamond 1998; Oppenheimer & Richards this volume). To build up reasonable models that explain the past with some guidance from genetic data is quite another matter.

Historical genetics thus appears to be 'preprocessual' when compared to archaeology. It lacks a nuanced theoretical base — or, to put it more drastically, it has no theory at all which would take into account the specific prehistoric issues. The few formalized migration models or coalescent models that come along with some cute mathematics are as 'applicable' to humans as they are to lizards. But would we really envision a prehistory of lizards?

Mind the gap

The predominant desire in historical genetics thus seems to be a craving for black boxes (genetic distance measures, mismatch distributions, principal components, population trees, synthetic maps, autocorrelograms, constant-size coalescent models) into which data are poured (Bertranpetit 2000) and whence fundamental truths emerge. They are perceived as adding a patina of rigorous model-testing to the discourse. However, in most cases the surface is easily scratched away to reveal an interpretative lacuna. A common approach is to construct a null hypothesis of almost no interest to the historical genetic programme and to reject it if possible; within an orthodox statistical framework, this is well and good. However, the miracle then happens when you are left to commune with the statistics you have evaluated and to weave them into an interpretation. The interpretations of correlograms within spatial autocorrelation analysis or of the pattern of statistics evaluated within nested cladistic analysis should be seen in this light. In both cases, the rejection of the trivial null of no geographical structure leaves one at the mercy of some interpretative key, in the latter case made painfully explicit (Templeton 1997). Granted, you can disguise the void between the train and the platform with a dose of simulation studies to see how your statistics behave under alternatives to the null. But without explicit models and at least an approximate estimate of the probability of the data given each of those models, the interpretation should be received with the same scepticism as a story one might tell about a synthetic map (Richards *et al.* this volume).

Aggregation of genetic information

Before thinking of a grand synthesis, which genetic data should be considered for historical genetics and how should they (if at all) be aggregated? Classical markers, large in number but each one typically meagre in information, bear only indirect evidence of genetic polymorphisms: only few alleles can be discerned, which in many cases were spread across the continents, albeit at different frequencies. By handling a large number of these markers as vectors of combined allele frequencies for perceived populations, Cavalli-Sforza *et al.* (1994) were able to visualize the dominant features of these allele distributions via Principal Component Analysis (PCA) and subsequent synthetic mapping. This has hence become the stance of aggregation of genetic data: compile and feed them into PCA or subject them as genetic distances to cluster analysis.

The assertion that 'HVR-1 data . . . *can and must* be treated like any other set of genetic data and be analyzed by the standard population-genetics methods' (Simoni *et al.* 2000) reflects this classical thinking. It ignores the fact that no other genetic system analyzed thus far bears the same fine-grained, deep hierarchical structure as mitochondrial DNA (although Y-chromosome information is starting to catch up), which allows one to tap into the phylogenetic information. Furthermore, as a technical point, the resolution offered by the first hypervariable segment ('HVR-1') alone does not suffice for one to be able to identify all of the important (monophyletic) clades of the matrilineal genealogy, even if one were able to reconstruct all recurrent mutational events.

It has been claimed repeatedly, too, that a mutation at a single locus is rather meaningless on its own since this was just a random event and only the aggregation of the variation observed at the genome would allow any inference about prehistory. This, however, is only an issue when the fictive populations are the sole target of investigation. Every single mutational event has its specific space-time coordinates, which may be difficult to reconstruct exactly, although broad regions and time intervals of origin can potentially be estimated within an archaeological/ecological model (Richards *et al.* 2000). Grouping numerous mutations with similar space-time coordinates could then help to postulate trajectories of contacts, which in turn may lead to a more refined modelling.

The grand synthesis

In order to arrive at some sort of synthesis of the results derived from different disciplines, it is mandatory that the analyses of the separate disciplines be carried out with an adequate level of proficiency (Renfrew 1999a). We have seen above that as far as genetics is concerned neither the sequencing (Bandelt *et al.* 2001) nor the data handling and analysis (Torroni *et al.* 2000) always meet minimal quality criteria, thus paving the way for phantasms to appear. Weak and highly controversial linguistic evidence (such as for the Nostratic hypothesis; cf. Trask 1999; Campbell 1999) would not be improved by tagging molecules onto it, which would suggest the desired timing for the spread quite wonderfully. In this sense, there is no application of genetics to historical linguistics (*pace* Renfrew 2000) — at least none in a direct way (Renfrew 1999b). For example, the fact that some mtDNAs may have been carried from the Near East to Europe with the early Neolithic (Richards *et al.* 2000) makes it plausible that some new languages were transported into Europe. Whether or not these included Proto-Indo-European is, however, far from clear, especially since most linguists would prefer a later date for the expansion of the Indo-European family. Again, although we could not find major traces of mtDNA input to Europe during the Mesolithic, a minor introgression of Proto-Indo-European speakers into the Balkans with the onset of the Holocene (Adams & Otte 1999) is not excluded by the mitochondrial record.

The (early and later) Neolithic may well have brought more than one language family to Europe (Sherratt & Sherratt 1988). Any leap-frog migration or small-scale movements must have brought people with (not necessarily related) languages into new territory, where the new languages — at a later stage — would come into competition with the already resident ones in the course of the formation of a unified regional culture. There is no compelling reason to believe that the Fertile Crescent itself, as a core area for Neolithic beginnings, was monolingual. One could therefore assume, by default, that (for example) the early spread of Neolithic cultures into the Balkans and along the Mediterranean was accompanied by quite different language families in each case. The western and central Mediterranean regions in fact do not show any signs of early Indo-European speech. On the other hand, the ancient languages of the Iberian and Italian peninsulas need not all be regarded as Palaeolithic leftovers (as is presumably the case with Basque). For instance, the related languages Raetic and Etruscan, which were replaced by Latin vernaculars, were in turn related to a language once spoken in the Aegean island of Lemnos (Rix 1998).

To stretch the origin of language families to the Fertile Crescent or nearby regions (Barbujani *et al.* 1993; 1994; Renfrew 1999a) may not explain the real processes, which could actually have run in the opposite direction or have involved other centres of origin. For example, the languages of the Altaic type most likely originated from a Manchurian spread zone, as was convincingly argued by Janhunen (1996). The steppes have repeatedly been zones of rapid spread in either direction (east or west) at climatically favourable periods. Further, in view of the growing evidence for an indigenous Neolithic in South Asia and the pre-agricultural subsistence of Proto-Dravidians (Fuller, this volume), there is no need to posit that the Dravidian language family was intrusive to India (whether or not Elamo-Dravidian is accepted).

A trans-disciplinary approach to prehistory, for which a synthesis — grand or not — may strive, would take account of the multi-facetted past by engendering a nuanced modelling process. It would tell the human geneticist that there exists a well established discipline, prehistoric archaeology, from which he or she could learn, forestalling the testing of irrelevant hypotheses with dubious methods and inappropriate data (Zvelebil 2000). It would stimulate the linguist to develop more complex models for the origin and spread of a specific language family and to investigate ancient *sprachbund* and other contact phenomena that could point to language meshes of the early Holocene or the late Upper Palaeolithic (Janhunen 1996; Dixon 1997; Fortescue 1998). It would encourage the archaeologist to embrace the human

genetic database, left notoriously poorly analyzed by the geneticist, and to explore its impact. A synthesis, however, would be going full circle — back to culture history — if it were to aim at a fallacious congruity of material culture, language and genes (Zvelebil 1995; Sims-Williams 1998). We should expect to see these spheres somehow inter-related (trivially or accidentally) but more often 'out of step' (as in Beringia: Fortescue 1998). It is then an understanding of the specific dynamics of these spheres and their disharmony that enables us to transcend syntheses framed as neat 'origins-of' packages, such as the speedboat-to-Polynesia or the three-wave scenario for American beginnings.

Acknowledgements

This work has been supported by a travel grant from the DAAD (Deutscher Akademischer Austauschdienst) to H-J. Bandelt and a Wellcome Trust Research Career Development fellowship to V. Macaulay.

References

Adams, J. & M. Otte, 1999. Did Indo-European languages spread before farming? *Current Anthropology* 40, 73–7.

Amorim, A., 1999. Archaeogenetics. *Journal of Iberian Archaeology* 1, 15–25.

Bandelt, H.-J. & P. Forster, 1997. The myth of bumpy hunter-gatherer mismatch distributions. *American Journal of Human Genetics* 61, 980–83.

Bandelt, H.-J., P. Lahermo, M. Richards & V. Macaulay, 2001. Detecting errors in mtDNA data by phylogenetic analysis. *International Journal of Legal Medicine* 115, 64–9.

Bandelt, H.-J., L. Quintana-Murci, A. Salas & V. Macaulay, 2002. The fingerprint of phantom mutations in mitochondrial DNA data. *American Journal of Human Genetics* 71, in press.

Barbujani, G., G. Bertorelle & L. Chikhi, 1998. Evidence for Paleolithic and Neolithic gene flow in Europe. *American Journal of Human Genetics* 62, 488–91.

Barbujani, G. & G. Bertorelle, 2001. Genetics and the population history of Europe. *Proceedings of the National Academy of Sciences of the United States of America* 98, 22–5.

Barbujani, G.A. & A. Pilastro, 1993. Genetic evidence on origin and dispersal of human populations speaking languages of the Nostratic macrofamily. *Proceedings of the National Academy of Sciences of the USA* 90, 4670–73.

Barbujani, G.A., A. Pilastro, S. de Domenico & C. Renfrew, 1994. Genetic variation in North Africa and Eurasia: Neolithic demic diffusion vs paleolithic colonisation. *American Journal of Physical Anthropology* 95, 137–54.

Bertranpetit, J., 2000. Genome, diversity, and origins: the Y chromosome as a storyteller. *Proceedings of the National Academy of Sciences of the United States of America* 97, 6927–9.

Campbell, L., 1999. Nostratic and linguistic palaeontology in methodological perspective, in Renfrew & Nettle (eds.), 179–230.

Cann, R.L., M. Stoneking & A.C. Wilson, 1987. Mitochondrial DNA and human evolution. *Nature* 325, 31–6.

Cavalli-Sforza, L.L., 1998. The DNA revolution in population genetics. *Trends in Genetics* 14, 60–65.

Cavalli-Sforza, L.L., P. Menozzi & A. Piazza, 1994. *The History and Geography of Human Genes.* Princeton (NJ): Princeton University Press.

Diamond, J., 1998. *Guns, Germs and Steel: a Short History of Everybody for the Last 13,000 Years.* London: Vintage.

Dixon, R.M.W., 1997. *The Rise and Fall of Languages.* Cambridge: Cambridge University Press.

Einstein, A., 1905. Zur Elektrodynamik bewegter Körper. *Annalen der Physik* 17, 891–921.

Finnilä, S., M.S. Lehtonen & K. Majamaa, 2001. Phylogenetic network for European mtDNA. *American Journal of Human Genetics* 68, 1475–84.

Forster, P., R. Harding, A. Torroni & H-J. Bandelt, 1996. Origin and evolution of Native American mtDNA variation: a reappraisal. *American Journal of Human Genetics* 59, 935–45.

Fortescue, M., 1998. *Language Relations Across Bering Strait: Reappraising the Archaeological and Linguistic Evidence.* London & New York (NY): Cassell.

Gamble, C., 2001. *Archaeology: the Basics.* London: Routledge.

Harpending, H. & A. Rogers, 2000. Genetic perspectives on human origins and differentiation. *Annual Review of Genomics and Human Genetics* 1, 361–85.

Hasegawa, M., A. Di Rienzo, T.D. Kocher & A.C. Wilson, 1993. Toward a more accurate time scale for the human mitochondrial DNA tree. *Journal of Molecular Evolution* 37, 347–54.

Hodder, I., 1982. *Symbols in Action.* Cambridge: Cambridge University Press.

Holden, C., 1996. Few founding Finns. *Science* 274, 507.

Horai, S., K. Murayama, K. Hayasaka, S. Matsubayashi, Y. Hattori, G. Fucharoen, S. Harihara, K.S. Park, K. Omoto & I.-H. Pan, 1996. mtDNA polymorphism in East Asian populations, with special reference to the peopling of Japan. *American Journal of Human Genetics* 59, 579–90.

Janhunen, J., 1996. *Manchuria, an Ethnic History.* Helsinki: The Finno-Ugrian Society.

Kallio, P., 2000. Posti's superstrate theory at the threshold of the new millenium, in *Facing Finnic. Some Challenges to Historical and Contact Linguistics*, ed. J. Laakso. Helsinki: The Finno-Ugrian Society, 80–99.

Kittles, R.A., A.W. Bergen, M. Urbanek, M. Virkkunen, M. Linnoila, D. Goldman & J.C. Long, 1999. Autosomal, mitochondrial, and Y chromosome DNA variation in Finland: evidence for a male-specific bottleneck. *American Journal of Physical Anthropology* 108, 381–99.

Menozzi, P., A. Piazza & L.L. Cavalli-Sforza, 1978. Synthetic maps of human gene frequencies in Europeans. *Science* 201, 786–92.

Nei, M. & W.H. Li, 1979. Mathematical model for studying genetic variation in terms of restriction endonucleases. *Proceedings of the National Academy of Sciences of the United States of America* 76, 5269–73.

Pääbo, S., 1996. Mutations in the mitochondrial microcosm. *American Journal of Human Genetics* 59, 493–6.

Peltonen, L., A. Palotie & K. Lange, 2000. Use of population isolates for mapping complex traits. *Nature Reviews Genetics* 1, 182–90.

Pfeiffer, H., R. Steighner, R. Fisher, H. Mörnstad, C.-L. Yoon & M.M. Holland, 1998. Mitochondrial DNA extraction and typing from isolated dentin-experimental evaluation in a Korean population. *International Journal of Legal Medicine* 111, 309–13.

Relethford, J.H., 2001. Genetic history of the human species, in *Handbook of Statistical Genetics*, eds. D. J. Balding, M. Bishop & C. Cannings. Chichester: Wiley, 813–46.

Renfrew, C., 1992. Archaeology, genetics and linguistic diversity. *Man* 27, 445–78.

Renfrew, C., 1999a. Nostratic as a linguistic macrofamily, in Renfrew & Nettle (eds.), 3–18.

Renfrew, C., 1999b. Reflections on the archaeology of linguistic diversity, in *The Human Inheritance: Genes, Language, and Evolution*, ed. B. Sykes. Oxford: Oxford University Press, 1–32.

Renfrew, C., 2000. Archaeogenetics: towards a population prehistory of Europe, in Renfrew & Boyle (eds.), 3–11.

Renfrew, C. & K. Boyle (eds.), 2000. *Archaeogenetics: DNA and the Population Prehistory of Europe.* (McDonald Institute Monographs.) Cambridge: McDonald Institute for Archaeological Research.

Renfrew, C. & D. Nettle (eds.), 1999. *Nostratic: Examining a Linguistic Macrofamily.* (Papers in the Prehistory of Languages.) Cambridge: McDonald Institute for Archaeological Research.

Richards, M., H. Côrte–Real, P. Forster, V. Macaulay, H. Wilkinson–Herbots, A. Demaine , S. Papiha, R. Hedges, H.-J. Bandelt & B. Sykes, 1996. Paleolithic and Neolithic lineages in the European mitochondrial gene pool. *American Journal of Human Genetics* 59, 185–203.

Richards, M., V. Macaulay, E. Hickey, E. Vega, B. Sykes, V. Guida, C. Rengo, D. Sellitto, F. Cruciani, T. Kivisild, R. Villems, M. Thomas, S. Rychkov, O. Rychkov, Y. Rychkov, M. Gölge, D. Dimitrov, E. Hill, D. Bradley, V. Romano, F. Calì, G. Vona, A. Demaine, S. Papiha, C. Triantaphyllidis, G. Stefanescu, J. Hatina, M. Belledi, A. Di Rienzo, A. Novelletto, A. Oppenheim, S. Nørby, N. Al-Zaheri, S. Santachiara-Benerecetti, R. Scozzari, A. Torroni & H.-J. Bandelt, 2000. Tracing European founder lineages in the Near Eastern mtDNA pool. *American Journal of Human Genetics* 67, 1251–76.

Richards, M.B., V.A. Macaulay, H.-J. Bandelt & B. C. Sykes, 1998. Phylogeography of mitochondrial DNA in western Europe. *Annals of Human Genetics* 62, 241–60.

Rix, H., 1998. *Rätisch und Etruskisch*. Innsbruck: Innsbrucker Beiträge zur Sprachwissenschaft (ed. C. Meid), Institut für Sprachwissenschaft.

Rogers A.R., 1995. Genetic evidence for a Pleistocene population explosion. *Evolution* 49, 608–15.

Sajantila, A., P. Lahermo, T. Anttinen, M. Lukka, P. Sistonen, M.-L. Savontaus, P. Aula, L. Beckman, L. Tranebjaerg, T. Gedde-Dahl, L. Issel-Tarver, A. Di Rienzo & S. Pääbo, 1995. Genes and languages in Europe — an analysis of mitochondrial lineages. *Genome Research* 5, 42–52.

Sajantila, A. & S. Pääbo, 1995. Language replacement in Scandinavia. *Nature Genetics* 11, 359–60.

Sajantila, A., A.-H. Salem, P. Savolainen, K. Bauer, C. Gierig & S. Pääbo, 1996. Paternal and maternal DNA lineages reveal a bottleneck in the founding of the Finnish population. *Proceedings of the National Academy of Sciences of the United States of America* 93, 12,035–9.

Sherat, A., 1981. Plough and pastoralism: aspects of the secondary products revolution, in *Pattern of the Past: Studies in Honour of David Clarke*, eds. N. Hammond, I. Hodder & G. Isaac. Cambridge: Cambridge University Press, 261–305.

Sherratt, A. & S. Sherratt, 1988. The archaeology of Indo-European: an alternative view. *Antiquity* 62, 584–95.

Simoni, L., F. Calafell, D. Pettener, J. Bertranpetit & G. Barbujani, 2000. Reconstruction of prehistory on the basis of genetic data. *American Journal of Human Genetics* 66, 1177–9.

Sims-Williams, P., 1998. Genetics, linguistics, and prehistory: thinking big and thinking straight. *Antiquity* 72, 505–27.

Su, B., J. Xiao, P. Underhill, R. Deka, W. Zhang, J. Akey, W. Huang, D. Shen, D. Lu, J. Luo, J. Chu, J. Tan, P. Shen, R. Davis, L. Cavalli-Sforza, R. Chakraborty, M. Xiong, R. Du, P. Oefner, Z. Chen & L. Jin, 1999. Y-chromosome evidence for a northward migration of modern humans into eastern Asia during the last ice age. *American Journal of Human Genetics* 65, 1718–24.

Sykes, B., 2001. *The Seven Daughters of Eve*. London: Bantam.

Templeton, A.R., 1997. Testing the Out of Africa replacement hypothesis with mitochondrial DNA data, in *Conceptual Issues in Modern Human Origins Research*, eds. G. A. Clark & C. M. Willermet. New York (NY): Aldine de Gruyter, 329–60.

Torroni, A., M. Richards, V. Macaulay, P. Forster, R. Villems, S. Nørby, M.-L. Savontaus, K. Huoponen, R. Scozzari & H.-J. Bandelt, 2000. mtDNA haplogroups and frequency patterns in Europe. *American Journal of Human Genetics* 66, 1173–7.

Trask, R.L., 1999. Why should a language have any relatives? in Renfrew & Nettle (eds.), 157–76.

von Haeseler, A., A. Sajantila & S. Pääbo, 1996. The genetical archaeology of the human genome. *Nature Genetics* 14, 135–40.

Ward, R.H., B.L. Frazier, K. Dew-Jager & S. Pääbo, 1991. Extensive mitochondrial diversity within a single Amerindian tribe. *Proceedings of the National Academy of Sciences of the United States of America* 88, 8720–24.

Watson, E., K. Bauer, R. Aman, G. Weiss, A. von Haeseler & S. Pääbo, 1996. mtDNA diversity in Africa. *American Journal of Human Genetics* 59, 437–44.

Weiss, G. & A. von Haeseler, 1998. Inference of population history using a likelihood approach. *Genetics* 149, 1539–46.

Zvelebil, M. 1986. Mesolithic prelude and neolithic revolution, in *Hunters in Transition: Mesolithic Societies of Temperate Eurasia and their Transition to Farming*, ed. M. Zvelebil. Cambridge: Cambridge University Press, 5–15.

Zvelebil, M., 1995. Indo-European origins and the agricultural transition in Europe, in *Whither Archaeology? Papers in Honour of Evzen Neustupny*, eds. M. Kuna & N. Venclová. Prague: Institute of Archaeology, 173–203.

Zvelebil, M., 2000. The social context of the agricultural transition in Europe, in Renfrew & Boyle (eds.), 57–79.

Part III

Regional Studies

A. *Western Asia and North Africa*

Chapter 10

The Natufian Culture and the Early Neolithic:
Social and Economic Trends in Southwestern Asia

Ofer Bar-Yosef

The primary transitions to agriculture formed major revolutions in the history of humankind. The processes that occurred in them differed from those which took place in secondary loci where farming was adopted. The latter processes of adoption can be more easily modelled as resulting from population infiltration, mass colonization, or transmission by contacts along geographic trajectories.

Investigating the primary core areas requires the development of a model that explicates how foragers became farmers, and the formulation of testable hypotheses. Among the assumptions and observations behind such a model are:

1. Calendrical time plays an important role in social evolution. Calibrated chronology facilitates the recognition of a regional sequence of inevitable locational shifts of the 'core area', and the establishment of secondary loci.

2. Population densities reflect geography and the conditions of availability, accessibility, and predictability of food resources. Food acquisition technologies and tools, the availability of weaning foods, reduction or increase in contagious diseases, degree of personal and communal cleanliness, and appropriate water resources, may determine the rhythm of population growth and the need to expand. Predictable mobility routes, the nature of the terrain, average distance between bands or villages, and the spread of a mating system are among the determinants of the social concept of 'demographic pressure'.

3. Changes in the subsistence system, whether based on wild progenitors or domesticated ones, were affected by the degree of human selection.

4. The impact of climatic fluctuations depended on the ecological locations of the villages concerned. Reactions to a series of good or bad years would vary according to the 'cultural filter' of the given

social entity, formed by the history of the group, its relationships with neighbours, and its particular environment.

As far as human impact considerations in the eastern Mediterranean are concerned, environmental degradation is dated to not earlier than the Early Bronze Age. There is no hard evidence that goat herding caused major environmental deterioration prior to this time, even in marginal environments. Triggered by the rapidly accumulating evidence, global warming and abrupt climatic changes are no longer solely the favoured subjects of palaeo-climatologists, but also of archaeologists and social scientists (Glantz et al. 1998; Weiss & Bradley 2001). In using abrupt climatic change as an explanation for modelling social disruption, we need to establish the causal sequence. In the present state of our understanding, climate change rather than human environmental impact seems to have been more important as a trigger for the social changes leading to the Southwest Asian Neolithic.

The palaeo-climatic record for Southwest Asia: a brief summary

Currently, the most reliable palaeo-climatic information for Southwest Asia is derived from marine pollen cores and stalagmites (van Zeist & Bottema 1991; Rossignol-Strick 1995; Bar-Mathews et al. 1999; Frumkin et al. 1999), and can be summarized as follows:

1. During the Last Glacial Maximum (LGM), c. 20,000–16,500 cal. BC, the entire region was cold and dry, but the hilly coastal areas enjoyed winter precipitation and were covered by forests.

2. Climatic improvement is indicated during the following millennia, c. 16,500–12,500 cal. BC, possibly first in the southern reaches of the Levant and later in Anatolia.

3. Precipitation over the entire region increased from about 12,500 cal. BC, peaking during the Bölling-Alleröd.

4. Rainfall decreased during the Younger Dryas period (*c.* 11,000/10,700–9600/9500 cal. BC).

5. Pluvial conditions returned around 9500/9300 cal. BC, but probably did not reach the previous Terminal Pleistocene peak in the Levant.

6. A wetter Early Holocene (9500–7000 cal. BC) allowed for the establishment of systematic cultivation during the Early Neolithic.

Finally, a gradual rise in sea level after the LGM, lasting until the mid-Holocene, reduced the flat sandy coastal plain of the Levant by a stretch 5–20 km wide and 500 km long. Given the poor aquatic resources of this section of the Mediterranean Sea, the sea rise affected mainly the size of foraging territories and the collection of marine shells of types often used for decoration.

From mobile hunter-gatherers to Natufian sedentary foragers

The archaeology of late Palaeolithic foragers is relatively well known. Cultural units are identified on the basis of detailed lithic analyses combined with other attributes such as site size, site structure, distribution of settlements and the reconstructed patterns of seasonal mobility. Sites of the Kebaran complex (*c.* 17,000–14,500 cal. BC) were limited geographically to the coastal Levant and isolated oases due the prevailing cold and dry climate. The Geometric Kebaran foragers took advantage of the climatic amelioration (14,500–13,000/12,500 cal. BC) and expanded into the formerly desertic belt, which became a lusher steppe. Ground stone mortars, bowls and cupholes, as well as bedrock mortars, were employed for vegetal food processing. Named as a prerequisite for the agricultural revolution, the 'Broad-Spectrum Revolution' (Flannery 1973; Stiner 2001) is manifested in the carbonized plant remains from a water-logged site, Ohalo II, dated to *c.* 19,000 cal. BC (Kislev *et al.* 1992). The assemblage here contains a rich suite of seeds and fruits, known also from the basal layers of Abu Hureyra dated to *c.* 11,500 cal. BC. Both collections reflect intensified gathering of *r*-selected resources from a variety of habitats and plant associations, which apparently began at least some 10,000 years before intentional cultivation came into practice.

The Natufian culture emerged either as a result of a short-term abrupt cold climatic spell immediately preceding the Bölling-Alleröd, or simply resulted from the improved ecological conditions which facilitated the establishment of semi- and fully sedentary communities. The archaeological record of this prehistoric entity is well known (Fig. 10.1; Valla 1995; Bar-Yosef & Valla 1991, and papers therein; Bar-Yosef 1998; Henry 1989; Belfer-Cohen & Bar-Yosef 2000; Goring-Morris & Belfer-Cohen 1997; Sellars 1998), and the following is just a brief summary.

The Natufian base camps in the 'homeland' area were located in the oak-pistachio woodland belt, where the herbaceous undergrowth contained high frequencies of cereals. The mountains of Lebanon and the Anti-Lebanon, the steppe areas of the Negev and Sinai, and the Syro-Arabian desert in the east accommodated only small Natufian occupations. This was due not only to a lower carrying capacity, but also to the presence of other groups of foragers conducting highly mobile exploitation strategies.

Natufian sites fall into various size categories and the largest are rarely greater in size than 1000 m², reflecting a small group size. Natufian dwellings are rounded pit-houses (about 3–6 m in diameter) with foundations of undressed stones and upper structures of brush and wood. Every base camp demonstrates rebuilding of pit-houses, indicating the repeated abandonment and re-occupation of the settlement, reflecting a state of semi- or full sedentism. There is one example of a public structure — probably for group gatherings or closed meetings of males (for feasting?) — in the form of a large semi-circular building in Eynan (Mallaha). For special use were also the small adjoining oval rooms inside Hayonim Cave. Only flimsy structures characterize the Late Natufian sites. Despite expectations to the contrary, storage installations are rare and it is possible that baskets were used for above-ground storage.

Most Natufian sites were excavated before systematic dry sieving and flotation were introduced in the late 1960s. Even in recent excavations, however, water floatation has failed to retrieve sufficient quantities of floral remains and, in some cases, the few recovered grains were AMS-dated to recent times. The poor preservation of vegetal remains results from the nature of the prevailing *terra rossa* soils.

Tools such as sickles and mortars, bowls and pestles are interpreted as evidence for the harvesting and processing of cereals and legumes. The few recovered seeds indicate that cereals, legumes, almonds, acorns and other fruits were gathered. The plant species in Mureybet IA and IB and the Epi-Palaeolithic deposits at Abu Hureyra indicate prolonged exploitation of a wide range of wild resources

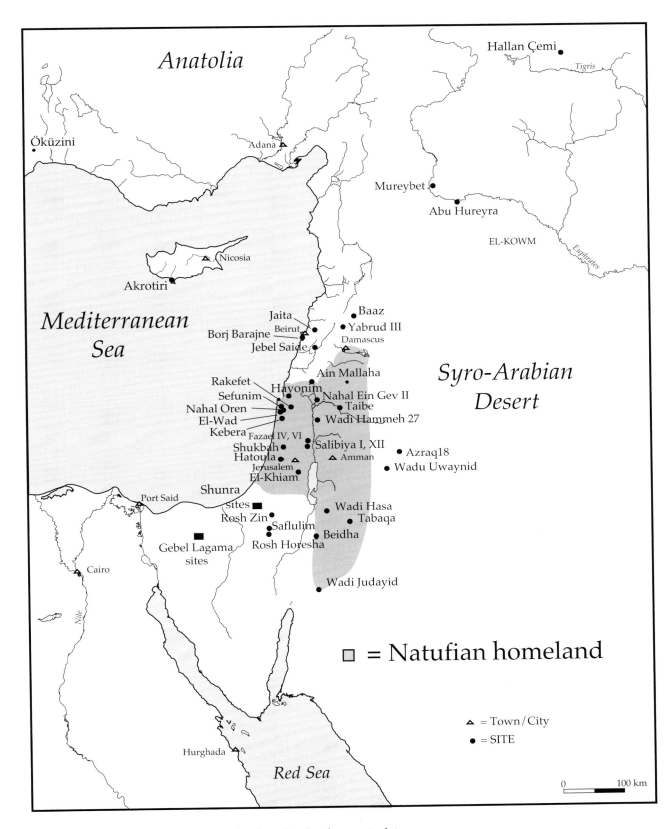

Figure 10.1. *Map indicating the Natufian homeland as known to date.*

since at least the time of Ohalo II (Colledge 1998; Hillman 2000).

Good bone preservation reflects the hunting of gazelle as well as other game, depending on the geographical location of each site, as well as smaller species such as tortoise and hare. In the coastal ranges, deer, cattle and wild boar were common, while in the steppe belt equids and ibex were typical prey. Waterfowl formed part of the Natufian diet, especially in sites along the Jordan Valley, where both migratory and nesting ducks were trapped during stress seasons, i.e. winter (December to March). Fresh water species of fish were caught seasonally in Lake Hula, while fishing seems to have been less important along the Mediterranean coast.

The Younger Dryas and the collapse of the Early Natufian

The climatic crisis of the Younger Dryas is recorded in deep-sea, pollen and ice cores (c. 10,900 to 9600 cal. BC). Complex hunter-gatherer societies such as the Early Natufian, which lasted for almost two millennia, are considered unstable social entities (Byrd 1998; Arnold 1996, and references therein). The climatic crisis caused the bearers of the Late Natufian industry to disperse and become more mobile. In the Negev and northern Sinai their final efforts to adapt to the new conditions through increased mobility created an entity named the Harifian culture (Goring-Morris 1987). The collapse of the Early Natufian was due to the incompatibility of sedentary modes of production and a growing population facing environmental deterioration, particularly in the marginal steppe areas and terebinth-almond woodland belts.

In the face of the uncertainties of the Younger Dryas, the Natufians and other social entities in the Near East had a variety of choices. In the Natufian homeland, increasing mobility into and out of base camps was a partial solution. Greater mobility during the Late Natufian is indicated by the disappearance of decorated burials, and the larger number of multi-individual graves (Belfer-Cohen & Bar-Yosef 2000). Kuijt (1996) considers the change as reflecting an attempt to erase social differentiation and to emphasize the unity of communities by giving similar treatment to all members.

A different socio-economic solution emerged in the eastern Taurus and Zagros foothills. In the open-air sites of Hallan Çemi Tepesi (10,900–8900 cal. BC) and Zawi Chemi Shanidar (c. 10,000–8200 cal. BC), groups shifted from more mobile hunting and gathering to semi-sedentary settlements. Their rounded pit-houses do not seem to have differed from those of the Natufian (Solecki 1981; Rosenberg et al. 1998).

The Neolithic Revolution and early villages

The 'Neolithic Revolution' (i.e. intentional cultivation) was begun during the Younger Dryas either by the Late Natufians or by contemporary foragers along the Middle Euphrates and Balikh river valleys (Fig. 10.2). One may hypothesize that the population which took this crucial step had previously survived on cereals exploited from natural stands. With the continuing cold and dry Younger Dryas conditions, C3 plants including cereals were affected by decreasing concentrations of atmospheric CO_2, which apparently resulted in declining yields of einkorn, emmer, rye and barley in their natural environments. Witnessing this decline and having, like all foragers, a knowledge of plants and their life cycles, a social decision was made. The options were: 1) increased mobility in order to search for resources; 2) movement into the northern neighbouring territories with the risk of physical conflict; or 3) cultivating naturally-wetted soils such as alluvial fans, riverine backswamps or shallow lakeside shores. As far as the latter cultivation option is concerned, grinding tools reflect the change in food processing. Natufians used mortars but their contemporaries in the Euphrates Valley employed flat grinding stone tools that herald the later types (Moore et al. 2000). In addition, as marginal areas became drier, it would be expected that kin-related groups relocated, causing population densities to mount within the fertile, coastal hilly belt of the Levant.

The Khiamian is the first Neolithic entity, but unfortunately, due to the paucity of excavated samples and radiocarbon dates, it is still poorly defined. Its estimated duration is a few centuries, c. 9700–9200 cal. BC (Aurenche & Kozlowski 1999; Kozlowski 1999; Gopher 1994; Goring-Morris & Belfer-Cohen 1997). This was probably when the mode of food production shifted. Ecological classification of the various species of wild cereals from Mureybet and Abu Hureyra by Colledge (1998) suggests that they were cultivated near the site. Hillman (2000) noted the increase of weedy grasses, which characterize cultivated fields in dry environments such as Abu Hureyra, at about 11,200–10,400 cal. BC. This rise was accompanied by the first appearance in Abu Hureyra of charred domesticated rye grains. If this indication is further supported, we may follow Cauvin (2000), who views this region of the northern Levant as the

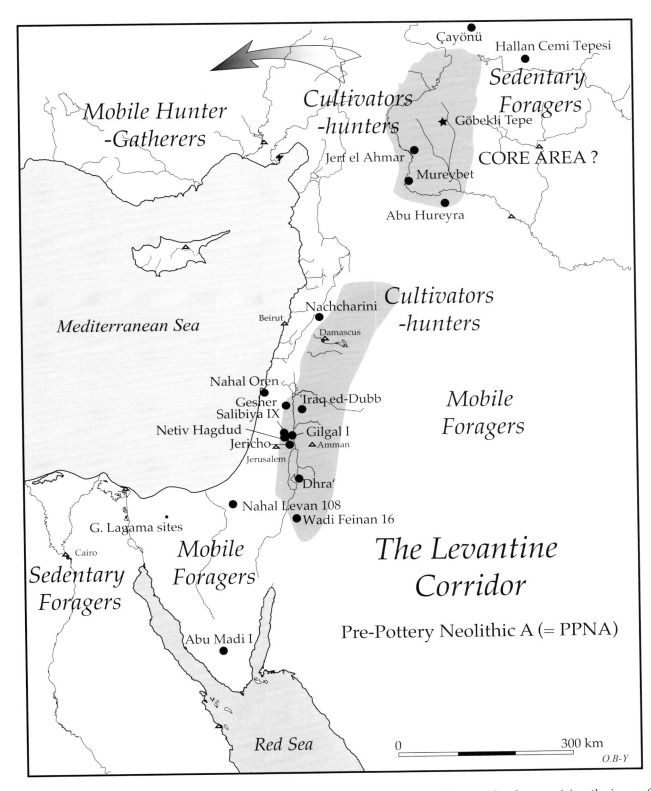

Figure 10.2. *Map of the Levant indicating the geographic location of the Levantine corridor, hence raising the issue of the original core area for early farming, whether in the Euphrates River Valley in Upper Mesopotamia or in the southern Levant.*

'core area'. Genetic studies of einkorn suggest that their oldest progenitors were in the northern Levant, while barley appears over the entire area (Badr *et al.* 2000; Heun *et al.* 1997). Wild barley was grown by PPNA communities in the Jordan Valley (Kislev 1997).

Population densities grew faster after the Younger Dryas. This is indicated by the rapid growth of site sizes. Most PPNA hamlets and villages are three to eight times larger than the largest Natufian sites (Bar-Yosef 1998). Their actual areas vary from 0.2 to 2.5 hectares.

Three cultural entities can be identified in the PPNA Levant: the Mureybetian in the north; the Aswadian in the centre; and the Sultanian in the south (Cauvin 2000; Aurenche & Kozlowski 1999). This subdivision does not include the material remains of those hunter-gatherers who continued to survive in semi-arid areas. The variability among the types of arrowheads across the region at this time is minimal, but the axe-adzes differ. Bifacially chipped axes-adzes are common in the southern Levant. Polished celts of limestone and basalt, common in the northern Levant, made their first appearance in the south at this time. In the Mureybetian, the adzes (*herminettes*) were shaped as unifaces from large and thick flakes. Microwear studies suggests that most axe-adzes were employed in woodworking activities such as building, domestic carpentry, and probably seacraft construction which in this region is attested from the early millennia of the Holocene when Cyprus was first colonized (Peltenburg *et al.* 2000). The earliest evidence for cordage and basketry was uncovered in PPNA Netiv Hagdud. Southern PPNA grinding stones include flat slabs with cupholes, rounded shallow grinding bowls and hand stones, often loaf-shaped (Wright 1994; Bar-Yosef & Gopher 1997).

Domestic architecture consists mainly of rounded to squarish pit-houses with stone foundations, and walls built of plano-convex unbaked mud-bricks or adobe. The best examples of communal building efforts are the walls and the tower of Jericho and its adjoining storage facilities. Originally interpreted by Kenyon (1957) as a defence system against raids by human groups, an alternative interpretation (Bar-Yosef 1986) suggests that the PPNA wall was erected on the western side of the site to protect the settlement against mudflows and flash floods. It also appears that there was only one tower in this settlement. The function of the 8.5 metre high tower with its interior steps is unknown, but it could have accommodated a small mud-brick shrine on its top. Although unequivocal evidence for public ritual is missing, the open space north of the tower had perhaps a similar function to the 'plaza' in Çayönü (Turkey), which served for public gatherings (Özdogan 1999).

Two unique buildings in Jerf el-Ahmar in the Euphrates valley (Stordeur *et al.* 2001) include a 'round house with cells', similar to the one uncovered in Mureybet IIIA, encircled by what seems to be a series of family houses. Below, an earlier communal building was uncovered. The 'house with slabs' (*le bâtiment aux dalles*) is a pit-house with a bench encircling the walls, with six column bases spread at equal distances around its edge. The outer face of the bench had a series of upright slabs incised with zigzag patterns.

Mortuary practices and figurines are considered indications of belief systems and rituals. In the Sultanian, most burials are single, with no grave goods. Skull removal was performed only on adults; child burials were left intact. Isolated crania are sometimes found in domestic areas or special purpose buildings. The entire array and sequence of mortuary practices of the period has been interpreted as a reflection of an egalitarian social structure (Kuijt 1996). However, differentiated treatment along age lines is a clear marker for an increasing presence of ranking, which stresses the departure from the Natufian tradition.

Human figurines shaped from limestone and clay are more frequent in PPNA contexts than in the Natufian and depict either standing or kneeling females. The 'seated woman' type may herald the elaborate manifestations of the same icon image in the succeeding PPNB. This explicit expression of gender, which was not evident in the Natufian culture, may indicate the emerging role of women in a society of farmers. Some suggest that this shift brought about the cult of the 'mother goddess, in later centuries (Cauvin 2000).

The economy of PPNA villages was based on a broad-spectrum exploitation pattern of hunting, trapping, gathering wild seeds and fruits, and cultivation of cereals and legumes. The common game animals in the northern Levant were equids and cattle. Wild cattle, gazelle, fox, fallow deer and wild boar occurred in the south (Tchernov 1994; Peters *et al.* 1999; Horwitz *et al.* 1999). There is ample evidence for import of obsidian from central Anatolia, and where excavated deposits were sieved, most of the marine shells recovered came from the Mediterranean rather than the Red Sea.

Competition is an expected component of the relationship between groups or even tribes. It would be naïve to assume that there were no conflicts within sedentary communities, either on an individual basis or along extended clan lines. Disagreements concerning access to land and water resources must have occurred. With the declining frequency of game animals, obtaining meat in marginal areas could have been the trigger for the use of improved bows and arrows. Such events, along with depletion of non-manured fields and natural population growth due to the availability of weaning foods and reduced mobility of females, led to the establishment of new villages. Archaeological evidence for inter-village clashes expressed in defensive walls first appears *c.* 6000 cal. BC in Tel as-Sawwan, immediately after the collapse of the PPNB civilization.

In sum, the regional archaeology of PPNA sites clearly demonstrates the emergence of a non-egalitarian society of cultivators-hunters. Public buildings are signs of increasing degrees of social organization, and the Jerf el-Ahmar structures resemble PPNB temples. Social ranking is expressed in mortuary practices. Indeed, the available data reflect emerging social complexity, the nature of which is clearer in the archaeology of PPNB sites.

The PPNB societies

Among PPNB agricultural activities, besides cultivation (e.g. Harris 1998; Zohary & Hopf 2000), are the incipient phases of goat, sheep, cattle and pig penning and eventual domestication. Contemporary foragers continued to hunt and gather while developing intricate relationships with farming communities. Their mutual relationships could have ranged from friendly encounters to violent conflicts, as is well-known from historical examples. Traditionally, the entire Levant can be considered a PPNB interaction sphere of both the 'sown land and the desert' (Bar-Yosef & Belfer-Cohen 1989).

Even though there has been intentional agriculture in the Levant and adjacent regions for over 10,000 years, it is difficult today, despite modern air photography, to identify prehistoric fields that have been buried by alluviation. Palaeo-climatic data point to a generally higher annual precipitation than today during the PPNB (Bar-Mathews *et al.* 1999). Van Zeist (1986) suspected that either winter precipitation was higher, or that irrigation was practised in the marginal eastern belt. Using stable carbon isotope analysis, seeds tested from PPNB contexts in Tell Halula on the Euphrates in Syria suggest that prehistoric crops enjoyed better water supplies than those available today through winter rain or irrigation (Araus *et al.* 2001).

The tool-kits of the early farmers included axe-adzes, which in the southern Levant were bifacially shaped with transverse blows producing a sharp cutting edge, and sometimes later modified by polishing. In the northern Levant and Anatolia polished celts were the standard. All these tools were employed in wood-working activities including tree-felling and clearing, shaping of wooden objects, and building of sea craft. Harvesting equipment included simple sickles, V-shaped bone tools for stripping the seed heads from straw, and later the threshing board or *tribulum* (Anderson 1998).

Storage facilities include special built-in installations and small rooms in houses or courtyards. Changes in the sizes and locations of storage facilities mark the shift from nuclear family consumption to larger social units and perhaps, already in some PPNB sites, to an institutionalized control of public granaries.

The Early PPNB (EPPNB) was the age of the transformation in the exploitation of animal resources. The process of husbandry began with the sheep during the EPPNB, with some hints that goats were also included (Peters *et al.* 1999; Zeder 1999; Horwitz *et al.* 1999). Later, during the Middle and Late PPNB (MPPNB and LPPNB), either goats and/or sheep were herded in the central and southern Levant (Martin 1999). A clear example of translocation of goat, sheep, cattle, and pigs (as well as the wild fallow deer) is documented in the PPNB Cypriote site of Shillourocambos (Vigne *et al.* 1999). These animals, not original species of the island, had to be transported on sea craft by colonizing farmers. Zooarchaeological analysis of the bone assemblages indicates that the earliest herded goats were morphologically wild (Peters *et al.* 1999). Thus, in sites located in the natural habitat of caprovines, the absence of morphological changes cannot be interpreted as evidence for continued hunting by farmers, since the process of penning could already have started. In areas where bones of wild goats are rarely found in Epi-Palaeolithic and PPNA contexts, any sudden shift to a high frequency of caprovines within a faunal spectrum will be a good indicator for the introduction of herding. In the semi-arid sites of the Syro-Arabian desert, goats became part of the economy only by 8000/7500 cal. BC and later (Martin 1999).

Domesticated cattle and pigs appeared during the PPNB period. The penning of aurochs and their ensuing domestication seems to have been first motivated by religious reasons (the 'bull-cult'; Cauvin 2000). Similar to other animals, cattle (mostly bulls) were sacrificed, possibly during ceremonial feasts.

Pigs were probably the last major domestic animal to be incorporated into the Levantine household. While there is a proposal for the penning of pigs in Hallan Çemi during the late Epi-Palaeolithic, early husbandry is reported only from the MPPNB sites.

In sum, the fully developed Neolithic economy, with its domesticated species of plants and animals, seems to have emerged earliest in the northern Levant. Due to geographic proximity, innovations did not escape notice by the inhabitants of the central and southern Levant, and the resulting regional network formed the PPNB interaction sphere (Bar-Yosef & Belfer-Cohen 1989).

Interactions between farmers-herders and contemporary mobile foragers played an important role, not yet fully researched. Societal interactions could have been in constant flux, either amicable, which may have led to intermarriage (generally with forager women marrying into farming communities), or hostile. Foragers could have also have acted as mobile 'traders'.

During the Early Neolithic, exchange relationships are indicated by marine shells from the Red Sea in inland farming communities, as well as by 'down the line' movement of obsidian from Central Anatolia into the Levant (Cauvin 1994). The exchange of commodities (such as grain) between foragers and farmers has been suggested, but not yet fully demonstrated (Bar-Yosef Mayer 1997). The transport of edibles is exemplified in Nahal Hemar cave, where fruits and seeds of plants occur that grow some 15–150 km away.

Among the other archaeological markers of farmer-forager interaction are the game drives known as 'desert kites'. These were probably laid out by PPNB foragers to hunt gazelle or onager *en masse*. Employing this technique, which is also known from other locations in the world, must mean that there was a need for the meat, hides and horns from more than a single animal. In one Jordanian site (Jilat 26; Garrard *et al.* 1994), a rectangular house in a foragers' camp of rounded dwellings might be interpreted as a 'merchant's temporary home'.

While the evidence is poor, it seems likely that some degree of conflict would have existed between hunter-gatherers and farming communities in the Near East, as in general in farmer–forager relationships (e.g. Ember & Ember 1997). Indeed, the boundaries between farmers-herders and foragers in semi-arid or mountain regions were evidently far from stable during the PPNB. By about 7500 cal. BC, the present economic dichotomy between farmers-herders and pastoral nomads had emerged and became more established in following millennia. Members of both economic regimes continued to hunt and trap, as well as gather wild plants, seeds and fruits for various purposes, including medicines.

Identifying the social territories and the collapse of the PPNB civilization

From the early PPNA to the first PPNB chiefdoms in southwestern Asia, a considerable number of organizational and economic shifts can be recognized (Cauvin 2000). Viewing social forces as the main energizers of change, Cauvin named the process the 'Revolution of Symbols'. While this is an attractive proposal, we do not feel that one can easily decouple the social realm from the economic arena. As human history tells us, economic decisions will have social implications, as much as decisions on social issues will have an impact on the economy. The view that one aspect is more important than the other has led to endless debate among historians, as well as archaeologists, on what determines the trajectory of cultural evolution. With the proliferation of palaeoclimatic data, radiocarbon dating, genetic studies of founder crops and the like, it is now becoming clearer that social decisions were made in face of a variety of environmental situations, some of which can be defined as 'climatic surprises' (Glantz *et al.* 1998). In the face of a natural disaster or social crisis, decisions in prehistoric societies would have been made by temporary or hereditary leaders through alliance building, verbal negotiation and communal feasting, all activities which will hardly leave any physical evidence. But what could have been an easy solution for a band of hunter-gatherers would have become more complex at the tribal level and increasingly so in chiefdoms and states.

One of the relevant issues for understanding the PPNA and PPNB, not yet fully explored for the Near Eastern Neolithic, is the rapidity of population growth, so evident from the growth in site sizes. This resulted from a combination of mounting total fertility of females, their reduced mobility, the availability of weaning foods and increasing investment in adolescents. It is expected in such situations, as shown by ethnic studies, that resulting population increase will ignite a tendency towards development of an inclusive identity. Large villages functioned as biological descent groups that developed the means for safeguarding and transmitting their own culture. Hence, recurring elements in material culture, mortuary practices, clay figurines and the like can facili-

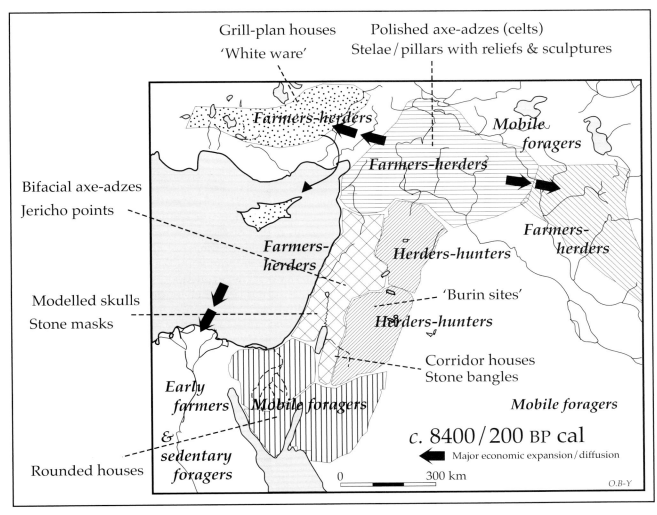

Figure 10.3. *Map indicating the suggested geographic spread of PPNB entities ('tribes') with the main cultural characteristics of each territory.*

tate tentative delineation of homelands, and ensuing directions of colonization and/or diffusion.

We therefore turn to mapping proposed tribal territories within the PPNB interaction sphere (Fig. 10.3). Among prominent markers of territory are ceremonial centres, architectural variations in house types, technological variations in the flaking of heavy-duty tools such as axes and adzes, variations in the frequencies of projectile point types, occurrences of modelled skulls, and the like. Within the newly forming interaction sphere one can identify similar beliefs and an overall cosmology. The modelled skulls found in various sites may hint at the presence of élite members or chiefly families. However, no uniquely rich tombs have been discovered to date and thus we cannot classify PPNB societies as chiefdoms. With ongoing field work, this may change

in a few years. Evidence for what should have been an organized effort and not just a family affair was the colonization of Cyprus. The building of seafaring craft, transport of animals and the crossing by several groups, as shown by the discovery of several early PPNB sites on this island, speaks to the presence of leaders.

Markers of personal property (of individuals or extended families?) are probably indicated by rare engraved flat pebbles, by markings on the backs of 'shaft straighteners' in the PPNA, as well as by stamp seals in the PPNB. The engravings on these objects, as noted by Cauvin (2000), resemble pictographs used in early writing. One may add here the tokens that are thought to be elements of a counting system (Schmandt-Besserat 1990). Traded or exchanged items indicate a much wider interaction sphere in which sources and producers were located beyond the permeable boundaries of the PPNB civilization. Among the better known exchanged materials are obsidian, chlorite bowls, asphalt, cinnabar, and marine shells.

During the two millennia of the PPNB, only a few settlements survived through many centuries. A stratigraphic gap between the PPNB and the Pottery Neolithic is well established in the Levant and on the Anatolian plateau (Aurenche & Kozlowski 1999; Gopher & Gophna 1993; Özdogan & Basgelen 1999), indicating widespread village abandonment. Given this observation, the proposal to explain the collapse of a major village such as 'Ain Ghazal in Jordan as due to local environmental over-exploitation (e.g. Rollefson *et al.* 1992) does not fit within the general geographic phenomenon of climatic crisis (Oba *et al.* 2001). The abrupt and adverse climatic change around 8400–8200 BP that is well-recorded in ice cores (Alley *et al.* 1997), in the stalagmites of Soreq Cave (Bar-Mathews *et al.* 1999), as well as in eastern Mediterranean pollen cores (Rossignol-Strick 1995; Baruch & Bottema 1999), was the main culprit. Affected by a series of droughts, tribal societies that subsisted on farming and herding, in which the demands of better-off individuals (or families) drove the flow of prestige goods, could not continue to accumulate the needed surpluses. Shifts in the patterns of seasonal precipitation necessitated a search for pastures further away and resulted in lower yields for summer harvests. The economic deterioration would have accelerated competition for leadership (Flannery 1999), resulting in an organizational change expressed in the disappearance of previously large villages and the establishment of smaller villages, hamlets and farmsteads. The new conditions probably enhanced reliance on a more flexible subsistence strategy of farming and herding, and increased the presence of pastoral societies after cal. 7000 BC. In sum, the collapse of the PPNB could have been the trigger for the colonization of the Nile Delta (Fig. 10.4), and through a 'domino effect' the dispersal by sea to the Mediterranean islands.

Discussion

Archaeological data from the Levant, Upper Mesopotamia and Anatolia raise various issues concerning the topic of the conference from which this book is derived, and I will deal with them one by one. Firstly, where was the location of the original 'core area' of the Neolithic Revolution? Did the centre of socio-economic change move from one 'core area' to a second or additional ones? Can we interpret movement outwards from the central locus to colonization via demic diffusion, as suggested by Ammerman & Cavalli-Sforza (1984), or to diffusional transmission of technology and ideas? Figure 10.4 illustrates a preliminary proposal regarding the location of the original core area. By placing the question mark on the Natufian homeland we indicate the need to uncover the still-unknown immediate 'pre-Neolithic' hunter-gatherer societies in the northern Levant and Upper Mesopotamia, where we see the later blooming of the PPNB civilization. Without a sound archaeological record we cannot determine the location of the original 'core area'. According to currently available evidence it was located in the central Levant. If this observation holds, then the northward displacement of the 'core area' that determined the ensuing development of the agricultural system heralds similar historical models that indicate geographic shifts in the centre of innovation from the onset of the Industrial Revolution until today.

Secondly, we must ask if the fragmentary archaeological record allows for a conclusion that population growth or 'demographic pressure' drove the evolution of farming societies and the need to take over new lands? It seems that the best available measure of changing population size is total site size through time. Needless to say, the translation of areas measured in hectares to numbers of people is not easy, but mound sizes can serve as a relative scale (e.g. Bar-Yosef & Meadow 1995, fig. 3.7). Population growth in Neolithic communities was supported by the availability of weaning foods, the high yield per acre of cultivated cereals (e.g. Araus *et al.* 2001) and the development of storage facilities. Any surplus could have been used for the purchase of precious goods, and enhanced social stratification. The geographic nature of Upper Mesopotamia, the northern Levant and the Anatolian plateau, with numerous intermontane valleys, allowed farmers to depart from their original village and establish new communities.

Thirdly, does the information from the region under discussion support the 'wave of advance' model, or the 'saltatory jumps' model proposed by van Andel & Runnels (1995)? I believe that these two models have a common denominator and are essentially the same. The wave of advance model draws the large picture and the average rate of continental movement, while the saltatory model deals with the detailed reality. Farmers move to arable lands, whether in intermontane valleys, along river valleys or up tributaries. By looking only for arable land they leave the more rugged or semi-arid areas for the foragers. One can easily imagine the complex

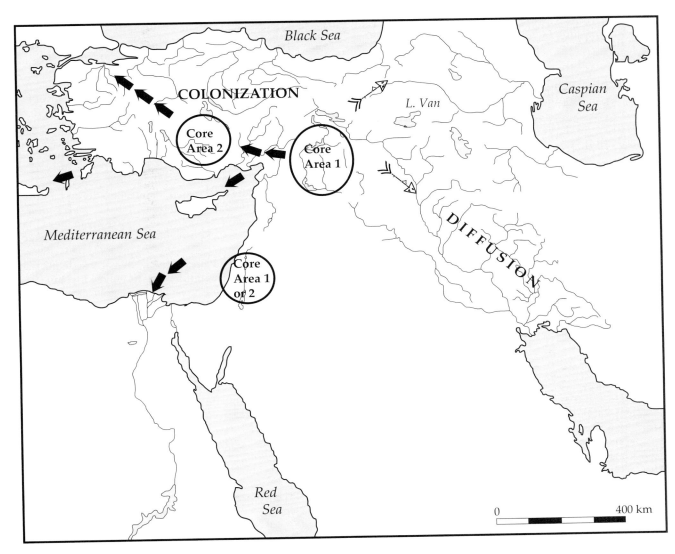

Figure 10.4. *Map of southwestern Asia indicating the dispersal of Early Neolithic economy by colonization and diffusion raising the issue of the exact location of the original core area of the Neolithic revolution.*

relationships within a reticulate settlement pattern, with either mutual or competing economies and social relations.

Finally, did the dispersal of the Neolithic economy depend on geographic axes (north–south versus east–west) as major determinants, as predicted by Diamond (1997)? The response, similar to that of Bellwood (2001, 187), is 'not necessarily so'. The spreads in the Levant and the Zagros foothills were along the north to south axis, while into Anatolia and Thessaly it was from east to west. It seems that farmers were attracted by the distribution of arable lands in various directions. Perhaps more important is the 'agricultural package', which was larger in southwestern Asia than almost any other region of

the world (see Harris this volume).

In conclusion, if the origin of the Indo-European languages can be located within the Anatolian region, perhaps we can more clearly locate the core area either on the Anatolian plateau or in the northern Levant–Upper Mesopotamia. This, however, will also necessitate discussion concerning the core area for the origins of the Afroasiatic languages, and their relationship to the dispersal of agriculture from the core area into northeast Africa.

Acknowledgements

Several ideas and interpretations presented in this paper were discussed with my colleagues A. Belfer-

Cohen (Hebrew University), N. Goring-Morris (Hebrew University), A. Gopher (Tel-Aviv University), R. Meadow (Harvard University), and C.C. Lamberg-Karlovsky (Harvard University). W. Fournier provided editorial assistance. Due to restrictions on space, I was unable to cite many of my colleagues whose work is both pertinent and deserving of mention. However, I am solely responsible for any shortcomings in this version.

References

Alley, R.B., P.A. Mayewski, T. Sowers, M. Stuiver, K.C. Taylor & P.U. Clark, 1997. Holocene climatic instability: A prominent, widespread event 8200 years ago. *Geology* 25(6), 483–6.

Ammerman, A.J. & L.L. Cavalli-Sforza, 1984. *The Neolithic Transition and the Genetics of Populations in Europe.* Princeton (NJ): Princeton University Press.

Anderson, P.C., 1998. History of harvesting and threshing techniques for cereals in the prehistoric Near East, in Damania *et al.* (eds.), 145–59.

Araus, J.L., G.A. Slafer, I. Romagosa, & M. Molist, 2001. Estimated wheat yields during the emergence of agriculture based on the carbon isotope discrimination of grains: evidence from a 10th millennium BP site on the Euphrates. *Journal of Archaeological Science* 28(4), 341–50.

Arnold, J.E. (ed.), 1996. *Emergent Complexity: the Evolution of Intermediate Societies.* Ann Arbor (MI): University of Michigan.

Aurenche, O. & S.K. Kozlowski, 1999. *La Naissance du Néolithique au Proche Orient ou Le Paradis Perdu.* Paris: Editions Errance.

Badr, A., K. Müller, R. Schäfer-Pregl, H. El Rabey, S. Effgen, H.H. Ibrahim, C. Pozzi, W. Rohde & F. Salamini, 2000. On the origin and domestication history of barley (*Hordeum vulgare*). *Molecular Biology and Evolution* 17(4), 499–510.

Bar-Mathews, M., A. Ayalon, A. Kaufman & G.J. Wasserburg, 1999. The eastern Mediterranean paleoclimate as a reflection of regional events: Soreq cave, Israel. *Earth and Planetary Science Letters* 166, 85–95.

Bar-Yosef Mayer, D.E., 1997. Neolithic shell bead production in Sinai (as950097). *Journal of Archaeological Science* 24(2), 97–112.

Bar-Yosef, O., 1986. The walls of Jericho: an alternative interpretation. *Current Anthropology* 27, 157–62.

Bar-Yosef, O., 1998. The Natufian culture in the Levant: threshold to the origins of agriculture. *Evolutionary Anthropology* 6(5), 159–77.

Bar-Yosef, O. & A. Belfer-Cohen, 1989. The Levantine 'PPNB' interaction sphere, in *People and Culture in Change*, ed. I. Hershkovitz. (BAR International Series 508(i).) Oxford: BAR, 59–72.

Bar-Yosef, O. & A. Gopher (eds.), 1997. *An Early Neolithic Village in the Jordan Valley*, part I: *The Archaeology of Netiv Hagdud.* Cambridge (MA): Peabody Museum Publications, Harvard University.

Bar-Yosef, O. & R.H. Meadow, 1995. The origins of agriculture in the Near East, in *Last Hunters, First Farmers: New Perspectives on the Prehistoric Transition to Agriculture*, eds. T.D. Price & A.B. Gebauer. (School of American Research Advanced Seminar Series D.) W. Schwartz, general ed. Santa Fe (NM): School of American Research Press, 39–94.

Bar-Yosef, O. & F.R. Valla (eds.), 1991. *The Natufian Culture in the Levant.* Ann Arbor (MI): International Monographs in Prehistory.

Baruch, U. & S. Bottema, 1999. A new pollen diagram from Lake Hula: vegetational, climatic, and anthropogenic implications, in *Ancient Lakes: Their Cultural and Biological Diversity*, eds. H. Kawanabe, G.W. Coulter & A.C. Roosevelt. Brussels: Kenobi Productions, 75–86.

Belfer-Cohen, A. & O. Bar-Yosef, 2000. Early sedentism in the Near East: a bumpy ride to village life, in *Life in Neolithic Farming Communities: Social Organization, Identity, and Differentiation*, ed. I. Kuijt. New York (NY): Plenum Press, 19–37.

Bellwood, P., 2001. Early agriculturalist population diasporas? Farming, languages and genes. *Annual Review of Anthropology* 30, 181–207.

Byrd, B.F., 1998. Spanning the gap between the Upper Paleolithic and the Natufian: the Early and Middle Epipaleolithic, in *The Prehistoric Archaeology of Jordan*, ed. D.O. Henry. (British Archaeological Reports S705.) Oxford: Archaeopress, 64–82.

Cauvin, J., 2000. *The Birth of the Gods and the Origins of Agriculture.* Translated by T. Watkins. Cambridge: Cambridge University Press.

Cauvin, M.-C., 1994. La circulation de l'obsidienne au Proche-Orient Néolithique, in *Neolithic Chipped Stone Industries of the Fertile Crescent: Proceedings of the First Workshop on PPN Chipped Lithic Industries*, eds. H.G. Gebel & S.K. Kozlowski. Berlin: Ex Oriente, 15–22.

Colledge, S., 1998. Identifying pre-domestication cultivation using multivariate analysis, in Damania *et al.* (eds.), 121–31.

Damania, A.B., J. Valkoun, G. Willcox & C.O. Qualset (eds.), 1998. *The Origins of Agriculture and Crop Domestication.* Aleppo, Syria: ICARDA.

Diamond, J.M., 1997. *Guns, Germs, and Steel: the Fates of Human Societies.* New York (NY): W.W. Norton.

Ember, C.R. & M. Ember, 1997. Violence in the ethnographic record: results of cross-cultural research on war and aggression, in *Troubled Times: Violence and Warfare in the Past*, eds. D.L. Martin & D.W. Frayer. (War and Society 3.) Amsterdam: Gordon & Breach Publishers; Overseas Publishers Association, 1–20.

Flannery, K.V., 1973. The origins of agriculture. *Annual Review of Anthropology* 2, 271–310.

Flannery, K.V., 1999. Chiefdoms in the early Near East: why it's so hard to identify them, in *The Iranian World: Essays on Iranian Art and Archaeology*, eds. A. Alizadeh, Y. Majidzadeh & S.M. Shahmirzadi.

Tehran: Iran University Press, 44–61.

Frumkin, A., D.C. Ford & H.P. Schwarcz, 1999. Continental oxygen isotopic record of the last 170,000 years in Jerusalem. *Quaternary Research* 51, 317–27.

Garrard, A.N., D. Baird, S. Colledge, L. Martin & K. Wright, 1994. *Prehistoric Environment and Settlement in the Azraq Basin: an Interim Report.*

Glantz, M.H., D.G. Streets, T.R. Stewart, N. Bhatti, C.M. Moore & C.H. Rosa, 1998. *Exploring the Concept of Climate Surprises: a Review of the Literature on the Concept of Surprise and How it is Related to Climate Change.* U.S. Department of Energy, Office of Energy Research.

Gopher, A., 1994. *Arrowheads of the Neolithic Levant: a Seriation Analysis.* (Dissertation Series 10.) Winona Lake (IN): Eisenbrauns.

Gopher, A. & R. Gophna, 1993. Cultures of the eighth and seventh millennium BP in southern Levant: a review for the 1990s. *Journal of World Prehistory* 7(3), 297–351.

Goring-Morris, A.N., 1987. *At the Edge: Terminal Pleistocene Hunter-gatherers in the Negev and Sinai.* (British Archaeological Reports International Series 361.) Oxford: BAR.

Goring-Morris, A.N. & A. Belfer-Cohen, 1997. The articulation of cultural processes and Late Quaternary environmental changes in Cisjordan. *Paléorient* 23(2), 71–94.

Harris, D.R., 1998. The origins of agriculture in Southwest Asia. *The Review of Archaeology* 19(2), 5–12.

Henry, D.O., 1989. *From Foraging to Agriculture: the Levant at the End of the Ice Age.* Philadelphia (PA): University of Pennsylvania Press.

Heun, M., R. Schäfer-Pregl, D. Klawan, R. Castagna, M. Accerbi, B. Borghi & F. Salamini, 1997. Site of einkorn wheat domestication identified by DNA fingerprinting. *Science* 278, 1312–14.

Hillman, G.C., 2000. Abu Hureyra 1: the Epipalaeolithic, in Moore *et al.* (eds.), 327–99.

Horwitz, L.K., E. Tchernov, P. Ducos, C. Becker, A. von den Driesch, L. Martin & A. Garrard, 1999. Animal domestication in the Southern Levant. *Paléorient* 25(2), 63–80.

Kenyon, K., 1957. *Digging Up Jericho.* London: Benn.

Kislev, M.E., 1997. Early agriculture and paleoecology of Netiv Hagdud, in Bar-Yosef & Gopher (eds.), 209–36.

Kislev, M.E., D. Nadel & I. Carmi, 1992. Epi-Palaeolithic (19,000 BP) cereal and fruit diet at Ohalo II, Sea of Galilee, Israel. *Review of Palaeobotany and Palynology* 71, 161–6.

Kozlowski, S.K., 1999. *The Eastern Wing of the Fertile Crescent: Late Prehistory of Greater Mesopotamian Lithic Industries.* (British Archaeological Reports International Series 760.) Oxford: Archaeopress.

Kuijt, I., 1996. Negotiating equality through ritual: a consideration of Late Natufian and Prepottery Neolithic A period mortuary practices. *Journal of Anthropological Archaeology* 15, 313–36.

Martin, L., 1999. Mammal remains from the Eastern Jordanian Neolithic, and the nature of caprine herding in the steppe. *Paléorient* 25(2), 87–104.

Moore, A.M.T., G.C. Hillman & A.J. Legge (eds.), 2000. *Village on the Euphrates: From Foraging to Farming at Abu Hureyra.* Oxford: Oxford University Press.

Oba, G., E. Post & N.C. Stenseth, 2001. Sub-saharan desertification and productivity are linked to hemispheric climate variability. *Global Change Biology* 7, 241–6.

Özdogan, A., 1999. Çayönü, in Özdogan & Basgelen (eds.), 35–64.

Özdogan, M. & N. Basgelen (eds.), 1999. *Neolithic in Turkey: Cradle of Civilization. New Discoveries.* Istanbul: Arkeoloji ve Sanat Yayinlari.

Peltenburg, E., S. Colledge, P. Croft, A. Jackson, C. McCartney & M.A. Murray, 2000. Agro-pastoralist colonization of Cyprus in the 10th millennium BP: initial assessments. *Antiquity* 74, 844–53.

Peters, J., D. Helmer, A. von den Driesch & M.S. Segui, 1999. Early animal husbandry in the northern Levant. *Paléorient* 25(2), 27–47.

Rollefson, G.O., A.H. Simmons & Z. Kafafi, 1992. Neolithic cultures at 'Ain Ghazal, Jordan. *Journal of Field Archaeology* 19, 443–70.

Rosenberg, M., R. Nesbitt, R.W. Redding & B.L. Peasnall, 1998. Hallan Çemi, pig husbandry, and post Pleistocene adaptations among the Taurus-Zagros Arc (Turkey). *Paléorient* 24(1), 25–41.

Rossignol-Strick, M., 1995. Sea–land correlation of pollen records in the eastern Mediterranean for the glacial-interglacial transition: biostratigraphy versus radiometric time-scale. *Quaternary Science Reviews* 14, 893–915.

Schmandt-Besserat, D., 1990. Accounting in the prehistoric Middle East. *Archeomaterials* 4, 15–23.

Sellars, J.R., 1998. The Natufian of Jordan, in *The Prehistoric Archaeology of Jordan*, ed. D.O. Henry. (British Archaeological Reports S705.) Oxford: Archaeopress, 83–101.

Solecki, R.L., 1981. *An Early Village Site at Zawi Chemi Shanidar.* (Bibliotheca Mesopotamica 13.) Malibu (FL): Undena Publications.

Stiner, M.C., 2001. Thirty years on the 'Broad-Spectrum Revolution' and paleolithic demography. *Proceedings of the National Academy of Sciences of the USA* 98(13), 6993–6.

Stordeur, D., M. Brenet, G. der Aprahamian & J.-C. Roux, 2001. Les bâtiments communautaires de Jerf el Ahmar et Mureybet horizon PPNA (Syrie). *Paléorient* 26(1), 29–44.

Tchernov, E., 1994. *An Early Neolithic Village in the Jordan Valley II: The Fauna of Netiv Hagdud.* (American School of Prehistoric Research Bulletin 44.) Cambridge (MA): Peabody Museum Publications, Harvard University.

Valla, F.R., 1995. The first settled societies — Natufian (12,500–10,200 BP), in *The Archaeology of Society in the Holy Land*, ed. T. Levy. London: Leicester University

Press, 169–89.

van Andel, T. & C.N. Runnels, 1995. The earliest farmers in Europe. *Antiquity* 69, 481–500.

van Zeist, W., 1986. Some aspects of Early Neolithic plant husbandry in the Near East. *Anatolica* 15, 49–67.

van Zeist, W. & S. Bottema, 1991. *Late Quaternary Vegetation of the Near East*. (Beihefte zum Tübinger Atlas des Vorderen Orients, Reihe A (Naturwissenschaft) 18.) Weisbaden: Dr Ludwig Reichert Verlag.

Vigne, J.-D., H. Buitenhuis & S. Davis, 1999. Les premiers pas de la domestication animale à l'Ouest de l'Euphrate: Chypre et l'Anatolie Centrale. *Paléorient*

25(2), 49–62.

Weiss, H. & R.S. Bradley, 2001. What drives societal collapse? *Science* 291, 609–10.

Wright, K.I., 1994. Ground stone tools and hunter-gatherer subsistence in southwest Asia: implications for the transition to farming. *American Antiquity* 59(2), 238–63.

Zeder, M.A., 1999. Animal domestication in the Zagros: a review of past and current research. *Paléorient* 25(2), 11–25.

Zohary, D. & M. Hopf, 2000. *Domestication of Plants in the Old World*. 3rd edition. Oxford: Clarendon Press.

Chapter 11

Archaeology and Linguistic Diversity in North Africa

Fekri A. Hassan

Africa, a vast continent, contains more languages than any other, with approximately 2000 spoken by over half a billion people. Most of these are spoken by small groups of people, the exceptions being Arabic, Berber and some Bantu languages. Faced with such bewildering diversity, linguists have attempted to classify African languages into families: Greenberg's 1966 grouping into four main families is often adopted by linguists, with some reservations concerning the boundaries of each of the families and the languages assigned to them (see Blench 1999 for a recent discussion of the classification of African languages).

Greenberg's families included groups named, on the basis of their regional spreads, Khoisan, Niger-Congo, Nilo-Saharan and Afroasiatic.[1] The Khosian languages are spoken in an enclave in the southern part of Africa in an area around the Kalahari Desert extending from Namibia to Botswana. This is the smallest language family in Africa, with fewer than 40 languages spoken by about 300,000 people. The Niger-Congo, by contrast, is the largest African language family, with around 1350 languages spread across Sub-Saharan Africa encircling the Khoisan region. Its northern boundary extends in a southeast–northwest direction from Tanzania and southern Kenya crossing Central Africa to Senegal. The Afroasiatic languages lie north of the Niger-Congo family and extend over most of North and Northeast Africa. Lastly, there are enclaves of Nilo-Saharan languages in Mali, Chad and western Ethiopia/southeastern Sudan/northern Uganda/western Kenya.

The regional extents of these families are believed to have resulted from historical factors. Greenberg (1966) attempted to make historical inferences from what was then known about the languages of sub-Saharan Africa. At that time, individual languages were assigned to families using the methodology of lexicostatistics, with time depth attributed through glottochronology. Although it is now recognized that these methodologies are dubious (Blench 1993, 126), attempts to provide absolute chronologies to linguistic taxonomies in Africa are strongly advocated by Ehret (1993; 1998). Ehret bases his classification on words of cultural significance, especially those related to cattle, sheep, cultivation and specific cultigens. His attempts to infer overall cultural linkages between languages, and further to assume that such languages belong to distinct groups of peoples (ethnic groups in contemporary jargon) who spread by migration from a core area, are fraught with danger. Such inferences are dangerous because they rest on assumptions that can be shown to be flawed both within and outside Africa.

The spread of words for cultigens, animals or food-processing activities need not be related to migrations, but to the diffusion of ideas and the adoption of subsistence practices. Although we do not exclude migration as a means by which languages have spread, we cannot disregard evidence, both ethnographic and archaeological, showing in many cases that food production spread as various hunting-gathering groups added selected elements of this novel subsistence strategy to their food-getting régimes.

Ehret (1993) also uses what he calls 'the principle of least moves' to explain the probable location of earlier speech communities. The problem here is that words may spread in a leapfrog pattern, bypassing certain regions on their way (as suggested for archaeological assemblages by van Andel & Runnels 1995), to reach environmental locales favourable for the activities which they denote. Communities may also be connected by watercourses, roads etc. (e.g. the Silk Road or the trade routes across the Sahara), thus establishing stronger links between very distant partners than between neighbouring groups outside the transportation arteries. Note, for example, the presence of Indo-European languages in southern Africa introduced by colonialists from afar.

Note also that archaeological evidence shows that cattle spread earlier over long distances westward across the Sahara than they did to the neighbouring Nile Valley.

Ehret's glottochronological inferences are based on an analogy with the presumed rate of change for Romance languages (on average two languages would have 86 per cent core vocabulary items in common after 1000 years). But the rate of change may differ — ritual or religious words may not be relinquished as easily as words used in secular domains. Moreover, chronologies based on words shared in common are subject to a greater margin of error the further back in time a link is estimated. Crystal (1998, 333) notes that, after 7000 years of divergence, there would be only 12 per cent cognacy. Thus, if just one cognate were misanalyzed, the resulting date would be 300 years in error. We may thus conclude that any pretense for accuracy or precision of glottochronology is illusory.

It is also regrettable that Ehret has either uncritically accepted, or selected, erroneous claims for archaeological events in order to lend credence to his chronological scheme, e.g. the claim (Ehret 1998, 11) that 'wheat, barley, and chick-peas from the Middle East passed to the suitably cool highlands of Eritrea and Ethiopia probably via the Red Sea Hills about the fifth or fourth millennium' (Note that Ehret's chronology is in years BC).

In their recent review of prehistoric agriculture in Ethiopia, archaeobotanist d'Andrea and her co-workers (1999, 106) state that the earliest unequivocal evidence for domesticated plants dates to at least 500 BC, and consists of hulled and naked barley, chickpea and several legumes recovered at Lalibela cave in central Ethiopia (Dombrowski 1970), as well as wheat and barley at Aksum (Ona Nagast) dated by association with charcoal to 390 cal. BC (Bard & Vattovich 1995). This also flies in the face of other claims by Ehret, who states (Ehret 1998, 10) that

> By as early as the sixth millennium, the Cushites who had moved into highland grasslands in Eritrea may have begun to switch over from supplementing their diet with wild-grain collection to the deliberate cultivation of two indigenous highland grains, t'ef and finger millet.

D'Andrea et al. (1999, 105) categorically state that the earliest evidence for finger millet, presumably of African origin on the basis of cytogenic studies, dates to the second millennium BC in India (with a reference to Harlan 1993). Unfortunately, Harlan cites no primary sources for this claim, but his statement may be traced back to Weber (1991), who produced

a dissertation on plants and Harappan subsistence at the site of Rojdi in the Saurashtra peninsular region of Gujarat. According to Weber, finger millet (*Eleusine coracana*) occurs in abundance in the earliest levels at Rojdi, dating to *c.* 2600 BC. Sorghum was found in the upper levels dating to *c.* 2000 BC. Weber (1991, 73–4) notes that although an African origin was proposed by Harlan for *E. coracana*, it could have evolved from recently-identified South Asian varieties (after Dixit *et al.* 1987).

Moreover, both finger millet and sorghum appear in conjunction with a broad spectrum of indigenous Asian domesticated plants. For example, Weber (1991, 174) notes that, while a number of species of *Panicum* were recovered at Rojdi, *P. miliare* was by far the most dominant at 2500 BC. The place of origin of this plant ranges from Southeast Asia to East Asia, with a most probable origin in South Asia. This led him to conclude that plants need not have been introduced from other regions of the world in order for farming communities to develop. The presence of both winter and summer cultivation by 2500 BC at Rojdi suggests that the adoption of domesticates (including varieties of millets such as *Eleusine coracana*) predates that time, and that the first South Asian domesticates were indigenous (see Fuller this volume). With the establishment and florescence of Harappan maritime trade, certain wild African cereals such as sorghum could have been introduced as exotic gourmet food and subsequently cultivated locally (H. Barakat pers. comm.). It is important to note that current evidence does not support any claims for domestication of sorghum in Africa before the first century BC (see below).

Cultural dynamics and linguistic change

The diversity of African languages cannot be adequately explained solely in terms of presumed linkages between peoples and migrations. Language as a means of communication is bound with social interaction within and between groups. Changes in language may occur as a result of differential innovation, retention or loss of linguistic items within society. Although innovations may emerge in a random fashion, they are fostered by specific practices and can be ignored, banned, shunned or restricted to specific domains or, by contrast, encouraged, favoured, endorsed and promoted on the basis of social motivations. Such motivations may be triggered by the need to communicate with others for economic or ritual purposes, to identify with one segment of society or with strangers, or to differentiate oneself from others for ritual, economic or political reasons. The work of William Labov in this context is informative (Crystal 1998, 334), when he notes, for example, that certain forms of pronunciation are favoured as markers of prestige, imitating those of higher status. He also notes that a people might exaggerate their mode of speech in order to distinguish themselves from an overwhelming, dominant speech pattern. This exaggerated form may then spread as a result of imitation by other groups in a similar situation. Labov also concludes that the process of language change can hardly be accurately represented using a family-tree model.

We may also assume that languages of the same origin, separated for one reason or another, will undergo some form of drift, and that the same language used over a broad region will show clinal changes. The inconstancy of social roles, the ever-changing dynamics of split and fusion especially common among hunter-gatherers, and the flexibility and fluidity of ethnic identities lead us to think that a simple linear model of language change is inadequate.

It may also be useful to consider the possibility of rapid and abrupt changes in language as a result of profound structural re-organization of subsistence régimes, social relations, technology or religious ideology. These may be triggered by responses to abrupt climatic changes, invasions, or internal political upheavals. The resilience of a language depends on its functional utility for survival and the welfare of those who speak it. In Egypt, Arabic was widely adopted by native Egyptians within three centuries of its introduction by Arab invaders from the Arabian Peninsula. Two centuries before the Arabs appropriated Egypt from its Byzantine overlords, three languages were in wide use: Egyptian, Latin and Greek (Bagnall 1993, 231). Latin had its importance for a career in the imperial civil service or the army. The higher one wished to climb the more one needed some Latin. Today, this applies to learning English. A generation ago it was French, and a few generations before that Turkish. The prestigious languages notwithstanding, within a few centuries after becoming vassals of Greece, Egyptians adopted Greek as a second language in their daily communications. Christian names also become widespread from the reign of Constantine. The use of Egyptian, Greek or Latin in the earlier Roman period in Egypt reflects not only the rapidity and selectivity of language change, but also the importance of residence, social and economic class, sex, and contingent personal factors in choosing a language.

Cattle, cultivation and culture in the later prehistory of Northeast Africa

The introduction of pastoralism and plant cultivation in Northeast Africa led to revolutionary changes in demographic patterns (size, permanency, composition, growth rates, movements of local and regional population units), social relations (solidarities, alliances, animosities, occupational differentiation, rank differentiation, sex-based differentiation), territoriality (ownership, defence, range, seasonality), and ecological choices (pastures, permanent and seasonal water holes and springs, oases and valleys). It also established new modes of food exchange, symbiosis and trade in order to safeguard against fluctuations in food yield. Such fluctuations are brought about by factors endemic to agricultural and pastoral economies, and are worse when adverse climatic events are involved.

The first radical transformation in African economy, on the basis of current evidence, began in the Eastern Sahara, in the southeastern corner of the Western Desert of Egypt (Gautier 1984; Wendorf et al. 1987; Close & Wendorf 1992). The core area of this radical change might have extended farther south to northern Sudan and as far west as the junction of Libya, Egypt, Chad and the Sudan — an area we will refer to later as the 'Four Corners'. In this region, as data from the Nabta Playa-Bir Kiseiba region in Egypt show, cattle keeping emerged as early as 8500 cal. BC.

Within a millennium, abrupt cold climatic events at 7500, 6600, and most significantly c. 5800 cal. BC, were crucial in the spread of cattle keeping westward across the Sahara. Pastoralist communities became established in better-watered range and basin areas associated with a series of highlands, such as the Ennedi, Tibesti, Tassili and Hoggar massifs (Hassan 1986; 1996; 1997; 2000a,b).

In Southwest Asia, the end of favourable rainy conditions and the onset of drier climate in various parts of the region at c. 6000 cal. BC (6100–5800 BC), coincident with a marked reduction in sea surface temperature at 5800 cal. BC (Rohling et al. 1997), was not anticipated. As a consequence, the agrarian communities established in the Levant (Pre-Pottery Neolithic B) collapsed. This collapse, according to Bar-Yosef (1998a), was not a local event. It affected the western slopes of the Mediterranean ranges in Palestine and the Lebanon as much as it affected the eastern side. Population dispersal out of the Levant, southwards into Arabia and westwards via the Sinai into Northeast Africa, became noticeable.

Droughts at this time are also manifest in many

records from North, East and Equatorial Africa (Gasse & van Campo 1994; Roberts *et al.* 1993). The abrupt series of events is clearly manifest in the record of Lake Malha in the Sudan (Mees *et al.* 1991). Severe cold and dry conditions are also recorded in the Egyptian Sahara at this time, and subsequently at *c.* 5000–4800 cal. BC (Hassan 1986). By 4700 cal. BC, the Egyptian Sahara assumed its current hyperarid regime and was no longer conducive to habitation, except in close proximity to oases with groundwater springs.

There is no evidence for agriculture in the Nile Valley before 4880 cal. BC, the date of the oldest solid evidence for food production from Merimde Beni Salama (Hassan 1988), a site on the western edge of the Delta. Bioarchaeological remains here include sheep and goat, wheat and barley. These food resources are not indigenous and were definitely introduced from the Levant. Immigrants from the southern fringe of Southwest Asia were apparently driven by droughts to the Nile Valley, where they settled and mixed with the local foraging-fishing communities to establish the first farming communities in Egypt. Other immigrants followed the Red Sea coast southward. Ovicaprids from the Levant have been identified at a site near Qusseir in Egypt at 5800 cal. BC (Veermersch *et al.* 1996). In the Egyptian Sahara, west of the Nile, ovicaprids also appear in Farafra Oasis and Nabta Playa at 5500 cal. BC, and in Dakhla Oasis *c.* 5700 cal. BC (Hassan 2000a, with references). Farther west, ovicaprids appear at Grotto Capeletti in Algeria at *c.* 4850 cal. BC.

The widespread diffusion of cattle keeping from an African cradle in the Eastern Sahara, and of domesticated sheep/goat from the Levant by 4000 BC, contrasts with the limited distribution of the domesticated Levantine cereals and pulses. Wheat and barley remained restricted to the Nile Valley and did not penetrate farther South into Ethiopia until 500 BC (see above).

Current evidence clearly demonstrates that one of the paramount transformations in the Eastern Sahara and the Sudan during the early Holocene was the intensive utilization of wild sorghum and pearl millet from *c.* 7500 to 4900 cal. BC (Barakat 1995; 2002; Barakat & Fahmy 1999; Magid 1989; 1995; Magid & Caneva 1998; Stemler 1990; Stemler & Falk 1981; Wasylikowa 1997). This early record of utilization notwithstanding, sorghum was not cultivated in Egypt until much later. The first firm evidence of domesticated sorghum (using DNA analysis) comes from first century AD Qasr Ibrim in Egypt (Rowley-Conwy 1991; Rowley-Conwy *et al.* 1997). In the Su-

dan, the first solid evidence for the domestication of sorghum comes from Meroe about 2000 years ago, according to Stemler & Falk (1981).

Nowadays, sorghum is widely cultivated in Central Sudan rather than in Egypt where, as a summer crop, it would require a higher temperature than that present nowadays, or after 5000 BC, in the lower Nile Valley. Moreover, in Egypt, the Nile Valley was favourable for Near Eastern cultivars which provide a much higher yield than sorghum and are more palatable. Sorghum is mostly used nowadays in Egypt as fodder.

In West Africa, the oldest domesticated pearl millet in Mauritania, at Dhar Tichitt, dates to *c.* 1800–1630 cal. BC. In Burkina Faso and the Chad Basin estmates ranged from 2100 to 110 cal. BC (Amblard 1996; Harlan 1992; Wetterstrom 1998). Recent investigations by Breunig & Neumann (2002), however, show that there were no indications for agriculture in Burkina Faso before 1200 cal BC. This appears to have been a development in response to the impact of adverse climatic conditions on foragers and pastoralists. Pastoralists were in Mali by 2500 cal. BC and Ghana and Mauritania by 1800 cal. BC. They could not advance much further to the west, were prevented from going north as the Sahara expanded, and would have found it difficult to move south on account of the tse-tse barrier (Hassan 2000a). The adverse climatic conditions in West Africa at that time were in all likelihood linked with a global climatic anomaly consisting of a cold, abrupt event dated from 2200 to 1880/1750 cal. BC.

In East Africa, the goats and sheep introduced down the coast of the Red Sea into the Sudan, as well as the cattle introduced to northern Sudan from the Sahara by 4800 cal. BC, reached southern Kenya and northern Tanzania by 2700–2500 cal. BC (Marshall 1998; Gifford-Gonzalez 2000; Owen *et al.* 1982). In parallel to West Africa, specialized pastoralism developed in East Africa after 2100 cal. BC, certainly by *c.* 1500–1400 cal. BC (Marshall 1998; Gifford-Gonzalez 2000).

Cattle, crops and linguistic changes in Africa

The glottochronological and historical linguistic claims by Ehret (1993) have been seriously questioned by Bender (1996) and Blench (1999). Ehret's chronology is certainly incongruent with archaeological data, as shown above. The data, however, support, in part, Blench's hypothesis that the diversity in all African language families developed before agriculture. With the exclusion of Nilo-Saharan, pre-agricultural linguistic reconstructions include Proto-Khosian in Sub-Saharan Africa, Proto-Niger-Congo in West and Central Africa, and Proto-Afroasiatic in Northeast Africa. These differentiations predate the Holocene and are related to regional environmental differences.

The emergence and spread of cattle from 8500 to 5800 cal. BC occurred within the domain of Nilo-Saharan languages, with subsequent differentiation as cattle-keeping groups became territorially based in favourable habitats in the Central Sahara. By 5900 BC, sheep/goat were introduced from the Levant, renewing links between Afroasiatic-speaking groups severed during the last glacial maximum when the Sinai and the southern Levant were hyperarid. The zone of Proto-Afroasiatic would have been along the Mediterranean coast, the Red Sea coast, and perhaps the lower Nile Valley. The spread of sheep and goat from 5800 to 2500 cal. BC, westward into West Africa and along the Red Sea coast and southwards up the Nile to Ethiopia and northern Kenya, would have been associated with the introduction of words for goat and sheep into Nilo-Saharan languages and the intrusion of Afroasiatic languages into Eastern Africa.

Claims for the introduction of words for grain cultivation in association with cattle in the absence of sheep and goat cannot be accepted on the basis of current evidence. Grain cultivation in the Nile Valley appears by c. 4700 cal. BC in conjunction with sheep/goat. Sheep and goats in the Egyptian Sahara, however, date to 5700–5500 cal BC and to 5900 cal BC in the Red Sea Hills. In the rest of Africa, sheep/goat spread after this time, before the adoption of grain cultivation at 2100 cal. BC in West Africa and c. 500 BC in Ethiopia.

The linguistic proxies for herding cattle in Proto-Eastern-Sudanic languages in Nubia (Bechhaus-Gerst 2000, 457), on the basis of archaeological evidence, may date to a time close to the first appearance of cattle in Northeast Africa in the Eastern Sahara and possibly the Four Corners Area at the junction of Libya, the Sudan, Egypt and Chad, c. 8500 BC. Linguistic evidence for sheep/goat in the Proto-Sahelian languages (Ehret 1993) and the Proto-Nubia-Tama-Nera language (Bechhaus-Gerst 2000, 457), using archaeological evidence, would have to date no earlier than 5900 cal. BC.

The Afroasiatic languages with words for goat and sheep in Africa, using current archaeological evidence, cannot be earlier than 5900 BC. The Proto-Afroasiatic language, with a Pleistocene homeland yet to be identified, split into the so-called 'Semitic' (Levantine) and Erythraic groupings, the latter descending from a language which spread along the Red Sea Coast by 5900 BC. In the Nile Valley, Ancient Egyptian emerged within the context of an agrarian society. Farther south, west of the Nile, specialized pastoralists developed Cushitic speech. East of the Nile along the Red Sea Coast of southern Egypt, in the Sudan and northern Ethiopia, the Beja language was developed also by pastoralists between 5900 and 2500 BC. Chadic and Berber languages, with words for sheep and goat, would also have to date after 5900 BC.

The appearance of cereal cultivation in Egypt after 5000 BC and the adoption of grain cultivation (barley, wheat) in Ethiopia by c. 500 BC indicate that the spread of founder crops from Southwest Asia was not in tandem with the spread of sheep/goat. Most probably, exchanges between Egypt and Kerma (2500–1500 BC) would have led to the introduction of words related to cereal cultivation in Cushitic speech. This accounts for the appearance of Cushite loan words from the domain of agriculture in the Nobiin language by 1500 BC. There is no archaeological evidence at the moment to suggest that Eastern Sudanic speakers played a role in the domestication of grain and the development of agriculture (*contra* Ehret 1993, but in agreement with the linguistic analysis by Bechhaus-Gerst 2000, 458).

Conclusions

Current attempts to construct a genealogy of African languages on the basis of family-trees using lexico-statistical and glottochronological methods are inadequate both on theoretical and empirical grounds. The appearance of cognate words related to food production, such as cattle, sheep, goat and cultivation, in various African languages may be explained in terms of a dynamic model of population dispersal and cultural borrowing. Cattle keeping is first recorded from the southeastern corner of the Egyptian Sahara. By 5700 cal. BC it had spread to the Ennedi, Tibesti and the Acacus. Later it spread in successive moves, first eastwards to the Nile Valley both in Egypt and the Sudan at the same time (c. 5000 cal. BC), and westwards to Adrar Bous and Adrar n'Kiffi. The subsequent moves were from the Sudan southwards to southern Kenya and northern Tanzania at 2700–2400 cal. BC, and westward from the Central Sahara to Mali, Ghana and Mauritania at 3600–1800 cal. BC.

Goats and sheep were added to the subsistence items from Southwest Asia around 5900 BC. They spread rapidly into the Nile Valley, the Sahara and the Red Sea Coast by 4800 BC. Zooarchaeological data suggest that cattle, sheep and goats were added to a broad-spectrum economy of foraging and that specialized pastoralism did not emerge until *c.* 2100 BC in East and West Africa. However, pastoralism appeared earlier in the Central Sahara, perhaps as early as 5400–5000 cal. BC. This suggests that the rock art showing pastoral scenes in North Africa is not earlier than that time, and that such scenes in East Africa are not earlier than 2100 BC. It also suggests that the appearance of terms for cattle in Nilo-Saharan languages post-dates 8500 BC, and that words for cattle and cattle-keeping spread into Nilo-Saharan and Afroasiatic languages between 6300 and 1800 cal. BC. The spread of sheep/goat from 5900 cal. BC began within Afroasiatic-speaking peoples. The dispersal of sheep/goat overlapped with the dispersal of cattle from the mid-Holocene onwards.

Distance and climatic changes led to drift and the development of regional languages. Before the appearance of specialized pastoralism, the dispersal of sheep and goats was a result of a dynamic interaction between struggling refugees and established communities of foragers, fishers and hunters, with cultural exchanges leading in different contexts to a diversity of syncretic, assimilated and transformed new cultural modalities. During droughts, a trickle of people from different areas may converge on a favourable region where, through cultural fusion, innovations, modes of speech and practices would emerge.

Terms denoting plant cultivation could not have been firmly adopted in Africa before 5000 BC, when imported cultigens from an Asiatic context are first recorded in the Nile Delta. In the rest of Africa, it was not until after 2200 BC that cultivation was practised. Therefore languages outside the Nile Valley with words for plant cultivation could not be earlier than that date.

Note

1. The distributions of these families are shown in Figure 2.2 of the chapter by Peter Bellwood.

References

Amblard, S., 1996. Agricultural evidence and its interpretation on the Dhars Tichitt and Oulata, south-eastern Mauritania, in Pwiti & Soper (eds.), 421–7.

Bagnall, R., 1993. *Egypt in Late Antiquity.* Princeton (NJ): Princeton University Press.

Bar-Yosef, O., 1998. Agricultural origins: caught between hypotheses and a lack of hard evidence, in Bar-Yosef (ed.) 1998b, 58–64.

Bar-Yosef, O. (ed.), 1998b. *The Transition to Agriculture in the Old World.* Special Issue of *The Review of Archaeology* 19.

Barakat, H., 1995. Middle Holocene vegetation and human impact in Central Sudan: charcoal from the Neolithic site at Kadero. *Vegetation History and Archaeobotany* 4, 101–8.

Barakat, H., 2002. Regional pathways to agriculture in northeast Africa, in Hassan (ed.), 111–22.

Barakat, H. & A.G. Fahmy, 1999. Wild grasses as 'Neolithic' food resources in the Eastern Sahara, in van der Veen (ed.), 33–53.

Bard, K. & R. Vattovich, 1995. The I.O.U./B.U. excavation at Bieta Giyorgis (Aksum): an interim report. *Nyame Akuma* 44, 25–7.

Bender, M.L., 1996. *The Nilo-Saharan Languages: a Comparative Essay.* Munich: Lincom Europa.

Bechhaus-Gerst, M., 2000. Linguistic evidence for the prehistory of livestock in Sudan, in Blench & MacDonald (eds.), 449–61.

Blench, R., 1993. Recent developments in African language classification and their implications for prehistory, in *The Archaeology of Africa*, eds. T. Shaw, P. Sinclair, B. Andah & A. Okpoko. London: Routledge, 126–38.

Blench, R., 1999. The languages of Africa: macrophyla proposals and implications for archaeological interpretation, in *Archaeology and Language*, vol. IV, eds. R. Blench & M. Spriggs. London: Routledge, 29–47.

Blench, R.M. & K.C. MacDonald (eds.), 2000. *The Origins and Development of African Livestock: Archaeology, Genetics, Linguistics and Ethnography.* London: UCL Press.

Breunig, P. & K. Neumann, 2002. From hunters and gatherers to food producers: new archaeological and archaeobotanical evidence from the West African Sahel, in Hassan (ed.), 123–56.

Close, A.E. & F. Wendorf, 1992. The beginnings of food production in the Eastern Sahara, in *Transitions to Agriculture in Prehistory*, eds. A.B. Gebauer & T.D. Price. (Monographs in World Archaeology 4.) Madison (WI): Prehistory Press, 63–72.

Crystal, D., 1998. *The Cambridge Encyclopedia of Language.* Cambridge: Cambridge University Press.

d'Andrea, C., D. Lyons, M. Haile & A. Butler, 1999. Ethnoarchaeological approaches to the study of prehistoric agriculture in the Highlands of Ethiopia, in van der Veen (ed.), 101–22.

Dixit, A.S, S.S. Dixit & Vishnu-Mitre, 1987. The occurrence of Eleusine africana in India and its significance in the origin of Eleusine coracana. *Proceedings of the Indian Academy of Sciences (Plant Sciences)* 97(1), 1–10.

Dombrowski, J.C., 1970. Preliminary report on excavations in Lalibela and Natchabiet caves. *Begemeder. Annales d'Ethiopie* 8, 21–9.

Ehret, C., 1993. *Nilo-Saharans and the Saharao-Sudanese Neolithic.* Cambridge: Cambridge University Press.

Ehret, C., 1998. *An African Classical Age: Eastern and South-*

ern Africa in World History, 1000 BC *to* AD *400.* Charlottesville (VA): University Press of Virginia.

Gasse, F. & E. van Campo, 1994. Abrupt post-glacial climate events in West Asia and North Africa monsoon domains. *Earth and Planetary Science Letters* 126, 435–56.

Gautier, A., 1984. Archaeozoology of Bir Kiseiba region, Eastern Sahara, in *Cattle Keepers of the Eastern Sahara: the Neolithic of Bir Kiseiba*, eds. A.E. Close, F. Wendorf & R. Schild. Dallas (TX): Southern Methodist University, 49–72.

Gifford-Gonzalez, D., 2000. Animal disease challenges to the emergence of pastoralism in Sub-Saharan Africa. *African Archaeological Review* 17(3), 95–139.

Greenberg, J.H., 1966. *The Languages of Africa*. The Hague: Mouton.

Harlan, J.R., 1992. Indigenous African agriculture, in *The Origins of Agriculture: an International Perspective*, eds. C.W. Cowan & P.J. Watson. Washington (DC): Smithsonian Institution Press, 59–70.

Harlan, J.R., 1993. The tropical African cereals, in *The Archaeology of Africa*, eds. T. Shaw, P. Sinclair, B. Andah & A. Okpoko. London: Routledge, 53–60.

Hassan, F.A., 1986. Desert environment and origins of agriculture in Egypt. *Norwegian Archaeological Review* 19, 63–76.

Hassan, F.A., 1988. The Predynastic of Egypt. *Journal of World Prehistory* 2, 135–85.

Hassan, F.A., 1996. Abrupt Holocene climatic events in Africa, in Pwiti & Soper (eds.), 83–9.

Hassan, F.A., 1997. Holocene palaeoclimates of Africa. *African Archaeological Review* 14, 213–30.

Hassan, F.A., 2000a. Climate and cattle in North Africa, in Blench & MacDonald (eds.), 61–86.

Hassan, F.A., 2000b. Holocene environmental change and the origins and spread of food production in the Middle East. *Adumatu* 1, 7–28.

Hassan, F.A. (ed.), 2002. *Drought, Food and Culture: Ecological Change and Food Security in Africa's Later Prehistory*. New York (NY): Kluwer Academic/Plenum Publishers.

Magid, A.A., 1989. *Plant Domestication in the Middle Nile Basin*. (British Archaeological Reports 523.) Oxford: BAR.

Magid, A.A., 1995. Plant remains and their implications, in *Aqualithic Sites along the Rivers Nile and Atbara, Sudan*, eds. R. Halland & A.A. Magid. Bergen: Alma Mater, 147–77.

Magid, A.A. & I. Caneva, 1998. Exploitation of food plants in the early Holocene central Sudan: a reconsideration, in *Before Food Production in North Africa*, eds. S. Di Lernia & G. Manzi. Forlí: ABACO, 79–89.

Marshall, D., 1998. Early food production in Africa. *The Review of Archaeology* 19, 47–58.

Mees, F., D. Verschuren, R. Nijs & H.J. Dumont, 1991. Holocene evolution of the crater lake at the Malha, Northwest Sudan. *Journal of Palaeolimnology* 5, 227–53.

Owen, R.B., J.W. Barthelme, R.W. Renaut & A. Vincens, 1982. Palaeolimnology and archaeology of Holocene deposits north-east of Lake Turkana, Kenya. *Nature* 298, 523–8.

Pwiti, G. & R. Soper (eds.), 1996. *Aspects of African Archaeology*. Harare: University of Zimbabwe Publications.

Roberts, N., M. Taieb, P. Barker, B. Damnati, M. Icole & D. Williamson, 1993. Timing of the Younger Dryas event in East Africa from lake-level changes. *Nature* 366, 146–8.

Rohling, E.J., F.J. Jorissen & H.C. De Stigter, 1997. 200-year interruption of Holocene saptopel formation in the Adriatic Sea. *Journal of Micropalaeontology* 16, 97–108.

Rowley-Conwy, P.A., 1991. Sorghum from Qasr Ibrim, Egyptian Nubia, *c.* 8000 BC–AD 1811: a preliminary study, in *New Light on Early Farming: Recent Developments in Palaeoethnobotany*, ed. J.M. Renfrew. Edinburgh: Edinburgh University Press, 211–34.

Rowley-Conwy, P.A., W.J. Deakin & C.H. Shaw, 1997. Ancient DNA from archaeological sorghum (*Sorghum bicolor*) from Qasr Ibrim, Nubia. Implications for domestication and evolution and a review of the archaeological evidence. *Sahara* 9, 23–33.

Stemler, A., 1990. A scanning electron microscopic analysis of plant impressions in pottery from Kadero, El Zakiab, Um Direiwa and Al Kadada. *Archéologie du Nil Moyen* 4, 87–105.

Stemler, A. & R.H. Falk, 1981. SEM of archaeological specimens. *Scanning Electron Microscopy* III, 191–6.

van Andel, T.H. & C.N. Runnels, 1995. The earliest farmers in Europe. *Antiquity* 69, 481–500.

van der Veen, M. (ed.), 1999. *The Exploitation of Plant Resources in Ancient Africa: Proceedings of the 2nd International Workshop on Archaeobotany in Northern Africa, held June 23–25 1997 in Leicester, England.* New York (NY) & London: Kluwer Academic.

Vermeersch, P., P. Van Peer, J. Moeyersons & W. Van Neer, 1996. Sodmein cave site, Red Sea Mountains (Egypt). *Sahara* 6, 31–40.

Wasylikowa, K., 1997. Flora of the 8000-years-old archaeological site E-75-6 at Nabta Playa, Western Desert, Southern Egypt. *Acta Palaeobotanica* 37(2), 99–205.

Weber, S.A., 1991. *Plants and Harappan Subsistence*. Boulder (CO): Westview Press.

Wendorf, F., A.E. Close & R. Schild, 1987. Early domestic cattle in the eastern Sahara. *Palaeoecology of Africa* 18, 441–8.

Wetterstrom, W., 1998. The origins of agriculture in Africa: with particular reference to sorghum and pearl millet, in Bar-Yosef 1998b (ed.), 30–46.

Chapter 12

The Prehistory of a Dispersal:
the Proto-Afrasian (Afroasiatic) Farming Lexicon

Alexander Militarev

Adduced below are more than thirty common Afrasian (Afroasiatic, Semito-Hamitic) terms, most of which obviously relate to farming, while some may relate to either farming or the collecting of wild cereals and fruit. Almost all of these terms are attested in more than two branches of the Afrasian linguistic family, a fact which proves their Proto-Afrasian origin. There are also several dozen other terms not included because of their narrower attestation; nevertheless they make a promising base for future research. In any case, the lexicon presented seems sufficient to assert that the Proto-Afrasians were a farming people.

The Proto-Afrasian language, on the verge of a split into daughter languages, should be roughly dated to the ninth millennium BC. This date is later than those which I proposed in Militarev 2000 (see Tree on p. 303), these being the tenth millennium BC for the separation between the Northern Branch of Afrasian (Egyptian, Semitic, Chadic and Berber) and the Southern Branch (Cushitic and Omotic), and the ninth millennium BC for successive separations between Egyptian and Semitic-Chadic-Berber, and between Semitic and Chadic-Berber, on the one hand, and Cushitic and Omotic, on the other.

My reasons for this correction are as follow. Starostin's method in glottochronology (see Starostin 2000) requires a thorough etymological analysis to detect and eliminate loanwords from the scores. The criteria and techniques used in detecting loanwords in a basic lexicon of Semitic, Egyptian and Berber are more or less satisfactory, something which cannot be said of Chadic, Cushitic and Omotic. With future progress in comparative Afrasian studies, an expected rise of revealed loans to be eliminated from the 100-word lists (resulting in the reduction of the number of items) of some if not many individual languages should increase the proportion of each of these languages' cognates with any other related language, thus decreasing the time span from the split of their common proto-language. Therefore, the time of the Proto-Afrasian split obtained from a formal comparison which ignores unrevealed loanwords has to be corrected towards a somewhat later date. However, since the 100-word list contains rarely-borrowed words, this correction should not be significant. I would estimate the expected average number of loanwords at 5–8, i.e. 5–8 per cent. This roughly corresponds to the ninth millennium BC as the most realistic and cautious dating for the split of Proto-Afrasian into Cushitic, Omotic, Egyptian, Semitic and Chadic-Berber (the latter being the only couple showing a conspicuous rise of common items in the diagnostic lists, which, with all reservations, seems to me somewhat more significant than a mere result of long linguistic contacts and, hence, both-way lexical borrowing).

The Proto-Afrasian speakers can be identified, with high probability, with the creators of the Natufian and Post-Natufian Early Neolithic archaeological culture of the Levant. We propose the following criteria for identifying habitats of reconstructed proto-language speakers characterized by a specific archaeological culture (or several cultures), in other words, for locating a proto-language's 'home' (see Militarev 1984b; Militarev & Shnirelman 1984; 1988; Militarev 1996). First, dates estimated by both linguistic and archaeological methods should generally coincide. Second, the two pictures of the material culture (as well as elements of the intellectual culture and social organization) and natural environment of the presumed homeland, one reconstructed on the evidence of the proto-language lexicon, the other on the archaeological data, should also basically coincide. Third, there must be traces of linguistic contacts between the proto-language in question and its early daughter dialects, on the one hand, and other proto-languages or ancient languages likely spoken in the same area during the corresponding periods, on the other. Fourth, presumed routes of the daughter dialects migration to their historically attested habitats should correspond to the directions of ethno-cultural expansion established archaeologically.

The identification of Proto-Afrasians as Natufians and Post-Natufians seems to satisfy all the four criteria. Besides the farming lexicon, there are sets of reconstructed Proto-Afrasian terms pointing to incipient animal-breeding (Militarev & Shnirelman 1984; 1988); a wide variety of dwelling and settlement types (Militarev & Shnirelman 1988; Militarev *et al.* 1989); a territory characterized by both desert and steppe-forest type of terrain and drying river-beds as well as deep permanent streams; a vegetation typical of such territory; and the animals whose bones have been found at the Natufian and Early Neolithic Post-Natufian sites (interestingly, there is a large number of common Afrasian terms denoting flocked ungulate animals usually inhabiting steppes and semi-deserts: see Militarev & Shnirelman 1988). A strong argument against the idea of an African homeland for Proto-Afrasian proposed by some authors (see Olderogge 1952; Diakonoff 1981; Ehret 1979) can be based on the linguistic contacts revealed between African (non-Semitic) Afrasian branches and North Caucasian, on the one hand (Militarev & Starostin 1984; Militarev 1996), and Sumerian on the other (Militarev 1984a; 1995; 1996). Finally, the Levant appears to be an attested region from where population began to spread starting in the Early Neolithic, covering not only wide tracts of Southwestern Asia, but also the adjacent parts of the Mediterranean and Africa.

As to the other primary farming centre in the Zagros (likely stemming from the Levant), it may be, albeit highly hypothetically, linked with the speakers of Proto-Sino-Caucasian, a language postulated and reconstructed by Sergei Starostin. There are two more Old World macro-family proto-languages dated approximately to the same period as the Afrasian one, whose cultural lexicon is reconstructed in general outline, namely Sino-Caucasian and Nostratic. According to Starostin (pers. comm.), while in Proto-Nostratic there seem to be no reliable farming terms, the Proto-Sino-Caucasian lexicon contains several such terms, though fewer than Proto-Afrasian. Since there is little doubt that all the three macro-families are eventually related, one may assume that the split of their common proto-language took place during the Natufian period prior to the 'Neolithic Revolu-

tion', after which the Proto-Nostratic-speaking group(s) left the Levant, while the Proto-Sino-Caucasian-speaking group(s) moved from the Levant to the Zagros area after agriculture and animal husbandry were introduced. Because there are very few agricultural terms common to Proto-Afrasian and Proto-Sino-Caucasian, one may assume that the Sino-Caucasian speakers left the Levant very soon after the 'Neolithic Revolution' took a start, carrying with them the attainments of incipient agriculture and only a few terms shared with Afrasian (borrowed from the latter or inherited from the common ancestor) to later develop an independent agricultural lexicon.

In the main, etymological, section of this paper (see below), I adhere to the general principles of comparative-historical method in linguistics and more specific approaches and positions in Semitic and Afrasian comparison expounded in the Introduction to Militarev & Kogan (2000).

Acknowledgements

I am indebted to L. Kogan, S. Starostin and O. Stolbova for valuable remarks. My thanks are also due to three foundations supporting my research in Semitic and Afrasian languages: The Russian State Foundation for the Humanities, The Russian Foundation for Sciences, and the Russian Jewish Congress.

Conventions:

- * marks a reconstructed proto-form;
- \- separates affixed elements from the stem;
- *V* in reconstructed forms conveys a non-specified vowel, e.g. *bVr- should be read 'either *a, or *i, or *u';
- *H* in reconstructed forms conveys a non-specified laryngeal or pharyngeal;
- *S* in reconstructed forms conveys a non-specified sibilant;
- / separating two symbols means 'or', e.g. **ʔi/abar*- should be read 'either *ʔibar- or *ʔabar-';
- ( ) a symbol in round brackets means 'with or without this symbol', e.g. **ba(w)r*- should be read '*bawr- or *bar-';
- ~ between reconstructed forms means 'and'.

Abbreviations of languages and language periods:
Adgh. - Adghaq; Af. - Afar; Afras. - Afrasian (Afroasiatic); Akk. - Akkadian; Al. - Alaba; Alg. - Alagwa; Amh. - Amharic; Amrn. - Amarna; Anf. - Anfilla; Ang. - Angas; Ank. - Ankwe; Arb. - Arabic;

Arg. - Argobba; Arm. - Aramaic; Aw. - Awiya; Bač. - Bačama; BD - Book of the Dead; Bib. - Biblical; Bil. - Bilin; Bid. - Bidiya; Bmrn. - Baamrani; Bnn. - Banana; Bol. - Bolewa; Brb. - Berber; Brj. - Burji; Bw. - Bworo; C. - Central; Can. - Canarian; Ch. - Chadic; Copt. (B F S) - Coptic (Bohairic, Fayyumic, Sahidic); CT - Coffin Texts; Cu. - Cushitic; Dah. - Dahalo; Dar. - Darasa; Daṭ. - Daṭina, Dem. - Demotic; Dff. - Daffa; Dgl. - Dangla; Dob. - Dobese; E. - East; Eg. - Egyptian; Emp. - Empire; End. - Endegeñ; Enn. - Ennemor; Eth. - Ethiopian; Gaa. - Gaʔanda; Gab. - Gabin; Gaf. - Gafat; Gel. - Geleba; Gez. - Geez; Ghdm. - Ghadames; Gid. - Gidole; Glmb. - Galambu; Glv. - Glavda; Goll. - Gollango; Gr. - Greek Period; Grnt. - Geruntum; Gur. - Gurage; Gwn. - Gwandara; Had. - Hadiya; Har. - Harari; Hbr. - Hebrew; Hgr. - Tahaggart; Hil. - Hildi; Hrs. - Harsusi; Hs. - Hausa; Iger. - Igerwan; Ir. - Iraqw; Izd. - Izdeg; Izy. - Izayan; Janj. - Janjero; Jib. - Jibbali; Jmb. - Jimbin; Jud. - Judaic; Kar. - Kariya; Kf. - Kafa; Khmr. - Khamir; Kmb. - Kambatta; Kon. - Konso; Krkr. - Karekare; Lex. - Lexical Texts; Log. - Logone; MA - Middle Assyrian; MB - Middle Babylonian; Mbr. - Mbara; Mč. - Moča; Med. - Medical Texts; Mhr. - Mehri; Mig. - Migama; MK - Middle Kingdom; Mnd. - Mandaic; Mndr. - Mandara; Mnj. - Munjuk; Mok. - Mokilko; Mpn. - Mupun; Mrg. - Margi; Ms. - Masqan; Msg. - Musgum; Mtkm. - Matakam; Mṭmṭ - Maṭmaṭa; Mw. - Mwulien; Mz. - Mzab; N. - North; Nak. - Nakači; Nan. - Nančere; NE - New Egyptian; Nfs. - Nefusi; Ngm. - Ngamo; Ngz. - Ngizim; Nj. - Njangi; Nkts. - Nakatsa; Nslm. - Taneslemt; Ntf. - Ntifa; OAkk. - Old Akkadian; OAss. - Old Assyrian; OB - Old Babylonian; OK - Old Kingdom; Om. - Omotic; Or. - Oromo, Pa. - Paʔa; pB. - post-Biblical; Ph. - Phoenician; Pi. - Piẑimbi; Pyr. - Pyramid Texts; Qbl. - Qabylian; Qbn. - Qabenna; Qw. - Qwadza; Qwr. - Qwara; Rnd. - Rendille; S. - South; Sa. - Saho; Sab. - Sabaic; Sam. - Samaritan; SB - Standard Babylonian; Sel. - Selti; Sem. - Semitic; Sghr. - Seghrušen; Shw. - Shawiya; Sid. - Sidamo; Smll. - Semlal; Smr. - Sumrai; Sod. - Soddo; Sok. - Sokoro; Som. - Somali; Soq. - Soqotri; Sum. - Sumerian; Syr. - Syriac; Tait. - Taitoq; Tfl. - Tifilalt; Tgr. - Tigre; Ṭmb. - Ṭembaro; Tna. - Tigriñña (Tigrai); Tng. - Tangale; Tum. - Tumak; Ugr. - Ugaritic; W. - West; Wlm. - Tawllemmet; Wln. - Wolane; Wmd. - Wamdiu; Wrj. - Warji; Wryn. - Ait Warain; Yaud. - Yaudi; Yem. - Yemen; Zgw. - Zeghwana; Zmr. - Zemmur; Zng. - Zenaga; Zw. - Zwai.

Abbreviations of references:
AHw = Soden, W. von., 1965–81. *Akkadisches Handwörterbuch*. Wiesbaden: Harassowitz.

Brock. = Brockelmann, C., 1928. *Lexicon Syriacum*. Halle: Max Niemeyer.

CAD = Oppenheim, L., E. Reiner & M.T. Roth (eds.), 1956–. *The Assyrian Dictionary of the Oriental Institute, the University of Chicago*. Chicago (IL): The Oriental Institute.

DLU = Del Olmo Lete, G. & J. Sanmartín, 1996–2000. *Diccionario de la lengua ugarítica* I–II. Barcelona: Editorial Ausa.

DM = Drower, E.S. & R. Macuch, 1963. *A Mandaic Dictionary*. Oxford: Clarendon Press.

Dull. = Amborn, H., G. Minker & H.-J. Sasse, 1980. Das Dullay: Materialen zu einer astkuschitischen Sprachgruppe. *Kölner Beiträge zur Afrikanistik* 6, 228–81.

EG = Erman, A. & H. Grapow, 1957–71. *Wörterbuch der aegyptischen Sprache* I–VII. B. Berlin: Akademie-Verlag.

HAL = Koehler, L. & W. Baumgartner, 1994–96, 1999–2000. *The Hebrew and Aramaic Lexicon of the Old Testament* I–III. Leiden, New York & Cologne: Brill. IV–V. Leiden, Boston & Köln: Brill.

HSED = Orel, V.E. & O.V. Stolbova, 1995. *Hamito-Semitic Etymological Dictionary: Materials for a Reconstruction*. Leiden, New York & Cologne: Brill.

Huds. = Hudson, G., 1989. *Highland East Cushitic Dictionary*. Hamburg: Buske.

Ja. = Jastrow, M., 1996. *A Dictionary of the Targumim, the Talmud Babli and Yerushalmi, and the Midrashic Literature*. New York (NY): The Judaica Press.

JJ = Johnstone, T.M., 1981 *Jibbāli Lexicon*. New York (NY): Oxford University Press.

JM = Johnstone, T.M., 1987. *Mehri Lexicon*. London: University of London.

Jung. CLR = Jungraithmayr, H. & D. Ibriszimow, 1994. *Chadic Lexical Roots* I–II. B. Berlin: Dietrich Reimer.

Kraft = Kraft, C.H., 1981. *Chadic Wordlists* I–III. Berlin: Dietrich Reimer.

Lamb. Wol. = Lamberti, M. & M.R. Sottile, 1997. The Wolaytta language. *Studia linguarum africae orientalis* 6, 1–563.

LGur. = Leslau, W., 1979. *Etymological Dictionary of Gurage (Ethiopic)*, vol. III. Wiesbaden: Otto Harassowitz.

LGz. = Leslau, W., 1987. *Comparative Dictionary of Geʕez (Classical Ethiopic)*. Wiesbaden: Otto Harassowitz.

LH = Littmann, E. & M. Höffner, 1956. *Wörterbuch der Tigre Sprache: Tigre-deutsch-englisch*. Wiesbaden: Franz Steiner Verlag GMBH.

LS = Leslau, W., 1938. *Lexique Soqoṭri (Sudarabique*

moderne) avec comparaisons et explications étymologiques. Paris: Librairie C. Klincksieck.

Sas. Bur. = Sasse., H.-J., 1982. *An Etymological Dictionary of Burji.* Hamburg: Helmut Buske Verlag.

SD = Beeston, A.F.L., M.A. Ghul, W.W. Müller & J. Ryckmans, 1982. *Sabaic Dictionary (English-French-Arabic).* Louvain-la-Neuve, Beyrouth: Peeters, Librairie du Liban.

A. Corn, beans, edible plants

1. Afras. **ʔary/w- ~ *(ʔV)w/yar-* **'corn, beans, edible plants'** (related to No. 15?)

(?) Sem.: Hbr. *ʔōrōt* (pl.) 'mallow, *Malva rotundifolia* (edible)' (HAL, 25); Arb. *ʔary-* '*manne,* substance végétale qui s'épaissit sur les feuilles des arbres' (BK 1, 27).

Brb.-Can. **Hawr-an/*Harw-an*: Ghdm. *aḇer-n,* Aujila *(a)ḇru-n,* Siwa, Shw. *ar-en,* Mzb. *wir-en,* Qbl. *awr-en* 'farine' (Kossmann 1999, 92; *ḇ* in Ghdm. and Aujila vs. *w/0* in N. Brb. may reflect a laryngeal in the vicinity of **w*); Tenerife *a-hor-en* 'farine d'orge rôti' (Wölfel 1965, 516).

Ch. W.: Fyer *worom* 'groundnuts', Dera *worom* 'beans' (Skinner 1996, 176); Bol. *are* 'seed' (Skinner 1996, 117); Pero *árùè* 'seed' (Frajzyngier 1985, 21; cf. also *árì* 'nut' Frajzyngier 1985, 20); Tsagu *waran* 'beans' (Skinner 1996, 176); C.: Bač. *warey* 'groundnuts' (Skinner 1996, 176); Fali **ʔyar,* Zgv. *wira* 'millet' (Skinner 1996, 83); Mada *ire* 'semence' (Barreteau & Brunet 2000, 231); *úwwár* '*Mucuna pruriens* (Fabaceae)' (Barreteau & Brunet 2000, 267); Lame *ʔurū* 'millet' (Skinner 1996, 46), Musey, Bnn. *ira* 'seed' (Skinner 1996, 117); E.: Dgl. *yorwa* 'sorghum' (Skinner 1996, 83); Kera *arway* 'graines poussant vite' (Skinner 1996, 117).

Eg.: *ịwry* 'Bohne' MK (EG I, 56), Copt. (SF) *aro* 'fève' (Vycichl 1983, 15).

Cu. C.: Bil. Khmr. Qw. Damot, Aw. *ar;* E.: Or. *arū* 'Korn, Getreide, Feldfruchte' (Reinisch 1887, 44), Brj. *wór-i* 'cereals (general)' (Sas. Bur., 190), (?) Som. *ara* 'fruits (de terre et d'arbre)' (Cohen 1947, 80; not in Abraham 1962 and Agostini *et al.* 1985).

Om. N.: Kf., Mč., S. Mao, Nao *yāro* 'seed' (Skinner 1996, 290).

2. Afras. **bar- > *bar-, baʔr* **'a cereal'** (any connec-

tion with No. 16?)

Sem.: Hbr. *bār* '(clean, threshed) grain' (HAL, 153); Arb. *burr-* 'froment' (BK 1, 103); Sab. *br* 'wheat' (SD, 31); Tgr. *barbaro* (redupl.) 'a kind of small, red durra' (LH, 277); Amh. *bǝr* 'stalk (of barley, wheat); straw'; Mhr. *barr* 'maize' (JM, 51; acc. to Johnstone, from Arb.); Soq. *bor* 'froment' (LS, 98).

Brb.: Hgr. *a-bôra* 'sorgho à gros grain' (Foucauld 1951–52, 84); E. Wlm. *a-bōra* 'sorgho' (Nicolas 1957, 22); Zng. *būru* 'pain' (Nicolas 1953, 180).

Ch. W.: Hs. *iburo* 'a cereal' (Bargery 1934, 472; *<*ʔibur-*); Ang. *ḇwèr* 'yam' (*<*buʔr-*), Pero *ḇwɔrɔ̀ŋ* 'millet' (Kraft; *<*buʔr-Vn,* cf. *ḇárà* 'stalk' Frajzyngier 1985, 21); C.: Log. *bāberā* 'maize' (HSED, No. 265; redupl. *<*barbVr-*); Bač. *byàra* 'groundnut' (Kraft; *<*bVyar-*); E.: Tum. *ḇar* 'Pennisetum millet' (*<*baʔr-*).

Eg.: *b:.t* 'eine Körnerfrucht' Pyr.- MK (EG I, 416, 418; *<*bVr-*); Copt. (S) *ebra,* (B) *bray* 'grain de céréales et d'autres plantes' (Vycichl 1983, 39).

Cu. E.: Or. *omborii* 'oats' (Gragg 1982, 305; *<*ʔV-mbVr-,* with a secondary *-m-*?); S.: Burunge *baru* 'grain (generic)' (Ehret 1980, 338); Dah. *ḇùru* 'maize' (Ehret *et al.* 1989, 34; *<*buʔr-*?).

Om. N.: Moča *bàro,* Anf. *baro* 'maize' (Leslau 1959, 22).

Cf. Militarev 1990, 79–80; HSED, Nos. 224, 265.

3. Afras. **ba/u(ʔ)r-ay-* **'flour, groats'** (relative adjective derived from No. 2 implying the meaning 'processed grain'?) ~ **ba/urba/ur-* (redupl.)

Sem.: Arb. *burbūr-* 'blé broyé' (Blachère *et al.* 1964, 495; redupl. stem).

Brb. **-bVray-*: Ghdm. *ta-bare-t* 'gâteau fait d'un pain' (Lanfry 1973, 27); Sghr. *i-bray-n* (pl.) 'rough flour' (Abdel-Massih 1971, 181); Smll. *i-briy-n* (pl.) 'farine grossière' (Destaing 1920, 124).

Ch. **bu/a(ʔ)r(ay)-*: W.: Hs. *buri, biri* 'the flour in which balls of *fura* are rolled' (Bargery 1934, 134, 111); Ngz. *barbari* 'gruel' (HSED, No. 224; redupl.); C.: Mw. *ḇúrô;* Bač. *ḇùrey* 'gruel' (Kraft; *<*buʔr-ay*); E.: Smr. *bura,* Tum. *bař* 'flour' (HSED, No. 224).

Eg.: *b:y* 'etw. Essbares aus Getreide', *b:y.t* 'ein

Backwerk' MK (EG I, 417; <*bVrVy, cf. brry 'Art Brot' NE, EG I, 466).

Cu. C.: Khmr. *bura* 'Mehlgrütze' (Reinisch 1884, 349); E.: Som. *bur* 'flour' (Abraham 1962, 36).

4. Afras. *baw/yar- ~ *?i/a-bar- 'fig-tree'

Sem.: Arb. *?ibrat-* 'figuier sycomore', *?br* 'féconder un palmier femelle par une greffe mâle' (BK 1, 3); Gez. *burāt* 'olive tree' (LGz., 108), Amh. *abʷar* 'tree like the *warka*' (Kane 1990, 1194; acc. to LGur., 9 a loan of Or. *habru, abru, harbū* 'sycamore', which is less likely; *warka* means 'sycamore' Kane 1990, 1508); Wln. *abro* 'k. of tree' (LGur., 9); End. *burat* 'k. of tree' (LGur., 156).

Brb.: Ghdm. *ebrər* 'être fécondé (palmier)', *aḫerīr* 'fleur de palmier mâle' (Lanfry 1973, 20); Aujila *še-brer* (caus.), Siwa *ss-urr* 'féconder un palmier', Hgr. *ehərər* id., pl. *ihərâr* (compared in Prasse 1969, 68 and Kossmann 1999, 118; <*?i/abVrir, with a partial reduplication of the stem).

Ch. W.: Hs. *ḇaure* 'fig-tree, fig-fruit' (Abraham 1965, 91; <*?Vbawr-); E.: Mig. *báàrá* 'figuier (rouge)' (Jungraithmayr & Adams 1992, 68; <*baw/yar-).

Cu. N.: Beja *bīr* 'Dumpalm' (Reinisch 1895, 50; <*bVyVr?); E.: Som. *báar* 'tree top; *Commelina* spec.', Rnd. *bàar* '*Hyphaene coracea* Gaertn., Palmae' (<*báar 'river palm' Heine 1979, 183); Som., Boni *beer* 'garden' (Heine 1978, 54; all <*baw/yar-); Or. *habru, abru, harbū* 'sycamore' (LGur., 9; the form *habru/abru* may continue *?abru or be an Amharism, which is less likely because of the difference in pattern).

5. Afras. *čVʕaw- 'grain, ear (of barley, wheat)'

Sem. *šVʕVʕ- 'barley, ear of corn; k. of beans': Akk. *šeʔu* 'barley, grain; pine nut' OAkk. on (CAD š1, 345; AHw, 1222; acc. to both sources, from Sum.; the reading quoted has been recently doubted by Huehnergard); *šuʔu* 'pulse, chickpea' Nuzi, MA, SB (CAD š3, 416), 'eine Getreideart' SB, NAss. (AHw, 1294); Jud. *šəʕūʕīt* 'a species of beans' (Ja., 1610); *šəʕīt-* id. (Ja., 1611); Arb. *šaʕaʕ-, šiʕaʕ-, šuʕaʕ-* 'barbe de l'épi', *šʕʕ* IV 'se remplir de grains (se dit des épis, des céréales)' (BK 1, 1234); Tgr. *säʕaʕ* 'oats' (LH, 194), *səʕsəʕa* (redupl.) 'épeautre' (LH, 194); Tna. *saʕaʕ* 'avena, sorta di biada' (Bassano 1918, 202); *saʕsəʕe* (redupl.) 'sorta di orzo che si semina nella stagione asciutta' (Bassano 1918, 201). Cf. metathetic *ʕay/wš-

'bread, corn food'; Jud. *ʕīs-* 'started dough, quantity of flour used for one person's meal' (Ja., 1072); *ʕāsāsīt* 'pounded wheat or peas' (Ja., 1098); Sab. *ʕys₂* '? cornland' (SD, 24), 'food, provision, produce' (Biella 1982, 363, 368); Arb. (Eg. dial.) *ʕayš-* 'pain' (BK 2, 420), (N. Yem. dial.) *ʕawš, ʕayš* 'Brot' (Behnstedt 1992-, 878, 884); Tgr. *ʕeš* 'bread (of the Europeans)' (LH, 481); Har. *ēs* 'oat' (Leslau 1963, 33).

Ch. W.: Siri *ŝawi* 'guinea corn' (Skinner 1977, 24). Cf. in Stolbova 1996, 53: W. *čaHwa 'guinea corn', Sura *šwáa*, Ang. *šwe*, Ank., Tng. *sua* compared to E.: Mig. *čiwwa* 'gros mil (sorgho)'.

Eg.: *šʕ.w.t* 'Kuchen, aus Spelt, Fett und Honig' Pyr. (EG IV, 421); *šʕ.t* 'Teil der Gerste' Med. (EG IV, 420); *šʕ.t.t* 'Art Brot' BD, Med. (EG IV, 418).

Cu. N.: Beja *šūš* '*Panicum turgidum*' (Reinisch 1895, 218; redupl.); C.: Kem., Qwr. *sewī* 'Aehre' (Rein. Qw., 119); E.: Sa. *suwā* 'grain that ripens' (LGz., 539; all these examples may or may not be loans from Eth., where the similarly looking forms, however, end in *-t-*: Gez. *ŝawit*, etc. - see LGz., 539); Had. *soʔo*, Ṭmb. *soha* 'barley' (-h- < *-ʕ-?), Sid. *šoʔē* 'ear of corn' (Dolgopolsky 1973, 120, with a different reconstruction). Cf. metathetic E.: Or. *ees* 'a k. of corn' (Sasse 1979, 44); Harso, Dob., Goll. *ʕawš-* 'reifen' (Dull., 263).

Cf. differently in Militarev 1990, 79; 1995, 117–18; HSED, No. 559.

6. Afras. *čarVy- 'barley'

Sem. (1) *šaʕVr- 'barley; grass, straw' (Dolgopolsky explains -ʕ- as the result of contamination with Sem. *šaʕr- 'hair'; otherwise influenced by Sem. *šVʕVʕ-, see No. 5): Ugr. *šʕrm* 'cebada' (DLU, 427); Hbr. *šəʕōrā* 'the hairy, grainy kernel-fruit, barley' (HAL, 1346); Jud. *səʕart* 'barley' (Ja., 1010); Syr. *səʕār-ət-* 'hordeum' (Brock., 489); Mnd. *sara* 'barley' (DM, 315); Arb. *šaʕīr-* 'orge' (BK 1, 1238); Sab. *s₂ʕr* 'barley' (SD, 268); Gez. *ŝaʕr* 'herb, herbage, grass, vegetation, straw' (LGz., 525); Tgr. *säʕar* 'grass, hay' (LH, 194; *šaʕir* 'barley', LH, 226 is likely an Arabism); Tna. *saʕri* 'erba, fieno' (Bassano 1918, 139); Amh. *sar* 'grass (either green or dried)' (Kane 1990, 482); *sororro* 'white *ṭef*' (Kane 1990, 486); Har. *säʔar, sār* 'grass' (Leslau 1963, 136); Gur. *saʔar* 'grass' (LGur., 530); Mhr. *ŝēr* 'straw' (JM, 370); Jib. *ŝáʕər* 'dry grass, straw' (JJ, 244). Cf. Mhr. *šəʕīr* (JM, 391); Jib. *šiʕír* 'barley' (JJ, 259); Soq. *šaʕir* 'orge' (LS, 420), very likely Arabisms.

139

Sem. (2): Eth. *šər(-n)ay- 'wheat' (borrowing from Cu. cannot be ruled out): Gez. šərnāy, Tgr. šərnay, šənray; Tna. sərnay, Amh. sənde, Gaf. səndä, Arg. sərray, Gur. *sәre 'wheat', Har. sərri 'thick bread made of wheat' (LGz., 534).

Ch. W.: Tng. sîr- 'yam' (s- in Tng continues several Afrasian sibilants, incl. *ĉ); C.: Bnn. šordà 'okra' (Kraft) <*ĉVr-d- <*ĉVr-t- (cf. kowànà 'son, daughter' ~ kòwàyendà 'sister', or čindà 'mahogany' <*tiʔn-t-, cf. No. 14 below, and Stolbova 1996, 136).

Eg.: šr.t 'Gerste' MK (EG IV, 524).

Cu. *ʔaĉar- (with *ʔa- prefixed): N.: Beja ešerri 'Mais' (Reinisch 1895, 33; cf. also ašratta 'eine lange Grasart' Reinisch 1895, 33); E.: Kmb. ašārú-ta, Ṭmb. ašaru 'barley' (Leslau 1959, 18). Cf. *SVr- 'wheat': N.: Beja serám 'Weizen' (Reinisch 1895, 205); E.: Som. saren 'wheat' (Abraham 1962, 218); Or. šuroo, široo 'k. of pap made out of well-ground peas' (Gragg 1982, 370); Had. sara-ta 'sorghum' (Huds., 139); Harso soro 'Weizen' (Dull., 279). Cf. also N.: Beja šinrǻy 'Weizen' (Reinisch 1895, 217); E.: Af. sirrǻy; Sa. sinrǻ; C.: Bil. šinrǻy id. (Reinisch 1886, 904), probably borrowed from or to Eth.

Om. N.: Mč. ašāro '(roasted) barley' (Leslau 1959, 18; a loan from E. Cu.?).

Cf. Militarev 1990, 79; HSED, No. 544: Sem. *šaʕā/īr-; Eg. šr.

7. Afras. *da/ingʷ- ~ *(ʔa-)da(n)g⁽ʷ⁾Vr- ~ *(ʔa-)dangʷal- 'beans, leguminous plants; corn'

7.1. *da/ing⁽ʷ⁾- 'k. of beans; corn'

Sem. *dVng⁽ʷ⁾- 'beans' ~ *dagan- 'corn, grain' (metathetic or <*da(n)g-an-): Soq. dengo 'haricots' (LS, 130); (?) Tgr. baldänga, bärdunga 'bean; Vicia faba Sill.' (LH, 273; <*bal/r-dung-, with an obscure first element; probably from Bil. or Sa.; cf. also Tna baldänun 'Bohne' LH, 273); Ugr. dgn 'grano, trigo' (DLU, 130); Ph. dgn, Hbr. dāgān, Arm. Eg. dgn 'corn, grain' (HAL, 214).

Brb. *digi(n): E. Wlm. ta-dəgin-it 'Bauhinia rufescens (gousses noires)' (Nicolas 1957, 37); Zng. ti-ḏīgi-d 'caroube, haricot' (Nicolas 1953, 265). Cf. Ayr te-dängǎw-t 'grenier de céréales' (Alojaly 1980, 24).

Ch. *da/ingw-: W.: Hs dangwa-mi 'a gruel made with

the mealy pulp found inside locust-bean pods' (Bargery 1934, 219); Ang. tang 'corn' (HSED, No. 620; <*dang-); E.: Nan. tínge 'bean' (<*ding-; cf. Jung. CLR, I, XXIII Sound correspondence table).

Eg.: ḏḏw 'kind of grain' OK (Faulkner 1962, 314; cf. EG V, 502) < *dVg(V)w.

(?) Cu. *bal/r-dangʷ- (the meaning of the first element of this composed word is not clear): C.: Bil. baldanguǎ 'Bohne, Faba' (Reinisch 1887, 78); E.: Sa. bardangǎ, baldangā 'eine bestimmte Bohnengattung' (Reinisch 1890, 86).

7.2. *(ʔa-)da(n)g⁽ʷ⁾Vr- 'k. of beans'

Sem. *dVgVr- 'beans': Syr. dagr-, Arb. daẑr-, duẑr-, duẑur-, Mhr. dêẑir, Jib. dəgərät, pl. dugur, Soq. dígir 'fèves' (Cohen et al. 1970–, 222). Cf. Tgr. ʔadungʷara, Tna. ʔadangʷəra, Amh. adängʷare, Gaf. adängʷarä, S. Arg. adongure, Gur. adängʷarre id. (Cohen et al. 1970–, 222), obviously Cushitisms.

Ch. E.: Sok. dagir 'millet' (HSED, No. 621).

Cu. *ʔa-da(n)gʷVr-: C.: Bil. Khmr. adogur, Damot, Aw. adangwari 'bean' (LGur., 17; Reinisch 1887, 15); E.: Som. digir 'fagioli' (Agostini et al. 1985, 186); Or. adanguar 'Bohne' (Reinisch 1887, 15; cf. also otongora 'beans' Gragg 1982, 307); Sa. adagur 'Bohnen' (Reinisch 1890, 11).

7.3. *(ʔa-)dangʷal- 'corn; beans'

Sem. *(ʔa-)dang⁽ʷ⁾al- ~ *dalgʷ-am-: Tgr. ʔädängäl 'bean(s)' (LH, 384; <Bil.? cf., however, ʔädäggäla, däggäla poet.; Tna. däggäla 'a sort of corn growing wild; Eleusine aegyptiaca' LH, 385); Har. dāngulle 'pea' (Leslau 1963, 57; < Or.); Gez. dəlgʷəmmā 'porridge', Amh. dälgʷäm 'a variety of sorghum' (LGz., 131).

Ch. *(ʔV-)da(n)gwVl-: W.: Krkr. dəgwəlì 'gruel' (Kraft); C.: Mada édiŋgèl 'tige de mil (dont on a coupé l'épi)' (Barreteau & Brunet 2000, 93); E.: Mig. dágàlááwé 'noix de palmier doum' (Jungraithmayr & Adams 1992, 76; metathetic <*dagwal-).

Cu. *(ʔa-)dangʷal-: C.: Bil. adängʷal 'Bohne' (Reinisch 1887, 15; LGur., 17; cf. adagalǎ 'eine essbare Pflanzensorte' Reinisch 1887, 13); E.: Or. dängulle 'bean' (LGur., 17).

Cf. Militarev 1990, 79; HSED, Nos. 620, 621, 653.

8. Afras. **g⁽ʷ⁾ỉ/ar- ~ *garga/ir-* 'grain; bean' (related to No. 20?)

Sem.: Hbr. *gērā* 'carob seed' (HAL, 200); pB. *gargēr* id. (Ja., 265); Jud. *gargēr-* id. (Ja., 265); Arb. *ǯarǯar-*, *ǯirǯir-* 'fève' (BK 1, 275).

Brb.: Hgr. *a-ḡḡar* 'gousse rempli de graines pas comestible (servent à tanner les peaux)' (Foucauld 1951–52, 478); Ayr, E.Wlm. *a-ggar* 'fruit de *ṭəggart*; tan' (Alojaly 1980, 57); Qbl. *ṭa-ǯʷrir-ṭ* 'papillonacée à petites gousses comestibles' (Dallet 1982, 271).

Ch. **(ʔa-)g⁽ʷ⁾a/ir- ~ *gargar-*: W.: Hs. *guro* 'okra', *gērō* 'bulrush millet' (Abraham 1965, 346, 315); Sura *gyewuro*, Dera *gerò*, Seya *gyoro* 'millet', Ang. *gürm* 'bean' (<**gʷir-m-*?), C.: Mndr. *gíre*, Glv. *ʔagùrà*, Zgw. *ŋgure*, Gava *ŋgurè*, Nkts. *ngūre* 'bean' (<**ʔa-gʷVr-*?), Misme (Zime) *guirany* 'guinea-corn' (<**gʷir-an-*?), Higi (Futu) *gòrwá* (all Kraft), Mtkm. *gagar* 'millet' (Kraft; <**gargar-*), Mada *aŋgar* 'niébé cultivé, haricot' (Barreteau & Brunet 2000, 220; <**ʔan-gar-*); *ŋgárŋgàr* '*Indigofera hirsuta* (Fabaceae)' (Barreteau & Brunet 2000, 221; <**ʔagarʔagar-*?); Log. *máágùréé* 'beans' (Jung. CLR, II, 11; <**ma-gʷVr-*?); E.: Smr. *giri*, *ǯìrī*; Jegu *giri*, *gír(k)* 'bean' (HSED, No. 933; Jung. CLR, II, 11); Mig. *gàgàrré* 'mil (à demi écrasé et mouillé)' (Jungraithmayr & Adams 1992, 86; <**gargar-*).

Cu. E.: Or. *garii* 'seed' (Gragg 1982, 169); Had. *ǯar-etta* id. (Huds., 130; *ǯ* <**g*?).

Cf. HSED, No. 933: Hbr., part of Ch.

9. Afras. **ḥVnṭ-* 'kind of cereal'

Sem.: Akk. *uṭṭatu* 'Getreide, Gerste, Korn' OAkk. on (AHw, 1446); Ugr. *ḥṭṭ*, Hbr. *ḥiṭṭā*, Jud. *ḥinṭat-*, Syr. *ḥeṭṭət-*, Arb. *ḥinṭat-*, Soq. *ḥinṭəh* 'wheat' (HAL, 307); Jib. *ḥiṭ* 'food; beans; any cereal' (JJ, 119).

Ch. W.: Hs. *gùnḍu* 'k. of short-headed bulrush-millet' (Bargery 1934, 408; <**ḥunṭ-*); (?) Tng. *kwonḍò* 'groundnut', Gera *handìmì* 'beans' (Kraft; sound correspondences not clear); Glmb. *ándi* id. (Stolbova 1987, 60; <**ḥanṭ-*?).

Cu. E.: Som. *haḍuḍ* 'corn, millet, sorghum' (Abraham 1962, 102); *ḥadud* 'corn, sorghum' (Dolgopolsky 1973, 222, quoted after Reinisch); Sid. *hayṭe* 'barley' (Huds., 24). Cf. Brj. *haṭ-*, Kmb. *haṭiid-* 'to cut crops, reap' (<**haṭ-* Huds., 46; may originate from **ḥaṭ-*).

10. Afras. **kabb- ~ *kib-t- ~ *kaHb-/*kabH-* 'kind of corn (wheat?)'

Sem.: Akk. *kibtu* 'wheat' OAkk. on (CAD *k*, 340; AHw, 472 = Sum. GIG(BA), but hardly a Sumerism); Tgr. *käbbä* 'Getreidebrei' (LH, 411).

Brb.: Hgr. *a-kəbbu* 'noyau (de fruit)' (Foucauld 1951–52, 728); Ayr, E. Wlm. *ekăbb* id. (Alojaly 1980, 87); *te-kəbbəkəb-t* (redupl.) 'épi de certaines plantes (blé etc.)' (Alojaly 1980, 88); Tait. *a-kəbbu* 'noyau (de datte)', Qbl. *a-kubab* 'épi de sorgho' (Laoust 1920, 475).

Ch. W. **kabH-/*kaHb-*: Hs. *kubewa* 'okra', *kabu* '*Fura* made of guinea-corn' (Bargery 1934, 625, 515). Cf. Gwn. *kóbo*, Glmb. *kằb*; Pero *kàppu*; Bole *kapp* (*-pp* <**-bb*) 'to plant, sow'; Tng. *kaabe* 'to sow' (Jungraithmayr 1991, 93).

Cu. E.: Gel. *kabbo* 'unleavened bread' (Huds., 31); Konso *kapp-a*, Gid. *kapp(-o)* 'wheat' (PEC, 57; *-pp* <**-bb* — see PEC, 55; acc. to Sasse, from **gazb-* PEC, 57, which is less likely); Dob. *kapoča* 'Gerste' (Dull., 244; <**kab-Vt-*).

Om. S.: Dime, Ari *kəbb* 'maize, corn' (Bender 1994, 154).

11. Afras. **lay/w- ~ *ʔ/Vl(l)- ~ *w/yVlal-* 'k. of corn (millet ?)'

Sem.: Akk. *lillânu* (*lilliannu*, *lālânu*) 'grain at its highest growth' SB (CAD *l*, 188; AHw, 553; <**laylay-an-*, reduplicated, with *-an* suffixed?).

Brb. **y/HVl(V)l-*: Ghdm. *ileli* 'millet', Ntf. *ill-an* (pl.), Zng. *ill-en* (pl.) 'sorgho' (Laoust 1920, 268).

Ch. **ʔi/ulaw- ~ *wVyal-*: W.: Dera *yila* 'nut, grain' (Skinner 1996, 246); C.: Peve *lo*, Gude *ʔəlaʔin* 'okra' (Kraft); E.: Mubi *wèyál* 'seed' (Jung. CLR, II 287); Mok. *ʔulo* 'grain' (Skinner 1996, 117). Cf. Bid., Dgl. *luw-* 'sémer' (Skinner 1996, 246); Mig. *lúwáw* id. (Jungraithmayr & Adams 1992, 104).

Cu. N.: Beja *óli* 'geröstetes Getreide' (Reinisch 1895, 14); *olli* 'Brei' (Reinisch 1895, 15); E.: Saho, Afar *iláû* 'Korn, Getreide, spec. *Durra*' (Reinisch 1886, 808); Brj. *álo* 'millet' (Sass. Bur., 25); Harso *älölo* '*Phaseolus vulgaris*' (Dull., 235), *wolalla* 'sorghum' (Dull., 269).

Om. N.: Koyra *allo* 'millet' (Sass. Bur., 25, quoted

after Hayward); S.: Ari *uula*, Hamer *ulla* 'maize, corn' (Bender 1994, 154). Cf. Kačama *ayl-* 'to sow' (Lamb. Wol., 308).

12. Afras. *sVnnVy/ʔ- 'seed, corn; standing crops'

Sem.: Akk. *ašnan (asnan)* 'grain, cereal (as a generic term)' (CAD *a*2, 450); *ašnanu* (AHw, 82) OB on (<*ʔa-šnan-*, with prefixed *ʔa-*); (?) Chaha *sənä*, Eža, Ms. *sənne*, Gyeto *sənay*, *səneʔä*, End. *səneʔ*, Enn. *səneʔä* 'wheat' (LGur., 558–9; acc. to LGur, 555, represents *səre* with *r:n*, which cannot explain -*ʔ* in part of the forms; cf. Har. *säñi*, Sel. *säñe*, Wol. *sänñe*, Zw. *säñi* 'seed, crop' LGur., 555, very likely from Cu.); Mhr. *mə-hnoy* 'farm near a town' (JM, 159); Jib. *mə-šnuʔ* 'garden on the mountain for *dhura* or beans', *ešné* 'to have a garden, field' (JJ, 263); Soq. *šane* 'semence, blé qui est sur les tiges', *héne* 'semer' (LS, 145).

Ch. (1) W. *sVnʔ-*: Ang. *šôŋ* 'millet' (Kraft); Tng. *siŋa* 'sp. of bread' (Jungraithmayr 1991, 145); C. (redupl.): Daba *sèsīn*, Kola *sísîn* 'seed' (Jung. CLR, II, 287).

Ch. (2): W.: Wrj. *sənána*, Tsagu *šínàn*, Kariya *sîn*, Pa. *sinna*, Siri *šinàwi*, Mburku *šíná*, Jmb. *sùná*; C.: Masa *síne*, Zime-Batna *sínē* 'fields (farm)' (Jung. CLR II, 134–5); Lame *šínì*, Peve *šìne*, Bnn. *senina* (Stolbova 1996, 39 and HSED, No. 2249 compare these forms to Ch. E. *sinya-* 'earth, sand' and Eg. *syn* 'clay' reconstructing Ch. *sina* 'field, earth': Stolbova 1996, 39, and Afras.*sin-* 'earth, clay' HSED, No. 2249).

Eg.: *sn.w* 'Opferbrote' MK (EG IV, 155).

Cu. E.: Som. *šuni* (LGur., 555); Or. *sañɲe*, Gel. *sanne*, Brj. *sañɲee* (Huds., 130); Dar. *sanne* (LGur., 555) 'seed'.

Om. S.: Hamer *isin* 'sorghum' (Bender 1994, 148; <*ʔV-sin*?).

13. Afras. *ŝV(m)bar- 'k. of corn; chickpea'

Sem.: *ŝₓabr(-Vm)-* (on Afras. *ŝ-* > Sem. *ŝₓ-* > Hbr *š* ~ Arb. *š-* see Militarev & Kogan 2000, xcviii–cv): Hbr. *šäbär* 'grain', Sam. *šabru*, *šabrimma id.* (HAL, 1405–6); Arb. *šubrum-* 'espèce de plante dont la graine resemble aux lentilles' (BK 1, 1184; metathetic of *ŝₓVmbVr-* or < *ŝₓVbr-*, with -*Vm* suffixed); (?) Tgr. *säbbära* '*Lathyrus sativus*' (LH, 183; with a meaning shift). Cf. Tna. *šəmbəra*, Amh., Arg., Har. *šumbura*, Gur *šəmbura* 'chickpea' (LGur., 579; likely Cushitisms, though borrowing into Cush. cannot be completely ruled out).

(?) Brb. (with a meaning shift?): Hgr. *é-səbər* 'natte d'*afeẓu*' (Foucauld 1951–52, 1803; *a-fəẓu* means '*Panicum turgidum*', a k. of millet: Foucauld 1951–52, 374); Ayr, E.Wlm. *e-säbăr* 'natte, tapis d'*afaẓo*' (Alojaly 1980, 169).

Ch. *ŝabur-* 'kind of corn': W.: Hs. *zábráá* 'millet'; C.: Mndr. *ẑébèrè*, *ẑəbùrè* 'ocra' (Stolbova 1996, 51); (?) Masa *ẑòònòra*, Lame (Peve) *ẑōr*, Heḍe, Zime *ẑor id.* (Stolbova 2001; <*ŝVmbVr-*?).

Cu. C.: Aw. *šəmbər-i* 'chickpea' (LGur., 579); Bil. *sabbar-á* 'Hülsenfrucht' (Reinisch 1887, 294); E.: Sa., Af. *sabbar-é* 'eine bestimmte Hülsenfrucht' (Reinisch 1886, 895); Or. *šumbur-ā*, Gel., Kmb. *šumbur-a*, Brj., Had., Sid. *šimbur-a* 'chickpea' (Huds., 39); Goll. *sumbur-o* 'Erbse' (Dull., 239).

14. Afras. *tiʔ(i)n- 'fig-tree' (<*tiʔ-n-? Cf. Akk. *tiʔu* and Janj. *teʔā*)

Sem. *tiʔin-*: Akk. *tittu, tiʔittu*, pl. *tīnātu* 'Feige(nbaum)' Lex., *tiʔu* 'Feige' SB (AHw, 1363); Hbr. *təʔēnā* 'fig, *Ficus carica*' (HAL, 1675); Jud. *tēnət-*, Syr. *teʔətt*, pl. *tēʔənē id.* (HAL, 1675); Mnd. *tina* 'fig-tree' (DM, 486); Arb. *tīn-* (coll.) 'figue', *tīnu-l-ʔafranǰi* 'espèce de cactus' (BK 1, 213); Har. *tīn, tīni* 'fruit of cactus' (acc. to Leslau 1963, 150, from Arb. *tīn* 'fig' of Aramaic origin; otherwise from Cu.).

Brb. *tiHVyn*: Hgr. *təyne*, Ayr *tayni, təyni, tini, tinəy*, Nslm. *tehəyne*, Smll. *tiyni* (Prasse 1969, 91); Zng. *təynih* (Nicolas 1953, 142) 'datte'.

Ch. *tiʔun-/*tiʔan-* 'mahogany, fig tree' (Stolbova 1996, 136): W.: Ang. *teung* 'tree, fig tree', Sura *tiŋ* 'tree', Gera *tyèniá*, Bol. *tàní*, Kirfi *tán*, Ngm. *tànì*; C.: Boka *tîîn-da*, Gab. *tiyìn-da*, Gaa *tîn-da*, Hona *tûnə*, Peve *mə-čin*, Bnn. *čin-dà* 'mahogany', Masa *čin-da* 'mahogany; tamarind' (Kraft).

Cu. E.: Som. *tin*, Or. *tīni* 'fruit of cactus' (Leslau 1963, 150; possibly from Arb.).

Om. N.: Janj. *teʔā* 'sicomoro' (Cerulli 1938, 85).

B. Cultivation of land

15. Afras. *ʔry/w ~ *ʔyr- ~ *ʔrr ~ *rʔ/w 'to gather, reap, cultivate' (related to No. 1?)

Sem.: Akk. *arû* 'to cut branches (of a date palm)' SB (CAD *a*2, 317; cf. also *arû* 'granary, storehouse' OAss.?

CAD *a2*, 313; AHw, 72); Hbr. *ʔry* 'to pluck', pB. 'to gather figs' (HAL, 82); Ph. *ʔry* 'to gather' (Tomback 1978, 30); Gez. *ʔarara* 'to reap, gather, harvest' (LGz., 39), *ʔaraya*, Tgr. *ʔarä*, Tna. *ʔaräyä* 'to gather, glean' (LGz., 40); Amh. *arrärä* 'to reap, mow' (LGz., 39).

Ch. **ʔirw-* ~ **raʔ-* ~ **rawraw-*: W.: Hs. *ror-* 'to gather, glean, harvest' (Skinner 1996, 220; redupl.); Ang. *er* 'to hoe', Dwot *ʔir* 'hoe' (Skinner 1996, 109); Ngz. *ruw* 'to cultivate, hoe, weed'; C.: Gude *ra* 'field, farm, plot' (Skinner 1996, 209); Lame *raʔa* 'ramasser' (Skinner 1996, 220); E.: Dgl. *rōre* 'faire le dernier sarclage' (Skinner 1996, 220; redupl.); Kera *erwi* 'sarcler' (Skinner 1996, 109).

Cu. C.: Aw. Bil. *ar* 'to gather, glean' (LGz., 40; possibly from Eth.); Khmr. *ayer* 'mähen, schneiden (Gras, Korn)' (Reinisch 1884, 345); E.: Sa. *arar* 'to glean' (LGz., 39); Af. *arar* 'sammeln, ernten' (Reinisch 1886, 816; two latter forms probably from Eth.); Som. *ururi*, Rnd. *urʼuuri*, Boni *eruuri* 'to gather, collect' (Heine 1978, 75; <**ʔVruri*, hardly from Eth. in view of the difference in vocalism); Sid. *roa, roʔira* (redupl.) 'to pluck vegetables' (Skinner 1996, 220), Dob.; Gorrose *ayre* 'Erntefest' (Dull., 239).

16. Afras. **by/wr* ~ **ʔbr* 'to cultivate, hoe', **bay/wr-* 'land (designed) for cultivation' (any connection with No. 2?)

Sem.: Akk. *aburru* 'rear, back (of a house or field); field or pasture by the city wall' OB on (CAD *a1*, 90; 'Flusswiese' in AHw, 9; <**ʔaburr-*, with prefixed *ʔ-*); Hbr. pB. *būr* 'to be empty, waste, uncultivated' (Ja. 148); Syr. *būr-* 'terra inculta' (Brock., 63); Arb. *bawr-* 'terrain qui n'est pas encore propre à être ensemencé; jachère' (BK 1, 177). Cf. Gez. *ma-bāro* 'means of digging (hoe, spade)'; Tna. *baräwä* 'to dig', *mä-baro* 'hoe' (LGz., 330).

Ch. W.: Bol. *bóóró* 'to plough' (Takács 2001, 27); C.: Mada *óbbòr* 'biner avant de semer' (Barreteau & Brunet 2000, 70; <**ʔVbVr*); E.: Mig. *bârče* 'jachère' (Jungraithmayer & Adams 1992, 69; <**bar-t-*); Bid. *beret* 'sarcler, biner' (Takács 2001, 26).

Eg. *b:* 'hacken' OK (EG I, 415); <**bVr*?

Cu. C.: Khmr. *baruw* 'auflockern die Erde mit einem Karst' (Reinisch 1884, 350; metathetic <**bwr*); E.: Som. *beer* 'campo coltivato; giardino; orto; seminare, piantare' (Agostini *et al.* 1985, 53), *abuur-*; Alaba *abuurr-*, Had. *abuull-* (-*ll* <**-rr*) 'to cultivate', Bayso

abar- 'to plant' (Lamb. Wol., 313); Brj. *bóyr-a* 'two-handed hoe', Kon. *payr-aa* 'two-tipped digging stick'; Gid. *pawr-a* 'two-bladed digging stick', Dob. *payr-e* 'two-pronged hoe' (Sas. Bur., 41; *p-* <**b-*); S.: Alg. *burabura* (redupl.) 'cultivated ground' (Ehret 1987, No. 387). Cf. Dah. *ḥur-* 'to cut grass, mow' (Ehret 1980, 138).

17. Afras. **ĉdd* ~ **ĉdʔ/*ĉʔd* 'to hoe (border-furrows); measure/survey/apportion field-plots', **ĉadw/y-* 'a (measured) plot of open country, cultivated land'

Sem. (1) **ŝady-* 'a (measured) plot of open country, cultivated land': Akk. *ŝadû* 'open country, steppeland' OAkk. on (CAD *ŝ1*, 49; AHw, 1124–5; the omonymous *ŝadû* 'mountain, mountain region' CAD *ŝ1*, 49, is to be compared to Ugr. *ŝd* 'monte' DLU, 431, and Arb. *sadd-* 'montagne' BK 1, 1068, to reconstruct a different Sem. root **ŝadd/w-* 'mountain' < Afras. **sad-*), *ŝiddu* '(long) side of a piece of immovable property; a measure of length or area (incl. a road)' OAkk. on, 'real estate grants and sales' MB on (CAD *ŝ2*, 403–5; AHw, 1230); Ugr. *ŝd* 'una franja, un largo de terreno, bancal; yugada / acre; campo abierto, campiña; campo, terreno, parcela, finca, explotacion agrícola; estepa' (DLU, 431, 433); Hbr. *ŝādā* 'pasture, open fields, land, acreage, arable land' (HAL, 1307–8); Ph. *ŝd* 'field, territory, cemetery, mainland' (Tomback 1978, 314); Amrn. *ŝa-te-e* 'field, plain' (HJ, 1110); Syr. *sadd-* 'sulcus; spatium sulci i.e. 400 ulnarum' (Brock., 460); Mnd. *sadia* 'field, open space, plain, desert' (DM, 310); Sab. *s₂dw* 'mountain or cultivated land?' (SD, 131; the correct meaning must be 'cultivated land', as the similar-looking Sem. root for 'mountain', **ŝadd/w-* adduced above has another sibilant in the *Anlaut* yielding Sab. *s₁*); Tgr. *səd* 'distance, frontier' (LH, 197); Amh. *säd(d)a* 'place having no fence, hedge or wall' (Kane 1990, 574).

Sem. (2) **ŝdd* ~ **ŝʔd* 'to hoe border-furrows; to measure a field, distribute plots': Akk. *ŝadādu* 'to measure, survey a field' OAkk. on (CAD *ŝ1*, 27; AHw, 1121); Hbr. *ŝdd* (pi.) 'to harrow, plough border-furrows' (HAL, 1306); pB. *ŝad* 'furrow' (Ja., 1523); Jud. *sdd* (pa.) 'to plough' (HAL, 1306); Har. *seʔada* to distribute', *ŝiža* (-*ž-* <**-d-*) 'part, share'; Gur. **sādä* 'to distribute, give a share' (LGur., 535).

Ch. W.: Wrj., Miya *ŝaḍ-*, Pa. *ŝaḍu*, Siri *ŝaḍa*, Kar. *ŝeyaŝeḍə* (redupl.) 'to hoe, cultivate' (Skinner 1977, 26; <**ĉadaH-* or **ĉaHad-*, see Stolbova 1987, 200); E.: Mok. *séḍḍó* 'recolter, moissonner' (Mok., 123;

<*ĉVddVH- or *ĉVHVdd-).

Eg.: šdw 'Grundstuck; als Teil des sḥ.t Feldes' MK (EG IV, 568); šdỉ 'to apportion field-plots' MK (Foulkner 1962, 273).

Cf. Militarev 1990, 75–6; differently in HSED, Nos. 522, 566.

18. Afras. *g⁽ʷ⁾'a/in(y/ʔ)- 'area, plot of land producing edible plants' (likely related to No. 19)

Sem. *ga/inn- 'garden': Ugr. gn 'jardín, huerto' (DLU, 148); Hbr. gan (HAL, 198), gannā, *ginnā (HAL, 199) 'garden'; Emp. gn (Cohen 1970–, 147); Jud. gīnnət-, gīn- (Ja., 240) id.; Syr. gannət- 'hortus' (Brock., 122); Mnd. ginta 'garden' (DM, 91); Arb. ǯannat- 'jardin' (BK 1, 333; considered a loan from Arm., see LGz., 199); Alg. dial. ǯannat 'campagne' (BK 1, 333); Sab. gnt 'garden, orchard' (SD, 50). Cf. Gez. gannat 'garden, paradise' (considered a loan from Syr.-Arm., see LGz., 199); Tgr. gänna, ǯännät, Tna ǯännät 'paradise', Amh. gannat 'garden, paradise', Mhr. gənnēt, Hrs. gennét, Jib. gént, Soq. gínnəh 'paradise' (Cohen 1970–, 147; all loanwords).

Brb.-Can.: Smll. ta-gän-t 'forêt' (Destaing 1920, 132), Demnat, Tazerwalt id. (Bronzi 1919, 31); Ferro gan 'el arbol santo' (Wölfel 1965, 448).

Ch. (1) *g⁽ʷ⁾anʔ- 'field, farm': W.: Hs. gṓnằ, Tng. kaŋ, Fyer hagón (metathetic), Dff., Sha goŋ; E.: Mig. gắn, Bid. gaŋ (Jung. CLR, II, 134–5; cf. HSED, No. 890, with a different reconstruction).

Ch. (2) *gwinay- 'edible fruit': Hs. guna 'melon', C. Gude gunaya 'tree sp. with edible fruit', Mafa-Mada group *-gwini 'papaya' (Skinner 1996, 91).

Ch. (3) W. *gangin- (redupl.) 'Deleb palm (Borassus aethiopum)': Hs. giginya, Dera gangiyo, Bol. ganga; Glmb. kanga (Skinner 1996, 84).

19. Afras. *g⁽ʷ⁾ny/w/ʔ 'to cultivate, till field; to crop' (likely related to No. 18)

Sem. *g⁽ʷ⁾ny/ʔ 'to gather, crop': Arb. ǯny 'cuellir des fruits', II 'abonder en produits qu'on cueille, qu'on récolte, comme plantes, céréales, etc.' (BK 1, 340); Daṯ. dial. ǯanā 'remove the honey from a beehive' (LGur., 318); Sab. t-gn 'to gather crop', gny 'crop' (SD, 50); Gez. gʷanʔa 'to heap up' (LGz., 196); Ms. ǯäññä 'to remove the honey from a beehive' (LGur., 318).

Ch. W. *g(V)wan-: Gwn. gwana; Fyer ŋgon 'to cultivate' (Skinner 1996, 88); C.: Nak. magigànà, Glv. magyigànà 'hoe' (redupl. stem with the instrumental prefix <*ma-gingan- 'instrument for tilling field'; cf. Takács 1999, 44); Masa guna 'hoe, mattock' (Kraft); E. *gawn-: Bid., Dgl. gaw(a)n (Skinner 1996, 88); Mig. gáwnò, Mubi gàwán 'to cultivate' (Jung. CLR, I 64).

Eg.: dny.w 'ein Gerät neben Hacken' CT (EG V, 575; Takàcs 1999, 44: <*gny); cf. also dnw 'Tenne' NE (EG V, 575).

20. Afras. *gʷar- or gu/ar- 'to collect, harvest' (related to No. 8?)

(?) Sem.: Gur. *gʷär 'season of agricultural activities, harvest' (LGur., 287; acc. to Leslau, from a Cu. term meaning 'time' and 'opportune time').

Brb.: Rif, Snhj. eǯru, Ntf. gru 'glaner, cueillir, gualer' (Laoust 1920, 417); Qbl. (Zwawa) ger 'donner un fruit' (Laoust 1920, 258); *a/i-mgir 'sickle' (with the instrumental m- prefix): Ntf. imgir (Destaing 1920, 124); Qbl. a-mžər (Dallet 1982, 490); Siwa a-mžīr (Laoust 1932, 236); Ghdm. a-mžīr (Lanfry 1973, 208); *mgr 'to harvest' (a denominal verb derived from *a/i-mgir 'sickle'?): Ntf. mgər (Destaing 1920, 189); Qbl əmžər (Dallet 1982, 489); Siwa mîžər (Laoust 1932, 261); Ghdms əmžər (Lanfry 1973, 208).

Ch. W.: Ang. gur 'to collect in great numbers', Bol. gar 'to reap' (Kraft); Pero gúurù 'sickle' (Frajzyngier 1985, 32).

Cu. E.: Rnd. gur-, Boni kur- 'to pick fruit' (Sas. Bur., 86); Som. gar- 'to harvest', Or. guur-, Kmb., Gid., Brj. guur- 'to pick up, gather' (Lamb. Wol., 435); Sid. gur- 'to pick coffee' (Huds., 69).

21. Afras. *(HV)g⁽ʷ⁾Vr- 'cultivated field; tilling, hoeing' (<*ʔV-gʷar- related to No. 20 *gʷar- or *gu/ar-, with *ʔV- prefixed, or < *hVgwVr- to compare to Eth. *garh-, with metathesis)

Sem.: Akk. ugāru 'Feldflur, Ackerland' OAkk. on (AHw, 1402; acc. to von Soden, from Sum., but more likely from Sem. *(ʔV-)g⁽ʷ⁾ar- or *hugar-); Arb. ǯawwār- 'laboureur' (BK 1, 353; nomen agentis <*gwr); Gez. garha 'to plough', garāht, garh 'field, arable land, farm. estate', Tgr. gärhat, Tna. gərat, pl. gərahəw 'field' (LGz., 202).

(?) Brb. *HigVr (otherwise from Lat. ager): Ntf. igər,

Sghr. Mṭmṭ *ižər* 'champ de céréales', Shw. *iḡr, iyər* 'terrain cultivé' (Laoust 1920, 258); Qbl. *ižər* 'champ labouré et ensemencé de céréales (orge, blé)' (Dallet 1982, 270).

Ch. W.: Pero *gbúgrò* 'to till the soil' (Frajzyngier 1985, 31; <*gwVgr- <*gwVrgVr-?); C.*ŋgwur(-um)- 'hoe' with an instrumental suffix; cf. Stolbova 1996, 71, where these examples are combined with Hs. *kŏrámé* and C. Ch. forms in k-, ẖ- and h- to reconstruct *qoram-): Higi (Gye) *ŋ̀gwuru*, Fali (Kiria) *ùŋwuru-mu*, Fali (Gili) *ŋ̀wur* 'hoe'.

Cu. E.: Af. *gawra* 'open space, fields, cultivated land' (Parker & Hayward 1985, 111).

22. Afras. *ḫa/ull- ~ *ḫVw/yal- 'hoe; farming'

Sem.: Akk. *allu* 'hoe' OAkk. on (CAD a1, 356; AHw, 37; acc. to von Soden, from Sum. *alAL, which is less likely); Sod. *wällät* 'forked digging stick' (acc. to LGur., 653, represents *wännät id.* with alternance l:n unless from Cu.).

Brb.: Shilḥ (Ntf. and other dialects) *a-wallu*, Sened, Nfs. *uilli* 'charrue' (Laoust 1920, 277).

Ch. W.: Grnt. *uwal* 'fields, farm' (Jung. CLR, II, 134); C.: Fali (Jilbu) *(w)ole* 'farm' (Kraft).

Eg.: *ḫnn* 'Hacke' Pyr. (EG III, 114; -*nn* may originate from *-ll).

Cu. E. *ḫayl- ~ *ḫull-: Sid. *heella-kko* 'small digging stick' (Huds., 50); Brj. *háyl-ee* 'neighbourhood help, i.e. mutual help in agricultural work' (Sas. Bur., 93–4); *ayliy-* 'to sow', Kon. *ayl-* 'to sow (seeds) and plough them under' (Sas. Bur., 29); Goll. *ḫullo* 'Erntefest' (Dull., 239).

Om. N.: Wol. *ayliyyᵃ* 'hoe', Kačama *ayl-* (Lamb. Wol., 308); Koyra *ayl-* (Sas. Bur., 29 quoted after Hayward, p.c.) 'to sow'.

23. Afras. *k(w)alaʔ/w- 'forage, fodder; pasture; mowing, cutting grass'

Sem.: Akk. *ukullû* 'Viehfutter; Verpflegung(sration), Verköstigung' OB on (AHw, 1406; <*kʷVllaʔ- ?); Arb. *klʔ* 'abonder en fourrage (se dit d'un pays)' (BK 2, 919); *kalaʔ-* 'fourrage (sec ou vert)' (BK 2, 920); Gez. *kʷālawa* 'to reap, mow' (LGz., 284); *makala, makkola* (acc. to LGz., 339, for *makkʷala*; secondary deriva-

tion with m- prefixed) 'to cut with a sickle, mow', Tgr. *mäklay* 'halm of durra, halm of corn', Tna. *mäkälä* 'to mow, cut' (LGz., 339); Amh. *kəlkəl* 'pasture' (Kane 1990; redupl.).

Brb. S. *klkl* (redupl. stem of intensive action): Hgr. *kelukelu* 'ramasser hâtivement çà et là (des brins de pailles, des brindilles de bois)' (Foucauld 1951–52, 800); Ayr, E. Wlm. *kələnkilet* 'ramasser, reunir completement' (Alojaly 1980, 92; t-stem with a secondary -n-).

Ch. W.: Hs. *kāla* 'gleaning, cutting grass' (Abraham 1965, 459); Mpn. *čál* 'field, grassy area' (Takács 1999, 68); Pero *kálà* 'place for growing plants, farming land', *kálù* 'to gather' (Frajzyngier 1985, 68, 35).

Cu. E.: Or. *kalō* 'pasture, leaves and grass, grazing area; property' (Gragg 1982, 244); Gel., Brj., Sid. *kalo*, Kmb. *kalu* 'pasture' (Huds., 111); (?) C.: Khmr. *kilkil* 'Wiese, Trift' (Reinisch 1884, 376; likely a loan of Amh. *kəlkəl*); Quara *kōla* 'das Tiefland, die Niederung' (Reinisch 1885, 83). Not to confuse with Afras. *kal(aʔ)-* 'earth, land': Sem.: Arb. *klʔ* II 'atterrir, approcher de la terre (un navire)', *kallāʔ-* 'rivage' (BK 2, 919–20); Brb.: Qbl. *a-kal* 'terre; sol; bien, propriété foncière (terrain cultivable)' (Dallet 1982, 401); Ntf. *a-kal* 'terre, sol, terrain', etc. (Laoust 1920, 359); Ch. W.: Tng. *kálau* 'soil, earth, ground'; E.: Tum. *kɔlɔ* 'earth' (Takács 1999, 68).

Cf. differently Takács 1999, 68.

24. Afras. *(ʔa-)kʷal- or *(ʔa-)kawal- 'k. of hoe, a hammer/axe-like tool, a pick-axe'

Sem.: Akk. *akkullu* (rather than *aqqullu*) 'a hammer-like tool, tool for field work' OAkk. on (CAD a1, 276); 'Dechsel, Picke' Bab., NAss. (acc. to AHw, 30, from Sum. ᵍⁱˢNIN-GUL; rather <*ʔa-kull-, with a secondary reduplication of -k-); *kullu* 'hoe' Lex. (CAD k, 508; not in AHw); Syr. *ʔakl-* 'malleus' (Brock., 17); Arb. *ʔaklat-* 'marteau, mailloche?' (Blachère *et al.* 1964, 166); S. Arg., Har. *kalka* 'axe' (according to Leslau 1997, 208, from Cu. E. *kalta* 'with an occasional alternance k:t'; rather redupl. <*kalkal; Sel. *kälta*; Wln. *kältä*; Zw. *halta* 'small axe' must be Cushitisms - see Cu. below and LGur., 342).

Ch. *kawal-*: W.: Hs. *káálài* 'a worn-out long-handled hoe' (considered a Kanuri loan-word, which is unlikely in view of other Ch. and Afras. data; cf. also *kalme* 'k. of small hoe' Abraham 1962, 462; *kal-mi*);

Krkr. *kàlà* 'hoe' (from Hs.?); Gera *kwalli*, Jimi *kwalo*; C.: Wmd. *kùl*, Hil. *kwùlū* id. (Stolbova 1996, 60).

(?) Eg.: *iknw* 'Hacke' MK (EG I, 140); *-n-* <*-l-*? (In Takács 1999, 216, *-n-* is otherwise interpreted as *-n-* and compared to Ch. W.: Ang. *čĕn*, Sura *čaan*, Mupun *čāan*; Jmb. *kəyaŋga* 'hoe', reconstructed as Afras. *ky-n*).

Cu. *kʷal-*: N.: Beja *kŭála-ni* 'Axt, Beil, Haue', *kŭaláy* 'Stock, Stab', *kūl-* 'hämmern, hauen' (Reinisch 1895, 142, 139); E. *kal-t-*: Brj. *kált-e* 'shaft (of plough); small axe' (Sas. Bur., 113), 'plough' (Huds., 114); Or., Qbn., Kmb. *kalta* 'small axe' (LGur., 342); Kon. *ḥali-tta* 'crutch, stick'; Baiso *kal-te* 'axe' (Lamb. Wol., 411); Dob. *takale* 'Grabstock ohne Klinge' (Dull., 245; <*ta-kale* or *ta-akale* <*ta-ʔakal-*, with prefixed *t-*?).

Om. N.: Wol., Kačama *kaal-ta* 'axe', Dawro, Gamu *kal-ta* id., Dače, Zaisse, Koyra *kallo* 'stick, club' (Lamb. Wol., 411).

25. Afras. *kwr (Ch., Cu.) ~ *ʔkr (Sem.) 'to cultivate', *ʔa/ikkār- 'labourer' (Sem, Eg.) ~ *kiry- ~ *kVw/ʔ Vr- 'garden, cultivated field' (Akk., Ch. W., Eg.)

Sem. (1): Akk. *ikkaru, inkaru* (Nuzi) 'ploughman, farm labourer; farmer, small farmer; plough animal (Nuzi)' OAkk on (CAD *i*, 49; AHw, 368; acc. to both sources, from Sum ENGAR, which is hardly so in view of the comparative data); Hbr. *ʔikkār* 'agricultural worker without land' (HAL, 47); Syr. *ʔakkār-* 'agricola', *ʔkr* 'arravit, agrum coluit' (Brock., 20); Mnd. AKR 'to plough, dig, cultivate' (DM, 18); *ʕkara* 'peasant, husbandman, tiller of soil' (DM, 349); Arb. *ʔakr-* 'action de creuser la terre, une fosse; action de laborer la terre', *ʔakkār-* 'qui creuse la terre, fossoyeur; laboureur' (BK 1, 42); *ʔkr* 'labourer (le sol), le creuser' (Belot 1929, 11); Amh. *akkärä* 'to renew the land by ploughing and sowing' (LGur., 593); Chaha *t-akärä*, Enn., Gyeto *t-ākärä*, End. *t-ākkärä* 'to build a house and cultivate the field around it for the first time' (LGur, 595). (The Hbr. and Arm. forms and, probably, Arb. *ʔakkār-* may eventually be Akk. loanwords, in which case the Arm. and Arb. verbs should be analyzed as an exceptional instance of an 'artificial' reverse primary verb derivation from an agent noun *ʔi/akkār-* derived, in its turn, from Sem. *ʔkr* 'to cultivate, plough' preserved in Amh. and Gur.)

Sem. (2): Akk. *kirû (kiriu)* 'garden, orchard, palm grove' OAkk. on (CAD *k*, 411; AHw, 485; acc. to von

Soden, from Sum.).

Ch. (1) W. **kVwVr-* ~ **kuHVr-* 'farm, fields': Bol. *koori*, Ngm. *kɔ̀rì* (Kraft); Tng. *korok* (Jungraithmayr 1992, 102; redupl. <*kVrkVr-*); Pero *kuurì* (Frajzyngier 1985, 68); Krf. *kuru* 'fields, farm' (Jung. CLR, II, 134).

Ch. (2) C. **kwr* ~ **krw* 'to hoe': Mofu *kərw*; Lame *kura* 'to hoe, prepare field for sowing' (HSED, No. 26).

Ch. (3) **kawira(-mi)-* 'hoe' (*-mi* is an instrumental suffix): W.: Hs. *kórámḗ* 'long-handled hoe' (Stolbova 1996, 71; reconstructed as **qoram-*, see No. 21 above); Ngz. *kùrəm*; C.: Hona *kūra*, Lame *kârúa*, Bnn. *kàwirà* (Kraft); Fali (Bwagira) *ta-kurmi-n* 'hoe' (in Stolbova 1996, 71 reconstructed as **qoram-*).

Ch. (4) W. **kwr* 'to reap': Bol. *kur* 'to reap', Tng. *korot* 'the clearing of fields' (Jungraithmayr 1991, 102); Pero *káwrò* 'to glean' (Frajzyngier 1985, 35); Ron **karat* 'to harvest' (Skinner 1996, 133).

Ch. (5) W. **kVwir-* 'sickle': Tng. *kwirì*, Brm. *kòr* (Kraft); C.: Mofu-Gudur *kərw* 'couper l'herbe avec une faucille pour préparer un nouveau champ'.

Eg. (1): *ikr* 'earth-god *Aker*' (determined with the ideogram 'patch of land') Pyr. (EG I, 22). Originally 'The Labourer'?

Eg. (2): *k:ry* 'Gärtner' late MK (EG V, 108).

Cu. S.: **kur-* 'to cultivate': Ir., Al. *kurumo* 'hoe', Asa *kurim-*, Maʔa *-kúru* 'to cultivate' (Ehret 1980, 247).

Cf. Militarev 1990, 75; differently in HSED, Nos. 26, 70, 1483 and Takács 1999, 68.

26. Afras. *ladd- ~ *lVʔVd- 'plot of land (of a specific status)'

Sem.: Akk. *ludû*, an administrative designation of a field (probably a field, on which specific work obligations have to be performed) OB on (CAD *l*, 1238); 'eine Art Saatfeld' (AHw, 561; <*lVdw/y-*); Arb. *ladīdat-* 'jardin couvert de verdure et de fleurs' (BK 2, 982; with a meaning shift?).

Ch. E.: Jegu *lóód* 'field' (Jung. 125; <*laHad-*).

Eg. *i:d.t* 'Art Feld' MK (EG I, 35), 'tract of land' (Faulkner 1962, 10), *i:dw.t* 'Viehweiden' 19 Din. (EG I, 35) < *lʔd*?

146

Cu. E.: Or. *laddaa* 'one person's area, property' (Gragg 1982, 259).

Cf. HSED, No. 1633: Jegu; Eg.; Or.

27. Afras. **mVrr-* 'hoe'; **mrr, *my/?r* 'to hoe, farm'

Sem.: Akk. *marru* 'spade, shovel' OB on (CAD *m*, 287; AHw, 612; acc. to both sources, from Sum. *MAR*; the Akk. term is commonly thought to be a loan in Syr. and Arb.; however, the obviously related, not borrowed, Amh. and Gur. as well as other Afras. forms confirm a Semitic and, eventually, Afrasian origin of the Akk. *marru* therefore to be regarded as a source for the Sum. *MAR*), *mayāru* 'to plough without seeder; land ploughed with the *m.*-plough' SB on (CAD *m*, 120; AHw, 587); Syr. *marr-*, *ma?r-* 'marra, pala ferrea vel ligo' (Brock., 400); Arb. *marr-* 'pelle en fer' (BK 2, 1083); Amh. *märämmärä* 'to dig', Gur. **mirämärä* 'to plough a field for the third time' (LGur., 422; redupl.).

Ch. W.: Bol. *mar-*, Dera *marra*, Ngm. *mira* (<**myr*) 'to hoe', Ang. *mār* 'to farm', Sura *máar* (<**maHar-*), Ank. *màr*, Ngm. *marra* 'farm', E.: Smr. *mîrí* 'hoe' (Jung. CLR, II, 134; Stolbova 1987, 233).

Eg.: *mr* 'als Schriftzeichen: die hölzerne Hacke' Old Eg. (EG II, 98).

Cu. E.: Had. *morāra* 'the hook of the plough' (LGur., 423).

Cf. Militarev 1984a, 60; differently in HSED, Nos. 1738, 1739.

28. Afras. **ngl* 'to reap' (> **mi/a-ngal-* 'sickle' Sem.) ~ **nVgi/ula(-t)-* 'sickle' (Ch.)

Sem.: Akk. *niggallu, ningallu* 'sickle' OB, OA on (CAD *n2*, 213; AHw, 787; acc. to both sources, from Sum.; likely <**mi-ngal-*); Hbr. *maggāl*, Jud. *maggəl-*, Syr. *maggalət-* id. (HAL, 545); Mnd. *manglia* 'sythes' (DM, 247); Arb. *nӡl* 'faucher (les céréales), labourer (la terre)' (Belot 1929, 807); *minӡal-* 'faucille de moissonneur' (BK 2, 1208). All <**mi/a-ngal-* 'sickle', an instrumental noun derived from the verb **ngl* 'to reap' likely preserved in Arb.

Ch. **nVgi/ul(-at)-*: W.: Miya *ngəlatə*, Wrj. *ngəlatə-na*, Kry. *ngaləta* 'sickle' (Skinner 1977, 39); C.: Nj. *ngîla* 'knife, sword', Gude *ŋgíla* 'knife' (Kraft); E.: Mig. *?àngùl* 'faucille' (Jungraithmayr & Adams 1992, 66;

with *?a-* prefixed).

29. Afras. **skk, *swk, *skw/y/?* 'to cultivate, to hoe and sow'

Sem.: Akk. *šakāku* 'to harrow' OA, OB on (CAD *š1*, 113; AHw, 1134), *šikkatu* 'harrowed land' OB (CAD *š2*, 433; AHw, 1234); (?) Sab. *s₁kt*, a proper name probably meaning 'plough' or 'harrow' (in: *?hl ḥrt s₁ktn* Conti Rossini 1931, 195; the interpretation of *s₁k-t* as 'plough' or 'harrow' and the whole context as 'folk ploughing with a plough or harrow' is highly hypothetic).

(?) Brb.: Zmr., Iger. *səkka*, Tfl. *ta-skki-t* 'soc de la charru', Mz. *skkə-t* 'charru', *skka* 'labourer' (Laoust 1920, 282, 285; all these forms may, or may not, be Arb. loans, cf. Arb. *sikkat-* 'soc de la charru' BK 1, 1112, likely borrowed from Arm. *sikkat-* 'peg, nail, ploughshare', cf. Kaufman 1974, 91, stemming from Sem. **sikk-at-* < Afras. **cikk-at-*).

Ch. **swk ~ *skw*: W.: Hs. *šuka* 'to sow (i.e. place seed in ground and cover with soil)' (Bargery 1934, 944); *sàkwa-mī* 'a long-handled hoe used at sowing time' (Bargery 1934, 888); *soke* 'to reap corn by uprooting the whole plant with a special instrument' (Bargery 1934, 951); Sura *sak* 'to hoe, plough', Tng. *suk* 'to plough' (Stolbova 1987, 177: <**sak⁽ʷ⁾-*); C.: Vulum *súki*, Msg. *suki, soká* 'faire le trou avant de semer', Mbr. *čók* 'to sow' (Takács 1999, 236); cf. Bura group **ŝakw-*, Gude *ŝakwa*, Lame *ŝukwēi* 'sickle' (Skinner 1996, 186; **ŝ-* <**s-* in C. Ch.? Cf. Stolbova 1996, 55). Cf. E. **sūk-* 'grenier': Bid., Mok. (Skinner 1996, 239).

Eg. *sk:* 'pflügen (mit dem Pflug, mit der Hacke)' Pyr. (EG IV, 315–16), 'der Ertrag der Feldbestellung, die Ernte' MK (EG IV, 316); *sty* 'säen, ausstreuen' Pyr. (EG IV, 346); <**sk?/y*.

Om. N.: Sheko *šookk-* 'säen', Kf. *šok* 'to sow', Bw. *šookà* 'Saat; Same' (Lamberti 1993, 374–5); Mč. *šòkki* 'seed' (Leslau 1959, 50).

30. Afras. **sVkay/w-* 'land not cultivated actually, fallow' (very likely related to No. 29)

Sem.: Tgr. *šeka, šekät* 'field, meadow, valley', Tna. *šäka* 'water-meadow' (LH, 222).

Brb. N.: **su/ik(V)y*: Bmrn. *i-ssuki*, Ntf., Zmr. *i-ssîki*, Tfl. *a-ssîki*, Izd. *isiki* (pl. *isak-at-ən*), Izy. *a-siki*, Qbl. *a-suki*, Shw. *a-m-suki* 'jachère' (Laoust 1920, 261–2).

Ch. W.: Hs. *šeka* 'a piece of waste, uncultivated land inside a compound' (Bargery 1934, 935); C.: Log. *skò* 'field, farm' (Jung. CLR, II, 135, after Bouny).

(?) Cu. C.: Bil. *šákā, šékā* 'Ebene, Steppe' (Reinisch 1887, 319; probably from Eth.).

31. Afras. *ȝVry/ʔ/ʕ- ~ *ɝVry/ʔ/ʕ- 'seed, sowing, sown field', *ȝry/wʔ/ʕ ~ *ɝry/w/ʔ/ʕ 'to sow, cultivate' (related to, or contaminated with, No. 32?)

Sem.: Akk. *zēru* (*zarʔu*) 'seed (of cereals and of other plants); acreage, arable land' OAkk. on (CAD *z*, 89); Ugr. *d/ḏrʕ* 'simiente, grano de siembta, sementera; semilla', *ḏrʕ* 'sembrar, diseminar' (DLU, 137); Hbr. *zrʕ* 'to sow', *zäraʕ* 'seed', Ph., Yaud. *zrʕ*, Arm. Bib. *zəraʕ*, Emp., Eg. *zrʕ* 'seed, descendance' (HAL, 1867–8); Jud. *drʕ* 'to sow', *dəraʕ, darʕ-* 'seed, produce, offspring' (Ja., 324), *zaraʕ, zarʕ-* 'seed', *zrʕ* 'to strew, sow' (Ja., 414); Syr. *zrʕ* 'seminavit', *zarʕā* 'semen' (Brock., 207); Mnd. *ZRA* 'to sow, scatter' (DM, 170); *zira* 'seed, semen' (DM, 167); Arb. *ḏry/w* 'répandre la semence (en semant), semer' (BK 1, 771); *ḏurat-* 'dorra, espèce de millet' (BK 1, 772); *ḏrʔ* 'ensemencer (la terre)' (BK 1, 767); *zrʕ* 'semer, répandre la semence; ensemencer un champ de quelque graine', *zurʕ-* 'semence; céréales sur pied, champ cultivé' (BK 1, 124); Sab. *m-ḏrʔ-t* 'sown field, sown ground' (SD, 40); Gez. *zarʔa, zarʕa* 'to seed, sow, scatter seed', *zarʔ* 'seed, seedling, plantation', Tgr. *zärʔa*, Tna *zärʔe*, Amh., Arg., Gur. **zärra*, Har. *zäraʔa*, Gaf. *zärrä* 'to seed, sow' (LGz., 642); Gur. **zär* 'grain, seed' (LGur., 713); Mhr. *zūra* '(plants) to grow', *ha-zrē* 'to cultivate', S. Mhr. *zərēt* 'plantation, cultivated area' (JM, 469); *dəráyyət* 'offspring' (JM, 81); Jib. *zéraʕ* '(plants) to grow', *ezóraʕ* 'to plant many seeds', *zéraʕ* 'farmer' (JJ, 320); *dərrít* 'progeny, offspring' (JJ, 47) (cf. also Mhr. *dərēt* (JM, 82); Jib. *dérét* 'sorghum, *dhurah*' (JJ, 47), likely Arabisms); Soq. *deri* 'semence' (LS, 135).

Ch. W.: Pero *ȝúrà* 'groundnuts' (Frajzyngier 1985, 34; no other voiced sibilant or affricate in Pero to render **ȝ* or **ɝ*).

Eg.: *z*: 'Bez. der achtel Arure, acht Aruren Acker' Gr., late Eg. (EG III, 411), 'Art Acker' Gr. (EG III, 414); <**ȝVr* or **ɝVr*.

Cu. **ȝVrʔ/y/w-* or **ɝVrʔ/y/w-* 'seed' ~ **ȝyr/*ȝry* or **ɝyr/*ɝry* 'to sow, cultivate': N.: Beja *deráʔ* 'Samen' (Reinisch 1895, 70; unless an Arabism; cf. *sérʔa* id., *seraʔ* 'säen' Reinisch 1895, 204; acc. to Takács 1999, 267–8, Afras. **ȝ* and **ɝ* yield Beja *d* and *y* while acc.

to Dolgopolsky 1973, 326, Afras. **ȝ* > Beja *s/š* and Afras. *ɝ* > Beja *d*); C.: Khmr. *zürû* 'Weizen' (Reinisch 1884, 411); *zir-* 'to sow', Kem. *zar-* id., Aw. *zer*; E.: Gid. *zare*, Kmb., Had. *zare-tta*, Alaba *zari-tᵃ*, Afar *diriyi*, Saho *dara* 'seed', *-idiriy-* 'to cultivate' (Lamb. Wol., 562).

(?) Om. N. **ȝVry-* or **ɝVry-* 'seed' ~ **ȝyr* or **ɝyr* 'to sow': Wol. *zer-* 'to spread, to seed'(Lamb. Wol., 561); *zere-tta*, Malo *zere-ts*, Gamu, Dače *zere-ttsi*, Bencho *zar* 'seed', Kačama *zeer-* 'to sow' (Lamb. Wol., 562). Acc. to Lamb. Wol., 561–2, all Cu. and Om. forms are borrowed from Eth., though a wide spread of these forms in three branches of Cu. rather speaks for their Afras. origin; borrowing of the Om. forms from Eth. or E. Cu. is possible.

32. Afras. *ɝrr/w/y/ʔ ~ *wɝr 'to scatter, spread (seed), winnow' (related to, or contaminated with, No. 31?)

Sem.: Akk. *zarû* 'to sow seed broadcast; scatter, sprinkle; winnow' OB on (CAD *z*, 70); Hbr. *zry* 'to scatter, winnow' (HAL, 280); Jud. *dry, drʔ* 'to scatter, strew; winnow' (Ja., 322); *zry, zrʔ* 'to scatter' (Ja., 413; borrowed from Hbr.?); Syr. *drʔ* 'sparsit, dispersit', *madrəy-* 'vannus' (Brock., 165); Mnd. *DRA* 'to scatter (e.g. the yearly harvest, the seed)' (DM, 114); Arb. *dry/w* 'vanner, nettoyer (le grain) en le lançant au vent avec une pelle ou avec un van' (BK 1, 771); Gez. *zarawa* 'to scatter, spread around, disperse'; Tna *zäräwä* 'to scatter', *(ʔa)zräwä, (ʔa)zräyä* 'to winnow'; Amh. *(a)zärra* 'to winnow, scatter' (LGz., 644); Har. *(a)zōra* 'to winnow' (Leslau 1963, 167); Gur. **(a)zärä* 'to winnow grain by letting it fall from above the head' (LGur., 713); Mhr. *dər* 'to spread out; to spread (gravy, curry, seed)' (JM, 47); Jib. *derr* 'to spread out', *dóttər* 'to be spread around (as, e.g. rice, sugar)' (JJ, 47; *-t-* stem).

Brb. **uzzar* 'vanner': Ntf. *a-z-úzzər* 'le vannage; action de séparer le grain de la paille broyée en le lançant en l'air à l'aide d'une fourche, puis d'une pelle', Zkara, Snus *s-úzzər* 'vanner', Zmr., Qbl. *a-zu-zər* 'vannage' (Laoust 1920, 392); Ayr, E.Wlm. *uzzar* 'ê. versé sur le sol ou sur une natte pour que le vent emportes les débris de paille/les déchets/la poussière (grains des céréales, après le battage); ê. versé (en général)' (Alojaly 1980, 216).

(?) Eg.: *dy.w.t* 'Arbeiterin auf dem Gut bei der Ernte: Worflerin' OK (EG V, 421) <**ɝVr-w-t*? For Eg. *d* ~ Sem. *d* <Afras. **ɝ*, cf.: (1) Eg. **ıdn* 'ear' OK ~ Sem. **ʔudin-* id.; (2) Eg. *dbḥ* '(food) offering' MK ~ Sem.

*ḏVbḥ- 'sacrifice' ~ Ch. E.: Bid. *ziib* 'faire les premiers sacrifices avant de manger les nouvelles récoltes' ~ Cu. E.: Som. *dabaaḥ* 'slaughter'; (3) Eg. *db* 'jackal' CT, *z:b id.* OK ~ Sem. *ḏiʔb-* 'wolf, jackal'.

References

Abdel-Massih, E., 1971. *A Computerized Lexicon of Tamazight.* Ann Arbor (MI): The University of Michigan.

Abraham, R.C., 1962. *Somali-English Dictionary.* London: University of London Press.

Abraham, R.C., 1965. *Dictionary of the Hausa Language.* London: University of London Press.

Agostini, F., A. Puglielli, C.M. Siyaad, R. Ajello, G. Banti, B. Bruno, L. Maffi & B. Panza (eds.), 1985. *Dizionario Somalo-Italiano.* Rome: Gangemi editore.

Alojaly, G., 1980. *Lexique touareg-français.* Copenhagen: Akademisk Forlag.

Bargery, G.P., 1934. *A Hausa–English Dictionary and English–Hausa Vocabulary.* London: Oxford University Press.

Barreteau, D. & A. Brunet, 2000. *Dictionnaire Mada.* Berlin: Dietrich Riemer.

Bassano, F. da, 1918. *Vocabolario tigray-italiano e repertorio italiano-tigray.* Rome: Casa editrice italiana & C. de Luigi.

Basset, R., 1909. *Mission au Sénégal,* tome I. (Étude sur le dialecte zenaga.) Paris: Ernest Leroux.

Behnstedt, P., 1992–. *Die nordjemenitischen Dialekte,* vol. 2: *Glossar.* Wiesbaden: Ludwig Reicher Verlag.

Belot, J.B., 1929. *Vocabulaire arabe-français à l'usage des étudiants.* Beyrouth: Librairie orientale.

Bender, M.L., 1994. Aroid (South Omotic) lexicon. *Afrikanistische Arbeitspapiere* 38, 133–62.

Biella, J.C., 1982. *Dictionary of Old South Arabic. Sabaean Dialect.* (Harvard Semitic Studies 25.) Chico (CA): Scholars Press.

Blachère, R., M. Chouémi & C. Denizeau, 1964–. *Dictionnaire arabe–français–anglais.* Paris: Maisonneuve and Larose.

Bronzi, P., 1919. *Frammento di fonologia berbera.* Bologna: Gamberini e Parmeggiani.

Cerulli, E., 1938. *Studi etiopici III. Il linguaggio dei Giangerò ed alcune lingue Sidama dell'Omo (Basketo, Ciara, Zaissè).* Rome: Instituto per l'Oriente.

Cohen, D., 1970–. *Dictionnaire des racines sémitiques ou attestées dans les langues sémitiques.* Paris: La Haye; Leuven: Peeters.

Cohen, M., 1947. *Essai comparatif sur le vocabulaire et la phonétique du chamito-sémitique.* Paris: Librairie ancienne Honoré Champion.

Conti Rossini, C., 1912. La langue des Kemant en Abyssine, in *Kaiserliche Akademie der Wissenschaften. Schriften der Sprachenkommission IV.* Vienna: Kommission bei Alfred Hölder, I–XII, 1–316.

Conti Rossini, K., 1931. *Chrestomathia arabica meridionalis epigraphica edita et glossario instructa.* Rome: Instituto per l'Oriente.

Dallet, J.-M., 1982. *Dictionnaire kabyle-français. Parler des At*

Mangellat (Algérie). Paris: Société d'études linguistiques et anthropologiques de France.

Destaing, E., 1920. *Etude sur la Tachelḥît du Soûs* I: *Vocabulaire français-berbère.* Paris: Ernest Leroux.

Diakonoff, I., 1981. Early Semites in Asia: agriculture and animal husbandry according to linguistic data (VIIIth–IVth Millennia BC). *Altorientalische Forschungen* VIII, 23–74.

Dolgopolsky, A., 1973. *Comparative-Historical Phonetics of Cushitic.* Moscow: Nauka.

Ehret, C., 1979. On the antiquity of agriculture in Ethiopia. *Journal of African History* 20, 2.

Ehret, C., 1980. *The Historical Reconstruction of Southern Cushitic Phonology and Vocabulary.* Berlin: Dietrich Reimer.

Ehret, C., 1987. Proto-Cushitic Reconstruction. *Sprache und Geschichte in Afrika* 8, 7–180.

Ehret, C., E.D. Elderkin & D. Nurse, 1989. Dahalo lexis and its sources. *Afrikanistische Arbeitspapiere* 18, 1–49.

Faulkner, R.O., 1962. *A Concise Dictionary of Middle Egyptian.* Oxford: Clarendon Press.

Foucauld, le père C. de., 1951–52. *Dictionnaire touareg-français* 1–4. Paris: Imprimerie nationale de France.

Frajzyngier, Z., 1985. *A Pero-English and English-Pero Vocabulary.* Berlin: Dietrich Reimer.

Gragg, G.B., 1982. *Oromo Dictionary.* East Lansing (MI): Michigan State University.

Heine, B., 1978. The Sam Languages: a history of Rendille, Boni and Somali. *Afroasiatic Linguistics* 6/2, 23–116.

Heine, B., 1979. Some cultural evidence on the early Sam-speaking people of Eastern Africa. *Sprache und Geschichte in Afrika* 3, 169–200.

Jungraithmayr, H., 1991 (in collaboration with N.A. Galadima & U. Kleinewillinghöfer). *A Dictionary of the Tangale Language.* Berlin: Dietrich Reimer.

Jungraithmayr, H. & A. Adams, 1992. *Lexique Migama.* Berlin: Dietrich Reimer.

Kane, T.L., 1990. *Amharic–English Dictionary.* Wiesbaden: Harassowitz.

Kaufman, S.A., 1974. *The Akkadian Influences on Aramaic.* Chicago (IL) & London: University of Chicago Press.

Kossmann, M., 1999. *Essai sur la phonologie du proto-berbère.* Cologne: Rüdiger Köppe.

Lamberti, M., 1993. *Die Shinassha-Sprache. Materialen zum Boro.* Heidelberg: Universitätsverlag C. Winter.

Lanfry, J., 1973. *Ghadamès II. Glossaire (Parler des Ayt Waziten).* Alger: Le Fichier Périodique.

Laoust, E., 1920. *Mots et choses berbères.* Paris: Augustin Challamel.

Laoust, E., 1932. *Siwa: son parler.* Paris: Librairie Ernest Leroux.

Leslau, W., 1959. *A Dictionary of Moča (Southwestern Ethiopia).* Berkeley & Los Angeles (CA): University of California Press.

Leslau, W., 1963. *Etymological Dictionary of Harari.* Berkeley & Los Angeles (CA): University of California Press.

Leslau, W., 1997. *Ethiopic Documents: Argobba. Grammar and Dictionary.* Wiesbaden: Harassowitz.

Militarev, A., 1984a. Afrasian–Sumerian contacts in lexicon, in *Preprints of the Conference 'Language Recon-struction and Prehistory of the East'* 1. Moscow: Nauka, 58–61.

Militarev, A., 1984b. Comparative-historical Afrasian stud-ies today: what light can they throw on the prehis-tory?, in *Preprints of the Conference 'Language Reconstruction and Prehistory of the East'* 3. Moscow: Nauka, 3–26.

Militarev, A., 1990. Evidence of Proto-Afrasian cultural lexicon, in *Proceedings of the Fifth International Hamito-Semitic Congress 1987*, vol. 1. Vienna: Institut für Afrikanistik, 73–86.

Militarev., A., 1995. Sumerians and Afrasians. *Journal of Ancient History* 2, 113–27.

Militarev, A., 1996. Home for Afrasian: African or Asian? Areal linguistic arguments, in *Cushitic and Omotic Languages: Proceedings of the Third International Sym-posium*, eds. C. Griefenow-Mewis & R.M. Voigt. Co-logne: Rüdiger Köppe Verlag, 13–32.

Militarev, A., 2000. Towards the chronology of Afrasian (Afroasiatic) and its daughter families, in Renfrew *et al.* (eds.), 267–307.

Militarev, A. & L. Kogan, 2000. *Semitic Etymogical Diction-ary*, vol. 1: *Anatomy of Man and Animals*. Münster: Ugarit Verlag.

Militarev, A. & V. Shnirelman, 1984. Towards the problem of locating the early Afroasiatic speakers, in *Preprints of the Conference 'Language Reconstruction and Prehis-tory of the East'* 2. Moscow: Nauka, 35–53.

Militarev, A. & V. Shnirelman, 1988. *The Problem of Proto-Afrasian Home and Culture: an Essay in Linguo-Ar-chaeological Reconstruction. Paper to be read at the 12th International Congress of Anthropological Sciences (Zagreb, Yugoslavia, 1988)*. Moscow: Nauka.

Militarev, A. & S. Starostin, 1984. Common Afroasiatic and North Caucasian cultural lexicon, in *Preprints of the Conference 'Language Reconstruction and Prehis-tory of the East'* 3. Moscow: Nauka, 34–43.

Militarev, A., V. Orel & O. Stolbova, 1989. Hamito-Semitic cultural lexicon: dwelling, in *Materials for Discussion at the International Conference 'Linguistic Reconstruc-tion and Prehistory of the East'* 1. Moscow: Nauka, 137–58.

Nicolas, F., 1953. *La langue berbère de Mauritanie*. Dakar: Institut Français d'Afrique Noire.

Nicolas, F., 1957. Vocabulaires ethnographiques de la Tamâjeq des Iullemmeden de l'est (Touâreg de la Colonie de Niger, Afrique Occidentale Française). *Anthropos* 52, 49–63, 564–80.

Olderogge, D., 1952. The origin of the peoples of Central Sudan. *Soviet Ethnography* 2, 23–38.

Parker, E.M. & R.J. Hayward, 1985. *An Afar–English–French Dictionary*. London: School of Oriental and African Studies, University of London.

Prasse, K.-G., 1969. *A propos de l'origine de H touareg*

(tahaggart). (Det Kongelige Danske Videnskabernes Selskab. Historisk-filosofiske meddelelser 43/3.) Copenhagen: the Royal Danish Academy of Sciences and Letters.

Reinisch, L., 1884. Die Chamir-Sprache in Abessinien II. Chamir-deutsches Wörterbuch. *Sitzungberichte der Kaiserlichen Akademie der Wissenschaften. Phil.-hist. Klasse* 106, 330–450.

Reinisch, L., 1885. Die Quarasprache in Abessinien II. Quarisch-deutsches Wörterbuch. *Sitzungberichte der Kaiserlichen Akademie der Wissenschaften. Phil.-hist. Klasse* 109/1, 3–152.

Reinisch, L., 1886. Die ʕAfar-Sprache II. *Sitzungberichte der Kaiserlichen Akademie der Wissenschaften. Phil.-hist. Klasse* 113.

Reinisch, L, 1887. *Die Bilin-Sprache 2. Wörterbuch der Bilin-Sprache*. Vienna: Alfred Hölder.

Reinisch, L., 1890. *Wörterbuch der Saho-Sprache*. Vienna: Alfred Hölder.

Reinisch, L., 1895. *Wörterbuch der Beḍauye-Sprache*. Vienna: Alfred Hölder.

Renfrew, C., A. McMahon & L. Trask (eds.), 2000. *Time Depth in Historical Linguistics*, vol. 1. (Papers in the Prehistory of Languages.) Cambridge: McDonald Institute for Archaeological Research.

Sasse, H.-J., 1979. The consonant phonemes of Proto-East-Cushitic (PEC): a first approximation. *Afroasiatic Lin-guistics* 7/1, 1–67.

Skinner, N., 1977. North Bauchi Chadic languages: com-mon roots. *Afroasiatic Linguistics* 4/1, 1–49.

Skinner, N., 1996. *Hausa Comparative Dictionary*. Cologne: Rüdiger Köppe Verlag.

Starostin, S., 2000. Comparative-historical linguistics and lexicostatistics, in Renfrew *et al.* (eds.), 223–65.

Stolbova, O., 1987. West Chadic comparative phonetics and lexicon, in *African Historical Linguistics*. Mos-cow: Nauka, 30–268.

Stolbova, O., 1996. *Studies in Chadic Comparative Phonol-ogy*. Moscow: Diaphragma publishers.

Stolbova, O., 2001. On Chadic Lateral Sibilants. Unpub-lished manuscript.

Takács, G., 1999. *Etymological Dictionary of Egyptian*, vol. 1: *a Phonological Introduction*. Leiden, Boston (MA) & Cologne: Brill.

Takács, G., 2001. *Etymological Dictionary of Egyptian*, vol. 2: *b-, p-, f-*. Leiden, Boston (MA) & Cologne: Brill.

Tomback, R.S, 1978. *A Comparative Semitic Lexicon of the Phoenician and Punic Languages*. PhD dissertation. Ann Arbor (MI): New York University.

Tourneux, H., C. Seignobos & F. Lafarge, 1986. *Les Mbara et leur langue*. Paris: Orstom.

Vycichl, W., 1983. *Dictionnaire étymologique de la langue copte*. Leuven: Peeters.

Wölfel, D.J., 1965. *Monumenta Linguae Canariae*. Graz: Akademische Druck- u. Verlagsanstalt.

Chapter 13

Transitions to Farming and Pastoralism in North Africa

Graeme Barker

In the case of North Africa, the 'demic diffusion' thesis for the beginnings of farming that was the focus of the 2001 Cambridge symposium was first explicitly formulated by J.D. Clark in 1962 and 1964, when he reviewed the first suite of radiocarbon dates from the region. Relatively few of the known Neolithic sites had at this time yielded radiocarbon dates, and fewer still had good C14 dates associated with clear evidence for farming in the form of bones and seeds of domestic species, so the agricultural status of the inhabitants often had to be assumed indirectly from inferences based on the presence of pottery and stone tools. In most of the areas where Neolithic sites had been found, the evidence for reliably-dated Mesolithic sites with good evidence for hunting, fishing, and gathering, was even poorer. Comparing the two sets of data, Clark concluded that the evidence indicated that farming began in North Africa as a result of a migration of a new people from the Near East who brought with them domesticated wheat, barley, sheep and goats. He argued that the dates indicated that these Neolithic colonists arrived at the Nile delta about 5000 BC, spread westwards into the Sahara by 4000 BC and southwards up the Nile valley to the Khartoum region by about 3000 BC, finally expanding into the Sahel by about 2000 BC. The environmental, demographic and social contexts of the initial dispersal were not clear but, as an explanation for the later spread, he postulated that desiccation in the Sahara would have pushed farmers southwards into the Sahel, an idea that has stayed firmly in the literature ever since (Clark 1984; Harlan 1989; 1993; Shaw 1984; Stemler 1980; 1984).

At about the same time, Greenberg published his major study of modern and historically-attested African languages, in which he grouped them into four major language groups on the basis of common lexical and grammatical elements: Afroasiatic, Nilo-Saharan, Niger-Congo, and Khoisan (Greenberg 1966). North Africa was the primary focus of the Afroasiatic language family (Fig. 13.1), the term proposed because of the links noted between North African languages within groups such as Berber, Egyptian, Cushitic and Chadic, and the Semitic languages of the Near East. Khoisan, the smallest of the four language groups defined by Greenberg, is spoken today by people in and around the Kalahari Desert in southern Africa who were or have recently been living as hunter-gatherers, and the absence of words for crops, animals, or agricultural activities was taken to indicate that the historical development of Khoisan had always been associated with people who were not farmers (Ehret 1976). This contrasted with the other three, much larger, language groups, all of which were characterized by a set of shared agricultural terms amongst their respective members (Ehret 1984; Ehret & Posnansky 1982). Hence successive linguists have concluded that the speakers of the originating languages from which the various members of these three language groups were ultimately descended were likely to have been acquainted with domestic crops and animals probably from the beginning. In the case of Afroasiatic, linguists have variously favoured the Near East or North Africa as the focus of origin (Blench 1993; Militarev this volume). A Near Eastern origin obviously chimes best with the archaeological model of Neolithic demic diffusion from the Near East into North Africa. In this model, the Neolithic farmers who spread into the Nile valley from the Near East and thence colonized the upper Nile and the Sahara, were Proto-Afroasiatic speakers, thus introducing the Afroasiatic language group into North Africa, a classic example of the agricultural/linguistic dispersal model that was the focus of the Cambridge symposium.

The primary focus of this chapter is to review the archaeological evidence for the beginnings of farming in North Africa (Fig. 13.2). As the title of my

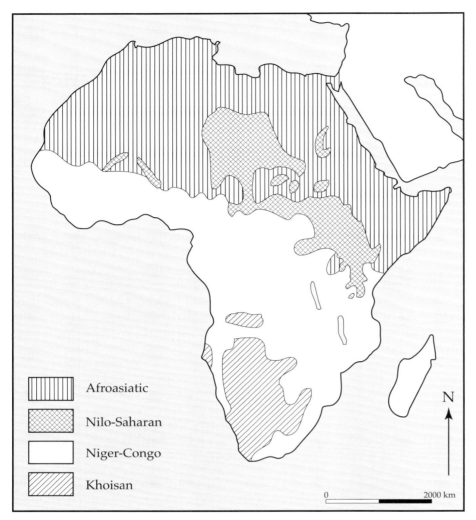

Figure 13.1. *The distribution of Africa's major language families. (Simplified after Greenberg 1966.)*

peratures were lower than to-day by nine degrees centi-grade, and Saharan dunefields extended some 500 kilometres further south than their present-day limit (Grove 1993). Large parts of the interior of the region became uninhabitable, and hunter-gatherers retreated to the better-watered regions bordering the Sahara, especially the Nile valley. The Nile at this time was a small sluggish river some fifteen metres higher than its present level, seasonally flooding a narrow band of marshes and meadows on either side.

Most late Palaeolithic sites in the Nile valley are very small, but there are indications that many locations were repeatedly occupied, presumably on a seasonal basis. A major activity was collecting plant foods from the marshes and meadows. The site of Wadi Kubbaniya caused a great stir in the 1970s when domesticated barley, chickpeas and lentils were reported from levels dated to 18,000 years ago (Wendorf *et al.* 1976; 1979), but they were uncharred and AMS dating since then of some of the seeds has made it clear that they were intrusive (Wendorf *et al.* 1989). However, detailed analysis by Hillman (1989; Hillman *et al.* 1989) of the charred remains, which are certainly of late Palaeolithic date, has found evidence for the exploitation of a suite of seeds, fruits and vegetables that grow wild today in the Nile valley, especially nut-grass (*Cyperus rotundus*), a type of sedge. This would have been a good staple food: harvesting it regularly would have automatically increased its yields, as removing old woody tubers stimulates the production of young palatable tubers, and if people had disturbed the ground around it and removed competing plants, it would have been even more productive (Hillman 1989). The starch found on the grinders from the site suggests that tubers were more important than seeds in the vegetable diet, and coprolites indicate that infants were

paper suggests, I shall seek to demonstrate that the evidence reveals a much more complex process than demic diffusion by Neolithic farmers from the Near East, a process which primarily involved changes in subsistence practices amongst the indigenous population of hunter-fisher-gatherers in North Africa. Having discussed the archaeological evidence, I shall then comment on the issue of correlating archaeological and linguistic models, and also on the genetic evidence that is the third strand of data that we must now bring into our discussions of the origins and early development of farming in this region.

Late Pleistocene foraging

In North Africa, hyperaridity characterized the maximum cold stage about 18,000 years ago: average tem-

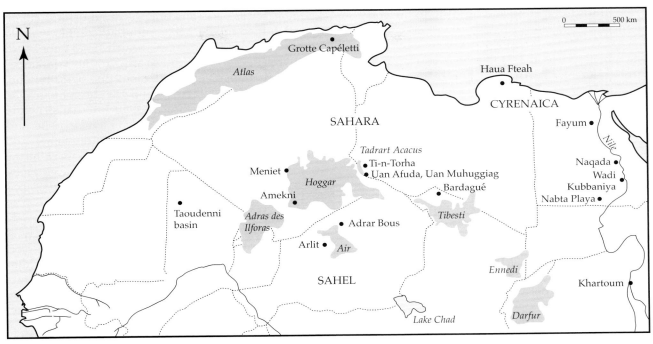

Figure 13.2. *North Africa, showing the principal regions and archaeological sites mentioned in the text.*

being weaned on a vegetable mush from plants like club-rush and chamomile (Hillman 1989).

The plants, however, were part of a broad-spectrum diet — people fished the river and hunted in the surrounding dunefields (Vermeersch *et al.* 1989). At Wadi Kubbaniya, for example, there were over 100,000 fishbones at the site, mainly of catfish (van Neer 1989). Birds were predominantly waterfowl such as ducks, coots and geese, probably caught variously by spears, nets and traps. Molluscs were collected such as *Unio*. The variety of game hunted included hare, ass, aurochs, gazelle, large antelopes and even hippopotamus (Gautier *et al.* 1980; Wendorf *et al.* 1988; 1989). Hillman (1989, 231) concluded from the wealth and diversity of the food remains at Wadi Kubbaniya that all-year-round occupation would have been possible at such sites, even if food was not stored.

Sites with similar artefact assemblages and faunas of game, waterfowl and fish, though without the abundance of plant remains of Wadi Kubbaniya, have been found from the Nile delta to the upper Nile and its tributaries such as the Atbara (Marks 1989; Marks *et al.* 1987; Peters 1990; Wendorf & Hassan 1980; Wendorf & Schild 1984). Pollen studies indicate that barley was growing in the lower Nile, and it is possible that in the Delta region at least barley was one of the grasses exploited by late Palaeolithic foragers (Williams 1984), but further south we must assume

that Nile marsh plants like those of Wadi Kubbaniya were the staple foods at this time.

Presumably coastal North Africa was also a refuge for late Palaeolithic populations, though most evidence for any such settlement will have been lost to subsequent sea-level rise. The occupants of the Haua Fteah cave in Cyrenaica hunted animals like hartebeest, aurochs, gazelle and, in particular, Barbary sheep (Higgs 1967; McBurney 1967), the latter also the main animal represented in the faunal samples at a number of contemporary sites in the Maghreb (Lubell 1984). Saxon *et al.* (1974) argued from sex and age ratios that people may have started to herd Barbary sheep at this time, but a detailed re-analysis of the Haua Fteah faunal material suggests that this is unlikely (Klein & Scott 1986): most of the sheep killed were young adult animals, but younger and older animals were also well represented in the faunal sample, a 'catastrophic' kill pattern thought to result from communal hunting methods such as driving animals over cliffs rather than individual hunters stalking selected animals, or herders selecting animals from a controlled flock. Similar kill patterns were found in the case of the Barbary sheep that formed the main prey at another Cyrenaican cave, Hagfet ed-Dabba. The Maghreb sites have also produced grinding stones and blades with 'sickle gloss', but unfortunately botanical remains have not been found to show what plants people were gathering (Lubell 1984).

Transitions to farming and herding in the early Holocene

The transition to the Holocene was characterized throughout North Africa by the relatively sudden development of significantly wetter climates than today, as the southern monsoonal belts shifted northwards. In the Taoudenni basin of northern Mali, for example, early Holocene rainfall was some 300–600 mm a year, compared with 5–50 mm today (Petit-Maire 1991). At the maximum, rainfall has been estimated variously at between five and fifteen times modern levels, and lakes were in places 100 metres higher than today (Grove 1993).

These extraordinary climatic shifts brought dramatic changes to the regime of the Nile, greatly increasing the force and unpredictability of its flooding cycle. People living along its banks had to become more mobile to respond to the dangers of flooding, but they continued to rely heavily on its fish, though harvesting them meant developing more sophisticated techniques of fishing involving deep-water fishing in the main channel as well as shallow-water techniques. Many faunal samples have numerous bones of Nile perch, a species that can grow to over 100 kilograms in weight (Hassan 1986; Vermeersch 1998; Wetterstrom 1993). Strong bone harpoons were developed for this fishing, though nets were probably used as well, and the large number of hearths at many camps suggests that much of the catch was smoked. The faunal samples show that hunting was practised both within the Nile valley and also on what are today the desert margins that were then savanna scrub and grassland — they include waterfowl, turtles, hare, gazelle, cattle, hartebeest, crocodile and hippopotamus.

The climatic amelioration allowed people to expand outwards from the Nile valley to depressions where permanent lakes formed, such as the Fayum and Nabta Playa, where they lived by a mix of hunting, fishing, and gathering plants such as sedges, *Polygonum* and *Rumex* (Wendorf & Schild 1980; Wenke & Casini 1989; Wenke *et al.* 1988). In Nabta Playa, though, there are indications of rather more substantial settlements, associated with pottery-making, by 6000 cal BC. Site E-76-6 here, for example, consisted of a series of hut floors, cooking hearths, and bell-shaped storage pits, arranged in two orderly lines (Wendorf *et al.* 1998). The first excavations yielded three cereals grains (of naked barley, and two- and six-row hulled barley), but since then some 40 varieties of plants have been identified, including legumes, *Scirpus*, *Rumex*, millet (*Panicum*),

Setaria, Zizyphus fruits and seeds, mustard, caper, unidentified tubers, and sorghum (Wasylikowa *et al.* 1993). The sorghum seeds, which have been AMS dated to *c.* 6000 cal BC and so are certainly contemporary with the settlement, are morphologically wild, but infra-red spectroscopy and gas chromatography show that they are closer in their internal structure to modern domesticated *Sorghum bicolor*. Wild sorghum grows in abundance today in the Sahel, and would have been as abundant in the Sahara in the early Holocene. It can be harvested efficiently by beating or shaking the seeds off the head into a basket (Harlan 1993), which would not have promoted the morphological changes that come with seed selection and planting. Given that modern wild and domestic sorghums are fully inter-fertile and cross-pollinate very easily, it seems very likely that wild sorghum was harvested by early Holocene foragers as a staple food plant for a very considerable period — without sickles, and without resultant morphological changes.

Like the debates regarding the wild or domestic (or intermediate) status of staple plant foods at this time, the early Holocene faunal samples from the eastern desert of Egypt also support conflicting views regarding the possibility of herding, in this case of cattle (Clutton-Brock 1989; Smith 1986; Wendorf *et al.* 1984). Gautier (1984) proposed that morphologically-domestic cattle were probably present here from very early in the Holocene, but the thesis was based on extremely fragmentary remains and Gautier later retracted the idea (Gautier 1987). Close & Wendorf (1992), however, have argued that, whilst the cattle bones at the early Holocene desert sites are of large animals, which would generally be taken as evidence of their belonging to wild cattle or aurochs (*Bos primigenius*), other factors suggest that they may have been herded. The frequency of animals such as hare and gazelle that need little water, and the absence of hartebeest which has roughly the same water needs as cattle, indicate that water was not abundant (later herders at Nabta Playa dug large wells to ensure an adequate water supply for their stock). Hence, Close & Wendorf concluded, the presence of cattle ought to imply that they were only there because people had brought them, from the Nile valley. The rarity of cattle bones, they argued, is because cattle were valued more alive than dead, though an argument based primarily on how few bones there are at this point gets rather tenuous!

The dramatic climatic amelioration of the early Holocene allowed Sahelian flora and fauna to colonize the interior of North Africa, and humans to follow, a process of 'forager demic diffusion' that seems to have been both rapid and comprehensive. Foraging populations colonized the better-watered highland areas of the Sahara, ranging from these onto the scrub and seasonal grassland of the intervening plains (Kuper 1993; Muzzolini 1993; Roset 1987; Smith 1980; 1984). Their material culture included microlithic flint industries, bone harpoons, and grindstones, associated with evidence for fishing, shellfish collection, and for hunting riverine animals like crocodiles, hippopotamus and turtles as well as savanna animals such as large and small antelopes and cattle. Plant foods collected included fruits, bulbs, nuts and grasses in the Maghreb (Roubet 1978), and grasses in the Sahara including wild sorghum and millet (Muzzolini 1993; Smith 1984). Pottery was also used from an early date, leading to debates years ago about whether these people should be classified as 'Mesolithic' or 'Neolithic', or as Sutton (1977) proposed for the Sahara and the Sahel at this time, 'Aqualithic'. Recent evidence, however, is producing major shifts in our understanding of the sophistication of the methods by which these early colonists of the Sahara were exploiting animals and plants.

Some of the most remarkable evidence has been retrieved from inter-disciplinary programmes of surveys and excavations by Italian teams in the Tadrart Acacus and the adjacent massif to its east, Messak Settafet (Barich 1984; 1987a,b; 1998; Cremaschi & di Lernia 1998a). In the early Holocene, caves in the Tadrart Acacus such as Uan Afuda and Thora were used as base camps by bands of foragers equipped with microlithic flint tools, who ranged out across the adjacent lowlands (now sand seas) to fish, kill waterfowl and other birds living near the lakes and pools, and hunt a range of small and medium-sized game, but especially Barbary sheep. By the seventh millennium BC, coinciding with the first drier oscillation, there are indications of more sedentary behaviour at Uan Afuda, with the construction of windbreaks and pen-like structures inside the cave. Furthermore, within the pen at Uan Afuda was a thick layer of ash, dung and straw, and micromorphological analysis showed that the dung derives from ovicaprids (di Lernia 1998a). The only ovicaprid bones in the faunal sample at this time are of Barbary sheep (Corridi 1998). The implication, as di Lernia (1998a,b) argues, is that these Saharan foragers were beginning to herd Barbary sheep, at least 500 years before other evidence for domestic animals in the locality.

The material remains left in the cave at this time included simple pottery decorated with im-pressed wavy lines, wooden tools (a suspension hook and a spatula), tools made of Barbary sheep horn, stone grinders, and fragments of baskets and cords, some of them with seeds of *Urochlea/Brachiaria* still attached to them. Partially-ground seeds were found in herbivore as well as human coprolites, further evidence for the stall-feeding of Barbary sheep (Castelletti *et al.* 1998). Other plant remains at the cave included wild millet (*Panicum/Setaria*), and there was a cache of stored Gramineae seed at Fozzigiaren cave. Cremaschi & di Lernia (1998b) therefore conclude that, as the first major arid phase of the Holocene developed in the seventh millennium BC, shrinking water sources and diminishing the amount of fish and marsh plant foods available, the foragers of the Tadrart Acacus not only intensified their use of seed plants but also started to manage Barbary sheep, stalling and feeding them when the natural food and water supplies for them were at their most meagre — the pollen in the dung at this and other caves indicates that it accumulated in the late winter and spring, the driest part of the year.

In short, the early Holocene foragers of the Nile valley and Saharan interior clearly fished, hunted, and gathered plants intensively, with pottery facilitating the storage and processing of these foods after about 6000 BC; they probably did not practise what we would recognize as horticulture and herding; but in both regions their attitudes to and manipulation of certain plants and animals seem to have had characteristics of both.

The developed commitment to farming and herding

In Egypt the first clear evidence for the systematic use of domestic plants and animals dates to the early fifth millennium BC, whilst comparable evidence further south is a thousand years later, in both cases as part of strategies that still relied heavily on fishing, hunting, and gathering wild plants (Hassan 1984; 1985; 1988; 1998; Wendorf & Hassan 1980; Wetterstrom 1993). By the early fourth millennium BC sites near Naqada have unequivocal evidence for herding in the form of pens floored with compacted dung, and emmer wheat, six-row barley and flax were grown, but again herding and cultivation were combined with fishing, hunting and gathering a range of wild plants (Litynska 1993; Wetterstrom 1993). At all these sites, 'domesticates offered merely another resource to be utilized in an overall generalized procurement strategy' (Brewer 1989, 171). In Egypt the major commitment to mixed farming only seems to have developed thereafter, in the early fourth millennium BC, alongside dramatic changes in settlement size and social complexity that presaged the emergence of the Pharoanic state a millennium later (Hassan 1984; Wengrow 2001).

In the Sahara there is evidence of a wetter oscillation or oscillations in the mid Holocene, though the overall trend was to increasing aridity, and the latter seems to have been the critical context in which the indigenous populations developed an increasing commitment to pastoralism. In the Tadrart Acacus, there were fragmentary remains of cattle from the sixth-millennium BC levels at Ti-n-Torha, the status of which is unclear, but domestic cattle, sheep and goats were certainly present at both Ti-n-Torha and Uan Muhuggiag in deposits dating to the fifth millennium BC (Gautier 1987; Gautier & van Neer 1982). However, pastoralism was practised alongside hunting, fishing, and gathering: the people using Ti-n-Torha and Uan Muhuggiag were eating fish, migratory birds, ungulates such as Barbary sheep, gazelle, and hartebeest, warthog and smaller game such as hyrax and porcupine (Corridi 1998), and they were collecting a range of plant foods including wild millet and sorghum, rhizomes, and various grasses, fruits, and seeds (Barich 1987a,b; Wasylikowa 1992; 1993). Although domestic cattle have also been reported from a sixth-millennium BC context at Bardagué in the Tibesti mountains (Barich 1998, 42), they do not seem to have been widespread in the Sahara until about 4000 BC or soon thereafter, when there are cattle not only in the Tadrart Acacus but also in the Aures mountains of Algeria (the Grotte Capélletti), Amekni and Meniet in southern Algeria, and Adrar Bous and Arlit in the Ténéré mountains of Niger (Gautier 1987).

The development of pastoralism seems to have been the context in which the interior basins of the Sahara were first used systematically, on a seasonal basis (Smith 1984). In many of these vast empty spaces there are enormous concentrations of what have been termed *Steinplatze* ('stone places'), small but dense collections of lithics, potsherds and grindstones, sometimes with charcoal and bone fragments of domestic animals (Aumassip 1987; Gabriel 1987; Muzzolini 1993). Some of these sites also have grooved stones which are thought to have been weights for rope traps or hobbles (Pachur 1991; Le Quellec 1990). There are pictures in Saharan rock art of both wild animals like giraffes and what are assumed to be domestic cattle with their legs haltered with such stones, and the Tuareg are known to have used weighted traps to catch game as well as to hobble stock. The balance of probability is that the

Neolithic pastoralists of the Sahara also used such stones for both trapping game and hobbling stock.

The most remarkable evidence left by these forager-herder societies, though, is their rock art (Caligari 1993). The wonderful images of animals such as crocodile and elephant were the first and most striking evidence for archaeologists that the Sahara had once been a verdant landscape far removed from its modern aridity. Most of the mountain massifs of the Sahara have rock walls, often associated with settlement sites such as rock shelters, decorated with incised and painted images. There is great variability in technique and motif. The primary classifications of these by Lhote (1959) and Mori (1960; 1965) suggested that the art began with incised images of wild animals such as buffalo, elephant, ostrich and crocodile being produced by early Holocene hunter-fisher-gatherers, so termed by Mori the Big Game, or Bubaline phase after the buffalo images. Later pastoralists, they argued, painted monochrome and then polychrome images of people herding livestock, especially cattle (the 'Pastoral' or 'Bovidian' phase), and within this broad repertoire there were also images of campsites, hunting, gathering, and of round-headed people dancing and performing what look like other rituals (hence Mori defined a 'Round Head' style or phase). The primary dating evidence for pastoralist art was the occurrence of fragments of painted rock that had fallen from painted images on the walls of the Uan Muhuggiag rock shelter into occupation deposits below dated to about 3000 BC.

In recent years, however, it has become increasingly clear from stylistic studies looking at details such as motif overprinting that there is no simple chronological separation between the images of wild and domestic animals — most are broadly contemporary, and date to the millennia of the mid Holocene when Saharan foragers were developing an increasing commitment to pastoralism (Le Quellec 1987; Muzzolini 1986; 1993). As Ingold (1988) has pointed out, the development by foragers of a commitment to herding animals is likely to have involved major transformations in the social relations of production and the ideology of prestige, for in most forager societies today hunters obtain prestige by demonstrating prowess in the hunt and generosity in distributing their kills to the rest of the band, whereas prestige in modern pastoralist societies comes from accumulating live animals and using them in competitive arrangements of gift-giving for bridewealth and such like. Whilst one-to-one analogies are clearly inappropriate, there is every reason to believe that

Saharan rock art, like recent San and Australian Aboriginal rock art (Lewis-Williams 1983; Lewis-Williams & Dowson 1990), was embedded in complex belief systems as the old ways of living became increasingly a 'landscape of memory' and the new ways of coping with an increasingly hostile environment meant both new ways of looking at the natural world and new kinds of social relationships. Smith (1993a,b) argues that Saharan pastoral art was probably produced by shamans in altered states of consciousness, perhaps in relation to initiation ceremonies of the kind undergone by young male Fulani pastoralists in recent times. Another recent study of central Saharan rock art has noted images of what seem to be rituals associated with baskets of seeds, others with tethered animals, males and females dancing together, people apparently levitating, and an image of a supernatural being spreading rain (Sansoni 1998).

It seems likely that Saharan pastoralism was combined with the gathering of seeds such as millet and sorghum between the fourth and the second millennia BC, but the extent to which, if at all, people also practised horticulture in the sense of preparing the ground, sowing seed, and nurturing the growing crop before harvest, is entirely unknown. The first evidence for significant agricultural intensification in the central Sahara is not until the beginning of the first millennium BC, when oases in southwest Libya became the foci for dense settlement by people we can identify as the Garamantes tribe known to us from the classical writers, whose cereal farming was sustained by irrigation using *foggara* (underground channel) technology (Mattingly *et al.* 1998; van der Veen 1992).

Discussion

Both Bar-Yosef and Hassan (this volume) favour the demic diffusion model for the North African Neolithic, arguing that domestic wheat and barley and domestic animals were introduced into Egypt about 6000 BC by PPNB farmers forced to evacuate the Levant in the face of climatic crisis. The extension of the model envisages this population then taking parts of that package (herding especially) westwards across the Sahara. It is true that there are significant environmental and cultural transformations in the archaeological record of Egypt and the Sahara at this time but, as I have discussed above, the longer-term perspective of forager behaviours in late Pleistocene and early Holocene North Africa does not chime easily with such a scenario for when,

how and why farming and pastoralism began in this region.

In the Nile valley, hunting, fishing and gathering sustained numerous and more or less sedentary populations in the closing millennia of the Pleistocene. With the climatic transformations of the early Holocene, these systems of forager subsistence rapidly incorporated intensive plant gathering, probably in part supported by 'horticulture-like' activities such as plant protection, selection, and/or tending (as in the case of recent Australian plant-collectors), though plant use was not of such a nature as to change the morphological characteristics of staple seed crops such as sorghum. If demic diffusion by PPNB farmers from the Levant was the primary process by which domesticates were introduced into Egypt, it is very odd that plant and animal agriculture then played such a minor role at the majority of 'their' Neolithic settlements compared with foraging. It is also striking that most people living in the Nile valley only developed a significant commitment to mixed farming much later, as one aspect of the post-Neolithic step changes in social complexity that presaged the emergence of the Pharoanic civilization.

The rapid colonization of the Sahara at the beginning of the Holocene was by foragers, not farmers, responding to the foraging opportunities created there by the sudden and dramatic development of a humid climate. The Tadrart Acacus data demonstrate that these foragers then responded to the beginnings of desertification two or three millennia later by intensifying plant gathering and trying new ways of managing key ungulates such as Barbary sheep and, perhaps, cattle. The ensuing short-lived wetter oscillation may have allowed a relaxation in these strategies, but the inexorable shift to aridity from the late seventh millennium BC onwards made the commitment to specialized pastoralism an increasingly attractive option. Given what we now know of the scale, ubiquity and adaptability of Saharan foraging through the early Holocene, the rapid, widespread and sudden development of pastoralism across the Sahara seems much more plausibly understood in terms of responses by these indigenous foraging populations to aridification than in terms of a westwards migration of pastoralists from the Nile valley. (And what happened to the existing forager population in the latter scenario?) The lack of evidence for such pastoralist societies in the Nile valley beforehand is noteworthy, as is the lack of evidence there for significant disjunctures in the settlement record suggesting either abandonment in the putative homeland, or the build up of population levels there as the trigger for a westwards migration. This is not to say that Nile valley and Saharan communities were not in contact with each other, far from it: the occurrence of Saharan materials such as ostrich egg shell and hippopotamus ivory in adjacent regions makes it clear that materials (and domesticates?) as well as ideas could move easily over enormous distances across North Africa at this time.

Although it has long been argued that domestic cattle were introduced first to the Nile valley from the Near East, and then spread westwards into the Sahara (Clark 1962; Clutton-Brock 1989; 1993; Hugot 1968), the appearance of bones of morphologically-domestic cattle in the Nile valley and the Sahara is in fact approximately synchronous, and wild cattle were present in both regions in the early Holocene (Smith 1980; 1986). Hence it is perfectly possible on the present evidence to argue that cattle were first domesticated in the Sahara and then were acquired by Nile populations, or vice versa, or that wild cattle were taken into domestication across the entire region as part of a single process (Chenal-Vélardé 1998). The situation regarding domestic sheep and goats is even less clear. It is often uncertain from publications of very fragmentary faunal remains whether Barbary sheep, or domestic sheep and goats, or both, are represented at a particular site. Domestic sheep and goats have normally been assumed to be exotic to North Africa and introduced from the Near East (Clutton-Brock 1993; Higgs 1967), but it is possible that they were being exchanged amongst hunter-gatherers in the central and western Mediterranean basin in the mid Holocene (Lewthwaite 1986), so it is possible that they entered North Africa via the Maghreb and the Sahara instead of or as well as from the Levant into the lower Nile. After decades of theorizing about how animal herding must have 'spread into' North Africa from the Near East, it is salutary to note that the discoveries of the Uan Afuda dung in the last few years, representing the earliest unequivocal evidence for herding in North Africa contemporary with PPNB villages in the Near East, are of the 'wrong' animal (the Barbary sheep) in the 'wrong' place (the central Sahara)!

In the same vein, wheat and barley may have been introduced to North Africa from the Near East, or they may have been indigenous to the lower Nile valley. Wetterstrom (1993; 1998) in fact has suggested that early Holocene foragers here may have started to cultivate these cereals to compensate for the unpredictability of the Nile flooding regime. This last point is particularly telling in terms of model-

ling transitions to farming as processes of change and acculturation rather than demic diffusion and replacement. Many theoretical discussions of the transition to farming start from the perspective that the advantages of farming would have been obvious to all but the most obdurate forager, and that under any kind of pressure they would have leapt at the opportunity to try to become farmers. Yet as Minnis (1985; 1992) and Wills (1992) have argued in the case of initial farming in the American Southwest, it is as likely that foragers incorporating aspects of plant and/or animal husbandry into their existing systems of subsistence were in fact endeavouring to maintain their existing way of life as trying to experiment with something new. Thus in the case of the cereals in the Nile valley, Wetterstrom suggested that 'domesticates were . . . a means to improve the foraging system by diversifying it rather than replacing it' (Wetterstrom 1993, 166). In this perspective the development of pastoralism by Saharan foragers would be regarded as a means to improve foraging systems there by specializing on animals well suited to coping with (increasing) aridity.

Like the archaeological evidence, the available genetic evidence appears to suggest specifically North African trajectories in terms of domestication histories. DNA studies of modern cattle suggest that African and European cattle diverged from a common ancestor over 20,000 years ago (Bradley & Loftus 2000). Both taurine (unhumped) and zebu (humped) cattle in Africa appear to have been domesticated in Africa, quite separate from cattle domestication in Europe, the Near East, and India (Loftus *et al.* 1994).

The linguistic evidence can also be reconciled with the 'non-demic diffusion' reading of the archaeological record. The disparate and contentious evidence for the date of the earliest Afroasiatic language ('Proto-Afroasiatic') points to an early Holocene or even late Pleistocene formation, certainly much earlier than the 6000 BC date identified by both Bar-Yosef and Hassan (this volume) as the context for PPNB Neolithic farmers migrating into North Africa from the Near East. Though linguistic scholars debate whether the language originated in North Africa or the Levant, we can at least point to the similarities in the respective archaeological records of the Natufian culture of the Levant and of contemporary foragers in coastal North Africa across the late Pleistocene and early Holocene boundary (Camps-Fabrer 1989; MacDonald 1998, 58). The theory that the earliest speakers of the language were agriculturalists rests on the assumption that terms identified in Proto-Afroasiatic such as grains and grasses and grinders must automatically refer to domesticated species and their processing rather than to wild plant collecting, whereas Blench (1993) and Ehret (this volume) point out that a correlation with wild grass collectors is in fact just as likely in the formative stages of this language group. Very similar arguments have also been put forward for the Nilo-Saharan languages: that their origin probably goes back to the Saharan populations of the early Holocene, and that the earliest usages of words for grain, grindstones, grazing animals, and so on are more likely to refer to foraging than to agricultural activities (Blench 1993; Ehret 1993, and this volume). In both language groups terminologies with indisputable agricultural connotations can only be identified in the more developed languages. These conclusions clearly chime well with the reading of the archaeological data presented here regarding late Pleistocene and early Holocene foragers in North Africa and their eventual commitment to agriculture and/or pastoralism.

Some 25 years ago, Thurston Shaw commented that, in comparison with other parts of the world, 'Africa lags behind . . . in relation to archaeological research and in knowledge about the beginnings of food production' (Shaw 1977. 108). Several years later, Ann Stahl qualified her review of the African evidence with exactly the same point: 'research into the origins of African agriculture lags ten to fifteen years behind studies of early agriculture elsewhere' (Stahl 1984, 19). It is heartening to see North African archaeology moving centre stage in debates about transitions to farming, with its growing evidence for complex processes of subsistence change in the late Pleistocene and through the Holocene very different from the predictions of the demic diffusion model first proposed by Desmond Clark on the basis of the fragmentary data base available to him in the early 1960s.

References

Aumassip, G., 1987. Neolithic of the basin of the Great Eastern Erg, in Close (ed.), 235–58.

Barich, B.E., 1984. Fieldwork in the Tadrart Acacus and the 'Neolithic' of the Sahara. *Current Anthropology* 25(5), 683–6.

Barich, B.E., 1987a. Adaptation in archaeology: an example from the Libyan Sahara, in Close (ed.), 189–210.

Barich, B.E., 1987b. *Archaeology and Environment in the Libyan Sahara: the Excavations in the Tadrart Acacus 1978–1983.* (British Archaeological Reports, International Series 368.) Oxford: BAR.

Barich, B.E., 1998. *People, Water and Grain: the Beginnings of Domestication in the Sahara and the Nile Valley.* Rome: 'L'Erma' di Bretschneider.

Blench, R., 1993. Recent developments in African language classification and their implications for prehistory, in Shaw *et al.* (eds.), 126–38.

Blench, R.M. & K.C. MacDonald (eds.), 2000. *The Origins and Dispersal of African Livestock: Archaeology, Genetics, Linguistics, and Ethnography.* London: UCL Press.

Bradley, D. & R. Loftus, 2000. Two Eves for *taurus*? Bovine mitochondrial DNA and African cattle domestication, in Blench & MacDonald (eds.), 244–50.

Brewer, D.J., 1989. *Fishermen, Hunters, and Herders: Zooarchaeology in the Fayum, Egypt (c. 8200–5000 bp).* (British Archaeological Reports, International Series 478.) Oxford: BAR.

Caligari, G. (ed.), 1993. *L'Arte e l'Ambiente del Sahara Preistorico: Dati e Interpretazioni.* (Memorie della Società Italiana di Scienze Naturali e del Museo Civico di Storia Naturale de Milano 26. Fascicolo II.) Milan: Società Italiana di Scienze Naturali.

Camps-Fabrer, H., 1989. Capsien du Maghreb et Natoufien du Proche Orient. *Traveaux du LAPMO* 1989, 1–104.

Castelletti, L., M. Cottini & M. Rottoli, 1998. Early Holocene plant remains from Uan Afuda cave, Tadrart Acacus (Libyan Sahara), in di Lernia & Manzi (eds.), 91–102.

Chenal-Vélardé, I., 1998. Les premières traces de boeuf domestique en Afrique du Nord: état de le recherche centré sur les données archéozoologiques, in *Animals and People in the Holocene of North Africa*, ed. A. Gautier. Grenoble: La Pensée Sauvage, 11–40.

Clark, J.D., 1962. The spread of food production in sub-Saharan Africa. *Journal of African History* 3, 211–28.

Clark, J.D., 1964. The prehistoric origins of African culture. *Journal of African History* 5, 161–83.

Clark, J.D., 1984. Prehistoric cultural continuity and economic change in the central Sudan in the early Holocene, in Clark & Brandt (eds.), 113–26.

Clark, J.D. & S.A. Brandt (eds.), 1984. *From Hunters to Farmers: the Causes and Consequences of Food Production in Africa.* Los Angeles (CA): University of California Press.

Close, A.E. (ed.), 1987. *Prehistory of Arid North Africa.* Dallas (TX): Southern Methodist University Press.

Close, A.E. & F. Wendorf, 1992. The beginnings of food production in the eastern Sahara, in Gebauer & Price (eds.), 63–72.

Clutton-Brock, J., 1989. Cattle in ancient North Africa, in *The Walking Larder*, ed. J. Clutton Brock. London: Unwin Hyman, 200–206.

Clutton-Brock, J., 1993. The spread of domestic animals in Africa, in Shaw *et al.* (eds.), 61–70.

Corridi, C., 1998. Faunal remains from Holocene archaeological sites of the Tadrart Acacus and surroundings (Libyan Sahara), in Cremaschi & di Lernia (eds.) 1998a, 89–94.

Cremaschi, M. & S. di Lernia (eds.), 1998a. *Wadi Teshuinat: Palaeoenvironment and Prehistory in South-western Fezzan (Libyan Sahara).* Florence: Insegna del Giglio.

Cremaschi, M. & S. di Lernia, 1998b. The geoarchaeological survey in central Tadrart Acacus and surroundings (Libyan Sahara): environment and cultures, in Cremaschi & di Lernia (eds.) 1998a, 243–96.

di Lernia, S., 1998a. Early Holocene pre-pastoral cultures in the Uan Afuda cave, Wadi Kessan, Tadrart Acacus (Libyan Sahara), in Cremaschi & di Lernia (eds.) 1998a, 123–54.

di Lernia, S., 1998b. Cultural control over wild animals during the early Holocene: the case of Barbary sheep in central Sahara, in di Lernia & Manzi (eds.), 113–26.

di Lernia, S. & G. Manzi (eds.), 1998. *Before Food Production in North Africa*. Forlì: Abaco.

Ehret, C., 1976. Linguistic evidence and its correlation with archaeology. *World Archaeology* 8, 5–18.

Ehret, C., 1984. Historical/linguistic evidence for early African food production in Africa, in Clark & Brandt (eds.), 26–35.

Ehret, C., 1993. Nilo-Saharans and the Saharo-Sudanic Neolithic, in Shaw *et al.* (eds.), 104–25.

Ehret, C. & M. Posnansky (eds.), 1982. *The Archaeological and Linguistic Reconstruction of African History.* Berkeley (CA): University of California Press.

Gabriel, B., 1987. Palaeoecological evidence from Neolithic fireplaces in the Sahara. *African Archaeological Review* 5, 93–103.

Gautier, A., 1984. Quaternary mammals and archaeozoology of Egypt and the Sudan: a survey, in *Origin and Early Development of Food-Producing Cultures in North-Eastern Africa*, eds. L. Krzyzaniak & M. Kobusiewicz. Poznan: Polish Academy of Sciences, 43–56.

Gautier, A., 1987. Prehistoric men and cattle in North Africa: a dearth of data and a surfeit of models, in Close (ed.), 163–87.

Gautier, A. & W. van Neer, 1982. Prehistoric fauna from Ti-n-Torha (Tadrart Acacus, Libya). *Origini* 11, 87–127.

Gautier, A., P. Ballman, & W. van Neer, 1980. Molluscs, fish, birds and mammals from the late Palaeolithic sites at Wadi Kubbaniya, in *Loaves and Fishes: the Prehistory of the Wadi Kubbaniya*, eds. F. Wendorf, R. Schild & A. Close. Dallas (TX): Southern Methodist University, 281–93.

Gebauer, A.B. & T.D. Price (eds.), 1992. *Transitions to Agriculture in Prehistory.* (Monographs in World Archaeology 4.) Madison (WI): Prehistory Press.

Greenberg, J.H., 1966. *The Languages of Africa*. Bloomington (IN): Indiana University.

Grove, A.T., 1993. Africa's climate in the Holocene, in Shaw *et al.* (eds.), 32–42.

Harlan, J.R., 1989. Wild-grass seed harvesting in the Sahara and sub-Sahara of Africa, in Harris & Hillman (eds.), 79–98.

Harlan, J.R., 1993. The tropical African cereals, in Shaw *et al.* (eds.), 53–60.

Harris, D.R. & G.C. Hillman (eds.), 1989. *Foraging and Farming: the Evolution of Plant Exploitation.* (One World Archaeology 13.) London: Unwin Hyman.

Hassan, F., 1984. Environment and subsistence in predynastic Egypt, in Clark & Brandt (eds.), 57–64.

Hassan, F., 1985. Radiocarbon chronology of Neolithic and Predynastic sites in Upper Egypt. *African Archaeological Review* 3, 95–116.

Hassan, F., 1986. Holocene lakes and prehistoric settlements of the western Faiyum, Egypt. *Journal of Archaeological Science* 13, 483–501.

Hassan, F., 1988. The predynastic of Egypt. *Journal of World Prehistory* 2, 135–85.

Hassan, F., 1998. Holocene climatic change and riverine dynamics in the Nile valley, in di Lernia & Manzi (eds.), 43–51.

Higgs, E.S., 1967. Environment and chronology: evidence from mammalian fauna, in *The Haua Fteah in Cyrenaica*, ed. C.B.M. McBurney. Cambridge: Cambridge University Press, 16–44.

Hillman, G.C., 1989. Late Palaeolithic plant foods from Wadi Kubbaniya in Upper Egypt: dietary diversity, infant weaning, and seasonality in a riverine environmen, in Harris & Hillman (eds.), 207–39.

Hillman, G.C., E. Madeyska & J. Hather, 1989. Wild plant foods and diet at late Palaeolithic Wadi Kubbaniya: the evidence from charred remains, in *The Prehistory of Wadi Kubbaniya*, vol. 2, eds. F. Wendorf & A.E. Close. Dallas (TX): Southern Methodist University Press, 162–242.

Hugot, H., 1968. The origins of agriculture: Sahara. *Current Anthropology* 9, 483–9.

Ingold, T., 1988. Notes on the foraging mode of production, in *Hunters and Gatherers: History, Evolution and Social Change*, eds. T. Ingold, D. Riches & J. Woodburn. Oxford: Berg, 269–85.

Klein, R.G. & K. Scott, 1986. Re-analysis of faunal assemblages from the Haua Fteah and other late Quaternary archaeological sites in Cyrenaican Libya. *Journal of Archaeological Science* 13, 515–42.

Krzyzaniak, L. & M. Kobusiewicz (eds.), 1989. *Late Prehistory of the Nile Basin and the Sahara.* Poznan: Poznan Archaeological Museum.

Krzyzaniak, L., M. Kobusiewicz & J. Alexander (eds.), 1993. *Environmental Change and Human Culture in the Nile Basin and Northern Africa until the Second Millennium BC.* Poznan: Poznan Archaeological Museum.

Kuper, R., 1993. Sahel in Egypt: environmental change and cultural development in the Abu Ballas area, Libyan desert in Krzyzaniak *et al.* (eds.), 213–23.

Le Quellec, J.-L., 1987. *L'Art Rupestre du Fezzan (Septentrional), Libye): Widyan Zreda et Tarut (Wadi Esh-Shati).* (British Archaeological Reports, International Series 365.) Oxford: BAR.

Le Quellec, J.-L., 1990. Pierres de Ben Barur et 'Radnetzen' au Fezzan (Libye). *L'Anthropologie* 94, 115–26.

Lewis-Williams, J.D., 1983. *The Rock Art of Southern Africa.* Cambridge: Cambridge University Press.

Lewis-Williams, J.D. & T.A. Dowson, 1990. Through the veil: San rock paintings and the rock face. *South African Archaeological Bulletin* 45, 5–16.

Lewthwaite, J., 1986. The transition to food production: a Mediterranean perspective, in *Hunters in Transition: Mesolithic Societies of Temperate Eurasia and their Transition to Farming*, ed. M. Zvelebil. Cambridge: Cambridge University Press, 53–66.

Lhote, H., 1959. *The Search for the Tassili Frescoes*. London: Hutchinson.

Litynska, M., 1993. Plant remains from the Neolithic site at Armant: preliminary report, in Krzyzaniak *et al.* (eds.), 351–4.

Loftus, R.T., D.E. MacHugh, D.G. Bradley, P.M. Sharp, & P. Cunningham, 1994. Evidence for two independent domestications of cattle. *Proceedings of the National Academy of Sciences of the USA* 91, 2757–61.

Lubell, D., 1984. Palaeoenvironments and Epi-palaeolithic economies in the Maghreb (c. 20,000 to 5000 BP), in Clark & Brandt (eds.), 41–56.

McBurney, C.B.M., 1967. *The Haua Fteah in Cyrenaica*. Cambridge: Cambridge University Press.

MacDonald, K.C., 1998. Archaeology, language and the peopling of West Africa: a consideration of the evidence, in *Archaeology and Language II: Correlating Archaeological and Linguistic Hypotheses*, eds. Blench & Spriggs. London: Routledge, 33–66.

Marks, A.E., 1989. The later prehistory of the central Nile valley: a view from the eastern hinterlands, in Krzyzaniak & Kobusiewicz (eds.), 443–50.

Marks, A.E., J. Peters & W. van Neer, 1987. Late Pleistocene and early Holocene occupations in the upper Atbara river valley, Sudan, in Close (ed.), 137–61.

Mattingly, D.J., M. al-Mashai, H. Aburgheba, P. Balcombe, E. Eastaugh, M. Gillings, A. Leone, S. McLaren, P. Owen, R. Pelling, T. Reynolds, L. Stirling, D. Thomas, D. Watson, A.I. Wilson & K. White, 1998. The Fezzan project 1998: a preliminary report on the second season of work. *Libyan Studies* 29, 115–44.

Minnis, P.E., 1985. Domesticating people and plants in the Greater Southwest, in *Prehistoric Food Production in North America*, ed. R.I. Ford. (Anthropological Papers 75.) Ann Arbor (MI): University of Michigan, Museum of Anthropology, 309–39.

Minnis, P.E., 1992. Earliest plant cultivation in the desert borderlands of North America, in *The Origins of Agriculture: an International Perspective*, eds. C.W. Cowen & P.J. Watson. Washington (DC): Smithsonian Institution Press, 121–41.

Mori, F., 1960. *Arte Preistorica del Sahara Libico*. Rome: De Luca.

Mori, F., 1965. *Tadrart Acacus*. Turin: Einaudi.

Muzzolini, A., 1986. *L'Art Rupestre Préhistorique des Massifs Centraux Sahariens*. (British Archaeological Reports, International Series 318.) Oxford: BAR.

Muzzolini, A., 1993. The emergence of a food-producing economy in the Sahara, in Shaw *et al.* (eds.), 227–39.

Pachur, H.-J., 1991. Tethering stones as palaeoenvironmental indicators. *Sahara* 4, 13–32.

Peters, J., 1990. Late palaeolithic ungulate fauna and landscape in the Plain of Kom Ombo. *Sahara* 3, 45–52.

Petit-Maire, N., 1991. Recent Quaternary climatic change

and Man in the Sahara. *Journal of African Earth Sciences* 12(1–2), 125–32.

Roset, J.-P., 1987. Paleoclimatic and cultural conditions of Neolithic development in the early Holocene of northern Niger (Aïr and Ténéré), in Close (ed.), 211–34.

Roubet, C., 1978. Une économie pastorale, pré-agricole en Algérie orientale: le Néolitique de tradition capsienne. *Anthropologie* 82(4), 583–6.

Sansoni, U., 1998. Indications about the economic strategies as indicated from the rock art of the central Sahara: the 'Round Heads' phase, in di Lernia & Manzi (eds.), 147–62.

Saxon, E.C., A.E. Close, C. Cluzel, V. Morse & N.J. Shackleton, 1974. Results of recent investigations at Tamar Hat. *Libyca* 22, 49–91.

Shaw, T., 1977. Hunters, gatherers and first farmers in West Africa, in *Hunters, Gatherers and First Farmers Beyond Europe*, ed. J.V.S. Megaw. Leicester: Leicester University Press, 69–125.

Shaw, T., 1984. Archaeological evidence and effects of food-producing in Nigeria, in Clark & Brandt (eds.), 152–7.

Shaw, T., P. Sinclair, B. Andah & A. Okpoko (eds.), 1993. *The Archaeology of Africa: Food, Metals and Towns*. (One World Archaeology 20.) London: Routledge.

Smith, A.B., 1980. Domesticated cattle in the Sahara and their introduction into West Africa, in Williams & Faure (eds.), 489–501.

Smith, A.B., 1984. Origins of the Neolithic in the Sahara, in Clark & Brandt (eds.), 84–92.

Smith, A.B., 1986. Cattle domestication in North Africa. *African Archaeological Review* 4, 197–203.

Smith, A.B., 1993a. New approaches to Saharan rock art, in Caligari (ed.), 467–8.

Smith, A.B., 1993b. New approaches to Saharan rock art of the Bovidian period, in Krzyzaniak *et al.* (eds.), 77–89.

Stahl, A.B., 1984. A history and critique of investigations into early African agriculture, in Clark & Brandt (eds.), 9–25.

Stemler, A.B., 1980. Origins of plant domestication in the Sahara and the Nile, in Williams & Faure (eds.), 503–26.

Stemler, A.B., 1984. The transition from food collecting to food production in northern Africa, in Clark & Brandt (eds.), 127–31.

Sutton, J.E.G., 1977. The African aqualithic. *Antiquity* 51, 25–34.

van der Veen, M., 1992. Garamantian agriculture: the plant remains from Zinchecra. *Libyan Studies* 23, 7–39.

van Neer, W., 1989. Fishing along the prehistoric Nile, in Krzyzaniak & Kobusiewicz (eds.), 49–56.

Vermeersch, P.M., 1998. Fishing along the Nile, in di Lernia & Manzi (eds.), 103–11.

Vermeeersch, P.M., E. Paulissen & W. van Neer, 1989. The late Palaeolithic Makhadma sites (Egypt): environment and subsistence, in Krzyzaniak & Kobusiewicz (eds.), 87–114.

Wasylikowa, K., 1992. Holocene flora of the Tadrart Acacus area, SW Libya, based on plant macrofossils from Uan Muhuggiag and Ti-n-Torha/Two Caves archaeological sites. *Origini* 16, 125–59.

Wasylikowa, K., 1993. Plant macrofossils from the archaeological sites of Uan Muhuggiag and Ti-n-Torha, southwestern Libya, in Krzyzaniak *et al.* (eds.), 25–41.

Wasylikowa, K., J.R. Harlan, J. Evans, F. Wendorf, R. Schild, A.E. Close, H. Krolik & R.A. Housley, 1993. Examination of botanical remains from early Neolithic houses at Nabta Playa, Western Desert, Egypt, with special reference to sorghum grains, in Shaw *et al.* (eds.), 154–64.

Wendorf, F. & F. Hassan, 1980. Holocene ecology and prehistory in the Egyptian Sahara, in Williams & Faure (eds.), 407–19.

Wendorf, F. & R. Schild, 1980. *Prehistory of the Eastern Sahara*. New York (NY): Academic Press.

Wendorf, F. & R. Schild, 1984. The emergence of food production in the Egyptian Sahara, in Clark & Brandt (eds.), 93–101.

Wendorf, F., R. Schild, R. Said, C.V. Haynes, A. Gautier & M. Kobusiewicz, 1976. The prehistory of the Egyptian Sahara. *Science* 193, 103–14.

Wendorf, F., R. Schild, N. El Hadidi, A.E. Close, M. Kobusiewicz, H. Wieckowska, B. Issawi & H. Haas, 1979. The use of barley in the Egyptian Late Palaeolithic. *Science* 205, 103–14.

Wendorf, F., R. Schild & A.E. Close (eds.), 1984. *Cattle-keepers of the Eastern Sahara: the Neolithic of Bir Kiseiba*. Dallas (TX): Southern Methodist University.

Wendorf, F., R. Schild, A.E. Close, G.C. Hillman, A. Gautier, W. van Neer, D.J. Donahue, A.J.T. Jull & T.W. Linick, 1988. New radiocarbon dates and late Palaeolithic diet at Wadi Kubbaniya, Egypt. *Antiquity* 62, 279–83.

Wendorf, F., R. Schild & A.E. Close (eds.), 1989. *The Prehistory of the Wadi Kubbaniya*. 2 volumes. Dallas (TX): Southern Methodist University.

Wendorf, F., R. Schild, K. Wasylikowa, J. Dahlberg, J. Evans & E. Biehl, 1998. The use of plants during the early Holocene in the Egyptian Sahara: early Neolithic food-economies, in di Lernia & Manzi (eds.), 71–8.

Wengrow, D., 2001. Rethinking 'cattle cults' in early Egypt: towards a prehistoric perspective on the Narmer Palette. *Cambridge Archaeological Journal* 11(1), 91–104.

Wenke, R.J. & M. Casini, 1989. The Epipalaeolithic–Neolithic transition in Egypt's Fayum depression, in Krzyzaniak & Kobusiewicz (eds.), 139–55.

Wenke, R.J., J.E. Long & P.E. Buck, 1988. Epipaleolithic and Neolithic subsistence and settlement in the Fayyum oasis of Egypt. *Journal of Field Archaeology* 15, 29–51.

Wetterstrom, W., 1993. Foraging and farming in Egypt: the transition from hunting and gathering to horticulture in the Nile valley, in Shaw *et al.* (eds.), 165–226.

Wetterstrom, W., 1998. The origins of agriculture in Africa: with particular reference to sorghum and pearl millet. *The Review of Archaeology* 19(2), 30–46.

Williams, M.A.J., 1984. Late Quaternary environments in the Sahara, in Clark & Bradford (eds.), 74–83.

Williams, M.A.J. & H. Faure (eds.), 1980. *The Sahara and the Nile*. Rotterdam: Balkema.

Wills, W.H., 1992. Foraging systems and plant cultivation during the emergence of agricultural economies in the prehistoric American Southwest, in Gebauer & Price (eds.), 153–76.

Chapter 14

Language Family Expansions: Broadening our Understandings of Cause from an African Perspective

Christopher Ehret

The relation of agricultural invention to language family expansion has been a lively topic for some years now (Bellwood 2001), and the papers in this book present evidence for a variety of cases. What I intend here is somewhat different. I propose to construct an interpretive framework, rudimentary but with aspirations of global applicability, as to how the possession of agricultural practices may or may not, in different historical and environmental circumstances, generate the spread of speech communities. For these proposals I draw on a body of information little used so far in the discussion, namely, our extensive knowledge of language family expansions in Africa.

Food producers, we can agree, have material advantages that tend to facilitate the expansion of their cultures, economies, and therefore languages, into regions previously occupied by hunting and gathering peoples. But the possessors of cultivation or pastoralism do not inevitably prevail over hunter-gatherers. And we have not looked widely enough at the human experience if we suppose that the possession of food production everywhere explains the expansions of the widespread language families, or if we fail to realize that other, quite different long-term features of deep culture may also set off recurrent language cum cultural expansions.

The history of the African continent provides an immense variety of test cases for this way of looking at the past. These examples tell us indeed of the spread of agriculturists' languages and cultures into former hunter-gatherer lands. But they also reveal instances of food-collecting ways of life able to contend successfully against the spread of agriculture; they give us cases of arrested and then renewed agricultural expansion; and they show us cases where alternative causation of recurrent language family expansion must be supposed.

African food production and the Nilo-Saharan language family

The earliest sub-Saharan African development of food production belongs to the ninth millennium BC. It is as old a development almost as the first food production in Southwest Asia. The locus of this surely independent African development lay hundreds of miles apart from the earliest Middle Eastern herding and cultivation, in the southeastern portions of what is today the Sahara. Between 9000 and 8500 BC, the inhabitants of this region began to tend native cattle, herding them in regions too dry for the animals to live without human assistance in obtaining water. (At least this early, and possibly even before 9000 BC, these same people invented pottery, the earliest occurrence of this technology outside East Asia.) For centuries living in ephemeral settlements, the communities of this region started sometime before 7000 BC to build larger, semi-permanent settlements with round houses, granaries, and wells and, we suspect, commenced to cultivate indigenous previously wild grains. At the third stage of this history, sometime after 7000 BC, goats and sheep, domesticated in the separate Middle Eastern centre of agricultural invention, spread finally southward to these already food-producing peoples (Wendorf & Schild 1998). A solid linguistic stratigraphy, correlating point for point with what the archaeology of that region reveals, plausibly connects this three-step sequence of developments with speakers of early languages of a specific branch of the Nilo-Saharan language family, the Northern Sudanic branch (Ehret 1993; 2000a) (Fig. 14.1).

Did these developments lead to the expansion of the Northern Sudanic speakers? The answer is a mixed one: over the short long run, the answer is, No; over the very long run indeed, we can say, Yes, unevenly. From each aspect of these subsequent ages of Nilo-Saharan agricultural history we can draw an insight pertinent to interpretive theory.

From 9000 till after 6500 BC, the possession of elements of an agricultural economy seems to have led to only relatively restricted expansion. As far as we can tell — although admittedly our archaeological knowledge leaves much to be desired — the cattle raising and, apparently from the later eighth millennium, the cultivating descendants of the Proto-Northern Sudanians continued to inhabit limited areas of the eastern Sahara around and south of the Tropic of Cancer. All across the rest of the southern Sahara as far west as the Hoggar Mountains, an alternative way of life, based on the gathering and hunting of aquatic food resources, what we can call the Aquatic Tradition of Middle Africa, predominated during those 2500 years (Fig. 14.1). This was a period of significantly wetter climate across the Sahara than today, with open savanna in the south and grass and bush steppe in the more central areas. Streams flowed out of the mountain ranges of the central Sahara, and lakes occupied basins and low areas today wholly dry. Areas with good grazing and cultivating potential must have abounded in areas today virtually uninhabitable in the Sahara. Yet the food-producing Northern Sudanic peoples spread to only a small part of this vast set of regions.

Why? One approach is to argue that the earliest Northern Sudanians, of the ninth and earlier eighth millennium, lived at the bare threshold of an agricultural way of life. They could be understood as hunter-gatherers who also tended some livestock. For the last 800–1000 years of the period 9000–6500 BC, of course, they became more fully agricultural, as their larger semi-permanent settlements with granaries require, and still they did not yet greatly expand. Now we could propose that a time lag perhaps ensued, as more extensive food-producing activities slowly built up a population adequate to sustain a great expansion of Northern Sudanic languages and culture. There is a problem with taking this view, though. The Khoekhoe of the late first millennium BC and early first millennium AD in southern Africa provide a powerful example of the capacity of livestock raising to impel rapid and extensive territorial expansion. Similarly to what we have supposed for the earliest Northern Sudanians, the Khoekhoe lacked cultivation but mixed livestock raising with food collecting.

So might there be another explanation for the initially slow dispersal of Northern Sudanic food producers? I think there is. Certain kinds of hunting and gathering, specifically certain aquatic-based systems, are capable of supporting what are, for food collectors, significantly denser populations and much more complex social formations than we could otherwise expect. The Northwest Coast Native Americans are the preeminent case of food-collecting societies with not only unusually dense local concentrations of people, but also with stratified social structures including nobility and slaves. The Aquatic Tradition of the African Sahara and Sudan of 9000–6500 BC was, I would suggest, such a case, not as complex certainly as the recent Northwest Coast peoples of North America, but nevertheless highly successful in exploiting the natural environment of its time and place. I suggest that it held its own for so long because it was every bit as productive as, and perhaps more productive than, the early Northern Sudanic peoples' herding and, later on, cultivation practices.

Sometime during the period 6500–5500 BC, however, the expansion of Sudanic agriculture, with its cattle raising and its cultivation of such crops as sorghum, took off, spreading as far west as Hoggar and south through all of the southern Sahara and into what is today the Sahel belt of Africa (Fig. 14.2). What happened during that period? For about 1000–1200 years, during just that period, African climate became drier than it had been for the previous 3000 years. Saharan rivers dried up or ran only for part of the year. The lakes and wetlands of the southern Sahara shrank, even as the areas of steppe and grassland expanded. As a result, the peoples of the Aquatic tradition nearly everywhere would have faced a severe food crisis. Climate change reversed the balance of opportunity during those 1000–1200 years, opening new lands to agricultural expansion and turning herding and cultivation into essential means of survival. By the later sixth and early fifth millennia BC, even in areas where aspects of the Aquatic economy persisted, such as along the Nile River, the raising of animals and the cultivation of crops now supplemented the old ways of life.

African food production and the Cushitic languages

The Nilo-Saharans belonging to the Northern Sudanic branch of that family were not the only innovators of food production in the southeastern Saharan regions before 5500 BC. An additional set of food-producing peoples, the Cushites, also played key roles in spreading this kind of agriculture. Cushitic forms one of the deep branches of the Afrasan (Afroasiatic) family.

The Proto-Cushites were clearly pastoralists; the Proto-Cushitic vocabulary contained words diagnostic of a well-developed live-stock economy, including terms referring to donkeys, goats and sheep, as well as cattle. The primary split in the Cushitic group, in most scholars' view, is between Beja, long spoken in the southern Red Sea Hills region, and a second branch comprising the three remaining sub-branches of Cushitic — Agaw, Eastern Cushitic and Southern Cushitic. At the second stage of Cushitic history, the common ancestral language of this second branch added a verb for 'to cultivate' and a noun for 'cultivated field' along with names for two grains, t'ef and finger millet, indigenous to the Ethiopian highlands. This development shows the Proto-Agaw/Eastern/Southern Cushitic people to have become grain cultivators as well as pastoralists and to have lived in or adjacent to northern or eastern parts of the highlands, where t'ef and finger millet were native (Ehret 1999a,b).

The simplest account of the territorial history of the early Cushites would place the Proto-Cushitic lands in or near modern-day Beja country (Fig. 14.1). The Proto-Cushites would then have expanded more widely, with the forebears of the speakers of the other Cushitic languages subsequently moving farther south through the Ethiopian highlands and eventually into northern East Africa (Fig. 14.2). Even though we as yet lack direct evidence in the form of archaeological cultures attributable to the earliest Cushites, we do have one strong indirect indicator of just how long ago the Proto-Cushitic period was. This same indicator by inference supports locating the Proto-Cushites in or near the south-

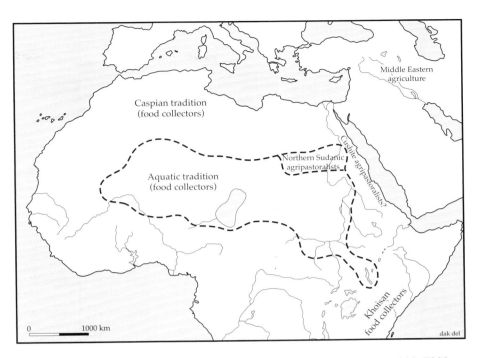

Figure 14.1. *Earliest Sudanic (and possibly Cushitic) agripastoralism, 9000–7000 BC.*

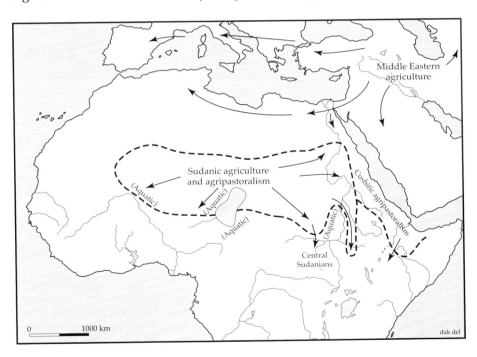

Figure 14.2. *Age of agriculture elaboration and spread, 6500–4000 BC.*

ern Red Sea Hills.

What is this evidence? It consists of a particular kind of stock terminology. The diagnostic data are the two earliest generic words for goat in the Northern Sudanic languages, *nay and *ay, both traceable back to the proto-language of the Sahelian sub-branch of Northern Sudanic.

The first of the two terms is found today only in the Beja branch of Cushitic, where it appears as *nʔay*. The dropping of the original glottal stop (ʔ) took place in Proto-Sahelian because that sound was not present in the early Northern Sudanic languages. This same linguistic criterion also reveals the direction of borrowing, showing us it passed from a Cushitic language source into Proto-Sahelian.

The second term derives from a Proto-Cushitic word for 'goat or sheep,' *ʔaz-, found in a wide scatter of Cushitic languages still today. Its pronunciation, though, shows a specifically Beja sound shift of Proto-Cushitic *z to y in non-initial position in words as well as the Beja narrowing of the meaning to 'goat' (Ehret 1983; 1987).

These two terms, in other words, appear to have come into Proto-Sahelian from an ancient form of Beja. This evidence in turn implies that the divergence of Proto-Cushitic into its two primary branches, Beja and Agaw/Eastern/Southern, had already begun before goats became known to the Proto-Sahelian descendants of the Proto-Northern Sudanians. The first ovicaprids in Northern Sudanic sites, according to the available archaeology, date after 6700 BC (Wendorf & Schild 1998), possibly to roughly sometime in the later seventh millennium. If this correlation holds, then the initial divergence and expansion of Cushitic peoples should date to before 6500 BC.

These considerations require the Proto-Cushites and Sahelian descendants of the Proto-Northern Sudanians of around the early seventh millennium BC to have been neighbours, and that fits well with other evidence. The Proto-Cushitic language on other grounds, as we saw, most probably was spoken in or near the southern Red Sea hills region. The early Northern Sudanic peoples and their immediate descendants, on the basis of our proposed archaeological correlations, would have lived in the plains of the southeastern Sahara extending westward from the Red Sea hills.

The evidence of reconstructed economic vocabulary tells us that both sets of peoples were keepers of cattle, and that raises the question of whether both were involved in initially bringing this development about. The borrowing of goat and sheep terms shows clearly the spread of these two animals from the Cushites to certain of the Northern Sudanians. But the cattle evidence does not indicate diffusion of this animal in either direction. The early Northern Sudanians borrowed no terms for cattle from the Cushites, but instead generated their bovine termi-

nology from earlier Nilo-Saharan root words: *yaːyr 'cow,' for instance, derives from Proto-Nilo-Saharan (PNS) *yaːy 'meat' plus a noun-deriving suffix in *r (Ehret 2001b). Similarly, the Cushitic vocabulary of cattle raising contains no certain instances of word borrowing from Northern Sudanic. We are forced to argue that the Proto-Northern Sudanians and Proto-Cushites must have taken to the tending of cattle as part of a shared regional development, dating to 9000–7000 BC — we cannot argue differently, given the neighbouring locations of the two. But each society must have evolved this economy within it own cultural context, surely aware of what its neighbours were doing, but — or so the linguistic evidence suggests — separately taking the same tack and so separately developing the vocabulary of cattle raising.

Cushites, similarly to the Northern Sudanic descendant societies, expanded much more widely once they had taken up their food-producing way of life. From the later patterns of language distributions, it appears that the Cushites spread initially into the far northern and the eastern parts of the Ethiopian highlands. The Agaw branch emerged in the northern areas, while the communities ancestral to the Proto-Eastern and Proto-Southern Cushites broke off to spread south along the Ethiopian Rift Valley (Ehret 1976a), where grasslands suitable to cattle raising would have existed at all periods (Fig. 14.2).

Agricultural and language spread in the Sudan Belt, 5500–1500 BC

After 5500 BC, the cattle-raising Sudanic and Cushitic types of agriculture advanced southward episodically, sometimes bringing associated Northern Sudanic and Cushitic languages along, sometimes not.

The first break in the coterminality of linguistic and agricultural spreads came about in the southwestern parts of the Middle Nile Basin, perhaps not long after 5000 BC. In that region, Central Sudanic peoples adopted key aspects of Sudanic agriculture from peoples of the Sahelian sub-branch of Northern Sudanic. The Central Sudanic languages belong to the Nilo-Saharan family, but form a distinct branch of Nilo-Saharan, separate from the Northern Sudanic branch. Agricultural knowledge and practice was transferred in this case without the accompanying adoption of a Northern Sudanic language (Ehret 1993; 2001b).

Why did a different history intervene at this point? The probable cause was environment in the broad sense. A vast expanse of wetlands and seasonally and perennially inundated areas covered the heart of the southern parts of the Middle Nile Basin between 9000 and 2000 BC. In the heart of this wetland zone as it existed before 2000 BC, Sudanic grains would not have thrived. The Sudanic agripastoral[1] tradition arose in steppe and dry open savanna north of that zone. The Proto-Central Sudanic people lived in the savannas immediately south of the western extension of the wetland zone, in a region we call today the Bahr-al-Ghazal (Fig. 14.2). The wetland zone, we can propose, brought the southward advance of the Northern Sudanians to a halt, giving the proto-Central Sudanians time to gradually adopt and incorporate these ideas into their own subsistence system. In subsequent periods the descendants of the Proto-Central Sudanic society then spread their own version of this agriculture into a variety of areas between the wetland zone and the rainforest to the south, as well as southward into areas along the northwest side of the Western Rift, where the modern countries of Uganda and Congo conjoin today (Ehret *et al.* 1974; Ehret 1998, chaps. 2 & 3) (Fig. 14.3).

Through a long, and at that time relatively narrow, stretch of dry land round the east side of the inundated lands of the upper Middle Nile Basin, Sahelian speech communities of the Northern Sudanic branch of Nilo-Saharan account for the continued spread of Sudanic agripastoralism. These areas, lying below the western edges of the Ethiopian highlands, would have formed a corridor of savanna vegetation, similar to that found farther north in the Middle Nile Basin, into which Sudanic agriculture spread between 6500 and 5500 BC (Fig. 14.2). The language evidence indicates the very early

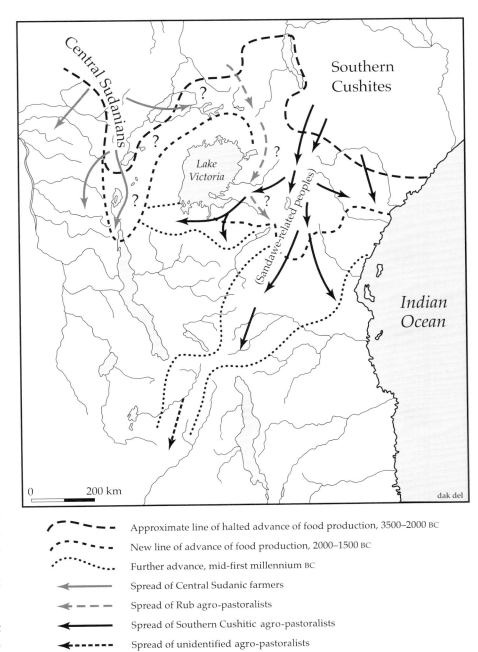

Figure 14.3. *Stages of agricultural advance in eastern Africa, 3500–500 BC.*

presence of two Sahelian-speaking populations, the Proto-Surmic and Proto-Rub, in the areas just west of the far southwestern fringe of the Ethiopian highlands, each bringing with them different elements of the inherited agricultural vocabulary of their earlier Northern Sudanic ancestors. Unfortunately, we have no archaeology from this region, with the exception of a site dating to perhaps the second millennium BC, which from the decorative styles of its pottery appears to have been a site of the Rub peoples (Ehret 1998, 90, arguing from Robertshaw & Collett 1983). So we lack direct evidence of when these two groups first arrived in the region. Linguistic dating of the internally diverse Surmic group implies that the arrival of Proto-Surmic society in the region goes back roughly to the fifth millennium BC (Bender 1971; Ehret 1983). But, until possibly as late as the second millennium, these Sahelian farmers and cattle raisers apparently spread no farther south than this stretch of land.

At the south end of the Ethiopian highlands there may have been a similar halt in agricultural advance and, in fact, more than one such halt. The language dating suggests that the Eastern and Southern Cushites diverged from a common ancestral society as early as the late sixth or early fifth millennium BC. The archaeological and linguistic dating agree in not requiring a further southward movement of the Southern Cushites into northern Kenya until between 3500 and 3000 BC. At that period, after spreading out widely across the areas east of Lake Turkana, the advance of the Southern Cushites again came to a halt. Here, the archaeological correlations are solid so the case seems especially clear. A thousand or more years later, in the early second millennium BC, the Southern Cushites opened a new episode of southward agricultural spread, through the Kenya highlands and all across the plains and plateaus of northern Tanzania (Ambrose 1982) (Fig. 14.3).

What caused these successive periods of delay in the spread of food production? The probable answer is, again, environment, but probably environment in a specific guise. Diane Gifford-Gonzalez (2000) makes a strong case that the southward advance of the agricultural frontier into eastern Africa encountered a succession of differing livestock disease environments. Each major stage of spread — for instance of Southern Cushites from the Ethiopian highland grasslands to the drier, hotter north of Kenya, and from there into the highland grasslands of central Kenya and northern Tanzania — required a period of adaptation for their domestic animals to new disease vectors. Each environmental belt, it turns out, was home to different wild herbivores that were intermediate hosts of diseases new to the cattle of the Cushites. Gifford-Gonzalez' arguments and evidence relate directly to the Kenya and Tanzania regions, but similar factors would have faced the Rub, Surmic and Central Sudanic food producers in the far southern Sudan and far northwestern Uganda.

A last interruption in the southward spread of the agricultural frontier took place between the later second and late first millennium BC. The holdup in this case was the wide belt of wooded savanna, home to tsetse-fly and thus trypanosomiasis as well as other livestock diseases, separating East Africa from those parts of Africa lying south of the Zambezi (Fig. 14.3). Sometime after 500 BC, however, this gap was breached — we as yet do not know just how or exactly when — and first sheep and then cattle began to be raised by southern Africans.

These last two cases of the arrested advance of the agricultural frontier allowed something else to take place. It gave a sort of historical breathing space, allowing time for certain hunter-gatherers to take up some of the practices of food production without adopting the languages associated with the full agricultural package. In Eastern Africa the notable case was the Sandawe (Fig. 14.3). Their ancestors were soon enough surrounded by the newly re-expanding Southern Cushites in the first millennium BC, so they could not embark on a large-scale agricultural expansion of their own. But they did become able to support a sufficiently substantial population to remain a distinctive people down to the present.

In southern Africa, the notable instances of adoption were by the Khoekhoe and the Kwadi, both peoples previously of Khoisan hunter-gatherer background. They added first sheep and then cattle to their existing food-collecting economy between about 500 and 200 BC, but in general did not take up cultivating. They nevertheless began rapidly to expand once they had added the raising of domestic animals. The Khoekhoe spread especially far afield, from northeastern Botswana to the far southern coast of the continent by the first century AD (Ehret 1982).

Overall patterns: a summary so far

Clearly, the African examples we have looked at to this point show the power of the possession of agriculture in spreading languages and cultures. But these cases also reveal limiting factors, and they allow us to propose a set of theoretical expectations.

1. *In the earliest stages of the shift to food production, when food collecting still provides the great majority of the food, different peoples living in the same broad region, but of different cultural backgrounds and different languages families, may each contribute to the seminal developments of the new economy.*

The notable example here is the probable common participation of the early Northern Sudanic and the Proto-Cushitic peoples of the ninth and eighth millennia BC in the domestication of African wild cattle. What may have enhanced their abilities separately to take advantage of this development was their habitation of neighbouring but climatically distinct kinds of grassy environment: the Proto-Cushites in the then Mediterranean steppe in the Red Sea hills, and the Proto-Northern Sudanians in the tropical steppe and desert steppe to the west in the lands around the Nile River (Fig. 14.1). Both groups were thus in a position to expand more widely as this economy fully took hold, each set of peoples spreading out in the environments to which their version of that economy was best adapted. I would argue that a similar multiplicity of participants created Middle Eastern agriculture in the same era — peoples of the Caucasic, Sumerian, and Elamo-Dravidian families, as well as, perhaps more peripherally, the ancestors of the Proto-Semites. In like fashion, speakers of more than one family of languages — among them presumably the linguistic forebears of the Austronesians — probably contributed to the emergence of southern East Asian agriculture.

2. *The possession of a food-producing economy does not automatically entail the expansion of the languages associated with it, at least in the periods when that economy is still taking shape. Certain kinds of especially productive food-collecting systems, particularly those relying on aquatic resources, for a time may be equally competitive in their ability to support a larger population.*

3. *Once a food-producing economy is more fully established, that economy tends to expand along with the languages and cultures in which it is embedded, until reaching an environmental barrier.*

4. *When such a barrier is encountered, the advance of the economy and its accompanying set of languages and cultures into new areas slows or comes to a halt.*

5. *If the adaptation of significant parts of the agricultural system to the new environmental challenges is possible, this process tends to take place over a period of centuries, after which the language cum agricultural advance may well resume.*

But the lag in these developments may allow an alternative history to come about.

6. *The intervening time lag gives food collectors ahead of the agricultural frontier a chance to adopt and readapt the agriculture or parts of it to their lands, if they so chose. In some instances, such people became themselves the new advancers of the food production frontier. In other instances, the productivity of a new mixed collecting and farming economy can support sufficient population growth to allow former hunter-gatherers to persist as a distinctive people in the face of renewed expansion of other agricultural peoples all around them.*

The histories of the Central Sudanic speakers and the Khoekhoe give us examples of the former outcome, namely, the secondary spread of food production cum language by former food collectors; the Sandawe exemplify the second possible outcome, the persistence of an erstwhile hunter-gatherer society in the midst of surrounding agricultural advance.

Generalizing subsistence expansion theory

What we have at this point is still a rather limited theory of the causation of language family expansion. We have shown African examples supportive of the idea that possession of food production can indeed sustain long-term, often episodic expansions of language families into the lands of hunter-gatherers. We have also encountered particular ways in which the forefront of expansion can shift from one group of speech communities to an entirely different one, as in the Central Sudanic instance.

But it is already evident from that very case that we need to set our sights wider. Central Sudanic is one of three deep-level branches of the Nilo-Saharan family, the other two being Northern Sudanic and Koman. Only Northern Sudanic can be correlated with the origination of food production. Central Sudanic and Koman both consist of sets of peoples whose ancestors long ago adopted agriculture, but 'adopted' is the operative word here. Both the Proto-Central Sudanic and the Proto-Koman languages borrowed some key words of their vocabulary of agriculture from later descendant languages of Proto-Northern Sudanic, showing their adoption of the ideas and practices from different Northern Sudanian peoples whose ancestors had long previously raised livestock and cultivated crops (Ehret 1993; 2001b).

So the Proto-Nilo-Saharans, the common ancestors of all three branches, were *not* food producers. Yet these three early branchings of the family occupied distant areas within the vast Middle Nile Basin from as far back as we can trace them. The Koman lived at the far eastern edge of the basin, near the Blue Nile and the foothills of the Ethiopian highlands; the Central Sudanians at the far southwest of the basin; and the earliest Northern Sudanians at the far north. If we draw a loop around these locations, we encompass a million and a half square kilometres. What set in motion the original Nilo-Saharan expansions accounting for these far-flung populations? We do not know, but it was not possession of food production.

We encounter the same kind of story if we look at the Afrasan (Afroasiatic) language family. But here we do have a plausible explanation of what it was that enabled the first several stages of the expansion of that family. It was a subsistence advantage, but not an advantage of food production.

We should get one point clear here. There is a common presumption in the literature that the Proto-Afrasans had food production in some form. This idea is *not* supported by the reconstruction of Proto-Afrasan subsistence vocabulary. The Proto-Afrasan vocabulary contains a large number of words relating to the exploiting of grasses/grains for food, but not a single term *diagnostic* of the *cultivation* of plants. And there are also no root words in Proto-Afrasan either that are *diagnostic* of livestock *raising* (Ehret 1999a,b).[2] In contrast, the vocabularies of the proto-languages of each of the major divisions of the family — that is, Proto-Cushitic, Proto-Chadic, Proto-Berber, and Proto-Semitic — do indeed contain significant numbers of verbs and noun explicitly connoting or implying herding and cultivating. Moreover, each branch separately developed its own words diagnostic of this kind of economy. The evidence is thus numerous and consistent in its indications that, only in significantly later periods than the Proto-Afrasan (Proto-Afroasiatic) era, did each of the descendant groups of the Proto-Afrasans separately take up food production. The earliest expansions of the Afrasan family, resulting in the dispersal of Afrasan speakers to regions as far apart as the Berbers of North Africa and the Cushites and Omotic peoples of Ethiopia and the Horn of Africa, thus took place in pre-food-producing times.

So why did these expansions come about? The vocabulary of subsistence in Proto-Afrasan shows the speakers of that language to have used grains/grasses as food, but it does not show any indication that they cultivated. They were, in other words, most likely the collectors of wild grains/grasses. The most probable archaeological correlation of the Proto-Afrasans is therefore with the early wild grass collectors of the far eastern Sahara and far northern Ethiopia, dating as long ago as 16,000–13,000 BC. This kind of economy would have provided a larger component of carbohydrate calories than any previous food collecting and so very probably could support more people on the same amount of land. It had spread before the eleventh millennium BC widely across northeastern Africa and even into the southwestern corner of Asia, and it soon spread still wider westward across the Sahara. The geography of its spread fits closely with that of Afrasan: the various regions of this kind of subsistence account for most of the expanse of lands in which languages of the

Afrasan family were spoken at the earliest times for which we have direct evidence.

So it appears that we need to expand our generalization about subsistence and language spread. What is it that gives agricultural production the potential of generating language and cultural expansion? Agriculture in all its forms produces more food from the same amount of land, therefore having the potential of supporting larger local populations and greater population overall. But food-collecting systems can differ from each other in the same manner. We can restate our hypothesis as follows:

> The development of any subsistence system, whether food collecting or food producing, that can provide more food than existing systems from the same amount of land, may set off a history of recurring expansions of the languages and cultures associated with the new system.

Institutions and institutionalized ideas and attitudes in language expansion

So far we have looked at instances of subsistence-change-driven language spread. But this category of cause by no means accounts for all the histories of long-term, recurrent language family spread. We move on now to a *longue durée* history in Africa where subsistence advantage is not adequate to explain what took place. Our example is the repeated expansions of the Nilotic languages.

The Proto-Nilotic language derived from the Proto-Sahelian descendant language of Proto-Northern Sudanic. It emerged as a distinct language at least eight and possibly ten stages later in the history of Northern Sudanic agricultural peoples than the Proto-Northern Sudanic period (Ehret 2001b, 70–71, 88–9). It was nevertheless spoken a long time ago, roughly, it appears, in the fifth or fourth millennium BC in the areas between the White and Blue Nile Rivers, not far north of the span of then-inundated lands in the southern Middle Nile Basin (to which we have already referred). Nilotic history since that time has been punctuated by repeated expansions of the Nilotic languages. In every case, with one possible exception, these expansions intruded into the lands of food producers and led to the assimilation and absorbing of those earlier food producers into Nilotic-speaking societies (Fig. 14.4).

In the early stages of this history, between roughly 4000 and 1500 BC, the Proto-Nilotes diverged into three successor societies, the Proto-Southern, Proto-Eastern, and Proto-Western Nilotes, and began the first era of their expansions.

The Proto-Southern Nilotes moved initially southward around the east side of the inundated lands of the southern Middle Nile Basin. They passed through the lands at the western edge of the Ethiopian highlands, arriving by no later than the second millennium in the modern-day borderlands of Uganda, Sudan, Ethiopia and Kenya (Ehret 1983). This location is confirmed by the large sets of word borrowings that entered Proto-Southern Nilotic from both the Surmic and the Rub languages (Heine 1976; Ehret 1983; 2001b). These, it will be remembered, were the languages of the earliest Northern Sudanic farmers to move into this part of Africa. The loanword sets in Proto-Southern Nilotic from both of these groups include agricultural terms, confirming that we are indeed dealing with the expansion of food producers into the lands of other food producers. In both cases large numbers of words passed into the Southern Nilotes' language from those of their predecessors, including even several words in the most basic vocabulary. This kind of borrowing is an especially strong indicator of the adoption by a pre-existing majority population of the language of an incoming minority (Ehret 1971; 1976b; 1981; 2000a).

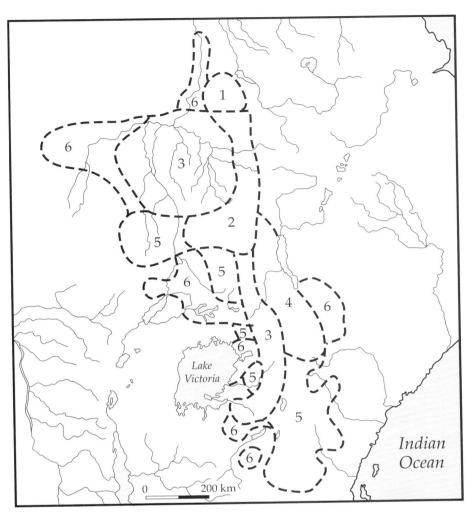

Figure 14.4. *Nilotic expansions, 4000 BC to AD 1800: 1) Proto-Nilotes, before 4000 BC; 2) Nilotic expansions, 3000–1000 BC; 3) Nilotic expansions, first millennium BC; 4) Nilotic expansions, AD 100–800; 5) Nilotic expanions, AD 800–1400 BC; 6) Nilotic expansions, AD 1400–1800.*

From the linguistic indications it appears that the adoption of Surmic loanwords into Southern Nilotic came before the even more intensive adoption of Rub loanwords. This loanword sequence fits the geographical picture of successively farther southward movements of the early Southern Nilotes. First they encountered Surmic peoples off the southwest edges of the Ethiopian highlands. They then progressed farther south into the early Rub lands, best located in the far northeastern part of present-day Uganda (Ehret 1983).

In the early first millennium BC — and for this period we have a strongly based archaeological correlation (Ambrose 1982) — the Proto-Southern Nilotes moved farther south, into the highlands of modern-day central Kenya, assimilating large numbers of erstwhile Southern Cushite food producers into their society. New major Southern Nilotic expansions, 600–300 BC, then brought about their divergence into two descendant societies, the Proto-Kalenjin and Proto-Tato. Advancing south across the plains of northern Tanzania, the Tato communities again displaced and assimilated many Southern Cushites. A final major period of Southern Nilotic expansion belongs to the period AD 800–1200, during which time Kalenjin communities spread around the eastern Kenya highlands and far south almost to the centre of Tanzania. At each stage of Southern Nilotic advance, numerous loanwords from Southern Cushitic languages entered the various Southern Nilotic tongues, in each instance including basic vocabulary indicative of the assimilation of large numbers of Southern Cushites into the Tato and Kalenjin societies (Ehret 1971; 1974).

The Proto-Eastern Nilotes of around the third millennium BC crossed beyond the inundated regions of the southern Middle Nile Basin, settling apparently in areas east of the Nile and just north of the present-day borders of Uganda. We can locate them there partly because the later distributions of Eastern Nilotic languages support this placement. But, more powerfully, this conclusion is required by the numbers of Central Sudanic loanwords adopted into Proto-Eastern Nilotic, words borrowed clearly from a language ancestral to the Central Sudanic languages spoken next door to that region today. Moreover, these word borrowings include agricultural terms, showing decisively that the Central Sudanians of the region were already farmers. The Central Sudanic loanwords were adopted into many other parts of Proto-Eastern Nilotic vocabulary as well (Ehret *et al.* 1974). This pattern of borrowing is one, as we have seen, that normally implies the shift of a former majority population to the language of an incoming minority.

The Eastern Nilotes then underwent a succession of divergences and expansions of their own over the next several thousand years. In every case, the loanword evidence tells us that these expansions intruded into the lands of other food-producing peoples.

The Proto-Eastern Nilotes diverged initially into two societies, the Proto-Bari and the Proto-Tung'a; the linguistic estimates of the timing of this development would place it around the third millennium BC (Ehret 2000b). The Proto-Bari spread into the lands of two competing food-producing societies. On the one hand, they continued the interactions of their Proto-Eastern Nilotic ancestors with Central Sudanic peoples, adopting large numbers of new Central Sudanic loanwords, again even in basic vocabulary. But more intriguingly they entered into an especially important encounter with a quite different Nilo-Saharan people, related in language to the Daju subgroup of the Sahelian sub-branch of Northern Sudanic. (The Daju of the past 1500 years of African history have been important pastoralists and farmers of the lands from the Nuba Mountains to Jebel Marra.) For lack of a better name, we will call these people the 'South Daju'. The South Daju appear most

probably to have moved, as the Proto-Eastern Nilotes had, directly across the inundated region to settle in the savanna zone to the south of it. From the South Daju the Proto-Bari also borrowed large numbers of words, including basic vocabulary (see Etymological Dictionary in Ehret 2001b), once more an indicator that the Proto-Bari must have begun as a minority intrusive element and yet ended up the dominant population.

The Proto-Tung'a broke up into the ancestral Ateker, Lotuko, and Maa-Ongamo societies over the course of the last millennium BC. The Proto-Ateker spread eastward, apparently into the far southeastern corner of the present-day country of Sudan, where initially they expanded at the expense of Surmic peoples (Dimmendaal 1983). In the later first millennium AD they began a new, wider expansion southward across the northeastern parts of Uganda, assimilating large numbers of former Rub people into their society (Ehret 1983). The Proto-Lotuko probably remained in the original lands of their Proto-Tung'a ancestors: their vocabulary shows no major period of contact influences from other peoples. But the Proto-Maa-Ongamo moved far away to the south in the first millennium AD, settling in the grassy plateaus north of Mount Kenya in about the eight century (we base this relatively precise date on a well established archaeological correlation, first established in Ambrose 1982). In these regions they encountered and apparently assimilated a substantial pre-existing Southern Cushitic population (Ehret 1974, 77–8 provides a small sampling of the evidence).

In subsequent centuries, two major spreads of Maa-Ongamo communities took place — of the Ongamo south to the plains around Mount Kilimanjaro in about the tenth century, and of the Maasai from 1500 onward southward through the Rift Valley of Kenya and all across the plains of northern Tanzania. The Ongamo may largely have displaced Southern Cushitic herders in the areas they settled; the Maasai, though, clearly advanced into the territories of Southern Nilotes, warring against both Kalenjin and Tato communities and assimilating significant numbers of these groups into their society (Ehret 2001a).

The remaining branch of the Nilotes, the Western Nilotes, similarly engaged in a long history of recurrent language and cultural expansion. The earliest spreading out of the Proto-Western Nilotes, diverging into the Proto-Burun and Proto-Jii groups, may date as early as the fourth millennium BC. But the first really major expansion of Western Nilotes belongs to the period of the second and first millennia BC. This expansion, of the Proto-Jii, appears to have followed the gradual shrinking back of the inundated areas of the southern Middle Nile Basin, after the close of the Holocene Wet Phase in the third millennium BC. It may actually be an example of the spread of food production into a last residual area of the old Aquatic livelihood.

But the next major period of Western Nilotic expansion, beginning in the first half of the second millennium AD, everywhere affected the lands of existing food producers. The Luo peoples, descendants of the Proto-Jii, spread all around the peripheries of the southern Middle Nile Basin before 1500, displacing and absorbing a variety of other Northern Sudanic peoples into their communities. Then, from the late 1400s into the eighteenth century, a succession of Luo expansions spread Luo dialects through large parts of northern Uganda and into western Kenya. There they moved amongst Central Sudanic peoples and the Eastern Nilotic Ateker (Atkinson 1994) and, in western Kenya, they settled among Bantu farmers (Ogot 1967; Ehret 1977), assimilating all these groups gradually into their societies. At the same period, another great expansion of a Jii people, the Dinka, took shape across many of the former Luo areas of the southern Middle Nile Basin. Then, in the nineteenth century, an almost equally great spread of still another Jii society, the Nuer, advanced across the heart of the Dinka lands.

Time and again, and stage by stage, Nilotic-speaking peoples established themselves across a vast set of territories over a 5000-year or longer period. At all but perhaps one early regional stage in this complex of histories, Nilotic expansion overtook areas already food producing in economy, usually non-Nilotic in the early periods, but often of related Nilotic language in more recent ages (Fig. 14.4).

The consistency of this pattern over a very long run of time makes chance vagaries of historical causation an insufficient explanation. Was there then some recurrent factor that we can isolate? With the exception of one grouping, there is such a factor. The Proto-Nilotes and all their descendant groups, except for the southern Luo of recent centuries, initiated their young men at adolescence into age-sets. The age-sets served as military companies, groups of young men permanently on a war footing. This is not to say that they were permanently *at war*. But when cause for battle arose, they formed a ready set of fighters, and the ideology of Nilotic age-sets, wherever we have information, encouraged the attitudes that go along with such preparedness. None of the

non-Nilotic food producers against whom the Nilotes successfully expanded had those institutions or ideologies. In other words, over the long term of their history, most Nilotes had an institution and apparently an attitude toward war that recurrently gave them the advantage over all their neighbours, except for other Nilotic peoples, whenever conflict arose. Even in the encounters of different Nilotes with each other, the possession of these institutions and their associated ideologies led to shifting balances of opportunity and power, allowing new expansions of Nilotes to take place at the expense of earlier established Nilotic populations.

I bring the Nilotic example particularly to our attention because it seems to me so like Indo-European history. Scholars nowadays eschew the overblown imagery of former European thinking about the Indo-Europeans, as being always warlike conquerors. And considering the terrible and racist uses to which these caricatured ideas were put in the twentieth century, the reaction is more than understandable. It seems to us, as well, an unsophisticated, mono-causal romanticism. But if we throw out caricature and romantic nonsense, we still are left with numerous cases, in both written records and written-down oral remembrances, of Indo-European-speakers prevailing over other peoples, including other Indo-Europeans, because of the violent suddenness of their attacks and the fierceness with which they fought. We find preserved in early myths and legends almost everywhere among Indo-Europeans a glorification of battle, and particularly of death in battle, not entirely unknown elsewhere in the world, but of an intensity not often matched. We also find widely in these stories a division of society that singles out warriors as an élite group. The Nilotes, too, anciently had a warrior group, although one that was differently fitted into the structure of society as a whole.

Similar also to the Nilotic situation, the linguistic evidence from each branch of Indo-European shows them to have been preceded everywhere, except possibly in Balto-Slavic areas, by other food producers. Nearly everywhere Indo-Europeans languages ended up, they borrowed fundamental old crop terms from other, no-longer-spoken languages. Just two grain terms, for rye and for possibly barley, can be reconstructed back to Proto-Indo-European, and even these terms were often displaced by words of non-Indo-European origin. Only in the vocabulary of livestock raising did Indo-European terminology tend to prevail, and even into this part of vocabulary loanwords could and did intrude from non-Indo-

European languages. (I am not referring here to the vocabulary of later crops, foods, and goods spread widely by Mediterranean trade, the borrowed words for which often spread widely from language to language in Classical and pre-Classical times.)

I do not adopt this view lightly — that the possession over the long term of history of institutions of war-readiness is one of the factors that can again and again sustain language expansion (cf. LeBlanc's paper in this volume). I see strong reasons for taking it seriously. On the other hand, I certainly see it as just one of the possible kinds of advantage that can impel the expansion of language families.

If our purview is the widest range of human experience, we can expect to find that quite different long-term advantages have impelled language expansion in different times and places. In addition to the possession of advantageous subsistence systems, either agricultural or pre-agricultural, the potential factors include the possession of persistent institutional advantage, such as institutions of military preparedness, and probably other long-term features of culture we have not yet even thought of.

Summing up

From these considerations, I adopt a broad statement of cause for the expansions of language families. It goes something like this:

Once the original settlement of Homo sapiens sapiens in any part of the globe had taken place, subsequent expansions of language families depended on the possession by the speakers of that family of a persistent long-term cultural advantage.

What do we mean by 'cultural advantage'?

One kind of advantage easy to define and identify is the possession of a subsistence system able to support a larger population in the same amount of land or able better to cope with or adapt to the natural world with which people contend. We more often can identify this kind of long-term causation because it is material: it leaves material remains in the archaeology. Earlier in this paper I laid out a series of expectations, numbered 1–6, based on African historical patterns, as to how agricultural frontiers might or might not have advanced in concert with the spread of linguistic frontiers. I then went on to generalize the insight to any subsistence advantage, whether agricultural or pre-agricultural, suggesting that subsistence advantage can be characterized as the capacity of a subsistence system to produce more food from the same amount of land than competing systems.

But just as important, the possession by people of a particular language family of certain kinds of long-term cultural attitudes and associated social institutions can also favour recurring or ongoing language family spread. One of these is the possession of attitudes and institutions persistently enhancing fighting capabilities. The various Nilotic peoples provide a strong set of instances in African history. So we ought not to back off from the clear implications both in mythology and the historical record that Indo-Europeans also long maintained, after their own fashion, institutions and a readiness for combat unparalleled in their predecessor populations in Europe and India both.

I would go further. There may well be other, quite different configurations of institutions cum ideology that can impel recurrent language family expansions, configurations that we have not yet thought of. There is no reason, either, to assume that cultural advantages of such a type would generate language expansions only after food production was well established. What of an early language family expansion, taking place *after* the initial human establishment in a part of the world, but long *before* agriculture? Would subsistence change always have been involved?

Summary of the proposed interpretive framework

Let us close by combining the interpretive claims brought forth in this article. We will invert their order of appearance and place them in outline format so as to move from the more general contentions to the more specific:

A. Once the original settlement of *Homo sapiens sapiens* in any part of the globe had taken place, subsequent expansions of language families depended on the possession by the speakers of that family of a persistent long-term cultural advantage.

B. If our purview is the widest range of human experience, we can expect to find that quite different long-term advantages have impelled language expansion in different times and places. In addition to the possession of advantageous subsistence systems, either agricultural or pre-agricultural, the potential factors include the possession of persistent institutional advantage, such as institutions of military preparedness, and probably other long-term features of culture we have not yet even thought of.

C. The development of any subsistence system, whether food collecting or food producing, that can provide more food than existing systems from the same amount of land may set off a history of recurring expansions of the languages and cultures associated with the new system.

D. Finally, when language expansion does accompany the spread specifically of agriculture, this historical process may pass through a succession of different stages over the very long term. For these stages, I refer readers back to the set of six theoretical expectations for population and language expansion proposed above.

Notes

1. Although 'agropastoral' is the common term in the literature, 'agripastoral' is to be preferred because it follows the rules of English coinage of words of this type. It combines a Latin formative element, *agri-* with a Latin-derived word *pastoral*. 'Agropastoral' violates the rules by adding 'agro-,' the Greek version of the same formative. I therefore consistently use 'agripastoral' in my writing.
2. It must be pointed out here, however, that Alexander Militarev in his article in this volume argues to the contrary and proposes examples of early Afroasiatic vocabulary that he feels are indicative of food production. Showing why these proposals do not make the case requires additional lengthy discussion, for which we unfortunately have no space to take up here. But the writer would be happy to correspond in detail on the specific problems he finds with Militarev's data.

References

Ambrose, S., 1982. Archaeology and linguistic reconstructions of history in East Africa, in Ehret & Posnansky (eds.), 104–57.

Atkinson, R., 1994. *The Roots of Ethnicity: the Origins of the Acholi of Uganda*. Philadelphia (PA): University of Pennsylvania Press.

Bellwood, P., 2001. Early agriculturalist population disaporas? Farming, languages and genes. *Annual Review of Anthropology* 30, 181–207.

Bender, M.L., 1971. The languages of Ethiopia. *Anthropological Linguistics* 13, 165–288.

Dimmendaal, G., 1983. Contacts between Nilotic and Surmic groups: linguistic evidence, in Mack & Robertshaw (eds.), 101–10.

Ehret, C., 1971. *Southern Nilotic History: Linguistic Approaches to the Study of the Past*. Evanston (IL): Northwestern University Press.

Ehret, C., 1974. *Ethiopians and East Africans: the Problem of Contacts*. Nairobi: East African Publishing House.

Ehret, C., 1976a. Cushitic prehistory, in *The Non-Semitic Languages of Ethiopia*, ed. M.L. Bender. East Lansing (MI): Michigan State University.

Ehret, C., 1976b. Linguistic evidence and its correlation with archaeology. *World Archaeology* 8, 5–18.

Ehret, C., 1977. Aspects of social and economic change in western Kenya, 500–1800, in *Kenya Before 1900*, ed. B.A. Ogot. Nairobi: East African Publishing House.

Ehret, C., 1981. The demographic implications of linguistic change and language shift, in *African Historical Demography II*, eds. C. Fyfe & D. McMaster. Edinburgh: University of Edinburgh, Centre of African Studies.

Ehret, C., 1982. The first spread of food production to southern Africa, in Ehret & Posnansky (eds.), 57–65.

Ehret, C., 1983. Population movement and culture contact in the southern Sudan, *c.* 3000 BC to AD 1000, in Mack & Robertshaw (eds.), 19–48.

Ehret, C., 1987. Proto-Cushitic reconstruction. *Sprache und Geschichte in Afrika* 8, 7–180.

Ehret, C., 1993. Nilo-Saharans and Saharo-Sudanese Neolithic, in *The Archaeology of Africa: Foods, Metals and Towns*, eds. T. Shaw, P. Sinclair, B. Andah & A. Okpoko. London & New York (NY): Routledge, 104–25.

Ehret, C., 1998. *An African Classical Age: Eastern and Southern Africa in World History, 1000 BC to AD 400*. Charlottesville (VA): University Press of Virginia.

Ehret, C., 1999a. Wer waren die Felsbildkünstler der Sahara?. *Almogaren* 20, 77–94. [German translation of 1999b.]

Ehret, C., 1999b. Who were the rock artists? Linguistic evidence for the Holocene populations of the Sahara, in Symposium: Rock Art and the Sahara, eds. A. Muzzolini & J.-L. Le Quellec, in *Proceedings of the International Rock Art and Cognitive Archaeology Congress News95*. Turin: Centro Studie Museo d'Arte Prehistorica. [Published as a CD.]

Ehret, C., 2000a. Language and history, in *African Languages: an Introduction*, eds. B. Heine & D. Nurse. Cambridge: Cambridge University Press, 272–97.

Ehret, C., 2000b. Testing the expectations of glottochronology against the correlations of language and archaeology in Africa, in *Time Depth in Historical Linguistics*, vol. 2, eds. C. Renfrew, A. McMahon & L. Trask. (Papers in the Prehistory of Languages.) Cambridge: McDonald Institute for Archaeological Research, 373–99.

Ehret, C., 2001a. The eastern Kenya interior, 1500–1800, in *African Historians and African Voices*, ed. E.S. Atieno Odhiambo. Basel: P. Schlettwein Publishers.

Ehret, C., 2001b. *A Historical-Comparative Reconstruction of Nilo-Saharan*. Cologne: Rüdiger Köppe Verlag.

Ehret, C., T. Coffman, L. Fliegelman, A. Gold, M. Hubbard, D. Johnson & D.E. Saxon, 1974. Some thoughts on the early history of the Nile-Congo watershed. *Ufahamu* 5, 85–112.

Ehret, C. & M. Posnansky (eds.), 1982. *The Archaeological and Linguistic Reconstruction of African History*. Berkeley & Los Angeles (CA): University of California Press.

Gifford-Gonzalez, D., 2000. Animal disease challenges to the emergence of pastoralism in Sub-Saharan Africa. *African Archaeological Review* 17(3), 95–139.

Heine, B., 1976. *The Kuliak Languages*. Nairobi: East African Publishing House.

Mack, J. & P. Robertshaw (eds.), 1983. *Culture History in the Southern Sudan*. (Memoire 8.) Nairobi: British Institute in Eastern Africa.

Ogot, B.A., 1967. *The History of the Southern Luo*. Nairobi:

East African Publishing House.

Robertshaw, P. & D. Collett, 1983. A new framework for the study of early pastoral communities in East Africa. *Journal of African History* 24, 289–301.

Wendorf, F. & R. Schild, 1998. Nabta Playa and its role in northeastern African prehistory. *Anthropological Archaeology* 20, 97–123.

Chapter 15

Language and Farming Dispersals in Sub-Saharan Africa, with Particular Reference to the Bantu-speaking Peoples

David W. Phillipson

A new and concise survey of African linguistics (Heine & Nurse 2000), refining Greenberg's (1963) classification, has recently appeared and may be taken as point of departure for the present discussion. Pre-colonial[1] African languages may, by common consent, be divided between four major families: Khoisan, Niger-Congo, Nilo-Saharan and Afroasiatic. It is assumed that readers are familiar with the composition and present distribution of these families. The following points should, however, be emphasized. Contrary to earlier opinion, an African origin is now commonly attributed to Afroasiatic.[2] Some authorities have suggested that Niger-Congo and Nilo-Saharan may share a common ancestor. The initial development of these three families may have taken place in contiguous regions lying between the Sahara and the equatorial forest (Blench 1993). The distribution of Khoisan, past and present, is more southerly.

Virtually all modern speakers of Niger-Congo, Nilo-Saharan and Afroasiatic languages, together with some of those who speak Khoisan, belong to societies which have traditionally based their livelihood on subsistence farming — on cultivation, on herding or on a combination of the two.[3] It is pertinent to enquire to what extent the developmental processes of these language families may have paralleled their speakers' adoption of farming practices (cf. Renfrew 1997).

Evaluation of methodologies

Attempts to reconstruct African prehistory from linguistic data began well before the archaeological investigation of sites south of the Sahara. For the last half-century, however, the two approaches have been conducted in parallel, generally by specialists who have only a rudimentary familiarity with the methodology and achievements of the other discipline. The present writer does not claim to be an exception to this generalization.

Linguistics
One underlying principle of the broader historical application of linguistic studies is that socio-political boundaries and linguistic ones are to a significant extent interdependent. Language has much to contribute to, and not infrequently exercises considerable control over, an individual's sense of identity and group-membership. It confirms a child's cultural affinity from an early age. Almost certainly, language divisions will more closely reflect socio-political groupings (but not necessarily economic groupings) than will the material remains which form the initial, if not the prime, focus of archaeological studies (cf. Huffman 1989; Vansina 1995).

There is nevertheless an important contrast to be made between the source material of the two disciplines, in the light of which their respective methodologies and conclusions must be evaluated. In the case of languages which, like most of those African ones with which we are here primarily concerned, were not committed to writing until comparatively recent times, the linguist's primary source material is restricted to records of languages as recently spoken, and to the recent geographical distribution of such languages. Archaeological remains, on the other hand, may have remained undisturbed since the time of their initial formation or deposition. Yet it is on the two sets of modern data noted above that the reconstructions of past linguistic forms, both lexical and grammatical, and of distant shifts in language distribution patterns are, of necessity, based. It will be apparent that these two endeavours are of somewhat different orders of complexity.

The first (reconstructing past language development) involves detailed linguistic comparisons that attempt to determine the form and content of ancestral languages from which one or more modern ones are derived. It will seek to demonstrate more-or-less regular sound-shifts and to identify shared cognates, changes in meaning and in grammatical form, and also borrowings from neighbouring languages, related or unrelated. At least in Africa, the majority of this research has been lexically based and has resulted in the accumulation of a vast and complex body of lexicostatistical analysis: only a few researchers have based their reconstructions upon the innovations which define individual subgroups. Both approaches, together or independently, have been used to establish hierarchical classifications (often in the form of dendrograms) of *reconstructed* languages: only those which have been recorded as spoken in recent times are demonstrable entities of known date. It cannot be emphasized too strongly that all the earlier ones are reconstructions; but if it is accepted that they have validity (and agreement on this is widespread but not universal), it follows that they must have been spoken by a certain population living in a certain area at a certain time.

The second study, focusing on geographical aspects of linguistic reconstruction, is of particular concern in the present context. A number of writers have been remarkably precise in postulating the location of reconstructed past language groups. Where reasons for such locations are offered, reference is almost invariably made to the so-called 'least moves principle', based upon present linguistic distributions and (when loan-word studies are involved) on the need to establish contiguity between donor and recipient languages. Toponymy is of clear relevance here, but has not yet received wide attention in Africa. This least moves principle, a sort of geographical Occam's razor, offers many pitfalls (Vansina 1995) and has given rise to a number of improbable reconstructions, as noted by David (1982a,b) in connection with Ehret's (1982; see also Ehret *et al.* 1974) postulated homeland for speakers of Proto-Central Sudanic. There has also, I suggest, been a tendency too narrowly to define past linguistic distributions, partly by underestimating the areas that may have been occupied by earlier linguistic groups.

A further problem which requires consideration in this context is the process of dialect differentiation and language separation. Contiguity and verbal intercourse will prolong mutual comprehension. The actual point of division can, in practice, be determined only arbitrarily. In certain circumstances, closely-related languages may show convergent evo-

lution. All these factors give rise to difficulties in the application of conventional simple models to the history of Bantu language development.

A focus on historical linguistic change and shifting distribution is hampered by the fact that surprisingly little research has been undertaken on similar processes in recent African societies. The writings of historical linguists contain remarkably few detailed references to the demographic and social processes inherent to their reconstructions. A useful exception is found in the *Language and Dialect Atlas of Kenya* (Heine & Möhlig 1980), where linguistic transmission through and between socio-political population groupings is carefully evaluated (see also Ehret 1981). In a more historical frame, the present writer has been able to show, in the context of nineteenth-century events which are profusely documented in Zambian oral tradition, that the linguistic reaction to population movement is dependent on the demographic composition of the immigrant group (Phillipson 1974).

The chronology which such studies can provide is purely relative. On the hypothesis that similar languages will have had a more recent common ancestor than ones which retain fewer shared features, a sequence can be established in which divergences, loans, sound shifts and the like can be set out in temporal order. The provision of a time-scale, however, — that is, the tentative transformation of such a relative chronology into an absolute one — is a difficult and controversial matter. The only substantial data available to us which throw light on speeds of linguistic change over periods of any significant duration necessarily relate to written languages or, exceptionally, to periods of contact with representatives of literate societies. There is no reason to believe that the speeds of change which are indicated in such circumstances will necessarily resemble those which may prevail in non-literate situations.

Nevertheless, many historical linguists persist in attempting to offer some sort of absolute time-scale for their reconstructed stages of linguistic change. It is noteworthy how infrequently the bases for these age-estimates are specifically stated (e.g. Ehret 1974b). Some depend upon the controversial principles of 'glottochronology'. Of necessity, the calculations on which this lexicostatistical numbers game is based have been derived from study of written languages; and many factors which must affect processes of linguistic change have been ignored altogether, notably the extent to which divergence may have been restrained by contiguity of related dialects (as in Indo-European and Bantu) or accelerated by geographical separation. On other occasions, time-estimates may be based upon supposed correlations, admitted or not, with archaeological evidence, as for the inception of metallurgy, the introduction of a foreign cultigen or some other event which may be assumed to have coincided with a specific lexical innovation. There are dangers of circular argument here, especially when the reasons for proposed linguistic chronologies are not explicitly stated. Another stumbling block is the apparent precision of glottochronological estimates. Most linguists (e.g. Ehret 1988) who apply this methodology are at pains to stress that it can give only a very general and approximate estimate which relates to the linguistic event (dialect separation or adoption of loan, for example), not to the inception of the process (dispersal or establishment of contact) which gave rise to it. Some historians nonetheless persist in presenting the results of glottochronological calculations to the nearest decade and expressing concern over apparent mis-matches of a few centuries (e.g. Vansina 1990). Such over-reliance on, and mis-use of, an at-best dubious methodology has no lasting value.

Archaeology

This is not the place for a general evaluation of archaeological methodology. In a paper focusing on farming dispersals in Africa it will be appropriate to take as the baseline for discussion the general overview offered by the present writer (Phillipson 1993a) with the summaries of more recent research edited for cultivation by van der Veen (1998) and for livestock herding by Blench & MacDonald (1998). In grossly over-generalized terms, this picture shows the gradual domestication of indigenous plants and some animals in sub-Saharan latitudes north of the equatorial forest, and the adoption there of other domestic animals and crops of non-African origin, by peoples who had no knowledge of metallurgy, during the period 5000–1000 BC. Subsequently, both cultivation and herding were adopted in more southerly parts of Africa, featuring almost exclusively species, both plant and animal, previously unknown there.

Some general points should, however, be emphasized. First is the extreme paucity of archaeological research in many regions of sub-Saharan Africa. Secondly, until very recently, very few archaeological research projects in Africa adopted methodologies specifically aimed at the recovery of archaeobotanical materials. Study of such materials as are available is hampered by the dearth of well-documented com-

parative collections in comparison with those in many other regions.[4] Thirdly, morphological change in plants or animals may not become readily discernible in archaeological materials until the domestication process is well advanced. The antiquity of *in situ* domestication may thus be seriously underestimated during the early stages of archaeological investigation, whereas the introduction of domestic species beyond the distribution of their wild prototypes will be more readily apparent.

What lessons may be learned from the critique presented above of historical linguistics in Africa about the juxtaposition of linguistic hypotheses with archaeological research? Firstly, we are dealing with independent variables and it is not to be expected that linguistic and material culture parameters will necessarily coincide. Both, however, are independent reflections of the past events and processes which it is the concern of the prehistorian to interpret. Secondly, language, like material culture, may only be understood in its socio-political and economic context. Thirdly, correlation between archaeological and reconstructed linguistic entities should not be seen as an end in itself but as a possible route to a more comprehensive understanding of past cultural processes.

Language and farming dispersals

It is now appropriate to compare the evidence that is emerging from linguistic and archaeological investigations. The initial establishment of semi-permanent settlements where incipient plant and animal domestication took place is generally attributed to fishing communities in what is now the southern Sahara at a time of widespread desiccation during the mid-Holocene. Sutton (1974) noted the broad similarity of these communities' distribution and the areas where Nilo-Saharan languages are currently spoken.[5] Farming developments in the Ethiopian highlands appear to have taken place largely independently of events in neighbouring African regions (Phillipson 1993b; Barnett 1999); they cannot yet be dated archaeologically but a high antiquity has been postulated by Ehret (1980), linked with early Afroasiatic language development. There are certainly strong indications that both plough-cereal agriculture and vegeculture were developed respectively in the northern and southern Ethiopian highlands before the advent of Semitic speech generally attributed to the early centuries of the last millennium BC.

In East Africa there is now secure archaeological evidence for the progressively more southerly adoption of herding and, possibly, cultivation also, during the last two and a half millennia BC. Since, almost without exception, the species involved were not indigenous to the region, a dispersal from a general northern or northwestern direction is strongly indicated. The region today is linguistically diverse, with representatives of all four African language families being spoken there. The East African Khoisan languages presumably represent remnants from an early hunter-gatherer continuum; the Bantu-speaking Niger-Congo representatives may be linked with the major sub-equatorial dispersal of farming peoples discussed below. It is generally accepted that the East African pre-metallurgical herders were speakers of Cushitic (Afroasiatic) and/or Nilotic (Nilo-Saharan) languages. Indeed, the linguistic indications that the earliest East African speakers of such languages may already have been familiar with domestic animals (and, less certainly, crops) provides a useful parallel indication of southwards dispersal.

The corresponding developments in West Africa remain very poorly understood (MacDonald 1998). Major differences are to be anticipated between developments in the equatorial forests and those in the more northerly savanna. This ecotone has shifted markedly, generally southwards, during the Holocene. Expectations that vegeculture in the forest may have an antiquity at least as great as cereal cultivation in the savanna have not yet received support from archaeology or Niger-Congo linguistic studies (Connell 1998).

To the south extends a huge area where there is no archaeological evidence that either cultivation or herding preceded the local adoption of metallurgy. Through most of this area the languages belong to the Bantu branch of Niger-Congo, discussed in somewhat greater detail below.

The Bantu languages

Similarities between languages spoken in widely separated regions of sub-equatorial Africa were recognized by outsiders long ago. To well-travelled inhabitants of the sub-continent itself, intercomprehensibility must of course always have been apparent. The first Portuguese navigators to enter the Indian Ocean round the Cape of Good Hope commented on the fact that languages spoken on the East African coast could be understood by someone versed in Angolan speech (Theal 1910, 160–61, cited by Vansina 1979, 325). The strong similarities of local African languages (other than those now desig-

nated Khoisan) were apparent to colonists in South Africa from at least the early nineteenth century (e.g. Archbell 1838). These observations were codified and extended by Bleek (1862–69), to whom is due credit for recognizing the distinctiveness of those languages which he designated 'Bantu', after the plural form of the word by which they almost invariably refer to a human being.

Detailed study of the distribution and diversity of the Bantu languages owes much to the pioneering work of Sir Harry Johnston (Oliver 1957) from the 1880s until the publication of his magisterial *Comparative Study of the Bantu and Semi-Bantu Languages* in 1919–22. At an early stage in his enquiries, Johnston (1886) drew attention to three crucial facts. For much of its extent, the northern boundary of the Bantu-language distribution was marked by a sharp distinction with largely unrelated languages. Only in the extreme northwest, in what is now western Cameroon and eastern Nigeria, did there occur languages (designated Semi-Bantu) which, while not fully Bantu, were nonetheless clearly related. It was similarly in the northwest that the Bantu languages themselves showed the greatest diversity.

During the 1950s two very significant developments took place. Greenberg developed an overall classification of African languages which, for the first time, permitted a view of how the Bantu languages fitted into an overall pattern. Although largely based on earlier work, Greenberg's results were definitively published only in 1963. Although Greenberg was not initially concerned with the historical implications of his linguistic classification, his work gave confirmation and fresh emphasis to two of Johnston's most important conclusions: the greater diversity of the northwestern Bantu languages and the affinity between them and their non-Bantu immediate neighbours. The Bantu languages were seen to represent a single sub-branch of a family, Niger-Congo, which included many West African languages (see also Greenberg 1972; 1974). Murdock (1959) published a wide-ranging and, in places, highly speculative account of traditional African societies in historical perspective which used linguistic affinity as a prime classificatory factor and, by implication, historical source. Although Murdock's approach, based on conventional 'tribal' divisions which Vansina (1989) has described as 'a colonial mirage', has been criticized and found to be in error on numerous points of detail, it did provide a valuable stimulus to research on the internal developments of sub-Saharan Africa's pre-literate past, as opposed to its reaction to external factors.

Internal divisions and linguistic reconstructions
As is the case in archaeology, the aims and methods of linguistic analysis are inextricably linked. A methodology can only be fairly evaluated, or criticized, through reference to the questions which it seeks to address. It is important to keep this point in mind when considering the work of Guthrie. Although he was the first scholar in the second half of the twentieth century to attempt a reconstruction of the history of Bantu-speaking peoples from exclusively linguistic sources, the prime flaw in his work was that its basic methodology had not been devised to address historical questions. Subsequent modifications never succeeded in rectifying this fundamental problem. Whereas Greenberg had been concerned with the position of Bantu on the overall language map of Africa, Guthrie (1962; 1967–71) took a narrower view. He sought a comparison between the Bantu languages throughout their area of distribution and based his classification first and foremost on a system of geographical zones which had been drawn up at an early stage in his research with only minimal reference to linguistic data. Guthrie's developing aims and methodology have been subjected to critical appraisal by Flight (1980; see also Ehret 1972), the details of whose arguments need not be repeated here.

The basic thrust of Guthrie's work was the belief that the Bantu languages fall into western and eastern divisions, that ancestral forms for each could be reconstructed, and that elements common to both were derived from a more remote Proto-Bantu. Modern languages which retained the greatest number of these ancestral forms were believed, for reasons never clearly set out, to mark the areas where the proto-languages had been spoken. This resulted in the conclusion, contrary to that reached by most researchers since Johnston and most recently propounded by Greenberg, that the 'homeland' from which the Bantu languages were as a whole derived was located not in the northwest (Cameroon) area but in an elliptical area stretching from west to east across the savanna to the south of the equatorial forest (see also Guthrie 1970).

Subsequent research on Bantu language development may conveniently be divided into that based on lexicostatistics, that which considers primarily loan-words from non-Bantu sources, and that which seeks to balance lexical and grammatical factors. The first group comprises the most numerous studies, some of which involve the reworking of Guthrie's own data, while others are independent. Several scholars applied different methodologies to the analysis of Guthrie's data (Dalby 1975; 1976; Henrici 1973; Mann 1970; 1980). All drew attention to sampling problems and to the conceptual straight-jacket imposed by the rigid system of geographical zones. They also cast doubt on the assumptions used to support the placement of a nucleus south of the forest, going so far as to point out that a high incidence of common elements is more likely to be brought about by recent interaction that by early dispersal. Others (Heine 1973; Heine *et al.* 1977) produced a lexical analysis independent of Guthrie. It supported an east/west division but was otherwise quite different. Both divisions were derived from a northwesterly source, but eastern Bantu was seen as a much more recent development than western Bantu. The former languages were seen as having originated south of the forest in an area which, perhaps coincidentally, lay in the general location of Guthrie's nucleus.

Möhlig (1977; 1979; 1981) took a completely independent stance. He recognized that phonology as well as vocabulary has comparative and historical significance. He also emphasized that the Bantu languages have for a very long time formed a web of interaction: there was no reason whatsoever to assume (as most other researchers seemed to do) that only one process, rather than a series of processes, had been involved in the development of the present pattern of Bantu language distribution. Möhlig thus proposed that linguistic development should be viewed as a series of superimposed layers, it being necessary for the researcher to reconstruct successive stages despite the fact that each such stage would tend to obscure its predecessors. The full potential value of this important conceptual advance was not achieved, however, since Möhlig was not able to systematize the plethora of data which he obtained and, in making the attempt, came to doubt the historical validity of his linguistic reconstructions.

Results in many ways similar were obtained by Ehret (1967; 1968; 1973; 1974a), using a methodology based on the recognition of loan-words. He was not primarily concerned with establishing the origins of Bantu, but with recognizing stages in its development and the external influences to which Bantu-speakers had at various times been subjected. He argued that many words of particular cultural significance, such as those relating to several domestic animals, were loans into certain (predominantly eastern) Bantu languages from non-Bantu sources which could sometimes be identified as Central Sudanic. The implication of such observations is that the items or cultural practices to which the loan-words refer were themselves acquired by Bantu-speakers from a Central Sudanic source at the same time as the vocabulary. By noting the extent to which loan-words had been subject to specifically Bantu sound-shifts, Ehret was able to suggest at what stages in Bantu language-development each particular loan had been acquired. As the present writer has pointed out (Phillipson 1977a; 1985), Ehret's historical reconstructions are marred by his apparent assumption that a loan must have taken place near the area where the loan-word is currently used, rather than elsewhere prior to movement through normal modes of language transmission. The bases for Ehret's proposed chronologies are not always stated, and may be glottochronological calculations or unadmitted correlations with an archaeological sequence.

Concern over the imprecisions of linguistic methodologies led several archaeologists (Lwanga-Lunyiigo 1976; Gramly 1978) to deny altogether the relevance of such studies to the study of the African past, and to suggest that the Bantu languages might have been spoken in eastern and/or southern Africa for a far longer period than other scholars had suggested. These suggestions have either been summarily dismissed (Ehret & Posnansky 1982) or ignored.

Archaeological/linguistic correlations
Systematic linguistic research in Bantu-speaking Africa was undertaken long before archaeologists began to pay attention to other than a very few isolated sites, mostly in Southern Rhodesia (Zimbabwe) and the former Belgian Congo. Early attempts at a historical overview were thus based almost exclusively on linguistic data. As noted above, Murdock (1959) was the first scholar who sought to combine the two approaches, and he was faced with an almost complete absence of reliable archaeological information. Soon afterwards, however, Merrick Posnansky (1961a,b) drew attention to typological similarities between the oldest pottery in the Lake Victoria and Zambezi basins, suggesting the possibility that these assemblages might mark sites of early Bantu-speaking inhabitants of the respective regions. These important papers, appearing at a time of economic and intellectual optimism when nations in most parts of Bantu-speaking Africa were attaining political independence, stimulated the growth of research on recent archaeology in several areas of anglophone eastern and south-central Africa. It became apparent that the period from the mid-first millennium BC to the mid-first millennium AD had seen major cultural changes over the greater part of sub-equatorial Africa. Although the innovations were demonstrably not precisely synchronous in all areas, this general period saw the first appearance throughout the areas where Bantu languages are now spoken of cultivation, herding and metallurgy, the practitioners of which occupied semi-permanent or permanent villages and produced pottery displaying marked stylistic similarity over a very wide region.

A pioneering attempt to combine new archaeological discoveries with the linguistic interpretations that were concurrently proliferating was made by Oliver (1966). The basic framework was still linguistic, comprising an attempt to combine the views of Greenberg who placed the Proto-Bantu nucleus in Cameroon, with those of Guthrie, who put it in southern Congo about 2500 kilometres to the southeast. Oliver suggested that an initial movement of Bantu-speakers had taken place from a Cameroon centre through the equatorial forest, giving rise to a second nucleus in the southern Congo location proposed by Guthrie, whence the new languages had dispersed through the savanna regions of eastern and southern Africa. Oliver accepted the idea that the Bantu-speakers had been responsible for the early pottery recognized by Posnansky, but suggested that this was more likely to have been introduced from the upper Zambezi to East Africa, rather than *vice versa*. Such a proposition was not contradicted by the few radiocarbon dates that were then available. The reconstruction was proposed specifically as an attempt to reconcile the two principal linguistic hypotheses that had been proposed during the previous decade. Archaeology was regarded as a secondary approach, with the particular role of providing dates. Little attention was paid to the questions of how the Bantu languages had been transmitted, or how their speakers may have related to previous inhabitants whom they encountered.

At this stage, archaeologists moved to the fore, requiring major modification to Oliver's initial model (cf. Oliver & Fagan 1975; 1978; see also Oliver 1979). Linguists were waiting for the long-promised publication of Guthrie's detailed research conclusions, which eventually appeared in four volumes between 1969 and 1972. In eastern and south-central Africa, several archaeologists were producing initial accounts of research on the farming peoples of the first millennium AD who had made pottery related to that provisionally attributed to the first Bantu-speakers. Posnansky (1968) in the Lake Victoria region, Soper (1967a,b) in Kenya and the present writer (Phillipson 1968) in Zambia all produced local archaeological syntheses, with radiocarbon dates, which demonstrated that varied farming communities had been widely distributed through the savannas since early in the Christian era (see Grundeman 1968).

Shortly afterwards, two independent attempts were made to synthesize this new archaeological information. Soper (1971) wrote from an East African perspective, while Huffman's (1970) viewpoint was centred south of the Zambezi. Although differing in their detailed conclusions, both recognized several regional traditions which shared some common affinity: Huffman applied an American model and attributed them to a single co-tradition. The dearth of archaeological investigations in the equatorial forest and other northwesterly regions continued to restrain attempts at an overall synthesis.

A few years later, the present writer (Phillipson 1976; 1977a,b) offered a more comprehensive synthesis which attempted to compare linguistic and archaeological reconstructions. The archaeological data were regarded as paramount, but were largely restricted to the savanna regions of eastern and southern Africa. They were essentially those previously discussed by Soper and Huffman, with additional subsequent discoveries mostly from Zambia and South Africa. The almost total lack of archaeological material from the northwest — indeed, from any part of the equatorial forest — was a serious impediment, as was the extreme scarcity of reliable information from the western savanna of Angola. By this time a large number of radiocarbon dates was available and a detailed examination of these (Phillipson 1975) had supported the view that the characteristic pottery was somewhat earlier in the Lake Victoria region than further to the south. An elaborate ten-stage reconstruction was offered (Phillipson 1977a, 227–30), arguing for the early development of Bantu speech in the Cameroon area c. 1000 BC by a stone-tool-using population which, at a relatively early date, obtained domestic goats and may have practised some form of agriculture. Subsequently, some of these Bantu-speakers dispersed eastwards along the northern fringes of the equatorial forest. In the process, they came into contact with mixed-farmers who may have been speakers of ancestral Central Sudanic languages and from them, through a relatively prolonged period of contact, adopted the herding of domestic cattle and sheep, as well as the cultivation of certain cereal crops, notably sorghum.

Almost certainly it was at this stage also that knowledge of metal-working techniques was acquired by Bantu-speaking people. They established an Early Iron Age culture in the interlacustrine region, where they are represented in the archaeological record by sites yielding Urewe ware. A second Bantu-speaking population penetrated southwards from Cameroon to the area south of the lower Congo. These were stone-tool-using people making pottery and ground-stone artefacts, and may have brought with them knowledge of those food-production techniques with which their ancestors had been acquainted in the Cameroon area. Some Urewe ware-makers spread around the flank of the equatorial forests to the southern savanna and then westwards, where they were responsible for introducing many aspects of Early Iron Age culture to the other group of Bantu-speakers who had moved directly southwards from Cameroon to the lower Congo area. This coalescence subsequently gave rise to the western stream of the Early Iron Age. An eastern stream meanwhile penetrated southwards and eastwards from the interlacustrine region to the coast of southern Kenya and northern Tanzania, establishing settlements characterized by Kwale ware. A major southward expansion of the eastern stream c. AD 300–400 from the interlacustrine region passed through the highlands west of Lake Malawi to the South African interior. A parallel southward expansion brought the eastern stream's lowland facies from the Kwale area, east of Lake Malawi, to southern Mozambique and Kwazulu / Natal. Slightly later, peoples of the western stream expanded eastwards into Shaba and western Zambia, establishing contact with the eastern-stream people.

This elaborate and premature attempt at a comprehensive synthesis received detailed criticism from several sources. Although at first, several archaeologists objected to the use of the term 'stream' to designate the main divisions, on the grounds that it implied a linear migration, the term has subsequently received surprisingly wide usage. Terminology aside, the main criticism of the detailed division concerned the attribution of the inland South African material to the eastern rather than the western stream. It was correctly observed by several critics that an archaeological synthesis which claimed to cover the whole of the sub-continent had been drawn up on the almost exclusive basis of discoveries in the eastern half of that area. Winter (1981) noted with justification that the synthesis was not based on an exhaustive comparative typological analysis of pottery assemblages. Several archaeologists felt that the work relied too heavily on linguistic sources. It is noteworthy, however, that the broad overall picture has, despite initial criticism, gained widespread but not unanimous, acceptance (but cf. Robertson & Bradley 2000).

In 1979 and 1980, Vansina published an exhaustive critique of the syntheses that had been proposed, without offering an alternative. In 1984, however, he produced a valuable paper, based almost entirely on recent lexicostatistical studies at Tervuren (e.g. Bastin *et al.* 1983), which provided new insights on the establishment of Bantu speech in the equatorial forest and adjacent regions, thus rectifying one of the main weaknesses of earlier syntheses. At the same time he was able to offer a revised and more precise plotting of the modern linguistic boundary between eastern and western Bantu than had previously been attempted. He emphasized that, through much of the southern savanna, the modern Bantu languages show a combination of both eastern and western features.

From this time onwards, a series of local studies began to provide much-needed detail and coherence both in southern Africa (Ehret *et al.* 1972; Ehret & Kinsman 1981) and in the east (Nurse & Philippson 1980; Hinnebusch *et al.* 1981; Wrigley 1987; Nurse 1988; Nurse & Hinnebusch 1993). The integration of linguistic studies with other methodologies still proved problematic, however, except in cases where emphasis was placed on a particular aspect of the past, such as the development of metallurgical techniques (e.g. de Maret & Nsuka 1977; Nsuka-Nkutsi & de Maret 1980).

During the 1980s and 1990s there became available for the first time a significant body of archaeological information from the equatorial forest of the Congo basin, as well as from Gabon and Cameroon. Reconnaissance led by Eggert (e.g. 1983) received definitive publication by Wotzka (1995). Wotzka specifically proposed that the archaeological evidence for the spread of pottery-making (or pottery-using) peoples through the forest marked the progress of Bantu-speakers, but he did not himself attempt a re-evaluation of the linguistic data. Vansina (1990), in a substantial work on the development of political tradition in equatorial Africa, greatly amplified his account of western Bantu expansion in the region. The work is marred by an unsophisticated use of chronometric data, glottochronological calculations and radiocarbon determinations both being attributed unwarranted precision. Far to the south the present writer (Phillipson 1989) drew attention to possible connections between a new archaeological reconstruction of the inception of herding in the Kalahari fringe and linguistic evidence for the early development of Khoikhoi dialects (see also Denbow & Campbell 1986). Subsequently, a revised synthesis (Phillipson 1993a) concentrated almost exclusively on archaeological data, making no attempt to further the debate on linguistic correlations. A further overview by Vansina (1995), stated to be based on the results of a major and long-awaited lexicostatistical study which has not yet been published in detail, reaffirms the division between eastern and western Bantu languages but makes disappointingly little use of archaeological data. Likewise, Ehret (1998) has offered an account of history in Bantu-speaking Africa which, while satisfying in itself, is extremely hard for the non-linguist to use and which fails adequately to relate with the increasing body of non-linguistic data now available.

Despite ongoing controversies, it is reasonable to claim that a broad consensus is emerging which combines archaeological and linguistic evidence for a major cultural and demographic discontinuity in most of subequatorial Africa between 2500 and 1500 years ago. The most readily discernible results of this were the adoption of Bantu languages, of herding and cultivation techniques, and of metallurgy. It would be facile to claim that all these innovations were precisely synchronous in view of the varying influences of earlier (perhaps mainly Khoisan-speaking) populations, and of environmental and other constraints on economic and technological development, but a broad overview, with major contrasts between west and east, between forest and savanna, is now beginning to emerge and receives further support as more in-depth local studies become available.

Notes

1. Note that parts of the continent have been colonized from Phoenician times onwards. It is arguable that the term 'pre-colonial African languages' should not embrace the Semitic languages of the Horn and much of northern Africa. Under this head I have, however, somewhat arbitrarily included Ge'ez, Tigre, Tigrinya and Amharic, while excluding Arabic.
2. An opposing view was expressed at the conference by Militarev (this volume).
3. Many African societies have traditionally based their subsistence exclusively on cultivation or on herding. The generalized concept of 'food production' is frequently, in an African context, misleading — not only because it confuses two independent processes, but also because there are important products of both cultivators and herders that are used for purposes other than food.
4. Note that the study by Zohary & Hopf (1994) of plant domestication in the Old World ignores sub-Saharan Africa.
5. The distribution of Nilo-Saharan languages is now notably discontinuous, presumably following expansion of Afroasiatic speakers.

References

Archbell, J., 1838. *A Grammar of the Bechuana Language.* Grahamstown: Meurant & Godlonton.

Barnett, T., 1999. *The Emergence of Food Production in Ethiopia.* (British Archaeological Reports International Series 763.) Oxford: BAR.

Bastin, Y., A. Coupez & B. de Halleux, 1983. Classification lexicostatistique des langues bantoues (214 relevés). *Bulletin de l'Académie royale des Sciences d'Outre-Mer* 27, 173–99.

Bleek, W., 1862–69. *A Comparative Grammar of South African Languages.* Cape Town: Solomon.

Blench, R., 1993. Recent developments in African language classification and their implications for prehistory, in Shaw *et al.* (eds.), 126–38.

Blench, R. & K. MacDonald (eds.), 1998. *The Origins and Development of African Livestock: Archaeology, Genetics, Linguistics and Ethnography.* London: UCL Press.

Blench, R. & M. Spriggs (eds.), 1997. *Archaeology and Language,* vol. I: *Theoretical and Methodological Orientations.* London: Routledge.

Blench, R. & M. Spriggs (eds.), 1998. *Archaeology and Language,* vol. II: *Archaeological Data and Linguistic Hypotheses.* London: Routledge.

Bouquiaux, L. (ed.), 1980. *L'expansion bantoue.* Paris: SELAF.

Connell, B., 1998. Linguistic evidence for the development of yam and palm culture among the Delta Cross River peoples of southeastern Nigeria, in Blench & Spriggs (eds.), 324–65.

Dalby, D. (ed.), 1970. *Language and History in Africa.* London: Frank Cass.

Dalby, D., 1975. The prehistorical implications of Guthrie's *Comparative Bantu*: I - problems of internal relationship. *Journal of African History* 16, 481–501.

Dalby, D., 1976. The prehistorical implications of Guthrie's *Comparative Bantu*: II - interpretation of cultural vocabulary. *Journal of African History* 17, 1–27.

David, N., 1982a. Prehistory and historical linguistics in Central Africa: points of contact, in Ehret & Posnansky (eds.), 78–95.

David, N., 1982b. The B.I.E.A. Southern Sudan Expedition of 1979: interpretation of the archaeological data, in Mack & Robertshaw (eds.), 49–57.

de Maret, P. & Y. Nsuka, 1977. History of Bantu metallurgy: some linguistic aspects. *History in Africa* 4, 43–66.

Denbow, J. & A. Campbell, 1986. The early stages of food production in southern Africa and some potential linguistic correlations. *Sprache und Geschichte in Afrika* 7.1, 83–103.

Eggert, M.K.H., 1983. Remarks on exploring archaeologically unknown rain forest territory: the case of Central Africa. *Beitrage zur Algemeinen und Verleichenden Archaologie* 5, 283–322.

Ehret, C., 1967. Cattle-keeping and Central Sudanic peoples in southern Africa. *Journal of African History* 8, 1–17.

Ehret, C., 1968. Sheep and Central Sudanic peoples in southern Africa. *Journal of African History* 9, 213–21.

Ehret, C., 1972. Bantu origins and history: critique and interpretation. *Transafrican Journal of History* 2, 1–19.

Ehret, C., 1973. Patterns of Bantu and Central Sudanic settlement in central and southern Africa. *Transafrican Journal of History* 3, 1–71.

Ehret, C., 1974a. Agricultural history in central and southern Africa. *Transafrican Journal of History* 4, 1–25.

Ehret, C., 1974b. *Ethiopians and East Africans: the Problem of Contacts.* Nairobi: East African Publishing House.

Ehret, C., 1980. On the antiquity of agriculture in Ethiopia. *Journal of African History* 20, 161–77.

Ehret, C., 1981. The demographic implication of linguistic change and language shift, in Fyfe & McMaster (eds.), 153–82.

Ehret, C., 1982. Population movement and culture contact in the Southern Sudan, *c.* 3000 BC–AD 1000: a preliminary linguistic overview, in Mack & Robertshaw (eds.), 19–57.

Ehret, C., 1988. Language change and the material correlates of language and ethnic shift. *Antiquity* 62, 564–74.

Ehret, C., 1998. *An African Classical Age.* Oxford: Currey.

Ehret, C. & M. Kinsman, 1981. Shona dialect classification and its implications for Iron Age history in southern Africa. *International Journal of African Historical Studies* 14, 401–43.

Ehret, C. & M. Posnansky (eds.), 1982. *The Archaeological and Linguistic Reconstruction of African History.* Berkeley (CA): University of California Press.

Ehret, C., M. Bink, T. Ginindza, B. Hall, M. Hlatschwayo, D. Johson & R.L. Powels, 1972. Outlining southern African history, AD 100–1500. *Ufahamu* 3, 9–27.

Ehret, C., T. Coffman, L. Fliegelman, A. Gold, M. Hubbard, D. Johnson & D. Saxon, 1974. Thoughts on the history of the Nile-Congo watershed. *Ufahamu* 5, 85–112.

Flight, C., 1980. Guthrie and the reconstruction of Bantu prehistory. *History in Africa* 7, 81–118.

Fyfe, C. & D. McMaster (eds.), 1982. *African Historical Demography 2.* Edinburgh: University of Edinburgh African Studies Centre.

Gramly, R.M., 1978. Expansion of Bantu-speakers *versus* development of Bantu language and African culture *in situ*. *South African Archaeological Bulletin* 33, 107–12.

Greenberg, J., 1963. *The Languages of Africa.* The Hague: Mouton.

Greenberg, J., 1972. Linguistic evidence concerning Bantu origins. *Journal of African History* 13, 189–216.

Greenberg, J., 1974. Bantu and its closest relatives, in Leben (ed.), 115–19.

Grundeman, T., 1968. Wenner-Gren conference on Bantu origins. *Bulletin of the African Studies Association of the United Kingdom* 13, 2–9.

Guthrie, M., 1962. Some developments in the prehistory of the Bantu languages. *Journal of African History* 3, 273–82.

Guthrie, M., 1967–71. *Comparative Bantu: an Introduction to the Comparative Linguistics and Prehistory of the Bantu*

Languages. Farnborough: Gregg.

Guthrie, M., 1970. Contributions from comparative Bantu studies to the prehistory of Africa, in Dalby (ed.), 20–33.

Heine, B., 1973. Zur genetischen Gliederung der Bantusprachen. *Afrika und Übersee* 59, 164–85.

Heine, B. & W.J. Möhlig (eds.), 1980. *Language and Dialect Atlas of Kenya*, vol. 1. Berlin: Reimer.

Heine, B. & D. Nurse (eds.), 2000. *African Languages: an Introduction.* Cambridge: Cambridge University Press.

Heine, B., H. Hoff & R. Vossen, 1977. Neuere Ergebnisse zur Territorialgeschichte der Bantu, in Möhlig *et al.* (eds.), 57–70.

Henrici, A., 1973. Numerical classification of Bantu languages. *African Language Studies* 14, 82–104.

Hinnebusch, T.J., D. Nurse & M. Mould (eds.), 1981. *Studies in the Classification of Eastern Bantu Languages.* Hamburg: Helmut Buske.

Huffman, T.N., 1970. The Early Iron Age and the spread of the Bantu. *South African Archaeological Bulletin* 25, 3–21.

Huffman, T.N., 1989. *Iron Age Migrations.* Johannesburg: Witwatersrand University Press.

Johnston, H.H., 1886. *The Kilima-Njaro Expedition: a Record of Scientific Exploration in Eastern Equatorial Africa.* London: Kegan Paul, Trench & Co.

Johnston, H.H., 1919–22. *A Comparative Study of the Bantu and Semi-Bantu Languages.* Oxford: Clarendon Press.

Leben, W.R. (ed.), 1974. *Papers from the Fifth Annual Conference on African Linguistics.* Los Angeles (CA): University of California.

Lwanga-Lunyiigo, S., 1976. The Bantu problem reconsidered. *Current Anthropology* 17, 282–5.

MacDonald, K., 1998. Archaeology, language and the peopling of West Africa: a consideration of the evidence, in Blench & Spriggs (eds.), 33–66.

Mack, J. & P. Robertshaw (eds.), 1982. *Culture History in the Southern Sudan.* Nairobi: British Institute in Eastern Africa.

Mann, W.M., 1970. Internal relationships of the Bantu languages: prospects for topological research, in Dalby (ed.), 133–45.

Mann, W.M., 1980. Similarity analyses and the classification of the Bantu languages, in Bouquiaux (ed.), 583–91.

Möhlig, W.J., 1977. Zur frühen Siedlungsgeschichte der Savannen-Bantu aus authistorischer Sicht, in Möhlig *et al.* (eds.), 166–93.

Möhlig, W.J., 1979. The Bantu nucleus: its conditional nature and its prehistorical significance. *Sprache und Geschichte in Afrika* 1, 109–42.

Möhlig, W.J., 1981. Stratification in the history of the Bantu languages. *Sprache und Geschichte in Afrika* 3, 251–316.

Möhlig, W.J., F. Rottland & B. Heine (eds.), 1977. *Zur Sprachgeschichte und Ethnohistorie in Afrika.* Berlin: Reimer.

Murdock, G.P., 1959. *Africa: its Peoples and their Culture History.* New York (NY): McGraw-Hill.

Nsuka-Nkutsi, F. & P. de Maret, 1980. Étude comparative de quelques termes métallurgiques dans les langues bantoues, in Bouquiaux (ed.), 731–41.

Nurse, D., 1988. The diachronic background to the language communities of south-western Tanzania. *Sprache und Geschichte in Afrika* 9, 15–116.

Nurse, D. & T.J. Hinnebusch, 1993. *Swahili and Sabaki: a Linguistic History.* Berkeley (CA): University of California Press.

Nurse, D. & G. Philippson, 1980. Historical implications of the language map of East Africa, in Bouquiaux (ed.), 685–714.

Oliver, R., 1957. *Sir Harry Johnston and the Scramble for Africa.* London: Chatto & Windus.

Oliver, R., 1966. The problem of the Bantu expansion. *Journal of African History* 7, 361–76.

Oliver, R. (ed.), 1978. *The Cambridge History of Africa*, vol. II. Cambridge: Cambridge University Press.

Oliver, R., 1979. Cameroun — the Bantu cradleland? *Sprache und Geschichte in Afrika* 1, 7–20 .

Oliver, R. & B.M. Fagan, 1975. *Africa in the Iron Age.* Cambridge: Cambridge University Press.

Oliver, R. & B.M. Fagan, 1978. The emergence of Bantu Africa, in Oliver (ed.), 342–409.

Phillipson, D.W., 1968. The Early Iron Age in Zambia: regional variants and some tentative conclusions. *Journal of African History* 9, 191–211.

Phillipson, D.W., 1974. Iron Age history and archaeology in Zambia. *Journal of African History* 15, 1–25.

Phillipson, D.W., 1975. The chronology of the Iron Age in Bantu Africa. *Journal of African History* 16, 321–42.

Phillipson, D.W., 1976. Archaeology and Bantu linguistics. *World Archaeology* 8, 65–82.

Phillipson, D.W., 1977a. *Later Prehistory of Eastern and Southern Africa.* London: Heinemann.

Phillipson, D.W., 1977b. The spread of the Bantu languages. *Scientific American* 236(4), 106–14.

Phillipson, D.W., 1985. An archaeological reconsideration of Bantu expansion. *Muntu* 2, 69–84.

Phillipson, D.W., 1989. The first South African pastoralists and the Early Iron Age. *Nsi* 6, 127–34.

Phillipson, D.W., 1993a. *African Archaeology.* 2nd edition. Cambridge: Cambridge University Press.

Phillipson, D.W., 1993b. The antiquity of cultivation and herding in Ethiopia, in Shaw *et al.* (eds.), 344–57.

Posnansky, M., 1961a. Bantu genesis. *Uganda Journal* 25, 86–93.

Posnansky, M., 1961b. Iron Age in East and Central Africa: points of comparison. *South African Archaeological Bulletin* 16, 134–6.

Posnansky, M., 1968. Bantu genesis: archaeological reflexions. *Journal of African History* 9, 1–11.

Renfrew, C., 1997. World linguistic diversity and farming dispersals, in Blench & Spriggs (eds.), 82–90.

Robertson, J.H. & R. Bradley, 2000. A new paradigm: the African Early Iron Age without Bantu migrations. *History in Africa* 27, 287–323.

Shaw, T., P. Sinclair, B. Andah & A. Okpoko (eds.), 1993.

The Archaeology of Africa. London: Routledge.

Soper, R., 1967a. Kwale: an Early Iron Age site in south-eastern Kenya. *Azania* 2, 1–17.

Soper, R., 1967b. Iron Age sites in north-eastern Tanzania. *Azania* 2, 19–36.

Soper, R., 1971. A general review of the Early Iron Age in the southern half of Africa. *Azania* 6, 5–37.

Sutton, J.E.G., 1974. The aquatic civilisation of middle Africa. *Journal of African History* 15, 527–46.

Theal, G.M., 1910. *The Yellow and Dark-Skinned People of Africa South of the Zambesi*. London: Sonnenschein.

van der Veen, M. (ed.), 1998. *Exploitation of Plant Resources in Ancient Africa*. Dordrecht: Kluwer.

Vansina, J., 1979. Bantu in the crystal ball - I. *History in Africa* 6, 287–333.

Vansina, J., 1980. Bantu in the crystal ball - II. *History in Africa* 7, 293–325.

Vansina, J., 1984. Western Bantu expansion. *Journal of African History* 25, 129–45.

Vansina, J., 1989. Deep-down time: political tradition in central Africa. *History in Africa* 16, 341–62.

Vansina, J., 1990. *Paths in the Rainforests: Toward a History of Political Tradition in Equatorial Africa*. London: James Currey.

Vansina, J., 1995. New linguistic evidence and the 'Bantu expansion'. *Journal of African History* 36, 173–95.

Winter, J.C., 1981. Bantu prehistory in eastern and southern Africa: an evaluation of D.W. Phillipson's archaeological synthesis in the light of ethnological and linguistic evidence. *Sprache und Geschichte in Afrika* 3, 317–56.

Wotzka, H.-P. 1995. *Studien zur Archäologie des zentralafrikanischen Regenwaldes*. Cologne: Heinrich-Barth-Institut.

Wrigley, C.C., 1987. Cattle and language between the lakes. *Sprache und Geschichte in Afrika* 8, 247–80.

Zohary, D. & M. Hopf, 1994. *Domestication of Plants in the Old World*. Oxford: Clarendon Press.

B. *Asia and Oceania*

Chapter 16

An Agricultural Perspective on Dravidian Historical Linguistics: Archaeological Crop Packages, Livestock and Dravidian Crop Vocabulary

Dorian Fuller

The Indian subcontinent is diverse both linguistically and agriculturally. Linguistically, the Indo-European, Austro-Asiatic, Dravidian and Tibeto-Burman languages are present in the subcontinent as well as a few unclassified languages (e.g. Parpola 1994; Tikkanen 1999). Subtracting crops introduced from the New World during the colonial period, one is still left with a staggering diversity of cereal species, pulse species, tubers, oilseeds and fruits which derive from origins in Africa, Southwest Asia, Central Asia, China, Southeast Asia and of course South Asia itself (see Fuller 2002; Fuller & Madella 2001). There has been something of a tacit acceptance that South Asian agriculture is derivative and secondary, either based on introduced taxa and systems or else on some local species inspired by the introduction of agriculture (e.g. Hutchinson 1976; MacNeish 1992; Harlan 1995). Within the context of the Renfrew/Bellwood hypothesis, the three major language groups of central and peninsular India have all been attributed to such language-farming dispersals, including Indo-European, Dravidian and Austro-Asiatic (the Munda sub-family) (e.g. Renfrew 1992; 1996; Bellwood 1996). These hypotheses, however, have not been considered in detail in relation to either the archaeological, archaeobotanical or linguistic evidence relating directly to early agriculture in South Asia. The present paper will do this, with a particular emphasis on peninsular India and Dravidian languages, by drawing upon the now considerable and growing data base of archaeobotanical data (Fuller 1999; 2002), as well as archaeozoological data (e.g. Thomas & Joglekar 1994; Meadow 1996).

The Neolithic cultures recognized in South Asia are generally later than those known from the Southwest Asian centre of origin or from China (Table 16.1). For the Neolithic of southern India, immigrant origins have been postulated from either the northeast or northwest. In the 1940s the known distribution of lithic materials, especially ground-stone axes and shouldered celts, was used to postulate general origins of India's Neolithic coming from the northeast, ultimately from Southeast Asia (Wheeler 1948, 295; 1959, 89; Worman 1949, 199). A detailed review of the available evidence, however, led Allchin to critique this, and establish the peninsular Neolithic as a tradition distinct from that emanating from northeastern India (Allchin 1957). Allchin (1960; 1963) discussed possible parallels for southern Neolithic pottery in Iran, implying either migration or diffusion from the northwest. He noted, however, that the lack of systematic archaeology in the intervening regions, especially the northern Peninsula, made this hypothesis vulnerable to revision (Allchin 1963, 160). Subsequent research favours independence since the Neolithic begins earlier here than in the northern Peninsula (Shinde 1994; Allchin & Allchin 1997; Korisettar *et al.* 2001). Indeed, an independent centre of plant domestication on the Indian Peninsula, and probably more than one in the subcontinent, is now suggested by botanical and archaeological evidence (Fuller 1999; 2001; 2002; Fuller *et al.* 2001).

Similarly, the distributions of Dravidian and Munda languages have suggested immigrations into India. While some authors have assumed that all language families came from the northwest, with Munda as a relict of early peopling (e.g. Gadgil *et al.* 1998), Munda is usually derived from the northeast due to its relationship to the largely Southeast Asian Austro-Asiatic family (e.g. Higham 1995; this volume; Bellwood 1996; Blust 1996). The presence of Brahui, a Dravidian language in Pakistan, and the

Table 16.1. *Comparative chronology of Neolithic/Chalcolithic cultures of South Asia and main sequences in Southwest Asia and China. There remains poor internal chronological evidence for the Mesolithic of South Asia and the beginnings of Neolithic sequences.*

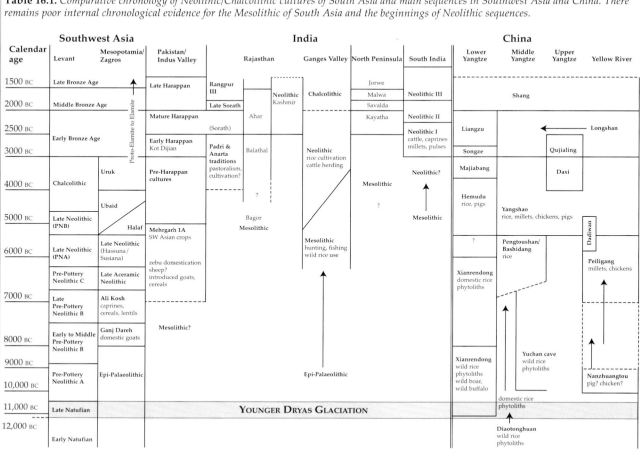

possibility of a relationship with ancient Elamite, have pointed towards a northwestern introduction for Dravidian languages (e.g. McAlpin 1981; Fairservis & Southworth 1989; Parpola 1994). While some authors have argued for the introduction of Dravidian languages later than the Neolithic, for example with the 'megalithic' burial traditions of the first millennium BC (Fürer-Haimendorf 1948; 1953; Maloney 1975), recent opinions tend to push this family back to the beginnings of agriculture (Renfrew 1992; 1996; Bellwood 1996; Cavalli-Sforza & Cavalli-Sforza 1995; Gadgil *et al.* 1998). Parpola (1994, 174) associates Dravidian speakers with the 'Chalcolithic phase' of the northern Peninsula (as well as the Harappan civilization) and therefore suggests an immigration into the Peninsula between 1700–1000 BC (i.e. *during* the latter half of the southern Neolithic tradition of Karnataka).

The current paper will develop an alternative model by building on empirical archaeological evidence and the linguistics of particular crops and agricultural terms. While most previous hypotheses have been based on broad-brush generalizations, such as geographical distributions of languages and chronological priority of archaeological cultures, this paper will start with empirical building blocks and smaller linguistic inferences. A starting point for understanding the origins of agriculture in South Asia is determining where particular species of crops (and livestock) are likely have originally been wild and domesticated. The available archaeological evidence for the presence of these species in different regions during different periods can then be considered to provide a geographical and chronological framework for the dispersal of these species, and to outline the existence of agricultural packages of different regions and different periods. There is now a sizeable data base of sites with archaeobotanical evidence, with just over 100 sites reviewed by Fuller (2002), as well as additional recent evidence.

With these outlined archaeo-agricultural packages as a starting point, I will then turn to the linguistic data for key species to see how far back they can be reconstructed for sub-groupings within the

Dravidian family, and how these might relate to geographical groupings. On the basis of the available evidence I will argue that much of the modern distribution and the diversification within the Dravidian languages, including South, South-Central and Central Dravidian subfamilies, can be argued to go back to the beginnings of food production but that the evidence suggests that the proto-Dravidians (including the North Dravidian Branch) were already in place on the Indian Peninsula as seed-using foragers and differentiating when agriculture began. Also a few implications for the prehistory of other language groups, such as Munda, will be outlined.

Crop packages of early South Asia

Before engaging with linguistic data, we can outline the picture of early regional agricultures provided by botanical and archaeological evidence. Over recent decades there has been an increasing quantity of archaeobotanical research with more widespread use of systematic flotation sampling (Kajale 1991; Fuller 2002). The archaeobotanical record is biased toward cereals and pulses, and it is therefore these staple categories for which we have the best sense of their ancient distribution. While the evidence on wild progenitors often requires further research, a rather dispersed literature provides insights into likely regions of origin (Fuller 1999; 2002). A synthetic map of early agricultural traditions in South Asia is given in Figure 16.1.

In northwestern South Asia, the dominant crops were derived from Near Eastern Neolithic founders (*sensu* Zohary 1996; Zohary & Hopf 2000). A fairly complete Southwest Asian agricultural package was well-established and presumably widespread by the time of Harappan urbanism (Meadow 1996; 1998; Fuller & Madella 2001), including wheats, barley, lentils, chickpeas/gram, peas, grass pea, and flax/linseed. It remains to be clarified whether these crops came to South Asia together at the period of agricultural beginnings, represented by the site of Mehrgarh where systematic flotation samples were not available (Costantini 1983), or whether the pulses and flax diffused separately over a much longer period, as might be suggested by the evidence from Miri Qalat (Tengberg 1999). These crops spread to some regions east of the Indus Valley in pre-Harappan times, before the end of the fourth millennium BC, as suggested by the emerging evidence from Ahar culture sites such as Balathal (cf. Kajale 1996a; Misra *et al.* 1997). They spread into the Ganges Valley during

the Harappan phase, i.e. 2500–2000 BC and their further diffusion into central or peninsular India may have occurred after the mid-third millennium BC, as stray finds from the site of Kayatha suggest.

In the northern Deccan Chalcolithic (Maharashtra) of the early second millennium BC, wheats, barley and southwest Asian pulses were important crops, while only wheats and barley made a limited impact on the Neolithic of the Southern Deccan, perhaps as early 2200 BC. In both South India and the Ganges Valley the early finds of the Southwest Asian (and Harappan) package of winter crops suggest that these species were added to existing agricultural systems based on other monsoonal crops, and did not get agriculture started.

In southern India, the archaeobotanical evidence (Fuller 1999; Fuller *et al.* 2001) indicates that a basic set of native staples occurred throughout the Southern Deccan (Table 16.2). Evidence from 11 sites indicates the predominance of mungbean (*Vigna radiata*), probably deriving from wild progenitor populations in the transitional vegetation zones east of the Western Ghats; horsegram (*Macrotyloma uniflorum*), presumably a savanna native in the Deccan (as well as elsewhere in India?); as well as browntop millet (*Brachiaria ramosa*) and bristley foxtail (*Setaria verticillata*), both grasses of uncommon but localized occurrence on wetter soils in the semi-arid Deccan savanna zones. There is also parenchyma tissue from all sampled sites and nearly all contexts, which suggests tuber use, possibly wild(?) yams. A wild *Cucumis* species was also utilized, although cucurbitaceous vegetables were probably of no great significance. In addition, a range of wild fruits, available during the dry season, are in evidence. Other millets of peninsular Indian origin have also been recovered in small quantities, although they may not have been cultivars, including little millet (*Panicum sumatrense*), kodo millet (*Paspalum scrobiculatum* L.), sawa millet (*Echinochloa colona* (L.) Link), and yellow foxtail millet (*Setaria pumila* (Poir.) Roem & Schultz, syn. *S. glauca* auct. pl.).

During the course of the South Deccan Neolithic and the North Deccan Chalcolithic a number of other crops originating elsewhere were added to the subsistence system (Table 16.3). Crops of African origin had arrived in India, although they had not apparently become of widespread importance, including sorghum, pearl millet, hyacinth bean and cowpea. To a more limited extent, some of these crops were also taken up in northwestern India. They apparently arrived in a piecemeal fashion, during the same general phase that wheats and barley were taken up in the

Table 16.2. *Early Neolithic food plants of South India, and their native habitat.*

Early Neolithic, Southern Deccan			Available wild fruits: Deccan Neolithic/Chalcolithic		
Ashmoud Tradition Phase I: 2800–2200 BC (& earlier?)					
Inferred basic package			Jujube	*Ziziphus mauritania*	dry deciduous/savanna
Mungbean	*Vigna radiata*	wet(–dry) deciduous forests	Sebestan plum	*Cordia dichotoma*	wet deciduous
			Emblic myrobalan	*Phylianthus emblica*	wet deciduous
Horsegram	*Macrotyloma uniflorum*	Peninsula: savanna	Cuddapah almond	*Buchnania lanzan*	dry deciduous
Browntop millet	*Brachiaria ramosa*	Peninsula: savanna	Indian jambos	*Syzigium cumini*	wet deciduous
Bristley Foxtail	*Setaria verticillata*	Peninsula: savanna	Figs	*Ficus* spp.	various
Wild(?) yams	*Dioscorea* sp.	wet(–dry) deciduous forests			

Table 16.3. *Food plants added to subsistence in peninsular India during the Neolithic/Chalcolithic, and their regions of origin.*

Middle Neolithic, Southern Deccan: Additional Crops			Malwa-Jorwe Chalcolithic, Northern Deccan		
Ashmoud Tradition Phase II: 2200–1800 BC			*1700–1000 BC*		
Hyacinth bean	*Lablab purpureus*	Africa	Mungbean	*Vigna radiata*	Peninsula: wet(–dry) deciduous
Pearl millet	*Pennisetum glaucum*	Africa	Urd	*Vigna mungo*	Peninsula: Wet(–dry) deciduous
Wheat	*Triticum* spp.	Southwest Asia, via Indus Valley	Horsegram	*Macrotyloma uniflorum*	Peninsula: savanna
Barley	*Hordeum vulgare*	Southwest Asia, via Indus Valley	Browntop millet?	*Brachiaria ramosa*	Peninsula: savanna
Grasspea?	*Lathyrus sativus*	Southwest Asia, via Indus Valley	Bristley Foxtail?	*Setaria verticillata*	Peninsula: savanna
			Little millet?	*Panicum sumatrense*	Peninsula: savanna
Late Neolithic, Southern Deccan: Additional Crops			Wheat	*Triticum* spp.	Southwest Asia, via Indus Valley
Ashmoud Tradition Phase III: 1800–1000 BC			Grasspea	*Lathyrus sativus*	Southwest Asia, via Indus Valley
Pigeonpea	*Cajanus cajan*	eastern Peninsula: Orissa	Pea	*Pisum sativum*	Southwest Asia, via Indus Valley
Hyacinth bean	*Lablab purpureus*	Africa	Lentil	*Lens culinaris*	Southwest Asia, via Indus Valley
Cotton	*Gossypium* cf. *arboreum*	Peninsula? or Indus Valley	Chickpea	*Cicer arietinum*	Southwest Asia, via Indus Valley
Linseed/flax	*Linum usitatissimum*	Southwest Asia, via Indus Valley	Hyacinth bean	*Lablab purpureus*	Africa
Finger millet?	*Eleusine coacana*	Africa	Cow pea	*Vigna unguiculata*	Africa
Present only at end of phase?			Pearl millet	*Pennisetum glaucum*	Africa
			Great millet	*Sorghum bicolor*	Africa

Southern Deccan. Additional crops from elsewhere in India are also first documented during this period, including pigeonpea, a native of Bastar and Orissa.

The situation in Gangetic India also indicates that possible native domesticates were being cultivated when the Southwest Asian crops were introduced. Recent sampling at Senuwar (Saraswat in press; see also, Saraswat 1992; Saraswat & Chanchala 1995) indicates that, during the first phase of this Neolithic site, wheat, barley, lentils and peas arrived later than rice (*Oryza sativa*) and yellow foxtail (*Setaria pumila*). This implies that a rice-millet cultivation system was already established before other crops were introduced from the west. Evidence from the upper and middle Ganges, as at Senuwar, indicates that some crops of African origin were adopted early in the second millennium BC, including hyacinth bean, cowpea and sorghum, while evidence

for pearl millet and finger millet is absent before the late second millennium BC (Fuller in press).

An important set of crops native to northern India, but still fairly poorly documented, are cucurbitaceous vegetables including cucumbers (*Cucumis sativus*), snake gourd (*Trichosanthes cucumerina*) and ivy gourd (*Coccinia grandis*). Although *Cucumis* sp. seeds have been reported fairly widely, specific identity remains elusive, with melons, cucmbers and wild species all possibilities. *C. grandis* has been recovered from Hulas in the upper Ganges basin at 1800–1300 BC.

The origins of Indian rice remain problematic, but a domestication event in north India is certainly possible. Rice was domesticated at least once in south China (Lu 1999; Anping 1998; Zhao 1998; Cohen 1998), probably along with chickens (West & Zhou 1988) and pigs (see Smith 1995). Some would tie it to a hypothetical 'Austric' package (*sensu* Blust 1996)

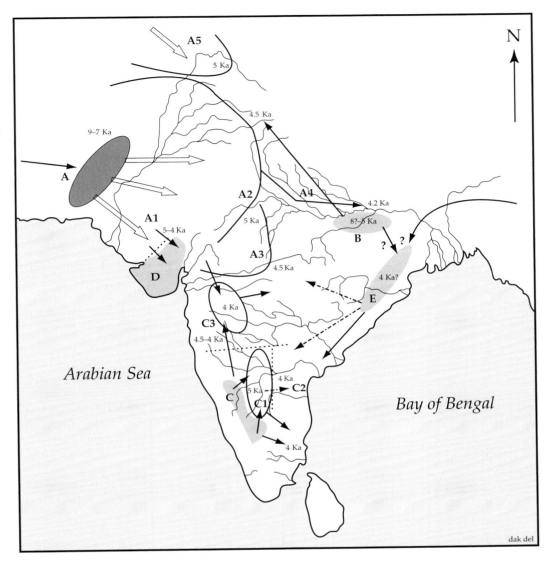

Figure 16.1. *A synthetic view of early agricultural origins and dispersals in South Asia. Regions of probable local domestications shaded. Dispersals indicated by arrows and prehistoric agricultural frontiers indicated by lines (solid = 'moving'; dotted = 'static'). Approximate minimum ages for frontiers and dispersals indicated in 1000s of years before present (calibrated). Important 'events' indicated by letters and numbers: A) early zone of agro-pastoralism of Southwest Asian origin, with some local domestications (zebu cattle, cotton, sheep?); A1) possible dispersal of pastoralism without Southwest Asian cultivars, pastoralism may spread further east and south; A2) frontier of Southwest Asian package with Early Harappan societies and Balathal/Ahar culture; A3) subsequent frontier with Kayatha culture; A4) dispersal of Southwest Asian crops and livestock into Gangetic plain, with existing cultivation system(s); A5) agriculture of Southwest Asian crops of the northern Neolithic may derive from Central Asia; B) middle Ganges centre of domestication, possibly of* indica *rice, also yellow foxtail(?), various cucurbits, horsegram (?) with possible dispersal west and south/east; C) southern domestication centre of small millets and pulses; C1) ashmound tradition, combining south Indian crop domesticates with domestic fauna, possibly introduced from north; C2) eastwards dispersal (diffusion) of Southern Neolithic agro-pastoralism into non-ashmound tradition; C3) northwards dispersal of South Indian crops, combined with Southwest Asian crops and livestock in Chalcolithic Maharshtra; D) Saurashtra where introduced livestock combine with millet cultivation (by the third millennium), possible native millet domestications; E) Orissa Neolithic, where rice could have been domesticated(?) along with pigeonpea and tuber crops (?) — this Neolithic is poorly documented and dated, and could derive from northeastern immigrants.*

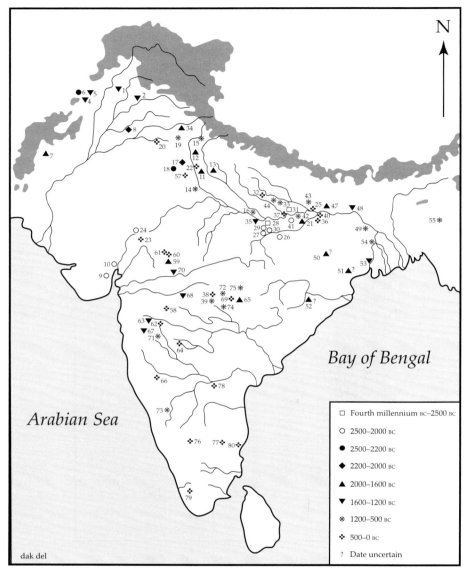

Figure 16.2. *Archaeological evidence for rice in South Asia indicated by chronological phase. (After Fuller 2002.)*

that dispersed by migration into northeastern India with the Austro-Asiatic (Munda) languages (e.g. Higham 1995; this volume; Glover & Higham 1996; Bellwood 1996). The current genetic evidence, however, is clear in indicating a minimum of two domestications for *Oryza sativa* (Sato *et al.* 1990; Sano & Morishima 1992; Chen *et al.* 1993; 1994; Wan & Ikehashi 1997), with the second domestication of *indica* cultivars conceivably in the Gangetic basin. Unfortunately, despite some suggestive early dates from contexts containing rice, which many accept as indicating the domestication of rice in the Vindhya Plateau of north-central India *c.* 6000–5000 BC (Sharma

et al. 1980; Saraswat 1992; Mehra 1997), the dating of the evidence is highly problematic (cf. Allchin & Allchin 1982; Sharma & Sharma 1987; Possehl & Rissman 1992; Glover & Higham 1996), with the mid-fourth to early third millennium BC representing a conservative estimate for evidence of rice use (but not necessarily cultivation) based on impressions in pottery from Chopanimando and subsequent Neolithic sites (Fuller 2002; cf. Chakrabarti 1999, 207). Systematic sampling and direct AMS dates are needed. In addition late Mesolithic (early third or fourth millennium BC) evidence from Damdama suggests wild rice use, together with other wild grasses (cf. *Eleusine indica, Dactylocitnum* sp.: Kajale 1990) by a society that may have been sedentary, although engaged in hunting (Chattopadyaya 1996). The subcontinental record for rice indicates diffusion of this species from the Ganges region starting in the late third millennium (Fig. 16.2).

Leaving aside the problem of rice, there are other crops clearly of Chinese (or perhaps Central Asian) origin that made their appearance in South Asia before 2000 BC. These include at least one of the 'Chinese' millets, common foxtail millet (*Setaria italica* (L.) Beauv.), with much more limited evidence for proso millet (*Panicum miliaceum* L.) and hemp (*Cannabis sativus* L.). Although it is clear that the two millets were important in early north Chinese agriculture, it seems likely that *S. italica,* and perhaps *P. miliaceum* as well, was domesticated more than once in Eurasia, with southeastern Europe and/or the Caucasus as possible regions (cf. Burkill 1953; Prasada Rao *et al.* 1987; Marnival 1992; Zohary & Hopf 2000). The *S. italica* cultivated in India today seems to derive in part from both Chinese and European genetic stock (Li *et al.* 1998). These crops are likely to have reached South Asia from the north or northwest via central Asia, perhaps as early as the Harappan period, although with clearest evidence from the Late Harappan (after 2000 BC). It should be noted, however, that the evidence suggests that each of these three species is likely to have followed its own course of diffusion. *S. italica* appears to have arrived first, as it is reported from Gujarat from the mid-third millennium BC (Weber 1991), whereas *P. miliaceum* appears in Baluchistan and Afghanistan only from sometime in the early second millennium BC (Costantini 1979; Willcox 1991). Thus, these species from Central Asia appear to have played a relatively minor role in the overall patterns of agriculture in early South Asia.

One of the more intriguing patterns is that of Gujarat, which despite being a region generally included in the Harappan civilization (see e.g. Possehl 1980; 1997; Kenoyer 1998; Chakrabarti 1999), shows a very different agricultural system from the Indus Valley (see Weber 1991; 1998; 1999; Reddy 1991; 1994; Chanchala 1994; Kajale 1996b; Fuller 2002). In part this can be attributed to local ecology since Gujarat lacks a perennial major river and instead must rely on monsoon rains — to which the summer-cultivated millets are better suited. Although the earliest archaeobotanical samples date back only to c. 2600 BC, sedentary sites with ceramics such as Padri suggest that cultivation was established by the end of the fourth millennium BC (Shinde 1998; cf. Possehl 1999). Although sites such as Rojdi and Kuntasi which date to the Mature Harappan phase have extremely limited evidence for wheat and barley in a few samples, the ubiquitous and dominant species are tropical millets, including indisputable identification of the native Indian little millet (*Panicum sumatrense*) which appears to dominate published sites, contrasting with the contemporaneous millets from elsewhere on the subcontinent. In addition there is evidence for foxtail millets, probably including *S. verticillata* and *S. pumila,* while *S. italica*, presumably introduced (from Central Asia?) had reached Gujarat by the mid-third millennium BC. While African finger millet (*Eleusine coracana*) has also been reported, details of identification are still awaited (see Fuller 2002; in press).

The fact that these small millets were being cultivated in this region by the middle of the third millennium BC suggests that they were domesticated, perhaps locally. Horsegram may also have been domesticated locally before 3000 BC, and the Southwest Asian winter pulses are in evidence in small quantities before 2000 BC. In general, despite the clear influence of Indus Valley material culture in Gujarat during the third millennium BC (the so-called Sorath Harappan), there appears to be a distinctly native cropping system.

Livestock origins and dispersals

Livestock have long played an important role in South Asian subsistence systems, and, as with crops, different regions of origin can be postulated. Sheep and goat were clearly domesticated in Southwest Asia by the time of the middle Pre-Pottery Neolithic B (Smith 1995; Bar-Yosef & Meadow 1995; Harris 1998; Zeder & Hesse 2000). Genetic and archaeozoological data point to the Zagros mountains of northern Iran for goat domestication (Zeder & Hesse 2000), and both species were present as domesticates by c. 6000 BC at Mehrgarh (Meadow 1996), with the possibility for separate sheep domestication still open (Meadow 1984; 1989; cf. Hiendleder *et al.* 1998). The dispersal of goats (and sheep?) together with wheat and barley (and winter pulses?) from the Fertile Crescent to Baluchistan does not appear to have included domestic cattle, and perhaps preceded their Southwest Asian domestication. In Baluchistan, as the bone evidence from Mehrgarh indicates, humped zebu cattle were independently domesticated (Meadow 1996; MacHugh *et al.* 1997; Bradley *et al.* 1998; Grigson 1985).

From Baluchistan, it is likely that pastoralism spread eastwards. Despite some claims for additional zebu domestications (e.g. Allchin & Allchin 1974; Alur 1990) and some suggestive proxy genetic indicators (Naik 1978), there are no clear archaeozoological or genetic sequence data in support (Pushpendra *et al.* in press). Nevertheless, the presence of large *Bos* bones, which suggest the existence of wild cattle populations in the Neolithic/Chalcolithic period in both Gujarat and South India (Thomas *et al.* 1997), makes additional zebu domestication(s) plausible. The evidence from Gangetic India is problematic, with the identification by Sharma *et al.* (1980) called into question by more recent research on Mesolithic fauna from Damdama, indicating an entirely wild fauna into the (mid?) third millennium BC (Thomas *et al.* 1995a).

Taking a more minimalist view, however, we can assume that cattle dispersed into India from Pakistan. The earliest established dates for the presence of cattle beyond Baluchistan and east of the Indus Valley are c. 4000 BC from northern Gujarat, where recent AMS collagen dates from Loteshwar (Patel 1999) confirm the earlier evidence from Bagor, and perhaps Adamgarh, for sheep/goat and cattle

Table 16.4. *Finds of* Gallus *bones in South Asian archaeological sites, with probable dates cal.* BC. *Those at right occur within the native range of* Gallus spp. *those at top within the range of Red Junglefowl, the ancestor of domestic chicken. Those at left occur outside the modern natural range and are likely domestic chickens. Peninsular finds, at lower right, show general consistency suggesting introduction in the mid-second millennium* BC. *(Data from Sahu 1988; Kane 1989; Venkatasubbaiah* et al. *1992; Joglekar & Thomas 1993; Thomas* et al. *1995a,b.)*

		Areas with wild *Gallus*	
	Areas with wild *Gallus gallus*	**Kashmir** Gufkral I (*c.* 2300 BC)	**Ganges** Damdama (4000–2000 BC) Mahadaha (2500-1000 BC) Bharatapur (2nd mill. BC?) Narhan (*c.* 1400–800 BC)
Areas without wild *Gallus*			
Indus (2500–2000 BC) Harappa Mohenjodaro Kalibangan II Rupar	**Rajasthan** Ahar IC (2100–2000 BC) **Gujarat** Rojdi (2500–2000 BC) Surkotada (2400–2000 BC) Shikarpur (2500–2000 BC)	**Northern Deccan** Daimabad V (1500–1100 BC) Nevasa (1500–1200 BC) Inamgaon (1700–1000 BC) Walki (1500–1000 BC) Thuljapur Garhi (1500–1000 BC)	**Southern Neolithic** Kodekal (1600–900? BC) Paiyampalli (1700–900 BC) Hallur (1400–1100? BC) Hanumantaraopeta (1500–1000? BC) Peddamudiyam (1500–1000? BC)

in Mesolithic contexts (Thomas & Joglekar 1994). A domestic fauna was well-established in Saurashtra by *c.* 3000 BC with the Padri culture (Joglekar 1997). Further east, across the Aravalli hills, the beginnings of the Ahar culture of Rajasthan can now be pushed back into the fourth millennium BC, with cattle and sheep/goat pastoralism (Thomas & Joglekar 1996) and presumably winter crop cultivation (cf. Kajale 1996a). The earliest evidence from the Peninsula remains the ashmounds of Karnataka from *c.* 2800 BC, with a noticeable gap in contemporary or earlier evidence in the intervening region of Maharashtra (Thomas & Joglekar 1994; Joglekar 1999; Korisettar *et al.* 2002; Joglekar in press).

The prehistory of the other animal domesticates in South Asia remains problematic. Archaeozoological evidence for buffalo, pigs and chickens is complicated by problems of identification, since populations of wild relatives still occur in the subcontinent (Meadow 1996). In the case of pigs, usually listed as domestic (cf. Thomas & Joglekar 1994), clear osteological criteria for domestic status are lacking. In the case of water buffaloes, differentiation of wild/domestic is not possible and for many bones it is problematic to separate them from cattle (but see Thomas *et al.* 1995b). Even when water buffalo are clearly present, the generally low frequencies may indicate that they were merely hunted, as Meadow (1998) has suggested for the Harappan period. The reasonably large proportion of buffalo bones in relation to definite cattle bones at Harappan Dholavira might suggest that both species were herded (Patel & Meadow 1997), and buffaloes have similarly been suggested to have been herded at Shikarpur, another Harappan site in Gujarat (Thomas *et al.* 1995b). While

water buffalo are also considered an early domesticate in China, present (but domesticated?) during the Hemudu phase (Smith 1995), additional domestication event(s) in South Asia remain a possibility.

The situation with chickens is similarly problematic in terms of determining domestic status and geographical origins. Wild *Gallus* spp. are well-known in South Asia, such as *G. sonnerati* in the Peninsula, while the wild progenitors of domestic chickens are distributed across north and northeast India. In addition, there are several other gallinaceous birds native to South Asia (Johnsgard 1986). Distinguishing chickens from these may prove complicated, just as MacDonald (1992) has shown to be the case in Africa. In China, the widespread occurrence of *Gallus*-type bones by the sixth–fifth millennia BC would seem to argue for husbandry/domestication (West & Zhou 1988). If we take a similar view of the numerous *Gallus* reports from South Asia, which are by and large restricted to agricultural periods (Table 16.4), we can suggest the pattern of chicken dispersal. In western regions (Gujarat and the Indus Valley), where the wild progenitor is absent today (although this need not have been in the case in prehistory), several finds point to chicken-keeping by the Mature Harappan phase. Similarly, most finds from north India also come from the second half of the third millennium BC, probably including Mesolithic Damdama, where chickens occur in reasonably large quantities during the later levels (Thomas *et al.* 1995a). Could this indicate emerging chicken husbandry amongst hunters, who were probably sedentary (cf. Chattopadyaya 1996) and using wild(?) rice (Kajale 1990)? In Peninsular India, despite the poor dating of some sites, most *Gallus* finds date from the mid to late second millennium BC and are often absent in earlier levels of the same sites. This would seem to indicate that chickens dispersed southwards as domesticates in the mid-second millennium, a hypothesis congruent with the Dravidian linguistic evidence (see below).

Dravidian historical linguistics and other languages

The four major Dravidian subgroups seem well-established (Fig. 16.3), although controversy surrounds the placement of Brahui (Fig. 16.4). While the location of Brahui has often been taken to indicate a dispersal of early Dravidian speakers from the northwest, with subsequent language shift to Indo-European languages, an alternative hypothesis suggests that the ancestral Brahui migrated westward more recently from a North Dravidian area in central India (Elfenbein 1987; 1998; Parpola 1994, 161).

A number of lines of evidence point to a more widespread distribution of Dravidian cultural groups in the past, with subsequent conversion to Indo-European languages (see Fig. 16.3; Trautman 1979; Fairservis & Southworth 1989; Parpola 1994). Southworth (1979), for example has traced village place-name endings typical of South India throughout Maharashtra and the Saurashtra Peninsula, and perhaps even Sindh (Fairservis & Southworth 1989; Southworth 1979; 1988; 1992). In these regions cross-cousin marriages are either typical or practised by some cultural/caste groups, as discussed by Trautman (1979; 1981). This implies that this characteristically Dravidian cultural practice has persisted in areas where Indo-Aryan languages are now spoken, although there appears to be no evidence that cross-

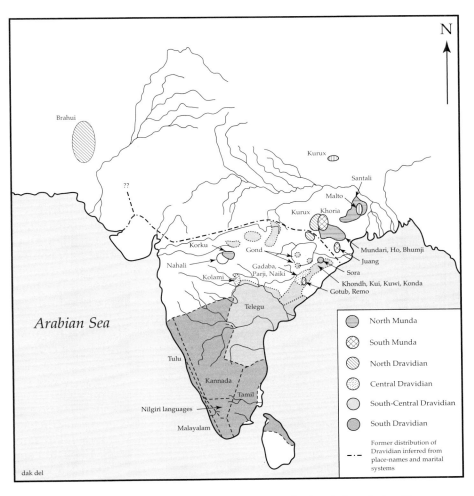

Figure 16.3. *Distribution of Dravidian languages, broken into sub-families, Munda languages, divided into North and South subfamilies, and Nahali (based on Bhattacharya 1975; Zide & Zide 1976; Singh 1994; Tikkanen 1999; Steever 1998a). Dashed-and-dotted line indicates general frontier region of former Dravidian linguistic/cultural influence as indicated by the occurrence of Dravidian kinship terminology/marital systems and Dravidian place-names (see Fairservis & Southworth 1989).*

cousin marriages were ever practised in Gangetic India. The practice of cross-cousin marriages within the North Dravidian sub-family remains problematic, with the practice only recorded amongst the Kuruk. It is worth considering that this practice of kin-group endogamy may have important implications for modelling the process of the dispersal of agriculture in peninsular India by comparison to other regions such as Europe where models assume exogamy between agriculturalists and hunter-gatherers (e.g. Zvelebil 1996).

The Munda language family includes a number of relatively small and often isolated languages in two main sub-groups (Bhattacharya 1975; Zide &

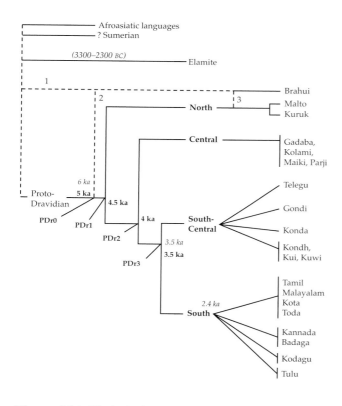

Figure 16.4. *Phyletic diagram of Dravidian languages incorporating various proto-language hypotheses, sub-grouping hypotheses, and date suggestions from linguistics/ glottochronology. Divergence dates indicated in thousands of years (ka) after Zvelebil (1970, 18) in italics and after Southworth (1995) in bold. Subgroupings follow Steever 1998 and Zvelebil 1990. Proto-language node numbers follow Southworth. Three hypotheses for the placement of Brahui indicated by boxed numbers: 1) after McAlpin 1981; 2) after Southworth 1995; Fairservis & Southworth 1989; 3) conventional, e.g. Zvelebil 1990; Steever 1998. Possible extra Dravidian relationships indicated by dashed lines (see Blazek 1999).*

Zide 1976): South Munda, including the Sora and Kharia languages, and North Munda, including Santali of northern Orissa and Bihar, and the grouping of Mundari, Ho and Bhumji, further south. The isolated Korku in Madhya Pradesh is also grouped more distantly with the northern group. This disjunct location of the Korkus suggests that the Mundaric dispersal westward preceded the northward expansion of Gondi (south-central Dravidian) speakers. Nahali, further west still, includes Munda elements but is now generally excluded from this group (Bhattacharya 1975; Tikkanen 1999). A few studies provide evidence for the agricultural vocabu-

lary of ancient Munda groups as well as the influence of their language on other groups in India (e.g. Zide & Zide 1976; Kuiper 1948; Masica 1979).

Beyond the modern languages, there is possible evidence for an extinct pre-Indo-European language group in Gangetic India (Deshpande 1995). Early texts indicate that Indo-Aryan speakers picked up retroflexion as they moved eastward in north India. While Dravidian languages are largely retroflex, Deshpande entertains the possibility that this was due to the influence of other languages. Of particular significance is the evidence for agricultural and botanical terminology borrowed into Indo-Aryan, and to a lesser extent Dravidian, which appears to be neither Dravidian nor Munda (Masica 1979; Fairservis & Southworth 1989, 137). As will be argued below, this evidence for an extinct North Indian agricultural language is compatible with our current understanding of early North Indian agriculture.

Historical linguistics of indigenous and introduced crop staples

While Dravidian etymological data fit the archaeological picture for early Indian agriculture outlined above, some provisos are needed. Various crops have been reconstructed to various proto-languages within the Dravidian family (e.g. Southworth 1976; 1979; 1988; 1995), but such reconstructions inevitably rely on recorded vocabulary. A perusal of the *Dravidian Etymological Dictionary* (Burrow & Emeneau 1984, abbreviated hereafter *DEDR*) makes it clear that, in many cases, the palaeolinguistic level to which a word can be reconstructed could reflect lack of recording, especially in North Dravidian and often Central Dravidian. For example, in the case of wheat, no word for this species is provided by the dictionary for any of the North or Central Dravidian language sub-families, even though wheat is grown in some of these regions. Nevertheless, I will suggest that the available linguistic evidence is congruent with the archaeological evidence outlined above.

There are some well-recorded Dravidian etyma for a South Indian Neolithic native crop package (Table 16.5). The two pulse taxa which can be traced furthest back in the Dravidian phylogeny are mung-bean and horsegram, both of which reconstruct to proto South-Central Dravidian (Southworth 1976; 1979; 1988; 1995). In addition, there are words for urd and pigeonpea, both recorded early from peninsular sites, and for wild fruits. The ancestors of the Central, South and South-Central (SC) Dravidian branches may well have been in place on the Penin-

Table 16.5. *Linguistic evidence for crops, excluding millets, and wild fruits of the early peninsular Neolithic. Proto-linguistic reconstructions given after Southworth (1988) when possible, with* DEDR *entry numbers from Burrow & Emeneau (1984). When no reconstruction has been published, words in representative languages are provided after Burrow & Emeneau. Italicized etyma in quotations are taken from the* Madras Flora *(Gamble 1921; 1935; Fischer 1928) or Watt's* Dictionary of the Economic Products of India.[1] *Additional names from Jain & Mudgal 1999.[2] Additional names from Haines (1921–25).*

	South Dravidian	South-Central Dravidian	Central Dravidian	North Dravidian
Horsegram	PDr-2 *kol(ut) [→ OIA *kulatthika*, Pmunda *kodaXj] (*DEDR* 2153)			No data
Mungbean	PDr-2 *payaru (*DEDR* 3941), cf. 'green' (*DEDR* 3821) ?→ S/SC 'dhal' (*DEDR* 3978), Ta. *paruppu*			No data
Urd	*DEDR* 690: Ta. *uruntu*, Ma. *urunnu*, Ka. *urdu, uddu*, Tu. *urdu*, Te. *uddulu*, Kol. *urunde*, Nk, *urnda* [→ Pkt. *udidi*]			No data
Urd	N/A	PDr-2 *minimu [→ Skt. *malada*] *DEDR* 4862: Pa. *midi*, Ga. *mindi*, Te. *minimu*		
Wild forest date	PDr.1 *kiintu (*DEDR* 2617)			
Jujube	*DEDR* 475: Ta. *iratti*, Ma. *ilanta*, Ka. *era, elaci*, Te. *regu*, Kol. *renga*, Nk. *rega*, Ga. *ren*, Go. *renga*, Pa. *rega*, Malto *ilkru*			
Sebestan plum	*DEDR* 3627: Ta. *naruvili, naruli*, Ma. *naruvari*, Te. *nekkera* *DEDR* 5408: Ta. *viracu*, Ma. *virisu*, Te. *virigi*		No data	No data
Indian jambos	*DEDR* 2914: Ta. *naval*, Ma. *naval*. *DEDR* 2917: Ma. *naral*, Ka. *neral*, Tu. *nerulu*, Te. *neredu*, Pa. *nadi*, Ga. *nendi*, Konda *nerre*			No data
Cuddapah almond	Ta. 'Morala', Ma. 'Munga pera', Ka. 'Nurkul', 'murkalu'	*DEDR* 2628: Kol. *sire*, Kui *sreko*, Kuwi *reko*, Nk, *sire*, Pa. *cir*, Pe. *reka*, Ma.Go. 'reka'[1], Go. 'edka'[1], 'Saraka, herka', Te. 'morli' (cf. Mah. 'Chironji', Or. 'Charu', Korku 'Taro', Sant. 'Tarop')	No data	
Emblic myrobalan	PDr.2 *nelli [including Parji, but in Konda, Kui, Kuwi = 'tamarind'] [?→ Skt. *Amalaka, amlika* 'Emblic' and 'Tamrind'.] (*DEDR* 3755). Also, Go. 'Isurkaya'[1]			No data
Emblic myrobalan	N/A	Te. *usirika*, Kol. *usurka*, Go. *Usirka*, Konda *usirka*, Pe. *hurka*, Kui *jurka*, Kui *jura*, Kuwi *juro* (*DEDR* 574)		N/A

sula when agriculture began, so that these widespread subfamilies might trace their geographical dominance in part at least to their locally-developed agricultural economy.

Unfortunately, good linguistic data are not available for the native small millets, although one might suggest equivalent antiquity. For most of these millets there are no entries in the *Dravidian Etymological Dictionary*, and we must rely on the vernacular names given by botanists (e.g. Watt 1889–93; Fischer 1928; Gamble 1921; 1935). This means that such names may not be recorded with linguistic accuracy (in this paper they are placed in quotation marks), but unlike the linguistic sources we can be confident of their botanical accuracy. For *S. verticillata*, for example, we have different compound grass names recorded for Tamil and Kannada only. It is possible that the South Dravidian *navane*, which is taken to refer to *Setaria italica* today, may in the past have referred to *S. verticillata* as grasses in this genus are largely the same and one can envisage the more productive *S. italica* being rapidly adopted to replace the indigenous and less productive variety of foxtail. While *navane* (*DEDR* 3614) also refers to rice in several languages, all are from regions where rice has become particularly important in recent times. The archaeobotanical record would argue that this represents semantic shift. In the case of *Brachiaria ramosa*, we have a few vernacular names that clearly link this species with other small millets, suggesting that it also acquired its name secondarily. This would appear to be the case for the name *Pedda sama* (Te.), reported from the Eastern Ghats, where *B. ramosa* is generally cropped along with *samai* (*Panicum sumatrense*) (De Wet *et al.* 1983; cf. Kimata *et al.* 2000).

Brachiaria ramosa, like several other millet species, can be referred to with an apparently widespread 'ragu' morpheme, a root for several small millet species in Dravidian languages (see Table 16.6). While the best-known crop name derived from this root today is *ragi*, finger millet, the archaeological evidence suggests this is a relative latecomer which must have taken over the name from one or more native millet species. Southworth could only recon-

Table 16.6. *Some linguistic evidence for the native millets. Italicized etyma in quotations are taken from the* Madras Flora (*Gamble 1921; 1935; Fischer 1928) or Watt's* Dictionary of the Economic Products of India.[1] *Additional names from Jain & Mudgal 1999.*[2] *Additional names from Haines (1921–25).*[3] Korali *is recorded by de Wet* et al. *1979 for* Setaria pumila.

	South Dravidian	South-Central Dravidian	Central Dravidian	North Dravidian
Setaria millets (including *S. italica, S. pumila*, perhaps *S. verticillata*)	DEDR 3614. Ta. Navarai (rice), Ma. Navira (*Paspalum scrobiculatum?*), Tu. *Navara* (a kind of grain), Ka. 'Navane' (*Setaria italica*), Te. *Nivari* (rice) [→ Skt. *nivara* (wild rice)]		?	?
	DEDR 2163: Ta. *kural,* Ko. *koyl,* Ka. *korale,* To. *korralu,* Te. '*koralu, korali*'[3] Go. Kohala, *kosra* [Ma.Go. *ko'la* (*Panicum sumatrense* and/or *P. miliaceum*), Ko.Go. *korra* (*Eleusine coracana*)], Kui *kueri,* Pa. *koyla* [→ Skt. *khangu;* cf. Pmunda **hoxy*]		No data
A general millet term, with variants or derivatives referring to *Panicum, Brachiaria ramosa, Setaria, Paspalum scrobiculatum*	'ragu' (root) [from PDr. **iraki*] (DEDR 812, 525, cf. 379, 5260): Ka. 'kadu baragu' (*B. ramosa*), 'kari baragu' (*S. italica*), 'baragu' (*P. miliaceum*), 'Haraku arikel' (*P. scrobiculatum*), Te. 'varagulu, wuragi' (*P. miliaceum*), 'Arugu, arikelu' (*P. scrobiculatum*), Ta. 'Varagu, karu varagu' (*P. scrobiculatum*), 'kalvaragu, kapai' (*E. coracana*) → DEDR 5287: 'rice grain', Ta. *raki,* Ma. *varru,* Kol. *val,* Nk. *val(ku).* [?→ Pmunda *e-rig*]. Differs from Sant. 'mota gundli' = *B. ramosa*[2]			
Uncertain original millet, compare with *Panicum sumatrense* and *Echinochloa colona* (below).	DEDR 3265: Ta. *tinai* (*Setaria*), *camai* (*P. sumatrense*), Ma. *tina,* Ka. *tene-gida* (*Setaria*), Ko. *ten* (ear of grain). Cf. Skt. *China* (*P. miliaceum*)	? (see below)	No data	No data
Panicum sumatrense ('little millet'). ? = DEDR 3265	Ta. '*shamai, samai, chamai*', Te. '*nella-shama, nella-shamalu, nalla-chamalu, saumai*', Cf. Mah. '*Warai*'. Cf. Sant. '*gundli*'[2]	No data	No data	
Echinochloa colona ssp. Frumentacea ('sawa millet'). ? = DEDR 3265	Ka. '*same, save*', Te. '*bonta-shama, sawa, bonta chamalu, chamalu, chama*' (→ Skt. *Shyamaka,* Or. *Samu*). Cf. Mah. '*Bavto*'	No data	No data	

struct *ragi* back to proto-South/SC Dravidian, but he also proposed a more general proto-Dravidian etymon, **iraki*, referring to some sort of food. Could this have been an early term for a millet, such as *B. ramosa*, or a more general millet-grass term? This root seems to have evolved into a wide range of grain-related words, via some semantic shifts, even referring to rice grains (*DEDR* 5287) in some Central and South Dravidian languages. The widespread similarity in the use of *ragi* in most modern languages, including Indo-Aryan languages, to refer to finger millet (*Eleusine coracana*) may represent some form of emergent standardization. Given the great difficulty that even trained botanists have in distinguishing some of the millets, and as is evident from vernacular names, there has surely has been much sharing and semantic shifting of millet terms between similar species in the past (for instance, the *samai, savai, sawa* names for *Panicum sumatrense* and *Echinochloa colona*, two species readily confused).

In contrast to the South Indian Neolithic crop package and the native fruits, species which were introduced later tend to reconstruct to later proto-languages, usually proto-South/SC Dravidian (PDr.3; see Table 16.7). Crops which Southworth has reconstructed for this stage include wheat, pearl millet, flax/linseed, cotton and finger millet. He has suggested that sorghum may date back to the previous stage (PDr.2), although his reconstruction appears to privilege the Tamil etymon as being more conservative whereas the possibility that this etymon is derived from borrowing from the Sanskrit *yavanala-*, itself derived by compounding a term for barley might indicate that the apparent cognation between central, south-central and south Dravidian derives from early borrowing between these languages. It is also possible that this term derives originally from some other millet as is apparently the case in Kuwi. For pigeonpea there are two distinct terms, one of which appears to go back to proto-South/Central, whereas the other is only proto-South/SC, but perhaps borrowed at this stage into (or from) Central Dravidian. A similar situation seems to hold with chickens in which proto-S/SC and Central have dif-

Table 16.7. *Linguistic evidence for crops and chickens added during the peninsular Neolithic/Chalcolithic. Proto-linguistic reconstructions given after Southworth (1988) when possible, with* DEDR *entry numbers from Burrow & Emeneau (1984). When no reconstruction has been published words in representative languages are provided after Burrow & Emeneau. Italicized etyma in quotations are taken from the* Madras Flora *(Gamble 1921; 1935; Fischer 1928) or Watt's* Dictionary of the Economic Products of India.

	South Dravidian	South-Central Dravidian	Central Dravidian	North Dravidian
Wheat	PDr-3 *koo-tumpai [=OIA *godhuma*]		No data	*Xolum*, separate borrowing from OIA *godhuma*?
Barley	*DEDR* 1106: Ko. *kaj*, To. *koj*, Ta. 'ganji' (cf. Pkt. *gajja*)	No data	No data	No data
Pearl millet	PDr-3 *kampu (*DEDR* 1242) (cf. Skt. *kambu*)		No data	No data
Sorghum	PDr-2 *connel (*DEDR* 2896). Ta. *colam, connal* (also maize), Ma. *colam*, To. *swi lm* (maize), Ka. *jola*, Kod. *jola*, To., *jola*, Te. *jonna*, Kol. *sonna*, Kol. *sonna*, Pa. *jenna*, Ga. *jonel*, Goo. *Jonnang*, Kuwi *Ka'wa zona* (millet), Nk. *sonna* [?= Skt. *yavanala*-]		No data	
Finger millet (see also, *Brachiaria ramosa* in Table 16.6, above)	PDr-3 *iraki, borrowed from 'raki'/'ragu millets'? [from PDr-1 *iraki 'food'] (*DEDR* 812, 525) [→ Skt. *raga, ragi*; → *DEDR* 5287 'rice grains']		?	No data
Hyacinth bean	*DEDR* 262: Ta. *avarai*, Ka. *avare*, *amare* [?→ skt. *saimbya*]	*eikkudu* (Te.) 'jata' (Go.)	No data	No data
Pigeonpea	*DEDR* 1213: *kanti* (Ta.), *kandulu* (Te.), *kandi* (Go.)		*DEDR* 1934: *ken* (Konda, Pe.), *kaánga* (Kui), *kayu* (Kuwi) [→ *kanga* (Mah.); ?→ *DEDR* 1213]. *Kandi* (Konda) [from Go.?]	No data
	DEDR 3353: *tuvarai* (Ta.), *tovari* (Ka.), *togari* (Te.), *turi* (Go.), *togar* (Kol.), *togari* (Nk.) [→ Skt. *tubarika*]			No data
Peas	Ta. 'patanie', Ka. 'batgadle', Te. 'patanlu' (cf. Mah. 'Vatana, patana', Guj. 'watana') [not from OIA *matara]		No data	No data
Lentils	Ta. 'Misurpurpur', Te. 'Misur-pappu, chiri sanagalu', Ka. 'Massur, chanangi' (from Skt. *Masura*)		No data	No data
Grasspea	No data, but Mah. 'Lakh', Guj. 'Lang' [not from Skt. *Khesari*]		No data	No data
Chickpea	*DEDR* 1120: Ta. *katalai*, Ma. *Katala*, Ko. *kacl*, Ka. *kadale*, Kod. *kadale*, Tu. *Kadale* [? = Skt. *cana(ka)*-]	Te. 'sannagalu, harimandhakam'	No data	No data
Flax/linseed	PDr-3 *akace [=OIA *atasi*-] (*DEDR* 3)		No data	No data
Cotton	PDr-3 *tuu...[from PDr-2 *tuu- 'feather, down'] (*DEDR* 3393) [→ Skt. *Tula*]		'feather, down'	No data
	DEDR 3976: Ta./Ma. *parutti*, Ka. *parti*, Kod. *parati*, Tu. *pati*, Te. *piratti*, Go. *parti*, Kui *parti*, Kuwi *pratti*		No data	No data
Chicken	*DEDR* 2248: *kori* (Ta., Ma, Ka.), *kodi* (Te.), *gogori* (Go.) [→ *gogori* (Nk.)]		*DEDR* 2160: *korr* (Pa.), *kor* (Nk.), *Koru* (Konda), *Koju* (Kui) [→ *korr* (Go.)]	*DEDR* 2013: *xer* (Kur.), *qeru* (Malt.)

ferent terms, but with clear borrowings between these branches. In general, the evidence for these species suggests that they were added very shortly after the divergence between Central and South/SC Dravidian, when these language groups were still in quite close contact. Based on archaeological evidence for the taxa involved, we would seem to be looking at the middle Neolithic and the pre-to-early Malwa

societies of the northern Peninsula (2200–1700 BC). For some of the winter pulses that were well-established in Chalcolithic Maharashtra, notably peas and grasspeas, non-Sanskrit names persist in Maharati and Gujarati. Were these derived from pre-existing Dravidian names?

There remain additional suggested cognates amongst Dravidian languages that could refer to

203

cultivars from an earlier stage in the language (Southworth 1988; 1992; 1995), although one might suggest that this indicates knowledge of wild progenitors instead. Amongst those discussed by Southworth (1992) are sesame (PDr-1 *el) and date (PDr-1 *cintu, DEDR 2617), which Southworth (1992) suggests may have given its name to Sindh, and possibly two words for rice. The two former species are known earliest in the northwest, with date stones dating back to the fifth millennium at Mehrgarh and sesame to the Mature Harappan (Fuller & Madella 2001; Tengberg 1999). Both could have been known in wild form on the Peninsula; wild Sesamum mulayanum occurs here, in addition to Punjab (Ilhenfeldt & Grabow-Seidensticker 1979; Patil 1999; Hiremath & Patil 1999; probably syn. S. orientale var. malabaricum of Bedigian & Harlan 1986), and the wild forest date (Phoenix sylvestris) can also be found (Barrow 1999).

The situation with rice is more problematic. Southworth maintains that familiarity with rice may derive from early Dravidian societies in Gujarat, on the periphery of the Harappan, 'which knew the use of rice' (Southworth 1992, 82), referring to chaff tempered potsherds reported from Rangpur and Lothal. Unfortunately, this is unconvincing evidence for serious rice cultivation, although some knowledge of rice is indicated. Systematic archaeobotany indicates emphatically that rice was not a staple food for most of the populations in these regions. Despite systematic sampling on sites in Gujarat, Rajasthan and the northern Deccan, rice is absent prior to the late second millennium BC, in contrast to the vast quantities of other cereals (Weber 1991; Reddy 1994; Kajale 1996a,b; Chanchala 1994). The recovery of three grains of rice from Jorwe period Inamgaon (in contrast to over 10,000 barley: see Kajale 1988), and a few negligible (and not clearly domesticated) grains from Neolithic Hallur (Fuller 1999), clearly point to the absence of widespread or significant rice cultivation systems in Gujarat/Peninsular India during the third–second millennia BC. It thus seems likely that rice, which has become culturally salient probably since the first millennium BC, has co-opted words that earlier referred to other cereals or had more general meanings. This is clearly the case with proto-Dravidian *vancik/ manci (DEDR 5265, 4639) as indicated by Southworth (1992), and presumably *ari (DEDR 215), which although often used in many languages to refer to rice grains can in some languages be used for any husked grain. Mahdi (1998, 398) has suggested that an early Dravidian reflex *urigi may be the source for the Sanskrit vrihi. Might this derive from an earlier millet term such as *iraki?

A number of terms reconstructed for proto-Dravidian that were considered agricultural by Southworth (1976) and McAlpin (1981, 133) read in fact like a range of activities that we would expect to precede agriculture. These operations would have been part of the behavioural repertoire of wild-grain-using (Mesolithic?) hunter-gatherers as much as for cultivators, and include skills that must have preceded domestication (see e.g. Harris 1984; 1996a; Hillman & Davis 1990; Willcox 1992; 1999). These include words for digging (or tilling) (DEDR 688 *ur-), reaping (DEDR 2119 *koy-), seed or sowing [but not necessarily sowing; the Malto derivative is glossed simply 'seed'] (DEDR 5401 vit(t)), as well as several terms relating to the processing of seed crops, such as words for winnowing (DEDR 2019 *KeR-, DEDR 3435 *tel-), threshing floor (DEDR 2119 *kal), to parch or roast grains (DEDR 4537 *por(i)-) and chaff or husks (DEDR 4491, 4562 *poll-, *pot-; and DEDR 637, *um). The last of these etyma is connected by McAlpin (1981, 96) to ancient Elamite umi ('to grind [grain]'). We might also point to an etymon for a grain-based porridge, usually made from Eleusine or rice but presumably of more generic origin, that goes back to PDr-1 (DEDR 174). Given that wild grasses (wild cereals) were utilized by Levantine foragers as early as 19,500 bp (Kislev et al. 1992) and have been inferred to have been used by Aboriginal Australians perhaps back to 30,000 bp (Cane 1989), we cannot assume that such activities are 'Neolithic'.

In addition, the Dravidian languages and hypothetical Elamo-Dravidian appear to have cognate words for sheep, goat and cattle, but only in restricted languages specifying herding. We can consider the possibility that livestock diffused among hunter-foragers prior to the development of cultivation, as can be suggested to have occurred in parts of Gujarat and Rajasthan by the late fifth millennium BC. Thus, in general we should probably see the proto-Dravidians as wild-grain-using foragers who might have become widespread already from Gujarat to the Peninsula without agriculture, although they may have been quick to adopt some livestock.

Linguistic evidence congruent with an early North Indian (Gangetic) agricultural complex comes from a range of agricultural terms found in Sanskrit, and sometimes in Dravidian languages, which appear to derive from extinct languages of unknown affiliation (see Masica 1979). These terms include cereals and pulses of Near Eastern origin, established in Rajasthan by c. 3000 BC and in the Ganges Valley by 2500–2200 BC, as well as several other crop plants which may be of Indian origin, such as cucurbits

Table 16.8. *Words of neither Dravidian nor Indo-European origin in Indo-Aryan, suggesting the former presence of extinct agricultural languages in North India. (After Masica 1979.)*

English	Botanical Latin	Indo-Aryan	Comments on origin
Southwest Asian Package			
Wheat	*Triticum* spp.	Skt. *godhuma*, cf. PDr-3 **koo-tumpai*, Br. *xolum*	Southwest Asian origin, established early in Northwest India, staples of Harappan Indus Valley. In Ganges by 2200 BC.
Grasspea	*Lathyrus sativus*	**k(h)esari*	"
Chickpea	*Cicer arietinum*	Skt. *cana(ka)-*	"
Pea	*Pisum sativum*	**mattara*	"
Lentil	*Lens culinaris*	Skt. *masura(ka)-*	"
Flax / linseed	*Linum usitatissimum*	Skt. *atasi-*, cf. PDr-3 **akace*	"
Potential North or Northwest Indian Natives			
Rice	*Oryza sativa*	Skt. *sali-*	North Indian domestication(?)
Foxtail millet	*Setaria* sp.	Skt. *kangu*, cf. Pmunda **(h)oxy*, also cf. *DEDR* 2163	*S. pumila* at Senuwar, *c.* 2500 BC
Mung	*Vigna radiata*	Skt. *mudga*	Multiple origins in India?
Urd	*Vigna mungo*	**udidda*	Multiple origins in India?
Cucumber	*Cucumis sativus*	Skt. *ksiraka*	North Indian origin, *Cucumis* sp. Finds back to *c.* 2500 BC
Bitter gourd	*Momordica charantia*	Skt. *karavella*	North Indian origin
Ivy gourd	*Coccinia grandis*	Skt. *kunduru*	North Indian origin, early find *c.* 1800 BC upper Ganges.
Luffa / Sponge gourd	*Luffa acutangula*	**tori*	North Indian origin
Okra	*Abelmoschus esculenta*	Skt. *bhinda-*	Several wild spp. In India
Indian Jambos	*Syzygium cumini*	Skt. *jambu-*	Wild throughout monsoonal India(?)
Jujube	*Ziziphus mauritania*	Skt. *badara-*	Wild throughout India(?)
Wild(?) date	*Phoenix sylvestris*	Skt. *kharjura-*	Wild throughout India
Cotton	*Gossypium arboreum*	Skt. *karpasa*	Domesticated in Baluchistan(?), at Mehrgarh by 5000 BC
Sesame	*Sesamum indicum*	Skt. *tila-*	Wild in Punjab and western Peninsula, earliest finds Harappan, middle Ganges *c.* 1500 BC
Related Terminology			
Bread		Skt. *rotika*	
Sow		Skt. *vap-*	
Chaff, straw		Skt. *busa-*	
Winnowing basket		Skt. *surpa-*	
Plough		Skt. *langala*, cf. N.Munda, Pmunda?, AA??	Early Harappan ardmarks (Kalibangan)
Sheep		Skt. *bhedra-*, cf. Pmunda **medra*	From Southwest Asia (and Baluchistan?)

(Table 16.8). This evidence also fits our archaeological picture of a separate early agricultural complex emanating from Gangetic India, which added Southwest Asian crops to its repertoire during the second half of the third millennium BC. The agricultural populations of this lost-language group came into contact with Peninsular Dravidians after the separation of Central Dravidian and during the same general period as the early borrowings between Central and proto-South/SC Dravidian, i.e. late third to early second millennium BC. They may also have interacted with proto-Munda speakers in eastern India (see below).

Proto-Munda agriculture: some considerations

A reconstructed proto-Munda agricultural vocabulary provides some intriguing hypotheses and problematic questions for future research (Zide & Zide 1976). At present we have no direct archaeobotanical evidence for the development of cultivation and agricultural systems in Orissa or eastern India where most Munda-speaking groups are found today. Terms for mortar and pestle reconstruct clearly for *proto*-South Munda, with likely cognates amongst Mon-Khmer languages. While this implies use of grain foods, such as millets or rice, they need not have been cultivated.

There are a number of potential wild food resources, namely fruits, which also reconstruct for proto-Munda, although most of these species were at some point brought into arboricultural cultivation in eastern India, including mangoes, wild dates, wild figs, Indian jambos (*Syzigium cumini*), as well as the tuber tumeric, and characteristic vegetation species, including two words for bamboo and one for the sal tree (*Shorea robusta*). The reconstructed etymon for tamarind is potentially problematic, if we accept the assumption of most botanists that this species is a native of Africa (e.g. Purseglove 1968; Rehm & Espig 1991, 221; although this assumption deserves a systematic botanical re-assessment). Nevertheless, semantic shift between species with similar tasting fruits (cf. Emeneau 1997), as suggested for the Dravidian and Sanskrit words for tamarind and emblic myrobalan, might be at work here. The word for tamarind might also have been adapted from the words for northern Southeast Asian native tree-legumes with sour edible fruits: *Dialium indum* L. and *Parkia speciosa* Hassk. (cf. Yaacob & Subhadrabandhu 1995). The only hard evidence for tamarind is wood charcoal throughout the sequence at Narhan (middle Ganges) starting *c.* 1300 BC (Saraswat *et al.* 1994). The fact that South and North Munda subfamilies do not share a clear root for rice, although both have rice roots that point to connections with other Austroasiatic languages, may suggest that although rice was known from the beginning it may not have been a dominant crop in their subsistence and thus rice vocabulary attrition occurred. Indeed, if early Mundaric groups were hill cultivators, rice may have been merely one of many cereals (treated more like a millet) that they used in a mixed millet, rain-fed system. Although some scholars, like Mahdi (1998) have suggested proto-Austroasiatic roots for rice, a recent tabulation of data by Blench (in press) indicates that there is no coherent rice vocabulary that can be traced across Austro-Asiatic sub-groups.

The presence of three proto-Munda roots for different millets, as well as several additional terms in some subfamilies, suggest that mixed millet cultivation was important to these peoples. The compilation of Zide & Zide (1976) suggests *Setaria italica* as a confident gloss for **(h)oxy* (cf. Skt. *kangu*), *Panicum sumatrense* or *Echinochloa colona* for **iri/ *e-rig*, and *Pennisetum* or *Sorghum* as possible identifications for **gan-gay*. As I have already indicated, identifying particular millets with particular words may be problematic and Zide & Zide (1976, 1311) suggest that some words have shifted meanings with changes in staple foodstuffs. It remains to be established how early *S. italica* reached India, but other *Setaria* spp. are probably equally likely to be the source of a reconstructible early word, such as *S. pumila*, now documented for the Middle Ganges by *c.* 2500 BC and presumably cultivated (Saraswat in press).

Some pulses of South Asian origin also feature in the proto-Munda vocabulary. There is a reconstructed root for black gram (*Vigna mungo*), probably native to the northern Peninsula or central India (Fuller 1999; 2002). The reconstructed root for horsegram, proto-Munda **kodaxj*, may be seen as borrowed from indigenous Central/SC Dravidians (PDr2 **kolut*). Another 'red pulse' might be *Cajanus cajan*, a native of the Orissan region. Archaeologically, this species occurs outside its wild range in Peninsular India by 1800–1500 BC, during the proposed period of early divergence and interaction between Central and South/SC Dravidian languages. Interactions with Dravidian and North Munda cultural groups are also indicated by other linguistic borrowings (Zide 1991).

Thus, proto-Munda speakers had probably reached eastern India by sometime in the first half of the second millennium BC. Although still very poorly dated, the emergence of the Neolithic culture of Orissa, as represented for example by the site of Kuchai, might date to this general period.

The presence of roots for a number of livestock terms, including chicken, suggests that proto-Munda speakers brought some domestic animals with them and may already have had draught animals. While a good root for pig is available for proto-South Munda it remains uncertain whether pigs were part of proto-Munda subsistence. The presence in proto-Munda of a word for goat presents no problem if we assume that the proto-Munda arrival was later than the spread of Southwest Asian agro-pastoralism across India, this presumably reaching the lower Ganges by the second half of the third millennium BC. Words for cattle are inherently more problematic due to the potential for confusing mithan, zebu and perhaps water buffalo. Zide & Zide (1976) suggest that water buffalo terms are cognate across the Munda sub-families. In addition, they reconstruct a proto-Munda term that may refer to draught cattle. Another word that refers to cattle is present for proto-South Munda. This suggests that buffalo, but perhaps not zebu, belonged to the proto-Munda repertoire and may have been used for ploughing. The widespread Indian word for plough in Indo-Aryan and Dravidian languages has long been regarded as a loan from proto-Munda, although it is only documented in Korku and North Munda (Kuiper 1948; Masica 1979; Southworth 1979; Burrow & Emeneau 1984). Could this have come from the hypothetical and now extinct Gangetic language family?

Discussion: testing alternative models

In this paper I have attempted to build a new model for the dispersal of Dravidian languages and subsistence systems in India as an alternative to those current in the literature. This new model relies heavily on recent archaeobotanical evidence and finds general congruence with our patchy understanding of Dravidian plant-name etymologies and evidence for word-borrowing with early Munda speakers. As maintained by Rouse (1986), inferences about prehistory can be strengthened by approaching them through multiple working hypotheses, and indeed the model proposed here should be seen as another hypothesis to be tested alongside others. Thus it is perhaps worth concluding by reiterating the main points of the present model and how they differ in their archaeological and linguistic expectations from existing hypotheses.

The existing model differs in terms of assumptions about the mode of subsistence of the proto-Dravidians. While most authors have pointed to Dravidians as fundamentally agriculturalist (e.g. Southworth 1976; McAlpin 1981; Parpola 1994), the reconstructed vocabularies point towards some of the practices that must have preceded agriculture amongst hunter-gatherer groups with traditions of wild seed (especially grass) and tuber use. Thus, the present model predicts that early Dravidians were essentially 'Mesolithic', but with the technology for threshing/de-husking, grinding and some degree of storage. This implies that in locating a proto-Dravidian homeland we need not be looking for an agricultural society, although these societies may already have had some domestic fauna. This differs from other models which have implied the need to find agricultural proto-Dravidians and have thus been drawn towards the Indo-Iranian borderlands.

Different models also differ in their reconstruction of the nature and biological basis of the first agricultural systems amongst Dravidian speakers. The present model suggests that the first agricultural systems amongst Dravidian groups, after some of the main language sub-families had already diverged, were based on suites of species domesticated within savanna environments of South Asia, in particular tropical pulses and small millets. Evidence for different early packages of such crops come from the Southern Neolithic and from the Saurashtra Peninsula (Gujarat), which might suggest two centres of plant domestication within Dravidian-speaking societies. Other hypotheses, whether Elamo-Dravidian (McAlpin 1981) is accepted or not, look to the northwest and thus necessarily imply that the earliest agriculture should have been based on the Southwest Asian suite of wheat, barley, winter pulses and flax, along with sheep and goats. Such agriculture was winter/spring in seasonality and is more likely to have been floodplain based within South Asia (east of the Indus) where winter rains are unavailable, whereas the native crops of the new model would have been rain-fed by the monsoons and not restricted to river valleys. The crops of South India fit linguistically with species that were probably known before the divergence of the Central Dravidian languages, whereas for other models we must assume the pre-existing knowledge of the Southwest Asian crops was lost, and is thus linguistically irretrievable. Given the preponderance of the Southwest Asian crops in the Indian archaeological record, the only region where one might argue for such a process of loss is Saurashtra, where wheat and barley appear by and large absent during the Harappan period.

The models differ fundamentally in predictions about the directions of the dispersal of Dravidian languages as well as the timing. My model sees proto-Dravidian somewhere within the core range of modern Dravidians, whereas others look outside South Asia, normally towards Elamite Iran. Whereas these other models see a fairly straightforward progressive movement eastward and southward with different language branches hiving off sequentially, starting in Baluchistan with Brahui, the present model implies more of a mosaic of differentiating and interacting language groups largely within peninsular India and Gujarat. The main directions of dispersal would have been out from the Deccan towards its peripheries and zones of isolation, such as the isolated hill regions (Nilgiris, Eastern Ghats, Satpuras), towards the hill zones of Orissa and Bihar, and at least one group to the northwest via Gujarat and Sindh (Brahui). Whereas the present model places the earliest differentiation only just prior to agriculture, probably sometime in the mid-Holocene (*c.* 4000 BC?), and thus agrees in general with glottochronology, an agricultural dispersal model from the northwest might imply a separation of Brahui considerably prior to this time (*c.* 6000 BC) with the establishment of the other Northern Dravidian languages (in Central India?) perhaps within the subsequent millennium. While the new model would place some important movements and differentiation into the poorly understood later Mesolithic of peninsular India and Gujarat, other models would look only at Neolithic (i.e. ceramic) societies. These better-documented periods, however, offer at best inconsistent evidence for a sequential dispersal from northwest to the Peninsula. The new model would predict processes of differentiation, spread and interaction between cultural groups during the Neolithic/Chalcolithic phases of the Deccan, and such processes are indeed suggested in the archaeological record.

There is much research to be done on the prehistory of India, in archaeology, historical linguistics, and indeed genetics (but see Kivisild this volume). There are many gaps to fill in the evidence. As the etymological tables indicate there is much linguistic recording of plant names that is needed, especially in consultation with a millet-savvy botanist. In addition, archaeological research needs to aim at establishing a better chronological framework for the Mesolithic and earliest Neolithic periods of India, as well as systematic recovery of subsistence data from these phases. The Neolithic of Orissa is particularly enigmatic, and the unresolved issues of the emergence of Neolithic societies in the Middle Ganges require renewed fieldwork. In addition, model-building of the impacts of Dravidian cross-cousin marriage on the diffusion of crops and language spread might prove fruitful. It is hoped at least that some of the issues have been constructively raised to suggest alternative perspectives to explore.

Acknowledgements

The author would like to thank David Harris, Roger Blench and Peter Bellwood for their constructive comments on earlier drafts of this paper. The final text has also benefited from the discussions during the conference.

Abbreviations

DEDR Dravidian Etymological Dictionary, Revised edition (Burrow & Emenaeau 1984)
Language abbreviations follow the above source: Br. (Brahui), Ga. (Gadba), Go. (Gondi), Ka. (Kannada), Ko. (Kota), Kod. (Kodagu), Kol. (Kolami), Kur. (Kurux, Oraon), Ma. (Malayalam), Malt. (Malto), Nk. (Naiki), Pa. (Parji), Ta. (Tamil), Te. (Telegu), To. (Toda), Tu. (Tulu), Skt. (Sanskrit), Pkt. (Prakrit), OIA (Old Indo-Aryan), Guj. (Gujarati), Mar. (Marathi).

PDr-0, PDr-1, PDr-2, PDr-3 are abbreviations for internal nodes in the reconstructed Dravidian Language tree following Southworth (see Fig. 16.4).

References

Allchin. B. & F.R. Allchin, 1982. *The Rise of Civilization in India and Pakistan.* Cambridge: Cambridge University Press.

Allchin, F.R., 1957. The Neolithic stone industry of the North Karnataka region. *Bulletin of the School of Oriental and African Studies* 19, 321–35.

Allchin, F.R., 1960. *Piklihal Excavations.* Hyderabad: Andhra Pradesh Government Publications

Allchin, F.R., 1963. *Neolithic Cattle Keepers of South India: a Study of the Deccan Ashmounds.* Cambridge: Cambridge University Press.

Allchin, F.R. & B. Allchin, 1974. Some new thoughts on Indian cattle, in *South Asian Archaeology 1973*, eds. J.E. van Lohuizen-de Leeuw & J.N. Ubaghs. Leiden: E.J. Brill, 71–7.

Allchin, F.R. & B. Allchin, 1997. *Origins of a Civilization: the Prehistory and Early Archaeology of South Asia.* New Delhi: Penguin Books India.

Alur, K.R., 1990. *Studies in Indian Archaeology and Palaeontology.* Dharwad: Shrihari Publications.

Anping, P., 1998. Notes on new advancements and revelations in the agricultural archaeology of early rice domestication in the Dongting Lake region. *Antiquity* 72, 878–85.

Bar-Yosef, O. & R. Meadow, 1995. The origins of agriculture in the Near East, in Price & Gebauer (eds.), 39–94.

Barrow, S., 1999. Systematic studies in *Phoenix* L. (Palmae: Coryphoideae). *Memoirs of the New York Botanic Garden* 83, 215–23.

Bedigian, D. & J.R. Harlan, 1986. Evidence for cultivation of sesame in the ancient world. *Economic Botany* 40, 137–54.

Bellwood, P., 1996. The origins and spread of agriculture in the Indo-Pacific region: gradualism, diffusion or revolution and colonization, in Harris (ed.) 1996b, 465–98.

Bhattacharya, S., 1975. *Studies in Comparative Munda Linguistics.* Simla: Indian Institute for Advanced Study.

Blazek, V., 1999. Elam: a bridge between Ancient Near

East and Dravidian India?, in Blench & Spriggs (eds.), 48–78.

Blench, R., in press. From the mountains to the valleys: understanding ethnoliguistic geography in SE Asia, in *Early Settlement of East Asia: Putting Together Archaeology, Linguistics and Genetics*, eds. R. Blench, L. Sagart & A. Sanchez-Mazas. London: Curzon Press.

Blench, R. & M. Spriggs (eds.), 1999. *Archaeology and Language*, vol. IV. London: Routledge.

Blust, R., 1996. Austronesian culture history: the windows of language, in *Prehistoric Settlement of the Pacific*, ed. W.H. Goodenough. Philadelphia (PA): American Philosophical Society, 28–35.

Bradley, D.G., R. Loftus, P. Cunningham & D.E. MacHugh, 1998. Genetics and domestic cattle origins. *Evolutionary Anthropology* 6, 79–86.

Burkill, I.H., 1953. Habits of Man and the origins of the cultivated plants of the Old World. *Proceedings of the Linnean Society, London* 164, 12–42.

Burrow, T. & M.B. Emeneau, 1984. *A Dravidian Etymological Dictionary*. Oxford: Clarendon Press.

Cane, S., 1989. Australian Aboriginal seed grinding and its archaeological record: a case study from the Western Desert, in *Foraging and Farming: the Evolution of Plant Exploitation*, eds. D.R. Harris & G. Hillman. London: Unwin & Hyman, 99–119.

Cavalli-Sforza, L.L. & S. Cavalli-Sforza, 1995. *The Great Human Diasporas: the History of Diversity and Evolution*. Reading (MA): Addison-Wesley.

Chakrabarti, D.K., 1999. *India: an Archaeological History*. New Delhi: Oxford University Press.

Chanchala, 1994. Harappan plant economy of Kutch, Gujarat. *Geophytology* 23, 227–33.

Chattopadyaya, U.C., 1996. Settlement pattern and the spatial organization of subsistence and mortuary practices in the Mesolithic Ganges Valley, North-Central India. *World Archaeology* 27, 461–76.

Chen, W.-B., I. Nakamura, Y.-I. Sato & H. Nakai, 1993. Distribution of deletion type in cpDNA of cultivated and wild rice. *Japanese Journal of Genetics* 68, 597–603.

Chen, W.-B., I. Nakamura, Y.-I. Sato & H. Nakai, 1994. Indica and Japonica differentiation in Chinese landraces. *Euphytica* 75, 195–201.

Cohen, D.J., 1998. The origins of domesticated cereals and the Pleistocene–Holocene transition in East Asia. *The Review of Archaeology* 19, 22–9.

Costantini, L., 1979. Plant remains at Pirak, in *Fouilles de Pirak*, eds. J.-F. Jarrige & M. Santoni. Paris: Diffusion de Boccard, 326–33.

Costantini, L., 1983. The beginning of agriculture in the Kachi Plain: the evidence of Mehrgarh, in *South Asian Archaeology 1981*, ed. B. Allchin. Cambridge: Cambridge University Press, 29–33.

de Wet, J.M.J., K.E. Prasada Rao & D.E. Brink, 1983. Systematics and domestication of Panicum sumatrense (Graminae). *Journal d'Agriculture Traditionelle et de Botanique Appliquée* 30, 159–68.

de Wet, J.M.J., J.L.L. Oestry-Stidd & J.I. Cunero, 1979. Origins and evolution of foxtail millets. *Journal d'Agriculture Traditionelle et de Botanique Appliquée* 26, 54–64.

Deshpande, M.M., 1995. Vedic Aryans, non-Vedic Aryans, and non-Aryans: judging the linguistic evidence of the Veda, in Erdosy (ed.), 67–84.

Deshpande, M.M. & P.E. Hook (eds.), 1979. *Aryan and Non-Aryan in India*. Ann Arbor (MI): Center for South and Southeast Asian Studies, University of Michigan.

Elfenbein, J., 1987. A periplus of the 'Brahui Problem'. *Studia Iranica* 16, 215–33.

Elfenbein, J., 1998. Brahui, in Steever (ed.) 1998b, 388–414.

Emeneau, M.B., 1997. Linguistics and botany in the Nilgiris, in *Blue Mountains Revisited: Cultural Studies on the Nilgiri Hills*, ed. P. Hoskins. New Delhi: Oxford University Press.

Erdosy, G. (ed.), 1995. *The Indo-Aryans of Ancient South Asia*. (Language, Material Culture and Ethnicity.) Berlin: Walter de Gruyte.

Fairservis, W.A. & F. Southworth, 1989. Linguistic archaeology and the Indus Valley culture, in *Old Problems and New Perspectives in the Archaeology of South Asia*, ed. J.M. Kenoyer. Madison (WI): Department of Anthropology, University of Wisconsin, 133–41.

Fischer, C.E.C., 1928. *Flora of the Madras Presidency*, vol. III. London: Adlard and Son.

Fuller, D.Q., 1999. The Emergence of Agricultural Societies in South India: Botanical and Archaeological Perspectives. Unpublished PhD thesis, University of Cambridge, Cambridge.

Fuller, D.Q., 2001. Fifty years of archaeobotanical studies in India: laying a solid foundation, in *Indian Archaeology in Retrospect*, vol. III: *Archaeology and Interactive Disciplines*, eds. S. Settar & R. Korisettar. New Delhi: Manohar, 247–363.

Fuller, D.Q., 2002. Ashmounds and hilltop villages: the search for early agriculture in southern Inda. *Archaeology International* 4 (2000/2001), 43–6.

Fuller, D.Q., in press. African crops in prehistoric South Asia: a critical review, in *Progress in African Archaeobotany, Proceedings of the Third International Workshop for African Archaeobotany, Frankfurt, 5–7 July 2000*, eds. K. Neumann, A. Butler & S. Kahlheber. Cologne: Heinrich Barth Institut für Archäologie und Geschichte Afrikas.

Fuller, D.Q. & M. Madella, 2001. Issues in Harappan archaeobotany: retrospect and prospect, in *Indian Archaeology in Retrospect*, vol. II: *Protohistory*, eds. S. Settar & R. Korisettar. New Delhi: Manohar, 317–90.

Fuller, D.Q., R. Korisettar & P.C. Venkatasubbaiah, 2001. Southern Neolithic cultivation systems: a reconstruction based on archaeobotanical evidence. *South Asian Studies* 17, 171–87.

Fürer-Haimendorf, C., 1948. Culture strata in the Deccan. *Man* 48, 87–90.

Fürer-Haimendorf, C., 1953. New aspects of the Dravidan problem. *Tamil Culture* 2, 127–35.

Gadgil, M., N.V. Joshi, U.V. Shambu Prasad, S. Manoharan

& S. Patil, 1998. Peopling of India, in *The Indian Human Heritage*, eds. D. Balasubramanian & N. Appaji Rao. Hyderabad: Universities Press, 100–129.

Gamble, J.S., 1921. *Flora of the Presidency of Madras*, vol. II. London: Adlard & Son.

Gamble, J.S., 1935. *Flora of the Madras Presidency*, vol. I. London: Adlard & Son.

Glover, I.C. & C.F.W. Higham, 1996. New evidence for early rice cultivation in South, Southeast and East Asia, in Harris (ed.) 1996b, 413–41.

Grigson, C., 1985. *Bos indicus* and *Bos namadicus* and the problem of autochthonous domestication, in *Recent Advances in Indo-Pacific Prehistory*, eds. V.N. Misra & P. Bellwood. New Delhi: Oxford and IBH, 425–8.

Haines, H.H., 1921–25. *Botany of Bihar and Orissa*. 6 parts. London: Adlard & Son and Newmand Ltd.

Harlan, J.R., 1995. *The Living Fields*. Cambridge: Cambridge University Press.

Harris, D.R., 1984. Ethnohistorical evidence for the exploitation of wild grasses and forbes: its scope and archaeological implications, in *Plants and Ancient Man. Studies in Paleoethnobotany*, eds. W. van Zeist & W.A. Casparie. Rotterdam: A.A. Balkema, 63–9.

Harris, D.R., 1996a. Introduction: themes and concepts in the study of early agriculture, in Harris (ed.) 1996b, 1–9.

Harris, D.R. (ed.), 1996b. *The Origins and Spread of Agriculture and Pastoralism in Eurasia*. London: UCL Press.

Harris, D.R., 1998. The origins of agriculture in Southwest Asia. *The Review of Archaeology* 19, 5–11.

Hiendleder, S., K. Mainz, Y. Plante & H. Lewalski, 1998. Analysis of mitochondrial DNA indicates that domestic sheep are derived from two different ancestral maternal sources: no evidence for contributions from urial and argali sheep. *The Journal of Heredity* 89, 113–20.

Higham, C., 1995. The transition to rice cultivation in Southeast Asia, in Price & Gebauer (eds.), 127–56.

Hillman, G. & M.S. Davis, 1990. Measured domestication rates in wild wheats and barley under primitive cultivation. *Journal of World Prehistory* 4, 157–222.

Hiremath, S.C. & S. Patil, 1999. Genome homology and putative progenitors of sesame (*Sesamum indicum* L.). *Journal of Cytology and Genetics* 34, 69–74.

Hutchinson, J.B., 1976. India: local and introduced crops. *Philosophical Transactions of the Royal Society, London* B 275, 129–41.

Ilhenfeldt, H.-D. & U. Grabow-Seidensticker, 1979. The genus *Sesamum* L. and the origin of cultivated sesame, in *Taxonomic Aspects of African Economic Botany*, ed. G. Kunkel. Las Palmas de Gran Canaria: Ayuntamiento de Las Palmas de Gran Canaria, 53–60.

Jain, S.K. & V. Mudgal, 1999. *A Handbook of Ethnobotany*. Dehra Dun: Bishen Singh Mahedra Pal Singh.

Joglekar, P.P., 1997. Faunal remains from Padri: second preliminary report. *Bulletin of the Deccan College Post-Graduate and Research Institute* 56–7, 55–68.

Joglekar, P.P., 1999. Re-examination of faunal remains from

Piklihal, Karnataka. *Bulletin of the Deccan College Post-Graduate and Research Institute* 58–9, 69–76.

Joglekar, P.P. & P.K. Thomas, 1993. Faunal diversity at Walki: a small Chalcolithic settlement in Western Maharashtra. *Bulletin of the Deccan College Post-Graduate and Research Institute* 53, 75–94.

Johnsgard, P.A., 1986. *Pheasants of the World*. Oxford: Oxford University Press.

Kajale, M.D., 1988. Plant economy, in *Excavations at Inamgaon*, eds. M.K. Dhavalikar, H.D. Sankalia & Z.D. Ansari. Pune: Deccan College Postgraduate and Research Institute, 727–821.

Kajale, M.D., 1990. Some initial observations on palaeobotanical evidence for Mesolithic plant economy from excavations at Damdama, Pratapgarh, Uttar Pradesh, in *Adaptation and Other Essays*, ed. N.C. Ghosh & S. Chakrabarti. Santiniketan: Visva Bharati Research Publications, 98–102.

Kajale, M.D., 1991. Current status of Indian palaeoethnobotany: introduced and indigenous food plants with a discussion of the historical and evolutionary development of Indian agriculture and agricultural systems in general, in *New Light on Early Farming: Recent Developments in Palaeoethnobotany*, ed. J.M. Renfrew. Edinburgh: Edinburgh University Press, 155–89.

Kajale, M.D., 1996a. Palaeobotanical investigations at Balathal: preliminary results. *Man and Environment* 21, 98–102.

Kajale, M.D., 1996b. Plant remains, in *Kuntasi: a Harappan Emporium on West Coast*, eds. M.K. Dhavalikar, M.R. Raval & Y.W. Pune: Deccan College Post-Graduate and Research Institute, 285–9.

Kane, V.S., 1989. Animal remains from Rojdi, in *Harappan Civilization and Rojdi*, eds. G.L. Possehl & M.H. Rawal. New Delhi: Oxford and IBH, 182–4.

Kenoyer, J.M., 1998. *Ancient Cities of the Indus Valley Civilization*. Karachi: Oxford University Press.

Kimata, M., E.G. Ashok & A. Seetharam, 2000. Domestication, cultivation and utilization of two small millets, *Brachiaria ramosa* and *Setaria glauca*, Poaceae in South India. *Economic Botany* 54, 217–27.

Kislev, M.E., D. Nadel & I. Carmi, 1992. Epipalaeolithic (19,000 bp) cereal and fruit diet at Ohalu II, Sea of Galilee, Israel. *Review of Palaeobotany and Palynology* 73, 161–6.

Korisettar, R., P.C. Venkatasubbaiah & D.Q. Fuller, 2001. Brahmagiri and beyond: the archaeology of the Southern Neolithic, in *Indian Archaeology in Retrospect*, vol. I: *Prehistory*, eds. S. Settar & R. Korisettar. New Delhi: Manohar

Korisettar, R., P.P. Joglekar, D.Q. Fuller & P.C. Venkatasubbaiah, 2002. Archaeological re-investigation and archaeozoology of seven southern Neolithic sites in Karnataka and Andhra Pradesh. *Man and Environment* 26(2), 47–66.

Kuiper, F.B.J., 1948. *Proto-Munda Words in Sanskrit*. Amsterdam: Noord-Hollandsche Uitgevers Maatschappij.

Li, Y., J. Jia, Y. Wang & S. Wu, 1998. Intraspecific and interspecific variation in Setaria revealed by RAPD analysis. *Genetic Resources and Crop Evolution* 45, 279–85.

Lu, T.L.D., 1999. *The Transition from Foraging to Farming and the Origin of Agriculture in China*. (British Archaeological Reports S774.) Oxford: BAR.

McAlpin, D.W., 1981. *Proto-Elamo-Dravidian: the Evidence and its Implications*. Philadelphia (PA): American Philosophical Society.

MacDonald, K.C., 1992. The domestic chicken (*Gallus gallus*) in Sub-Saharan Africa: a background to its introduction and its osteological differentiation from indigenous fowls (Numinidinae and *Francolinus* sp.). *Journal of Archaeological Science* 19, 303–18.

MacHugh, D.E., M.D. Shriver, R.T. Loftus, P. Cunningham & D.G. Bradley, 1997. Microsatellite DNA variation and the evolution, domestication and phylogeography of taurine and zebu cattle (*Bos taurus* and *Bos indicus*). *Genetics* 146, 1971–86.

MacNeish, R.S., 1992. *The Origins of Agriculture*. Norman (OK): University of Oklahoma.

Mahdi, W., 1998. Linguistic data on transmission of Southeast Asian cultigens to India and Sri Lanka, in *Archaeology and Lanaguage, vol. II: Archaeological Data and Linguistic Hypotheses*, eds. R. Blench & M. Spriggs. London: Routledge, 390–415.

Maloney, C., 1975. Archaeology in South India: accomplishments and prospects, in *Essays on South India*, ed. B. Stein. Honolulu (HI): University of Hawaii, 1–40.

Marnival, P., 1992. Archaeobotanical data on millets (*Panicum miliaceum* and *Setaria italica*) in France. *Review of Palaeobotany and Palynology* 73, 259–70.

Masica, C.P., 1979. Aryan and non-Aryan elements in North Indian agriculture, in Deshpande & Hook (eds.), 55–151.

Meadow, R., 1984. Animal domestication in the Middle East: a view from the Eastern Margin, in *Animals in Archaeology*, vol. 3: *Early Herders and their Flocks*, eds. J. Clutton-Brock & C. Grigson. (British Archaeological Reports S202.) Oxford: BAR, 309–37.

Meadow, R., 1989. Prehistoric wild sheep and sheep domestication on the eastern margin of the Middle East, in *Early Animal Domestication and its Cultural Context*, eds. P.J .Crabtree, D. Campana & K. Ryan. Philadelphia (PA): MASCA, The University Museum of Archaeology and Anthropology, 24–36.

Meadow, R., 1996. The origins and spread of agriculture and pastoralism in northwestern South Asia, in Harris (ed.) 1996b, 390–412.

Meadow, R., 1998. Pre- and Proto-historic agricultural and pastoral transformations in Northwestern South Asia. *The Review of Archaeology* 19, 12–21.

Mehra, K.L., 1997. Biodiversity and subsistence changes in India: the Neolithic and Chalcolithic age. *Asian Agri-History* 1, 105–26.

Misra, V.N., V. Shinde, R.K. Mohanty, L. Pandey & J. Kharakwal, 1997. Excavations at Balathal, Udaipur District, Rajasthan (1995–97), with special reference to Chalcolithic architecture. *Man and Environment* 22, 35–59.

Naik, S.N., 1978. Origin and domestication of zebu cattle (*Bos indicus*). *Journal of Human Evolution* 7, 23–30.

Parpola, A., 1994. *Deciphering the Indus Script*. Cambridge: Cambridge University Press.

Patel, A.K., 1999. New radiocarbon determinations from Loteshwar and their implications for understanding settlement and subsistence in North Gujarat and adjoining areas. Paper presented at Fifteenth International Conference on South Asian Archaeology, Leiden University, July 5–9, 1999.

Patil, S., 1999. Genomic studies and seed oil analysis in some species of *Sesamum* L. (Pedaliaceae). Unpublished PhD thesis. Karnatak University, Dharwad.

Possehl, G.L., 1980. *Indus Civilization in Saurashtra*. Delhi: B. R. Publishing Corp.

Possehl, G.L., 1997. The transformation of the Indus civilisation. *Journal of World Prehistory* 11, 425–72.

Possehl, G.L., 1999. *Indus Age: the Beginnings*. Philadelphia (PA): University of Pennsylvania Press.

Possehl, G.L. & P. Rissman, 1992. The chronology of prehistoric India from earliest times to the Iron Age, in *Chronologies in Old World Archaeology*, ed. R.W. Ehrich. Chicago (IL): University of Chicago Press, I: 465–90; II: 47–74.

Prasada Rao, K.E., J.M.J. de Wet, D.E. Brink & M.H. Mengesha, 1987. Infraspecific variation and systematics of cultivated *Setaria italica*, foxtail millet (Poaceae). *Economic Botany* 41, 108–16.

Price, T.D. & A.B. Gebauer (eds.), 1995. *Last Hunters-First Farmers: New Perspectives on the Prehistoric Transition to Agriculture*. Santa Fe (NM): School of American Research.

Purseglove, J.W., 1968. *Tropical Crops. Dicotyledons*. London: Longmans.

Pushpendra, K., A.R. Freeman, R.T. Loftus, C. Gaillard, D.Q. Fuller & D.G. Bradley, in press. Admixture analysis of South Asian Cattle. *Animal Genetics*.

Reddy, S.N., 1991. Archaeobotany at Oriyo Timbo 1989–1990: a post urban site in Gujarat. *Man and Environment* 16, 73–84.

Reddy, S.N., 1994. Plant Usage and Subsistence Modeling: An Ethnoarchaeological Approach to the Late Harappan of Northwest India. Unpublished PhD thesis, University of Wisconsin.

Rehm, S. & G. Espig, 1991. *The Cultivated Plants of the Tropics and Subtropics: Cultivation, Economic Value, Utilization*. Weikersheim: Verlag Josef Margraf.

Renfrew, A.C., 1992. World languages and human dispersals: a minimalist view, in *Transition to Modernity: Essays on Power, Wealth and Belief*, eds. J.A. Hall & I.C. Jarve. Cambridge: Cambridge University Press, 11–68.

Renfrew, A.C., 1996. Language families and the spread of farming, in Harris (ed.) 1996b, 70–92.

Renfrew, J.M. (ed.), 1991. *New Light on Early Farming: Recent Developments in Palaeoethnobotany*. Edinburgh: Edinburgh University Press.

Rouse, I., 1986. *Migrations in Prehistory*. New Haven (CT): Yale University Press.

Sahu, B.P. 1988. *From Hunters to Breeders (Faunal Background of Early India)*. Delhi: Anamika Prakashan.

Sano, R. & H. Morishima, 1992. Indica-Japonica differentiation of rice cultivars viewed from variations in key characters of isozyme, with species reference to Himilayan hilly areas. *Theoretical and Applied Genetics* 84, 266–74.

Saraswat, K.S., 1992. Archaeobotanical remains in ancient cultural and socio-economical dynamics of the Indian subcontinent. *Palaeobotanist* 40, 514–45.

Saraswat, K.S., in press. Plant economy of early farming communities at Senuwar, Bihar, in *Senuwar Excavations*, ed. B.P. Singh. Varanasi: Banares Hindu University.

Saraswat, K.S. & Chanchala, 1995. Palaeobotanical and pollen analytical investigations. *Indian Archaeology 1990–91: a Review*, 103–4.

Saraswat, K.S., N.K. Sharma & D.C. Saini, 1994. Plant economy at Ancient Narhan (*c.* 1300 BC–AD 300/400), in Singh (ed.), 255–346.

Sato, Y-I., R. Ishikawa & H. Morishima, 1990. Non-random association of genes and characters found in indica x japonica hybrids of rice. *Heredity* 65, 75–9.

Sharma, D.P. & M. Sharma, 1987. A reappraisal of the chronology of Mesolithic and Neolthic cultures of the Vindhyas and middle Ganga Valley, in *Archaeology and History: Essays in Memory of Shri A. Ghosh*, eds. B.M. Pande & B.D. Chattopadyaya. Delhi: Agam Kal Prakashan, 57–66.

Sharma, G.R., V.D. Misra, D. Mandal, B.B. Misra & J.N. Pal, 1980. *Beginnings of Agriculture (Epi-Palaeolithic to Neolithic: Excavations at Chopani-Mando, Mahadaha, and Mahagara)*. Allahabad: Abinash Prakashan.

Shinde, V., 1994. The Deccan Chalcolithic: a recent perspective. *Man and Environment* 19, 169–78.

Shinde, V., 1998. Pre-Harappan Padri culture in Saurashtra: the recent discovery. *South Asian Studies* 14, 173–82.

Singh, P. (ed.), 1994. *Excavations at Narhan (1984–1989)*. Varanasi: Banaras Hindu University.

Smith, B.D., 1995. *The Emergence of Agriculture*. New York (NY): Scientific American Library.

Southworth, F., 1976. Cereals in South Asian prehistory: the linguistic evidence, in *Ecological Backgrounds of South Asian Prehistory*, eds. K.A.R. Kennedy & G.L. Possehl. Ithaca (NY): South Asia Program, Cornell University, 52–75.

Southworth, F., 1979. Lexical evidence for early contacts between Indo-Aryan and Dravidian, in Deshpande & Hook (eds.), 191–233.

Southworth, F., 1988. Ancient economic plants of South Asia: linguistic archaeology and early agriculture, in *Languages and Cultures: Studies in Honor of Edgar C. Polome*, eds. M.A. Jazayery & W. Winter. Amsterdam: Mouton de Gruyter, 649–88.

Southworth, F., 1992. Linguistics and archaeology: prehistoric implications of some South Asian plant names, in *South Asian Archaeology Studies*, ed. G.L. Possehl. New Delhi: Oxford and IBH, 81–5.

Southworth, F., 1995. Reconstructing social context from language: Indo-Aryan and Dravidian prehistory, in Erdosy (ed.), 258–77.

Steever, S.B., 1998a. Introduction to Dravidian linguistics, in Steever (ed.) 1998b, 1–39.

Steever, S.B., 1998b. *The Dravidian Languages*. London: Routledge.

Tengberg, M., 1999. Crop husbandry at Miri Qalat, Makran, SW Pakistan (4000–2000 BC). *Vegetation History and Archaeobotany* 8, 3–12.

Tewari, R., R.K. Srivastava, K.S. Saraswat & K.K. Singh, 2000. Excavations at Malhar, District Chandauli (U.P.) 1999: a preliminary report. Pragdhara. *Journal of the Uttar Pradesh State Archaeology Department* 10, 69–98.

Thomas, P.K., 1992. The faunal assemblage and subsistence strategies at Tuljapur Garhi. *Man and Environment* 17, 71–4.

Thomas, P.K. & P.P. Joglekar, 1994. Holocene faunal studies. *Man and Environment* 19, 179–203.

Thomas, P.K. & P.P. Joglekar, 1996. Faunal remains from Balathal, Rajasthan: a preliminary report. *Man and Environment* 21, 91–7.

Thomas, P.K., P.P. Joglekar, V.D. Mishra, J.N. Pandey & J.N. Pal, 1995a. A preliminary report of the faunal remains from Damdama. *Man and Environment* 20, 29–36.

Thomas, P.K., P.P. Joglekar, A. Deshpande-Mukherjee & S.J. Pawankar, 1995b. Harappan subsistence patterns with special reference to Shikarpur, a Harappan site in Gujarat. *Man and Environment* 20, 33–41.

Thomas, P.K., P.P. Joglekar, Y. Matsushima, S.J. Pawankar & A. Deshpande, 1997. Subsistence based on animals in the Harappan culture of Gujarat, India. *Anthropozoologica* 25–26, 767–76.

Tikkanen, B., 1999. Archaeological-linguistic correlations in the formation of retroflex typologies and correlating areal features in South Asia, in Blench & Spriggs (eds.), 138–48.

Trautman, T.R., 1979. The study of Dravidian kinship, in Deshpande & Hook (eds.), 153–73.

Trautman, T.R., 1981. *Dravidian Kinship*. Cambridge: Cambridge University Press.

Venkatasubbaiah, P.C., S.J. Pawankar & P.P. Joglekar, 1992. Neolithic faunal remains from the Central Pennar Basin, Cuddapah District, Andhra Pradesh. *Man and Environment* 17, 55–9.

Wan, J. & H. Ikehashi, 1997. Identification of two types of differentiation in cultivated rice (*Oryza sativa* L.) detected by polymorphism of isozymes and hybrid sterility. *Euphytica* 94, 151–61.

Watt, G., 1889–93. *A Dictionary of the Economic Products of India*. London: W.H. Allen and Co.

Weber, S.A., 1991. *Plants and Harappan Subsistence: an Example of Stability and Change from Rojdi*. New Delhi: Oxford and IBH.

Weber, S.A., 1998. Out of Africa: the initial impact of millets in South Asia. *Current Anthropology* 39, 267–74.

Weber, S.A., 1999. Seeds of urbanism: palaeoethnobotany

and the Indus civilization. *Antiquity* 73, 813–26.

West, B. & B.-X. Zhou, 1988. Did chickens go north? New evidence for domestication. *Journal of Archaeological Science* 15, 515–33.

Wheeler, R.E.M., 1948. Brahmagiri and Chandravalli 1947: megalithic and other cultures in Mysore state. *Ancient India* 4, 180–230.

Wheeler, R.E.M., 1959. *Early India and Pakistan*. London: Thames & Hudson.

Willcox, G., 1991. Carbonised plant remains from Shortugai, Afghanistan, in J.M. Renfrew (ed.), 139–53.

Willcox, G., 1992. Archaeobotanical significance of growing Near Eastern progenitors of domestic plants at Jales (France), in *Préhistoire de l'Agriculture: nouvelles approches expérimentales et ethnographiques*, ed. P.C. Anderson. Paris: Editions CNRS, 159–77.

Willcox, G., 1999. Agrarian change and the beginnings of cultivation in the Near East: evidence from wild progenitors, experimental cultivation and archaeobotanical data, in *The Prehistory of Food: Appetites for Change*, eds. C. Gosden & J. Hather. London: Routledge, 478–500.

Worman, E.C.J., 1949. The Neolithic problem in the prehistory of India. *Journal of Washington Academy of Sciences* 39, 181–201.

Yaacob, O. & S. Subhadrabandhu, 1995. *The Production of Economic Fruits in South-East Asia*. Kuala Lampur: Oxford University Press.

Zeder, M.A. & B. Hesse, 2000. The initial domestication of goats (*Capra hircus*) in the Zagros Mountains 10,000 years ago. *Science* 287, 2254–7.

Zhao, Z., 1998. The Middle Yangtze region in China is one place where rice was domesticated: phytolith evidence from the Diaotonghuan Cave, Northern Jaingxi. *Antiquity* 72, 885–97.

Zide, A.R.K. & N.H. Zide, 1976. Proto-Munda cultural vocabulary: evidence for early agriculture, in *Austroasiatic Studies*, part II, eds. P.N. Jenner, L.C. Thompson & S. Starosta. Honolulu (HI): University of Hawaii Press, 1295–334.

Zide, N.H., 1991. Possible Dravidian sources of some Munda demonstrative bases, in *Studies in Dravidian and General Linguistics: a Festschrift for B. Krishnamurti*, eds. B. Lakshmi Bai & B. Ramakrishna Reddy. Hyderabad: Centre of Advanced Study in Linguistics, Osmania University, 349–64.

Zohary, D., 1996. The mode of domestication of the founder crops of Southwest Asian agriculture, in Harris (ed.) 1996b, 142–58.

Zohary, D. & M. Hopf, 2000. *Domestication of Plants in the Old World*. Oxford: Oxford University Press.

Zvelebil, K.V., 1970. *Comparative Dravidian Phonology*. The Hague: Mouton.

Zvelebil, K.V., 1990. *Dravidian Linguistics: an Introduction*. Pondicherry: Pondicherry Institute of Linguistics and Culture.

Zvelebil, M., 1996. The agricultural frontier and the transition to farming in the circum-Baltic region, in Harris (ed.) 1996b, 323–45.

Chapter 17

The Genetics of Language and Farming Spread in India

Toomas Kivisild, Siiri Rootsi, Mait Metspalu, Ene Metspalu,
Jüri Parik, Katrin Kaldma, Esien Usanga, Sarabjit Mastana,
Surinder S. Papiha & Richard Villems

Most maternal lineages of present-day Indians derive from a common ancestor in mtDNA haplogroup M that split into Indian, eastern Asian, Papuan, and Australian subsets 40,000–60,000 mtDNA-years ago. The second major component in Indian maternal heredity lines traces back to the split of haplogroup U into Indian, western Eurasian and northern African variants approximately at the same time. The variation in these two ancient Indian-specific sets of lineages is the main modifier in the heterogeneity landscape of Indian populations, defining the genetic differences between caste groups and geographic regions in the sub-continent. The difference between regional caste groups is accentuated furthermore by the presence of a northwest to south decline of a minor package of lineages of western Asian or European origin.

In contrast, the majority of Indian paternal lineages do not share recent ancestors with eastern Asian populations but stem from haplogroups common to (eastern) European or western Asian populations. This finding has recently been interpreted in favour of the classical Indo-Aryan invasion hypothesis. Here, we show that this interpretation is probably caused by a phylogeographically-limited view of the Indian Y-chromosome pool, amplified because of current inconsistencies in the interpretation of the temporal scale of the variability in the non-recombining part of the Y chromosome (NRY). It appears to us that the high variability of STRs in the background of NRY variants in India is consistent with the view of largely autochthonous pre-Holocene genetic diversification — a conclusion reached earlier for the Indian maternal lineages (Kivisild *et al.* 1999a).

While interpreting the genetic aspects of farming/language dispersal in the Indian context, it is easy to get lost in its 'multitude of endogamous pockets' (Cavalli-Sforza *et al.* 1994). Yet a forest can hopefully be seen behind the trees, provided that the conclusions to be drawn derive from a phylogeographically representative analysis of the people of the sub-continent. Perhaps new ideas, analogous to the recently introduced 'SPIWA' model for Europe (see Renfrew this volume), are needed when developing new farming/language dispersal models for India.

The earliest 'agricultural package' in the Indian subcontinent — a combined presence of wheat, barley, cattle, sheep and goat domestication — is found in Mehrgarh, Baluchistan, and dates to about 9000 years before present (BP). It spread first into an area extending from the Punjab in the northwest to Uttar Pradesh in the east and to Gujarat in the south. It took another 4000 years before it eventually reached southern Peninsular India (Chakrabarti 1999). In this northwestern early agricultural region lie the roots of the Indus Civilization, and any later cultural influence or human migration from the northwest or west had to pass through this area in order to reach the rest of India.

Neolithic communities in India did not start on empty ground. Cultural complexes belonging to a comparatively short Mesolithic episode developed from the preceding Middle and Upper Palaeolithic cultures and continued to exist through the Neolithic, Bronze and Iron Ages, with microlithic tools continuing in use here and there in some communities even today. The advent of agriculture in India, although largely reflecting local developments, is to be understood against the background of agricultural growth in its geographic neighbourhood, encompassing the Iranian plains and the Fertile Crescent in the west, and Southeast Asia — as far as rice is concerned — in the east (Chakrabarti 1999).

Three quarters of the Indian population today speak Indo-European (IE) languages. Next, in terms of the number of speakers, is the Dravidian language family, spread now mostly over the southern parts of the Indian peninsula, with Telugu, Tamil, Kannada and Malayalam being the most important languages spoken today. Besides these two major groups, Austroasiatic and Tibeto-Burman languages are spoken in the central and eastern parts of India. The introduction of all these four major language families to India is thought to be related to relatively recent immigration episodes.

IE languages in India are commonly thought to originate from either the invasion of Indo-Aryan tribes during the post-Harappan period, or possibly from the spread of Neolithic populations (Renfrew 1987). Supposedly, Dravidian too had its closest linguistic relatives in western Asia (ancient Elamite?) (Ruhlen 1991) and was brought into India before the IE languages, together with or before the spread of farming. Alternatively, the Dravidian languages may turn out to be native to South India, as argued by Fuller (this volume). Neolithic origins, albeit not from the northwest but from the northeast, are claimed also for the spreads of the Austroasiatic and Tibeto-Burman languages.

Thus, according to these linguistic hypotheses, the ancestors of close to 100 per cent of the indigenous languages spoken in India today came to India during the Holocene. Consequently, all the preceding pre-Neolithic languages were totally replaced. If this is indeed so, how extensive was the genetic replacement caused by these events?

Linguistic affiliations, although suggestive of some level of gene flow (as argued by Bellwood this volume), do not always or necessarily correlate with the genetic affinities of the populations. A well-known example of language change by élite dominance is the represented by the Turkish population in Anatolia, which clusters in genetic analyses with populations from the Middle East and Europe, rather than with the linguistically-related Altai populations. Analyses of mtDNA and Y chromosomes reveal that Turks share only about 5–10 per cent of their maternal and paternal lineages with their linguistic relatives in Altai, while the rest of their lineages belong to western Eurasian lineage families (Rolf *et al.* 1999; Tambets *et al.* 2000).

Mitochondrial DNA continuity of Indian populations: identifying and quantifying ancient and recent gene flow

In India, where palaeoanthropological findings from the Middle and Upper Palaeolithic are very rare and no ancient DNA study has proven successful (Kumar *et al.* 2000), evidence for the beginning of the settlement of modern humans comes from mtDNA and Y-chromosomal studies (Mountain *et al.* 1995; Passarino *et al.* 1996; Kivisild *et al.* 1999a; Quintana-Murci *et al.* 1999; Underhill *et al.* 2000; 2001; Bamshad *et al.* 2001).

Haplogroup M is the most frequent mtDNA cluster in present-day Indian populations and, because it is nearly absent in western Eurasia, it stands out as a separate cluster from the African haplogroup L3. It has been suggested that M represents the earliest wave of the migration of anatomically modern humans (AMH) out of Africa (Kivisild *et al.* 1999a; 2000; Quintana-Murci *et al.* 1999), following the suggested earlier 'southern route' (Cavalli-Sforza *et al.* 1994; Lahr & Foley 1994). The Indian haplogroup M lineages differ substantially from those found in eastern and central Asian populations and most likely represent *in situ* diversification in the sub-continent since the Palaeolithic (Kivisild *et al.* 1999b; Bamshad *et al.* 2001). It is important to note that this ancient cluster is present at frequencies above 50 per cent all over India. Its sub-clusters, as with the Indian mtDNA tree in general (Mountain *et al.* 1995), are not subdivided according to linguistic (Indo-European, Dravidian) or caste affiliations (Kivisild *et al.* 2000; Bamshad *et al.* 2001), although there may occur (sometimes drastic) population-wise differences in frequencies of particular sub-clusters.

Another profound peculiarity of the Indian mtDNA pool lies in the high frequency (~14 per cent on average in India) and great diversity of narrowly Indian-specific lineages deriving directly from the phylogenetic node R, otherwise ancestral to HV, JT, and U found in western Eurasia, and B and F in eastern Eurasia (Kivisild *et al.* 1999b). The coalescence age of this node is similar to that for haplogroup M and its presence in India suggests, once again, *in situ* differentiation of maternal lineages since the Upper Palaeolithic.

Furthermore, two sub-clusters of western Eurasian specific haplogroup U, these being U2 and U7, occur in India in relatively high frequencies. Because of their deep coalescence times, their presence was interpreted as testifying another Palaeolithic human migration to the Indian subcontinent from the west (Kivisild *et al.* 1999a). However, patterns of the spread of U2 and U7 differ in an interesting way. The lineages of the first group are restricted mainly to the Indian subcontinent and form a set of an Indian-specific sub-cluster U2i (Kivisild *et al.* 1999a). Although U2i is spread in a decreasing frequency from northwest to south and east in India, its presence in nearby western Asian populations is marginal (<1 per cent).

Quite a different phylogeographic picture emerges for U7 lineages. Its world-wide frequency is the highest among Iranians (we lack reliable data on Afghani populations) and U7 is also common among the Arabic-speaking western Asian populations (Table 17.1). On the one hand, its frequency in India is about four to five times lower than in Iran. On the other hand, considering the frequency of U7 among the subset of the western Eurasian lineages present in the Indian mtDNA pool, i.e. excluding from comparisons Indian-specific lineages of M, R, and U2i clusters, U7 appears over twice as frequently in Indians as in Iranians (Table 17.1). Most importantly however, we have observed that haplotype sharing between the Indian and western Asian U7 lineages occurs only through common founder motifs. On average, Indian U7 HVS-I sequences differ from the common founder motifs by one transition (~20,000 years), suggesting their split around the time of the Last Glacial Maximum (LGM). Hence, one may speculate that global cooling and the accompanying extensive spread of deserts separated mtDNA haplogroup U7 carriers into two branches — the western and the eastern. There is an analogy with U2 (U2e and U2i), except that this split occurred about twice as early. An analogy can be seen also in the spread and diversity of haplogroup W lineages (Kivisild *et al.* 1999b).

Thus, what we see as specific to Indian subcontinent is the presence of diverse sub-clusters of haplogroups M, R, and U that are virtually absent elsewhere. All these sub-clusters show coalescent times at around 50,000 BP. Given their high overall frequency in India this suggests a very limited gene flow — at least as far as maternal lineages are concerned — beyond the subcontinent over a long time span, likely since its initial colonization.

The Holocene

To focus on lineages that might be tentatively associated with the spread of Neolithic and Bronze Age cultures, Dravidian and Indo-European languages in West and South Asia, we ignore the lineage clusters that reveal clear signs of an 'early' (~15,000 years or longer) differentiation between Indians and western Asians. Our task becomes less sophisticated than it was in separating 'autochthonous' European mtDNA lineages from those present in the Levant (Richards *et al.* 2000).

First, it would be interesting to compare whether 'recent western' lineages among the present-day Indians correlate in their founder frequencies with those postulated to have been imported to Europe during and since the Neolithic. As shown in Table 17.1, a fraction of about 8 per cent of the Indian maternal gene pool can be assigned to a status of 'a putative recent import from the west' (PRIFW) — i.e. in time scale throughout the Neolithic, Bronze and Iron Ages to more recent times. In space, it begins with a possible impact from Iran and Afghanistan, extending to potential migrations from further west and north.

Of course, here we should mention a possibility that some of the lineage clusters we have marked above as 'pre-Holocene', such as U7 and W, could have contributed to more recent gene flow(s) into India as well. Yet any possible difference such a scenario would make is likely to be rather small because of the comparatively low overall frequency of such lineages in the extant Indian mtDNA pool.

It would be extremely difficult if not impossible to discern Neolithic and Bronze Age migrations to India apart from each other, especially if they originated from the same source population/geographically restricted pool of mtDNAs. Compared to the composition of the mtDNA pool of Europeans, the PRIFW component in Indians differs in higher frequencies of HV and U1 and lower frequencies of H and U5 — a pattern similar to that observed for Anatolians and Iranians (Table 17.1). Nevertheless, some differences between Indians and western Asians can be noted, like the absence of U3 and the significantly lower frequency of K ($p < 0.05$) in the former, while the Indian share of PRIFW lineages comprises haplogroups I and U4. These are frequent also in Eastern Europe and present in Central Asian populations at higher frequencies than in Iran, Anatolia and in Arabians (Table 17.1). A notable difference lies also in the pre-HV lineages, characterized by 16217C, which reveal similar diversity and patterns of spread as haplogroup U7 lineages in India and western Asia (Table 17.1).

Currently, the western Asian Neolithic component assigned to the present-day mtDNA pool of Europeans is thought to consist mostly of haplogroups J, U3 and T1. It has been suggested that female carriers of these lineage clusters migrated from the Near East to Europe, probably at the same time and possibly as a consequence of the spread of farming (Richards *et al.* 2000). In this context, it is specifically interesting to note that, like U3 and J, T1 lineages are also found in a comparatively low frequency in Indians (compare a T1 to T ratio of 2/14 in India versus 15/38 in Iran). It is possible, then, that Iranians ob-

Table 17.1. *MtDNA haplogroup composition in Indians compared to western Asian populations.*

	India				Iran			Anatolia			Arabia		
	n	All	Fr.1	Fr.2	*n*	All	Fr.2	*n*	All	Fr.2	*n*	All	Fr.2
A–G, M, N9	862	66.3%	–	–	28	6.2%	–	20	5.2%	–	30	7.7%	–
I	8	0.6%	5.1%	7.7%	9	2.0%	2.6%	9	2.3%	2.7%	3	0.8%	1.0%
N1a	1	0.1%	0.6%	1.0%	2	0.4%	0.6%	5	1.3%	1.5%	1	0.3%	0.3%
N1b	0	0.0%	0.0%	0.0%	2	0.4%	0.6%	3	0.8%	0.9%	11	2.8%	3.7%
W	19	1.5%	12.2%	–	9	2.0%	–	15	3.9%	–	7	1.8%	–
X	2	0.2%	1.3%	1.9%	13	2.9%	3.8%	17	4.4%	5.0%	7	1.8%	2.4%
N*	3	0.2%	1.9%	2.9%	10	2.2%	2.9%	0	0.0%	0.0%	8	2.1%	2.7%
pre-HV[1]	1	0.1%	0.6%	1.0%	6	1.3%	1.8%	9	2.3%	2.7%	58	14.9%	19.7%
pre-HV[2]	5	0.4%	3.2%	4.8%	5	1.1%	1.5%	2	0.5%	0.6%	1	0.3%	0.3%
HV	8	0.6%	5.1%	7.7%	25	5.5%	7.4%	14	3.6%	4.1%	14	3.6%	4.8%
H	31	2.4%	19.9%	29.8%	77	17.1%	22.6%	97	25.0%	28.7%	50	12.9%	17.0%
(pre-)V	0	0.0%	0.0%	0.0%	3	0.7%	0.9%	1	0.3%	0.3%	1	0.3%	0.3%
J	10	0.8%	6.4%	9.6%	61	13.5%	17.9%	42	10.8%	12.4%	81	20.8%	27.6%
T	14	1.1%	9.0%	13.5%	38	8.4%	11.2%	46	11.9%	13.6%	18	4.6%	6.1%
U1	7	0.5%	4.5%	6.7%	12	2.7%	3.5%	17	4.4%	5.0%	6	1.5%	2.0%
U2I	101	7.8%	–	–	2	0.4%	–	1	0.3%	–	5	1.3%	–
U2e	2	0.2%	1.3%	1.9%	5	1.1%	1.5%	3	0.8%	0.9%	2	0.5%	0.7%
U3	0	0.0%	0.0%	0.0%	12	2.7%	3.5%	21	5.4%	6.2%	5	1.3%	1.7%
U4	6	0.5%	3.8%	5.8%	5	1.1%	1.5%	4	1.0%	1.2%	2	0.5%	0.7%
U5	7	0.5%	4.5%	6.7%	15	3.3%	4.4%	21	5.4%	6.2%	2	0.5%	0.7%
U6	0	0.0%	0.0%	0.0%	1	0.2%	0.3%	0	0.0%	0.0%	4	1.0%	1.4%
U7	33	2.5%	21.2%	–	40	8.9%	–	6	1.5%	–	9	2.3%	–
K	2	0.2%	1.3%	1.9%	34	7.5%	10.0%	25	6.4%	7.4%	14	3.6%	4.8%
U*	0	0.0%	0.0%	0.0%	5	1.1%	1.5%	2	0.5%	0.6%	6	1.5%	2.0%
R*	178	13.7%	–	–	22	4.9%	–	7	1.8%	–	3	0.8%	–
L1–L3	0	0.0%	–	–	10	2.2%	–	1	0.3%	–	41	10.5%	–
	1300	100.0%	12.0%	8.0%	451	100.0%	75.4%	388	100.0%	87.1%	389	100.0%	75.6%

[1] 73A, 11719G, 14766T, 16126C, 16362C
[2] 73G, 11719G, 14766C, 16217C
Fractions 1 and 2 (Fr.1; Fr.2) are defined excluding haplogroups indicated by dash (–), see text for details.

tained most of their U3, K, J, T1 and also X lineages only after a substantial diffusion of 'Proto-Iranian' lineages to the Indian mtDNA pool had taken place.

One should not forget that India is large

As has already been observed for classical markers (Cavalli-Sforza *et al.* 1994), changes in the Indian genetic landscape do not occur gradually but are structured as a 'multitude of endogamous pockets'. At first glance, the same might seem to be the case for mtDNA and Y-chromosomal markers as well, because of strong founder effects and drift in genetically semi-isolated communities. Therefore, the frequency of any specific lineage in India can vary profoundly. Yet, there are a few general patterns of change.

The geographic distribution of lineages belonging to the 'western loan' fraction is concentrated mainly toward the north and west, declining from a high of 25 per cent in the Punjab (northwest) and 15 per cent in Gujarat (west) to a low of 4 per cent in western Bengal and Andhra Pradesh. There is no significant difference, however, in the frequency of this fraction of maternal lineages between Hindi speakers from Uttar Pradesh (6 per cent) and Dravidian speakers (4 per cent) from Andhra Pradesh (Kivisild *et al.* 1999a). Contrary to a prediction, deriving from a hypothesis that a higher frequency of 'western' gene lineages should discriminate higher castes from lower castes, it was found (Bamshad *et al.* 2001) that the difference between 'upper', 'middle' and 'lower' caste Dravidian-speaking Telugus is more strongly stratified in terms of the two Indian-specific maternal lineage clusters M3 (19 per cent in 'upper', 4 per cent in 'middle', and 1 per cent in 'lower' castes) and U2i (17 per cent - 10 per cent - 6 per cent, respectively), rather than by those of recent western Asian origin (5 per cent - 2 per cent - 1 per cent, respectively). The five-fold frequency difference for the latter can be interpreted in terms of a selective western impact on the mtDNA pools of upper castes (Bamshad *et al.* 2001). However, the fact that just the two autochthonous Indian mtDNA clusters, out of a much larger variety, comprise about a third of all maternal lineages of the upper castes of

Dravidian-speaking Telugus suggests strongly that the origin of the endogamous caste system should not be traced to a simple model of a putative Indo-Aryan invasion some 4700 years ago.

If one wants to maintain an Aryan invasion scenario, then one must at least assume that the incoming female lineages were absorbed selectively into an *already existing* profound stratification. One should also keep in mind possible differences in sizes of migrant/local populations: for example, if the entire population of the British Isles would *in corpore* emigrate today to India, it would, assuming random admixture, leave a genetic impact of no more than 5 per cent on average.

Table 17.2. *Some Y-chromosomal haplogroup frequencies in India, western Asia and Europe.*

	DYS257 92R7 HG1	M89 HG2	SRY1532 HG3	12f2 HG9	M130 HG10	M9 HG26	M20 HG28	YAP HG21
Punjab	67	9.0	4.5	50.7	20.9	3.0	0	11.9	0
Gujarat	29	10.3	13.8	24.1	20.7	17.2	3.4	10.3	0
Andhra Pradesh	36	41.7	11.1	8.3	5.6	16.7	0	0	0
Western Bengal	31	29.0	16.1	38.7	9.7	3.2	3.2	0	0
Sri Lanka	87	24.1	20.7	23.0	16.1	0	0	16.1	0
India[1]	250	21.6	12.4	30.4	15.6	6.8	0.8	12.4	0
AP, higher castes[2]	55	9.1	n.d.	45.5	9.1	1.8	12.7	0	
AP, middle castes[2]	111	12.6	n.d.	16.2	12.6	2.7	21.6	0	
AP, lower castes[2]	74	12.2	n.d.	20.3	5.4	5.4	13.5	0	
Iran[1]	83	8.4	13.3	10.8	41.0	1.2	3.6	7.2	14.5
Anatolia[1] and Caucasus[3]	323	24.8	26.3	4.6	32.2	0.9	3.7	1.2	4.3
Eastern Europe[4]	302	10.9	n.d.	47.0	3.3	n.d.	0.6	5.0	
Western Europe[5]	327	66.4	n.d.	3.7	3.9	n.d.	0.9	5.5	

[1] - this study
[2] - Andhra Pradesh (Bamshad *et al.* 2001)
[3] - including Armenians and Georgians from (Rosser *et al.* 2000).
[4] - including Polish, Russian, Byelorussian, and Ukrainian populations (Rosser *et al.* 2000).
[5] - including French, Belgian, Scottish, Basque, and Spanish populations (Rosser *et al.* 2000).

A recent massive western Y-chromosomal invasion of India?

Phylogeography of the mtDNA haplogroup M suggests that it spread during the Palaeolithic by the southern route taken by modern humans during their initial colonization of Eurasia (Quintana-Murci *et al.* 1999; Kivisild *et al.* 1999a). Because haplogroup M makes up the largest fraction (>50 per cent) of maternal lineages, both in India and eastern Asia, in population-wise comparisons, Indian maternal lineages cluster more closely with populations of East Asia (Bamshad *et al.* 2001). In the paternal history of present-day Indian populations, RPS4Y (M130) has been suggested to have been carried by the southern route migrants (Underhill *et al.* 2001). Yet its frequency in India is quite low (7 per cent). In fact, most Indian Y chromosomes cluster in haplogroups that are typical of European and western Asian populations (Rosser *et al.* 2000), but infrequent or even absent in eastern Asia (Su *et al.* 1999). Another NRY cluster, characterized by M52 and M69 mutations, has been suggested to accompany an early (likely pre-LGM) eastward expansion of Levantine mtDNA sub-cluster(s) of haplogroup U to India (Underhill *et al.* 2001).

There are differences in caste affinities for European Y-chromosomal varieties — in Telugus, higher castes reveal shorter distances from Europeans (Bamshad *et al.* 2001). This sex-specific difference may be interpreted as resulting from a predominantly male-specific recent gene flow into the upper castes, not necessarily from Europe as such, but perhaps from western and/or central Asia. More specifically, Quintana-Murci *et al.* (2001) suggested that NRY marker 12f2 (haplogroup 9) indicates a Neolithic spread of farmers into India that is, with a short tandem repeat (STR) diversity in the background of M9^G-SRY1532^A (haplogroup 3), consistent with an Indo-Aryan migration from Central Asia. Thus, both these studies suggest a substantial western male-specific gene flow to India during the Holocene.

However, several aspects of these genetic distance and haplogroup-wise comparisons should be considered with caution. First, the affinities of higher caste Telugus to European populations are not informative alone in telling from which source and when a putative migration took place. When comparing the Y-chromosomal affinities of Indian, western Asian and European populations in detail (Bamshad *et al.* 2001), it becomes apparent that 'higher' caste Telugus have, in contrast to 'lower' and 'middle' castes, a higher frequency (45.5 per cent) of haplogroup 3. Further typing of NRY markers in Indian populations has now revealed that a high frequency of this haplogroup is, however, characteristic not only of (eastern) European populations, but also of northwest India, where haplogroup 3 is characteristic of about half of the male population and is also frequent among western Bengalis (Table 17.2). Therefore, the Y-chromosomal origin of 'higher' caste Telugus (i.e. high frequency of this particular NRY lineage among them) is not necessarily related to migration to India from outside and least likely from Iran and/or Anatolia, where haplogroup 3 is apparently much less frequent than among most of the Indian populations investigated in this respect.

Second, great caution is required when interpreting the dates deriving from Y-chromosomal STR coalescent calculations. Table 17.3 reveals that profoundly inconsistent time estimates can be reached when different calibration methods are used. Hence, it seems safer to operate with raw diversity estimates — to determine the polarity of the movement — leaving the time of origin question unanswered until reliable dating methods for Y-chromosomal STR diversity are worked out. Yet, even if time estimates are avoided, there are some problems introduced by sampling strategies and differences in demographic histories. For example, in the study by Quintana-Murci et al. (2001), a decline in diversity stretching from Iran to India was observed in haplogroups 3 and 9 and the authors rushed to interpret this empirical observation in favour of directional gene flow to India during Neolithic period (haplogroup 9). They linked this finding to the introduction of Indo-European languages (haplogroup 3) to India. Time estimates for their spread were derived from the STR clock.

Here, however, the clock is just a secondary problem — the first being 'the Indian reference sample' used. Indeed, the Indians included in this study consisted of a (limited) sample from Gujarat — one of the western maritime provinces of India. When extending the Indian sample with collections from different states, a quite different, even opposite, pattern emerges (Table 17.3). Indians appear to display the higher diversity both in haplogroups 3 and 9 — even if a pooled sample of eastern and southern European populations was considered. If we were to use the same arithmetic and logic (sensu haplogroup 9 is Neolithic) to give an interpretation of this table, then the straightforward suggestion would be that both Neolithic (agriculture) and Indo-European languages arose in India and from there, spread to Europe. We would also have to add that inconsistencies with the archaeological evidence would appear and disappear as we change rate estimates (Table 17.3).

Thirdly, it has been suggested that the Neolithic spread of farmers to Europe included, above 12f2, also Y chromosomes carrying markers M35 (at the background of YAP+) and M201 (Semino et al. 2000;

Underhill et al. 2001). But note that while in Europe, Anatolia and the South Caucasus as well as in Iran, both M35 (haplogroup 21) and 12f2 (haplogroup 9) are present — and could even be called friendly co-inhabitants of the corresponding Y-chromosomal pools (Table 17.2) — this does not hold for India (Table 17.2). Indians, in contrast to their neighbours, generally lack the Alu insertion in their Y chromosomes (Kivisild et al. 1999b, and references therein), while possessing haplogroup 9 Y chromosomes in a substantial frequency. Thus, here we observe a situation, analogous to that indicated above for mtDNA. One does not find a strong correlation between the identity of European and Indian (putatively) 'Neolithic' components, having supposedly spread out from Levant/Middle East. In particular, the lack of YAP+ chromosomes in India (although found in some Pakistani populations), contrary to their presence in Europe, suggests that Y chromosomes carrying the M35 marker arrived in the Near and Middle East (likely from northern Africa) only after a putative earlier gene flow from Iran to India had taken place — but obviously earlier than the spread of a certain fraction of the Near Eastern Y chromosomes to Europe. One may see here an obvious analogy to a certain set of maternal lineages, such as K, U3, T1 and J.

However, in general, this lack of symmetry of possible eastwards and westwards Neolithic spreads from the Fertile Crescent should not be seen as a contradiction. Indeed, why should one assume that the initial area of the beginning of agriculture was itself geographically narrow and genetically homogeneous (see e.g. Bar-Yosef this volume)?

Y chromosomes and mitochondrial DNA — not necessarily together, not necessarily apart

Besides the example of parallelism in the patterns of the spread of Y-chromosomal markers RPS4Y and M52 with mitochondrial haplogroups M and U (Underhill et al. 2001), noted above, there might be other links of interest and worth further exploring. One involves M20 in NRY and haplogroups U7 and pre-HV^2 (see Tables 17.1 & 17.2) in mtDNA, which seem to co-decrease in frequencies from India and Iran to the Caucasus and the southern Mediterranean.

Clear differences in the genetic impact of a (probable) Neolithic component in Europeans and Indians, both in their mtDNA and Y-chromosome pools, are not easily explained with the simplest model of a single narrow source region — be it Anatolia or the Fertile Crescent — from which

Table 17.3. *Variance and coalescent time estimates on Y-chromosomal STRs.*

| | | Age estimates | |
	Variance[1]	Pedigree rate[2]	Phylogenetic rate[3]
Haplogroup 9			
Europe	0.44	6100	42,200
India	0.51	7100	48,900
Haplogroup 3			
Europe	0.24	3300	23,100
India	0.37	5200	35,700

[1] - the variances were calculated using five STR loci (DYS19, DYS388, DYS390, DYS391, and DYS393)
[2] - using rate of 1.8×10^{-3} based on most recent pedigree studies (Quintana-Murci *et al.* 2001)
[3] - using rate of 2.6×10^{-4} based on phylogenetic calibration (Forster *et al.* 2000).
Note that each calibration involves large error margins.

Table 17.4. *Stratification of mtDNA lineages according to their probable sequence of appearance in the Indian sub-continent.*

Time period	MtDNA cluster	Frequency
Primarily early UP	M	66%
	U2i	8%
	R	14%
		88%
Primarily late UP	W	1–2%
	U7	2–3%
		~4%
Neolithic and later	H, T, J, I, HV, U1, U5, U4, pre-HV, X, K, U2e, and N1	~8%

'Neolithic genes' moved in European and Indian directions. Other models should be sought and tested for explanation. But given the relatively low frequency of recent western lineages in the Indian mtDNA pool, a great number of samples from a wide variety of diverse Indian populations should be analyzed to collect a representative sample of sufficient size for a rigorous founder analysis. Similarly, massive founder analysis is desirable for the Y-chromosome because, as we have demonstrated, interpretations deriving solely from haplogroup frequency and even from combined SNP-STR diversity distributions can be misleading. It appears likely that more informative markers in this context are needed as well.

Concluding remarks

When discussing the genetics of Indian populations, different authors have now and then stressed the enormous complexity of their social systems, perhaps dating back much longer than written evidence. While that is certainly true, it nevertheless seems to us that knowledge accumulated thus far allows us not only to draw the first reasonably well-supported conclusions concerning what one may call the basic time-and-space oriented landmarks of the Indian maternal and paternal lineages, but also to avoid the pitfalls so easily created by an obvious desire 'to tell an exciting tale'. Table 17.4 brings together our current understanding of the arrival of maternal lineages to India — as far as it can be deduced from the approximately 1300 extant mtDNAs analyzed.

Unfortunately, here we cannot provide an 'equally simple' table for the NRY markers for reasons given above (see Table 17.3), but it would be very surprising indeed if present-day Indians, possessing at least 90 per cent of what we think of as autochthonous Upper Palaeolithic maternal lineages, were to carry but a small fraction of equally old paternal lineages.

References

Bamshad, M., T. Kivisild, W.S. Watkins, M.E. Dixon, C.E. Ricker, B.B. Rao, J.M. Naidu, B.V. Prasad, P.G. Reddy, A. Rasanayagam, S.S. Papiha, R. Villems, A.J. Redd, M.F. Hammer, S.V. Nguyen, M.L. Carroll, M.A. Batzer & L.B. Jorde, 2001. Genetic evidence on the origins of Indian caste populations. *Genome Research* 11(6), 994–1004.

Cavalli-Sforza, L.L., P. Menozzi & A. Piazza, 1994. *The History and Geography of Human Genes.* Princeton (NJ): Princeton University Press.

Chakrabarti, D.K., 1999. *India: an Archaeological History. Palaeolithic Beginnings to Early Historic Foundations.* Oxford: Oxford University Press.

Comas, D., F. Calafell, E. Mateu, A. Perez-Lezaun, E. Bosch, R. Martinez-Arias, J. Clarimon, F. Facchini, G. Fiori, D. Luiselli, D. Pettener & J. Bertranpetit, 1998. Trading genes along the silk road: mtDNA sequences and the origin of Central Asian populations. *American Journal of Human Genetics* 63(6), 1824–38.

Forster, P., A. Rohl, P. Lunnemann, C. Brinkmann, T. Zerjal, C. Tyler-Smith & B. Brinkmann, 2000. A short tandem repeat-based phylogeny for the human Y chromosome. *American Journal of Human Genetics* 67(1), 182–96.

Kivisild, T., M.J. Bamshad, K. Kaldma, M. Metspalu, E. Metspalu, M. Reidla, S. Laos, J. Parik, W.S. Watkins, M.E. Dixon, S.S. Papiha, S.S. Mastana, M.R. Mir, V. Ferak & R. Villems, 1999a. Deep common ancestry of Indian and western-Eurasian mitochondrial DNA lineages. *Current Biology* 9(22), 1331–4.

Kivisild, T., K. Kaldma, M. Metspalu, J. Parik, S.S. Papiha & R. Villems, 1999b. The place of the Indian mitochondrial DNA variants in the global network of maternal lineages and the peopling of the Old World, in Papiha *et al.* (eds.), 135–52.

Kivisild, T., S.S. Papiha, S. Rootsi, J. Parik, K. Kaldma, M. Reidla, S. Laos, M. Metspalu, G. Pielberg, M. Adojaan, E. Metspalu, S.S. Mastana, Y. Wang, M. Gölge, H. Demirtas, E. Schnekenberg, G.F. de Stefano, T. Geberhiwot, M. Claustres & R. Villems, 2000. An Indian ancestry: a key for understanding human diversity in Europe and beyond, in Renfrew & Boyle (eds.), 267–79.

Kumar, S.S., I. Nasidze, S.R. Walimbe & M. Stoneking, 2000. Discouraging prospects for ancient DNA from India. *American Journal of Physical Anthropology* 113(1), 129–33.

Lahr, M. & R. Foley, 1994. Multiple dispersals and modern human origins. *Evolutionary Anthropology* 3, 48–60.

Mountain, J.L., J.M. Hebert, S. Bhattacharyya, P.A. Underhill, C. Ottolenghi, M. Gadgil & L.L. Cavalli-Sforza, 1995. Demographic history of India and mtDNA-sequence diversity. *American Journal of Human Genetics* 56(4), 979–92.

Papiha, S., R. Deka & R. Chakraborty (eds.), 1999. *Genomic Diversity: Application in Human Population Genetics.* New York (NY): Kluwer Academic/Plenum Publishers.

Passarino, G., O. Semino, L.F. Bernini & A.S. Santachiara-Benerecetti, 1996. Pre-Caucasoid and Caucasoid genetic features of the Indian population, revealed by mtDNA polymorphisms. *American Journal of Human Genetics* 59(4), 927–34.

Quintana-Murci, L., O. Semino, H.-J. Bandelt, G. Passarino, K. McElreavey & A.S. Santachiara-Benerecetti, 1999. Genetic evidence of an early exit of *Homo sapiens* sapiens from Africa through eastern Africa. *Nature Genetics* 23(4), 437–41.

Quintana-Murci, L., C. Krausz, T. Zerjal, S.H. Sayar, M.F. Hammer, S.Q. Mehdi, Q. Ayub, R. Qamar, A. Mohyuddin, U. Radhakrishna, M.A. Jobling, C. Tyler-Smith & K. McElreavey, 2001. Y-chromosome lineages trace diffusion of people and languages in southwestern Asia. *American Journal of Human Genetics* 68(2), 537–42.

Renfrew, C., 1987. *Archaeology and Language: the Puzzle of Indo-European Origins.* London: Jonathan Cape.

Renfrew, C. & K. Boyle (eds.), 2000. *Archaeogenetics: DNA and the Population Prehistory of Europe.* (McDonald Institute Monographs.) Cambridge: McDonald Institute for Archaeological Research.

Richards, M., V. Macaulay, E. Hickey, E. Vega, B. Sykes, V. Guida, C. Rengo, D. Sellitto, F. Cruciani, T. Kivisild, R. Villems, M. Thomas, S. Rychkov, O. Rychkov, Y. Rychkov, M. Golge, D. Dimitrov, E. Hill, D. Bradley, V. Romano, F. Calí, G. Vona, A. Demaine, S. Papiha, C. Triantaphyllidis, G. Stefanescu, J. Hatina, M. Belledi, A. di Rienzo, A. Novelletto, A. Oppenheim, S. Norby, N. Al-Zaheri, S. Santachiara-Benerecetti, R. Scozzari, A. Torroni & H.-J. Bandelt, 2000. Tracing European founder lineages in the near eastern mtDNA pool. *American Journal of Human Genetics* 67, 1251–76.

Rolf, B., A. Röhl, P. Forster & B. Brinkmann, 1999. On the origin of the Turks: study of six Y-chromosomal short tandem repeats, in Papiha *et al.* (eds.), 75–83.

Rosser, Z.H., T. Zerjal, M.E. Hurles, M. Adojaan, D. Alavantic, A. Amorim, W. Amos, M. Armenteros, E. Arroyo, G. Barbujani, G. Beckman, L. Beckman, J. Bertranpetit, E. Bosch, D.G. Bradley, G. Brede, G. Cooper, H. Corte-Réal, P. de Knijff, R. Decorte, Y.E. Dubrova, O. Evgrafov, A. Gilissen, S. Glisic, M. Golge, E.W. Hill, A. Jeziorowska, L. Kalaydjieva, M. Kayser, T. Kivisild, S.A. Kravchenko, A. Krumina, V. Kucinskas, J. Lavinha, L.A. Livshits, P. Malaspina, S. Maria, K. McElreavey, T.A. Meitinger, A.V. Mikelsaar, R.J. Mitchell, K. Nafa, J. Nicholson, S. Norby, A. Pandya, J. Parik, P.C. Patsalis, L. Pereira, B. Peterlin, G. Pielberg, M.L. Prata, C. Previdere, L. Roewer, S. Rootsi, D.C. Rubinsztein, J. Saillard, F.R. Santos, G. Stefanescu, B.C. Sykes, A. Tolun, R. Villems, C. Tyler-Smith & M.A. Jobling, 2000. Y-chromosomal diversity in Europe is clinal and influenced primarily by geography, rather than by language. *American Journal of Human Genetics* 67, 1526–43.

Ruhlen, M., 1991. *A Guide to the World's Languages.* London: Edward Arnold.

Semino, O., G. Passarino, P.J. Oefner, A.A. Lin, S. Arbuzova L.E. Beckman, G. de Benedictis, P. Francalacci, A. Kouvatsi, S. Limborska, M. Marcikiae, A. Mika, B. Mika, D. Primorac, A.S. Santachiara-Benerecetti, L.L. Cavalli-Sforza & P.A. Underhill, 2000. The genetic legacy of paleolithic *Homo sapiens sapiens* in extant Europeans: a Y-chromosome perspective. *Science* 290, 1155–9.

Su, B., J. Xiao, P. Underhill, R. Deka, W. Zhang, J. Akey, W. Huang, D. Shen, D. Lu, J. Luo, J. Chu, J. Tan, P. Shen, R. Davis, L. Cavalli-Sforza, R. Chakraborty, M. Xiong, R. Du, P. Oefner, Z. Chen & L. Jin, 1999. Y-chromosome evidence for a northward migration of modern humans into Eastern Asia during the last Ice Age. *American Journal of Human Genetics* 65(6), 1718–24.

Tambets, K., T. Kivisild, E. Metspalu, J. Parik, K. Kaldma, S. Laos, H.-V. Tolk, M. Gölge, H. Demirtas, T. Geberhiwot, S.S. Papiha G.F. de Stefano & R. Villems, 2000. The topology of the maternal lineages of the Anatolian and Trans-Caucasus populations and the peopling of the Europe: some preliminary considerations, in Renfrew & Boyle (eds.), 219–35.

Underhill, P.A., P.D. Shen, A.A. Lin, L. Jin, G. Passarino, W.H. Yang, E. Kauffman, B. Bonné-Tamir, J. Bertranpetit, P. Francalacci, M. Ibrahim, T. Jenkins, J.R. Kidd, S.Q. Mehdi, M.T. Seielstad, R.S. Wells, A. Piazza, R.W. Davis, M.W. Feldman, L.L. Cavalli-Sforza & P.J. Oefner, 2000. Y-chromosome sequence variation and the history of human populations. *Nature Genetics* 26, 358–61.

Underhill, P.A., G. Passarino, A.A. Lin, P. Shen, M. Mirazon Lahr, R. Foley, P.J. Oefner & L.L. Cavalli-Sforza, 2001. The phylogeography of Y-chromosome binary haplotypes and the origins of modern human populations. *Annals of Human Genetics* 65(1), 43–62.

Chapter 18

Languages and Farming Dispersals: Austroasiatic Languages and Rice Cultivation

Charles Higham

There were two major transitions to agriculture in the Old World. One took place in the Levant and involved wheat, barley, cattle and sheep. The other was centred in the Yangtze and Yellow River basins of China, where rice and millet were brought under cultivation in association with cattle and pig domestication. Both took place at about the same time and under parallel climatic changes. In the western centre, much research has been devoted to exploring possible links between the expansion of agricultural communities from the Near East and the present distribution of Indo-European languages. Archaeogenetic research has been deployed as a testing mechanism for the broad models generated. East and Southeast Asia lag well behind this move, but the region is important not only on its own terms, but also as a means of seeking possible similarities with the spread of Indo-European languages.

This paper identifies first a series of cognates for rice cultivation which link the Austroasiatic languages of Southeast Asia and eastern India. It then seeks archaeological evidence for the expansion of rice farmers south and west from the centre of domestication in the Yangtze Valley, and finds an encouraging conformity between the distribution of Austroasiatic (AA) languages and the spread of Neolithic settlement based on rice, and the raising of domestic cattle, pigs and the dog. It then considers the possible adoption of Austroasiatic languages by indigenous hunter-gatherers. The concluding model is proposed and means of testing it are explored.

AA languages fall into two major divisions, Munda and Mon-Khmer, and are found from eastern India to Vietnam, south to peninsular Malaysia and the Nicobar Islands. The Kurku are the westernmost group of AA speakers, living south of the Narmada River in Maharashtra. Norman & Mei (1976) have identified a possible AA substrate in

southern China which suggests that this language family once had an even wider distribution. The most northerly known AA language is P'u-man, recognized in 1899 in the village of Xiao Qin in Yunnan. This is a particularly vital location, for it lies on the strategic Mekong about 100 km south of lake Dali. Apart from Vietnamese and Khmer, the national languages of Vietnam and Cambodia, the distribution of AA speakers consistently takes the form of isolated enclaves. This is, at least in part, due to more recent, historically-documented intrusions. The Thai, for example, have taken up much of the Chao Phraya Valley, thus isolating the speakers of Mon (an AA language) to remote, usually upland enclaves. The Kuay people of the lower Thai provinces of the Khorat Plateau are islands surrounded by speakers of Lao. The Burmese have marginalized the Mon, while Munda languages persist as enclaves surrounded by Indo-European languages. No AA speakers survive in Lingnan (southern China) in the face of the expansion of Sino-Tibetan.

AA languages have, for almost a century, been linked in various ways with other language families. Schmidt (1906) was foremost in suggesting that AA and Austronesian (AN) languages belong to a phylum he named Austric. This linkage was not widely supported until Reid (1994) found evidence in the Nancowry language of the Nicobar Islands for a link based not so much on cognates, but on morphemes in which conservative AN structures survived in AA languages due probably to the remote island location. The notion that the Munda languages were intrusive to India was suggested by Heine-Geldern (1932), who further linked their arrival from Southeast Asia with the distribution of the polished shouldered adze and the spread of agriculture. Wheeler (1959) joined him in identifying an eastern source for the Neolithic of eastern India.

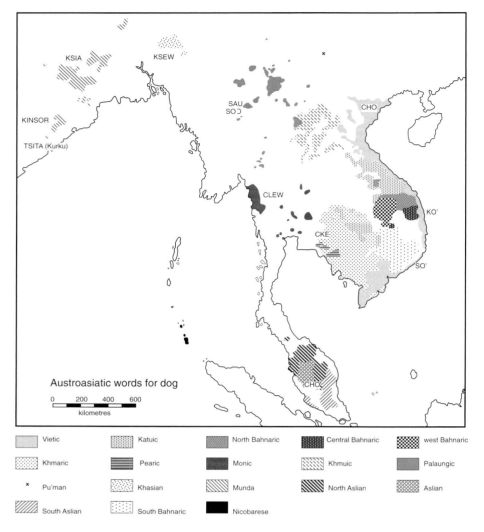

Figure 18.1. *Austroasiatic words for dog.*

The word for dog, for example, is likely to be important. There is, in Southeast Asia, no native wolf from which to derive the domesticated dog. Yet the cranial characteristics of the prehistoric dog reveal, beyond doubt, a lupine ancestry. The nearest possible sources for the wolf are *Canis lupus chanco* in China, and *C.l. pallipes* in India. Figure 18.1 shows the word for dog in a variety of AA languages. It is clear that cognates are present over the entire area of AA language distribution, even into Central India. The word for child (Fig. 18.2) is virtually identical between Kurku in Central India, and Bahnar on the eastern seaboard of Vietnam, a distance of almost 3000 km, equivalent to that from the Konya Plain in Turkey to Skara Brae in Scotland. Fish is another key word for any expansionary group of farmers in Southeast and South Asia. As can be seen in Figure 18.3, this too is clearly cognate across the area of AA languages, linking small islands of speakers.

But perhaps the key words in the vocabulary are those for rice in its various forms. Luce (1985) has considered the word for husked rice. In Old Mon it is *sno'*, Old Khmer *ranko*, Danaw *ko*, in the P'u-man language of Yunnan it is *'n-k'u* and in Khasi, it is *khaw*. The word for rice plant (Fig. 18.4) in Sakai is *ba'ba'* or *ba'*, in Stieng, Biat, Gar and Bahnar it is *ba*, in Khasi is becomes *kba* and in Mundari, it is *baba*. Luce concluded with these words: 'What can be the cause of this startling diffusion? I can only think of one adequate explanation: wet rice cultivation' (Luce 1985, 3). At a time when archaeological research had hardly begun, he suggested that rice cultivation began in the Red River Valley, whence agriculturalists moved up stream to Yunnan, across to the headwaters of the Brahmaputra and so into India. As will be seen, his first idea has been largely sustained by further linguistic research,

Any consideration of this possible link between AA languages and the spread of agriculture should most logically commence by considering cognate words for rice cultivation across the broad spectrum of AA languages. As with all aspects of the Southeast Asian past, such studies lag behind comparable research in other parts of the world. However, in a series of lectures delivered to the École des Langues Orientales Vivantes in Paris in 1966, Gordon Luce provided a pioneering analysis of the implications of the distribution of AA languages for the spread of rice cultivation (Luce 1985). He began by considering a number of key cognates linking the widely-scattered speakers of AA. These form such a key platform for any further consideration of this issue that they need to be briefly summarized. In doing so, I have chosen certain words relevant to the spread of agriculturalists.

but his archaeological correlates need drastic revision.

Thus, Zide & Zide (1976) have considered the Proto-Munda vocabulary, and compared the reconstructed words with those found in other AA languages in Southeast Asia. Their results reveal that, on the basis of the reconstructed Proto-Munda word list, the Munda were more advanced agriculturally than archaeologists had previously thought. Whereas it was widely assumed that the more advanced Munda, speaking Sora, Mundari or Santali, received their knowledge of agriculture from intrusive Indo-Aryan speakers, the linguistic evidence revealed that they would have been rice farmers at the time of their arrival in eastern India. Indeed, the reconstruction of plant names provides a dimension to Munda prehistory not available so far from archaeology. Bamboo and bamboo shoot have cognates between Sora and Gorum in Munda, and in Old Mon.

There are Proto-Munda names for rice and uncooked husked rice which have cog-

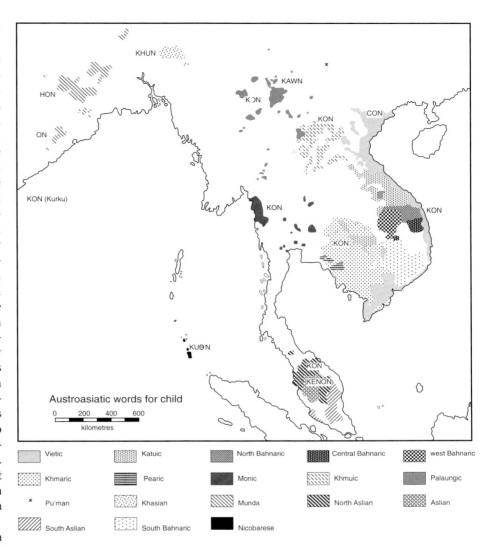

Figure 18.2. *Austroasiatic words for child.*

nates in Mon-Khmer, Lawa, Rumai and Khmu. Lawa is spoken in the Ping River valley of northern Thailand, while Khmu speakers are found in upland Laos. The north Munda form has cognates in Kharia, Mon-Khmer, Khasi and Semang. The word for pestle might be cognate in Kurku and Mon, Khmer and Proto-MK, while alcohol and inebriation have widespread AA cognates. There is also a reconstructable word for dog with cognate forms in Mon-Khmer. The Munda word for bull seems to have been borrowed from Indo-Aryan, whereas there is a possible cognate for cow with Proto-Munda and Mon-Khmer. Zide & Zide have concluded that at least 3500 years ago, at a conservative estimate, the Proto-Munda speakers practised subsistence agriculture, cultivating rice, millet and at least three legumes. They also used husking pestles and mortars which go back to

Proto-AA. But they developed some cultigens or plant resources in India, for there are no AA cognates for mango or turmeric.

This situation is supported by Mahdi (1998), who has found that the Proto-AA word for rice can be reconstructed in Munda, Mon-Khmer, Palaung-Wa, Viet-Muong, Old Mon and Lamet. Pejros & Shnirelman (1998) have also deployed linguistic evidence in suggesting that neither the Austroasiatic nor Austronesian proto-languages reveal evidence for a tropical origin, but rather point to inland beginnings north of the tropical zone of eastern Eurasia. They identify the middle Yangtze Valley as a likely homeland, and feel that Proto-Austric began to divide in the ninth to eighth millennia BC. Within AA, Munda and Mon-Khmer split from each other by the end of the fifth millennium BC. By the end of the

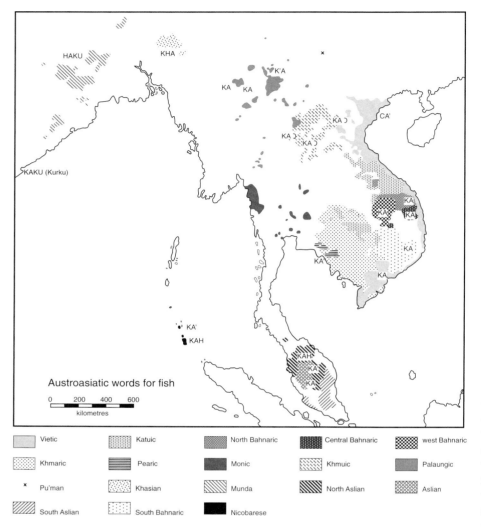

Austroasiatic words for fish

Vietic	Katuic	North Bahnaric	Central Bahnaric	west Bahnaric
Khmaric	Pearic	Monic	Khmuic	Palaungic
Pu'man	Khasian	Munda	North Aslian	Aslian
South Aslian	South Bahnaric	Nicobarese		

Figure 18.3. *Austroasiatic words for fish.*

fourth millennium, Mon-Khmer began to divide into Khmer, Bahnaric and Viet-Muong.

The linguistic evidence summarized above is compatible with an original Austric homeland in the middle Yangtze Valley, from which at least the ancestors of the AA and AN languages originated and spread, the former largely by land, and the latter by sea. Linguists seem to agree that a considerable time depth is necessary to account for the differences between the Munda and Mon-Khmer languages, and rather less for the divergence between the individual languages of the latter division.

Robert Blust (1996) followed Reid's conclusion on the validity of Austric by proposing, purely on linguistic evidence, that the distribution of AA languages in South and Southeast Asia results from a series of intrusive movements which took advan-

tage of riverine routes of expansion. From a source in the upper Yangtze valley, he suggested that Proto-Munda speakers followed the course of the Brahmaputra River into India, while speakers of Proto-Mon-Khmer followed the Irrawaddy into Burma, the Chao Phraya and Mekong into Thailand and Cambodia, and the Red River into Vietnam. This proposal called upon prehistorians to review the archaeological data available, to see if the evidence supported such a model. This involves consideration of the climate and archaeological sequence in the Yangtze Valley, based on evidence only assembled over the last few years.

The early Holocene climate of the Yangtze Valley underwent a series of profound changes incorporating the end of the Pleistocene Ice Age and the oscillations in temperature and rainfall. Recent evaluations of pollen spectra and faunal assemblages there reveal a climate 4–10°C cooler and much drier than now between 20,000 and 15,000 BC (Higham & Lu 1998). Rainfall was probably 1000 mm per annum below its present level of 1600 mm, accounting for the predominance of drought-resistant plants in the pollen spectra. From 15,000 to about 13,700 years BP the climate moderated, encouraging the spread of oak and pine, elm and willow. But thereafter, and until 10,000 BP, there was a reversal to cold conditions described across Eurasia as the Younger Dryas period. Thereafter, it again became warmer and moister. Broad-leaved trees colonized the Yangtze Valley and the fauna became subtropical. Increased rainfall fed rivers and lakes, and wild rice spread out from refugia.

It is against this environmental kaleidoscope that we can measure the significance of recent finds from deep excavations in the caves which fringe the lacustrine lowlands. The sequence at Diaotonghuan, for example, spans the later Pleistocene into the early

Neolithic period. This cavern overlooks a small, swampy basin in Jiangxi Province (Zhao 1998). The excavators have identified 16 sequential zones of occupation and recovered samples of rice phytoliths, the hard silica bodies found in the rice plant. There was, for example, a surge in the numbers of rice glume phytoliths in zone G, which is tentatively dated to the terminal Pleistocene. These are seen as evidence for the collection of wild rice during the mild phase which characterized that period. Rice phytoliths were extremely rare during zone F, which corresponds to the Younger Dryas cold phase. However, rice was again abundantly represented during zone E, which is thought to date between 10,000–8000 BP. About half the sample conforms with a domestic variety of rice. This context also provided the first evidence for pottery in the form of very crude, sometimes cord-marked vessels which could well have been made in order to cook rice.

A lack of reliable radiocarbon dates makes this a tentative framework, but it gains support from similar sequences in other caves. Xianrendong is located only 800 m from Diaotonghuan, and again has a Palaeolithic occupation under a Neolithic horizon containing rice phytoliths. Yuchanyan also overlooks low-lying wetlands, and has provided a sample of fish, turtle and mammalian bone as well as rice husks said to be transitional to the domestic form. Potsherds from this site are dated in the vicinity of 12,500 BP (Yuan & Zhang 1999). Bashidang is a village site which covers about three hectares. Its lower layers date to about 8000 BP, and excavations in 1993–97 uncovered waterlogged deposits which had preserved over 15,000 rice grains. These have been ascribed to a cultivated variety (Pei 1998). Water caltrop and lotus, both of which can easily be propagated in

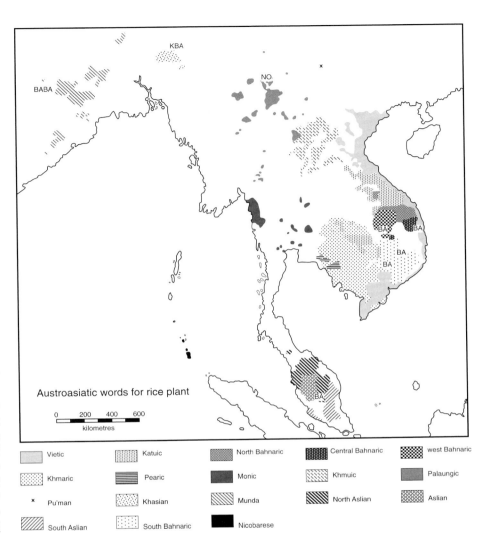

Figure 18.4. *Austroasiatic words for rice plant.*

marshes and lakes, were also abundantly represented in this settlement, together with hunted and probably domestic animals, pottery vessels, wooden spades and pestles, the foundations of pile dwellings and over 100 human burials. Bashidang is similar in many respects to the settlement of Pengtoushan, found only 20 km to the southwest. Here, we encounter a cemetery in which the dead were interred with complete pottery vessels and exotic stone ornaments. The clay used for making pots was tempered with rice chaff. Again, there are the remains of houses and every sign of a successful adaptation to the rich resources offered in the middle Yangtze Lakeland. Two radiocarbon determinations obtained from the rice used as a tempering agent are 6420–6990 BC and 5780–6380 BC (calibrated: Crawford & Chen Shen 1998).

This accumulating body of evidence indicates that the Yangtze Valley was one of the very few areas in Eurasia that witnessed a Neolithic Revolution, the transition from hunting and gathering to agriculture. Population growth is a recurrent characteristic of sedentary agricultural communities. As settlements grow, there is a strong incentive for a segment to move and found a new community. This appears to have followed the establishment of such sites as Pengtoushan and Bashidang. Fenshanbao, which was occupied within the period 8000–7500 BP, lies east of Lake Dongting, and excavations have revealed 50 burials and pottery tempered with rice. To the west, we find agriculture spreading upstream to Chengbeixi in the Three Gorges. In an easterly direction, the famous site of Hemudu in Zhejiang Province was a base for lakeside rice cultivation by 7000 BP.

This sequence has a strong bearing on the Neolithic settlement of Southeast Asia, because it is now possible to trace the expansion of agricultural communities progressively further to the south. Several rivers provide access from the Yangtze Valley to the rich hot lowlands of Lingnan. The Gan and Xiang flow north to Lakes Poyang and Dongting, while the Bei flows south. The first evidence we have for the establishment of rice farmers is, not unexpectedly, in the headwaters of this last river, where the sites Shixia, Xincun, Chuangbanling and Niling date from the early third millennium BC. Shixia in its earliest phase included a cemetery in which grave goods included jade *cong* (tubes) of a type known to have been of deep ritual significance in the Liangzhu culture to the north, as well as bracelets, pendants and split rings. The subsequent Nianyuzhuan culture sites reflect a further spread of agricultural settlement, but began to encounter and interact with rich hunter-gatherer groups commanding the delta of the Zhu River.

The Bei is just one of the rivers which ultimately connects the Yangtze Valley with Southeast Asia. In general, these rivers flow south and radiate out from a hub in the eastern Himalayan foothills. From east to west, they include the Red, Mekong and Chao Phraya systems. Further to the west, this configuration is repeated in the form of the Irrawaddy, Chindwin and Brahmaputra Rivers. Given the dense canopied forests that would then have dominated the lowlands of Southeast Asia, the rivers were the principal arteries for communication and movement.

Yunnan is a key area for documenting any expansionary movement of this nature, because it has links with the Yangtze, the Mekong and the Red Rivers. Baiyangcun is a site which lies within strik-

ing distance of all three. It has a deep stratigraphic sequence, involving over four metres of accumulated cultural material. The initial settlement has been dated to between 2400–2100 BC, and excavations over an area of 225 square metres have revealed the remains of eleven houses and a cemetery. Many of the human remains were found with no cranium, and grave goods were also absent, but the pottery from this phase was decorated with a distinctive series of patterns, incorporating parallel incised lines infilled with impressions (YPM 1981). The nearby site of Dadunzi is rather later, the single radiocarbon date suggesting a mid second-millennium BC occupation. Again, house plans were noted, often superimposed over earlier structures, and 27 burials were encountered. Adults were buried in extended positions with no preferred orientation, and infants were interred in mortuary jars. The style of pottery decoration matched that found earlier at Baiyangcun.

Archaeological research in the major river valleys of Southeast Asia has revealed a compelling pattern in which new agricultural villages were established between 2500–2000 BC. In the Red River valley, this phase is seen in many sites of the Phung Nguyen culture. In the Mekong catchment, we find Neolithic phases of occupation at Ban Chiang, Non Kao Noi, Ban Non Wat and Ban Lum Khao. In the valley of the Chao Phraya River, Ban Kao, Non Pa Wai and Ban Tha Kae indicate settlement towards the end of the third millennium BC. A common inhumation burial ritual, the bones of domestic pigs, cattle and dogs, and a similar technique of decorating pottery vessels link these sites. In eastern India, rice remains and rice-tempered pottery have been found at Chirand, dated probably to the third millennium BC, while Allchin & Allchin (1982) have described sites further east, such as Sarutaru and Daojali Hading, which contain cord-marked pottery recalling wares from Southeast Asia and southern China. There is, therefore, a consistent horizon of third-millennium BC settlement sites incorporating evidence for rice cultivation, from southern China to Eastern India. It is difficult not to see this pattern as being similar to the expansion of the Linearbandkeramik sites of the European loess lands.

There is, however, as in Europe, a need to consider the presence of established hunter-gatherer communities long since settled in the area which saw such proposed intrusive Neolithic peoples. There are at least two aspects to the hunter-gatherer settlement of mainland Southeast Asia. The first involved settlement in the interior, where the remains are largely confined to rockshelters, such as Lang

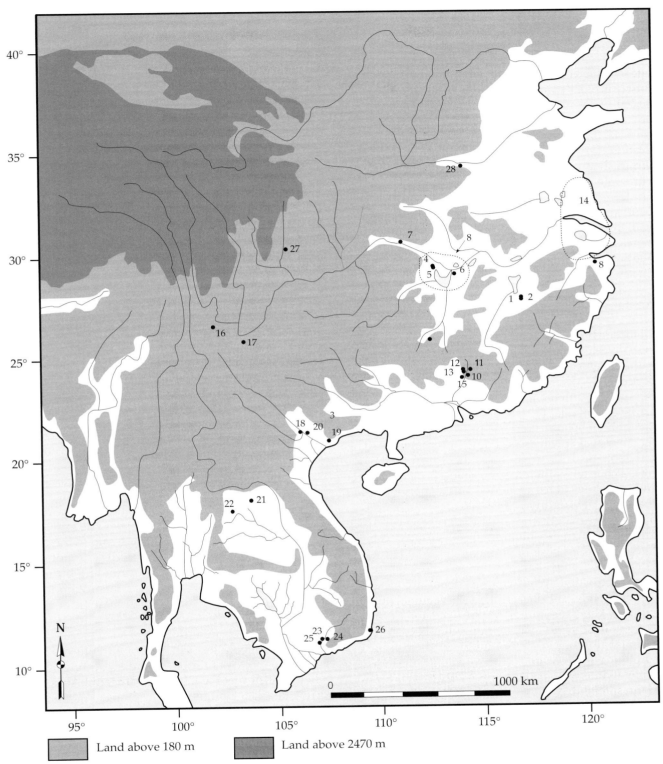

Figure 18.5. *The distribution of sites mentioned in the text: 1) Diaotonghuan; 2) Xianrendong; 3) Yuchanyan; 4) Bashidang; 5) Pengtoushan; 6) Fenshanbao; 7) Chengbeixi; 8) Hemudu; 9) area of the Tangjiagan culture; 10) Shixia; 11) Xincun; 12) Chuangbanling; 13) Niling; 14) area of the Liangzhu culture; 15) Nianyuzhuan; 16) Balyancun; 17) Dadunzi; 18) Phung Nguyen; 19) Trang Kenh; 20) Lung Hoa, Xom Ren; 21) Ban Chiang; 22) Non Nok Tha; 23) Cu Lao Rua; 24) Cau Sat; 25) Ben Do; 26) Xom Con; 27) Sanxingdui; 28) Erlitou.*

Rongrien in peninsular Thailand where the earliest layers go back to about 38,000 BP. Recent investigations, particularly in Vietnam, have identified numerous regional groups of hunter-gatherers, the earlier ones having considerable time depth. The Nguom industry is older than 23,000 BP, the Dieu sites date from 30,000 BP and the Son Vi from 23,000–13,000 BP. Very few sites are found in interior river valleys, but this could be the result of subsequent environmental modification. The number of occupied inland rockshelters diminished markedly from the third millennium BC, but some sites continued in occupation, and forest hunter-gatherers continue to occupy small tracts of peninsular Thailand and Malaysia. These hunter-gatherers present an interesting biological question, because in contrast to the agricultural population of Southeast Asia they are short, dark and have a distinctly Australo-Melanesian phenotype.

The second hunter-gatherer adaptation was coastal, and it has failed to survive into the present. However, the raised beaches which mark the Holocene high sea levels from southern China to the Gulf of Siam harbour hundreds of former hunter-gatherer sites. The rich bio-productivity of the shore, particularly where it forms an estuary, encourages permanent settlement, and some of these coastal sites are large and deeply stratified. However, none antedates about 4000 BC, because prior to that period the sea level was lower than today, but rising fast. The archaeological record is therefore confronted with coastal hunter gatherers who made pottery vessels and polished adzes from the initial period of archaeological visibility.

Unfortunately, the situation has been confused by the Vietnamese naming these groups 'coastal Neolithic' on the basis of pottery making and ground-stone tools rather than any biological evidence for food production. What emerges from a consideration of the relevant sites is a series of regional hunter-gatherer-fishers, some of whom lived long enough at their base for a considerable depth of cultural material to accumulate, who buried their dead by inhumation in a seated, crouched position, in association with mortuary offerings. Very little is known of the spatial organization within these sites, except for the site of Nong Nor, which has been almost completely excavated (Higham & Thosarat 1998). This site was located on the shore of an extensive marine embayment of the Gulf of Siam. The faunal remains indicate deep-water fishing for large sharks and eagle rays, hunting marine mammals, as well as fishing for smaller species and the collection of shellfish. Specific areas for making pottery vessels and

working stone have been isolated. No evidence for rice cultivation or animal domestication has been found in this site, dated to about 2300 BC.

The form and decoration on the pottery vessels, as well as the adze and bone industry at Nong Nor, are virtually identical with those from the base of a much larger estuarine settlement known as Khok Phanom Di, 14 km to the north. This enigmatic site was occupied from about 2000–1500 BC, and its precise relationship to the intrusion of Neolithic groups into Central Thailand is not yet finally resolved. The material culture of the basal layers in all respects follows the local fisher-hunter-gatherer tradition. Over the ensuing five centuries, however, there were many developments. Burials followed the same pattern as that seen in inland agricultural communities, with extended inhumation replacing the former seated, crouching position. Rice remains were found from fairly early in the sequence, but at a time when local conditions would have either ruled out cultivation or made it highly marginal. A handful of sherds were tempered with rice chaff, but all were of exotic origin. Initially, there were no dogs at the site, but these appeared after a century or so of occupation. Domestic dogs must have been derived from an ultimately exotic source that included native wolves. The closest such source of wolves to Thailand is in China.

During the third and fourth of the seven mortuary phases, local conditions saw a reduction in sea level and the formation of freshwater swamps. At this juncture, the presence of hoes and reaping knives, as well as changes in dental health, are compatible with local rice cultivation. But a later rise in sea level saw a return to marine conditions, and to the end of the reaping knives and hoes. While the potters of Khok Phanom Di fashioned outstanding burnished mortuary vessels, and decorated them with incised banded designs not totally dissimilar from the inland repertoire, the forms of pot are quite different from those of the inland farmers.

Again, parallels can be drawn with the situation in Northwest Europe, where expanding agricultural groups met local hunter-gatherers. At present, Khok Phanom Di could be interpreted as a site where there was a vigorous exchange in valued goods between coastal hunter-gatherers and inland farmers, an exchange which certainly involved shell jewellery, stone adzes and ceramic vessels, but which could equally have incorporated people. The anvil, for example, associated with the richest female potter interred there, was made of an exotic clay and was inscribed with an owner's mark. Her presumed daughter buried in an adjacent grave, aged 18 months at death, was accompanied by a miniature anvil made of the local clay (Vincent pers. comm.). It would be unusual if there were not such interactions at the contact between two such different groups of people. The intriguing question posed concerns the course of language change under such circumstances.

Geoffrey Benjamin (1976) has reported on a detailed study of the languages spoken by the Aslian (AA-speaking) hunter-gatherers of Malaysia. The Semang are a group of Negrito hunter-gatherers adapted to the inland forested habitat. They speak AA languages (Aslian subgroup), and in particular, their vocabularies for domesticated plants and animals are derived from AA. Benjamin has suggested that their ancestors originally would have spoken a language related to Andamanese, and adopted their AA languages from intrusive agriculturalists, with whom they would have been in exchange contact. He turned to archaeology for the dating evidence that suggests a beginning in the third millennium BC. Reid (1994) adopted a similar interpretation for the Nicobarese AA languages when he identified Nancowry as a conservative relic language, into which the original Negrito inhabitants contributed much of the non AA lexical component before being completely assimilated.

Conclusions

Bellwood (1993) has proposed a characteristically succinct interpretation of a complex issue by suggesting that the original hunter-gatherers of Southeast Asia now survive as Negrito groups in the Andaman Islands, the Philippines and peninsula Thailand and Malaysia. They may even be descended from Hoabinhian occupants of the very caves where to this day, hunter-gatherers still gather seasonally. Their ancestral language is not known but possibly related ones could be investigated on the Andamans. The intrusive agriculturalists were of southern Mongoloid biological stock and introduced AA languages. Acculturation in much of Southeast Asia then saw the widespread adoption of AA. A broad swathe of interacting groups of AA agriculturalists, whose settlements stretched from Lingnan to Orissa, and from Yunnan to southern Thailand, were later themselves overtaken by other intrusive groups, including the Thais (Austro-Tai languages), the Chams (Austronesian), the Burmese (Sino-Tibetan) and the speakers of Indo-Aryan languages in India. Thus developed the kaleidoscope of languages spoken in Southeast Asia today, a mix first noted by Simon de la Loubère in 1693.

This model stands for testing. It has brought some opprobrium on the author of this paper, but it results from a genuine attempt to seek a consistent and logical pattern. Critics are invited to provide an alternative. However, testing must proceed, and the most promising avenue is seen in the new subject of archaeogenetics. Already, the study of dog DNA hints at links between the prehistoric Southeast Asian and Chinese canids. A research initiative to study ancient human DNA is being planned.

Acknowledgements

I wish to thank Colin Renfrew and Peter Bellwood for inviting me to attend this meeting.

References

Allchin, R. & B. Allchin, 1982. *The Rise of Civilization in India and Pakistan*. Cambridge: Cambridge University Press.

Bellwood, P., 1993. Cultural and biological differentiation in peninsular Malaysia: the last 10,000 years. *Asian Perspectives* 32, 37–60.

Benjamin, G., 1976. Austroasiatic subgroupings and prehistory in the Malay Peninsula, in Jenner *et al.* (eds.), 37–128.

Blench, R. & M. Spriggs (eds.), 1998. *Archaeology and Language*, vol. II: *Correlating Archaeological and Linguistic Hypotheses*. London: Routledge.

Blust, R., 1996. Beyond the Austronesian homeland: the Austric hypothesis and its implications for archaeology, in *Prehistoric Settlement of the Pacific*, ed. W.H. Goodenough. (Transactions of the American Philosophical Society 86.) Philadelphia (PA): American Philosophical Society, 117–40.

Crawford, G.W. & Chen S., 1998. The origins of rice agriculture: recent progress in East Asia. *Antiquity* 72, 858–66.

De la Loubère, S., 1693. *A New Historical Relation of the Kingdom of Siam*. London: Tho. Horne.

Heine-Geldern, R. von, 1932. Urheimat und fruheste wanderungen der Austronesier. *Anthropos* 27, 543–619.

Higham, C.F.W. & T.L.-D. Lu, 1998. The origins and dispersal of rice cultivation. *Antiquity* 72, 867–77.

Higham, C.F.W. & R. Thosarat (eds.), 1998. *The Excavation of Nong Nor: a Prehistoric Site in Central Thailand*. Oxford: Otago University Anthropology Department and Oxbow Books.

Jenner, P.N., L.C. Thompson & S. Starosta (eds.), 1976. *Austroasiatic Studies*, vol. II. (Oceanic Linguistics Special Publication 13.) Honolulu (HI): University Press of Hawaii.

Luce, G.H., 1985. *Phases of Pre-Pagan Burma*. Oxford: Oxford University Press.

Mahdi, W., 1998. Linguistic data on transmission of Southeast Asian cultigens to India and Sri Lanka, in Blench & Spriggs (eds.), 390–415.

Norman, J. & T. Mei, 1976. The Austroasiatics in ancient South China; some lexical evidence. *Monumenta Serica* 32, 274–301.

Pei, A., 1998. Notes on new advancements and revelations in the agricultural archaeology of early rice domestication in the Dongting Lake region. *Antiquity* 72, 878–85.

Pejros, I. & V. Schirelman, 1998. Rice in Southeast Asia: a regional interdisciplinary approach, in Blench & Spriggs (eds.), 379–89.

Reid, L.A., 1994. Morphological evidence for Austric. *Oceanic Linguistics* 33, 323–44.

Schmidt, W., 1906. Die Mon-Khmer Völker: ein Bindeglied Zwischen Völkern Zentralasiens und Austronesiens. *Archiv der Anthropologie (Braunschweig)* n.s. 5, 59–109.

Wheeler, R.E.M., 1959. *Early India and Pakistan to Asboka*. London: Thames & Hudson.

YPM (Yunnan Provincial Museum), 1981. The Baiyangcun site at Binchuan County, Yunnan Province . *Kaogu Xuebuo* 1981, 349–68. [In Chinese.]

Yuan, J. & C. Zhang, 1999: The origins of pottery and rice cultivation in China. *Newsletter of the Grant-in-Aid Program for COE Research Foundation of the Ministry of Education, Science, Sports and Culture in Japan* 2(1), 3–4.

Zhao, Z., 1998. The middle Yangtze region in China is one place where rice was domesticated: phytolith evidence from Diaotonghuan cave, northern Jiangxi. *Antiquity* 72, 885–97.

Zide, A.R.K. & N.H. Zide, 1976. Proto-Munda cultural vocabulary: evidence for early agriculture, in Jenner *et al.* (eds.), 1295–334.

Chapter 19

Tibeto-Burman Phylogeny and Prehistory: Languages, Material Culture and Genes

George van Driem

As Auguste Comte once observed, 'on ne connaît pas complétement une science tant qu'on n'en sait pas l'histoire'[1] (1830, 82).

The return of the original Tibeto-Burman theory

The Tibeto-Burman theory dates back to the eighteenth century, when scholars observed that Tibetan was genetically related to Burmese. Later, in 1823, the contours of the Tibeto-Burman family were delineated by Julius Heinrich Klaproth, who showed on the basis of common roots that the language family comprised Chinese, Tibetan and Burmese and those languages which could be demonstrated to be genetically related to these three, whilst he explicitly excluded Thai and other Daic languages as well as Vietnamese, Mon and other Austroasiatic languages. The Tibeto-Burman theory has in principle always remained agnostic about subgrouping within the family, whilst it encompassed all those languages which could be shown to be related to the key defining member languages — Chinese, Tibetan and Burmese. Early proponents of the Tibeto-Burman theory, such as Carl Richard Lepsius and Wilhelm Grube, mooted reflexes of Tibeto-Burman historical morphology in Chinese. The Tibeto-Burman theory became widely accepted and was soon taken for granted. Tibeto-Burman even became an ingredient in grander theories of linguistic relationship, such as Turanian and Indo-Chinese (Fig. 19.1).

For most of the nineteenth century, Friedrich Max Müller championed the Turanian theory, which grouped together into a single large Turanian family all of the 'allophylian' languages of the world, i.e. languages which were neither Indo-European nor Afroasiatic. Yet Müller expressed uncertainty about how to group Sinitic, for he could not decide whether Sinitic belonged to the northern branch of Turanian,

together with the phyla which we know today as Uralic and Altaic, or to Southern Turanian, along with Tibetan and the languages of Southeast Asia. After enjoying much popularity, particularly in the British Isles, Turanian was discredited, and Müller himself abandoned the theory before he died in 1900. Scholars who propounded the Turanian theory, such as Hodgson (1849) and Müller (1855), removed Sinitic from the original Tibeto-Burman family and so created a new truncated 'Tibeto-Burman' at variance with the original Tibeto-Burman theory.

Another equally vague theory of linguistic relationship was Indo-Chinese, widely known today by the name 'Sino-Tibetan', which, according to John Casper Leyden who conceived it, encompassed most of the languages spoken by 'the inhabitants of the regions which lie between India and China, and the greater part of the islanders in the eastern sea' (1808, 158). The shape and girth of Indo-Chinese would wax and wane to accommodate the hunches and impressions of whichever scholar used the term. However, in the nineteenth century, adherents of the Indo-Chinese theory such as Ernst Kuhn (1889) and August Conrady (1896) not only adopted the Turanian approach toward Sinitic by treating it as a subgroup distinct from the rest of the Tibeto-Burman family, but went a step further and grouped Sinitic together with Daic. The 'Tibeto-Burman' subgroup which became an ingredient in the Indo-Chinese or Sino-Tibetan theory is therefore not equivalent to the original Tibeto-Burman language family, but represents a truncated construct from which Sinitic has been excised.

In the 1880s, German scholars such as Emile Forchhammer and Ernst Kuhn knew enough to be able to distinguish the Austroasiatic languages as representing a distinct phylum. When their insights gained widespread acceptance a few decades later, Indo-Chinese was reduced to 'Tibeto-Burman' and

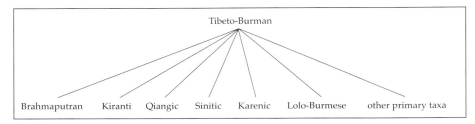

Figure 19.1. *The Tibeto-Burman theory.*

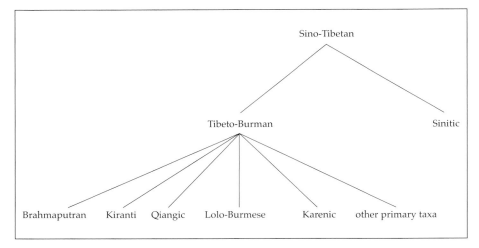

Figure 19.2. *The Sino-Tibetan or rump Indo-Chinese theory, incorporating the truncated Tibeto-Burman hypothesis. The latter presumes that all of 'Tibeto-Burman' underwent defining shared unitary developments independently of Sinitic.*

Sino-Daic. The separate treatment meted out to Sinitic by proponents of Indo-Chinese and the inclusion of the genetically distinct Daic languages can in retrospect be attributed to the misguided emphasis placed on typological features, the ignorance of Sinitic historical phonology, the inability at the time to distinguish between borrowed from inherited vocabulary in Thai, and the fact that the limited repertoire of reflexes of Tibeto-Burman morphological processes in Chinese had not yet been generally recognized. Indo-Chinese was renamed 'sino-tibétain' by Jean Przyluski in 1924, and the name entered the English language in 1931 as 'Sino-Tibetan' when Przyluski and the British scholar Gordon Hannington Luce wrote an etymological note on the 'Sino-Tibetan' root for the numeral 'hundred'. From the mid nineteenth century to the Second World War, an essential feature of the Indo-Chinese or Sino-Tibetan theory was that Daic was seen as the closest relative of Sinitic, very much at variance with Klaproth's original Tibeto-Burman theory, which saw Sinitic, but not Daic, as part of Tibeto-Burman.

In the United States, Alfred Kroeber and Robert

Shafer adopted the new term 'Sino-Tibetan' for Indo-Chinese. Shafer soon realized, however, that Daic did not belong in the Indo-Chinese or Sino-Tibetan family and in 1938 'prepared a list of words showing the lack of precise phonetic and semantic correspondence' between Daic and other Indo-Chinese languages. Armed with this list, Shafer travelled to France before the outbreak of the Second World War 'to convince Maspero that Daic was not Sino-Tibetan' (1955, 97–8). Instead, Henri Maspero managed in the end to convince Shafer to retain Daic within Sino-Tibetan. When Paul Benedict moved to Berkeley in 1938 to join Kroeber's Sino-Tibetan Philology project, he likewise abandoned the name Indo-Chinese for 'Sino-Tibetan'. Benedict (1942), however, was more resolute than Shafer in ousting Daic from the family. This operation resulted in rump Sino-Tibetan. After this operation, the defining difference between the Sino-Tibetan or Indo-Chinese theory and the Tibeto-Burman theory was the heuristic artefact that proponents of Sino-Tibetan treated Sinitic as a separate trunk of the language family.

For a brief spate in the 1970s, proponents of Sino-Tibetan even propagated a phylogenetic model consisting of a Sinitic trunk and a Tibeto-Karen construct, which in turn was divided into a Karen branch and an even more mutilated 'Tibeto-Burman'. Great significance was ascribed to superficial criteria such as word order. Later, Karen was put back into 'Tibeto-Burman', but Sinitic has, for advocates of the Sino-Tibetan phylogenetic model, remained the primaeval 'other half' of the family to this day. Jim Matisoff adopted this model from his mentor Paul Benedict in 1968 and has been its most outspoken proponent ever since (Benedict 1972) (Fig. 19.2).

The last decade of the twentieth century saw a paradigm shift in scholarly thinking about Tibeto-Burman subgrouping, heralding a return to the original Tibeto-Burman theory and its ascendance above the Sino-Tibetan or Indo-Chinese phylogenetic model. The explicit assumption built into the Sino-Tibetan theory, that all of truncated 'Tibeto-Burman' was a valid subgroup which collectively underwent shared unitary innovations independently of Sinitic, is now recognized to be false. The Sino-Tibetan or Indo-Chinese theory has now effectively been superseded by the original Tibeto-Burman theory because: 1) the Tibeto-Burman character of Sinitic has been amply demonstrated; 2) no uniquely shared innovations have been adduced which could define Proto-Tibeto-Burman as a separate coherent taxon that would exclude Chinese and be coordinated with Proto-Sinitic; 3) evidence has been adduced, suggesting that Sinitic is in fact more closely allied with certain Tibeto-Burman groups, e.g. Bodic or Kiranti, than with others; and 4) evidence in the form of isoglosses has been identified which may represent possible lexical innovations indicating that a more primary bifurcation in the language family is between certain other subgroups, e.g. Brahmaputran or 'Sal', and the rest of the Tibeto-Burman family including Sinitic. This fourth emerging insight has recently been bolstered by the identification of uniquely shared morphological innovations in Brahmaputran.

The Sino-Tibetan hypothesis, that the first split in the language family at its greatest time depth was between Sinitic and the rest of the family, remains unsupported. No evidence has ever been adduced to demonstrate the existence of shared innovations which define Tibeto-Burman excluding Sinitic as a unified group. Sinitic shows greater affinity with certain Tibeto-Burman subgroups such as Bodic, and it is amply evident today that certain Tibeto-Burman

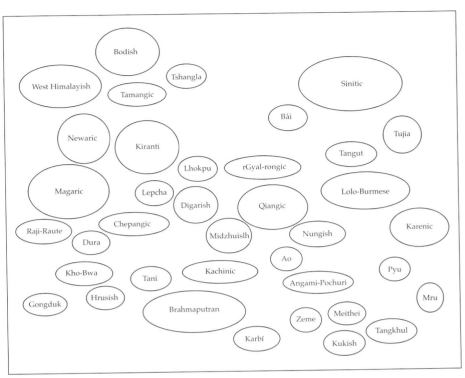

Figure 19.3. *This patch of leaves on the forest floor has fallen from a single tree, which we know as Tibeto-Burman. We cannot see the branches of the tree, but we are beginning to see the shadows they cast between the leaves on the forest floor. This schematic geographical representation provides an informed but agnostic picture of Tibeto-Burman subgroups. The extended version of the Brahmaputran hypothesis includes Kachinic, but for the sake of argument this diagram depicts the short variant of Brahmaputran, viz. excluding Kachinic. Kachinic comprises the Sak languages and the Jinghpaw dialects. Likewise, Tangut is separately depicted, although Tangut is likely to be part of Qiangic. Digarish is Northern Mishmi, and Midzhuish is Southern Mishmi, i.e. the Kaman cluster. Bái is listed as a distinct group, whereas it may form a constituent of Sinitic, albeit one heavily influenced by Lolo-Burmese. Tujia is a heavily sinicized Tibeto-Burman language of indeterminate phylogenetic propinquity spoken by about three million people in an area which straddles the provinces of Sichuan, Hubei, Hunan and Guizhou. The Sino-Bodic hypothesis encompasses at least the groups called Sinitic, Kiranti, Bodish, West Himalayish, rGyal-rongic, Tamangic, Tshangla and Lhokpu and possibly Lepcha. Other hypotheses, such as the inclusion of Chepang and perhaps Dura and Raji-Raute within Magaric, are discussed in my handbook (van Driem 2001).*

subgroups such as Gongduk show greater divergence from mainstream Tibeto-Burman features than Sinitic does. These insights have led to the abandonment of the Sino-Tibetan theory in favour of the older Tibeto-Burman theory.

Tibeto-Burman phylogeny

Indo-Chinese or Sino-Tibetan had always been a more pretentious conglomerate of subgrouping hypotheses with a more chequered history than the more agnostic Tibeto-Burman theory. Since 1823, Chinese, Tibetan and Burmese have been the three defining members of the Tibeto-Burman family, but the Tibeto-Burman theory is still essentially as agnostic about subgrouping today as it was in the days of Julius Klaproth. The Tibeto-Burman phylogenetic model also provides the empirically best-supported and most neutral framework within which to test new higher-order subgrouping proposals within the language family. The Tibeto-Burman phylogenetic model can be represented as a bubble diagram (Fig. 19.3) rather than as an articulated family tree. This representation reflects our present ignorance about the relative chronology of branching within the language family. The various empirically-indefensible family trees have been replaced by a patch of leaves on the forest floor which have fallen from a single tree. Not only is the branching pattern of the tree not within view, the constituent language subgroups of the family were only finally exhaustively identified in the last decade of the twentieth century with the discovery in Bhutan of the last hitherto unreported Tibeto-Burman languages.

A number of the subgroups within Tibeto-Burman proposed by Sten Konow (Grierson 1909) and the prolific Robert Shafer (1953; 1955; 1966; 1967; 1968; 1974) are still recognized to be viable today. A differentiated view of Tibeto-Burman subgroups leaps from the pages of the many older British sources and recently a differentiated picture of Tibeto-Burman subgroups in northeastern India and the Indo-Burmese borderlands has been presented by Geoffrey Edward Marrison (1967; 1989), Walter French (1983), Robbins Burling (1983; forthcoming) and myself (van Driem 2001; 2002).

The added value of this new, more candid, but at the same time also more comprehensive view of the language family is that the emphasis will now shift from the periphery to the heartland of Tibeto-Burman linguistic diversity. Moreover, scholars will be confronted with the immediate need to search for and identify the evidence which could support empirically defensible higher-order subgroups within Tibeto-Burman, analogous to Italo-Celtic and Balto-Slavic in the Indo-European language family. The antiquated Indo-Chinese framework provided a far too polarized view which split the family up into a Sinocentric and an Indocentric cluster of subgroups. The empirically unsupported Sino-Tibetan model has not only put a generation of linguists on a wrong footing, this framework has even misled population geneticists in their attempt to conduct a balanced and informed sampling of language communities for haplotype studies, as we shall see below. The model of fallen leaves exhaustively identifies the constituent subgroups of the family and draws the focus of attention back to the centre of Tibeto-Burman linguistic diversity, which lies in the Indo-Chinese borderlands.

The patch of fallen leaves on the forest floor provides a more informative framework than a false tree. The recognition of the primary branches of Tibeto-Burman makes it possible to target sample population groups for genetic assays in an ethnolinguistically informed manner. No shared innovations have been found which could support 'truncated Tibeto-Burman' (i.e. Tibeto-Burman minus Sinitic), 'Kamarupan', 'Jiburish', 'Rung' or similar obsolete constructs. Instead, grammatical and lexical studies have led to the identification of many language groups of the Himalayas and northeastern India as high-order branches of the language family. The Tibeto-Burman situation is precisely analogous to the Austronesian situation. Whilst most primary branches of Austronesian are confined to Formosa, the Malayo-Polynesian branch corresponds to the greatest geographical spread. Likewise, Sinitic, a single Tibeto-Burman subgroup, accounts for the greatest geographical spread outside of the region where all other primary taxa of Tibeto-Burman are concentrated. Geographically, only Tujia is tellingly intermediate between the historical locus of Sinitic and the Tibeto-Burman core area. The fallen leaves of Tibeto-Burman are analogous to the primary branches of Austronesian on Formosa, which are sometimes represented as branches emanating from a single node. We shall return to this comparison below.

Figure 19.4 illustrates· the distribution not of Tibeto-Burman languages, but of the historical geographical centres of primary taxa or subgroups of languages of the Tibeto-Burman family. In order to present a fairer picture of the internal diversity of Brahmaputran, the Dhimalish, Bodo-Koch and Konyak subgroups have each been represented by a separate diamond. Likewise, two separate diamonds indicate Kiranti and Newaric, the two constituent subgroups within the internally highly diverse and hypothetical Mahakiranti subgroup. The extinct Tangut language, however, is treated as a member of Qiangic. When the linguist Bob Blust pointed out that nine primary branches of the Austronesian family were represented by Formosan language groups spoken on Taiwan and that a tenth branch is represented by all other Austronesian languages which

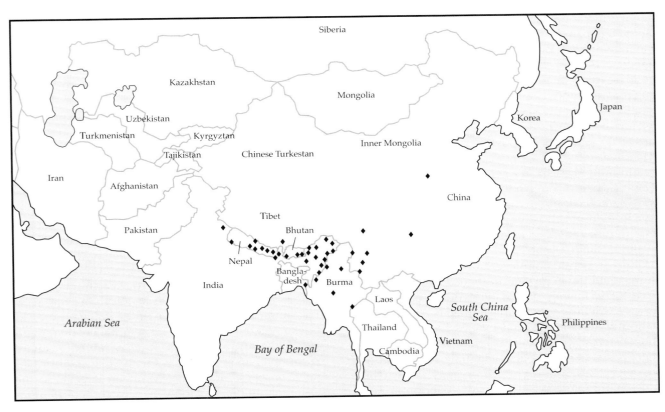

Figure 19.4. *In this clutch of 39 diamonds, each diamond represents not a language, but the historical geographical centre of a primary taxon or subgroup of languages of the Tibeto-Burman family. In order to present a fair picture of the internal diversity of the Brahmaputran branch, the Dhimalish, Bodo-Koch and Konyak subgroups have each been represented by a diamond. Likewise, two separate diamonds indicate Kiranti and Newaric, the two constituent subgroups within the hypothetical and internally highly diverse Mahakiranti branch. The extinct Tangut language, however, is treated as a member of Qiangic.*

have spread over a vast part of the globe, archaeologists drew their conclusions and quite logically proceeded to search for correlates for the spread of this one ubiquitous branch in the form of identifiable cultural assemblages. It is relevant to point out that this task was relatively easy in case of the dispersal of the Oceanic branch of Malayo-Polynesian, where the spread of language and culture coincided perfectly in many places because the linguistic ancestors of the modern language communities colonized hitherto uninhabited insular domains in the Pacific. Tibeto-Burman represents an analogous case in that the historical geographical centres of primary taxa are likewise concentrated in an easily circumscribed geographical region, i.e. the eastern Himalayas, northeastern India, the Indo-Burmese borderlands, Yunnan and Sichuan. Yet both the ethnolinguistic and archaeological picture of the East Asian heartland is far more complex than in the Austronesian case. Tibeto-Burman shares the East Eurasian heartland with many other linguistic stocks, such as Daic, Austroasiatic, Altaic, Indo-European, Dravidian, Hmong-Mien and a number of isolates. Sinitic, which is a lower-order subgroup within Tibeto-Burman, or at least not the first group to have split off from Tibeto-Burman, represents a secondary spread over a vast expanse of territory. The sinification of southern China during the second half of the first millennium BC is relatively recent, and the earlier spread of Sinitic as a whole may be one of the best candidates for a language spread associated with a farming dispersal (van Driem 2001). Moreover, both northeastern India as well as Yunnan and Sichuan are key regions in the understanding of Tibeto-Burman population prehistory, and both areas have been sorely neglected by archaeologists.

A number of Australian linguists have recently argued against the *Stammbaum* model as the only model of language relationship. Bob Dixon invokes the concept of a diffusion zone as well as the evolutionary metaphor of punctuated equilibria (1997). According to Dixon, conventional family tree phylogenies work well under circumstances of linguistic evolution characterized by 'punctuation', i.e. by the expansion and branching of an original language community, but the language family model would purportedly not work during periods of equilibrium characterized by cultural and linguistic stasis. Structural and lexical features diffuse and the genetic affinities of languages blur when language communities coexist in a state of cultural and demographic stasis through a vast expanse of time. Dixon considers Australia to be the 'prototypical example of a long-term diffusion zone', in which egalitarian communities engaged in low-key interaction for tens of thousands of years, and he also considers such prolonged periods of stasis to have been the norm rather than the exception in the history of hominid prehistory. Pawley & Ross (1995) argued that it is easier to identify subgroups defined by shared innovation when the ancestral groups have travelled a long distance from their original habitat or when there has been intermediate language extinction, and that elsewhere a mesh of groups may result where innovations may have developed in overlapping sets. In this context, Pawley and Ross distinguish between innovation-linked and innovation-defined groups. If the initial spread was rapid and geographically extensive, Ross (1997) and Pawley (1999) argue that a chain of subgroups that exhibit a 'rake-like' phylogeny results. The notion of the diffusion or spread zone has also been applied to the Eurasian heartland by Johanna Nichols (1992; 1998), but Michael Fortescue (1998) has shown that such notions can only be meaningfully and productively implemented when the comparative method has first been rigorously applied.

This has certainly not been done in the case of Tibeto-Burman. Therefore, the use of a bubble diagram to schematically represent the language family should not be construed as indicating that a family tree is an inappropriate phylogenetic model for Tibeto-Burman. The reticulate structure of Tibeto-Burman language groups in northeastern India, the Indo-Burmese borderlands and the eastern Himalayas is most probably not the result of a single linguistic expansion. As recently as the early second millennium AD, the now extinct Tibeto-Burman group Pyu was supplanted by the Burmese. Moreover, the complex ethnolinguistic composition of northeastern India, the Indo-Burmese borderlands and the eastern Himalayas must be seen against the background of the complex topography and original ecol-

ogy of the region as well as the gradient of endemic disease barriers in the area, which were no doubt exacerbated by the gradual conversion of the dense jungles, which used to blanket areas like the Brahmaputran plain, into agricultural land.

Genes, material culture and linguistic dispersals

The Neolithic Revolution and the spread of agriculture are widely thought to have been important factors in the dispersal of ancient populations and the spread of language families. However, the Fertile Crescent itself attests to the fact that agriculture was adopted by ethnolinguistically unrelated populations and that agriculture spread effortlessly across ethnolinguistic boundaries without affecting them in any significant way. Sumerian, Elamite, Akkadian, Hurrian, Hattic and other languages of early agricultural civilizations which have left no surviving linguistic descendants bear witness to the permeability of linguistic boundaries for the dissemination of agriculture. Certainly, a Neolithic wave of advance cannot be a universal explanation for the dispersal of language families, and Indo-European is perhaps the best illustration. Not only is a hypothetical Indo-European homeland in Anatolia linguistically problematic (D'jakonov 1968; Zvelebil & Zvelebil 1988; Mallory 1989; 1997; Mallory & Adams 1997; van Driem 2001; *pace* Gamkrelidze & Ivanov 1995), but the model of an Indo-European demic wave of advance originating from Anatolia singularly neglects to account for the social conditions under which the dispersal of Indo-European is most likely to have taken place, based on what is known about Indo-European culture and linguistic palaeontology. Moreover, an Indo-European demic wave of advance emanating from Anatolia does not fit well with what is known about the complex ethnolinguistic composition of Anatolian populations at the time that such a homeland would have existed. Instead, the Neolithic and Bronze Age of Asia Minor and Mesopotamia is characterized by a very long period of incursive population movements into, rather than out of Anatolia and the Fertile Crescent, driven or lured, it seems, by the relative affluence of urban centres supported by agricultural surplus. Not just Indo-European population groups such as the Hittites and Mitanni were drawn in by the allure of the good life. Gutaeans, Amorites, Kassites and other peoples likewise came to settle in the Fertile Crescent and Anatolia. Toponymical evidence and details about the cults of certain deities have been used to argue that even the Sumerians originally migrated from an earlier northern homeland to lower Mesopotamia, where they adopted agriculture from a resident population. This hypothesis is corroborated by the fact that the Sumerians appear to have borrowed agricultural terms such as *agar* 'field', *apin* 'seeder plough' and *apsin* 'furrow' from a substrate language.

Those who secondarily adopt a technique, tradition or cultural institution often improve upon it and excel in its exploitation beyond the attainments of its original innovators. In Dutch this is known as *de wet van de remmende voorsprong*, i.e. the 'law' that the very group which has managed to get ahead of other groups by virtue of an innovation is also more prone to get bogged down at a later stage by shortcomings inherent to the prototypical version of the technology which originally gave them the edge over other groups. Meanwhile, other groups who did not have to invest the resources and effort to develop and implement the technology in the first place forge ahead by introducing a more refined and streamlined version of the innovation and are unhampered by having to replace or revamp an obsolete infrastructure. O'Connor (1995) and Blench (2001) have argued that irrigated rice agriculture in the Southeast Asian lowlands does not correlate with a spread at the language family level, but with spreads at a lower phylogenetic level. Irrigated rice cultivation is what enabled a single group to seize control of the plains. The adoption of agriculture on flood plains by the Khmer, Pyu, Cham and Mon and, much later, by the intrusive Thai, Burmese and Vietnamese, accounts for the correlation between these expansive ethnic groups and historical polities and modern nation states. A high level of ethnic diversity is the regional norm, but the original ethnolinguistic diversity is maintained in upland areas that had hitherto been more favourable habitats until wet cultivation transformed the lowlands from epidemiologically undesirable places to live into bountiful habitats.

By contrast, perhaps what the incursive Indo-Europeans did may have been nothing other than land theft. Nevertheless, the spread of specific, well-defined Neolithic cultural assemblages remains a powerful tool in the reconstruction of ancient population movements and, more particularly, in the possible early dispersal of language families. The hypothesis that an agricultural dispersal may reflect the ancient spread of a language community underlies my reconstruction of the spread of the Sino-Bodic branch of Tibeto-Burman (van Driem 1998; 1999; 2001). The distribution of primary branches of Tibeto-Burman suggests that it may be that the urban affluence of pre-Tibeto-Burman agricultural

populations was what drew the linguistic ancestors of early Sinitic civilization to the Yellow River and North China Plain in the first place, just as Gutaeans, Kassites, Amorites and Indo-Europeans were drawn to the Fertile Crescent and Anatolia. Benedict once proposed that the Shang may not have been Sinitic at all and that the Zhou, who came from the west, may have been the bearers of the Proto-Sinitic language to the Yellow River basin, where they adopted the Shang ideograms devised by a pre-Tibeto-Burman population (1972, 197), though the prosperous agricultural civilization on the North China Plain may have lured the linguistic forebears of Sinitic, or perhaps Sino-Bodic, long before the Shang period. Quite often the archaeological record may not directly reflect such linguistic intrusions. Instead, archaeology shows the regional discrepancies in technical advancement which may have motivated foreign linguistic intrusions, both in the case of the early displacement of Sinitic outside of the Tibeto-Burman core area as well as in the case of the advent of Indo-European groups to the Near East, such as the Hittites in Anatolia and the Mitanni in the Jazirah. Not only did agriculture spread across linguistic boundaries from the very outset, the direction of linguistic intrusions in many episodes of prehistory may have been diametrically opposed to the direction of the spread of agriculture.

My reconstruction is based on a family tree model of Tibeto-Burman, which presumes a clustering of groups and suggests a relative chronology. Yet the model is not purely a *Stammbaum* as such. The problem with Tibeto-Burman family tree models proposed to date is that uniquely shared innovations are scarce, and higher-level subgroups are often defined by what later turn out to be shared retentions. Neither is the family tree in Figure 19.5 just a geographically-inspired schema, for it incorporates subgroups which were discerned by Shafer and are still recognized on the basis of phonological and morphological criteria and lexical isoglosses. The model also incorporates Sino-Bodic, a higher-level subgrouping hypothesis involving Sinitic and those languages within Tibeto-Burman which appear to be more immediately related to Sinitic than either are to, for example, Brahmaputran, Karbí, Gongduk and other genetically remote groups.

Although Sino-Bodic is associated with my name (van Driem 1995; 1997), earlier versions of the Sino-Bodic hypothesis had previously suggested themselves to Walter Simon (1929), Robert Shafer (1955; 1966; 1967; 1968; 1974) and Nicholas Bodman (1980), on the basis of uniquely-shared lexical items.

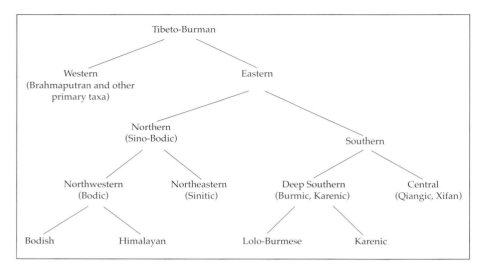

Figure 19.5. *Linguistically-inspired archaeological interpretation of the geographical dispersal of Tibeto-Burman groups, incorporating the Sino-Bodic and Brahmaputran linguistic hypotheses.*

In addition to the limited set of lexical isoglosses, I have described morphological features that appear to bolster the identification of Sino-Bodic as a subgroup (van Driem 1997). Recently, Laurent Sagart reconstructed an Old Chinese 'voicing prefix' *<N-> (1994, 279–81). This reconstruction was also adopted by William Baxter (Baxter & Sagart 1998, 45), thus replacing Baxter's earlier *<ɦ-> (1992). Starostin has told me on several occasions that this prefix is best reflected in Kiranti, Bodish, Sinitic and West Himalayish. If this is correct, this morphological element bolsters the case for Sino-Bodic. However, if the feature is a shared retention rather than a shared innovation, then the distribution of the phenomenon is merely suggestive.

By contrast, the constellation of subgroups which I collectively name Western Tibeto-Burman represents a number of primary branches which I assume had split off at an early stage and settled in northeastern India, originating from a Tibeto-Burman proto-homeland which I locate in Sichuan. British scholars in the nineteenth century had already located the Tibeto-Burman homeland in Sichuan, even though they could not yet have known the linguistic, archaeological and genetic evidence which today argues for a Tibeto-Burman homeland in Sichuan. Here I shall briefly outline the model again and adduce additional supporting arguments from recent research on haplotypes on the Y chromosome. I shall also point out linguistic and archaeological weaknesses in the model, which leave room for an alternative version of the reconstructed linguistic dispersal.

Though primarily linguistically-inspired, my theory represents an interpretation of the archaeological record in light of Tibeto-Burman subgrouping hypotheses and the geographical distribution of modern and historically attested Tibeto-Burman language communities. The theory depicted schematically in Figure 19.5 is illustrated in Figures 19.6 to 19.9. The differences between Figures 19.3 and 19.5 illustrate the linguistic and the archaeological view between which some correlation is sought. Western Tibeto-Burman in particular is not just a linguistic hypothesis, but an archaeological theory about the population history of the Tibeto-Burman area informed by linguistic insights about the primary nature of subgroups in the Himalayas and northeastern India. From a phylogenetic perspective, Western Tibeto-Burman is analogous to the Formosan language groups within Austronesian. Like Formosan, Western Tibeto-Burman is not a single taxon, but a collection of primary taxa within the family. Rather, it is the remaining branch, Eastern Tibeto-Burman, which may constitute a possible genetic unit, just as Malayo-Polynesian is a single primary branch within Austronesian. It is therefore more fitting to speak of an Eastern than of a Western Tibeto-Burman hypothesis, if there is such a thing.

The various ways of reconstructing prehistory, i.e. archaeology, linguistics and genetics, measure three independent quantities which are merely probabilistically correlated and which, moreover, may divide into taxa which may correspond to quite different time depths. Discrepancies between the chromosomal and the linguistic pictures of the past indicate that in some cases a larger incursive population may have adopted a language of a smaller population already resident in the area which they had settled, e.g. the case of Bulgarian, whereas some languages borne by ruling élites have been adopted by a larger dominated resident population, e.g. the case of Hungarian. The racial heterogeneity of Tibeto-Burman populations in northeastern India, particularly the phenotypic difference between Brahmaputran language communities and other Tibeto-Burman

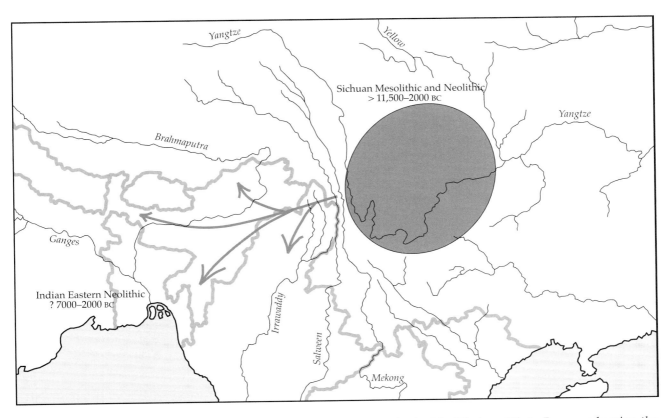

Figure 19.6. *Lower Brahmaputra basin and surrounding hill tracts colonized by Western Tibeto-Burmans bearing the technologies from Sichuan which were to become known as the Indian Eastern Neolithic, an* Auswanderung *possibly set in motion before the seventh millennium* BC.

groups in the northeast, has been noted ever since the earliest British accounts of the area.

In genetic terms, two apparently conflicting sets of findings have recently been obtained by teams of geneticists looking at Tibeto-Burman populations in China and the greater Himalayan region. Yet the discrepancy between these findings may be more apparent than real and may very well correspond to different realities situated at different time depths. The hypothesis of a Tibeto-Burman homeland in Sichuan has recently found unexpected corroboration in the findings of the Chinese Human Genome Diversity Project, whose ethnolinguistically informed assays of population groups in China have shown that the Chinese did not originate in the Yellow River basin but migrated to this area in a northeasterly direction from southwestern China (Chu *et al.* 1998). This information was still unavailable when I first proposed that the Tibeto-Burman homeland lay in Sichuan on linguistic grounds. Another team of geneticists has found a strong genetic affinity amongst population groups of the Tibeto-Burman language family in the form the prevalence of a T to C muta-

tion at Y-chromosome locus M122, whereas the extremely high frequency of H8, a haplotype derived from M122C, reflects the results of a genetic bottleneck effect that occurred during an ancient southwesterly migration (Su *et al.* 2000). The latter group of geneticists attempted to relate the geographical distribution of Tibeto-Burman populations with a migration from the middle Yellow River basin about 10,000 years ago, and to conjecture that the earliest Neolithic cultures of this area might have been associated with the putative Tibeto-Burman homeland. However, there are two flaws in this interpretation. First of all, the study by Su *et al.* (2000) sampled only six individuals from the pivotal, ethnolinguistically most heterogeneous Tibeto-Burman heartland in northeastern India. The samples from this area were limited to a 'Kachari' individual, a Rabha, a Naga, an Adi, a Nishi and an Apatani. Their study left most key Tibeto-Burman population groups untouched. Conjectures were advanced about prehistoric migrations to the Himalayas but, other than the three samples from Arunachal Pradesh, no Himalayan populations were tested. Fifteen samples, con-

241

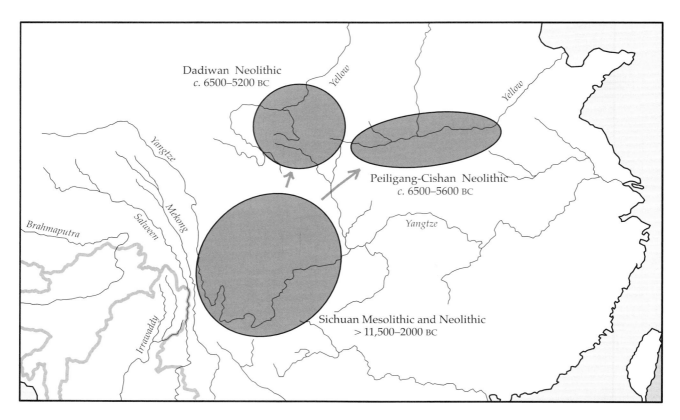

Figure 19.7. *The establishment of the early Neolithic Peiligang-Cishan and Dadiwan civilizations in the Yellow River basin by Northern Tibeto-Burmans before the beginning of the sixth millennium* BC.

stituting half of the test material, were obtained from individuals representing Hàn Chinese populations settled in various provinces of China. The remaining samples were from several Tibeto-Burman populations resident in China, i.e. Nakhi, Bái, Yi , Jinuo, Jinghpaw, Yunnan Lahu and Tujia. Finally, there were two Tibetan samples, one from Lhasa and one from Yunnan, and a single Karen sample from Southeast Asia. The assay was therefore limited and did not sample most of the key Tibeto-Burman language communities in the Himalayas about whose ancestors inferences were made. The second problem is that the interpretative framework was based on the phylogenetic model presented by Matisoff (1991), in which an Indo-Chinese or 'Proto-Sino-Tibetan' *Ursprache* at its deepest time depth is presumed to have split east–west into 'Proto-Chinese' and 'Proto-Tibeto-Burman'. Problems with this model have been discussed above.

At a far greater time depth, ethnolinguistically informed assays of the population of eastern Asia on the basis of thirty microsatellites made by Chu *et al.* (1998) have shown that the ethnolinguistic composition of China is reflected in the genetic complexity,

and that the peopling of eastern Asia probably occurred in a northward movement from Southeast Asia. These results have been corroborated in a study of nineteen biallelic loci on the Y chromosome, which demonstrated that northern populations in eastern Asia only represent a subset of the haplotypes found in southern populations, which show greater polymorphism on the whole than northern populations (Su *et al.* 1999).

Craniometric and skeletal evidence is still routinely used by archaeologists and palaeontologists to reconstruct population history. For example, Brown (1998) and Demeter (2000) argue for major morphological changes in population in the Far East between various phases of the post-Pleistocene or between the Mesolithic and Neolithic periods. Hopefully, it will be possible in future to make such findings square with the new insights of genomic studies. Particularly in view of the phenotypic variation sometimes observed within single populations, it will hopefully be undertaken to extract DNA from such crania for study. Recent work by Ding *et al.* (2000) has also shown that northern and southern haplotype clusters blend across a cline without any abrupt

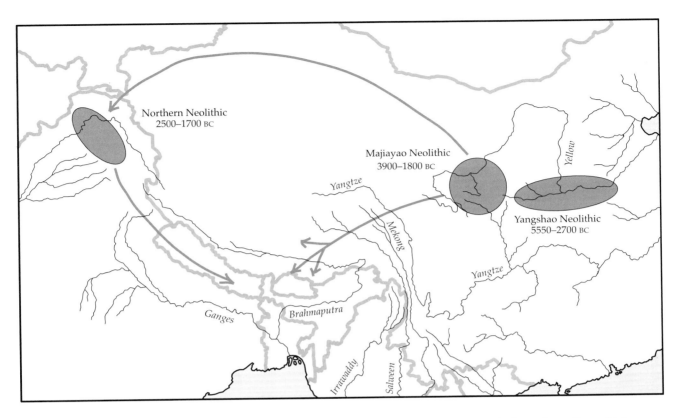

Figure 19.8. *One offshoot of the late Neolithic Majiayao cultural complex migrates south through northern Sichuan and eastern Tibet into Sikkim, whereas another offshoot migrates to the southwest across the Himalayas to establish the Northern Neolithic civilization in Kashmir. Northwestern Tibeto-Burmans peopled the Himalayas, both from the northeast, colonizing Sikkim and Nepal, and from the west, colonizing the western Himalayas and the Tibetan plateau.*

change, so that there is little genetic support in evidence for linguistic theories connecting Chinese to Caucasian, e.g. the Sino-Caucasian theory advocated by Starostin, or for connecting Chinese genetically with Indo-European, as Pulleyblank does. Yet all these investigations have merely scratched the surface of a vast terrain which lies to be charted and have begun to make possible an integrated vision of the genetic, linguistic, historical, archaeological and anthropological data.

Three arguments support the identification of Sichuan as the Tibeto-Burman homeland. The first is the centre of gravity argument based on the present and historically attested geographical distribution of Tibeto-Burman language communities. Sichuan encompasses the area where the upper courses of the Brahmaputra, Salween, Mekong and Yangtze run parallel to each other within a corridor just five hundred kilometres in breadth. The second argument is that archaeologists identify the Indian Eastern Neolithic, associated with the indigenous Tibeto-Burman populations of northeastern India and the

Indo-Burmese borderlands, as a Neolithic cultural complex which originated in Sichuan and spread into Assam and the surrounding hill tracts of Arunachal Pradesh, the Meghalaya, Tripura, the Chittagong, Mizoram, Manipur and Nagaland before the third millennium BC.

Archaeologists have estimated the Indian Eastern Neolithic to date from between 10,000 and 5000 BC (Thapar 1985; Sharma 1989). If these estimates are taken at face value, it would mean that northeastern India had shouldered adzes at least three millennia before they appeared in Southeast Asia. Whilst some archaeologists may give younger estimates for the Indian Eastern Neolithic, a solid stratigraphy and calibrated radiocarbon datings are still unavailable for this major South Asian cultural assemblage. The Indian Eastern Neolithic appears intrusively in the northeast of the Subcontinent and represents a tradition wholly distinct from the other Neolithic assemblages attested in India. Assuming that the Indian Eastern Neolithic was borne to the Subcontinent by ancient Tibeto-Burmans, then if the younger esti-

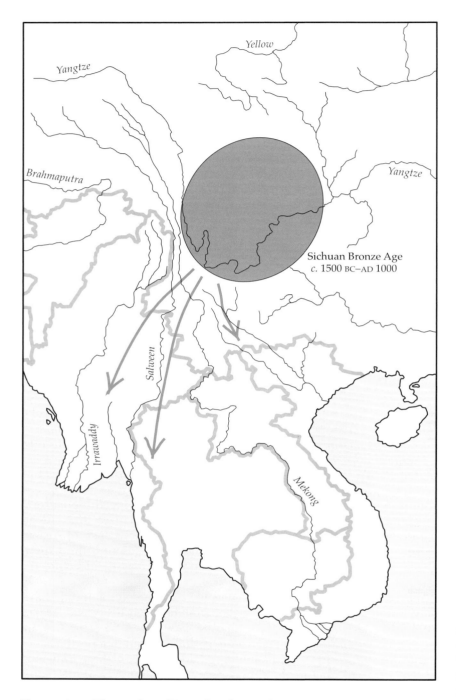

Yellow

Yangtze

Brahmaputra

Yangtze

Sichuan Bronze Age
c. 1500 BC–AD 1000

Salween

Irrawaddy

Mekong

Figure 19.9. *The exodus of Deep Southern Tibeto-Burmans into peninsular Southeast Asia had begun by the first millennium BC, and the process seems to have never completely come to a halt, as Lolo-Burmese groups have continued to trickle into Thailand from Yunnan in recent history.*

before (van Driem 1998; 2001).

The third argument is that archaeologists have argued that southwestern China would be a potentially promising place to look for the precursors of the Neolithic civilizations which later took root in the Yellow River Valley (Chêng 1957; Chang 1965; 1977; 1986; 1992). The Dadiwan culture in Gansu and Shanxi and the contiguous and contemporaneous Peiligang-Císhan assemblage along the middle course of the Yellow River share common patterns of habitation and burial and employed common technologies, such as hand-formed tripod pottery with short firing times, highly worked chipped stone tools and non-perforated semi-polished stone axes. The Dadiwan and Peiligang-Cishan assemblages, despite several points of divergence, were closely related cultural complexes, and the people behind these civilizations shared the same preference for settlements on plains along the river or on high terraces at confluences. Whereas the Sichuan Neolithic represented the continuation of local Mesolithic cultural traditions, the first Neolithic agriculturalists of the Dadiwan and Peiligang-Cishan cultures may be identified tentatively with innovators who migrated from Sichuan to the fertile loess plains of the Yellow River basin. The technological gap between the earlier local microlithic cultures and the highly advanced Neolithic civilizations which subsequently come into flower in the Yellow River basin remains striking. Yet a weakness in this third argument lies in the archaeological state of the art. Just as it is difficult to argue for a possible precursor in Sichuan in face of a lack of compelling archaeological evidence, neither can the inadequate state of the art in Neolithic archaeology in southwestern China serve as an argument for the absence of such a precursor.

Moreover, agricultural dispersals and linguis-

mates for this cultural assemblage can be substantiated by solid dating, the linguistic fracturing of subgroups would have to have occurred earlier in Sichuan before the migrations, as I have suggested tic intrusions may be distinct issues altogether. The concentration within a contiguous geographical region of all major high-order Tibeto-Burman subgroups other than Tujia and Sinitic constitutes a linguistic argument for an early Tibeto-Burman linguistic intrusion into the area that today is northern China. If the Dadiwan culture in Gansu and Shanxi and the contiguous Peiligang-Cishan assemblage along the middle course of the Yellow River are indeed primary Neolithic civilizations, then the eccentric location of Sinitic and Tujia may even trace the route of the early migration out of Tibeto-Burman homeland to the affluent and more technologically advanced agricultural societies in the Yellow River basin. In other words, since the linguistic evidence puts the Tibeto-Burman heartland in southwestern China and northeastern India, an archaeological precursor in Sichuan for the Dadiwan and Peiligang-Cishan cultures would fit the hypothesis that the displacement of Sinitic to northern China was the result of an early Tibeto-Burman archaeological dispersal. The absence of any such precursor in Sichuan would fit a theory of early migration from the northern end of the ancient Tibeto-Burman dialect continuum to the affluent areas of pre-Tibeto-Burman agricultural civilizations along the Yellow River.

I collectively refer to the ancient Tibeto-Burman populations, who either bore with them from Sichuan to the loess plateau the technologies of polished stone tools and cord-marked pottery or were enticed to the loess plateau by the affluence of the technologically more advanced agricultural civilizations there, as 'Northern Tibeto-Burmans'. I identify these Northern Tibeto-Burmans as the likely linguistic ancestors of the Sino-Bodic groups. Subsequent technological developments were both innovated and introduced comparatively rapidly in the north, whereas relatively egalitarian small-scale agricultural societies persisted in southwestern China until the Bronze Age. This hypothesis places the split between Northern and Southern Tibeto-Burman in the seventh millennium BC, just before the dawn of the Dadiwan and Peiligang-Cishan civilizations.

I identify the spread of Bodic groups from Gansu with the dispersal of the Majiayao and Yangshao Neolithic cultures and the cultivars broomcorn millet *Panicum mileaceum* and foxtail millet *Setaria italica*, first domesticated on the North China Plain, into the Himalayan region in the third millennium BC. Sino-Bodic would have split up into Sinitic and Bodic before this date. This dispersal proceeded along two routes. The Majiayao Neolithic culture spread westward along the main ancient Inner Asian

trade route across the Himalayas to establish the genetically related Northern or Kashmir Neolithic in Kashmir and Swat. At the same time, the Majiayao cultural assemblage spread southward from Gansu through eastern Tibet into southeastern Tibet, Bhutan and Sikkim to establish the Neolithic cultures of Chab-mdo and northern Sikkim, both of which have been identified as colonial exponents of the Majiayao Neolithic. Moreover, these colonial exponents make their appearance in Kashmir, eastern Tibet and Sikkim in the second half of the third millennium BC, so that the final phase of these movements coincides precisely with the Banshan phase of the Majiayao cultural assemblage, which covers the period between 2200 and 1900 BC and is characterized by a marked geographical contraction of the original Majiayao core territory.

My reconstruction of Tibeto-Burman dispersals, presented in greater detail elsewhere (van Driem 1998; 1999; 2001), is outlined here in Figures 19.6 to 19.9. On the whole, this reconstruction still fits the known facts well. Yet the weaknesses in this model must be recognized. First of all, Sichuan and southwestern China in general remains archaeologically inadequately researched, despite the significance of the area's prehistory. A second problem is that the linguistic state of the art gives us no real relative chronology for the splitting off of the main taxa of the language family, as shown in Figure 19.3. Nevertheless, the sheer number of high-order subgroups in the Himalayan region and the northeast of the Subcontinent provides a good idea of where and when it would be most fruitful to look for likely archaeological correlates for the dispersal of ancient Tibeto-Burman populations. The lopsided geographical distribution of most major Tibeto-Burman groups in the Himalayas and northeastern India, the likely linguistic affinity of Sinitic with Bodic, and the possible affinity of 'Deep Southern' with 'Central' Tibeto-Burman groups have inspired the tree schema outlined in Figure 19.5.

An alternative proposal to a Tibeto-Burman homeland in Sichuan would be to identify the earliest Neolithic cultures along the Yellow River basin and on North China Plain with the Tibeto-Burman homeland. However, if the Tibeto-Burman homeland were to have lain in the Yellow River basin, then we would be hard pressed to find a plausible archaeological correlate for the spread of Brahmaputran language communities, which once extended beyond Assam and the Meghalaya and formerly covered much of the area that is now Bangladesh and West Bengal. It must be kept in mind that the early

Neolithic civilization on the Yellow River is distinct from the cultural assemblages of the middle Yangtze basin, the succeeding stages of which ultimately spread as far afield as Oceania in the course of the millennia. Both the Yellow River and the middle Yangtze civilizations represent ancient agricultural societies nearly as old as those of the Fertile Crescent.

Clearly, the first and foremost *desiderata* are that the archaeology of Sichuan and northeastern India be better understood, that a fine-grid and ethno-linguistically informed genome study of the greater Himalayan region be carried out, and that a new look be taken at subgroups within Tibeto-Burman, whereby the same methodological rigour of sound laws and shared innovation is applied which has characterized Indo-European studies. My reconstruction of Tibeto-Burman language dispersals, outlined synoptically here in Figures 19.6 to 19.6 and in much more detail elsewhere (van Driem 1998; 1999; 2001), will remain sensitive to revision and modification based on new data and new insights.

Finally, it is germane to this discussion to mention one interesting theory which has been proposed involving a remote linguistic relationship with Tibeto-Burman. The Sino-Austronesian theory proposed by Laurent Sagart (1990) connects Tibeto-Burman with Austronesian. The epistemological basis for this theory is still not very large, but the evidence is tantalizing. Of course, it is possible that the lexical correspondences between Austronesian and Tibeto-Burman adduced by Sagart (1994; 2001) could represent ancient loans exchanged during contact between early Sino-Bodic and early Austronesian peoples. However, the vocabulary items adduced by Sagart include over thirty very basic items which decidedly reflect core vocabulary, such as 'head', 'brain', 'body hair', 'earth', 'fire', 'belly', 'snake' and so forth. In favour of the evidence it must be noted that the sound correspondences between the Proto-Austronesian, Old Chinese and Proto-Tibeto-Burman forms appear to be regular, though the total number of roots which have thus far been adduced is limited. Sino-Austronesian has not been conclusively demonstrated, but neither can the theory be dismissed as fanciful or far-fetched.

Because Sagart initially recognized possible Sino-Austronesian correspondences in Chinese material more than in Tibeto-Burman, he was originally inclined to identify the Sino-Austronesian unity with the Longshan cultural horizon. In recent years, however, Sagart has recognized that the correspondences appear to obtain between Austronesian and Tibeto-Burman as a whole. Therefore he is now inclined to

assume a greater time depth for the Sino-Austronesian unity and currently holds that the most probable archaeological correlate for Sino-Austronesian are the earliest millet-cultivating cultures along the Yellow River, on the North China Plain and in Shandong. Sagart argues that the early Neolithic culture on Formosa would represent an early civilization of Sino-Austronesian millet cultivators who had settled the island from the mainland. In this context, Sagart argues that rice cultivation on Formosa is a late acquisition dating from the third millennium BC which came to the island from the middle Yangtze valley via a southerly route. In order to maintain this view, Sagart must assail the soundness of the historical linguistic evidence adduced by Robert Blust for rice as a cultivar known to the early Austronesians and also its presence on Formosa by at least 3000 BC (Tsang 2001).

However, there is an alternative way of viewing the Sino-Austronesian evidence and the archaeological record. The Longshan coastal interaction ensued upon a northward expansion of Proto-Austronesian or Austro-Tai culture from its ancient homeland in southern and southeastern China, and this northward expansion of early Austronesians would have brought them into contact with early Northern Tibeto-Burmans. The ensuing contact situations between Austronesian and the Sino-Bodic branch of Tibeto-Burman could have involved the ancient exchange of vocabulary between the two language families. The way to test this would be to determine whether items shared by Austronesian and Tibeto-Burman are indeed limited to the Sino-Bodic branch of Tibeto-Burman, including rice terms such as Malay *beras* and Tibetan *'bras*, a correspondence already pointed out by Hendrik Kern in 1889 (Kern 1889, 5). The Longshan interaction sphere is an obvious candidate in terms of time and place for early contacts between ancient Austronesians and ancient Tibeto-Burmans, particularly the Dawenkou Neolithic of Shandong with its well-established ties both with the other coastal cultures of the Longshan interaction sphere as well as with the ancient Northern Tibeto-Burman Yangshao Neolithic civilization.

However, the archaeological record presents earlier possible correlates for contact between ancient Daic or Austro-Tai and ancient Northern Tibeto-Burman culture. For one, impressions of rice contained within the walls of ceramic vessels from the sixth millennium BC indicate that the Yangshao Neolithic maintained some degree of interaction with the probably Daic rice-cultivating civilizations south of the Qinling mountains along the Yangtze. However, the first reported instance of recovery of actual rice remains in the Yellow River basin dates from the beginning of the second millennium BC, associated with the Longshan culture of Henan (Wu 1996). A much later candidate for an archaeological reflection of intense interaction between ancient Northern Tibeto-Burmans on the Yellow River and ancient Daic peoples on the middle Yangtze, some time after the Longshan horizon, is the Qujialing and Shijiahe culture, which expanded from the middle Yangtze into peripheral regions rapidly and on a grand scale, even replacing the Yangshao culture in southern and southeastern Henan in the middle of the third millennium BC (Zhang 1996).

Notes

1. The acute accent where there should now be a grave accent is an original feature of the orthography of the period. I thank William Hubbard Baxter for pointing out the appropriateness of this remark for the present juncture in the history of Tibeto-Burman linguistics.

References

Baxter, W.H., 1992. *A Handbook of Old Chinese Phonology.* Berlin: Mouton de Gruyter.

Baxter, W.H. & L. Sagart, 1998. Word formation in Old Chinese, in *New Approaches to Chinese Word Formation: Morphology, Phonology and the Lexicon in Modern and Ancient Chinese*, ed. J.L. Packard. Berlin: Mouton de Gruyter, 35–76.

Benedict, P.K., 1939. Semantic differentiation in Indo-Chinese. *Harvard Journal of Asiatic Studies* 4, 213–29.

Benedict, P.K., 1942. Thai, Kadai, and Indonesia: a new alignment in southeastern Asia. *American Anthropologist* 44, 576–601.

Benedict, P.K., 1972. *Sino-Tibetan: a Conspectus.* Cambridge: Cambridge University Press.

Blench, R.M., 2001. From the Mountains to the Valleys: Understanding Ethnolinguistic Geography in Southeast Asia. Paper presented at the Colloque «Perspectives sur la Phylogénie des Langues d'Asie Orientales» at Périgueux, France, 30 August 2001.

Blench, R. & M. Spriggs (eds.), 1997. *Archaeology and Language*, vol. I: *Theoretical and Methodological Orientations.* London: Routledge, 209–61.

Blench, R. & M. Spriggs (eds.), 1998. *Archaeology and Language*, vol. II: *Archaeological Data and Linguistic Hypotheses.* London: Routledge.

Bodman, N.C., 1980. Proto-Chinese and Sino-Tibetan: data towards establishing the nature of the relationship, in *Contributions to Historical Linguistics: Issues and Material*, eds. F. van Coetsem & L.R. Waugh. Leiden: E.J. Brill, 34–199.

Brown, P., 1998. The first Mongoloids? Another look at Upper Cave 101 and Minatogawa 1. *Acta Anthropologica Sinica* 17, 260–75.

Burling, R., 1983. The Sal languages. *Linguistics of the Tibeto-Burman Area* 7(2), 1–31.

Burling, R., forthcoming. The Tibeto-Burman languages of Northeastern India, in *The Sino-Tibetan Languages*, eds. G. Thurgood & R. LaPolla. London: Curzon Press.

Chang, K.-C. (i.e. Zhang, G.), 1965. Relative chronologies of China to the end of Chou, in *Chronologies in Old World Archaeology*, ed. R.W. Ehrich. Chicago (IL): Chicago University Press, 503–26.

Chang, K.-C. (i.e. Zhang, G.), 1977. *The Archaeology of Ancient China.* 3rd edition. New Haven (CT): Yale University Press.

Chang, K.-C. (i.e. Zhang, G.), 1986. *The Archaeology of Ancient China.* 4th edition, revised and enlarged. New Haven (CT): Yale University Press.

Chang, K.-C. (i.e. Zhang, G.), 1992. China, in *Chronologies in Old World Archaeology*, ed. R.W. Ehrich. 3rd edition, 2 vols. Chicago (IL): Chicago University Press, vol. 1, 409–15; vol. 2, 385–404.

Chêng, T., 1957. *Archaeological Studies in Szechwan.* Cambridge: Cambridge University Press.

Chu, J.Y., W. Huang, S.Q. Kuang, J.M. Wang, J.J. Xu, Z.T. Chu, Z.Q. Yang, K.Q. Lin, P. Li, M. Wu, Z.C. Geng, C.C. Tan, R.F. Du & L. Jin. 1998. Genetic relationship of populations in China. *Proceedings of the National Academy of Sciences of the USA* 95, 11,763–8.

Comte, A., 1830. *Cours de philosophie positive*, tome I. Paris: Rouen Frères.

Conrady, A., 1896. *Eine indochinesische Causativ-Denominativ-Bildung und ihr Zusammenhang mit den Tonaccenten: Ein Beitrag zur vergleichenden Grammatik der indochinesischen Sprachen, insonderheit des Tibetischen, Barmanischen, Siamesischen und Chinesischen.* Leipzig: Otto Harrassowitz.

Demeter, F., 2000. Histoire du peuplement humain de l'Asie extrême-orientale depuis le pléistocène supérieur récent. Sorbonne à Paris, thèse de doctorat, 19 décembre 2000.

Ding, Y.-C., S. Wooding, H.C. Harpending, H.-C. Chi, H.-P. Li, Y.-X. Fu, J.-F. Pang, Y.-G. Yao, J.-G. Xiang Yu, R. Moyzis & Y. Zhang, 2000. Population structure and history in East Asia. *Proceedings of the National Academy of Sciences of the USA* 97(25) [25 December 2000], 14,003–6.

Dixon, R.M.W., 1997. *The Rise and Fall of Languages.* Cambridge: Cambridge University Press.

D'jakonov, I.M., 1968. *Predystorija Armjanskogo Naroda: Istorija Armjanskovo Nagorya s 1500 po 500 g. do n.è., Xurrity, Luvijcy, Protoarmjane.* Erevan: Akademija Nauk Armjanskoi Sovetskoi Socialisticheskoi Respubliki.

Fortescue, M., 1998. *Language Relations across Bering Strait: Reappraising the Archaeological and Linguistic Evidence.* London: Cassell.

French, W.T., 1983. Northern Naga: a Tibeto-Burman Mesolanguage. 2 vols. Unpublished doctoral dissertation, City University of New York.

Gamkrelidze, T.V. (i.e. T. Gamqreliże) & V.V. Ivanov, 1995. *Indo-European and the Indo-Europeans: a Reconstruction and Historical Analysis of a Proto-Language and a Proto-Culture.* 2 vols. Berlin: Mouton de Gruyter.

Grierson, G.A. (ed.), 1909. *Linguistic Survey of India,* vol. III, part I: *Tibeto-Burman Family: Tibetan Dialects, the Himalayan Dialects and the North Assam Group.* Calcutta: Superintendent of Government Printing, India.

Grube, W., 1881. *Die sprachgeschichtliche Stellung des Chinesischen.* Leipzig: T.O. Weigel.

Hodgson, B.H., 1849. On the Aborigines of North-eastern India. *Journal of the Asiatic Society of Bengal* 203 (May 1849), 451–60.

Kern, H., 1889. Het stamland der Maleisch-Polynesische volken. *Tijdschrift voor Nederlandsch-Indië* 18(2), 1–9.

Klaproth, J.H., 1823. *Asia Polyglotta.* Paris: A. Schubart.

Klaproth, J.H., 1826. *Mémoires relatifs à l'Asie, contenant des recherches historiques, géographiques et philologiques.* 2 vols. Paris: Société Asiatique de Paris.

Kroeber, A.L., 1938. Editorial foreword, in *Sino-Tibetica 1: Prefixed n-, ng- in Tibetan,* ed. R. Shafer. Berkeley (CA): Sino-Tibetan Philology Project, 1–3.

Kuhn, E., 1889. Beiträge zur Sprachenkunde Hinterindiens (Sitzung vom 2. März 1889), in *Sitzungsberichte der Königlichen Bayerischen Akademie der Wissenschaften.* (Philosophisch-philologische Classe II.) Munich: Royal Bavarian Academy of Sciences at Munich, 189–236.

Lepsius, C.R., 1861. Über die Umschrift und Lautverhältnisse einiger hinterasiatischer Sprachen, namentlich der Chinesischen und der Tibetischen [sic]. *Abhandlungen der Königlichen Akademie der Wissenschaften zu Berlin,* aus dem Jahre 1860, 449–96.

Leyden, J.C., 1808. On the languages and literature of the Indo-Chinese nations. *Asiatic Researches* X, 158–289.

Mallory, J.P., 1989. *In Search of the Indo-Europeans.* London: Thames & Hudson.

Mallory, J.P., 1997. The homelands of the Indo-Europeans, in Blench & Spriggs (eds.), 93–121.

Mallory, J.P. & D.Q. Adams, 1997. *Encyclopaedia of Indo-European Culture.* London: Fitzroy Dearborne Publishers.

Marrison, G.E., 1967. The Classification of the Naga Languages of North-East India. 2 vols. Unpublished PhD dissertation, University of London.

Marrison, G.E., 1989. The Adi-Dafla group of languages of north-east India: a sketch, in *Prosodic Analysis and Asian Linguistics: to Honour R.K. Sprigg,* eds. D. Bradley, E.J.A. Henderson & M. Mazaudon. Canberra: Pacific Linguistics, 205–22.

Matisoff, J.A., 1991. Sino-Tibetan linguistics: present state and future prospects. *Annual Review of Anthropology 1991* 20, 469–504.

Müller, F.M., 1855. *Languages of the Seat of War in the East, with a Survey of the Three Families of Language, Semitic, Arian, and Turanian* (frontispiece title: *Max Müller's Survey of Languages*). 2nd edition. London: Williams and Norgate.

Nichols, J., 1992. *Linguistic Diversity in Time and Space.* Chicago (IL): Chicago University Press.

Nichols, J., 1998. The Eurasian spread zone and the Indo-European spread, in Blench & Spriggs (eds.), 220–66.

O'Connor, R.A., 1995. Agricultural change and ethnic succession in Southeast Asian states: a case for regional anthropology. *Journal of Asian Studies* 54(4), 968–96.

Pawley, A.K., 1999. Chasing rainbows: implications of the rapid dispersal of Austronesian languages, in *Selected Papers from the Eighth International Conference on Austronesian Linguistics,* eds. E. Zeitoun & P. Li. Taipei: Academia Sinica, 95–138.

Pawley, A.K. & M. Ross, 1995. The prehistory of the Oceanic languages, in *The Austronesians: Historical and Comparative Perspectives,* eds. P. Bellwood, J.J. Fox & D. Tryon. Canberra: Australian National University, 39–74.

Przyluski, J., 1924. Le sino-tibétain & Les langues austroasiatiques, in *Les Langues du Monde,* eds. A. Meillet & M. Cohen. Paris: Librairie Ancienne Édouard Champion, 361–403.

Przyluski, J. & G.H. Luce, 1931. The number 'a hundred' in Sino-Tibetan. *Bulletin of the School of Oriental Studies* VI(3), 667–8.

Ross, M., 1997. Social networks and kinds of speech-community event, in Blench & Spriggs (eds.), 209–61.

Sagart, L., 1990. Chinese and Austronesian are Genetically Related. Paper presented at the 23rd International Conference on Sino-Tibetan Languages and Linguistics (5 to 7 October), University of Texas at Arlington.

Sagart, L., 1994. Proto-Austronesian and Old Chinese evidence for Sino-Austronesian. *Oceanic Linguistics* 33(2), 271–308.

Sagart, L., 2001. Lexical Evidence for Austronesian-Sino-Tibetan Relatedness. Paper presented at the Conference on Connections across the Southern Pacific, Hong Kong City University, 18 January 2001.

Shafer, R., 1953. Classification of the northern-most Naga languages. *Journal of the Bihar Research Society* 39(3), 225–64.

Shafer, R., 1955. Classification of the Sino-Tibetan languages. *Word: Journal of the Linguistic Circle of New York* 11, 94–111.

Shafer, R., 1966. *Introduction to Sino-Tibetan,* part I. Wiesbaden: Otto Harrassowitz.

Shafer, R., 1967. *Introduction to Sino-Tibetan,* part II. Wiesbaden: Otto Harrassowitz.

Shafer, R., 1968. *Introduction to Sino-Tibetan,* part III. Wiesbaden: Otto Harrassowitz.

Shafer, R., 1974. *Introduction to Sino-Tibetan,* part IV. Wiesbaden: Otto Harrassowitz.

Sharma, T.C., 1989. Neolithic: Eastern region, vol. 1, in *An Encyclopaedia of Indian Archaeology,* ed. A. Ghosh. 2 vols. New Delhi: Munshiram Manoharlal Publishers, 58–60.

Simon, W., 1929. Tibetisch-chinesische Wortgleichungen, ein Versuch. *Mitteilungen des Seminars für Orientalische Sprachen an der Friedrich-Wilhelms-Universität zu Berlin* 32(1), 157–228.

Su, B., J. Xiao, P. Underhill, R. Deka, W. Zhang, J. Akey, W. Huang, D. Shen, D. Lu, J. Luo, J. Chu, J. Tan, P. Shen, R. Davis, L. Cavalli-Sforza, R. Chakraborty, M. Xiong, R. Du, P. Oefner, Z. Chen & L. Jin, 1999. Y-chromosome evidence for a northward migration of modern humans into eastern Asia during the last Ice Age. *American Journal of Human Genetics* 65, 1718–24.

Su, B., C. Xiao, R. Deka, M.T. Seielstad, D. Kangwanpong, J. Xiao, D. Lu, P. Underhill, L. Cavalli-Sforza, R. Chakraborty & L. Jin, 2000. Y-chromosome haplotypes reveal prehistorical migrations to the Himalayas. *Human Genetics* 107(6), 582–90.

Thapar, B.K., 1985. *Recent Archaeological Discoveries in India*. Paris: United Nations Educational Scientific and Cultural Organization.

Tsang, C., 2001. Recent Discoveries of the Tap'enkeng Culture in Taiwan: Implications for the Problem of Austronesian Origins. Paper presented at the Colloque «Perspectives sur la Phylogénie des Langues d'Asie Orientales» at Périgueux, France, 30 August 2001.

van Driem, G., 1995. Black Mountain verbal agreement morphology, Proto-Tibeto-Burman morphosyntax and the linguistic position of Chinese in Yoshio Nishi, in *New Horizons in Tibeto-Burman Morphosyntax* eds. J.A. Matisoff & Y. Nagano. (Senri Ethnological Studies 41.) Osaka: National Museum of Ethnology, 229–59.

van Driem, G., 1997. Sino-Bodic. *Bulletin of the School of Oriental and African Studies* 60(3), 455–88.

van Driem, G., 1998. Neolithic correlates of ancient Tibeto-Burman migrations in Blench & Spriggs (eds.) 1998, 67–102.

van Driem, G., 1999. A new theory on the origin of Chinese in *Bulletin of the Indo-Pacific Prehistory Association Bulletin*, vol. 18, eds. P. Bellwood & I. Lilley. (*Indo-Pacific Prehistory: The Melaka Papers*, vol. 2). Canberra: Australian National University, 43–58.

van Driem, G., 2001. *Languages of the Himalayas*. 2 vols. Leiden: Brill.

van Driem, G., 2002. Tibeto-Burman replaces Indo-Chinese in the 1990s: review of a decade of scholarship. *Lingua* 110, 79–102.

Wu, Y., 1996. Prehistoric rice agriculture in the Yellow River valley, in *Indo-Pacific Prehistory: The Chiang-Mai Papers*, vol. 2, eds. I.C. Glover & P. Bellwood. (Proceedings of the 15th Congress of the Indo-Pacific Prehistory Association, Chiang Mai, Thailand, 5 to 12 January 1994.) Canberra: Australian National University, 223–4.

Zhang, C., 1996. The rise of urbanism in the middle and lower Yangtze river valley, in *Indo-Pacific Prehistory: The Chiang-Mai Papers*, vol. 3, eds. P. Bellwood & D. Tillotson. (Proceedings of the 15th Congress of the Indo-Pacific Prehistory Association, Chiang Mai, Thailand, 5 to 12 January 1994.) Canberra: Australian National University, 63–8.

Zvelebil, M. & K.V. Zvelebil, 1988. Agricultural transition and Indo-European dispersals. *Antiquity* 62, 574–83.

Chapter 20

The Austronesian Dispersal:
Languages, Technologies and People

Andrew Pawley

My brief in this paper is to review research on the dispersal of the Austronesian (An) languages (Fig. 20.1), including the question of whether archaeological, demographic and biological correlates of the language spread can be identified.[1] The largest part of the discussion (sections 1–3) will be devoted to comparing the testimonies of archaeology and historical linguistics. The demographic and biological history of the An-speaking peoples of Oceania will be touched on in section 4.

The question arises how one can correlate the languages of prehistoric societies with archaeological assemblages. Bellwood (2001) proposes several desiderata for connecting the spread of a linguistic family with the spread of farming: a) strong sets of lexical reconstructions relating to crops and agricultural activities and perhaps to domestic animals; b) evidence of early rapid spread of languages over a large area; c) time depths corresponding to early agricultural dispersals attested in the archaeological record; d) other markers which allow particular languages to be connected with particular archaeological assemblages with a high degree of confidence, such as sets of cognates for distinctive elements of the material culture and a sudden, horizon-like appearance of the archaeological cultures.

In regions inhabited and invaded by diverse peoples in late prehistoric times, such as Europe, such correlations have proved difficult to make with any assurance. At first glance the Austronesian-speaking world might seem to pose equal difficulties: the peoples show great diversity in their ways of life and biological makeup. But it also happens that parts of the An-speaking world offer a combination of circumstances that are very favourable to making such correlations. Austronesian is unusual among language families in several respects:

1. It is extremely numerous. Of the world's established language families, the two with by far the largest memberships are An and Niger-Congo, each containing over 1000 languages.[2]

2. It is exceptionally far flung, extending two-thirds of the way around the tropical and subtropical world, from Madagascar to Easter Island, and over 70 degrees of latitude, from 25 degrees N (Taiwan) to 48 degrees S (the southern tip of New Zealand). Until the global migrations of the last two centuries, only Indo-European after Columbus had a wider distribution.

3. It is the only major language family that is predominantly spoken on islands. In some cases languages and subgroups are isolated by ocean gaps of several hundreds, even thousands, of kilometres.

4. An speakers were the first people to colonize certain regions of the earth, namely Madagascar and much of the Pacific. The colonization of these regions was quite recent, within the last 3500 years and, in much of Polynesia, only within the last 800 to 1200 years.

5. The archaeological record for Island Southeast Asia and the Pacific Islands shows clear evidence of the first entry and dispersal of Neolithic cultures, with cultural content and directions of movement which rather closely match those independently inferred from linguistic evidence. Archaeological dating of these events provides a much more robust time frame for points in the An dispersal than that which linguistics alone can supply.

6. An has a deeply stratified family tree and there is a fair degree of agreement about many of the key subgroupings.

7. The abundance of independent witnesses, in combination with the geographic dispersion of many of the subgroups, is an enormous advantage when

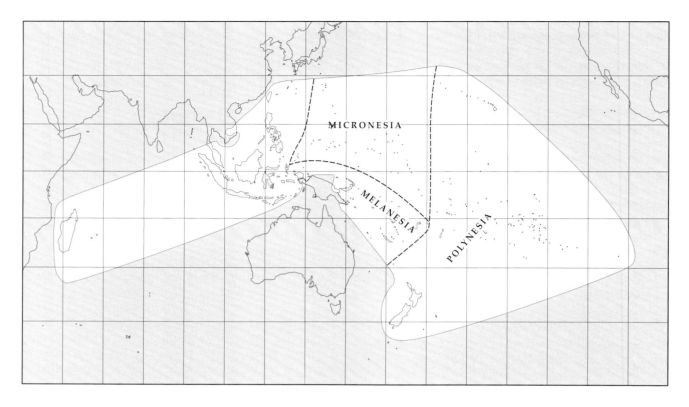

Figure 20.1. *The geographical distribution of Austronesian and its major subgroups.*

it comes to doing reconstruction. For certain stages of An, for example, it has been possible to reconstruct several thousand lexical items, including detailed terminologies for domains of material culture, social organization and physical environment.[3] The outlines of the Austronesian family were recognized 300 years ago by the Dutch scholar Hadrian Reland (Reland 1708), who compared words from Malay, Malagasy and Polynesian (the Formosan languages were not included until the nineteenth century). By the 1860s, linguists were beginning systematic comparative studies of certain languages of the Indo-Malaysian Archipelago and the Philippines. In 1889, Hendrik Kern used cognate sets for flora and fauna to infer the probable location of the primary dispersal centre of the An languages.[4] Otto Dempwolff's influential three volume reconstruction of Proto-Austronesian (PAn) phonology and of a PAn lexicon of some 2200 roots appeared in 1934–38. Systematic archaeological research in Southeast Asia and the Pacific Islands was slower to get under way. Intensive subsurface archaeology began in Polynesia in the 1950s, a time in which Oceanic historical linguistics also began to blossom. Since then there has been regular dialogue between historical linguists and archaeologists and, to a lesser extent, between

these and researchers in other historical disciplines.

What may be termed the standard view of the An dispersal — the location of its primary centre and its directions, dating and mechanisms — took shape between 1960 and 1980. Over the last 20 years, additional research has for the most part strengthened the grounds for this view while modifying a number of details. Some of the core ideas had already emerged by 1964, when an issue of *Current Anthropology* carried papers by a linguist, George Grace, and two archaeologists, K.C. Chang and Wilhelm Solheim II, on 'Movements of the Malayo-Polynesians 1500 BC to AD 500'. The question of the role of agriculture in both enabling and restricting the spread of An languages in Oceania was in the air by 1970. Scholars had realized the possible primacy of the Lapita culture in the settlement of Remote Oceania (Fig. 20.2) and the central role of agriculture, arboriculture, and sailing and fishing technology in the successful first colonization of Remote Oceania, a point repeatedly emphasized by Roger Green (Green 1979; 1991a,b; Pawley & Green 1973; 1984). In 1970, the Kuk site in the New Guinea Highlands was discovered, yielding evidence that agriculture was developed in New Guinea before its introduction from Southeast Asia.

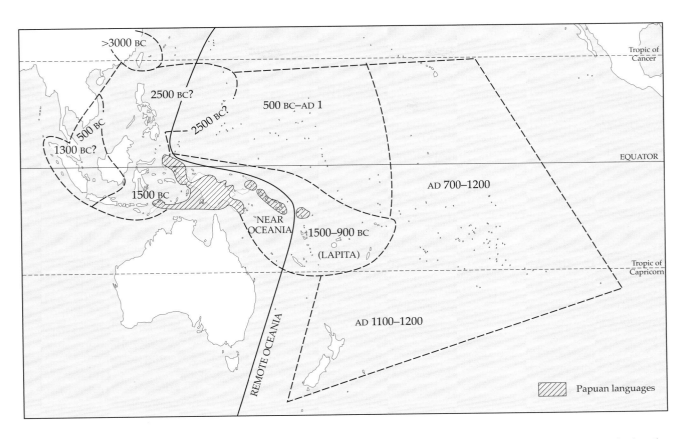

Figure 20.2. *Near Oceania, Remote Oceania, and approximate dates for initial Austronesian colonization, calculated from archaeological and linguistic data. The Lapita cultural complex occurs on the islands within the zone labelled 1300–800 BC.*

In 1975, Richard Shutler and Jeff Marck (an archaeologist and a linguist) explicitly connected the initial An dispersal with horticulture. In 1976, the linguist Robert Blust published the first of several papers in which he summarizes and updates his views on the reconstructed culture of the early An speakers, compared with evidence from archaeology and the distributions of plants and animals (Blust 1976; 1982; 1985; 1995a). Other recent surveys by linguists are Pawley & Ross (1993; 1995) and Zorc (1994).

Probably the best-known interdisciplinary syntheses centring on the An region are several books by archaeologists: Bellwood (1978; 1985; 1997), in his later books and in many articles (e.g. Bellwood 1995; 2000) has emphasized the role of agriculture in the initial An expansion. Irwin (1992), Kirch (1997; 2000) and Spriggs (1997) focus on Oceanic prehistory, developing variants of the standard view. Terrell (1986) gives a contrary interpretation. At the Australian National University we have for the last decade been looking at lexical terminologies in Proto-Oceanic and

at what these can tell us about early An material culture, society and environment (Pawley & Ross 1993; Ross *et al.* 1998; forthcoming). Two archaeologists have recently published a major synthesis of linguistic and archaeological research in Polynesia (Kirch & Green 2001).

So I am following a well-trodden path. I will attempt to describe the bases of the standard view, beginning with that region where circumstances are most favourable for making correlations: Remote Oceania. I will also look at some dissenting opinions, and point to some of the methodological issues which researchers in the field face. But coverage will necessarily be sketchy and selective. Austronesian is a huge language family and the relevant archaeological and linguistic literature is massive.

1. Archaeology and language in Remote Oceania

1.1. Near Oceania vs Remote Oceania
Oceania is often divided into three main regions: Melanesia, Polynesia and Micronesia. However, a

more useful primary division for understanding the history of plants, animals and humans in the Pacific is between *Near Oceania* and *Remote Oceania*.[5]

Near Oceania is that part of the Southwest Pacific whose chief landmasses are New Guinea, the Bismarck Archipelago and the main islands in the Solomons chain, while excluding Australia. The islands of Near Oceania for the most part form an intervisible series, which in turn continues the chain of island stepping-stones that begin in Island Southeast Asia. The largest gaps between the main islands in Near Oceania are currently on the order of 130 km, except for Manus, which is about 240 km west of the St Matthias Group. The east–west boundary between Near and Remote Oceania is the ocean gap of some 350 km separating the main Solomons chain from the small Santa Cruz group. In the Polynesian Triangle, whose apices are Hawaii, New Zealand and Easter Island, some of the island groups are extremely isolated, across ocean gaps of between 1000 and 3000 kilometres. Micronesia consists of several extensive and widely separated groups of small islands (Marianas, Carolines, Marshalls, Kiribati), most of them atolls.

There is no archaeological evidence that any part of Remote Oceania was settled before the late second millennium BC. Presumably the ocean gaps were too great to cross against the prevailing southeast trade winds with the technology available to earlier populations resident in the Solomons. Also, permanent settlement on small Remote Oceanic islands, with their restricted flora and land fauna, would have been very difficult if not impossible to sustain without agriculture and without the capacity to make regular two-way long-distance voyages to replenish the population and other key resources.

1.2. The Lapita diaspora (Fig. 20.2)

In the second millennium BC there were at least three independent movements of Neolithic cultures into Remote Oceania. Around 1500 BC, a highly distinctive archaeological tradition, known as Lapita, appeared suddenly in the Bismarck Archipelago (Kirch 1997; 2000; Spriggs 1997). Upwards of 200 Lapita sites have now been found, although only a minority have been excavated. The earliest sites are in the region of the St Matthias Group, New Britain and New Ireland. Within three or four centuries Lapita spread widely across the Southwest Pacific into Santa Cruz, New Caledonia and Vanuatu.[6] By 1000–900 BC Lapita was present in Fiji and Tonga and within another century or so in Samoa, Futuna and 'Uvea, some 4000 km to the east of the Bismarcks.

The most prominent markers of the Lapita culture are well-made earthenware with a characteristic variety of vessel shapes, including water jars, globular cooking vessels and flat-bottomed dishes, including some vessels decorated by very distinctive, elaborate dentate-stamped geometric motifs. In the more completely excavated Lapita sites the pottery is part of a cluster of features — artefacts, settlement patterns and architecture — which Green (1979) termed the 'Lapita cultural complex'. Settlements are in the hamlet to village range and nearly always situated on small offshore islands or on the coasts of large islands. In at least some settlements houses were built on piles below high-tide level. The Lapita tool kit frequently contains ground and polished stone and shell adzes; obsidian and chert flake tools, often imported from remote sources; one-piece shell fishhooks; pearlshell knives and scrapers; various kinds of cone shell disks and pendants. Earth ovens are present. Middens are typically full of lagoon fish and turtle bones, attesting to the importance of fishing and to a variety of fishing techniques (Walter 1989). Bones of dog, chicken and pig indicate that these animals (none of which are native to Near Oceania) were kept as domesticates.

The bearers of Lapita culture were, it seems, the first people to settle Santa Cruz, Vanuatu and New Caledonia. They were almost certainly the first people to reach Fiji and Western Polynesia. Once there they did not maintain regular links with peoples to the west. In Western Polynesia there is no archaeological evidence of intrusive cultures from outside the Fiji–West Polynesia area in the period of some 2600 years between the Lapita colonization and first European landfall in 1615. In Fiji, however, there is some evidence for intrusions of cultural elements and clear evidence for intrusion of people bringing new genes (in both cases probably from Vanuatu). In Fiji and Western Polynesia the Lapita archaeological culture evolved into a set of local cultures which remained very similar to one another until about 2200 BP, when the two regions begin to diverge markedly (Green 1979; Kirch & Green 2001).

In Western Polynesia, there was a 'pause' of a millennium or more before speakers of Polynesian languages successful colonized Eastern Polynesia. There are at present few solid archaeological grounds for thinking that the first permanent settlement of East Polynesia (the Society Islands, Cook Islands, Marquesas and Tuamotus) occurred before the fourth century AD. The earliest dates accepted by Spriggs & Anderson (1993) are in the ranges AD 300–600 for the Marquesas, AD 650–850 for Hawaii, AD 700–1000 for the Society Islands and Southern Cooks and AD 400–1270 for Easter Island.

Why was there such a long standstill in Western Polynesia? One can point to the greater distances between island groups that had to be traversed against the prevailing SE trade winds (Irwin 1992). There is debate as to whether the Lapita people had vessels suitable for carrying people, animals and plants on voyages of thousands of kilometres. At first European contact the large-platformed double-hulled canoe was the favoured vessel of Polynesians and Fijians for long ocean voyages. But Blust (1999) suggests that it was not developed until after well after the initial colonization of Fiji and West Polynesia. The linguistic evidence (Pawley & Pawley 1994) is equivocal; see section 3.5.7. A second pause, lasting several centuries, evidently occurred in Central East Polynesia before bearers of the distinctive classical East Polynesian cultures settled marginal regions of East Polynesia such as Hawaii (probably around AD 800) and New Zealand (around AD 1200).

1.3. What language(s) did the Lapita settlers of Remote Oceania speak?

We come now to the equation of archaeological cultures with language in Remote Oceania. Some 180–190 distinct languages were spoken in Remote Oceania at first European contact. About 110–115 are spoken in Vanuatu, about 25 in the New Caledonia–Loyalties Group and about 10 in Santa Cruz and other outlying islands in the Solomons. Some 16 languages are spoken in the Polynesian Triangle and between 13 and 17 (depending how one treats dialect chains) in Micronesia. The Fiji group contains at least two languages, each a dialect chain of great internal diversity. Rotuman, spoken on Rotuma 260 miles to the north of Fiji, is a separate language. All these languages are An with the possible exception of three on Santa Cruz Island in the eastern Solomons.[7] Furthermore, almost all belong to a single subgroup, Oceanic.

The Oceanic group was established by Dempwolff (1934–38) on the basis of a number of shared innovations in phonology. Subsequent research has refined Dempwolff's claims and added some new arguments, chiefly from morphology and irregular changes in some lexical forms. Oceanic consists of all 500 or so of the An languages spoken in Oceania with the following exceptions: 1) Chamorro, spoken in the Marianas; and 2) Belau, spoken on Belau (Palau) Island at the western margin of the Carolines, are unclassified members of the Malayo-Polynesian subgroup; 3) at the western end of New Guinea,

west of 136 degrees east, there are about 30 An languages which belong to subgroups closely related to Oceanic (see 3.2).

Although Oceanic is very large (containing about 40 per cent of all the languages in the An family), it is no more than a fourth-order branch of An. For reasons that will be given in section 3, I believe that Proto-Oceanic was probably spoken in the Bismarck Archipelago by bearers of the Lapita culture and that it began to break up in the middle of the second millennium BC when carriers of that culture began to disperse widely.

Polynesian, Fijian and Rotuman form a subgroup apart from all other Oceanic languages. This subgroup, known as Central Pacific is, however, only weakly defined (Grace 1959; 1967; Pawley 1972; 1996a; Geraghty 1983; 1986; 1996). It appears that Proto-Central Pacific was a chain of dialects spoken in Fiji. These evidently underwent only a short period of common development apart from their nearest relatives (probably the languages of Central and Northern Vanuatu) before a branch ancestral to Polynesian and certain dialects of Eastern Fiji (Geraghty 1983), and a branch ancestral to Rotuman and certain dialects of northwest Fiji (Pawley 1996a), diverged from the rest. Reconstruction of the lexicon of Proto-Central Pacific and Proto-Polynesian yields extensive terminologies for canoe parts and sailing, for agricultural technology and domesticated plants, for domesticated animals and for fishing gear (see section 3.5). The reconstructed lexicon closely matches what we would expect from the content and context of the foundation archaeological culture in Fiji and Western Polynesia (Kirch & Green 2001).

The degree of lexical and grammatical divergence between Polynesian, Fijian and Rotuman is consistent with separation around 3000 years ago or somewhat earlier (Grace 1967; Pawley 1972). The Polynesian languages form an extremely well-defined subgroup. They share several phonological innovations, dozens of morpho-syntactic innovations (Clark 1979; Pawley 1996b) and hundreds of lexical innovations (Marck 2000). Polynesian shows an internal diversity in core vocabulary and grammar slightly greater than the Romance or Germanic families.[8] This degree of diversity suggests that Proto-Polynesian broke up roughly 2000 years ago. For what it is worth, the glottochronological method yields an estimate of about 1300 years as the period of common development for Polynesian after its separation from Fijian and Rotuman. As it happens, both these estimates agree fairly well with current archaeological evidence.

The Lapita colonization of Remote Oceania, in which humans, plants and animals were transported across a series of large ocean gaps, over 4000 km from the Bismarck Archipelago to western Polynesia, in the space of about four or five centuries, was Mankind's most spectacular seafaring accomplishment up to that time. It is difficult to avoid the conclusion that the Lapita settlers of Remote Oceania spoke an An language of the Oceanic branch. And there can hardly be any doubt that the people who first colonized Fiji, Rotuma and the Polynesian Triangle were speakers of the ancestor of the present day Central Pacific languages.

1.4. Multiple settlements of Micronesia

At least two and probably three other movements into Remote Oceania occurred about the same time as the Lapita expansion, but independently of it. All were into western Micronesia. The Mariana Islands, forming the northwest margin of Micronesia, were settled by 1500 BC (Bonhomme & Craig 1987). Belau (Palau), at the western margin of the Carolines, was settled by at least 3000 years ago (Welch in press). The sources of these movements were probably the Philippines and/or eastern Indonesia. Early assemblages in the Marianas show a red slip decorated earthenware remarkably similar to that found in the northern Philippines — and to the Lapita tradition. (See 2.3 concerning the languages.) It is likely that Yap (Western Carolines) was also settled very early. The highly divergent Yapese language is Oceanic but cannot on present evidence be subgrouped with any other member of Oceanic (Ross 1996).

The remaining languages of Micronesia derive from a fourth movement which occurred well after the Lapita settlement of Remote Oceania. All the languages of Micronesia except for Chamorro, Belauan and Yapese form a closed subgroup. This Nuclear Micronesian group is fairly well-defined though much less well-marked than Polynesian (Bender 1971; Bender & Wang 1985; Jackson 1983). Its centre of genetic diversity is in the east, in the region of Kiribati, Kosrae, Pohnpei and the Marshalls. Blust (1984) argues that the immediate relatives of Nuclear Micronesian are the Southeast Solomonic languages. The earliest archaeological dates in Nuclear Micronesia are on the order of 2000 BP, for sites with plain and rim-notched pottery that could be derived from late Lapita (Athens 1980).

1.5. Origins of Lapita and the Oceanic group

So far so good. But what is the relationship between the earliest Lapita cultures, those of the Bismarck Archipelago and An languages? This has been a matter of lively debate and it is convenient to consider it within the wider context of the origins of other Neolithic cultures found in Island Southeast Asia and Near Oceania.

2. The Neolithic horizon in Island Southeast Asia and Near Oceania

2.1. The pre-Neolithic in Island Southeast Asia and the Pacific

Until a few thousand years ago, all human populations in Island Southeast Asia, from Taiwan to Timor, lived exclusively or principally by hunting and gathering. The archaeological assemblages show a complete absence of artefacts associated with agriculture — there is no pottery, no fully ground and polished adzes, no signs of permanent villages (Bellwood 1997). From 18,000 BC, until as recently as 1000 BC in some places, stone technologies consisted of flaked tools with some edge ground-tools. Populations were probably sparse and nomadic. Borneo, most of which was covered in rainforest, was probably very lightly inhabited. Sumatra and Java, with more extensive grasslands, probably had larger hunter-gather populations. People may have planted or tended some trees for their nuts and fruit but true agriculture was still unknown in the region. When Neolithic cultures do appear in Island Southeast Asia they do so as a sharply defined horizon.

2.2. The beginnings of the Neolithic in East Asia

The early stages of agriculture in East Asia probably go back at least 10,000 years. Rice is thought to have been domesticated from wild rice (*Orzyza rufipogon*) in the swampy regions around the middle and lower Yangtze River. By 8000 years ago some groups living in the temperate regions of central and northern China were practising full scale field agriculture, with economies based on rice (Yangtze Valley) or foxtail and broomcorn millet (Yellow River Basin) and domestic animals (Chang 1986; Shih 1993; Yan 1993). These farmers lived in villages and made pottery.

An important early Neolithic site at Hemudu, just south of Hangzhou Bay in Northeast Zhejiang Province, contains a waterlogged level, dated to 5200–4900 BC, which is associated with a village of well-built rectangular houses raised on small timber piles, among which clumps of rice grains were found. A wide range of pottery vessels were found, along with pot stands and sherds containing rice husks as temper. Bellwood (1997, 211) writes that the Hemudu tradition 'shows that the totality of potting knowledge found in the early cultures of Taiwan was already present in this region a millennium before the beginnings of An expansion'. Other artefacts included bone hoes, wooden spades, stone adzes and knee-shaped adze hafts of the type commonly found in An cultures of Oceania. Although a wide range of animals were represented, including chicken and dog, 90 per cent of the bones are of pig, indicating domestication of this animal.

Bellwood (1995, 97) argues that four major language families, An, Thai-Kadai, Hmong-Mien and Austroasiatic, 'seem to have arisen by . . . dispersal out of subtropical southern China and northern mainland China, where the cultivation of rice and other crops developed widely between about 6000 and 3000 BC'.

2.3. The early Neolithic in Taiwan (Fig. 20.3)

In Island Southeast Asia, the first appearance of Neolithic cultures, by at least 3500 BC, is on the large island of Taiwan. The oldest Taiwan Neolithic culture, known as the Ta-p'en-k'eng (TPK), has distinctive cord-marked and incised pottery (Chang 1969; 1986), associated with rice cultivation, shell reaping knives, pottery spindle whorls, polished stone adzes, stone barkcloth beaters and net sinkers, and polished slate points (Tsang Cheng-hwa pers. comm. to P. Bellwood). TPK assemblages are also found on the Pescadores (P'eng-hu) Islands, between Taiwan and the Asian mainland (Tsang 1995). Between 3500 and 2500 BC, variants of the TPK culture are present in fairly homogeneous form in coastal sites around Taiwan. In terms of origin, no specific location can be pin-pointed, but pottery similar to TPK is found in sites in Fujian and Guangdong Provinces on the Chinese mainland dating to the fifth and fourth millennia BC (Chang 1995).

After about 2500 BC, the TPK on Taiwan developed into later cultures that show a number of common features, and also increasing diversity. The Yuan-shan assemblages of northern Taiwan contain pottery decorated with red slip and incision, but without cord-marking. Artefacts similar to the TPK continue, with the addition of fishhooks in bone and shell, bone harpoons and cone shell ring ornaments. Absent in Yuan-shan are the slate reaping knives found by this time in western Taiwan, perhaps indicating a shift to bamboo reaping knives. The Peinan culture of eastern Taiwan (Lien 1993) appears to have much in common with Yuan-shan. Taiwan archaeologists currently regard these post-TPK assemblages, which also occur along the western coast and

around the southern tip of the island, as derived in Taiwan by regional transformations of the TPK (Bellwood pers. comm.).

2.4. The spread of the Neolithic in Island Southeast Asia south of Taiwan (Fig. 20.3)

Four things are striking about the early Neolithic in Island Southeast Asia south of Taiwan. First, there was a long pause before Neolithic technology crossed the Bashi Channel, the 350 km stretch of ocean, dotted with small islands, that separates Taiwan from Luzon in the northern Philippines. The pause was, on present evidence, not less than 1000 years. This delay indicates that the initial Neolithic peoples of Taiwan lacked the sailing technology to make this crossing (Blust 1995a).

Second, it is the post-TPK assemblages of Taiwan, especially the Yuan-shan (although the apparent prominence of Yuan-shan may reflect in part the high intensity of archaeological research in the Taipei Basin), that most resemble those found in early Neolithic sites in the Philippines, Indonesia and Oceania (Bellwood 1997; Kirch 1995). Between 2500 and 1500 BC, assemblages with plain and red-slipped pottery resembling post-TPK Neolithic materials appeared widely in northern Luzon. At Dimolit in Isabela Province, red-slipped pottery was found together with postholes for wooden houses. Shell middens in the fertile Cagayan Valley have yielded similar pottery, some with pedestal-supported bowls with dentate-stamped decoration resembling Lapita pottery. New research in the Batanes Islands is yielding similar red-slipped pottery (Bellwood pers. comm.) and the sites here, together with the burial assemblages from Arku cave in the Cagayan Valley, contain many other artefacts closely matching Taiwanese assemblages.

The third striking feature is the swiftness of the spread of Neolithic traditions after they reached the Philippines. The archaeological record for the early Neolithic in the Indo-Malaysian region is very spotty, especially for Java and Sumatra, but a fairly consistent overall pattern has emerged across the region. Bellwood (1997, 232–3) believes that there were probably no Neolithic cultures in the Indo-Malaysian Archipelago before about 2500 BC, and most early dated sites fall closer to 1500 BC. Currently, securely-dated Neolithic assemblages appear more or less simultaneously in North Borneo, Sulawesi, Halmahera, Timor, the Bismarck Archipelago and various parts of Remote Oceania, with dates ranging from 1500 to 1000 BC and with assemblages carrying markers of close relationship. Earlier Neolithic sites dating to

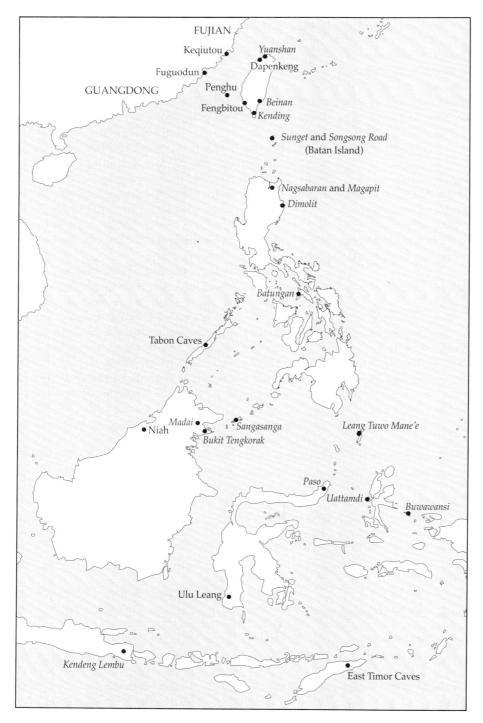

Figure 20.3. *Neolithic sites in the Islands of Southeast Asia. (Courtesy P. Bellwood.)*

stamped decoration, along with a complex of shell and stone tools and ornaments. In terms of Oceanic connections, the Uattamdi rockshelter site on Kayoa Island, northern Moluccas, is of special interest. It contains materials dated to 1500 BC or a bit later, including a range of pottery vessel forms and a suite of tools and ornaments extremely similar to those found on early Lapita sites in the Bismarck Archipelago.

A fourth remarkable feature of the Neolithic in Island Southeast Asia is the strong association that can be made with Austronesian languages, a matter which we will return to in section 3. It is noteworthy that Neolithic cultures associated with the An dispersal do not arrive on the Southeast Asian mainland until considerably later Iron Age times — about 500 BC in South Vietnam and perhaps later in the Malay Peninsula (Bellwood 1997).

2.5. Origins of Lapita
Some archaeologists confidently assign a Southeast Asian origin to most components of the Lapita culture (Bellwood 1997; Kirch 1997; 2000; Spriggs 1996; 1997). Kirch (1997, 282) writes 'the early Lapita assemblages fit comfortably within the range of variation . . . for cultural complexes dating to the second and third millennia B.C. in island southeast Asia'. Although the Island Southeast Asian traditions 'lack the particular extremely complex artistic style characteristic of Lapita, we should view the early Lapita sites of the Bismarcks as an eastward extension of a "polythetic" set of related cultures of presumably An-speaking peoples that

between 2500 and 2000 BC are present in Sarawak, but the relationships of these sites to An dispersal are uncertain. In eastern Indonesia, Neolithic sites contain red-slipped pottery, some with incised or underwent rapid expansion in the period between 3,000–1,000 B.C.'

Others have argued for a predominantly local origin of Lapita in the Bismarck Archipelago (Allen & Gosden 1996; Allen & White 1989; Terrell & Welsch 1997; White 1996). There are precedents for some elements of Lapita technology and trade patterns in the pre-Lapita period there, including lagoon fishing, trochus shell armrings, earth ovens, and an inter-island trade in obsidian. In New Guinea itself there is evidence of an independent development of agriculture in the central highlands by 4000 BC and possibly earlier (Golson 1977; 1991; Swadling & Muke forthcoming), an agriculture evidently based on root crops, presumably taro and, at lower altitudes, probably bananas. It is a reasonable hypothesis that the initial spread of agriculture in New Guinea was the driving force behind the remarkable expansion of one family of Papuan languages, Trans New Guinea, which extends over much of New Guinea and Alor, Pantar and parts of Timor, in eastern Indonesia, and contains some 450 to 500 languages. It is possible that a version of this agricultural tradition, supplemented by tree crops, was practised in the Bismarcks before the arrival of An speakers. However, there is as yet no evidence of pre-Lapita agriculture in the Bismarcks. Critics of the local origin hypothesis point out that the early Neolithic in New Guinea, so far attested only in the central highlands, was of a markedly different character from that which developed in China and spread into Island Southeast Asia and, soon after, into Near and Remote Oceania (Spriggs 1997).

Green (1991b; 2000) has proposed a less polarized model to explain the origins of the Lapita culture. This is the Triple-I model of 'intrusion', 'integration' and 'innovation'. 'Intrusion' refers to elements of Lapita which enter Near Oceania from outside, specifically from Island Southeast Asia, 'integration' refers to elements having antecedents in Near Oceania (and eastern Wallacea), and 'innovations' to features unique to Lapita. Green clearly thinks of Lapita as having a core complex of technology, settlement patterns and social organization which An speakers carried with them when they entered Near Oceania. This intrusive technology included red-slipped pottery, seagoing outrigger canoes, the two-boom triangular sail, and both quadrangular sectioned and ovoid to lenticular sectioned polished stone adzes. Green considers the earth oven and possibly the heavy, hinge-portioned *Tridacna* adze as coming most likely from a Near Oceanic source. Following Yen's conclusion (Yen 1973; 1991)

that a number of tree crops and plant domesticates such as Australimusa bananas, breadfruit, coconut and sugarcane were Near Oceania domesticates, Spriggs (1997), Kirch (1996) and Green suggest that these may have been added to the Lapita suite of crops as a result of contact with non-Lapita populations. (But see 3.5.2 for linguistic arguments against this view.) Green (2000) proposes a dual origin (Southeast Asia and New Guinea) for bananas and sugarcane, and thinks that the coconut and betel nut are most likely of Southeast Asian provenance.

The inter-island trade in obsidian practised by Lapita peoples was almost certainly based on trade systems that had existed in the Bismarcks since the Upper Pleistocene, but shows significant changes in the range and frequency of the trade and in technology (Summerhayes 2000). The distinctive decorative style on Lapita pottery is deemed to be an innovation (although it may have had antecedents in tattooing and the decoration of perishable artefacts such as bark cloth), as are the planilateral and plano-convex sectioned stone adze types. Under probable local innovations of Lapita, Green would also place certain developments in canoe building and sailing techniques. Green's Triple I model has been widely accepted in principle. The area of debate remains the relative importance of each of the three 'I's.

Not until a good deal later do An-associated cultures show up clearly in the (admittedly very scanty) archaeological record for the New Guinea mainland. The earliest such well-established sequence begins around 2000 BP in the Central Province of Papua. For obvious geographic reasons there must have been somewhat earlier settlements made on the north coast of New Guinea and around the eastern tip. But on the New Guinea mainland Austronesians encountered established populations speaking Papuan languages, many of them probably cultivators, and Oceanic languages in New Guinea are largely confined to the coast.

3. Linguistic evidence for the Austronesian dispersal and the fit with archaeology

3.1. Methodological preliminaries: the Comparative Method

Two main kinds of linguistic evidence can be adduced concerning the homeland and directions of spread of a family of languages. One is subgrouping by shared innovations (cladistic classification). The most likely primary dispersal centre ('homeland') for a genetic group, biological or linguistic, is the area of its greatest genetic diversity, where the highest-order branchings in the family tree are found. The other kind of evidence consists of lexical reconstructions to do with technology and social organization and with flora and fauna.

Both sorts of evidence derive chiefly from applications of the so-called 'Comparative Method' of historical linguistics. This is a reconstructive method, designed to distinguish between innovations, shared retentions and borrowings, and to yield a relative chronology for innovations, which in turn forms the basis for subgrouping. The method is based on certain crucial facts about language: all languages change over time, sound-form pairings in ordinary words (as opposed to sound symbolic words) are essentially arbitrary, and sound change tends to be regular. The applications of the method do not yield precise and reliable reconstructions under all conditions — the data may be intractable, or too limited, or the method may be badly applied. But given rich data it is a powerful method.

It should be noted that, from the standpoint of genetic continuity, the lexicon of a set of related languages divides into two components. One component consists of the lexical units that the daughter languages inherit from their common ancestor X (the cognates). The other consists of material that has been added to each language later, chiefly borrowings and newly-coined words. The quantity of material that each daughter language retains from X will decrease over time.

Austronesianists have generally assumed that it will be possible to establish a clear sequence of splits for the earlier stages of the An diaspora, such that each contemporary language or dialect falls into only one subgroup. Having a well-defined and highly stratified family tree greatly simplifies the tasks of phonological, lexical and grammatical reconstruction. It is well known, however, that conventional family tree diagrams seldom represent accurately the manner in which languages have diverged. Rather, they are (like maps) understood to be convenient approximations. Most of the time, the divergence of sister languages is not a sudden clean split that yields perfectly discrete subgroups. More often it is a gradual and untidy affair. A *linkage*, in the sense of Ross (1988), is a subgroup formed by a chain of dialects differentiating *in situ*, rather than by sharp geographic separation.

3.2. On the higher-order subgroups of Austronesian and directions of dispersal

In a series of papers, Blust (1977; 1978a,b; 1982; 1983–84; 1991; 1993; 1995b; 1999) has developed a fairly detailed classification of the upper parts of the An family tree (Fig. 20.4). The conjunction of linguistic and archaeological evidence indicates that the splits posited for this part of the tree occurred 3500 years ago or earlier (see section 3). Blust's overall classification is not a unitary hypothesis. To some extent, he builds on previous subgrouping hypotheses, but his tree as given here contains a number of new proposals.

3.2.1. The top of the tree

The most controversial part of Blust's tree is at the top. Two radically different hypotheses about the first order divisions within An have been proposed by senior Austronesianists: (A) The Philippine languages subgroup with the rest of An, apart from the Formosan languages. The non-Formosan branch is termed Malayo-Polynesian. (B) The Philippine languages subgroup with the Formosan languages apart from at least the Oceanic languages and possibly apart from most of the languages of the Indo-Malaysian Archipelago.[9]

Subgrouping A — call it the Malayo-Polynesian hypothesis — has been advanced by Blust (1977; 1995b) on the basis of a number of putative innovations in phonology and morphology. A similar subgrouping was foreshadowed by Dyen (1965), but was first advocated on the basis of shared phonological innovations by Dahl (1973). Blust's innovations differ in kind and extent from Dahl's. Blust (1995b; 1999) finds that there is no convincing body of shared innovations uniting the Formosan languages against the rest of An. He concludes that Proto-An broke up into ten first-order branches, one of them Malayo-Polynesian, the other nine confined to Formosa.

Subgrouping B — call it the Formosan-Philippine hypothesis — has been proposed by both Dyen (Dyen 1990; 1995; Dyen & Tsuchida 1991) and Wolff (1995), chiefly on the basis of the large number of uniquely shared cognate sets and, in Wolff's case, on structural resemblances in morphosyntax. Dyen and Wolff argue that some of these cognate sets (they cannot say which ones) must reflect lexical innovations common to the languages of Taiwan and the Philippines.

The quantity of innovations defining Malayo-Polynesian is small compared with the large number that defines the Polynesian group. However, their quality is respectable and the Malayo-Polynesian hypothesis has been preferred to the Philippine-Formosan hypothesis by most Austronesianists who have taken a position on this issue (e.g. Ross 1992;

1995; Pawley 1999; Reid 1982; Zorc 1994). A serious objection to the Formosan-Philippines hypothesis is that it does not distinguish between shared retentions and shared innovations (Blust 1990). Thus, all the uniquely-shared resemblances may be the result of common heritage from Proto-An by relatively conservative languages. When only two primary subgroups are posited it is hard to determine what has replaced what when the two branches disagree (the 'directionality of change problem'). In such cases of indeterminacy, Blust (1995b) and Ross (1992) have appealed to the naturalness or otherwise of particular directions of change. The likelihood of linguistic contact and diffusion across the Bashi Channel after the Formosan and Philippines languages split is a factor that proponents of both subgroupings A and B must allow for.

3.2.2. The branching of Proto-Malayo-Polynesian

Blust (1993, 244–5) finds that both Central Malayo-Polynesian (CMP) and Central-Eastern Malayo-Polynesian (CEMP) are linkages (see 3.1) rather than discrete subgroups. Although he has sometimes (e.g. Blust 1983–84; 1993) spoken of Western MP as a subgroup of MP, Blust (1999, 68) has recently stated that he regards this term as standing for a residual collection of unclassified groups. It appears that all the languages of the Philippines, together with certain neighbouring languages of North Sulawesi, and Yami (spoken on Lan-yu Island, Taiwan) form a closed subgroup (Zorc 1986; Blust 1991). But Blust is uncertain whether this Greater Philippines group belongs in a branch of Malayo-Polynesian together with such putative groups as Malayic (Adelaar 1992; Nothofer 1988), Malayo-Javanic (Nothofer 1975), Malayo-Chamic (Blust 1981; 1994) and the group which comprises the Malagasy languages and the Barito group of South Borneo (Dahl 1951; 1977).

Eastern Malayo-Polynesian rests on a small but generally persuasive set of innovations (Blust 1978a), suggesting a short period of unified development. The Oceanic subgroup is not disputed (see 2.3), nor is South Halmahera-West New Guinea.

3.3. The directions and dating of the early stages of Austronesian dispersal

In the case of a proto-language with just two primary subgroups, the favoured homeland is the zone where the two subgroups meet. If the Formosan-Philippine hypothesis is accepted, the most likely homeland for An is the Philippines and contiguous areas of Indonesia. If the Malayo-Polynesian hypothesis is accepted, the most likely dispersal centre is

Taiwan. Plainly, the archaeological evidence favours the latter. Proponents of a Taiwan dispersal centre do not exclude the possibility that branches of An were once spoken on the south coast of China as well, but were later extinguished by the southwards expansion of Han Chinese civilization.

Blust's internal classification of MP, together with the data on lexical replacement and the evidence that some of the interstages were extensive dialect chains, implies the following scenario.

1. For some centuries PMP probably persisted as a chain of dialects stretching around the coastal regions of the Philippines and extending into Sulawesi and Borneo.
2. The disintegration of this dialect chain probably occurred when one stream of MP speakers moved southeast into the Moluccas and became separated from the other PMP dialects. The Moluccan branch in turn expanded into a chain of dialects extending in an arc from Halmahera south to the Central Moluccas and then west along the Lesser Sundas from Timor. This dialect chain was ancestral to CEMP.
3. The dialect chain centred in the Philippines gradually disintegrated into several languages as Malayo-Polynesian speakers settled extensively around the coasts of Borneo, Sumatra, Java and Sulawesi.
4. A decisive break in the CEMP dialect chain probably occurred when one group of speakers moved to the Cenderawasih Bay area at the neck of the Bird's Head of New Guinea, where Proto-Eastern Malayo-Polynesian (PEMP) developed in isolation from the rest of CEMP. Cenderawasih Bay is the most likely homeland of the EMP subgroup for reasons discussed below (this section and 3.4).
5. PEMP broke up into two branches when some of its speakers moved to the eastern part of New Guinea or the Bismarck Archipelago (see section 2.4).

Historical linguistics lacks reliable methods of absolute dating. Its chief method is glottochronology, which uses a set of 100 or 200 core concepts with estimated standard replacement rates for each set. Glottochronology is problematic in a number of respects, but when applied to large language families yields matrices of results that are sometimes strongly suggestive. Blust (1993; 1999) has reconstructed 200 word basic vocabularies for various stages of An. From these it is possible to estimate time intervals between nodes of his family tree, using a replacement rate of almost 2 per cent per century. The estimated intervals for individual comparisons should

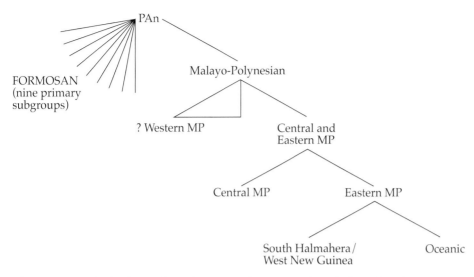

Figure 20.4. *The higher order subgroups of Austronesian. (After Blust.)*

CEMP *Central Eastern Malayo-Polynesian, containing about 600 languages, and encompassing CMP and EMP.*

CMP *Central Malayo-Polynesian, comprising over 100 languages, mainly in the Lesser Sundas and south Moluccas, with a few languages on the Bomberai Peninsula of Irian Jaya.*

EMP *Eastern Malayo-Polynesian, made up of the Oceanic and SHWNG groups.*

Formosan *There are 26 recorded Formosan languages, of which 14 are still spoken.*

MP *Malayo-Polynesian, containing about 1000 languages.*

Oceanic *Some 450–500 languages, all located east of 132°E and, in Melanesia, east of 136°E.*

SHWNG *South Halmahera-West New Guinea, made up of about 50 languages spoken in South Halmahera and in the Cenderawasih Bay area of Irian Jaya, and on islands between Halmahera and New Guinea.*

WMP *A residual category, consisting of those MP languages that are not CEMP: those of the Philippines, Borneo, Sumatra, Vietnam, the Malay Peninsula, the Lesser Sundas as far east as mid-Sumbawa, and Madagascar, some 400–500 in all.*

not begin until people moved from Taiwan to the Philippines. However, it is also possible that Malayo-Polynesian began to diverge in Taiwan. If the latter was the case, we might expect to find that some Formosan languages subgroup with Malayo-Polynesian. Blust does not think that any such languages have survived (excluding Yami of Lan-yu or Botel Tobago Island, a recent interloper from the Philippines), but they might have died out.

The glottochronological evidence indicates that there were only short intervals between PMP and the immediately following proto-languages depicted in Figure 20.4:

Systematic attempts to reconstruct Swadesh 200-item lists at various time-depths show clearly that Proto-Central-Eastern Malayo-Polynesian was hardly distinct from Proto-Malayo-Polynesian (98 per cent similar). A comparable relationship holds for Proto-Central Malayo-Polynesian in relation to Proto-Central-Eastern Malayo-Polynesian (96 per cent). The comparison of other pairs of these protolanguages yields only moderately lower values: PCMP and PMP (94 per cent), [Proto-Oceanic] and PCEMP (93 per cent), [Proto-Oceanic] and PMP (88 percent), [Proto-Oceanic] and PCMP (84 per cent). These figures reveal internal inconsistencies that hinder straightforward interpretation. (Blust 1993, 245)

These figures indicate time depths of roughly the following order: from PMP to PCEMP (100–150 years), PCEMP to PCMP (200–300 years), PMP to Proto-Oceanic (600–700 years) and PCEMP to Proto-Oceanic (300–400 years). Only the Oceanic group is indicated to be the product of a unified interstage lasting more than a couple of centuries.

The overall pattern of the glottochronological data is consistent with the archaeological evidence,

not be taken too seriously. For one thing, rates of lexical replacement are known to fluctuate and for another, the breakup of a language is usually a gradual process. But the overall pattern is indicative.

A comparison of the PAn list and the PMP list shows between 15 and 30 per cent replacement between these two stages, depending on how one scores certain variables. The lower figure converts to a most probable interval of about 800 years, the higher figure to an interval of around 1800 years. These rough estimates are not inconsistent with the archaeological evidence for a long pause (at least 1000 years) between the arrival of the Neolithic cultures in Taiwan and their appearance in the northern Philippines. It is possible that the whole of that pause was associated with the formation of PAn itself and that the development of a Malayo-Polynesian branch did which indicates a swift dispersal of Neolithic cultures from the Philippines across north and eastern Indonesia and into northwest Melanesia. It is likely that Eastern MP speakers undertook reconnoitering movements before 1500 BC eastwards along the north coast of New Guinea, leading to settlements on small islands or on the coast. But east of 136°E only one such settlement survived, linguistically. This was a movement to the Bismarck Archipelago, expressed archaeologically by the Far Western Lapita horizon, now firmly dated to 1500–1300 BC. The archaeological record tells us that, within a century or two, Lapita colonies were quickly established in many parts of the New Britain, New Ireland and St Matthias groups. However, bearers of the Lapita culture encountered populations of non-An speakers on the main islands of the Bismarck Archipelago, and for this and other reasons their settlements were largely confined to offshore islands. The Far Western Lapita people spoke a language of, or ancestral to, the Oceanic branch of Eastern MP. The stay-at-home branch in Cenderawasih Bay diversified into the South Halmahera-West New Guinea group.

There are strong grounds for placing the breakup of Proto-Oceanic at between 1500 and 1200 BC (see section 3.4). Taking 1500 BC as the baseline for Proto-Oceanic and using Blust's lexicostatistical percentages, we arrive at the following glottochronological estimates for the breakup of earlier stages: around 2000 BC for Proto-Central-Eastern Malayo-Polynesian, around 2200–2100 BC for Proto-Malayo-Polynesian and somewhere between 3000 and 4000 BC for PAn itself. At present the earliest secure dates for Neolithic sites in the eastern part of the Indonesian Archipelago are no earlier than the period 1500–1300 BC. As there are established dates of this order from various Lapita sites in Near Oceania, which can be connected with the Oceanic subgroup, there ought to be dates associated with the pre-Oceanic colonization of eastern Indonesia that are at least a few hundred years earlier.

3.4. Directions and dating of the Oceanic dispersal

The innovations defining Oceanic are numerous enough to indicate a few centuries of common development following the split from SHWNG and before the breakup of Proto-Oceanic. The innovations of Proto-Oceanic could have accumulated either in the Bismarck Archipelago or during a preceding period, when pre-Oceanic speakers were in moving along the north coast of New Guinea, or in both contexts.

On subgrouping grounds, the likeliest primary dispersal centre for Oceanic is in the Bismarck Archipelago (Blust 1978a; Ross 1988; cf. also Grace 1961; 1964). The subgrouping grounds are two: (1) The Oceanic branch has its immediate relatives around Cenderawasih Bay and in South Halmahera, and its next closest relatives are in the Moluccas and Lesser Sundas. (2) The centre of greatest genetic diversity within Oceanic itself appears to be in the Bismarck Archipelago.

Ross (1988) recognizes at least two and possibly three primary branches of Oceanic in the Bismarck Archipelago. One is the Admiralties group. Another is the widely dispersed Western Oceanic linkage. A third may be Mussau and other languages of the St Matthias group, to the north of New Ireland, for which evidence is limited. Ross divides Western Oceanic into three large linkages, which between them include all the An languages of New Guinea from Jayapura east, and all those of New Britain, New Ireland and the western Solomons. Each of the three large linkages appears to derive from an old dialect network. Blust (1978b) argues for a first two way split between the Admiralties and the rest of Oceanic, on the grounds that the rest all merge Proto-Oceanic *c and *j.

No very widely dispersed subgroups have been clearly identified elsewhere in Melanesia. Although a wider 'Eastern Oceanic' group, comprising at least Central Pacific plus Northern and Central Vanuatu and Southeast Solomonic has been mooted (Geraghty 1983; Lynch & Tryon 1985; Pawley 1972), the evidence for such a group is not, in my view, convincing.

By 1200 BC, Lapita colonists had settled Santa Cruz, Vanuatu and New Caledonia and, perhaps, Manus. These movements give a latest possible date for the breakup of Proto-Oceanic. There is reason to think that the peoples who first settled various parts of Remote Oceania spoke dialects of Proto-Oceanic rather than well-differentiated languages. That interpretation is based chiefly on the observation that there is no well-defined higher order subgroup of Oceanic that embraces both some languages of eastern Near Oceania and some of Remote Oceania. Such a subgroup might have developed had there been pauses on the way — say in the Solomons — long enough for a significant body of innovations to accumulate. As it is, the structure of the Oceanic family tree points to a rapid linguistic movement from Near Oceania across the southwest Pacific as far east as Fiji and Western Polynesia. This is supported by a second consideration. A representative sample of languages from Remote Oceania yields constructions of a proto-phonology and a proto-morpho-syntax that differ only slightly from reconstructions based on a sample representing the entire Oceanic subgroup.

3.5. Lexical reconstructions concerning early An technology

Detailed summaries and interpretations of the linguistic evidence for early An technology, social organization and cosmology are given by Blust (1995a) and Zorc (1994). The following account touches on only a few domains that are particularly relevant to the concerns of this paper, and draws mainly on Blust. I follow Blust's practice of showing the approximate regional and subgrouping distribution of reflexes of each reconstruction by adding regional names in parentheses after the reconstruction. The following abbreviations (in addition to those introduced in Fig. 20.1) are used: A = Admiralties, CP = Central Pacific, EI = Eastern Indonesia, M = Nuclear Micronesian, O = Oceanic, P = Philippines, T = Taiwan, WI = Western Indonesia, WO = Western Oceanic. I refer only in selected cases to the intra-Oceanic distribution of reflexes.

3.5.1. Grain crops

There is an extensive terminology for grain crops attributable to PAn: *pajay 'rice plant, rice in the field' (T, P, WI, EI), *beRas 'harvested rice, husked rice' (T, P, WI, EI), *Semay 'cooked rice' (T, P, WI), *baCaR 'millet sp.' (T, P, WI, EI), *beCeŋ 'millet sp., prob. foxtail millet' (T, P, WI, EI), *zawa 'millet sp.' (T, P, WI).

Existence of names for plants does not in itself establish that people cultivated the plants. As Blust (1995a, 469) observes, what places the linguistic evidence for PAn cultivation of grain crops beyond question is the array of related terms which pertain to cultivation. The following PAn terms are reconstructable: *binSiq 'seed rice' (T, P, WI, EI), *buRaw 'chase away, drive off, esp. birds or animals from the fields' (T, P, WI, EI), *eRik, iRik 'thresh grains by trampling' (T, WIN), *lepaw 'granary' (T, WI, EI), *lesuŋ 'mortar' (T, P, WI), *qaSelu 'pestle' (T, P, WI, EI), *paspas 'thresh grains by beating' (T, P), *qani 'to harvest, usu. rice' (T, P, WI), *qeCa 'rice husk' (T, P, WI), *tapeS 'winnow' (T, P, WI) and *zaRami 'rice straw, rice stalks left standing after harvest' (T, P, WI).

No terms for grain crops persist in Oceanic, indicating that this component of early An agriculture was lost by the An speakers who settled in Near Oceania, where root and tree crops were the staples.

3.5.2. Other crops and terms for gardening

Only one root crop can be attributed to PAn: *biRaq 'giant taro, *Alocasia* sp.' (T, P, WI, EI, WO, CP), and this refers to a famine food rather than a staple. However, other root crop names can be reconstructed for PMP and Proto-Oceanic: *qubi '*Dioscorea* yam' (P, WI, EI, A, WO, CP), *tales 'taro, *Colocasia esculenta*' (WI, EI, A, WO, CP) and *laqia 'ginger' (P, WI, EI, WO, CP).

Reflexes of PAn *CebuS 'sugarcane' are ubiquitous in the An-speaking world (T, P, WI, EI, WO, CP). The distinctive Formosan reflexes make it unlikely that the term was borrowed by Formosan speakers from MP speakers. Note also PMP *qusqus 'chew on sugarcane' (P, WI, O).

The fruit or edible parts of a number of tropical plants are important to An speakers south of Taiwan and reconstructions can be made to the PMP level, e.g. *punti 'banana' (P, WI, EI, A, WO, CP), *kuluR 'breadfruit' (P, WI, A, WO, CP, M), *niuR 'coconut' (P, WI, EI, A, WO, CP), *Rambia 'sago' (WI, EI, A, WO). (Except for bananas, none of these grows well in Taiwan.) The linguistic evidence for continuity from PMP to Proto-Oceanic to Proto-Central Pacific thus does not support the suggestion (see 2.5) that Lapita people added bananas, breadfruit and coconuts to their suite of crops in Near Oceania. They might, however, have incorporated locally-domesticated varieties into their repertoire.

A number of other terms for gardening are attributable to PAn or to PMP: PAn *tebaS 'cut, clear vegetation for cultivation' (T, P, WI, O), PAn *qumah 'swidden garden, cultivated area' (T, P, WI, EI, O), PMP *qucaN 'fallow land' (P, WI, O) (in POC *qutan 'bushland'), PMP *talun 'fallow land' (P, WI, O), *tanem 'to plant' (P, WI, O), PMP *hasek 'dibble' (P, WI, O), PMP *babaw 'to weed' (P, WI, O), PMP *zeket 'burn (fields etc.)' (P, WI, O).

3.5.3. Domesticated animals

PAn terms for three domestic animals are reconstructable: *asu or *wasu 'dog' (T, P, WI, EI), *beRek 'pig' (T, P, WI, O), *babuy 'pig' (T, P, WI, EI), *manuk 'fowl (*Gallus gallus*)' (P, WI, EI, O). *manuk was evidently polysemous, being the generic term for 'bird' as well as denoting fowls, but PMP *laluŋ 'cock, rooster' (P, WI, EI) refers specifically to fowls. The use of these terms alone does not guarantee that these animals were all domesticated but the occurrence of PAn *babuy-an 'pig pen' (T, F) suggests that pigs were kept; the evidence of archaeology and zoogeography supports such a view, also for dogs. Blust (1976) also proposes a distinction between PAn *beRek 'domesticated pig' and *babuy 'wild pig' (T, P, WI, EI), on the grounds that only the term *beRek is found east of the Wallace Line, and that pigs were probably first introduced to Near Oceania by An speakers. No pig species are native to Near Oceania (Groves 1995). Asian water buffalo, which today play an important part in wet-rice farming in An speaking regions, have probably been introduced from mainland Southeast Asia within the last 2000–3000 years. Words resembling Malay *kerbau* are widespread but appear to be loans from a Mon-Khmer source (Blust 1995a).

3.5.4. Pots and cooking
Four terms for kinds of earthenware cooking pots are reconstructable for PMP: *kuden 'cooking pot' (T, P, WI, EI, A, WO, CP), *balaŋa 'shallow cooking pot' (P, WO), *banaq 'pot, cooking vessel' (P, WI, WO) (which yields Proto-Oceanic *bwaŋa 'k.o. large pot') and *kalalaŋ 'narrow-necked water jar'. It is noteworthy that at least the first three terms are continued by some Oceanic languages and that a possible reflex of the fourth, *kalalaŋ, is found in Western Oceanic (Osmond & Ross 1998). Cooking pots rested on a *dalikan 'trivet, three stone support' (P, EI, EI). Only one of these terms, *kuden, is also reconstructable for PAn, but we can infer from the archaeological record that PAn speakers made earthenware vessels in a variety of forms and functions.

Among the several PMP terms for methods of cooking, one is of particular interest: *qumun 'earth oven' (EI, O, Belau), referring to the cooking of food between layers of leaves and hot stones in a pit. This method is rare in Indonesia but common in Near Oceania and it has been suggested (see 2.5) that earth ovens may have been added to the Lapita culture in Near Oceania. But the fact that reflexes of *qumun are also found in Central Malayo-Polynesian languages and in Belau indicates that the method was known to PCEMP speakers but fell out of use in Island Southeast Asia.

3.5.5. Weaving
Several terms relating to weaving with a loom are securely attributable to PAn: *tenun, *tinequn 'weave' (T, P, WI, EI), *baRija 'batten of the loom' (T, P, WI, EI), *qatip and *qatip-an 'part of the loom, prob. the breast-beam' (T, P, WI) , *qaŋi '?weaving spindle' (T, EI). Note also PAn *tapis 'skirt-like garment probably made of woven cloth' (T, P, WI, EI). Spindle whorls are now reported from TPK sites in Taiwan.

Houses: Terms for several kinds of dwelling are reconstructable for PAn and/or PMP: PAn *Rumaq 'dwelling house' (T, P, WI, EI, O), PMP *balay 'open-sided building' (WI, EI, O) (taking on the sense 'dwelling house' in CP), PMP *kamaliR 'men's house' (P, WI, O). The following terms provide evidence that PMP- (and probably PAn) speakers built sturdy gable-roofed thatched houses: PAn *qatep 'thatch of sago leaves' (F, P, WI, EI, O), PAn *SadiRi 'housepost' (T, P, WI, EI, O), PMP *bubuŋ 'ridgepole, ridge on the roof' (P, WI, EI, O), PMP *ataŋ 'cross-beam' (P, WI, EI), PMP *kasaw 'rafter' (P, WI, EI, O, PMP *turus 'house post' (P, WI, EI, O). Note also PMP *haRezan 'notched log ladder' and Proto-Oceanic *gabwari 'space under a house' (A, WO), which point to houses raised on posts and entered by a ladder.

3.5.6. Vessels and sailing
There can be no doubt that PMP speakers had the outrigger canoe complex, including the five-part canoe hull, with dugout underbody, built up by adding strakes and bow and stern pieces, and thwarts, outrigger, sail and steering paddle. The following terms are attributable to PMP (Blust 1976; Pawley & Pawley 1994): *(cs)a-R-man 'outrigger float' (WI, EI, A, WO, CP, M), PMP *seŋkar 'thwart or cross-seat in a boat' (P, WI, EI, CP, M), *papan 'plank, strake' (WI, EI, WO, CP, M), PMP *layaR 'sail' (T, WI, EI, WO, CP), *quli(n, ŋ) 'steering oar, steer' (P, WI, EI, A, WO, CP), *laŋe(nN) 'rollers, skids or blocks for raising or moving' (P, EI, CP, M), *limas 'bailer' (P, WI, EI, WO, CP, M), *lujan, *ujan 'load a vessel, cargo' (P, WI, A, WO, CP, M), *be(R)(c,s)say 'a paddle, to paddle' (P, WI, EI, A, WO, CP, M), *pa-luja ' a paddle, to paddle' (T, P, WI, O), *teken 'punting pole' (P, WI, EI, WO, CP). Proto-Oceanic *kati(R) 'small outrigger canoe, canoe hull' (WO) has cognates in the Philippines and Indonesia which generally refer to the outrigger float, so that the precise reference of PMP *katiR is uncertain.

The following terms are so far reconstructable only for PCEMP or PEMP: PCEMP *waŋka 'outrigger canoe' (EI, A, CP, M), PEMP *patotV 'sticks connecting outrigger to boom' (EI, WO, CP), PEMP *ta(d,r)i 'steer a course' (EI, WO).

A number of canoe types and terms for parts of the canoe or rigging are attributable to Proto-Oceanic but not on present evidence to earlier stages: *jila 'boom or yard of (triangular) sail' (A, WO, CP), *kiajo 'outrigger boom' (A, WO, M, CP), *katae, katea 'free side of canoe, opposite the outrigger' (WO, M, CP), *patar 'platform erected over hull and outrigger' (A, WO, CP), *ijuŋ 'projecting headboard of prow, often ornately carved' (A, WO, CP), *(q)oRa 'washstrake, prob. topstrake' (WO, CP), *muqa 'bow of boat (A, WO, CP), *muri 'stern' (A, WO, CP), *tola '?large canoe, canoe with hull built up by adding planks' (A, WO).

It is not possible to say whether speakers of the Formosan languages lost the outrigger complex or whether they never had it. The only terms in the boat domain that have Formosan as well as MP reflexes are *layaR 'sail' and *paluja 'paddle' (see above) and *qabaŋ 'canoe, poss. a dugout' (T, P, WI, EI, O). In historical times none of the Formosan peoples used outrigger canoes. But since the Chinese colonization of Taiwan in the seventeenth century many Formosan languages that were once spoken on the coast have disappeared or retreated inland. At any rate, the pattern of An movements in the period 2000 to 1000 BC (dated by the appearance of related Neolithic cultures) indicates that important advances in boat-building and sailing technology probably took place in the Philippines, Indonesia and Oceania.

3.5.7. Fishing
An extensive vocabulary of fish names and terms for fishing gear and techniques testify to the importance of fishing in early An communities. The following terms for fishing gear can be attributed to PMP and certain later interstages: *apuŋ apuŋ 'fishnet float' (WI, O), *bitik 'fishing pole' (P, WI, EI, O), *hapen 'fishing line' (P, WI, EI, O), *kebuR 'fish drive' (P, WI, O), *lawaq 'net, ?dipnet' (WI, O), *puket 'dragnet' (P, WI, EI, O), *saruk 'type of net' (WI, O), *tuba 'derris root fish poison' (P, WI, EI, O), *bubu 'basket, trap for fish' (T, P, WI, EI, O), *kawil 'fishhook' (T, P, WI, EI, O), *paen 'bait' (T, P, WI, O).

Only the last three of these terms are also attributable to PAn but it is certain that much maritime terminology has been lost by speakers of Formosan languages (see section 3.5.7).

3.6. Animal terms as evidence for the linguistic homeland
Blust (1982) notes that the distribution of terms for placental mammals provides evidence that PAn and PMP speakers lived west of the Wallace Line (Fig. 20.2), dividing the Southeast Asian and Australian faunal zones. Reflexes of PAn *luCuŋ 'monkey' (P, WI), *buhet 'squirrel' (P, WI), *qaRem 'scaly anteater' (T, WI) are found in Formosan and in WMP languages. Similarly, the distribution of terms for marsupial mammals indicates that PCEMP, PCMP and PEMP speakers lived east of the Wallace Line. Reflexes of PCEMP *kandoRa 'cuscus (*Phalanger* spp.) and *mandar 'bandicoot marsupial rat' are found in

the northern Moluccas and in certain Oceanic languages of the Admiralties and Western Oceanic subgroups. As the cuscus and bandicoot are not found in Remote Oceania, the same evidence can be used to narrow down the primary dispersal centre of Oceanic to Near Oceania.

3.7. Technology from PAn to Proto-Oceanic: continuity and change
There is a great deal of continuity in terminologies for various domains of technology and social organization between the PMP, Proto-Oceanic and Proto-Central Pacific stages, and to a lesser extent between PAn and PMP. This persistence of terminologies is powerful evidence that the speech communities associated with these stages of An maintained a considerable degree of cultural continuity. There is some linguistic evidence consistent with the addition of some components of technology and the loss of others at particular stages, but these changes are, to the linguist, less impressive than the continuity.

4. Notes on the demography and biology of the An language dispersal

The matter of 'Austronesian' origins is, fundamentally, a question about the history of languages and elements of culture encoded in language. By definition, there was genetic continuity in the transmission of speech among the communities who carried An languages from Taiwan to Polynesia, but the speakers need not have maintained genetic continuity in the biological sense. Nevertheless, anthropologists and geneticists have long been interested in the biological origins of Pacific Island peoples, especially the Polynesians.

Renfrew and Bellwood have raised interesting questions about the sociology and demography of the spread of farming and the spread of language families in prehistoric times. Did farming typically spread over large areas by migrating communities of farmers, who took their languages with them, or were the ideas and technology (and sometimes the languages) of the immigrants often adopted by autochthonous hunter-gatherer communities who were able to hold onto their territories?

In the case of Remote Oceania, no one disputes the primacy of An-speaking farmers. Bellwood has argued, I think entirely persuasively, that the spread of the Neolithic in Island Southeast Asia was also mainly the result of farming communities migrating rather than of the aboriginal hunter-gatherer populations adopting farming. The linguistic record for continuity in many domains of lexicon in large part supports his position. It would be astonishing, however, if there were no gene flow and cultural exchange between the immigrants and the autochthones at various stages in the dispersal of An-speaking farmers.

Large scale incursions of peoples of southern Mongoloid stock into Island Southeast Asia appear nowhere to have begun before 6000 to 7000 BP (Bellwood 1997). Who, then, were the peoples who occupied Island Southeast Asia in the early Holocene? A reasonable inference is that the inhabitants of this region 7000 years ago were most closely related to one or more of the following contemporary populations: the so-called Negrito peoples, who still occupy parts of the Philippines, the Malay Peninsula and the Andaman Islands; the Australians, and the Melanesian peoples who occupy much of Near Oceania. It is also possible that some degree of gene flow from the Asian mainland had occurred into Indonesia by this time.

What was the fate of the pre-Neolithic populations and cultures of Island Southeast Asia after the arrival of farming peoples? In several parts of the Philippines and in the Malay Peninsula, Negrito peoples continued to co-exist as separate communities with distinctive cultures, though they did not retain tenure over prime lands. All the surviving Negrito communities in the Philippines have adopted An languages (Reid 1991; 1994). Much less is known about developments in Indonesia. In Eastern Indonesia, two stocks of non-An (Papuan) languages are spoken in the Timor-Moluccas region. These have their immediate relatives among the West Papuan and Trans New Guinea families of New Guinea, respectively. Both appear to stem from relatively recent movements (probably within the last four millennia) from the western end of New Guinea. No other non-An languages survive in Indonesia from the pre-An era, and all we can say is that the pre-Neolithic populations there eventually ceased to exist as separate communities from the incoming farmers.

In Near Oceania the situation was different. Pre-Austronesian agriculture existed in New Guinea and when An speakers arrived they probably found the best coastal lands already well populated. The fact that Lapita settlements in the Bismarck Archipelago were mainly on offshore islands suggests that the main islands in this region remained the dominion of the established non-An communities, for at least the first few centuries. The encroachment by

An languages against Papuan languages in the larger Bismarck and Solomon islands was almost certainly a slow process. Papuan languages still predominate in the southern half of Bougainville and a few remain in New Britain, New Ireland and the central Solomons. It is hard to know to what extent the expansion of the territories of An languages was the result of language shift, or of An expansion coupled with intermarriage (for studies of language contact in the New Guinea area see Dutton & Tryon 1994; Bradshaw 1997; Thurston 1987).

Anthropologists have entertained the possibility that the peoples of Polynesia may be among the best living witnesses to the genetic makeup of early An-speaking peoples in Island Southeast Asia. One may suppose that: a) the ancestors of the Polynesians reached Polynesia from Southeast Asia without much interbreeding with other populations; and b) once in Polynesia they were isolated and so largely unaffected by gene flow from external sources. Supposition (b) is generally accepted, but certain qualifiers must be added to it. Serjeantson & Gao (1995) emphasize the importance of founder effects, selection, mutation and drift in changing the genetic profile of the Polynesians. Studies of haplotype diversity within the Cook Island sample indicate a marked reduction in diversity some 2200 years ago pointing to a population bottleneck at that time, presumably in Western Polynesia (Kayser et al. 2001). Skeletal remains associated with Lapita burials from St Matthias, Watom, Fiji and Tonga show certain features indicative of close relationship to Polynesians: relatively tall stature, rocker jaw, slight to moderate incisor shovelling, and a cluster of other traits. But in certain other features the Lapita skeletons differ from all contemporary Pacific Islanders (Pietrusewky 1989a,b). It is clear that Polynesians and other Pacific Island populations have undergone extensive changes in the last 2000–3000 years.

Supposition (a) is not strongly supported by the evidence from skeletal and genetic studies. Serjeantson (1989) and Hertzberg et al. (1989) discuss early evidence supporting a Southeast Asian origin of a number of genetic subsystems prominent in Polynesian populations. More recently, Golstein and Capelli and their co-workers (Capelli et al. 2001) found that the Y-chromosome haplogroup L, which is present in about a third of their Polynesian sample, and in Melanesia, has its highest frequency and diversity in Southern China and in Taiwan. But they also found two other markers, haplogroups C and F, that are common in Polynesians, less common in Near Oceania, rarer in Southeast Asia and rarer still in Taiwan.

Kayser and Stoneking and their associates found that the distribution of mtDNA 9 base pair deletion markers prevalent in Polynesia suggest a Taiwanese origin for this marker (Kayser *et al.* 2001). However, several recent studies using Y-chromosome data tell a more complicated story. Kayser and Stoneking studied the distribution of Y-chromosome polymorphisms, examining the distribution of two diagnostic mutations in haplotypes present in a sample of Polynesians from the Cook Islands. They conclude that one mutation probably arose in Melanesia about 11,000 years ago and another in Asia about the same time. Most Polynesians show a combination of mutations in mtDNA that are found in some 'Melanesians' and East Indonesians but which are absent in the Philippines and Taiwan. Oppenheimer and Richards propose an eastern Indonesian origin, more than 10,000 years ago, for this suite of mt DNA markers (see their paper in this volume).

Recent popular portrayals of competing models of the origins of the Polynesians in terms of an 'express train' versus a 'slow boat' from Southeast Asia are likely to bring more confusion than enlightenment. The new genetic studies are confirming what most anthropologists have long assumed: that the Polynesians are biologically of mixed origins. An *languages* travelled from Taiwan to western Polynesia in less than 2000 years. But the *people* who colonized western Polynesia brought with them some genetic markers that travelled from Taiwan and other markers that travelled from Indonesia and Near Oceania. It is safe to assume that, while the details may differ, the same generalization will be true of most other populations speaking an Oceanic language.

5. Conclusions

Linguistics and archaeology tell very similar stories concerning, respectively, the broad outlines of the An dispersal and the spread of the Neolithic in Island Southeast Asia and the South Pacific. Instances of sharp contradiction are few. However, the two disciplines have complementary strengths so that a union of the two tells a fuller story than either discipline can tell alone. The following synthesis, while it represents a personal view in some details, is essentially the standard interpretation.

While agriculture in all its varied forms provided the *necessary* conditions for the rapid colonization by Austronesian speakers of all the major islands of the Philippines, the Indo-Malaysian Archipelago and the South Pacific, and, later, Madagascar, it was

a continued set of improvements in the voyaging capacity that provided the *sufficient* conditions. Without sophisticated sailing technology no amount of agriculture would have led to the remarkable Austronesian diaspora. The first inter-island movements, in the region of Taiwan, were perhaps accomplished with the sailing raft and dugout canoe but the subsequent spread of Malayo-Polynesian languages was enabled by the outrigger canoe complex, perhaps developed in the Central Philippines.

PAn was spoken in Taiwan, which is both the area of the highest concentration of first-order subgroups and the site of the earliest Neolithic cultures in Island Southeast Asia. It may also have been spoken on the facing coast of South China but left no descendants there. Speakers of PAn cultivated a range of crops including rice, millet, taro and yams and kept fowls, pigs and dogs. They made pottery, wove cloth using the backstrap loom and were fishermen. They paddled dugout canoes and used sails but it is uncertain whether they had the outrigger canoe complex.

PAn broke up no later than some time in the third millenium BC, when some An speakers crossed from Taiwan to the Philippines. The migrants continued to cultivate the full range of grain and root crops known to PAn speakers as well as cultivating a number of tree crops that were possibly unknown or of little importance in Taiwan, including bananas, breadfruit and the coconut (see Paz this volume). They employed a wide range of fishing techniques, made red-slipped pottery in a variety of vessel shapes, and developed (if they did not bring with them) the outrigger complex. For a few centuries they probably remained concentrated in the Philippines, occupying the best coastal niches, and continued to speak variants of a single language, Proto-Malayo-Polynesian. But the development of efficient craft for ocean sailing, combined with a economy based jointly on farming and fishing, paved the way for their subsequent rapid spread across the Indo-Pacific region.

A decisive split in the Proto-Malayo-Polynesian dialect chain occurred when one stream of MP speakers moved southeast into the Moluccas and another stream or streams moved south and west, into Sulawesi and Borneo. These movements probably occurred no later than 2000 BC and in due course yielded at least two extensive dialect chains. One, Central-Eastern MP, extended in an arc from Halmahera to Timor and west along the Lesser Sundas. The other, nuclear Western Malayo-Polynesian, extended around the coasts of Borneo and Sulawesi and, probably later, to Sumatra, Java and Bali. Much later, around AD 700 to 1000, An speakers from western Indonesia were the first settlers of Madagascar. In the second millenium BC there were independent first settlements by MP speakers of two islands in western Micronesia — Guam and Belau.

In Island Southeast Asia An speakers encountered already established communities of foragers. In a few parts of the Philippines and the Malay Peninsula and in larger parts of the Timor and Halmahera regions these communities have survived as separate cultural entities, although in the Philippines they have adopted An languages. Elsewhere these foraging communities disappeared or lost their separate cultural identities.

The Central-Eastern MP dialect chain probably broke up when one group of speakers moved to the Cenderawasih Bay area on the Bird's Head of New Guinea, where Proto-Eastern MP developed. This movement must have taken place before 1500 BC. Speakers of PEMP did not retain grain crops. It is likely that, in the second millennium BC, Eastern MP speakers moved east along the north coast of New Guinea and established a number of settlements there, but only one such movement has left surviving linguistic descendants. This was a movement to the Bismarck Archipelago, expressed archaeologically by the Far Western Lapita culture, which appears there by 1500–1300 BC and which led to the well-marked Oceanic branch of Eastern MP.

On the main islands of the Bismarck Archipelago the bearers of the Lapita culture encountered well-established populations of non-Austronesian speakers and for this and other reasons their settlements were largely confined to offshore islands and patches of coastal territory. Some exchanges of technology and genes took place. Within a century or two, Lapita colonies were quickly established in many parts of the New Britain, New Ireland and St Matthias groups. By 1200–1100 BC, Lapita colonists had settled Santa Cruz, Vanuatu and New Caledonia and, no doubt, Manus (Admiralty Islands). These movements marked the latest possible date of the breakup of Proto-Oceanic. Within another couple of centuries, Lapita people had made the crossing to Fiji and soon after to western Polynesia. It was not until a good deal later, probably in the first millennium BC, that speakers of Oceanic languages established themselves firmly on the New Guinea mainland (and nearby small islands) east of 136°E. There they encountered established populations speaking Papuan languages, many of them probably cultivators. Oceanic languages in New Guinea remain largely confined to the coast.

Millennia of interaction with Papuan speakers in the Bismarck Archipelago and on the New Guinea mainland brought about profound changes in the culture and biology of An speakers in these regions. By contrast, once Lapita people reached the Central Pacific they remained relatively isolated. The distinctive ancestral Polynesian language, culture and genetic pattern developed in Western Polynesia between about 1000 BC and perhaps AD 400, when Polynesian speakers began to colonize Central and Eastern Polynesia. During much of this long period the Pre-Polynesians probably interacted with people of very similar language and biological type in Fiji but had no other outside contacts. The islands that make up 'Nuclear Micronesia' were probably not settled until late in the first millennium BC.

There is a high degree of continuity in terminologies for various domains of technology and social life between PMP, Proto-Oceanic and Proto-Central Pacific, and to a lesser extent between PAn and PMP. There is some linguistic evidence consistent with the addition of some components of technology and the loss of others at various stages, but these changes are to the linguist less impressive than the continuity.

Notes

1. I am particularly indebted to Peter Bellwood, Robert Blust and Roger Green for helpful discussions and comments on sections of this paper.
2. The next largest language family is probably Trans New Guinea (see 2.5), with 450–500 members.
3. The two largest sets of reconstructions with supporting cognate sets are those for Proto-Polynesian — some 3500 sets compiled by Biggs & Clark (in progress) — and for Pan or PMP and later interstages, with over 4000 sets compiled by Blust (in progress). Very substantial sets exist for Proto-Central and North Vanuatu (Clark in progress), Proto-South Hebridean (Lynch 2001), Proto-Micronesian (Bender *et al.* 1983) and Proto-Oceanic (Ross *et al.* 1998; forthcoming).
4. Kern observed that flora and fauna with a distinctive geographic distribution were a possible source of clues as to the homeland. He concluded that the immediate common ancestor of the family was spoken near the sea and on or near the Asian mainland.
5. Green (1991a) gives an extended discussion. For the record, the terms 'Near Oceania' and 'Remote Oceania' were first used in Pawley & Green (1973). The conceptual contrast was Green's, the names mine.
6. The earliest dates for Vanuatu are around 3000 BP. However, on logical grounds, it is likely that Vanuatu as settled at least as early as New Caledonia.
7. The Santa Cruz languages appear to contain both an

Oceanic and a Papuan layer (Lincoln 1978; Wurm 1978). The Papuan layer is presumably from a now extinct Papuan language of the main Solomons chain.

8. The lowest cognate percentages between Polynesian languages on the 200 meaning list are between 35 and 45 (Biggs 1978; Pawley 1996a). Compare English and German, which show 60 per cent cognation.

9. Dyen (1995) and Tsuchida (1976) propose a variant of this hypothesis in which the ancestor of Philippine-Formosan group was part of a chain which also includes at least some western Indo-Malaysian languages. Dyen labels this larger group 'Indo-Formosan'. The question is whether a dialect chain could have been maintained over a chain of islands as far flung as those of Taiwan, the Philippines and parts of western Indo-Malaysia and if so, for how long.

References

Adelaar, K.A., 1992. *Proto-Malayic: a Reconstruction of its Phonology and Parts of its Morphology*. Canberra: Pacific Linguistics C-119.

Aikins, C.M. & S.N. Rhee (eds.), 1993. *Pacific Northeast Asia in Prehistory*. Pullman (WA): Washington State University Press.

Allen, J. & C. Gosden, 1996. Spheres of interaction and integration: modelling the culture history of the Bismarck Archipelago, in Davidson *et al.*, 183–97.

Allen, J. & P. White, 1989. The Lapita homeland: some new data and an interpretation. *Journal of the Polynesian Society* 98(2), 129–46.

Athens, J.S., 1980. Pottery from Non Madol, Ponape, Eastern Caroline Islands. *Journal of the Polynesian Society* 89(1), 95–9.

Bellwood, P., 1978. *Man's Conquest of the Pacific*. London: Collins.

Bellwood, P., 1985. *Prehistory of the Indo-Malaysian Archipelago*. Sydney: Academic Press Australia.

Bellwood, P., 1995. Austronesian prehistory in Southeast Asia: homeland, expansion and transformation, in Bellwood *et al.* (eds.), 96–111.

Bellwood, P., 1997. *Prehistory of the Indo-Malaysian Archipelago*. (2nd edition.) Honolulu (HI): University of Hawaii Press.

Bellwood, P., 2000. The time depth of major language families: an archaeologist's perspective, in Renfrew *et al.* (eds.), 109–40.

Bellwood, P., 2001. Early agricultural population diasporas? Farming, language and genes. *Annual Review of Anthropology* 30, 181–207.

Bellwood, P., J. Fox & D. Tryon (eds.), 1995. *The Austronesians: Historical and Comparative Perspectives*. Canberra: Department of Anthropology, Research School of Pacific and Asian Studies, Australian National University.

Bender, B.W., 1971. Micronesian languages, in *Current Trends in Linguistics*, vol. 8: *Linguistics in Oceania*, ed. T. Sebeok. The Hague: Mouton, 426–65.

Bender, B.W. & J. Wang, 1985. The status of Proto-Micronesian, in Pawley & Carrington (eds.), 53–92.

Bender, B.W., R. Hsu, F. Jackson, K. Rehg, S. Trusell & J. Wang, 1983. Proto-Micronesian Cognate Sets. Unpublished printout, Department of Linguistics, University of Hawaii.

Biggs, B., 1978. The history of Polynesian phonology, in Wurm & Carrington (eds.), 691–716.

Biggs, B. & R. Clark, in progress. POLLEX. Proto-Polynesian lexicon. Computer files. Department of Maori Studies, University of Auckland.

Blust, R., 1976. Austronesian culture history: some linguistic inferences and their relations to the archaeological record. *World Archaeology* 8, 19–43.

Blust, R., 1977. The Proto-Austronesian pronouns and Austronesian subgrouping: a preliminary report. *University of Hawaii Working Papers in Linguistics*, 9.2, 1–15.

Blust, R., 1978a. Eastern Malayo-Polynesian: a subgrouping argument, in Wurm & Carrington (eds.), 181–234.

Blust, R., 1978b. *The Proto-Oceanic Palatals*. (Monograph 43.) Auckland: Polynesian Society.

Blust, R., 1981. The reconstruction of proto-Malayo-Javanic: an appreciation. *Bijd. tot de Taal-, Land -en Volkenkunde* 137, 456–69.

Blust, R., 1982. The linguistic value of the Wallace line. *Bijd. tot de Taal, Land- en Volkenkunde* 138.2–3, 231–50.

Blust, R., 1983–84. More on the position of the languages of eastern Indonesia. *Oceanic Linguistics* 22–23, 1–28.

Blust, R., 1984. Malaita-Micronesian: an Eastern Oceanic subgroup? *Journal of the Polynesian Society* 93, 99–140.

Blust, R., 1985. The Austronesian homeland: a linguistic perspective. *Asian Perspectives* 26, 45–67.

Blust, R., 1990. Summary report: linguistic change and reconstruction methodology in the Austronesian language family, in *Linguistic Change and Reconstruction Methodology*, ed. P. Baldi. (Trends in Linguistics Studies and Monographs 54.) Berlin: Mouton de Gruyter, 133–53.

Blust, R., 1991. The Greater Central Philippines hypothesis. *Oceanic Linguistics* 30, 73–129.

Blust, R., 1993. Central and Central Eastern Malayo-Polynesian. *Oceanic Linguistics* 32.2, 241–93.

Blust, R., 1994. The Austronesian settlement of mainland Southeast Asia, in *Papers from the Second Annual Meeting of the Southeast Asian Linguistics Society*, eds. K.L. Adams & T.L. Hudak. Tempe (AZ): Program for Southeast Asian Studies, Arizona State University, 25–83.

Blust, R., 1995a. Prehistory of the Austronesian-speaking peoples. *Journal of World Prehistory* 9.4, 453–510.

Blust, R., 1995b. The position of the Formosan languages: method and theory in Austronesian comparative linguistics, in Li *et al.* (eds.), 585–650.

Blust, R., 1999. Subgrouping, circularity and extinction: some issues in Austronesian comparative linguistics, in Zeitoun & Li (eds.), 31–94.

Blust, R., in progress. Austronesian Comparative Dictionary. Computer file. Department of Linguistics, University of Hawaii.

Bonhomme, T. & J. Craig, 1987. Radiocarbon dates from Unai, Baipot, Saipan: some implications for the prehistory of the Mariana Islands. *Journal of the Polynesian Society* 96(1), 95–106.

Bradshaw, J., 1997. The population kaleidoscope: another factor in the Melanesian diversity vs. Polynesian homogeneity debate. *Journal of the Polynesian Society* 106(2), 222–49.

Capelli, C., J.F. Wilson, M. Richards, M.P. Stumpf, F. Gratrix, S. Oppenheimer, P. Underhill, V.L. Pascali, T.M. Ko & D.B. Goldstein, 2001. A predominantly indigenous paternal heritage for the Austronesian-speaking peoples of insular Southeast Asia and Oceania. *American Journal of Human Genetics* 68(2), 432–43.

Chang, K.C., 1969. *Fengpitou, Tapenkeng and the Prehistory of Taiwan.* (Publications in Anthropology 73.) New Haven (CT): Yale University.

Chang, K.C., 1986. *The Archaeology of Ancient China.* (4th edition.) New Haven (CT): Yale University Press.

Chang, K.C., 1995. Taiwan Strait archaeology and Proto-Austronesian, in Li *et al.* (eds.), 161–83.

Clark, R., 1979. Language, in Jennings (ed.), 249–70.

Clark, R., in progress. Proto North and Central Vanuatu reconstructions. Computer files. Institute of Linguistics, University of Auckland.

Dahl, O., 1951. *Malgache et Maanjan: une comparison linguistique.* Oslo: Egeede-Instituttet.

Dahl, O., 1973. *Proto-Austronesian.* (Monograph Series 15.) Lund: Scandinavian Institute of Asian Studies.

Dahl, O., 1977. La subdivision de la famille Barito et la place du Malgache. *Acta Orientalia* 38, 77–134.

Davidson, J., F. Leach, G. Irwin, A. Pawley & D. Brown (eds.), 1996. *Oceanic Culture History: Essays in Honour of Roger Green.* Wellington: New Zealand Archaeological Association.

Dempwolff, O., 1934–38. *Vergleichende Lautlehre des austronesichen Wortschatzes.* 3 vols. Berlin: Reimer.

Dutton, T.E. & D.T. Tryon (eds.), 1994. *Language Contact and Change in the Austronesian World.* Berlin: Mouton de Gruyter.

Dyen, I., 1965. Formosan evidence for some new Proto-Austronesian phonemes. *Lingua* 14, 285–305.

Dyen, I., 1990. Homomeric lexical classification, in *Linguistic Change and Reconstruction Methodology*, ed. P. Baldi. Berlin/New York: Mouton de Gruyter, 211–30.

Dyen, I., 1995. Borrowing and inheritance in Austronesianistics, in Li *et al.* (eds.), 455–519.

Dyen, I. & S. Tsuchida, 1991. Proto-Philippine as the nearest relative of Proto-Formosan, in Harlow (ed.), 85–101.

Geraghty, P., 1983. *The History of the Fijian Languages.* (Special Publication 19.) Honolulu (HI): Oceanic Linguistics.

Geraghty, P., 1986. The sound system of Proto-Central-Pacific, in Geraghty *et al.* (eds.), 289–312.

Geraghty, P., 1996. Problems with Proto-Central Pacific,

in *Oceanic Studies: Proceedings of the First International Conference on Oceanic Linguistics*, ed. J. Lynch. Canberra, Pacific Linguistics C-133, 83–91.

Geraghty, P., L. Carrington & S.A. Wurm (eds.), 1986. *FOCAL II: Papers from the Fourth International Conference on Austronesian Linguistics.* Canberra: Pacific Linguistics.

Golson, J., 1977. No room at the top: agricultural intensification in the New Guinea Highlands, in *Sunda and Sahul: Prehistoric Studies in Southeast Asia, Melanesia and Australia*, eds. J. Allen, J. Golson & R. Jones. New York (NY): Academic Press, 601–38.

Golson, J., 1991. Bulmer phase II: early agriculture in the New Guinea Highlands, in Pawley (ed.), 484–91.

Grace, G.W., 1959. *The Position of the Polynesian Languages within the Austronesian (Malayo-Polynesian) Language Family.* (International Journal of American Linguistics, Memoir 16.) Bloomington (IN): Waverly Press.

Grace, G.W., 1961. Austronesian linguistics and culture history. *American Anthropologist* 63, 359–68.

Grace, G.W., 1964. Movement of the Malayo-Polynesians 1500 BC to AD 500: the linguistic evidence. *Current Anthropology* 5, 361–8, 403–4.

Grace, G.W., 1967. Effect of heterogeneity on the lexicostatistical test list: the case of Rotuman, in *Polynesian Culture History: Essays in Honor of Kenneth P. Emory*, eds. G.A. Highland, R.W. Force, A. Howard, M. Kelly & Y.H. Sinoto. (Special Publication 56.) Honolulu (HI): Bishop Museum, 289–302.

Green, R.C., 1979. Lapita, in Jennings (ed.), 27–60.

Green, R.C., 1991a. Near and Remote Oceania — disestablishing 'Melanesia' in culture history, in Pawley (ed.), 491–502.

Green, R.C., 1991b. The Lapita cultural complex: current evidence and proposed models. *Bulletin of the Indo-Pacific History Association* 12, 295–305.

Green, R.C., 2000. Changes over Time: Steps in the Human Colonisation of the Pacific Ocean. Printout circulated by the author.

Groves, C., 1995. Domesticated and commensal animals of Austronesia and their histories, in Bellwood *et al.* (eds.), 152–63.

Halim, A., L. Carrington & S.A. Wurm (eds), 1982. *Papers from the Third International Conference on Austronesian Linguistics, vol. 2: Tracking the Travellers.* Canberra: Pacific Linguistics, C-75.

Harlow, R. (ed.), 1991. *VICAL 2: Western Austronesian Languages. Papers from the Fifth International Conference on Austronesian Linguistics*, parts 1–2. Auckland: Linguistic Society of New Zealand.

Hertzberg, M., K.N.P. Mickleson, S.W. Serjeantson, J.F. Prior & R.J. Trent, 1989. An Asian-specific 9-bp deletion of mitochondrial DNA is frequently found in Polynesians. *American Journal of Human Genetics* 44, 504–10.

Hill, A.V.S. & S.W. Serjeantson (eds.), 1989. *The Colonization of the Pacific: a Genetic Trail.* Oxford: Oxford University Press.

Irwin, G., 1992. *The Prehistoric Exploration and Colonisation of the Pacific*. Cambridge: Cambridge University Press.

Jackson, F.H., 1983. The Internal and External Relationships of the Trukic Languages of Micronesia. Unpublished PhD dissertation, Department of Linguistics, University of Hawaii.

Jennings, J.D. (ed.), 1979. *The Prehistory of Polynesia*. Cambridge (MA) & London: Harvard University Press.

Kayser, M., S. Brauer, G. Weiss, P. Underhill, L. Roewer, W. Schiefenhovel & M. Stoneking, 2001. Melanesian origin of Polynesian Y chromosomes. *Current Biology* 10(20), 1237–46.

Kern, H., 1889. Taalkundige gegevens ter bepaling van het stamland der Maleisch-Polynesische volken. *Verglagen en Medelelungen der Kominlijke Akademie van Wetennschappen atdeeling Letterkunde* 3, 270–87.

Kirch, P.V., 1995. The Lapita culture of Western Melanesia in the context of Austronesian origins and dispersal, in Li *et al.* (eds.), 255–94.

Kirch, P.V., 1996. Lapita and its aftermath: the Austronesian settlement of Oceania, in *Prehistoric Settlement of the Pacific*, ed. W.H. Goodenough. (Transactions of the American Philosophical Society 86 part 5.) Philadelphia (PA): American Philosophical Society, 57–70.

Kirch, P.V., 1997. *The Lapita Peoples: Ancestors of the Oceanic World*. Oxford: Blackwell.

Kirch, P.V., 2000. *On the Road of the Winds: an Archaeological History of the Pacific Islands before European Contact*. Berkeley (CA): University of California Press.

Kirch, P.V. & R.C. Green, 2001. *Hawaiki, Ancestral Polynesia: an Essay in Historical Reconstruction*. Cambridge: Cambridge University Press.

Li, P., J.-K.C. Tsang, Y. Huang, D. Ho & C. Tseng (eds.), 1995. *Austronesian Studies Relating to Taiwan*. (Institute of History and Philology Symposium Series 3.) Taipei: Academia Sinica.

Lien, C., 1993. Pei-nan: a Neolithic village, in *People of the Stone Age*, ed. G. Burenhult. San Francisco (CA): Harper, 132–3.

Lincoln, P., 1978. Santa Cruz asAustronesian, in Wurm & Carrington (eds.), 929–67.

Lynch, J., 1981. On Melanesian diversity and Polynesian homogeneity: the other side of the coin. *Oceanic Linguistics* 20(2), 95–129.

Lynch, J. & D. Tryon, 1985. Central-Eastern Oceanic: a subgrouping hypothesis, in Pawley & Carrington (eds.), 31–52.

Marck, J., 2000. *Polynesian Language and Culture History*. Canberra: Pacific Linguistics.

Nothofer, B., 1975. *The Reconstruction of Proto-Malayo-Javanic*. (Verhandelingen van het Koninlijk Instituut voor Taal-, Land- en Volkenkunde 73.) The Hague: Martinus-Nijhoff.

Nothofer, B., 1988. A discussion of two Austronesian subgroups: Proto-Malay and Proto-Malayic, in *Rekonstruksi dan cabang-cabang bahasa Melayu induk*, eds. M. Ahmad & Z.M. Zain. Kuala Lumpur: Dewan Bahasa dan Putuska, Kementerian Pendidikan Malaysia, 34–58.

Nothofer, B. (ed.), 1996. *Reconstruction, Classification, De-*

scription – Festschrift in Honor of Isidore Dyen. Hamburg: Abera-Verlag.

Osmond, M. & M. Ross, 1998. Household artefacts, in Ross *et al.* (eds.), 67–114.

Pawley, A., 1972. On the internal relationships of Eastern Oceanic languages, in *Studies in Oceanic Culture History*, vol. 3, eds. R.C. Green & M. Kelly. (Pacific Anthropological Records 13.) Honolulu (HI): Bishop Museum, 1–142.

Pawley, A. (ed.), 1991. *Man and a Half: Essays in Pacific Anthropology and Ethnobiology in Honour of Ralph Bulmer*. Auckland: Polynesian Society.

Pawley, A., 1996a. On the position of Rotuman, in Nothofer (ed.), 85–120.

Pawley, A., 1996b. The Polynesian subgroup as a problem for Irwin's continuous settlement hypothesis, in Davidson *et al.* (eds.), 387–410.

Pawley, A., 1999. Chasing rainbows: implications of the rapid dispersal of Austronesian languages for subgrouping and reconstruction, in Zeitoun & Li (eds.), 95–138.

Pawley, A. & L. Carrington (eds.), 1985. *Austronesian Linguistics at the 15th Pacific Science Congress*. Canberra: Pacific Linguistics C-88.

Pawley, A. & R.C. Green, 1973. Dating the dispersal of the Oceanic languages. *Oceanic Linguistics* 12, 1–67.

Pawley, A. & R.C. Green, 1984. The Proto-Oceanic language community. *Journal of the Pacific History* 19, 123–46.

Pawley, A. & M. Pawley, 1994. Early Austronesian terms for canoe parts and seafaring, in Pawley & Ross (eds.), 329–61.

Pawley, A. & M. Ross, 1993. Austronesian historical linguistics and culture history. *Annual Review of Anthropology* 22, 425–59.

Pawley, A. & M. Ross (eds.), 1994. *Austronesian Terminologies: Continuity and Change*. Canberra: Pacific Linguistics C-127.

Pawley, A. & M. Ross, 1995. The prehistory of Oceanic languages: a current view, in Bellwood *et al.* (eds.), 39–74.

Pietrusewsky, M., 1989a. A study of the skeletal and dental remains from Watom Island and comparisons with other Lapita people. *Records of the Australian Museum* 41, 235–92.

Pietrusewsky, M., 1989b. A Lapita-associated skeleton from Natunuku, Fiji. *Records of the Australian Museum* 41, 297–325.

Reid, L., 1982. The demise of Proto-Philippines, in Halim *et al.* (eds.), 201–16.

Reid, L., 1991. The Alta languages of the Philippines, in *VICAL 2: Western Austronsian Languages: Papers from the Fifth International Conference on Austronesian Linguistics parts 1–2*, ed. R. Harlow. Auckland: Linguistic Society of New Zealand, 265–97.

Reid, L., 1994. Unravelling the history of the Negrito languages, in Dutton & Tryon (eds.), 363–88.

Reland, H., 1708. *Dissertatio de linguis insularum quarundem orientalun, partes tres*. Trajecti ad Rhenum, 55–139.

Renfrew, C., A. McMahon & L. Trask (eds.), 2000. *Time Depth in Historical Linguistics*. (Papers in the Prehistory of Languages.) Cambridge: McDonald Institute for Archaeological Research.

Ross, M., 1988. *Proto-Oceanic and the Austronesian Languages of Western Melanesia*. Canberra: Pacific Linguistics, C-98.

Ross, M., 1992. The sound of Proto-Austronesian: an outsider's view of the Formosan evidence. *Oceanic Linguistics* 31, 23–64.

Ross, M., 1995. Some issues in Austronesian comparative linguistics, in *Comparative Austronesian Dictionary*. vol. 1, ed. D.T. Tryon. Berlin: Mouton de Gruyter, 45–120.

Ross, M., 1996. Is Yapese Oceanic?, in Nothofer (ed.), 121–66.

Ross, M., A. Pawley & M. Osmond, 1998. *The Lexicon of Proto Oceanic*, vol. 1: *Material Culture*. Canberra: Pacific Linguistics.

Ross, M., A. Pawley & M. Osmond, forthcoming. *The Lexicon of Proto Oceanic*, vol. 2: *The Physical Environment*; vol. 3: *Flora and Fauna*; vol. 4: *Proto-Oceanic Society*. Canberra: Pacific Linguistics.

Serjeantson, S.W., 1989. HLA genes and antigens, in Hill & Serjeantson (eds.), 120–73.

Serjeantson, S.W. & X. Gao, 1995. *Homo sapiens* is an evolving species: origins of the Austronesians, in Bellwood *et al.* (eds.), 165–80.

Shih, X-B., 1993. Neolithic cultural systems in China, in Aikins & Rhee (eds.), 125–32.

Shutler, R. & J.C. Marck, 1975. On the dispersion of the Austronesian horticulturalists. *Archaeology and Physical Anthropology in Oceania* 10(2), 81–113.

Spriggs, M., 1996. What is Southeast Asian about Lapita?, in *Prehistoric Mongoloid Dispersals*, eds. T. Akazawa & E. Szathmary. Oxford: Oxford University Press, 324–48.

Spriggs, M., 1997. *The Island Melanesians*. Cambridge (MA) & Oxford: Blackwell.

Spriggs, M. & A. Anderson, 1993. Late colonisation of East Polynesia. *Antiquity* 67, 200–217.

Summerhayes, G.R., 2000. *Lapita Interaction*. (Terra Australia 15, Department of Archaeology and Natural History and the Centre for Archaeological Research.) Canberra: Australian National University.

Swadling, P. & J. Muke, forthcoming. *9000 years of Gardening: Kuk and the Archaeology of Agriculture in Papua New Guinea*. Port Moresby: Papua New Guinea National Museum.

Terrell, J., 1986. *Prehistory in the Pacific Islands: a Study of Variation in Language, Customs and Human Biology*. Cambridge: Cambridge University Press.

Terrell, J. & R. Welsch, 1997. Lapita and the temporal geography of prehistory. *Antiquity* 71, 548–72.

Thurston, W., 1987. *Processes of Change in the Languages of North-western New Britain*. Canberra: Pacific Linguistics B-99.

Tsang, Cheng-hwa, 1995. New archaeological data from both sides of the Taiwan Straits and their implications for the controversy about Austronesian origins and expansion, in Li *et al.* (eds.), 185–225.

Tsuchida, S., 1976. *Reconstruction of Proto-Tsouic Phonology*. Tokyo: Institute for the Study of Languages and Cultures of Asia and Africa.

Walter, R., 1989. Lapita fishing strategies: a review of the archaeological and linguistic evidence. *Journal of Pacific Studies* 13(1), 127–49.

Welch, D., in press. Archaeological and paleoenvironmental evidence of early settlement in Palau. *Bulletin of the Indo-Pacific Prehistory Association* 22.

White, J.P., 1996. Rocks in the head. Thinking about the distribution of obsidian in New Oceania, in Davidson *et al.* (eds.), 199–209.

Wolff, J., 1995. The position of the Austronesian languages of Taiwan within the Austronesian group, in Li *et al.* (eds.), 521–83.

Wurm, S., 1978. Reefs-Santa Cruz: Austronesaian but!, in Wurm & Carrington (eds.), 969–1010.

Wurm S. & L. Carrington (eds.), 1978. *Second International Conference on Austronesian Linguistics: Proceedings*. Canberra: Pacific Linguistics C-61, 691–716.

Yan, W., 1993. Origins of agriculture and animal husbandry in China, in Aikins & Rhee (eds.), 113–24.

Yen, D., 1973. The origins of Oceanic agriculture. *Archaeology and Physical Anthropology in Oceania* 8(10), 68–85.

Yen, D., 1991. Domestication: the lesson from New Guinea, in Pawley (ed.), 558–69.

Zeitoun, E. & P. Li, 1999. *Selected Papers from the Eighth International Conference on Austronesian Linguistics*. Taipei: Academia Sinica, Institute of Linguistics.

Zorc, D., 1986. The genetic relationships of Philippine languages, in Geraghty *et al.* (eds.), 147–73.

Zorc, D., 1994. Austronesian culture history through reconstructed vocabulary, in Pawley & Ross (eds.), 541–94.

Chapter 21

Island Southeast Asia: Spread or Friction Zone?

Victor Paz

The tone-setting papers by Colin Renfrew (2000) and Peter Bellwood (Bellwood this volume) discuss correlations between language and farming dispersal in antiquity, the main theme of the McDonald symposium. They rightly clarify that there are different scales in looking at the past, and the scale where one observes best, in space and time, a pattern linking language and agricultural dispersal may be a very large one. In Bellwood's paper, he adopts the terms 'spread' and 'friction' zone to describe two differing kinds of agricultural dispersal (see Bellwood this volume, Table 2.1). Island Southeast Asia, in the total scheme of dispersing agriculturalist Austronesian speakers, is wholly considered a 'spread zone', as opposed to the 'friction zone' status of New Guinea and northern Sahul in general (see also Hurles in this volume).

This paper weighs this observation against the current archaeobotanical data of Island Southeast Asia, as a starting-point towards addressing the wider question of an Austronesian language family spread by agriculturists. On a smaller scale of analysis, as presented in this work, the picture is more complex, and leads to possibilities of rethinking or reshaping of established ideas.

Island Southeast Asia is in the direct path of the language-farming spread from Eurasia towards the Pacific, articulated as the Austronesian dispersal hypothesis. According to this hypothesis, the movement of people from Mainland Southeast Asia to Taiwan took place around 5000 BP and carried on to the Philippine Islands starting around 4000 BP (Bellwood 1991; 1997; Spriggs 1995; Kirch 1997). The expansion continued to the easternmost islands of Oceania, and also to the west, to the island of Madagascar off the coast of Africa. The engines of this dispersal are recognized as manifold, but the explanation for the first leg has usually focused on cereal agriculture, together with a founder-focused ideology observed widely in current and historical

ethnographies from the region (Bellwood 1996; Fox & Sather 1996).

Not all scholars working in this part of the world agree with the timing and direction of the Austronesian dispersal. Details of the debate have been articulated in several papers and will not be repeated here (see Oppenheimer 1998 for recent critique & Bellwood 2000 for response). Suffice it to say that most criticisms focus on one aspect of the hypothesis and seldom consider the whole Austronesian picture (for instance, Solheim (1996; 1964) and Meacham (1988; 1995) for Island Southeast Asia, Terrell *et al.* (2001; Terrell 2000) for Sahul and Melanesia). This perhaps may be the reason why the current 'Out-of-Taiwan' hypothesis for Austronesian dispersal is so widely accepted. Its ability to connect and address trends for both Island Southeast Asia *and* Oceania is its main strength as a model, which makes its components good case studies for testing and scrutiny.

While the debate on the nature of Austronesian dispersal has been toned down from its peak in the 1980s (Solheim 1988; Meacham 1988; Bellwood 1988; Spriggs 1989), and while the current Out-of-Taiwan hypothesis is the dominant view, there is still room to aspire for greater clarity in our understanding of the processes involved. This is especially so for questions of the specific origin of the spread, its time depth, and the actual engines that promoted Austronesian dispersal so rapidly across such a vast area.

The current dominant narrative is argued from two main disciplinary data sets: archaeology (Kirch & Green 2001; Bellwood 1997) and linguistics (Blust 1976; 1995a,b; Pawley & Ross 1993). It is supported in part by a third data set derived from population genetics (Melton *et al.* 1995; Sykes *et al.* 1995). The first stage of the Austronesian dispersal into Island Southeast Asia is stated to reflect a 'spread zone' situation by Bellwood (Bellwood this volume), whereas coastal New Guinea is considered a friction

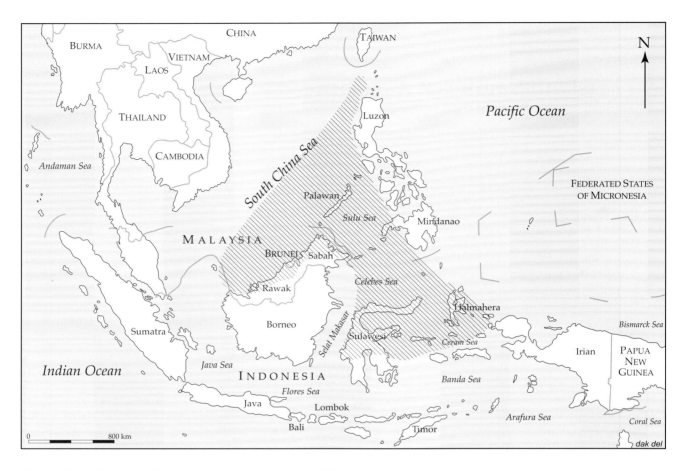

Figure 21.1. *The general extent of the 'spread zone' in Island Southeast Asia.*

zone (Bellwood this volume), where the rate of dispersal is seen to be slower. Our current understanding of the spread of the Austronesians thus has rapid dispersal from Taiwan down to Luzon via the Batanes islands, then going south to the Visayan islands and Mindanao, and moving further southeast towards Melanesia and southwest to Borneo. The rapidity of the dispersal was mainly due to the probably low population densities of the gathering and hunting communities encountered in its path (Bellwood 1997; this volume). It may also be possible that, in some cases, remote and small islands in the path of the dispersal were previously uninhabited. Intervisibility between islands located in calm inner seas allowed effective and rapid travel in single-hulled outrigger canoes.

The Austronesian dispersal is articulated mainly through historical linguistic reconstructions based on the comparison of existing languages in Island Southeast Asia and Oceania. The archaeological data base reveals distinct horizons where one can infer a regional shift, commencing in the north about 5000 BP

and continuing to 3500 BP in the south, from preceramic complexes predominantly of pebble or flake tools (Reynolds 1993) to a complex of red-slipped pottery (some decorated) and uni-bevelled stone adzes (Bellwood 1997, 202).

Agriculture, specifically cereal agriculture, is argued for in this hypothesis mainly through the comparative linguistic reconstruction of proto-languages e.g. Malayo-Polynesian (Blust 1979). It is, for example, possible to reconstruct specific words relating to food processing, tools and field systems (Wurm & Wilson 1975; see Pawley, this volume). The linguistic data also set the homeland of the early Austronesian languages and the directions of their spread. Archaeology provides the time depth for this narrative. Though there are limited reports of cereal remains in Taiwanese sites (see Bellwood 1997, 211–12; Tsang 1995), the presence of the red-slipped pottery and uni-bevelled adzes are sometimes seen as part of a package that was carried with cereal agriculture.

With the linguistic conclusions fitting the general archaeological picture of a north–south spread of red-slipped pottery, polished adzes and domestic animals, all secured temporally by unproblematic radiocarbon dates, the hypothesis of Austronesian expansion is relatively well anchored in its early stages, and also in its later stages in Oceania. Unfortunately, however, the same secure temporal anchoring cannot be said to apply in most of Island Southeast Asia, where there are limited sites with secure dates (Spriggs 1989). The presence of cereal agriculture beyond Taiwan, in this period, is therefore argued more from the totality of the Austronesian dispersal hypothesis than from direct data.

My concerns are not at the level of whether or not there was an Austronesian dispersal, but over the nature of this dispersal and its chronology. I accept that Austronesian speakers most likely spread through Island Southeast Asia around 4000 BP, but my data question the seemingly homogeneous view scholars take when looking at this region, and at the same time cast doubt on the significance of cereal agriculture in the early stages, especially around the northern half of the Philippine archipelago.

Relevant archaeobotanical data

Archaeobotanical data must play an important role in clarifying questions about the spread of cereal agriculture. We can state that millet has never been found in secure archaeological contexts in Island Southeast Asia. There are claims, as for Bekes in Luzon (Bodner 1986) and East Timor (Glover 1979; 1986), but they are based on weak determinations. We concentrate therefore on the archaeobotanical data for rice (*Oryza sativa* L.).

So far, only two sites in Island Southeast Asia (excluding Taiwan) have rice remains and pottery in secure association (Fig. 21.2). The oldest is Gua Sireh, a cave in western Sarawak with a Neolithic phase starting 4500 years ago. This site yielded pottery with carved, cord-wrapped or basketry-wrapped paddle-impressed surfaces; red slip and incision were both rare (Bellwood 1997, 237; Datan & Bellwood 1991). Rice remains were recovered from the soil matrix and as pottery fabric inclusions. A charred rice grain inclusion in one sherd was AMS C14-dated to 3850±260 BP (*c.* 2334 cal BC [CAMS 725] (Beavitt *et al.* 1996, 29; Datan & Bellwood 1991, 391).

The other site is Ulu Leang in the Maros district of south Sulawesi, a cave with early deposits characterized by preceramic Toalian stone tools. After 2500 BC this stone tool assemblage was joined by plain non-slipped globular earthenware pottery (Glover 1976). Ulu Leang has the largest quantity of recov-

ered charred rice remains in Island Southeast Asia (Glover 1976; 1979), from or near a hearth feature. Unfortunately, however, there has been unobserved disturbance, as reflected in the large discrepancies in the C14 dates for this context. There has also been no opportunity for AMS dating since no grains survived after the identification (Glover & Higham 1996, n. 10). However, in randomly choosing one of the Ulu Leang environmental samples stored in the Institute of Archaeology in London, I recovered a grain broken before charring and two fragments of charred rice hull from a context in Trench C, approximately 10 metres from the previously discoveries. The nearest recorded disturbance is approximately 2 metres away (Glover 1977, fig. 12), so hopefully these specimens can be AMS dated in the future.

In the site of Sembiran in northern Bali, rice phytoliths were identified in soil samples, associated with an assemblage of Indian pottery, metal implements and black-slipped pottery with rice inclusions. The site is dated typologically by the Indian pottery to 200 BC to AD 300, but rice husk in one black-slipped sherd has been AMS C14-dated to 2660±100 BP (*c.* 800 cal BC [CAMS 723]: Ardika & Bellwood 1991, 225).

In the Philippines, two sites with reported rice grains are Bekes in the Cordillera mountains of Luzon (Bodner 1986) and Santiago Church in Panay island (Gunn 1997). Unfortunately, in both cases the grains were uncharred and their identification is not secure. There is, however, one secure discovery of rice in the Philippines, from the open site of Andarayan in the Cagayan Valley, Luzon. Rice hull and stem fragments occur in the fabrics of red-slipped earthenware sherds, one of which was AMS-dated to 3400±125 BP. An associated piece of wood charcoal gave a traditional C14 date of 3240±160 BP [SFU-86], or *c.* 1500 BC (Snow *et al.* 1986, 9). Another site with possible rice inclusions in pottery is Unto on Negros, but there is only one reported sherd with plant inclusions and the determination of '*Oryza* sp.' is tentative (Bacus 1997; Bacus & Lucero 1999).

In East Malaysia, apart from Gua Sireh, rice inclusions have been identified in 3 sherds from Bukit Tengkorak in Sabah, and in 32 sites from Sarawak (excluding Gua Sireh and Niah which I discuss separately). These contexts date generally between 3000 and 400 BP (Doherty *et al.* 2000). In the case of the Niah West Mouth in Sarawak, where several pottery sherds were recovered with rice inclusions, preliminary work on the environmental bulk samples taken in the 2000 season (see Barker *et al.* 2000) reveals no macro-remains of rice (Paz, unpubl. report). Any

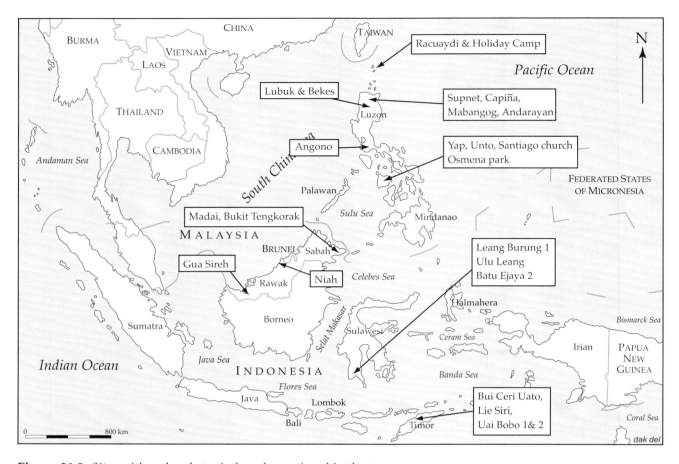

Figure 21.2. *Sites with archaeobotanical work mentioned in the text.*

argument that the cave was ever used for rice process-ing has yet to be proven convincingly.

There are several ways to explain the presence of rice inclusions in pottery, some being as follows:

1. The community created pots and produced rice at the same time. With this possibility, there is always a good chance for rice processing by-prod-ucts to enter the clay used for pottery making. Chaff can also be added deliberately to the clay matrix to serve as temper.

2. The rice was a trade good, but was consumed and processed near the pottery production area. Such situations can be observed in recent ethno-graphies (personal experience with pottery com-munities in Maripipi island, Philippines; see Hunter-Anderson *et al.* 1995, 75; Ushijima & Zayas 1994).

3. The pottery was traded into a site that did not produce its own pottery from a community that produced/consumed rice. Not all settlements could produce pots, limited as they were by the availability of clay sources.

To differentiate between these three possibilities, one can examine the ratio of pottery with rice inclusions to the total recovered pottery (as has been done for the Sarawak sites), determine the source of the pot-tery from fabric analyses, search for macro rice-plant remains in the soil, and record any presence of rice phytoliths. A positive result for two out of four of these processes may support an argument for rice production in a site. As it stands, the presence alone of pottery with rice inclusions/impressions need not necessarily mean rice was cultivated in the immedi-ate area of the site.

Looking at the results of archaeobotanical in-vestigation in Island Southeast Asia, it is worth stress-ing that most sites with pottery have not produced macro-remains of rice. For sites within the relevant time frame for Austronesian dispersal there are sev-eral examples. In the Cagayan Valley, Luzon, there are three sites with archaeobotanical data sets — one cave site in the foothills called Mabangog (Ogawa 1998; 1999) and two shell midden sites near the Cagayan river called Supnet and Capiña (Tsang 1998;

Paz 2001). In these sites, red-slipped pottery has been recovered within the general time frame of interest, but no rice or millet remains came out of the environmental flot samples (Paz 2001). We had the same negative results with a rock-shelter site in Angono, Rizal province, Luzon.

In Sabah, the cave site of Madai 1 did not reveal any rice remains. However, several charred remains of plant tubers were identified, including *Dioscorea alata* and probably *Colocasia esculenta* (Paz 2001). In Leang Burung-1, South Sulawesi, red-slipped pottery and remains of tubers also occurred, but the latter are at the weaker end of the scale of confidence, e.g. cf. *Dioscorea* sp. and probably *Colocasia esculenta*. In eastern Timor, the cave sites of Bui Ceri Uato, Lie Siri, Uai Bobo 1 and 2 produced many plant remains (Glover 1977; 1979; 1986), but no rice (Bellwood 1997; Glover 1986). A possible Job's tears seed (*Coix* sp.) and one determined as *Setaria* sp. (foxtail millet) were recovered, but identified at very low levels of confidence (Glover 1979, table 4).

Turning to sites in more recent periods, it is interesting to see that rice macro-remains are also absent while pottery is ubiquitous. The test excavation at Holiday Camp, in the Batanes Islands, produced red-slipped sherds but no rice. This site has a single AMS C14 date of cal. AD 70 to 330 (Paz 2001). Phytolith extraction and determination methods were applied in the investigation of the site to look for diagnostic rice phytoliths, but with no positive results. The Batanes settlement site of Rakwaydi was inhabited between the fourteenth and nineteenth centuries AD, but no rice remains were recovered, even in an excavated kitchen hearth (see Paz 2001; Paz *et al.* 1998). The same is true for the two settlement sites of Unto and Yap on Negros, both argued to have been occupied by chiefdom communities (see Bacus 1997; Bacus & Lucero 1999; Paz 2001). The later deposits in Batu Ejaya cave in South Sulawesi are also positive for pottery but have a total absence of rice (Di Lello 1997, app. A; Paz 2001).

All in all, in Island Southeast Asia, there are 23 sites where archaeobotanical sampling has been applied. Only one, Gua Sireh, has reported rice phytoliths from the matrix of the site. There are at least 36 sites with reported rice inclusions in pottery fabrics; one in Luzon, one in Negros island, one in Sabah (Bukit Tengkorak) and the rest in Sarawak.

One may argue that the current data set is insufficient and deals in most cases with archaeological deposits too young to be relevant for understanding Austronesian dispersal. Likewise, people may argue that rice remains do not survive or that it

is a weak position to argue from negative evidence. But rice has fairly robust seeds and hulls, even when charred, as seen in numerous sites in Thailand (Thompson 1996), in South Asia (see Glover & Higham 1996, 418), and in more than 100 sites in China (An 1999; Yan 1991). Thus, it is safe to say that if rice was consumed by a community in association with hearths or combustion areas, then rice macro-remains will most likely survive (see Paz 2001; Stevens 2000; Fuller 1999 for discussions on taphonomic processes concerning cereal preservation). In processing rice for everyday consumption, pounding and winnowing is done in the habitation space, as we can see from ethnographic and historical data from eastern South Asia and Island Southeast Asia (see Paz 2001 for a review).

The following observations and conclusions can now be formulated:

1. In Wallacea, a pottery-rice agriculture correlation for the period of early Austronesian dispersal cannot be supported. The only region that partially supports such a correlation is Sarawak. But here, the associated pottery is not red-slipped but paddle-impressed.

2. The data set dispels long-held ideas that plant remains hardly ever survive in tropical conditions. The ability to locate plant remains in Southeast Asia is ever-growing, especially for seed/ fruits and tubers.

3. The successful identification of root crops and tubers (at different scales of confidence) in sites such as Madai 1, Leang Burung 1, Capiña, Supnet, and younger sites such as Rakwaydi, allows us better to investigate plant utilization, introductions, and the spreads of agricultural systems.

4. There is a recognition of the utility of using plant biogeographic knowledge to approach central questions of research. For instance, recognizing yam (*Dioscorea alata*) as an indicator of human dispersal requires biogeographic understanding of its origins and suggests that it could only have spread to Wallacea and beyond through human agency (see Paz 1999).

Possible fine-tuning of the Austronesian dispersal hypothesis

Remembering that the 'Out-of-Taiwan' view is the basic premise for discussion, how does the regional archaeobotanical data set affect understanding? Whatever package of materials and ideas was brought at first by Austronesian migrants, the package might have been broken up rapidly. As a consequence of this thinking, whilst accepting that cereal agriculture may have spread with the initial Austronesian dispersal, it questions whether it ever became widely established. The doubts are based on the absence of rice macro-remains in sites with pottery. Furthermore, in the rare cases when both rice and pottery were present in the same context, 2 out of 3 times (Gua Sireh & Ulu Leang) the pottery was not of red-slipped design.

So if we are to hold to the Taiwan origin for the initial dispersal of Austronesians, I propose that the dispersal may have been of the 'spread' type through a narrow corridor, at least towards Oceania. I would argue that this possible corridor of rapid spread lay between the western Philippine Islands and eastern Borneo/northern Sulawesi, where at a later time rice-based cultures took deep roots (Fig. 21.1). I argue this hypothesis from the following points:

1) Environmental variables

Most of the Philippine Islands would have been friction zones for spreading Austronesian agriculturalists because of thick rainforest cover. Even as recently as 1900, 70 per cent of the islands were still covered in old growth forest (Heaney & Regalado 1998, 63). There is also the issue of the photoperiod-sensitive nature of domesticated rice. Transporting rice varieties from the higher latitudes of southern China/ Taiwan to southern lands, where the daylight pattern through the year is different, must have created real difficulties in the first instance (Eckardt 2000; Poonyarit *et al.* 1989; Oka 1988). Rice would also be susceptible to pests and the expected annual typhoons. It only takes a successive failure of crops for a family of new settlers to lose their capacity to produce seed rice for another cycle. Perhaps two consecutive failures would spell total disaster for the entire rice crop of a new community, which had no easy way of acquiring more seed.

2) Conflict and contact with early populations

The existence of established communities of pre-Austronesian ethnolinguistic groups would have slowed down the spread. Most if not all islands in Southeast Asia were already inhabited by likely ancestors of the various Agta and other Australo-melanesian populations (see Bellwood 1997, 71–3; Reed 1904, 14 for review). The Agta languages of Luzon reveal a body of non-Austronesian terms, perhaps a residue of an early pidgin or trade language formed to facilitate interaction between Agta ancestors and in-migrating Austronesians (Reid 1994b). Eventually, the Agta shifted to an Austronesian lan-guage, which supports the possibility that the two groups had to negotiate their relationships constantly with each other. Some of these interactions may have been violent, since historical accounts show a wider distribution of Agta than now and the Spanish often recorded them in conflict with agriculturalists (e.g. Reed 1904; Medina 1973 [1630]). In my own ethno-historical work in remote Agta communities in the Sierra Madre Mountains of Luzon, I was able to document cases of raids (*kayaw*) which took place in the later half of the twentieth century. In one instance, the mourning ceremony for an important member of an Agta community triggered the organization of a raiding party that crossed the Sierra Madre mountain range to the Cagayan Valley and attacked an unsuspecting unrelated Agta riverside camp. Until the 1970s, further raids also extended to non-Negrito communities (see Paz 1999). It is not difficult to imagine that, during the initial dispersal of the Austronesians, their relations with the original population might have hindered rapid and easy dispersal.

3) A linguistic observation

In the sub-grouping of the Austronesian language family, the languages of the Philippine Islands and those found in Sundaland are grouped as Western Malayo-Polynesian (Blust 1980; Dyen 1965; 1971, in Bellwood 1997). The speed of early Malayo-Polynesian dispersal is argued to have been rapid, producing networks of weakly-differentiated dialects over large geographic areas (Pawley 1999). Because of this, there is great difficulty in clearly reconstructing defined proto-languages or an order of subgroup formation within Western Malayo-Polynesian. Thus, in the Philippine Islands, there is no clear sequence of linguistic development through space. In Luzon (Reid 1994a; 1996) and in the Visayas (Zorc 1977), one can make a phylogenetic tree of most languages, but linking the two regions into one tree is yet to be done convincingly. This concern is still very much an on-going project of Philippine linguists (see Constantino 1998). However, the rapidity of the dispersal of early Malayo-Polynesian languages and their speakers does not contradict the idea that, in the wake of the main corridor of spread, groups were left behind who became transformed as a result of interaction with indigenous populations.

4) Observations from ethnohistory and ethnography

We have already examined the archaeobotanical data. One way to extend these data is to focus on the terms for rice and the associated products from processing rice. There seems to be a divide here between, on the one hand, ethnolinguistic groups with rice as a main staple who have detailed terminologies for rice processing traceable to early Austronesian proto-languages, who make rice alcoholic beverages and rice sweets; and, on the other hand, groups who do not have the complete repertoire of rice products and terminology and who use other crops, such as maize or tubers, as their major staple. The following ethnolinguistic groups are examples of the first category of rice-dependent populations: the Bontoc and Ifugao of the Mountain province of Luzon (Conklin 1980; Barton 1938; Jenks 1905), the Tagbanwa of northern Palawan (Fox 1982), the Subanon of Zamboanga (Finley & Churchill 1913), the Iban of Sarawak (Jensen 1974), the Kelabit and Murut of interior Borneo (Harrisson 1959), the Dusun of Sabah (Jensen 1974), and the Makasarese and Sadang of Sulawesi (Kennedy 1953). For many other existing ethnolinguistic groups the repertoire is incomplete. Usually they lack rice beverages, using sugarcane or palm wine instead, or rice sweets.

An interesting point is the insight acquired from looking at the term for 'cooked rice'. Listed Early Austronesian reconstructions are *imay, *hemay or *semay (Blust 1995; Wurm & Wilson 1975). Of the rice-dependent groups listed above coming from the Philippines, only the Subanon of Zamboanga have a close-sounding term (gemai). What I think is significant is that, in Tagalog and several other languages in Luzon, 'cooked rice' is Kanin or Kanén; in the neighbouring Kapampangan group the term is nasi. In Visayan languages it is Kan'on, but Kanin can also mean cooked ground corn (Zea mays). This is also true for the Itawes in the Cagayan Valley in Luzon. These are illustrative examples and my search was not exhaustive; I am not in a position to go into details as to why we have this linguistic division. Suffice to say that rice terms in well-established agricultural groups such as the Tagalog and Kapampangan do not sound like early Austronesian reconstructions. In the past, rice may have been significant for these cultures, but was not deeply imbedded. Several sites excavated in the Visayas, for instance, Unto, Yap, Santiago church and Osmena park, have tenth- to seventeenth-century AD deposits and the absence of rice may be understood in the light of the above argument: rice was significant, but not wholly integrated in the culture and in the economy.

Another element to add to the discussion relates to the fermentation starters used in making rice alcoholic beverages (see Haard et al. 1999). It is interesting to see that the studied Island Southeast Asian starters (e.g. bubod in the Philippines, ragi in Indonesia) resemble those from China (chu) in ingredient (rice flour), shape (cake) and the active micro-organisms present (the fungi Rhizopus spp. and Amylomyces spp.). They differ in at least two of the three listed elements from fermentation starters studied in Korea (nuruk), Japan (koji), Thailand (loopang) and India (marchaa) (Haard et al. 1999, table 2). These data may relate to cultural dispersal, and I am inclined to see them as part of the later establishment of a rice-based economy in the region. This is because there are no terms reconstructed for 'rice wine/beer' in early Austronesian proto-languages (Blust 1995; Zorc 1994; Wurm & Wilson 1975). This is a curious point, given the role played by these beverages in known cultures, and thus suggests perhaps a much later date of introduction.

A last element worth mentioning in this discussion pertains to the current distribution of Sea Nomads (Orang Laut) in Southeast Asia. It has been argued that the sea nomadic life may have been an important characteristic of early Austronesian culture (see Sather 1993). This is, of course, supported by a great deal of proto-language reconstruction (Pawley & Pawley 1994), and the rapid dispersal of Austronesian speakers could only have been undertaken by peoples with close affinities to the sea. Of the three main groupings of Sea Nomads in Southeast Asia, the Moken and Orang Laut are currently located in the Malay Peninsula and Sumatra, but the Bajau are spread across the Sulu archipelago, Sabah and Sulawesi (Lenhart 1995), within the corridor of spread articulated in this paper.

Conclusion

Based on the above discussion, one can argue that, in the initial stages of Austronesian dispersal, most of the Philippine islands served as a friction zone for cereal-agriculture based communities. Thus, the spread of agriculture with early Austronesians may have been much more limited than previously accepted. Western Luzon, Palawan, western Mindanao, Sarawak and Sulawesi seem to have had a deeper rice culture, with the oldest secure evidence for rice and pottery existing in Sarawak where the pertinent archaeological suite of materials is supplemented by the ethnographic and linguistic data discussed above. To summarize, the proposed sequence discussed in this paper is as follows:
1. An initial dispersal of Austronesian speakers arriving in Island Southeast Asia with a cultural package, including cereal agriculture, around 4000 BP.

2. The package breaks up and its components spread at different rates, with pottery representing the faster-spreading element. Cereal agriculture had difficulties spreading — rice was hindered by the new climatic conditions, even in the narrow spread zone. For most islands the dispersal was slow, especially when indigenous populations were encountered. Apart from the western coast of Luzon, the islands facing the China sea, Sabah, western Mindanao and Sulawesi, moving towards Sahul, were mostly friction zones for these incoming groups.

3. Rice agriculture entered the region with greater strength at the same time as metal technology, after 500 BC. This is similar to 'stage 3' in the large scale reconstruction of the general stages of Austronesian agricultural prehistory articulated by Bellwood (1997, 249–51).

It will be interesting to see the results of future excavations carried out with a sensitivity to archaeobotanical data recovery down the western coastlines of the Philippine Islands, specifically in the Batanes, western coast of northern Luzon and northern Palawan (see Bellwood & Anderson 2001). Chances are, these sites will suggest the pattern described in this paper. It will also be of interest to see where linguistics and population genetics take the discussion, especially on questions of small-scale directional movement in antiquity. The next few years will hopefully usher in a new research dynamism in the islands of Southeast Asia.

Acknowledgements

I would like to acknowledge Peter Bellwood for his very constructive comments; to Mathew Hurles for our interesting discussions; to Colin Renfrew and Katie Boyle for inviting me to participate in this conference; and to Martin Jones and the Pitt-Rivers laboratory group, for their support and encouragement.

References

An, Z., 1999. Origin of Chinese rice cultivation and its spread east. http//www.admissions.carleton.ca/¬bgordon/Rice/papers/zhimin99.htm.

Ardika, I.W. & P. Bellwood, 1991. Sembiran: the beginnings of Indian contact with Bali. *Antiquity* 65, 221–32.

Ardika, I.W. & P. Bellwood, 1999. Prestige and potency: political economies of protohistoric Visayan polities, in Bacus & Lucero, 67–87.

Bacus, E., 1997. The Unto site: excavations at a late first millennium BC and mid-second millennium AD habi-

tation site in southeastern Negros Island, the Philippines. *Asian Perspectives* 36, 106–41.

Bacus E. & L. Lucero (eds.), 1999. *Complex Polities in the Ancient Tropical World*, vol. 9. Washington (DC): American Anthropological Association.

Barker, G., H. Barton, P. Beavitt, S. Chapman, M. Derrick, C. Doherty, L. Farr, D. Gilbertson, C. Hunt, W. Jarvis, J. Kirgbaum, B. Maloney, S. Mclaren, P. Pettit, B. Pyatt, T. Reynolds, G. Rushworth & M. Stephens, 2000. The Niah caves project: preliminary report on the first (2000) season. *The Sarawak Museum Journal* 55, 111–50.

Barker, G., D. Badang, H. Barton, P. Beavitt, M. Bird, P. Daly, C. Doherty, D. Gilbertson, I. Glover, C. Hunt, J. Manser, S. McLaren, V. Paz, B. Pyatt, T. Reynolds, J. Rose, G. Rushworth & M. Stephens, 2001. The Niah Cave Project: the second (2001) season of fieldwork. *The Sarawak Museum Journal* 56, 37–120.

Barton, R.F., 1938. *Philippine Pagans: the Autobiographies of Three Ifugaos*. London: Routledge and Sons Ltd.

Beavitt, P., E. Kurui & G. Thompson, 1996. Confirmation of an early date for the presence of rice in Borneo: preliminary evidence for possile Bidayuh/Asian links. *Borneo Research Bulletin* 27, 29–38.

Bellwood, P., 1988. A hypothesis for Austronesian origins. *Asian Perspectives* 26, 107–17.

Bellwood, P., 1991. The Austronesian dispersal and the origin of languages. *Scientific American* 256, 70–75.

Bellwood, P., 1996. Hierarchy, founder ideology and Austronesian expansion, in Fox & Sather (eds.), 18–40.

Bellwood, P., 1997. *Prehistory of the Indo-Malaysian Archipelago*. Revised edition. Honolulu (HI): University of Hawaii.

Bellwood, P., 2000. Some thoughts on understanding the human colonisation of the Pacific. *People and Culture in Oceania* 16, 5–17.

Bellwood, P. & A. Anderson, 2001. Report on Archaeological Reconnaissance in Cagayan, Ilocos Norte and Batanes Provinces, Northern Philippines, January–February 2001. Unpublished manuscript, Australian National University.

Bellwood, P., J. Fox, & T. Darrell (eds.), 1993. *The Austronesians: Historical and Comparative Perspectives*. Canberra: Australian National University.

Blust, R., 1976. Austronesian homeland: a linguistic perspective. *Asian Perspective* 26, 107–17.

Blust, R., 1979. Proto Western Malayo-Polynesian vocatives. *Bijdragen tot de Taal-, Land- en Volkenkunde* 135, 205–51.

Blust, R., 1980. Austronesian etymologies. *Oceanic Linguistics* 19, 1–181.

Blust, R., 1995a. The position of the Formosan languages: method and theory in Austronesian comparative linguistics, in Li *et al.* (eds.), 585–650.

Blust, R., 1995b. The prehistory of the Austronesian-speaking peoples: a view from language. *Journal of World Prehistory* 9, 453–510.

Bodner, C.C., 1986. On the Evolution of Agriculture in

Central Bontoc. Unpublished PhD, University of Missouri.

Burkill, I.H., 1966. *A Dictionary of the Economic Products of the Malay Peninsula*, vols. 1–2. Singapore: Government printer.

Conklin, H.C., 1957. *Hanunoo Agriculture: a Report on an Integral System of Shifting Cultivation in the Philippines*. Rome: Food and Agriculture Organization of the U.N.

Conklin, H.C., 1980. *Ethnographic Atlas of Ifugao*. New Haven (CT): Yale University Press.

Constantino, E., 1998. Current Topics in Philippine Linguistics. Paper read at the meeting of the linguistics society of Japan held in Yamaguchi University, Japan October 31: Http://www.geocities.com/CollegePark/Field/4260/book/papers_current.html.

Datan, I. & P. Bellwood, 1991. Recent research at Gua Sireh (Serian) and Lubang Angin (Gunung Mulu National Park, Sarawak). *Bulletin of the Indo-Pacific Prehistory Association* 10, 386–405.

Di Lello, A., 1997. A Use-wear Analysis of Stone Artefacts from South Sulawesi. Unpublished Bachelor of Arts dissertation, University of Western Australia.

Doherty, C., P. Beavitt & E. Kurui, 2000. Recent observations of rice temper in pottery from Niah and other sites in Sarawak. *Bulletin of the Indo-Pacific Prehistory Association* 19, 147–52.

Dyen, I., 1965. A lexicostatistical classification of the Austronesian languages. *International Journal of American Linguistics* 31(1) supplement.

Eckardt, N.A., 2000. Giving rice the time of day: molecular identification of a major photoperiod sensitivity quantitative trait locus. *Plant Cell* 12, 2299–301.

Finley, J.P. & W. Churchill. 1913. *The Subanu: Studies of a Sub-Visayan Mountain Folk of Mindanao*. Washington (DC): Carnegie Institution of Washington.

Fox, J.J. & C. Sather (eds.), 1996. *Origins, Ancestry and Alliance: Explorations in Austronesian Ethnography*. Canberra: Department of Anthropology, Australian National University.

Fox, R., 1982. *Tagbanwa Religion and Society*. Manila: National Museum.

Fuller, D.Q., 1999. The Emergence of Agricultural Societies in South India: Botanical and Archaeological Perspectives. Unpublished PhD dissertation, University of Cambridge.

Glover, I.C., 1976. Ulu Leang cave, Maros: a preliminary sequence of post-Pleistocene cultural development in south Sulawesi. *Archipel* 11, 113–54.

Glover, I.C., 1977. The late Stone Age in eastern Indonesia. *World Archaeology* 9, 42–61.

Glover, I.C., 1979. Prehistoric plant remains from Southeast Asia: with special reference to rice, in *South Asian Archaeology 1977*, ed. M. Taddei. Naples: Instituto Universitario Orientale, 5–37.

Glover, I.C., 1986. *Archaeology in Eastern Timor*, vol. 11: *Terra Australis*. Canberra: Department of Prehistory, Research School of Pacific Studies.

Glover, I.C. & C.F.W. Higham, 1996. New evidence for early rice cultivation in South, Southeast and East Asia, in *The Origins and Spread of Agriculture and Pastoralism in Eurasia*, ed. D.R. Harris. London: UCL Press, 413–41.

Gunn, M.M., 1997. The Development of Social Networks: Subsistence Production and Exchange between the Sixth and Sixteenth Centuries AD in the Tanjay Region, Negros Oriental, the Philippines. Unpublished PhD dissertation, University of Hawaii.

Haard, N.F., S.A. Odunfa, C.-H. Lee, R. Quintero-Ramirez, A. Lorence-Quñones & C. Wacher-Radarte, 1999. *Fermented Cereals: a Global Perspective*. (FAO Agricultural Services Bulletin 138.) Rome: Food and Agriculture Organization.

Harrisson, T., 1959. The Kelabits and Muruts, in *The Peoples of Sarawak*, ed. T. Harrisson. Sarawak: Sarawak Museum, 57–72.

Heaney, L.R. & J.C.J. Regalado, 1998. *Vanishing Treasures of the Philippine Rain Forest*. Chicago (IL): Field Museum.

Hunter-Anderson, R., G.B. Thompson & D.R. Moore, 1995. Rice as a prehistoric valuable in the Mariana islands, Micronesia. *Asian Perspectives* 34, 69–89.

Jenks, A.E., 1905. *The Bontoc Igorot*. (Ethnological Survey Publications 1.) Manila: Bureau of Public Printing.

Jensen, E., 1974. *The Iban and their Religion*. (Oxford Monograph on Social Anthropology.) Oxford: Oxford University Press.

Jones, R., 1999. Dating the human colonisation of Australia: radiocarbon and luminescence revolutions, in *World Prehistory: Studies in Memory of Grahame Clark*, eds. J. Coles, R. Bewlye & P. Mellars. Oxford: The British Academy & Oxford University Press, 37–65.

Kennedy, R., 1953. *Field Notes on Indonesia: South Celebes, 1949–50*. New Haven (CT): Human Relations Area Files.

Kirch, P.V., 1997. *The Lapita Peoples: Ancestors of the Oceanic World*. London: Blackwell.

Kirch, P.V. & R.C. Green, 2001. *Hawaiki, Ancestral Polynesia: an Essay in Historical Anthropology*. Cambridge: Cambridge University Press.

Lenhart, L., 1995. Recent research on Southeast Asian sea nomads. *Nomadic Peoples* 36/37, 245–60.

Li, P.J.-K., D.-A. Ho, Y.-K. Huang, C.-H. Tsang & C.-Y. Tseng (eds.), 1995. *Austronesian Studies Relating to Taiwan*. Taipei: Academica Sinica.

Meacham, W., 1988. On the improbability of Austronesian origins in South China. *Asian Perspectives* 26, 89–106.

Meacham, W., 1995. Austronesian origins and the peopling of Taiwan, in Li *et al.* (eds.), 227–94.

Medina, J.D., 1973 [1630]. History of the Augustinian order in the Filipinas islands, in *The Philippines Islands, 1493–1898*, vol. 23, eds. E.H. Blair & J.A. Robertson. Mandaluyong: Cacho Hermanos, 119–298.

Melton, T., R. Peterson, J. Redd, N. Saha, A.S.M. Sofro, J. Martison & M. Stoneking, 1995. Polynesian genetic affinities with Southeast Asian populations as identified by mtDNA analysis. *American Journal of Human Genetics* 57, 403–14.

Ogawa, H., 1998. Problems and hypotheses on the prehistoric Lal-lo, Northern Luzon, Philippines — archaeological study on the prehistoric interdependence between hunter-gatherers and farmers in the tropical rain forest. *Journal of Southeast Asian Archaeology* 18, 122–66.

Ogawa, H., 1999. *Archaeological Research on the Prehistoric Interdependent Relationship Between Hunter-gatherers and Lowlanders — Preliminary Report on the Excavation of Mabangog Cave, San Mariano Lal-lo, Cagayan, northern Luzon, Philippines.* Tokyo: Tokyo University of Foreign Studies.

Oka, H.-I., 1988. *Origin of Cultivated Rice.* Amsterdam: Elsevier.

Oppenheimer, S., 1998. *Eden in the East: the Drowned Continent of Southeast Asia.* London: Weidenfeld and Nicholson.

Pawley, A., 1999. Chasing rainbows: implications of the rapid dispersal of Austronesian languages for subgrouping and reconstruction, in *Selected Papers from the Eighth International Conference on Austronesian Linguistics*, eds. E. Zeitoun & P.J.-K. Li. Taipei: Academia Sinica, 95–138.

Pawley, A. & M. Pawley, 1994. Early Austronesian terms for canoe parts and seafaring, in *Austronesian Terminologies: Continuity and Change*, series-C-127, eds. A. Pawley & M.D. Ross. Canberra: Australian National University, 329–62.

Pawley, A. & M. Ross, 1993. Austronesian historical linguistics and cultural history. *Annual Review of Anthropology* 22, 425–59.

Pawley, A. & M. Ross (eds.), 1994. *Austronesian Terminologies: Continuity and Change.* (Pacific Linguistics C-127.) Canberra: The Australian National University.

Paz, V., 1999. Neolithic human movement to Island Southeast Asia: the search for archaeobotanical evidence. *Bulletin of the Indo-Pacific Prehistory Association* 2, 151–8.

Paz, V., 2001a. Archaeobotany and Cultural Transformation: Patterns of Early Plant Utilisation in Northern Wallacea. Unpublished PhD dissertation, University of Cambridge.

Paz, V., 2001b. Report on the Analysis of Environmental Samples from Niah Cave. Submitted to Greame Barker. George Pitt-Rivers Laboratory, University of Cambridge. [see abridged version in Barker *et al.* 2001.]

Paz, V., A. Mijares, G. Barretto, J. Cayron, Y. Hara & D. Galang, 1998. Batanes Expedition Report. Unpublished manuscript, Archaeological Studies Program, University of the Philippines.

Poonyarit, M., D.J. Mackill & B.S. Vergara, 1989. Genetics of photoperiod sensitivity and critical day length in rice. *Crop Science* 29, 647–52.

Reed, W.A., 1904. *Negritos of Zambales.* (Ethnological Survey Publications 11, part 1.) Manila: Bureau of Public Printing.

Reid, L.A., 1994a. Terms for rice agriculture and terrace building in some Cordilleran languages of the Philippines, in Pawley & Ross (eds.), 363–88.

Reid, L.A., 1994b. Possible non-Austronesian lexical elements in Philippine Negrito languages. *Oceanic Linguistics* 33, 37–71.

Reid, L.A., 1996. The current state of linguistic research on the relatedness of the language families of East and Southeast Asia. *Bulletin of the Indo-Pacific Prehistory Association* 15, 87–91.

Renfrew, C., 2000. At the edge of knowability: towards a prehistory of languages. *Cambridge Archaeological Journal* 10(1), 7–34.

Reynolds, T.E., 1993. Problems in the Stone Age of southeast Asia. *Proceedings of the Prehistoric Society* 59, 1–15.

Roberts, R.G., R. Jones, N.A. Spooner, M.J. Head, A.S. Murray & M. Smith, 1994. The human colonisation of Australia: optical dates of 53,000 and 60,000 years bracket human arrival at Deaf Adder Gorge, Northern Territory. *Quaternary Science Reviews* 13, 575–83.

Ross, M., A. Pawley & M. Osmond (eds.), 1998. *The Lexicon of Proto-Oceanic: the Culture and Environment of Ancestral Oceanic Society*, vol. I: *Material Culture.* (Pacific Linguistics C-152). Canberra: Australian National University.

Sather, C., 1993. Sea nomads and rainforest hunter-gatherers: foraging adaptations in the Indo-Malaysian archipelago, in Bellwood *et al.* (eds.), 229–68.

Snow, B.E., R.J. Shutler, D.E. Nelson, J.S. Vogel & J.R. Southon, 1986. Evidence of early rice cultivation in the Philippines. *Philippine Quarterly of Culture and Society* 14, 3–11.

Solheim, W.G.I., 1964. *The Archaeology of Central Philippines.* (National Institute of Science & Technology Monograph 10.) Manila: National Institute of Science & Technology.

Solheim, W.G.I., 1988. The Nusantao hypothesis: the origin and spread of Austronesian speakers. *Asian Perspectives* 26, 77–88.

Solheim, W.G.I., 1996. The Nusantao and the north–south dispersal. *Indo-Pacific Prehistory Association Bulletin* 15, 101–9.

Solheim, W.G.I., 1998. Southeast Asian Earthenware Pottery and its Spread. Revised paper presented at the IPPA Conference, Melaka, Malaysia, August 1998.

Spriggs, M., 1989. The dating of the Island Southeast Asian Neolithic: an attempt at chronometric hygiene and linguistic correlation. *Antiquity* 63, 587–613.

Spriggs, M., 1995. The Lapita' culture and Austronesian prehistory in Oceania, in Bellwood *et al.* (eds.), 112–33.

Stevens, C., 2000. Cultural taphonomic pathways to charred assemblages. Submitted to *Journal of Archaeological Science.*

Sykes, B., A. Leiboff, J. Low-Beer, S. Tetzner & M. Richards, 1995. The origins of the Polynesians: an interpretation from mitochondrial lineage analysis. *American Journal of Human Genetics* 57, 1463–75.

Terrell, J.E., 2000. A 'tree' is not a 'train': mistaken analogies in Pacific archaeology. *Antiquity* 74, 331–3.

Terrell, J.E., K.M. Kelly & P. Rainbird, 2001. Forgone conclusions? In search of 'Papuan' and 'Austronesians'. *Current Anthropology* 42, 97–124.

Thompson, G.B., 1996. *The Excavation of Khok Phanom Di: a Prehistoric Site in Central Thailand*, vol. IV: *Subsistence and Environment: the Botanical Evidence (the Biological Remains*, part II). (Research Report LIII edition.) London: Society of Antiquaries.

Tsang, C.-H., 1995. New archaeological data from both sides of the Taiwan Straits and their implications for the controversy about Austronesian origins and expansion, in Li *et al.* (eds.), 185–226.

Tsang, C.-H., 1998. Preliminary report on archaeological surveys and excavations on the Northern Luzon coast of the Philippines. *Newsletter of the Southeast Asian Studies* 6, 17–33.

Ushijima, I. & C.N. Zayas (eds.), 1994. *Fishers of the Visayas.* (Visayas Maritime Anthropological Studies I, 1991–1993.) Quezon City: University of the Philippines Press.

Wurm, S.A. & B. Wilson, 1975. *English Finderlist of Reconstructions in Austronesian Languages*, vol. 33. (Pacific Linguistics Series C.) Canberra: The Australian National University.

Yan, W., 1991. China's earliest rice agricultural remains. *Indo-Pacific Prehistory Association Bulletin* 10, 118–26.

Zorc, D.P., 1977. *The Bisayan Dialects of the Philippines: Subgrouping and Reconstruction.* (Pacific Linguistics C-44.) Canberra: The Australian National University.

Zorc, D.P., 1994. Austronesian culture history through reconstructed vocabulary (an overview), in Pawley & Ross (eds.), 541–94.

Chapter 22

Polynesians: Devolved Taiwanese Rice Farmers or Wallacean Maritime Traders with Fishing, Foraging and Horticultural Skills?

Stephen Oppenheimer & Martin Richards

Most linguists and archaeologists support a migration model for the origins of Polynesians, but until recently there was little relevant genetic evidence with which to test this view. Archaeologists may reconstruct material culture and date it but, in the absence of written texts and skeletal remains, they have less success identifying the origins of the *manufacturers* of the assemblages. Similarly, linguists can reconstruct the branching history of their languages, but have no direct evidence for the origins of the *speakers* of those languages. Here, we discuss the new genetic evidence on human dispersals into the Pacific. At the same time, we question the mutually-dependent structure of evidence from archaeology and linguistics that is used to support a farming-fuelled range expansion all the way from South China out into the Pacific.

Because languages change at a variable rate, both Indo-European and Austronesian farming dispersal models derive their dates and cultural horizons primarily from archaeology. However, linguistic palaeontology remains extremely influential in the reconstruction of prehistoric dispersals (Mallory 1989; Bellwood 1997), even though this practice has been condemned by Renfrew (1987, 77–86). Even the ghost of glottochronology seems to linger. For example, comparative linguists often argue that, because of lexical decay, language families cannot be traced back more than about 6000–8000 years; in other words, not before the Neolithic transition (Trask 1996, 377). Bellwood (2001) has recently argued that this figure may not have arisen by chance, but may after all be telling us that the major language families were spread by farming dispersals. But although the great modern language families may have only become recognizable in the modern reconstructed record within the past 8000 years, this does not have to imply they sprang suddenly into life *de novo* at that time.

As an example, Dixon (1997, 46–8) has suggested that present evidence does not preclude Proto-Indo-European dating back 10,500 BP, or perhaps even 12,000 years ago. If this were the case, language and demic expansion congruity could also be fitted to the major post-glacial climatic amelioration following the Younger Dryas event *c.* 11,500 BP (Dansgaard *et al.* 1993). This raises the possibility that demic expansion occurred as much as a result of climate improvement as of the fecundity of agricultural societies (e.g. Adams & Otte 1999). Since accumulating genetic evidence from both mitochondrial DNA (mtDNA) (Richards *et al.* 2000) and the Y chromosome (Semino *et al.* 2000) in Europe have suggested that post-glacial expansions and recolonizations had a much greater impact on gene pools than Neolithic immigration, this seems to be a possibility worth considering for Asia as well.

Polynesian origins

There are two main clusters of homeland hypotheses attempting to explain Austronesian and/or Polynesian origins and dispersals: mainland farming dispersal (Bellwood 1997; Blust 1984–85), or offshore, non-farming-dependent dispersal (Dyen 1965; 1971; Terrell & Welsch 1997; Terrell *et al.* 2001; see also Meacham 1984–85; Solheim 1994; 1996 for arguments for an Austronesian homeland in Island Southeast Asia).

Both mainland and offshore models have relied on combinations of linguistic palaeontology and archaeology. This approach has been criticized, however, on grounds of the relative mobility of cultural and linguistic markers when compared with the large source populations that nurtured them (Terrell 2001). Such mobility depends on small numbers of people, for instance relays of sailors, who may transmit language and culture through long-distance trade networks. Not surprisingly the migrationist view presented on the basis of language trees has only produced a true consensus on the final stages of Polynesian expansion to occupy the uninhabited islands of the Pacific.

Since the models concern the movements of people, we argue that they are best tested using the evidence of the genes which, unlike cultures and languages, are transmitted exclusively vertically down the generations.

Asian mainland origin and 'Out-of-Taiwan'

Archaeologist Peter Bellwood (1997) and linguist Robert Blust (1984–85; 1996) have been closely associated for the past 20 years with refining the mainland origins archaeolinguistic model. This was christened by Diamond (1988), as the 'Express Train to Polynesia', but is perhaps better referred to as the 'Out-of-Taiwan' model, in order to emphasize the central contention of a Taiwanese origin for the Austronesian family. It argues that the ancestors of Polynesians were the vanguard of a demic expansion of Austronesian-speaking, rice-growing agriculturists originating in South China, around 6000 years ago. This maritime wave of advance spread successively south to Taiwan, the Philippines and Indonesia, and then east to Melanesia, reaching Fiji by 3000 years ago, subsequently radiating across the Pacific to fill the Polynesian triangle by 1000 years ago. Under this model, the expanding Neolithic diaspora from South China largely replaced the local hunter-gatherer populations of Island Southeast Asia who, on first contact, would have been of Australo-Melanesian extraction (Bellwood 1997). A less extreme version allows for genetic input from mainland Southeast Asia prior to this dispersal, but nevertheless still argues for a complete linguistic replacement (Bellwood 1997, 91–2).

Late Holocene replacement?

According to the strong version of the theory (Bellwood 1997), until about 4000 years ago Island Southeast Asia was entirely inhabited by non-Austronesian-speaking 'Australoid' hunter-gatherers. Today, apart from a few Papuan tongues spoken in the eastern Indonesia, every single language in ISEA is now Austronesian. This implies that there was a near complete linguistic and ethnic replacement. It is extraordinary that such an ethnic sweep — as this was supposed to be — should have left no

relicts, linguistic or otherwise, of the former hunter-gatherer inhabitants of the huge island of Borneo, which ranks with New Guinea as one of the great island tropical wildernesses. If Austronesian languages had such difficulty replacing (let alone dominating) the pre-existing languages of Australia and New Guinea, how were they so extraordinarily successful in Island Southeast Asia?

In traditional societies of Southeast Asia and the Pacific, the rigid conceptual dichotomy of one culture *versus* another breaks down. Complementary and parallel development seem to be more the rule. While there are a few societies that are more or less exclusively nomadic hunter-gatherers, trading with more settled folk, many farming societies that live on the edge of, or within, the forest derive the bulk of their protein and vegetables from hunting and gathering. Polynesians show no evidence, present or past, of rice-growing and grow the same root crops as Melanesians. Maritime foraging and boat skills, on the other hand, seem to have been important all the way from Southeast Asia to Polynesia. To describe modern Southeast Asian forest hunter-gatherers and Pacific marine foragers as 'devolved agriculturists' would seem to weaken the basis of the farming premise. In any case there are no attested cases of hunter-gatherer devolution in Borneo (Sather 1995).

Linguistic argument

The 'Out-of-Taiwan' model has relied primarily on linguistics for the structure and geographic integrity of its migration route, although there are no Austronesian languages or accepted precursors of Austronesian languages in the South Chinese mainland (Meacham 1984–85). Under the Austric hypothesis, now supported by Blust (1996), the nearest modern family to Austronesian is Austroasiatic, which is found in Mainland Southeast Asia and not anywhere near the East China coast.

The direction and structure of the phylogeny of Malayo-Polynesian Austronesian languages, stretching from Western Malayo-Polynesian in Island Southeast Asia to the Polynesian group (part of the Central Pacific branch of Oceanic) in the Pacific, is hardly disputed. Blust (1984–85; 1996; 1999), however, supports an ultimate Taiwanese rather than Island Southeast Asian origin for Austronesian languages, since he identifies an increasing number of innovation-defined primary branches of Austronesian, all but one of which are spoken only in Taiwan (see also Diamond 2000). But as Meacham (1984–85) has pointed out, there is no evidence in Taiwan for any

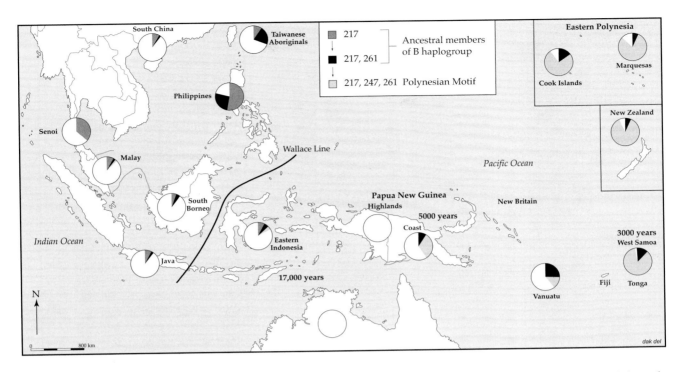

Figure 22.1. *Distribution of the defining mtDNA (maternal) 'Polynesian motif' and its ancestors in eastern Asia and the Pacific. (Data combined from: Redd* et al. *1995; Melton* et al. *1995; Sykes* et al. *1995.)*

representatives of the largest branch, the Malayo-Polynesian group (MP) which encompasses the rest of Austronesian languages, i.e. most of Island Southeast Asia — and the remote Pacific. The base of the tree is thus un-rooted. Consistent with this uncertainty, an alternative phylo-linguistic view, 'the Formosan-Philippine hypothesis', vies with Blust's Malayo-Polynesian hypothesis (discussed in Pawley this volume).

This means that Taiwan could equally have been colonized from Southeast Asia prior to the emergence and dominance of the Malayo-Polynesian branch. The small handful of Taiwanese Austronesian languages are certainly very unlike the others, and also each other. However, the lack of equivalent deep-branch diversity in parts of Southeast Asia such as the Philippines may have resulted from the linguistic phenomenon of 'levelling' during the Neolithic or Metal Age. If Taiwan had simply been an Austronesian backwater, as argued on the basis of the archaeological evidence by Meacham (1984–85), earlier levels of diversity might well have survived through isolation.

Archaeological evidence

Meacham (1984–85) has also enumerated archaeological reasons for regarding Taiwan as an isolated backwater rather than the Austronesian homeland. Terrell (1999) has also recently challenged its validity. The South Chinese technology, proposed by Bellwood (1997) to motivate the expansion to Taiwan, was rice farming. Yet the only islands in the Pacific that ever grew rice were the Marianas, and this practice could have resulted from a later, direct, end-point colonization from the nearby Philippines. The domesticated foodstuffs that the Pacific Austronesian speakers took out with them were not rice, which spread only to Eastern Indonesia, but yams, bananas, breadfruit, sago, betel-nuts, coconuts and chickens. Such root and tree crops and indeed the chicken (*Gallus gallus*) are indigenous to Southeast Asian and Melanesian cultures. Like terms for boat-building, none of the names for these ancient Southeast Asian and Pacific foodstuffs appear in the reconstructed hypothetical Proto-Austronesian vocabulary of Taiwan, although they are there in Blust's (1984–85) reconstructed hypothetical ancient Proto-Malayo-Polynesian language. Only details of cereal agriculture can be consistently reconstructed back to Proto-Formosan. This means that the 'Out-of-Taiwan' argument entails that the entire subsistence basis of the advancing Austronesian speakers dramatically changed *en route* through Island Southeast Asia (Bellwood 1997, ch. 7; Mahdi 1994); yet the

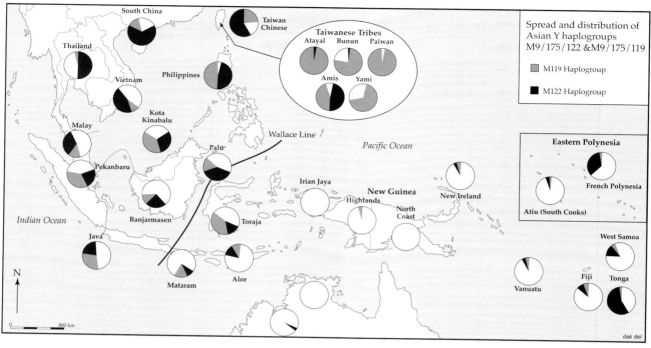

Figure 22.2. *Distribution of M122 and M119 haplogroups of the Y chromosome in eastern Asia and the Pacific. (Data combined from: Kayser et al. 2000; 2001; Su et al. 2000; Capelli et al. 2001.)*

subsistence base is intended to have driven the expansion in the first place. The case is weakened still further by the sheer paucity of evidence in Island Southeast Asia for the spread of rice agriculture alongside red-slipped pottery and the lack of clear origins for red-slipped pottery further back than the Philippines.

An insular Polynesian homeland

The principal alternative view is that Austronesian languages and the cultures of those that speak them evolved offshore from the Asian mainland, somewhere in the region they are spoken today (Meacham 1984–85; Solheim 1994). This suggests that we should be looking for the genetic origins of Polynesian peoples somewhere either in Island Southeast Asia and/or Melanesia.

Coastal Melanesia, Wallacea and Island Southeast Asia are all potential offshore homelands for the ancestors of today's Polynesian peoples. All these sites have indeed also been proposed as Austronesian linguistic homelands (Dyen 1971; Wolff 1995; Meacham 1984–85). However, we should be wary of conflating Austronesian and Polynesian origins. Whilst the 'Out-of-Taiwan' view provides a simple dispersal narrative with Austronesian origins at one end and the Polynesian expansion at the other, these alternative models may uncouple the two, so that the origins of the Polynesian dispersals may not follow on directly from the earlier history of the bulk of the Austronesian speakers in Island Southeast Asia.

Terrell & Welsch (1997) have also argued that the ancestors of the Polynesians originated within the 'voyaging corridor' between Wallacea and the Solomon Islands, defined by Irwin (1992). Terrell has been a fierce critic of what he regards as deterministic models of racial migration based on language trees and archaeologically-defined culture zones, and his work has emphasized the effects of reticulated cultural slipstreams such as those formed along trade-routes.

Solheim (1994; 1996) has also stressed the importance of development of long-distance trade networks in Early Holocene Austronesian prehistory, but he has taken the concept right on from Southeast Asia round the coastline of East Asia to Japan. Like Terrell, he is cautious not to predicate the whole structure on a linguistic/racial mono-culture, saying merely that at any one time the majority language type in this cultural network, which he calls the 'Nusantao', was probably Malayo-Polynesian. Solheim perceives the most likely area of genesis of the Nusantao in the boundary zone between Wallacea,

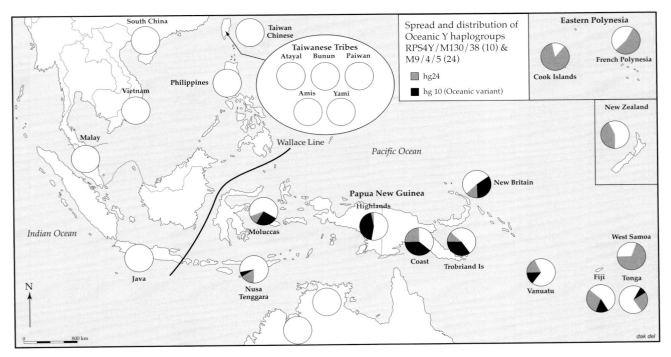

Figure 22.3. *Distribution of Oceanic-variant haplogroup 10 (DYS390.3del/ RPS4Y711T) and haplogroup 24 (M4/ M5) of the Y chromosome in eastern Asia and the Pacific. (Data combined from Kayser et al. 2000; 2001; Su et al. 2000; Capelli et al. 2001. DYS390 repeats of 21 or fewer are used where other markers are lacking.)*

Sabah and the Sulu Sea, dating from before 5000 BC, at the time of the final sea-level rise. He also argues that marine technology and horticulture both had local origins in Island Southeast Asia (Solheim 1994; 1996). The 15-year-old 'Out-of-Taiwan' hypothesis is now being rejected by other archaeologists, even some former adherents (Gibbons 2001). So how does the genetic evidence affect interpretation?

The genetic evidence

The 'Out-of-Taiwan' model for the origins of Polynesians, and Austronesian speakers more generally, belongs to a family of 'farming dispersal' models initially proposed by Renfrew (1987), and including the Indo-European and Bantu languages. The offshore homeland models suggest a more stable local demographic evolution, at least in Island Southeast Asia and Near Oceania, with cultural fertilization through relays of long-distance marine trading networks. Whilst using cultural and linguistic evidence, farming-dispersal models were initially felt to require a substantial demographic component in order to spread languages widely in the absence of the cultural élites that only emerged in the Bronze Age (Renfrew 1987). The emerging genetic picture in

Southeast Asia and the Southwest Pacific however seems to support a more stable demographic picture during the Holocene with limited spread occurring from way-stations rather than all along the line.

Much of the early genetic study in Southeast Asia met with the problem that the classical autosomal markers being used were common to many populations, varying only slightly in frequency from one population to another. Work in the 1980s on protein products of rare allelic variants and highly-specific mapped globin gene abnormalities from Melanesia and Polynesia started to change that.

Globin gene deletions
The mapping of globin genes in the 1980s indicated two unique α-globin gene deletions, resulting in forms of α-thalassaemia, found throughout coastal and lowland Melanesia with potential as migration markers (Oppenheimer *et al.* 1984; Oppenheimer 1998, 182–93). One of these, the $\alpha^{3.7III}$ type, deletes one of the two genes that encode for the α-globin part of the haemoglobin molecule. The $\alpha^{3.7III}$ type constitutes 60 per cent of α-deletions found in the Austronesian speakers of the Bismarck Archipelago. It is also the dominant type found throughout the rest of Island Melanesia and is also found in Poly-

nesia, although at lower rates than in Melanesia. It is, however, only found in Oceania and is rare in the highlands of New Guinea. The other type, $\alpha^{4.2}$, deletes the other of the two α-globin genes. In Melanesia, the latter is the dominant type in non-Austronesian speakers, especially of the north coast of New Guinea, where it is found either as a heterozygote or homozygote in 80 per cent of the population. It also occurs throughout Austronesian speakers of Island Melanesia but at lower rates than the $\alpha^{3.7III}$-deletion. The $\alpha^{4.2}$-deletion is notably *not* found in Polynesia (Flint *et al.* 1986; Hill *et al.* 1985).

In the case of both of these α-thalassaemia deletions, the flanking DNA sequences indicate that they are local mutations (i.e. not recently derived from Southeast Asia) (Flint *et al.* 1986). In other words, the $\alpha^{3.7III}$-deletion may have travelled with Austronesian speakers right out to eastern Polynesia, but it arose locally, somewhere along the voyaging corridor, around or off the north coast of New Guinea. Not only are they local, but these deletions may also be quite ancient. The unique $\alpha^{3.7III}$-deletion has been around northern Island Melanesia long enough to acquire a further mutation that produces a variant haemoglobin molecule called Hb J Tongariki, which is found in some people on Karkar Island, off the north coast of New Guinea (Old *et al.* 1980; Hill *et al.* 1985).

These observations suggest that the Polynesians' ancestors, if they were not local, must have stopped somewhere in northern Melanesia long enough to intermarry locally. If the Polynesians' ancestors ever stopped on the north coast of New Guinea long enough to pick up the $\alpha^{3.7III}$-deletion, however, they failed to pick up the $\alpha^{4.2}$-deletion although it is present in over 80 per cent of the people now living there. The alternative is that they travelled out to the Pacific 3500 years ago via offshore islands such as the Bismarck Archipelago, where the $\alpha^{3.7III}$-deletion is the dominant variant today. Such a bypass interpretation certainly fits the aspect of the common archaeological model that identifies the Proto-Polynesians with Lapita pottery because, with one exception, there are no Lapita pottery sites anywhere on the New Guinea mainland.

Mitochondrial DNA
For greater power to resolve prehistoric migrations by genetic means, however, we must turn to the non-recombining, uniparental loci: the mitochondrial DNA (mtDNA) and the Y chromosome. Early work on mtDNA in the control region highlighted what came to be known as the 'Polynesian motif'

(Hagelberg & Clegg 1993; Redd *et al.* 1995). This is a unique suite of four substitutions, at nucleotide positions 16189, 16217, 16247 and 16261, in the non-coding control region of mitochondrial DNA. These four substitutions identify a sub-group of haplogroup B — a widespread East Asian clade of mitochondrial lineages characterized by an intergenic 9-base-pair deletion.

The Polynesian motif, so-called because it reaches high rates in Polynesian populations, is actually distributed at varying frequencies throughout the coastal populations of Oceania, including Micronesia and coastal Melanesia (Cann & Lum 1996; Melton *et al.* 1995; Redd *et al.* 1995; Sykes *et al.* 1995; Merriwether *et al.* 1999). This unique Oceanic marker, which is not found in highland New Guinea, is, however, virtually absent in Asia to the west of Wallace's Line (Redd *et al.* 1995; Richards *et al.* 1998). The distribution of the marker thus also follows Austronesian linguistic boundaries. The distribution excludes virtually all populations speaking Western Malayo-Polynesian languages — in other words the whole of Island Southeast Asia west of Wallace's Line (Oppenheimer 1998, 193–203) (Fig. 22.1).

Although the Polynesian motif is not found in the Philippines, Taiwan or China, we do find its immediate ancestor type in these regions, with only three of the four substitutions (at nucleotide positions 16189, 16217 and 16261). This places the ancestors of the motif on the Southeast Asian mainland, and led to the initial interpretation that the mtDNA variation supported the 'Out-of-Taiwan' model (Melton *et al.* 1995; Redd *et al.* 1995; Sykes *et al.* 1995). But further study suggests that this view may have been mistaken.

Since eastern Indonesia is the westernmost Asian region in which the full motif type, defined by the substitution at position 16247, is now found, then the 16247 mutation must have arisen in that region. This means that the age of the motif can be estimated using the molecular clock by dating the variation accumulated on the motif branch. The age of the most recent common ancestor of lineages with the motif is very approximately 17,000 years (95 per cent credible region: 5500–34,500 years) (Richards *et al.* 1998).

As evidence of internal validation, genetic dates for the Pacific dispersals of the motif obtained using the same method place their arrival in Samoa at around 3000 years ago and in Eastern Polynesia at around 1000 years ago — consistent with the archaeological evidence. The dates derived for the arrival of the Polynesian motif along the north coast of

New Guinea are interesting since they come out at 5000 years ago (but note the 95 per cent credible region: 1500–10,000 years) (Richards *et al.* 1998). Swadling (1997) has recently suggested a date of around 5800 years ago for the introduction of exotic foodstuffs (e.g. betel-nut) and shell technology to the Sepik region of the north New Guinea coast. Curiously, this is also closer to the time depth estimated by Dyen (1971) for Austronesian languages of Melanesia.

It therefore appears that the motif is at least 5000 years old, and probably considerably older. However, the 'Out-of-Taiwan' model is chronologically constrained by the appearance in eastern Indonesia of red-slipped pottery: it argues for an arrival in the Moluccas around 2000–1500 BC (Bellwood 1997, 232–3, 242). In other words, the motif probably originated long before farmers of Taiwanese origin could have arrived in the Moluccas.

Polynesian populations are quite unlike any other populations in Southeast Asia (or indeed most populations world-wide) in being overwhelmingly dominated by the Polynesian motif sequence type and, to a much lesser extent, by its immediate one-step ancestor. This shows clear evidence of strong founder effects on the way out into the Pacific. With the exception of the minority ancestral haplogroup B haplotype — which is universally present in Southeast and East Asia — none of the other minority Polynesian mtDNA lineages show any evidence of being derived from Taiwan (Sykes *et al.* 1995).

The mtDNA data, then, seem more consistent with models for Polynesian origins within tropical Island Southeast Asia: what might be termed a 'slow boat model', in contrast with Diamond's 'express train to Polynesia' (Oppenheimer & Richards 2001; see also Kayser *et al.* 2000). It also has implications for models of Austronesian origins, since it implies that one of the main insular mtDNA clusters, haplogroup B, has been present in the archipelago for more (probably considerably more) than 5000 years.

The Y chromosome
Since the first genetic arguments in favour of the 'slow boat' model three years ago (Richards *et al.* 1998), there has been a revolution in the study of the second non-recombining uniparental genetic system, with the identification of almost 200 new markers (Underhill *et al.* 2000). This has led to the publication of a series of studies of the male line of descent in Southeast Asia and the Pacific (Su *et al.* 2000; Capelli *et al.* 2001; Kayser *et al.* 2000; 2001; Underhill *et al.*

2001). These have fuelled further doubts about the 'Out-of-Taiwan' model for the origin of the Polynesians, and returned to an earlier twist in the story: namely, the size of the Melanesian contributions to the Polynesian gene pool. Working from largely similar data sets, but using markers of varying resolution and equivalence, a range of interpretations have been proposed, ranging from predominantly Melanesian origins to predominantly Insular Southeast Asian origins for Polynesians. It is worth trying to put these results together to see whether a picture emerges.

As with mtDNA, Polynesian Y chromosomes show dramatic reductions in diversity, indicating strong founder effects. Just two Y chromosome haplogroups dominate the Polynesian scene. One of these, defined by marker M122 ('haplogroup L' of Capelli *et al.* 2001), is clearly derived from East Asia or Southeast Asia, since it is common throughout those regions but absent from the New Guinea highlands (Kayser *et al.* 2000; 2001; Capelli *et al.* 2001) (Fig. 22.2). It occurs at highest frequencies, approximately 60 per cent, on the south Chinese mainland (and also in Han Taiwanese), and at around 50 per cent in both Vietnam and the Philippines. It is almost absent from Taiwan aborigines, with the exception of the Ami where a few types have been elevated to almost 50 per cent. It is present at around 30 per cent in northern Borneo and Sulawesi, falls to around 15–20 per cent in southern Sulawesi, southern Borneo, Java and Sumatra, and falls away to very low levels along the coast of New Guinea and Island Melanesia. It is absent from inland Irian Jaya and highland Papua New Guinea. However, it occurs at low levels in Samoa and the Cook Islands, but at much higher levels in Tonga (almost 60 per cent) and French Polynesia (35 per cent).

The most likely explanation for this distribution is that this haplogroup originated on the mainland and dispersed into Island Southeast Asia (Kayser *et al.* 2000; Capelli *et al.* 2001). Thus it could represent a marker for dispersal of either the Neolithic or even Austronesian languages into the archipelago, or both, in agreement with the 'Out-of-Taiwan' model. On the other hand a more ancient dispersal (perhaps corresponding to that of mtDNA haplogroup B) from the mainland is also possible, and this might equally have been from South China, or Indo-China, or even both. The presence of shared microsatellite haplotypes (more rapidly evolving markers) within this haplogroup indicates a more recent dispersal than that of haplogroup 10 (see below), but does not preclude a pre-Neolithic, post-glacial entry. Unfortunately, microsatellite dating is not yet sufficiently refined for a reliable age estimate for the dispersal; recent work has indicated that earlier estimates may require significant re-evaluation.

A further haplogroup, defined by M119 (referred to as 'haplogroup H' in Capelli *et al.* 2001), may also be implicated in a dispersal from or via Taiwan, as argued by Kayser *et al.* (2001), although the evidence is more equivocal than for the M122 clade (Capelli *et al.* 2001). This cluster is less common on the mainland, especially in Indo-China, but occurs at extremely high frequencies within Taiwan itself, and is also common in the Philippines (Fig. 22.2). It occurs at lower frequencies in other parts of the archipelago, and is rarely found further east than Alor. It should be noted, however, that if both haplogroups were taken to represent northern agriculturists, these lineages would signify a substantial demographic impact within Southeast Asia.

Whether or not these haplogroups may indicate a Neolithic or pre-Neolithic expansion from the mainland into the archipelago, they do not serve as a significant markers for the Polynesian expansion. The M119 group is absent from Polynesia. The M122 group's presence in Tonga may well represent the earliest stages of the Polynesian expansion, but its presence further east is likely to be a red herring. Median-joining networks suggest that, whilst the Tongan types form a starburst and are shared with Melanesians and Indonesians (and indeed are closely related to several lineages from the Ami in Taiwan), the vast majority of the French Polynesian lineages form a diverse, heterogeneous group each member of which is closely related to extant southern Chinese types. The implication is that these are likely to derive from recent Chinese immigrants, who form 12 per cent of the modern population of French Polynesia.

The dominant Y haplogroup in Polynesians, comprising about 80 per cent of Cook Island lineages and the vast majority of remaining lineages in French Polynesia, is defined by an RPS4Y variant and the M216 marker (Underhill *et al.* 2001), corresponding to haplogroup 10 in the widely-used nomenclature of Jobling & Tyler-Smith (2000) ('haplogroup C' in Capelli *et al.* 2001). It is defined further locally, and uniquely in Oceania, by a further mutation M38, which is consistently associated with a unique microsatellite deletion, DYS390.3del (Forster *et al.* 1998; Kayser *et al.* 2000; Underhill *et al.* 2001).

The distribution of this sub-group of haplogroup 10 is striking (Fig. 22.3). It is confined to eastern Indonesia, coastal Melanesia, and Polynesia but is rare in the New Guinea highlands; indeed, it is the only form of the clade to be found in Melanesia and Polynesia, and the more common form found in eastern Indonesia. This distribution is reminiscent of the mtDNA 'Polynesian motif' described above, which is also restricted to eastern Indonesia, coastal Melanesia and Polynesia. As with the mtDNA haplogroup B, the distribution of variation within haplogroup 10 strongly suggests an ancient Asian ancestry, with the mutations to the derived types occurring in eastern Indonesia during the Pleistocene. Kayser *et al.* (2000) estimate that the derived type appeared very approximately 11,500 years ago, which is likely to be an under-estimate given the problems associated with microsatellite dating.

Kayser *et al.* (2000; 2001) propose that this result supports a primarily Melanesian origin for the Polynesians. Disregarding the geographic distribution, they argue this point on the basis that microsatellite diversity within the derived RPS4Y subclade is higher within Melanesia than in eastern Indonesia (Kayser *et al.* 2000). In fact, though, the diversity information is equivocal; the geographical distribution would tend to suggest an eastern Indonesian origin. The principal Polynesian lineages (derived from 'Polynesian Modal Haplotype B' in the scheme of Capelli *et al.* 2001) all then derive from a single one of these Melanesian types (in a cluster found so far only in north coastal New Guinea). Hence, as with mtDNA haplogroup B, it appears that haplogroup 10 may be intrusive into Melanesia, but have an ancient ancestry within eastern Indonesia. It remains to be seen, however, whether the time depths for the two systems in Melanesia can be matched up. Superficially, the time depth of the haplogroup 10 Y-chromosome lineages ancestral to those of Polynesia appear to be more ancient than the 5000 years or so of the mtDNA Polynesian motif. If so, this may point to a sex-related pattern of dispersal in the early stages of the Polynesian expansion; alternatively, it may simply highlight the confounding effects of genetic drift in both systems.

A notable absence in Polynesia is the unique and characteristically Melanesian Y haplogroup 24, defined by variants M4 and M5 (Hurles *et al.* 1998). This haplogroup is the main characteristic cluster identified so far for the New Guinea highlands, and is also present at moderate levels on the New Guinea coast and in Island Melanesia (Fig. 22.3). It resembles the distribution of the $\alpha^{4.2}$-globin deletion distribution both in its predominance in non-Austronesian speakers in New Guinea and its absence from Polynesia. Whilst the absence of both from Polynesians may simply be the result of founder effects, they may also point to an offshore route (or origin) for the ancestors of the Polynesians, and may again support an east Indonesian or west Melanesian origin for the majority of Polynesian lineages.

Summary of genetic evidence

The genetic evidence suggests that the ancestors of Austronesian speakers have been in Island Southeast Asia for longer than can be allowed by the tightly constrained dates of the 'Out-of-Taiwan' model, and the linguistic evidence seems at least compatible with such a view. If we put the results from these various genetic marker systems together, certain features emerge. On the one hand, there is no genetic support for the majority of modern Polynesians sharing recent common ancestors with modern aboriginal Taiwanese; on the other hand there is evidence for an ancient genetic corridor from Wallacea into lowland and coastal Oceania. Several common haplotypes in this corridor are not shared to a great extent either with highland New Guineans or with Australians. Just how ancient this corridor is may be inferred from the fact that Wallace's Line defines a clear discontinuity in both maternal and paternal lineages. The principal markers defining the recent Polynesian expansions are all derived from east of the line and one at least (the Polynesian motif) dates, locally in Wallacea, back to the late Pleistocene.

Conclusion

We are left with the conclusion that even if there were a Neolithic dispersal from the Asian mainland, via Taiwan, into the Indo-Malaysian archipelago (the Y-chromosome evidence is equivocal on this, and the mtDNA evidence is not yet in), the mtDNA and Y-chromosome evidence both suggest that any dispersing populations were not the ancestors of the majority of the Polynesian islanders. Therefore, if the Polynesians were connected in some direct way with the earlier dispersals, it must have been via acculturation. Here, however, the archaeological record suggests something of a paradox. Although there may be evidence for dispersals involving rice farming from South China into Taiwan, there was a shift within the archipelago such that the ancestors of the Polynesians dispersed with a completely different technological package. The main link between Polynesia at one end of the chain, and Taiwan at the other, would therefore seem to be the Austronesian languages. Yet neither genetics nor archaeology can, of themselves, provide clear information about the spread of language families.

Language and technology well may have moved rapidly along trade corridors up to Taiwan and out to the Solomons during the Holocene; but on the basis of the genetic evidence, large-scale movements of people seem unlikely. Where gene flow has occurred along the 'voyaging corridor', Southeast Asian lineages may have been spreading to lowland Melanesia from before the mid-Holocene. Polynesians lineages seem to derive primarily from east of the Wallace Line, in Wallacea and to some extent also Melanesia. It seems likely, however, that resolving the 'origin of the Polynesians' has little bearing on the linguistic question of the 'Austronesian homeland'.

Acknowledgements

The authors wish to thank Graeme Barker, Waruno Mahdi and John Terrell for their useful comments on the manuscript. A modified version of this manuscript appeared in volume 84 of *Science Progress*. We thank the publishers for their consent for us to reproduce three of the figures here.

References

Adams, J. & M. Otte, 1999. Did Indo-European languages spread before farming? *Current Anthropology* 40, 73–6.

Bellwood, P., 1997. *Prehistory of the Indo-Malaysian Archipelago.* Revised edition. Honolulu (HI) University of Hawaii Press. [First edition: Academic Press Australia 1985.]

Bellwood, P., 2001. Early agriculturalist population diasporas? Farming, languages and genes. *Annual Review of Anthropology* 30, 181–207.

Blust, R., 1984–85. The Austronesian homeland: a linguistic perspective. *Asian Perspectives* 26, 45–67.

Blust, R., 1996. Beyond the Austronesian homeland: the Austric hypothesis and its implications for archaeology, in Prehistoric settlement of the Pacific, ed. W.H. Goodenough. *Transactions of the American Philosophical Society* 86(5), 117–40.

Blust, R., 1999. Subgrouping, circularity and extinction: some issues in Austronesian comparative linguistics, in *Selected Papers from the Eighth International Conference on Austronesian Linguistics*, eds. E. Zeitoun & P.J. Li. (Symposium Series of the Institute of Linguistics (Preparatory Office) Academia Sinica Number 1.) Taipei: Academia Sinica, 31–94.

Cann, R.L. & J.K. Lum, 1996. Mitochondrial myopia: reply to Bonatto *et al. American Journal of Human Genetics* 59, 256–8.

Capelli, C., J.F. Wilson, M. Richards, M.P.H. Stumpf, F. Gratrix, S.J. Oppenheimer, P. Underhill, V.L. Pascali, Tsang-Ming Ko & D.B. Goldstein, 2001. A predominantly indigenous paternal heritage for the Austronesian-speaking peoples of insular Southeast Asia and Oceania. *American Journal of Human Genetics* 68, 432–43.

Dansgaard, W., S.J. Johnsen, H.B. Clausen, D. Dahl-Jensen, N.S. Gundestrup, C.U. Hammer, C.S. Hvidberg, J.P. Steffensen, A.E. Sveinbjörnsdottir, J. Jouzel & G. Bond, 1993. Evidence for general instability of past climate from a 250-kyr ice-core record. *Nature* 364, 218–20.

Diamond, J.M., 1988. Express train to Polynesia. *Nature* 336, 307–8.

Diamond, J.M., 2000. Taiwan's gift to the world. *Nature* 403, 709–10.

Dixon, R.M.W., 1997. *The Rise and Fall of Languages.* Cambridge: Cambridge University Press.

Dyen, I., 1965. *A Lexicostatistical Classification of the Austronesian Languages.* (Memoir 19.) Baltimore (MD): International Journal of American Linguistics.

Dyen, I., 1971. The Austronesian languages and Proto-Austronesian, in *Current Trends in Linguistics, no. 8: Linguistics in Oceania,* ed. T.A. Sebeok. The Hague: Mouton, 5–54.

Flint, J., A.V.S. Hill, D.K. Bowden, S.J. Oppenheimer, P.R. Sill, S.W. Serjeantson, J. Bana-Koiri, K. Bhatia, M.O. Alpers, A.J. Boyce, D.J. Weatherall & J.B. Clegg, 1986. High frequencies of alpha thalassaemia are the result of natural selection by malaria. *Nature* 321, 744–50.

Forster, P., M. Kayser, E. Meyer, L. Roewer, H. Pfeiffer, H. Benkmann & B. Brinkmann, 1998. Phylogenetic resolution of complex mutational features at Y-STR DYS390 in aboriginal Australians and Papuans. *Molecular Biology and Evolution* 15, 1108–14.

Gibbons, A., 2001. The peopling of the Pacific. *Science* 291, 1735–7.

Hagelberg, E. & J.B.Clegg, 1993. Genetic polymorphisms in prehistoric Pacific islanders determined by analysis of ancient bone DNA. *Proceedings of the Royal Society of London* 252, 163–70.

Hill, A.V.S., D.K. Bowden, R.J. Trent, D.R. Higgs, S.J. Oppenheimer, S.L. Thein, K.N.P. Mickleson, D.J. Weatherall & J.B. Clegg, 1985. Melanesians and Polynesians share a unique alpha thalassaemia mutation. *American Journal of Human Genetics* 37, 571–80.

Hurles, M.E., C. Irven, J. Nicholson, P.G. Taylor, F.R. Santos J. Loughlin, M.A. Jobling & B.C. Sykes, 1998. European Y-chromosomal lineages in Polynesians: a contrast to the population structure revealed by mtDNA. *American Journal of Human Genetics* 63, 1793–806.

Irwin, G., 1992. Pleistocene voyaging and the settlement of Greater Australia and its near Oceanic neighbours, in *The Prehistoric Exploration and Colonisation of the Pacific,* ed. G. Irwin. Cambridge: Cambridge University Press, 18–30.

Jobling, M.A. & C. Tyler-Smith, 2000. New uses for new haplotypes. *Trends in Genetics* 6, 235–62.

Kayser, M., S. Brauer, G. Weiss, P. Underhill, P. Roewer, W. Schiefenhövel & M. Stoneking, 2000. Melanesian origin of Polynesian Y chromosomes. *Current Biology* 10, 1237–46.

Kayser, M., S. Brauer, G. Weiss, W. Schiefenhövel, P. Underhill & M. Stoneking, 2001. Independent histories of human Y chromosomes from Melanesia. *American Journal of Human Genetics* 68, 173–90.

Mahdi, W., 1994. Some Austronesian maverick protoforms with culture-historical implications - II. *Oceanic Linguistics* 33, 431–90.

Mallory, J.P., 1989. *In Search of the Indo-Europeans.* London. Thames and Hudson.

Meacham, W., 1984–85. On the improbability of Austronesian origins in South China. *Asian Perspectives* 26, 89–106.

Melton, T., R. Peterson, A.J. Redd, N. Saha, A.S.M. Sofro, J. Martinson & M. Stoneking, 1995. Polynesian genetic affinities with Southeast Asian populations as identified by mtDNA analysis. *American Journal of Human Genetics* 57, 403–14.

Merriwether, D.A., J.S. Friedlaender, J. Mediavilla, C. Mgone, F. Gentz & R. Ferrell, 1999. Mitochondrial DNA variation is an indicator of Austronesian influence in Island Melanesia. *American Journal of Physical Anthropology* 110, 243–70.

Old, J.M., J.B. Clegg, D.J. Weatherall & P.B. Booth, 1980. Hb J Tongariki is Associated with a Thalassaemia. *Nature* 273, 319–20.

Oppenheimer, S.J., 1998. *Eden in the East.* London: Weidenfeld & Nicolson.

Oppenheimer, S.J. & M. Richards, 2001. Polynesian origins: slow boat to Melanesia? Brief communications. *Nature* 410, 166–7.

Oppenheimer, S.J., D.R. Higgs, D.J. Weatherall, J. Barker & R.A. Spark, 1984. Alpha thalassaemia in Papua New Guinea. *Lancet* I, 424–6.

Redd, A.J., N. Takezaki, S.T. Sherry, S.T. McGarvey, A.S.M. Sofro & M. Stoneking, 1995. Evolutionary history of the COII/tRNA(Lys) intergenic 9-base-pair deletion in human mitochondrial DNAs from the Pacific. *Molecular Biology and Evolution* 12, 604–15.

Renfrew, C., 1987. *Archaeology and Language: the Puzzle of Indo-European Origins.* London: Jonathan Cape.

Richards, M., S.J. Oppenheimer & B. Sykes, 1998. MtDNA suggests Polynesian origins in Eastern Indonesia. *American Journal of Human Genetics* 63, 1234–6.

Richards, M., V. Macaulay, E. Hickey, E. Vega, B. Sykes, V. Guida, C. Rengo, D. Sellitto, F. Cruciani, T. Kivisild, R. Villems, M. Thomas, S. Rychkov, O. Rychkov, Y. Rychkov, M. Golge, D. Dimitrov, E. Hill, D. Bradley, V. Romano, F. Calí, G. Vona, A. Demaine, S. Papiha, C. Triantaphyllidis, G. Stefanescu, J. Hatina, M. Belledi, A. di Rienzo, A. Novelletto, A. Oppenheim, S. Norby, N. Al-Zaheri, S. Santachiara-Benerecetti, R. Scozzari, A. Torroni & H.-J. Bandelt, 2000. Tracing European founder lineages in the Near Eastern mtDNA pool. *American Journal of Human Genetics* 67, 1251–76.

Sather, C., 1995. Sea nomads and rainforest hunter-gatherers: foraging adaptations in the Indo-Malaysian archipelago, in *The Austronesians Historical and Comparative Perspectives*, ed. P. Bellwood. Canberra: The Australian National University, 229–68.

Semino, O., G. Passarino, P.J. Oefner, A.A. Lin, S. Arbuzova, L.E. Beckman, G. de Benedictis, P. Francalacci, A. Kouvatsi, S. Limborska, M. Marcikiæ, A. Mika, B. Mika, D. Primorac, A.S. Santachiara-Benerecetti, L.L. Cavalli-Sforza & P.A. Underhill, 2000. The genetic legacy of Paleolithic *Homo sapiens sapiens* in extant Europeans: a Y-chromosome perspective. *Science* 290, 1155–9.

Solheim II, W., 1994. Southeast Asia and Korea from the beginnings of food production to the first states, in *The History of Humanity*, ed. S.J. De Laet. London: Routledge, 468–81.

Solheim II, W., 1996. The Nusantao and north–south dispersals, in *The Chiang Mai Papers*, vol. 2, ed. P. Bellwood. *Bulletin of the Indo-Pacific Prehistory Association* 15, 101–9.

Su, B., J. Li, P. Underhill, J. Martinson, N. Saha, S.T. McGarvey, M.D. Shriver, J. Chu, P. Oefner, R. Chakraborty & R. Deka, 2000. Polynesian origins: insights from the Y chromosome. *Proceedings of the National Academy of Sciences of the USA* 97, 8225–8.

Swadling, P., 1997. Changing shorelines and cultural orientations in the Sepik-Ramu, Papua New Guinea: implications for Pacific prehistory. *World Archaeology* 29(1), 1–14.

Sykes, B., A. Leiboff, J. Low-Beer, S. Tetzner & M. Richards, 1995. The origins of the Polynesians — an interpretation from mitochondrial lineage analysis. *American Journal of Human Genetics* 57, 1463–75.

Terrell, J.E., 1999. Pacific lizards or red herrings. *Archaeology* 52(3), 24–5.

Terrell, J.E., 2001. The uncommon sense of race, language, and culture, in *Archaeology, Language, and History: Essays on Culture and Ethnicity Archaeology, Language, and History: Essays on Culture and Ethnicity*, ed. J.E. Terrell J.E. Westport (CT): Bergin & Garvey.

Terrell, J.E. & R.L. Welsch, 1997. Lapita and the temporal geography of prehistory. *Antiquity* 71, 548–72.

Terrell, J.E., K.M. Kelly & P. Rainbird, 2001. Foregone conclusions?: in search of 'Papuans' and 'Austronesians'. *Current Anthropology* 42, 97–124.

Trask, R.L., 1996. *Historical Linguistics*. London. Arnold.

Underhill, P.A., P.D. Shen, A.A. Lin, L. Jin, G. Passarino, W.H. Yang, E. Kauffman, B. Bonné-Tamir, J. Bertranpetit, P. Francalacci, M. Ibrahim, T. Jenkins, J.R. Kidd, S.Q. Mehdi, M.T. Seielstad, R.S. Wells, A. Piazza, R.W. Davis, M.W. Feldman, L.L. Cavalli-Sforza & P.J. Oefner, 2000. Y-chromosome sequence variation and the history of human populations. *Nature Genetics* 26, 358–61.

Underhill, P.A., G. Passarino, A.A. Lin, S. Marzuki, P. Oefner, L.L. Cavalli-Sforza & G.K. Chambers, 2001. Maori origins, Y-chromosome haplotypes and implications for human history in the Pacific. *Human Mutation* 17, 271–80.

Wolff, J., 1995. The position of the Austronesian languages of Taiwan within the Austronesian group, in *Austronesian Studies Relating to Taiwan*, eds. P.J. Li, J.-K.C. Tsang, Y. Huang, D. Ho & C. Tseng (eds.), 1995. *Austronesian Studies Relating to Taiwan*. (Institute of History and Philology Symposium Series 3.) Taipei: Academia Sinica, 521–83.

Chapter 23

Can the Hypothesis of Language/Agriculture Co-dispersal be *Tested* with Archaeogenetics?

Matthew Hurles

It is a rare opportunity for a biologist to be able to escape from the shackles of peer-reviewed journals and discuss issues in greater depth. To be able to do so with such an eminent readership and in response to the two thought-provoking articles by Peter Bellwood (2001) and Colin Renfrew (2000) is a double pleasure.

Having been given this opportunity, I want to explore a number of seemingly disparate strands in considering the integration of the study of extant genetic diversity with the investigation of the hypothesis of the co-dispersal of language and agriculture.

The first of these strands is a reformulation of published and unpublished data on genetic diversity in Southeast Asia and the Pacific and of recently published data in Europe. Initially, I shall concentrate on the former region and consider how the story from genetic data has changed over the past ten years. Then I shall move on to a comparative analysis of the two regions above, both of which are hypothesized to have undergone language/agriculture co-dispersal. Specifically I wish to draw from Peter Bellwood's depiction of 'friction zones' (Bellwood 2001) and attempt to demonstrate how such zones might appear to the geneticist.

The second strand is a consideration of what is required to attempt hypothesis *testing* as opposed to merely demonstrating hypothesis *compatibility*. My scientific background leads me to try to falsify hypotheses. It is entirely possible to weave a narrative from genetic data alone. However, as John Brookfield cautions (Brookfield 2000): 'The conjunction of extraordinary interest and largely uninformative data combine to make inference about human origins one of the more speculative branches of the biological sciences.'

The third strand is a consideration of how the evolution of our multi-disciplinary field and the nature of the individual disciplines may lead us to skewed interpretations. There are probably fewer people less qualified than I am to discuss such sociological phenomena. I am aware, however, that my position as a geneticist at an archaeological institute affords a rather unique view. I see the different nature of our data and the publishing cultures of our fields as being barriers to effective communication, and thus welcome the present bringing together of disciplines.

Patrick Kirch notes, probably very accurately, that (Gibbons 2001): 'What struck me in reading the genetics papers is they cite my book on the Lapita peoples, but they haven't read it.'

It is an unspoken truth that the nature of peer-reviewed journals, impact factors and the prevailing academic culture reward academics who write papers more than they read them! John Terrell laments the over-simplistic rendering of Pacific prehistory given in the introduction to genetic papers (Terrell *et al.* 2001), not realizing that rather than being an authorial preference for dichotomization, it is a publishing necessity for brevity, however much we might wish it were not so. (As an intellectual exercise, try rendering a consensus settlement history for Southeast Asia and the Pacific in a single paragraph without appearing to dichotomize the issues.)

My desire to explore this novel realm is stimulated by the fact that, to my mind, the manner in which genetic data have sometimes been integrated with more established archaeological and linguistic data sets in the Pacific has been to some degree conditioned upon poor communication between the disciplines rather than patterns in the data. My implicit assumption is that, as equal partners in this multidisciplinary enterprise, we should attempt to generate interpretations that are free from such historical contingencies. It is undeniable that prehistoric interpretation of extant genetic diversity is a relatively young and rapidly changing field. However, the utility of present data, specifically that which does not accord with expectation, should not be ignored on the basis of perceived immaturity. An immature field is one that panders to preconceived expectations and outside influence and is thus incapable of generating its own hypotheses. A mature field is one that does not suffer these faults and can generate results stable to future advances, not one that has ceased data gathering and generating new analytical methodologies.

A point which I feel has been poorly appreciated is that genetics has to start from its own foundations, not those set for it by more established disciplines that investigate related but not identical prehistories. After all, *a priori*, biological and cultural origins need not be coupled at all. If genetic research had over a century worth of illustrious history to draw upon whereas archaeology was a recent and dynamic innovation, we would not wish archaeologists to start where we left off, exploring what we might think were only those realms of inference into which our own data cannot lead. Rather, we would want archaeology to work from first principles, building up an entirely independent picture that can be latterly integrated with other disciplines. Premature integration proceeds at the expense of independence. That is why it is important for major genetic studies to start from first principles and why some papers will appear to other disciplines as revisiting an already settled consensus.

Throughout this paper I shall attempt to supply explanations of why genetic data are analyzed as they are. Whilst full comprehension of all fields within multi-disciplinary syntheses can never be realized, a greater understanding of both the nature of the data and the methodologies used will hopefully be useful to both archaeologists and linguists. Peter Bellwood points out that (Bellwood 2001, 192): 'archaeologists . . . often have unrealistic views about how languages are transmitted throughout time and space'.

The same is undoubtedly true of the transmission of genetic information. In many senses, although genetics is the Johnny-come-lately to the archaeo-linguistic party, it is linguistics and genetics that have the most striking similarities in terms of the nature of their data. Both of these disciplines deal primarily with extant diversity, with patterns that represent the outcomes of processes that may or may not be represented in the archaeological record. It can be argued that both are strongly resistant to horizontal transmission. In looking at outcomes, linguists and geneticists are afforded a different perspective on prehistory, one that emphasizes the output of 'compound interest' intergenerational processes.

The hypothesis

According to Peter Bellwood the farming/language co-dispersal hypothesis is (his italics, Bellwood 2001, 195): 'the *foundation* dispersals of the major agriculturalist language families . . . have a high chance of being directly associated with the **spreads of initial farming populations** through regions previously occupied by hunter-gatherers'. As phrased above, what in this hypothesis is testable for the archaeogeneticist? What can be falsified with genetic data? Bellwood is careful not to suggest mechanisms of dispersal, but merely an association. However, he does include the phrase which I have highlighted in bold which clearly indicates a requirement for directional gene flow, but how much gene flow? Owing to the lack of specification such a hypothesis can only be falsified if it can be proved that absolutely no gene flow has occurred. This is clearly false. Amongst other clear indications, there are clinal patterns of diversity at multiple loci that have been noted radiating from multiple centres of Neolithic innovation (Cavalli-Sforza *et al.* 1994; Kayser *et al.* 2001; Rosser *et al.* 2000; Semino *et al.* 2000). Selection could not be expected to be acting on all loci (Barbujani 2000).

An interesting point that illustrates the need to consider dispersal mechanisms is the directionality of clinal patterns. In Europe, opposing clines, most notably of the Y-chromosomal haplogroups 1 and 9 (Rosser *et al.* 2000; Semino *et al.* 2000), have been noted. It has traditionally been assumed that haplogroup 9, in proceeding from high frequency in Southwest Asia to low frequency in Northwest Europe, is indicative of Neolithic gene flow, whereas haplogroup 1, with a diametrically opposed frequency distribution, represents Palaeolithic 'resistance' (Semino *et al.* 1996). Yet when we look at Polynesia we see the supposedly Neolithic mitochondrial DNA (mtDNA) 9bp deletion with a clinal pattern at highest frequency at the extremity of the putative dispersal (Melton *et al.* 1995; Sykes *et al.* 1995). Thus the direction of a cline need not indicate its point of origin. The crucial difference may be in the mechanism of spread. The successive founder effects of island colonization can lead to a cline that increases as it moves away, rather than towards, the point of origin. The wave-of-advance model for European Neolithic dispersal predicts a cline that decreases away from its point of origin (Ammerman & Cavalli-Sforza 1984). However, others have suggested that saltatory jumping between suitable environments is a more reasonable model for the spread of European agriculture (Van Andel & Runnels 1995), and as such would be closer in kind to a island colonization model, despite Europe's continental contiguity. Thus *a priori* we can not use the direction of a cline to indicate its origin. Furthermore, some consideration of dispersal mechanism is required for us to predict what patterns of extant genetic diversity might be expected for a given 'spread zone'.

The tendency for commentators on putative dispersals to hedge their bets on mechanisms leaves little for the geneticist to test. Thus, we are left with reading between the lines to seek testable hypotheses. The alternative is to resort to weaving narratives from genetic data. Here I want to raise the issue of the degree of genetic continuity between those at the origin of agricultural dispersals and those at the periphery of the 'spread' zone. My motivation is that there seems to be a wide range of differing expectations within archaeology. Within the Austronesian 'spread zone', Bellwood believes the majority of Polynesian genetic ancestry lies within Southeast Asian Neolithic dispersals that originated in Southeast China and Taiwan (Bellwood 2001), whereas Terrell believes that the majority of Polynesian genes derive from sources in and around coastal Papua New Guinea (Terrell *et al.* 1997). Roger Green would seem to predict a position intermediate between these opposing views (Green 1991). Note that these views as represented here are entirely of the author's derivation and I apologize for any misrepresentations. Note also that the opposing views of Bellwood and Terrell are not represented as qualitative dichotomies but rather lie at opposite ends of a quantitative spectrum, a 'continuum of reality' (Bellwood 2001).

Using frequency as a guide to origin is not the only tool available to the geneticist (Barbujani 2000). The study of non-recombining portions of the human genome allows us to explore chronologies contained within genetic data. This information generally comes from one of two sources. The simplest is the relative chronology that is provided by the phylogenetic tree that underpins variation at non-recombining loci. The more complex is the analysis of intra-lineage diversity.

At this point I must reiterate the difference between population dendrograms and a true phylogeny, as there seems to be much misunderstanding on this issue. Dendrograms of the form commonly used to show relationships between populations result from hierarchical clustering procedures and simply record the order in which populations were clustered together by the algorithm. They imply a bifurcating, non-reticulate, *model* of population evolution with zero gene flow, which is clearly violated

by almost every known population. As such, a population tree is merely a display tool for a statistical analysis of diversity. In contrast, a phylogeny of a non-recombining portion of a genome (a 'gene tree') is not a statistical summary but is a recapitulation of the mechanistic path or paths by which extant variation arose. In the case of the perfect phylogeny of Y-chromosomal haplotypes (the most detailed of which has been documented by Peter Underhill: Underhill *et al.* 2000), the gene tree is a phylogeny which encapsulates the precise unequivocal *mechanism* by which the extant variation arose from a most recent common ancestor. Thus the relative chronology implied by the topology of the tree cannot be violated.

Further investigation of the mtDNA 9bp deletion in the Pacific led to the delineation of a nested phylogeny of haplotypes, the youngest being the so-called 'Polynesian motif' (CGT) which accounts for the vast majority of mtDNA types in the Pacific. Its directly ancestral haplotype (CAT) could be traced all the way back along the putative axis of Neolithic dispersal and the ancestor of that haplotype (CAC) was found all over Southeast Asia, but not in the Pacific (Melton *et al.* 1995; Sykes *et al.* 1995). Thus, the relative chronology of the Polynesian motif and its ancestral haplotypes appeared to represent a similar structure to the nested clades of Austronesian languages over the same region (Pawley & Ross 1993; Gray & Jordan 2000). In 1995, this result was widely taken as support for the idea of a rapid movement of agricultural peoples spreading the Austronesian languages into the Pacific with little admixture with populations that had been resident in the 'transit' regions since the first settlement by our species. I would argue that the reaching of this conclusion reflected both the lack of an analytical method for determining an absolute chronology and a lack of independence of the field as data became prematurely shoe-horned into a narrative already predominant in other more established disciplines.

A monophyletic lineage, by definition, originates in a single individual with zero diversity. Through the late 1990s a number of analytical methods became available to generate chronologies from diversity within such lineages (Forster *et al.* 1996; Thomas *et al.* 1998; Wilson & Balding 1998). At its simplest level this represents a relative chronology; the greater the diversity, the older the history of that lineage (within the population in which it is found). Diversity presents an alternative and more reliable means by which to determine the spatial origin of a cline. At a more complex level this chronology can be calibrated by a variety of means to obtain an absolute chronology. These methods require that the mutation rate be known. For sequence evolution, this is often determined indirectly through comparisons between human and chimps and calibrated using the fossil record. The mutation rate of faster mutating markers, such as Y-chromosomal microsatellites, can be determined directly in human pedigrees (Heyer *et al.* 1997; Kayser *et al.* 2000b).

Strikingly, these new methods showed that the Polynesian motif, which is not found in the Philippines or Taiwan, is much older (~17,000 years old, with a 95 per cent credible range of 5500–34,500 years) than would be expected if it were a mutation that occurred in transit during the Austronesian dispersal (Richards *et al.* 1998). It appears that the relative chronology apparent in the phylogeny is indicative of prior settlement of the region rather than Neolithic dispersals, which (as in Europe) followed a similar trajectory from the Asian mainland. Any investigation of origins must include some consideration of time depth, otherwise we are all Africans.

At present, published dates from genetic data come with wide confidence limits, which often do not allow us to exclude competing explanations. In the previous case we were distinguishing between a Neolithic dispersal which should have reached eastern Indonesia ~4000 years ago and an initial settlement that started an order of magnitude earlier, a substantial difference that allows genetic evidence to discriminate between the two scenarios.

It is worthwhile considering the sources of error within such determinations of absolute chronology. The first source is inescapable, the stochasticity of evolution. If we observe a certain number of 'tails' when spinning a coin, how accurately can we know how many times the coin was spun? Six 'tails' suggests the coin has been spun twelve times, but it could easily have been eleven or thirteen (read mutations for 'tails' and generations for 'spins'). Thus, we have to generate confidence limits around our central estimates. Unfortunately, it appears that the confidence limits depend on the demography of the population. Thus, our second source of error is our uncertainty of the prehistoric demography. It is a moot point as to how accurately such parameters can ever be known. The decline in recent absolute age estimates noted by Bellwood (2001, 199) results from two independent developments in two different dating methodologies. One class of methods, those involving coalescent simulation, have been improved to incorporate simple models of population expansion rather than a constant population size (Hurles *et al.* 1999; Thomson *et al.* 2000). Unlike

other analyses the central estimates of these methods are also sensitive to the population model being used. My feeling is that, as these methods incorporate ever more realistic population models (e.g. subdivided populations), we may see a slight adjustment upward in age estimates and not the further reduction that Bellwood hopes for. A second class of method, 'rho dating', has also seen a reduction in age estimates for European mitochondrial lineages as a result of greater sampling in the 'Near Eastern mtDNA pool' (Richards *et al.* 2000). Again, further dramatic age reductions are unlikely. The third source of error results from uncertainty in the parameters that are used to relate diversity to years, namely mutation rate and generation time. As more data are accumulated, the former parameter is becoming known with greater and greater precision (Kayser *et al.* 2000b). However, the possibly unknowable uncertainty in prehistoric demography leads me to think that genetic dating will never approach the precision of radiocarbon dating, although some improvement can be expected. As a consequence, I do not expect that the estimated age of the mtDNA Polynesian motif will fall such that it could have arisen as recently as the Southeast Asian Neolithic.

What does the Y chromosome tell us about Polynesian origins? Whilst there is not one single lineage that predominates to the level of the mtDNA Polynesian motif, my own research has identified that the most common paternal lineage in Polynesia, which accounts for approximately half of genuine Polynesian Y chromosomes (post-contact European admixture excluded: Hurles *et al.* 1998), can only be traced as far back as coastal Papua New Guinea (PNG). A number of recent Y-chromosomal studies have identified very similar, phylogenetically overlapping, lineages which again can only be traced back to coastal PNG and eastern Indonesia (Capelli *et al.* 2001; Kayser *et al.* 2000a). A common feature of these closely related lineages from independent studies, apart from their absence from Taiwan and the Philippines, is that estimates for their age are all older than the settlement history of the Neolithic in these regions.

Eastern Indonesia and coastal New Guinea as an Austronesian friction zone

Given that many genetic studies, including all those described above, have shown a large degree of genetic continuity throughout island Southeast Asia, can we consider the transit of Neolithic culture from eastern Indonesia to the western Pacific as having passed through a 'friction zone'?

Bellwood (2001, 187–9) introduces the concept of 'friction zones' with:

> Clearly, early agricultural economies and their associated material cultures could spread extremely rapidly . . . But environmental boundaries and transitions slowed down the process by creating friction, . . . such 'friction zones' served as likely arenas of major reticulation and reformulation within linguistic and genetic realms, as well as in material (archaeological) culture.

It is important to remember here in the context of phylogenetics that the use of 'reticulate' refers to a *model* of processes of population interaction. The underlying *mechanism* by which non-recombining portions of the genome accumulate diversity remains unequivocally non-reticulate.

We might assume that a friction zone will reveal itself to the geneticist as a region in which, due to temporal stalling (amongst other factors), there is substantially more admixture between incoming agriculturalists and indigenous hunter-gatherers. Such zones are traditionally visualized as being at the fringes of spread zones, as in Northern and Western Europe (Bellwood 2001).

However, in special cases innovations may allow the periphery of prior settlement to be traversed. This prior periphery, when viewed from the perspective of the final distribution of settlement, may appear to be a zone of 'friction'. This clearly seems to have occurred during the period of Polynesian origins with the role of the outriggered and later double types of sailing canoe in the colonization of the Pacific (Pawley & Pawley 1994). In an analogous fashion we might consider that the colonization of the New World resulted from cumulative European innovations that allowed spread through a prior periphery in Iberia. The only difference would be that it took Europeans some 3500 years to innovate but the Proto-Lapita peoples only 500–1000 years. This metaphor could be explored further in terms of the concomitant spread of Romance languages, European agricultural practices and, to a lesser extent, genes to the Americas.

It is important to note that a friction zone can only ever be a relative term when defined in terms of a slowing down relative to the speed of Neolithic movement through the surrounding areas. The defining of a friction zone in this way is entirely dependent on the dimensions of the region being considered. If one was to define the surrounding area as the present-day geographical distribution of cultures owing ancestry to the Southeast Asian Neolithic, and to consider in which region was the greatest genetic change noted, that region would be eastern Indonesia and coastal PNG. This suggests that present-day populations lying to the east of this friction zone, including Polynesians, should bear a genetic imprint of such 'friction'. This does not deny the existence of more locally distributed friction zones within the Austronesian expansion.

Disassembling biological and cultural suites in the Austronesian expansion

It is vital that extant genetic diversity is viewed as a suite of prehistoric signals of different time depths. Whereas cultural characteristics are often assembled into suites when they occur in a spatially and temporally congruent fashion more often than can be expected by chance, the nature of genetic data is that the suite has to be disassembled into its component parts. It is impossible to collect 'stratified' genetic data to make inferences solely about a given time period. Each allele has its own history, which may be a mixed one. Each locus contains multiple alleles and therefore a set of stories. Hence, the geneticist's predilection for 'populations'; an individual can only reveal part of *one* story and there is no guarantee that that you will get parts of the *same* story if you sample one individual from each location. An entire population must be assayed to get a fuller picture of each history that has contributed to the whole.

An even more important feature of genetic heritage is that genomic regions are readily dissociable by recombination. Different parts of any single genome will have independent histories. The following vastly oversimplified scenario illustrates the powerful implications of the above phenomenon. Imagine that just 1 per cent of British genetic diversity derives from Neolithic influx, so that this equates to about 300 of the estimated 30,000 genes in the human genome. If some of these genes just happen to affect skin colour and bone morphology, what might we infer from anthroposcopy and anthropometrics? It is extremely unlikely that the set of genes encoding our physical phenotype would be a representative sample of the entire genome.

Peter Bellwood points out that modern genetic diversity is a proxy for ancient genetic heritage (Bellwood 2001, 197), however, these proxies are of single loci, with quantifiable selective biases, distinguishable individual 'histories', definitive relative chronologies and a rough absolute chronology. By contrast, ancient bone morphometrics is a proxy for an unknown number of ancient genes that under-

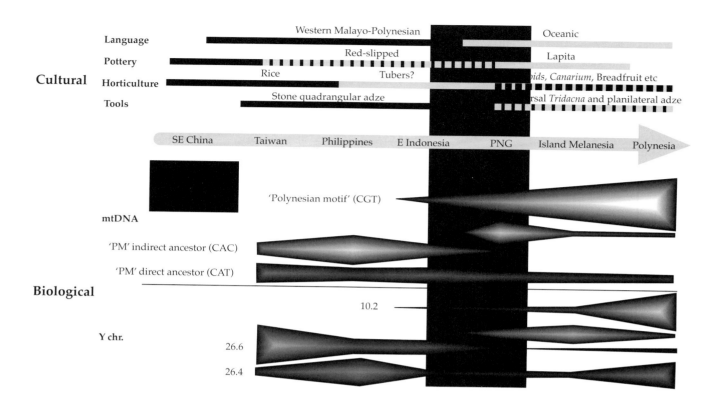

Figure 23.1. *Disassembling biological and cultural Austronesian 'suites'. The spatial distributions of cultural and biological characteristics are shown either side of an axis of Neolithic spread in SE Asia and the Pacific. MtDNA lineage data come from Melton et al. 1995 and Sykes et al. 1995, and are labelled according to the nomenclatures in those papers. Y-chromosomal data are from unpublished data (Hurles et al. 2002). The shaded inset shows the phylogenetic structure of the mtDNA Polynesian Motif (PM) and its ancestral lineages. The vertical box indicates a common geographical region of rapid change. Cultural comparisons come from Green 1991 and Kirch 1999. Dashed grey lines within the culture suites indicate supplementary changes, solid lines indicate replacement.*

went unknown selection pressures, both environmental and social. As such, a number of competing 'histories', both selective and population-based, are likely to be encapsulated within the one phenotype. At most, one predominant story is likely to be readable through the lens of these largely non-dissociable 'histories'. Whether this history is accurately recorded or represents in an unbiased manner the weight of multiple stories is likely to remain a moot point, although the inability to reconstruct the known primate phylogeny from craniodental morphology is a notable recent result (Collard & Wood 2000).

Figure 23.1 shows the spatial distribution of cultural characters belonging to several of the Neolithic suites alongside the major maternal and paternal lineages of the region. The spatial axis chosen is the commonly proposed route of Austronesian spread from Southeast Asia to Polynesia (from Taiwan, via the Philippines and Indonesia, then north

of New Guinea and through Melanesia). MtDNA and the Y chromosome exhibit highly similar if quantitatively variant sets of lineages. Concordant patterns from independent loci argue against selection as a causal factor (Barbujani 2000). Broadly speaking, there are four main patterns of Neolithic lineage distribution along this axis. The predominant lineages in Polynesia can only be traced back as far as eastern Indonesia or coastal PNG within the Neolithic. There are two types of lineages that are at appreciable frequency across Southeast Asia. The first can be found at diminished frequencies in the Pacific, the second dies out abruptly in eastern Indonesia. Finally there are lineages present at low frequency in Polynesia which most likely originate in highland Papuans.

To my mind the clearly multiple genetic origins of Polynesians negate serious discussion of a single 'biological' homeland. Thus the region of greatest

Erratum

In Chapter 23 (Can the Hypothesis of Language/Agriculture Co-dispersal be *Tested* with Archaeogenetics? by Matthew Hurles), Figure 23.1 on p. 304 lost some vital information in pre-press and it should actually appear as below:

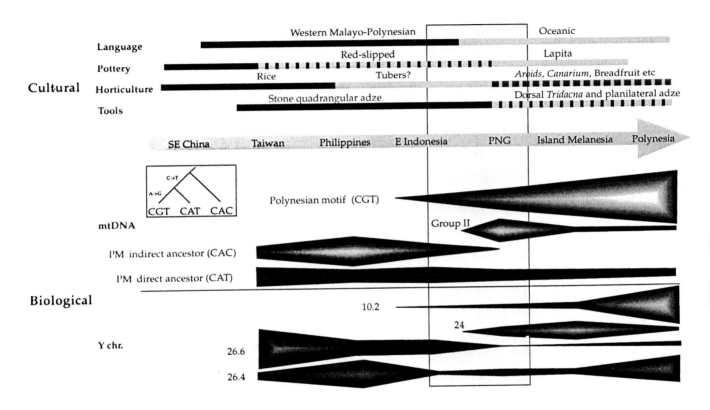

Figure 23.1. *Disassembling biological and cultural Austronesian 'suites'. The spatial distributions of cultural and biological characteristics are shown either side of an axis of Neolithic spread in SE Asia and the Pacific. MtDNA lineage data come from Melton et al. 1995 and Sykes et al. 1995, and are labelled according to the nomenclatures in those papers. Y-chromosomal data are from unpublished data (Hurles et al. 2002). The shaded inset shows the phylogenetic structure of the mtDNA Polynesian Motif (PM) and its ancestral lineages. The vertical box indicates a common geographical region of rapid change. Cultural comparisons come from Green 1991 and Kirch 1999. Dashed grey lines within the culture suites indicate supplementary changes, solid lines indicate replacement.*

genetic change along the whole axis occurs between eastern Indonesia and the islands off the northeastern coast of New Guinea. These genetic changes are mirrored by substantial changes in tool use, voyaging technologies, agricultural crops and pottery (Green 1991). All of these cultural features appear to be surprisingly uniform between Taiwan and eastern Indonesia. Moreover, this geographical region of major change is also home to the only major rake-like structure within the phylogeny of Austronesian languages. This kind of comparison emphasizes spatial discontinuities, whereas Bellwood focuses his attention upon temporal transitions. Yet when space and time are closely correlated, as is the case in dispersals, the two become to some degree interchangeable.

The geographical discontinuities evident in both the cultural and biological records between eastern Indonesia and the Bismarck Archipelago would seem to indicate that a greater degree of integration has occurred in this region between incoming and indigenous peoples than occurred either previously or subsequently along this spatial axis. It appears, on both temporal and spatial grounds, that the periods of time during which (i) the Lapita cultural complex was being assembled and (ii) genes were flowing relatively more rapidly from indigenous peoples into Austronesian-speaking populations, are congruent. These concordant discontinuities reflect closely the expectations of the Triple-I model of *intrusion, integration* and *innovation* underpinning the origins of the Lapita cultural complex proposed by Roger Green (1991).

It is tempting to equate these changes to a possible stalling of the spread of Austronesians represented by the gap in accepted radiocarbon dates between the earliest Neolithic occupation of eastern Indonesia and the first Lapita sites (Spriggs 1989). However, Irian Jaya remains poorly characterized archaeologically and the whole region requires better-documented dates before such a correlation can be regarded as anything stronger than conjecture.

Additionally, there is growing preliminary evidence from both Y-chromosomal (Hurles *et al.* 2002) and mtDNA studies (Lum & Cann 2000) that Nuclear Micronesians (Carolines, Marshalls, Kiribati) have a clearly distinct set of lineages to those found in Polynesia. These lineages also seem to originate proximally in Melanesia and eastern Indonesia, suggesting a distinct founder pool to Polynesians. Thus, these early data seem to mimic intriguingly the rake-like pattern of linguistic diversity observed in the Oceanic subfamily (Pawley & Ross 1993).

Comparing the Neolithic trajectories of Southeast Asia and Europe

It is harder to perform a similar spatial analysis of European maternal and paternal lineages, despite the larger data sets that have accumulated over recent years (Richards *et al.* 2000; Rosser *et al.* 2000; Semino *et al.* 2000). Y-chromosomal studies of European diversity lag behind those of Island Southeast Asia, in the sense that no published data exist with which to generate *reliable* absolute chronologies for the multiple and clearly clinal paternal lineages. In contrast, much work has gone into dating the major mtDNA lineages apparent in Europe, with the result that most seem to predate the putative arrival of Neolithic immigrants (Richards *et al.* 2000). However, there appears to be little discernible spatial pattern to the distribution of these major lineages within Europe (Simoni *et al.* 2000; M.E. Hurles unpublished analyses). It remains to be seen whether there are more geographically substructured sublineages of these major maternal clades. The reticulate nature of present mtDNA data sets makes defining monophyletic sublineages problematic. Thus, in the absence of large temporally-structured datasets from ancient DNA work, it seems that it will also not be possible to define potential friction zones in Europe using the spatial approach adopted above, due to the almost homogeneous distribution of major maternal lineages.

With the above caveats in mind I have attempted to examine the spatial distribution of some notable European paternal lineages (Rosser *et al.* 2000). Figure 23.2 shows a comparison of paternal lineage distributions along a Southeast–Northwest European axis of putative Neolithic and Indo-European dispersal, alongside those from the Austronesian axis examined above.

What is noticeable is the lack of a single region of rapid change in Europe analogous to that found between eastern Indonesia and the islands Northeast of New Guinea. If the hypothesis that haplogroup 1 represents a Palaeolithic remnant is proven by absolute chronology (or by further phylogenetic resolution leading to a more detailed relative chronology), then it would appear that, rather than representing friction zones *per se*, the Northern and Western limits of Europe represent the endpoints of reasonably strong processes of genetic integration that had been operating at relatively similar rates across the entire continent. Such a model might explain the low frequency of definitively Neolithic maternal lineages. Under such a model I would estimate the level of

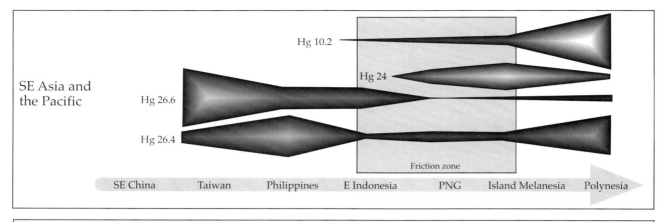

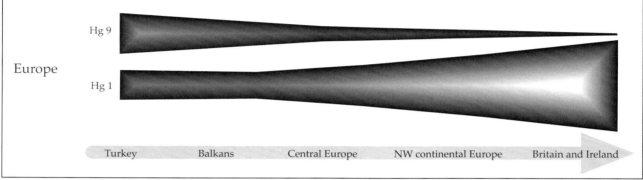

Figure 23.2. *Comparing the clinal paternal lineages of Europe and Island SE Asia and the Pacific. Spatial distributions of Y-chromosomal lineages against the Neolithic spread axes of Europe and SE Asia and the Neolithic. European data come from Rosser* et al. *2000 and is labelled according to their nomenclature.*

European genetic admixture to be intermediate between the low levels occurring in Island Southeast Asia and the high levels encountered during the pre-Lapita gestation in eastern Indonesia and the Islands Northeast of New Guinea. Undoubtedly there is bound to be some variation in the amount of 'friction' experienced by the different primary Neolithic cultures in Europe, and a recent genetics study claims to have shown this, albeit with questionable corroborating evidence (Semino *et al.* 2000). An alternative scenario to explain the lack of obvious friction zones in Europe might be that the local heterogeneities in the genetic landscape resulting from such Neolithic 'friction zones' have been 'levelled' by substantial amounts of gene flow, enabled by such a continental landmass.

Conclusions

Bellwood has suggested that in the Pacific it is; 'the genetics that is causing headaches' (Gibbons 2001), presumably because the majority of Pacific peoples seem to trace their maternal and paternal origins, within the Neolithic, to a more proximal 'homeland' than that indicated by both their agricultural history and their languages. Yet there is by no means a perfect congruence between the agricultural and linguistic 'homelands'. A suite of cultural characteristics is defined through its *relative* congruence in terms of both spatial and temporal distribution. However, such congruence is rarely perfect. I know of no evidence that Austronesian languages were ever spoken on the Asian mainland, from where rice agriculture clearly originates. In addition the birth of agriculture in southwestern Asia is thought to have sponsored the dispersal of multiple languages (Barbujani *et al.* 1994; Bellwood 2001), so clearly there is no 1:1 relationship here either. It remains to be seen whether it is a general rule that the peripheries of agriculturally-sponsored spread zones owe the majority of their genetic heritage to more indigenous sources within the Neolithic, thus representing a substantial residue of indigenous Palaeolithic peoples. Moreover, it would be interesting to investigate to what degree agricultural 'starbursts' are capable of co-dispersing languages of neighbouring 'early-adopters' as well as the language of the innovators themselves.

At a more general level, there does seems to be clear genetic evidence for contemporaneous gene flow accompanying the spread of Neolithic cultures and their associated languages both in Europe and in Southeast Asia and the Pacific. Whilst it would seem to validate the expectation of a tighter fit between genes, languages and culture during such episodes, there is a substantial difference here between saying that, during agricultural dispersals, biology and culture will be coupled more closely than during other cultural episodes, and saying that the *majority* of genes at the edge of spread zones trace their origin to the population of agricultural innovators.

It remains to be seen whether the archaeological record, which is so successful at allowing the reconstruction of ancient societies, identities and ways of life, under-represents to some degree the 'compound interest' of inter-generation admixture that seems to be critical in understanding the spatial and temporal distribution of genetic diversity. The relative impenetrability of temporal trajectories of linguistic reconstruction to such processes results from the infrequent nature of language shift. By contrast, the ability of a population to contain *multiple* genetic lineages at no fitness cost (as opposed to the communication costs associated with having multiple languages) renders the genetic record more sensitive to detecting such admixture.

Suggestions for the future integration of archaeogenetics and archaeology

I propose a model similar to Roger Green's Triple I model for a truly multi-disciplinary investigation of the Language/Agriculture co-dispersal hypothesis. We have recently seen the *intrusion* of genetics into prehistorical studies. Now that genetics has achieved a more independent footing, we need a more active process of *integration* and *innovation*. It would help enormously if experts writing about their own discipline could explicitly suggest testable hypotheses to be explored by the others. Computer modelling of prehistoric processes should prove indispensable, both to test and generate new hypotheses, and to explore the limits of knowability, specifically with regard to prehistoric demography. Such models should ideally draw upon the complementary strengths of the different disciplines.

References

Ammerman, A.J. & L.L. Cavalli-Sforza, 1984. *Neolithic Transition and the Genetics of Populations in Europe.* Princeton (NJ): Princeton University Press.

Barbujani, G., 2000. Geographical patterns: how to identify them, and why. *Human Biology* 72, 133–53.

Barbujani, G., A. Pilastro, S. Dedomenico & C. Renfrew, 1994. Genetic-variation in North Africa and Eurasia: Neolithic demic diffusion vs Paleolithic colonization. *American Journal of Physical Anthropology* 95, 137–54.

Bellwood, P., 2001. Early agriculturalist population diasporas? farming, languages and genes. *Annual Review of Anthropology* 30, 181–207.

Brookfield, J.F.Y., 2000. How recent were the Y chromosome ancestors? *Current Biology* 10, R722–3.

Capelli, C., J.F. Wilson, M. Richards, M.P.H. Stumpf, F. Gratrix, S. Oppenheimer, P. Underhill, V.L. Pascali, T.M. Ko & D.B. Goldstein, 2001. A predominantly indigenous paternal heritage for the Austronesian-speaking peoples of insular Southeast Asia and Oceania. *American Journal of Human Genetics* 68, 432–43.

Cavalli-Sforza, L.L., P. Menozzi & A. Piazza, 1994. *The History and Geography of Human Genes.* Princeton (NJ): Princeton University Press.

Collard, M. & B. Wood, 2000. How reliable are human phylogenetic hypotheses? *Proceedings of the National Academy of Sciences of the USA* 97, 5003–6.

Forster, P., R. Harding, A. Torroni & H.-J. Bandelt, 1996. Origin and evolution of Native American mtDNA variation: a reappraisal. *American Journal of Human Genetics* 59, 935–45.

Gibbons, A., 2001. The peopling of the Pacific. *Science* 291, 1735–7.

Gray, R.D. & F.M. Jordan, 2000. Language trees support the express-train sequence of Austronesian expansion. *Nature* 405, 1052–5.

Green, R.C., 1991. The Lapita cultural complex: current evidence and proposed models. *Indo-Pacific Prehistory Association Bulletin* 11, 295–305.

Heyer, E., J. Puymirat, P. Dieltjes, E. Bakker & P. de Knijff, 1997. Estimating Y-chromosome specific microsatellite mutation frequencies using deep rooting pedigrees. *Human Molecular Genetics* 6, 799–803.

Hurles, M.E., C. Irven, J. Nicholson, P.G. Taylor, F.R. Santos J. Loughlin, M.A. Jobling & B.C. Sykes, 1998. European Y-chromosomal lineages in Polynesians: a contrast to the population structure revealed by mtDNA. *American Journal of Human Genetics* 63, 1793–806.

Hurles, M.E., R. Veitia, E. Arroyo, M. Armenteros, J. Bertranpetit, A. Pérez-Lezaun, E. Bosch, M. Shlumukova, A. Cambon-Thomsen, K. McElreavey, A. López de Munain, A. Röhl, I.J. Wilson, L. Singh, A. Pandya, F.R. Santos, C. Tyler-Smith & M.A. Jobling, 1999. Recent male-mediated gene flow over a linguistic barrier in Iberia suggested by analysis of a Y-chromosomal DNA polymorphism. *American*

Journal of Human Genetics 65, 1437–48.

Hurles, M.E., J. Nicholson, E. Bosch, C. Renfrew, B.C. Sykes & M.A. Jobling, 2002. Y-chromosomal evidence for the origins of oceanic-speaking peoples. *Genetics* 160, 289–303.

Kayser, M., S. Brauer, G. Weiss, P. Underhill, L. Roewer, W. Schiefenhovel & M. Stoneking, 2000a. Melanesian origin of Polynesian Y chromosomes. *Current Biology* 10, 1237–46.

Kayser, M., L. Roewer, M. Hedman, L. Henke, J. Henke, S. Brauer, C. Kruger, M. Krawczak, M. Nagy, T. Dobosz, R. Szibor, P. de Knijff, M. Stoneking & A. Sajantila, 2000b. Characteristics and frequency of germline mutations at microsatellite loci from the human Y chromosome, as revealed by direct observation in father/son pairs. *American Journal of Human Genetics* 66, 1580–88.

Kayser, M., S. Brauer, G. Weiss, W. Schiefenhovel, P. Underhill & M. Stoneking, 2001. Independent histories of human Y chromosomes from Melanesia and Australia. *American Journal of Human Genetics* 68, 173–90.

Kirch, P.V., 1999. *The Lapita Peoples*. Oxford: Blackwells.

Lum, J.K. & R.L. Cann, 2000. MtDNA lineage analyses: origins and migrations of Micronesians and Polynesians. *American Journal of Physical Anthropology* 113, 151–68.

Melton, T., R. Peterson, A.J. Redd, N. Saha, A.S.M. Sofro, J. Martinson & M. Stoneking, 1995. Polynesian genetic affinities with Southeast Asian populations as identified by mtDNA analysis. *American Journal of Human Genetics* 57, 403–14.

Pawley, A. & M. Pawley, 1994. Early Austronesian terms for canoe parts and seafaring, in *Austronesian Terminologies: Continuity and Change*, eds. A.K. Pawley & M.D. Ross. (Pacific Linguistics Series C 127.) Canberra: Research School of Pacific and Asian Studies, 329–61.

Pawley, A. & M. Ross, 1993. Austronesian historical linguistics and culture history. *Annual Review of Anthropology* 22, 425–59.

Renfrew, C., 2000. At the edge of knowability: towards a prehistory of languages. *Cambridge Archaeological Journal* 10(1), 7–34.

Richards, M., S. Oppenheimer & B. Sykes, 1998. MtDNA suggests Polynesian origins in eastern Indonesia. *American Journal of Human Genetics* 63, 1234–6.

Richards, M., V. Macaulay, E. Hickey, E. Vega, B. Sykes, V. Guida, C. Rengo, D. Sellitto, F. Cruciani, T. Kivisild, R. Villems, M. Thomas, S. Rychkov, O. Rychkov, Y. Rychkov, M. Golge, D. Dimitrov, E. Hill, D. Bradley, V. Romano, F. Calí, G. Vona, A. Demaine, S. Papiha, C. Triantaphyllidis, G. Stefanescu, J. Hatina, M. Belledi, A. di Rienzo, A. Novelletto, A. Oppenheim, S. Norby, N. Al-Zaheri, S. Santachiara-Benerecetti, R. Scozzari, A. Torroni & H.-J. Bandelt, 2000. Tracing European founder lineages in the near eastern mtDNA pool. *American Journal of Human Genetics* 67, 1251–76.

Rosser, Z.H., T. Zerjal, M.E. Hurles, M. Adojaan, D.

Alavantic, A. Amorim, W. Amos, M. Armenteros, E. Arroyo, G. Barbujani, G. Beckman, L. Beckman, J. Bertranpetit, E. Bosch, D.G. Bradley, G. Brede, G. Cooper, H. Corte-Réal, P. de Knijff, R. Decorte, Y.E. Dubrova, O. Evgrafov, A. Gilissen, S. Glisic, M. Golge, E.W. Hill, A. Jeziorowska, L. Kalaydjieva, M. Kayser, T. Kivisild, S.A. Kravchenko, A. Krumina, V. Kucinskas, J. Lavinha, L.A. Livshits, P. Malaspina, S. Maria, K. McElreavey, T.A. Meitinger, A.V. Mikelsaar, R.J. Mitchell, K. Nafa, J. Nicholson, S. Norby, A. Pandya, J. Parik, P.C. Patsalis, L. Pereira, B. Peterlin, G. Pielberg, M.L. Prata, C. Previdere, L. Roewer, S. Rootsi, D.C. Rubinsztein, J. Saillard, F.R. Santos, G. Stefanescu, B.C. Sykes, A. Tolun, R. Villems, C. Tyler-Smith & M.A. Jobling, 2000. Y-chromosomal diversity in Europe is clinal and influenced primarily by geography, rather than by language. *American Journal of Human Genetics* 67, 1526–43.

Semino, O., G. Passarino, A. Brega, M. Fellous & A.S. Santachiara-Benerecetti, 1996. A view of the Neolithic demic diffusion in Europe through two Y-chromosome-specific markers. *American Journal of Human Genetics* 59, 964–8.

Semino, O., G. Passarino, P.J. Oefner, A.A. Lin, S. Arbuzova L.E. Beckman, G. de Benedictis, P. Francalacci, A. Kouvatsi, S. Limborska, M. Marcikiae, A. Mika, B. Mika, D. Primorac, A.S. Santachiara-Benerecetti, L.L. Cavalli-Sforza & P.A. Underhill, 2000. The genetic legacy of paleolithic *Homo sapiens sapiens* in extant Europeans: a Y-chromosome perspective. *Science* 290, 1155–9.

Simoni, L., F. Calafell, D. Pettener, J. Bertranpetit & G. Barbujani, 2000. Geographic patterns of mtDNA diversity in Europe. *American Journal of Human Genetics* 66, 262–78.

Spriggs, M., 1989. The dating of the Island Southeast Asian Neolithic: an attempt at chronometric hygiene and linguistic correlation. *Antiquity* 63, 587–613.

Sykes, B., A. Leiboff, J. Low-Beer, S. Tetzner & M. Richards, 1995. The origins of the Polynesians: an interpretation from mitochondrial lineage analysis. *American Journal of Human Genetics* 57, 1463–75.

Terrell, J.E., T.L. Hunt & C. Gosden, 1997. The dimensions of social life in the Pacific: human diversity and the myth of the primitive isolate. *Current Anthropology* 38, 155–95.

Terrell, J.E., K.M. Kelly & P. Rainbird, 2001. Foregone conclusions? in search of 'Papuans' and 'Austronesians'. *Current Anthropology* 42, 97–124.

Thomas, M.G., K. Skorecki, H. Ben-Ami, T. Parfitt, N. Bradman & D.B. Goldstein, 1998. Origins of Old Testament priests. *Nature* 384, 138–40.

Thomson, R., J.K. Pritchard, P.D. Shen, P.J. Oefner & M.W. Feldman, 2000. Recent common ancestry of human Y chromosomes: evidence from DNA sequence data. *Proceedings of the National Academy of Sciences of the USA* 97, 7360–65.

Underhill, P.A., P.D. Shen, A.A. Lin, L. Jin, G. Passarino, W.H. Yang, E. Kauffman, B. Bonné-Tamir, J.

Bertranpetit, P. Francalacci, M. Ibrahim, T. Jenkins, J.R. Kidd, S.Q. Mehdi, M.T. Seielstad, R.S. Wells, A. Piazza, R.W. Davis, M.W. Feldman, L.L. Cavalli-Sforza & P.J. Oefner, 2000. Y chromosome sequence variation and the history of human populations. *Nature Genetics* 26, 358–61.

Van Andel, T. & C. Runnels, 1995. The earliest farmers in Europe. *Antiquity* 69, 481–500.

Wilson, I.J. & D.J. Balding, 1998. Genealogical inference from microsatellite data. *Genetics* 150, 499–510.

Chapter 24

Agriculture and Language Change in the Japanese Islands

Mark Hudson

The Japanese islands provide us with an important case study for understanding the relationships between agriculture, population dispersals and language change. Full-scale farming in Japan was a secondary introduction from the Asian mainland that occurred many thousands of years after the first agricultural societies developed in China. The fact that the transition from foraging to farming is relatively recent in the Japanese islands, however, means that the relevant archaeological and human biological records are extremely good. Linguistically, only a little over a thousand years separate the beginning of agriculture from the first historical records in Old Japanese. The Japanese sequence can only inform us about the spread of a very small language family which is here termed 'Japonic', yet the sociocultural processes behind the expansion of this family can be studied at a much more detailed level than is possible for many of the case studies discussed in this book.[1]

This chapter develops the hypothesis first proposed by Hudson (1994) that there is a relationship between the spread of Japonic and the expansion of agricultural populations in the Japanese islands. After a brief summary of this hypothesis, I discuss recent developments relating to the spread of Japonic into the Ryukyu islands. I then attempt an analysis of why Ainu was not replaced by Japonic until the twentieth century; this part of the chapter proposes an extension to the farming/language dispersal hypothesis which takes account of complex interactions between agricultural cores and their foraging peripheries. A final section presents some speculations on the position of Japonic within Northeast Asia as a whole.

Foraging to farming in the Japanese islands

In Japan, as in many other parts of the world, scholars working on the origins of farming can be broadly divided into two camps depending on whether they give more emphasis to continuity and gradual evolution or to sudden, decisive change. My own view is that the Japanese sequence provides unambiguous support for the latter approach which sees the beginning of farming as an agricultural revolution, or at least a transformation that was revolutionary in its outcomes. Like Spriggs (1996), Tsuneki (1999) and others, my definition of agriculture goes beyond the presence of cultivation and/or domestication and is primarily based on social criteria. I define agriculture as a socioeconomic system which is *expansionary*, *exploitative*, and is based on principles of social *exclusion* (Hudson in press; in prep.). Despite growing evidence for the management of various plant and animal species in the Jomon period, such a socioeconomic system did not develop in Japan until the following Yayoi period.

Limitations of space preclude a discussion of the archaeological evidence relating to the foraging–farming transition in the Japanese islands in this chapter. English summaries of some of the relevant material can be found in Crawford (1992a,b; 1997), D'Andrea (1999), Hudson (1990; 1999; in press), Imamura (1996) and Nishida (1983). By no means all of the reported evidence can be taken at face value; despite reports of rice from several Jomon sites, for example, Kazahari in Aomori Prefecture is the only site at which rice remains have been dated directly (see D'Andrea *et al.* 1995). Nevertheless, it is my belief that the record of small-scale, non-intensive plant and animal management known from the Jomon period is broadly consistent with that known from many other hunter-gathering societies in temperate latitudes. Despite the diversity in subsistence adaptations within the Jomon tradition, there is no evidence that Jomon societies were evolving toward a qualitatively different socioeconomic system. If anything, plant cultivation in the Jomon seems to have served to maintain 'traditional' cultural practices (Hudson 1997).

When full-scale agriculture began in the Japanese islands at the beginning of the Yayoi period, it was associated with an influx of migrants from the Korean Peninsula and the rapid expansion of immigrant populations within Japan. The biological evidence for these population dispersals is some of the best from anywhere in the prehistoric world (see Hudson 1999, 59–81). It is not surprising, therefore, that this process of immigration and population expansion should have a very clear linguistic signature. Whatever its ultimate origins, there is no doubt that farming entered the Japanese islands from the Korean Peninsula as a whole economic, social and ideological package. Since many of the plants known in the Yayoi already appear to have been cultivated to some extent in the Jomon, the new social and ideological factors may have been the most crucial part of this Yayoi agricultural package.

The late arrival of agriculture in the Japanese islands affords us unique perspectives on the demography of the foraging/farming transition there. By the seventh century AD — only about a thousand years after the arrival of farming — we can use documentary records to estimate population for at least the areas under the control of the Yamato state. These estimates suggest a massive increase in population from about 75,000 in the Final Jomon to 5.4 million by the seventh century (Koyama 1978). Within Japan there has been considerable debate as to what proportion of this increase was due to immigration. If one uses a low rate of population increase then one is forced to argue for high levels of immigration, and Hanihara (1987) proposed that as many as 1 to 3 million migrants may have reached Japan in the Yayoi and Kofun periods. Such figures are, of course, highly unlikely. Using cemetery studies, Nakahashi has argued for an annual growth rate of 1.3 per cent in the Yayoi, although such a rate would not have been maintained during the period as a whole (Nakahashi & Iizuka 1998; Nakahashi 2000). Aoki & Tuljapurkar (2000) have attempted more complex demographic modelling using variable growth rates (see also Aoki *et al.* 1996). While debate still surrounds this issue, it seems safe to assume that quite high rates of population increase — probably over 1 per cent per annum — must have existed at certain stages in the Yayoi period.

The language situation in the Japanese islands

The starting point for our discussion here must be the striking lack of linguistic diversity in the Japanese islands. The islands are low in what Nettle

(1999, 10) terms 'language diversity', 'phylogenetic diversity' and 'structural diversity'. While there are many dialects of Japanese, there are only three indigenous languages known in the islands: Ainu, Japanese and Ryukyuan. Some Japanese linguists assume Japanese has a long history stretching back into the Jomon period for 10,000 years or more (e.g. Sakiyama 19o2, 169; Koizumi 1998); the present linguistic diversity of the islands, however, is not easily reconciled with such a time depth.

Of the three Insular languages, Ryukyuan clearly holds a very close genetic relationship with Japanese. It is widely accepted that Ryukyuan and Japanese are derived from a common source (Chamberlain 1895; Grootaers 1983; Hattori 1961). Based on glottochronological estimates and rough comparisons with the rates of divergence of the Romance languages, linguists have argued that Proto-Japonic (PJ) was spoken *about* two thousand years ago (Hattori 1961, 25–6). Hattori (1954) proposed a glottochronological date for the separation of the Kyoto and Shuri dialects of Japanese and Ryukyuan at between about 1450 and 1700 years ago (cf. Lees 1956). He later revised this to between 1500 and 2000 years ago (Hattori 1976). Discounting a move in the opposite direction, Hattori argued that the split between the two languages was caused by a population movement from mainland Japan (Hattori 1976, 43–5). Hokama (1977, 192–4) agrees with Hattori's basic conclusions, noting that Ryukyuan has attributes of eighth century or even earlier Japanese, implying a similar date of separation to the glottochronological estimates, i.e. between the second and seventh centuries AD (Hokama 1981, 266–7; 1986, 94–6). Hattori (1976, 21) elsewhere argues that Ryukyuan and mainland Japanese cannot be derived from the eighth-century Nara dialects of the early historical records: their common parent language must have existed *before* the Nara period.

Our historical understanding of Japanese dialects in the main islands is complicated by the strong influence of the speech of Kyoto which became the capital of Japan in AD 794 (Miller 1967, 141–71; Shibatani 1990, 185–214). In a study which attempts to go beyond the historical influence of Kyoto speech forms, Inoue (1996) compared the amount of independent dialectical forms with the degree of usage of 'standard' Japanese for each prefecture. Within mainland Japan he found that Kyushu and the Tohoku region (northeast Honshu) both made the least use of standard speech. Of these two, however, the Tohoku region also had a low level of divergent dialectical forms. Ruling out geographical and social factors, Inoue convincingly explains this situation as a result of the comparatively late settlement of the Tohoku by Japanese speakers associated with the expansion of the Yamato state in the Kofun, Nara and Heian periods.

This linguistic evidence from the Japanese islands is clearly not consistent with the retention of the high linguistic diversity that we can assume for the Jomon period, nor does it support the creolization proposed by Maher (1996). Rather, it suggests language replacement by Japonic in relatively recent times. Glottochronology and internal reconstruction using historical texts provide us with a rough estimate for the split of Japonic into its two major branches at between 1500 and 2000 years ago. Proto-Japonic (PJ) has to date to before this and the suggestion — based purely on the archaeological evidence for the start of the Yayoi — that it dates to around 2400 BC would seem to be broadly consistent with the linguistics. If Japonic spread through the islands beginning in the Yayoi period, then it seems highly probable that it was associated with the agricultural colonization known from the archaeological and anthropological records.

As agriculture spread first from the Korean Peninsula to northern Kyushu, we might expect that the north Kyushu dialects should be the oldest form of Japanese. If one follows Miller's (1980) theory that PJ arrived in Kyushu in the Early Jomon, but only spread to the rest of Japan in the Yayoi, then we would expect quite noticeable variations between Kyushu and other dialects. The lack of such major variations implies that PJ arrived in Kyushu at the beginning of the Yayoi and then spread almost immediately to the other islands. This would agree with the biological evidence for immigration at that time. The alternative scenario espoused by Hattori (1961, 27–8), that PJ had been spoken in north Kyushu for millennia but later became somehow fused with Yayoi people and culture involves all sorts of complex conjectures and premises, such that Hattori (1961, 27-8) himself ended up by concluding that '"Proto-Japanese" is but a hypothetical concept . . . which does not accord with the historical facts'!

Okinawa and Ryukyuan

As noted already, the language spoken in the Ryukyu or Okinawa islands is very closely related to Japanese and is thought to have spread from Kyushu sometime in the early centuries AD. Traditionally it has been argued that the people of Okinawa are ethnically different from the mainland Japanese and

are derived — together with the Ainu — from Jomon ancestors (von Baelz 1911; Hanihara 1991).[2] In my 1994 paper I proposed that we need to consider the possibility that the speakers of Ryukyuan did in fact arrive from Kyushu in the Yayoi period or later and were not the direct descendants of Jomon populations (Hudson 1994). This suggestion — which was quite controversial at the time — has been supported by recent work in biological anthropology which has demonstrated that Okinawan populations from the medieval Gusuku period onwards are much closer to the mainland Japanese than to prehistoric Okinawan groups (Dodo et al. 1998; Hatta et al. 1999; Pietrusewsky 1999; Doi 2000). Owing to the scarcity of skeletal samples from the centuries immediately preceding the Gusuku period, however, it is not yet known when or how this medieval morphology became established.

Nakamoto (1981) suggested that the spread of Proto-Ryukyuan through the Okinawan chain can be linked with the spread of rice farming, but archaeological evidence for both the introduction of agriculture and population movement into the Ryukyu islands remains poorly understood and thus it is at present difficult to reconcile the linguistic expectation of the spread of a new language in the late Yayoi or Kofun periods with the archaeological record. Takamiya (1997) has found evidence for the cultivation of wheat and barley at Naazakibaru, Okinawa Island in the eighth century. Earlier (sixth century) remains of rice from the Nagabaru Higashi site on Iejima Island may have been introduced through trade (Takamiya 2001). Hudson & Takamiya (2001) have attempted to look at palaeopathological evidence for the transition to farming in Okinawa, but small samples have prevented us from obtaining clear results. Despite these problems, the Ryukyu islands provide an important case study where the independent use of linguistic, archaeological and biological data has provided us with powerful models with which to study the past.

Agriculture, underdevelopment and language change: the case of Ainu

In a mountainous archipelago such as Japan there must have been great linguistic diversity through the ten thousand years of the Jomon period. Almost none of this presumed diversity, however, appears to have survived the expansion of Japonic in the Yayoi and later periods. Linguists commonly argue that there is very little sub-stratum influence from pre-Japonic languages in the islands (e.g. Unger 2001), and this includes the Ryukyus. The exception to this generalization is Ainu, a language which survived in Hokkaido and surrounding regions until agricultural colonization by the Japanese and Russians in the eighteenth to twentieth centuries.

In the absence of historical records, we cannot prove that Ainu — or an earlier form of Ainu — was actually spoken in the Jomon period. The antiquity of Ainu as a language, however, is suggested by place names in the Tohoku region of northern Honshu which are derived from Ainu words (Tamura 2000, 269–71). Most common are names ending in -*nai* and -*betsu* which are derived from two Ainu words for 'river', *nai* and *pet*. Around 400 examples of the -*nai* form are known in Aomori, Akita and Iwate Prefectures (Imaizumi 1992, 167). Kudo (1989, 135) writes that there is no possibility that Tohoku Ainu place names were formed in the medieval or later periods; it seems safe to assume, therefore, that a language spoken in Tohoku from at least the eighth century was an earlier form of Ainu. Bearing in mind the cultural continuities visible over this general time period, it does not seem too much of a leap in the dark to suggest that this ancestor of Ainu may have been spoken in the Jomon period. The very fact that the earliest evidence for Ainu comes from the south of its later historical distribution suggests that Ainu did not spread from the north in historic times.

The case of Ainu gives us an excellent opportunity to look at the persistence of a hunter-gatherer language on the borders of a farming society. It is clear that the Ainu language did not survive because Ainu society was completely isolated from Japonic-speaking farmers to the south. Very intense trading contacts were, in fact, developed between Japanese farmers and the Ainu from as early as the Yayoi/Epi-Jomon period and this trade continued until the actual colonization of Hokkaido by Japanese farmers began in the late nineteenth century (see Hudson 1999, 206–32). Population movement associated with the expansion of agricultural societies appears to have been the primary factor behind the eventual spread of Japonic into the Ainu Moshir (the 'Land of the Ainu').[3] Other chapters in this book argue that the same process was responsible for the expansion of many other language families. As well as the initial dispersals associated with early farming societies, however, we should not ignore the broader role of agricultural systems in causing language change. Most agricultural societies were not only expansionary but by their very nature also engendered complex social and political processes of exploitation, conflict and underdevelopment.

Bellwood (2001, 189) has used the term 'friction zones' to refer to areas at the borders of agricultural expansion zones. These friction zones were sites of complex reticulation and regional continuity where agricultural expansion became 'diluted' through contact and conflict with hunter-gatherers. Bellwood's approach mirrors linguistic models of language contact which propose that increased contact leads to increased change (e.g. Thomason 2001, 70–71). At least in the case of Ainu, however, it is clear that increased *social* interaction between two speech communities does not automatically lead to greater linguistic convergence or to language death. Instead, the process of language change was structured by core/periphery hierarchies in the wider world system. The argument here, then, is that a world-systems perspective may prove a useful extension to the farming/language dispersal hypothesis in helping us to model change on the borders of agricultural societies. The incorporation of border regions as economic peripheries by agricultural cores led to changes in the former societies which cannot be understood simply by studying levels of diffusion from centre to edge.

The linguistic influences of Japanese on Ainu probably reflect levels of contact — and in particular levels of bilingualism — in the regular fashion suggested by Thomason (2001) and others.[4] At the macro-sociological level, however, the 'development of underdevelopment' of Ainu society (Hudson 1999, 206–32) had wide-ranging linguistic implications that have not been predicted by existing analyses of archaeology and linguistics. Not only was Ainu not immediately replaced by Japonic, but it actually expanded from Hokkaido into surrounding regions and appears to have undergone significant processes of standardization. Asai (1974) and others have proposed three main dialect groups within Ainu: Hokkaido, Sakhalin and the Kurils. Since Ainu populations do not appear to have inhabited Sakhalin and the Kurils prior to about the twelfth century AD, this three-fold dialect division almost certainly derives from Ainu expansion from Hokkaido to Sakhalin and the Kuril islands in the early medieval era.

The Ainu dialects of Hokkaido itself do not display especially high levels of diversity. Vovin writes that his reconstruction of Proto-Ainu 'probably corresponds to the last centuries of the first millennium AD, when Ainu began to move northward from northern Honshu under Japanese pressure' (Vovin 1993, 155). Janhunen (2001) also argues that the Ainu language spread from northern Honshu into Hokkaido as a result of the expansion of Yayoi farmers. I believe this to be an extremely interesting suggestion which deserves further research. Whether or not the Ainu language spread from Honshu or just within Hokkaido, however, it seems clear that there was a considerable degree of language replacement and/or standardization as a result of the Satsumon expansion of late Antiquity.

Table 24.1. *Some suggested processes behind language standardization in northeast Asia.*

Language	Approximate Time depth	Processes behind spread/standardization
Ainu	Early medieval	Expansion resulting from peripheral underdevelopment?
Proto-Japonic	2500 BP	Agricultural expansion
Proto-Ryukyuan	1500 BP?	Agricultural expansion?
Korean	Protohistoric	Élite dominance

Agriculture and language in northeast Asia

If, as argued above, Japonic arrived in the Japanese islands with agriculture in the Yayoi period, can the expansion of that family be related to broader processes of agricultural dispersals in Northeast Asia? A full consideration of this problem is beyond the scope of the present paper, but the excellent archaeological and biological records from Japan enable us to test some of the available theories. Japonic is most closely related to the languages of the Korean Peninsula, especially to Old Koguryo, a protohistoric northern peninsular language known only from fragments recorded in later texts (Lewin 1976; Miller 1979; Unger 2001).[5] Wider affiliations with families such as Altaic and Austronesian have been widely discussed but remain highly controversial. In the West, the Altaic hypothesis has received a great deal of exposure in archaeological circles through the many publications of American linguist Roy Andrew Miller (e.g. 1980; 1986; 1989; 1990). Recently, however, growing linguistic criticisms of the Altaic hypothesis (e.g. Unger 1990) have been matched by doubts over Miller's interpretation of the archaeological data (Hudson 1994, 236–7). One of the most basic problems is how to reconcile the presumed time depth of Altaic with the traditional link between nomadic pastoralism and the spread of the Altaic family, and Miller (1989, 14; 1990, 16) himself is forced to argue that Japanese speakers arrived in Japan over a thousand years *before* Proto-Altaic began moving east from its original homeland to the Altai Mountains!

While it would be premature — especially for an archaeologist — to totally dismiss the Altaic hypothesis, there is at present insufficient agreement over the nature of Altaic for us to use the traditional family tree model in culture-historical reconstructions. The removal of Altaic as a broad classificatory concept has thrown the linguistic diversity of Northeast Asia into focus once again. Janhunen (1998, 199) notes that 'The small genetic units of Northeast Asia stand in sharp contrast with the large and highly diversified language families distributed to the west and south, notably Indo-European and Sino-Tibetan'. For Janhunen, this situation is normal: 'the ethnohistorical situation in Northeast Asia is probably more natural than that in most other parts of the Eurasian continent, where exceptionally favourable cultural and demographic circumstances have resulted in extraordinarily large and diversified language families' (Janhunen 1998, 199). From an anthropological perspective, however, it is doubtful whether the situation in Northeast Asia is any more 'natural' than it is anywhere else. In fact, several quite distinctive historical processes would seem to lie behind the apparently contradictory phenomena of high linguistic diversity over the region as a whole but relatively low levels of internal differentiation within each language family. Some of these processes are summarized in Table 24.1.

In this table, 'approximate time depth' refers in the case of Proto-Japonic and Proto-Ryukyuan to the time when that language was actually spoken, but in the case of Ainu and Korean to the time when there appears to have been considerable standardization within those respective languages. Of the four, only the spread of PJ can currently be explained through agricultural dispersals. The hypothesis that Proto-Ryukyuan also spread with the agricultural colonization of the Okinawan islands awaits further testing. Modern Korean derives primarily from the language of the protohistoric kingdom of Silla and the dominance of this language must be explained by the unification of the Peninsula by Silla in the early eighth century. Of course, this élite dominance model does not rule out earlier language changes associated with agricultural dispersals on the Peninsula, but the existence or nature of such changes are still unknown. The social dynamics behind the apparent standardization of Ainu in the medieval era are also unknown but may relate to trade and/or intensive cultivation in the late Satsumon era.

The low level of language diversity known from post-Yayoi Japan suggests that Japonic has only one geographical source. Both the linguistic and the archaeological records independently place that source on the Korean Peninsula. The poor skeletal record from the relevant period in Korea has so far ruled out further support from physical anthropology but the combined use of linguistic, archaeological and biological data has already proven to be of invaluable use in understanding the population history of Northeast Asia.

Conclusions

This chapter has argued that the expansion of Japonic through the Japanese islands can be linked with agricultural colonization from the Yayoi period onwards. The language of the Yayoi farmers quickly replaced the previous Jomon languages except for Ainu in the north. This expansion of Japonic is, I believe, one of the clearest cases of a link between agricultural dispersals and language change from anywhere in the world since it is based on linguistic data supported by independent archaeological and anthropological evidence for the immigration and expansion of farming populations from the Korean Peninsula. The argument here is that language change at the broad level of the Japanese archipelago resulted primarily from the physical expansion and demographic growth of farming populations.

While the link between language and agricultural expansions is clear in the case of mainland Japan, however, the situation in neighboring areas is at present less well understood. The status of Ryukyuan and Korean are still problematic because we lack good archaeological data relating to the beginning of farming and any associated changes in human biology. In the case of Korean, we know that later 'elite dominance' mechanisms were important but these are unlikely to be the whole story.

This chapter has also argued that the farming/language dispersal hypothesis needs to give more consideration to the processes of language change on the periphery of agricultural societies. The case of Ainu demonstrates that peripheral hunter-gatherer languages could undergo expansion and other major changes as a result of contact with their farming neighbours. The world-systems model sketched in this chapter has the potential to provide one approach to the 'macro sociolinguistics' that Renfrew (this volume) correctly notes has been largely absent from the field so far.

Notes

1. The term 'Japonic' was coined by Leon Serafim of the University of Hawaii (Serafim pers. comm.).

2. Early researchers such as von Baelz, of course, simply linked the Ryukyuans with the Ainu. It was only later proposed that they both stemmed from a common ancestor.

3. By the late nineteenth century, the Japanese were not just agricultural but were rapidly developing an industrial economy. For our purposes, however, the industrial stage can be seen as an advanced form of agricultural society

4. Many linguists have noted similarities between Ainu and Japanese but it is not clear how or when those similarities came about. Refsing (1986, 57) argues that Japanese influence on Ainu has been especially strong over the last one hundred years when most Ainu have been bilingual. This may be true since the Ainu were forbidden from learning Japanese through much of the Tokugawa era (1600–1868). Ainu bilingualism is likely to have been higher than the official records suggest, however, especially in southwest Hokkaido where an official Japanese colonial enclave existed from 1550. Janhunen (2001) and others have also argued for a layer of very ancient borrowings from Japanese into Ainu.

5. The relationship with Old Koguryo appears to have been very close and Janhunen (1998, 201) argues that 'Japonic as a genetic unit was once spoken on the Korean Peninsula, from where it was only secondarily relocated to Japan'.

References

Aoki, K. & S. Tuljapurkar, 2000. Hanihara's conundrum revisited; theoretical estimates of the immigration into Japan during the 1000 year period from 300 BC to AD 700. *Anthropological Science* 108(4), 305–19.

Aoki, K., M. Shida & N. Shigesada, 1996. Travelling wave solutions for the spread of farmers into a region occupied by hunter-gatherers. *Theoretical Population Biology* 50, 1–17.

Asai, T., 1974. Classification of dialects: cluster analysis of Ainu dialects. *Hoppo Bunka Kenkyu* 8, 45–136.

Bellwood, P., 2001. Early agriculturalist population diasporas? Farming, languages, and genes. *Annual Review of Anthropology* 30, 181–207.

Chamberlain, B.H., 1895. Essay in aid of a grammar and dictionary of the Luchuan language. *Transactions of the Asiatic Society of Japan* 23 (Supplement).

Crawford, G.W., 1992a. Prehistoric plant domestication in East Asia, in *The Origins of Agriculture: an International Perspective*, ed. C.W. Cowan & P.J. Watson. Washington (DC): Smithsonian Institution Press, 7–38.

Crawford, G.W., 1992b. The transitions to agriculture in Japan, in *Transitions to Agriculture in Prehistory*, ed. A.B. Gebauer & T.D. Price. Madison (WI): Prehistory Press, 117–32.

Crawford, G.W., 1997. Anthropogenesis in prehistoric northeastern Japan, in *People, Plants, and Landscapes: Studies in Paleoethnobotany*, ed. K.J. Gremillion.

Tuscaloosa (AL): University of Alabama Press, 86–103.

D'Andrea, A.C., 1999. The dispersal of domesticated plants into north-eastern Japan, in *The Prehistory of Food: Appetites for Change*, ed. C. Gosden & J. Hather. London: Routledge, 166–83.

D'Andrea, A.C., G.W. Crawford, M. Yoshizaki & M. Kudo, 1995. Late Jomon cultigens in northeastern Japan. *Antiquity* 69, 146–52.

Dodo, Y., N. Doi & O. Kondo, 1998. Ainu and Ryukyuan cranial nonmetric variation: evidence which disputes the Ainu-Ryukyu common origin theory. *Anthropological Science* 106, 99–120.

Doi, N. 2000. Skeletal morphology and the Ryukyu Islanders, in Hudson (ed.), 14.

Grootaers, W.A., 1983. Dialects, in *Kodansha Encyclopedia of Japan*, vol. 2, ed. G. Itasaka. Tokyo: Kodansha, 91–3.

Hanihara, K., 1987. Estimation of the number of migrants to Japan: a simulative study. *Journal of the Anthropological Society of Nippon* 95(3), 391–403.

Hanihara, K., 1991. Dual structure model for the population history of the Japanese. *Japan Review* 2, 1–33.

Harris, D.R. (ed.), 1996. *The Origins and Spread of Agriculture and Pastoralism in Eurasia*. London: UCL Press.

Hatta, Y., J. Ohashi, T. Imanishi, H. Kamiyama, M. Iha, T. Simabukuro, A. Ogawa, H. Tanaka, T. Akaza, T. Gojobori, T. Juji & K. Tokunaga, 1999. HLA genes and haplotypes in Ryukyuans suggest recent gene flow to the Okinawa islands. *Human Biology* 71, 353–65.

Hattori, S., 1954. On the method of glottochronology and the time depth of proto-Japanese. *Gengo Kenkyu* 26–27, 29–77. [In Japanese with English summary.]

Hattori, S., 1961. The affinity of Japanese: phonetic law and lexicostatistical 'sounding'. *Acta Asiatica* 2, 1–29.

Hattori, S., 1976. Ryukyu hogen to hondo hogen [Ryukyu dialects and mainland dialects], in *Okinawagaku no Reimei* [*The Dawn of Okinawan Studies*]. Tokyo: Okinawa Bunka Kyokai, 7–55.

Hokama, S., 1977. Okinawa no gengo to sono rekishi [The language of Okinawa and its history], in *Iwanami Koza Nihongo*, vol. 11 [*The Iwanami Course on Japanese*, vol. 11], ed. S. Ono & T. Shibata. Tokyo: Iwanami, 181–233.

Hokama, S., 1981. *Nihongo no Sekai*, vol. 9: *Okinawa no Kotoba* [*The World of Japanese*, vol. 9: *The Language of Okinawa*]. Tokyo: Chuo Koronsha.

Hokama, S., 1986. *Okinawa no Rekishi to Bunka* [*The History and Culture of Okinawa*]. Tokyo: Chuo Koronsha.

Hudson, M.J., 1990. From Toro to Yoshinogari: changing perspectives on Yayoi period archeology, in *Hoabinhian, Jomon, Yayoi, Early Korean States: Bibliographic Reviews of Far Eastern Archaeology 1990*, ed. G.L. Barnes. Oxford: Oxbow, 63–111.

Hudson, M.J., 1994. The linguistic prehistory of Japan: some archaeological speculations. *Anthropological Science* 102(3), 231–55.

Hudson, M.J., 1997. Noko o kobanda Jomonjin [The Jomon

peoples's rejection of agriculture]. *Nihonjin to Nihon Bunka* ['*Interdisciplinary Study on the Origins of Japanese Peoples and Cultures*' Newsletter] 2, 19.

Hudson, M.J., 1999. *Ruins of Identity: Ethnogenesis in the Japanese Islands*. Honolulu (HI): University of Hawaii Press.

Hudson, M.J., 2000. *Interdisciplinary Study on the Origins of Japanese Peoples and Cultures*. Kyoto: Ministry of Education, Science, Sport & Culture Project on 'Interdisciplinary Study on the Origins of Japanese Peoples and Cultures'.

Hudson, M.J., in press. The agricultural threshold in the Japanese islands, in *From Jomon to Star Carr*, eds. L. Janik, S. Kaner, A. Matsui & P. Rowley-Conwy. Oxford: BAR.

Hudson, M.J., in prep. *Articulating the Islands: an Anthropology of the World System*.

Hudson, M.J. & H. Takamiya, 2001. Dental pathology and subsistence change in late prehistoric Okinawa. *Bulletin of the Indo-Pacific Prehistory Association* 21, 68–76.

Imaizumi, T., 1992. Ritsuryo kokka to Emishi [The Emishi and the Ritsuryo state], in *Shinpan 'Kodai no Nihon' 9: Tohoku, Hokkaido* [*New Edition 'Ancient Japan'*, vol. 9: *Tohoku and Hokkaido*], ed. K. Tsuboi & K. Hirano. Tokyo: Kadokawa, 163–98.

Imamura, K., 1996. Jomon and Yayoi: the transition to agriculture in Japanese prehistory, in Harris (ed.), 442–64.

Inoue, F., 1996. Isolated dialectical forms and language substratum in Japan, in *Interdisciplinary Perspectives on the Origins of Japanese*, ed. K. Omoto. Kyoto: International Research Center for Japanese Studies, 293–308.

Janhunen, J., 1998. Ethnicity and language in prehistoric Northeast Asia, in *Archaeology and Language*, vol. II: *Correlating Archaeological and Linguistic Hypotheses*, eds. R. Blench & M. Spriggs. London: Routledge, 195–208.

Janhunen, J., 2001. On the chronology of the Ainu ethnic complex. Paper presented at the 16th International Abashiri Symposium, Abashiri, Hokkaido, October 20–21.

Koizumi, T. 1998. *Jomongo no Hakken* [*The Discovery of the Jomon Language*]. Tokyo: Seidosha.

Koyama, S., 1978. Jomon subsistence and population. *Senri Ethnological Studies* 2, 1–65.

Kudo, M., 1989. *Josaku to Emishi* [*Forts and the Emishi*]. Tokyo: New Science Press.

Lees, R.B., 1956. Shiro Hattori on glottochronology and proto-Japanese. *American Anthropologist* 58, 176–7.

Lewin, B., 1976. Japanese and Korean: the problems and history of a linguistic comparison. *Journal of Japanese Studies* 2(2), 389–412.

Maher, J.C., 1996. North Kyushu Creole: a language-contact model for the origins of Japanese, in *Multicultural Japan: Palaeolithic to Postmodern*, ed. D. Denoon, M. Hudson, G. McCormack & T. Morris-Suzuki. Cambridge: Cambridge University Press, 31–45.

Miller, R.A., 1967. *The Japanese Language.* Chicago (IL): University of Chicago Press.

Miller, R.A., 1979. Old Japanese and the Koguryo fragments: a re-survey, in *Explorations in Linguistics: Papers in Honor of Kazuko Inoue*, eds. G. Bedell, E. Kobayashi & M. Muraki. Tokyo: Kenkyusha, 348–68.

Miller, R.A., 1980. *Origins of the Japanese Language.* Seattle (WA): University of Washington Press.

Miller, R.A., 1986. Linguistic evidence and Japanese prehistory, in *Windows on the Japanese Past*, ed. R. Pearson. Ann Arbor (MI): Center for Japanese Studies, University of Michigan, 101–20.

Miller, R.A., 1989. Where did Japanese come from? *Asian and Pacific Quarterly of Cultural and Social Affairs* 21(3), 1–25.

Miller, R.A., 1990. Archaeological light on Japanese linguistic origins. *Asian and Pacific Quarterly of Cultural and Social Affairs* 22(1), 1–26.

Nakahashi, T., 2000. Population movements in the Yayoi period, in Hudson (ed.), 12–13.

Nakahashi, T. & M. Iizuka, 1998. Anthropological study of the transition from the Jomon to the Yayoi periods in northern Kyushu using morphological and paleodemographic features. *Anthropological Science Jap. Ser.* 106(1), 31–53. [In Japanese with English summary.]

Nakamoto, M., 1981. *Nihongo no Genkei: Nihon Retto no Gengogaku* [*The Original Form of Japanese: The Linguistics of the Japanese Islands*]. Tokyo: Kinkeisha.

Nettle, D., 1999. *Linguistic Diversity.* Oxford: Oxford University Press.

Nishida, M., 1983. The emergence of food production in Neolithic Japan. *Journal of Anthropological Archaeology* 2, 305–22.

Pietrusewsky, M., 1999. A multivariate craniometric study of the inhabitants of the Ryukyu islands and comparisons with cranial series from Japan, Asia, and the Pacific. *Anthropological Science* 107(4), 255–81.

Refsing, K., 1986. *The Ainu Language: the Morphology and Syntax of the Shizunai Dialect.* Aarhus: Aarhus University Press.

Sakiyama, O., 1992. Formation of the Japanese language in connection with Austronesian languages, in *Prehistoric Mongoloid Dispersals*, ed. T. Akazawa & E. Szathmary. Oxford: Oxford University Press, 349–58.

Shibatani, M., 1990. *The Languages of Japan.* Cambridge: Cambridge University Press.

Spriggs, M., 1996. Early agriculture and what went before in Island Melanesia: continuity or intrusion?, in Harris (ed.), 524–37.

Takamiya, H., 1997. Subsistence Adaptation Processes in the Prehistory of Okinawa. Unpublished PhD dissertation, UCLA.

Takamiya, H., 2001. Nagarabaru Higashi kaizuka shutsudo no shokubutsu itai (2000 nendo) [Plant remains from the Nagarabaru Higashi shell midden (2000 season)]. *Archaeological Report, University of Kumamoto* 36, 50–57.

Tamura, S., 2000. *The Ainu Language.* Tokyo: Sanseido.

Thomason, S.G., 2001. *Language Contact: an Introduction.* Edinburgh: Edinburgh University Press.

Tsuneki, A., 1999. Yosho: noko tanjo [Introduction: the birth of agriculture], in *Shokuryo Seisan Shakai no Kokogaku* [*The Archaeology of Food-Producing Societies*], ed. A. Tsuneki. Tokyo: Asakura Shoten, 1–21.

Unger, J.M., 1990. Japanese and what other Altaic languages?, in *Linguistic Change and Reconstruction Methodology*, ed. P. Baldi. Berlin & New York: Walter de Gruyter.

Unger, J.M., 2001. Layers of words and volcanic ash in Japan. *Journal of Japanese Studies* 27(1), 81–111.

von Baelz, E., 1911. Die Riu-Kiu-Insulaner, die Aino und andere kaukasierhanliche Reste in Ostasien. *Korrespondenzblatt der Deutschen Gesellschaft für Anthropologie, Ethnologie und Urgeschichte* 42, 187–91.

Vovin, A., 1993. *A Reconstruction of Proto-Ainu.* Leiden: E.J. Brill.

C. Mesoamerica and the US Southwest

Chapter 25

Contextualizing Proto-languages, Homelands and Distant Genetic Relationship: Some Reflections on the Comparative Method from a Mesoamerican Perspective

Søren Wichmann

The general argument of this paper is that comparative linguistics, narrowly defined as the practice of the comparative method, has to be combined with theories modelled on other principles or imported from other disciplines if it is to be applied in any interesting way to questions of homelands and migrations. An attempt will be made to characterize as precisely as possible the possible differences between a proto-language and the 'real' language which a proto-language is seen as representing. It is also argued that the logic of the comparative method, when used for devising scenarios for the way that language families split up and subgroups and individual languages disperse, is not necessarily adequate. Finally, some recent proposals concerning long-distance relationships involving Mesoamerican languages are discussed. Again it will be argued that we need to refer to theories external to that of the comparative method in order to evaluate or explain the results of its application to cases of possible long-distance relations.

The nature of proto-languages

Before using reconstructions produced by means of the comparative method as representations of an early language state for the purpose of archaeological or other external correlations, it is wise to consider the nature of such reconstructions as compared with the real-life languages that they are taken to represent. In the following I shall refer to the 'real-life' early language as 'eLg' (for 'early language'). The more conventional abbreviation 'pLg' stands for 'proto-language' in the strict sense of the construct resulting from the application of the comparative method. In this paper I shall stress that the pLg is

both impoverished and partly anachronistic in comparison with the eLg. It is impoverished because it must exclude items that are either innovated or retained by just one dialect, as well as items that were carried through to the eLg but did not make it to any descendants. It is anachronistic because it collapses potentially very old items that may have been innovated any time in prehistory, items that were innovated during the time of the eLg, and some items that were innovated even after the eLg stage.

Given the great success of the comparative method and the absence of a better method of reconstruction we are usually content to think about proto-languages as fairly good approximations of real languages. We are perhaps not inclined to see discontinued trajectories, insufficient attestation and late diffusion as factors that seriously threaten the adequacy of the proto-language as an image of the real language. It would be nice, however, to gain a more precise impression of the sorts of differences one might expect between a reconstructed pLg and the eLg that it is supposed to represent. Such a comparison offers itself in the case of the Ch'olan subgroup of the Mayan languages. Ch'olan speakers were the foremost group responsible for maintaining the writing system with the longest history among the writing systems of the Americas: Maya writing. Comparison of the attested hieroglyphic language and Proto-Ch'olan, as reconstructed bottom-up, will allow us to flesh out the general observations made above.

While the language which had emerged by the end of the 1990s from the decipherment of the ancient Mayan script looked like a mildly impoverished version of Proto-Ch'olan, the proto-language ancestral to an important group of Lowland Mayan languages (reconstructed, in part, by Kaufman & Norman 1984), things have taken a drastic new turn since 1998. New discoveries have resulted in a reversion, such that the hieroglyphic language now presents a richer picture than the proto-language, not only in terms of grammar and lexicon, but also in phonological contrasts. The inventory of known affixes has increased to around 80 (Wichmann forthcoming a, ch. 5). By a conservative count, the lexical inventory has swollen to about the same size as the one reconstructed for Proto-Ch'olan by Kaufman & Norman (1984), but is by no means identical and is in reality greater, considering all the items that have yet to be identified. With the discovery (Grube forthcoming) that the writing system not only distinguished velar and glottal fricatives, which had already been reconstructed for Proto-Ch'olan (Kaufman & Norman 1984) and were expected (e.g. Justeson 1989) to be distinguished in the writing system, but also vowel length (Houston *et al.* 1998) and glottal stops (Lacadena & Wichmann forthcoming b), the phonological system of the written language has grown richer than reconstructed Proto-Ch'olan.

At the same time, a more refined picture of the language distribution in the so-called Classic Maya period (the time of the monumental inscriptions, *c.* AD 250–900) has emerged which shows that we have full texts in two different languages; Yucatecan in the far central and northeast regions of Yucatan, and Ch'olan in the rest of the lowlands (Lacadena & Wichmann 2002; forthcoming a; Lacadena 2000). Within the Ch'olan area there are dialect differences and a dynamic situation of diffusion, and on its western fringe we can identify substrate features of Tzeltalan (Lacadena & Wichman forthcoming a). There are reasons to believe that all four of the Ch'olan languages that we recognize today had begun to crystallize by the Classic period. In earlier studies (Robertson 1992; 1998), it was assumed that the Ch'olti' language, which is only known through descriptions dating to the end of the seventeenth century, was a forerunner of modern Ch'orti', but it now appears (Wichmann 2002) that the two, rather than standing in a mother–daughter relationship, are related as aunts and nieces, descending from sisters that had already begun to emerge as distinct from one another during the last part of the Classic period.

Thus, the linguistic epigraphy of the Maya script is at a critical juncture where epigraphically identified lexical, grammatical or phonological data are not necessarily expected to match Proto-Ch'olan re-

constructions, but may go beyond, matching Proto-Mayan reconstructions that are not licensed for bottom-up reconstructed Proto-Ch'olan by data in the alphabetically-attested Ch'olan languages. The very notion of 'Proto-Ch'olan' is beginning to lose sense since its impoverished and anachronistic nature is becoming more and more apparent. As the language of the hieroglyphic Ch'olan inscriptions reveals an increasingly greater part of its nature and the grip on the decipherment becomes steadily stronger, this language must begin to count as a set of data in its own right. Even Proto-Mayan may in some respects not provide verification of linguistic interpretations of the Maya script since there could easily be features of hieroglyphic Ch'olan that are only attested in this language, but nevertheless have Proto-Mayan ancestry, which, given the uniqueness of attestation, would be undetectable.

A comparison of Proto-Ch'olan and hieroglyphic Ch'olan will reveal exactly the sorts of differences that we expect to exist between a proto-language (pLg) and the early language (eLg) that the pLg is supposed to represent. Let us summarize in tabular form some of the differences that separate all pLgs and eLgs and then exemplify these differences by reference to the Ch'olan case.

	pLg	eLg
1	Is essentially unitary (although in some cases a few dialect differences, fuzzily defined geographically, may be detected).	Has a number of dialect differences with specific, geographic distributions.
2	Includes some late diffused items as belonging to the entire entity.	Diffused items will appear as such.
3	Excludes discontinued items.	Includes discontinued items.
4	Excludes features attested in one branch only.	Includes features only attested in one branch if they are attested, even if only dialectally, at the given stage of the eLg.
5	Is placed in space within a relatively confined 'homeland', normally defined as corresponding to a particular ecological or otherwise geographically-defined region.	May be spoken across different ecological zones, like any language.

Each of the five differences listed can be exemplified by findings from recent epigraphic research:
1. Hieroglyphic Ch'olan has dialect differences. These begin to be attested around AD 400. From around 700, features from the western dialect be-

gin to spread to the eastern vernacular zone. The attested differences are slight, relating to a single derivational affix, some lexical items, and the phonological area of vowel length, but may in reality have been greater. It is not certain to what degree the writing system covers up differences under norms deriving from one or more high Ch'olan variant(s). Some epigraphers (Houston *et al.* 2000) have gone so far as to claim that one language of special prestige, namely a direct ancestor of modern Ch'orti', is identifiable as *the* language of the Mayan hieroglyphic inscriptions and that all variation in the script must be interpreted as stemming from vernacular substrates. Even if it is too early to say whether this model is acceptable in its entirety, it is certainly the case that no writing system has ever been found to increase the degree of linguistic differentiation. If there are any effects from writing on language at all they will always pull in the opposite direction of greater uniformity. So the fact that we are looking at the eLg (in this case eCh'olan) through the writing system should alert us that the variation found is only a fraction of the vernacular variation.

2. An example of a late diffused item that has been reconstructed for Proto-Ch'olan is the suffix *-wa:n*, whose function has been reconstructed as marking the completive of the class of intransitive verbs known in Mayan linguistics as positionals (Kaufman & Norman 1984, 106–7). Hruby & Child (forthcoming) point out that this suffix first appears in the Western Maya lowlands around the middle of the seventh century and later spreads to sites in the eastern lowlands, following the same direction of spread as several other dialectal features identified by Lacadena & Wichmann (2002).

3. Items that are discontinued in Proto-Ch'olan but found to recur in Hieroglyphic Ch'olan are among the most interesting finds of recent epigraphy. The first item of this kind is actually not so recent, but it has taken time to become widely accepted. This is the vowel-harmonic *-Vʔw* affix that serves to indicate the declarative status of the class of transitive verbs that have the structure consonant-vowel-consonant (CVC). This suffix was recognized by Bricker (1986, 126), who identified it as 'some kind of transitive suffix' that goes with 'root transitive verbs' (roughly the same as CVC transitives), and related it to Tojolab'al *-V(w)*, a transitive verbal marker. For the first time a grammatical marker had to be reconstructed for Proto-Ch'olan from evidence

attested for Ch'olan only in the script, supported by non-Ch'olan evidence. More recent examples are two markers for the absolutive status of different classes of nouns, *-ax* (Houston *et al.* 2001, 43) and *-is* (Zender forthcoming). The first of these appears in Q'anjob'alan, Mamean and K'iche'an languages but not in Ch'olan, apart from the script. The second shows up only in the script and in the Poqom languages Poqomam and Poqomchi' within the K'iche'an subgroup.

As for phonology, a contrast between velar and glottal fricatives was consistently recorded in the script (Grube forthcoming). Without the inscriptions it would not be fully reconstructible for Proto-Ch'olan without drawing upon evidence from Mayan languages beyond the Ch'olan group. Similarly, vowel length was recorded in the script (Houston *et al.* 1998), a distinction no longer reconstructible for Proto-Ch'olan except for the /a/:/a:/ contrast, which is reflected as two different qualities in the Western Ch'olan languages. Finally, there are a number of lexical items that show a certain syllable nucleus type involving a glottal stop both in the script as well as in some non-Ch'olan languages, but not in the modern Ch'olan languages where this complex nucleus type is reduced to a plain, short vowel (Lacadena & Wichmann forthcoming b). It is interesting that the losses of the /h/:/x/ contrast, vowel length and the glottal stop in the afore-mentioned syllable nucleus type all begin to get recorded in the script at roughly the same time, around the beginning of the eighth century AD. At this time the Maya collapse, although it was to begin only one to two centuries later, had not yet set in and literacy was still vigorous, so it is more natural to explain the changes attested in the script as real language changes than as the results of decreased literacy or the breakdown of orthographic norms.

In sum, Hieroglyphic Ch'olan records a significant number of features that cannot be reconstructed for Proto-Ch'olan. The current tendency is for an ever-increasing number of such features to be identified. With each year, Proto-Ch'olan as reconstructed from the alphabetically-recorded languages and as a model of a real language spoken by real people, becomes increasingly less meaningful.

4. As an example of a feature which cannot be reconstructed bottom-up for Ch'olan because it is only attested in one branch we may cite the (vowel-harmonic) transitivizer of positional verbs *-b'u/-b'a*. Today this suffix occurs in the Eastern

branch only, but the script shows it to have been in use throughout the Ch'olan area. We might reconstruct it for Proto-Ch'olan using evidence from the Tzeltalan subgroup, but the point here is to see what Proto-Ch'olan would look like if we did not have any cognate languages outside the group, i.e. as a picture of a reconstructed ancestor to an entire family, and then compare it to the real language of the inscriptions.

5. The methodology of homeland identification invites one to search out confined geographical (often ecologically defined) regions as candidates. When mapped on to space, the idea of a family tree splitting up brings with it the image of an ever-expanding zone occupied by members of the language family and, conversely, the image of an area which is ever-more refined as one goes back in time to the proto-language. A major problem with this type of logic is that the speakers of some of the most widespread and well understood language families in terms of their historical development were farmers (Bellwood 1994; 1997; 2001). Since farming is expected to produce a demographic boom with concomitant geographical spread of the population, many proto-languages would also be expected to be spoken in larger regions. The observation of Bellwood that some of the best-established language families correlate with farming dispersal leads to the possible hypothesis that subsistence patterns license family tree structures that make possible detailed reconstructions of most areas within the proto-language. If this hypothesis is correct, the same conditions that produce the possibility for us to reconstruct a proto-language also produce a pattern of settlement over large areas, which is at variance with the traditional conception of a narrowly defined homeland. The pLg, then, is not even a tolerable approximation of the eLg in what concerns geographical correlates, it is rather its reverse. The more refined the proto-language, the more widespread the eLg must have been geographically and the more dialect variation we must posit for the eLg.

The hypothesis that an eLg may have been more widespread than the idea of a proto-language would have led us to assume is again borne out by the comparison of Proto-Ch'olan and the eLg represented by the Ch'olan hieroglyphic inscriptions. Whereas the former should theoretically have been spoken in a quite restricted area, the latter spread out across a large part of southern Mesoamerica, occupying the southern part of the Yucatan peninsula as well as a large area to the south of it.

The question of homelands: some Mesoamerican examples

In the above I have sought to argue that a pLg should be used as a model of an eLg only with extreme caution. In terms of structure the pLg is inevitably an impoverished and anachronistic model of the eLg, and in terms of mapping on to space the eLg is more likely to be the reverse of a pLg, The eLg will tend to have a rather indefinite extension, whereas a pLg will tend to be viewed almost as a point in space. Two studies concerning homelands by Terrence Kaufman exemplify different takes on the problem. In an early attempt to pinpoint the homeland of Proto-Mayan, Kaufman (1976) presents various 'working principles' of his approach, specifically designed to suit the Mayan case. One of them is a 'least moves' principle, i.e. a model that requires a minimum of dislocation with respect to the current location of the Mayan languages. Another working principle is the following:

> Proto-Mayan has terms for both highland and lowland flora and fauna. In this area, lowland people are ignorant of highland products, but highland people are aware of lowland products. Therefore, the Proto-Mayan homeland was in a highland not far from the lowlands. (Kaufman 1976, 104)

It appears that Kaufman was working from the assumption that Proto-Mayan could not have been spoken over more than one ecological zone. Without this assumption, the conclusion would simply be that the Proto-Mayans were located both in the highlands and the lowlands. Instead, Kaufman goes on to envisage a highland location close to lowlands and near rivers flowing north, east, and west, which, when followed the easiest way, i.e. downstream, would facilitate the dispersal of the Proto-Mayans and suggests one particular homeland area (the Soloma area).

This sort of approach is very similar to comparative linguistics itself. 'Least moves' resembles parsimony in the explanation of linguistic developments. The least effort assumption motivating the placement of the Proto-Mayan upstream and having them move downstream as they disperse resembles the assumption of directionality in phonological changes (e.g. lenition, assimilation, etc.). The single location resembles linguistic reconstruction, for instance of proto-phonemes that will later mutate or even split up. There is an important difference between a proto-language and a homeland, however, namely that the former is a model accounting for descendant phenomena and not a real entity in its own right, whereas a homeland is something assumed to be real.

In another work, written about a decade later, Kaufman (n.d.) looks at another of the large Mesoamerican language families, namely Oto-Manguean, again setting out to determine the homeland. This time the proposal, although presented in a less optimistic tone, is realistic and probably closer to the truth. Kaufman sees no reason for locating the Proto-Oto-Mangueans in any particular narrowly defined area and simply projects a large part of the area occupied today by Oto-Manguean languages back in time:

> the maximum extent of the pOM might have been as follows: the Valley of Mexico, the Valley of Morelos, the Balsas Basin, the Valley of Puebla, the Tehuacán Valley, the Valley of Oaxaca, and the Mixteca Alta. The Tehuacán Tradition, an archaeological horizon that extends from 5000 to 2300 BC, brackets the probable time period for the break-up of pOM (c. 4000–4500 BC). The Tehuacán Tradition has a geographical spread that includes all of the above regions, as well as the Chinantla, the Valley of Querétaro, and the Pachuca-Mezquital Valley. Locating the pOM homeland within this area seem[s] unavoidable. *We may doubt whether a single protolanguage could have been spoken over such a large area*, but associating the pOM homeland with a specific subarea within the distribution of the Tehuacán Tradition is not at the moment feasible. The Tehuacán Tradition occupies a highland habitat. (Kaufman n.d.; my emphasis)

The speakers of the Mayan and Oto-Manguean languages are farmers and evidence, as long as we can trace it, points to considerable populations of the speakers of both language families. For both, I would assume that the eLgs were quite widespread, having distributions not radically different from those of the current families.

In conclusion, we should not assume that the logic of making linguistic reconstruction applies equally well when we are dealing with the spatial distribution of the languages that we reconstruct. The criticism I have voiced against mapping the root node of a family tree on to a narrow region in space also applies to the translation of nodes of the tree into migration in space. If we allow ourselves to envisage a proto-language as being extended over a large area we do not necessarily in all cases need migrations to account for the development of branches further down the tree. Demographic conti-

nuity may easily combine with increased linguistic differentiation. In other words, the forefathers of the speakers of different related languages may well have been in the same areas as their descendants even if the languages of the descendants have become differentiated from the language of the forefathers. It is difficult to refrain from projecting latter-day differentiation back into the past, but doing so leads to the absurdity of a linguistic map of the World's languages of some 5000–8000 years ago where the forefathers of today's major language families were just points in space.

New perspectives on some recently proposed long-distance relationships involving Mesoamerican languages

In recent work Jane Hill (2001; this volume) has followed a suggestion by Peter Bellwood (1994; 1997) and argued that speakers of the Uto-Aztecan languages were emigrants from Mesoamerica who moved north as a result of population expansion in the wake of the development of agriculture. I prefer to remain agnostic about this theory since it rests largely on the probability of the general language-agriculture expansion theory in general and has very little hard linguistic evidence to support it (Campbell this volume). Nevertheless, I will here give it the benefit of the doubt and try to look at how the hypothesis of the Uto-Aztecan expansion from the south, as well as the language-farming hypothesis in general, fit into a larger view of Mesoamerican languages.

In a paper written and circulated in 1993 and published in a working paper series (Wichmann 1999) I propose that Uto-Aztecan (UA) is related to Mixe-Zoquean (MZ), a language family whose speakers reside in the heart of Mesoamerica. The proposal is based on 80 comparisons of proto-forms from the two language families, including 11 grammatical markers (8 affixes and 3 particles). Although today I would throw out some of the comparisons altogether, I still believe that the evidence is quite good. In the following, I cite the most convincing comparisons without attempting to reconstruct the forms ancestral to the two proto-languages (this is done in the original article). A number of correspondences that involve changes in one of the proto-languages are demonstrated: an *a : *o correspondence (1–3), an *ng : *w correspondence (4–6), loss of initial *p in MZ (3, 7–11), an *s : *tz correspondence (12–13), loss of medial *s in MZ (14–16) and subsequent change of *i, if present, to a glide (14–15), loss of final *k in UA

(18–21) (in the practical orthography used 'ä' represents a high, central vowel, 'ng' a velar nasal, and 'tz' an unvoiced alveolar affricate; 'X' is a symbol for an indeterminate element and 'V' for an indeterminate vowel). Some of the similarities may be due to chance, but chance can hardly explain all of them, given that the lists of reconstructed forms from which the comparisons are drawn are quite limited.

The Uto-Aztecan reconstructions are from a number of authors, but mostly Kaufman (1981), and the Mixe-Zoquean ones are from Wichmann (1995). In most cases the reconstructions go back to the deepest level of either language family, although some of them pertain to intermediate stages.

	UA	**MZ**
(1)	*ʔahyä 'good'	*ʔoya 'good'
(2)	*naʔa/i 'to burn, kindle'	*noʔ 'to light, set fire to'
(3)	*paakaa 'reed'	*ʔook(wiʔn) 'reed'
(4)	*nga.. 'to cry'	*wanʔ 'to sing; want'
(5)	*ngo.. 'to bend back'	*woy 'to roll'
(6)	*ngaa 'root'	*wa-tzi 'root-diminutive'
(7)	*paa-tzi 'elder brother-dim.'	*ʔahtzi 'elder brother'
(8)	*po(o)tzi 'navel'	*ʔotz-i 'folded or rolled'
(9)	*(p)äwi 'to sleep'	*ʔäw 'to sing; sleep'
(10)	*punku 'dog'	*ʔuku 'agouti' or 'dog'
(11)	*pala 'leaf'	*ʔay 'leaf'
(12)	*sik 'to cut'	*tzik 'to cut, harvest, peal'
(13)	*suma 'to tie'	*tzum 'to tie'
(14)	*ku(X)si 'wood'	*kuy 'tree'
(15)	*nasii 'ashes'	*nayi 'wax'
(16)	*kʷäsä 'to take, catch'	*käʔ 'hand, arm'
(17)	*nihyá 'to name, call'	*näyä 'name'
(18)	*kopa 'forehead'	*ko-pak 'head'
(19)	*kutaa 'neck'	*ko- 'pertaining to head', *tak(us) 'walking stick'
(20)	*maana 'female child'	*manäk 'son, daughter'
(21)	*tongoo 'knee'	*tongko 'heel'
(22)	*wiku 'to whistle'	*wiikʔ 'to whistle'
(23)	*ʔahpä '(grand)father'	*ʔapu 'grandfather'
(24)	*ʔaawV 'to tell'	*ʔaw 'mouth'
(25)	*määtza 'moon'	*maatzaʔ 'star'
(26)	*ya 'die'	*yah 'end'
(27)	*soho 'cottonwood'	*soho 'oak'
(28)	*toʔka 'spider'	*toʔk 'to spread out on the ground'
(29)	*wohi 'to bark, yell, howl'	*woh 'to bark'
(30)	*hää 'yes'	*hää 'yes'
(31)	*ka 'negative'	*kaah 'no'
(32)	*sivi 'now, today'	*sääw 'day, sun'
(33)	*hota 'to dig'	*hot 'to dig a hole'
(34)	*makoi '10'	*ma(h)k(V)y '10'
(35)	*koomV 'pitcher, jug, pot'	*kom 'to put in'
(36)	*soon 'many'	*sone 'much, many'
(37)	*suyi- 'sting'	*suy 'sew, fish with hook'
(38)	*huuki 'bunchgrass'	*huk 'to tie together'
(39)	*-i 'nominalizer (result)'	*-i 'nominalizer (product)'
(40)	*naa- 'reciprocal'	*nay- 'reciprocal'
(41)	*pää 'distributive'	*-pä 'distributive'
(42)	*-mä 'plural'	*ta-m 'plural'
(43)	*-tzi 'diminutive'	*-tzi 'diminutive'

The proposal is presented as an alternative to the better-known Macro-Mayan hypothesis, according to which the Mesoamerican families Mixe-Zoquean, Mayan and Totonacan are related (some scholars also include Huave, but data in support of this suggestion have never been presented, so it is of little interest). For proposals of Macro-Mayan that present actual — though in all cases scanty — data in support, see Radin (1924), Swadesh (1954), Kaufman (1964, paper not seen by the present author), Brown & Witkowski (1979), and Greenberg (1987). For disagreements with the hypothesis see Wonderly (1953) and Hamp (1979). Lyle Campbell and Terrence Kaufman (most recently Campbell 1997, 323–4, Kaufman & Golla 2000) have both, for around a quarter of a century, voiced the opinion that the hypothesis is shaky but worthy of investigation, but neither of them have ever made any larger attempts to either dismantle or support it. I have always been sceptical about the Macro-Mayan hypothesis (Wichmann 1994a, 243) and more recently, as I have begun to work more intensely on comparative Mayan, I have not come across good evidence for it.

Kaufman (in press) has made a good case for a relation between Oto-Manguean and Hokan (where Hokan is said to include Pomoan, Chimariko, Yana-Yahi, Karok, Shastan, Achumawi-Atsugewi, Washo, Salinan, Yuman, Seri, Tequistlatec, Jicaque, and perhaps some other languages that are poorly documented). Kaufman's evidence is also based on the comparison of reconstructed forms and he provides 115 such comparisons, including 23 grammatical markers (13 affixes or clitics and 10 particles). There are thus more comparisons than in my Uto-Aztecan–Mixe-Zoquean proposal and the number of good semantic matches is greater. On the other hand, in Kaufman's comparisons no systematic correspondences of non-identical segments are demonstrated and the items compared are in many cases short (CV), yielding a greater possibility of chance resemblance. Finally, Kaufman does not cite his Hokan data, but only reconstructions (introduced by '#' instead of '*', probably to indicate that they are not fully worked out reconstructions). Thus, the weights of the two proposals could be roughly equal. It is likely that they are both good examples of the limits of what the comparative method has to offer in terms of establishing long-distance relationship.

The geographical separation of Oto-Manguean and Hokan is similar to that of Mixe-Zoquean and Uto-Aztecan. One may wonder how the two cases relate to the language-farming dispersal hypothesis. Since both Oto-Manguean and Hokan have a great time depth, as evidenced by a high degree of diversity in the descendant languages, comparable to that of Indo-European, it is unlikely that the expansion of their common ancestor could be late enough to be related to farming. Presumably, the geographical link between the two families is the Pacific coast, since speakers of several of the California Hokan languages have a coastal adaptation. It is not easy to determine which way the migration would have gone, but if we follow the lead of Blust (1991b), Fortescue (1997), and Ross (1991) (all cited in Bellwood 2001, 185) we may perhaps wage a hypothesis. The authors mentioned agree on the observation that the languages of migrants tend to more rapidly undergo linguistic changes than the languages of those who stay home. Now, in the case of Hokan–Oto-Manguean, Kaufman argues that Oto-Manguean has undergone a greater number of changes. Applying the standard theory of tonogenesis he mentions the possibility that tones in Oto-Manguean developed from the loss of morpheme-final consonants. Additionally, Kaufman notes that the VO word order in Oto-Manguean could have developed from the OV type word order found in Hokan. He argues that 'VO syntax is an areal trait in Mesoamerica, and while universal and perhaps original in OM, is probably not original in the common ancestor of OM and Hokan' (Kaufman in press). In support of Kaufman's assumption that OV is the older order is the highly unusual typological combination in Tlapanec, one of the Oto-Manguean languages, of a reference-tracking system related to switch-reference and VSO word order (Wichmann 1994b) (a similar system may exist in other Oto-Manguean languages as well, but this has so far not been documented). Switch-reference, which is a common phenomenon among Hokan languages and many other languages of North America, is almost universally associated with a verb-final word order so we must explain the Tlapanec phenomenon as a change prompted by a change from verb-final to verb-initial word order. This would seem to suggests that Oto-Manguean underwent a change under the influence of other Mesoamerican languages, perhaps as a result of an entrance into Mesoamerica.

On the other hand, it is difficult to tell what a Mesoamerican linguistic area might have looked like at the time of Proto-Oto-Manguean, Oto-Manguean being the largest and oldest family in the area. In-deed, it probably does not make sense to talk about such an area at all at the time concerned. Brown (1996) makes a good case that some of the features argued by Campbell *et al.* (1986) to define the Mesoamerican linguistic area may be due to a very late influence, mainly from Nahuatl of the Aztec empire, i.e. several thousand years after a possible Oto-Manguean immigration. Thus, the linguistic evidence cannot determine whether the Oto-Manguean–Hokan ancestor came from Mesoamerica or from some place, say, in or around present-day California, although it does perhaps weigh in favour of the latter view. It is not impossible that the language-farming dispersal hypothesis might explain the expansion of Oto-Manguean within Mesoamerica, but before this expansion we might perhaps imagine that speakers of a branch of Hokan–Oto-Manguean, for whatever other reason, migrated to the south, perhaps along the Pacific coast. A similar migration much later took speakers of Tequistlatec, a Hokan language, to southern Mexico where, today, they are surrounded by speakers of Oto-Manguean languages.

The time depths of both Uto-Aztecan and Mixe-Zoquean are shallower than those of Hokan and Oto-Manguan, so their presumed ancestor would also be younger than the presumed Hokan–Oto-Manguean ancestor. It is not clear at all whether the invention of agriculture could be simultaneous with a common Uto-Aztecan–Mixe-Zoquean expansion. But perhaps it might explain the case of Uto-Aztecan. The family's current distribution represents an enormous area, and if we consider the possibility that some of the extinguished languages of northern Mexico were Uto-Aztecan, the prehistoric territory would have been even vaster. If there ever were a continuity between Hokan and Oto-Manguean, the Uto-Aztecans would have encroached upon the area that today separate Hokan and Oto-Manguean. On the other hand, if there ever were geographical continuity between Uto-Aztecan and Mixe-Zoquean, this could have been broken by the Oto-Manguean expansion. Mixe-Zoquean is not very expansive, but this fact is not difficult to explain, since the Proto-Mixe-Zoqueans would have been surrounded by other sedentary peoples, mostly notably the Mayans to the east and the Oto-Mangueans to the west, who would all have taken up farming at roughly the same time as the Proto-Mixe-Zoqueans.

To sum up, we may imagine a picture of thousands of years of initial migrations by Palaeoindians and their descendants followed by the maximal expansion of groups who took up farming. Within Mesoamerica, different groups would have taken up farming at roughly the same time, in most cases reducing the possibilities of particular groups to expand at the expense of others. To the north of Mesoamerica, however, there would be space to invade which was not already occupied by farmers.

Conclusion

It is clear that the comparative method, while a back-bone of any serious attempt to device language histories at shallower levels and even still useful for first-order distant relationships (i.e. demonstrating relationship between well-established language families but not beyond that), is not in itself a sufficient tool when it comes to correlating linguistic history with space, time, and archaeologically defined horizons. Proto-languages are impoverished and anachronistic, homeland hypotheses generated by a logic similar to that of the comparative method may be inaccurate if not sometimes misleading, and in the case of long-distance comparison the comparative method often can not tell us which way the migration went. Thus, models of human interaction, dispersal, etc. from other disciplines should be fused with the results of the application of the comparative method if we are to arrive at firm and interesting hypotheses concerning human prehistory. As a case study we have been looking at the major language families in and to the immediate north of Mesoamerica. It seems that the language-farming hypothesis could help explain the current distributions of these language families. To be sure, there is no currently available alternative theory that explains them better.

References

Bellwood, P., 1994. An archaeologist's view of language macrofamily relationships. *Oceanic Linguistics* 33, 391–406.

Bellwood, P., 1997. Prehistoric cultural explanations for widespread language families, in McConvell & Evans (eds.), 123–34.

Bellwood, P., 2000. The time depth of major language families, in *Time Depth in Historical Linguistics*, vol. 1, eds. C. Renfrew, A. McMahon & L. Trask. (Papers in the Prehistory of Languages.) Cambridge: McDonald Institute for Archaeological Research, 109–40.

Bellwood, P., 2001. Early agriculturalist population diasporas? Farming, language and genes. *Annual Review of Anthropology* 30, 181–207.

Blust, R. (ed.), 1991a. *Current Trends in Pacific Linguistics*. (Pacific Linguistics, Series C-117.) Canberra: Research School of Pacific and Asian Studies, The Australian National University.

Blust, R., 1991b. Sound change and migration distance, in Blust (ed.) 1991a, 27–42.

Bricker, V., 1986. *A Grammar of Mayan Hieroglyphs*. (Middle American Research Institute, Publ. 56.) New Orleans (LA): Tulane University.

Brown, C.H., 1996. How Mesoamerica Became a Linguistic Area. Unpublished manuscript in possession of the author.

Brown, C.H. & S.R. Witkowski, 1979. Aspects of the phonological history of Mayan-Zoquean. *International Journal of American Linguistics* 45, 34–47.

Campbell, L., 1997. *American Indian Languages: the Historical Linguistics of Native America*. New York (NY) & Oxford: Oxford University Press.

Campbell, L., T. Kaufman & T.C. Smith-Stark, 1986. Meso-America as a linguistic area. *Language* 62, 530–70.

Fortescue, M., 1997. Dialect distribution and small group interaction in Greenlandic Eskimo, in McConvell & Evans (eds.), 111–22.

Greenberg, J., 1987. *Language in the Americas*. Stanford (CA): Stanford University Press.

Grube, N., forthcoming. The orthographic distinction between velar and glottal spirants in Maya hieroglyphic writing, in Wichmann (ed.) forthcoming b.

Hamp, E.P., 1979. A glance from here on, in *The Languages of Native America: Historical and Comparative Assessment*, eds. L. Campbell & M. Mithun. Austin (TX) & London: University of Texas Press, 1001–15.

Hill, J., 2001. Proto-Uto-Aztecan: a community of cultivators in central Mexico? *American Anthropologist* 103(4), 913–34.

Houston, S., D. Stuart & J. Robertson, 1998. Disharmony in Maya hieroglyphic writing: linguistic change and continuity in Classic cociety, in *Anatomía de una civilización. Aproximaciones interdisciplinarias a la cultura maya*, eds. A. Ciudad, M. Garcia, J. Iglesias, A. Lacadena & L. Sanz. (Publicaciones de la S.E.E.M. 4.) Madrid: Sociedad Española de Estudios Mayas, 275–96.

Houston, S., J. Robertson & D. Stuart, 2000. The language of Classic Maya inscriptions. *Current Anthropology* 41.3, 321–56.

Houston, S., J. Robertson & D. Stuart, 2001. *Quality and Quantity in Glyphic Nouns and Adjectives*. (Research Reports on Ancient Maya Writing 47.) Washington (DC): Center for Maya Research.

Hruby, Z.X. & M.B. Child, forthcoming. Chontal linguistic influence in ancient Maya writing: intransitive positional verbal affixation, in Wichmann (ed.) forthcoming b.

Justeson, J.S., 1989. The representational conventions of Mayan hieroglyphic writing, in *Word and Image in Maya Culture: Explorations in Language, Writing, and Representation*, eds. W.F. Hanks & D.S. Rice. Salt Lake City (UT): University of Utah Press, 25–38.

Kaufman, T., 1964. Evidence for the Macro-Mayan Hypothesis. Unpublished manuscript, pp. 20, not seen by the author.

Kaufman, T., 1976. Archaeological and linguistic correlation in Mayaland and associated areas of Mesoamerica. *World Archaeology* 8.1, 101–18.

Kaufman, T., 1981. Comparative Uto-Aztecan Phonology. Ms. in possession of the author.

Kaufman, T., in press. Tlapaneko-Subtiaba, OtoMangue, and Hoka: where Greenberg went wrong, in *Language and Prehistory in the Americas*, ed. A. Taylor. Stanford (CA): Stanford University Press.

Kaufman, T., n.d. Early OtoManguean Homelands and Cultures: Some Premature Hypotheses. Unpublished manuscript in possession of the author.

Kaufman, T. & V. Golla, 2000. Language groupings in the New World: their reliability and usability in cross-disciplinary studies, in *America Past, America Present: Genes and Languages in the Americas and Beyond*, ed. C. Renfrew. (Papers in the Prehistory of Languages.) Cambridge: McDonald Institute for Archaeological Research, 47–57.

Kaufman, T. & W.M. Norman, 1984. An outline of Proto-Cholan phonology, morphology and vocabulary, in *Phoneticism in Mayan Hieroglyphic Writing*, eds. J. Justeson & L. Campbell. (Institute of Mesoamerican Studies Publ. 9.) Albany (NY): State University of New York at Albany, 77–166.

Lacadena, A., 2000. Nominal syntax and the linguistic affiliation of Classic Maya texts, in *The Sacred and the Profane: Architecture and Identity in the Classic Maya Lowlands. 3rd European Maya Conference, University of Hamburg, November 1998*, eds. P.R. Colas, K. Delvendahl, M. Kuhnert & A. Schubart. Markt Schwaben: Verlag Anton Sauerwein, 119–28.

Lacadena, A. & S. Wichmann, 2002. The distribution of Lowland Maya languages in the Classic Period, in *La organización social entre los mayas. Memoria de la Tercera Mesa Redonda de Palenque*, vol. 2, eds. V. Tiesler, R. Cobos & M. Greene Robertson. México D.F.: Instituto Nacional de Antropología e Historia & Universidad Autónoma de Yucatán, 275–314.

Lacadena, A. & S. Wichmann, forthcoming a. The dynamics of language in the western Lowland Maya region. Paper presented at the 2000 Chacmool conference. Calgary, November 9–11, 2000. To be published in the proceedings.

Lacadena, A. & S. Wichmann, forthcoming b. On the representation of the glottal stop in Maya writing, in Wichmann (ed.) forthcoming b.

McConvell, P. & N. Evans (eds.), 1997. *Archaeology and Linguistics*. Melbourne: Oxford University Press.

Radin, P., 1924. On the relationship of Maya to Zoque-Huave. *Journal de la Société des Américanistes de Paris* 16, 317–24.

Robertson, J.S., 1992. *The History of Tense/Aspect/Mood/Voice in the Mayan Verbal Complex*. Austin (TX): University of Texas Press.

Robertson, J.S., 1998. A Ch'olti'an explanation for Ch'orti'an grammar: a postlude to the language of the Classic Maya. *Mayab* 11, 5–11.

Ross, M., 1991. How conservative are sedentary languages?, in Blust (ed.) 1991a, 433–57.

Swadesh, M., 1954. Perspectives and problems of Amerindian comparative linguistics. *Word* 10, 306–32.

Wichmann, S., 1994a. MixeZoquean linguistics: a status report, in *Panorama de los estudios de las lenguas indígenas de México*, eds. L. Manrique, Y. Lastra & D. Bartholomew. (Colección Biblioteca Abya-Yala 16.) Quito: Ediciones Abya-Yala, 193–267.

Wichmann, S., 1994b. Topic Switch-Reference in Azoyú Tlapanec and the Local-Global Parameter. Paper presented at the 6th International Conference on Functional Grammar, York.

Wichmann, S., 1995. *The Relationship among the Mixe-Zoquean Languages of Mexico*. Salt Lake City (UT): University of Utah Press.

Wichmann, S., 1999. On the relationship between Uto-Aztecan and Mixe-Zoquean. *Kansas Working Papers in Linguistics* 24.2, 101–13.

Wichmann, S., 2002. *Hieroglyphic Evidence for the Historical Configuration of Eastern Ch'olan*. (Research Reports on Ancient Maya Writing 51.) Washington (DC): Center for Maya Research.

Wichmann, S., forthcoming a. *Mayaernes Skrift - Introduktion og Håndbog*. Copenhagen: C.A. Reitzels Forlag.

Wichmann, S. (ed.), forthcoming b. *The Linguistics of Maya Writing*. Salt Lake City (UT): University of Utah Press.

Wonderly, W.L., 1953. Sobre la propuesta filiación lingüística de la familia totonaca con las familias zoqueana y mayense, in *Huastecos, totonacos y sus vecinos*, eds. I. Bernal & D. Dávalos Hurtado. *Revista Mexicana de Estudios Antropológicos* 13, 105–13.

Zender, M., forthcoming. On the morphology of intimate possession in Mayan languages and Classic Mayan glyphic nouns, in Wichmann (ed.) forthcoming b.

Chapter 26

Proto-Uto-Aztecan Cultivation and the Northern Devolution

Jane H. Hill

Until very recently, most scholars held that the ancestral community for Uto-Aztecan, a language family that extends from Idaho to El Salvador and from California to east Texas, was made up of bands of foragers occupying the uplands of Arizona and Northwest Mexico at around 5000 BP. Maize cultivation was thought to have spread north from Mesoamerica and been adopted by all southern Uto-Aztecan descendants and, at an early date, by the Hopi, after the breakup of the proto-community. The northern groups, including the Takic and Tubatulabal of California and the Numic peoples of the Great Basin, under this model exhibit the archaic foraging subsistence pattern (cf. Fowler 1983; Miller 1983). Only Romney (1957) argued for cultivation in the proto-community.[1]

Bellwood (1997; 2001) proposes that the geography of the Uto-Aztecan family suggests an agricultural expansion of primary cultivators from Mesoamerica into the U.S. Southwest. Northern Uto-Aztecan subsistence patterns would in this model constitute an innovation, a 'devolution' from cultivation to hunting and gathering. In this essay I seek evidence, especially historical-linguistic evidence, to test this idea. I restrict the discussion to the Numic-speaking peoples. The distribution of Numic-speaking groups in the Great Basin is shown in Figure 26.1.

Early Uto-Aztecan cultivation: lexical evidence

Linguistic evidence for Bellwood's model includes a ten-item lexicon for maize cultivation and processing reconstructed for Proto-Uto-Aztecan (PUA), using the Comparative Method from historical linguistics (Hill 2001). This maize vocabulary displays regular sound correspondence among the daughter languages and is attested in northern (including Hopi and Southern Numic) as well as southern languages. The vocabulary of the maize cultivation complex, with its very regular sound correspondences, can be distinguished from the words for 'squash' and 'beans', which were borrowed among daughter languages after the breakup of the proto-language. This parallels the archaeological evidence, which suggests that squash and beans arrived in the Southwest later than maize. The linguistic evidence suggests dating the breakup of the community between 4000 and 3000 BP, after the arrival of maize in the southwest, with considerable intergroup contact as late as the arrival of squash and gourds around 2900 BP, but with quite a high level of divergence of the daughter groups before the arrival of beans in the southwest at about 2500 BP.

The problem of devolution: if and when

Cultivation surely was practised from a very early period by all southern Uto-Aztecan groups and the Hopi. However, cultivation among Southern Numic groups such as the Chemehuevi and San Juan Paiute has been understood as the result of more recent contact with nearby cultivators. I review here ethnohistoric, archaeological, ethnographic and linguistic evidence against the idea that the Numic peoples acquired cultivation by contact, and in favour of the idea that cultivation among them maintains an archaic adaptation.

Ethnohistoric evidence

Cultivation is attested at a very early date in the historic period for many Numic groups. Liljeblad & Fowler (1986), drawing on Steward (1930; 1933), quote observations of quite intensive cultivation in the mid-nineteenth century among the Owens Valley Paiute, speakers of Mono (a Western Numic language):

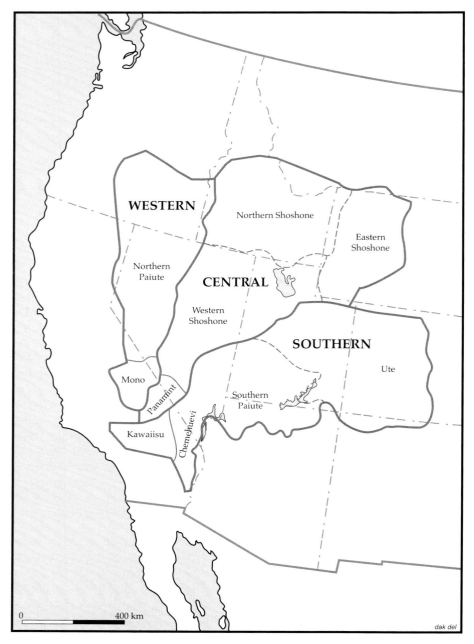

Figure 26.1. *Modern distribution of the Numic languages in the Great Basin. (After Madsen & Rhode 1994. I thank the University of Utah Press for permission to reproduce this map.)*

The Owens Valley Paiute managed miles of canals, controlling the flow of water with check dams supervised by committees of senior men. While they did not cultivate maize (the Owens Valley lies beyond the northwestern limits of the summer rainfall regime that permits maize cultivation with archaic techniques), their intensive irrigation is strongly reminiscent of practices in other Uto-Aztecan groups, where canal and check-dam irrigation is attested from early in the first millennium BC (Hill 2001). Liljeblad & Fowler (1986) summarize arguments that this water management system is an indigenous development. Owens Valley Paiute practices are usually categorized as 'incipient cultivation' or 'proto-agriculture'. A similar interpretation has been given to practices like broadcasting wild seeds, reported for several bands of the Western Shoshone (Fowler 1986, 93). I would argue for a different interpretation, that among Uto-Aztecan groups in marginal climates these practices represented the last vestiges of an earlier commitment to cultivation.

Among the Central Numic, Fowler points out that the Tumpisha Shoshone (living in and around Death Valley and in contact with the Las Vegas Paiute) practised garden horticulture; she believed that they had borrowed gardening from the Paiutes 'in early post-contact times' (Fowler 1986, 94). In Western Shoshone territory, cultivation was identified as having been practised in the immediate pre-contact period 'as far north as Spring, Snake, Antelope, and Steptoe valleys' (Fowler 1986, 94). Among the Southern Numic, we have cultivation lexicon from the Chemehuevi, Las Vegas Paiute, Kaibab Paiute and San Juan Paiute bands. The

Whole fields, miles in extent, of this grass [mainly *Cyperus esculentus*, but perhaps also *Dichelostemma pulchella* and *Eleocharis* spp. [(Fowler 1986, 94)] are watered with great care. Digging the tubers, destroys the fields, and the 'nuts' are reproduced by planting (Liljeblad & Fowler 1986, 412).

Besides *Cyperus*, the Owens Valley Paiute 'irrigated, cultivated, and pruned' tobacco (Fowler 1986, 94).

Chemehuevi cultivated intensively and used canal irrigation. Scholars have argued that they borrowed cultivation from the Yuman-speaking Mohave. However, Chemehuevi *ha?wiv(i)* 'corn', does not resemble Mohave *tadiich* 'corn'. Instead, the Chemehuevi word resembles Las Vegas Paiute *hawíp* 'corn', *hawíiv* 'corn cob' (from John Wesley Powell's 1873 vocabulary; Fowler & Fowler 1971, 155).

Roberts (2000) finds that Europeans who contacted Southern Paiute groups, from the Escalante expedition in 1776 down to the 1850s, consistently recorded cultivation, including the use of irrigation canals, among the Paiute bands of the St George Basin (Paroosits, Tonoquints and Shivwits). Roberts argues that cultivation only ended in this area after 1865, when Mormon settlers captured Paiute lands and water sources, reducing them to indigency. Powell collected maize cultivation vocabulary in 1873 from the Uintah Utes in northeastern Utah (Fowler & Fowler 1971, 173). Among the Weeminuche Utes (living in the triangle between the Colorado and San Juan Rivers), 'exceptional families planted varieties of maize' before the arrival of Whites. The Utes at Moab, at the confluence of the Colorado and Green Rivers, were cultivating in the early nineteenth century (Callaway *et al.* 1986, 343).

Archaeological evidence

Contemporary Numic groups occupy regions on the Colorado Plateau and in the eastern Great Basin where archaeology attests the ancient presence of cultivators. Cultivation appears on the Colorado Plateau perhaps as early as 3300 BP for maize and 2900 BP for squash (Smiley 2000; Matson this volume; Matson prefers a more conservative date of *c.* 2300 BC for maize dependence on the Plateau). In the eastern Basin, maize cultivation was practised at Steinaker Gap in northern Utah by 2100 BP (Talbot & Richens 1996).[2] The Fremont peoples, living in the eastern Basin between AD 400 and AD 1300 (Marwitt 1986), practised sedentary cultivation.[3] Between AD 900 and AD 1150, the archaeological record identifies intensive cultivation and high population densities on the Colorado Plateau (Jones *et al.* 1999).

In the eastern Great Basin and on much of the Colorado Plateau, cultivation ceased well before the historic period, as a major warming and drying of the climate shifted the northern limits of the summer rains that are crucial for maize cultivation south to a line roughly defined by the San Juan River. In the north, the Uintah Basin was abandoned by Fremont cultivators before AD 1000 (Marwitt 1986, 170). Jones *et al.* (1999) review episodes of abandonment on the

Colorado Plateau climaxing in the 'Great Drought' of AD 1276–1299.

Abandonment processes: ancestral Puebloan retreat and Numic invasion, or ancestral Puebloan retreat and Numic devolution?

What happened to the populations of cultivators who abandoned the eastern Great Basin and the northern Colorado Plateau? Most scholars have assumed that they either succumbed *in situ* to starvation and disease, or retreated southward. This 'abandonment' model assumes that newly-unoccupied lands were claimed by bands of Numic-speaking hunters and collectors, moving in from the southwest corner of the Great Basin in the notorious 'Numic Spread' (Matson, this volume, implicitly endorses this model).

This 'abandonment/Numic Spread' model is probably oversimplified, and I propose that it be supplemented by a 'Numic ethnogenesis *in situ*' model. First, it seems likely that at least some of the cultivators of the Colorado Plateau and the eastern Great Basin were Northern Uto-Aztecans. Hill (in press) proposes a suite of loan words for maize cultivation from Proto-Northern Uto-Aztecan into Proto-Kiowa Tanoan, which, if confirmed, must involve a contact situation dating roughly to the period that Matson (1991; and this volume) suggests for contact between the Western and Eastern Basketmaker II in the Four Corners region of the Colorado Plateau. The Numic peoples are descendants from a Northern Uto-Aztecan community, and, if this proposal holds up, are therefore descendants of cultivators. Marwitt (1986) points out that the 'Fremont Culture' was highly variable; he distinguishes five geographic variants, which may reflect ethnolinguistic differentiation. In the southern Basin and neighbouring Colorado Plateau, the Virgin Anasazi constituted a distinctive component of the larger Ancestral Puebloan (Anasazi) complex. The Virgin Anasazi exhibited obvious 'Shoshonean' components as early as AD 1000. Fowler & Madsen (1986) suggest that Southern Numic peoples acquired cultivation from Puebloan elements of the Virgin Anasazi at this period. However, the revised picture of Uto-Aztecan prehistory summarized above permits us to consider an alternative scenario: rather than a 'Numic Spread' into areas inhabited by vulnerable cultivators, a Numic ethnogenesis occurred *in situ*, as climatic stress differentiated the Northern Uto-Aztecans into subgroups that increasingly emphasized hunting and collecting versus subgroups that retained an emphasis on cultivation and either died out or retreated southward, such as some components of the Hopi.

The linguistic evidence, which will be considered in more detail below, supports this picture, and does not support the hypothesis of the borrowing of cultivation. For instance, Southern Numic *kumia 'corn', attested in Kaibab Paiute, San Juan Paiute, and Uintah Ute, is not a borrowing from Hopi (which has kokoma, 'maize with dark red kernels'), but is instead a regular development of PUA **ku:mi/u 'to nibble food in small particles, especially corn'.

Marwitt (1986) points out that some archaeologists have long argued that the Central Numic derive from the Fremont cultures of the eastern Great Basin, and the Virgin River Anasazi have been suggested as ancestors of Southern Numic. These proposals have generally been rejected, based on the widely-held belief that the linguistic evidence for a 'Numic Spread' from the Death Valley area is 'transparent[ly]' (Bettinger 1994, 45) visible in the historic geographical distribution of the Numic languages: the famous 'Numic Fan' with three small, sharply differentiated languages in the southwestern corner in California, and enormous, relatively undifferentiated dialect continua extending from these across the Basin (see Fig. 26.1).

But the 'Numic Fan' is not 'transparent' evidence for a Numic spread. While the sharp differentiation of the southwestern languages (Kawaiisu in Southern Numic, Tumpisha Shoshone in Central Numic, and Mono in Western Numic) has generally been taken to exemplify the 'maximum diversity' that signals great antiquity in the region, other evidence contradicts this proposal. Shaul (1998) points out that there is no mutual intelligibility between Kawaiisu and the other Southern Numic languages. However, Tumpisha Shoshone is highly inter-intelligible with the rest of Shoshone. He thus suggests that Southern Numic, spoken in a belt across the southern Basin and the northern Colorado Plateau, represents the oldest layer of Numic occupation. The high diversity of the three southwesternmost languages at the base of the fan can be explained as the result of their incorporation into the Californian 'residual' or 'accretion zone' (Nichols 1992; Golla 2000). In accretion zones, the linguistic processes that Thurston (1987) calls 'esoterogeny' result from a local linguistic and ethnic ecology in which involutional processes of linguistic differentiation come to dominate processes that favour wider communication. Golla (2000) has made this argument for California Athabascan. In northern California and Oregon, several small Athabascan languages are sharply differentiated from one another and from the rest of Athabascan. Athabascan, like Numic, out-

side of California consists of enormous dialect continua that exhibit low internal differentiation.

The archaeological record reveals no definitive discontinuities in the history of the Great Basin that clearly attest to a 'Numic Spread'. Bettinger (1994) identifies a shift to 'processing' in the westernmost Great Basin around 1400 BP, that for him signals the arrival of Numic peoples. However, Bettinger's model remains controversial (see papers in Madsen & Rhode 1994 for extensive discussion). The proposal advanced here suggests that some 'processing' innovations might well be seen as practices left over from former cultivation, rather than the intensification of foraging techniques.

A few groups of cultivators in the eastern Basin and the Colorado Plateau must have successfully retreated to more favourable habitats when climatic deterioration forced abandonment of their homelands. However, these successful refugees would have been a small percentage of the population. The potential refugia were all fully occupied by peoples who were quite capable of defending their territories (cf. LeBlanc 1999; this volume; Wilcox 1996; Wilcox & Haas 1994). Some refugees perhaps survived as clients in communities that were willing to offer patronage. But not all could have been accommodated. As the climate in the Basin deteriorated, most groups must have remained more or less *in situ*, increasingly emphasizing foraging over cultivation and nomadism over sedentism, shifting to the subsistence practices observed in much of the Basin in the historic period, with considerable intensive management of wild plants, the use of seed beaters for collection of labour-intensive wild seeds, and pine nuts as a major food crop. This is the 'processor' form of foraging that Bettinger & Baumhoff (1982; 1983) argued was the diagnostic Numic adaptation. The larger home ranges required by even the most intensive 'processing' in comparison to cultivation would yield the 'spread' of the Numic into their attested range across the entire Great Basin, a spread that probably emanated simultaneously from the west, south and east, and of course involved the reoccupation after about AD 1300 of former cultivator zones in the Fremont areas of the eastern Basin and in the Anasazi region on the Colorado Plateau north of the San Juan River (although recall that the ethnohistoric record shows cultivation into the nineteenth century by Paiute and Ute groups in the latter area).

Ethnographic models
Other cases of devolution from cultivation to foraging are attested ethnographically. Cases include the

South Island New Zealand Maori, the Austronesian-speaking Penan/Punan of Borneo, buffalo hunters on the North American plains, and probably some hunters and gatherers affiliated with the Tupí-Guarani language family in South America (Balée 1994). Nevertheless, in order to sustain a proposal of a devolution for the Numic of the Great Basin-Colorado Plateau, we require models of this process. One model comes from the work of Levy (1992) on the Hopi town of Oraibi. Here, access to cultivable land was controlled by senior clans, who favoured other high-ranking clans and relegated low-ranking ones to marginal lands. Takic groups in California were also divided between high-ranking lineages who controlled access to lands and 'common people' who did not (Hill & Nolasquez 1973). Thus, a division between 'landed' and 'landless' kin groups may have been part of the Northern Uto-Aztecan common heritage. In such a system, social discrimination could have forced low-ranking lineages to emphasize foraging. Such marginalized groups would have been likely (and more competent) to adopt a 'devolution' rather than a 'refugee' strategy, given that they would have been accustomed to foraging and that their low status would have made them unattractive to potential patrons.

Another Uto-Aztecan adaptation involved the presence of subsistence strategies specialized among social components of a regional system. The Upper Pimans distinguished River People, cultivating along permanent streams, Two-Village People, moving between winter water tanks and summer rainfall fields, and Sand Papago, foragers who occupied regions too dry for cultivation. These groups all spoke the same language. Sand Papago and Two-Village people occasionally worked for River People in exchange for access to food and water (Hackenberg 1983). Peoples living in the same areas inhabited in historic times by the Sand Papago participated in the trade in shells from the Gulf of California during the Hohokam period in the first millennium AD. In this Upper Piman system, the foragers, semi-sedentary cultivators and fully sedentary cultivators (some of whom were Yuman speakers: Shaul & Hill 1998) all played a role. If a similar adaptation characterized the margins of the Great Basin, forager groups in clientage to cultivators (like the Sand Papago) would have had no reason to retreat as refugees with their patrons during the period of climatic deterioration when these patrons could no longer be generous. Instead, they could simply remain *in situ*. Thus, Numic ethnogenesis might have become final when groups of cultivator symbionts gradually abandoned ties of

clientage that had become increasingly unreliable.

In summary, there are several ethnographic models for Numic ethnogenesis and devolution. Under the deteriorating climatic regime of the second millennium AD, some relatively high-ranking groups would have failed as refugees and would have been forced into foraging. Groups that were already marginalized, perhaps permitted access to cultivable lands only in very favourable years, could have maximized their skills as foragers and made this a permanent adaptation. Groups who were foragers in symbiosis with patron cultivators could have broken those ties as their patrons departed or became impoverished. But it is important to remember that the 'devolution' was only partial; many Numic groups continued to cultivate into the historic period.

The linguistics of devolution

In this section, I examine semantic change in the Northern Uto-Aztecan (NUA) subsistence lexicon, seeking evidence that cultivation was archaic among these people.

Northern Uto-Aztecan maize vocabulary

The *Hopi Dictionary* (Hill *et al.* 1998) includes at least 49 Hopi roots (many occurring in dozens of derived lexical items) having to do with the maize complex, or, if the Hopi root is not in the maize complex, other Uto-Aztecan languages attest a cognate with a meaning within it. Of these Hopi roots, 22 have cognates or resemblants[4] in other NUA languages. The data for these are summarized in Table 26.1. While additional research may yield more sets, the present sample will give us some idea of what is going on.

The complete inventory of 49 Hopi maize words includes the Hopi residue of the Proto-Northern Uto-Aztecan (PNUA) maize lexicon. The PNUA community must have existed roughly between 3000 and perhaps 2000 BP. The (admittedly unreliable) glottochronological constant predicts that at least 40 per cent of the PNUA lexicon has been replaced. The identification of 22 cognates of the 49 Hopi items in sister NUA languages is reasonably consistent with this dating.

Among the sets in Table 26.1, two types suggest semantic histories that are crucial for my purposes. First are those for which we can argue that the original meaning was within the maize complex, even though in some languages the meaning has shifted. These are sets (11), (15) and (22). The second are those for which all attestations are in the maize complex. These are (2), (3), (7), (8) and (9). It is only

Table 26.1. *Northern Uto-Aztecan maize vocabulary.*[5]

1. HO àaki 'for an ear of corn to come off stalk, pick corn' (comb. aki): KA kopaki- 'break off', kovaki 'break' (cf. TS kopiah 'break flexible object into pieces', CH koʔpok(i) 'snap, break stick' (cf. Miller 1988, 110, ko-115 'to break, to cut').

2. HO hàako- 'grind corn coarsely'. Possibly CH haʔwiv(i) 'corn', SP (Las Vegas) hawíp 'corn', SP (Kaibab) awív 'corn kernels' (Shaul 2001). Cf. HO hakwurkwa 'grind corn to a coarse meal'.

3. HO haani 'corn flour ground fine'; CM haniíbi 'maize' (the combining form, hani-, appears in many compound expressions). It seems likely that this set is related to set (2); cf. also HO haahalviki 'a snack made from blue corn flour batter'.

4. HO hooma 'ceremonial cornmeal'; CM homopɨ 'powder, flour'.

5. HO höqni 'harvested corn crop' < hö:qö 'harvest' -ni; TS hongopi(-ttsi) 'flour'.

6. HO himi- 'shell corn'; CA hemi 'collapse crumbling'.

7. HO i:ya 'to plant'; NP masɨa 'plant'; NP ɨappɨ, SH iʔapv *Chenopodium* spp.' (literally, 'something planted'; the word means 'corn' in some SP dialects (Kelly & Fowler 1986, 371)); TS iʔa 'plant', KA iʔa 'to plant', SP ia 'to plant', UT ɨay 'trap, plant' (PUA **ica 'to plant').

8. HO kokoma 'dark red, almost purple corn', komo *Amaranthus cruentus'* (a dye plant); SP (Kaibab) qumia 'old Indian name for corn, rarely used now' (Sapir 1932, 641); SP (San Juan) kumwi *Zea mays'* (Franklin & Bunte 1987, 28; note also SP (San Juan) kumut *Amaranthus caudatus',*); UT (Uintah) kuma 'corn', kumwi 'corn kernels', kumuivaia 'corn cob'; probably CM kukɨmepɨ 'corn, toasted', kukɨmerɨ 'parch' (PUA **ku:mi/u 'to nibble small pieces of food, especially corn on the cob or popcorn').

9. HO kicvavɨ (comb. kicvap) 'kernels of roasted sweet corn that has been dried and stored, then shelled'; CM hani koca-pɨ 'cornmeal mush'.

10. HO kitɨki 'parched corn'; KA kikɨtɨ-bɨ 'plant sp.' (cf. Tepiman *kɨrivi 'to shell corn'; not cognate with HO but resemblant — a loan?).

11. HO öövi ('at) 'butt end of corn cob', qaa'ö 'dried corn' (prototypical form, many combining forms, from qaa- 'öö); SP qa'ooˢ- 'pine cone' -vi (abs); SP (Kaibab) o'ok 'corn cob'; KA ʔono-ci 'hooked stick used to pull down pinyon cones', TS onno(-cci) 'pine cone harvesting hook', KA 'ono-ci 'hooked stick used to pull down pinyon cones', ookorosi 'small cone-shaped basket for pinyons' (??); CM hani-wo'ora 'corncob' (PUA **oʔra/*oʔri 'corn, cob').

12. HO paacama 'hominy'; possibly SP páasɨ 'Amaranth' (Fowler 1972, 93); TB pa:sil 'Chia seeds' (Fowler 1972, 167); SR pahinat 'Chia', Proto-Cupan *pasal (Fowler 1972, 289); CH paʔs(a) 'field, pasture' (PUA **paʔci 'ear of corn, corn kernel, seed').

13. HO piiki 'piki bread'; KA pigi-vɨ 'cake of acorn meal, juniper, etc.'; TS piki 'mesquite flour (especially in blocks)'; SP -pik.iˢ- 'semi-liquid mass', e.g. mu-p:iki:i 'nasal mucus'; piq:o 'yant [*Agave* spp.] cake, made out of the roasted heart of the cabbage-like head of the yant'; SP (Kaibab) pikiv 'bread', ɨpigiv 'cakes of cactus apple' (Fowler & Fowler 1971, 143).

Table 26.1. *(cont.)*

14. HO sami 'fresh, uncooked, unshucked corn' (comb. samii); CH samita?ap(i) 'bread', sami-kar(i). The Hopi form is probably related to the Numic word for 'raw', e.g. SH sa:m-pi:ccih 'raw (of food)'; Takic *sawi/-; (cf. M sa-13: Miller 1988). If this is the case then the CH-HO resemblance may be due to chance. But note also Takic *šaw- 'bread, tortillas'; Tepiman *saw- 'to make bread,' Aztecan *ša:mV- 'tortilla, baked thing'.

15. HO sööŋö 'corn cob', TS -soni 'grass' [archaic] cf. pisoni 'loincloth' (piᴳ- 'butt', -soni 'grass'); MN sona; SH, CM soni-pɨ 'grass'; SP son:i 'tinder' (PUA **sono 'maize byproducts such as cobs, leaves, cane').

16. HO tawakci (comb. tawa 'sun'- kɨc-) 'Hopi sweet corn, associated with the nadir'; possibly CM hani-kotasapɨ 'cornmeal mush'.

17. HO tɨma 'griddle'; SR tɨ:ʔ- 'to roast, bake'; KA tɨʔma-, tuʔma 'to roast, bake', SP tɨʔma- 'to roast under ashes'. See also HO tɨhpe 'bake, roast in pit oven', tɨʔc- 'roast corn'. Are there perhaps two etyma here? (PUA **tɨma 'tortilla, tamale, cake-like preparation of maize').

18. HO tɨi- 'corn, food'; MN tɨhɨtta 'deer'; NP (Yerington) tɨhɨdda, NP (McDowell) tɨhɨtya; KA tɨhɨya 'deer', tɨ-tiha 'dry meat, make jerky, to butcher', also tɨhani; SP tɨ-ˢ 'deer, game', tɨnna 'to pursue'; TS tɨhɨya 'deer', tɨhanni 'butcher'; SH tɨhɨyan(A) 'deer'; CH tɨʔhij(a) 'deer'; possibly TB tohi:l 'deer', LU ton-la 'antelope'.

19. HO toʔavi 'chaff, dregs, loose dirt, sediment'; TB tuʔil 'type of flour', SR toʔa-i 'pound, grind into flour', toaʔt 'flour'.

20. HO wihkʸa 'digging stick'; TB wi:ginat/'iwi:gin 'to stir' (PUA **wika 'digging stick').

21. HO wɨtaqa 'a gruel made from blue or white corn flower and boiling water', HO wihi-ta 'be sifting (using wind), winnowing' [e.g. corn kernels]; TS wɨppu'ah 'winnow'; KA wɨ-tɨʔni 'to shake out, dust off, winnow' [wɨ- 'with an instrument' [in other languages, the instrumental prefix for a long, flexible instrument); TS wɨppu'ah 'winnow' (PUA **wɨra 'to shell corn'; this set needs a lot of work).

22. HO yoowi(-'at) 'corn silk, loose strands of fiber on edges of yucca leaves'; Takic (Cupan only) *yu:- 'hair, head'.

fair to point out that at least two sets, (1) and (12), exhibit probable change from non-maize-related to maize-related meanings. (1), an obvious specialization in Hopi, is not important for our case. For (12), the earliest Proto-Uto-Aztecan meaning was probably 'seed in general' — perhaps 'edible seed' — with some daughter languages retaining this meaning. In the case of (13) and (17), their specific Hopi meanings reflect advances in maize preparation that reached the Southwest in the thirteenth century; however, it is likely that their earlier meanings were also within the maize complex.

Cultivation is attested historically for the Southern Paiute and Tumpisha Shoshone; for Kawaiisu, only 'semicultivation' of tobacco is recorded (Fowler 1986, 94). Tumpisha Shoshone and the Kawaiisu/

Southern Paiute are in two different branches of Numic (Central and Southern respectively), yet they share many of the same semantic correlations with Hopi. Of special interest are the sets for 'corn cob' = 'pine cone' (11); 'corn seed' = 'amaranth' (12); 'piki bread' = 'cake or block of acorn flour, mesquite flour' (13); 'corncob' = 'grass' (15), and 'corn, food' = 'deer, meat' (18). Where the same semantic changes are shared by two of the three Numic sub-groups, if we can show that they are innovations, then they occurred at a very early stage of Numic ethnogenesis — and suggest that an increasing emphasis on foraging was part of that ethnogenesis. For sets (11) and (15) we can make that argument (but not for set 22 since it involves Takic, not Numic).

For set (11), I argue for a change 'corn cob, corn

ear' > 'pine cone', as follows. The first part of the argument is that the meaning 'corn cob, corn ear' is more widely distributed. It is attested in the southern Uto-Aztecan languages as well as in Hopi. Furthermore, a reflex of the PUA **oʔra, Kaibab Southern Paiute *oʔok, was recorded by Powell with the meaning 'corn cob'. Comanche, outside the pine nut zone, has *hani woʔora* 'corn cob.' Finally, Hopi itself exhibits a reflex of PUA *oʔra in *öö-vi* 'butt end of corn cob'. The second part of the argument is that, while pine-nut harvesting was probably not a major activity in the Proto-Uto-Aztecan community, it was a major source of food for NUA groups, who share a common word for 'piñon nut', PNUA *tipa(h). This word is not shared with any of the southern languages (Fowler 1983, 237). Words for 'piñon' are attested in the south only for Northern Tepehuan and Tarahumara; the words are independent developments that are not resemblant or cognate.

In Hopi, *qaaʔö* 'dried ear of corn' is the 'prototypical' word for corn, the most important food source. Interestingly, the Hopi word has a secondary meaning in *qaaʔö-at* 'green cone of pine', literally, 'its corn ear' (Emory Sekaquaptewa pers. comm.). It seems very likely that as foraging was increasingly emphasized, Numic-speaking peoples shifted the semantic 'centre' for this word away from the ear of maize and over to the pine cone, source of the most highly valued vegetable food for Numic peoples. The semantic shift is facilitated by the fact that the habit of growth of the piñon nuts in the pine cone is not dissimilar to that of the maize kernels on their cob. In addition, there is a parallel management technique; just as the tassels of the maize plant are cut off to promote growth of the ears of corn, the Tumpisha Shoshone broke off the tips of piñon branches to 'produce more cones in subsequent years' (Fowler 1986, 94).

We cannot preclude the possibility that the semantic change was PUA **kaⁿ-oʔra 'hard-ear of corn' > NUA *qaaʔ-o 'pine cone' (hard-ear) > HO *qaaʔö* 'dried ear of corn'. However, we would still have to explain the presence in Hopi of another corn word formed with *öö* from PUA *oʔra, *öövi* 'butt end of corncob', and, of course, we would have to explain the precious attestation of Kaibab *oʔok* 'corncob', and the *woʔora* part of Comanche *hani woʔora* 'corncob'. Thus on balance, the argument favors the Hopi maize-releated meanings for *qaaʔö*, *öövi* as the archaism.

A second example where a change from the maize-specific meaning to a secondary, foraging-related meaning in Numic seems more likely is set

(15). The Hopi meaning, 'corncob', is specialized in comparison to the likely PUA meaning 'corn waste' (including stalks and leaves), based on meanings attested in the southern languages. The Numic meaning, 'grass, tinder', would easily be derived from the more generalized PUA sense. In contrast, it would be very difficult to derive Hopi 'corncob' from a generalized 'grass'. A corncob is certainly a type of waste by-product from maize, but it is not a kind of grass. Corncobs can be used for fuel, but 'grass' is used for many of the same purposes as corn waste.

Among the sets where all attestations are within the maize complex, (2), (3), (4), (7), (8) and (9) have correspondences or resemblances between Hopi and Comanche. Comanche has maize-related meanings in (3), (4), (8) and (9). Comanche also has the meaning 'corncob' for (11). Comanche split from Eastern Shoshone as recently as the eighteenth century. The Eastern Shoshone appear in the ethnographic record as Plains-assimilated buffalo hunters, but presumably originated in the eastern Great Basin. On the forager-origin model, the Comanche should have no history as cultivators. Why, then, do they share five cognates or resemblants with Hopi where the Comanche words continue to refer precisely to maize, and do not show the semantic shifts seen, for instance, in Tumpisha Shoshone, the closest relative to Comanche in the lists above? Only in (15) does Comanche share a non-maize meaning with the other Numic languages.

One possibility is that the Comanche borrowed their maize words when, in the mid-eighteenth century, they raided Tanoan and Keresan pueblos on the upper Rio Grande. However, none of the Comanche maize vocabulary looks like any attested Tanoan or Keresan words. Instead, it exhibits cognates or resemblances with Hopi forms. The Comanche never raided west as far as Hopi, so late contact with Hopi is an unlikely source. Under the archaic cultivation model, this conundrum can be clarified. If the Comanche are descendants of the easternmost Shoshone, then before their move on to the Plains they would have been in the eastern Great Basin, where cultivation is continuously attested archaeologically from about 2100 BP until as late as 600 BP. The Comanche are excellent candidates for participants in the Fremont (Dave Wilcox, pers. comm.). Thus, Comanche ancestors probably preserved the NUA cultivation complex until a relatively late date. The high rate of retention of the cultivation vocabulary in the maize-related meanings is probably due to continuing contact with Tanoan and Keresan cultivators.

Conclusion

I have reviewed above ethnohistoric, archaeological, ethnographic, and linguistic arguments for a hypothesis that the hunting and gathering adaptation of many of the Numic peoples results from a devolution from cultivation. While I do not believe that the case is proven, I hope to have shown that the suggestion is an interesting one. I urge a fresh look at the archaeological evidence, testing the possibility that: a) the Northern Uto-Aztecan proto-community included cultivators; and b) the distribution and subsistence habits of the Numic peoples and the contrast between them and the Puebloans are the result in part of an ethnogenesis *in situ* on the Colorado Plateau and adjacent regions of the Great Basin, and not of a migration of archaic foragers into zones abandoned by cultivators.

Notes

1. I am grateful for help on this project from Dave Shaul, Dave Wilcox, and Rick Ahlstrom, and of course from my husband Kenneth C. Hill.
2. Matson (this volume) suggests that the earliest dates may be on forms of maize where canes, not cobs, were used for food, but considers that a full commitment to cultivation on the Plateau dates to as early as 2300 BP. Furthermore, it must be emphasized that *Zea mays* propagates only with human intervention; the appearance of any form of this plant signals the presence of cultivators.
3. LeBlanc (this volume) points out that archaeological evidence of several types suggests that early cultivators in the eastern-most part of this northern zone, the Eastern Basketmaker, were not Uto-Aztecans, but local foraging groups, possibly ancestral Tanoans, who adopted cultivation by contact.
4. I have not yet worked out for some of the sets in Table 26.1 whether they exhibit regular sound correspondence or are merely resemblant. Space limitations rule out full discussion of the etymological issues here, but many of the sets seem quite regular.
5. Abbreviations in Table 26.1 are as follows: CA = Cahuilla; CH = Chemehuevi; CM = Comanche; comb. = combining form; HO = Hopi; KA = Kawaiisu; LU = LuiseZo; MN = Mono; NP = Northern Paiute; PUA = Proto-Uto-Aztecan; SH = Shoshone; SP = Southern Paiute; SR = Serrano; TB = Tubatulabal; TS = Tumpisha Shoshone; UT = Ute.

References

Balée, W., 1994. *Footprints of the Forest: Ka'apor Ethnobotany - The Historical Ecology of Plant Utilization by an Amazonian People*. New York (NY): Columbia University Press.

Bellwood, P., 1997. Prehistoric cultural explanations for widespread language families, in *Archaeology and Linguistics*, eds. P. McConvell & N. Evans. Melbourne: Oxford University Press, 123–34.

Bellwood, P., 2001. Archaeology and the historical determinants of punctuation in language family origins, in *Areal Diffusion and Genetic Inheritance: Problems in Comparative Linguistics*, eds. A. Aikhenvald & R. Dixon. Oxford: Oxford University Press, 27–43.

Bettinger, R.L., 1994. How, when, and why Numic spread, in Madsen & Rhode (eds.), 44–55.

Bettinger, R.L. & M.A. Baumhoff, 1982. The Numic spread: Great Basin cultures in competition. *American Antiquity* 47(3),485–503.

Bettinger, R.L. & M.A. Baumhoff, 1983. Return rates and intensity of resource use in Numic and Pre-Numic adaptive strategies. *American Antiquity* 48(4), 830–84.

Callaway, D., J. Janetski & O.C. Stewart, 1986. Ute, in D'Azavedo (ed.), 336–67.

D'Azavedo, W.L. (ed.), 1986. *Handbook of North American Indians*, vol. 11: *Great Basin*. Washington (DC): Smithsonian Institution Press.

Fowler, C.S., 1972. Comparative Numic Ethnobiology. Unpublished PhD dissertation, University of Pittsburgh.

Fowler, C.S., 1983 Lexical clues to Uto-Aztecan prehistory. *International Journal of American Linguistics* 49, 224–57.

Fowler, C.S., 1986. Subsistence, in D'Azavedo (ed.), 64–97.

Fowler, D.D. & C.S. Fowler (eds.), 1971. *Anthropology of the Numa: John Wesley Powell's Manuscripts on the Numic Peoples of Western North America, 1868–1880*. (Smithsonian Contributions to Anthropology 14.) Washington (DC): Smithsonian Institution.

Fowler, D.D. & D.B. Madsen. 1986. Prehistory of the southeastern area, in D'Azavedo (ed.), 173–82.

Franklin, R.J. & P.A. Bunte, 1987. *From the Sand to the Mountain: Change and Persistence in a Southern Paiute Community*. Lincoln (NE): University of Nebraska Press.

Golla, V., 2000. Language history and communicative strategies in aboriginal California and Oregon, in *Languages of the North Pacific Rim*, vol. 5, eds. O. Miyaoka & M. Oshima. Suita: Faculty of Informatics, Osaka Gakuin University, 43–64.

Hackenberg, R., 1983. Pima and Papago ecological adaptations, in Ortiz (ed.), 161–77.

Hill, J.H., 2001. Proto-Uto-Aztecan: a community of cultivators in central Mexico? *American Anthropologist* 103(4), 913–34.

Hill, J.H., in press. Toward a linguistic prehistory of the Southwest: 'Azteco-Tanoan' and the arrival of maize cultivation. *Journal of Anthropological Research*, December.

Hill, J.H. & R. Nolasquez, 1973. *Mulu'wetam: the First People*. Banning (CA): Malki Museum Press.

Jones, T.L., G.M. Brown, L.M. Raab, J.L. McVickar, W.G. Spaulding, D.J. Kennett, A. York & P.L. Walker, 1999. Environmental imperatives reconsidered: Demographic crises in western North American during the Medieval Climatic Anomaly. *Current Anthropology* 40(2), 137–70.

Kelley, I.T. & C.S. Fowler, 1986. Southern Paiute, in D'Azavedo (ed.), 368–97.

LeBlanc, S.A., 1999. *Prehistoric Warfare in the American Southwest.* Salt Lake City (UT): The University of Utah Press.

Levy, J., 1992. *Orayvi Revisited.* Santa Fe (NM): School of American Research Press.

Liljeblad, S. & C.S. Fowler, 1986. Owens Valley Paiute, in D'Azavedo (ed.), 412–34.

Madsen, D.B. & D. Rhode (eds.), 1994. *Across the West: Human Population Movement and the Expansion of the Numa.* Salt Lake City (UT): University of Utah Press.

Marwitt, J.P., 1986. Fremont cultures, in D'Azavedo (ed.), 161–72.

Miller, W.R., 1983. Uto-Aztecan Languages, in Ortiz (ed.), 113–24.

Miller, W.R., 1988. Computerized Data Base for Uto-Aztecan Cognate Sets. University of Utah ms.

Nichols, J., 1992. *Linguistic Diversity in Space and Time.* Chicago (IL): University of Chicago Press.

Ortiz, A. (ed.), 1983. *Handbook of North American Indians,* vol. 10: *Southwest.* Washington (DC): Smithsonian Institution Press.

Roberts, H., 2000. Settlement and Subsistence Strategies of the Southern Paiute in the St George Basin, Southwestern Utah. Paper presented at the 27th Great Basin Anthropological Conference, Ogden, UT, October, 2000.

Romney, A.K., 1957. The genetic model and Uto-Aztecan time perspective. *Davidson Journal of Anthropology* 3, 35–41.

Sapir, E., 1932. Southern Paiute, a Shoshonean language,

parts 1 & 2. *Proceedings of the American Academy of Arts and Sciences* 65(1), 1–296; 65(2), 297–536.

Shaul, D.L., 1998. The Numic Unspread: Bad Linguistics, Convenient Archaeology. University of Arizona ms.

Shaul, D.L. & J.H. Hill, 1998. Tepimans, Yumans, and other Hohokam. *American Antiquity* 63, 375–96.

Smiley, F.E., 2000. First farmers: New Basketmaker II research on the Colorado Plateau. Paper presented at the 65th Annual Meeting of the Society for American Archaeology, Philadelphia, PA, April 8, 2000.

Steward, J., 1930. Irrigation without agriculture. *Papers of the Michigan Academy of Science, Arts, and Letters* 12, 149–56.

Steward, J., 1933. Ethnography of the Owens Valley Paiute. *University of California Publications in Anthropology, Archaeology, and Ethnology* 33(3), 233–350.

Talbot, R.K. & L.D. Richens, 1996. *Steinaker Gap: an Early Fremont Farmstead.* (Occasional Papers 2.) Provo, UT: Brigham Young University Museum of Peoples and Cultures.

Thurston, W.R., 1987. *Processes of Change in the Languages of North-Western New Britain.* (Pacific Linguistics Series b 99.) Canberra: Department of Linguistics, Research School of Pacific Studies, The Australian National University.

Wilcox, D.R., 1996. Pueblo III people and polities in relational context, in *The Prehistoric Pueblo World,* AD 1150–1350, ed. M.A. Adler. Tucson (AZ): University of Arizona Press, 241–54.

Wilcox, D.R. & J. Haas, 1994. The scream of the butterfly, Competition and conflict in the prehistoric southwest, in *Themes in Southwestern Prehistory: Grand Patterns and Local Variations in Culture Change,* ed. G.J. Gumerman. Santa Fe (NM): School of American Research Press, 211–38.

Chapter 27

The Spread of Maize Agriculture into the U.S. Southwest

R.G. Matson

How did maize agriculture come to the U.S. Southwest? Over the years there have been a number of answers to this question and, as new information comes available, the explanations continue to change. The locus of investigation has changed, as well. The archaeology of the Anasazi, the ancestors of the present-day Pueblo people on the Colorado Plateau, was — and is — better known than that to the south, in the Basin and Range Province (Fig. 27.1). The initial investigations of early agriculture centred on the Colorado Plateau and it is still best understood there, but the focus in the last 15 years has shifted to the Basin and Range Province and, most recently, to northern Mexico.

Here I review the history and the accumulating evidence for the occurrence of early agriculture, as well as the changing locus of investigation. The pattern of evidence is, I believe, the result of both migration and indigenous development. I end with an example of how the abandonment of agriculture led to a migration and a new linguistic spread, the Athapaskan migration from Canada into the U.S. Southwest, and some comments on how Southwestern developments compare with those elsewhere.

Background

The domestication of maize occurred in Central Mexico. Most investigators believe that maize evolved from a variety of teosinte native to the Rio Balsas (Iltis 2000; Benz 2001; Long *et al.* 1989; Smith 1997). Since teosinte is not found anywhere near the Southwest culture area, we must assume that this area did not participate in its original domestication.

Our understanding of the origins of Southwestern agriculture has changed dramatically in the last 15 years. Perhaps most dramatic has been the redating of domesticated Tehuacan Valley maize from Central Mexico to no older than 4700 radiocarbon years, rather than the 7000 that has been conventional wisdom for the previous 30 years (Long *et al.* 1989). Very recently two cobs have been dated from Guila Naquitz which extend this to 5400 years ago (Benz 2001; Piperno & Flannery 2001). When this redating is combined with the Huckells' 1984 discovery of the agricultural-based Milagro San Pedro site in Tucson, Arizona (Fig. 27.1) (Huckell & Huckell 1984; Huckell *et al.* 1995; Huckell 1990), which dates to 2900 radiocarbon years ago, the time between the earliest dated domesticated maize in Mexico and the first clear agricultural settlements in the U.S. Southwest is dramatically condensed. Instead of around 5000 years as previously thought (7000 BP maize in Mexico, 2000 BP Basketmaker II in the Southwest), we have an interval of no more than 2400 years (5400–3000 BP).

The late development of domesticated maize is supported by Smith's (1997) recent redating of ancient maize from Tamaulipas to no more than 3930 radiocarbon years. These earliest forms of maize are unlikely foundations for an agricultural-based economy as the cobs, kernels and inferred yields are all very small. The earliest dates for agricultural villages in Mexico are no more than 3500 years ago, and some say no more than 3200 radiocarbon years. Maize was likely not in widespread use as a cereal grain until shortly before then, when more productive varieties were developed. The extensive use of maize arrived very shortly after this in the southern portions of the greater Southwest, no less than 3000 radiocarbon years ago.

The Southwestern background

Culture History in the U.S. is often dated to the Pecos synthesis in 1927, which in turn followed closely Kidder's 1924 book. The earlier parts of the sequence relied extensively on work carried out by Kidder & Guernsey (1919) and Guernsey & Kidder (1921) in northeastern Arizona ('Kayenta' on Fig. 27.2) (Matson 1991, 14–21). Kidder & Guernsey were

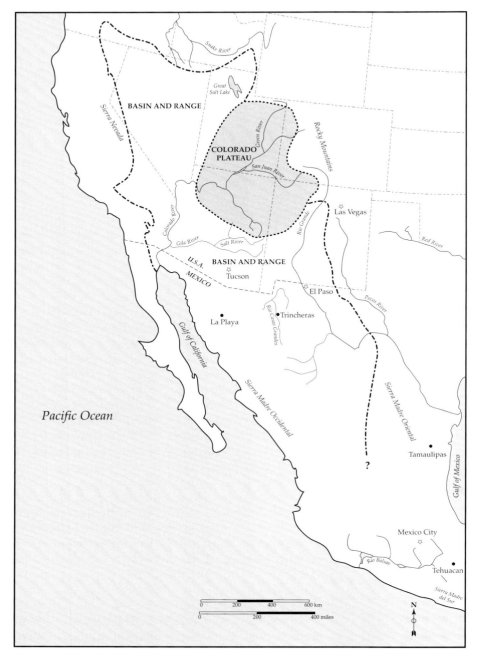

Figure 27.1. *The geographical context. The Colorado Plateau, the Basin and Range Province, the Southwest and northern Mexico.*

tery users found in the same area. By the time of the Pecos conference, a complete Anasazi sequence from the preceramic 'Basketmakers' to the contemporary Pueblo Indians (Pueblo V) had been developed for the Colorado Plateau. The Pecos conference defined seven evolutionary stages: Basketmaker II, Basketmaker III and Pueblo I–IV, and the hypothetical Basketmaker I. The Basketmaker III was not preceramic but had both plain and painted pottery, the first Anasazi stage to do so, but did not have above-ground living structures — 'Pueblos' — while the later stages did.

The Basketmaker I stage remained undefined and undiscovered. Thus, the subject of this paper might be redefined as 'who were the Basketmaker I?' And the answer to this question is there are multiple 'whos'.

An indigenous origin for the Basketmaker II was specified in the Pecos conference report:

> There was practical unanimity as to the course of development, i.e. that agriculture was taken up by a previous resident, long-headed, nomadic or semi-nomadic people, who did not practice skull-deformation, and who already made excellent coiled basketry, twined-woven bags, sandals, and used the atlatl; but whose dwellings were of perishable nature (Kidder 1927, 556).

In 1915, however, Kidder (1917, 110) presented a paper to the 19th International Congress of Americanists in Washington in which he reviewed both a migration model and an indigenous origin model for the Basketmaker II. He concluded that their culture was most likely an 'intrusive one'. Nevertheless, the Pecos position on agricultural adop-

guided in their efforts by John Wetherill, who assisted his brother Richard Wetherill in the 1890s in Southeastern Utah ('Cedar Mesa' on Fig. 27.2), where the earliest member of the Anasazi tradition, the Basketmaker II, was discovered (Matson 1991, 14–15; McNitt 1966).

Richard Wetherill called this culture the 'Basketmakers', contrasting them with the later pot-

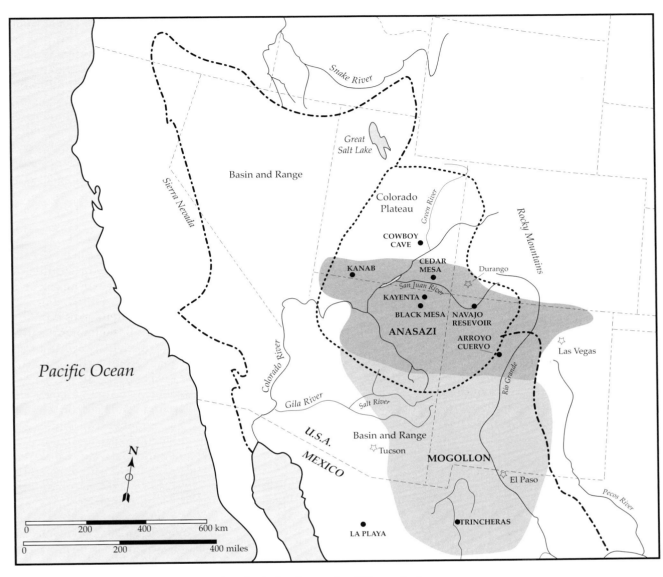

Figure 27.2. *The U.S. Southwest. Archaeological cultures, localities and sites.*

tion became the conventional wisdom for the next sixty years in Southwestern Archaeology.

Our modern understanding of Basketmaker II (Matson 1991) includes dates ranging from 400 BC to AD 400. They were an *atlatl*-using people, who practiced maize agriculture extensively, used rockshelters for storage in sandstone slab-lined cists and bell-shaped hardpan cists, and sometimes reused these facilities for burials. Pottery is generally absent (Fig. 27.4, cols. 2 & 3). In addition to maize, cucurbits (pumpkin and squash) were cultivated. Pit-houses are present and are found in hamlets or small villages after AD 100. This conventional description is heavily biased towards the remains in Southeastern

Utah, where they were originally discovered, and in adjacent Northeastern Arizona where Kidder and Guernsey carried out their investigations.

Morris & Burgh's report (1954) on the Durango or Los Pinos Basketmakers located to the east (Fig. 27.2) was the first clear challenge to the Pecos position. Their careful comparison between Basketmaker II and two other well-known (by that time) cultures to the south, the early Mogollon and San Pedro Cochise, called into question the conventional indigenous development idea.

The Mogollon (Fig. 27.2) is another archaeological tradition, found on the southern Colorado Plateau and spilling over to the adjacent Basin and

Range. The Mogollon also contributed to the present day Pueblo, but are usually represented as being heavily influenced by the Anasazi after about AD 1000, during Pueblo II times. Early Mogollon appears to have a number of similarities with the Basketmaker II, as Morris and Burgh pointed out.

The Cochise is a regional sequence of Archaic, or hunting and gathering cultures defined in the Southern Basin and Range by Sayles (1983) and Sayles & Antevs (1943). Later work (Huckell & Huckell 1984; Huckell 1996) indicates that the general distinctiveness of the Cochise sequence from other Southwestern Archaic cultures can not be maintained (Matson 1991). The San Pedro Cochise, however, is the last part of this sequence, best known in the Tucson, Arizona area, and distinctive for its large, side-notched *atlatl* points and lack of ceramics. Unlike other units of the Cochise sequence, the San Pedro was not widely recognized over the rest of the Southwest.

Morris & Burgh conclude their comparisons by stating (1954, 85) that San Pedro Cochise 'may have been' parental to both BM II and early Mogollon, thus introducing the idea that the Anasazi BM II resulted from a migration from the south. They also carried out a detailed trait comparison between Durango and 'Classic' BM II from northeastern Arizona and southeastern Utah, showing a 70 per cent agreement between the two. Although they conclude that there are differences, they determine that both are of the 'same culture', albeit different variants. Today, looking at the perishables, a conclusion of two different ethnicities is self evident, as I review below.

The Pecos view of an indigenous origin of the Anasazi had a strong proponent in C. Irwin-Williams (1973; 1985). She developed a sequence at Arroyo Cuervo, west of Albuquerque, on the edge of the Basin and Range Province, which she saw as being ancestral to the Anasazi (Fig. 27.2). This is a local Archaic sequence that is inferred to have similarities with early Anasazi. It is the Eastern, or Durango, Basketmakers that C. Irwin-Williams (1973) compares with her Arroyo Cuervo material, not the Western Basketmakers, accepting an ethnic difference within the BM II (Irwin-Williams 1967).

Berry (1982) and Berry & Berry (1986) put forward an explicit model for the derivation of the Basketmaker II (in general) from the San Pedro Cochise, going so far as to lump them together as the 'San Pedro/Basketmaker II'. They also make an argument for the San Pedro being agricultural, a position which soon became validated, with the discovery

of the 'Milagro' phenomenon (Huckell 1990; Huckell & Huckell 1984; Huckell *et al.* 1995). The Berrys' position can be viewed as a strong presentation of the Morris and Burgh view, with the inference of maize agriculture being the mechanism for this process.

Thus there has a been broad range of interpretations for the origins of the Anasazi and the coming of maize to the Southwest. The 'facts' though, have changed with time, and neither of these opposed positions can really explain the full range of what is known today.

Early maize use

Our understanding of early use of maize in the Southwest has also changed. Previously many Southwestern archaeologists believed that maize was not a critical part of the subsistence pattern until relatively late, maybe even as late as Pueblo II, AD 1000 (Plog 1979). Even today, one can read recent accounts that appear to support this view (Cordell 1997). Although some have long argued that certain Basketmaker II variants were agriculturally based (Eddy 1972), now it is apparent from settlement patterns, coprolite analysis, midden analysis and stable carbon isotope analyses that the major Basketmaker II variants were approximately as dependent on maize agriculture as their later Pueblo descendants (Matson & Chisholm 1991; Chisholm & Matson 1994; Martin *et al.* 1991; Martin 1999; Matson 1991; 1999). This is true for BM II at Black Mesa, Cedar Mesa, Kanab area, Navajo Reservoir, as well as canyon variants in the Cedar Mesa area (Fig. 27.2). By at least 2000 years ago on the Colorado Plateau the early users of maize were not 'modified hunters and gatherers' but committed and dependent maize agriculturalists.

Although the best evidence does not extend to the beginning of the BM II (conservatively 400 BC[1]), it appears to be a reasonable inference that the agricultural dependence does go back that far. If this is so, what about the earlier maize dates and the possibility that they are the result of indigenous Archaic people developing maize agriculture? Some reported Southwestern maize dates are well over 3000 radiocarbon years ago, although one reported recently from McEuen Cave (Huckell *et al.* 1999) is now seen as likely to be unreliable (B. Huckell pers. comm. 2001).

Even if these early maize dates are confirmed, I am not certain that they will change anything. There are intriguing hints that teosinte was originally domesticated not as a cereal but as a source of sugar

(Iltis 2000, 30; Smalley & Blake n.d.). The recently-dated Guila Naquitz maize can be interpreted as supporting this new idea, as Benz (2001) points out that these cob remains do not appear to be different from the later (4700–4400 BP) San Marcos Cave examples. This is hard to understand if the cobs were under intense selective pressures, but would be reasonable if the stalks were the important part and the cobs, at that time, only used for reproduction. This idea might explain some maize dates in the Southwest that appear to be earlier than any agricultural villages in the New World (Mabry n.d.). In any event, maize that could be the basis of a sedentary, agricultural lifeway, dates far later (*c.* 3200–3400 BP) than these small cob forms, which are less than 5 cm long.

The earliest Southwestern agricultural villages

The situation in the more southern Basin and Range Province is not quite as clear as on the Colorado Plateau, but I believe the evidence is in accord with very early maize dependence. Huckell's (1990) dissertation presents the evidence for extensive maize use in the 'Milagro' phenomenon of the San Pedro Cochise in a convincing fashion, although the isotopic and coprolite corroboration available for the BM II on the Colorado Plateau is not present.

Hard & Roney (1999) have shown that the Trincheras site on the Rio Casas Grandes in Northern Chihuahua, a large site adjacent to a river flood plain, must have also been agricultural (Figs. 27.1 & 27.2). Carpenter *et al.* (n.d.) have shown that the Las Playas site in Northern Sonora (Figs. 27.1 & 27.2), is very similar. Both sites date to 3000 BP and have abundant maize remains, and their multi-hectare sizes leave little doubt about the importance of maize. Roney and Hard, however, also report the presence of a domesticated amaranth, which has not been reported elsewhere in the Southwest. The dates of the Milagro version of the San Pedro, the Trincheras sites in Chihuahua and the Playa site all appear to begin about 3000 radiocarbon years ago (most dates are on maize), or 1200 BC in calendar years. Cucurbits are the only other domesticates present at this time.

In contrast with the view 20 years ago, we now recognize a preceramic period with extensive use of maize both on the Plateau and in the Basin and Range Provinces. William Lipe has called this the PPN, Pre-Pottery Neolithic, a term that emphasizes both the pre-ceramic and agricultural aspects of this stage. Since the reference is to the Americas, a more appropriate term would be PPF, Pre-Pottery Formative. Given the recent compression of the period between the first known use of maize and agricultural villages in Mexico and agricultural villages in the Southwest, the likelihood of 'independent indigenous development' of agriculture in the Southwest has become less likely.

A rapid spread of the PPF into the Southwest would be in accord with agricultural villages expanding into all niches not occupied by dense populations of hunters and gatherers, where corn could be grown under the central Mexican regime of planting after the first monsoon rain in the summer (Matson 1991, 209). Given the apparent source of maize from Rio Balsas teosinte, we can see this spread occurring in all directions (Iltis 2000). As maize moves north, we can see the change from direct rainfall dry-farming to floodwater farming and planting after the first flood (Matson 1991, 210). The earliest agricultural villages in the Basin and Range Province are located in such environments (despite Cordell 1997, 140 to the contrary). According to current dates, this spread of maize-based Formative villages from the Rio Balsas neighbourhood (3500–3200 BP) to the southwestern Basin and Range under the Mogollon rim took less than 500 years, and it could have happened in only 200 years (3200–3000 BP).

Competing models

Let us review the two competing models for the origins of the Anasazi and other Southwestern Cultures. If the Anasazi were the result of a single migration, ultimately from Mexico, one would expect something like the Numic situation in the Great Basin, a large area covered with the descendants of a single language, with a time depth of less than 3000 years. Instead, we find a variety of languages and language families at contact times, with only two, Hopi and Pima/Papago, having any clear relationship with Mexican languages (Fig. 27.3). Furthermore, there are many traits, deeply rooted in early Anasazi, such as kivas (circular, subterranean ceremonial rooms with cribbed log roofs), which could not be derived from Mexico or any area south of the Colorado Plateau. So the Anasazi can not be seen as originating entirely by migration from south of the Colorado Plateau. At the same time, though, there are other lines of evidence which do support Mexican connections and there appears to be increasing evidence for these.

In fact, the Uto-Aztecan language family to which the Hopi and Pima/Papago belong extends in a long 'Tepiman' corridor from southern Arizona south to central Mesoamerica (Fig. 27.3), as Wilcox

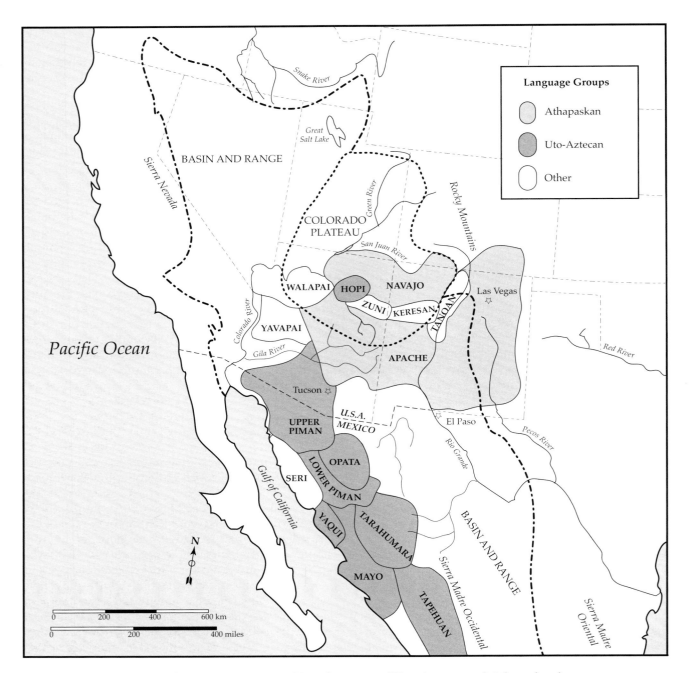

Figure 27.3. *Southwestern languages at contact. Note the extent of Uto-Aztecan and Athapaskan languages.*

(1983) delineated nearly 20 years ago and as Shaul & Hill (1998) have recently revisited. Hill (2001; this volume) argues that the Uto-Aztecan languages spread north with agriculture, in contrast to the previous view expressed by Miller (1983), which placed Uto-Aztecan origins in southeastern California. The current language pattern can be understood if Anasazi origins are the results of *both* migrations from further south and indigenous developments,

given that the Colorado Plateau also includes the non-Uto-Aztecan Zuñi, Keres, and Tanoan languages.

Basketmaker II ethnicity

The ethnic divisions likely resulting from migrationary and indigenous origins can be seen in the first Anasazi, the Basketmaker II. The Western or 'Classic' Basketmaker II have affinities with the San Pedro

Cochise, as recognized by the Berrys. The Durango, or Los Pinos (Navajo Reservoir area on Fig. 27.2) BM II, however, have affinities with local Archaic cultures, as argued by Cynthia Irwin-Williams (1973). This is exactly what would be expected if the Western Basketmaker II evolved from the San Pedro Cochise and the Durango Basketmakers derived from the local Archaic, while being influenced by the Western BM II.

The perishable textiles have long been seen as the part of the artefactual record most sensitive to ethnic differences (Adovasio & Pedler 1994). Coiled basketry foundations are illustrated in Figure 27.4.

At Durango (Table 27.1), 95 per cent of the basketry was either one rod and bundle or the closely related half rod and bundle form (Webster & Hays-Gilpin 1994, 318). Many collections in the west have only two rod and bundle forms. A total of 138 pieces of two-ply cordage found at Durango were examined by Morris & Burgh (1954, 65), and of those only two were Z twist. In contrast, at the Turkey Pen site, in Grand Gulch, Utah, 1058 pieces of Z twist 2 ply cordage were reported and only 47 of S twist (Powers 1984).

A total of four *tule* (bulrush) twilled sandals are reported from Durango (Morris & Burgh 1954, 64); none are reported from Western Basketmaker sites. In the west, Kidder and Guernsey Type Ib (crushed yucca leaves, four warp wickerwork) and Type III (multiple warp yucca cord sandal) are the common types (Matson 1991, 22). Type Ia (uncrushed yucca leaves, four warp wickerwork) is also found in the west, but rarely. Morris & Burgh (1954, 65) suggest that Kidder and Guernsey report only three of these. A single example is found at Durango (Morris & Burgh 1954, 65). This type now has added significance because Geib (2000, 521) has suggested a mechanism through which it could have been derived from early Archaic sandal types.

Although only a single 'open loop' cradle board is found at Durango, nothing like it is known from the west, although there are a number of 'full loop' cradle boards reported.

Even the house structures are different (Fig. 27.4). The earliest western houses appear to be round constructions, lacking slab-lined entrance ways, but with interior bell-shaped storage pits (Black Mesa: Matson 1991, 114; and Rainbow Plateau: Geib *et al.* 1997; Geib & Spurr 2000). Slab-lined entrance ways are found later at Cedar Mesa (Matson 1991). In the east, both cribbed roofs and antechambers are found, which are absent in the west. The cribbed roofs persevere into later Anasazi kivas. Even projectile points differ, with distinct side-notched points only abun-

Table 27.1. *Basketmaker II perishables.*

ITEM	Western BM II	Eastern BM II
Coiled basketry foundations	Two rod and bundle	One rod and bundle
Cordage	Z twist	S twist
Sandals	Four ply wickerwork, cord	Tule twilled, One Kidder and Guernsey Type Ia
Cradle board	Full loop	Open loop

dant in the west, and various relatively broad-notched corner-notched forms dominating in the east. These differences are numerous, indicating that we are seeing the remains of two different ethnic groups.

Furthermore, the similarities between the Western BM II and the San Pedro Cochise are numerous, in house form, projectile forms, basketry foundations, and even to some degree in sandal technology (Fig. 27.4). All these are consistent with a derivation from the San Pedro culture. The case for the relationship between the Eastern/Los Pinos Basketmaker and the local Archaic is not quite as strong, in part because the best-known Archaic is located to the west of the Western Basketmaker! Still, cribbed roofs structures are found in the Archaic of the Gunnerson Basin further north on the Colorado Plateau (Stiger 1997), and the basketry and cordage from Durango are very similar to late Archaic material found in Cowboy Cave (Jennings 1980). The projectile points also are similar to the local Archaic, as pointed out by C. Irwin-Williams (1973). The Archaic perishables were not available to Morris and Burgh at the time of their investigation, but they did point out the similarities between the Eastern Basketmakers and the Fremont, now usually seen as derived from the local Archaic (Geib 1996).

The evidence, including the most sensitive category of perishables (Adovasio 1980; Adovasio & Pedler 1994), supports three propositions: an east/west ethnic division among the BM II; the similarity of the Eastern BM II with earlier Colorado Plateau Archaic; and of the Western BM II with the San Pedro Cochise. Let us turn now to the limited biological evidence.

Christy Turner's (1993) contributions

Earlier biological investigations usually grouped all BM II samples together and so are not informative for these issues. Christy Turner (1993) has carried out investigations using a number of dental characteristics looking at a broad range of Southwestern

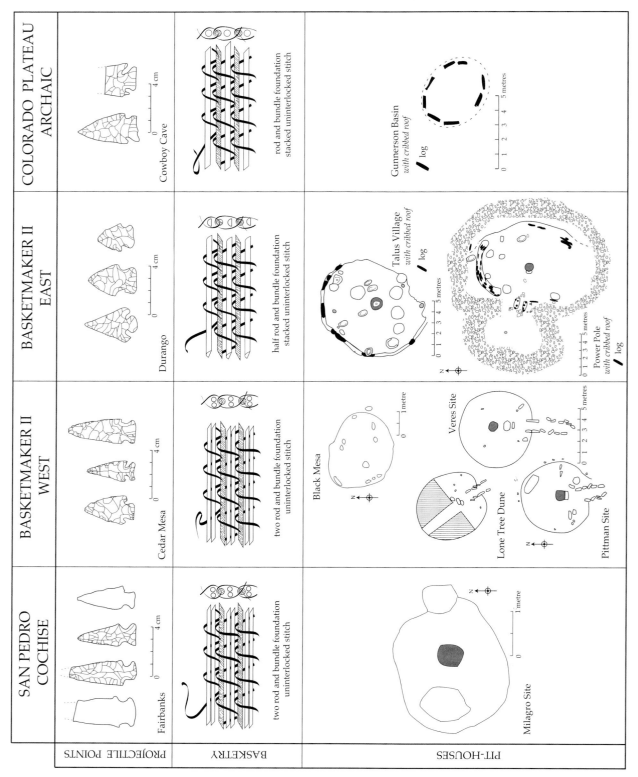

Figure 27.4. *Archaeological traits of San Pedro Cochise, Western Basketmaker II, Eastern Basketmaker II, and Colorado Plateau Archaic.*

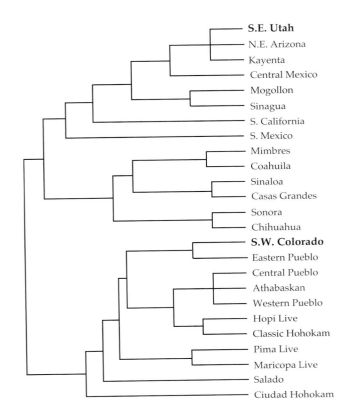

S.E. Utah
N.E. Arizona
Kayenta
Central Mexico
Mogollon
Sinagua
S. California
S. Mexico
Mimbres
Coahuila
Sinaloa
Casas Grandes
Sonora
Chihuahua
S.W. Colorado
Eastern Pueblo
Central Pueblo
Athabaskan
Western Pueblo
Hopi Live
Classic Hohokam
Pima Live
Maricopa Live
Salado
Ciudad Hohokam

Figure 27.5. *Cluster analysis based on dental characteristics (after Turner 1993). SE Utah sample is primarily Western Basketmakers; SW Colorado is mostly Durango Basketmakers.*

samples. Although the samples are not grouped in an ideal way for our purposes, the 'SE Utah' samples are mainly Western Basketmakers and the 'SW Colorado' samples are mostly Eastern Basketmakers, as shown in the redrawn cluster analysis in Figure 27.5. It is striking how the SW Colorado sample is linked with modern eastern Pueblos, while the Western Basketmakers are closely linked with other archaeological remains (and no modern Pueblo group), demonstrating little dental affinity between the two Basketmaker samples. This distribution indicates that the ethnic division between the two Basketmaker II groups is also a biological one. The Western BM II are most closely linked with the Kayenta Anasazi which eventually developed into the Hopi. Further, the Central Mexico sample (Fig. 27.5) is closely linked to the Western Basketmakers/Kayenta Anasazi samples, which is expected if their ultimate origin were early Mexican maize-using immigrants. The only link that remains to be discovered is between the Colorado Plateau Archaic and the Eastern Basketmakers.

The relationship between the indigenous Ar-

chaic peoples and the Basketmakers can be examined if one is willing to assume that the Fremont are descended from Colorado Plateau Archaic, as most do today (Geib 1996). If so, then one can accept the Fremont human remains as a proxy for the Archaic and use Reed's (Lister 1997, 142; Reed 1955) modest study of the Fremont for the comparison. Reed points out that the cranial shape of his small Fremont population sample is very similar to that of the Durango Basketmakers and quite different from the Western Basketmakers, supporting a link between the indigenous Colorado Plateau Archaic and the Eastern Basketmakers.

Summary of evidence

The evidence presented shows that the Eastern Basketmakers have material affinities with the previous Archaic and significant differences from Western Basketmakers. The latter share a number of traits with San Pedro Cochise. Although the perishables are the most sensitive stylistic items, the very public rock art (Matson & Cole 1992) also differs significantly between the two Basketmaker variants. The link between the Western Basketmakers and the Kayenta Anasazi is well known (and supported by Turner's analysis), and the Kayenta Pueblo V are the Hopi, who speak a Uto-Aztecan language. The Eastern Pueblos, who speak Tanoan languages, do not have such linguistic links with Mexico and are most likely derived from indigenous Archaic people via the Eastern BM II.

The available biological evidence is neither grouped in the most useful fashion, nor is it very broadly based, but it does support a tight relationship between the Eastern Basketmakers and eastern Pueblos on the one hand, and between Western Basketmakers, early Kayenta Anasazi and Mexican populations on the other.

A scenario for Anasazi origins

Given the above mosaic of archaeological cultures, biological variants and modern languages, what events could have produced it? First, a migration of Mexican agriculturalists, at least some of whom were Uto-Aztecan speakers, appears to have been the basal event. One might expect that such an event would result in conflict with the indigenous hunters and gatherers. We now have abundant evidence of conflict (Hard & Roney 1999; Wilcox 1978) during the early PPF and in the BM II (Matson & Cole in press; Farmer 1997), although it is not clear which populations were involved.

During such a process we would expect agriculture to spread first where previous cultivation procedures could be used with little modification (Matson 1991, 210), as shown with the earliest floodwater sites in the Basin and Range PPF. Only later would the modifications in farming techniques and plant biology permitting maize cultivation on the Colorado Plateau be developed (Matson 1991, 207–16). These procedures were brought up on to the Plateau by the Western Basketmakers, and the indigenous Archaic people quickly adopt similar techniques to become the Eastern Basketmakers.

Interestingly enough, the early Mexican contribution must have been swamped by later events, as Turner's work indicates little biological connection between the Hopi and Mexico. I earlier (Matson 1991, 320) pointed out that the Anasazi Basketmaker III period on the Colorado Plateau looks much more like Eastern Basketmaker than Western, indicating blending. Other linguistic evidence (Shaul & Hill 1998; Hill 1999) suggests a multi-ethnic model for the Hohokam in the Basin and Range, which I think is also a good fit for both the early (Basketmaker) and late (Pueblo) Anasazi.

The PPF situation

Implicit in the model presented above is the idea that Mexican migrations formed the source of the San Pedro Cochise and the PPF Trincheras sites, and resulted in the presence of Uto-Aztecans in the Southwest. The process responsible for this event is simply the much greater population density that comes with maize agriculture, and the inevitably of the potential becoming the actual (Hayden 1981). For example, we estimate a population of between 500 and 800 people in the surveyed area (300 sq.m) of Cedar Mesa (Fig. 27.2) during the two hundred years of the Grand Gulch Basketmaker II phase (Matson *et al.* 1988). This BM II population density is about 16 times that of the mainly hunting-gathering Walapai (*c.* 1000 people in about 8000 square miles (McGuire 1983, 25; Martin 1985), who occupied similar environments in northwestern Arizona in the nineteenth century (Fig. 27.3).

The connections between the Basin and Range PPF and central Mexico ought to be clearer than those between the Western Basketmaker II and Mexico, although they are only now being recognized (Carpenter *et al.* n.d.; Mabry n.d.) and detailed studies of biology and perishables found on the Colorado Plateau are not yet available. One detailed study,

though, supports the inferred process (Hyland *et al.* 1998; Hyland & Adovasio 2000).

Hyland & Adovasio (2000) report on the domesticates and perishables from the area north of El Paso, Texas (Fig. 27.2). They conclude that there is a disjuncture in perishable industries that corresponds with the first widespread occurrence of cultigens and that this is best explained by a migration of agriculturalists from Mexico. Further, recent reports indicate that San Pedro Cochise-like projectile points are found in northern Mexico. Finally, Webster (2001) reports that 'looped string bags', which are found both in the Basin and Range and in the BM II, but not earlier on the Colorado Plateau, have a definite central Mexican origin, the first perishables to be so linked.

Reservations

The migration hypothesis is more than plausible, it is compelling according to current evidence (Matson 1991). However, the 'current evidence' may well change. Older maize may appear in Mexico; the recent redating of maize is from collections 30 to 50 years old. Earlier agricultural villages in Mesoamerica may well exist as the 'PPF' stage is not well known in Mexico. Most early Formative villages in Mexico were identified through ceramics, although I understand that the PPF stage is now recognized in western Mexico. Finally the provenience and dating of much of the original Basketmaker material from Durango is uncertain (Lister 1997). One of the possible reasons this material may be so similar to the Colorado Plateau Archaic is that it truly is Archaic, rather than Basketmaker as assumed. Radiocarbon dates run recently on material intimately associated with the human remains, however, are of Basketmaker age (LeBlanc pers. comm. 2001), reducing this possibility.

The Pueblo III collapse and the entry of the Athapaskans

I now turn to an example how a system collapse, the failure of agriculture (Renfrew 2000) in the northern Anasazi area and western plains precipitated the spread of a new language and a long distance Athapaskan migration from Canada into the Southwest. Southwestern archaeology has long puzzled over the abandonment of the San Juan river region in Pueblo III times. In a recent paper, Lipe (1995) presents compelling evidence that this region began to be abandoned about AD 1250 and was completely deserted by 1281. In the succeeding 150 years the

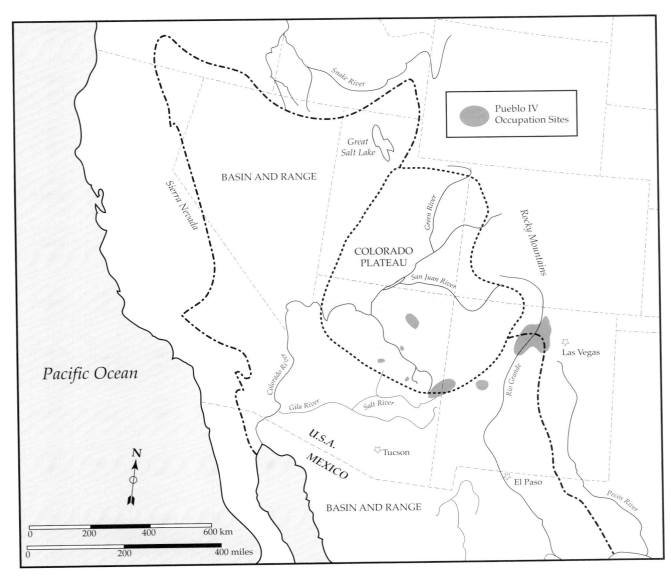

Figure 27.6. *Areas occupied by Pueblos (Anasazi) in Pueblo IV (AD 1300–1450).*

area occupied by the Pueblo Indians shrank to that of today (Fig. 27.6). Lipe (1995) argues convincingly that at least 10,000 people were found north of the San Juan alone in AD 1250, compared with estimates of 30,000 to 60,000 for the total Pueblo population at the time of Spanish contact. Deteriorating environmental conditions were clearly an important factor (Ahlstrom *et al.* 1995). Thus, space was made available which was later occupied by the Athapaskan-speaking Navajo and Apache peoples.

It has long been recognized that the Navajo and Apache (Apachean language speakers) were linguistically closely related to the Athapaskans in Canada (Fig. 27.7) (Dyen & Aberle 1974). Generally, the clos-

est linguistic relationships are with Chipewyan and Sarsi, with separation dates of 900–1000 years (Dyen & Aberle 1974, 12). Although a number of routes have been suggested for this migration, most evidence points to the eastern slopes of the Rocky Mountains (Magne 2001). Similarly, although there is disagreement for the earliest date of Athapaskan arrival in the Southwest (Towner 1996), all substantiated claims are post AD 1400.

Questions have been often raised about the conditions that would have allowed the Athapaskans to travel the distances involved within such a short period. These can be answered by the environmental consistency along the eastern flank of the Rocky

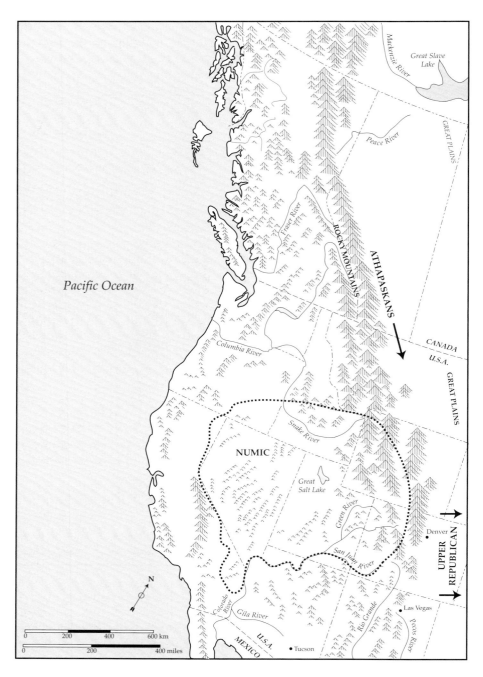

Figure 27.7. *Western North American physiography and the distribution of Numic languages. Note the lineal extent of the eastern edge of the Rocky Mountains.*

way down. It appears clear that the proto-Apacheans had such an adaptation in Canada.

How and why did they move south? Around AD 1300 the collapse of the Upper Republican culture left the eastern slopes of the Rocky Mountains uninhabited. The Upper Republican culture was a pit-house, maize-using culture located in the river valleys flowing east from the Rocky Mountains. Around AD 1300, the range of this culture contracted, probably moving downstream towards the east (J. Wood 1967; W. Wood 1998), presumably because of the same environmental changes that resulted in the abandonment of the northern Southwest by the Anasazi (although the Upper Republican is not as well dated).

The Upper Republican adaptation, like that of other plains agriculturalists, also relied on large game hunting (Wood 1967). Prior to the introduction of the horse in the 1700s, the hunting area of the Plains agriculturalists was very limited. Thus, the AD 1300 contraction left the eastern flanks of the Rockies unused, which encouraged the proto-Apacheans to travel down this corridor, resulting in their entry into the Southwest (Figs. 27.3 & 27.7).

The Numic expansion into the Great Basin,[2] briefly referred to above (Fig. 27.7), probably resulted from the collapse of the agricultural Fremont cultures at the same

Mountains and the collapse of the Upper Republican tradition. To large-mammal hunters, the eastern slopes of the Rockies are very much alike from the Peace River south to Las Vegas, New Mexico (Fig. 27.7). An adaptation at one end works at the other as bison are present, along with elk and deer, all the

time and for the same reasons (Lipe 1995). The Numic cultures are all very similar in terms of language, and it is an open question whether Navajo and Apache have differentiated enough to be considered separate languages. The Numic and Apachean language distributions thus have the exact pattern expected for a recent agricultural driven migration — a large group of people with similar language(s) and similar cultures spread through a large area — although they are actually cases of a reverse process, an agricultural-collapse-driven migration by hunter-gatherers!

The Southwest in perspective

The Southwestern situation is complicated. Maize agriculture appears to be associated with at least one migration from Mexico, and it is likely that several were involved. Indigenous people, however, ended up dominating the population, and a great deal of blending took place. The most definite cases for migration appear to occur after AD 1300, with the Athapaskan migration from the north and the Numic expansion from the west, both resulting from the collapse of agricultural adaptations and the abandonment of the northern Southwest by the Anasazi.

The Western BM II is the best-documented previous Southwestern migration, involving agriculture, ethnicity and biology. It derived from the San Pedro Cochise and moved on to the Colorado Plateau. The evidence includes two biological analyses, numerous diagnostic perishables, and good subsistence analyses for establishing dependence on maize. However, for the Basin and Range, the equivalent biological and isotopic information is not yet available, nor are the perishables as well dated or studied. Moreover, the potential source area, somewhere further south in Mexico, remains virtually unknown archaeologically. All these factors mean that the migration of agricultural people to the southern Basin and Range area, however plausible, is less definite than that for the migration which lead to the origins of the Anasazi on the Colorado Plateau.

In reviewing the culture history of the Southwest, one is reminded of the words of Boas on race, language, and culture; these are not bonded together, but are relatively independent. Lipe (1996, 4) has recently restated this as 'genes, culture traits, and language are not inherited in neat tribal packages, but spread, contract, and change fairly independently over time'.

Although I originally thought that Southwest prehistory differed from that of other areas, through the McDonald seminar I reached the understanding that the differences were in detail rather than process. The initial spread of agriculture resulted in a mosaic, as indigenous hunters and gatherers coexisted with the newly-arrived agriculturalists in areas where their resistance was possible or where agriculture was not as feasible. Over time the mosaic

became a blend, as seen in the Southwest after the Basketmaker II stage. The 'blending mosaic' process occurred several times in the Southwest and is recognized in other areas of the world in this volume, for instance, for Western Europe by Scarre.

This process is compatible with the Renfrew 'chain model' (this volume), with the individual links being forged by the various temporary stops in different environments. LeBlanc's comments at the symposium pointed to how over time, a mosaic of say 50 per cent 'new farmer linguistic groups' and 50 per cent indigenous groups would end up as 100 per cent new linguistic group. In both sets, different communities will become culturally extinct, but when a unique indigenous group becomes extinct that language is dead, while the 'new linguistic group' will still be present, although some of the languages within it will have died. The Southwest appears to have several examples of this process — Fremont, Cohonino, Virgin Anasazi — these all being archaeological cultures that apparently have left no clear descendants. In conversations with J. Hill and S. LeBlanc at the seminar it was striking how we all thought that Southwestern linguistic diversity would have decreased further if independent developments had not been truncated by the Spanish.

The Southwest is not an exception, but instead an example of the general pattern of farming-migration-induced change recognized at the symposium. It was frozen at an unusually diverse stage, partly because, unlike temperate Europe, arable land (which in the Southwest is defined by deep soils and either the presence of enough rainfall or floodwater) is very discontinuously distributed. This 'patchy' nature reinforced the mosaic-like nature of cultural distribution. Further, during Pueblo IV (AD 1281–1450) times, the population was aggregated into a few large communities. Locations that would support these larger communities were few and far between, further isolating them. LeBlanc (this volume and elsewhere) has demonstrated that conflict had an important role in establishing these larger communities. Once communities were aggregated for defence, it was not possible to go back to the earlier pattern of smaller, dispersed communities. It was this empty, abandoned niche which was colonized by the Apacheans.

The precision dating and abundant perishables in the Southwest make the mosaic more visible than is typical in other regions in prehistory. These factors mean that the mosaic stage lasted longer and is more visible in the Southwest, a mosaic of cultures which is consistent with the emerging biological information and the recognition of the independence of biology, language and culture.

Notes

1. BM II is defined by either the perishable assemblages or lithic assemblages shown in Figure 27.4. Dates on maize or pumpkins that lack these associations go back to about 2800 radiocarbon years on the Colorado Plateau. Until good artefactual associations are discovered the meaning of these dates remains unclear, but they could indicate the beginning of the BM II.

2. Hill (this volume) presents an argument for the Numa having been present in the Great Basin for thousands of years. The perishables, in particular the 'utter dissimilarity' (Adovasio & Pedler 1994, 121) between those of the Numa and the Fremont, show this can not have been the case for the eastern Great Basin.

References

Adovasio, J.M., 1980. Fremont: an artifactual perspective, in *Fremont Perspectives*, ed. D.B. Madsen. (Antiquities Section, selected papers 7(16).) Salt Lake City (UT): Division of State History, 35–40.

Adovasio, J.M. & D.R. Pedler, 1994. A tisket, a tasket: looking at the Numic speakers through the 'lens' of a basket, in *Across the West: Human Population Movement and the Expansion of the Numa*, eds. D. Madsen & D. Rhode. Salt Lake City (UT): University of Utah Press, 114–23.

Ahlstrom, R., C. van West & J. Dean, 1995. Environmental and chronological factors in Mesa Verde-Northern Rio Grande migration. *Journal of Anthropological Archaeology* 14, 125–42 [Special Issue, ed. by C. Cameron, Migration and the Movement of Southwestern Peoples.]

Benz, B., 2001. Archaeological evidence of teosinte domestication from Guila Naquitz, Oaxaca. *Proceedings of the National Academy of Sciences of the USA* 98, 2104–6.

Berry, C. & M. Berry, 1986. Chronological and conceptual models of the Southwestern archaic, in *Anthropology of the Desert West: Essays in Honor of Jesse D. Jennings*, eds. C.J. Condie & D.D. Fowler. (Anthropological Papers 110.) Salt Lake City (UT): University of Utah, 253–327.

Berry, M., 1982. *Time, Space and Transition in Anasazi Prehistory*. Salt Lake City (UT): University of Utah Press.

Cameron, C. (ed.), 1995. Migration and the movement of Southwestern peoples. *Journal of Anthropological Archaeology* 14, 99–250. [Special Issue.]

Carpenter, J., G. Sanchez & M.E. Villalpando C., n.d. The Late Archaic/Early Agricultural Period in Sonora, Mexico. MS in possession of author, Departmento de Antropologia, Universidad de las Americas-Puebla, Cholula, Puebla 72820, Mexico.

Chisholm, B. & R.G. Matson, 1994. Carbon and nitrogen isopic evidence on Basketmaker II diet at Cedar Mesa, Utah. *Kiva* 60, 239–56.

Cordell, L.S., 1997. *Archaeology of the Southwest*. 2nd edition. San Diego (CA): Academic Press, Inc.

Dyen, I. & D. Aberle, 1974. *Lexical Reconstruction: the Case of the Proto-Athapaskan Kinship System*. Cambridge: Cambridge University Press.

Eddy, F.W., 1972. Culture ecology and the prehistory of the Navajo Reservoir District. *Southwestern Lore* 38(1,2), 1–75.

Farmer, J.D., 1997. Iconographic evidence of Basketmaker warfare and human sacrifice: a contextual approach to early Anasazi art. *Kiva* 62, 391–420.

Geib, P., 1996. *Glen Canyon Revisited*. (Anthropological Papers 119.) Salt Lake City (UT): University of Utah Press.

Geib, P., 2000. Sandal types and archaic prehistory on the Colorado Plateau. *American Antiquity* 65, 509–24.

Geib, P. & K. Spurr, 2000. The Basketmaker II–III transition on the Rainbow Plateau, in *Foundations of Anasazi Culture*, ed. P. Reed. Salt Lake City (UT): University of Utah Press, 175–200.

Geib, P., J. Huffman, K. Spurr, L.T. Neff, V. Clark, M. Warburton & K. Hays-Gilpin, 1997. *Excavations at Nine Sites along Segment 4 of N16*. (Navajo Nation archaeology Report 95-131.) Flagstaff (AZ): Northern Arizona University Branch Office.

Guernsey, S.J. & A.V. Kidder, 1921. *Basket-Maker Caves of Northeastern Arizona*. (Papers of the Peabody Museum of American Archaeology and Ethnology 8(1).) Cambridge (MA): Peabody Museum.

Hard, R. & J. Roney, 1999. A massive terraced village complex in Chihuahua, Mexico dated to 3000 years before present. *Science* 279, 1661–4, March 13.

Hayden, B., 1981. Research and development in the stone age: technological transitions among hunter-gatherers. *Current Anthropology* 22, 519–48.

Hill, J.H., 1999. Linguistics. *Archaeology Southwest* 13(1), 8.

Hill, J.H., 2001. Proto-Uto-Aztecan: a community of cultivators in central Mexico? *American Anthropologist* 103(4), 913–34.

Huckell, B.B., 1990. Late Preceramic farmer-foagers in Southeastern Arizona: a Cultural and Ecological Consideration of the Spread of Agriculture into the Arid Southwestern United States. Unpublished PhD dissertation. Faculty of Arid Lands Resource Sciences, University of Arizona, Tucson.

Huckell, B.B., 1996. The Archaic prehistory of the North American Southwest. *Journal of World Prehistory* 10, 305–73.

Huckell, B.B. & L. Huckell, 1984. Excavations at Milagro, a Late Archaic Site in the Eastern Tucson Basin. Unpublished report on file, Arizona State Museum, Tucson.

Huckell, B.B., L. Huckell & S.K. Fish, 1995. *Investigations at Milagro, a Late Preceramic Site in the Eastern Tucson Basin*. (Technical Report 94-5.) Tucson (AZ): Center for Desert Archaeology.

Huckell, B.B., L. Huckell & S. Shackley, 1999. McEuen Cave. *Archaeology Southwest* 13(1), 12.

Hyland, D.C. & J.M. Adovasio, 2000. The Mexican connection: a study of sociotechnical change in perishable manufacture and food production in Prehistoric New Mexico, in *Beyond Cloth and Cordage*, eds. P. Drooker & L. Webster. Salt Lake City (UT): University of Utah Press, 141–59.

Hyland, D.C., J.M. Adovasio & R.E. Taylor, 1998. Corn, Cucurbits, Cordage, and Colonization: an Absolute Chronology for the Appearance of Mesoamerican Domesticates and Perishables in the Jornada Basin, New Mexico. Unpublished paper presented at the 63rd Annual Meeting of the Society for American Archaeology, Seattle

Iltis, H., 2000. Homeotic sexual translocations and the origin of maize (*Zea mays*, Poaceae): a new look at an old problem. *Economic Botany* 54, 7–42.

Irwin-Williams, C., 1967. Prehistoric Cultural and Linguistic Patterns in the Southwest Since 5000 BC. Unpublished paper presented at the 32nd Annual Meeting of the Society for American Archaeology, Ann Arbor, Michigan, May, 1967.

Irwin-Williams, C., 1973. *The Oshara Tradition: Origins of the Anasazi Culture.* (Contributions in Anthropology 5(1).) Portales: Eastern New Mexico University, 1–28.

Irwin-Williams, C., 1985. Review of *Time, Space, and Transition in Anasazi Prehistory*, by M.S. Berry. *Kiva* 51, 44–8.

Jennings, J., 1980. *Cowboy Cave.* (Anthropological Paper 104.) Salt Lake City (UT): University of Utah.

Kidder, A.V., 1917. Prehistoric cultures of the San Juan drainage, in *Proceedings of the 19th International Congress of Americanists* (Washington 1915), 108–13.

Kidder, A.V., 1924. *An Introduction to the Study of Southwestern Archaeology.* (Papers of the Southwestern Expedition 1.) New Haven (CT): Published for the Phillips Academy by Yale University Press.

Kidder, A.V., 1927. Southwestern Archaeological Conference. *El Palacio* 23, 554–61.

Kidder, A.V. & S.J. Guernsey, 1919. *Archaeological Explorations in Northeastern Arizona.* (Bulletin 65.) Washington (DC): Bureau of American Ethnology.

Lipe, W.D., 1995. The depopulation of the northern San Juan: conditions in the turbulent 1200s. *Journal of Anthropological Archaeology* 14, 143–69. [Special Issue, ed. by C. Cameron, Migration and the Movement of Southwestern Peoples.]

Lipe, W.D., 1996. Letter to the editor of the *New York Times* (Oct. 4, 1996). Reprinted in the *SAA Bulletin* 14(5), 4, November 1996.

Lister, F., 1997. *Prehistory in Peril: the Worst and the Best of Durango Archaeology.* Niwot (CO): University Press of Colorado.

Long, A., B.F. Benz, D.J. Donahue, A.J.T. Jull & L.J. Toolin, 1989. First direct AMS dates on early maize from Tehuacan, Mexico. *Radiocarbon* 31, 1035–40.

Mabry, J., 1998. *Archaeological Investigations at Early Village Sites in the Middle Santa Cruz Valley: Analyses and Synthesis.* (Anthropological Papers 19.) Tucson (AZ): Center for Desert Archaeology.

Mabry, J., n.d. The First Sixty-Five Years: Archaeologists's Changing Knowledge and Ideas about the First Farmers in Southeastern Arizona. MS in possession of Author, Desert Archaeology Inc., Tucson, Arizona.

McGuire, T., 1983. Hualapai, in *Southwest*, vol. 10: *Handbook of North American Indians*, ed. A. Ortiz. Washington (DC): Smithsonian Institution, 25–38.

McNitt, F., 1966. *Richard Wetherill: Anasazi.* Revised edition. Albuquerque (NM): University of New Mexico Press.

Magne, M., 2001. Plateau and Plains Athapaskan Movements in Late Prehistoric and Early Historic Times: a View from the Middle. Unpublished paper presented in Migration, Then and Now Symposium, Society for American Archaeology Annual Meetings, April 18–22, New Orleans.

Martin, D.L., A.H. Goodman, G.J. Armelagos & A.L. Magennis, 1991. *Black Mesa Anasazi Health: Reconstructing Life from Patterns of Death and Disease.* (Center for Archaeological Investigations, Occasional Paper 14.) Carbondale (IL): Southern Illinois University.

Martin, J., 1985. The prehistory and ethnohistory of Havasupai-Hualapaie relations. *Ethnohistory* 32, 135–53.

Martin, S.L., 1999. Virgin Anasazi diet as demonstrated through the analysis of stable carbon and nitrogen isotopes. *Kiva* 64, 495–514.

Matson, R.G., 1991. *The Origins of Southwestern Agriculture.* Tucson (AZ): University of Arizona Press.

Matson, R.G., 1999. The spread of maize to the Colorado Plateau. *Archaeology Southwest* 13(1), 10–11.

Matson, R.G. & B. Chisholm, 1991. Basketmaker II subsistence: carbon isotopes and other dietary indicators from Cedar Mesa, Utah. *American Antiquity* 56, 444–59.

Matson, R.G. & S. Cole, 1992. Ethnicity and Conflict among the Basketmaker II of the U.S. Southwest. Unpublished paper presented at the 25th annual Chacmool Conference, Calgary.

Matson, R.G. & S. Cole, in press. Ethnicity and conflict among the Basketmaker II of the U.S. Southwest, in *The Archaeology of Contact: Processes and Consequences*, ed. B. Kulle. Calgary: Archaeological Association of the University of Calgary.

Matson, R.G., W.D. Lipe & W. Haase, 1988. Adaptation continuities and occupational discontinuities: the Cedar Mesa Anasazi. *Journal of Field Archaeology* 15, 245–64.

Miller, W.R., 1983. Uto-Aztecan languages, in *Handbook of North American Indians*, vol. 10: *Southwest*, ed. A. Ortiz. Washington (DC): Smithsonian Institution, 113–24.

Morris, E. & R. Burgh, 1954. *Basket Maker II Sites near Durango, Colorado.* (Carnegie Institution of Washington Publication 604.) Washington (DC): Carnegie Institution of Washington.

Piperno, D.R. & K.V. Flannery, 2001. The earliest archaeological maize (*Zea mays* L.) from highland Mexico: new accelerator mass spectrometry dates and their implications. *Proceedings of the National Academy of Sciences of the USA* 98, 2101–3 (February 13, 2001).

Plog, F.T., 1979. Prehistory: Western Anasazi, in *Handbook of North American Indians*, vol. 9: *Southwest*, ed. A. Ortiz. Washington (DC): Smithsonian Institution, 108–30.

Powers, M., 1984. *The Salvage of Archaeological Data from Turkey Pen Ruin, Grand Gulch Primitive Area, San Juan County, Utah.* (Contributions to Anthropology Series 808.) Farmington (NM): Division of Conservation Archaeology, San Juan County Museum Association.

Reed, E., 1955. Human skeletal remains form the Turner-Look site, in *A Reappraisal of the Fremont Culture*, by H.M. Wormington. (Proceedings 1.) Denver (CO): Denver Museum of Natural History, 38–43.

Renfrew, C., 2000. At the edge of knowability: towards a prehistory of languages. *Cambridge Archaeological Journal* 10(1), 7–34.

Roney, J., 1996. Cerro Juanaquena: a Late Archaic Cerro de Trincheras in Northwestern Chihuahua. Unpublished paper presented at the Conference on the Archaic Prehistory of the North American Southwest. Oct. 25, 1996, Albuquerque.

Sayles, E.B., 1983. *The Cochise Cultural Sequence in Southeastern Arizona.* (University of Arizona Anthropological Papers 42.) Tucson (AZ): University of Arizona Press.

Sayles, E.B. & E. Antevs, 1943. *The Cochise Culture.* (Medallion Papers 29.) Gila Pueblo (AZ): Globe.

Shual, D. & J. Hill, 1998. Tepimans, Yumans, and other Hohokam. *American Antiquity* 63, 375–96.

Smalley, J. & M. Blake, n.d. Sweet Beginnings. Unpublished MS in possession of the authors, Laboratory of Archaeology, University of British Columbia, Vancouver.

Smith, B.D., 1997. Reconsidering the Ocampo Caves and the era of incipient cultivation in Mesoamerica. *Latin American Antiquity* 9, 342–83.

Stiger, M., 1997. Unpublished paper on Gunnison Basin Archaeology. In possession of the Author.

Towner, R.H. (ed.), 1996. *The Archaeology of Navajo Origins.* Salt Lake City (UT): University of Utah Press.

Turner, C.G. II, 1993. Southwest Indian teeth. *National Geographic Research & Exploration* 9(1), 32–53.

Webster, L., 2001. Mogollon and Zuni Perishable Materials: Textiles, Basketry, and Wooden Ceremonial Objects. Unpublished paper presented at the Mogollon-Zuni Seminar, Museum of Northern Arizona, Oct. 14–19, Flagstaff.

Webster, L. & K. Hays-Gilpin, 1994. New trails for old shoes: sandals, textiles, and baskets in Basketmaker culture. *Kiva* 2, 313–27.

Wilcox, D., 1978. Warefare implications of dry-laid masonry walls on Tunamoc Hill. *Kiva* 45, 15–38.

Wilcox, D., 1983. *Hohokam Ballcourts and their Interpretations.* (Archaeological Series 160.) Tucson (AZ): State Museum.

Wood, J.J., 1967. Archaeological Investigations in Northeasterrn Colorado. Unpublished PhD Dissertation, University of Colorado, Boulder.

Wood, J.J. & R.G. Matson, 1973. Two models of sociocultural systems and their implications for the archaeological study of change, in *The Explanation of Culture Change*, ed. C. Renfrew. London: Duckworth, 673–83.

Wood, W.R. (ed.), 1998. *Archaeology on the Great Plains.* Lawrence (KA): University Press of Kansas.

Chapter 28

Conflict and Language Dispersal:
Issues and a New World Example

Steven A. LeBlanc

Anthropologists and archaeologists underestimate the intensity, ubiquity and consequences of warfare in the past, including conflict among non-complex societies, and especially among initial farmers. A revised model of initial farmer spread is presented that includes competition. The farming spread from Mesoamerica to the American Southwest is examined in this light.

Language-distribution maps from almost anywhere in the world show speakers of one language separated by people speaking other languages, together with language isolates, and large areas occupied by people speaking closely-related languages. The question is obvious: how could such patterns have come about? Few explanations explicitly include the role of conflict and competition. Yet, I believe conflict and competition are the very mechanisms that are primarily responsible for such observed linguistic patterns.

Conflict is not only ubiquitous, but it is patterned. It differs with the type of society, and especially when competition is between societal types. So, how do different forms of competition result in different types of linguistic pattern? In particular, how did competition affect the nature of the farming spread on a world-wide basis? The better scholars understand how and why this conflict took place, the more their models will be realistic and relevant, so a brief description of the nature of conflict in the past and why it took place is useful.

Warfare in the past

There is an unwillingness to recognize the extent and importance of conflict in the past because of several broadly held misconceptions. This topic has recently received some attention and the following is a brief summary of ideas presented by Keeley

(1996), LeBlanc (1999), and Read & LeBlanc (2003). In short, all humans can reproduce at rates that will double the population in less than a century, and in many circumstances in only 30–40 years. This is true for foragers, early farmers and other non-state societies. Even foragers with the lowest reproductive rates known have more than four births per woman (Howell 1979), and some foragers have rates almost twice that (Hill & Hurtado 1995; Kelly 1995). Virtually all farmers, even the most marginal ones such as the Yanomamo, have seven to eight births per woman on average (Early & Peters 1990; Hassan 1981). No society, until very recently, has ever developed mechanisms to produce a zero growth rate (Bates & Lee 1979; Divale 1972). As a consequence, all societies, except for those in terrible environments, quickly approach the carrying capacity.[1]

While population can ultimately be controlled by disease and starvation, or societies can try to increase the carrying capacity by new technology and intensification of agriculture, warfare is an option for dealing with limits of the carrying capacity. People will fight before they starve, and people will often fight before they work very hard to increase the carrying capacity (e.g. Vayda 1960; 1961). Therefore, if warfare is the consequence of pressing the carrying capacity, then warfare will be the norm most of the time.[2]

The spread of agriculturalists, our current topic, would have involved people organized at a tribal level of social organization competing with peoples either organized as foraging bands or as very simple tribes. Thus, it is to those types of societies that we must turn for useful examples of warfare. Virtually all foragers engaged in warfare, virtually everywhere: the Bushmen, Australian Aborigines, and Eskimos (Burch 1974; Denbow 1984; Eibl-Eibesfleldt 1975; Jones 1974; Knuckey 1992). The European Mesolithic had considerable conflict, including massacres (Villa

1992; Frayer 1997).[3] The intensity of warfare among non-complex farming societies, such as Highland New Guinea and the Yanomamo, are well attested (Chagnon 1968; Berndt 1964; Meggitt 1977; Morren 1984).

One commonly finds that 25 per cent of the adult males were killed in warfare in forager and simple farmer societies, both ethnographically, as in Highland New Guinea (Berndt 1964; Meggitt 1977; Morren 1984; Sillitoe 1977) and elsewhere (Chagnon 1968), or archaeologically (Walker & Lambert 1989; Milner et al. 1991; Bridges, 1996). Soltis et al. (1995) show that group extinctions can reach 30 per cent per century, while about 10 per cent of all groups were exterminated per century in the New Guinea highlands. Thus, competition between foragers and farmers results in considerable demographic consequences. Rarely does one side command a military-technology advantage. Raids and ambushes each result in only a few deaths, but they are so frequent that overall deaths are high. Therefore, warfare tends to be attritional and relative numbers of people in each competing society do count — the largest group almost always wins. Relative reproductive success is a key determinant of who is the long-term winner in these conflicts.

There is a general pattern to the fate of women in such conflicts. Men are rarely taken captive, but women are frequently captured and incorporated into the victorious group. Children are rarely taken captive by foragers, but farmers will capture them as they can be economically useful. Girls are more likely to be taken captive than boys, but both will be taken.

Farmer birth-spacing is reduced due to sedentism and other factors.[4] So, while all human populations can grow significantly over the long run, sedentary farmers can grow much faster than foragers. As I discuss below, however, some wild-food acquisition and processing technologies allow non-farmers to act demographically like farmers.

To summarize: Human population growth is potentially more rapid than we generally credit. Population pressure almost always assures that resource limits are reached and conflict results. Thus, competition is the world-wide norm. And, the group with the largest numbers wins in the absence of a military-technology advantage.

As Renfrew (1996) and Bellwood (1991), among others, have pointed out, the transition to agriculture provided a significant demographic advantage. However, much of the basis for the advantage was sedentism, not food production *per se*. Thus, in trying to understand why some peoples were replaced by farmers and others are not, we must make a distinction between foragers and hunter-gatherers. Peo-

ple who are not farmers, but are demographically like farmers, I refer to as *sedentary collectors*. These include people who focus on plants — California acorn gatherers, palm processors of the Orinoco delta or the Moluccas — or animals — Northwest Coast salmon fishers, and Eskimo whalers. Other sedentary collectors include the Natufians of the Levant, the shell-mound dwellers of the Ohio drainage, and littoral collectors from Florida to the Baltic. Their focus is on a few key resources which are intensely harvested and often stored, and considerable time is spent in processing food. Such resources are valuable and so are defended. Women spend less time travelling to find food and more time collecting and processing it; therefore they are less mobile and can space children closer together. In addition, preserved foods can be used to wean children earlier, thereby further shortening the birth interval.

So, sedentary collectors can be demographically equivalent to farmers, and the competitive advantage does not necessarily fall always to the farmers. As the above examples suggest, coastal people are particularly likely to be sedentary collectors. The point is that true foragers are always at a demographic disadvantage when compared to farmers or to sedentary collectors. But neither of these latter two types of groups is automatically advantaged over the other.

A model of farmer dispersal that includes competition

The following is a modification of the Bellwood-Renfrew model of farming dispersal. Initial farmers spread at the expense of foragers, primarily by replacement not absorption, and foragers do not easily accept the 'idea of farming'. Foragers are usually replaced because of their competitive disadvantage, but not always. Some foragers survive, either in areas that are not farmable (or herdable) such as the Kalahari Desert, the Arctic or dense tropical forests. However, these surviving foragers are almost always incorporated in some way into the farming social and economic systems (Headland & Reid 1989; Denbow 1984; Wilkie & Curran 1993). Such demographic symbiosis has a distinct demographic consequence: forager women are often taken as wives by farmer men, but the reverse does not happen. Thus, gene flow is from forager to farmer, not the reverse. However, farmers do not easily spread in the face of sedentary collectors. Sedentary collectors were often so like farmers that the latter have no biological and hence military advantage. Moreover, sedentary collectors are 'pre-adapted' to farming because they have already developed storage technologies, permanent structures, social rules for land ownership, sharing of stored foods and other cultural features that are necessary for farming societies to function. To put it another way, sedentary collectors have farmer lifestyles without domesticates, and when domesticates are made available they are likely to be rapidly adopted.

Thus, we should expect initial farming to spread rapidly, but with pockets of 'resistance' which may be occupied by: 1) foragers left in inhospitable localities or incorporated into the overall farming economy by exploiting non-farmable areas; or 2) sedentary collectors who can maintain enough population density to limit the intrusion of farmers. At the same time, the true farmers will periodically be expected to reach the biological limits of adaptability of their domesticates. Genetic selection can overcome these biological limits over time, but it does allow for a new dynamic between farmers and foragers or sedentary collectors to develop, and increase the likelihood that the domesticates will be adopted by sedentary collectors.

Initially, farmers would be expected to capture forager women and some children. Moreover, some foragers would form symbiotic relationships with farmers resulting in forager women marrying into the farming groups. Over time, the farmers would replace the foragers, but as a three-step process: 1) competition, with female gene flow to farmers; 2) some symbiosis, with primarily female gene flow; and 3) forager extinction. I believe this model accounts for much of the demographic/cultural patterning observed for the Near East to Europe farmer expansion.

If Bar-Yosef (this volume) is correct and initial domestication did not take place on the Anatolian plateau, then the earliest farming sites there must also represent farmer expansion into new territory. Sites such as Çatalhöyük, Hacilar, Hoca Çeşme, Aşikli and Hallan Çemi (Mellaart 1975; Özdogan & Basgelen 1999) have evidence for conflict. In spite of the limitations of the data and contrary to much popular belief, the evidence of conflict with the Linearbandkeramik (LBK) expansion is not simply *present* in Belgium (Keeley & Cahen 1989), but is *widespread* (Keeley pers. comm.). Gronenborn (1999) and Bogucki (1988) summarize additional evidence. Moreover, one can go back to the very initial point of farmers moving into Southeast Europe (Zvelebil & Lillie 2000) and see evidence for conflict there as well (Horvath 1989). Until all the possible evidence

for warfare is reviewed, it is premature to assume that the process of farmers spreading out of the Fertile Crescent was entirely peaceful.

Scandinavia may have been beyond an ecological threshold for the early farmers, who were not initially able to penetrate farther north because their domesticates were not adequately adapted. Perhaps more likely, the availability of marine resources in Scandinavia resulted in a high reproductive capacity and density there during the Mesolithic, and while the LBK was expanding, so that the LBK expansion was slowed for some time (see Bogucki 2000 and other papers in Price 2000). That is, the Mesolithic Scandinavians may have been sedentary collectors and with the ensuing high reproductive capacity and high density were not easily susceptible to competition from farmers. This 'stalemate' would have allowed for the interaction and subsequent evolution seen between the two types of societies (see Price *et al.* 1995).

The above discussion may paint an overly simplistic picture. We would expect, and there is evidence summarized by Gronenborn (1999), that some Mesolithic populations may have been incorporated into the LBK economy as foragers. Other localized Mesolithic people may also have been sedentary and therefore demographically capable of not being easily displaced. And, some pockets of true foragers, as in the Alps, may have persisted for some time. Another possible example of these principles is from Portugal and is described by Zilhão (2000) and Scarre (this volume). There, we find farming populations in enclaves well-spaced from the Mesolithic people who lived along the major drainages and estuaries. We would expect to find sedentary collectors in these environments and so they were not easily replaced by farmers. The presence of empty zones — excellent evidence for conflict elsewhere in the world — implies competition between farmers and sedentary collectors, and not rapid replacement of foragers by farmers.

A less known case of farmer expansion in the New World provides a good example of initial farmer spreading, and also involves conflict and patchy language distributions.

The Mesoamerica to Southwest farming expansion

Mesoamerica is a core area of domestication (summarized by McClung de Tapia 1992). However, an accepted date of when a fully functional domesticated economy was in place there is not well established. The domestication of various plants seems to have taken place between 5000 and 3000 BC, but it is not obvious when the process was far enough along to result in a demographic expansion. Farming-dependent villages do not seem to appear until after 2000 BC, although pre-ceramic farming villages have not been intensely looked for. Nevertheless, there was finally a population radiation out of the core area.

A case can be made that the original Meso-american farmers spoke ancestral languages in one of four large families (and some language isolates which are ignored here): Uto-Aztecan, Mayan, Mixe-Zoquean and Oto-Manguean. Proto-languages containing agricultural terms, especially maize terms, have been reconstructed for all four families (Jane Hill pers. comm.). We can see rather easily from linguistic distribution maps that Mayan spread to the eastern lowlands including, ultimately, the Yucatan Peninsula. The language homogeneity there suggests a very rapid filling in of the Yucatan Peninsula, which must previously have been inhabited by very low-density foragers who seem to have been replaced in their entirety. Oto-Manguean and Mixe-Zoquean did not spread far, much like Sumerian did not spread in the Near East. Finally, and for our purposes most importantly, Uto-Aztecan speakers spread north, ultimately to the American Southwest and even beyond, with an almost continuous distribution from Mesoamerica northwards. There has been some question of whether Uto-Aztecan spread north or south from an initial core area, but it now seems clear that it spread north (Hill this volume), with some Uto-Aztecan speakers moving south at a later time.

The spread of agriculture into the American Southwest

For many years, the generally accepted model for the adoption of corn farming in the American Southwest was of corn 'diffusing' up the flanks of the Sierra Madre Occidental that linked Mesoamerica with the Southwest. This model had foragers slowly adopting corn into their lifestyle, taking well over 1000 years to convert from a foraging to sedentary farming way of life. The voluminous literature on this topic is summarized by Minnis (1992). Owing to the stunning revelations from recent extensive contract-based excavations, primarily and most impressively in southern Arizona, this slow indigenous model of the adoption of farming is now seen to be quite wrong, and a very different formulation is emerging. This is described by Matson (this volume) and need not be repeated in detail here.

The earliest agriculture in the Southwest is seen in 'villages' along low-elevation drainages such as the Santa Cruz River near Tucson, Arizona (Mabry 1998), and near El Paso, Texas (O'Laughlin 1980). Similar, lower and warmer locations were also occupied by farmers in northern Chihuahua (Roney 1996) and Sonora, Mexico (Carpenter *et al.* 1999). The Tucson-area sites contain small but well-made pit-houses and have large internal and external storage pits. Although pottery is absent, maize is ubiquitous in these sites and there is evidence for small-scale irrigation works by around 1100 BC. In short, these people were farmers. But it appears that this was not the case in the mountain highlands and high Colorado Plateau to the east and northeast of these sites. It appears that the initial farmers in the Southwest were intrusive into the region and that they initially used areas that were most like the environments to the south. The dating of these early farmers in the greater Southwest is still uncertain, but an initial date of *c.* 1500 BC seems a reasonable interpretation of the current evidence. After some hundreds of years, some of the low-elevation farmers moved into the higher, western Colorado Plateau area where they are known as Western Basketmakers. At the same time, on the eastern edge of the Colorado Plateau, people who may be referred to as Eastern Basketmakers seem to have adopted agriculture *in situ*. These two populations of Basketmakers were culturally distinct, as described by Matson (this volume).

Current ongoing research seems to suggest that the two groups were also biologically distinct, based on overall morphometrics (Doug Owsley pers. comm.) and discrete dental traits (Turner 1993). In the case of the dental traits, the Western Basketmakers linked to groups in Mexico, and the Eastern Basketmakers did not. The Eastern Basketmakers shared dental similarities (and various cultural traits) with the Archaic people of the more arid province to the north.

In sum, the Western Basketmakers migrated on to the Colorado Plateau from southern Arizona, and the Eastern Basketmakers adopted agriculture in place. The time lag between the appearance of farming in the low desert and on the northern Colorado Plateau is explained by the need to readapt the maize to the shorter growing season, and to develop new technologies to deal with the need to dry-farm instead of to irrigate or flood-water farm. It seems that the adaptation process was gradual enough that there was enough time for some indigenous people, presumably ones with the greatest degree of sedentism and density to begin with, to convert to farming before they could be replaced by the migrant farmers. That is, the Eastern Basketmakers may be the functional equivalent to the Scandinavian Mesolithic populations, and the Western Basketmakers to LBK. Other highland areas in the Southwest continued to hold pockets of indigenous foragers long after the spread of the farmers, as also occurred in Europe.

Interestingly, the western side of the Southwest was dominated historically by Uto-Aztecan speakers, a language family extending down into the Mesoamerican core area, as we have seen, while the eastern Southwest was dominated by Tanoan speakers (and some linguistic isolates) who have no definite Mesoamerican linguistic links (see Fig. 27.3).

One interpretation of the above is that the Mesoamerican farming complex reached a level that enabled the farmers to spread out of the core area, and that they were sedentary enough to out-compete foragers reproductively. They expanded up the mountain flanks of present-day northwestern Mexico, usually replacing foragers and reaching the limits of the Mesoamerican environment in southern Arizona, northern Chihuahua and west Texas. After a pause, the expansion continued leading to the Western Basketmaker migration into the northern Southwest, replacing foragers there. This pause allowed enough time for some indigenous populations to adopt agriculture, and we have linguistically, biologically and culturally distinct farmers from about 500 BC onwards. In addition, there seem to have been populations that remained as foragers for some time in areas that were marginal for maize farming, and there was also competition between farmers and foragers in some areas.

Conflict and farmer expansion in the Greater Southwest

The farmer expansion into the Southwest was not a peaceful process. The most impressive evidence of

Figure 28.1. *An aerial view of the early agricultural site of Cerro Juanaqueña in northern Chihuahua. This is one of at least seven sites clustered near each other with defensive terraces. Good farm land and ample room for habitation can be seen at the foot of the hill, demonstrating that the hilltop was not used because of a shortage of land or that the terraces were for farming. (Photo by Adriel Heisey, courtesy of John Roney and Robert Hard.)*

warfare associated with the early farmers comes from northern Chihuahua (Roney 1996). Cerro Juanaqueña is the best known of at least seven hilltop sites, which date to around 1150 BC. These sites contain up to 400 low terraces per site that form a barrier to movement up the hill and form flat places for houses and domestic activities (Fig. 28.1). These habitation sites are located adjacent to very good river-bottom farmland, and the only viable explanation for the terraced hilltop sites is defence. The bow and arrow did not reach the Southwest until the first few centuries AD, so the primary weapon was the spearthrower (*atlatl*), and hilltops are a good defence against this (LeBlanc 1999). Similar terraced hilltop sites are known from southeast Arizona, and although they were also used much later in time, they were first occupied *c.* 500 BC (Fish *et al.* 1986). That is, we have evidence for warfare during the initial colonization of the low areas of the Southwest.

We also have evidence for warfare in the Western Basketmaker area to the north (Matson & Cole in press; LeBlanc 1999). Western Basketmaker sites are sometimes built in defensible locations and some have far more burned structures than we would ex-

Table 28.1. *Comparison of the spread of farming from the Near Eastern and Mesoamerican core areas.*

	Near East	Mesoamerica
Time between initial domestication and expansion	*c.* 3000 years	More than 2000 years
Language families in core area	Indo-European, Afroasiatic, Elamite, Sumerian	Uto-Aztecan, Mayan, Mixe-Zoquean, Otomanguean
Population expansions		
Major	To Europe	To Southwest
Minor	To Indus valley	Maya area
Trivial	Nile Delta	–
Resultant language isolates	Basque, Etruscan?	Keres, Zuñi
Local populations converting to farming	Sardinians, Scandinavians, Basques	Tanoans, Keres, Zuñi
Friction zones	Baltic, Indus, Upper Nile?	Low desert
Rate of spread	2.5 km/year	3.7 km/year
Conflict	Anatolian Highlands, extreme SE Europe, LBK	Low desert, both groups of Basketmakers, Basin and Range

pect from just accidental fires. Dry caves in the area have preserved a great amount of evidence for conflict. In 1894, Wetherill's Grand Gulch expedition 'found remains of arms and hands from elbows, and legs and feet from knees, showing evidence of having been cut off before burial' (Blackburn & Williamson 1997). Adults from the Utah Green Mask Cave and nearby Red Canyon had wounds to the head, apparently resulting in their deaths (Christy Turner pers. comm.). The Green Mask Cave is of particular interest because there is a Western Basketmaker-style pictograph that Cole (1993) convincingly argues depicts the flayed and painted skin from a human head. A trophy-head skin, clearly curated, carefully sewn up and painted in the same manner as the pictograph, was found by Kidder & Guernsey (1919) in northeastern Arizona. Woodchuck Cave yielded 20 burials of all ages and sexes, all missing skulls (Lockett & Hargrave 1953). And some 13 individuals were apparently killed at Battle Cave; although there is a full representation of ages and sexes, there are too few children and women compared with a typical population — just what we would expect if the men had been killed, but reproductive-aged women and some children had been taken captive. Other examples of violence and trophy head-taking are known (Guernsey & Kidder 1921; Morris 1933; LeBlanc 1999). The numbers of individuals and the numbers of incidents are truly staggering considering the low population densities one would anticipate from such a marginal environment.

The Eastern Basketmaker situation is harder to interpret, because there has been far less excavation. There are Eastern Basketmaker sites in caves, and some additional rather defensive-looking sites ter-

raced into hillsides (Fenenga & Wendorf 1956; Morris & Burgh 1954). To the north of the Basketmaker area, people continued to be foragers at this time. There, Howard & Janetski (1992) describe scalps and basketry scalp-stretchers. The basketry scalp-stretchers are quite similar to each other and seem to represent a rather standard artefact used just for this one purpose. This implies both that scalp-taking was common and that the associated behaviours were quite codified. Of final note, a well-developed spear thrower-fending stick complex was present at this time, which was clearly used for fighting and not hunting (Heizer 1942). This complex has been found over much of the greater Southwest and is not restricted to one of the Basketmaker groups. Thus, not only do the farmers show evidence for the practice of warfare, but so do adjacent foragers.

Two more lines of evidence are relevant. One is the rate of the initial expansion from Mesoamerica to the Southwest. Taking 2000 BC as a start date for the expansion, and an arrival in the Southwest around 1500 BC, about 1850 km was traversed in 500 years — a rate of 3.7 km/year. Bellwood (2001, 187) summarizes other rates. However, I believe his calculation for the Fertile Crescent to India should be taken from the eastern edge of the Fertile Crescent, not the western, resulting in 3.2 km/year instead of the 5.0 km/year calculated by Bellwood. Therefore, Bellwood's (2001, 187) three expansions over land are 2.5, 3.2, and 3.5 km/year, a close fit with the 3.7 km/year calculated here for Mesoamerica to the Southwest.

Genetic evidence for expansion is a final issue. Unfortunately, there are far fewer New World mtDNA data than for the Old, and the Southwest is poorly sampled — for example, there are almost no genetic data for Hopi, the farthest north Uto-Aztecan farmers. And there are no data from the area between the Mesoamerican core and the Southwest. At present, the Southwest appears rather homogeneous genetically, regardless of language group, and distinct from Mesoamerica (Lorenz & Smith 1997; Carlyle *et al.* 2000). However, there was a major population bottleneck *c.* AD 1300 followed by a recombination of much of the Southwest's population, which probably reduced genetic variability. There are not enough Y-chromosome data to say anything. In all, it is premature to interpret the genetic data.

So these two cases of early farming dispersal — Europe and the US Southwest — have a great number of parallels that are summarized in Table 28.1. Each case has evidence for conflict, producing patterns one would expect from the demographic consequences of such competition. In particular, the nature of the gene flow, the presence of friction zones, the patchy conversion of non-farmers to farming, and the presence of language isolates, fit with a model of farming dispersal that had a conflict component.

Conclusion

The model of farmers replacing foragers fits with the demographic consequences of farming and the nature of non-state warfare. Farmers and foragers will not long occupy the same space without reaching carrying capacity. Warfare will occur and the farmers will always win in the long run. Early farmers spread from Mesoamerica to the American Southwest, a case that strongly parallels events in the Near East/Europe. This does not imply that agriculture always results in such biological expansion, as the events in the Eastern United States attest. Consideration of the demographic situations of foragers, sedentary collectors and true farmers results in several different expectations when they confront each other. These scenarios have important linguistic, biological and cultural consequences.

The situation for the New World is far from well-investigated, and more careful evaluation of the extant information will undoubtedly provide additional insights into the general process of initial farming expansion and linguistic spread.

Notes

1. The concept of carrying capacity is much more complex than eluded to here; see Dewar (1984).
2. One must distinguish between the proximate causes and underlying causes of warfare. In the long term the underlying cause of warfare seems to be competition over scarce resources (Durham 1976; Ember & Ember 1992).
3. One problem with dealing with warfare is definitional. If warfare is defined as involving armies and specialized fighters, then the early past becomes peaceful by definition. However, if one sees warfare as conflict between politically independent social groups, and does not use the methods or the numbers of combatants as criteria for warfare, then one can consider warfare cross-culturally, which is what is done here. See Morren (1984) for a further discussion of the definition of warfare.
4. Processed food would allow earlier weaning and more closely spaced births; the sick and injured are more likely to survive with sedentism, and stored food reduces famine episodes.

References

Bates, D. & S. Lees, 1979. The myth of population regulation, in *Evolutionary Biology and Human Social Behavior*, eds. N. Chagnon & W. Irons. North Scituate (MA): Duxbury, 273–89.

Bellwood, P., 1991. Austronesian dispersal and the origins of language. *Scientific American* 265, 88–93.

Bellwood, P., 2001. Early agriculturalist population diasporas? Farming, langagues, and genes. *Annual Review of Anthropology* 30, 181–207.

Berndt, R., 1964. Warfare in the New Guinea Highlands. *American Anthropologist* 66(4), 183–203.

Blackburn, F. & R. Williamson, 1997. *Cowboys and Cave Dwellers: Basketmaker Archaeology in Utah's Grand Gulch.* Santa Fe (NM): School of American Research Press.

Bogucki, P., 1988. *Forest Farmers and Stockherders: Early Agriculture and its Consequences in North-Central Europe.* Cambridge: Cambridge University Press.

Bogucki, P., 2000. How agriculture came to north-central Europe, in Price (ed.), 197–218.

Bridges, P., 1996. Warfare and mortality at Koger's Island, Alabama. *International Journal of Osteoarchaeology* 6, 66–75.

Burch, E., 1974. Eskimo warfare in Northwest Alaska. *Anthropological Papers of the University of Alaska* 16(2), 1–14.

Carlyle, S.W., R.L. Parr, G. Hayes & D.H. O'Rourke, 2000. Context of maternal lineages in the Greater Southwest. *American Journal of Physical Anthropology* 113, 85–101.

Carpenter, J., G. Sanchez de Carpenter & E.C. Villalpando, 1999. Preliminary investigations at La Playa, Sonora, Mexico. *Archaeology Southwest* 13(1), 6.

Chagnon, N., 1968. Yanomamo social organization and warfare, in *War: the Anthropology of Armed Conflict and Aggression*, eds. M. Fried, M. Harris & R. Murphy. New York (NY): Natural History Press, 109–59.

Cole, S., 1993. Basketmaker rock art at the Green Mask Site, Southeastern Utah, in *Anasazi Basketmaker: Papers from the 1990 Wetherhill-Grand Gulch Symposium*, ed. V.M. Atkins. (Cultural Resource Series 24.) Salt

Lake City (UT): Bureau of Land Management, 193–222.

Cowan, C.W. & P.J. Watson (eds.), 1992. *The Origins of Agriculture: an International Perspective.* Washington (DC) & London: Smithsonian Institution Press.

Denbow, J., 1984. Prehistoric herders and foragers of the Kalahari: the evidence for 1500 years of interaction, in *Past and Present in Hunter-gatherer Studies,* ed. C. Schrire. Orlando (FL): Academic Press, 175–93.

Dewar, R., 1984. Environmental productivity, population regulation, and carrying capacity. *American Anthropologist* 86, 601–14.

Divale, W.T., 1972. Systematic population control in the Middle and Upper Paleolithic: inferences based on contemporary hunter-gatherers. *World Archaeology* 42(2), 222–41.

Durham, W., 1976. Resources, competition and human aggression, part I: a review of primitive war. *The Quarterly Review of Biology* 51, 385–415.

Early, J. & J. Peters, 1990. *The Population Dynamics of the Mucajai Yanomamo.* New York (NY): Academic Press.

Eibl-Eibesfeldt, I., 1975. Aggression in the !Ko-Bushmen, in *War: Its Causes and Correlates,* eds. M. Nettleship, R. Givens & A. Nettleship. The Hague: Mouton, 281–96.

Ember, C. & M. Ember, 1992. Resource unpredictability, mistrust, and war: a cross-cultural study. *Journal of Conflict Resolution* 36(2), 242–62.

Fenenga, F. & F. Wendorf, 1956. Excavations at the Ignacio, Colorado, field camp: site LA2605, in *Pipeline Archaeology,* eds. F. Wendorf, N. Fox & O. Lewis. Santa Fe (NM) & Flagstaff (AZ): Laboratory of Anthropology and Museum of New Mexico.

Fish, P., S. Fish, A. Long & C. Miksicek, 1986. Early corn remains from Tumamoc Hill, southern Arizona. *American Antiquity* 51, 563–72.

Frayer, D., 1997. Ofnet: evidence for a Mesolithic massacre, in *Troubled Times: Violence and Warfare in the Past,* eds. D. Martin & D. Frayer. Amsterdam: Gordon and Breach, 181–216.

Gronenborn, D., 1999. A variation on a basic theme: the transition to farming in southern Central Europe. *Journal of World Prehistory* 13(2), 123–210.

Guernsey, S. & A. Kidder, 1921. *Basket-Maker Caves of Northeastern Arizona: Report on the Explorations, 1916–1917.* Cambridge (MA): Harvard University Press.

Hassan, F., 1981. *Demographic Archaeology.* New York (NY): Academic Press.

Headland, T. & L. Reid, 1989. Holocene foragers and interethnic trade: a critique of the myths of isolated independent hunter-gatherers, in *Between Lands and State: Interaction in Small-Scale Societies,* ed. S. Gregg. Carbondale (IL): Southern Illinois Press, 333–40.

Heizer, R., 1942. Ancient grooved clubs and modern rabbit-sticks. *American Antiquity* 8(1), 41–56.

Hill, K. & A. Hurtado, 1995. *Ache Life History: the Ecology and Demography of a Foraging People.* New York (NY): Aldine de Gruyter.

Horvath, F., 1989. A survey on the development of Neolithic settlement pattern and house types in the Tisza region, in *Neolithic of Southeastern Europe and Near Eastern Connections,* ed. S. Bökönyi. (Varia Archaeologica Hungarica II Redigit.) Budapest: Publicationes Institute Archaeologici Academiae Scientiarum Hungaricae, 85–101.

Howard, J. & J. Janetski, 1992. Human scalps from eastern Utah. *Utah Archaeology* 5(1), 125–32.

Howell, N., 1979. *Demography of the Dobe !Kung.* New York (NY): Academic Press.

Jones, R., 1974. Tasmanian tribes, in *Aboriginal Tribes of Australia: Their Terrain, Environmental Controls, Distribution, Limits and Proper Names,* ed. N. Tindale. Berkeley (CA): University of California Press, 319–54.

Keeley, L., 1996. *War Before Civilization.* New York (NY) & Oxford: Oxford University Press.

Keeley, L. & D. Cahen, 1989. Early Neolithic forts and villages in northeastern Belgium: a preliminary report. *Journal of Field Archaeology* 16, 157–76.

Kelly, R., 1995. *The Foraging Spectrum: Diversity in Hunter-gatherer Lifeways.* Washington (DC): Smithsonian Institution Press.

Kidder, A. & S. Guernsey, 1919. *Archaeological Explorations in North-eastern Arizona.* Washington (DC): Government Printing Office.

Knuckey, G., 1992. Patterns of fracture upon Aboriginal crania from the recent past. *Proceedings of the Australasian Society for Human Biology* 5, 47–58.

LeBlanc, S., 1999. *Prehistoric Warfare in the American Southwest.* Salt Lake City (UT): University of Utah Press.

Lockett, H. & L. Hargrave, 1953. *Woodchuck Cave, a Basketmaker II Site in Tsegi Canyon, Arizona.* (Bulletin 26.) Flagstaff (AZ): Museum of Northern Arizona.

Lorenz, J.G. & D.G. Smith, 1997. Distribution of sequence variation in the mtDNA control region of Native North Americans. *Human Biology* 69(6), 749–76.

Mabry, J.B., 1998. *Archaeological Investigations at Early Village Sites in the Middle Santa Cruz Valley: Analyses and Synthesis.* (Anthropological Papers 19.) Tucson (AZ): Center for Desert Archaeology.

McClung de Tapia, E., 1992. The origins of agriculture in Mesoamerica and Central America, in Cowan & Watson (eds.), 143–72.

Matson, R.G. & S.J. Cole, in press. Ethnicity and conflict among the Basketmaker II of the U.S. Southwest, in *The Archaeology of Contact: Processes and Consequences,* ed. B. Kulle. Calgary: Archaeological Association of the University of Calgary.

Meggitt, M., 1977. *Blood is Their Argument.* Palo Alto (CA): Mayfield.

Mellaart, J., 1975. *The Neolithic of the Near East.* New York (NY): Charles Scribner's Sons.

Milner, G., E. Anderson & V. Smith, 1991. Warfare in late prehistoric West-Central Illinois. *American Antiquity* 56, 581–603.

Minnis, P., 1992. Earliest plant cultivation in the desert borderlands of North America, in Cowan & Watson (eds.), 121–42.

Morren, G., 1984. Warfare on the highland fringe of New

Guinea: the case of the mountain ok, in *Warfare, Culture, and Environment*, ed. R. Ferguson. Orlando (FL): Academic Press.

Morris, A., 1933. *Digging in the Southwest*. Chicago (IL): Cadmus Books, E.M. Hale & Co.

Morris, E. & R. Burgh, 1954. *Basket Maker II Sites Near Durango, Colorado*. Washington (DC): Carnegie Institution of Washington.

O'Laughlin, T., 1980. *The Keystone Dam Site and Other Archaic and Formative Sites in Northwest El Paso, Texas*, vol. 8. El Paso (TX): University of Texas.

Özdogan, M. & N. Basgelen (eds.), 1999. *Neolithic in Turkey: the Cradle of Civilization/New Discoveries*. Istanbul: Arkeoloji Ve Sanat Yayinlari.

Price, T.D. (ed.), 2000. *Europe's First Farmers*. Cambridge: Cambridge University Press.

Price, T., A. Gebrauer & L. Keeley, 1995. The spread of farming into Europe north of the Alps, in *Last Hunters-First Farmers: New Perspectives on the Prehistoric Transition to Agriculture*, eds. T. Price & A. Gebrauer. Santa Fe (NM): School of American Research Press, 95–126.

Read, D. & S. LeBlanc, 2003. Population growth, carrying capacity, and conflict. *Current Anthropology* 44(1).

Renfrew, C., 1996. Language families and the spread of farming, in *The Origins and Spread of Agriculture and Pastoralism in Eurasia*, ed. D. Harris. London: UCL Press, 70–92.

Roney, J., 1996. Late Archaic Cerros de Trincheras in Northwestern Chihuahua. 61st annual meeting of the Society for American Archeology, New Orleans, 1996b.

Sillitoe, P., 1977. Land shortage and war in New Guinea. *Ethnology* 16, 71–81.

Soltis, J., R. Boyd & P.J. Richerson, 1995. Can group-functional behaviours evolve by cultural group selection? An empirical test. *Current Anthropology* 36, 473–94.

Turner, C.G. II, 1993. Southwest Indian teeth. *National Geographic Research and Exploration* 9(1), 32–53.

Vayda, A., 1960. *Maori Warfare*. Wellington: The Polynesian Society.

Vayda, A., 1961. Expansion and warfare among swidden agriculturalists. *American Anthropologist* 63, 346–58.

Villa, P., 1992. Cannibalism in prehistoric Europe. *Evolutionary Anthropology* 1(3), 93–104.

Walker, P. & P. Lambert, 1989. Skeletal evidence for stress during a period of cultural change in prehistoric California, in *Advances in Paleopathology*, ed. L. Capasso. Chieti, Italy: Marino Solfanelli, 207–11.

Wilkie, D. & B. Curran, 1993. Historical trends in forager and farmer exchange in the Ituri rain forest of northeastern Zaire. *Human Ecology* 21(4), 389–417.

Zilhão, J., 2000. From the Mesolithic to the Neolithic in the Iberian peninsula, in Price (ed.), 144–82.

Zvelebil, M. & M. Lillie, 2000. Transition to agriculture in eastern Europe, in Price (ed.), 57–92.

D. Europe

Chapter 29

Issues of Scale and Symbiosis:
Unpicking the Agricultural 'Package'

Martin Jones

In many fields of enquiry researchers are becoming acutely aware of the relationship between pattern and scale. A pattern that is conspicuous and crystal clear on one scale of analysis may disappear completely on another, while some entirely new pattern emerges. That relationship is a familiar feature of ecology. An expanse of grassland that seems uniform from a distance, becomes a changeable mosaic of hummocks and hollows viewed close up, and under the microscope reassembles into new patterns of tissues and cells. This pattern and heterogeneity on different scales then connects with the ecology of different species that live on equivalent scales. Something similar applies to archaeology and timescale. Phenomena that are striking on the millennial timescale dissolve as the resolution sharpens. As millennia make way for centuries and then decades, the global patterns dissolve while quite new local patterns appear.

The search for the beginnings of agriculture has illustrated this well. Viewed globally and over the millennial timescale, human ecology falls easily into two contrasting modes, the hunter-gatherer and farming modes, one procuring food, the other producing it. The difference is striking and informs most aspects of the study of human societies. Childe (1936; 1942) assembled a whole series of cultural traits separating one from the other: nomadic versus settled life, catering for the moment versus planning ahead, low versus high population growth, and absence versus presence of craft specialization, trade and urban civilization. His analysis helped set an agenda for those seeking the transition in particular places and times, in the search for agricultural origins.

What transpired, however, when archaeologists placed this transition under the 'magnifying glass' of fieldwork and excavation, was that individual components of the striking global pattern began to

disaggregate. As the chronological resolution increased, so the cultural differences that sharpened the boundary of transition dispersed into different centuries, sometimes into different millennia. The first Southwest Asian communities to sow wheat and barley would have lost all memory of the first fixed settlements or the earliest obsidian exchange, and certainly of the first time their ancestors gathered and stored cereal seeds from the wild. Those things were already ancient. Conversely, they had no inkling of the first pottery production in the region, and certainly not of urban specialization. These things were far into the future.

This critical feature of the relationship between pattern and scale has sometimes eluded the attention of archaeologists. Much 'origin-seeking' still works on the premise that some global, millennial transition may in principle be discovered as a microcosm, unearthed within the local, biographical traces of an excavation. Something similar is repeatedly happening within the young and promising field of archaeogenetics. This field also starts with global, millennial patterns, the long-term accumulation of human genetic diversity and its disaggregation across space. The patterns so produced are also striking, and as papers in this volume reveal, have become a considerable source of information about the human past. As in conventional archaeology however, there has sometimes been a tendency to seek one-to-one relationships between these large-scale archaeogenetic patterns and small-scale historical episodes.

For effective analysis, such scale-free equations need to be superseded by the concept of 'emergent structure' (cf. Prigogine & Stengers 1984). This refers to structure on one scale of analysis that is the logical consequence of quite separate structures in place on another scale. Patterns on a global scale, such as a sharp contrast between two ways of life, or the spatial boundary that separates them, resolve not to the same thing in microcosm, but instead to a distinct series of local patterns, for example the relationships between successive generations of a family in terms of their difference in numbers, how far they tend to move and what they tend to take with them. The aim of this paper is to explore the relationship between one element of local structure, namely the biographical patterns of movement within communities, and a disaggregation that is becoming apparent from recent studies of domestication. That is, divergence in the archaeological and genetic patterns in the domestication of plants and animals.

The anatomy of agricultural spread

In relating the spread of farming to general principles, several researchers have alluded to emergent structure, as in the case of the once fashionable 'demic diffusion' model. The original version drawn upon by Ammerman & Cavalli-Sforza (1973) is in fact a simple and elegant example of the principle of emergent structure (Kendall 1965; Skellam 1951). This ecological model works from few initial conditions, one being that offspring move away from their parents. This movement doesn't need to be in any specified direction or form. A second premise is that population growth is greater than zero, in other words that the parents and offspring prove to be ecologically 'fit' in the context of their competitors and predators. In fact, these two premises are enough, along with the general rules of ecology and reproduction, to gradually create a pattern of radiating bands with the initial parents at the centre. So long as the initial conditions remain unchanged, the outward spread becomes uniform. The radiating bands constitute an emergent structure — the movements of individuals that generate it have their own separate structure.

In fact, this model remains perfectly plausible and is presumably going on in many places the entire time, in all genetic lines not immediately headed for extinction. However, in moving from 'demic diffusion' to the 'wave of advance' model, to its application in archaeology, there was a tendency for this element of emergent structure to recede. Although Ammerman & Cavalli-Sforza, in their initial formulation, drew a clear distinction between this model and the kind of politically-structured colonizations known from the historical era, there has been a constant tendency for the 'wave of advance' to merge conceptually with something like the nineteenth-century American Frontier. Lines on a map, in reality

corresponding to some kind of genetic abstraction, became populated with pioneer farmers or horse-riding warriors, actively and consciously moving that wave forward. The model also became associated with ideas of extreme population pressure, and of a landscape 'bursting at the seams' with farmers. Such an idea is neither consistent with contemporary environmental evidence (Jones *et al.* 1996; Willis & Bennett 1994) nor is it necessary for the operation of demic diffusion, which instead arises from the more modest condition of population growth greater than zero. A conflict has also been posited between the original demic diffusion model and the 'saltation' model of Van Andel & Runnels (1995). However, the manner of movement is not specified in the demic diffusion model, and indeed most ecological systems involve some element of 'patch-jumping'. Whether or not demic diffusion is the most useful model in all or part of the world, its original exploration of emergent structure is a useful guide to the need to look for patterns on the local scale, such as intergenerational mobility, that may feed in to distinct patterns on a larger scale.

I shall now move on to consider patterns of mobility in the context of genetic and archaeological evidence for some of the domesticated plants and animals linked to the spread of populations. A number of the key domesticates have been explored through molecular phylogeny, first through analysis of variation within proteins, then within modern and ancient DNA (cf. Jones & Brown 2000, for a recent review). The general goals of such analyses have been to search for genetic bottlenecks, and then to relate any bottlenecks to spread from putative centres of origin. The patterns fall along a spectrum between two extremes. At one extreme, the phylogeny of the domesticate may be described as 'clustered'. From protein variation, and on occasion from AFLP analysis of DNA, this clustering manifests itself as an isolated branch of the wild gene pool corresponding to the domesticated gene pool, encouraging many botanists to favour the single origin model. Within such clusters, however, analysis of specific DNA sequences has repeatedly isolated a plural number of clades, sometimes with distinct biogeographies, but relating to a relatively contained region. Typical examples of these include emmer wheat, rice and maize, key founder crops in the important centres of origin in West Asia, East Asia, and Central America, respectively.

At the other extreme, rather than being tightly clustered, the phylogeny of the domesticate instead reflects a considerable genetic breadth inconsistent with recent bottlenecks. The convergence point of these domesticate gene pools leads instead to much earlier bottlenecks, for example, Pleistocene movements between land masses. Typical examples of these include dog, horse and cattle. In other words, we can recognize two contrasting groups of domesticates. Blumler (1992) has characterized these as illustrating 'stimulus diffusion', in which a very localized revolutionary origin triggers cross-continental diffusion and transformation, as opposed to 'independent invention', in which more widely dispersed evolutionary pressures lead to multiple origins. Although by no means a hard and fast rule, a number of key crop plants have tended towards a more clustered phylogeny, and a number of key domestic animals have tended towards a more dispersed phylogeny.

Four key plants and three key animal species are considered below, bringing together elements of their genetics and archaeology, in order to consider how these different patterns of domestication might relate to different patterns of intergenerational mobility. The list is selective and is biased, largely towards domesticates which have been subjected to a range of genetic analyses, including protein variations, modern and ancient DNA studies. There are other critical species, such as the goat and sheep in the Old World, and camelids in both the Old World and the New. With such species, either the archaeogenetic analyses are less well advanced, or they have generated less clear pictures. The global list of domesticated plants runs to several thousand species, and so any pretence at full representation would be unwise. However, the patterns discerned in those domesticates that have received intensive archaeogenetic study allow some hypotheses to be explored about the effects on patterns of mobility of a range of domestication symbioses between humans and other species.

Dogs

From skeletal evidence alone, dogs have often been recognized as the first domesticates of all, their short-snouted skulls distinguishing them from their wolf ancestors. Such skulls have been found in Mesolithic and Upper Palaeolithic contexts from Europe to Siberia. The antiquity of this domestication has been stretched yet further by the mitochondrial DNA analyses of Vilà et al. (1999). As with the majority of DNA studies of animal domestication, the target sequence Vilà used lay within the mitochondrial control region. This is a rapidly evolving region of the mammalian genome, and mutations accumulate at a

pace suitable for the study of within-species change on an archaeological timescale. 162 wolves and 140 breeds of domestic dog were thus examined. The latter clustered into 26 mitochondrial haplotypes. Taken together, the wolves and dogs form four clades, whose common origin is estimated to be in the order of 135,000 years ago. Each of these clades contains at least some of the 26 domesticated dog haplotypes. Of particular note is that one of these clades is made up entirely of domesticated dogs. The most parsimonious explanation of this pattern is that wolves may have been domesticated a number of times, that and one of those domestication trajectories has an antiquity that goes back further than Palaeolithic rock art and other records of modern human behaviour.

A key feature of these data was how they applied to New World dogs. A number of indigenous breeds are known, some of which survive today. Vilà's student, Jennifer Leonard, sought out dog bones that had been excavated from archaeological deposits pre-dating Columbus (Leonard 2000; Leonard et al. in press). She managed to track down seven different pre-Columbian dogs from Bolivia and Mexico, and to amplify their DNA. They were quite diverse; the seven dogs generated six haplotypes which could then be positioned on Vilà's phylogenetic for modern dog DNA.

All these pre-Columbian dogs clustered together with their domesticated Old World relatives, and evidently shared a common ancestry. Their ancestors of these particular dogs did not make the long journey from Asia to America as wolves, they came with their owners, as domesticated dogs. Moreover, they did so several thousand years before the term 'domestication' could be applied to any other species, in any part of the world. 14,000 years ago is about the latest that it could have happened, and many would argue that 30,000 BP would be quite plausible. The human expansion northeastwards into Siberia and Beringia from the heart of Asia was much earlier (Merriwether et al. 1996). Indeed, estimates derived from the mitochondrial clock for the convergence point of all New World humans on the one hand, and all dog breeds in Vilà's fully domestic clade on the other, share a similar order of magnitude.

These data allow us to venture the following hypothesis. First, the 'domestication' of the dog, or at the least the very close symbiosis between two hunter/scavenger species, was an early event in the prehistory of anatomically modern humans. Second, this symbiosis constituted the precondition for a new kind of human mobility. Prior to this domestication, that mobility had not extended to the harshest environments of Asia. However, in partnership with dogs, Siberia and Beringia became feasible, in turn a precondition for moving south into the New World.

Wheat and barley

While the very ancient domestication of an animal which could perhaps be used for both traction and as a hunting partner does seem to correspond with a new pattern of mobility, the relationship between the earliest recorded domestication of plants and mobility is more open to question. The movement of an agricultural 'package' across Europe, which is prominent in the debate addressed in this conference, involved both plants and animals. Within Southwest Asia, however, the dates for domestication of these same plants and animals segregate into different millennia. This enables us to separate the consequences of plant domestication from animal domestication, by looking specifically at the period before the advent of pottery and of animal domestication.

At the site of Ohalo in Israel, Kislev *et al.* (1992) examined a group of charred barley grains that were 19,000 years old. Along with the grains were some of the rachis fragments, displaying the clean, natural break that marked them out as wild cereals. He also noticed four rachis fragments lacking that clean break. This is a pattern normally associated with domestication. Nine thousand years on, at another grass gatherers' site, Netiv Hagdud, over 100 barley rachis fragments out of a few thousand lacked the clean break (Bar-Yosef *et al.* 1991). Dating from the next few centuries, assemblages occur in which all the rachis fragments recovered lacked the clean break. The gatherers of Ohalo and Netiv Hagdud were following an ecological path rather similar to others that had been taken across the world. At the end of the Pleistocene, they shifted to dependable, fast turnaround foods in changing environments, in the process fostering the 'tough rachis' mutation that has became identified with 'domestication'.

The Levantine corridor, where Netiv Hagdud is located, is not the only contender region within Southwest Asia for the first plant domestication. Southeast Anatolia has also, in sites such as Çayönü, yielded early evidence of domesticated cereals, and also lies close to the wild cereal populations that seem closely related to domesticates (Heun *et al.* 1997). While some have argued that there must be a single earliest centre, and that one of these two regions must fall to a secondary position, work on wheat DNA sequences suggests that both centres

may be primary. Allaby *et al.* (1999) have collated glutenin DNA sequence data from modern wheats and related grasses representing all three ploidy levels, and from ancient specimens from the Aegean Bronze Age and sub-Alpine Neolithic. Within the B-genome, which forms a component part of most tetraploid and hexaploid wheat genomes, a clear pattern of internal polymorphism was discerned, consistent with a very distant convergence of lineages. The authors concluded that tetraploid emmer wheat and the hexaploid bread wheat (*Triticum aestivum*) each comprise multiple lineages with respect to this region, whose common ancestor is found much earlier than the earliest agriculture. Interestingly, of two key clades found in modern emmer wheat, in stands of its wild ancestor, *Triticum dicoccoides*, one clade is found near the Levantine Corridor, the other near Southwest Anatolia. Wheat may provide a good example of a 'clustered' domestication, taking place at a number of points within a fairly restricted region. It is worth emphasizing how small the distances involved are, and these two centres, for example, could be covered in a few days' walk.

The transition in Southwest Asia from gathering wild grasses to cultivating cereals was not marked by any immediate upheaval. Gatherers and farmers continued to live within walking distance of each other in not dissimilar settlements for two thousand years or more. The transition was apparently smooth, yet one more adaptation in a species accustomed to constant change. Byrd (1992) has reviewed evidence of the spread of domesticates within the Levantine region itself. He noted how restricted the sites containing plant domesticates within Pre-Pottery Neolithic A (10,300–9300 uncal. BP) actually are. The occupants of Jericho and Netiv Hagdud may have received obsidian from Central Anatolia, and shells from the Mediterranean coast, but it was several centuries before their new crops moved overland a distance of a few hundred kilometres, and 2000 years before they spread right across the Levant. Rather than following the obsidian pathway at this stage, Byrd (1992) argued that such an insignificant trickle is consistent with the gradual incorporation of a novel resource or two by neighbouring hunter-gatherers, who, in any case, were well used to coping with a coarse-textured temporality of climate and ecology by switching around between fast regenerating plant resources. Although cereal production is widely seen as the primary fuel of demographic expansion, the earliest archaeological evidence of plant domestication, prior to the domestication of animals, is more consistent with the lack of mobility of a very localized phenomenon.

Cattle

In contrast to this apparent immobility of the first recorded exploiters of domestic plants, this whole field has been greatly stimulated by the idea that Indo-European languages and the spread of an Old World farming package are interlinked. However, that package is the later package incorporating a range of animals, rather than the earlier package of cereals and legumes alone. In discussing the European element of the spread, Renfrew (1999) places emphasis upon Central Anatolia, and sites such as Çatalhöyük, substantially more recent than such sites as Çayönü and Netiv Hagdud and noteworthy for its economic and symbolic reference to cattle. In a separate paper on farming, language and genes, Bellwood (2001) cites four examples of Old World farming expansion that are notable for their relatively rapid spread. One of these is a spread largely over water, and obviously mediated by boat transport. The remaining three cases of rapid spread, from the Hungarian Plain to Alsace in the sixth millennium BC, from the Levant to northwestern Pakistan in the eighth millennium BC, and from the East African Lakes to South Africa, in the first millennium BC, have in common two features. One is the use of cattle by each of the populations involved. The other is some component of savannah/steppe/parkland steppe along the path (most tentatively in the Hungarian Plain, but clearly in the other two regions). Could it be that, much as the human–dog partnership could have had a particular mobility in the Arctic Steppe of Siberia and Beringia, the human–cattle partnership also had a particular mobility in more southerly seasonal grasslands?

Cattle genetics has been subject to intensive studies at Dublin and elsewhere (Bailley *et al.* 1996; Bradley *et al.* 1996; 1998; Loftus *et al.* 1994). For evidence of the wild progenitors, we are entirely dependent upon ancient DNA from wild cattle (aurochsen), which to date has only been explored from a restricted region of northwest Europe. Such data as exist shows this aurochsen range to be very narrow in comparison with the range for domesticated cattle. Within the latter group there is a deep split within the mitochondrial DNA phylogeny, converging between 200,000 and one million years ago. This separates Asian humped 'zebu' cattle from European and North African 'taurine' cattle. There is a second, shallower split within the taurine group, converging around 25,000 years ago, suggesting independent domestications in Europe and

North Africa. In other words, the domestication of cattle is dispersed through all three continents of the Old World. The genetic evidence also revealed other interesting aspects of cattle mobility, in particular the late prehistoric exchange between South Asia and East Africa, involving amongst other things, the eastward movement of sorghum and the westward movement of zebu cattle. It was crosses between Asian zebu bulls and African taurine cows that played an important role in the third of Bellwood's fast track terrestrial expansions, from the East African Lakes to South Africa in the first millennium BC.

Rice

Moving further east than the Asian home of zebu cattle, rice offers another instance of plant utilization independent of animals. At a subsequent stage in the spread of rice farming it is accompanied by pigs and dogs, while key elements of the mobility of rice farming are mediated by boat transport. However, in the earliest stages of rice farming, its mobility may be independently observed. As with wheat, DNA sequence analysis has separated multiple genetic pathways into domestication, involving both the 'Eastern Fertile Crescent', a region spanning Burma, Thailand and Laos, where wild rice species are currently widespread, and the Middle Yangtze Valley, from where wild rice has now disappeared (Chen 1993; Chen *et al.* 1993; Nakamura & Sato 1991a,b; Sato 1990; 1997). These analyses allowed Sato's group to argue for the former existence in the Yangtze Basin of a wild rice giving rise to the *japonica* strains. He inferred that the domestication of *indica* strains at some distance to the southwest relates to a separate pathway to domestication.

So far as we know, the earliest dates for rice exploitation come from the Middle Yangtze and Huai valleys, from such sites as Pengtoushan and Jaihu, where rice has been recorded from at least 8500 BP. Less than 1000 km to the south, archaeological sites in Thailand have been subject to a sustained search for early rice. Yet the accepted Thailand dates fall within the last 5000 years (see Higham this volume). In other words, the southerly expansion of rice from its earliest use seems to have occurred at perhaps 250 metres a year, a mere fraction of what Bellwood (2001, 186) estimates is the typical 'slow' rate of between 0.5 and 1.25 km per year. Like Levantine exploitation of wheat and barley, early rice exploitation does not seem to have been associated with exceptional mobility.

Horse

Probably the most contentious animal in relation to the theme of this volume is the horse. A number of philologists, geneticists and archaeologists have followed Maria Gimbutas (1952; 1970) in holding the horse, or more precisely its riders, responsible for the spread of the early Indo-European languages. Gimbutas argued that the domestication of the horse, in the wooded steppe north of the Black and Caspian seas, was both the cause and the means for a series of westward waves of horse-rider warrior societies. These waves took them across Europe, where they overran the more peaceful and harmonious matriarchal societies of Neolithic Europe. Prehistoric settlements like Dereivka in Russia and Botai in Kazakhstan yielded horse bones in considerable numbers. From here, her three waves of 'kurgan' (mound-building) cultures moved westward, spreading a new language, culture, technology and masculine ideology across western Eurasia. Kurgan waves have been repeatedly cited in archaeogenetic arguments, for example to account for the third principal component in the analysis of European genes by Cavalli-Sforza et al. (1994), and for some of the principal Asian Y haplotypes (cf. Underhill 1999).

This account of a radiation of the horse from an Asian centre of origin, taking with it the cultural package of its riders, is open to question on various fronts. Levine et al. (1999) have queried its basis in the archaeology and historical ecology of the horse. Renfrew (1987; 1999) has questioned the evidence for the various 'kurgan' migrations. Patterns of horse domestication have also been re-examined through DNA sequencing of modern and ancient specimens. Modern breeds seem phenotypically diverse, something that has led others to speculate about two, perhaps three separate domestications. These would separately account for breeds described as 'light' or 'warm-blooded' and those described as 'heavy' or 'cold-blooded'. The first group includes the rather elegant, fast and spirited animals such as the Arabian so favoured by horse racers. The second includes the massive hard workers such as the Shire Horse and Suffolk Punch. Between these lie many crosses and intermediates, and there are the so-called 'native ponies' on the moors of southwest England, for example. According to one morphological argument, the light breeds derive from wild horses from the heart of Asia, and the heavy breeds arose independently from a European wild forest horse. Another argument gives native ponies their own local ancestry.

Working from a horse–zebra split between two to four million years ago, in this case based on a rich and detailed fossil record, the variations in mitochondrial DNA among living horse breeds and recently disappearing or extinct remnants from wild stock, such as the tarpan and Przewalski's horse, stem from a common maternal ancestor that lived in the region of 880,000 years ago (Lister et al. 1999). As with both dogs and cattle, the horse phylogeny is too deep to be contained within the archaeologically attested timescale for domestication. A rather similar conclusion was reached more recently by Vilà et al. (2001), who also examined mitochondrial DNA from modern and archaeological horse specimens, a survey further extended by Jansen et al. (2002). Those early Central Asian sites, yielding the earliest archaeological evidence for intensive horse management, go back five thousand years at most. There is no way that the sequence divergence measured by Lister could be contained within this abbreviated timescale. Neither was there a genetic division between light and heavy breeds. Two heavy breeds, the Suffolk Punch and Shire, are on completely different branches, and such breeds as the Thoroughbred and Shetland Pony are scattered among different branches. The Przewalski's horses do indeed cluster together, but not in a way that might suggest a long and separate history.

Lister's key finding was that the date for the common maternal ancestry of all living horses, including Przewalski's horse, corresponds well with the fossil record date for the first entry of horse into Eurasia (Lister et al. 1999). Following this entry, and the genetic bottleneck associated with it, a huge range soon developed, and over the millennia a great deal of variation built up in their mitochondrial DNA, which is rather randomly distributed among modern horse breeds. The more detailed study of Jansen et al. (2002) have shown this distribution to be less random than at first seemed, with a number of breeds and geographical groupings showing up as distinct clades. While the various episodes of kurgan migration may be open to question, the eventual impact of this dispersed domestication of the horse certainly had a significant influence upon patterns of human mobility.

Maize

This brief review of domesticates opened with the dog, and particular reference to its presence in the New World. The movement of people southwards from Beringia across the length of the New World, it now seems in partnership with domesticated dogs, has provided a important axis for exploration of, and debate about, language and genes. Interestingly, the subsequent partnership with domesticated plants is relatively inconspicuous in that debate, even though the domesticates concerned, maize in particular, were to become as prominent in the New World as wheat, barley and rice in the Old World.

The centripetal movement of maize has been charted in detail by archaeobotanists. The preserved cobs trace bands of diminishing antiquity, radiating from Mexico into North and South America, resonant with the kind of bands similarly charted for wheat and barley around Southwest Asia. Not only does this centripetal pattern feature little in discussions of continental human genetics, but more detailed bio-archaeology has diminished its significance in human dietary terms. Maize does appear to move relatively quickly, particularly into South America, but a number of lines of evidence now suggest that it remained a minor dietary component for a considerable period of time. These lines include isotopic evidence of human bones (Vogel & van der Merwe 1977) and starch and phytolith inclusions in residues on the surfaces of grinding tools (Piperno & Holst 1998). In both North and South America, maize does eventually become the familiar dominant component of the food chain, but not until the first millennium AD, several thousand years after its initial domestication.

There are other elements that resonate with the patterns seen in wheat and rice. Sequence analysis of maize does appear to fit well with a clustered domestication model (Goloubinoff et al. 1993; Jones & Brown 2000), with some botanists arguing for a singular event (Doebley 1990; 1992; 1995). Just as wheat and barley exploitation in Southwest Asia had a long 'run-in' without major visible demographic impact, so Flannery (1986) has argued, in the context of his work at Guila Naquitz, for a similar long trajectory for maize. He argues that until maize selection was at a fairly advanced stage, the yield advantage against gathering *Prosopis* (mesquite) pods, for example, would have been open to question.

Conclusions and inferences

From this selection of domesticates, each of which has played a key role in Holocene human ecology, a contrast emerges. On the one hand, we find a series of key cereal crops that have gone on to dominate the human food chain, each tracing back to a cluster of localized domestication events within a relatively

restricted region. Where we can separate evidence of their cultivation from the domestication of animals, we find that expansion from the core was relatively slow. In contrast to these, we also encounter a series of key multi-purpose animals, each of which could be exploited as a source of food, companionship, or as a beast of burden. Their domestication follows a different pattern, with widely dispersed elements of the wild genome being domesticated across a large geographic area. Beyond the three domesticated animals considered here, the most recent DNA studies are suggesting that goat, sheep, pig and water buffalo will also follow a dispersed pattern (Luikart et al. 2001; MacHugh & Bradley 2001). A combination of empirical evidence and logical reasoning associates the multi-purpose animals considered in this paper with a qualitatively altered mobility.

This altered mobility need not simply relate to the possibility of using dog, horse and cattle for traction and load-carrying when on the move, although that may often be significant. It certainly is not confined to the past episodes of pastoral nomadism, real and imagined, that have dominated some discussions of this theme. In the ancient case of dog domestication, it presumably relates to a new range of hunting/scavenging possibilities and the hitherto inhospitable niches that open up for exploitation. In the subsequent cases of cattle and horse domestication, it may in many cases have related to the spatial ecology of mixed farmers who thought of themselves as attached to one particular place. However, their maintenance of domesticated animals linked them to larger units of land than cultivators and horticulturalists alone, and necessitated seasonal movements between different grazing lands. The maintenance of a viable and balanced herd, and any training of animals within that herd, would also have involved co-operation with larger human groups. Within any single generation, the setting up of a new settlement 'on the periphery' would have had a different meaning and different consequence than it did in the smaller scale landscape of the cultivator-horticulturalist and the larger-scale mixed farmers. These differences in pattern would be a familiar and enduring part of the landscape on a local scale. As successive generations followed one another, so patterns would emerge from the successive establishments of new settlements on new peripheries. Over the very long term, these emergent patterns would manifest themselves through their material, genetic and linguistic attributes. These are patterns of which the original agents may have been relatively unaware.

References

Allaby, R.G., M. Banerjee & T.A. Brown, 1999. Evolution of the high-molecular-weight glutenin loci of the A, B, D and G genomes of wheat. *Genome* 42, 296–307.

Ammerman, A.J. & L.L. Cavalli-Sforza, 1973. A population model for the diffusion of early farming in Europe, in *The Explanation of Culture Change: Models in Prehistory,* ed. A.C. Renfrew. London: Duckworth, 343–57.

Bar-Yosef, O., A. Gopher, E. Tchernov & M.E. Kislev, 1991. Netiv Hagdud: an early Neolithic village site in the Jordan Valley. *Journal of Field Archaeology* 18, 405–24.

Bellwood, P., 2001. Early agriculturalist population diasporas? Farming, languages and genes. *Annual Review of Anthropology* 30, 181–207.

Blumler, M.A., 1992: Independent inventionism and recent genetic evidence on plant domestication. *Economic Botany* 46, 98–111.

Bradley, D.G., D.E. MacHugh, E.P. Cunningham & R.T. Loftus, 1996. Mitochondrial diversity and the origins of African and European cattle. *Proceedings of the National Academy of Sciences of the USA* 93, 5131–5.

Bradley, D.G., R.T. Loftus, E.P. Cunningham & D.E. MacHugh, 1998. Genetics and domestic cattle origins. *Evolutionary Anthropology* 6(3), 79–86.

Byrd, B., 1992. The dispersal of food production across the Levant, in *Transitions to Agriculture in Prehistory,* eds. A.D. Gebauer & T.D. Price. Madison (WI): Prehistory Press, 49–61.

Cavalli-Sforza, L.L., P. Menozzi & A. Piazza, 1994. *The History and Geography of Human Genes.* Princeton (NJ): Princeton University Press.

Chen, W.B., 1993. Indica-Japonica Differentiation and its Relevance to Domestication Process in Rice: Bio-archaeological and Molecular Genetic Studies. Unpublished PhD dissertation, Gifu University, Gifu, Japan.

Chen, W.B., I. Nakamura, Y.I. Sato & H. Nakai, 1993. Distribution of deletion type in CpDNA of cultivated and wild rice. *Japanese Journal of Genetics* 68, 597–603.

Childe, V.G., 1936. *Man Makes Himself.* London: Watts & Co.

Childe, V.G., 1942. *What Happened in History.* New York (NY): Penguin Books.

Doebley, J.F., 1990. Molecular evidence and the evolution of maize, in New perspectives on the origin and evolution of New World domesticated plants, ed. K. Bretting. *Economic Botany* 44, 6–28.

Doebley J.F., 1992. Molecular systematics and crop evolution, in *Molecular Systematics of Plants,* eds. S. Soltis, D.E. Soltis & J.J. Doyle. New York (NY) & London: Chapman & Hall, 202–22.

Doebley, J.F., 1995. Genetics, development, and the morphological evolution of maize, in *Experimental and Molecular Approaches to Plant Biosystematics,* eds. C. Hock & A.G. Stephenson. St Louis (MI): Missouri Botanic Gardens, 57–70.

Flannery, K., 1986. *Guila Naquitz: Archaic Foraging and Early Agriculture in Oaxaca, Mexico.* Orlando (FL): Academic Press.

Gimbutas, M., 1952. On the origin of north Indo-Europeans. *American Anthropologist* 54(4), 602–11.

Gimbutas, M., 1970. Proto-Indo-European culture: the Kurgan culture during the 5th to 3rd millennia BC, in *Indo-European and Indo-Europeans,* eds. G. Cardona, H.M. Koeningswald & A. Senn. Philadelphia (PA): University of Pennsylvania Press, 155–98.

Goloubinoff, P., S. Pääbo & A.C. Wilson, 1993. Evolution of maize inferred from sequence diversity of an Adh2 gene segment from archaeological specimens. *Proceedings of the National Academy of Sciences of the USA* 90, 1997–2001.

Heun, M., R. Schafer-Pregl, D. Klawan, R. Castagna, M. Accerbi, B. Borghi & F. Salamini, 1997. Site of einkorn wheat domestication identified by DNA fingerprinting. *Science* 278, 1312–14.

Jansen, T., P. Forster, M.A. Levine, H. Oelke, M. Hurles, C. Renfrew, J. Weber & K. Olek, 2002. Mitochondrial DNA and the origins of the domestic horse. *Proceedings of the National Academy of Sciences of the USA* 99, 10,905–10.

Jones, M.K. & T. Brown, 2000. Agricultural origins: the evidence of modern and ancient DNA. *Holocene* 10(6), 775–82.

Jones, M.K., T.A. Brown & R.G. Allaby, 1996. Tracking early crops and early farmers: the potential of biomolecular archaeology, in *The Origins and Spread of Agriculture and Pastoralism in Eurasia,* ed. D.R. Harris. London: University College London, 93–100.

Kendall, D.G., 1965. Mathematical models of the spread of infection, in *Mathematics and Computer Science in Biology and Medicine,* ed. Medical Research Council. London: HMSO, 213–325.

Kislev, M.E., D. Nadel & I. Carmi, 1992. Epipalaeolithic (19,000 BP) cereal and fruit diet at Ohalo II, Sea of Galilee, Israel. *Review of Palynology* 73, 161–6.

Leonard, J.A., 2000. Origin of Domestic Dogs, a Separate Domestication? Paper presented to the 5th International Ancient DNA conference, Manchester, July 2000.

Leonard, J.A., R.K. Wayne, J. Wheeler, R. Valadez, S. Guillén & C. Vilà, in press (2002). Ancient DNA evidence for Old World origin of New World dogs. *Science.*

Levine, M., Y. Rassamakin, A. Kislenko & N. Tatarintseva, 1999. *Late Prehistoric Exploitation of the Eurasian Steppe.* (McDonald Institute Monographs.) Cambridge: McDonald Institute for Archaeological Research.

Lister, A.M., M. Kaldwell, L.M. Kaagan, W.C. Jordan, M.B. Richards & H.F. Stanley, 1999. Ancient and modern DNA in a study of horse domestication. *Ancient Biomolecules* 2(2), 267–80.

Loftus, R.T., D.E. McHugh, D.G. Bradley, P.M. Sharp & E.P. Cunningham, 1994. Evidence for two independent domestications of cattle. *Proceedings of the Na-*

tional Academy of Sciences of the USA 91, 2757–61.

Luikart, G., L. Gielly, L. Excoffier, J.D. Vigne, J. Bouvet & P. Taberlet, 2001. Multiple maternal origins aand weak phylogeographic structure in domestic goats. *Proceedings of the National Academy of Sciences of the USA* 98, 5927–32.

MacHugh, D.E. & D.G. Bradley, 2001. Livestock genetic origins: goats buck the trend. *Proceedings of the National Academy of Sciences of the USA* 98, 5382–4.

Merriwether, D.A., W. Hall, A. Vahlne & R.E. Ferrell, 1996. MtDNA variation indicates Mongolia may have been the source for the founding population for the New World. *American Journal of Human Genetics* 59(1), 204–12.

Nakamura, I. & Y.I. Sato, 1991a. Amplification of chloroplast DNA fragment from a single ancient rice seed. *Rice Genetics (IRRI Manila, Philippines)* 2, 802–5.

Nakamura, I. & Y.I. Sato, 1991b. Amplification of DNA fragments isolated from a single seed of ancient rice (AD 800) by polymerase chain reaction. *Chinese Journal of Rice Science* 5, 175–9.

Piperno, D.R. & I. Holst, 1998. The presence of starch grains on prehistoric stone tools from the Humid neotropics: indications of early tuber use and agriculture in Panama. *Journal of Archaeological Science* 25(8), 765–76.

Prigogine, I. & I. Stengers, 1984. *Order Out of Chaos: Man's New Dialogue with Nature*. London : Fontana Paperbacks.

Renfrew, A.C., 1987. *Archaeology and Language: the Puzzle of Indo-European Origins*. London: Jonathan Cape.

Renfrew, A.C., 1999. At the edge of knowability: towards a prehistory of languages. *Cambridge Archaeological Journal* 10(1), 7–34.

Sato, Y.I., 1990. Non-random association of genes and characters found in *Indica x Japonica* hybrids of rice. *Heredity* 65, 75–9.

Sato, Y.I., 1997. Cultivated rice was born in the lower and middle basins of the Yangtze River. *Nikkei Science* 1, 32–42.

Skellam, J.G., 1951. Random dispersal in theoretical populations. *Biometrika* 38, 198–218.

Underhill, P.A., 1999. Y-chromosome biallelic haplotype diversity: global and European perspectives, in *Abstracts. Human Diversity in Europe and Beyond: Retrospect and Prospect (Third Biennial Euroconference of the European Human Genome Diversity Project, 9–13 September 1999)*, eds. K. Boyle & P. Forster. Cambridge: McDonald Institute for Archaeological Research, 35–6.

Van Andel, T. & C. Runnels, 1995. The earliest farmers in Europe. *Antiquity* 69, 481–500.

Vilà, C., J.E. Maldonado & R.K. Wayne, 1999. Phylogenetic relationships, evolution, and genetic diversity of the domestic dog. *Journal of Heredity* 90(1), 71–7.

Vilà, C., J.A. Leonar, A. Götherströ, S. Marklund, K. Sandberg, K. Lidén, R.K. Wayne & H. Ellegren, 2001. Widespread origins of domestic horse lineages. *Science* 291, 474–7.

Vogel, J.C. & N.J. van der Merwe, 1977. Isotopic evidence for early maize cultivation in New York State. *American Antiquity* 42, 238–42.

Willis, K.J & K.D. Bennett, 1994. The Neolithic transition — fact or fiction? Palaeoecological evidence from the Balkans. *The Holocene* 4(3), 326–30.

Chapter 30

Demography and Dispersal of Early Farming Populations at the Mesolithic–Neolithic Transition: Linguistic and Genetic Implications

Marek Zvelebil

The origins of the Neolithic are inevitably connected with the introduction of farming to Europe. Traditionally, the Neolithic, as a period and as a way of life, is defined by the practice of farming. Although this defining criterion has been questioned by some archaeologists (i.e. Hodder 1990; Thomas 1988; 1991), agro-pastoral farming remains for most the main feature, which separates the Neolithic farmers from the preceding hunter-gatherers of the Mesolithic. This basic distinction raises two key questions: 1) when was agro-pastoral farming introduced to Europe; 2) how was it introduced?

There can be little doubt that agro-pastoral (Neolithic) farming originated in the Levant and Anatolia some 10,000 years ago. It then spread throughout Europe over the next 4000 years, mostly between 8000 and 4000 years ago. In some regions, such as the east Baltic, northwest Russia and most of peninsular Scandinavia, farming did not develop until the Iron Age (Zvelebil 1981; 1985; 1998; Taavitsainen 1998; Antanaitis 1999). So, to answer the first question, at the continental scale the introduction of farming was a very long process indeed.

How was it introduced to Europe? Archaeologically, three major points of view can be identified:

1. The *immigrationist explanation* represents the traditional, established view formulated by Gordon Childe (1925; 1957; also Piggott 1965; Clark 1966). According to this interpretation, farmers, migrating from the Near East, colonized hitherto unfarmed areas of Europe, replaced indigenous hunter-gatherers and introduced farming into Europe. This process was driven by the rapid population growth experienced by Neolithic farming populations.

2. The *indigenist explanation* adopts the opposite perspective (Dennell 1983; Barker 1985; Whittle 1996). The adoption of farming in Europe and the origins of the Neolithic came about exclusively through frontier contact and cultural diffusion. Migration from the Near East had little or no role to play. Genetically, then, populations of Near Eastern origin had little or no contribution to make, and any spread of languages would have occurred through processes other than population dispersal. This view is based on strict interpretation of archaeological evidence, where the burden of proof is placed on the presence of clear archaeological markers of migration: a requirement difficult to meet on archaeological grounds alone.

3. The *integrationist explanation* regards both types of processes — those involving a population transfer and those that do not — as being responsible for the agricultural transition (Zvelebil 1986a,b; 1989; 1995a,b; 1996a; Chapman 1994; Thorpe 1996; Price 1987; 1991; 1996; Zilhão 1993; 1997; Auban 1997). The importance of the relative contributions of each process differs from author to author. The varying interpretations of these three groups are of a degree rather than categorical, but the implications for population history, genetic patterning and linguistic change at the agricultural transition are quite major.

Demography and population growth of early farmers as an explanation for agricultural transition

The rationale most often cited for the immigration of Neolithic farmers from the Near East to Europe by demic diffusion is the rapid population growth brought about by the emergence and development

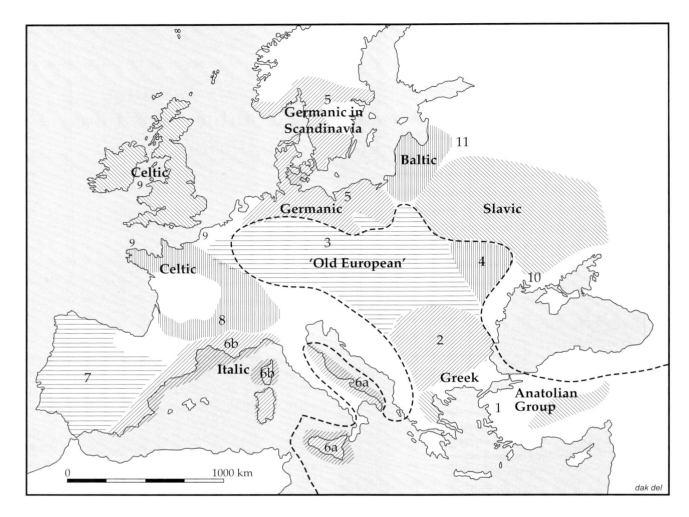

Figure 30.1. *First Neolithic cultures and the spread of Indo-European language groups in Europe. The broken line denotes southeastern and central Europe where farming was introduced by demic diffusion mostly. (Partly based on Renfrew 1987. For further explanation, see main text and note 2.)*

of farming (i.e. Renfrew 1987; 1996), regarded by some as 'demographic explosion' (Cavalli-Sforza & Cavalli-Sforza 1995, 133–4). The shift to agriculture brought about an increasingly sedentary existence, improved diet, and rise in the economic value of child labour. This in turn reduced the need for population controls; having more children became both possible and desirable. In consequence, farming populations grew rapidly, colonized adjacent regions and replaced hunter-gatherer communities, whose population growth was negligible or nil.

In the present paper, my main proposition is this: there is no clear support for rapid population growth of early farming populations at the Meso-lithic–Neolithic transition in Europe, either from direct evidence or in the supporting arguments. If true, this proposition removes a central assumption un-

derpinning the spread of farming into Europe by demic diffusion.

Archaeologically, there is no evidence for sustained and wide-ranging immigration that would support either the demic diffusion hypothesis or a major continent-wide migration (Dolukhanov 1979; Dennell 1983; 1992; Barker 1985; Zvelebil 1986b; 1989; 1995a,b; Thomas 1996; Midgley 1992; Larsson 1990). There is, however, clear evidence for the introduction of agro-pastoral farming, and of regionally variable, associated cultural traits, in a clear chronological gradient from the southeast to the northwest of Europe (Clark 1966; Dennell 1983; Ammerman & Cavalli-Sforza 1984; Renfrew 1987; Pinhasi *et al.* 2000).

Although clear traces of population migrations are difficult to identify in the archaeological record (Renfrew 1987; 1999; Chapman & Dolukhanov 1992;

Anthony 1990), there is simply too much cultural continuity across the Mesolithic–Neolithic transition to validate the immigrationist hypothesis across Europe. This cultural continuity is manifested at a regional level in the location of settlements, resource-use patterns, technological traits in lithic assemblages, stylistic features and decorative patterns in ceramics and other artefacts, burial patterns, domestic architecture, distribution of raw materials and exchange networks. Many authors have now debated the similarities and differences between the last hunter-gatherers and first farming communities region by region, and there is no need to revisit these discussions here (Dolukhanov 1979; Bogucki 1988; Midgley 1992; Thomas 1996; Zvelebil 1981; 1986b; 1998; Price 2000). Very crudely, however, two major cultural zones at a continental scale can be perceived, separated by major frontier boundaries. In southeast and central Europe, there is evidence in most regions of a clear break in cultural traditions between the communities of the Mesolithic and those of the Neolithic. In other parts of Europe, patterns of continuity and innovation vary from one regional unit to another, with continuity in cultural traditions most clearly evident in the circum-Baltic region, and in northern and eastern Europe (Fig. 30.1).

These regionally variable archaeological patterns have led me to suggest in earlier publications that in southeast and central Europe, agro-pastoral farming was principally introduced through 'leap-frog colonisation' (as advanced by Arnaud 1982 and Zilhão 1993 also for the western Mediterranean), while in other parts of Europe, the transition to farming was accomplished principally through contact and limited, socially-embedded gene exchange through intermarriage ('frontier mobility') (Zvelebil 1995a; 2000a; Zvelebil & Lillie 2000).

Demographically, there is no evidence for population pressure sufficient to encourage first farmers to migrate, nor is there evidence for rapid population growth. Archaeological evidence does not record rapid saturation of areas colonized by Neolithic farmers, or demographic expansion, with the single possible exception of the core area of the Linear Pottery Culture in central Europe (but see Whittle 1996; Gronenborn 1998; Zvelebil 2000b).

Number, distribution and size of archaeological sites are routinely adopted as a rough guide to estimating population density and dynamics of communities in question (Naroll 1962; Plog 1975; Polgar 1975; Cohen 1977; 1989; Hassan 1975; 1978; 1985). In one of the most recent such studies, Pinhasi *et al.* (2000) and Lahr *et al.* (2000) attempted to estimate the sizes of the indigenous Mesolithic and intrusive Neolithic populations and their relative contributions to the neolithization of Europe. Their conclusions point to the major genetic impact of the Neolithic in Turkey and Greece, a major genetic impact of the Neolithic with minor Mesolithic 'admixture' in central and eastern Europe and northern Italy, and to an equal or greater genetic contribution of the Mesolithic communities in western and northern Europe. These conclusions, which are not markedly different from earlier scenarios outlined by the 'integrationists' (Zvelebil 1986a,b; 1995a,b; 2000a; more recently Renfrew 1999; 2000a,b), nevertheless illustrate the problems associated with estimating population densities from regionally variable archaeological settlement evidence.

Recent surveys, whether in Ireland (Zvelebil *et al.* 1992; 1996b; Woodman & Anderson 1990; Cooney 1999), Denmark (Price 2000), Greece (van Andel & Runnells 1995), or indeed any other region of Europe, have all resulted in the discovery of many additional Stone Age sites within the target regions, clearly showing just how under-represented our record of Mesolithic and Neolithic sites is. For example, in one small part of Ireland around Waterford, the number of Mesolithic and Neolithic sites increased from 0 to 16 and from 5 to 31 respectively as a result of systematic survey (Green & Zvelebil 1990; Zvelebil *et al.* 1992). So any relationship between the density of sites and population numbers has to be calibrated by the history of research in different regions.

To this requirement we must add a range of other variables, including mobility patterns, settlement-generating behaviour and the taphonomic processes which transform and obscure site-generating human activities. Roughly compared, remains of Mesolithic sites have significantly smaller chances of identification than those of the Neolithic for reasons of taphonomy and recognition (Zvelebil 1998; Jochim 1998; Bottema *et al.* 1990).

With generally poor preservation conditions in the more southern areas of Europe, the recognition of Mesolithic settlements depends on non-organic materials, especially chipped stone tools. The only lithic artefacts generally recognized as belonging to the late Mesolithic are narrow-bladed microliths and, arguably, micro-blade cores. How often can a site be identified chronologically by such narrow criteria? Relatively infrequently. This is true especially in central and southeastern Europe. We may be identifying only those sites where microliths were used, and missing or mis-identifying those sites where microliths were not used or where trapeze-dominated and/or broad-bladed industries replaced microlith use. This is often the case in the final stages of the Mesolithic in Western Europe. These observations call into the question the general assumption that there is a direct relationship between the distribution of archaeological sites and human population densities that is robust and reliable on the present evidence (*contra* Pinhasi *et al.* 2000, 48).

Even in Southeast Europe, the presumed core area for early farming demographic expansion (i.e. Cavalli-Sforza 1997; Pinhasi *et al.* 2000; Lahr *et al.* 2000), the demographic saturation process appears to have been slow and incomplete. This is shown, for example, through the work of van Andel & Runnels in Thessaly. Even though they argue in favour of demic diffusion for the spread of farming (1995, 494–8), their own calculations fail to substantiate the population growth rates necessary for such model to operate. They conclude that the Early and Middle Neolithic periods 'seemed to have been a time of steady but not very rapid population growth' so that 'even the Larisa basin, region of major growth, required some 1500 years, from about 9000 to 7500 BP to reach saturation' (1995, 497). This is a far cry from the 'demographic explosion' of Cavalli-Sforza, but in complete agreement with the recent palynological work carried out by Willis & Bennett (1994) showing that even in southeast Europe (including Greece) the impact of agriculture is not evidenced until *c.* 6000 BP, suggesting that the introduction of farming 'was not of sufficient intensity to be detected upon a landscape scale' (1994, 327; see also Zvelebil 1995a, 118; Zvelebil & Lillie 2000, 68–72).

At the same time, archaeological evidence for the Mesolithic in much of Europe (except central and southeast Europe) records stable, relatively affluent, often semi-sedentary communities that would have been capable of maintaining relatively high population densities (see below, Rowley-Conwy 1983; 1999; Price 1987; Price & Brown 1985a; Zvelebil 1986a; 1996b; Tilley 1996; Finlayson & Edwards 1997; Voytek & Tringham 1989; Renouf 1998).

Archaeological evidence for the early Neolithic in much of Europe records partly mobile communities which relied on a mixture of farming, hunting, gathering and animal husbandry (except for southeast and central Europe: Barker 1985; Bogucki 1988; Tilley 1994; 1996; Thomas 1991; 1996; Whittle 1996; Thorpe 1996; Barclay 1997; Deitz 1988). Consequently, the differences in economy and sedentism between hunters and farmers, which are held responsible for differences in population growth of the two types of communities, were much reduced during the time in question, removing the rationale for 'demographic explosion' and 'the growth-migration cycle' (Cavalli-Sforza 1997, 386).

In aggregate, these arguments point to two conclusions:

1. Because of its complexity and uneven quality, the current archaeological evidence makes any numerical estimates of likely population densities unreliable (although attempts have been made, i.e. Zvelebil 1983; Ammerman & Cavalli-Sforza 1984; English Heritage 1999), while any relative or graded estimates must be calibrated by regionally variable taphonomies, prehistoric mobility patterns, and histories of research to build a more accurate picture of the demographic landscape at the Mesolithic–Neolithic transition.

2. Current studies so far have tended to underestimate to various degrees the size and density of Mesolithic populations, thereby failing to acknowledge the full extent of their cultural and genetic contribution to the formation of the early Neolithic communities.

Ecologically, there is no evidence for sustained woodland clearances after the initial phase, and for the level of environmental degradation indicative of extensive agriculture, providing a rationale for population expansion before the Late Neolithic (Willis & Bennett 1994; Willis *et al.* 1998; Smith 1981; Edwards & Whittington 1997; Berglund 1990; Vera 2000). The evidence for this surprisingly enduring pattern comes from an increasing number of regions within Europe, including Greece, Slovenia (Willis & Bennett 1994), Hungary (Willis *et al.* 1998), Bohemia, Poland, Germany, Switzerland, Holland (Keeley 1992; Beneš 1995; 1998; Vera 2000; Nowak 2001; Zvelebil *et al.* 1998), Britain (Smith 1981; Edwards & Whittington 1997) and southern Scandinavia (Berglund 1990, Andersen 1993). For the latter, Price summarized the evidence as follows:

> The early Neolithic then was a 600-year-long period that saw the gradual adoption of farming. Settlements are small and there is no substantial forest clearance or extensive cultivation until 3300 BC (Price 2000, 272).

> It is not until the beginning of the Middle Neolithic around 3300 BC — at least 600 years after the first appearance of the Funnel Beaker culture — that significant agricultural activities are seen in the landscape of southern Scandinavia (Price 2000, 284).

At the same time, the ecology of Europe was favourable for supporting greater than average densities of hunter-gatherer populations, especially in coastal and lacustrine regions and along major rivers (Clarke 1976; Price 1987; Zvelebil 1986a; 1996b).

To summarize, then, both the ecological conditions prevailing in Europe at the time of the Mesolithic–Neolithic transition, as well as the resource use patterns of both the Mesolithic and the early Neolithic communities indicate that the sustainable population densities for Mesolithic hunter-gatherers and Neolithic farmers were much closer than generally postulated in literature.

Sustainable densities, however, do not tell the whole story. In reality, actual population densities and growth rates reflect historical contingencies, social conditions, prevailing ideologies and the biological health of the population. Careful use of ethnographic analogies can shed some light on such conditions, even though they can provide only a rough guidance for the historically specific situation of the Mesolithic–Neolithic transition.

Ethnographically, in this regard, the choice by the migrationist school of selected examples as analogues for the historical situation at the Mesolithic–Neolithic transition is inappropriate (Piggott 1965; Ammerman & Cavalli-Sforza 1984; Cavalli-Sforza & Cavalli-Sforza 1995). In fact, more general ethno-historical evidence shows that there is a wide overlap in population densities between hunter-gatherers and subsistence farmers, further eroding the demographic basis of the farming colonization hypothesis. The ethnographic sample shows that hunter-gatherer population densities range from 0.01 to about 34.00 per sq.km (Hassan 1975, 29; 1985) with the more sedentary groups in coastal, lacustrine and riverine environments having the greater population densities (see also Keeley 1988; 1992 demonstrating the link between sedentism and population density among hunter-gatherers). For example, Birdsell (1953) notes that in Australia, aboriginal populations in riverine zones were 20–40 times higher than in surrounding areas (see also Lourandos 1985; Webb 1995, 274–92). Given their patterns of mobility and subsistence, Mesolithic communities were likely to approximate the higher population densities found among the Californian and Northwest Coast Indians.

There are good biological reasons for this pattern. Recent research indicates that consumption of n-3 fatty acids, found in marine fish, shellfish and other marine food resources, as well as in oily freshwater fish, increases human reproductive potential. A study by Olsen of pregnant Danish women showed that those who consumed regularly fish rich in n-3

fatty acids had significantly reduced rate of pre-term delivery (1.9 per cent as opposed to 7.1 per cent for those who did not eat fish), while the birth weight was significantly higher among the fish-eaters (Olsen 2002). The importance of fat in hunter-gatherer diets is well-known, and the differential access to fat among men and women in hunter-gatherer communities can have major health implications (Speth 1990; Moss 1993; Zvelebil 2000b). The benefits of access to fat-rich marine resources and the considerable effort expended in procuring them among some communities, for example among the Bardi of Western Australia, have been described by Rouja (2002). Without going into the detail of social and cultural variation associated with fatty marine and freshwater food consumption (shellfish, fish and mammals), it is possible to state that a female diet rich in n-3 fatty acids would have enhanced the reproductive capacities of hunter-gatherer communities. In coastal and riverine zones in Mesolithic Europe, such diet, focused towards the consumption of marine and freshwater resources was fairly common (Tauber 1981; Price 1989; Meiklejohn & Zvelebil 1991; Meiklejohn *et al.* 2000; Bonsall *et al.* 1997; 2000; Schulting 1999; Schulting & Richards 2001; Lillie 1997; etc.).

By comparison, the population densities of farmers engaged in subsistence agriculture ranged from 3 per sq.km in Laos and Zimbabwe to 30 in the Philippines and to 300 in New Guinea, while the rural population of Lorraine and of Belgium in the mid fifteenth century was 10–25 and 30–70 people per sq.km respectively. The population of England in 1086 was calculated as 78 per sq.km (Hassan 1975). Difficult as it may be to compare these poorly standardized figures, there does seem to be some overlap between foragers and subsistence farmers in the ethnographic record.

Population density is, of course, just one key demographic variable influencing population growth. To it we can add fertility, reproductive span, infant and child mortality, and adult survival rate. Studies by Pennington (2001) show that modern hunter-gatherer fertility rates range from 2.6 to 8.0 children with an average around 6 live births, 'which is typical of women in any traditional society', including subsistence farmers (Pennington 2001, 179). Pennington concludes that sedentarization as such has no marked effect on the fertility rate (2001, 179–81, 185, 195).

Infant and child mortality patterns are clearly influenced by diet and community ecology, and this is discussed by a great number of researchers (Cohen & Armelagos 1984; M. Cohen 1977; 1989; this volume; J. Cohen 1995; Hassan 1975; 1981; Pennington

2001). In summary, the following conclusions are relevant. Both increased sedentism and a shift to an agricultural diet increase infant survivorship, arising from the increased length of the lactation period, better diet for mothers, and improved weaning diets for children. However, at the same time, a shift to a farming way of life increases child mortality principally because of reduced hygienic conditions and rise in density-dependant infectious diseases. As Pennington notes with respect to Agta:

> The Agta data indicate that things got better, then worse, when the Agta way of life changed. The differences in survival among children are large and indicate that infant mortality declined dramatically at the expense of very high early childhood mortality. As a result, many fewer children survive to reproductive age in the 'peasant' population (2001, 195).[1]

Global and regional population growth rates among hunter-gatherers, suggested by such demographic data and, more recently, by genetic evidence (Pennington 2001; Bandelt & Foster 1997; Harpending *et al.* 1998), do not support the notion of a very slow population growth which took off only with the invention of agriculture. Rather, they suggest a more rapid population growth among prehistoric hunter-gatherers, marked by the occurrence of 'boom and bust' cycles before the adoption of farming. Hammel (1996, 228) notes that the current evidence suggests no major change in mortality rates between the Palaeolithic and the eighteenth century AD, and that rapid population growth took off only 300 years ago, 'when doubling times generally dropped below a millennium' (Hammel 1996, 221; also Pennington 2001; J. Cohen 1995). Mark Cohen (this volume) goes on to suggest that Neolithic dispersal 'is unlikely to have resulted from population growth that, on average, must have been trivial in the short run and only very marginally greater than that of hunter-gatherers'.

At the same time, it is clear that hunter-gatherer populations are capable of rapid population increase: among the Ache, the current growth rate of nearly 3 per cent per annum will double the population in 25 years (Pennington 2001, 198). Pennington suggests a growth rate of 0.008 per cent per year in the 90,000 years prior to the beginning of plant and animal domestication (2001, 172–3, 195), a figure consonant with the hunter-gatherer reproductive rates of 0.004 to 0.008 proposed by Binford for postglacial Europe (2001, 441–2). The global population of hunter-gatherers 10,000 years ago is variously estimated between 5 and 20 million souls (Hassan 1981; Binford 2001; Cohen 1995; this volume). This is based

on the assumption of a slow and steady population increase, rather than cycles of growth and decline suggested by the fertility figures and reproductive rates.

The ethnographic sample upon which most of the hunter-gatherer demographic data is based may be actually *underestimating* hunter-gatherer population densities and demographic potential. As many authors note, such information comes from foraging societies living in marginal conditions and suffering from disease and persecution. For example, Pennington (2001) and Froment (2001) elucidate the extent to which diseases, introduced through contact with farming populations and their livestock, prejudiced the survival and reproductive potential of hunter-gatherer communities. And Layton notes that

> Current hunter-gatherer population densities may be doubly misleading. Up to 95% of the Aboriginal population in the Darwin hinterland and Victoria River district was killed during the early colonial era of the late nineteenth and early twentieth centuries and the survivors lived precariously attached to white buffalo shooters or on the fringes of towns and mining camps (Layton 2001, 305)

> Population densities in Arnhem Land, protected from the devastation of intense colonisation, are as high as those sustained by farming or stock-raising in northern Australia (Layton 2001, 299, quoting Jones 1981, 108).

All these considerations do suggest in aggregate a more even demographic playing field between foragers and farmers in prehistoric Europe. Although agricultural economies have the capacity to be far more productive than hunting and gathering ones (by as much as 50 to 100 times, according to some estimates, i.e. Hassan 1985; Renfrew this volume), such productivity can be attained only in limited, optimal areas under simple farming regimes. Although the population growth rates for farmers were likely to be greater than for hunter-gatherers, the differences must have been considerably smaller than often projected (for example, a 50-fold increase from 0.1 to 5 persons per sq.km with the arrival of farmers in Europe by Ammerman & Cavalli-Sforza 1984, 134). The population densities of prehistoric foragers and farmers in Europe may have partly overlapped as they do in the ethnographic sample.

Genetic implications: who were the first farmers of Europe?

The arguments I have presented so far lead to the conclusion that the agricultural transition in Europe and the origin of the Neolithic communities can only be understood in a social and historical context that involved both the resident hunter-gatherer Mesolithic populations and the immigrating communities of early farmers.

What of the genetic evidence? There is an ongoing debate among geneticists about the interpretation of modern genetic evidence, the dating and projection of modern genetic patterns into the past, and about the interpretation of genetic variation in terms of population histories. In general, however, increasing genetic support can be adduced for an integrationist hypothesis combining limited immigration and the indigenous adoption of farming as two major processes responsible for the origins of farming in Europe (Renfrew & Boyle 2000; Richards *et al.* 1996; 1998a,b; 2000; this volume; Evison 1999; 2001; Julku & Wiik 1998; Künnap 2000; Semino *et al.* 1996; 2000; Torroni *et al.* 1998; Simoni *et al.* 2000; Underhill *et al.* 2000; 2001).

Studies of modern human DNA (and some prehistoric DNA too) show quite clearly that the modern gene pool in Europe is mostly a consequence of three major demographic events (although their relative contributions in terms of population numbers are still matters of debate):

1. The initial colonization by anatomically modern humans, who entered Europe from North Africa/Near East between 40,000 and 25,000 years ago. There are at least two migration horizons, indicated by mitochondrial and Y-chromosomal evidence (Otte 1990; Torroni *et al.* 1998; Semino 1999; Richards *et al.* 1996; 1998a; 2000).

2. The Late Glacial population expansion and colonization of areas freed by deglaciation in northern Europe between 15,000 and 10,000 year ago. Combining archaeological and genetic evidence, it is increasingly clear that re-settlement originated from three source areas (also known as glacial refuges): southwest France/northern Spain, northern Balkans and northeast Ukraine. Arguably, this was the most significant demographic event in shaping the genetic map of modern Europeans (Richards *et al.* 1996; 1998; 2000a; Torroni *et al.* 1998; Evison 1999; Evison *et al.* 1999; Simoni *et al.* 2000; Semino *et al.* 2000; Underhill *et al.* 2000; Dolukhanov 1996; Housley *et al.* 1997).

3. The post-glacial penetration of Europe by the first farmers from the Near East; introducing farming to Europe. This penetration is documented by three sets of data:
   a) Principal component analysis of the 'classical markers'. The first principal component explains,

according to Cavalli-Sforza (Ammerman & Cavalli-Sforza 1984; Cavalli-Sforza & Cavalli-Sforza 1995), about 26–28 per cent of the modern genetic variation of Europe, mapped as a gradual distribution in values between the Near East and northwest Europe (although the directionality of spread could be from either margin).
   b) Mitochondrial DNA analysis, which shows a similar trend but accounts for only 10–20 per cent of mitochondrial sequences (Richards *et al.* 1996; 1998a; 2000, 1271) over all of Europe. Richards *et al.* conclude that, on the maternal side, the incoming lineages were 'in the minority, in comparison with the indigenous Mesolithic lineages whose bearers adopted the new way of life' (Richards *et al.* 2000, 1271). However, acculturation may have occurred in southeast Europe and 'there was considerable replacement in central Europe' (Richards *et al.* 2000, 1271).
   c) Y-chromosomal DNA analysis gives results which fall between the nuclear and the mitochondrial evidence: the frequency of Y-chromosome haplotypes originating in the Near East averages about 20 per cent, with more than 25 per cent in the Balkans and the Mediterranean, and less than 10 per cent in northern and western Europe (Semino *et al.* 1996; 2000). Recent studies by King & Underhill (2002) come broadly to the same conclusions. The difference between greater male (Y-chromosome) and lesser female (mitochondrial) genetic contribution to this process is significant in itself, indicating male exogamy and long-distance travel on one hand, and female matrilocality and regional endogamy on the other, among communities who were in the initial process of becoming farmers (for further elaboration and supporting evidence, see Zvelebil 1995a; Zvelebil & Lillie 2000; Niskanen 1998; Künnap 2000; Villems 1998).

In my opinion, four major processes contributed to the generation of southeast–northwest genetic gradient patterns. In aggregate, these processes present a more plausible explanation than population-driven, human colonization at the beginning of the Neolithic through demic diffusion or folk migration:

1. In general, the pattern we see today represents an 'incremental palimpsest' of small-scale population movements progressing from southeast Europe to the northwest over millennia. Such movements cover the entire course of modern human prehistory — from the Upper Palaeolithic to the Romans — and together account for the strong southeast to northwest gradient observed

in the genetic data. This is not surprising given that Europe is a northwestern peninsular extension of Asia.

2. More specifically, at the onset of the Neolithic we can postulate 'targeted', 'leapfrog' or 'pioneer' settlement of selected areas by small numbers of incoming farmers from the Near East/Anatolia to southeast, central and Mediterranean Europe, resulting in the foundation of agricultural 'enclaves' within landscapes occupied by hunter-gatherers (see Alexander 1978; Zvelebil 1986b; 1996a; Zvelebil & Lillie 2000; Zilhão 1993; 2000; Tichy 1999; 2001).

3. This event was followed by the adoption of farming by indigenous foragers in individual regions of Europe through contact, intermarriage and socially regulated mobility between foraging and farming communities within frontier zones.

4. A 'star-burst' pattern of regional demic expansion followed, which I outlined above (infilling of locally available niches by a genetically mixed population comprising local hunter-gatherers and some immigrant farmers). Arguably, this might produce more faithfully the graded variation pattern observed in the modern genome than would demic diffusion.

A balanced assessment of both the archaeological and genetic evidence lead to the same conclusion: the first farmers of Europe originated genetically and culturally from interbreeding of intrusive Near Eastern and indigenous Mesolithic populations, with the continuation of hunter-gatherer genetic inheritance and cultural traditions predominant in regions outside southeastern and central Europe (see also Barbujani & Dupanloup this volume; Richards *et al.* this volume; King & Underhill 2002).

Linguistic implications: the role of language shift

The notion of linguistic dispersal by migration has a long and distinguished tradition in both linguistics and archaeology. Using earlier linguistic and genetic research, Colin Renfrew (1987) presented his language-farming hypothesis, arguing that agriculture arrived in Europe principally by a gradual migration of farming populations from the Near East, and that these farming populations were the first Indo-European (IE) speakers to settle in Europe, their reproductive success fuelled by the practice of agro-pastoral farming. Renfrew's hypothesis reinvigorated the debate about Indo-European origins (Sherratt & Sherratt 1988; Zvelebil & Zvelebil 1988; Zvelebil 1995a; 2000a,b; Robb 1993; Sims-Williams 1998;

MacEachern 2000; Renfrew 1992; 1996; 1999; this volume; Renfrew & Boyle 2000).

How does my argument here influence the language-farming hypotheses about IE origins? If the first farmers to enter Europe 8500 years ago were indeed Proto-IE speakers (and this remains one among several key hypotheses), then the degree of population continuity across the Mesolithic–Neolithic transition implies that the IE linguistic dispersals must have been brought about by a combination of immigration and contact-induced language change.

In 1995, I tentatively suggested that the adoption of farming in western, eastern and northern parts of Europe was associated with a contact-induced language shift, resulting in the differentiation of IE speech into Celtic, Germanic and Balto-Slavic groups. In other words, local hunter-gatherers of the Mesolithic adopted IE speech, together with farming practices, which replaced in time their original mother tongue (Fig. 30.2; Zvelebil 1995a,b).

In contrast to others who have considered contact as a significant force in the spread of Indo-European languages (Dolukhanov 1986; 1989; Sherratt & Sherratt 1988; Robb 1993), the model I propose for the dispersal of Indo-European languages represents a specific attempt to apply the linguistic construct of contact-induced language change (Thomason & Kaufmann 1988; Emeneau 1980; Ross 1999) to the original Renfrew hypothesis (1987). This hypothesis accepts the notion of Asia Minor as the original homeland of PIE speakers, but rejects the idea that IE language dispersals must have principally occurred through demic diffusion or folk migration. While accepting that demic diffusion must have ushered the Neolithic into parts of Europe, this was not the case everywhere. While in southeastern and central Europe (broadly the areas covered by the first Balkan Neolithic and the Linear Pottery cultures), Indo-European languages were introduced principally by the colonizing farming populations, in the remaining regions of Europe, contact-induced language shift played the major role. This is fully in keeping with the archaeological, demographic and genetic arguments presented above.

In this latter zone outside southeast and central Europe, a farming economy was adopted and altered in response to local needs by the hunter-gatherer communities of the Mesolithic. During the later part of this period, this process was aided by the secondary colonization of sub-optimal farming habitats and by the development of dairy farming, the plough, and other aspects of the secondary products 'revolution' (Sherratt 1981).

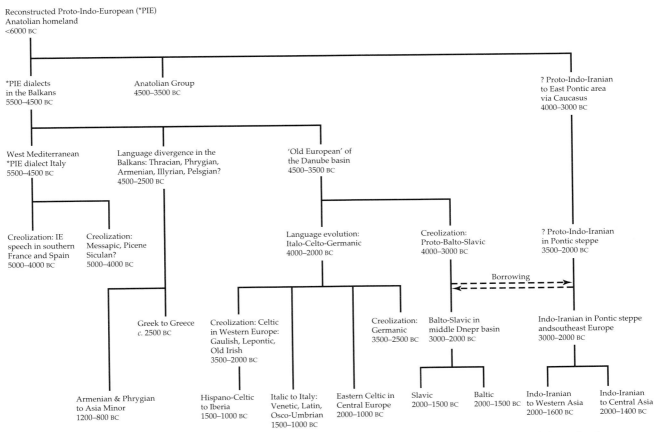

Figure 30.2. *The differentiation of Indo-European languages arising from the contact-indiced shift hypothesis as presented here. (For further explanation, see text and note 2.)*

These developments gave rise to Neolithic cultures with roots in the local Mesolithic, or local Mesolithic traditions combined with new Neolithic traits. Such cultures are represented by the west Mediterranean Impressed Ware (Fig. 30.1:6b), the Iberian Neolithic (Fig. 30.1:7), the Chassey-Cortalloid cultures of France and Switzerland (Fig. 30.1:8), the Neolithic of the British Isles (Fig. 30.1:9), the Funnel Beaker cultures (Fig. 30.1:5), the Boat Axe / Corded Ware cultures in the east Baltic (Fig. 30.1:11) and the Dnepr-Donets culture (Fig. 30.1:10). Each of these cultural traditions included several regional groups and engendered later derivative cultures. Each of these traditions may have absorbed enclave-forming, limited immigration from farming communities in central Europe or the east Mediterranean; this is evident in the regional variation within these traditions (i.e. Zilhão 1993; Bogucki 1988). Since the process of agricultural transition was chronologically uneven and relatively slow (see above, *contra* Ammerman & Cavalli-Sforza 1984; Cavalli-Sforza 1997), it lasted for 4000 calendar years or longer as a whole.[2]

Against this cultural background, and within the social context of enduring agricultural frontier zones, Indo-European languages would diffuse through contact, inter-marriage and limited (individual, kin-based) migration, rather than demic diffusion or folk movement. Contact-induced language change is likely to have occurred where an Indo-European speech was adopted as a standard inter-community speech between the immigrant farming communities and several hunter-gatherer groups along the agricultural frontier, probably in situations of social asymmetry (see note 2; Zvelebil 1995b; 1996a; 1998).

The adoption of a common intercommunity speech in such a situation may have been an advantage. Instead of creating their own pidgin language, the Mesolithic communities may have been encouraged to adopt an Indo-European dialect for three reasons. First, such a language was probably uniform over the large area of distribution of the Linear Pottery Ware (at least initially), allowing the local foraging communities to communicate with the world of the farmers. Second, the wide distribution of such a language along the agricultural frontier in the centre of Europe would maximize its potential as a *lingua franca* among the hunter-gatherer communities as well. And third, the language of the farmers, as a language of innovation and of desired resources, would have enjoyed, at least temporarily, prestige status (see also Robb 1993).

The uncoupling of language dispersal and population movement has three important consequences:
1. the need is removed for finding archaeological evidence for population movements sufficiently widespread to explain Indo-European dispersals;
2. the contact-induced shift hypothesis does not require a parity between genetic and linguistic dispersal. On the contrary, in cases of language adoption through contact, the gene pool of the adopting population should be heterogeneous and/or different from the donor population;
3. cultural continuity may be preserved even if there is a language shift.

Conclusion

In conclusion, then, the assumption of marked population differences between prehistoric hunter-gatherers and Neolithic farmers is based on a misunderstanding of hunter-gatherers as always mobile and organisationally simple — yet in Mesolithic Europe there is evidence of socio-economic complexity and sedentism. Neolithic farmers were always assumed to be sedentary and very productive: yet in Neolithic Europe they were often transhumant or mobile, with mixed hunting-farming economies.

We have become far too used to the stereotypic notion of super-productive cereal farmers and livestock keepers, sedentary in white-washed villages amid the sea of wind-swept yellow corn. This image has more to do with Vincent van Gogh, or modern agriculture fed by EC subsidies, than with Neolithic farming. The evidence I present here shows that prehistoric reality may have been quite different. To paraphrase Mortimer Wheeler (1954), Neolithic farmers might have been 'as miserable a huddle of disease-ridden crofters as nature could encompass', while successful hunter-gatherers could pick and choose what they needed from the original Neolithic package of innovations in the process of creating their own, indigenous native farming community.

So, who were we 6000 years ago? At the broadest level, these studies tell us something about the identity of those first Neolithic farmers. They show that many of them — most in the north temperate and northern Europe — were in fact the local hunter-gatherers turned farmers. The evidence suggests that their genes, language and culture were not the same — they did not come from the same source, nor did they share the same ancestry. So for example, a Neolithic farmer from the north European plain might have been speaking a Proto-Germanic speech, but his genetic inheritance might have been Iberian and Uralic: his material culture was a mixture of indigenous Mesolithic and borrowed Neolithic elements. Or, an early farmer in Finland might have used a Proto-Finnic or Finno-Ugric language, but, especially if a woman, her genetic inheritance would have been mainly European, derived from the initial colonization of Scandinavia, and her material culture would have little in common with the materiality of the Neolithic world - it would have been almost entirely based on the local hunter-gatherer traditions.

Notes

1. This, however, may be due to specific historical conditions, which the Agta have to endure at the hands of the lowland Filipino population, who make the Agta subservient, take their land and currently are driving them into cultural and linguistic extinction (Bellwood pers. comm.). I am grateful to Peter Bellwood for this communication. See Headland 1997; Early & Headland 1998.

2. In northern Europe, the well-attested contacts between Linear Pottery and later derived traditions on the one hand and the local hunter-gatherer groups on the other led to the adoption of the 'Old European' speech and its evolution to an ancestral Germanic proto-language between 5500 and 4500 BP, in the context of the TRB culture. In eastern Europe, contacts between the Tripolye 'Old European' speakers and the Dnepr-Donets and related groups led to the adoption of farming and of the IE language, with subsequent evolution into a language ancestral to the Indo-Iranian and Balto-Slavic groups under the influence of the local population between 6000 and 5500 BP. With the development of nomadic pastoralism in southern Ukraine, the Indo-Iranian branch split off from the common ancestor and its speakers penetrated at first the lower Danube basin, and then later central and western Asia in the fourth millennium BP. Balto-Slavic continued to develop *in situ* in the middle Dnepr basin, the divergence between the two families occurring probably around 4000 BP or later with the adoption of farming in the East Baltic at the end of the Corded Ware/Boat Axe cultural horizon (Zvelebil 1995a; see Wiik 2000 for a similar framework)

The notions of the development of the Germanic and Balto-Slavic language communities through creolization and contact-induced language shift are now supported by an increasing number of linguists and archaeologists (Wiik 1999; 2000; Dolukhanov 1996; Renfrew 1999). Studies by Wiik, describing the borrowing (*lingua franca*) phase and shifting (adoption) phase in situations of enduring contact between communities of different language speakers, correspond very well to my own perception of hunter-gatherer communities in contact with farmers passing through three phases: availability, substitution and consolidation. Wiik lists at least 12 phonetic features in Germanic languages, grammatical features, and substrate elements of vocabulary as evidence that the original hunter-gatherer language in the northern part of Europe was Uralic, and that contact-induced language shift occurred in these regions from a Uralic speech to an IE one. At the same time, many linguists have drawn attention to the existence of substrate, non-Indo-European words in Celtic, Germanic and Italic languages which, in some cases, are linked by meaning into 'semantic fields'. It is significant, perhaps, that some native European flora and fauna are known in the IE languages of Europe by non-IE terms (such as apple or snake), or have a dual set of names, one of which is not IE (such as pig: Hamp 1987). Polomè (1987), draws attention to non-IE terms pertaining to hunting-gathering, such as 'spawn of a fish', dill, clover, dove; or geographical features important in hunting and fishing activities, such as 'narrow bay', or 'water hole in a marsh', while farming terminology is essentially Indo-European (Polomè 1987, 232). In summary, if this scenario is correct, the original speakers of a linguistic unit which gave rise to Germanic, Baltic and Slavic were genetically part of the same population as Uralic-speakers. They adopted Indo-European speech as a *lingua franca* or prestige language through contact-induced language shift.

References

Alexander, J., 1978. Frontier studies and the earliest farmers in Europe, in *Social Organisation and Settlement*, eds. D. Green, C. Haselgrove & M. Spriggs. (British Archaeological Reports International Series 47.) Oxford: BAR, 13–29.

Ammerman, A.J. & L.L. Cavalli-Sforza, 1984. *The Neolithic Transition and the Genetics of Population in Europe.* (Addison-Wesley Module in Anthropology 10.) Princeton (NJ): Princeton University Press.

Andersen, S.H., 1993. Mesolithic coastal settlement, in *Digging into the Past: 25 years of Archaeology in Denmark*, eds. S. Hvass & B. Storgaard. Jutland: Jutland Archaeological Society, 65–8.

Antanaitis, I., 1998. Interpreting the meaning of East Baltic Neolithic symbols. *Cambridge Archaeological Journal* 8(1), 55–68.

Antanaitis, I., 1999. Concerning the transition to farming in the East Baltic. *Documenta Praehistorica* 26, 89–100.

Anthony, D.W., 1990. Migration in archaeology: the baby and the bathwater. *American Anthropologist* 92, 895–914.

Arnaud, J.M., 1982. Neolithique ancien et processus de néolithisation dans le sud du Portugal. *Archeologie en Languedoc, no. special, Actes du Colloque International de Prehistoire*, 29–48.

Auban, J.B., 1997. Indigenism and migrationism: the neolithization of the Iberian Peninsula. *Porocilo* 24, 1–18.

Bandelt H.-J. & P. Forster, 1997. The myth of hunter-gatherer mismatch distributions. *American Journal of Human Genetics* 61, 980–83.

Barclay, G.J., 1997. The Neolithic, in Edwards & Ralston (eds.), 127–50.

Barker, G., 1985. *Prehistoric Farming in Europe.* Cambridge: Cambridge University Press.

Beneš, J., 1995. Erosion and accumulation processes in the Late Holocene of Bohemia, in relation to prehistoric and medieval landscape occupation, in *Whither Archaeology?*, eds. M. Kuna & N. Venclová. Prague: Institute of Archaeology, 133–44.

Beneš, J., 1998. Keramika ornice a reliéf. Vyzkum polykulturního osídlení v Kozlech, o. Louny (SZ Cechy), *Archeologické rozhledy* 50, 170–91.

Berglund, B.E. (ed.), 1990. *The Cultural Landscape During 6000 Years in Southern Sweden — the Ystad Project.* (Ecological Bulletin 41.) Copenhagen: Munksgaard.

Binford, L., 2001. *Constructing Frames of Reference: an Analytical Method for Archaeological Theory Building using Ethnographic and Environmental Data Aets.* Berkeley (CA): University of California Press.

Birdsell, J.B., 1953. Some environmental and cultural factors influencing the structuring of Australian Aboriginal populations. *American Naturalist* 87, 169–207.

Bogucki, P.I., 1988. *Forest Farmers and Stock Herders: Early Agriculture and its Consequences in North-Central Europe.* (New Studies in Archaeology.) Cambridge: Cambridge University Press.

Bonsall, C., R. Lennon, K. McSweeney, C. Stewart, D. Harkness, V. Boroneant, L. Bartosiewicz, R. Payton & R. Chapman, 1997. Mesolithic and early Neolithic in the Iron Gates: a palaeodietary perspective. *Journal of European Archaeology* 5.1, 50–92.

Bonsall, C., G. Cook, R. Lennon, D. Harkness, M. Scott, L. Bartosiewicz & K. McSweeney, 2000. Stable isotopes, radiocarbon and the Mesolithic–Neolithic transition in the Iron Gates. *Documenta Praehistorica* XXVII, 119–32.

Bottema, S., A. Entjes-Nieborg & W. van Zeist, 1990. *Man's role in the Shaping of Eastern Mediterranean Landscape.* Rotterdam: Bolkema.

Cavalli-Sforza, L.L., 1997. Genetic and cultural diversity in Europe. *Journal of Anthropological Research* 53, 383–404.

Cavalli-Sforza, L.L. & F. Cavalli-Sforza, 1995. *The Great Human Diasporas: the History of Diversity and Evolution.* New York (NY): Addison-Wesley.

Chapman, J., 1994. The origins of farming in South East Europe. *Préhistoire Européenne* 6, 133–56.

Chapman, J. & P. Dolukhanov, 1992. The baby and the bathwater: pulling the plug on migrations. *American*

Anthropologist 94, 169–75.

Childe, V.G., 1925. *The Dawn of European Civilisation.* 4th edition. London: Keegan Paul.

Childe, V.G., 1957. *The Dawn of European Civilisation.* 6th edition. London: Routledge & Kegan Paul.

Clark, J.G.D., 1966. The invasion hypothesis in British archaeology. *Antiquity* 40, 172–89.

Clarke, D.L., 1976. Mesolithic Europe: the economic basis, in *Problems in Economic and Social Archaeology*, eds. I. Sieveking, I.J. Longworth & K.E. Wilson. London: Duckworth, 449–81.

Cohen, J.E., 1995. *How Many People Can the Earth Support?* New York (NY): Norton.

Cohen, M.N., 1977. *The Food Crisis in Prehistory.* New Haven (CT): Yale University Press.

Cohen, M.N., 1989. *Health and the Rise of Civilization.* New Haven (CT): Yale University Press.

Cohen, M.N. & G.J. Armelagos, 1984. *Paleopathology at the Origins of Agriculture.* New York (NY): Academic Press.

Cooney, G., 1999. *Landscapes of Neolithic Ireland.* London: Routledge.

Deitz, M., 1988. A molluscan perspective on the role of foraging in Neolithic farming communities, in *The Archaeology of Prehistoric Coastlines*, eds. G. Bailey & J. Parkington. Cambridge: Cambridge University Press, 116–24.

Dennell, R., 1983. *European Economic Prehistory.* London: Academic Press.

Dennell, R., 1992. The origin of crop agriculture in Europe, in *The Origins of Agriculture: an International Perspective*, eds. C.W. Cowan & P.J. Watson. Washington (DC): Smithsonian Institution Press, 71–100.

Dolukhanov, P.M., 1979. *Ecology and Economy in Neolithic Eastern Europe.* London: Duckworth.

Dolukhanov, P.M., 1986. Natural environment and the holocene settlement pattern in the north-western Part of the USSR. *Fennoscandia archaeologica* 3, 3–16.

Dolukhanov, P.M., 1989. Cultural and ethnic processes in prehistory as seen through the evidence of archaeology and related disciplines, in *Archaeological Approaches to Cultural Identity*, ed. S.J. Shennan. London: Unwin Hyman, 267–77.

Dolukhanov, P.M., 1993. Foraging and farming groups in north-eastern and north-western Europe: identity and interaction, in *Cultural Transformations and Interactions in Eastern Europe*, eds. J. Chapman & P. Dolukhanov. Aldershot: Avebury Press, 122–45.

Dolukhanov, P.M., 1996. The Mesolithic/Neolithic transition in Europe: the view from the East. *Porocilo* 23, 49–60.

Early, J.D. & T. Headland, 1998. *Population Dynamics of a Philippine Rainforest People.* Talahassee (FL): University of Florida Press.

Edwards, K.J. & I.B.M. Ralston (eds.), 1997. *Scotland: Environment and Archaeology, 8000 BC–AD 1000.* Chichester: John Wiley & Sons.

Edwards, K.J. & G. Whittington, 1997. Vegetation history, in Edwards & Ralston (eds.), 63–82.

Emeneau, M.B., 1980. *Language and Linguistic Area.* Stanford (CA): Stanford University Press.

English Heritage, 1999. Research Frameworks for the Palaeolithic and Mesolithic of Britain and Ireland. A report by the Working Party for the Palaeolithic and Mesolithic Annual Day meeting and the Council of the Prehistoric Society.

Eronen, M., 1974. The history of the Litorina sea and asociated events. *Societas Scientiarum Fennica Commentationes Physico-Mathematicae* 44(4), 79–195.

Evison, M., 1999. Perspectives on the Holocene in Britain: human DNA. *Quaternary Proceedings* 7, 615–23.

Evison, M., 2001. Population studies using HLA. *Ancient Biomolecules* 4, 1–14.

Evison, M., N. Fieller & D.M. Smillie, 1999. Ancient HLA: a preliminary survey. *Ancient Biomolecules* 3, 1–28.

Finlayson, B. & K.J. Edwards, 1997. The Mesolithic, in Edwards & Ralston (eds.), 109–26.

Froment, A., 2001. Evolutionary biology and health of hunter-gatherer populations, in Panter-Brick *et al.* (eds.), 239–66.

Green, S.W. & M. Zvelebil, 1990. The Mesolithic colonization and agricultural transition of south-east Ireland. *Proceedings of the Prehistoric Society* 56, 57–88.

Gronenborn, D., 1998. Altestbandkeramische Kultur, La Hoguette, Limburg, and . . . What else — contemplating the Mesolithic–Neolithic transition in southern Central Europe. *Documenta Praehistorica* 25, 189–202.

Hammel, G., 1996. Demographic constraints in population growth of early humans. *Human Nature* 7(3), 217–55.

Hamp, E.P., 1987. The pig in ancient northern Europe, in *Proto-Indo-European: the Archaeology of a Linguistic Problem*, eds. S.N. Skomal & E.C. Polomè. Washington (DC): Institute for the Study of Man, 185–90.

Harpending, H.C., M.A. Batzer, M. Gurven, L.B. Jorde, A.R. Rogers & S.T. Sherry, 1998. Genetic traces of ancient demography. *Proceedings of the National Academy of Sciences of the USA* 95, 1961–7.

Harris, D. (ed.), 1996. *The Origin and Spread of Agriculture and Pastoralism in Eurasia.* London: UCL Press.

Hassan, F., 1975. Determination of the size, density, and growth rate of hunting-gathering populations, in Polgar (ed.), 27–53.

Hassan, F., 1978. Demographic archaeology, in *Advances in Archaeological Method and Theory* vol. 1, ed. M. Schiffer. New York (NY): Academic Press, 49–103.

Hassan, F., 1985. *Demographic Archaeology.* New York (NY): Academic Press.

Headland, T., 1997 Limitation of human rights – Agta Negritos. *Human Organisation* 56, 79–90.

Hodder, I., 1990. *The Domestication of Europe.* Oxford: Blackwell.

Housley, R.A., C.S. Gamble, M. Street & P. Pettitt, 1997. Radiocarbon evidence for the Lateglacial Human Recolonisation of Northern Europe. *Proceedings of the Prehistoric Society* 63, 25–54.

Jochim, M.A., 1998. *A Hunter-Gatherer Landscape: South-*

west Germany in the Late Paleolithic and Mesolithic. New York (NY): Plenum Press.

Julku, K. & K. Wiik (eds.), 1998. *The Roots of Peoples and Languages of Northern Eurasia,* vol. I. Turku: Societas Historiae Fenno-Ugricae.

Keeley, I., 1988. Hunter-gatherer economic complexity and population pressure: a cross-cultural analysis. *Journal of Anthropological Archaeology* 7, 343–411.

Keeley, L.H., 1992. The introduction of agriculture to the western North European Plain, in *Transitions to Agriculture in Prehistory,* eds. A.B. Gebauer & T.D. Price, (Monographs in World Archaeology 4.) Madison (WI): Prehistory Press, 81–97.

King, R. & P.A. Underhill, 2002. Congruent distribution of Neolithic painted pottery and ceramic figurines with Y-chromosome lineages. *Antiquity* 73, 707–14.

Künnap, A. (ed.), 2000. *The Roots of Peoples and Languages of Northern Eurasia,* vols. II & III. Tartu: Societas Historiae Finno-Ugricae.

Lahr, M.M., R.A. Foley & R. Pinhasi, 2000. Expected regional patterns of Mesolithic–Neolithic human population admixture in Europe based on archaeological evidence, in Renfrew & Boyle (eds.), 81–8.

Larsson, L., 1990. The Mesolithic of southern Scandinavia. *Journal of World Prehistory* 4(3), 257–91.

Layton, R.H., 2001. Hunter-gatherers, their neighbours and the nation state, in Panter-Brick *et al.* (eds.), 292–321.

Lillie, M.C., 1997. Women and children in prehistory: resource sharing and social stratification at the Mesolithic–Neolithic transition in Ukraine, in *Invisible People and Processes: Writing Gender and Childhood into European Archaeology,* eds. J. Moore & E. Scott. London: Leicester University Press, 213–28.

Lourandos, H., 1985. Intensification and Australian prehistory, in Price & Brown (eds.) 1985b, 385–423.

MacEachern, S., 2000. Genes, tribes and African history. *Current Anthropology* 41(4), 357–86.

Mieklejohn C. & M. Zvelebil, 1991. Health status of European populations at the agricultural transition and the implications for the adoption of farming, in *Health in Past Societies: Biocultural Interpretations of Human Skeletal Remains in Archaeological Contexts,* eds. H. Bush & M. Zvelebil. (British Archaeological Reports International Series 567.) Oxford: BAR, 129–45.

Meiklejohn, C., E. Brinch Petersen & V. Alexandersen, 2000. The anthropology and archaeology of Mesolithic gender in the western Baltic, in *Gender and Material Culture in Archaeological Perspective,* eds. M. Donald & L. Hurcombe. Basingstoke: MacMillan Press Ltd, 222–37.

Midgley, M., 1992. *TRB Culture.* Edinburgh: Edinburgh University Press.

Moss, T.L., 1993. Shellfish, gender and status on the northwest coast: reconciling archaeological, ethnographic and ethnohistorical records of the Tlingit. *American Anthropologist* 95, 631–52.

Naroll, R., 1962. Floor area and settlement population. *American Antiquity* 27, 587–9.

Needham, S. & M.G. Macklin (eds.), 1992. *Alluvial Archaeology in Britain.* (Oxbow Monograph 27.) Oxford: Oxbow.

Neustupny, E., 1982. Prehistoric migrations by infiltration. *Archeologické rozhledy* 34, 278–93.

Niskanen, M., 1998. The genetic relationships of northern and central Europeans in light of craniometric measurements and gene frequencies, in Julku & Wiik (eds.), 133–49.

Nowak, M., 2001. The second phase of Neolithization in east-central Europe. *Antiquity* 75, 582–92.

Nuñez, M., 1990. On subneolithic pottery and its adoption in late Mesolithic Finland. *Fennoscandia archaeologica* 7, 27–50.

Nuñez, M., 1997. Finland's settling model revisited. *Helsinki Papers in Archaeology* 10, 93–102.

Otte, M., 1990. The Northwestern European plain around 18,000 BP, in *The World at 18,000 BP,* vol. 1: *High Latitudes,* eds. O. Soffer & C. Gamble. London: Unwin Hyman, 54–68.

Panter-Brick, C., R.H. Layton & P. Rowley-Conwy (eds.), 2001. *Hunter-gatherers: an Interdisciplinary Perspective.* Cambridge: Cambridge University Press.

Pennington, R., 2001. Hunter-gatherer demography, in Panter-Brick *et al.* (eds.), 170–204.

Piggott, S., 1965. *Ancient Europe.* Edinburgh: Edinburgh University Press.

Pinhasi, R., R.A. Foley & M.M. Lahr, 2000. Spatial and temporal patterns in the Mesolithic–Neolithic archaeological record of Europe, in Renfrew & Boyle (eds.), 45–56.

Plog, F., 1975. Demographic studies in southwestern prehistory, in Population Studies in Archaeology and Biological Anthropology, ed. A.C. Swedlund. *Society for American Archaeology Memoirs* 30, 94–103.

Polgar, S. (ed.), 1975. *Population Ecology and Social Evolution.* Chicago (IL): Mouton.

Price, T.D., 1987. The Mesolithic of Western Europe. *Journal of World Prehistory* 1, 225–332.

Price, T.D., 1989. The reconstruction of Mesolithic diets, in *The Mesolithic in Europe,* ed. C. Bonsall. Edinburgh: John Donald Publishers, 48–59.

Price, T.D., 1991. The Mesolithic of western Europe. *Annual Review of Anthropology* 20, 211–33.

Price, T.D., 1996. The first farmers of southern Scandinavia, in Harris (ed.), 346–63.

Price, T.D. (ed.), 2000. *Europe's First Farmers.* Cambridge: Cambridge University Press.

Price, T.D. & J.A. Brown, 1985a. Aspects of hunter-gatherer complexity, in Price & Brown (eds.) 1985b, 3–20.

Price, T.D. & J.A. Brown (eds.), 1985b. *Prehistoric Hunter-Gatherers: the Emergence of Cultural Complexity.* Orlando (FL): Academic Press.

Renfrew, C., 1987. *Archaeology and Language: the Puzzle of Indo-European Origins.* London: Jonathan Cape.

Renfrew, C., 1992. Archaeology, genetics and linguistic diversity. *Man* 27, 445–78.

Renfrew, C., 1996. Language families and the spread of farming, in Harris (ed.), 70–93.

Renfrew, C., 1998. Word of Minos: the Minoan contribution to Mycenaean Greek and the linguistic geography of the Bronze Age Aegean. *Cambridge Archaeological Journal* 8(2), 239–64.

Renfrew, C., 1999. Time depth, convergence theory and innovation in Proto-Indo-European: 'Old Europe' as a PIE linguistic area. *Journal of Indo-European Studies* 27, 257–93.

Renfrew, C., 2000a. At the edge of knowability: towards a prehistory of languages. *Cambridge Archaeological Journal* 10(1), 7–34.

Renfrew, C., 2000b. Archaeogenetics: towards a population prehistory of Europe, in Renfrew & Boyle (eds.), 1–11.

Renfrew, C. & K. Boyle (eds.), 2000. *Archaeogenetics: DNA and the Population of Prehistory of Europe.* (McDonald Institute Monographs.) Cambridge: McDonald Institute for Archaeological Research.

Renouf, M.A.P., 1998. Sedentary coastal hunter-fishers: an example from the Younger Stone age of Northern Norway, in *The Archaeology of Prehistoric Coastlines,* eds. G. Bailey & J. Parkington. Cambridge: Cambridge University Press, 102–16.

Richards, M. & C. Macaulay, 2000b. Genetic data and the colonization of Europe: genealogies and founders, in Renfrew & Boyle (eds.), 139–52.

Richards, M., H. Côrte-Real, P. Forster, V. Macaulay, A. Demaine, S. Papiha, R. Hedges, H.-J. Bandelt & B. Sykes, 1996. Palaeolithic and Neolithic lineages in the European mitochondrial gene pool. *American Journal of Human Genetics* 59, 185–203.

Richards, M., V.A. Macaulay, H.-J. Bandelt & B.C. Sykes, 1998a. Phylogeography of mitochondrial DNA in western Europe. *Annals of Human Genetics* 62, 241–60.

Richards, M., S. Oppenheimer & B. Sykes, 1998b. MtDNA suggests Polynesian origins in eastern Indonesia. *American Journal of Human Genetics* 63, 1234–6.

Richards, M., V. Macaulay, E. Hickey, E. Vega, B. Sykes, V. Guida, C. Rengo, D. Sellitto, F. Cruciani, T. Kivisild, R. Villems, M. Thomas, S. Rychkov, O. Rychkov, Y. Rychkov, M. Golge, D. Dimitrov, E. Hill, D. Bradley, V. Romano, F. Calí, G. Vona, A. Demaine, S. Papiha, C. Triantaphyllidis, G. Stefanescu, J. Hatina, M. Belledi, A. di Rienzo, A. Novelletto, A. Oppenheim, S. Norby, N. Al-Zaheri, S. Santachiara-Benerecetti, R. Scozzari, A. Torroni & H.-J. Bandelt, 2000. Tracing European founder lineages in the near eastern mtDNA pool. *American Journal of Human Genetics* 67, 1251–76.

Robb, J., 1993. A social prehistory of European languages. *Antiquity* 67, 747–60.

Ross, M., 1999. Social networks and kinds of speech-community event, in *Archaeology and Language,* vol. I: *Theoretical and Methodological Orientations,* eds. R. Blench & M. Spriggs. (One World Archaeology.) London & New York (NY): Routledge.

Rouja, P.M., 2002. Fishing for Fat: the Link between Sustainable Marine Resource Use and Human Health in the Bardi Fishery. Unpublished paper given at CHAGS conference, Edinburgh, September 2002.

Rowley-Conwy, P., 1983. Sedentary hunters, the Ertebølle example, in *Hunter-Gatherer Economy in Prehistory,* ed. G.N. Bailey. Cambridge: Cambridge University Press, 111–26.

Rowley-Conwy, P., 1999. Economic prehistory in Southern Scandinavia. *Proceedings of the British Academy* 99, 125–59.

Schulting, R., 1999. Slighting the sea: stable isotope evidence for the transition to farming in north-western Europe. *Documenta Praehistorica* XXV, 5th Neolithic Studies, 203–18.

Schulting, R. & M.P. Richards, 2001. Dating women and becoming farmers: new palaeodietary and AMS dating evidence from the Breton Mesolithic Cemeteries of Téviec and Hoëdic. *Journal of Anthropological Archaeology* 20(3), 314–44.

Semino, O., G. Passarino, A. Brega, M. Fellous & A.S. Santachiara-Benerecetti, 1996. A view of the neolithic demic diffusion in Europe through two Y chromosome-specific markers. *American Journal of Human Genetics* 59, 964–8.

Semino, O., G. Passarino, P.J. Oefner, A.A. Lin, S. Arbuzova L.E. Beckman, G. de Benedictis, P. Francalacci, A. Kouvatsi, S. Limborska, M. Marcikiae, A. Mika, B. Mika, D. Primorac, A.S. Santachiara-Benerecetti, L.L. Cavalli-Sforza & P.A. Underhill, 2000. The genetic legacy of paleolithic *Homo sapiens sapiens* in extant Europeans: a Y-chromosome perspective. *Science* 290, 1155–9.

Sherratt, A.G., 1981. Plough and pastoralism: aspects of the secondary products revolution, in *Pattern of the Past: Studies in Honour of David Clarke,* eds. I. Hodder, G. Isaac & N. Hammond. Cambridge: Cambridge University Press, 261–305.

Sherratt, A.G. & S. Sherratt, 1988. The archaeology of Indo-European: an alternative view. *Antiquity* 62, 584–95.

Simoni, L., F. Calafell, D. Pettener, J. Bertranpetit & G. Barbujani, 2000. Geographic patterns of mtDNA diversity in Europe. *American Journal of Human Genetics* 66, 262–78.

Sims-Williams, P., 1998. Genetics, linguistics and prehistory: thinking big and thinking straight. *Antiquity* 72, 505–27.

Smith, A.G., 1981. The Neolithic, in *The Environment in British Prehistory,* eds. I.G. Simmons & M. Tooley. London: Duckworth, 125–8, 133–83, 199–209.

Speth, J.D., 1990. Seasonality, resource stress, and food sharing in so-called 'egalitarian' foraging societies. *Journal of Anthropological Archaeology* 9, 148–88.

Taavitsainen, J.-P., 1998. Cultivation history beyond the periphery: early agriculture in the north European boreal forest. *Journal of World Prehistory* 12(2), 199–253.

Tauber, H., 1981. C13 evidence for dietary habits of prehistoric man in Denmark. *Nature* 292, 332–3.

Thomas, J., 1988. Neolithic explanations revisited: the Mesolithic–Neolithic transition in Britain and south Scandinavia. *Proceedings of the Prehistoric Society* 54,

59–66.

Thomas, J., 1991. The hollow men? A reply to Steve Mithen. *Proceedings of the Prehistoric Society* 57(2), 15–20.

Thomas, J., 1996. The cultural context of the first use of domesticates in continental Central and Northwest Europe, in Harris (ed.), 310–22.

Thomason, S.G. & T. Kaufman 1988. *Language Contact, Creolization, and Genetic Linguistics*. Berkeley (CA): University of California Press.

Thorpe, I.J., 1996. *The Origins of Agriculture in Europe*. London: Routledge.

Tichy, R., 1999. *Monoxylon II. Plavba po 8000 letech*. Nachod: JB Production.

Tichy, R., 2001. *Expedice Monoxylon. Pochazime z mladsi doby kamenne*. Spolecnost experimentalni archeologie a JB Production, Hradec Kralove.

Tilley, C., 1994. *A Phenomenology of Landscape*. Oxford: Berg.

Tilley, C., 1996. *An Ethnography of the Neolithic*. Cambridge: Cambridge University Press.

Torroni, A., H.-J. Bandelt, L. D'Urbano, P. Laherno, P. Moral, D. Sellito, C. Rengo, P. Forster, M.-L. Savontaus, B. Bonné-Tamir & R. Scozzari, 1998. MtDNA analysis reveals a major Late Palaeolithic population expansion from southwestern to northeastern Europe. *American Journal of Human Genetics* 62, 1137–52.

Underhill, P.A., P.D. Shen, A.A. Lin, L. Jin, G. Passarino, W.H. Yang, E. Kauffman, B. Bonné-Tamir, J. Bertranpetit, P. Francalacci, M. Ibrahim, T. Jenkins, J.R. Kidd, S.Q. Mehdi, M.T. Seielstad, R.S. Wells, A. Piazza, R.W. Davis, M.W. Feldman, L.L. Cavalli-Sforza & P.J. Oefner, 2000. Y chromosome sequence variation and the history of human populations. *Nature Genetics* 26, 358–61.

Underhill, P.A., G. Passarino, A.A. Lin, P. Shen, M.M. Lahr, R.A. Foley, P.J. Oefner & L.L. Cavalli-Sforza, 2001. The phylogeography of Y chromosome binary haplotypes and the origins of modern human populations. *Annals of Human Genetics* 65, 43–62.

van Andel, T.H. & C.N. Runnells, 1995. The earliest farmers in Europe. *Antiquity* 69, 481–500.

Vencl, S., 1995. K otazce verohodností svedectví povrchovych pruzkumu. *Archeologicke rozhledy* 47, 11–51.

Vera, F.W.M., 2000. *Grazing Ecology and Forest History*. Oxford: CABI Publishing

Villems, R., 1998. Reconstruction of maternal lineages of Finno-Ugric speaking people and some remarks on their paternal inheritance, in Julku & Wiik (eds.), 180–200.

Voytek, B. & R. Tringham, 1989: Rethinking the Mesolithic: the case of Southeast Europe, in *The Mesolithic in Europe*, C. Bonsall. Edinburgh: John Donald, 492–500.

Webb, S., 1995. *Palaeopathology of Aboriginal Australians*. Cambridge: Cambridge University Press.

Wheeler, M., 1954. *Archaeology from the Earth*. Harmondsworth: Penguin Books.

Whittle, A., 1996. *Europe in the Neolithic*. Cambridge: Cambridge University Press.

Wiik, K., 1999. Some ancient and modern linguistic processes in northern Europe, in *Time Depth in Historical Linguistics*, eds. C. Renfrew, A. McMahon & L. Trask. (Papers in the Prehistory of Languages.) Cambridge: McDonald Institute for Archaeological Research, 463–79.

Wiik, K., 2000. European *Lingua Francas*, in Künnap (ed.), 202–36.

Willis, K.J. & K.D. Bennett, 1994. The Neolithic transition — fact or fiction? Palaeoecological evidence from the Balkans. *The Holocene* 4, 326–30.

Willis, K.J., P. Sümeg, M. Braun, K.D. Bennett & A. Toth, 1998. Prehistoric land degradation in Hungary: who, how and why? *Antiquity* 72, 111–13.

Woodman, P. & E. Anderson, 1990. The Irish later Mesolithic: a partial picture?, in *Contributions to the Mesolithic in Europe*, eds. P.M. Vermeersch & P. Van Peer. Leuven: Leuven University Press.

Zilhão, J., 1993. The spread of agro-pastoral economies across Mediterranean Europe: view from the far west. *Journal of Mediterranean Archaeology* 6, 5–63.

Zilhão, J., 1997. Maritime pioneer colonisation in the Early Neolithic of the west Mediterranean. Testing the model against the evidence. *Porocilo* 24, 19–42.

Zilhão, J., 2000. From the Mesolithic to the Neolithic in the Iberian peninsula, in Price (ed.), 144–82.

Zvelebil, M., 1981. *From Forager to Farmer in the Boreal Zone*. (British Archaeological Reports, International Series, 115.) Oxford: BAR.

Zvelebil, M., 1983. Site catchment analysis and hunter-gatherer resource use, in *Ecological Models in Economic Prehistory*, ed. G. Bronitsky. (Anthropological Research Papers 29.) Tempe (AZ): Arizona State University, 73–114.

Zvelebil, M., 1986a. Postglacial foraging in the forests of Europe. *Scientific American* 254(5), 104–15.

Zvelebil, M. (ed.), 1986b. *Hunters in Transition: Mesolithic Societies of Temperate Eurasia and their Transition to Farming*. Cambridge: Cambridge University Press.

Zvelebil, M., 1989. On the transition to farming in Europe, or what was spreading with the Neolithic: a reply to Ammerman (1989). *Antiquity* 63, 379–83.

Zvelebil, M., 1995a. Neolithization in Eastern Europe: a view from the frontier. *Porocilo* 22, 107–50.

Zvelebil, M., 1995b. At the interface of archaeology, linguistics and genetics: Indo-European dispersals and the agricultural transition in Europe. *Journal of European Archaeology* 3(1), 33–70.

Zvelebil, M., 1996a. Agricultural frontier and the transition to farming in the circum-Baltic area, in Harris (ed.), 323–45.

Zvelebil, M., 1996b. Ideology, society, and economy of the Mesolithic communities in temperate and northern Europe. *Origini. Preistoria E Protostoria delle Civiltà Antiche* 20, 39–70.

Zvelebil, M., 1998. Agricultural frontiers, Neolithic origins, and the transition to farming in the Baltic Basin, in Zvelebil *et al.* (eds.), 9–28.

Zvelebil, M., 2000a. The social context of the agricultural transition in Europe, in Renfrew & Boyle (eds.), 57–79.

Zvelebil, M., 2000b. Les dernieres chasseur-collecteurs d'Europe temperee [The last hunter-gatherers of temperate Europe], in *Les Derniere Chasseurs-cueilleurs d'Europe occidentale*, eds. C. Cuppilard & A. Richard. Besancon: Presses Universitaires de Franche-Comte, 360–406.

Zvelebil, M. & M. Lillie, 2000. Transition to agriculture in eastern Europe, in Price (ed.), 57–92.

Zvelebil, M. & K.V. Zvelebil, 1988. Agricultural transition and Indo-European dispersals. *Antiquity* 62, 574–83.

Zvelebil, M., S.W. Green & M.G. Macklin, 1992. Archaeological landscapes, lithic scatters and human behaviour, in *Space, Time and Archaeological Landscapes*, eds. J. Rossignol & L. Wandsnider. New York (NY) & London: Plenum Press, 193–226.

Zvelebil, M., M.G. Macklin, D.G. Passmore & P. Ramsden, 1996. Alluvial archaeology in the Barrow Valley, southeast Ireland: the 'Riverford culture' re-visited. *Journal of Irish Archaeology* 7, 13–40.

Zvelebil, M., R. Dennell & L. Domanska (eds.), 1998. *Harvesting the Sea, Farming the Forest*. Sheffield: Sheffield Academic Press.

Chapter 31

Pioneer Farmers?
The Neolithic Transition in Western Europe

Chris Scarre

Many recent interpretations of the Neolithic transition in Europe have tended to take a polemical approach: arguing that the process should be seen as one of indigenous acculturation. Such indigenist approaches have been favoured especially by several British archaeologists, who see little rôle for demographic movements, especially in western Europe. Models of demographic displacement have indeed come to be widely mistrusted through their association with an earlier and less critically-aware period of archaeological interpretation in which diffusionism and invasion were frequently invoked to explain cultural and economic change. It was not until the 1960s that a more anthropologically-informed approach seriously began to question the value of invasion and migration as explanatory models in archaeology (e.g. Clark 1966; Renfrew 1969). Paradoxically, however, it was at around the same time that an influential series of articles began to appear which argued that the spread of farming across Europe, as revealed by the newly available C14 dates, could be explained by a 'wave of advance' model of demographic growth and expansion (Ammerman & Cavalli-Sforza 1971; 1973; 1984).

The 'wave of advance' model of farming-spread, beginning in Southeast Europe and ending at the northern and western fringes, has subsequently been invoked to explain patterns of linguistic change (notably the spread of the Indo-European languages: Renfrew 1987) and genetic composition (Cavalli-Sforza et al. 1994). Such models have their attractions: it is clear that the domestic plants and animals used by early European farmers did originate ultimately from wild forms present in the Near East. It is also generally accepted that Indo-European languages were most likely first spoken somewhere in eastern Europe or western Asia. In both cases, an east–west movement is implied. The problem from

an archaeological perspective, however, has been the mechanisms invoked to account for these movements. What may seem a plausible hypothesis in the abstract — that farming and Indo-European languages reached western Europe through demic diffusion of the farmers or language-speakers themselves — breaks down when confronted with the archaeological evidence for the nature of the Neolithic transition in individual regions. It is difficult to argue that the Indo-European language distribution in Europe is the result of a single uniform Indo-European 'process'.

Thus, the first problem is the disconformity between continent-wide explanations of linguistic and genetic change, and the regional or local archaeological sequences which seek to study changes happening to specific prehistoric communities within short spans of time: generations, centuries, or perhaps even decades where dendrochronology allows such precise dating. One example where close dating is possible is the Combe d'Ain, a narrow steep-sided valley in the Jura Mountains of eastern France. Here research by Pétrequin and colleagues has illustrated the detailed sequence of colonization, growth and abandonment of Neolithic farming settlements around the shores of Lakes Chalain and Clairvaux. In the period 3200–2900 BC the number of villages rose from one per lakeside to a total of nine in c. 2980 BC, before declining sharply again until the area was totally abandoned by 2900 BC (Pétrequin et al. 1998). It might be objected that the Alpine foothills are marginal to the principal farming zones of western Europe, and furthermore that this steep-sided valley was particularly vulnerable to rising lake levels and local environmental degradation. On the other hand, research in other areas supports the view that such cycles of colonization and abandonment, involving small-scale movements of people, were a regular

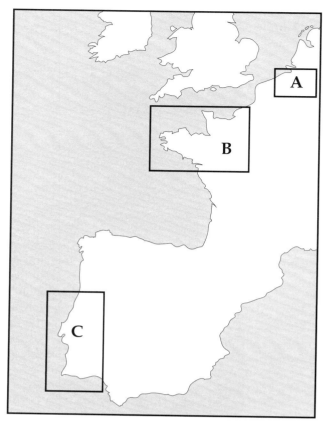

Figure 31.1. *Western Europe showing location of the three study-areas. A) Rhine-Meuse estuary; B) Northern France; C) Portugal.*

feature of the West European Neolithic (Scarre 2001). It furthermore brings to the fore the concept of space: that western Europe may not have been densely populated at this time, and that less attractive areas may have been settled and abandoned several times before permanent, continuous occupation ensued.

We may therefore be justified in assuming small-scale population movements throughout the Neolithic period. It remains nonetheless extremely difficult — outside exceptional contexts such as the Alpine lakeland — to recognize such movements with any degree of confidence in specific patterns of archaeological evidence. For many previous generations of archaeologists, pottery types, as markers of 'cultures', have traditionally been associated with the notion of 'peoples', and their distributions, expansions and contractions have been held to chart ethnic movements. Such views command little support today, unless backed up by other evidence. Yet the opposite extreme, in which demic diffusion is rejected almost as an article of faith, is equally unsatisfactory. The reality, I suggest, is likely to lie some-

where in between. It is also necessary to consider whether patterns of language and genetics might be the cumulative outcome of numerous small-scale events, rather than regional or even continent-wide phenomena. This applies especially to interpretations that link these changes to the Neolithic transition and the spread of farming. The Neolithic transition in western Europe is now widely regarded as a mosaic-type event, in which the movement of colonist-farmers (perhaps in small numbers, or over relatively short distances) was interspersed with the indigenous adoption of pottery and domesticates by Mesolithic hunter-gatherers.

1. The mosaic pattern of Neolithic transition: the Rhine/Meuse delta

The mosaic-type pattern of Neolithic transition may be demonstrated by the Rhine/Meuse delta (Fig. 31.1), which illustrates the pattern of early farming settlement across contrasting environmental zones. The southern edge of the Rhine delta is marked by fertile, well-drained loams (part of the classic loess lands) in the south, bordered by low-lying, relatively infertile sandy soils to the north. North of the sands are the wetlands of the Rhine delta proper, which, like the sands, were unattractive to early cultivators. The fertile loess soils of the south, on the other hand, were prime agricultural territory, and were exploited by farming communities of Linearbandkeramik (LBK) tradition from as early as *c.* 5500 BC. Yet these farmers were not the only communities of the region, for the sandy and estuarine areas to the north had long been occupied by hunter-gatherers (Fig. 31.2). It is clear that there were contacts between the farmers and their hunter-gatherer neighbours — LBK material (in the form notably of adzes) began to circulate among the Mesolithic hunter-gatherer communities of the sandy zone — but each retained their separate identities.

The absence of known Mesolithic sites from the loess lands of this region may reflect their preference for the sandy or estuarine areas, or could be attributed to processes of erosion consequent upon the intensive cultivation of the loess. Hence it is possible that Mesolithic communities were actively exploiting the loess lands before the LBK long-house communities became established. Whatever the case, the LBK communities appear very rapidly to have either displaced or absorbed the Mesolithic loess-land communities; earlier claims for Mesolithic influence on the LBK flintwork of the region (Newell 1970) have recently been dismissed (Vermeersch 1991) though

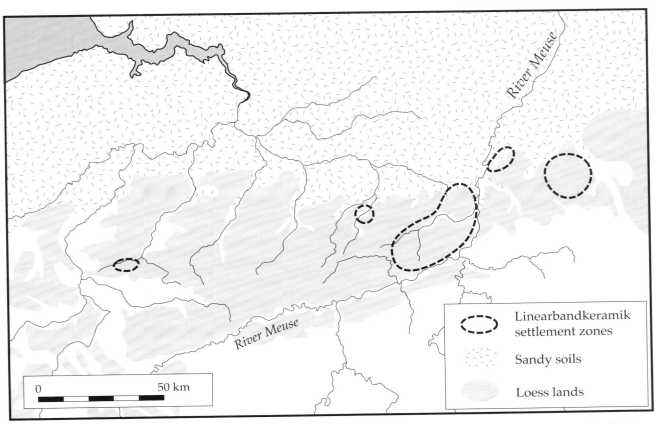

Figure 31.2. *Location of Bandkeramik settlement zones on loess lands south of the Rhine-Meuse estuary; Mesolithic groups continued to occupy sandy soils to the north.*

hybrid populations, combining indigenes and new-comers, remain a possibility (Lodewijckx & Bakels 2000).

The Neolithic transition in the sandy zone be-longs to a much later period, and is associated with Michelsberg (Middle Neolithic) material (from *c.* 4600 BC). Michelsberg material is characteristic of the Mid-dle Neolithic arable settlements of the loess land that succeed the LBK. It is also found at sites in the sandy zone that are interpreted as temporary camps. These camps may indicate that farming communities were now beginning to exploit the sandy zones, perhaps in a seasonal pattern in which cattle were pastured on the sandy soils in the summer, and brought back to the major loess-land settlements in the winter. Alongside such seasonal transhumance, there is evi-dence for increased contact between farmers and foragers in the circulation of flint from the mines at Rijkholt-Sint-Geertruid (Gronenborn 1999, 168). Vermeersch suggests that seasonal exploitation of the sandy zones led to deforestation and the incor-poration of the remaining Mesolithic communities into Neolithic communities, through the recruitment

of the hunter-gatherers as herders (Vermeersch 1991, 477). The result may have been a degradation of the environment which at the same time diminished or deprived the Mesolithic hunter-gatherers of their tra-ditional wild resources (Arias 1999, 434). The inte-gration of Mesolithic populations in the Michelsberg farming communities is suggested by flint assem-blages from loess-land Michelsberg settlements such as Thieusies, where the blades are identical to those of Final Mesolithic assemblages and there is also a microlithic element (Vermeersch 1991, 475).

This model assumes that the LBK settlement of the loess lands was the consequence of colonist farm-ers, who first co-existed with and then absorbed the indigenous hunter-gatherers. Elsewhere in Belgium, in the Hesbaye region, a case has been made for confrontation of a violent nature between LBK and Mesolithic groups (Keeley & Cahen 1989; Cahen *et al.* 1990). Distribution patterns show tight clusters of LBK sites in areas largely devoid of Late Mesolithic material. Excavation at Darion, one of these LBK sites, revealed a settlement surrounded by a sub-stantial V-sectioned enclosure ditch backed by an internal palisade. In the southern part of the enclosure were postholes of four classic LBK long-houses; the rest of the enclosure was interpreted as protected pasture. Excavations at the nearby LBK settlements of Longchamps and Oleye revealed a similar arrangement, with long-houses standing inside a ditched and palisade enclosure. At Oleye, the houses had been burned although it was not possible to say whether this was a result of hostile action. Nonetheless, at both Darion and Oleye Mesolithic arrowheads were found in pits, and Keeley and colleagues interpret these sites as fortified enclosures intended to provide protection for colonizing farmers against indigenous hunter-gatherers (Keeley & Cahen 1989, 171). A similar interpretation has been proposed for the enclosure at Esbeck, on the northern edge of the LBK zone (Fansa & Thieme 1985).

Persuasive though it may be, especially when coupled with imaginative reconstruction drawings of the defensive arrangements (Bosquet 1993), the interpretation of Darion and the other sites is not beyond question. In the Langweiler area, just across the border into western Germany, enclosures appear in a late stage of the LBK sequence and are not associated with an initial colonizing movement into hostile terrain (Stehli 1989). Furthermore, closer scrutiny of the plans of the Belgian Hesbaye enclosures raises other doubts. At Oleye and Longchamps, LBK houses were located both within and outside the enclosure, though this may represent occupation over multiple phases. Lüning has questioned whether the houses and enclosures are contemporary at any of these Belgian sites, or whether the enclosures belong to a later stage (Lüning 1998). Furthermore, at Darion, the discontinuous nature of the ditch and the width of the entrances detract from the impression that this might be a defensive enclosure. Alternative interpretations may be proposed, including use as a livestock kraal or for ritual purposes. Other LBK enclosures have been interpreted in these ways (Bogucki & Grygiel 1993).

Leaving aside the interpretation of LBK enclosures, the colonist interpretation of the LBK as a whole has come under increasing scrutiny in recent years from those who favour an indigenist model. One view suggests that the expansion of LBK settlements may represent the transformation of central European woodland populations, and the long-house interior, 'busy with wood', could be construed as the 'enculturation' of the surrounding forest of trees, associated perhaps with 'the animistic concerns of forager beliefs' (Whittle 1996, 25). That LBK houses with their large internal posts were overbuilt in engineering terms is well-established (Coudart 1998), and the visualization of the long-house interior as a forest of posts is a valuable insight, though there is no reason why this should relate to an indigenous acculturation model, rather than to colonist forest-farmers. Other 'indigenist' arguments draw on the level of diversity within the LBK:

> In the final analysis, the regional variations on the uniform LPC [Linearbandkeramik] theme were already distinguishable in the earliest phase . . . Such a pattern is only conceivable when a background already exists. The framework could only have been provided by the Mesolithic peoples who were familiar with organizing in bands. (Modderman 1988, 130)

Yet most authors place greatest emphasis on the regularities within the LBK, such as the uniformity of settlement locations and house forms across a broad band of territory from Moravia to eastern France, which Bogucki & Grygiel interpret as the mark of an essentially conservative frontier society:

> Even on the North European Plain, in an environment quite different from the loess belt, the settlements at Brzesc Kujawski and elsewhere in central Poland represent attempts to initially replicate the socio-economic patterns found elsewhere in temperate Europe. (Bogucki & Grygiel 1993, 421)

If the balance of evidence still favours the colonist model of LBK origins, that does not in itself explain the fate that befell the indigenous Mesolithic communities. The scarcity of Mesolithic material in LBK settlements could be attributed to a difference in terrain preferences: the Mesolithic communities preferring wetlands and areas of poor soil, the LBK communities opting for the fertile well-draining loess (Modderman 1988, 128). On the western edge of the LBK zone, however, there is clear evidence for interaction with non-LBK groups, in the form of Late Mesolithic flintwork, and non-LBK pottery styles (Limburg and La Hoguette). Furthermore, contact between LBK groups and their neighbours can be shown from the use of Rijkholt and Louisberg flint from Holland by earliest LBK communities, whose closest settlements at this stage still lay over 100 km to the east. The likeliest explanation is exchange between LBK farmers and non-LBK groups (Gronenborn 1999, 168). Other evidence for contact and cultural borrowing is the use of red ochre in certain LBK burials in Alsace and the Paris basin, a practice they may have adopted from local Mesolithic traditions (Jeunesse 1997).

That members of LBK communities were not static, tied to the same settlement throughout their entire lives, is revealed by strontium analysis of human skeletal remains from two Rhineland LBK cemeteries. These reveal that residential mobility was a major aspect of LBK life, though the movements that are indicated appear to have been between local LBK groups, or between LBK groups and neighbouring hunter-gatherer communities, rather than the result of any directional colonization of new territory by LBK farmers (Price *et al.* 2001).

At the same time, new explanations seek to understand the LBK expansion in terms of small-scale choices and decisions. Gone is the notion that either declining soil fertility or explosive population growth powered the continent-wide movement of farming communities. Instead, individual households are seen as the prime decision-making units, exploiting new territories beyond the existing settled zone as information became available; what Bogucki has termed a 'complex adaptive system' (Bogucki 2000, 215). We may perhaps venture beyond this, and speculate on the specific social practices which lay behind such an expansion; one being perhaps the abandonment of individual long-houses to the ancestors on the deaths of important individuals. Bradley has observed how LBK houses may have been left to decay when their owners died (Bradley 1998). If the life of the long-house is tied to the lifetimes of individuals, the demise of complete settlements might also be linked to key life or death events in the community inhabiting a particular settlement. The abandonment of settlement areas would create the need for more space to accommodate both former communities and living communities. Such a process could explain the pattern of settlement and abandonment seen at LBK sites of the Langweiler group (Stehli 1989).

The most valuable insight to arise from such an approach is that of the LBK expansion as the product of human decisions at the scale of individuals or households, 'the outcome of a dynamic web of individual and small-group interests' (Bogucki 2000, 215), rather than as some great amorphous process sweeping across central Europe. The scattered nature of the resulting settlement would provide ample room for the continued existence of indigenous hunter-gatherers, who were ultimately either driven out or absorbed by the LBK groups. A similar mosaic pattern of LBK farmers and local hunter-gatherers has recently been proposed by Nowak for east-central Europe; there again, as in Belgium, farming enclaves persisted surrounded by areas occupied by hunter-gatherer communities for over 1000 years before the general adoption of pottery and domesticates in the TRB phase (Nowak 2001). As the western limits of LBK expansion were reached, however, the contribution of local Mesolithic communities appears to have become ever more marked. This process would have continued in the expansion of farming groups across northern France, their encounter with other ceramic and non-ceramic traditions, and the ultimate formulation of new local traditions from the combination and recombination of these diverse features.

2. Pioneer farmers?: the Neolithic transition in northern France

The domestic setting offers one of the most powerful catalysts of social identity, and the symbolic importance accorded to houses makes them particularly potent indicators of continuity or change. In houses, the sets of values, principles and dispositions that structure social life become metaphorically transformed into an objectified spatial order which, through the routines of daily practice, comes to constitute uncontested 'reality' (Brück 1999).

The key role of houses in forming and transforming Neolithic social life and social relations was emphasized in Ian Hodder's concept of the domus:

> . . . a set of ideas and practices which focus on the house. The very fabric and practices of the house created Neolithic society because they involved bonds, dependencies and boundaries between people. The domestic social unit was constructed in the practices of the house. (Hodder 1994)

Bourdieu and others have highlighted the cosmological importance of house layout:

> As a microcosm organized according to the same oppositions which govern all the universe, the house maintains a relation with the rest of the universe which is that of a homology. (Bourdieu 1977, 104)

Thus we might expect that the significance of the Neolithic long-house resides not only in its architecture but in the particular way of life and way of thinking that it represents.

The main features of the classic LBK long-house are well known: a heavily-built rectangular structure with outer wall lines and three internal rows of substantial timber posts supporting a pitched roof. These houses are found throughout central Europe from Hungary and Poland to Dutch Limburg and the Netherlands. So standardized is their design that they must represent a particular manner of inhabitation, linked to social practices, gender divisions and economic needs. The monumentality of the long-

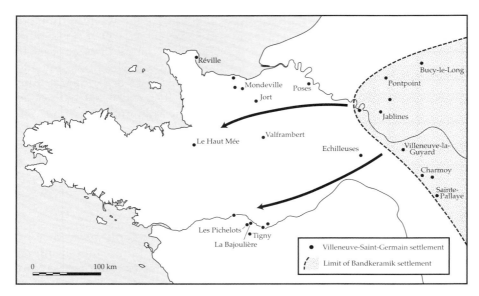

Figure 31.3. *Expansion of Villeneuve-Saint-Germain farming settlements across northern France.*

house suggests that it held a significance far beyond that of simply a setting for domestic activities; that it was indeed a cultural symbol. As Whittle has observed,

> From the beginning . . . the long-house may have encouraged formalized patterns of behaviour, emphasizing repetition, routine and conformity (Whittle 1996, 25).

Its significance persisted beyond the end of the LBK, and long-houses remained a feature of many of the LBK-successor groups such as Rössen in the Rhineland and Lengyel in central Europe. Among the changes seen at this period are the higher frequencies of smaller buildings known as 'Nebenbauten' alongside the long-houses, and the reduction within the long-houses in the number of internal partitions (Last 1996).

On the western fringes of the LBK zone, the successor groups are named after the sites of Blicquy and Villeneuve-Saint-Germain. The last ten years have seen much new evidence for the Villeneuve-Saint-Germain presence in northern France. In Normandy, Villeneuve-Saint-Germain sites are known not only in the lower Seine Valley at Léry and Poses, but also at Valframbert near Alençon, at Mondeville and Colombiers-sur-Seulles near Caen, and at Réville near the tip of the Cotentin peninsula (Verron 2000, 91–101) (Fig. 31.3). Further south, the distribution of Villeneuve-Saint-Germain material extends along the Loire Valley as far to the west as Saumur and possi-

bly Ancenis (Cassen *et al.* 1999).

A dozen or so small Villeneuve-Saint-Germain settlements have yielded reasonably complete house plans. The majority have remains of only a single house, or two at most; the site of Poses 'sur la Mare', with ten houses arranged in two separate rows, is exceptional (Bostyn *et al.* 1997). How many of the houses at Poses were in contemporary occupation is uncertain, and for the most part the Villeneuve-Saint-Germain settlements may be characterized as representing small groups of one or two households.

In their architecture, the Villeneuve-Saint-Germain houses are closely similar to each other (Fig. 31.4), and therefore lend themselves to the same analysis in terms of social and cosmological homogeneity as the houses of the preceding LBK, from which they are derived. In the Paris basin, the Villeneuve-Saint-Germain settlements are the direct lineal descendants of the LBK communities, and in some instances LBK and Villeneuve-Saint-Germain houses are found on the same site, demonstrating residential continuity. What is striking about the overall distribution of the Villeneuve-Saint-Germain settlements, however, is their expansion westward, beyond the limits of the former LBK zone, reaching as far as Le Haut Mée which is technically (though by only a few kilometres) within the administrative territory of Brittany. Furthermore, the social identity of the Villeneuve-Saint-Germain settlements is indicated by the movement of raw materials. A characteristic feature is the production (and no doubt the wearing) of perforated stone disks or bracelets made mainly of schist.

The principal source of schist in northern France was the Breton massif of primary rocks and adjacent parts of Normandy. Petrographic study has confirmed that this was the source of schist bracelets from Villeneuve-Saint-Germain sites in the Yvelines département on the western edge of Paris (Giligny *et al.* 1998). From an early stage in the establishment of Villeneuve-Saint-Germain settlements, schist for the manufacture of bracelets was being quarried at a series of extraction sites on the eastern edge of the Breton massif and transported eastwards. There it

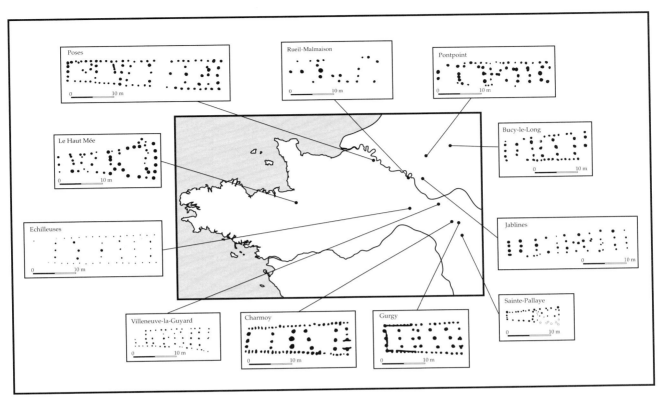

Figure 31.4. *Villeneuve-Saint-Germain long-houses.*

provided the raw material for the bracelet manufacture that is documented at many Villeneuve-Saint-Germain settlements located in the tertiary landscape of the Paris basin (Cassen *et al.* 1998). That some of this movement may have involved transport along the Loire is suggested by the analysis of schist from the bracelet production centre at Marcilly-Villerable, which was shown to come from the Angers region some 130 km to the west (Gruet, in Bailloud & Cordier 1987). Even more striking is the discovery, in a grave at the Villeneuve-Saint-Germain site of Les Longues Raies at Jablines east of Paris, of a polished stone bracelet of amphibolite. The probable source is the island of Groix off the south coast of the Morbihan. This lies significantly outside the known distribution of Villeneuve-Saint-Germain settlements and must hence have been acquired from Mesolithic communities beyond their borders (Bulard *et al.* 1993).

Thus the Villeneuve-Saint-Germain settlements — of which many more no doubt remain to be discovered — represent a network of small farming communities that remained in contact with each other though spread perhaps fairly thinly over extensive tracts of northern France. The similarities in house plan, and in material culture generally, strongly support the notion that they should be regarded as pioneer farmers. The lifespan of this settlement pattern was, however, relatively short — two or three centuries at most — and the period which follows sees a general change across northern France in which the distinctive features of Villeneuve-Saint-Germain are altered, absorbed and ultimately lost in a general and much more geographically widespread Neolithic transition. Thus the pioneer farming phase is followed by integration and acculturation among indigenous communities, themselves in the process of adopting domesticates and ceramics. The breakdown of community is illustrated by the fate of the Villeneuve-Saint-Germain long-house. House plans from the centuries immediately following the Villeneuve-Saint-Germain period are comparatively rare, which may in itself indicate the changing character and symbolism of the domestic context. Such house plans as are documented present a diversity of plans, including square and circular, as well as occasionally rectangular or trapezoidal (Valais 1995; Verjux 1998; Prodeo *et al.* 1997). The uniformity of domestic context has been lost as pioneer farmers were absorbed within a wider and more diversified cultural world.

Thus northern France presents a pattern of farmer-forager contact which is the converse of that on the southern edge of the Rhine-Meuse delta. In

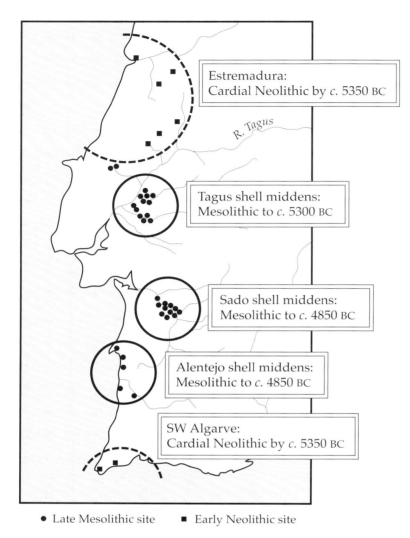

Estremadura:
Cardial Neolithic by *c.* 5350 BC

R. Tagus

Tagus shell middens:
Mesolithic to *c.* 5300 BC

Sado shell middens:
Mesolithic to *c.* 4850 BC

Alentejo shell middens:
Mesolithic to *c.* 4850 BC

SW Algarve:
Cardial Neolithic by *c.* 5350 BC

● Late Mesolithic site   ■ Early Neolithic site

Figure 31.5. *Early Neolithic settlement enclaves and Mesolithic communities in Portugal. (After Zilhão 2000.)*

3. Atlantic Portugal

The model of pioneer farming communities put forward for northern France must be considered of strictly limited application. It is not a general explanation which can automatically be applied to account for the Neolithic transition in other regions of Europe. Even within France, it does not fit the evidence from the far Northwest, from western and southern France south of the Loire, or from the Alpine foreland. In all those regions, indigenous acculturation with little population movement provides a more plausible alternative. There is, however, one other area of western Europe where a colonist explanation is currently proposed. In western Iberia, Zilhão has argued that the pattern of archaeological evidence supports a pioneer maritime colonization model for the introduction of pottery and domesticates (Zilhão 1993; 2000).

Zilhão bases his case on the pattern of radiocarbon dates and the respective distributions of Late Mesolithic and Early Neolithic sites (Fig. 31.5). In Central Portugal, he notes that the Late Mesolithic is represented by the well-known middens of the Tagus and Sado estuaries, whereas the earliest Neolithic sites are located on the limestone massif of the Estremadura. This suggests the exploitation of complementary landscape zones by contemporary farming and foraging groups, much as the LBK of Belgium settled the loess uplands while indigenous Mesolithic communities continued to exploit the sandy lowlands. That the Portuguese communities were indeed distinct populations, not merely seasonal aspects of a single mobile lifestyle, is indicated by stable isotope analysis of burials. Those from the Tagus shell middens indicate a diet high in marine foods; the Early Neolithic burials from the cave of Gruta da Caldeirão in the Estremadura, by contrast, had an almost exclusively terrestrial diet (Jackes & Lubell 1992; Lubell *et al.* 1994). The model is backed up by chronological evidence. Pottery from Caldeirão is of late Cardial type and is associated with radiocarbon dates overlapping in the range 5300–5080 BC (Zilhão 1992, 78). Early Neolithic sites spread into the interior in the following Epicardial phase, which began shortly before 5000 BC. By 4750 BC the Neolithic transition had

the latter area, hunter-gatherer groups appear to have been absorbed within intrusive farming communities; in northern France, however, evidence suggests it was the pioneer farming communities who were absorbed by the surrounding hunter-gatherer populations. These north France hunter-gatherers were themselves, however, in process of transition, adopting 'Neolithic' features such as pottery and domesticates, perhaps from the pioneer farmers, but equally possibly through long-standing exchange networks with the Mediterranean (Scarre 2002). There is scope for a model of fusion between farmers and hunter-gatherers in this case, but the likelihood that some early farming expansions were simply unsuccessful and failed, leaving little lasting legacy, must also be borne in mind.

reached the inland region of Trás-os-Montes, and the last hunter-gatherers of the Sado Valley disappeared (Zilhão 2000).

Zilhão notes close parallels between the earliest Neolithic pottery of western Portugal and that of south Spanish Early Neolithic sites such as Cova de l'Or. Furthermore, he observes that the Early Neolithic of the Estremadura appears earlier than that of intervening regions such as the Alentejo. He accordingly couches his explanation in the form of a leapfrogging model of maritime pioneer colonization, with small groups of farmers moving along the coast and settling areas such as the Estremadura which were suitable for agriculture but largely devoid of Mesolithic settlement. Similar enclaves are posited in his model for southern France and southern Spain (Zilhão 1993).

It is perhaps not surprising that this interpretation has been strongly contested on several grounds. Jackes and colleagues have argued that the differences in skeletal morphology and dentition between Portuguese Mesolithic and Neolithic populations are inconsistent with the thesis of population replacement since they are not abrupt but indicate slow changes in dietary regimes, fertility levels and activity patterns that were already under way before the end of the Mesolithic (Jackes et al. 1997; Lubell et al. 1994). This would imply indigenous uptake of domesticates and pottery by local Mesolithic groups. Arias notes that in inland Alentejo, the oldest megaliths are closest to the principal zones of Mesolithic settlement, and uses this along with other evidence to argue that the initial farming societies of the region were descended from local Mesolithic groups (Arias 1999). Calado takes a similar approach, observing that the Central Alentejo is the natural hinterland of the Tagus and Sado estuaries. He proposes that the Mesolithic communities of these estuaries were responsible for the Early Neolithic settlement of the Central Alentejo, and for the erection of the first megalithic monuments, through a process of social and economic transformation that is paralleled in other regions of Atlantic Europe (Calado 2002).

Thus the pioneer maritime farming model for the earliest Neolithic in western Iberia remains contentious. Whether or not it proves ultimately convincing, however, it has the merit of highlighting once again two key observations concerning the character of the Neolithic transition in western Europe: first, the mosaic-like patterning of the process; and second, the probable role, in certain regions, of small-scale population displacements. These displacements, however, are very different in both the numbers of people involved, and the distances moved, from those implied by broad-sweep demic diffusion models of agricultural origins.

Conclusion

This short paper has sought to elucidate the rôle of population movements in the Neolithic transition in Western Europe through two principal observations:

1. that in certain regions of Europe it may be possible to identify the presence of pioneer farming settlements on the basis of archaeological evidence; and that such an attempt gains increased support from the general likelihood that small-scale, short-range population movements were an inherent feature of European prehistory;

2. that the nature of the Neolithic transition should be envisaged as a mosaic process in which the indigenous adoption of pottery and domesticates occurred alongside the expansion of small pioneering farming communities. It is equally clear that in any individual case, the archaeological evidence will be capable of divergent interpretations, but this should not be allowed to obscure the probability that across western Europe as a whole, the Neolithic transition involved a combination of both these processes.

It remains briefly to consider what these observations might imply for patterns of languages and genetics.

First, the small-scale nature of these events, involving small numbers of people, must be sharply distinguished from the continent-wide interpretations of linguistic and genetic change derived from studies of modern (or recent historic) populations — the modern populations sampled by geneticists, or the linguistic information from living languages or texts which in the European case go back little more than 3000 years. There is an enormous gulf between the movements of real communities that we have sought to detect in the archaeological evidence, and the establishment of genetic or linguistic patterns or regularities.

Second, the interactions between indigenes and newcomers will have been highly diverse, including confrontation and violence, the absorption of the indigenes by the farming communities or the absorption of the latter by indigenous populations. These interactions would leave a variety of genetic and linguistic signatures. Among the possibilities, we may envisage genetic and linguistic replacement, where the indigenes were driven out or killed, and genetic interchange coupled with language replacement where indigenous groups intermarried into farming communities and abandoned their language. Such might apply in the case of the Mesolithic peoples of northern Belgium absorbed into the Michelsberg farming communities.

Third, it is important to consider the temporality of the event: pioneer farmers in northern France may have been so few in numbers that they were absorbed by the local (formerly hunter-gatherer) communities within two or three centuries; or conversely, the pioneer settlements themselves may have failed. In these circumstances there is no demographic explosion, with farmers multiplying in numbers and taking control of ever-expanding territories by virtue of sheer population size. Rather, the impact of many of these early farming groups in either linguistic or genetic terms may have been both too short-lived and too small-scale to have left an enduring legacy.

Fourth, even where the archaeological evidence supports a model of population movement, the distances moved may have been small — a few tens or hundreds of kilometres. Here again the key concept is scale: and it should also be borne in mind that the populations moving into an area may not have been either linguistically or genetically very different from the local hunter-gatherers, all of them descended from the same original Palaeolithic population. It is clear that, whatever the frequency of small-scale movements of this kind, there is no archaeological evidence to support either directional (east–west) demic diffusion or farming migration as the principal factors behind the Neolithic transition at a continent-wide level (Zvelebil 2000). The pattern as it stands must be the end-product of many small-scale events. This leaves as the key question the mechanism which caused the general pattern of European languages to shift in the direction of the Indo-European languages. An association with farming remains a strong possibility, though this must not automatically be equated with colonist farmers.

This disparity between large-scale interpretations of European prehistory from genetic or linguistic patterns and the 'actualist' perspectives drawn from observation and evaluation of specific archaeological data sets may at first sight be considered a fundamentally negative conclusion. That is certainly not the intention. What I have sought to show in this paper is that population movement very probably did occur in the European Neolithic, not least since Neolithic population levels may have remained relatively low, and certain areas of the landscape 'unfilled' at certain periods. Opportunities and decisions

taken at community level may have encouraged groups to move into new or more marginal areas, in response to changing demographic, environmental and social circumstances. Equally, as the evidence from the Combe d'Ain illustrates, they may sometimes have subsequently abandoned those areas. Nor we must ignore the possibility that a pioneer ethic developed among some of these communities, encouraging them to seek new lands and new opportunities. In the Polynesian colonization of the Pacific islands the motivation may have been provided by the phenomenon of founder rank enhancement, in which those establishing a new settlement achieved enhanced social standing (Bellwood 1996). Such a pioneer ethic might have lain behind the LBK expansion, but beyond the LBK zone in western and northern Europe, and perhaps occasionally within it, the Neolithic transition appears to have been a primarily indigenous transformation. There is nothing in such a process to bring large-scale linguistic or genetic change to France or Iberia, still less to Britain and Ireland.

For the Indo-European languages, we are left with two alternative conclusions. Either such languages were already spoken by Mesolithic communities of western Europe; or their arrival is not marked by clear archaeological evidence. The geographical coincidence between haplotype V and the Basque language of the Pyrenees (Renfrew 2000, 7) may suggest that the original Palaeolithic and Mesolithic languages of western Europe were, like Basque, not members of the Indo-European family. If that understanding is correct, the spread of Indo-European languages must be considered a Neolithic and/or post-Neolithic phenomenon. Rather than a single expansion event, however, it may instead be more appropriate to envisage a whole series of individual language shifts, some perhaps associated with pioneer farmers, others the result of small-scale population displacements or social and economic interactions. The aggregated outcome of such events, operating perhaps over several millennia, and observed in detailed archaeological cases, offers a more plausible scenario, operating at a more human scale, than 'waves of advance' or demic diffusion.

Finally the case-studies presented above illustrate how detailed archaeological evidence may be able to address the divergent outcomes of farmer–forager interaction. In the Belgian example, foragers may have been absorbed into farming communities; in northern France, small pioneer farming communities appear to have lost their separate identity after two or three centuries and been integrated within an indigenous pattern of change. These interpretations remain controversial, and their detail and complexity may deter those seeking more general explanations of linguistic or genetic patterning, but they do have the advantage of considering the question at the level of real prehistoric communities rather than generalized processes.

It is essentially the question of *scale* that distinguishes these different perspectives. Analyses based on present-day genetic data or post-prehistoric linguistic patterns inevitably remain coarse-grained. By concentrating on patterns that must be the cumulative end-product of thousands of years of social and demographic change, the processes that genetic and historical linguistics evoke are inevitably large-scale in their nature and operation. The difficulty is to distinguish between supra-regional patterning evident in the present day or recent past that may be the result of specific large-scale processes such as colonization events, and patterning that though geographically widely spread is merely the end-product of numerous accretional small-scale shifts. Furthermore, recent Y-chromosome study supports the conclusions from mtDNA in indicating that, for western Europe at least, the contribution of West Asian genes to the population remained relatively small (Chikhi *et al.* 2002). A large-scale process such as the spread of farming may seem to provide an obvious explanation for many aspects of present-day genetic and linguistic patterning. Such explanations, however, fail sufficiently to recognize the alternative scenarios that the dimensions of the timescale oblige us to consider. Farming was adopted in southeastern Europe during the seventh millennium BC; the widespread distribution of Indo-European languages only becomes apparent with the expansion of literacy during the first millennium BC. Over the thousands of years between, the Indo-European languages and their speakers would have needed only a modest social or economic advantage to supplant other native European languages. Archaeological evidence of the kind presented in this paper accords much more readily with such an interpretation, where the diversity of local circumstances may have made for very different and indeed unique transitions to Indo-European languages.

References

Ammerman, A.J. & C.S. Cavalli-Sforza, 1971. Measuring the rate of spread of early farming in Europe. *Man* 6, 674–88.

Ammerman, A.J. & C.S. Cavalli-Sforza, 1973. A population model for the diffusion of early farming in Europe, in *The Explanation of Culture Change*, ed. C. Renfrew. London: Duckworth, 34–57.

Ammerman, A.J. & C.S. Cavalli-Sforza, 1984. *The Neolithic Transition and the Genetics of Population in Europe*. Princeton (NJ): Princeton University Press.

Arias, P., 1999. The origins of the Neolithic along the Atlantic coast of Continental Europe: a survey. *Journal of World Prehistory* 13, 403–64.

Bailloud, G. & J. Cordier, 1987. Le Néolithique ancien et moyen de la vallée de la Brisse (Loir-et-Cher). *Revue Archéologique du Centre de la France* 26, 117–63.

Bellwood, P., 1996. Hierarchy, founder ideology and Austronesian expansion, in *Origins, Ancestry and Alliance: Explorations in Austronesian Ethnography*, eds. J.T. Fox & C. Sather. Canberra: Australian National University, 18–40.

Bogucki, P., 2000. How agriculture came to north-central Europe, in Price (ed.), 197–218.

Bogucki, P. & R. Grygiel, 1993. The first farmers of Europe: a survey article. *Journal of Field Archaeology* 20, 399–426.

Bosquet, D., 1993. Essai de reconstitution des dispositifs d'entrée de deux villages fortifiés du Rubané de Hesbaye. *Notae Praehistoricae* 12, 123–5.

Bostyn, F., M.-F. André, Y. Lanchon, E. Martial & Y. Praud, 1997. Un nouveau site d'habitat du groupe de Villeneuve-Saint-Germain à Poses 'Sur la Mare' (Eure), in Le Néolithique danubien et ses marges entre Rhin et Seine. Actes du XXIIe Colloque Interrégional sur le Néolithique, ed. C. Jenuesse. *Cahiers de l'Association pour la promotion de la Recherche Archéologique en Alsace*, Supplément no. 3., 447–66.

Bourdieu, P., 1977. The Berber house, in *Rules and Meanings: the Anthropology of Everyday Knowledge*, ed. M. Douglas. Harmondsworth: Penguin, 98–110.

Bradley, R., 1998. *The Significance of Monuments: on the Shaping of Experience in Neolithic and Bronze Age Europe*. London: Routledge.

Brück, J., 1999. Houses, lifecycles and deposition on Middle Bronze Age settlements in southern England. *Proceedings of the Prehistoric Society* 65, 145–66.

Bulard, A., J. Degros, C. Drouhot, P. Duhamel & J. Tarrête, 1993. L'habitat des Longues-Raies à Jablines, in *Le Néolithique au quotidien. Actes du XVIe Colloque Interrégional sur le Néolithique*, eds. J.-C. Blanchet, A. Bulard, C. Constantin, D. Mordant & J. Tarrête. Paris: Documents d'Archéologie Française, 41–62.

Cahen, D., L.H. Keeley, I. Jadin & P.-L. van Berg, 1990. Trois villages fortifiés du Rubané récent en Hesbaye Liègoise, in *Rubané et Cardial*, eds. D. Cahen & M. Otte. Liège: ERAUL, 125–46.

Calado, M., 2002. Standing stones and natural outcrops, in *Monuments and Landscape in Atlantic Europe*, ed. C. Scarre. London: Routledge, 17–35.

Cassen, S., C. Audren, S. Hinguant, G. Lannuzel & G. Marchand, 1998. L'habitat Villeneuve-Saint-Germain du Haut-Mée (Saint-Etienne-en-Coglès, Ille-et-Vilaine). *Bulletin de la Société Préhistorique Française* 95, 41–75.

Cassen, S., G. Marchand, L. Ménanteau, B. Poissonnier, R. Cadot & Y. Viau, 1999. Néolithisation de la France de l'Ouest. Témoignages Villeneuve-Saint-Germain, Cerny et Chambon sur la Loire angevin et atlantique. *Gallia Préhistoire* 41, 223–51.

Cavalli-Sforza, L., P. Menozzi & A. Piazza, 1994. *The History and Geography of Human Genes*. Princeton (NJ): Princeton University Press.

Chikhi, L., R.A. Nichols, G. Barbujani & M.A. Beaumont, 2002. Y genetic data support the Neolithic demic diffusion model. *Proceedings of the National Academy of Sciences of the USA* 99, 11,008–13.

Clark, J.G.D., 1966. The invasion hypothesis in British archaeology. *Antiquity* 40, 172–89.

Coudart, A., 1998. *Architecture et société néolithique. L'unité et la variance de la maison danubienne*. Paris: Maison des Sciences de l'Homme.

Darvill, T. & J. Thomas (eds.), 1996. *Neolithic Houses in Northwest Europe and Beyond*. Oxford: Oxbow Books.

Fansa, M. & H. Thieme, 1985. Eine Siedlung und Befestigungsanlage der Bandkeramik auf dem 'Nachtwiesen-Berg' bei Esbeck, Stadt Schöningen, Landkreis Helmstedt, in *Ausgrabungen in Niedersachsen, Archäologische Denkmalpflege 1979–1984*, ed. K. Wilhelmi. Stuttgart: Theiss, 87–92.

Giligny, F., E. Martial & I. Praud, 1998. Premiers éléments sur l'occupation des Yvelines au Néolithique. *Internéo* 2, 43–55.

Gronenborn, D., 1999. A variation on a basic theme: the transition to farming in southern Central Europe. *Journal of World Prehistory* 13, 123–210.

Hodder, I., 1994. Architecture and meaning: the example of Neolithic houses and tombs, in *Architecture and Order: Approaches to Social Space*, eds. M. Parker Pearson & C. Richards, 1994. London: Routledge, 73–86.

Jackes, M. & D. Lubell, 1992. The Early Neolithic human remains from Gruta do Caldeirão, in Zilhão (ed.), 259–95.

Jackes, M., D. Lubell & C. Meiklejohn, 1997. Healthy but mortal: human biology and the first farmers of western Europe. *Antiquity* 71, 639–58.

Jeunesse, C., 1997. *Pratiques funéraires au Néolithique ancien. Sépultures et nécropoles danubiennes 5500–4900 av. J.C.* Paris: Errance.

Jochim, M., 2000. The origins of agriculture in south-central Europe, in Price (ed.), 183–96.

Keeley, L.H. & D. Cahen, 1989. Early Neolithic forts and villages in NE Belgium: a preliminary report. *Journal of Field Archaeology* 16, 157–76.

Last, J., 1996. Neolithic houses — a central European perspective, in Darvill & Thomas, 27–40.

Lodewijckx, M. & C. Bakels, 2000. The interaction between early farmers (Linearbandkeramik) and indigenous people in central Belgium, in *The Prehistory and Early History of Atlantic Europe: Papers from a Session held at the European Association of Archaeologists Fourth Annual Meeting in Göteborg 1998*, ed. J.C. Henderson. (British Archaeological Reports International Series 861.) Oxford: Archaeopress, 33–46.

Lubell, D., M. Jackes, H. Schwarcz, M. Knyf & C. Meiklejohn, 1994. The Mesolithic–Neolithic transition in Portugal: isotopic and dental evidence of diet. *Journal of Archaeological Science* 21, 201–16.

Lüning, J., 1998. L'organisation régionale des habitats rubanés: sites centraux et sites secondaires (groupements de sites), in *Organisation néolithique de l'espace en Europe du Nord-Ouest. Actes du XXIIIe Colloque Interrégional sur le Néolithique*, eds. N. Cauwe & P.-L. van Berg. *Anthropologie et Préhistoire* Supplément 109, 163–85.

Lüning, J., U. Kloos & S. Albert, 1989. Westliche Nachbarn der bandkeramischen Kultur: La Hoguette und Limburg. *Germania* 67, 355–93.

Modderman, P.J.R., 1988. The Linear Pottery Culture: diversity in uniformity. *Berichten van de Rijksdienst voor het Oudheidkundig Bodemonderzoek* 38, 63–139.

Newell, R.R., 1970. The flint industry of the Dutch Linearbandkeramik. *Analecta Praehistorica Leidensia* 3, 144–83.

Nowak, M., 2001. The second phase of Neolithization in east-central Europe. *Antiquity* 75, 582–92.

Pétrequin, P., R.-M. Arbogast, C. Bourquin-Mignot, C. Lavier & A. Viellet, 1998. Demographic growth, environmental changes and technical adaptations: responses of an agricultural community from the 32nd to the 30th centuries BC. *World Archaeology* 30, 181–92.

Price, T.D. (ed.), 2000. *Europe's First Farmers*. Cambridge: Cambridge University Press.

Price, T.D., R.A. Bentley, J. Lüning, D. Gronenborn & J. Wahl, 2001. Prehistoric human migration in the Linearbandkeramik of Central Europe. *Antiquity* 75, 593–603.

Prodeo, F., C. Constantin, R. Martinez & C. Toupet, 1997. La culture de Cerny dans la région Aisne-Oise, in *La Culture de Cerny. Nouvelle économie, nouvelle société au Néolithique*, eds. C. Constantin, D. Mordant & D. Simonin. Nemours: Mémoires du Musée de Préhistoire de l'Ile de France 6, 169–86.

Renfrew, C., 1969. The autonomy of the south-east European copper age. *Proceedings of the Prehistoric Society* 35, 12–47.

Renfrew, C., 1987. *Archaeology and Language: the Puzzle of Indo-European Origins*. London: Cape.

Renfrew, C., 2000. Archaeogenetics: towards a population prehistory of Europe, in Renfrew & Boyle (eds.), 3–11.

Renfrew C. & K. Boyle (eds.), 2000. *Archaeogenetics: DNA and the Population Prehistory of Europe*. (McDonald Institute Monographs.) Cambridge: McDonald Institute for Archaeological Research.

Scarre, C., 2001. Modelling prehistoric populations: the case of Neolithic Brittany. *Journal of Anthropological Archaeology* 20, 283–313.

Scarre, C., 2002. Contexts of monumentalism: regional diversity at the Neolithic transition in north-west France. *Oxford Journal of Archaeology* 21, 23–61.

Stehli, P., 1989. Merzbachtal - Umwelt und Geschichte einer bandkeramischen Siedlungskammer. *Germania* 67, 51–76.

Valais, A., 1995. Deux bâtiments atypiques associés à du matériel Cerny (Herblay - Val d'Oise), in *Evreux 1993. Actes du XXe Colloque Interrégional sur le Néolithique*, ed. C. Billard. *Revue Archéologique de l'Ouest*, Supplément 7, 57–63.

Verjux, C., 1998. Des bâtiments circulaires du Néolithique moyen à Auneau (Eure-et-Loir) et Orval (Cher). Note préliminaire. *Revue Archéologique du Centre* 37, 179–90.

Vermeersch, P., 1991. Y-a-t-il eu co-existence entre le Mésolithique et le Néolithique en Basse et Moyenne Belgique? in *Mésolithique et Néolithisation en France et dans les Régions Limitrophes. Actes du 113e Congrès National des Sociétés Savantes*. Paris: Comité des Travaux Historiques et Scientifiques, 467–79.

Verron, G., 2000. *Préhistoire de la Normandie*. Rennes: Editions Ouest-France.

Whittle, A., 1996. Houses in context: buildings as process, in Darvill & Thomas (eds.), 13–26.

Zilhão, J., 1992. *Gruta do Caldeirão O Neolitico Antigo*. Lisbon: Instituto Português do Património Arquitectónico e Arqueológico.

Zilhão, J., 1993. The spread of agro-pastoral economies across Mediterranean Europe: a view from the Far West. *Journal of Mediterranean Archaeology* 6, 5–63.

Zilhão, J., 2000. From the Mesolithic to the Neolithic in the Iberian peninsula, in Price (ed.), 144–82.

Zvelebil, M., 2000. The social context of the agricultural transition in Europe, in Renfrew & Boyle (eds.), 57–79.

Chapter 32

Farming Dispersal in Europe and the Spread of the Indo-European Language Family

Bernard Comrie

The hypothesis that the spread of at least some of the largest language families, in terms of geographic extent, is to be correlated causally with the dispersal of farming is an attractive proposal which is certainly deserving of merit. Indeed, some of the cases presented at the symposium in Cambridge in August of 2001 seem to me to provide convincing instances of such a combined movement of people, farming and language, for instance the identification of the Austroasiatic family with the first agriculturalists in Southeast Asia (Charles Higham, this volume). My aim in the present paper is to examine whether such a correlation is possible, perhaps even necessary, in connection with the spread of Indo-European languages in Europe, a possibility that has been at the forefront of attention since the publication of Renfrew (1987). But before turning to the examination of this central question, a number of preliminary points, some of them methodological, need to be discussed.

1. The hypothesis

First, I will make a terminological distinction between primary and secondary farming dispersal. By a primary farming dispersal, I mean the spread of agriculture into an area that had previously not known agriculture. By a secondary dispersal, I mean a change by the practitioners of agriculture in a particular region either to a new population group or to a new language. An obvious example of secondary dispersal would be Spanish-speaking agriculturalists in Mesoamerica. We know that Mesoamerica was agricultural before the arrival of Spanish-speakers from around AD 1500, so the primary agricultural dispersal in Mesoamerica long preceded the arrival of Spanish-speakers, who thus constituted a secondary agricultural dispersal. This makes it clear that

we must distinguish two possible interpretations of the claim that the spread of Indo-European languages in Europe correlated with farming dispersal, since this might in principle refer either to primary or to secondary farming dispersal. Indeed, I shall try to argue that the balance of evidence is against Indo-European speakers as the instigators of primary farming dispersal in Europe, but in favour of their correlation with secondary farming dispersal.

The strongest form of the hypothesis correlating extensive language spread with farming dispersal would be that this a one-one correlation, at least in the pre-industrial world, i.e. that having agriculture would inevitably lead to spread and that not having agriculture would inevitably preclude spread. Clearly, this strong form of the hypothesis is incorrect. We know of areas which have been agricultural for thousands of years but where there has been no significant language spread, for instance New Guinea. Indeed, as became apparent at the Cambridge conference, even some instances which at first seemed paradigm examples of the correlation may in fact involve agriculture with little language spread, as in the case of the Mayan language family, whose geographical extent is actually quite restricted (Lyle Campbell this volume). Conversely, there are some instances of language spread that were not conditional upon agriculture. Examples include the Eskimo branch of the Eskimo-Aleut language family, spread from eastern Siberia to Greenland, though here there is a clear special factor, namely the superb adaptation of the Eskimo to a particularly inhospitable environment, one for which they had no effective human competition in pre-technological times. More mysterious is the spread of the Pama-Nyungan languages to occupy almost all of Australia, at least if Pama-Nyungan is indeed a well-defined language family, as argued by most, but not quite all specialists in Australian languages. The spread of the Athabaskan languages to the American Southwest (also discussed by Lyle Campbell in this volume) may well have required the partial collapse of agriculture in the American Southwest to make it possible, and the survival of the Athabaskan-speaking groups in that area was also dependent on their adoption of agriculture, a kind of secondary dispersal scenario to which I will return below, most explicitly in section 5. However, the claim does seem plausible that nearly all instances of language spread in the pre-industrial world involved either primary or secondary farming dispersal, with special explanations being required for exceptions.

2. Methodological preliminaries

In order to approach the linguistic side of the correlation proposed as a hypothesis in section 1, it is necessary to look in a little more detail at some of the linguistic methods to be used in addressing the problem.

We are dealing with the ancestor language of the Indo-European languages, conventionally called Proto-Indo-European, a language that is nowhere attested and indeed is separated by at least millennia from the earliest-attested Indo-European language, but whose existence is nonetheless necessary in order to account for the striking and systematic similarities among the attested Indo-European languages. In particular, we are concerned with the vocabulary of Proto-Indo-European as a reflection of the material culture of the speakers of that language, more especially the ways in which it reflects their degree of familiarity with agriculture. How can we tell what the vocabulary of Proto-Indo-European was like, in this or any other domain? The standard tool used by historical linguists, indeed the only tool that substantially addresses this question, is so-called linguistic palaeontology (also sometimes called linguistic archaeology). Essentially, this method asks whether it is possible to reconstruct the word for a particular concept in the proto-language; if so, then there is a *prima facie* case for reconstructing the concept back to the community that spoke the proto-language.

The method is by no means foolproof, for instance in that in some instances the later dissemination of a word across a group of related languages might erroneously lead us into attributing this word to the proto-language, but when combined with the usual stringent checks of the comparative method in linguistics it is reasonably robust as a way of reconstructing what words must have been present in the proto-languages. It is considerably less robust in determining the precise meaning of the reconstructed words, since semantic change is not subject to the same kinds of restrictions as changes in the form of a word. This turns out to be a particular stumbling block in studying agricultural terminology, since certain semantic changes are especially likely in this domain, in particular the transfer of the name of a wild plant or animal to its domesticated variant: a classic example is the possibility of reconstructing a word for 'horse' to Proto-Indo-European without knowing whether this necessarily referred to a domesticated variety. (Indeed, cross-linguistically, the only animal for which there seems to be a universal designation distinct from that of the wild forebear is 'dog' in relation to 'wolf'.) There are other possibilities for semantic shifts, for instance the name of a plant or animal being transferred to a similar but distinct species (witness the terms *corn* and *robin* in North American English), or a similar extension with words which later come to refer to agricultural practices, as when the Proto-Indo-European word reconstructed with the meaning 'to sow' has related meanings 'send, throw, drop'. Faced with such problems, linguistic palaeontology will probably never give an absolutely decisive answer, but where a particular overall pattern emerges it is unlikely that all aspects of the pattern will merely have converged by chance. And where one is dealing with a language family with as much internal diversification as Indo-European, it is unlikely that precisely the same shift will have taken place independently in all or several branches of the family — except perhaps for such natural semantic shifts as the transference of a term from a wild to a domesticated variety.

It should also be noted that linguistic palaeontology cannot be used with any degree of reliability to conclude from the absence of a reconstructed term in a proto-language that the corresponding concept must have been absent, since it is certainly possible that different descendants of the proto-language may independently have replaced the original term. There is no Proto-Indo-European term for 'hand', but one would hardly conclude from this that speakers of Proto-Indo-European lacked hands. Rather, different branches of Indo-European, or even different individual languages have innovated terms that have replaced whatever was present before, either by generalizing terms for parts of the hand (e.g. 'palm') or by deriving a noun from a verbal root with a meaning like 'seize, take, collect' (Buck 1949, 238–9). Thus, from the absence of a particular item of agricultural vocabulary in our reconstruction of Proto-Indo-European, one cannot conclude that no such word existed, and whence that the corresponding concept was absent. But again, the presence of general patterns can serve to mitigate this problem, as when Benveniste (1969, 245–53) concludes from the systematic reconstructability of Proto-Indo-European words for the husband's kin and the systematic non-reconstructability of words for the wife's kin that Proto-Indo-European society was virilocal, with the wife needing terms for her husband's ever-present kin, while the husband did not need corresponding terms for his wife's usually absent kin.

The application of linguistic palaeontology actually presupposes a prior methodological issue, namely a decision concerning the basis on which we decide that a word is to be attributed to Proto-Indo-European. Clearly, just finding a word in one Indo-European language, say English, would be insufficient, since it might simply reflect an innovation peculiar to English. Equally, finding it in just one branch of the Indo-European family, say Germanic, would not be evidence for reconstructing the word back to Proto-Indo-European, since this could be an innovation unique to Germanic. Finding a word in all branches of Indo-European, with regular relations as required by the comparative method, would justify reconstructing the word, but is surely too stringent a criterion, since a word might well have been lost in one or two branches but retained in all others, providing sufficient proof of its inheritance from the proto-language; in practice, rather few words are attested in all branches of Indo-European. What is needed is rather a criterion along the lines that the word should be attested in a reasonable number of branches of Indo-European. A rule of thumb which is sometimes invoked is that attestation in three branches is needed for reconstruction to the proto-language.

But this rule of thumb cannot be applied mechanically. In particular, it is clear that some branches of Indo-European are most closely linked to one another, perhaps having gone through a period of symbiosis after other branches of the family had split off. Given this, the clearest evidence for reconstructability would be attestation in the most widely separated branches of Indo-European, in terms of chronological separation from the main stock of the language family. Unfortunately, there is no consensus among Indo-Europeanists on even the relative dating of the separation of particular branches from the main stock of the family. Perhaps the most widely, but still not universally, accepted view is that the Anatolian branch was the first to separate, so that attestation in Anatolian as well as elsewhere in Indo-European

would be a strong indication of reconstructability. Tocharian is also, though perhaps less widely, considered to have been an earlier splinter group (though later than Anatolian), so that Mallory & Adams (1997, 640), for instance, consider a word for 'wheel' shared by only Hittite (by far the best-attested Anatolian language) and the two Tocharian languages to be sufficient evidence to reconstruct that word back to Proto-Indo-European. The Indo-Aryan languages, represented in the most ancient period by Vedic (usually subsumed under Sanskrit in English-language terminology), are also useful in that they were clearly geographically separated from the bulk of Indo-European quite early on, so that attestation in Sanskrit as well as in other branches (with the exception of Iranian, which actually forms a single Indo-Iranian branch with Indo-Aryan) can also be used, though somewhat less reliably, as a test of reconstructability. What is emphatically not reliable, however, is to rely exclusively on the testimony of the European languages (Celtic, Italic, Germanic, Balto-Slavonic, Greek, Albanian), or even worse on just the northern/western European languages (Celtic, Italic, Germanic, Balto-Slavonic). Indeed, with a number of agricultural terms we face precisely the problem that they are attested only in the European or northern/western European languages, and therefore cannot be reliably projected back to the proto-language; see, for instance, the last paragraph of the article 'Agriculture' in Mallory & Adams (1997, 8).

Finally, I turn to the vexed question of dating Proto-Indo-European. Let us suppose that we have, using the comparative method, reconstructed a particular word or set of words back to Proto-Indo-European and the corresponding concept back to the culture whose members spoke that language. An obvious question that arises, before we try correlating our linguistic conclusions with archaeological evidence, is the time to which our linguistic reconstructions relate, or more generally the time-depth question, as discussed from various perspectives in Renfrew et al. (2000); more specifically for Indo-European, see also Mallory & Adams (1997, 583–7). The majority of historical linguists are sceptical of any general principle regulating the rate of change of any part of a language, be it grammar or vocabulary, but nonetheless feel that a certain range of possibilities can be established by the examination of actual cases of language change. Cases of an attested ancestor language with attested descendants are rare, though not quite unknown, so that one can for example compare Latin with the modern Romance languages and see roughly what degree of change might take place in about two millennia; and indeed, in most respects, one finds a range, from more conservative languages like Tuscan Italian to more innovative languages like French. One can also trace the degree of change that has taken place over the history of languages that have a recorded history, including languages that have undergone rapid change, such as English, and those that have undergone slower change, such as Georgian, the Kartvelian language that is the major language of the Republic of Georgia; both have a recorded history of about one and a half millennia. This method is necessarily somewhat impressionistic — languages A and B differ from one another to a certain extent and have a known time depth, so languages C and D, which differ from one another to roughly the same extent, can be assigned roughly the same time depth — but it does provide limits within which historical linguistics work. And, as Mallory writes in Mallory & Adams (1997, 585): 'even assuming that all prehistoric Indo-European languages changed as slowly as Lithuanian has changed, extremely "high" dates for Proto-Indo-European (say, more than 7000 BC) would be impossible'. It should be emphasized that the limit of 7000 BC really is an extreme, assuming that the whole of Indo-European before its historical attestation changed at the rate of its slowest known changer; more plausible dates, assuming closer to average rates of change, would be later by millennia. Moreover, if Indo-European of the period were actively spreading, for instance with the dispersal of farming, into new areas, one would if anything expect a more rapid rate of change than usual.

Some linguists believe that there are certain parts of a language, in particular basic vocabulary, that change at a constant rate, thus giving rise to the method known as glottochronology, whereby rate of change in vocabulary is used as a measure of time depth. While recent developments in glottochronology, such as those developed in Starostin (2000), answer some of the criticisms made of earlier versions, I remain, like most historical linguists, sceptical of the overall reliability of the method. But for what it is worth, glottochronology has consistently given shallower time depths for Proto-Indo-European, not going back beyond about 4000 BC.

3. Population, agriculture and language in prehistoric Europe

Europe and its border areas present an interesting region for investigation of the correlation of linguistics, archaeology and genetics. Most of Europe is at present occupied by speakers of Indo-European languages, although there are border areas, in particular, where other languages are spoken, most noticeably Basque in the Pyrenees, the Caucasian families in the Caucasus, Uralic languages in the north and east (and, exceptionally, in the heart of the continent, in the case of Hungarian), and Turkic languages in the east and southeast. Europe has been populated by anatomically modern humans for around 40,000 years, yet the Indo-European languages clearly entered Europe at a significantly more recent date than this, even if, as discussed in section 2, linguists (and others) may still debate the precise timing of this expansion. Hungarian and the Turkic languages are clearly rather recent arrivals in their respective European territories, a point to which I return in section 5, while the Uralic and Caucasian families essentially define the limits of Indo-European expansion, rather than being specifically 'pre-Indo-European'; in addition, there is a good possibility that Indo-European and Uralic may ultimately be related as part of a larger language family, a possibility entertained even by linguists who are sceptical about such macro-groupings as Nostratic or Eurasiatic. The only well-attested descendant of a pre-Indo-European language of Europe is Basque. The other somewhat extensively attested non-Indo-European language of antiquity is Etruscan, which forms a small family with the barely attested Rhetian and Lemnian, but it is quite possible that Etruscan may itself be a relative newcomer to Europe, having arrived in northern Italy not significantly, if at all, earlier than Indo-European languages. Though other non-Indo-European languages can be identified (such as Iberian), and there is a possibility that Afroasiatic languages may have formed part of the pre-Indo-European picture, the evidence is either sparse or indirect or both. Toponyms are certainly suggestive of pre-Indo-European languages, for instance it is known that many place names characteristic of Greece (such as those in -*inthos*) cannot be given an Indo-European etymology, and Vennemann has recently suggested in a number of publications that many European place names can be given plausible Vasconic (his name for a family including Basque) etymologies; see, for instance Vennemann (1999). But overall, our picture of the pre-Indo-European linguistic landscape of Europe remains unclear, even if we can say definitively that there were people in Europe for thousands of years before the introduction of Indo-European languages and that these people must have spoken something.

The introduction of agriculture to Europe has

been much easier to date, with a clear pattern of the spread of agriculture from the southeast (Anatolia) into Europe starting around 7000 BC. If one accepts the earlier dates for the spread of Indo-European languages into Europe, then the assumption of a direct connection between the spread of Indo-European languages and agriculture is plausible, though as noted in section 2 this really does involve assuming the earliest possible date for the expansion of Indo-European to Europe.

Studies of the prehistoric population of Europe have gained an immense boost in recent years from the study of human genetics. Much of the pioneering work on the distribution of genetic variables across Europe and elsewhere, as reflected for instance in Cavalli-Sforza *et al.* (1994), relied on classical markers, which has the unfortunate result that, as in linguistics and unlike archaeology, precise dating is not possible and correlations between similar patterns across disciplines may lack a clear chronological underpinning. Data from mitochondrial DNA, tracing the female line, and from Y-chromosome DNA, tracing the male line, provide the possibility of dating, and are thus potentially more useful as one tries to draw closer comparisons between archaeological and genetic patterns, although the chronologies from genetics are often subject to quite broad confidence intervals, as was discussed intermittently at the Cambridge symposium. With respect to Europe, the mitochondrial DNA material is particularly interesting here (e.g. Sykes 1999), suggesting that there has been substantial continuity of European population going back 25–40,000 years. However, one of the female lineages that has been identified as widespread in Europe, namely haplotype J, goes back to a common ancestor around 10,000 years ago — it is by far the youngest of the seven widespread female lineages — which would provide a good fit with the dispersal of agriculture into Europe. Semino *et al.* (2000) provide a similar picture for Y-chromosome DNA.

This suggests that much of the population of Europe goes back further than the Neolithic, with only a certain component being provided by gene flow that took place around the divide between Palaeolithic and Neolithic. At the symposium in Cambridge, there was lively discussion of just what the respective contribution of established Palaeolithic and incoming Neolithic populations might be to the current population of Europe, with estimates ranging from around 80:20 to around 30:70, a substantial difference. But even with the second figure, it is clear that a substantial population in Europe is 'pre-Neolithic' and adopted agriculture from one or more incoming Neolithic populations. This has implications also for linguistics. If a substantial part of the population of Europe descends from a pre-Neolithic population, then a fortiori it also descends from a pre-Indo-European population. Yet their descendants living today nearly all speak an Indo-European language. There must thus have been substantial shift from non-Indo-European to Indo-European languages as part of the spread of Indo-European languages to Europe. This makes it necessary to say a few words about language shift.

'Language shift' is a term used by Thomason & Kaufmann (1988) to refer to the process whereby members of a community abandon one language in order to speak another. Its meaning is the same as the term 'language replacement' used in some recent literature on population genetics, although I will keep to the former term, now well established in linguistics. Many examples of language shift are attested in historical periods; for instance, over the past two hundred years most of Ireland has shifted from being Irish-speaking to being English-speaking. Until recently, although cases of language shift have often been posited for prehistoric times (or for times with insufficient direct historical records), it has been virtually impossible actually to test claims about language shift. The interface of linguistics and genetics provides new tools for this kind of investigation: if population Y is more closely related to population X in terms of genetics, but to population Z in terms of language, then we have a *prima facie* case of language shift, as when Southern Chinese show greater genetic affiliation to Tai-speaking populations but greater linguistic affiliation to Chinese-speaking groups.

There is often an assumption, especially among non-linguists, and especially among speakers of major world languages such as English, that language shift is somehow an unusual, even quite exceptional phenomenon. In fact, language shift is a frequent phenomenon across the world today, and while it is impossible to establish that this was certainly so in earlier periods for which we lack adequate documentation, there is equally no reason to believe that the situation was significantly different. Indeed, in an age when most languages were spoken by only small communities, one might well imagine that language shift might have been more frequent. Part of the problem of perspective on the part of speakers of major world languages is that they tend to think of the problem in terms of questions like 'what on earth would induce me to abandon my language in favour of some other — I'd have to go to the trouble of learning that other language, and I'd never be as at home in it as in my native language?' But this is rarely how language shift takes place. Typically language shift can occur within a few generations, certainly within a single family, for example starting with a monolingual generation, followed by a generation with passive competence in the encroaching language, followed by a generation with active competence in both languages, followed by a generation with only passive competence in the traditional language, followed by a generation monolingual in the encroaching language. In some cases, the process can be accelerated — I have met people from traditional Celtic-speaking communities who are themselves monolingual speakers of English or French and who report growing up being unable to communicate with their grandparents (or specifically, grandmothers), who were monolingual in the local Celtic language. Moreover, the crucial change-over from being basically a speaker of the traditional language to being basically a speaker of the encroaching language may be so subtle as to be barely detectable. Parent and child both seem to be fully bilingual in languages X and Y, but closer inspection shows that the parent is dominant in X, while the child is dominant in Y. The scene is set for X to recede ever further into the background. (See Cutler *et al.* (1992) for the subtle methods that may need to be used to test which language is actually dominant in an apparent balanced bilingual.)

To conclude this section, and before returning to the Indo-Europeans, it may be worth expanding slightly on the role of the Basques in the present discussion of the relation between language, agriculture, and genetics. The Basque language is certainly pre-Indo-European in Europe, and therefore the question arises of whether the Basques can be identified specifically as a pre-agricultural population and moreover one with a genetic signature that predates the gene flow from the southeast, the latter to an extent that is significantly different from that of any other populations in Europe. When classical markers provided the only available genetic material, it did indeed look as if the Basques might be distinct, with such clear genetic characteristics as an unusually, by European standards, high incidence of blood group O. However, even within the investigation of classical markers, there is another possible explanation for this distinct genetic signature, namely genetic drift. In particular given that investigation of classical markers provides no reliable chronology, the distinct genetic signature could be the result an

ancient difference, but could equally be the result of changes spreading rapidly through a small, relatively isolated population. The isolation would also, of course, have been a factor in the preservation of the pre-Indo-European language when almost all other such languages were disappearing. The mitochondrial DNA evidence provides a better chronology, and indeed it turns out that the lineage J, which provides a good chronological fit with the introduction of agriculture to Europe, is particularly rare among the Basques. But it is certainly not the case that the lineages that are found among the Basques are rare elsewhere in Europe. Thus lineage H, with a time depth of around 25,000 years and thus well before the introduction of agriculture, has its highest frequency among the Basques, but is also the most frequent in Europe overall. All of this makes it plausible that there is a correlation among the facts that the Basques were among the last groups to adopt agriculture, that they largely avoided the gene flow that accompanied the introduction of agriculture, and that they also avoided the language shift to Indo-European. But the difference in language family does not correspond to anything like a similar degree of genetic difference, since the Basques are similar to large numbers of other individual Europeans in terms of their genetic profile, in particular to large numbers of Europeans who adopted agriculture earlier and who shifted to an Indo-European language.

4. Proto-Indo-European and agriculture

We may now turn specifically to the evidence for the reconstruction of agricultural vocabulary to Proto-Indo-European. Ideally, this section should have been written by an Indo-Europeanist, especially given that Indo-European studies are currently an area of rapid development. I have based my discussion essentially on the article on 'Agriculture' in (and by) Mallory & Adams (1997, 7–8), though consultation of a more recent research paper, Krell (1998), suggests few if any modifications, interestingly so given the rather different ideological perspectives of the two sets of authors. While most of this section will be devoted, like this volume in general, to arable farming, section 4.1 will provide a brief discussion of animal husbandry.

4.1. Animal husbandry
Although Mallory & Adams (1997) do not provide a single article on animal husbandry to parallel their article on (arable) agriculture, relevant information

can be gleaned from articles scattered throughout the encyclopaedia, and these provide solid evidence for at least a substantial pastoralist component of Proto-Indo-European society. Perhaps the clearest evidence is the distinction between two terms, both reconstructable to Proto-Indo-European, referring respectively to 'wild animal' versus 'livestock'; the latter term, showing up in a slight modification of their transcription of Proto-Indo-European as *pék'u (with the conventional asterisk receding a reconstructed form), is found not only in the European languages but also in Sanskrit (Mallory & Adams 1997, 23). The article 'Milk' (Mallory & Adams 1997, 381–3) notes that 'we can reconstruct a rich vocabulary for PIE [= Proto-Indo-European — BC] concerning milk and milk products, a testimony to the importance of these things to a people who were heavily dependent on animal husbandry for sustenance'. A verb *h₂melg'- 'to milk', for instance, is reconstructable not only for the European languages but also for Tocharian. (The Hittite for 'to milk' is not attested, i.e. we cannot say that it was not cognate (or, of course, that it was); none of the other items cited in this article is provided with Anatolian cognates.) A reconstructable verb *demh- 'to tame' is attested in the European languages (English *tame* derives from this etymon) and in Sanskrit, though here we run into the problem discussed in section 2 of identifying the precise sense of the original word, since it is also found in some languages with the general meaning of 'to subdue', and only the related sense 'presses, pushes' is found in Hittite (Mallory & Adams 1997, 565).

4.2. *Arable farming*

While various problems remain concerning the precise meaning of some of the terms reconstructable to Proto-Indo-European in the area of agriculture, including both crops, tools, and activities, the picture is sufficiently clear to allow us to conclude with Mallory & Adams (1997, 8) that

> there is no case whatsoever for assuming that the ancestors of all the Indo-European stocks did not know cereal agriculture . . . terms for the plow, cultivated field, and techniques appropriate to the processing of domestic cereals whose home range lay outside of most of Europe, suggest that *all* the earliest Indo-Europeans knew agriculture before the dispersals.

Likewise, Krell (1998, 274) concludes that 'speakers of PIE were familiar with the basic techniques of agriculture and did indeed grow certain crops for their own consumption'.

'Perhaps the most specific of the solidly reconstructed terms' for cereals, in the expression used by Mallory & Adams (1997, 7), is *yéwos, which they gloss as 'grain (particularly barley)', found in the European languages, Sanskrit, and perhaps Tocharian (Mallory & Adams 1997, 236). If the term did originally mean 'barley', then one would expect a word for 'wheat', since none of agricultural packages attested in relevant parts of Eurasia have barley without wheat, but no such word is reconstructable with reasonable certainty, suggesting here an instance of the danger of drawing conclusions from negative evidence, as discussed in section 2. There is also no reliable reconstruction of terms for other cereals, since the reconstructable terms are either geographically restricted (to Europe, or to the Mediterranean), or arguably originally referred to wild varieties (as with 'oats'), although there is also a reconstructable word for 'ryegrass', one of the primary weeds of the early Neolithic, domesticated as rye only from around 2000 BC.

Several words for agricultural activities can be reconstructed back to the proto-language, for instance *melh₂- 'to grind' (with reflexes also in Hittite), *seh₁- 'to sow' (with reflexes also in Hittite), *peis- 'to thresh' (with reflexes also in Sanskrit) (Mallory & Adams 1997, 247, 534, 581). While such items are typically also attested with meanings that are not specifically agricultural, for instance 'throw, drop' as well as 'sow', or 'crush' as well as 'grind', the fact that precisely these formations are found with precisely these agricultural senses outside the European languages, including sometimes in Anatolian and Tocharian, strongly suggests that the agricultural senses should be reconstructed to the proto-language, rather than being independent parallel innovations of the individual branches.

But surely the most striking instance of reconstruction of a clearly agricultural term, with no ascertainable pre-agricultural use, to Proto-Indo-European is the verb 'to plough' (Mallory & Adams 1997, 434–6), namely *h₂érh₃ye/o-, attested not only in the European languages but also in Armenian and, most strikingly, Tocharian. Mallory & Adams (1997, 434) suggest that a cognate is also found in Hittite, though noting that the Hittite word has also been explained as a loan from the Semitic language Akkadian. (Note that the noun 'plough' is a derivative of the verb across much of Indo-European.) However, if this term is reconstructable to Proto-Indo-European, then a potential chronological question arises. According to Mallory & Adams (1997, 435–6), the earliest clear evidence for ploughs in Europe dates from the fourth millennium BC, the earliest evidence even in the Middle East to about the sixth millennium BC. The plough is thus considerably later in Europe than the introduction of agriculture. The existence of a common word for 'plough' across virtually the whole of Indo-European suggests that the term must predate the break-up of the language family, and more specifically the dispersal of Indo-European languages to Europe; but this is then difficult or impossible to reconcile with the correlation between the dispersal of Indo-European languages and the dispersal of farming in Europe, since as noted in section 3 agriculture started spreading into Europe about 7000 BC. Perhaps perversely, what may be the most solid piece of evidence for agriculture among the Proto-Indo-Europeans is also easier to interpret as evidence against their having introduced agriculture to Europe.

5. Secondary dispersals

The combined discussion of sections 3 and 4 points to certain problems for the hypothesis that the spread of Indo-European languages to Europe accompanied the primary dispersal of agriculture to that area. In particular, this assumption requires the postulation of an unusually slow rate of language change between Proto-Indo-European and the attested Indo-European languages, and the indubitable existence of a Proto-Indo-European word for 'to plough' likewise suggests that the date for Proto-Indo-European must be later than that of the primary farming dispersal. This leaves open the possibility, indeed virtually the necessity, that the spread of Indo-European languages was an instance of secondary dispersal. More specifically, agriculture would already have been in place before the spread of Indo-European languages to Europe. In principle, either a new Indo-European population could have by and large replaced the original population but taken over from them the agricultural way of life, or large segments of the original population could have shifted to the encroaching Indo-European speech. The genetic evidence discussed in section 3 suggests that the second was at least an important, and perhaps the major factor.

From a general cultural perspective, this should not be surprising, since there are many instances of a particular cultural element or package being used most successfully by a group other than the group that originally developed it, with obvious examples being monotheistic religions, the manufacture of televisions, and, to take a linguistic example, writing systems. In the modern world the Latin, Cyrillic and Arabic writing systems have virtually monopolized the field, with other writing systems either extinct (such as Phoenician, the basis of the Greek and thus of the Latin and Cyrillic alphabets) or restricted to a single language (such as Greek, the world's first nearly phonemic writing system consistently representing both consonants and vowels, but long since eclipsed by its upstart offspring, the Latin and Cyrillic writing systems).

Turning back to agriculture, we may ask if there are attested examples of secondary farming dispersals that have led to the replacement of the language (whether by language shift or otherwise) of those who introduced the primary farming dispersal. Southeast Asia seems to provide one good example, as the Austroasiatic languages are now subordinate across much of the area to the languages of groups that came later to agriculture, such as speakers of Tai and Sino-Tibetan languages (Charles Higham this volume). But there are also close parallels from the later history of Europe. Of course, any parallel from a different time can only be partial, and I am not claiming that the cases to be discussed in the remainder of this paragraph offer close analogues for the details of possible secondary farming dispersal in Europe. Rather, they illustrate the general principle that an incoming population or language can 'piggy-back' its way into a dominant position by exploiting an agricultural society, albeit, at least in pre-industrial times, by buying into the agricultural package.

Although the spread of Indo-European languages represents the historical event that has had the greatest influence on the current linguistic profile of Europe, there are some later developments that have had local impacts, especially at the eastern edge of the continent, and it is to these that I wish to turn now. They concern primarily the interaction, well after the establishment of Indo-European languages across most of Europe, with speakers of other languages coming from the steppes and bringing languages of non-Indo-European families, in particular Turkic languages and Hungarian. These interactions are interesting in that they point to instances where Indo-European languages spoken at the time by sedentary agricultural populations have subsequently yielded to the non-Indo-European languages spoken by originally nomadic pastoralist incomers.

I will start with the case of Hungarian. The Hungarian language, a member of the Uralic family, entered the general area of present-day Hungary towards the end of the ninth century AD. From various sources, including not only direct records but also the legacy of place-names, we can tell that the area they entered, then called Pannonia, was largely Slavonic-speaking. (For a recent survey of linguistic issues concerned with the arrival of the Magyars in Pannonia, see Kovács & Veszprémy 1997.) Yet a thousand years later, the area in question is overwhelmingly Hungarian-speaking, though its traditional mode of subsistence remained sedentary agriculture. In other words, it was the language of the pastoralist newcomers that prevailed. In terms of mode of subsistence, it was that of the earlier agricultural population. We can now add genetics to this picture: genetically, the Hungarians do not stand out markedly from neighbouring populations (Cavalli-Sforza et al. 1994, 273 — though I would be less committal on some of the details). We thus have an incoming population speaking a language that ultimately predominated, but with the overall continuation of the pre-existing population (defined biologically) and its mode of subsistence.

This is thus a classic example of élite dominance, i.e. a language that is brought in by a small élite but which, because of the dominance of this élite, ultimately comes to prevail in the community over which they exercise this dominance. The precise mechanism by which this comes about is perhaps not reconstructable in its details, but we can imagine a prestigious core of Hungarian-speakers gradually assimilating a periphery, a process that was still underway in the nineteenth century and was perhaps only stopped by the loss of power that Hungarian underwent relative to neighbouring languages as a result of the break-up of the Austro-Hungarian Empire.

The spread of Turkic languages to Europe and its periphery must have involved a similar overall scenario, with the establishment of élites speaking Turkic languages and the gradual linguistic assimilation of speakers of other languages, though without any substantial change of the agricultural mode of subsistence or, necessarily, the biological composition of the population. (It should of course be noted that there is nothing inevitable about this particular outcome. The Turkic-speaking Bulgars were at least influential enough to give the people the Bulgarians and the country Bulgaria their names, but in this case it was the original Slavonic language that prevailed.) While various Turkic-speaking speech communities on the periphery of Europe could in principle serve as illustrations of this process, I shall actually concentrate on one particular case that relates to ongoing work by the geneticists and lin-

guists at my institute, and which involves the introduction of Azeri (Azerbaijani) to the Caucasus and its spread there; work published to date includes Nasidze et al. (2001) and Nasidze & Stoneking (2001).

The Caucasus represents a veritable mosaic of languages, and while there are disagreements about many issues concerning macro-families and also concerning sub-grouping within well-established language families, at a certain level of linguistic genealogical classification there is a consensus concerning the language families represented there, taking for convenience the time before the arrival of Russian on the scene. Three groups of languages have no close relatives outside the Caucasus, namely the Kartvelian (South Caucasian) languages (including Georgian), the Northwest (West) Caucasian languages (including Abkhaz and Circassian), and the Northeast (East) Caucasian (Nakh-Daghestanian) languages (including Chechen and Avar). In addition, there are representatives of the Indo-European family, namely Armenian (a separate branch of the family) and Iranian languages (including Ossetian), and Turkic languages, namely representatives of the Oghuz branch (including Azeri) and the Kipchak branch (including Kumyk). Genetically, the Caucasus is also a region of considerable variation, considerably greater than in the whole of (the rest of) Europe put together. (Geographers and historians may argue over whether the Caucasus forms part of Europe. An inspection of the genetic variation suggests rather the question whether or not Europe should be considered part of the Caucasus!) In some cases there is good correlation between linguistic and genetic classifications, in that a particular group of languages that form a genealogical unit also correspond to a contiguous part of the genetic profile of the area. But there are also substantial discrepancies, providing prima facie evidence of language shift and meriting more detailed historical analysis and interpretation.

One of these cases of disagreement between linguistic and genetic affiliations concerns the Armenian and Azeri speech communities. (I am concerned here only with Azeri living in the Caucasus, not with those living in northwestern Iran, concerning whom I am not aware of any genetic studies. It thus remains an open question to what extent the Azeri of the Caucasus and of Iran are related genetically, although it is clear that they speak closely related varieties of the same language.) Linguistically, Armenian and Azeri are quite different, reflecting, as stated above, a branch of Indo-European versus a member of the Oghuz branch of the Turkic language family. Yet the work by Nasidze & Stoneking shows that in terms of mitochondrial DNA, the Armenian and Azeri populations are virtually indistinguishable from one another. As in Europe, the genetic material here reflects a long-standing continuity of population. This is an interesting result, since it not only flies against the linguistic classification, but may also seem surprising given the traditional animosity of the two speech communities. In this particular case, however, the historical explanation is relatively straightforward. We know from the historical record that the nomadic pastoralist speakers of Turkic languages entered the Caucasus about a thousand years ago, with Azeri gaining ascendancy in the early second millennium AD. Thus as a language Azeri is clearly a relative newcomer to the area. Nonetheless, in a relatively short period it succeeded in establishing itself as the major language of what is now Azerbaijan. The genetics shows that there was not a major shift in the biological basis of the population, at least insofar as the female line is concerned — it would of course be interesting to have comparable material for Y-chromosome DNA to see whether or not there was more population replacement within the male line. Moreover, the mode of subsistence of the Azeri is primarily agriculture, as it was before the arrival of speakers of Turkic languages. We thus have clear evidence for a language shift, from whatever was spoken before in present-day Azerbaijan to Azeri, without significant population change (at least as regards the female line) or change in mode of subsistence.

One may now ask just what was spoken in Azerbaijan before the arrival of Azeri. The answer is almost certainly Northeast Caucasian languages. The ancient kingdom of Caucasian Albania overlapped the territory of modern Azerbaijan, and its still poorly understood language, Caucasian Albanian, seems to be an ancestral form of present-day Udi, a Northeast Caucasian spoken in northern Azerbaijan. Indeed, the assimilation of smaller Northeast Caucasian languages to Azeri remains an ongoing process, especially in northern Azerbaijan, where a number of Northeast Caucasian languages now form small enclaves in Azeri-speaking territory. (It might be noted in passing that Azeri in northwestern Iran plays a similar role in assimilating speakers of smaller Iranian languages, although the situation here is somewhat complicated by the, relatively recent, introduction of Persian as a socially even higher-level language.) Interestingly, it is not the general case (though there may be exceptions) that the territory of present-day Azerbaijan was Armenian-speaking before the arrival of Azeri, so the question

also presents itself of the relation between the Indo-European linguistic affinity of Armenian-speakers and their genetic affinity not so much with speakers of other Indo-European languages as with other populations of the Caucasus, a question that probably requires more information, especially concerning genetic variation within Armenian populations, before it can be answered other than speculatively.

I have discussed the cases of Hungarian and Azeri in some detail because they provide important scenarios that need to be kept in mind as we consider the more general question of the spread of languages and agriculture, including in relation to gene flow. We have here two instances where a nomadic pastoral élite has succeeded in imposing its language on a sedentary agricultural population without significantly affecting the mode of subsistence of that population and without leaving any genetic signature even remotely comparable to its linguistic signature. Of course, we may argue that these are exceptional cases relative to Europe as a whole, but equally one can counter-argue, first, that we lack comparable direct evidence for earlier periods in Europe and, second, that the establishment of Hungarian and Azeri have been remarkably successful in a very short time (around 1000 years), so that given a longer time-span one might expect even greater levels of success. At the very least it leaves open the possibility that at least some branches of Indo-European might have established themselves in Europe not as a result of the spread of agriculture, but as the result of the subsequent imposition of the language of incomers on an agricultural population.

Of course, this leaves open the question of what factors led speakers of pre-Indo-European languages in Europe to shift to Indo-European languages, and in the absence of more direct evidence it may well be impossible to answer this question, although there is certainly a range of possibilities that one could consider (including, for instance, a partial agricultural collapse of the kind that seems to have allowed Athabaskan languages to gain a foothold in the American Southwest). I would, however, emphasize the point made in section 3 above, namely that language shift is not a 'big deal' in human history. Incoming Indo-European languages may have had some slight perceived advantage that induced speakers of other languages first to learn them as second languages, perhaps quite unaware that they were initiating a process that would lead to the extinction of their own languages.

418

6. Conclusions

I have tried to show that while there is good evidence for assuming that speakers of Proto-Indo-European were a population familiar with agriculture, there are problems with assuming that they were the population that first brought agriculture to Europe, both from the purely linguistic side (too slow an assumed rate of language change) and from the perspective of the linguistics–archaeology interface (a word for 'to plough' that is attributable to the proto-language but cannot, on the archaeological evidence, be early enough to have accompanied the primary farming dispersal). While it cannot absolutely be excluded, by stretching the chronological bounds to their limits, that speakers of Indo-European drove the primary farming dispersal in Europe, a more plausible hypothesis is that they entered a Europe already committed to agriculture, triggering a language shift process that led to the near-universal dominance of Indo-European languages in Europe but without too great a level of population replacement and without any major shift in the agricultural basis of subsistence.

References

Benveniste, É., 1969. *Le vocabulaire des institutions indo-européennes*, vol. 1: *Économie, parenté, société*. Paris: Les Éditions de Minuit.

Buck, C.D., 1949. *A Dictionary of Selected Synonyms in the Principal Indo-European Languages: a Contribution to the History of Ideas*. Chicago (IL): Chicago University Press.

Cavalli-Sforza, L.L., P. Menozzi & A. Piazza, 1994. *The History and Geography of Human Genes*. Princeton (NJ): Princeton University Press.

Cutler, A., J. Mehler, D. Norris & J. Segui, 1992. The monolingual nature of speech segmentation by bilinguals. *Cognitive Psychology* 24, 381–410.

Kovács, L. & L. Veszprémy (eds.), 1997. *Honfoglalás és nyelvészet*. Budapest: Balassi Kiadó.

Krell, K.S., 1998. Gimbutas' Kurgan–PIE homeland hypothesis: a linguistic critique, in *Archaeology and Language*, vol. II: *Archaeological Data and Linguistic Hypotheses*, eds. R. Blench & M. Spriggs. London: Routledge, 267–82.

Mallory, J.P. & D.Q. Adams, 1997. *Encyclopedia of Indo-European Culture*. London & Chicago (IL): Fitzroy Dearborn.

Nasidze, I. & M. Stoneking, 2001. Mitochondrial DNA variation and language replacements in the Caucasus. *Proceedings of the Royal Society of London* B 268, 1197–206.

Nasidze, I., G.M. Risch, M. Robichaux, S.T. Sherry, M.A. Batzer & M. Stoneking, 2001. Alu insertion polymorphisms and the genetic structure of human populations from the Caucasus. *European Journal of Human Genetics* 9, 267–72.

Renfrew, C., 1987. *Archaeology and Language: the Puzzle of Indo-European Origins*. London: Jonathan Cape.

Renfrew, C., A. McMahon & L. Trask (eds.), 2000. *Time Depth in Historical Linguistics*. 2 vols. (Papers in the Prehistory of Languages.) Cambridge: McDonald Institute for Archaeological Research.

Semino, O., G. Passarino, P.J. Oefner, A.A. Lin, S. Arbuzova, L.E. Beckman, G. De Benedictis, P. Francalacci, A. Kouvatsi, S. Limborska, M. Marcikic, A. Mika, B. Mika, D. Primorac, A.S. Santachiara-Benerecetti, L.L. Cavalli-Sforza & P.A. Underhill, 2000. The genetic legacy of Paleolithic *Homo sapiens sapiens* in extant Europeans: a Y chromosome perspective. *Science* 290, 1155–9.

Starostin, S.A., 2000. Comparative-historical linguistics and lexicostatistics, in Renfrew *et al.* (eds.), 223–59.

Sykes, B., 1999. Using genes to map population structure and origins, in *The Human Inheritance: Genes, Language, and Evolution*, ed. B. Sykes. Oxford: Oxford University Press, 93–117.

Thomason, S.G. & T. Kaufman, 1988. *Language Contact, Creolization, and Genetic Linguistics*. Berkeley (CA): University of California Press

Vennemann gen. Nierfeld, T., 1999. Volksetymologie und Ortsnamenforschung. Begriffsbestimmung und Anwendung auf ausgewählte, überwiegend bayerische Toponyme. *Beiträge zur Namenforschung* 34, 269–322.

Chapter 33

DNA Variation in Europe:
Estimating the Demographic Impact of Neolithic Dispersals

Guido Barbujani & Isabelle Dupanloup

Most anthropologists are convinced that anatomically modern Europeans are not descended from Neanderthal ancestors. Both morphological (Stringer & Andrews 1988; Foley 1998) and genetic evidence (Tishkoff *et al.* 1996; Krings *et al.* 1997; 2000; Ovchinnikov *et al.* 2000; Ingman *et al.* 2000; Underhill *et al.* 2000) point to a clear discontinuity between the two groups. Although it is still impossible to rule out completely the presence of any Neanderthal genes in the contemporary genome (Relethford 2001), the uncertainty really concerns whether Neanderthals contributed a minimal fraction of the European gene pool, or none at all. In both cases, the current European gene diversity can safely be viewed as the product of demographic processes occurring in the last 35,000 or 40,000 years, after the first Upper Palaeolithic colonizers arrived. Previously, the Europeans (or, more exactly, the ancestors of today's Europeans) did not live in Europe.

What happened next is, on the contrary, controversial. Many changes are documented in the material culture of the European populations. Some occurred on a local scale, others seem to have affected a large part of the continent. Of the latter, the inception of agriculture and animal breeding, or Neolithic transition, is probably the most dramatic. In the course of some 5000 years, farming economies developed over much of Europe, replacing hunting and gathering as the main subsistence technique. But archaeological evidence, however accurate, cannot tell us if these changes in the material culture mean that the same people adopted a different lifestyle (Zvelebil & Zvelebil 1988), or if new immigrants introduced the new lifestyle (Ammerman & Cavalli-Sforza 1984). Analysis of genetic diversity in contemporary populations and, more recently, in ancient specimens, has become an indispensable complement to the study of archaeology, for addressing questions of this kind (von Haeseler *et al.* 1996; Renfrew 2000b).

Although genetic data tend to be less ambiguous than, for instance, osteological data, their interpretation is not straightforward either. A well-known problem concerns the role of selection. Almost every conceivable pattern of genetic diversity may be explained both by a selection mechanism, and by the interplay between genetic drift and gene flow (see e.g. Tajima 1989a,b). And even for neutral genes, identical levels of population diversity, as measured by the standardized genetic variance, F_{st}, may reflect either extensive gene flow among small isolates, or limited gene flow among large populations, because F_{st} is inversely related to the product of the effective population size, N_e, by the migration rate, m (Wright 1951). Selective pressures are likely to affect just one or a few loci, whereas migration should have the same effect on the entire genome. Therefore, comparing patterns of variation across several loci is indispensable, at least to understand whether selection is necessary to explain the data (Piazza *et al.* 1981). But there is no easy recipe for reconstructing episodes of the human past, even using abundant DNA data.

The problem is clearly worse when the DNA data are not abundant, especially if a single locus is considered (Cavalli-Sforza & Minch 1997; Hilton & Hey 1997; Edwards & Beerli 2000; Stumpf & Goldstein 2001). In that case, disentangling the signals of population processes from sampling and stochastic variation may become very complicated (Takahata & Tajima 1991). Despite those potential difficulties, many investigators are currently attempting to reconstruct prehistory from genetic data, using the many DNA markers that can now be typed.

Here we shall outline only schematically the two main demographic scenarios that have been pro-

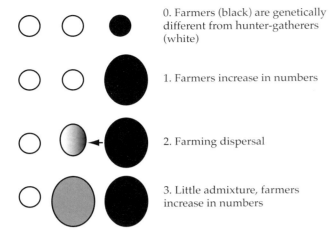

0. Farmers (black) are genetically different from hunter-gatherers (white)

1. Farmers increase in numbers

2. Farming dispersal

3. Little admixture, farmers increase in numbers

Figure 33.1. *Conditions for the origin of clines under demic diffusion. A schematic synthesis of the DD model, as proposed by Ammerman & Cavalli-Sforza (1984), using three populations.*

posed to account for the Neolithic transition in Europe. The interested reader will find much more in the original sources, and elsewhere in this volume. The demic diffusion (DD) model (Ammerman & Cavalli-Sforza 1984) considers the spread of technologies for food production as a consequence of the dispersal of the first farmers from the Levant; the farmers moved, and their technologies (as well as their genes) moved with them. On the contrary, the cultural diffusion (CD) model (Zvelebil & Zvelebil 1988) considers the spread of agriculture essentially as the spread of a cultural innovation, with limited consequences in the populations' build-up. Therefore, the two models predict different impacts of the Neolithic transition upon the genes of the Europeans. We understand that, under the CD model, the continental patterns of genetic variation should reflect demographic processes that occurred before the Europeans turned to agriculture. Therefore, the CD and the DD predict geographic patterns that may be attributed, respectively, to Palaeolithic and to Neolithic dispersal.

The purpose of this paper is to reconsider what genetic data have to say about the DD and the CD models. In particular, we shall claim that a persisting confusion between molecular evolution and demographic history has generated the unwarranted belief that mtDNA and Y-chromosome data suggest a strong genetic continuity between Palaeolithic and contemporary Europeans. We shall suggest an alternative, although certainly not new, way to look at those data, through the admixture coefficient, and we shall present some preliminary results.

Genetic diversity in Europe

The first genetic evidence for a major Neolithic contribution to the European gene pool comes from studies of protein markers. Menozzi *et al.* (1978) described broad gradients spanning much of Europe, and radiating North and West from the Levant. Such allele-frequency gradients affect several tens of loci (Sokal & Menozzi 1982; Sokal *et al.* 1989; Barbujani *et al.* 1994; Cavalli-Sforza *et al.* 1993; 1994; *contra* Fix 1999), and parallel the patterns of spread of farming, as inferred from archaeological evidence (Sokal *et al.* 1991). Cultural transmission is not expected to have genetic consequences, and so Ammerman & Cavalli-Sforza (1984) proposed that that parallelism reflects a common cause, that is, farming spread because the farmers expanded. Needless to say, genetic patterns, no matter whether identified at the protein or DNA level, do not carry a date with them. Therefore, any demographic process affecting Europe on a global scale can potentially generate the observed patterns. However, at least two things are clear, namely: 1) that process must have entailed extensive gene flow (otherwise no recognizable pattern would have been generated); and 2) it must have affected the whole continent (or else its consequences would not be evident over the whole continent).

Note that migration, by itself, does not create gradients. If some people just move from one place to another, the genetic similarity between those localities will increase, but intermediate localities will not be affected. Broad clines spanning, as in Europe, an entire continent, can only result from more complex processes. The DD model lists four conditions for their occurrence, namely: 1) that the expanding (i.e. farming, in our case) and the previously settled population differ genetically; 2) that the expanding population increases in numbers; 3) that that increase prompts a centrifugal dispersal, in the search for new arable land; and 4) that the dispersing farming communities and the local hunters and gatherers do not form a single group right away, but remain separated, although perhaps dwelling in the same area (Fig. 33.1).

The initial genetic difference is crucial because any exchange of genes among identical communities would be impossible to detect *a posteriori* (see Renfrew 2001). Conditions (2) and (3), namely the demographic growth of the farmers and their range expansion, are among the expected consequences of the shift to a food-producing economy. What may not be obvious is the importance of condition (4). Ammerman & Cavalli-Sforza (1984) have shown that if the hunter-gatherers merge *immediately* with the farmers, all members of the new community will benefit from the increased food available, the off-spring of the farmers will have no advantage over the offspring of the former hunter-gatherers, and so the farmers' genes will not travel too far from their geographic origin. On the contrary, if only the de-scendants of the first farmers can produce food, they will also be the only ones who keep growing in numbers. In this way, their alleles will tend to in-crease in frequency and to disperse, whereas the hunter-gatherers' alleles will not. This is the mean-ing of the low 'acculturation' parameter, g, in Ammer-man & Cavalli-Sforza (1984).

Computer simulations have confirmed that these processes do result in broad clines, under vari-ous rates of demographic growth, of farmers' dis-persal, and of successive gene flow (Rendine *et al.* 1986; Barbujani *et al.* 1995). Although these studies were not asking explicitly which fraction of the Eu-ropean gene pool is represented by genes of the farmers' descendants, clines resembling those ob-served in field studies were generated when at least 66 per cent, and up to 100 per cent, of the genes came in through dispersal of people who did not dwell in Europe, but in the Levant, at the beginning of the Neolithic.

The highest figure, 100 per cent, implies that continent-wide gradients can also be generated by a complete replacement of the previously settled popu-lation, and therefore, also by an expansion in a pre-viously unoccupied territory, such as the one that led to the initial, Palaeolithic peo-pling of Europe. In both such cases, bottlenecks, rather than demographic growth and range expansion, are the main factor determining clines. In the dispersal of small groups of individuals, repeated bot-tlenecks may lead to fixation of alleles. Later, the alleles lost may be reintroduced by short-range gene flow in geographically intermediate localities. This generates gra-dients that look much like those determined by demic diffusion (Barbujani *et al.* 1995; Fix 1997).

Thus, the allele-fre-quency clines are consistent with the DD model, but do not necessarily imply that model (see also Renfrew 2000a). When Richards *et al.* (1996) observed little geographical structuring in their analysis of mtDNA variation, they proposed that the clines observed at the protein level had been generated during the first, Palaeolithic colonization of Europe, and that Neolithic processes have had, in fact, a much smaller demographic impact than pre-viously believed.

In several studies (Richards *et al.* 1996; 1998; 2000; Sykes 1999), these authors typed the hyper-variable region I of the mitochondrial genome in various European groups. They then proceeded to estimate the ages of the main lineages, a procedure they called founder analysis (Richards *et al.* 2000). To that end, evolutionary networks (Bandelt *et al.* 1995) were constructed, the mutations characterizing the deepest branches of the networks were identified, and groups of haplotypes sharing those deep-root-ing mutations, or haplogroups, were defined. The estimates of the ages of the founder haplogroups have changed through time (Table 33.1), but most of them clearly exceed 10,000 years. It is on the basis of those dates that Richards *et al.* (2000) infer a largely Palaeolithic origin of the Europeans; Neolithic farm-ers were estimated to have contributed less than 20 per cent of the total European founder mtDNAs. A recent study of the Y chromosome reached similar conclusions, estimating at 22 per cent the Neolithic contribution to the European gene pool (Semino *et al.* 2000).

Table 33.1. *Estimated ages of the European founders of mitochondrial lineages (thousands of years). In the first column, the numbers in parentheses refer to the haplogroup designation in Richards et al. (1996). The figures in the fourth column represent ranges of possible values, on the assumption that each haplogroup was introduced in Europe not by one founder, but by founders who differed by not more than one mutation (Sykes 1999). Owing to the frequent changes of haplogroup definitions, the same haplogroup name does not necessarily indicate an identical set of haplotypes in different papers.*

Haplogroup	Richards *et al.* 1996	Richards *et al.* 1998	Sykes 1999	Richards *et al.* 2000
H (1)	23.5	20.5	11.0–14.0	15.0–17.2
HV				29.3–37.6
J (2A)	23.5	28.0	8.5	6.9–10.9
T (2B)	35.5	46.5	11.0–14.0	9.6–17.7
T1				6.1–12.8
T2				9.3–16.2
IWX (3)	50.5	35.0–18.0	11.0–14.0	
X			20.0	
I				19.9–32.7
K (4)	17.5	15.5	11.0–14.0	10.0–15.5
U (5)	36.5	52.5		44.6–54.4
U4				16.1–24.7
U5			50.0	

Those results were viewed as supporting the CD model, which, however, has not yet been tested by simulation. It would be interesting, for example, to see how likely it is that the mutations generating a new haplogroup are immediately followed by population expansions (as assumed by Richards *et al.* 2000, 1256), the only way whereby the age of a founder would approximate the timing of a migration. However, in Richards *et al.* (2000), the assumptions and predictions of the founder analysis were made explicit. Based on both archaeological (Barker 1985; Whittle 1996) and genetic (Torroni *et al.* 1998) evidence, and taking into account the possibility of back migration and repeated mutation at the same site, Richards *et al.* (2000) argued that genetic variation in Europe mostly reflects founder effects at the Last Glacial Maximum (LGM), some 18,000 years ago, followed by northward expansions of the survivors' lineages. In this way, geographic variation in Europe would have been determined essentially by gene flow from glacial refugia, probably located south of the Pyrenees, Alps and Balkans. This model, therefore, does not predict the existence of extensive southeast–northwest clines. Older gradients, established during the Palaeolithic peopling of the continent, should have been erased by population movements into the glacial refugia and then out of them, before and after the LGM; newer gradients would be unlikely, given the very limited Neolithic contribution envisaged. Semino *et al.* (2000) interpreted in much the same way the European Y-chromosome variation, although their statistical analysis was less elaborated.

In the last decade, however, clines were shown to be the rule in Europe, not only at the protein, but at the DNA level as well (Table 33.2). The Y chromosome, in particular, shows highly significant gradients from the Levant into Western and Northern Europe, both at the microsatellite level (Casalotti *et al.* 1999) and for biallelic markers (Semino *et al.* 1996; Quintana-Murci *et al.* 1999; Rosser *et al.* 2000). The exception seems to be mtDNA, for which a clinal structure was detected only around the Mediterranean Sea, but not in northern Europe (Simoni *et al.* 2000; Richards *et al.* 2002). The reasons why mtDNA shows a different pattern should be further investigated, but they may include selection (Excoffier 1990; Wise *et al.* 1998). On the other hand, nuclear DNA variation is compatible with the effects of both a Palaeolithic colonization of the continent, and of the Neolithic demic diffusion, but not with a substantial impact of Mesolithic re-expansions on the European genetic variation. Also, gradients radiating from the putative glacial refugia have not been described so far, to the best of our knowledge. In particular, studies of both modern populations (Simoni *et al.* 2000; Richards *et al.* 2002) and of ancient DNA (Izagirre & De la Rua 1999) have failed to identify evidence of an expansion from Iberia of people carrying the mitochondrial haplogroup V, as proposed by Torroni *et al.* (1998).

Haplogroups, populations

It seems fair to say that most studies based on allele genealogies have been interpreted as suggesting a minor contribution to the European gene pool of early Neolithic farmers, and hence as supporting a CD model of the European Neolithic. Conversely, most analyses of geographic variation have been interpreted as suggesting that the Neolithic contribution was, in fact, large, and that the DD model is correct. Is there any way to reconcile those results?

In a previous paper, we argued that it is important to maintain a distinction between processes affecting genes and processes affecting populations (Barbujani *et al.* 1998). Genes mutate and recombine, whereas populations expand, shrink, split, become extinct and exchange genes with one another. Both classes of phenomena determine genetic diversity, within and between populations, but the age of an allele genealogy only depends on the moment at which a certain mutation occurred. If we are asking questions about population history, the answer must be sought in population data, not in the ages of molecules, although the latter are much easier to estimate.

When a new allele, let us call it A, is generated by a mutation, it finds itself in total linkage disequilibrium with all other markers. In the course of time, recombination will reduce linkage dis-

Table 33.2. *Summary of analyses of geographic DNA variation in Europe.*

Authors	No. of Loci	Markers	Results
Semino *et al.* 1996	2	Y-chromosome RFLPs	SE–NW clines
Chikhi *et al.* 1998a,b	7	Nuclear STRs, minisatellites, and sequence polymorphisms	6 SE–NW clines
Casalotti *et al.* 1999	7	Y-chromosome STRs and YAP insertion	6 SE–NW clines
Simoni *et al.* 2000	1	Mitochondrial sequences	Clinal only in southern Europe
Rosser *et al.* 2000	11	Y-chromosome SNPs	SE–NW and N–S clines
Richards *et al.* 2002	1	mtDNA	SE–NW and E–W clines

equilibrium, and adjacent sites will also mutate. As a consequence of both phenomena (only of the latter, for non-recombining DNA regions), the diversity at sites linked to A, initially zero, will tend to increase. Genetic drift and/or selection will eliminate many newly arisen alleles. However, if A makes it through the first few generations, chances are it will exceed the frequency threshold (1 per cent or 5 per cent) at which it will be officially declared polymorphic by geneticists. When the mutation rate is known, the count of the mutations observed along the branches of the evolutionary tree provides an estimate of the age of that lineage, also referred to as the time to the most recent common ancestor, or coalescence time. The ρ-statistic (Forster *et al.* 1996), often used in mitochondrial studies, is an estimate of the age of a group of alleles.

What is the relationship between the age of a founder lineage, and the age of the population where it is found? In Figure 33.2 we outline what happens when an ancestral group splits into two descendent populations at time τ. The coalescence times for a locus, T, is expected to be $4N_e$, and the differences between two loci, T_1 and T_2, depend on the randomness of the coalescent process (Hudson 1990). Gene flow may complicate the pattern. However, in the simplest case of no ancestral polymorphism, on average the time since gene divergence exceeds τ roughly by a quantity $2N_e$ (Edwards & Beerli 2000), namely the expected time for the coalescence of the two alleles that have generated the genealogies in the two derived populations. If there is ancestral polymorphism, more than two alleles will have to coalesce, and that difference may be larger. By using T_1 and T_2 as a proxy for τ, the populations' ages are necessarily going to be overestimated, unless N_e (and therefore $2N_e$) is equal to 0. In other words, the only way whereby the age of a founder may approximate a population age is when the population originated through a drastic bottleneck.

Thus, the allele genealogies provide ready-to-use information on population history only if that history begun at extremely small (strictly speaking, zero) population sizes. That seems unlikely in Europe, for several reasons. First, systematic founder effects result in the presence of different alleles in different populations; had founder effects been common, many if not most alleles should be population-specific (see Heyer 1999). On the contrary, extensive allele sharing is documented in Europe, at the nuclear (Kidd *et al.* 2000; Rosser *et al.* 2000; Semino *et al.* 2000), as well as at the mitochondrial (Richards *et al.* 2000) level. Note also that establishing whether a

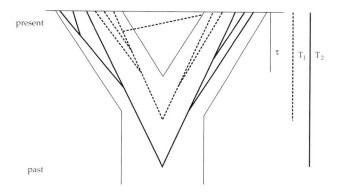

Figure 33.2. *What we want to know, and what we actually get, in population studies based on allele genealogies. An ancestral population (thin lines) splits into two descendent populations at time τ. The thick lines represent genetic divergence of alleles at two loci; an episode of gene flow is represented by the dashed line connecting the two populations. Unless a drastic founder effects has eliminated all genetic variation at the moment of the split, the coalescence time of the genealogy precedes the population split.*

mitochondrial allele is really absent from a population requires far greater sample sizes than currently available (Helgason *et al.* 2000), of the order of several thousands of individuals. Second, if a mutation rate of 1 transition every 20,180 years (Forster *et al.* 1996) is not an underestimate, the current mtDNA differentiation in Europe is too high to be compatible with bottlenecks in the last 10,000 years (Barbujani & Bertorelle 2001).

If, as a rule, the European populations did not originate through repeated and extreme founder effects, some initial polymorphism existed at most loci in most populations. This phenomenon has been described, for instance, in Caribbean individuals of African ancestry, who brought with them part of their original, African genetic diversity (Torroni *et al.* 1995). These are the cases, in other words, in which allele genealogies are older than the populations in which they occur, as discussed above. Edwards & Beerli (2000) also point out that the degree of overestimation of τ becomes much greater when the population of interest is not panmictic, but is structured into multiple, semi-isolated subpopulations. Once again, that seems the case for the prehistoric population of Europe.

One possible source of confusion may lie in the words we use. A lineage that originated during the Palaeolithic may be called 'Palaeolithic', but then one must be aware that Palaeolithic (or earlier) lineages may have arrived in a population at any later time. Well-known examples are the nucleotide substitutions shared by human and chimp alleles of the HLA system, which must have occurred prior to the human–chimpanzee split (Ayala *et al.* 1995). On the other hand, few alleles can be labelled as Neolithic, because the last 10,000 years are a short lapse of time, in mutational terms, with respect to the whole mutational history of the human population.

In short, the vast majority of human polymorphic alleles, or allelic lineages, arose during the Palaeolithic, or even much earlier, and this comes as no surprise. But this timing of a (molecular) phenomenon, a nucleotide substitution during the DNA replication preceding a meiosis, is independent from the (demographic) process whereby that molecular variant spreaded in the geographic space. We have seen that the coalescence times of human genes may go back to periods at which there was no such thing as a human being. It does not seem safe to assume that, on the contrary, the coalesce times of European mitochondrial lineages tell us the history of the first Europeans.

Three questions

The considerations outlined above lead us to suspect that the assumption of repeated, strong founder effects in the history of most European populations may lead to unwarranted inferences, including a systematic overestimation of the age of population splits. This is a complicated subject, and for the sake of clarity we summarize our views in the form of three very schematic questions. Their purpose is to stress that the dates of demographic changes and the ages of gene genealogies need not be correlated (on this subject, see also the review papers by Nichols 2001 and Hurles & Jobling 2001). We shall be glad to reconsider our views, should somebody answer these questions, or show that they make no sense. We hope that this may help reduce, or at least better define, the areas of disagreement.

1. If the alleles' ages provide a reasonable estimate of a population's age, why do the former differ so much among loci (Hey 1997; Lum *et al.* 1998)? In particular, why do autosomal and X-linked loci show much larger values than mitochondrial DNA and the Y chromosome (800,000 years for Beta-globin: Harding *et al.* 1997; 311,000 years for APO-E: Fullerton *et al.* 2000; 535,000 years for the Xq13-3 region: Kaessmann *et al.* 1999; 3 million years for the AB0-Secretor locus: Koda *et al.* 2000)? Which ones should we trust?

2. The overall coalescence time of mtDNA in Europe must be more than 50,000 years, since 50,000 years is the estimated age of one haplogroup, U(5) (Richards *et al.* 2000). If coalescence times provide reasonable estimates of a population's age, why should we not use that global age, rather than the age of arbitrarily-defined haplogroups, to estimate the age of the European population? This would support the view that Neanderthals, the only inhabitants of Europe at the time, did transmit their genes to contemporary Europeans.

3. If the coalescence time of haplogroups provides a reasonable estimate of a population's age, why should we not equate the coalescence time of the AB0-Secretor alleles, or of the HLA alleles, with the age of the world's population, thus rejecting the model of recent African origin of humankind?

Quantifying the contribution of parental populations to the European gene pool

The Y-chromosome haplogroup 9 (Fig. 33.3) has been proposed as a marker of Neolithic expansions, because it is clinally distributed with maximum frequency in the Near East (Semino *et al.* 1996; Quintana-Murci *et al.* 1999; Rosser *et al.* 2000) and because it seems relatively young (Semino *et al.* 2000). Its frequency, along with the frequencies of other similarly-distributed haplogroups, has been taken as a measure of the Neolithic component in the European gene pool (Semino *et al.* 2000).

Among the populations of the Levant, however, only 30 per cent of Y chromosomes belong to haplogroup 9. The average frequency of that haplogroup all over Europe is around 15 per cent. Now, the Basques, considered as the paradigm of a population that has received very limited input, if any, from Neolithic immigrants, do not show haplogroup 9 at all. It takes only a proportional calculation (30:100 = 15:X) to show that a haplogroup frequency of 15 per cent can be obtained by mixing 50 per cent, of people from the Levant, with an equal proportion of people whose Y chromosomes were like those of contemporary Basques. That 50 per cent is the admixture rate (see e.g. Chakraborty 1975).

It seems obvious to us that the debate on the Palaeolithic or Neolithic origin of the European gene pool is really a discussion on the amount of Neolithic admixture. Figure 33.4 shows a model of such admixture. The contributions, m_1 and m_2, of two paternal populations to a hybrid population can be estimated from the mean coalescence times of pairs of genes, drawn either within each population, or between the admixed and the parental populations (Bertorelle & Excoffier 1998; Dupanloup & Bertorelle 2001). This model also takes into account the effects of genetic drift after hybridization, and so it seems suitable for quantifying Neolithic and pre-Neolithic components in the European gene pool.

A crucial factor, which may potentially bias these estimates, is the definition of the parent populations. In our case, however, many authors have identified the Basque population as at most closely related to the Palaeolithic inhabitants of Europe (Calafell & Bertranpetit 1994; Bertranpetit *et al.* 1995; Hurles *et al.* 1999; Hill *et al.* 2000), while it is known that the early Neolithic farmers, whatever their number, came in from the Levant (Menozzi *et al.* 1978; Richards *et al.* 2000). Each locus represents a distinct realization of the same admixture process, and so, once again, robust estimates can only be based on several genes. As a preliminary phase in the application of this method to broader European data bases, however, we present here some results, relative to the analysis of one mitochondrial data set (Simoni *et al.* 2000, updated with Syrian, Greek and Anatolian sequences from our lab), and two data sets of Y-chromosome biallelic polymorphisms (Rosser *et al.* 2000; Semino *et al.* 2000).

Some DNA-based admixture estimates

We estimated the contributions of two ancestral populations to the gene pool of 12 European regions. The gene pools of the putative parental populations were assumed to contain the alleles now observed, respectively, in the Basque and in the Levant populations, at the same frequencies. Table 33.3 summarizes the admixture estimates obtained for each of the 12 regions, and for each data base studied.

Most standard errors are between 5 and 15 per cent; occasional higher values (e.g. for mtDNA in Portugal) depend on small sample sizes. Three estimates are greater than 1, reflecting more extreme genetic characteristics than those of the Levant population. The two Y-chromosome data sets contain different samples of individuals, and hence they are statistically independent.

There are large differences between estimates obtained from different data sets for the same region, thus stressing once again the inadequacy of single-locus approaches for robust inferences on population history. However, no systematic trend is evident in these differences. The m_L estimate is higher in the mtDNA data set for 5 regions, and in the Y-chromosome data set from Rosser *et al.* (2000) for

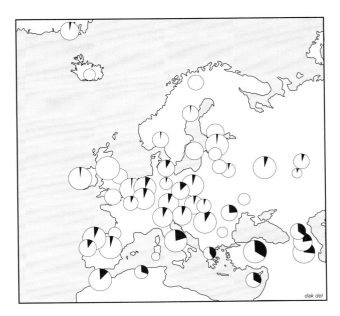

Figure 33.3. *Frequency of Y-chromosome haplogroup 9 in Europe (from Rosser* et al. *2000). The pie sizes are proportional to sample sizes.*

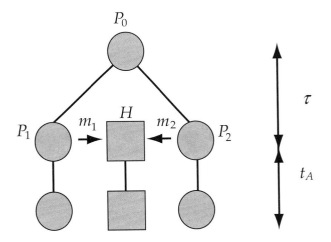

Figure 33.4. *A model of admixture.* P_1, *and* P_2 *are two populations that separated from a common set of ancestors, who lived in population* P_0. *After* t *generations, the parental populations mix, giving rise to a hybrid population,* H. *The contributions of the parental populations are, respectively,* m_1 *and* m_2 *(and their sum is 1). After admixture, the parental and the hybrid populations undergo genetic drift for* t_A *generations.*

seven regions (sign test insignificant).

More loci are necessary in order for these estimates to be reliable. Also, for four regions there were no data in the Semino *et al.* (2000) data set.

Table 33.3. *Estimated contribution of parental populations from the Levant, m_L, to the gene pool of 12 European regions. Values are percentages with their standard errors. YR: data from Rosser et al. (2000); YS: data from Semino et al. (2000).*

	m_L mtDNA	std. err.	m_L YR	std. err.	m_L YS	std. err.
Balkans	99.54	13.50	108.21	7.30	87.15	5.11
East Europe	48.13	13.55	110.47	8.71	89.78	5.18
Italy South	41.02	19.93	58.94	9.70	68.80	10.25
Italy North	95.11	12.17	28.97	12.00	31.33	9.60
Sardinia	37.68	22.93	62.68	27.88	79.63	7.43
Central Europe	68.10	12.40	53.77	11.05	29.04	13.20
France, Belgium	65.47	9.32	30.16	8.83	41.82	9.54
British Isles	41.61	13.83	8.93	10.69		
Spain	42.13	15.06	15.60	11.10	20.48	9.15
Portugal	12.68	27.83	29.28	8.84		
Scandinavia	62.06	21.61	90.77	9.30		
Finland	65.91	16.25	120.89	10.00		

33.5). Approximate though they must be, these results overlap with those of previous simulation studies (Rendine *et al.* 1986; Barbujani *et al.* 1995). The Near Eastern contribution to the current gene pool seems greater in northern than in southern Italy, in agreement with archaeological evidence suggesting that Neolithic technologies spread there from the north (Lahr *et al.* 2000).

Adding further loci to the analysis will reduce the standard errors and will provide us with more robust estimates. Aside from that, we envisage three reasons why these estimates may be imprecise, namely:

i) Gene flow from other sources. Other parental populations, e.g. from North Africa or from northern Asia, may have contributed to the gene pool of certain European regions. This possibility, which may also account for the admixture estimates greater than 1 described above, will be incorporated in further analyses.

ii) Successive gene flow into the parental populations. The current characteristics of the Basques and the Levant populations may not correspond to those existing at the moment of the putative admixture episode we are studying. The method we used would underestimate the contribution of the population that has received a higher input of foreign genes after admixture. Note, however, that successive gene flow is expected to affect in that manner all studies in which Neolithic phenomena have been inferred from modern Near Eastern and Basque samples (e.g. Richards *et al.* 2000; Semino *et al.* 2000; Wilson *et al.* 2001).

iii) Selection. Had selection affected more deeply either parental population after admixture, its contribution to the hybrid populations would be underestimated.

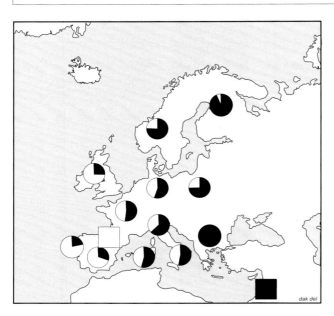

Figure 33.5. *Estimated contributions of alleles that can be attributed to admixture between the Basque (white) and the Near Eastern (black) populations, in various regions of Europe. Admixture estimates are weighted averages of the proportions estimated from one mitochondrial and two Y-chromosome data sets (Table 33.3). Solid squares are putative parental population.*

However, the average m_L values, calculated giving equal weight to mitochondrial and Y-chromosome information, exceed 70 per cent in Eastern Europe, and are close to 50 per cent in Sardinia and France. Only in the British Isles (confirming previous findings by Hill *et al.* 2000) and in Iberia does m_L approach the figures proposed for all of Europe by Richards *et al.* (2000) and Semino *et al.* (2000) (Fig.

At this stage, and if the assumptions of this analysis are approximately correct, these results suggest higher rates of Neolithic gene flow from the Near East than previously inferred from the same data (Richards *et al.* 2000; Semino *et al.* 2000). An independent analysis of the chromosome, based on a Bayesian approach, led to very similar conclusions (Chikhi *et al.* 2002).

What next?

We need more data. So far, only a handful of loci have been typed in a sufficient number of European samples. More polymorphisms need be studied, and populations that have not been thoroughly characterized, such as those of East Europe, must be better sampled. New markers may show different patterns from the ones described so far, and that may result in changes, perhaps even significant ones, in our perception of European genetic diversity.

We also need to refine our methods of data analysis. It is crucial to fully understand the implications and the assumptions of the statistical approaches being used, and their limitations. In addition, it has become evident that the inferences we draw need not only to be broadly consistent with some archaeological data, but also to be supported by computer simulations. Only in this way shall we know whether logically plausible conclusions are also compatible with the available information on past demography, rates of mutation and gene flow, etc. (Harpending 2001). Simulations based on the coalescent have become rather easy to run, and an efficient algorithm has been implemented in the Arlequin software package for genetic data analysis (Schneider et al. 2000).

Better integration with archaeology also seems indispensable. The European archaeological and historical records are comparatively very complete ones; as Sokal et al. (1996) remarked, it is not difficult to find some degree of support for almost any population phenomenon our data might suggest. Thus, we must find better ways to test hypotheses based on archaeology, or linguistics. A sensible idea seems to define in advance the genetic consequences of alternative historical processes, and then check by some form of likelihood-ratio test which model agrees best with the data. When analyzing population data, we must be aware that evolutionary related alleles might occur in distant populations because of individual movements that have nothing to do with the main demographic phenomena we try to understand. Once again, the acid test can only be at the multilocus level. If some form of large-scale migration has brought related alleles to different locations, that result should be evident at many loci.

Of course, each population has had a much more complex history than one can hope to reconstruct by analyZing Europe as a whole. The discussion on the relative merits of the CD and DD models should not obscure the fact that, above and beyond the large-scale, presumably prehistoric processes that

shaped European genetic diversity, many other processes occurred, and likely left marks on genetic diversity at the regional level. Only more detailed studies, especially if supported by non-biological evidence (see Wilson et al. 2001), may identify specific phenomena operating at the small geographic scale.

The studies of published by Richards et al. (1996; 1998; 2000) and by Semino et al. (2000) have significantly contributed to our understanding of mitochondrial and Y-chromosome variation. We now know that not all variable sites in these genome regions are equally good for evolutionary inferences, and we have a clearer idea of the hierarchical structure of molecular variation for those non-recombining parts of the genome. However, the founder ages and coalescence times which these studied estimated simply do not seem to serve the purpose of establishing the relative merits of the CD and DD models.

Recent developments in the technologies for assessing sequence variation on a genome-scale will soon permit broader comparative analyses in human populations (Chakravarti 1999; Przeworski et al. 2000). As we previously stressed, historical inferences based on comparisons of several loci are more reliable (Mountain & Cavalli-Sforza 1997; Stumpf & Goldstein 2001), and that also applies to the admixture estimates of this paper, of course. It may be that, by analyzing larger data sets and by further increasing the spatial resolution of our analyses, new patterns will emerge. For the time being, however, these estimates support a large contribution of Neolithic farmers to the current European gene pool. Under the CD model it is also difficult to justify the strong southeast to northwest patterning of protein and DNA variation in Europe, unless one is willing to conclude that that reflects the initial colonization of Europe (Fix 1997). This possibility cannot be ruled out. Accordingly, though, one should also conclude that neither post glacial expansions nor Neolithic dispersal have altered those clines. Conversely, the DD model is in good agreement with the observed patterns of genetic variation, with computer simulations, and with our new admixture estimates.

As any cultural product, the DD model is liable to be improved, and it would be surprising if it could explain all aspects of European population history. For instance, a stronger persistence of alleles coming directly from the first, Palaeolithic inhabitants of Europe is to be expected somewhere, especially in geographic isolates. And it may well be that more complex models of Neolithic dispersal (see Renfrew 2001) will yield predictions in closer agreement with the data. Studies of ancient DNA are still in their infancy, but they may also prove very informative, once a larger number of samples will have been carefully (Cooper & Poinar 2000) typed. At present, we think there are good reasons to take sides with the earlier (Ammerman & Cavalli-Sforza 1984) rather than with the later (Semino *et al.* 2000) studies by Cavalli-Sforza's group, and to maintain that a large fraction of the European gene pool is derived from the genes of ancestors who did not live in Europe, but in the Levant, until the Neolithic.

Acknowledgements

We thank Lorena Madrigal and Giorgio Bertorelle for critical reading of this manuscript. During the development of this study, G.B. was partly supported by the programme Short-Term Mobility of the Italian National Research Council (CNR).

References

Ammerman, A.J. & L.L. Cavalli-Sforza, 1984. *The Neolithic Transition and the Genetics of Populations in Europe.* Princeton (NJ): Princeton University Press.

Ayala, F.J., A. Escalante, C. O'Huigin & J. Klein, 1995. Molecular genetics of speciation and human origins, in *Tempo and Mode in Evolution*, eds. W.M. Fitch & F.J. Ayala. Washington (DC): National Academy Press, 187–211.

Bandelt, H.-J., P. Forster, B.C. Sykes & M.B. Richards, 1995. Mitochondrial portraits of human populations using median networks. *Genetics* 141, 743–53.

Barbujani, G. & G. Bertorelle, 2001. Genetics and the population history of Europe. *Proceedings of the National Academy of Sciences of the USA* 98, 22–5.

Barbujani, G., A. Pilastro, S. De Domenico & C. Renfrew, 1994. Genetic variation in North Africa and Eurasia: neolithic demic diffusion vs. Paleolithic colonisation. *American Journal of Physical Anthropology* 95, 137–54.

Barbujani, G., R.R. Sokal & N.L. Oden, 1995. Indo-European origins: a computer-simulation test of five hypotheses. *American Journal of Physical Anthropology* 96, 109–32.

Barbujani, G., G. Bertorelle & L. Chikhi, 1998. Evidence for Paleolithic and Neolithic gene flow in Europe. *American Journal of Human Genetics* 62, 488–92.

Barker, G., 1985. *Prehistoric Farming in Europe.* Cambridge: Cambridge University Press.

Bertorelle, G. & L. Excoffier, 1998. Inferring admixture proportions from molecular data. *Molecular Biology and Evolution* 15, 1298–311.

Bertranpetit, J., J. Sala, F. Calafell, P.A. Underhill, P. Moral & D. Comas, 1995. Human mitochondrial DNA variation and the origin of Basques. *Annual of Human Genetics* 59, 63–81.

Calafell, F. & J. Bertranpetit, 1994. Principal component analysis of gene frequencies and the origin of Basques. *American Journal of Physical Anthropology* 93, 201–15.

Casalotti, R., L. Simoni, M. Belledi & G. Barbujani, 1999. Y-chromosome polymorphism and the origins of the European gene pool. *Proceedings of the Royal Society of London* B 266, 1959–65.

Cavalli-Sforza, L.L. & E. Minch, 1997. Paleolithic and Neolithic lineages in the European mitochondrial gene pool. *American Journal of Human Genetics* 61, 247–54.

Cavalli-Sforza, LL, P. Menozzi & A. Piazza, 1993. Demic expansions and human evolution. *Science* 259, 639–46.

Cavalli-Sforza, L.L., P. Menozzi & A. Piazza, 1994. *The History and Geography of Human Genes.* Princeton (NJ): Princeton University Press.

Chakraborty, R., 1975. Estimation of race admixture: a new method. *American Journal of Physical Anthropology* 42, 507–11.

Chakravarti, A., 1999. Population genetics — making sense out of sequence. *Nature Genetics* 21(Suppl.), 56–60.

Chikhi, L., G. Destro-Bisol, V. Pascali, V. Baravelli, M. Dobosz & G. Barbujani, 1998a. Clinal variation in the nuclear DNA of Europeans. *Human Biology* 70, 643–57.

Chikhi, L., G. Destro-Bisol, G. Bertorelle, V. Pascali & G. Barbujani, 1998b. Clines of nuclear DNA markers suggest a largely Neolithic ancestry of the European gene pool. *Proceedings of the National Academy of Sciences of the USA* 95, 9053–8.

Chikhi, L., R. Nichols, G. Barbujani & M. Beaumont, 2002. Y genetic data support the Neolithic demic diffusion model. *Proceedings of the National Academy of the Sciences of the USA* 99, 10,008–13.

Cooper, A. & H.N. Poinar, 2000. Ancient DNA: do it right or not at all. *Science* 289, 1139.

Dupanloup, I. & G. Bertorelle, 2001. Inferring admixture proportions from molecular data: extension to any number of parental populations. *Molecular Biology and Evolution* 18, 672–5.

Edwards, S.V. & P. Beerli, 2000. Gene divergence, population divergence, and the variance in coalescence time in phylogeographic studies. *Evolution* 54, 1839–54.

Excoffier, L., 1990. Evolution of human mitochondrial DNA: evidence for departure from a pure neutral model of populations at equilibrium. *Journal of Molecular Evolution* 30, 125–39.

Fix, A.G., 1997. Gene frequency clines produced by kin-structured founder effects. *Human Biology* 69, 663–73.

Fix, A.G., 1999. *Migration and Colonization in Human Microevolution.* Cambridge: Cambridge University Press.

Foley, R., 1998. The context of human genetic evolution. *Genome Research* 8, 339–47.

Forster, P., R. Harding, A. Torroni & H.-J. Bandelt, 1996. Origin and evolution of Native American mtDNA variation: a reappraisal. *American Journal of Human*

Genetics 59, 935–45.

Fullerton, S.M., A.G. Clark, K.M. Weiss, D.A. Nickerson, S.L. Taylor, J.H. Stengard, V. Salomaa, E. Vartiainen, M. Perola, E. Boerwinkle & C.F. Sing, 2000. Apolipoprotein E variation at the sequence haplotype level: implications for the origin and maintenance of a major human polymorphism. *American Journal of Human Genetics* 67, 881–900.

Harding, R.M., S.M. Fullerton, R.C. Griffiths, J. Bond, M.J. Cox, J.A. Schneider, D.S. Moulin & J.B. Clegg, 1997. Archaic African and Asian lineages in the genetic ancestry of modern humans. *American Journal of Human Genetics* 60, 772–89.

Harpending, H.C., 2001. Book review of *Archaeogenetics: DNA and the Population Prehistory of Europe* edited by C. Renfrew & K. Boyle. *American Journal of Physical Anthropology* 116, 177–8.

Helgason, A., S. Siguretardottir, J.R. Gulcher, R. Ward & K. Stefansson, 2000. MtDNA and the origin of the Icelanders: deciphering signals of recent population history. *American Journal of Human Genetics* 66, 999–1016.

Hey, J., 1997. Mitochondrial and nuclear genes present conflicting portraits of human origins. *Molecular Biology and Evolution* 14, 166–72.

Heyer, E., 1999. One founder/one gene hypothesis in a new expanding population: Saguenay (Quebec, Canada). *Human Biology* 71, 99–109.

Hill, E.W., M.A. Jobling & D.G. Bradley, 2000. Y-chromosome variation and Irish origins. *Nature* 404, 351–2.

Hilton, H. & J. Hey, 1997. A multilocus view of speciation in the *Drosophila virilis* species group reveals complex histories and taxonomic conflicts. *Genetic Research* 70, 185–94.

Hudson, R.R., 1990. Gene genealogies and the coalescent process, in *Oxford Surveys in Evolutionary Biology*, vol. 1, eds. D. Futuyma & J. Antonovics. Oxford: Oxford University Press, 1–40.

Hurles, M.E. & M. Jobling, 2001. Haploid chromosomes in molecular ecology: Lessons from the human Y. *Molecular Ecology* 10, 1599–613.

Hurles, M.E., R. Veitia & E. Arroyo, 1999. Recent male-mediated gene flow over a linguistic barrier in Iberia suggested by analysis of a Y-chromosomal polymorphism. *American Journal of Human Genetics* 65, 1437–48.

Ingman, M., H. Kaessmann, S. Pääbo & U. Gyllensten, 2000. Mitochondrial genome variation and the origin of modern humans. *Nature* 408, 708–13.

Izagirre, N. & C. de la Rua, 1999. An mtDNA analysis in ancient Basque populations: implications for haplogroup V as a marker for a major Paleolithic expansion from southwestern Europe. *American Journal of Human Genetics* 65, 199–207.

Kaessmann, H., F. Heissig, A. von Haeseler & S. Pääbo, 1999. Nucleotide DNA sequence variation in a non-coding region of low recombination on the human X chromosome. *Nature Genetics* 22, 78–81.

Kidd, K.K., J.R. Kidd, A.J. Pakstis, B. Bonné-Tamir & E.

Grigorenko, 2000. Nuclear genetic variation of European Populations in a global context, in Renfrew & Boyle (eds.), 109–17.

Koda, Y., H. Tachid, M. Soejima, O. Takenaka & H. Kimura, 2000. Ancient origin of the null allele se(428) of the human ABO-secretor locus (FUT2). *Journal of Molecular Evolution* 50, 243–8.

Krings, M., A. Stone, R.W. Schmitz, H. Krainitzki, M. Stoneking & S. Pääbo, 1997. Neandertal DNA sequences and the origin of modern humans. *Cell* 90, 19–30.

Krings, M., C. Capelli, F. Tschentscher, H. Geisert, S. Meyer, A. von Haeseler, K. Grossschmidt, G. Possnert, M. Paunovic & S. Pääbo, 2000. A view of Neanderthal genetic diversity. *Nature Genetics* 26, 144–6.

Lahr, M.M., R.A. Foley & R. Pinhasi, 2000. Expected regional patterns of Mesolithic–Neolithic human population admixture in Europe based on archaeological evidence, in Renfrew & Boyle (eds.), 81–8.

Lum, J.K., R.L. Cann, J.J. Martinson & L.B. Jorde, 1998. Mitochondrial and nuclear genetic relationships among Pacific Island and Asian populations. *American Journal of Human Genetics* 63, 613–24.

Menozzi, P., A. Piazza & L.L. Cavalli-Sforza, 1978. Synthetic maps of human gene frequencies in Europeans. *Science* 201, 786–92.

Mountain, J.L. & L.L. Cavalli-Sforza, 1997. Multilocus genotypes, a tree of individuals, and human evolutionary history. *American Journal of Human Genetics* 61, 705–18.

Nichols, R., 2001. Gene trees and species trees are not the same. *Trends in Ecological Evolution* 7, 358–64.

Ovchinnikov, I.V., A. Götherstrom, G.P. Romanova, V.M. Kharitonov, K. Liden & W. Goodwin, 2000. Molecular analysis of Neanderthal DNA from the Northern Caucasus. *Nature* 404, 490–93.

Piazza, A., P. Menozzi & L.L. Cavalli-Sforza, 1981. Synthetic gene frequency maps of man and selective effects of climate. *Proceedings of the National Academy of Sciences of the USA* 78, 2638–42.

Przeworski, M., R.R. Hudson & A. di Rienzo, 2000. Adjusting the focus on human variation. *Trends in Genetics* 16, 296–302.

Quintana-Murci, L., O. Semino, E. Minch, G. Passarimo, A. Brega & A.S. Santachiara-Benerecetti, 1999. Further characteristics of proto-European Y chromosomes. *European Journal of Human Genetics* 7, 603–8.

Relethford, J.H., 2001. Absence of regional affinities of Neandertal DNA with living humans does not reject muliregional evolution. *American Journal of Physical Anthropology* 115, 95–8.

Rendine, S., A. Piazza & L.L. Cavalli-Sforza, 1986. Simulation and separation by principal components of multiple demic expansions in Europe. *American Nature* 128, 681–706.

Renfrew, C., 2000a. At the edge of knowability: towards a prehistory of languages. *Cambridge Archaeological Journal* 10(1), 7–34.

Renfrew, C., 2000b. Archaeogenetics: towards a population prehistory of Europe, in Renfrew & Boyle (eds.), 3–11.

Renfrew, C., 2001. From molecular genetics to archaeogenetics. *Proceedings of the National Academy Sciences of the USA* 98, 4830–32.

Renfrew, C. & K. Boyle (eds.), 2000. *Archaeogenetics: DNA and the Population Prehistory of Europe*. (McDonald Institute Monographs.) Cambridge: McDonald Institute for Archaeological Research.

Richards, M.B., H. Corte-Real, P. Forster, V. Macaulay, H. Wilkinson-Herbots, A. Demaine, S. Papiha, R. Hedges, H.-J. Bandelt & B. Sykes, 1996. Paleolithic and Neolithic lineages in the European mitochondrial gene pool. *American Journal of Human Genetics* 59, 185–203.

Richards, M.B., V.A. Macaulay, H.-J. Bandelt & B.C. Sykes, 1998. Phylogeography of mitochondrial DNA in Western Europe. *American Journal of Human Genetics* 62, 241–60.

Richards, M.B., V. Macaulay, E. Hickey, E. Vega, B. Sykes, V. Guida, C. Rengo, D. Sellitto, F. Cruciani, T. Kivisild, R. Villems, M. Thomas, S. Rychkov, O. Rychkov, Y. Rychkov, M. Golge, D. Dimitrov, E. Hill, D. Bradley, V. Romano, F. Calí, G. Vona, A. Demaine, S. Papiha, C. Triantaphyllidis & G. Stefanescu, 2000. Tracing European founder lineages in the Near Eastern mtDNA pool. *American Journal of Human Genetics* 67, 1251–76.

Richards, M.B., V. Macaulay, A. Torroni & H.-J. Bandelt, 2002. In search of geographical patterns in European mitochondrial DNA. *American Journal of Human Genetics* 71.

Rosser, Z.H., T. Zerjal, M.E. Hurles, M. Adojaan, D. Alavantic, A. Amorim, W. Amos, M. Armenteros, E. Arroyo, G. Barbujani, G. Beckman, L. Beckman, J. Bertranpetit, E. Bosch, D.G. Bradley, G. Brede, G. Cooper, H.B. Corte-Real, P. de Knijff, R. Decorte, Y.E. Dubrova, O. Evgrafov, A. Gilissen, S. Glisic, M. Golge, E.W. Hill, A. Jeziorowska, L. Kalaydjieva, M. Kayser, T. Kivisild, S.A. Kravchenko, A. Krumina, V. Kucinskas, J. Lavinha, L.A. Livshits, P. Malaspina, S. Maria, K. McElreavey, T.A. Meitinger, A.V. Mikelsaar, R.J. Mitchell, K. Nafa, J. Nicholson, S. Norby, A. Pandya, J. Parik, P.C. Patsalis, L. Pereira, B. Peterlin, G. Pielberg, M.J. Prata, C. Previdere, L. Roewer, S. Rootsi, D.C. Rubinsztein, J. Saillard, F.R. Santos, G. Stefanescu, B.C. Sykes, A. Tolun, R. Villems, C. Tyler-Smith & M.A. Jobling, 2000. Y-chromosomal diversity in Europe is clinal and influenced primarily by geography, rather than by language. *American Journal of Human Genetics* 67, 1526–43.

Schneider, S., D. Roessli & L. Excoffier, 2000. *Arlequin ver. 2.0: a software for population genetic data analysis*. University of Geneva, Switzerland

Semino, O., G. Passarino, A. Brega, M. Fellous & A.S. Santachiara-Benerecetti, 1996. A view of the Neolithic demic diffusion in Europe through two Y chromosome-specific markers. *American Journal of Human Genetics* 59, 964–8.

Semino, O., G. Passarino, P.J. Oefner, A.A. Lin, S. Arbuzova, L.E. Beckman, G. De Benedictis, P. Francalacci, A. Kouvatsi, S. Limborska, M. Marcikiae, A. Mika, B. Mika, D. Primorac, A.S. Santachiara-Benerecetti, L.L. Cavalli-Sforza & P.A. Underhill, 2000. The genetic legacy of Paleolithic *Homo sapiens sapiens* in extant Europeans: a Y-chromosome perspective. *Science* 290, 1155–9.

Simoni, L., F. Calafell, D. Pettener, J. Bertranpetit & G. Barbujani, 2000. Geographic patterns of mtDNA diversity in Europe. *American Journal of Human Genetics* 66, 262–78.

Sokal, R.R. & P. Menozzi, 1982. Spatial autocorrelation of HLA frequencies in Europe supports demic diffusion of early farmers. *American Nature* 119, 1–17.

Sokal, R.R., R.M. Harding & N.L. Oden, 1989. Spatial patterns of human gene frequencies in Europe. *American Journal of Physical Anthropology* 80, 267–94.

Sokal, R.R., N.L. Oden & C. Wilson, 1991. Genetic evidence for the spread of agriculture in Europe by demic diffusion. *Nature* 351, 143–5.

Sokal, R.R., N.L. Oden, J. Walker, D. di Giovanni & B.A. Thomson, 1996. Historical population movements in Europe influence genetic relationships in modern samples. *Human Biology* 68, 873–98.

Stringer, C.B. & P. Andrews, 1988. Genetic and fossil evidence for the origin of modern humans. *Science* 239, 1263–8.

Stumpf, M.P. & D.B. Goldstein, 2001. Genealogical and evolutionary inference with the human Y chromosome. *Science* 291, 1738–42.

Sykes, B., 1999. The molecular genetics of European ancestry. *Philosophical Transactions of the Royal Society of London* B 354, 131–9.

Tajima, F., 1989a. Statistical method for testing the neutral mutation hypothesis by DNA polymorphism. *Genetics* 123, 585–95.

Tajima, F., 1989b. The effect of change in population size on DNA polymorphism. *Genetics* 123, 597–601.

Takahata, N. & F. Tajima, 1991. Sampling errors in phylogeny. *Molecular Biology and Evolution* 48, 198–221.

Tishkoff, S.A., E. Dietzsch, W. Speed, A.J. Pakstis, J.R. Kidd, K. Cheung, B. Bonné-Tamir, A.S. Santachiara, P. Moral, M. Krings, S. Pääbo, E. Watson, N. Risch, T. Jenkins & K.K. Kidd, 1996. Global patterns of linkage disequilibrium at the CD4 locus and modern human origins. *Science* 271, 1380–87.

Torroni, A., M.D. Brown, M.T. Lott, N.J. Newman & D.C. Wallace, 1995. African, Native American, and European mitochondrial DNAs in Cubans from Pinar del Rio Province and implications for the recent epidemic neuropathy in Cuba. *Human Mutations* 5, 310–17.

Torroni, A., H.-J. Bandelt, L. d'Urbano, P. Lahermo, P. Moral, D. Sellitto, C. Rengo, P. Forster, M.L. Savontaus, B. Bonné-Tamir & R. Scozzari, 1998. MtDNA analysis reveals a major late Paleolithic population expansion from southwestern to northeastern Europe. *American Journal of Human Genetics* 62, 1137–52.

Underhill, P.A., P. Shen, A.A. Lin, L. Jin, G. Passarino, W.H. Yang, E. Kauffman, B. Bonné-Tamir, J. Bertranpetit, P. Francalacci, M. Ibrahim, T. Jenkins, J.R. Kidd, S.Q. Mehdi, M.T. Seielstad, R.S. Wells, A. Piazza, R.W. Davis, M.W. Feldman, L.L. Cavalli-Sforza & P.J. Oefner, 2000. Y chromosome sequence variation and the history of human populations. *Nature Genetcs* 26, 358–61.

von Haeseler, A., A. Sajantila & S. Pääbo, 1996. The genetical archaeology of the human genome. *Nature Genetics* 14, 135–40.

Whittle, A., 1996. *Europe in the Neolithic.* Cambridge: Cambridge University Press.

Wilson, J.F., D.A. Weiss, M. Richards, M.G. Thomas, N. Bradman & D.B. Goldstein, 2001. Genetic evidence for different male and female roles during cultural transitions in the British Isles. *Proceedings of the National Academy of Sciences of the USA* 98, 5078–83.

Wise, C.A., M. Sraml & S. Easteal, 1998. Departure from neutrality at the mitochondrial NADH dehydrogenase subunit 2 gene in humans, but not in chimpanzees. *Genetics* 148, 409–21.

Wright, S., 1951. The genetical structure of populations. *Annals of Eugenics* 15, 323–54.

Zvelebil, M. & K. Zvelebil, 1988. Agricultural transition and Indo-European dispersal. *Antiquity* 62, 574–83.

Chapter 34

Admixture and the Demic Diffusion Model in Europe[1]

Lounès Chikhi

Population genetics aims at describing the patterns of genetic diversity within and between existing populations and uses these patterns (if any) to infer their recent evolutionary history. While the first step may be relatively straightforward, the inferential step can be much more controversial. One reason for this is that many factors can affect the patterns observed in contemporary populations and it is quite difficult to separate them. The limits of genetic data to infer ancient demographic events have therefore to be kept in mind.

In the present paper I address the problem of estimating the genetic impact of Neolithic farmers, some 10,000 to 5000 years ago, on the hunter-gatherers who had already settled across Europe some 30,000 years before the arrival of farming (Ammerman & Cavalli-Sforza 1984). To do this I first give some background information justifying the use of an admixture approach. Then, I present a new admixture method which was developed and tested in collaboration with Mark Beaumont (University of Reading), Mike Bruford (Cardiff University) and Richard Nichols (Queen Mary and Westfield College). Simulation results are presented to stress important points regarding the amount of genetic information present in single-locus data. I then apply the method to the Y-chromosome data of Semino *et al.* (2000). I discuss some of their results and show that significantly different inferences can be drawn when a specific admixture method is used.

The rationale for an admixture approach

It is widely recognized that the discovery and development of agriculture in the Near East triggered a cultural change that brought farming and associated technologies across Europe in the last 5000–10,000 years commencing at about 6500 BC in the southeast (Ammerman & Cavalli-Sforza 1984; Renfrew 1987). Europe was already inhabited by hunter-gatherers

and the process of cultural and demographic change linked to agriculture and animal domestication has been described using two extreme demographic scenarios. The Demic Diffusion model (DDM), first proposed by Ammerman & Cavalli-Sforza (1973; 1984), suggests that the spread of technologies was caused by a movement of people (the early farmers) and implies a significant genetic input of Near Eastern genes from Neolithic farmers to the current European gene pool. In its most extreme version, it can be seen as a replacement model. Under the Cultural Diffusion model (CDM), on the contrary, the transition to agriculture is regarded essentially as a cultural phenomenon, involving the movement of ideas and practices rather than people. Consequently, it would not imply major changes at the genetic level. In practice, most specialists would probably agree that there is a spectrum of intermediate scenarios that are essentially admixture models: settlements were founded by a mixture of indigenous hunter-gatherers and farmers whose ancestors originally came from the Near East. For instance, Semino *et al.* (2000), while concluding against a large contribution of Neolithic farmers, write that 'Various types of evidence suggest that the present European population arose from the merging of local Palaeolithic groups and Neolithic farmers arriving from the Near East after the invention of agriculture in the Fertile Crescent'.

The exact details of admixture processes are likely to have varied across Europe. There must have been areas of Europe where farming practices were mostly transmitted culturally (Zvelebil & Zvelebil 1988; Zvelebil 2000), while in others such as the LBK (Linearbandkeramik) the movement of people may have been the leading force (e.g. Price *et al.* 2001). Genetic data are likely to play a key role in our understanding of the details of these admixture processes. In particular, mitochondrial DNA (mtDNA) and the non-recombining Y (NRY) chromosome are

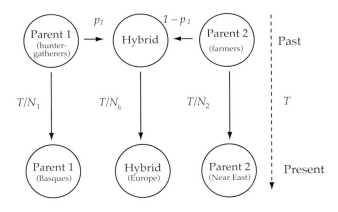

Figure 34.1. *The admixture model. We assume a single admixture event,* T *generations ago (see text). The three populations are allowed to have different sizes:* N_1*,* N_2 *and* N_h*. The contribution of Parent 1 is* p_1*.*

providing us with detailed pictures of present-day patterns (Semino *et al.* 1996; Simoni *et al.* 2000; Casalotti *et al.* 1999; Rosser *et al.* 2000; Pereira *et al.* 2001). Studies based on these markers are therefore of great importance. However, a number of conclusions that have been drawn from these markers are based on *ad hoc* methods whose assumptions are not always explicitly stated (Richards *et al.* 1996; 1998; Barbujani & Bertorelle 2001). Moreover, these markers are sometimes used to link specific haplotypes to particular prehistoric cultures (Semino *et al.* 2000). It is not clear how justified such claims are. Model-based methods, such as the one presented below, allow us to state assumptions explicitly and control for parameters.

A new method for estimating admixture proportions.

The admixture method used in the present paper is a Markov chain Monte Carlo (MCMC) method based on the simple model shown in Figure 34.1. The model assumes that two independent parental populations, P_1 (representing the hunter-gatherers, for instance) and P_2 (representing the farmers) of size N_1 and N_2, respectively, mixed T generations in the past with respective proportions p_1 and p_2 $(= 1 - p_1)$. During this admixture event, an admixed or hybrid population H (representing European populations) of size N_h was created. At the time of hybridization, the gene frequency distributions of P_1 and P_2 are, respectively, represented by x_1 and x_2. Consequently, the gene frequency distribution in the hybrid population is $p_1 x_1 + p_2 x_2$ at the moment of admixture. After

the admixture event the three populations P_1, P_2, and H are assumed to evolve independently by genetic drift, in such a way that some alleles may be lost in the process. Therefore, x_1 and x_2 are allowed to represent all observed alleles today, even though they may not be observed in all populations.

Even though T, the time since admixture, is by definition the same for the three populations, the model allows for them to be subjected to different amounts of drift. The time scaled by the effective size of each population can be different and is parameterized as $t_1 = T/N_1$, $t_2 = T/N_2$, and $t_h = T/N_h$. These times represent the amount of drift between present-day samples and the populations involved in the admixture. The technical details can be found in Chikhi *et al.* (2001; see also Ciofi *et al.* 1999; and Beaumont 2000). Suffice it to say that the method allows us to estimate the distribution of p_1, t_1, t_2, and t_h.

The model assumes no migration events after admixture. It also assumes that mutations are negligible and that the markers used are not under selection. These points are discussed below.

Single-locus data and information content: results from simulations

Simulations were used to test the method. In the present paper, hybrid populations were generated using $p_1 = 0.3$, meaning that 30 per cent of the genes in H came originally from P_1 and 70 per cent from P_2 (see Chikhi *et al.* 2001 for details). The sample size was $n = 200$ for each of the three populations (i.e. a total of 600) and each locus had 10 alleles in all simulations.

Figure 34.2 shows results of some of these simulations (the true value of p_1 is represented by the dashed vertical line in Figs. 34.2a & 34.2b). In Figure 34.2a, I have plotted the posterior p_1 distributions obtained for two groups of five independent loci simulated under different drift conditions. Each curve represents the probability density of p_1, with the mode being the most probable value. The solid lines represent cases where the amount of drift was extremely limited ($t_1 = t_2 = t_h = 0.001$), corresponding to one or ten generations of drift for a population size, N_i of 1000 or 10,000, respectively. The dashed lines correspond to a much larger amount of drift ($t_1 = t_2 = t_h = 0.1$) corresponding to 100 or 1000 generations of drift for $N_i = 1000$ and 10,000, respectively. The five solid curves show modal values that are distributed around and close to the true value (a reassuring result) but they also show differences, and above all, each curve shows that the amount of

Figure 34.2. *Effect of drift on admixture estimates. a) The solid curves represent the posterior p_1 distribution for five independent loci for $t_i = 0.001$. The five dashed curves correspond to five independent loci for $t_i = 0.1$. The vertical dashed line corresponds to $p_1 = 0.3$ (the value under which the data were simulated). The solid horizontal line corresponds to the uniform distribution between 0 and 1, to indicate the expected distribution if we had no data. As can be seen, some dashed distributions do not provide much more information. b) The five dashed lines correspond to the five solid lines form Figure 34.2a. They are plotted for comparison with the previous figure. The solid line corresponds to the use of five loci together. The uniform distribution is plotted for comparison. c) This figure represents the t_i distributions obtained from five independent loci, simulated for $t_i = 0.1$. The true value is plotted (vertical dashed line) together with the uniform between 0 and 1. One of the t_i distributions is not represented because convergence had not been reached.*

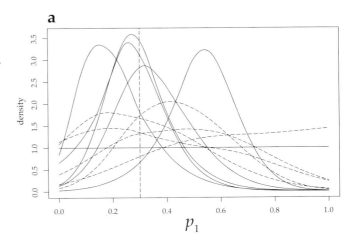

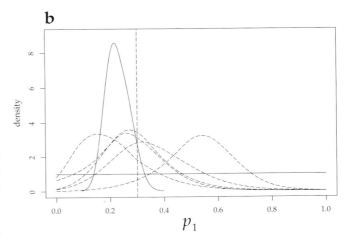

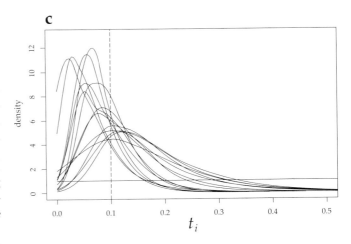

uncertainty around the mode is rather large. This is of course particularly clear when drift increases (dashed vs solid curves).

This indicates that, even when drift is limited, the modal value should be considered with caution. Based on simulations of 20 independent loci it has been shown that, excluding the five per cent most extreme values of the distribution (2.5 per cent lowest and largest p_1), the average width of the remaining interval is 0.56, 0.63 and 0.78 for $t_i = 0.001$, 0.01, 0.1, respectively (Chikhi *et al.* 2001). In other words, one locus (with 10 alleles) only allows us to reject 44 per cent of the range of p_1 values at the 5 per cent level, when $t_i = 0.001$. When $t_i = 0.1$, the values that can be safely rejected represent only about 22 per cent of the range.

The same simulations (i.e. with $p_1 = 0.3$) indicated that, for $t_i = 0.1$, as many as six of the 20 independent loci had a median which was larger than 0.5, three had a median > 0.6 and two had a median > 0.7. In other words, the chances of believing that $p_1 > 0.5$ when it is actually 0.3 are around 30 per cent. This result is dependent on the true value of p_1 being 0.3 (for smaller values, the risk of error would decrease) but this is certainly an effect that has to be taken into account.

As expected, the precision of admixture estimates decreases as genetic drift increases. There are two solutions to this problem. One is to increase the sample size, and the other is to increase the number of loci. It has been shown that increasing the sample size has only very limited effect beyond the sample sizes presented here (e.g. Mountain & Cavalli-Sforza 1994). For instance, the interval containing the 95 per cent central values of the distribution is only reduced from 0.81 to 0.78 when the sample size increases from $n = 50$ to $n = 200$ (for $t_i = 0.1$). We found

(Chikhi *et al.* 2001) that increasing the sample size appears to be effective only for very small t_i values. On the contrary, the improvement due to the use of multiple loci data is quite impressive. With only five loci, the range of values that could be rejected at the 5 per cent level was 77 per cent, 73 per cent and 53 per cent of the whole range for $t_i = 0.001$, 0.01 and 0.1, respectively. For the case with limited drift there is a tremendous increase in power, but even in the case of large drift (five loci and $t_i = 0.1$) we found that we could reject considerably more values than with one locus when $t_i = 0.001$. In other words, using five loci after 100 generations of drift (for $N = 10,000$) gives more power than one locus after 1 generation of drift. This means that patterns of admixture are better estimated with five loci after 2500 years than with single-locus data after 25 years (assuming a generation time of 25 years). Considering that mtDNA and NRY are about four times more subject to drift than nuclear loci, this indicates that five polymorphic loci might be more informative after 10,000 years than mtDNA will be after only one generation of drift.

The previous figures should be taken as a rule of thumb. Historical processes have certainly complicated admixture patterns. However, these results do hold as long as the model is able to capture important features of reality.

To conclude this section, I have plotted (Fig. 34.2c) the t_1, t_2 and t_h distributions for the previous five loci simulated with large drift ($t_i = 0.1$). The figure shows that there can be significant variation between the 15 distributions around the true value (dashed vertical line). We will come back to this point.

Application to Y-chromosome data

The simulation results, as well as common sense, suggest that whenever possible, multiple loci should be used. In practice, it is still difficult to get sequences from independent loci in many populations. MtDNA and NRY data are therefore likely to represent invaluable sources of information for a long time but increasing the sample size of particular populations is unlikely to be helpful. Thus, it appears that spatial information obtained by using as many samples as possible is the best way to increase the amount of information available.

Data used and suitability for the model
Semino *et al.* (2000) have recently presented genetic data on 22 binary markers from the non-recombining Y chromosome (NRY) in a large number of Euro-

pean populations ($n = 1007$ chromosomes from 25 samples, Table 34.1). These markers are considered to be the result of unique mutational events and are called unique-event polymorphisms (UEPs: Thomas *et al.* 1998; Stumpf & Goldstein 2001). They are thought to be rare enough to have occurred only once in the recent history of human populations. The presence of these UEPs in different populations is thus unlikely to indicate recurrent mutation but rather common ancestry, migration, selection or admixture events.

While this property is likely to hold for single UEPs it is important to estimate the number of new mutations which are actually expected when as many as 22 independent binary markers are analyzed in a large sample. Given the mutation rate of binary markers ($c. 10^{-8}$ per year: Jobling *et al.* 1997), and the short period of time since admixture (less than 10^4 years), we only expect that the expected number of new mutations in the sample will be $c. 22 \times 10^4 \times 10^{-8} \times 1007 \approx 2$. This represents 0.2 per cent of all haplotypes sampled. This is an overestimate since this calculation assumes independence of the 1007 individuals sampled. We can thus be confident that the assumption that mutation has negligible effect is appropriate for the markers used here and that drift and admixture are likely to explain most of the patterns observed. The data in Semino *et al.* (2000) provide a unique opportunity to apply the admixture method to a broad set of hybrid populations. Some results will be presented and discussed here; further analyses are in progress (Chikhi *et al.* 2002).

Choice of parental populations
The French and Spanish Basque samples ($n = 45 + 22$) were used to represent present-day descendants of hunter-gatherers. Indeed, linguistics, archaeology and classical genetic markers suggest that it is the European population that has been least influenced by the Neolithic expansion (e.g. Wilson *et al.* 2001).

Recent studies (e.g. Richards *et al.* 1998) have used samples from Turkey, Iraq, Iran, Lebanon or Syria. We have therefore combined the three samples available from these areas, namely Turkey ($n = 30$), Lebanon ($n = 31$) and Syria ($n = 20$), to represent the Near East. These three samples were genetically similar indicating that they could be grouped on a reasonable basis.

All European populations from Semino *et al.* (2000)'s paper were analyzed with the exception of the Saami ($n = 24$), Udmurt ($n = 43$) and Mari ($n = 46$) samples because of their geographical location far from the supposed route of Neolithic immigrants.

Table 34.1. *Absolute frequencies of the haplotypes found by Semino* et al. *(2000). The original table gave relative frequencies (in per cent) making it difficult to isolate singletons. The last two columns give the heterozygosity for each population (HET), and the combined frequency of the four haplotypes Eu-4, 9, 10, 11 (corresponding to the Neolithic contribution and therefore called Freq(Neo)).*

	n	Eu1	Eu3	Eu4	Eu6	Eu7	Eu8	Eu9	Eu10	Eu11	Eu12	Eu13	Eu14	Eu15	Eu16	Eu17	Eu18	Eu19	Eu20	Eu21	HET	Freq(Neo)
Andalusian	29	0	0	3	0	1	0	2	1	0	0	0	0	2	0	1	19	0	0	0	0.57	0.21
Sp. Basque	45	0	0	1	0	1	2	0	1	0	0	0	0	0	0	0	40	0	0	0	0.21	0.04
Fr. Basque	22	0	0	0	0	0	2	1	0	0	0	0	0	0	0	0	19	0	0	0	0.26	0.05
Catalan	24	0	0	1	0	1	0	1	0	2	0	0	0	0	0	0	19	0	0	0	0.38	0.17
French	23	0	0	2	0	4	0	3	1	0	0	0	0	0	0	0	12	0	1	0	0.7	0.26
Dutch	27	0	0	1	0	6	0	0	0	0	0	0	0	0	0	0	19	1	0	0	0.47	0.04
German	16	0	0	1	0	6	0	0	0	0	0	0	0	0	0	0	8	1	0	0	0.64	0.06
Czech & Slovaq.	45	0	0	1	0	7	0	4	0	2	0	0	1	1	1	0	16	12	0	0	0.78	0.16
Cent.–North. Italian	50	0	0	1	0	4	0	7	0	5	0	0	0	0	0	0	31	2	0	0	0.59	0.26
Calabrian	37	0	1	5	0	0	0	8	4	3	0	0	0	0	1	2	12	0	1	0	0.83	0.54
Sardinian	77	1	0	8	1	2	27	4	4	11	0	0	0	1	0	0	17	0	0	1	0.8	0.35
Croatian	58	0	0	4	0	26	0	3	0	1	0	0	0	0	1	0	6	17	0	0	0.71	0.14
Albanian	51	0	1	11	0	10	0	12	2	1	0	0	0	0	0	0	9	5	0	0	0.83	0.51
Greek	76	0	1	17	1	6	0	16	1	2	0	0	0	1	0	1	21	9	0	0	0.82	0.47
Macedonian	20	0	0	3	0	4	0	3	1	0	0	0	0	0	0	0	2	7	0	0	0.82	0.35
Polish	55	0	0	2	0	13	0	0	0	0	0	0	0	0	0	0	9	31	0	0	0.61	0.04
Hungarian	45	0	0	4	0	5	0	1	0	1	0	0	0	0	0	1	6	27	0	0	0.61	0.13
Ukrainian	50	0	0	2	0	9	0	3	0	2	1	0	3	1	0	0	1	27	1	0	0.68	0.14
Georgian	63	0	0	0	0	0	0	21	2	19	0	0	0	1	1	1	9	5	0	4	0.78	0.67
Turkish	30	0	1	4	0	1	0	12	1	2	0	0	1	1	1	1	2	2	1	0	0.83	0.63
Lebanese	31	0	0	8	1	1	0	9	5	1	0	0	0	0	0	1	2	3	0	0	0.83	0.74
Syrian	20	0	2	2	0	1	0	3	6	0	1	0	0	0	0	0	3	2	0	0	0.87	0.55
Saami	24	0	0	0	0	10	0	0	0	0	0	0	10	0	0	0	2	2	0	0	0.67	0
Udmurt	43	0	0	2	0	3	0	0	2	0	0	1	12	0	2	0	5	16	0	0	0.78	0.09
Mari	46	0	0	0	0	2	0	0	3	0	0	2	30	0	3	0	0	6	0	0	0.56	0.07
TOTAL	1007	1	6	83	3	123	31	113	34	52	2	3	57	8	10	8	289	175	4	5	–	0.28

These populations' gene pool is likely to contain a significant contribution from populations other than the two parental groups considered here. The total sample size analyzed here is therefore $n = 894$.

Distribution of admixture estimates across Europe

Figure 34.3a shows the p_1 distributions for some of the 17 European populations considered. I have selected seven distributions for the sake of clarity but the whole set can be found in Chikhi *et al.* (2002). Some general features can be noticed. First, there seems to be some geographical pattern. Populations closer to the Near East show distributions whose modes indicate small Palaeolithic contributions, while Western Europe populations have larger p_1 values. Indeed, the proportion of Neolithic genes $(1 - p_1)$ seems to decrease from modal values around 85–100 per cent in Albania, Macedonia or Greece to around 15–30 per cent in France, Holland or Germany (not shown). Second, the distributions are rather wide. For instance, even for populations as far from the Near East as Holland or France, we cannot exclude a p_1 of 0.2 at the 10 per cent level. This probably indicates a large amount of drift since the admixture event but also confirms the simulations results presented above: large standard errors are to be expected when inferring admixture from a single locus *in particular populations*.

In order to test whether p_1 values decrease along with distance from the Near East, the following approach was chosen. First, each sample was attributed a geographic distance from an average point between Lebanon and Syria (as in Semino *et al.* 2000). For simplicity, the linear distance was used. Then, for each population, one value was randomly selected from the corresponding p_1 distribution. A linear regression was then applied to these two sets of data and the regression was plotted. This process was repeated 1000 times allowing us to construct the distribution of the regression of p_1 on geographic distance.

If there is no association of p_1 with geographic distance from the Near East, we expect that, by chance, some regressions will exhibit a positive slope while others will have a negative one. On average, though we should see no particular geographic trend. In Figure 34.3b I have plotted the result of this process (instead of p_1, I have plotted $1 - p_1$, the Neolithic contribution). The figure shows a significant geographical trend indicating a decrease of Neolithic contribution from values around 80–100 per cent in the Near East to 20–40 per cent in Western Europe.

Average Neolithic contribution: limits of a single number

Semino *et al.* (2000) have suggested that four haplotypes (Eu4, Eu9, 10, 11) 'represent the male contribution of a demic diffusion of farmers from the Middle East to Europe' because these haplotypes exhibit a 'decreasing clinal pattern from the Middle East to Europe'. Consequently, they suggested that the male contribution of Neolithic people was about 22 per cent, the sum of the four haplotypes' frequencies.

It is not clear why the proportion of haplotypes exhibiting a clinal pattern visible in present-day populations should represent the contribution made by Neolithic farmers some 5000 to 10,000 years ago. In the case of an admixture between Europe and the Near East, a clinal pattern is expected only for those alleles that exhibit differentiation at the moment of admixture between the two groups of populations (e.g. Ammerman & Cavalli-Sforza 1984). Even for these alleles, gradients are likely to fade away with time due to drift. Another problem comes from the large number of alleles that are observed at low frequencies in different samples (Table 34.1). For instance, haplotype Eu17 is observed twice in the Near Eastern and Calabrian samples, and once in the Georgian, Greek, Andalusian and Hungarian samples. For this kind of haplotype no *visible* spatial pattern is likely to be as evident as that shown by the four haplotypes mentioned above, yet they certainly convey relevant information about the ancient demography. How much information is lost by not taking into account these alleles is unclear but Table 34.1 shows that more than 60 per cent of occurrences (non-empty cells) are singletons, doublets or triplets. The total frequency of these rare occurrences represents more than 15 per cent $(63 \times 1) + (31 \times 2) + (14 \times 3)/1007 = 167/1007 \approx 0.17)$.

These arguments indicate that there are grounds to question the meaning of this 22 per cent estimate and its relevance to objectively quantify the Neolithic contribution. This can be seen by plotting the regression obtained using the frequency of Eu4, –9, –10, –11 across Europe (represented by the dashed line with circles in Fig. 34.3b). This regression is significantly outside the region defined by the 1000 regressions obtained using the randomization approach described above. Consequently, this allows us to reject both the regression and the associated 22 per cent estimate for the Neolithic contribution ($P < 0.001$).

While a single number is unlikely to capture the complexity of admixture processes in Europe, it is possible to estimate the average p_1 value across all samples for comparison. The average Neolithic contribution is about 50 per cent (across all samples). This suggests that alleles (rare or not) that do not exhibit a clear gradient pattern do actually contain significant information.

This figure should be interpreted with care. First, it is not always relevant to summarize a spatial pattern by a single figure. Second, this figure represents average contribution across Europe, and therefore does not tell us much about the historical transition to farming in Europe. Indeed, it is important to keep in mind that the original question was whether the dispersing farmers were few (as in the CDM) or many (as in the DDM). The question regarding the overall genetic impact of the farmers across the whole continent is a related but different matter. This can be easily understood by assuming a very simple admixture process across Europe.

Fitting admixture patterns and processes

Let us assume that admixture took place in the form of a series of steps, such that at each step a group of farmers moves to the next location and mixes with local hunter-gatherers. If P_N is the proportion of farmers in admixed populations (assuming for simplicity that the process is repeated at each step), the Neolithic contribution will decrease geometrically from 1 to P_N^n, where n is the number of steps or admixture events taking place as populations move towards Western Europe. In Figure 34.4, the decrease of P_N with geographic distance from the Near East is plotted. The three curves represent a particular case where $P_N = 0.9$ (i.e. 90 per cent of farmers mix with 10 per cent of hunter-gatherers) for $n = 10$, 25 and 50 steps. Yet, the curves do not exhibit the same geographical pattern, nor do they exhibit the same average contribution (62, 36 and 21 per cent, respectively). The figure shows that, for a given value of P_N, the curve becomes very curvilinear as n increases, leading to a reduced genetic impact and to a lack of pattern as well. This simple dilution effect suggests that the lack of pattern or a low estimate of overall contribution described in some real data sets does not mean a rejection of a significant demic diffusion.

Using the trend observed in Figure 34.3b it is possible to find values of n and P_N compatible with the data. For instance, none of the three curves in Figure 34.4 would fit the data well, since the averages were 21, 36 and 62 per cent. We have seen above that for a given P_N value, the average Neolithic contribution decreases with n. This means that for a

Figure 34.3. *Contributions of Palaeolithic hunter-gatherers across Europe. a) Posterior distributions of* p$_1$ *for 7 selected European populations. b) Linear regression of* p$_1$ *against geographic distance from the Near East for all European populations. The geographic distance was calculated from the middle point between Syria and Lebanon (see Semino* et al. *2000). For each of the European samples, one* p$_1$ *value was randomly sampled from the corresponding posterior distribution obtained during the Markov chain. The set of* p$_1$ *values is regressed against the corresponding set of geographic distances. This process was repeated 1000 times to obtain the distribution of linear regressions. Fitted values are plotted and can therefore occur outside the range of* p$_1$. *The line with the circles represents the regression obtained using Eu4, –9, –10 and –11 as suggested by Semino* et al. (2000). *It is significantly different from the regressions we obtain using all the allelic information (*P < 0.001).

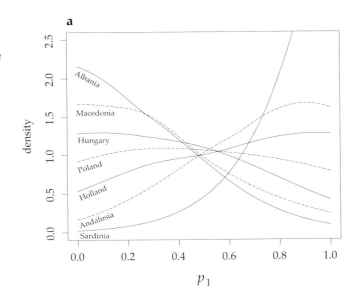

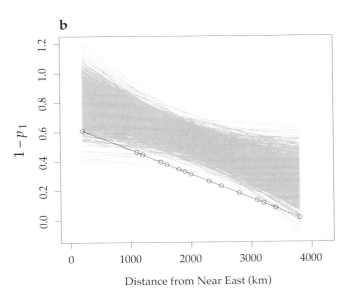

given average Neolithic contribution, larger P_N are required when n increases. In other words, $1 - P_N$ is maximized when n is small. As it appears, even when $n = 3$, P_N would have to be ~0.7 to explain the trend (mean and slope) observed in Figure 34.3b. More steps imply a much smaller contribution of the hunter-gatherers at the time of admixture. The archaeological evidence suggests a much more gradual process across Europe (i.e. larger n values). The trend observed in the data therefore indicates that the proportion of hunter-gatherers who were incorporated in the communities of dispersing farmers was less than 30 per cent at each location. By fitting values of P_N and n to the regressions obtained in Figure 34.3b, it appears that P_N is most likely between 0.8 and 0.95. It seems difficult to be more precise than that, given that we only have one locus. It is interesting and certainly reassuring that these values are in agreement with simulation studies (Rendine *et al.* 1986; Barbujani *et al.* 1995), showing that, in order to generate gradients similar to those observed in proteins, the genetic contribution of Neolithic farmers had to be between 66 and 100 per cent.

It has been suggested that the introgression of Near Eastern genes might be larger in Southern European populations along the Mediterranean shores (e.g. Simoni *et al.* 2000, using mtDNA). The overall contribution of Neolithic farmers was thus estimated using the NRY data by separating Mediterranean and Central and Northern samples. It appears to be larger in the Mediterranean samples (56 per cent vs 44 per cent in other samples), but the difference is not very large.

Admixture, drift and the case of Sardinia
Drift is a major factor in the distribution of NRY haplotypes in Europe as we have seen. For example, if one of the ancestral populations has remained relatively small and isolated since admixture (as might be the case for the Basques) it is expected to deviate more from its ancestral frequencies than another population which would have been demographically expanding. It is crucial to be able to separate the effects of drift and of admixture. For instance, two European populations may appear genetically similar today either because they have randomly drifted to similar allelic compositions or because their gene pools reflect admixture of the same parental

441

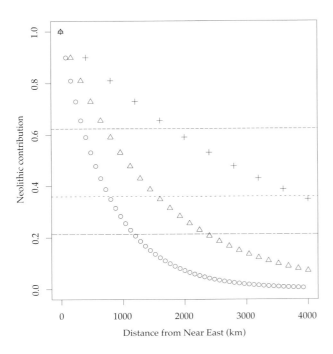

Figure 34.4. *Decrease of Neolithic contribution with geographic distance. The decrease of the Neolithic contribution is shown using the* n*-step admixture model described in the text for three values of* n *(*n = 10*,* n = 25 *and* n = 50 *represented by crosses, triangles and circles respectively). The process represented assumes that in each location settlements are created with 90 per cent of farmers and 10 per cent of hunter-gatherers. The horizontal lines represent the average contribution across the 4000 km between the Near East and Western Europe (62, 36 and 21 per cent, represented by dashed, dotted and dot-dashed lines, respectively).*

populations in similar proportions. In fact, various combinations of these two factors could generate the same picture. Our analysis of the European data shows that the admixture method, by parameterizing drift and admixture independently, allows us to separate their respective effects (see also Chikhi *et al.* 2001; 2002). Figure 3 of Semino *et al.* (2000) shows, for instance, that the Sardinian, Albanian and Greek samples are genetically similar in the PCA plot. These three populations appear to cluster in the centre of the plot, far from both the Near East and Basque samples. This would suggest that: i) the three populations have similar admixture estimates; and ii) that p_1 distributions would probably be centred on or close to $p_1 = 0.5$. The admixture analysis does not support any of these points. Figure 34.3a indicates that the most probable values for p_1 are at the opposite ends ($p_1 = 0$ for Albania and Greece, $p_1 = 1$

for Sardinia). Archaeological data show that Greece and Albania are among the first places of Europe where agriculture arrived and that Sardinia was submitted to limited Neolithic immigration (e.g. Ammerman & Cavalli-Sforza 1984).

These results suggest that the genetic differentiation observed between Basques and Sardinians today is not due to different levels of Neolithic immigration. Rather, substantial drift from common Mesolithic or Palaeolithic ancestors, with little input of genes from the Near East, explains the position of the Sardinian sample in the PCA plot. This can be tested further by using the Sardinian sample as a putative parental population. Only nine populations (Albania, Andalusia, Calabria, North Italy, Netherlands, France, Germany, Hungary and the Basques) were analyzed because of the time required to run the analyses. The results confirm those obtained with the Basques samples and actually indicate an even greater Neolithic contribution across Europe (62 vs 50 per cent). The geographical pattern is also confirmed when we generate regressions similar to those of Figure 34.3b (not shown). Again it is possible to significantly reject the regression obtained by Semino and colleagues ($P < 0.001$, recalculated on the same 9 populations).

Time since the admixture event and the effect of drift
The admixture method also generates estimates of the t_i values (t_1, t_2, t_h). As noted above, these time estimates represent the amount of genetic drift since the admixture event (small values indicate larger population sizes for a given number of generations). They do not represent absolute times unless we have some idea of the population sizes. It is possible to represent the distributions of t_1 (dashed lines) and t_2 (solid lines) for all European populations (Fig. 34.5a). Each curve corresponds to the analysis of a particular hybrid (European) population. The t_2 distributions suggest that drift was very limited in the Near Eastern populations since the admixture event. In other words, all 17 European samples, while having different p_1 distributions, agree in suggesting that rather large long-term population sizes characterize Near Eastern samples since the admixture event. On the contrary, the same samples agree in saying that the Basque population has undergone a large amount of drift. The exact amount of drift seems less precise than for the Near East (t_1 vs t_2 Fig. 34.5a), but the variation observed is similar, and actually less than that observed for simulated data (Fig. 34.2c, for $t_i = 0.1$).

Comparing the t_1 and t_2 distributions clearly indicates that the two sets of estimates are extremely different. This type of difference is exactly what we

Figure 34.5. *Distribution of time since the admixture event. a) Posterior distributions of* t_1 *and* t_2 *All* t_1 *curves are centred on t = 0.15, while all* t_2 *curves point toward values close to zero. While we observe some variation among the* t_1 *or among the* t_2 *distributions, this variation is well within the amount of variation expected from simulations (see Fig. 34.2c). The differences between any* t_1 *and any* t_2 *distribution are, on the contrary, very significant. b)* t_h *posterior distributions. Same as 34.2a. but for the hybrid populations. c) Linear regression of* t_h *against geographic distance. For each of the admixed population samples, one* t_h *value was randomly sampled from the corresponding posterior distribution (shown in b). A linear regression was then estimated between this set of values and the set of geographic distances from the Near East. This process was repeated 1000 times in order to obtain the regressions of* t_h *against geographic distance. Fitted values are plotted and can therefore occur outside the range of* t_h. *Calibrated radiocarbon dates representing the 95 per cent limit for the earliest date of arrival of agriculture are plotted (circles). These dates are based on locations for which there were more than 30 available data points (S. Shennan pers. comm.).*

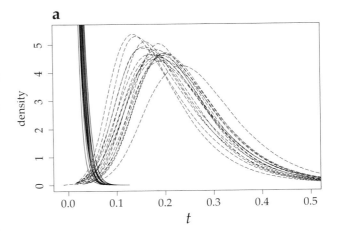

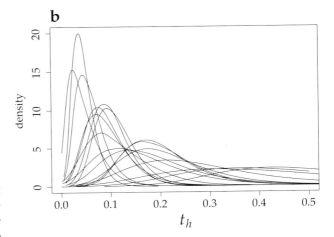

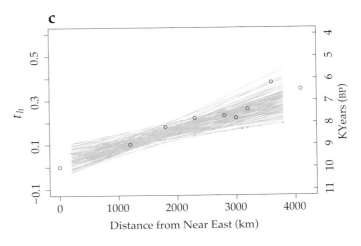

expect under a model of admixture where an expanding population (here, the one from the Near East) disperses into a scarcely populated area.

The t_h distributions, on the contrary, are not expected to exhibit much similarity. Indeed, the timing of the admixture event has varied across Europe and each population is likely to have been subjected to different amounts of drift, since it acquired agriculture at different times. Yet, it is possible to draw randomly from the t_h distributions and regress the values obtained with geographic distance. Figure 34.5c shows that a significant trend is obtained, which is consistent with the effects of an expansion from the Near East: t_h values increase as distance from the Near East increases, indicating that drift was greater where the archaeological record suggests a later arrival of agriculture.

As noted above, an absolute dating scale is difficult to obtain. However, we can plot calibrated radiocarbon dates of the first arrival of agriculture in a number of populations across Europe (S. Shennan pers. comm.). Again, it is reassuring that assuming a starting date around 10,000 years BP and an average rate of 1 km/year, the radiocarbon dates fit well with the trend of t_h values. This fitting procedure also means that for a generation time of 20–25 years, N has to be around 4000–5000 (i.e. 8000–10,000 diploid individuals). These values are in agreement with our current knowledge of human history (e.g. Pritchard & Rosenberg 1999; Pritchard & Przeworski 2001).

Pre-admixture differentiation and the choice of parental populations

Admixture studies rely on the assumption that the so-called parental populations have been properly chosen. This is a serious issue (Chakraborty 1986; Chikhi *et al.* 2001), which has to be discussed. The choice of the Basques is based on the fact that it is the best (or, perhaps more accurately, the least controversial) sample we can get in Europe of a population that has been little affected by Neolithic immigration (e.g. Wilson *et al.* 2001). In practice, it is highly unlikely that they have been able to maintain a complete isolation from neighbouring populations for thousands of years. This means that by using the Basque samples the Palaeolithic contribution has actually been overestimated. Similarly, the Near East is likely to have been subjected to some gene flow from Asia and perhaps Africa, making Near East samples more different from Europe that expected under pure drift. This is expected to reduce the estimated contribution of the Near East in Europe. For both reasons, p_1 values are likely to be overestimates and the Neolithic impact is underestimated.

Another problem comes from the fact that hunter-gatherer populations were probably genetically differentiated from each other before their contact with the early Neolithic farmers. Thus, using the Basques to represent descendants of the Palaeolithic ancestor for all European populations may be problematic. Fortunately, the admixture method does take into account this pre-admixture differentiation. This is done through the t_i and x_i parameters that are allowed to vary randomly during the MCMC step. In the model, the t_i and x_i values are not constrained. In practice, this means that different x_i distributions are explored to estimate the likelihood of the data. Consequently, the estimates encompass different demographic scenarios *prior* to admixture.

In practice, it is expected that the combined effect of pre-admixture differentiation and of drift since admixture should produce different t_1 distributions in the analysis of different European populations. The fact that the t_1 distributions are similar and are at the same time very different from the t_2 distributions suggests that the amount of genetic differentiation between the Mesolithic ancestors of all Europeans was not necessarily high when compared to the amount of drift that has taken place in the last 5000 to 10,000 years.

Concluding remarks

Admixture events are known to have been important in recent human history (Chakraborty 1986) and there are no reasons to think that this was not the case during our prehistory (e.g. Renfrew 1987; Mallory 1989). The model presented here is necessarily simple but, by separating the effects of drift and admixture, it should capture essential features of European prehistory. It is also the first step towards more complex demographic modelling of spatial processes. The results of the present study do not confirm the claims that agriculture was transmitted culturally. Rather, a significant movement of people (of males at least) seems to have taken place.

The controversy between the DDM and CDM was originally fuelled by a number of analyses using mtDNA. These studies originated in the group of Brian Sykes (Richards *et al.* 1996; 1998) and represented the first large-scale analyses of mtDNA across Europe. By criticizing the work of Cavalli-Sforza and co-workers these authors have triggered a very useful reappraisal of the evidence for the DDM and have been very influential. While these studies certainly represent a turning point in our understanding of Europe's mtDNA patterns, their conclusions have failed to convince many population geneticists (e.g. Harpending 2001). The reason for this is that, despite the huge amount of data, little is done to use them in a population genetics framework. *Ad hoc* methods have sometimes been employed without being tested using simulations. For instance, it was shown that the methods used to analyze the data in Richards *et al.* (1996) confused the issues of the age of molecules and the ages of populations where those molecules are found (Barbujani *et al.* 1998), a problem known to population geneticists (e.g. Nei & Li 1979; Tajima 1983). More recently, Barbujani & Bertorelle (2001) have stressed that an implicit assumption in many of these studies was that a drastic founder effect was at the origin of the European populations. Using simulations, they showed that such a bottleneck was not supported by the data.

Given that a number of studies have confirmed the existence of clinal patterns at the DNA level (Chikhi *et al.* 1998a,b), or have shown that the DDM was actually supported by Y-chromosome data (Semino *et al.* 1996; Casalotti *et al.* 1999), and by mtDNA in southern Europe (Simoni *et al.* 2000), the claims against the enormous work done by Cavalli-Sforza, Sokal and others were surprisingly strong. As the large data set published by Semino *et al.* (2000) appears to support the DDM, it is reasonable to suggest that current data do support the movement of people and that future studies are unlikely to give more credit to the CDM (with the exception of specific European regions, of course).

While mtDNA or NRY markers will keep playing a key role in human population genetics because of their ability to provide detailed gene genealogies, migration affects individuals, and hence all loci in their genome. Accordingly, multi-locus information seems particularly suited to address questions concerning past demography, population dispersal and other forms of gene flow. Recent genomic research indicates that our genome consists of large blocks of non-recombining DNA separated by regions with high recombination rates (Goldstein 2001 and references therein). This suggests that we might be able (within perhaps five or ten years) to have access to the equivalent of independent 'nuclear mtDNAs or NRY' markers.

Future population genetics will also depend on our ability to use linkage disequilibrium (LD: the statistical association between alleles from different loci). While the importance of independent loci was stated above, the information extracted from LD might prove crucial (Pritchard & Rosenberg 1999; Pritchard & Przeworski 2001; Reich *et al.* 2001). For instance, patterns of LD across the genome appear to provide unique information on our past history and do not seem to support the hypothesis of a dramatic demographic expansion (Wall & Przeworski 2000; Przeworski *et al.* 2000). The patterns observed seem to be consistent with significant population differentiation and admixture. If this proves to be correct, which is still debated, that might be bad news for mtDNA studies. Indeed the star phylogenies observed in mtDNA studies indicate either demographic expansions or selective sweeps. If mtDNA proves to be under strong selection (e.g. Wise *et al.* 1998), a number of conclusions based on this marker might have to be reconsidered.

To conclude, it is important to note that while Cavalli-Sforza and his collaborators have described gradients of allelic frequencies (see Cavalli-Sforza *et al.* 1994), the present study demonstrates the existence of a gradient in admixture proportions. This is a significant difference since we have seen that similar allele frequencies can lead to significantly different admixture estimates.

Acknowledgements

I am very grateful to Professors Colin Renfrew and Peter Bellwood for inviting me to the conference. I was able to attend the meeting thanks to the financial support provided by the BBSRC grant (Number 31/G13580 attributed to Prof. Ziheng Yang, UCL, London) and to the McDonald Institute for Archaeological Research. A number of the ideas presented here derive from discussions with Guido Barbujani, Mark Beaumont, Giorgio Bertorelle, Richard Nichols and Stephen Shennan. Finally, Stephane Aris-Brosou, Guido Barbujani and Mark Thomas are thanked for helpful comments on earlier versions of this text. Finally this contribution was also possible thanks to the patience of Katie Boyle, whom I would like to thank.

Note

1. All statistical analyses performed in the paper were done using the R language (Ihaka & Gentleman 1996). The densities were estimated using the program Locfit (Loader 1996) as implemented in the locfit package for R (v. 1.1). The admixture analysis can be performed using the program LEA (Likelihood-based Estimation of Admixture, Langella *et al.* 2001, freely available at http://www.cnrs-gif.fr/pge/bioinfo/lea).

References

Ammerman, A.J. & L.L. Cavalli-Sforza, 1973. A population model for the the diffusion of early farming in Europe, in *The Explanation of Cultural Change*, ed. C. Renfrew. London: Duckworth, 343–57.

Ammerman, A.J. & L.L. Cavalli-Sforza, 1984. *The Neolithic Transition and the Genetics of Populations in Europe*. Princeton (NJ): Princeton University Press.

Barbujani, G. & G. Bertorelle, 2001. Genetics and the population history of Europe. *Proceedings of the National Academy of Sciences of the USA* 98, 22–5.

Barbujani, G., G. Bertorelle & L. Chikhi, 1998. Evidence for Palaeolithic and Neolithic gene flow in Europe. *American Journal Human Genetics* 62, 488–91.

Barbujani, G., R.R. Sokal & N.L. Oden, 1995. Indo-European origins: a computer simulation test of five hypotheses. *American Journal of Physical Anthropology* 96, 109–32.

Beaumont, M.A., 2000. Conservation genetics, in *Handbook of Statistical Genetics*, eds. D.J. Balding, M. Bishop & C. Cannings. London: Wiley, 779–812.

Casalotti, R., L. Simoni, M. Belledi & G. Barbujani, 1999. Y-chromosome polymorphisms and the origins of the European gene pool. *Proceedings of the Royal Society, B, Biological Sciences* 266, 1959–65.

Cavalli-Sforza, L.L., P. Menozzi & A. Piazza, 1994. *The History and Geography of Human Genes*. Princeton (NJ): Princeton University Press.

Chakraborty, R., 1986. Gene admixture in human populations: models and predictions. *Yearbook of Physical Anthropology* 29, 1–43.

Chikhi, L., G. Destro-Bisol, G. Bertorelle, V. Pascali & G. Barbujani, 1998a. Clines of nuclear DNA markers suggest a largely Neolithic ancestry of the European gene pool. *Proceedings of the National Academy of Sciences of the USA* 95, 9053–8.

Chikhi, L., G. Destro-Bisol, V. Pascali, V. Baravelli, M. Dobosz & G. Barbujani, 1998b. Clinal variation in the nuclear DNA of Europeans. *Human Biology* 70, 643–57.

Chikhi, L., M.W. Bruford & M.A. Beaumont, 2001. Estimation of admixture proportions: a likelihood-based approach using Markov Chain Monte Carlo. *Genetics* 158, 1347–62.

Chikhi, L., R. Nichols, G. Barbujani & M. Beaumont, 2002. Y-chromosome data support the Demic Diffusion Model. *Proceedings of the National Academy of Sciences of the USA* 99, 11,007–13.

Ciofi, C., M.A. Beaumont, I.R. Swingland & M.W. Bruford, 1999. Genetic divergence and units for conservation in the Komodo dragon *Varanus komodoensis*. *Proceedings of the Royal Society of London B* 266, 2269–74.

Goldstein, D.B., 2001. Islands of linkage disequilibrium. *Nature Genetics* 29, 109–11.

Harpending, H.C., 2001. Book review on *Archaeogenetics: DNA and the Population Prehistory of Europe*, edited by C. Renfew & K. Boyle. *American Journal of Physical Anthropology* 116, 177–8.

Ihaka, R. & R. Gentleman, 1996. R: a language for data analysis and graphics. *Journal of Computer Graphics and Statistics* 5, 299–314.

Jobling, M.A., A. Pandya & C. Tyler-Smith, 1997. The Y chromosome in forensic analysis and paternity testing. *International Journal of Legal Medecine* 110, 118–24.

Langella, O., L. Chikhi & M.A. Beaumont, 2001. LEA (Likelihood-based estimation of admixture): a program to simultaneously estimate admixture and the time since admixture. *Molecular Ecology Notes* 1(4), 357–8.

Loader, C.R., 1996. Local likelihood density estimation. *Annals of Statistics* 24, 1602–18.

Mallory, J.P., 1989. *In Search of the Indo-Europeans: Language, Archaeology and Myth*. London: Thames and Hudson.

Mountain, J. & L.L. Cavalli-Sforza, 1994. Inference on human evolution through cladistic analysis of nuclear DNA restriction polymorphisms. *Proceedings of the National Academy of Sciences of the USA* 91, 6515–19.

Nei, M. & W.H. Li, 1979. Mathematical model for studying genetic variation in terms of restriction endonucleases. *Proceedings of the National Academy of Sciences of the USA* 76, 5269–73.

Pereira, L., I. Dupanloup, Z.H. Rosser, M.A. Jobling & G. Barbujani, 2001. Y-chromosome mismatch distributions in Europe. *Molecular Biology and Evolution* 18(7), 1259–71.

Price, T.D., R.A. Bentley, J. Luning, D. Grononborn & J. Wahl, 2001. Prehistoric human migration in the Linearbandkeramik of Central Europe. *Antiquity* 75, 593–603.

Pritchard, J.K. & M. Przeworski, 2001. Linkage disequilibrium in humans: models and data. *American Journal of Human Genetics* 69, 1–14.

Pritchard, J.K. & N.A. Rosenberg, 1999. Use of unlinked genetic markers to detect population stratification in association studies. *American Journal of Human Genetics* 65, 220–28.

Przeworski M., R.R. Hudson & A. di Rienzo, 2000. Adjusting the focus on human variation. *Trends in Genetics* 16, 279–325.

Reich, D.E., M. Cargill, S. Bolk, J. Ireland, P.C. Sabeti, D.J. Richter, T. Lavery, R. Kouyoumjian, S.F. Farhadian, R. Ward & E.S. Lander, 2001. Linkage disequilibrium in the human genome. *Nature* 411, 199–204.

Rendine, S., A. Piazza & L.L. Cavalli-Sforza, 1986. Simulation and separation by principal components of multiple demic expansions in Europe. *American Naturalist* 128, 681–706.

Renfrew, C., 1987. *Archaeology and Language: the Puzzle of Indo-European Origins*. London: Cape.

Richards, M., H. Côrte-Real, P. Forster, V. Macaulay, H. Wilkinson–Herbots, A. Demaine, S. Papiha, R. Hedges, H.-J. Bandelt & B. Sykes, 1996. Palaeolithic and Neolithic lineages in the European mitochondrial gene pool. *American Journal of Human Genetics* 59, 185–203.

Richards, M., V.A. Macaulay, H.-J. Bandelt & B.C. Sykes, 1998. Phylogeography of mitochondrial DNA in western Europe. *Annals of Human Genetics* 62, 241–60.

Rosser, Z.H., T. Zerjal, M.E. Hurles, M. Adojaan, D. Alavantic, A. Amorim, W. Amos, M. Armenteros, E. Arroyo, G. Barbujani, G. Beckman, L. Beckman, J. Bertranpetit, E. Bosch, D.G. Bradley, G. Brede, G. Cooper, H.B. Corte-Real, P. de Knijff, R. Decorte, Y.E. Dubrova, O. Evgrafov, A. Gilissen, S. Glisic, M. Golge, E.W. Hill, A. Jeziorowska, L. Kalaydjieva, M. Kayser, T. Kivisild, S.A. Kravchenko, A. Krumina, V. Kucinskas, J. Lavinha, L.A. Livshits, P. Malaspina, S. Maria, K. McElreavey, T.A. Meitinger, A.V. Mikelsaar, R.J. Mitchell, K. Nafa, J. Nicholson, S. Norby, A. Pandya, J. Parik, P.C. Patsalis, L. Pereira, B. Peterlin, G. Pielberg, M.J. Prata, C. Previdere, L. Roewer, S. Rootsi, D.C. Rubinsztein, J. Saillard, F.R. Santos, G. Stefanescu, B.C. Sykes, A. Tolun, R. Villems, C. Tyler-Smith & M.A. Jobling, 2000. Y-chromosomal diversity in Europe is clinal and influenced primarily by geography, rather than by language. *American Journal of Human Genetics* 67, 1526–43.

Semino, O., G. Passarino, A. Brega, M. Fellous & A.S. Santachiara-Benerecetti, 1996. A view of the Neolithic demic diffusion in Europe through two Y chromosome-specific markers. *American Journal of Human Genetics* 59, 964–8.

Semino, O., G. Passarino, P.J. Oefner, A.A. Lin, S. Arbuzova, L.E. Beckman, G. De Benedictis, P. Francalacci, A. Kouvatsi, S. Limborska, M. Marcikiae, A. Mika, B. Mika, D. Primorac, A.S. Santachiara-Benerecetti, L.L. Cavalli-Sforza & P.A. Underhill, 2000. The genetic legacy of Palaeolithic *Homo sapiens* in extant Europeans: a Y chromosome perspective. *Science* 290, 1155–9.

Simoni, L., F. Calafell, D. Pettener, J. Bertranpetit & G. Barbujani, 2000. Geographic patterns of mtDNA diversity in Europe. *American Journal of Human Genetics* 66, 262–78.

Stephens, M. & P. Donnelly, 2000. Inference in molecular population genetics. *Journal of the Royal Statistical*

Society B 62, 605–35.

Stumpf, M.P.H. & D.B. Goldstein, 2001. Genealogical and evolutionary inference with the human Y chromosome. *Science* 291, 1738–42.

Tajima, F., 1983. Evolutionary relationship of DNA sequences in finite populations. *Genetics* 105, 437–60.

Thomas, M.G., K. Skorecki, H. Ben-Ami, T. Parfitt, N. Bradman & D.B. Goldstein, 1998. A genetic date for the origin of Old Testament Priests. *Nature* 394, 138–40.

Wall, J.D. & M. Przeworski, 2000. When did the human population size start increasing. *Genetics* 155, 1865–74.

Wilson, J.F., D.A. Weiss, M. Richards, M.G. Thomas, N. Bradman & D.B. Goldstein, 2001. Genetic evidence for different male and female roles during cultural transitions in the British Isles. *Proceedings of the National Academy of Sciences of the USA* 98, 5078–83.

Wise, C.A., M. Sraml & S. Easteal, 1998. Departure from neutrality at the mitochondrial NADH dehydrogenase subunit 2 gene in humans, but not in chimpanzees. *Genetics* 148, 409–21.

Zvelebil, M., 2000. The social context of the agricultural transition record in Europe, in *Archaeogenetics: DNA and the Population Prehistory of Europe*, eds. C. Renfrew C. & K. Boyle. (McDonald Institute Monographs.) Cambridge: McDonald Institute for Archaeological Research, 45–56.

Zvelebil, M. & K.V. Zvelebil, 1988. Agricultural transition and Indo-European dispersals. *Antiquity* 62, 574–83.

Chapter 35

Complex Signals for Population Expansions in Europe and Beyond

Kristiina Tambets, Helle-Viivi Tolk, Toomas Kivisild, Ene Metspalu, Jüri Parik, Maere Reidla, Michael Voevoda, Larissa Damba, Marina Bermisheva, Elsa Khusnutdinova, Maria Golubenko, Vadim Stepanov, Valery Puzyrev, Esien Usanga, Pavao Rudan, Lars Beckmann & Richard Villems

François Jacob, in his brilliant 'The possible and the actual' (Jacob 1982), reminds us that 'scientific investigation begins by inventing a possible world, or a small piece of a possible world'. One may add that the space allowed for *the possible* is likely to be in strong positive correlation with the level of our ignorance. What chance, then, when discussing language/farming/gene dispersals, do we have to identify *the actual* from a plethora of *possible* scenarios?

Since the presentation of 'African Eve' (Cann *et al.* 1987; Vigilant *et al.* 1991), the last decade has demonstrated an increasingly better understanding of the phylogeny and phylogeography of mtDNA and of the Y chromosome. Here, the first influential achievement was a series of papers from Emory (reviewed in Wallace 1995) where, *inter alia*, it became obvious that human maternal lineages world-wide are very clearly structured geographically. This knowledge came thanks to phylogenetic analysis of the coding part of the mtDNA genome. Secondly, as Richards *et al.* (1996) have shown, the mtDNA hypervariable 1 (HVR 1) region offers an increased resolution of a phylogenetic tree, in particular as far as Europeans are concerned. Although mtDNA hypervariable region sequences started to accumulate in quantities (thanks largely to forensics), it soon became obvious that the results coming from RFLP analysis or the HVR sequence(s) alone were not informative enough to go further. Quite the opposite; it became clear that trees, based on HVR 1 sequence alone, were often phylogenetically wrong. However,

a synthesis of what is known about polymorphisms in the coding region (extensive RFLP as a tool) and HVR (direct sequencing) removes most of the ambiguities and leads to a much better understanding of the details of the topology of the phylogenetic tree of mtDNA (e.g. Macaulay *et al.* 1999). This analysis owes much to the use of median networks as an approach (Bandelt *et al.* 1995).

In this contribution we demonstrate that coalescence age calculation of the monophyletic branches of the mtDNA phylogenetic tree, applied together with a detailed phylogeographic knowledge, is an instrument which provides new insight into demographic processes of the past and, in particular, allows to see informative differences there, where mere haplogroup frequency calculations are able only to register flat landscapes.

General

How much further can one go in resolution? It is obvious that 'the ultimate' answer lies in analyzing, in all collected samples, all 16,500 plus nucleotides of the mtDNA genome — to carry out total (high fidelity!) re-sequencing. There are now at least a thousand fully sequenced mtDNA genomes at hand and this body of data, although rather time-consuming to analyze, is very useful in 'fine-tuning' phylogenetic analysis (Richards & Macaulay 2001). However, when we speak about many thousands of samples, total re-sequencing is not yet a viable approach and would probably be unnecessary either. While extensive re-sequencing did reveal a number of new polymorphisms very useful for fine-scale analysis, and allowed the resolution of a number of ambiguities, it did not create a need to revise the basic topology of the mtDNA tree as it had been deduced in relatively fine detail already. It does not mean, though, that an additional total or partial re-sequencing of mtDNAs is not needed any more, specifically where hitherto less understood variants are concerned.

Perhaps the most valuable aspect of mtDNA diversity analysis as an 'archaeogenetic tool' lies in the possibility of estimating coalescence ages of individual lineage clusters. In saying 'valuable', it is only fair to add that there are different views on the reliability of the mtDNA clock. Although coalescence estimates for human mtDNA lineage clusters (haplogroups) are often presented with rather large standard deviations and are prone to possible systematic errors in special circumstances, the approach as such is a tool to be polished further, not discarded.

One complicated question, though, is whether the diversity within a particular clade which we observe at present, among a population or a group of populations in a contiguous area, has arisen *in situ* or was, at least partially, already present among some ancestral population and then carried to new places by a large enough number of people to keep the pre-existing diversity 'alive'. This is a valid question universally (e.g. compare the coalescence ages of Amerindian mtDNA lineage clusters of more than 20,000 years with the much younger archaeological evidence for the peopling of the Americas), and to give a satisfactory answer is usually not easy. A thorough analysis of the phylogeography of individual lineage clusters with a reliable identification of founder haplotypes may help here.

It is justifiable to expect that the main driving forces behind the ancient demographic behaviour of human populations were more or less directly related to the availability of food and hunting and gathering territories. Consequently, one may presume that pre-Neolithic population expansions, on a Eurasian scale, could be largely attributed and traced to periods when large 'virgin' land areas first became available. The first colonization of Eurasia by modern humans and, particularly for Europe, the postglacial re-colonization of formerly glaciated territories, are two obvious examples. Less discussed in the western Eurasian context are other possible re-colonizations, particularly of lands deserted because of the extreme aridity that accompanied the LGM and made large areas of northern Africa and the

Near and Middle East inhospitable for humans. And then there was the Younger Dryas, with its very abrupt return to cold and dry conditions, possibly even more dangerous for human survival than equally harsh but much slower environmental changes.

That food production (agriculture) allows for higher population densities than hunting and gathering certainly seems to be self-evident. However, the historic context is always concrete and such general statements should be weighed against specific archaeological evidence (Bellwood 2001; Renfrew 2000). As far as Neolithic Europe is concerned, the literature addressing the influence of Neolithic Anatolian/Near Eastern genes in the extant gene pool of Europeans is already extensive and widely known. We refer here only to Richards *et al.* (2000) where, for the first time, a more complex model of gene flow between the Near East and Europe was considered in the interpretation of the phylogeography of mtDNA lineages. This model assumes reciprocal movements of people and is probably more realistic than one assuming only a one-way flow.

Modern humans started to colonize Europe about 40,000–50,000 years ago. Population density underwent many profound changes. How these phases of expansion/stabilization and regression/re-occupation may have influenced the linguistic situation is discussed by Renfrew (2000). He pays attention mostly to the more recent periods, whereas we will try to start 'from the beginning'. In the Eurasian context, it would be possible to consider the first expansion phase (i.e. the first colonization of Eurasia by modern humans) as having generated the first language spread zone. Next, one may ask how a drastic shrinkage of the area inhabited during the LGM (particularly in Europe) influenced the linguistic situation. While several much shorter post-LGM cold phases like the Younger Dryas arose and disappeared abruptly, within perhaps a few generations (van Andel 2000), it seems that the LGM itself developed in cold intensity much more slowly — a process that might well have allowed time for 'an organized retreat' into refugia. What proportion of the pre-LGM mtDNA and Y-chromosomal diversity survived in these refugia? And what was happening with languages?

However remote the pre-LGM period may seem to us — but notice a recent confirmation of sophisticated Aurignacian cave art in France (Valladas *et al.* 2001) — it lasted for more than 15,000 years and was a period when some of the most remarkable pan-European cultures like the Aurignacian and

Gravettian flourished. Could the following glacial maximum period (roughly 24,000–16,000 BP) represent a strong convergence phase for the pre-LGM languages in refuge areas, coupled with a simultaneous and profound divergence enforced by the geographic isolation of the principal refugia? And how complete was this isolation?

For example, was the 'Periglacial refugium' (Dolukhanov 2000) in Eastern Europe indeed isolated for millennia from other (likely) refugia in France and Iberia, in southern Siberia, in the Balkans, and along the eastern Black Sea coast? And were the latter two isolated from eastern Anatolia and the Levant, or was there in fact traffic, the migration of humans, forth and back? What influence would such traffic have had on the then-existing patterns of languages? Is this question at all relevant for the emergence of language families as we know them at present? Is it beyond knowability? If so, then archaeology and genetics can operate free of linguistic constraints over the time frame under discussion. Is it meaningful to explore, just for the sake of curiosity, an alternative working hypothesis according to which (some) language families which are currently spread across western Eurasia may have had their origins in a convergence phase during the LGM, where refugia brought together languages which earlier, during perhaps the preceding 15,000 years (or even much longer), were subject to a 'spread zone' scenario?

It may well be that the conventional methods of historical linguistics and glottochronology do not normally allow us to penetrate deeper than, say, 5000–8000 years. Sometimes it seems that this chronological barrier is understood to mean that a particular language family indeed arose at this time depth, while it may be just a time-line beyond which further reconstruction is impossible. Therefore, should one immediately reject currently unorthodox ideas, such as linking the Proto-Finno-Ugric languages to the 'Periglacial refugium' period, as some have suggested (e.g. Wiik 2000; Dolukhanov 2000)?

Below we discuss a few 'case studies', in order to illustrate why does it seem to us that the genetic interpretation of demographic and probably linguistic histories needs a time span at least back to the late Pleistocene. From these case studies we wish, first of all, to illustrate what can be considered as one of the key questions in the understanding of present-day variation in the human mtDNA pool in Europe. Namely, bearing in mind a detailed topology of the mtDNA phylogenetic tree, what does it tell us about the beginnings of expansion of various of its sub-

clusters? Following a phylogeographic approach, can we perhaps classify such signals over a variety of haplogroups and geographic regions? More to the point: are there significant differences in expansion times for mtDNA monophyletic clades, specific for different regions of Europe? And if yes, are there any patterns?

Out of a large number of possible examples, we first concentrate on U4 and U5 within a major western Eurasian haplogroup U. Both of them are recognized as Upper Palaeolithic, largely European varieties of mtDNA (Macaulay *et al.* 1999; Richards *et al.* 2000).

Case study: U5

U5 is a 'prototype' western Eurasian lineage cluster with a coalescence age of around 45,000–55,000 BP (Richards *et al.* 2000). Its phylogenetic tree does not suggest a star-like expansion from the founder (e.g. Richards *et al.* 2000; Finnilä *et al.* 2001). But our analysis of a large number of U5 mtDNAs revealed the presence of about a dozen putative sub-founders, most of which exhibit nice star-like expansions (Fig. 35.1). More importantly, we have found that almost all of them exhibit coalescence ages around 11,000–13,000 BP and only a few, like 'the Saami U5', seem to have started to expand significantly more recently. The 'Saami motif' — 16,270; 16,189, 16,144 — (labelled as S in Fig. 35.1, but the figure is here drawn without Saami variants) is rare outside northeastern Scandinavia: its topology in Scandinavia suggests recent severe bottleneck(s) in the demographic history of their carriers.

This nearly synchronous series of coalescence ages makes sense: it is much easier to imagine (specifically for a such an ancient branch) that an expansion phase hit all U5 twigs and limbs nearly simultaneously, than to assume a complicated pattern of a dozen or so widely irregular beginnings. Specifically, before the beginning of farming, a likely reason for an expansion may be traced to favourable climatic changes. A particular time frame before the beginning of the Holocene is highly likely, since this period corresponds (Younger Dryas and other cold events here excluded) to a rapid warming of climate after the LGM, and, therefore, to a re-occupation of large areas of northern Europe by humans as well varieties of animals and plants. We return to this question below.

Case study: U4

U4 is even more 'European' than U5: while U5 is relatively frequent all over western Eurasia, U4 is,

Figure 35.1. *Skeleton topology of the human mtDNA haplogroup U5 hypervariable 1 phylogenetic tree for western Eurasia. Circle sizes are proportional to numbers of individuals per haplotype. 'S' corresponds to a haplotype, most frequent among Saami population (HVR 1 motif 16,144; 16,189; 16,270).*

frequency exceeds that of U5.

In spite of this, we have not found any U4b mtDNA genomes among Finno-Ugric and Volga region people (*N* > 1000). This sub-cluster is largely, though not solely, typical for Germanic-speaking populations, being yet another highly characteristic example of a steep cline in the distribution of maternal lineages in Europe. The coalescence age of U4 is around 16,000–24,000 BP (Richards *et al.* 2000). With geographically more representative data at hand, it is interesting to estimate coalescence ages not only for each sub-division of U4 (i.e. U4*, U4a and U4b), but also for different linguistic/geographic entities within a sub-cluster. We found the answers intriguing. For the Baltic Finno-Ugric and Volga people (note that Hungarians differ here from the Finnic-speaking people), the coalescence ages both for U4* and U4a are around the maximum of the LGM, at 20,000–22,000 BP. Furthermore, taking U4c tentatively as monophyletic for this particular region, the corresponding sub-clade lineages in the FU–Volga area coalesce at about 19,000 BP — coinciding within the limits of error with U4* and U4a.

with a few interesting exceptions, more frequent in eastern Europe and is either absent or very rare in the Near East and elsewhere. In the European north, an interesting exception is the Saami mtDNA pool, where U4 is virtually absent.

We have constructed a HVR1–based phylogenetic tree for U4, using information from ~80 populations comprising a total of ~400 U4 genomes (Fig. 35.2). The topology of the U4 cluster is relatively simple, revealing the presence of a limited number of sub-founders. Of these, U4a and U4b are likely monophyletic, while U4c, determined by a transition at np 16,362, might be polyphyletic, at least in a pan-western Eurasian context. The highest frequencies of U4 (both in absolute terms and as a percentage of Hg U) can be observed actually not in Europe, but among Obi-Ugric Khantys and Mansis, living in northwestern Siberia. It is also frequent among the Finnic-speaking populations and in Volga Basin Turkic speakers, where, in some instances, its

Postulating the beginning of expansion during the LGM seems strongly counter-intuitive at first glance. Here, however, comes an equally unexpected archaeological finding (Dolukhanov 2000), that actual population density (calculated from the number of precisely dated settlements) rose considerably after about 25,000 BP in a periglacial area of northern Ukraine–southern Russia, reaching its maximum around the peak of the LGM. It is of course highly speculative, but nevertheless tempting to bring these two completely independent findings together and to suggest that the eastern 'Periglacial refugium' postulated by archaeological data, and beginning of the expansion of U4 among eastern Europeans, can be attributed to the same prehistoric people.

Next, we calculated coalescence ages of U4*,

U4a and U4b for the Germanic-speaking people (Germans, Norwegians, Swedes, Icelanders, Scots, German-speaking Swiss). Here the other interesting observation came. As indicated above, they share U4* and U4a with FU–Volga people, whereas the latter lack U4b. Nevertheless, the coalescence ages for all three indicated clades/sub-clades for the Germanic-speaking people are close and lie around 10,000–14,000 BP, suggesting that the beginning of their expansion was:

a) in the late Pleistocene, corresponding to the period of fast regression of continental ice cover in northern Europe and the general 'improvement' of climate;

b) much later (for U4* and U4a) than for people living in the adjacent geographic area of northeastern Europe.

One may ask about U4 in Mediterranean Europe. While U4a is so rare there that no meaningful calculation can be performed, the coalescence age for U4* for the Mediterranean is again about 13,000 BP.

Notice that this time scale (late Pleistocene) overlaps with that which one observes for the majority of the nicely star-like sub-clades of U5, discussed above. There is, of course, a profound difference between the spreads of U4 and U5 in western Eurasia. U5 is one of the major pan-western Eurasian maternal lineage clades, present in northwestern Africa, in the Near and Middle East and in Central Asia, while U4 is largely a northeastern-central European variety of mtDNA, found also in western Siberia/Altai and, in low frequencies, in Mediterranean Europe and the Near East. Interestingly, we have found a few U4 lineages even in India (see Kivisild *et al.* this volume).

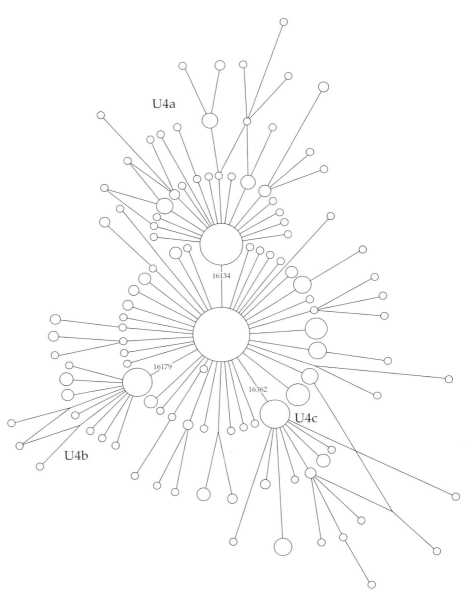

Figure 35.2. *Skeleton topology of the human mtDNA haplogroup U4 hypervariable 1 phylogenetic tree. The three sub-founders discussed (U4a, U4b and U4c) differ from the central node (referred as U* in the text) as indicated. About 400 U4 mtDNAs from about 15,000 mtDNAs were used to construct the tree.*

This pattern of a late Pleistocene expansion of population might be a general one. The coalescence age of largely European-specific (in contrast to western Eurasian U5) haplogroup V lies in late Pleistocene as well, and its expansion is explained in terms of the re-peopling of those parts of Europe deserted during the LGM (Torroni *et al.* 1998). For Hg V, this expansion seems to radiate from the Iberian peninsula (Torroni *et al.* 1998). Here, it is fair to refer to recent debate on this issue (Simoni *et al.* 2000; Torroni *et al.* 2000), clarified recently (Torroni *et al.* 2001). Furthermore, in Richards *et al.* (2000), coalescence ages of several other mtDNA haplogroups/sub-clusters display summary coalescence ages within a 'Mesolithic' time span (defined in this paper to lie approximately between 9000 and 14,000 BP).

To conclude; both for mtDNA and for the Y chromosome (e.g. Semino *et al.* 2000; Malaspina *et al.* 2000), it begins to appear that, although many lineage clusters currently visible in the European gene pool were likely present in Europe before the LGM, their present-day phylogeography is largely determined by demographic events after the LGM — during a period when re-peopling *before farming* seems to emerge as one of the most profound determinants of the present-day variability of European maternal lineages.

Several authors have rightfully stressed that a lineage cluster for individuals living in a given contiguous area cannot be assumed to have developed its diversity entirely or even largely in the area where it is found at present (e.g. Barbujani & Bertorelle 2001). In many instances it can be demonstrated that such cannot be so, in principle. After all, many northern European populations live at present in areas repopulated only after the LGM. This may mean that for Hg U5, widely spread also in the Near and Middle East, one can argue that its variability in Europe (which suggests coalescence ages for its sub-clades around 11,000–14,000 BP, see above) had already developed to a large extent in the Levant, Anatolia, the Caucasus, even in Egypt — wherever U5 is present today. All that is required is to assume that the founding migrants should have been numerous enough to carry the variants with them to Europe. Problems like this have been quantitatively treated in Richards *et al.* (2000), but it appears that the findings now seem to support the hypothesis that there was near-simultaneous expansion of sub-clusters of U5 around the late Pleistocene (in the late Upper Palaeolithic–Mesolithic), *together* with Hg V and sub-clusters of U4 among people whose maternal lineage descendants include Germanic language group Europeans. Because all three haplogroups are of a likely 'European' origin, the observation lends strong credence to a pan-European, late Pleistocene population expansion, traceable to the re-peopling of the region after the LGM.

Quite a few more examples may be added. Within European haplogroup H, we have:
1. a sub-cluster characterized by an additional transition at np 16,261 with a star-like phylogenetic

tree. From its pan-European data bank (this lineage cluster is very rare outside Europe) we have at present, with $N = 79$, a coalescence age of 12,900±1800 BP; for the FU–Volga area 12,300±3300 BP, and for Germanic language group populations 12,800±3300 BP;
2. a sub-cluster of Hg H, characterized by an additional transition at np 16,209 with a coalescence age of 12,600±3000 BP.

A detailed knowledge of the phylogeography of U4 offers several other avenues for speculation. It is nearly absent among Iranians, Ossetes and Kurds — i.e. among three Indo-Iranian-speaking populations. Neither have we found it in a limited sample of Tadjiks, yet another Indo-Iranian-speaking population. In contrast, U4 is present among some South Caucasus populations, in particular among Kartvels (Georgians), but again infrequent among Turks (Tambets *et al.* 2000). Although there is not enough space to discuss all of the conclusions stemming from these findings here, they seem to suggest the absence of any massive maternal gene flow from eastern Europe (where U4 is one of the oldest and most frequent mtDNA clades) to the Middle East since the end of the LGM. One may add that the opposite is also doubtful, argued on the basis of a near, although not complete, absence of U7 in northern and eastern Europe, while this cluster is most frequent worldwide in the Middle and Near East as well as in western India (Kivisild *et al.* 1999; see also Kivisild *et al.* this volume).

Nevertheless, if one favours scenarios with massive migrations from the Middle East to eastern Europe (present in many maps as a bold arrow originating in the Middle East, turning around the eastern Caspian and pointing west), then it is necessary to postulate that U7 reached Iran only after this putative northwards expansion. This is not an easy and straightforward assumption, because, as already mentioned, Iran is rich in U7, at least at present, and there is no obvious 'homeland' for U7 elsewhere. On the other hand, the presence of U7 in the Balkans suggests gene flow into Europe via Anatolia.

Some 'mini-cases' signal expansions in the Neolithic and Bronze Age

From the previous case studies, one may obtain an impression that we wish to synchronize the coalescence ages of all mtDNA lineage clusters/sub-clusters/sub-sub-clusters with demographic events in the Pleistocene, in particular with the post-LGM re-peopling of Europe. That is not so. One complication with more recent events is that they might well be 'hidden' — i.e. assimilated as 'new boosts' with the beginning of food production — into expansions which began earlier, in the late Pleistocene. Therefore, more recent events (expansions) can be best detected in cases where *de novo* sub-founders arose and produced star-like expansions.

With some fear of making the issue even more complex, we add here several such 'mini-cases' exhibiting coalescence ages well within the time span of food production.

Sub-haplogroup T1 - HVR I motif from T* - 16,163; 16,186; 16,189

1. For the European Finno-Ugric and Volga–South Ural Turkic-speaking people, the coalescence age of sub-haplogroup T1 is about 4000 BP. However, it appears to be even more recent for the Baltic-Finnic people (Finns, Estonians, Karelians). If these are removed from the calculations, then the coalescence age of T1 for the Volga-Uralic people (here: Maris, Mordvin, Komis, Udmurts, Tatars, Chuvashis, Bashkirs) rises to ~6500 BP.

2. For Germanic-language group people plus Scots, the coalescence age of sub-haplogroup T1 is about 4000 BP. This calculation ignores all putative reversions in mtDNA HVR 1 sequence data bases. If one accepts them, the coalescence age rises to about 6500 BP.

3. For Anatolia, South Caucasus, the Near and Middle East and northeast Africa, the overall coalescence age for T1 is very much older — around 17,000 BP.

Sub-haplogroup T1 is one of the clearest examples of a lineage cluster with a much earlier expansion in the Near and Middle East and South Caucasus than in Europe. Most importantly, it may possibly testify to the arrival of Neolithic farmers in Europe (e.g. Metspalu *et al.* 1999; Tambets *et al.* 2000; Richards *et al.* 2000). However, our new inspection, based on a more extensive study of the Near Eastern mtDNA pool, shows that the 'really old' part for T1 within western Asian seems to be the South Caucasus, Anatolia and Syria, possibly including also southeastern Mediterranean Europe and Egypt, where the corresponding tree coalesces about 26,000–29,000 BP. Furthermore, like the late Pleistocene series of coalescence ages for U5 and U4 in Europe, the western Asian coalescence ages for T1 pre-date significantly the beginnings of farming and animal domestication in Anatolia and the Fertile Crescent and may have been trigged by an early post-LGM climatic change, or by even more remote and unknown events before the LGM.

Interpretation of the coalescence ages for T1 in regionally/linguistically divided Europe is also not as obvious. While there seems to be one time frame corresponding roughly to an early expansion of agriculture, there are also signs of a significantly later expansion in northern Europe. There is not yet a powerful-enough data base for northern Russians, but the coalescence age for T1 among northeastern Komis and Udmurts is as recent as it is for the Baltic Finnic-speaking people — about 3000 to 4000 BP. This suggests a late arrival of females carrying T1 mtDNA to northeastern Europe.

Sub-cluster of Hg J – 16,069; 16,126; 16,145; 16,261; 16231

Although haplogroup J belongs to the list of putative Neolithic arrivals, this particular sub-clade of J is yet another largely 'northern European' variety of mtDNA lineage, very probably arisen in Europe and its coalescence age is around 7000 BP ($N = 58$; 7000 ± 1600 BP). This might be an overestimate: subtracting a putative sub-clade node at np 16,189, the coalescence age drops to about 5000 BP.

Thus, provided a sufficiently large data bank is at hand, one may 'collect' a long list of 'mini-clades' which coalesce around 4000–7000 BP. A relatively large standard deviation makes any detailed interpretation of the results complicated, but taking 4000–6000 BP as an average, the coalescence ages (signs of the beginning of an expansion of a particular clade) do fall into a time frame, corresponding to the 'consolidation and further expansion' of agriculture in Europe (Pinhasi *et al.* 2000). Identifying such mini-clades all over the main mtDNA lineage clusters supports a suggestion that we are dealing here with a general phenomenon.

Concluding remarks

It might sound unimaginative, but it appears that for further significant progress in finding answers to the 'big question' (defined as by Renfrew 2000), it will be necessary to gather more data and better data. As far as genetics is concerned, the *best* data are those which allow a detailed phylogeographic analysis to be carried out. In other words, this means making the best use of a fortunate situation for the researcher who is dealing with non-recombining, uniparentally inherited DNA. At least at the present, the barrier to *knowability* is hopefully still some unknown distance ahead. One may expect that most remaining problems in the phylogenetic analysis of mtDNA data will soon reach maturation as far as the topology of the corresponding tree (at least for western Eurasia) is concerned, and that the problems identified here will be largely solved, or shown to remain ambiguous forever because of built-in limitations resulting from the length of mtDNA.

What is much less clear is how we can reach significantly better temporal resolutions. Take, for example, U5: a cluster coalescing around 40,000–50,000 BP but consisting, as we interpret it now, of a number of sub-founders coalescing about 12,000 BP. Even though U5 mtDNAs are frequent in the western Eurasian mtDNA pool, to identify numerous sub-clusters within it one does need to operate with large sample sizes. For less frequent mtDNA varieties, only very large data bases, consisting of data about tens of thousands of mtDNAs, will allow a detailed temporal analysis, in particular for a time frame when important farming/language dispersal events took place. But there is clearly a light visible and, as already mentioned (Torroni *et al.* 2000; Helgason *et al.* 2001), deeper phylogenetic analysis reveals that there is no uniformity in the spread of maternal lineages in Europe. Now that genetics is approaching an increasingly finer phylogeographic resolution, including the temporal component, it depends increasingly on better coverage and resolution of time and density maps of archaeological sites (e.g. Pinhasi *et al.* 2000; Zvelebil this volume).

References

Bandelt, H.-J., P. Forster, B.C. Sykes & M.B. Richards, 1995. Mitochondrial portraits of human populations using median networks. *Genetics* 141, 743–53.

Barbujani, G. & G. Bertorelle, 2001. Genetics and the population history of Europe. *Proceedings of the National Academy of Sciences of the USA* 98, 22–5.

Bellwood, P., 2001. Early agricultural diasporas? Farming, languages and genes. *Annual Review in Anthropology* 30, 181–207.

Cann, R.L., M. Stoneking & A.C. Wilson, 1987. Mitochondrial DNA and human evolution. *Nature* 325, 31–6.

Dolukhanov, P., 2000. 'Prehistoric revolutions' and languages in Europe, in *The Roots of Peoples and Languages of Northern Eurasia II and III*, ed. A. Künnap, Tartu: Tartu University Press, 71–84.

Finnilä, S., M.S. Lehtonen & K. Majamaa, 2001. Phylogenetic network for European mtDNA. *American Journal of Human Genetics* 68, 1475–84.

Forster, P., R. Harding, A. Torroni & H.-J. Bandelt, 1996. Origin and evolution of Native American mtDNA variation: a reappraisal. *American Journal of Human Genetics* 59(4), 935-45.

Helgason, A., E. Hickey, S. Goodacre, V. Bosnes, K. Stefansson, R. Ward & B. Sykes, 2001. MtDNA and the islands of the North Atlantic: estimating the proportions of Norse and Gaelic ancestry. *American Journal of Human Genetics* 68, 723–37.

Jacob, F., 1982. *The Possible and the Actual*. New York (NY): Pantheon Books.

Kivisild, T., M.J. Bamshad, K. Kaldma, M. Metspalu, E. Metspalu, M. Reidla, S. Laos, J. Parik, W.S. Watkins, M.E. Dixon, S.S. Papiha, S.S. Mastana, M.R. Mir, V. Ferak & R. Villems, 1999. Deep common ancestry of Indian and western-Eurasian mitochondrial DNA lineages. *Current Biology* 9, 1331–4.

Macaulay, V.A., M.B. Richards, E. Hickey, E. Vega, F. Cruciani, V. Guida, R. Scozzari, B. Bonné-Tamir, B. Sykes & A. Torroni, 1999. The emerging tree of west Eurasian mtDNAs: a synthesis of control-region sequences and RFLPs. *American Journal of Human Genetics* 64(1), 232–49.

Malaspina, P., F. Cruciani, P. Santolamazza, A. Torroni, A. Pangrazio, N. Akar, V. Bakalli, R. Brdicka, J. Jaruzelska, A. Kozlov, B. Malyarchuk, S.Q. Mehdi, E. Michalodimitrakis, L. Varesi, M.M. Memmi, G. Vona, R. Villems, J. Parik, V. Romano, M. Stefan, M. Stenico, L. Terrenato, A. Novelletto & R. Scozzari, 2000. Patterns of male-specific inter-population divergence in Europe, West Asia and North Africa. *Annals of Human Genetics* 64(5), 395–412.

Metspalu, E., T. Kivisild, K. Kaldma, J. Parik, M. Reidla, K. Tambets & R. Villems, 1999. The Trans-Caucasus and the expansion of the Caucasoid-specific human mitochondrial DNA, in *Genomic Diversity*, eds. S. Papiha, R. Deka & R. Chakraborty. New York (NY): Kluwer Academic/Plenum Publishers, 121–34.

Pinhasi, R., R.A. Foley & M.M. Lahr, 2000. Spatial and temporal patterns in the Mesolithic–Neolithic archaeological record of Europe, in Renfrew & Boyle (eds.), 45–56.

Renfrew, C., 2000. At the edge of knowability: towards a prehistory of languages. *Cambridge Archaeological Journal* 10(1), 7–34.

Renfrew, C. & K. Boyle (eds.), 2000. *Archaeogenetics: DNA and Population Prehistory of Europe*. (McDonald Institute Monographs.) Cambridge: McDonald Institute for Archaeological Research.

Richards, M. & V. Macaulay, 2001. The mitochondrial gene tree comes of age. *American Journal of Human Genetics* 68, 1475–84.

Richards, M., H. Corte-Real, P. Forster, V. Macaulay, H. Wilkinson-Herbots, A. Demaine, S. Papiha, R. Hedges, H.-J. Bandelt & B. Sykes, 1996. Paleolithic and Neolithic lineages in the European mitochondrial gene pool. *American Journal of Human Genetics* 59(1), 185–203.

Richards, M., V. Macaulay, E. Hickey, E. Vega, B. Sykes, V. Guida, C. Rengo, D. Sellitto, F. Cruciani, T. Kivisild, R. Villems, M. Thomas, S. Rychkov, O. Rychkov, Y. Rychkov, M. Golge, D. Dimitrov, E. Hill, D. Bradley, V. Romano, F. Calí, G. Vona, A. Demaine, S. Papiha, C. Triantaphyllidis, G. Stefanescu, J. Hatina, M. Belledi, A. di Rienzo, A. Novelletto, A. Oppenheim, S. Norby, N. Al-Zaheri,

S. Santachiara-Benerecetti, R. Scozzari, A. Torroni & H.-J. Bandelt, 2000. Tracing European founder lineages in the near eastern mtDNA pool. *American Journal of Human Genetics* 67, 1251–76.

Saillard, J., P. Forster, N. Lynnerup, H.-J. Bandelt & S. Nørby, 2000. MtDNA variation among Greenland Eskimos: the edge of the Beringian expansion. *American Journal of Human Genetics* 67(3), 718–26.

Semino, O., G. Passarino, P.J. Oefner, A.A. Lin, S. Arbuzova L.E. Beckman, G. de Benedictis, P. Francalacci, A. Kouvatsi, S. Limborska, M. Marcikiae, A. Mika, B. Mika, D. Primorac, A.S. Santachiara-Benerecetti, L.L. Cavalli-Sforza & P.A. Underhill, 2000. The genetic legacy of Paleolithic *Homo sapiens sapiens* in extant Europeans: a Y-chromosome perspective. *Science* 290, 1155–9.

Simoni, L., F. Calafell, D. Pettener, J. Bertranpetit & G. Barbujani, 2000. Geographic patterns of mtDNA diversity in Europe. *American Journal of Human Genetics* 66, 262–78.

Tambets, K., 2000. The topology of the maternal lineages of the Anatolian and Trans-Caucasus populations and the peopling of Europe: some preliminary considerations, in Renfrew & Boyle (eds.), 219–35.

Tambets, K., T. Kivisild, E. Metspalu, J. Parik, K. Kaldma, S. Laos, H.-V. Tolk, M. Gölge, H. Demirtas, T. Geberhiwot, S. Papiha, S., G.F. De Stefano & R. Villems, 2000. The topology of the maternal lineages of the Anatolian and Trans-Caucasus populations and the peopling of the Europe: some preliminary considerations, in Renfrew & Boyle (eds.), 219–35.

Torroni, A., H.-J. Bandelt, L. D'Urbano, P. Lahermo, P. Moral, D. Sellitto, C. Rengo, P. Forster, M.L. Savontaus, B. Bonné-Tamir & R. Scozzari, 1998. MtDNA analysis reveals a major late Paleolithic population expansion from southwestern to northeastern Europe. *American Journal of Human Genetics* 62(5), 1137–52.

Torroni, A., M. Richards, V. Macaulay, P. Forster, R.

Villems, S. Nørby, M.L. Savontaus, K. Huoponen, R. Scozzari & H.-J. Bandelt, 2000. MtDNA haplogroups and frequency patterns in Europe. *American Journal of Human Genetics* 66(3), 1173–7.

Torroni, A., H.-J. Bandelt, V. Macaulay, M. Richards, F. Cruciani, C. Rengo, V. Martinez-Cabrera, R. Villems, T. Kivisild, E. Metspalu, J. Parik, H.V. Tolk, K. Tambets, P. Forster, B. Karger, P. Francalacci, P. Rudan, B. Janicijevic, O. Rickards, M.L. Savontaus, K. Huoponen, V. Laitinen, S. Koivumaki, B. Sykes, E. Hickey, A. Novelletto, P. Moral, D. Sellitto, A. Coppa, N. Al-Zaheri, A.S. Santachiara-Benerecetti, O. Semino & R. Scozzari, 2001. A signal, from human mtDNA, of postglacial recolonization in Europe. *American Journal of Human Genetics* 69(4), 844–52.

Valladas, H., J. Clottes, J.-M. Geneste, M.A. Garcia, M. Arnold, H. Cachier & N. Tisnerat-Laborde, 2001. Palaeolithic paintings: evolution of prehistoric cave art. *Nature* 413, 479.

van Andel, T.H., 2000. Where received wisdom fails: the mid-Palaeolithic and early Neolithic climates, in Renfrew & Boyle (eds.), 31–9.

Vigilant, L., M. Stoneking, H. Harpending, K. Hawkes & A.C. Wilson, 1991. African populations and the evolution of human mitochondrial DNA. *Science* 253, 1503–7.

Wallace, D., 1995. Mitochondrial DNA variation in human evolution, degenerative disease, and aging. *American Journal of Human Genetics* 57, 201–23.

Wiik, K., 2000. Some ancient and modern linguistic processes in northern Europe, in *Time Depth in Historical Linguistics*, eds. C. Renfrew, A. McMahon & L. Trask. (Papers in the Prehistory of Languages.) Cambridge: McDonald Institute for Archaeological Research, 463–79.

Zvelebil, M., 2000. The societal context of the agricultural transition in Europe, in Renfrew & Boyle (eds.), 31–9.

Chapter 36

Analyzing Genetic Data in a Model-based Framework: Inferences about European Prehistory

Martin Richards, Vincent Macaulay & Hans-Jürgen Bandelt

Our view of the genetic history of Europe has been dominated by what Renfrew (2000) has recently described as 'phase 1' of research. Cavalli-Sforza and his colleagues, using principal component (PC) analysis (Cavalli-Sforza *et al.* 1994; Menozzi *et al.* 1978), and supported by the work of Sokal and his colleagues, using spatial autocorrelation analysis (Sokal *et al.* 1989; 1991), developed approaches to aggregating allele frequency data from many genetic loci (the so-called 'classical markers') and searching for gradients, or clines. They found that the strongest component of the variation in European populations was a southeast–northwest gradient, which resembled maps of radiocarbon dates for the expansion of agriculture from the Near East into Europe. This was taken as strong support for the hypothesis that the spread of the Neolithic into Europe was driven by the movement of people from the Near East, bringing their new technologies with them. Specifically, they proposed that this was a result of 'demic diffusion' by means of a 'wave of advance', that is, the result of surplus-fuelled population growth accompanied by random migration into new territory (Ammerman & Cavalli-Sforza 1984). They argued that the existence of genetic gradients implied that the newcomers were gradually incorporating the genetic pool of the indigenous Mesolithic Europeans as they expanded, so that the mechanism was a mixture of demic diffusion and acculturation.

Whilst this early presentation of the hypothesis was carefully honed and modest, later ones became more and more robustly expressed as the interpretation crystallized, and the thrust of the argument became that the main contribution to the European gene pool was from the Near Eastern immigrants. By 1994 it was described as follows: 'This pattern agrees with a model of diffusion of farmers and partial admixture with local hunter–gatherers, who

were gradually absorbed by the much more numerous population of farmers, which could grow to higher population densities' (Cavalli-Sforza *et al.* 1994, 108). What is more, these analyses also suggested that much of the remaining variation was the result of *subsequent* migration events into Europe.

This view was very influential, and a consensus emerged concerning the overwhelming demographic impact of the Neolithic. Although Renfrew (1987) was initially extremely careful not explicitly to rely upon the genetic work, it haunts his re-evaluation of the spread of Indo-European languages, and, for that matter, Bellwood's (1997; this volume) work on the dispersals of the Austronesian language family (cf. Oppenheimer & Richards this volume; and Hurles this volume). Yet, although the view persisted, there were problems with this interpretation. The major gradients themselves appeared to be robust, but their interpretation was more problematic than at first assumed.

The first problem was the idea of 'one-PC–one-migration'. Zvelebil (1989; 1998) pointed out that there was no strong reason for associating the first PC solely with the Neolithic expansion. Europe, as a small peninsula of the Eurasian landmass, is likely to have been a sink for many such expansions throughout prehistory. It seems likely that many subsequent waves (or perhaps trickles) of population movement may have spread into Europe via Anatolia (Zvelebil 2000). Hence the suggestion arose that the gradients identified by principal component analysis might represent an 'incremental palimpsest' of migrations, of which the Neolithic may have been only one (and not necessarily even the most significant) (Zvelebil 2000). Just as an example, Richards *et al.* (1997) pointed out that the radiocarbon evidence suggested that the spread of the Early Upper Palaeolithic into Europe followed essentially the same pathway as the Neolithic (see also Sims-Williams 1998).

This draws attention to a major drawback of the classical approach: the lack of any means of dating. Cavalli-Sforza *et al.* (1994) arranged principal components in succession, according to their magnitude. The components were likened to the stratigraphic record of archaeology, and regarded as providing relative, if not absolute, dating of demic expansions, on the basis that each fresh expansion would be entering territory already marked by the gradients of previous expansions and would therefore have a lower impact (Cavalli-Sforza 1996). But the assumption that the magnitude of the PCs reflected their age was clearly questionable.

A further problem with this approach was that there was no way of knowing how the magnitude of the PC related to that of the expansion. The difficulty is that we don't know how genetically different the expanding populations were from the peoples that they dispersed into in any particular case; yet the magnitude of the PC depends on both the proportion of newcomers *and* how different they were from the aboriginals. Of course, if the PCs represent a palimpsest of processes, the issue becomes even more problematic.

Phylogeography and farming dispersals

Molecular approaches to these issues were first applied in the mid-1990s (Richards *et al.* 1996). Both Stoneking & Wilson (1989) and Torroni *et al.* (1993) had proposed a 'founder analysis' approach to phylogeography, in which variation in probable source and sink populations was compared in order to identify founder lineages and date individual migration events. The approach was elaborated in some detail in Stoneking *et al.* (1992). Another powerful statement, applied to the colonization of the Americas, and underpinned by a new phylogenetic-network method (Bandelt *et al.* 1995), was presented by Forster *et al.* (1996).

The idea is as follows. The genetic diversity of a population, for which there are any number of summary statistics, is not, in general, a reflection of the age of that population, even on the basis of a simple population-genetics model of population formation (by fission of earlier populations) in which the population is assumed meaningfully to have an age. The diversity partly reflects both the population size and the diversity of those other populations that contributed to its formation. In particular, many of the mutational variants contributing to the diversity of a

population may have occurred long before the formation of the population itself, in an earlier population, which may have resided elsewhere. Founder analysis is an attempt to correct the variation in the extant population by allowing for this pre-existing diversity. It does this by comparing putative source and descendant populations, in order to identify the fraction of the variation that had already arisen and to subtract this from the total (Richards & Macaulay 2000). The analysis can therefore offer a time span for the entry of each mtDNA type into the region of study. It needs to be stressed, though, that an analysis based purely on genetic data cannot alone serve as a predictor for the cultural (let alone linguistic) affiliation of its carrier. For example, we can test the magnitude of immigration from the Near East dating to the time of the spread of the Neolithic, but there is nothing in the genetic evidence *per se* that will associate the two.

An important aspect of this approach is therefore its use of explicit models, especially archaeological models. Genetic data can be very useful for distinguishing between different possibilities within a given context, but are unlikely to be very helpful in the absence of any framework. In our most recent and detailed analyses, we have used a number of models when applying the founder analysis to the settlement of Europe. Firstly, we analyzed the data within a model of prehistoric colonization based on archaeological and palaeoclimatological, as well as genetic, evidence. We specifically looked for signs of immigration at particular times during the European past when such immigration seemed likely on both genetic and non-genetic grounds. On the genetic side, we looked at the distribution of ages of the ten or so most frequent founder clades in Europe (accounting for about three-quarters of the data). Several clades were dated at ~9000 years ago, five fell at about 13,000–16,000 years ago, and one clade was almost 50,000 years old. Several fell between 20,000 and 35,000 years ago. From the archaeological and climatological side we took dates of 9000 years ago for the earliest Neolithic in Europe, 14,500 years ago for Late Upper Palaeolithic warming, and 45,000 years ago for the first Upper Palaeolithic colonization, each of which roughly corresponded with the major founder clade ages. We added a Middle Upper Palaeolithic age of 26,000 years ago to capture the clades in the 20,000–35,000-year range. This model then allowed us to assess the proportion of founder clades most likely to have arrived at around each of these times. We varied the model by allowing for a potential Mesolithic episode at 11,500 years ago, following the brief Younger Dryas cold period, but rejected the usefulness of this when few lineages were partitioned into this time period. Thus, if one has a framework for the analysis, it does not have to be treated rigidly; several lines of evidence can corroborate it, and the effect of varying the framework can be studied.

Demographic assumptions are also necessary to motivate the founder analysis. Some are unavoidable: for example, each founder clade was assigned (albeit with a certain probability) to a single migration episode. Common founder types in the Near East may of course have migrated more than once (another case of the 'palimpsest effect': Zvelebil 2000). However, the distribution of types in the Near East suggested that this was unlikely to be a major problem, since, unlike Europe, the Near East has not experienced a major bottleneck (at the LGM) leading to the presence of certain high-frequency types. For the commonest type, which occurs in the Near East at ~6 per cent, we repartitioned the outcomes to explore heuristically the effect of possible multiple migrations. The analysis also assumes a rapid expansion of founders as soon as they enter the sink region. This is supported by the star-like phylogeny of most of the founder clades. Further assumptions have to be made about back-migration into the source area, and back-mutation of derived types, not to mention the molecular clock and the calibration of the mutation rate. But in each case it is possible to explore the effects of the assumptions on the analysis. A particularly acute issue, that of sampling, can be explored by resampling procedures.

In our approach, we aim to rely on the population concept, in its technical, population-genetic, sense, as little as possible. We do not subscribe to the belief (common amongst geneticists) that there are such entities as 'human populations', which are the units of study and whose 'population history' it is our mission to discover (see Bandelt *et al.* this volume; cf. Barbujani & Dupanloup this volume; Chikhi *et al.* this volume). Although we have to distinguish between source and sink regions, we otherwise use the term only loosely, in its ordinary sense. We freely recognize that the different 'populations' from which we have taken samples have been defined in a variety of mutually incompatible ways — including geographical, national, ethnic and linguistic. We favour a regional definition, such as that used by Gamble (1986), and where possible have grouped our data into such regions for analysis. In the Near East in particular, however, sampling is as yet not adequate for such an approach. For our present studies we

have simply combined all Near Eastern data into a single unit.

When a rudimentary founder analysis was first applied to European mtDNA variation, the result was unexpected and rather striking (Richards *et al.* 1996). Rather a small proportion of the lineages appeared to have arrived from the Near East in the Neolithic — only ~15 per cent. The majority of European lineages appeared to descend from founders in the Middle or Late Upper Palaeolithic, and it was suggested that these very star-like clades were mainly the result of dramatic re-expansions in the post-glacial period.

These results were initially rather sketchy, partly due to reliance on the hypervariable part of the control region (HVS-I), and more especially due to lack of adequate sampling in the Near East. However, subsequent work by Richards *et al.* (1998; 2000), as well as further work on the mtDNA tree itself (Macaulay *et al.* 1999), have filled in the details. Furthermore, the important rôle of post-glacial expansion has been emphasized by the genealogical disentanglement of haplogroup V from haplogroup H (using coding-region restriction sites) and the mapping of its particular distribution and diversity (Torroni *et al.* 1998; 2001). These results suggested an expansion from a southwest European refugium after the Last Glacial Maximum involving mitochondrial haplogroup V, probably accompanied by lineages from haplogroup H. Again, since H is the commonest European haplogroup, this suggested a major rôle for post-glacial expansions in shaping the modern genetic landscape of Europe, although since haplogroup H itself predates the LGM, it remains unclear to what extent the regional mtDNA pools of Europe could be traced back to the expansion from the southwest.

In the most recent analyses, Richards *et al.* (2000) have used an improved Near Eastern mtDNA data base and new statistical analyses in order to make more quantitative estimates of the proportions of lineages surviving from the various major colonization and expansion phases in European prehistory. The Near East (in which we include Anatolia, Egypt and the southern Caucasus: cf. Kuhrt 1995) shows a similar haplogroup composition to Europe (Macaulay *et al.* 1999). However, it displays marked differences in haplogroup frequency and a higher diversity, including the presence of related haplogroups not (or only rarely) found in Europe. This supports the archaeological view that the Near East is the main source for migrations into Europe, at least in the Early Upper Palaeolithic (Mellars 1992) and the Neolithic (Henry 1989). The analysis further hinted at an entry *via* Eastern Europe or the Caucasus during the Middle Upper Palaeolithic, although more data from those regions are needed to evaluate and quantify this influence. There was also evidence for considerable gene flow back from Europe into the Near East, especially in the more peripheral parts bordering onto Europe or the Caucasus, such as Anatolia and Armenia. This had to be taken into account as far as possible when evaluating the results. The founder analysis was therefore carried out under a variety of different criteria for founder identification, to allow for the effects of both back-migration and recurrent mutation (which is a common problem in the mtDNA control region).

The results were remarkably consistent across criteria. They indicated a Neolithic component of 12–23 per cent, and an Early Upper Palaeolithic component of 2–17 per cent. Approximately 55–64 per cent could be attributed to late-glacial expansions, although there was some evidence that these had arrived earlier, during the Middle Upper Palaeolithic, and suffered bottlenecks at the Last Glacial Maximum, in agreement with the refugium hypothesis (Gamble 1986; Housley *et al.* 1997). Strikingly, under the most plausible assumptions, 76 per cent of extant lineages were encompassed by eleven major founder clades in Europe (Richards *et al.* 2000, fig. 1).

Regional comparisons within Europe

We also carried out the founder analysis at the regional level, to estimate the proportion of extant lineages dating to each founder event in each region. There were some striking differences with regard to the impact of Neolithic immigrants from region to region. The highest impact was on southeast Europe, north-central Europe, northwest and northeast Europe, which showed values of 15–22 per cent. The introduction of farming into southeast and central Europe by means of colonization is the most usual interpretation of the archaeological record (Bogucki 2000; Tringham 2000; Zvelebil 2000), although even here acculturation has been suggested (Whittle 1996). The mtDNA results suggest that colonization did occur, but that even so the majority of surviving lineages (about 80 per cent) appear to be the result of acculturation of indigenous Mesolithic people, along the lines of the 'integrationist' position in archaeology (Zvelebil 2000). Whether these lineages were recruited from the interior forests of central Europe, or perhaps from further to the south and east followed by a phase of expansion into much less populated territory, is open to question.

Resolving the details becomes more problematic the further we move away from the Near Eastern source. A number of archaeologists have argued (Price 2000; Zvelebil 2000; Zvelebil & Dolukhanov 1991) that agriculture was introduced to both northwest and northeast Europe predominantly by contact, rather than by immigration. Yet the values for descendants of Neolithic founders in these regions are again around 20 per cent. Whether these values represent new arrivals in the Neolithic, or are the result of subsequent exchanges with central Europe, is not clear. However, the lack of a gradient of Neolithic Near Eastern lineages on the southeast–northwest axis of Europe clearly distinguishes the mtDNA evidence from that of the first PC of classical markers. Rather than a demic diffusion, with a gradual incorporation of Mesolithic lineages as the wave advanced, it more readily suggests a rapid dispersal towards the northwest without gene flow in the early stages between the newcomers and the indigenous people. If the gradient of the first PC of classical markers (and the Y chromosome: see below) were to be regarded as primarily due to Neolithic demic diffusion, then this might point to sex-specific patterns of interaction in the early Neolithic forests. On the other hand, the autosomal and Y-chromosome data might be interpreted differently, as discussed below. If 'Neolithic' gradients were to evaporate for both sexes, then demic diffusion as a mechanism for the Neolithic spread could be firmly ruled out even for central Europe, and something akin to leap-frog colonization (Zvelebil 2000) could take its place.

The pattern along the Mediterranean is quite distinct: ~10 per cent of lineages from each region of the Mediterranean coastline in Europe are derived from Near Eastern Neolithic pioneers. This supports the archaeological picture of some colonization accompanied by acculturation of relatively dense, flourishing Mesolithic communities (Barnett 2000; Zilhão 2000). An especially striking result is the huge amount of recent (post-Neolithic) gene flow around the eastern Mediterranean basin; in agreement with the high levels of back-migration identified in the Near East, about 20 per cent of lineages in eastern Mediterranean Europe have a recent Near Eastern origin. This has implications for the interpretation of Y-chromosome data and autosomal allele frequencies, which we discuss below. The region with the lowest Neolithic component in our analysis is the Basque country (at ~7 per cent), in agreement with the Basques' putatively pre-Indo-European and possibly pre-agricultural language (Renfrew 1987), and their extreme position in autosomal studies of Europe (Cavalli-Sforza *et al.* 1994). The Saami are an even more extreme outlier, due to extensive drift (Lahermo *et al.* 1996; Torroni *et al.* 1998), and were excluded from our analysis for that reason. Scandinavia, which also is unlikely to have received many Neolithic immigrants when farming was first introduced, has ~10 per cent Neolithic lineages.

Comparisons with the Y chromosome

Recently, Y-chromosome data have become available at a much higher level of genealogical resolution than previously (Underhill *et al.* 2000), and as a consequence are also making a major contribution to the debate on European prehistory. Earlier work had already identified both a major Palaeolithic component of European Y-chromosome variation, haplogroup 1 (Lucotte & Hazout 1996; Semino *et al.* 1996), and a candidate Neolithic component from the Near East, haplogroup 9 (Semino *et al.* 1996) (for the haplogroup nomenclature, see Jobling *et al.* 1997), which declines in frequency from the Near East to Europe.

Both Rosser *et al.* (2000) and, using newly developed marker systems, Semino *et al.* (2000) have now identified complex patterns in Y-chromosome distributions in Europe, showing much sharper genetic clines than previously seen in mtDNA haplogroups. Because of these clear patterns, a certain amount can be inferred from their distribution without further genealogical resolution or founder analysis. Haplogroup 1 (Rosser *et al.* 2000, fig. 3C; shown in green in fig. 1 of Semino *et al.* 2000) is present in the Near East at fairly low levels, and the predominant haplogroups present there are 9 and 21 (shown in red and yellow respectively in figure 1 of Semino *et al.* 2000; Rosser *et al.* 2000, figs. 3D & 3E). Both of these haplogroups are also present in Europe at declining frequencies as one moves away from the Near East. Semino *et al.* (2000) interpret both as being markers for colonizing Neolithic men, thereby estimating the overall Neolithic contribution to Europe on the male side at ~20 per cent. Haplogroup 1 is concentrated in Atlantic Europe, suggesting a postglacial expansion from a southwestern refugium analogous to that proposed for mtDNA haplogroup V, and possibly supported by the second principal component of classical markers (see also Hill *et al.* 2000; Malaspina *et al.* 1998; Torroni *et al.* 1998; 2001; Wilson *et al.* 2001). This appears to be in good agreement with the results of the mtDNA analyses outlined above.

Some caution is needed, even so. There is a tendency in recent Y-chromosome studies towards a position of 'one-haplogroup–one-migration' that mirrors the 'one-PC–one-migration' of earlier work (indeed, this is made explicit in the analysis of Semino *et al.* 2000). The mtDNA founder analysis suggests rather that, as one would imagine, there is no one-to-one correlation between migrations and major clades. For example, a striking difference between the Y-chromosome and mtDNA patterns for inferred Neolithic dispersals in Europe is that on the mtDNA side the immigrant lineages are concentrated in southeast and central Europe, whereas in the Y-chromosome analysis they are concentrated along the Mediterranean. Remember that the mtDNA founder analysis for eastern Mediterranean Europe indicated a very high frequency (20 per cent) of recent gene flow, as compared with only about 10 per cent Neolithic input. It would be necessary to perform a similar founder analysis (using, for example, a large panel of fast-evolving microsatellites) to see whether or not a proportion of the putative Neolithic types on the paternal side in Europe are actually of more recent origin. However, it is already suggestive that the frequency of haplogroup 21, inferred as Neolithic by Semino *et al.* (2000), appears at particularly high levels in the western Mediterranean in the more extensive sample of Rosser *et al.* (2000, fig. 3E). As they suggest, this may imply gene flow from North Africa (where haplogroup 21 reaches its highest frequency) rather than from the Near East.

Perhaps then, only a fraction of the haplogroup 9 (and perhaps also haplogroup 21) lineages present in modern Europeans may result from the Neolithic expansion; the appearance of a gradient may partly be the result of recent gene flow into eastern and central Mediterranean Europe. This would reconcile the Y-chromosome and mtDNA pictures, and by implication the autosomal picture too, and remove from the running the wave of advance as a mechanism, even in central Europe. On the other hand, if the Y-chromosome interpretation holds up, a more complex picture of sex-specific processes may be required.

Modelling prehistoric processes

It needs to be emphasized that all of this evidence inevitably concerns the contribution of various immigration events during the prehistory of Europe to the modern genetic pool. Inferring the demographic impact at the time is another matter. Even so, there seems to be an emerging consensus that the globe filled up early, especially during the expansions following the Last Glacial Maximum 20,000 years ago. This would seem to undercut farming-dispersal hypotheses for the origins of major language families such as Indo-European. Models of these origins have usually been regarded as requiring large-scale demic diffusion as the mechanism for language spread, because of the lack of the social hierarchy and central organization necessary for an élite dominance model (Renfrew 1987). Renfrew (2001; this volume) has recently pointed out that, as Ammerman & Cavalli-Sforza (1984, 126–30) showed by simulation, population growth following gene flow between newcomers and indigenes can lead to substantial local demic diffusion. Although the indigenous genetic contribution would rapidly overwhelm that of the newcomers, this could nevertheless provide the basis for a demic-based model for the spread of languages (the 'Staged Population-Interaction Wave of Advance'). This model would be compatible with the rapid decline in Near Eastern Y-chromosome lineages as the distance from the source increases (Semino *et al.* 2000). It is more difficult to reconcile with the mtDNA evidence, in which strong southeast–northwest clines are lacking. It might therefore be more fruitful to abandon the wave of advance as a general working hypothesis and look for new, less monolithic, models for the Neolithic spread.

It is now widely acknowledged that Indo-European did not spread throughout Europe at a uniform rate, but is likely to have displaced other languages in a long process, extending possibly as far back as the Neolithic, up until as recently as the medieval period (Zvelebil & Zvelebil 1988). Perhaps something akin to demic diffusion was involved in some stages, for example between the Balkans and central Europe, where evidence of preceding Mesolithic populations remains scanty, though even here the genetic evidence suggests that the newcomers were in a minority. Furthermore, if the lack of specifically Neolithic clines in central Europe in mtDNA were corroborated by more detailed analyses of the Y chromosome, any remaining arguments for a wave of advance would seem to have dissipated. The patterns might rather suggest successive leap-frog colonization, followed by frontier mobility and perhaps what Zvelebil (2000) describes as 'starburst' demic diffusion, largely involving the acculturated Mesolithic population.

If Indo-European languages were indeed spread with farming, it therefore seems likely that contact-induced change and language shift must have been the critical factor. Both Sherratt & Sherratt (1988) and Zvelebil (1995) have proposed modifications of

the farming-dispersal view that allow for non-genetic linguistic transmission, for example in the formation of Indo-European-based creole languages amongst the Mesolithic communities adopting aspects of farming at the agricultural frontier (Zvelebil 1995). Renfrew himself (1998) has given his blessing to this line of argument. It might even seem more consistent with both the linguistic and genetic evidence to move the contact-induced language shift further back, to Proto-Indo-European speakers acculturated to farming by Near Eastern pioneers in southeast Europe before the expansions into the LBK zone. Given the thrust of the evidence the molecular genetics is beginning to provide, in conjunction with the dissatisfaction that many archaeologists feel with the more traditional explanations for Indo-European spread, this would appear to be the most fruitful direction for the study of Indo-European origins to take. Farming dispersal models may yet have a rôle to play in explaining language expansions. But grand syntheses based on demic diffusion and the wave of advance, in which farming, languages and genes all expand together, should become a thing of the past.

Acknowledgements

VM is a Wellcome Trust Research Career Development Fellow. This work was further supported by a travel grant to H-JB from the Deutscher Akademischer Austauschdienst (DAAD).

References

Ammerman, A.J. & L.L. Cavalli-Sforza, 1984. *The Neolithic Transition and the Genetics of Populations in Europe.* Princeton (NJ): Princeton University Press.

Bandelt, H.-J., P. Forster, B.C. Sykes & M.B. Richards, 1995. Mitochondrial portraits of human populations using median networks. *Genetics* 141, 743–53.

Barnett, W.K., 2000. Cardial pottery and the agricultural transition in Mediterranean Europe, in Price (ed.), 93–116.

Bellwood, P., 1997. *Prehistory of the Indo-Malaysian Archipelago.* Honolulu (HI): University of Hawaii Press.

Bogucki, P., 2000. How agriculture came to north-central Europe, in Price (ed.), 197–218.

Cavalli-Sforza, L.L., 1996. The spread of agriculture and nomadic pastoralism, in *The Origins and Spread of Agriculture and Pastoralism in Eurasia*, ed. D.R. Harris. London: University College London Press, 51–69.

Cavalli-Sforza, L.L., P. Menozzi & A. Piazza, 1994. *The History and Geography of Human Genes.* Princeton (NJ): Princeton University Press.

Forster, P., R. Harding, A. Torroni & H.-J. Bandelt, 1996. Origin and evolution of Native American mtDNA variation: a reappraisal. *American Journal of Human Genetics* 59, 935–45.

Gamble, C., 1986. *The Palaeolithic Settlement of Europe*. Cambridge: Cambridge University Press.

Henry, D.O., 1989. *From Foraging to Agriculture: the Levant at the End of the Ice Age*. Philadelphia (PA): University of Pennsylvania Press.

Hill, E.W., M.A. Jobling & D.G. Bradley, 2000. Y-chromosome variation and Irish origins. *Nature* 404, 351–2.

Housley, R.A., C.S. Gamble, M. Street & P. Pettitt, 1997. Radiocarbon evidence for the lateglacial human recolonisation of northern Europe. *Proceedings of the Prehistoric Society* 63, 25–54.

Jobling, M.A., A. Pandya & C. Tyler-Smith, 1997. The Y chromosome in forensic analysis and paternity testing. *International Journal of Legal Medicine* 110, 118–24.

Kuhrt, A., 1995. *The Ancient Near East*, vol. I. London: Routledge.

Lahermo, P., A. Sajantila, P. Sistonen, M. Lukka, P. Aula, L. Peltonen & M.-L. Savontaus, 1996. The genetic relationship between the Finns and the Finnish Saami (Lapps): analysis of nuclear DNA and mtDNA. *American Journal of Human Genetics* 58, 1309–22.

Lucotte, G. & S. Hazout, 1996. Y-chromosome DNA haplotypes in Basques. *Journal of Molecular Evolution* 42, 472–5.

Macaulay, V., M. Richards, E. Hickey, E. Vega, F. Cruciani, V. Guida, R. Scozzari, B. Bonné-Tamir, B. Sykes & A. Torroni, 1999. The emerging tree of West Eurasian mtDNAs: a synthesis of control-region sequences and RFLPs. *American Journal of Human Genetics* 64, 232–49.

Malaspina, P., F. Cruciani, B.M. Ciminelli, L. Terrenato, P. Santolamazza, A. Alonso, J. Banyko, R. Brdicka, O. García, C. Gaudiano, G. Guanti, K.K. Kidd, J. Lavinha, M. Avila, P. Mandich, P. Moral, R. Qamar, S.Q. Mehdi, A. Ragusa, G. Stefanescu, M. Caraghin, C. Tyler-Smith, R. Scozzari & A. Novelletto, 1998. Network analyses of Y-chromosomal types in Europe, northern Africa, and western Asia reveal specific patterns of geographic distribution. *American Journal of Human Genetics* 63, 847–60.

Mellars, P., 1992. Archaeology and the population-dispersal hypothesis of modern human origins in Europe. *Philosophical Transactions of the Royal Society of London Series B* 337, 225–34.

Menozzi, P., A. Piazza & L.L. Cavalli-Sforza, 1978. Synthetic maps of human gene frequencies in Europeans. *Science* 201, 786–92.

Price, T.D. (ed.), 2000. *Europe's First Farmers*. Cambridge: Cambridge University Press.

Renfrew, C., 1987. *Archaeology and Language*. London: Jonathan Cape

Renfrew, C., 1998. The origins of world linguistic diversity: an archaeological perspective, in *The Origins and Diversification of Language*, eds. N.G. Jablonski & L.C. Aiello. San Francisco (CA): California Academy of Sciences, 171–92.

Renfrew, C., 2000. Archaeogenetics: towards a population prehistory of Europe, in Renfrew & Boyle (eds.), 3–11.

Renfrew, C., 2001. From molecular genetics to archaeogenetics. *Proceedings of the National Academy of Sciences of the USA* 98, 4830–32.

Renfrew, C. & K. Boyle (eds.), 2000. *Archaeogenetics: DNA and the Population Prehistory of Europe*. (McDonald Institute Monographs.) Cambridge: McDonald Institute for Archaeological Research.

Richards, M. & V. Macaulay, 2000. Genetic data and the colonization of Europe: genealogies and founders, in Renfrew & Boyle (eds.), 139–51.

Richards, M., H. Côrte-Real, P. Forster, V. Macaulay, H. Wilkinson-Herbots, A. Demaine, S. Papiha, R. Hedges, H.-J. Bandelt & B. Sykes, 1996. Paleolithic and neolithic lineages in the European mitochondrial gene pool. *American Journal of Human Genetics* 59, 185–203.

Richards, M., V. Macaulay, B. Sykes, P. Pettitt, R. Hedges, P. Forster, H.-J. Bandelt, 1997. Palaeolithic and neolithic lineages in the European mitochondrial gene pool: a reply to Cavalli-Sforza and Minch. *American Journal of Human Genetics* 61, 251–4.

Richards, M., V.A. Macaulay, H.-J. Bandelt & B.C. Sykes, 1998. Phylogeography of mitochondrial DNA in western Europe. *Annals of Human Genetics* 62, 241–60.

Richards, M., V. Macaulay, E. Hickey, E. Vega, B. Sykes, V. Guida, C. Rengo, D. Sellitto, F. Cruciani, T. Kivisild, R. Villems, M. Thomas, S. Rychkov, O. Rychkov, Y. Rychkov, M. Gölge, D. Dimitrov, E. Hill, D. Bradley, V. Romano, F. Calì, G. Vona, A. Demaine, S. Papiha, C. Triantaphyllidis, G. Stefanescu, J. Hatina, M. Belledi, A. Di Rienzo, A. Novelletto, A. Oppenheim, S. Nørby, N. Al-Zaheri, S. Santachiara-Benerecetti, R. Scozzari, A. Torroni & H-J. Bandelt, 2000. Tracing European founder lineages in the Near Eastern mitochondrial gene pool. *American Journal of Human Genetics* 67, 1251–76.

Rosser, Z.H., T. Zerjal, M.E. Hurles, M. Adojaan, D. Alavantic, A. Amorim, W. Amos, M. Armenteros, E. Arroyo, G. Barbujani, G. Beckman, L. Beckman, J. Bertranpetit, E. Bosch, D.G. Bradley, G. Brede, G. Cooper, H.B.S.M. Côrte-Real, P. de Knijff, R. Decorte, Y.E. Dubrova, O. Evgrafov, A. Gilissen, S. Glisic, M. Gölge, E.W. Hill, A. Jeziorowska, L. Kalaydjieva, M. Kayser, T. Kivisild, S.A. Kravchenko, A. Krumina, V. Kučinskas, J. Lavinha, L.A. Livshits, P. Malaspina, S. Maria, K. McElreavey, T.A. Meitinger, A.-V. Mikelsaar, R.J. Mitchell, K. Nafa, J. Nicholson, S. Nørby, A. Pandya, J. Parik, P.C. Patsalis, L. Pereira, B. Peterlin, G. Pielberg, M.J. Prata, C. Previderé, L. Roewer, S. Rootsi, D.C. Rubinsztein, J. Saillard, F.R. Santos, G. Stefanescu, B.C. Sykes, A. Tolun, R. Villems, C. Tyler-Smith & M.A. Jobling, 2000. Y-chromosomal diversity in Europe is clinal and influenced primarily by geography, rather than language. *American Journal of Human Genetics* 67, 1526–43.

Semino, O., G. Passarino, A. Brega, M. Fellous & A.S.

Santachiara-Benerecetti, 1996. A view of the Neolithic demic diffusion in Europe through two Y chromo-some-specific markers. *American Journal of Human Genetics* 59, 964–8.

Semino, O., G. Passarino, P.J. Oefner, A.A. Lin, S. Arbuzova, L.E. Beckman, G. De Benedictis, P. Francalacci, A. Kouvatsi, S. Limborska, M. Marcikae, A. Mika, B. Mika, D. Primorac, A.S. Santachiara-Benerecetti, L.L. Cavalli-Sforza & P.A. Underhill, 2000. The genetic legacy of Paleolithic *Homo sapiens sapiens* in extant Europeans: a Y chromosome per-spective. *Science* 290, 1155–9.

Sherratt, A. & S. Sherratt, 1988. The archaeology of Indo-European: an alternative view. *Antiquity* 62, 584–95.

Sims-Williams, P., 1998. Genetics, linguistics, and prehis-tory: thinking big and thinking straight. *Antiquity* 72, 505–27.

Sokal, R.R., R.M. Harding & N.L. Oden, 1989. Spatial pat-terns of human gene frequencies in Europe. *Ameri-can Journal of Physical Anthropology* 80, 267–94.

Sokal, R.R., N.L. Oden & C. Wilson, 1991. Genetic evi-dence for the spread of agriculture in Europe by demic diffusion. *Nature* 351, 143–5.

Stoneking, M. & A.C. Wilson, 1989. Mitochondrial DNA, in *The Colonization of the Pacific: a Genetic Trail*, eds. A.V.S. Hill & S. Serjeantson. Oxford: Oxford Uni-versity Press, 215–45.

Stoneking, M., S.T. Sherry, A.J. Redd & L. Vigilant, 1992. New approaches to dating suggest a recent age for the human mtDNA ancestor. *Philosophical Transac-tions of the Royal Society of London Series B* 337, 167–75.

Torroni, A., T.G. Schurr, M.F. Cabell, M.D. Brown, J.V. Neel, M. Larsen, D.G. Smith, C.M. Vullo & D.C. Wallace, 1993. Asian affinities and continental ra-diation of the four founding Native American mtDNAs. *American Journal of Human Genetics* 53, 563–90.

Torroni, A., H.-J. Bandelt, L. D'Urbano, P. Lahermo, P. Moral, D. Sellitto, C. Rengo, P. Forster, M.-L. Savantaus, B. Bonné-Tamir & R. Scozzari, 1998. MtDNA analysis reveals a major late Paleolithic population expansion from southwestern to north-eastern Europe. *American Journal of Human Genetics* 62, 1137–52.

Torroni, A., H.-J. Bandelt, V. Macaulay, M. Richards, F. Cruciani, C. Rengo, V. Martinez-Cabrera, R. Villems, T. Kivisild, E. Metspalu, J. Parik, H.-V. Tolk, K.

Tambets, P. Forster, B. Karger, P. Francalacci, P. Rudan, B. Janicijevic, O. Rickards, M.-L. Savontaus, K. Huoponen, V. Laitinen, S. Koivumäki, B. Sykes, E. Hickey, A. Novelletto, P. Moral, D. Sellitto, A. Coppa, N. Al-Zaheri, A.S. Santachiara-Benerecetti, O. Semino & R. Scozzari, 2001. A signal, from hu-man mtDNA, of postglacial recolonization in Eu-rope. *American Journal of Human Genetics* 69, 844–52.

Tringham, R., 2000. Southeastern Europe in the transition to agriculture to Europe: bridge, buffer or mosaic, in Price (ed.), 19–56.

Underhill, P.A., P. Shen, A.A. Lin, L. Jin, G. Passarino, W.H. Yang, E. Kauffman, B. Bonné-Tamir, J. Bertranpetit, P. Francalacci, M. Ibrahim, T. Jenkins, J.R. Kidd, S.Q. Mehdi, M.T. Seielstad, R.S. Wells, A. Piazza, R.W. Davis, M.W. Feldman, L.L. Cavalli-Sforza & P.J. Oefner, 2000. Y chromosome sequence variation and the history of human populations. *Nature Genetics* 26, 358–61.

Whittle, A., 1996. *Europe in the Neolithic*. Cambridge: Cam-bridge University Press.

Wilson, J.F., D.A. Weiss, M. Richards, M.G. Thomas, N. Bradman & D.B. Goldstein, 2001. Genetic evidence for different male and female roles during cultural transitions in the British Isles. *Proceedings of the Na-tional Academy of Sciences of the USA* 98, 5078–83.

Zilhão, J., 2000. From the Mesolithic to the Neolithic in the Iberian peninsula, in Price (ed.), 144–82.

Zvelebil, M., 1989. On the transition to farming in Europe, or what was spreading with the Neolithic: a reply to Ammerman (1989). *Antiquity* 63, 379–83.

Zvelebil, M., 1995. Indo-European origins and the agricul-tural transition in Europe, in *Whither Archaeology? Papers in Honour of Evzen Neustupny*, eds. M. Kuna & N. Venclová. Prague: Institute of Archaeology, 173–203.

Zvelebil, M., 1998. Genetic and cultural diversity of Eu-rope: a comment on Cavalli-Sforza. *Journal of An-thropological Research* 54, 411–17.

Zvelebil, M., 2000. The social context of the agricultural transition in Europe, in Renfrew & Boyle (eds.), 57–79.

Zvelebil, M. & P. Dolukhanov, 1991. The transition to farming in eastern and northern Europe. *Journal of World Prehistory* 5, 233–78.

Zvelebil, M. & K.V. Zvelebil, 1988. Agricultural transi-tions and Indo-European dispersals. *Antiquity* 62, 574–83.

Postscript

Concluding Observations

Peter Bellwood & Colin Renfrew

Enlightenment or obfuscation? Some afterthoughts
PETER BELLWOOD

I am writing these words in the Institute of History and Philology in Academia Sinica in Taipei, six months after the Cambridge meeting and a few days after leaving the Batanes Islands in the northern Philippines, where I have been conducting field archaeology on Neolithic sites. The Batanes are immediately to the south of Taiwan, an island which may have played a highly significant role in the genesis of the dispersal of the Austronesian-speaking peoples. I will return later to what we have discovered in the Batanes because the experience has motivated me to contribute this short postscript.

We might first ask where the papers in this volume are leading us. It is clear that there is no consensus on the merits of the farming/language dispersal hypothesis — some contributors support it strongly, others regard it with deep suspicion. Many also follow a middle road, allowing that the hypothesis works for some situations, but not all.

The latter sentiment perhaps indicates the way out of the morass. As I have often stated, the farming/language dispersal hypothesis is not intended to explain the distributions of all language families and major language subgroups in all periods of human history. Were I to try to demonstrate that the modern distributions of the Romance and Germanic languages reflected purely Neolithic population dispersals I would be unlikely to attract many supporters. But even the most dubious would probably agree that the Hispanic- and English-speaking population dispersals since AD 1500 were founded upon the expansion of systems of post-medieval European agriculture, without which they could hardly have taken place with such remarkable speed or to such remarkable extents. Those who doubt even this should consider Crosby's eloquent commentary on the matter (Crosby 1986). Yet agriculture was not the sole causal factor behind the dispersals of the Hispanic and English-speaking populations — it was merely one, albeit an important one, of many historical contingencies which allowed the expansions to take place (cf. Diamond 1997).

So too with the Neolithic and the Formative — the development of agriculture alone could never have been the *sole* causative factor behind any dispersal and we must consider a variety of other social and ecological factors. Some agricultural populations intensified production at home, others extensified production abroad. Some developed specialized pastoralism and thereby spread, as discussed by Colin Renfrew below. Others perhaps developed new forms of transport (e.g. boats), intimidation, or even outright ideologies whereby the foundation of new settlements gave increased prestige to the founders (Bellwood 1996a). Nevertheless, it is in my view impossible to ignore the productive process altogether. For instance, agriculture might not have been the sole cause of the dispersal of the ancestral speakers of Austronesian languages through Southeast Asia and Oceania, but it was surely a major player in the whole drama, and in the hierarchy of causality we may suspect that it operated at a significant level.

This brings me back to the real content of the farming/language dispersal hypothesis. It is a global hypothesis in that it can be invoked to explain broad patterns, at the level of the language family rather than the individual language, and at the level of the regional Neolithic/Formative expression rather than that of the single site. But it is not intended to explain *all* broad patterns in human history, and it is a hypothesis which depends on historical contingency, on specific cultural and ecological factors in specific places at specific times in the past. In some regions, prior conditions allowed historical patterns to unfold which fit well with the hypothesis, in other regions they did not. Just why prior conditions should have differed from place to place is of course a matter for fine-grained regional analysis, rather than global generalization.

The hypothesis thus states that farming dispersal was significant at certain times and places in world history, that these times and places tend to overlap with the archaeological record for the development and spread of agriculture, and that they also overlap non-randomly with the dispersal histories of major portions of some of the largest language families of temperate and tropical latitudes. In temporal terms, the hypothesis favours a series of relatively short-term punctuations within an eternal process of more gradual change. The factor which links farming spread and language spread is basically the movement of *individuals* speaking the ancestral languages concerned — hence the significance of demic diffusion or even outright migration, as debated by many in this volume. At the whole language family level, foundation dispersal purely by the secondary learning of foreign languages is not a convincing explanation, especially in Neolithic circumstances, although as many of the papers presented above make clear, this does not mean that the native-speaking population within a broadly-spread language family remained genetically homogeneous for all time, or even descended entirely from one localized founding source population.

It will be realized that any absolute demonstration of the efficacy of the farming/language dispersal hypothesis will for ever elude us. The immensity and complexity of the human past will always allow other hypotheses to exist, as it will also allow the existence of situations within which the hypothesis manifestly does not work. Critics of the hypothesis will always be able to rub their hands with glee as yet another non-matching situation is hauled out of the annals of archaeology or anthropology and paraded before an awed audience of non-believers. We will never reconstruct the human past *in toto* — our only hope, if we are to understand the deeper reasons for our present cultural and linguistic condition, is to test global hypotheses such as that examined here from a world-wide data base. This requires an overtly *deductive* approach, an emphasis which might awaken memories of the New Archaeology of the 1960s and 1970s (Binford 1968, 16–18), but I think the canvas has changed unrecognizably in the intervening decades. The farming/language dispersal hypothesis would have been unthinkable in the 1960s — archaeology at that time had little conceptual apparatus for dealing with comparative historical inferences on a global scale, or of research in combination with the disciplines of comparative

linguistics and the then-nascent science of genetics.

And so to my final theoretical observations. Hypothesis testing from a world-wide data base is one direction in which research must proceed. But the other side of the coin is of course the strength and reliability of the data base itself. This is where the main disciplines come into their own — archaeologists need firm and reliable dates and contexts, linguists need strong and unambiguous reconstructions, geneticists need to know precisely how modern gene distributions can reveal the structure of populations who lived and died many millennia ago. Yet, no matter how refined the data bases might become, the overall process of understanding will not proceed very far unless scholars in all disciplines pay attention to the two major historical processes which underlie similarity and difference, these being shared inheritance (phylogeny) and what I have elsewhere termed 'reticulation' (or ethnogenesis in the terminology of Moore 1994) (see Bellwood 1996b; 2000; 2001; Kirch & Green 2001; Shennan 2000). Human societies form descent-based relationships through time and contact-based relationships through contemporary space. Of course, in reality it is impossible to separate the results of these two processes in the formation of an individual society or archaeological culture, but the concepts are nevertheless of great significance on the global scale of the farming/language dispersal hypothesis. The Austronesian language family represents an immense edifice of shared ancestral relationship, whatever might be the histories of individual peoples in individual regions. The historical explanation of such sharing, both for Austronesians and for many other peoples, is an enterprise which links all the contributors to this book. On this scale, the observation that genes and languages do not always correlate as precisely as simple mass-migration models might suggest does not in any way negate the overall validity of the farming/language dispersal hypothesis — it simply brings it into the realm of reality.

My final observation is on a local rather than a global scale, but it could have global consequences at the level of the overall history of the Austronesian language family and its archaeological background. My recent research in the Batanes Islands[1] has been a tiny drop in a vast pool of world archaeology, but it has allowed greater archaeological strength to the hypothesis that the dispersal of the Malayo-Polynesian languages (i.e. the Austronesian languages except for Formosan) occurred initially out of Taiwan, hand in hand with the dispersal of the manufacture of a very specific and recognizable type of red-slipped pottery which is found all the way from southeastern Taiwan through the Batanes and northern Luzon, through Sabah and eastern Indonesia, through Island Melanesia and finally to western Polynesia, between 3500 and 3000 years ago. The Batanes Neolithic assemblages, helpfully stratified between deep volcanic marker layers of ash and tephra and thus potentially well datable, provide an essential archaeological link between southeastern Taiwan and northern Luzon — a link essential in the success of the farming/language dispersal hypothesis as it can be applied to the Malayo-Polynesian world. Of course, we have a long way to go with respect to the archaeological record — vast regions of Island Southeast Asia still remain unknown — but at least the existing data are acquiring a chronological axis, a geographical patterning and a level of stylistic coherence which fit increasingly well with the Austronesian language subgroup dispersal patterns obtained independently from comparative linguistics.

In my view, the farming/language dispersal hypothesis will gain in strength as it endures criticism, and especially as it overcomes such criticism as new data come to hand. Some criticism of course will not be overcome, and as this occurs so the hypothesis will be modified, both in general terms and with respect to specific regions. Hopefully the debate will continue with clarity, historical maturity and disciplinary breadth — a dogmatically-structured human past is just as unattractive a prospect as is one totally without any cross-cultural common structure whatsoever. The trees should not render the forest invisible, the local should not dominate the global. Neither would we wish the reverse.

* * *

Outstanding problems
Colin Renfrew

> Human settlement around the Black Sea has a delicate, complex geology accumulated over three thousand years. But a geologist would not call this process simple sedimentation, as if each new influx of settlers neatly overlaid the previous culture. Instead, the heat of history has melted and folded peoples into one another's crevices, in unpredictable outcrops and striations. Every town and village is seamed with fault-lines. Every district display a different veining of Greek and Turkic, Slav and Iranian, Caucasian and Kartvelian, Jewish and Armenian and Baltic and Germanic (Ascherson 1996, 244–5).

To review our Symposium after six months, towards the conclusion of the editorial process, seems to lead in two directions. On the one hand little was definitively agreed, and a multiplicity of viewpoints was presented, taking note of the particularities of each geographic and linguistic context. Yet on the other hand the broad questions remain, and one is left with an acute sense of problem. For there is such evident patterning in the linguistic record, and such widespread agreement among linguists on various key issues, that one feels that some general principles must indeed be at work. These issues involve the validity, indeed the reality, of most of the language families reviewed, and a consensus upon the likelihood that the constituent languages of most of them are the lineal descendents of real (if no longer securely knowable) proto-languages which were spoken by real people at specific times in specific areas — even if these times and areas may difficult to establish today.

Even from my desk in Cambridge (for subsequent study has not taken me so far afield as my co-editorial colleague), several critical themes can be discerned which will require more intensive and systematic review in the future. One of these becomes more evident to me as I prepare for a forthcoming visit to the Black Sea, and confront again the complex issues of ethnicity and language which underlie the histories of the troubled lands surrounding it. These are themes which are admirably brought out in the recent book *Black Sea* by Neal Ascherson (1996), which provides the quotation at the head of this section. The changing nature of ethnicity through time, and the relationship of ethnicities with languages in varying social formations, clearly requires more coherent exploration. And specifically the different ways in which ethnicities may change at a time of social transformation brought about by the spread of a new subsistence economy remain to be systematically addressed. The farming/language dispersal hypothesis is in its infancy, and it will not mature until these matters are more coherently considered in relation to it.

Another feature of our Symposium was the systematic juxtaposition, in some cases for the first time, of well-founded archaeogenetic data to be set aside properly documented presentations of linguistic distributions and (so far as they are available) linguistic histories. My impression is that some initial inferences from what seem to be comparable patternings are not yet very well substantiated. So that whether we are dealing with a 'fast train to Polynesia' or a series of slow boats from Indonesia, more subtle methods of analysis, and probably much larger data sets, will be needed before the population histories of individual regions, such as the insular Pacific, can be regarded as well substantiated.

Underlying all of this is my growing conviction that in our discussion we have not yet learnt to distinguish with sufficient clarity between the life histories of individual languages and the rather different issues surrounding the life histories of language families. Very often it is assumed that the dynamics of change for a language family may be inferred from what seems appropriate for the dynamics of change for an individual language, or group of languages. Yet matters may be very much more complicated than that. The potential difficulties which arise from failing to make such distinctions is already inherent in the rather promiscuous listing of languages and families in the quotation from Ascherson given above.

Moreover I remain convinced that the nub of many of the arguments which are set out in this volume relates to issues of time depth, and to the assumptions which many scholars still find it easy to make about ages and periods of development, where languages and language families are concerned. The phrase 'accumulated over three thousand years' in the passage quoted above reflects the easy assumption so widely implied that we have available to us a valid if approximate notion of time scales for language change, and that these may remain roughly constant when other factors vary. But for time depth in archaeogenetics as much as for time depth in historical linguistics such assumptions remain to be investigated.

Later farming dispersals
In my original outline of the farming/language dispersal model (Renfrew 1989, 118; see also 1987, 124) I wrote more generally of a *demography/subsistence* model, emphasizing that:

a new group of persons (speaking a different language) will not find it easy to become established within the territory in question unless it has available to it something which will allow it to compete successfully, in terms of subsistence procurement, with the existing population.

In general the incoming group will need to be possessed of a subsistence technology which allows it to compete successfully with the pre-existing group, whether by occupying a different ecological niche, or by competing in the original one. For if the new group is to survive and its language ultimately to replace the preceding one, it must have the economic means to allow a population increase. There must be reasons why its numbers would increase while those of the pre-existing group remain constant or decline.

The discussion thus suggests that for an incoming group to achieve linguistic dominance without simply achieving it by force of arms, it will usually need to have economic advantage, often an innovation in the field of subsistence technology.

It is perhaps useful to retain this broader perspective for part of the discussion rather than to focus exclusively upon the initial spread of a farming economy. For within this broader perspective we may situate such later subsistence episodes as the development of nomad pastoralism (which commonly comes about in areas where some degree of farming is already established), and the spread of European farming technologies during the colonial period to regions, such as the Americas, where indigenous farming technologies were already present. This point is already well made by Peter Bellwood in his comments above, when he speaks of 'Romance and Germanic dispersals' in post-Neolithic Europe. It has, however, been most systematically addressed by Daniel Nettle in his chapter 'Neolithic Diversity: Changes in Time' (Nettle 1999, 97–114), in which he speaks of 'The Palaeolithic Equilibrium', 'The Neolithic Punctuation', and 'The Neolithic Aftershock'. This he describes (Nettle 1999, 108) as 'the expansion of Eurasian farmers into the rest of the temperate world'. His term 'Neolithic punctuation' for the initial farming/language dispersal episode derives of course from the terminology of Dixon (1997) which itself draws heavily (perhaps more heavily than he acknowledges — see Renfrew 2000a, 13) upon the farming/language dispersal model. But Wettle's notion of the 'Neolithic aftershock' very neatly encapsulates the very much later consequences of what, as he suggests, may reasonably be considered a later episode or phase of essentially the same process. For in much of the world today, in North and South America, in Australia and New Zealand, in South Africa, indeed in many of the former European colonies where Indo-European languages are now spoken, their presence is as much due to the effectiveness of European farming practices as it is to the gunpowder and the social structures of imperial domination. It is in this sense that the farming/language dispersal model underlies also much of the argumentation of Jared Diamond's widely read *Guns, Germs and Steel* (Diamond 1997). It is however the basic staples of the European farming economy — the wheat and barley, the pulse crops, the sheep, cattle and pigs — which Europe in turn derived from Anatolia and Western Asia eight thousand years ago, which underlie that process.

Of course there is implicit here the awareness that the models for language replacement do not necessarily work in isolation: they may work together. For the general impression that European colonization was a matter of élite dominance is of course not entirely erroneous. The success of the *conquistadores* in Mexico was very much a matter of such dominance, where gunpowder and the military use of the horse were important agents. But the enduring success of the colonists in North America, while initially aided by just those factors, was sustained by their own farming economy. The subsequent spread of the 'frontier' was as much a spread of that new farming economy as it was a matter of expanding imperial power. And much the same was true of the 'Overlanders' in Australia. What we see in the American Mid West today is more a product of prehistoric Anatolian and Western Asian domesticates (cereals, cattle) than it is of post-medieval British administrative virtue.

Interestingly much the same observations may hold for what I often taken as an outstanding episode of élite dominance, namely the spread of the Indo-Iranian languages on the European steppe lands and into Iran and the Indian sub-continent. For the success of nomadic pastoralism in central Eurasia was established there well before the horse was systematically used for military purposes. The development of nomadic pastoralism brought about the rearing of livestock — sheep, goat, cattle and horses — as well as of cereal cultivation in a more effective way than had previously been possible. It did so, however, drawing upon the resources long since available through the original spread of a mixed farming economy. That is one factor which facilitated the spread eastwards from the Balkans and the Ukraine of the Indo-European language family which (I have

argued) had already been established in Europe for some millennia prior to the third millennium BC.

Progress in archaeogenetics

In reviewing the current situation it is, I think, pertinent to note that the discipline of archaeogenetics is still in its infancy. The initial formulations of Cavalli-Sforza and his colleagues, based upon classical genetic markers (Menozzi *et al.* 1978), have been substantially modified in the light of mtDNA studies (Renfrew 2000b). And of course the methodology which they initially applied to Europe and later used in their ambitious global overview (Cavalli-Sforza *et al.* 1994), with the very wide use of principal components analysis, is thereby called into question, so that these methodological revisions have wider implications. But at the same time it is pertinent to note that the initial mtDNA observations for Europe which had such a significant impact upon the application of the Ammerman and Cavalli-Sforza wave-of-advance/demic diffusion model for the inception of farming in Europe (Richards *et al.* 1996) were within a few years significantly revised and placed upon a more precise chronological basis (Sykes 1999). The initial conclusions were thus quite rapidly modified. And once again they themselves are seen in a new light, now that Y-chromosome analyses are available and open to interpretation in a coherent context (Semino *et al.* 2001).

Moreover the majority of archaeogenetic studies so far undertaken work upon a rather large-scale geographical canvas. For the Americas, for instance, the majority of papers so far contributed deal with the initial peopling of the Americas at a continental level. Just a few papers (e.g. Merriwether *et al.* 2000) are now available which deal in detail with individual tribal groups, seeking to establish their affinities and relationships, and considering more recent time depths, over the past few centuries, rather than contemplating the millennial perspectives of initial colonization. We need more studies such as these if we are to feel that we are obtaining a real grasp of local population histories.

The challenge of time depth

Underlying many of the controversies in the present volume are uncertainties about chronology. For in most cases where the intention is to compare linguistic, genetic and archaeological data, the difficulty lies in seeking points of equivalence. Patterns may emerge in one discipline, but they are difficult to compare with those in another unless secure chronological frameworks are available.

The geophysical techniques now available to archaeology have permitted the construction of reasonably precise and fairly reliable time scales. But this is because actual material remains are available which were found in secure archaeological contexts with the artefacts under discussion, and which may themselves be dated by chronometric techniques usually dependent upon standard patterns of radioactive decay.

In molecular genetics, improved techniques of network analysis are allowing the development of techniques for dating both individual mutations and their subsequent demographic dispersals. But each of these chronological assessments is dependent upon a number of frameworks of reasoning, most of which ultimately rest upon conclusions (or more often assumptions) about mutation rates for particular gene loci. Here the genetic mutation rate is the analogue for the radioactive decay rate of specific elemental isotopes in the field of physics. But it is already clear that the mutation rate for specific gene loci is dependent upon their location in the molecule, and it is not possible here to make valid statements which have the same generality as those of isotopic physics. This is one area which needs further investigation, and indeed one which we hope to examine further at a forthcoming symposium at the McDonald Institute.

In historical genetics the difficulties are even more acute. The original claims for glottochronology (Swadesh 1955) have been very widely rejected (see Blust 2000; Matisoff 2000). They were of course based upon a decay rate (for word loss) which itself was closely modelled upon the isotopic decay rate patterns of atomic physics, such as sustain the radiocarbon method and the other radiometric methods used in archaeological science. But it is not at all clear why there should be a constant decay rate, nor what factors might significantly modify it. At a recent symposium some scholars took a more positive approach towards the potential of some form of lexicostatistics for offering coherent frameworks over great time depths (e.g. Embleton 2000; Baxter & Manaster Ramer 2000; Starostin 2000). But many other scholars prefer the approach outlined, for instance by Kaufman, whereby the historically-attested examples of time depth for languages and language families are compared, and used to suggest a framework which runs up against a knowability barrier of up to 12,000 to 14,000 years for the oldest attested language families (Kaufman & Golla 2000, 47).

These are problems which require further and more sustained research. They will not go away, and it is difficult to see how further advances can take place until they are further resolved.

Changing ethnicities

Sometimes in contemplating the histories of individual languages and of the specific populations which have spoken them one is nearly overwhelmed by the impression of constant flux and of almost random change. Certainly when one reads Neal Ascherson's excellent *Black Sea* (Ascherson 1996), mentioned at the outset of this paper, that is the impression which one may come away with. And of course there is no doubt that language and ethnicity are closely related. As recent studies have emphasized (e.g. Jones 1997) ethnicity is largely a matter of group self-awareness. To a large extent an ethnic group is what its members wish it to be. And language is one of the most powerful instruments which group members have available to them to establish and emphasize their own identity. For this reason ethnicity and linguistic distinctiveness often go hand in hand, a point as valid for hunter-gatherers (Dixon 1980) as for agriculturalists.

At the same time, however, we should note how our own perception of the phenomenon of ethnicity has been very much shaped by our own experience of a more recent variety of it, namely nationalism. As Ernest Gellner (1983) has shown, that was very much a product of the eighteenth and nineteenth centuries: the spatial division of the world into a number of clearly-defined nation states is of relatively recent origin. We should note also how the 'primordialist' view of ethnicity (Smith 1986, 7) so prevalent in the nineteenth century has now been displaced, in the thinking of anthropologists if not of demagogic political leaders, by an 'instrumentalist' view, where ethnicity, as noted above, is not a given quality, inherited with one's blood or imbibed with one's mother's milk, but something that can be deliberately assumed or negotiated. The view, for instance, that there was an inherent ethnicity among 'the Celts' can be seen as erroneous and it seems more appropriate today to take a processual view (Renfrew 1987, 214; see Jones 1997).

There is often a close correlation between a specific ethnicity and a specific language, and this was probably even more generally valid before the notion of the nation state, as noted above, usurped the nature of ethnicity. In many case a single language may be equated with a single ethnic group, and often likewise a single ethnic group with a single language. This pattern of overlapping language groups, as outlined by Ascherson, is largely equivalent to one of overlapping ethnicities.

It is possible, however, to suggest that these patterns of great mobility and of overlying strata of ethnicities may not be a universal feature of history. Many of the situations described by Ascherson are the product of military interventions undertaken by great powers in recent centuries, some of them indeed by the mighty Soviet state itself during the twentieth century. Such large-scale displacements are characteristic of empires, where there may be large armies capable of imposing population shifts by force of arms. Indeed the armies often contributed to new populations with their own personnel. Thus when we speak of a 'Migration Period' at the end of the Roman Empire we are probably speaking of something which was specific to the historical circumstances prevailing at that time, indeed to a phenomenon which I have described as 'system collapse' (Renfrew 1987, 133; 1989, 125).

Around the Black Sea the mobility factor may also reveal the influence of mounted warriors. As I have sought to show elsewhere, the riding of the horse for military purposes is in effect a feature which began with the first millennium BC (and perhaps a few centuries earlier in the Eurasian steppe lands).

Ethnicity, then, may not be regarded as a universal though time. Its very nature will have altered with the changing social structures accompanying the inception of farming, and again with the development of larger and more hierarchical social units, for instance at the outset of the European Iron Age (Renfrew 1996). The models appropriate to the discussion of language replacement are thus time-dependent. Cross-cultural generalizations about them are likely to be flawed.

Language distributions versus language family distributions
The point with which I should like to conclude these observations is a simple one, but one that is much ignored. Models appropriate to outlining the origins of a single language, or to the description of a specific case of language replacement, cannot readily be generalized or broadened to encompass the genesis of an entire language family, or the replacement of the languages of one family by those of another. It can be argued that the rather atheoretical stance adopted by many historical linguists in discussing time depth (in the sense that they reject general formulations for time depth but often prefer to work intuitively) is matched by the assumption that the description of how one specific language has replaced another in a given territory may be used as the basis for some notion of how entire language families have come to be replaced.

Two authors who are unusual in dealing with this issue systematically are Johanna Nichols (1992) and Daniel Nettle (1999). Nettle, in particular, in his chapter on 'Phylogenetic Diversity' builds upon Nichols' approach and adopts her terminology of *stocks*. She defines the stock as the deepest phylogenetic node that is reconstructable by the standard comparative method of historical linguistics (Nichols 1992, 24–5). In effect the term 'stock' is equivalent to the concept of the large-scale 'language family' as commonly used in historical linguistics, since Nichols does not adopt the concept of the 'macrofamily' nor the large groupings favoured by Greenberg and his colleagues and by the Russian Nostratic school.

Nettle makes an interesting point which it is useful to keep in view:

> It is important to stress that stocks and other lineages of languages are of no significance to the people who speak them in the here and now. A person's social and geographic opportunities are affected by how many other people speak his language . . . It makes no difference to anyone, however, how many other languages there are in his language stock. The other languages of the stock will be, by definition, mutual unintelligible with his own, and that is enough to exclude him from them, whether they belong to the same lineage or not (Nettle 1999, 116).

This was the notion I had in mind when writing an article with the subtitle 'Don't let's be beastly to the Hungarians' (Renfrew 1996), in suggesting that the identity of the Hungarians as Europeans by comparison with the citizens of other European nations is not impaired by the circumstance that their language is a non-Indo-European one.

The controversy between Nettle and Nichols centres upon her notion that the number of stocks in a large geographical area will increase linearly with time, where Nettle holds that 'the disappearance of stocks will if anything increase as time goes by owing to increased inter-group interaction and area convergence' (Nettle 1999, 122). He goes on to state:

> The phylogenetic diversity of areas with a clear Neolithic punctuation still appears to us, today, to be low, because there has not been time since the Neolithic for the languages spread by Neolithic transition to become so different that we count them as different stocks (Nettle 1999, 124).

Here, however, it is not the issue of the number of stocks that interests us, but the phenomenon of language replacement at the level of the stock or language family rather than at that of the single language. That is a different issue, and one which has not, so far as I am aware, been discussed in detail at all in the literature of historical linguistics.

Here we are beginning to enter hitherto uncharted areas of geo-linguistic theory. We need to ask more carefully how it could be that whole large areas could switch their languages from one stock or language family to another. In some cases this may have come about by the wide and rapid spread of a proto-language ancestral to the various subsequent constituent languages of the stock. But we need to ask more carefully just what it is that gives these constituent languages their survival value in comparison to the languages of other stocks. This is hardly likely to have been simply product of random process, as some have suggested. For the contiguous arrangement of different but related languages within the geographical distribution of a stock or language family is itself highly non-random.

These considerations leave me, then, with an acute sense of problem. There is, I feel, something remarkable, something which needs to be explained, when we look at these very wide geographical distributions. Whether it is the Austronesian stock, or the Niger-Kordofanian, or the Afroasiatic or the Indo-European, or indeed any of the other widespread language families discussed in our symposium, there is certainly something to explain. Of course the explanation does not have to be the same one in every case. Probably there will be several explanations operating at once for the particular details of the distribution of any specific stock or family. But are there not some underlying general processes at work to produce these highly non-random patternings? I feel that in our discussions we did begin to approach some of these central issues. So while our symposium may not have produced many definitive answers I have the feeling that it may have asked some of the right questions.

Note

1. Carried out with colleagues from the Australian National University, the National Museum of the Philippines and the University of the Philippines (the latter including Victor Paz, a contributor to this volume).

References

Ascherson, N., 1996. *Black Sea, the Birth of Civilisation and Barbarism*. London: Vintage.

Baxter, W.H. & A. Manaster Ramer, 2000. Beyond lumping and splitting: probabilistic issues in historical linguistics, in Renfrew *et al.* (eds.), 167–88.

Bellwood, P., 1996a. Hierarchy, founder ideology and Austronesian expansion, in *Origin, Ancestry and Alliance*, eds. J. Fox & C. Sather. Canberra: Department of Anthropology, Comparative Austronesian Project, ANU, 18–40.

Bellwood, P., 1996b. Phylogeny and reticulation in prehistory. *Antiquity* 70, 881–90.

Bellwood, P., 2000. Descent-based and Reticulate Perspectives on Human Colonization and Diversity. Unpublished paper presented at NSF Conference on Entering New Landscapes, School of American Research, Santa Fe, September 2000 (volume in preparation).

Bellwood, P., 2001. Archaeology and the historical determinants of punctuation in language family origins, in *Areal Diffusion and Genetic Inheritance*, eds. A. Aikhenvald & R. Dixon. Oxford: Oxford University Press, 27–43.

Binford, L., 1968. Archaeological perspectives, in *New Perspectives in Archaeology*, eds. S. Binford & L. Binford. Chicago (IL): Aldine, 5–32.

Blust, R., 2000. Why lexicostatistics doesn't work: the 'universal constant' hypothesis and the Austronesian languages, in Renfrew *et al.* (eds.), 311–32.

Cavalli-Sforza, L.L., P. Menozzi & A. Piazza, 1994. *The History and Geography of Human Genes*. Princeton (NJ): Princeton University Press.

Crosby, A., 1986. *Ecological Imperialism*. Cambridge: Cambridge University Press.

Diamond, J., 1997. *Guns, Germs and Steel*. New York (NY): Norton.

Dixon, R.W., 1980. *The Languages of Australia*. Cambridge: Cambridge University Press.

Dixon, R.W., 1997. *The Rise and Fall of Languages*. Cambridge: Cambridge University Press.

Embleton S., 2000, Lexicostatistics/glottochronology: from Swadesh to Sankoff to Starostin to future horizons, in Renfrew *et al.* (eds.), 143–66.

Gellner, E., 1983. *Nations and Nationalism*. Oxford: Oxford University Press.

Jones S., 1997. *The Archaeology of Ethnicity: Constructing Identities in the Past and Present*. London: Routledge.

Kaufman, T. & V. Golla, 2000, Language groupings in the New World: their reliability and usability in cross-disciplinary studies, in Renfrew (ed.), 47–58.

Kirch, P.V. & R.C. Green, 2001. *Hawaiki, Ancestral Polynesia*. Cambridge: Cambridge University Press.

Matisoff, J., 2000. On the uselessness of glottochronology for the subgrouping of Tibeto-Burman, in Renfrew *et al.* (eds.), 333–72.

Menozzi P., A. Piazza & L.L. Cavalli-Sforza, 1978. Synthetic map of human gene frequencies in Europe. *Science* 210, 786–92.

Merriwether, D.A., B.M. Kemp, D.E. Crews & J.V. Neel, 2000. Gene flow and genetic variation in the Yanomama as revealed by mitochondrial DNA, in Renfrew (ed.) 2000c, 89–125.

Moore, J., 1994. Putting anthropology back together again: an ethnogenetic critique of cladistic theory. *American Anthropologist* 96, 925–48.

Nettle, D., 1999. *Linguistic Diversity*. Oxford: Oxford University Press.

Nichols, J., 1992. *Linguistic Diversity in Space and Time.* Chicago (IL): University of Chicago Press.

Renfrew, C., 1987. *Archaeology and Language: the Puzzle of Indo-European Origins.* London: Jonathan Cape.

Renfrew, C., 1989. Models of change in language and archaeology. *Transactions of the Philological Society* 87, 103–55.

Renfrew, C., 1996. Prehistory and the identity of Europe, or Don't let's be beastly to the Hungarians, in *Cultural Identity and Archaeology*, eds. P. Graves-Brown, S. Jones & C. Gamble. London: Routledge, 125–37.

Renfrew, C., 2000a. At the edge of knowability: towards a prehistory of languages. *Cambridge Archaeological Journal* 10(1), 7–34.

Renfrew, C., 2000b. Archaeogenetics: towards a population prehistory of Europe, in Renfrew & Boyle (eds.), 3–11.

Renfrew, C. (ed.), 2000c. *America Past, America Present: Genes and Languages in the Americas and Beyond.* (Papers in the Prehistory of Languages.) Cambridge: McDonald Institute for Archaeological Research.

Renfrew, C. & K. Boyle (eds.), 2000. *Archaeogenetics: DNA and the Population Prehistory of Europe.* (McDonald Institute Monographs.) Cambridge: McDonald Institute for Archaeological Research.

Renfrew, C., A. McMahon & L. Trask (eds.), 2000. *Time Depth in Historical Linguistics.* (Papers in the Prehis-

tory of Languages.) Cambridge: McDonald Institute for Archaeological Research.

Richards, M.R., H. Côrte-Real, P. Forster, V. Macaulay, H. Wilkinson-Herbots, A. Demaine, S. Papiha, R. Hedges, H.-J. Bandelt & B. Sykes, 1996. Palaeolithic and neolithic lineages in the European mitochondrial gene pool. *American Journal of Human Genetics* 599, 185–203.

Semino, O., G. Passerino, P.J. Oefner, A.A. Lin, S. Arbuzova, L.E. Beckman, G. De Benedictis, P. Francalacci, A. Kouvatsi, S. Limborska, M. Marcikiae, A. Mika, D. Primorac, A.S. Santachiara-Benerecetti L.L. Cavalli-Sforza & P.A. Underhill, 2001. The genetic legacy of Palaeolithic *Homo sapiens sapiens* in extant Europeans: a Y-chromosome perspective. *Science* 290, 1155–9.

Shennan, S., 2000. Population, culture, and the dynamics of culture change. *Current Anthropology* 41, 811–35.

Smith, A.D., 1986. *The Ethnic Origins of Nations.* Oxford: Blackwell.

Starostin, S., 2000. Comparative-historical linguistics and lexicostatistics, in Renfrew *et al.* (eds.), 223–66.

Swadesh, M., 1955. Towards greater accuracy in lexicostatic dating. *International Journal of American Linguistics* 21, 121–37.

Sykes, B., 1999. The molecular genetics of European ancestry. *Philosophical Transactions of the Royal Society, Biological Sciences* 354, 131–40.

Index

compiled by Dora Kemp

L

O

DEMCO

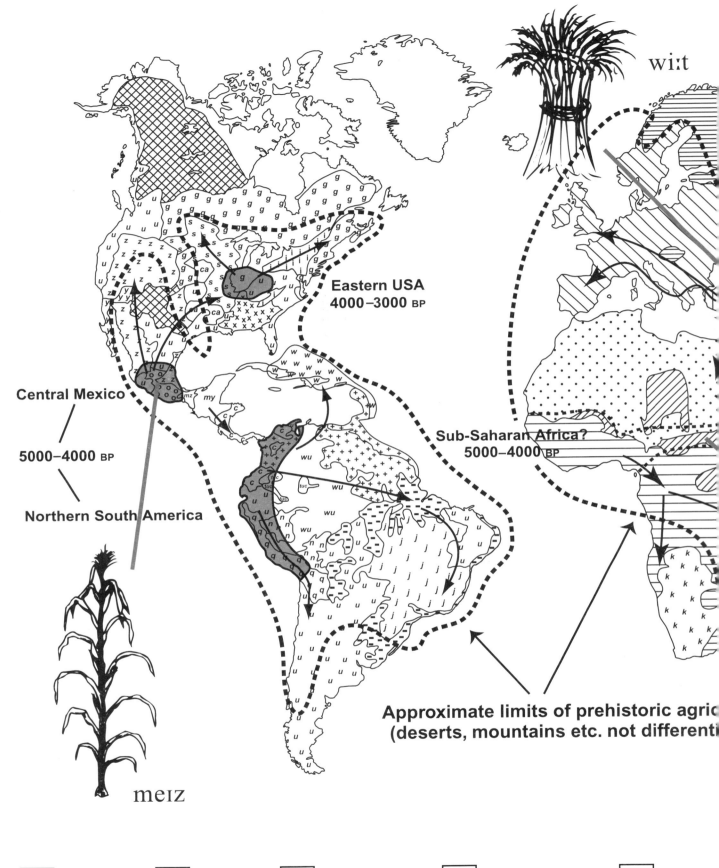

wi:t

Eastern USA
4000–3000 BP

Central Mexico

5000–4000 BP

Northern South America

Sub-Saharan Africa?
5000–4000 BP

Approximate limits of prehistoric agric
(deserts, mountains etc. not different

meɪz